I0220332

Acknowledgement

This transcription is dedicated to my wife Josephine "Fena" Marie Manibusan-Punzalan, children and grandson: Brandon Joseph Manibusan Punzalan & Sherezada Young-Punzalan, and my first-born grandson Jayden Joseph; Bryant Joshua Manibusan Punzalan & Melissa Gutierrez-Punzalan; Bernard Timothy Punzalan II; and Flaka Marie Punzalan. Throughout my journey of researching and documenting our families' Chamorro heritage they have been very patient, understanding and supportive of my time and effort on the Chamorro Roots Genealogy Project.

I am also grateful to Elizabeth "Lisa" Martinez Bitanga for proofreading this transcription and for the countless of selfless hours and contributions as a primary associate researcher and collaborator on the Chamorro Roots Genealogy Project.

About this transcription

This transcription of the 1920 population census of Guam is fairly straightforward. It begins with an overview and some of my observations of the census in general. There are no copies of the original images included within this book; with the exception of a modified copy of the title page. Each census page contained herein is simply a transcription from what was handwritten and transcribed into a type written format. It serves as a tool to make it a little easier for fellow genealogy researchers during the course of their work.

This book is copyright 2012 by Bernard T. Punzalan (author and publisher) of the Chamorro Roots Genealogy Project (www.chamorroroots.com). All rights reserved. No part of this book may be reproduced or transmitted in any form or by any means, electronic or mechanical, including photocopying, recording, or by any information storage and retrieval system, without the written permission of the author. (**ISBN 978-0-9851257-0-7**)

Table of Contents

Overview

In 1920, Guam was included for the first time in the census of the United States since it became a U.S. Territory in 1898. Census day began on January 1, 1920; however, the actual enumeration of census for Guam did not commence until February 24, 1920 with the final recording ending on April 24, 1920. The population schedule used for Guam is distinct and differs from the population schedule used for a State.

Copies of the *Fourteenth Census of the United States: 1920-Population, The Island of Guam* are on Microfilm[1] # T625-2032 and can be purchased at the National Archives and Records Administration website (www.archives.gov). Digital images may also be accessed for a fee at several genealogy websites; or, you can search for names that have also been transcribed and inputted into the Chamorro Roots Genealogy Project database and website (www.chamorroroots.com). Other methods of accessing census records include some major public libraries in the U.S.

Each enumerated census is actually comprised of two sets; totaling 50 names. The first sheet set contains individuals from 1 through 25 (referred to as Sheet A), and then a subsequent sheet allows the enumerator to record individuals from 26 to 50 (Sheet B). Therefore, as you view the beginning forms of each district or subdistrict, the forms will normally begin with Sheet 1A, followed by Sheet 1B, Sheet 2A, Sheet 2B and so on. I intentionally excluded some sheets that were blank ("B" sheets) when the Enumerators completed the enumeration of a particular area on a Sheet "A."

I have also noticed another number that appears to be stamped on the upper right side of the form. This number seems to be the numerical sequence number for the entire Guam census records to help arrange and organize the records. These stamped numbers also served as the basis for my attempt to reconcile the population numbers officially recorded and presented by the Census Bureau. Be mindful that these numbers are assigned on to the first document of each set (individuals 1 through 25 – Sheet A). The stamped numbers were helpful in my quest to organize and transcribe the information into the Chamorro Roots database. Some on-line genealogy sites have not been able to accurately organize this feature image by image and the pitfall to that can result in an erroneous transcription of family composition when family information is split between census sheets.

---

[1] Microfilm roll # T625-2032 contains copies of the Census for Guam and American Samoa. It does not include the military stationed and living at the Naval Station, Marine Barracks and receiving ship. The military that were considered by the US "stationed abroad" were recorded under a separate Census.

Island of Guam Population Summary

Census publications regarding the population statistics of Guam for the 1920 census record an official total population count of 13,275. However, in transcribing and reconciling the data there were actually 13,279 names recorded in the census, which leaves a difference of four (4).

Five primary districts were recorded for Guam and are comprised of the following localities, population count and enumerators:

1920 Population: Island of Guam		
District	Population	No. of Sheets
District 1	4,189	169
District 2	4,140	169
District 3	1,809	74
District 4	1,739	72
District 5	1,377	58
Total[2]	13,254	542

District 1			
Name of Place	Population	No. of Sheets	Enumerator
Agana City [San Nicolas area]	1142	46	Joaquin Torres
Agana City [San Ramon area]	362	15	Albert P. Manley
Dededo Barrio	369	16	Jose Kamminga
Barrigada Barrio	180	8	Jose Kamminga
Sinajana Barrio	204	9	Jose Kamminga
Machanao Barrio	28	2	Jose Kamminga
Agana City [San Antonio area][3]	1763	71	Jose Kamminga
Pago-Sinajana Barrio	30	2	Jose Kamminga
Total[4]	4,189	174	

---

[2] Total population does not include the military and their families residing on military installations/reservations. The Census for military was performed separately and on a separate population form.
[3] Although the subdistrict of the Agana City was labeled as the San Antonio Area, included in these sheets were the areas of Yigo Road, Barrigada Road, and Mongmong Road.
[4] Five census sheets that consisted of 111 people within District 1 (stamped Sheet numbers 44 through 46) were almost completely illegible are not transcribed within this book.

District 2			
Name of Place	Population	No. of Sheets	Enumerator
Anigua - Agana (City)	721	29	Vicente Tydingco
Agana (City)	3,335	135	Arthur W. Jackson
Tutujan (subdistrict)	56	3	Arthur W. Jackson
Maina (subdistrict)	28	2	Arthur W. Jackson
Total	4,140	169	

District 3			
Name of Place	Population	No. of Sheets	Enumerator
Asan Barrio	345	14	Vicente Tydingco
Tepungan Barrio	240	10	Vicente Tydingco
Piti Town	429	18	Vicente Tydingco
Sumay Town	795	32	Vicente Tydingco
Total	1,809	74	

District 4			
Name of Place	Population	No. of Sheets	Enumerator
Agat Town	757	31	Albert P. Manley
Umatac Barrio	327	14	Albert P. Manley
Merizo Town	655	27	Albert P. Manley
Total	1,739	72	

District 5			
Name of Place	Population	No. of Sheets	Enumerator
Inarajan Town	612	25	Joaquin Torres
Aga-Inarajan District	27	2	Joaquin Torres
Malolos-Inarajan District	39	2	Joaquin Torres
Bubulao-Inarajan District	60	3	Joaquin Torres
Talofofo Barrio	215	9	Joaquin Torres
Yona Municipality	424	17	Joaquin Torres
Total	1,377	58	

Race	#
Blank	1
Black	14
Chamorro	12,151
Chinese	58
Filipino	401
Japanese	200
Mix	43
Mulatto	8
Other	12
White	280

Interesting Facts, Observations & Tips

Age Range

Age/Range	0	1	2	3	4	5	6	7	8	9	
0-17 yrs	413	423	473	435	463	399	421	348	338	321	
	10	**11**	**12**	**13**	**14**	**15**	**16**	**17**			**Total**
	341	312	366	308	321	295	316	282			**6,575**

Age/Range	18	19	20	21	22	23	24	25	26	27	
18-37 yrs	276	271	290	192	217	194	247	230	216	201	
	28	**29**	**30**	**31**	**32**	**33**	**34**	**35**	**36**	**37**	**Total**
	194	176	193	121	135	148	136	159	148	124	**3,868**

Age/Range	38	39	40	41	42	43	44	45	46	47	
38-57 yrs	134	114	156	84	140	117	141	124	109	106	
	48	**49**	**50**	**51**	**52**	**53**	**54**	**55**	**56**	**57**	**Total**
	129	103	111	74	104	86	69	92	73	64	**2,130**

Age/Range	58	59	60	61	62	63	64	65	66	67	
58-77 yrs	73	57	71	20	37	17	27	44	17	16	
	68	**69**	**70**	**71**	**72**	**73**	**74**	**75**	**76**	**77**	**Total**
	18	21	41	8	8	6	7	21	10	6	**525**

Age/Range	78	79	80	81	82	83	84	85	86	87	
78-97 yrs	9	11	14	3	5	2	4	3	4	3	
	88	**89**	**90**	**91**	**92**	**93**	**94**	**95**	**96**	**97**	**Total**
	1	4	2	0	1	0	1	1	0	2	**70**

Gender & Average Age

Gender	Count	Avg. Age
Females	6,738	23
Males	6,430	21
Illegible	111	
Total	**13,279**	**22**

Oldest Residents

Manuel Sococo, a Chinese gentleman residing with his family in Asan, and Francisco B. Baliesta, a Filipino gentleman residing with his family in Sumay, were both 97 years old and are the oldest recorded in the 1920 Census for Guam. The oldest woman is Dolores G. Cruz, age 95, residing with her family at Dionicio Street, Umatac.

Newborns & Children[5]

There are 413 babies recorded with the age of less than one year. Nearly half the entire population of the names and information I was able to transcribe are children aged 17 and below.

Top 10 Common Names

There are 522 unique surnames that I was able to transcribe from census. Below are the top 10 most common surnames, first names and the number of times each occurs in my transcription; from highest to lowest.

COMMON SURNAMES	
Surname	**#**
Cruz	898
Santos	449
San Nicolas	343
Perez	312
Leon Guerrero	301
Camacho	285
Castro	276
Aguon	242
Mendiola	238
Salas	238

COMMON FIRST NAMES			
Male	**#**	**Female**	**#**
Jose	1,133	Maria	1,234
Juan	698	Ana	688
Vicente	572	Dolores	344
Jesus	446	Rosa	332
Joaquin	386	Antonia	213
Francisco	382	Carmen	195
Antonio	302	Josefa	195
Manuel	252	Rita	185
Pedro	244	Concepcion	164
Ignacio	187	Joaquina	134

And not so surprising as well, is a list of the top 10 common surnames with first names and number occurrences found in my transcription that often presents a genealogy research challenge when very little information on the individuals is available.

COMMON LAST NAMES WITH FIRST NAMES	#
Cruz, Maria	96
Cruz, Jose	88
Cruz, Juan	53
Santos, Maria	48
Cruz, Ana	44
San Nicolas, Maria	38
Cruz, Vicente	37
Santos, Jose	34
Camacho, Maria	33
Leon Guerrero, Maria	33

---

[5] The age transcription for children less than a year, appear in decimal format vice the original recording of months old.)

Potential Duplicate Recording of Individuals

Another discovery is that a few names appear to be duplicate recordings of the same individual; based on name, age and potential family affiliation of two separate dwellings. In addition, some individuals, particularly those who may have served as Cooks or Servants at other households may have been inadvertently recorded twice. Therefore, if the name matched and the age was within plus or minus one year, I have additionally flagged these individuals as potential duplicates. It also appears that one San Nicolas household family of four may have been a duplicate recording in two separate localities: Agana and Maina.

NAME	AGE	CENSUS INFORMATION
Ada, Joaquin S.	7	1920 Census Island of Guam	District 2	Agana (City)	San Ignacio Street	Sheet 41A / 145	Line: 10	Lodger	Marital Status: S	Occupation: None
Ada, Joaquin S.	7	1920 Census Island of Guam	District 2	Agana (City)	Santa Cruz Street	Sheet 42A / 146	Line: 14	Grandson	Marital Status: S	Occupation: None
Aguon, Soledad P.	16	1920 Census Island of Guam	District 2	Agana (City)	Cristobal Colon Street	Sheet 66A / 170	Line: 16	Daughter	Marital Status: S	Occupation: None
Aguon, Soledad P.	15	1920 Census Island of Guam	District 1	Agana City	General Terrero Street	Sheet 48B / 17	Line: 27	Cook	Marital Status: S	Occupation: Cook
Babauta, Francisco S.N.	13	1920 Census Island of Guam	District 4	Agat Town	Serain Street	Sheet 6A / 218	Line: 1	Son	Marital Status: S	Occupation: None
Babauta, Francisco S.N.	12	1920 Census Island of Guam	District 1	Agana City	San Victores Street	Sheet 35B / 66	Line: 47	Servant	Marital Status: S	Occupation: None
Blas, Consuelo M.	2	1920 Census Island of Guam	District 1	Agana City	Yigo Road	Sheet 53B / 84	Line: 37	Daughter	Marital Status: S	Occupation: None
Blas, Consuelo M.	2	1920 Census Island of Guam	District 3	Piti Town	Agana Piti Road	Sheet 17A / 192	Line: 5	Niece	Marital Status: S	Occupation: None
Charfauros, Andres C.	14	1920 Census Island of Guam	District 1	Agana City	Calle de San Ramon	Sheet 38A / 24	Line: 11	Servant	Marital Status: S	Occupation: Servant
Charfauros, Andres C.	13	1920 Census Island of Guam	District 4	Agat Town	Serain Street	Sheet 8B / 220	Line: 31	Son	Marital Status: S	Occupation: None
Francisco, Joaquin C.	14	1920 Census Island of Guam	District 1	Agana City	Gerona Street	Sheet 46A / 15	Line: 17	Brother-in-law	Marital Status: S	Occupation: None

NAME	AGE	CENSUS INFORMATION
Francisco, Joaquin C.	14	1920 Census Island of Guam | District 1 | Agana City | San Nicolas Street | Sheet 45A / 76 | Line: 2 | Son | Marital Status: S | Occupation: Farm laborer home farm
Franquez, Rita C.	6	1920 Census Island of Guam | District 1 | Agana City | Isabela la Catolica Street | Sheet 37B / 6 | Line: 50 | Daughter | Marital Status: S | Occupation: None
Franquez, Rita C.	5	1920 Census Island of Guam | District 2 | Agana (City) | Maria Ana de Austria Street | Sheet 54A / 158 | Line: 22 | Granddaughter | Marital Status: S | Occupation: None
Mendiola, Margarita M.	14	1920 Census Island of Guam | District 2 | Agana City | Legaspi Street | Sheet 44A / 96 | Line: 20 | Sister | Marital Status: S | Occupation: Servant
Mendiola, Margarita M.	14	1920 Census Island of Guam | District 2 | Agana (City) | Maria Ana de Austria Street | Sheet 54B / 158 | Line: 42 | Servant | Marital Status: S | Occupation: None
Pablo, Concepcion V.	10	1920 Census Island of Guam | District 2 | Agana (City) | Soledad Street | Sheet 3A / 107 | Line: 25 | Servant | Marital Status: S | Occupation: Servant
Pablo, Concepcion V.	11	1920 Census Island of Guam | District 1 | Machanao Barrio | Machanao Barrio | Sheet 21A / 52 | Line: 20 | Daughter | Marital Status: S | Occupation: None
Rosario, Silvestre C.	14	1920 Census Island of Guam | District 1 | Agana City | Paz Street | Sheet 43B / 29 | Line: 29 | Brother-in-law | Marital Status: S | Occupation: None
Rosario, Silvestre C.	14	1920 Census Island of Guam | District 1 | Agana City | Calle de Madrid Street | Sheet 44A / 30 | Line: 21 | Son | Marital Status: S | Occupation: None
San Nicolas, Vicente I.	26	1920 Census Island of Guam | District 2 | Agana (City) | Dr. Hesler Street | Sheet 50A / 154 | Line: 13 | Head | Marital Status: M | Occupation: Farmer
San Nicolas, Vicente I.	26	1920 Census Island of Guam | District 2 | Maina (sub-District) | | Sheet 71A / 175 | Line: 1 | Head | Marital Status: M | Occupation: Farmer
San Nicolas, Maria M.	25	1920 Census Island of Guam | District 2 | Agana (City) | Dr. Hesler Street | Sheet 50A / 154 | Line: 14 | Wife | Marital Status: M | Occupation: None
San Nicolas, Maria M.	25	1920 Census Island of Guam | District 2 | Maina (sub-District) | | Sheet 71A / 175 | Line: 2 | Wife | Marital Status: M | Occupation: None
San Nicolas, Trinidad M.	4	1920 Census Island of Guam | District 2 | Agana (City) | Dr. Hesler Street | Sheet 50A / 154 | Line: 15 | Daughter | Marital Status: S | Occupation: None
San Nicolas, Trinidad M.	3	1920 Census Island of Guam | District 2 | Maina (sub-District) | | Sheet 71A / 175 | Line: 3 |

NAME	AGE	CENSUS INFORMATION
		Daughter | Marital Status: S | Occupation: None
San Nicolas, Beatrice M.	1/12	1920 Census Island of Guam | District 2 | Agana (City) | Dr. Hesler Street | Sheet 50A / 154 | Line: 16 | Daughter | Marital Status: S | Occupation: None
San Nicolas, Beatrice M.	4/12	1920 Census Island of Guam | District 2 | Maina (sub-District) | | Sheet 71A / 175 | Line: 4 | Daughter | Marital Status: S | Occupation: None
Tenorio, Delfina G.	3	1920 Census Island of Guam | District 1 | Sinajana Barrio | Sinajana Barrio | Sheet 17B / 48 | Line: 33 | Niece | Marital Status: S | Occupation: None
Tenorio, Delfina G.	2	1920 Census Island of Guam | District 2 | Agana (City) | Cristobal Colon Street | Sheet 66B / 170 | Line: 43 | Daughter | Marital Status: S | Occupation: None

Surname Search Tips

Abbreviations. The only surname that was sometimes abbreviated in some cases was S. Nicolas (San Nicolas) in District 3. In some cases, first names were abbreviated with an initial by enumerators. However, this seems more prevalent and particular to some of the Japanese people that were recorded.

Spelling. There are some variations in the way the different enumerators spelled last names. However, here is a list of potentially misspelled prospects, as opposed to how I have observed some surnames spelled today. Below are some, but not all, examples:

Surname – Recorded Surname	Surname – Recorded Surname
Agualo – Aguahlo, Aguajlo	Malijan – Mariyan
Alvarez – Albarez	Megofna – Migofna
Alicto – Alecto	Mesa – Meza
Artero – Altero	Naputi – Naputy
Apuron – Afaron, Aparon	Nededog – Nededoc
Aquiningoc – Aguiningoc, Aquinigoc, Aquininog	Ninete – Nenete
Champaco – Chupaco	Pocaigue – Pocahigui
Charfauros – Chafauros	Quidachay – Qiudachay, Quidaguay
Chargualaf – Chagulaf, Chargulaf	Quitugua – Quidagua, Quiduagua, Quituguac
Cheguina – Chiguina	Quitano – Quitanoc
Concepcion – Conception	Respecio – Respicio
Demapan – Dimapan	Rodriguez – Rodriges
Desa – Deza	Salucnamnam – Saluznamnam
Dias – Diaz	Siguenza – Singuenza
Dydasco – Dy-dasco	Susuico – Susuica
Fegurgur – Fergurgur	Techaira – Tachira
Isezaki – Isizaki	Taienao – Taenao
Maguadog – Maguadoc, Magudoc	Taintongo – Taeantongo

Mother's Maiden Surname vs. Father's Surname. Researchers should also be aware that some families, particularly siblings, may not have the same surnames due in part to one sibling having retained his/her mother's maiden name as a surname and the father's surname becoming the middle name. During this period of the Census it was very common for a person to carry his/her mother's maiden surname as a middle name. During the Spanish occupation, it was also very common for a person to have his/her name recorded with the first name, father's surname (almost as if it was his/her middle name) followed by the mother's surname (in some cases with the use of a Spanish article "y" succeeding the father's surname and preceding the mother's maiden surname). If one did not understand this Spanish tradition, a translation/transcription error would likely occur within an official document and would then become the basis (likely for consistency) on how one's name would be recorded in the future. This was a transition challenge[6] of tradition from the Spanish to the American custom.

For example in the 1920 Census I have observed the following enumerations:

Albarez[Alvarez], Joaquin Q., age 31, whose occupation is recorded as an Enlisted Man US. Navy. Joaquin was residing with his brother Quitugua, Jose A.[Alvarez], age 37, and Jose's family.

Leon Guerrero, Vicenta de, Head
Guerrero, Jose D.L., Son (Occupation: Enlisted Man USN)
Leon Guerrero, Maria de, Daughter

---

[6] Naval Captain William W. Gilmer, a governor of Guam, introduced a contemporary genealogy challenge on March 4, 1920. Governor Gilmer decreed that all residents of Guam sixteen years and older must register and obtain a cèdula personal, which was basically a certificate of identification. The purpose for creating these identifications was to enable a person's identity to perform transactions with the government such as tax payments, land transfers, birth registrations, court matters, and so on. Another purpose was to reduce the centuries-old Spanish custom of a child bearing the father's last name first and the mother's maiden name second and reduce the practice of double names, (i.e. changing the name of what may once been "Juan de la Cruz y Torres" to "Juan Torres Cruz"), bringing names in line with the Western tradition of the father's name being recorded last. (Rodgers, 1995)

District 1

(CHAMORRO ROOTS GENEALOGY PROJECT ™ TRANSCRIPTION)
(COMPILED/TRANSCRIBED BY BERNARD T. PUNZALAN / HTTP://WWW.CHAMORROROOTS.COM)

SHEET NO. _32A_

FOURTEENTH CENSUS OF THE UNITED STATES: 1920–POPULATION
ISLAND OF GUAM

DISTRICT 1
NAME OF PLACE **Agana City**
[Proper name and, also, name of class, as city, town, village, barrio, etc]

ENUMERATED BY ME ON THE 27th DAY OF March, 1920

Joaquin Torres ENUMERATOR

Street, avenue, road, etc.	Number of dwelling house in order of visitation	Number of family in order of visitation	NAME	RELATION	Sex	Color or race	Age at last birthday	Single, married, widowed or divorced	Attended school any time since Sept. 1, 1919	Whether able to read.	Whether able to write.	Place of birth of this person.	Place of birth of father of this person.	Place of birth of mother of this person.	Whether able to speak English.	OCCUPATION
	2	3	4	5	6	7	8	9	10	11	12	13	14	15	16	17
	1	1	Leon, Jose M	Head	M	Cha	34.0	M		Y	Y	Guam	Guam	Guam	Y	Farmer
	1	1	Leon, Francisca I	Wife	F	Cha	32.0	M		Y	N	Guam	Guam	Guam	N	None
	1	1	Leon, Eziquel I	Son	M	Cha	21.0	S	N	Y	Y	Guam	Guam	Guam	Y	Storekeeper
	1	1	Leon, Francisco I	Son	M	Cha	17.0	S	N	Y	Y	Guam	Guam	Guam	Y	Cook
	1	1	Leon, Jesus I	Son	M	Cha	13.0	S	Y	Y	Y	Guam	Guam	Guam	Y	None
	2	2	Siguenza, Vicente S	Head	M	Cha	34.0	M		Y	Y	Guam	Unknown	Guam	Y	Blacksmith
	2	2	Siguenza, Dolores C	Wife	F	Cha	25.0	M		Y	Y	Guam	Guam	Guam	Y	None
	2	2	Siguenza, Jose C	Son	M	Cha	4.0	S				Guam	Guam	Guam		None
San Juan De Lettran Street	2	2	Siguenza, Juan C	Son	M	Cha	3.0	S				Guam	Guam	Guam		None
	3	3	Dy-dasco, Rosa F	Head	F	Cha	32.0	Wd		Y	Y	Guam	Guam	Guam	N	None
	3	3	Dy-dasco, Jesus F	Son	M	Cha	19.0	S	N	Y	Y	Guam	Guam	Guam	Y	Carpenter
	3	3	Dy-dasco, Jose F	Son	M	Cha	17.0	S	N	Y	Y	Guam	Guam	Guam	Y	Farm laborer home
	3	3	Dy-dasco, Joaquin F	Son	M	Cha	13.0	S	N	Y	Y	Guam	Guam	Guam	Y	Farm laborer home
	3	3	Dy-dasco, Ana F	Daughter	F	Cha	12.0	S	Y	Y	Y	Guam	Guam	Guam	Y	None
	3	3	Dy-dasco, Concepcion F	Daughter	F	Cha	9.0	S	Y			Guam	Guam	Guam		None
	3	3	Dy-dasco, Felix F	Son	M	Cha	7.0	S	N			Guam	Guam	Guam		None
	3	3	Dy-dasco, Gregorio F	Son	M	Cha	2.0	S				Guam	Guam	Guam		None
	3	3	Dy-dasco, Juan F	Son	M	Cha	1.0	S				Guam	Guam	Guam		None
	4	4	Pangelinan, Jose C	Head	M	Cha	30.0	M		Y	Y	Guam	Guam	Guam	Y	Carpenter
	4	4	Pangelinan, Antonia B	Wife	F	Cha	25.0	M		Y	Y	Guam	Unknown	Guam	Y	None
	5	5	Iglesias, Jose L	Head	M	Cha	24.0	M		Y	Y	Guam	Guam	Guam	Y	Enlisted man USN
	5	5	Iglesias, Ana D	Wife	F	Cha	20.0	M		Y	Y	Guam	Guam	Guam	Y	None
	5	5	Iglesias, Joseph D	Son	M	Cha	0.7	S				Guam	Guam	Guam		None
	6	6	Iglesias, Jesus F	Head	M	Cha	37.0	M		Y	Y	Guam	Guam	Guam	Y	Teamster
	6	6	Iglesias, Consolacion G	Wife	F	Cha	25.0	M		Y	Y	Guam	Unknown	Guam	Y	None

(CHAMORRO ROOTS GENEALOGY PROJECT ™ TRANSCRIPTION)
(COMPILED/TRANSCRIBED BY BERNARD T. PUNZALAN / HTTP://WWW.CHAMORROROOTS.COM)

FOURTEENTH CENSUS OF THE UNITED STATES: 1920—POPULATION
ISLAND OF GUAM

ENUMERATED BY ME ON THE 27th DAY OF March, 1920

Joaquin Torres ENUMERATOR

DISTRICT 1
NAME OF PLACE Agana City
[Proper name and, also, name of class, as city, town, village, barrio, etc]

	Dwelling No.	Family No.	NAME	RELATION	Sex	Color or race	Age	Marital	Attended school since Sept. 1, 1919	Read	Write	Place of birth of person	Place of birth of father	Place of birth of mother	Speak English	OCCUPATION
26	6	6	Iglesias, Jose G	Son	M	Cha	3.0	S				Guam	Guam	Guam		None
27	6	6	Iglesias, Francisco G	Son	M	Cha	1.0	S				Guam	Guam	Guam		None
28	6	6	Iglesias, Juan G	Son	M	Cha	0.0	S				Guam	Guam	Guam		None
29	7	7	Iglesias, Enrique F	Head	M	Cha	31.0	M		Y	Y	Guam	Guam	Guam	Y	Teamster
30	7	7	Iglesias, Josefa A	Wife	F	Cha	31.0	M		Y	Y	Guam	Guam	Guam	Y	None
31	7	7	Iglesias, Antonio A	Son	M	Cha	9.0	S	Y			Guam	Guam	Guam		None
32	7	7	Iglesias, Maria A	Daughter	F	Cha	7.0	S	Y			Guam	Guam	Guam		None
33	7	7	Iglesias, Tomas A	Son	M	Cha	5.0	S	N			Guam	Guam	Guam		None
34	8	8	Iglesias, Rita F	Head	F	Cha	72.0	Wd		Y	N	Guam	Guam	Guam	N	None
35	8	8	Iglesias, Ana F	Daughter	F	Cha	29.0	S		Y	Y	Guam	Guam	Guam	N	Laundress
36	9	9	Quitugua, Jose A	Head	M	Cha	37.0	M		Y	Y	Guam	Guam	Guam	Y	Farmer
37	9	9	Quitugua, Milagros P	Wife	F	Cha	36.0	M		Y	Y	Guam	Guam	Guam	N	None
38	9	9	Quitugua, Maria P	Daughter	F	Cha	16.0	S	N	Y	Y	Guam	Guam	Guam	Y	None
39	9	9	Quitugua, Jose P	Son	M	Cha	12.0	S	Y	Y	Y	Guam	Guam	Guam	Y	None
40	9	9	Quitugua, Ignacio P	Son	M	Cha	10.0	S	Y	Y	Y	Guam	Guam	Guam	Y	None
41	9	9	Quitugua, Vicente P	Son	M	Cha	8.0	S	Y	Y	Y	Guam	Guam	Guam	Y	None
42	9	9	Quitugua, Joaquin P	Son	M	Cha	6.0	S	N			Guam	Guam	Guam		None
43	9	9	Quitugua, Ana P	Daughter	F	Cha	3.0	S				Guam	Guam	Guam		None
44	9	9	Albarez, Joaquin Q	Brother	M	Cha	31.0	S		Y	Y	Guam	Guam	Guam	Y	Enlisted man USN
45	9	9	Quitugua, Ana B	Sister	F	Cha	28.0	S		Y	Y	Guam	Guam	Guam	Y	None
46	10	10	Manibusan, Jose D	Head	M	Cha	41.0	M		Y	Y	Guam	Guam	Guam	Y	Carpenter
47	10	10	Manibusan, Maria C	Wife	F	Fil	52.0	S		Y	Y	Guam	Philippine Islands	Guam	N	None
48	10	10	Manibusan, Ana N C	Daughter	F	Cha	10.0	S	Y	Y	Y	Guam	Guam	Guam	Y	None
49	11	11	Franquez, Vicente I	Head	M	Cha	37.0	M		Y	Y	Guam	Guam	Guam	Y	Silversmith
50	11	11	Franquez, Rosa C	Wife	F	Cha	37.0	M		Y	Y	Guam	Guam	Guam	N	None

Street: San Juan De Letran Street

14

(CHAMORRO ROOTS GENEALOGY PROJECT ™ TRANSCRIPTION)
(COMPILED/TRANSCRIBED BY BERNARD T. PUNZALAN / HTTP://WWW.CHAMORROROOTS.COM)

FOURTEENTH CENSUS OF THE UNITED STATES: 1920-POPULATION
ISLAND OF GUAM

DISTRICT 1
NAME OF PLACE **Agana City**
[Proper name and, also, name of class, as city, town, village, barrio, etc]

ENUMERATED BY ME ON THE 27th DAY OF March, 1920

Joaquin Torres ENUMERATOR

Street, avenue, road, etc.	Number of dwelling house in order of visitation	Number of family in order of visitation	NAME of each person whose place of abode on January 1, 1920, was in the family.	RELATION Relationship of this Person to the head of the family.	Sex	Color or race	Age at last birthday	Single, married, widowed or divorced	Attended school any time since Sept. 1, 1919	Whether able to read.	Whether able to write.	Place of birth of this person.	Place of birth of father of this person.	Place of birth of mother of this person.	Whether able to speak English.	OCCUPATION Trade, profession, or particular kind of work done, as salesman, laborer, clerk, cook, merchant, washerwoman, etc.
1	2	3	4	5	6	7	8	9	10	11	12	13	14	15	16	17
	11	11	Franquez, Jesus P	Son	M	Cha	14.0	S	Y	Y	Y	Guam	Guam	Guam	Y	None
	11	11	Franquez, Emiliana P	Daughter	F	Cha	11.0	S	Y	Y	Y	Guam	Guam	Guam	Y	None
	11	11	Franquez, Maria P	Daughter	F	Cha	9.0	S	Y			Guam	Guam	Guam		None
	11	11	Franquez, Antonia C	Daughter	F	Cha	2.0	S				Guam	Guam	Guam		None
	11	11	Franquez, Remedios C	Daughter	F	Cha	1.0	S				Guam	Guam	Guam		None
	11	11	Franquez, Lorenzo C	Son	M	Cha	0.0	S				Guam	Guam	Guam		None
	12	12	Villagomez, Elena C	Head	F	Cha	46.0	S		Y	Y	Guam	Guam	Guam	N	None
	12	12	Villagomez, Rosa C	Sister	F	Cha	39.0	S		Y	Y	Guam	Guam	Guam	N	None
	12	12	Villagomez, Juana C	Sister	F	Cha	36.0	S		Y	Y	Guam	Guam	Guam	N	None
	12	12	Villagomez, Carlos C	Brother	M	Cha	31.0	S		Y	Y	Guam	Guam	Guam	Y	Farmer
	12	12	Villagomez, Ignacia C	Sister	F	Cha	28.0	S		Y	Y	Guam	Guam	Guam	Y	None
	12	12	Villagomez, Maria C	Adopted daughter	F	Cha	1.0	S				Guam	Unknown	Guam		None
	12	12	Villagomez, Jose C	Nephew	M	Cha	24.0	S		Y	Y	Guam	Unknown	Guam	Y	Bookkeeper
	12	12	Manibusan, Jose P	Servant	M	Cha	13.0	S	N	N	N	Guam	Guam	Guam	N	Servant
	13	13	Flores, Lorenzo A	Head	M	Cha	48.0	Wd		Y	Y	Guam	Guam	Guam	N	Farmer
	13	13	Flores, Maria R	Daughter	F	Cha	25.0	S		Y	Y	Guam	Guam	Guam	Y	None
	13	13	Flores, Jose R	Son	M	Cha	21.0	S	N	Y	Y	Guam	Guam	Guam	Y	Carpenter
	13	13	Flores, Lorenzo R	Son	M	Cha	18.0	S	N	Y	Y	Guam	Guam	Guam	Y	Enlisted man USN
	13	13	Flores, Dolores R	Daughter	F	Cha	13.0	S	N	Y	Y	Guam	Guam	Guam	Y	None
	13	13	Rivera, Joaquin D	Nephew	M	Cha	23.0	S		N	N	Guam	Unknown	Guam	N	Farm laborer home farm
	13	13	Acosta, Mariano C	Farm laborer	M	Cha	55.0	Wd		N	N	Guam	Guam	Guam	N	Farm laborer
	14	14	Aguon, Juan G	Head	M	Cha	36.0	S		Y	Y	Guam	Guam	Guam	Y	Enlisted man USN
San Juan De Letran Street	14	14	Aguon, Remedios A	Daughter	F	Cha	13.0	S	Y	Y	Y	Guam	Guam	Guam	Y	None
	14	14	Aguon, Adriano A	Son	M	Cha	7.0	S	Y			Guam	Guam	Guam		None
	14	14	Aguon, Tomasa A	Daughter	F	Cha	5.0	S	N			Guam	Guam	Guam		None

15

(CHAMORRO ROOTS GENEALOGY PROJECT ™ TRANSCRIPTION)
(COMPILED/TRANSCRIBED BY BERNARD T. PUNZALAN / HTTP://WWW.CHAMORROROOTS.COM)

FOURTEENTH CENSUS OF THE UNITED STATES: 1920—POPULATION
ISLAND OF GUAM

DISTRICT 1
NAME OF PLACE Agana City

ENUMERATED BY ME ON THE 29th DAY OF March, 1920

Joaquin Torres ENUMERATOR

	Number of dwelling house in order of visitation (2)	Number of family in order of visitation (3)	NAME (4)	RELATION (5)	Sex (6)	Color or race (7)	Age at last birthday (8)	Single, married, widowed or divorced (9)	Attended school any time since Sept. 1, 1919 (10)	Whether able to read (11)	Whether able to write (12)	Place of birth of this person (13)	Place of birth of father of this person (14)	Place of birth of mother of this person (15)	Whether able to speak English (16)	OCCUPATION (17)
26	15	15	Finona, Jose Q	Head	M	Cha	54.0	M		N	N	Guam	Guam	Guam	N	Farmer
27	15	15	Finona, Rita G	Wife	F	Cha	46.0	M		N	N	Guam	Unknown	Guam	N	None
28	15	15	Finona, Manuel G	Son	M	Cha	22.0	S		Y	Y	Guam	Guam	Guam	Y	Farm laborer home
29	15	15	Finona, Jesus G	Son	M	Cha	17.0	S	N	Y	Y	Guam	Guam	Guam	Y	Farm laborer home
30	15	15	Finona, Maria G	Daughter	F	Cha	15.0	S	N	N	N	Guam	Guam	Guam	N	None
31	16	16	Finona, Jose G	Head	M	Cha	24.0	M		Y	Y	Guam	Guam	Guam	Y	Farmer
32	16	16	Finona, Ignacia T	Wife	F	Cha	23.0	M		Y	Y	Guam	Guam	Guam	Y	None
33	16	16	Finona, Vicente T	Son	M	Cha	4.0	S				Guam	Guam	Guam		None
34	16	16	Finona, Eliza T	Daughter	F	Cha	2.0	S				Guam	Guam	Guam		None
35	16	16	Finona, Rosalia T	Daughter	F	Cha	1.0	S				Guam	Guam	Guam		None
36	16	16	Finona, Ana F	Sister	F	Cha	32.0	S		Y	N	Guam	Guam	Guam	N	None
37	17	17	Finona, Francisco G	Head	M	Cha	26.0	M		N	N	Guam	Guam	Guam	N	Farmer
38	17	17	Finona, Antonia T	Wife	F	Cha	24.0	M		N	N	Guam	Guam	Guam	N	None
39	17	17	Finona, Rosario T	Daughter	F	Cha	0.3	S				Guam	Guam	Guam		None
40	18	18	Camacho, Ana O	Head	F	Cha	58.0	Wd		N	N	Guam	Guam	Guam	N	None
41	18	18	Camacho, Carmen O	Daughter	F	Cha	22.0	S		Y	Y	Guam	Guam	Guam	N	Salt maker
42	18	18	Camacho, Maria O	Daughter	F	Cha	21.0	S	N	Y	Y	Guam	Guam	Guam	Y	Laundress
43	18	18	Camacho, Concepcion O	Daughter	F	Cha	18.0	S	N	Y	Y	Guam	Guam	Guam	Y	Laundress
44	18	18	Camacho, Joaquin O	Son	M	Cha	17.0	S	N	Y	Y	Guam	Guam	Guam	Y	Laborer
45	18	18	Camacho, Enrique O	Grand-son	M	Cha	6.0	S				Guam	Unknown	Guam		None
46	18	18	Camacho, Jesus O	Grand-son	M	Cha	4.0	S				Guam	Unknown	Guam		None
47	18	18	Camacho, Antonia O	Grand-daughter	F	Cha	2.0	S				Guam	Unknown	Guam		None
48	18	18	Camacho, Josephine O	Grand-daughter	F	Cha	0.1	S				Guam	Unknown	Guam		None
49	17	19	Pablo, Juan P	Head	M	Cha	59.0	Wd		Y	Y	Guam	Guam	Guam	N	Farmer
50	17	19	Pablo, Manuel C	Son	M	Cha	27.0	S		Y	Y	Guam	Guam	Guam	Y	Carpenter

Street: San Juan De Letran Street

(CHAMORRO ROOTS GENEALOGY PROJECT ™ TRANSCRIPTION)
(COMPILED/TRANSCRIBED BY BERNARD T. PUNZALAN / HTTP://WWW.CHAMORROROOTS.COM)
FOURTEENTH CENSUS OF THE UNITED STATES: 1920—POPULATION
ISLAND OF GUAM

ENUMERATED BY ME ON THE 29th DAY OF March, 1920

Joaquin Torres ENUMERATOR

DISTRICT 1
NAME OF PLACE Agana City

[Proper name and, also, name of class, as city, town, village, barrio, etc]

	PLACE OF ABODE			NAME	RELATION	PERSONAL DESCRIPTION					EDUCATION			NATIVITY					OCCUPATION
Street, avenue, road, etc.	Number of dwelling house in order of visitation	Number of family in order of visitation		of each person whose place of abode on January 1, 1920, was in the family. Enter surname, firs, then given name and middle initial. If any. Include every person living on January 1, 1920. Omit children born since January 1, 1920.	Relationship of this Person to the head of the family.	Sex	Color or race	Age at last birthday	Single, married, widowed or divorced	Attended school any time since Sept. 1, 1919	Whether able to read.	Whether able to write.	Place of birth of this person.	Place of birth of father of this person.	Place of birth of mother of this person.	Whether able to speak English.	Trade, profession, or particular kind of work done, as salesman, laborer, clerk, cook, merchant, washerwoman, etc.
1	2	3		4	5	6	7	8	9	10	11	12	13	14	15	16	17
	18	20	1	Cruz, Joaquin C	Head	M	Cha	42.0	M		Y	Y	Guam	Guam	Guam	N	Farmer
	18	20	2	Cruz, Josefa G	Wife	F	Cha	34.0	M		Y	Y	Guam	Guam	Guam	N	None
	18	20	3	Cruz, Demetrio G	Son	M	Cha	16.0	S	N	Y	Y	Guam	Guam	Guam	Y	Blacksmith
	18	20	4	Cruz, Eliza G	Daughter	F	Cha	14.0	S	N	Y	Y	Guam	Guam	Guam	Y	None
	18	20	5	Cruz, Juan G	Son	M	Cha	12.0	S	Y	Y	N	Guam	Guam	Guam	N	None
San Juan De Letran Street	18	20	6	Cruz, Maria G	Daughter	F	Cha	10.0	S	Y	Y		Guam	Guam	Guam	N	None
	18	20	7	Cruz, Engracia G	Daughter	F	Cha	8.0	S	Y			Guam	Guam	Guam		None
	18	20	8	Cruz, Jesus G	Son	M	Cha	7.0	S	N			Guam	Guam	Guam		None
	18	20	9	Cruz, Ana G	Daughter	F	Cha	5.0	S	N			Guam	Guam	Guam		None
	18	20	10	Cruz, Jose G	Son	M	Cha	3.0	S				Guam	Guam	Guam		None
	18	20	11	Cruz, Isabel G	Daughter	F	Cha	1.0	S				Guam	Guam	Guam		None
	19	21	12	Mateo, Jose C	Head	M	Fil	32.0	S		Y	Y	Guam	Philippine Islands	Guam	N	Farmer
	19	21	13	Mateo, Pedro C	Brother	M	Fil	26.0	S		Y	Y	Guam	Philippine Islands	Guam	Y	Storekeeper
	19	21	14	Mateo, Tomasa C	Sister	F	Fil	23.0	S		Y	Y	Guam	Philippine Islands	Guam	Y	Nurse
	19	21	15	Mateo, Antonio C	Brother	M	Fil	20.0	S	N	Y	Y	Guam	Philippine Islands	Guam	Y	Farm laborer home
	19	22	16	Cruz, Francisco C	Head	M	Cha	21.0	M	N	Y	Y	Guam	Guam	Guam	Y	Enlisted man USN
	19	22	17	Cruz, Maria M	Wife	F	Fil	26.0	M		Y	N	Guam	Philippine Islands	Guam	N	None
	19	22	18	Ogo, Esperanza O	Boarder	F	Cha	7.0	S	Y			Guam	Unknown	Guam		None
	20	23	19	Rivera, Dolores D	Head	F	Cha	63.0	S		N	N	Guam	Unknown	Guam	N	None
	20	23	20	Rivera, Maria D	Daughter	F	Cha	28.0	S	N	Y	N	Guam	Unknown	Guam	N	Laundress
	20	23	21	Rivera, Biatris D	Grand daughter	F	Cha	6.0	S				Guam	Unknown	Guam		None
	20	23	22	Rivera, Maria D	Grand daughter	F	Cha	2.0	S				Guam	Unknown	Guam		None
	21	24	23	Muna, Juan D	Head	M	Cha	44.0	M		Y	Y	Guam	Guam	Guam	N	Farmer
	21	24	24	Muna, Rosa F	Wife	F	Cha	44.0	M		Y	Y	Guam	Guam	Guam	N	None
	21	24	25	Muna, Vicente F	Son	M	Cha	18.0	S	N	Y	Y	Guam	Guam	Guam	Y	Farm laborer home

17

(CHAMORRO ROOTS GENEALOGY PROJECT ™ TRANSCRIPTION)
(COMPILED/TRANSCRIBED BY BERNARD T. PUNZALAN / HTTP://WWW.CHAMORROROOTS.COM)

FOURTEENTH CENSUS OF THE UNITED STATES: 1920–POPULATION
ISLAND OF GUAM

ENUMERATED BY ME ON THE 30th DAY OF March, 1920

Joaquin Torres ENUMERATOR

DISTRICT 1
NAME OF PLACE Agana City

	PLACE OF ABODE		NAME	RELATION	PERSONAL DESCRIPTION				EDUCATION			NATIVITY				OCCUPATION
Street	Dwelling house no.	Family no.	Name	Relationship to head	Sex	Color or race	Age	Single, married, widowed, divorced	Attended school since Sept. 1, 1919	Read	Write	Place of birth of person	Place of birth of father	Place of birth of mother	Whether able to speak English	Trade, profession
1	2	3	4	5	6	7	8	9	10	11	12	13	14	15	16	17
	21	24	Muna, Francisco F	Son	M	Cha	13.0	S	Y	Y	Y	Guam	Guam	Guam	Y	None
	21	24	Muna, Ana F	Daughter	F	Cha	12.0	S	Y	Y	Y	Guam	Guam	Guam	Y	None
	21	24	Muna, Juan F	Son	M	Cha	9.0	S	N			Guam	Guam	Guam	Y	None
	21	24	Muna, Dolores F	Daughter	F	Cha	5.0	S	N			Guam	Guam	Guam		None
	22	25	Suarez, Antonio C	Head	M	W	39.0	M		Y	Y	Guam	Spain	Guam	Y	Commissioner
	22	25	Suarez, Teresa M	Wife	F	Cha	17.0	M	N	Y	Y	Guam	Guam	Guam	Y	None
	22	25	Suarez, Maria G	Daughter	F	Cha	1.0	S				Guam	Guam	Guam		None
	22	25	Taijiron, Gertrudes C	Servant	F	Cha	13.0	S	N	Y	Y	Guam	Guam	Guam	Y	Servant
	22	26	Mendiola, Antonia B	Head	F	Cha	53.0	M		Y	Y	Guam	Guam	Guam	N	Farmer
	22	26	Mendiola, Maria B	Daughter	F	Cha	23.0	S	N	Y	Y	Guam	Guam	Guam	N	None
	22	26	Gogue, Joaquin B	Son	M	Cha	19.0	S	N	Y	Y	Guam	Unknown	Unknown	Y	Farm laborer home
	22	26	Gogue, Magdalena B	Daughter	F	Cha	17.0	S	N	Y	Y	Guam	Unknown	Unknown	Y	None
	22	26	Gogue, Ignacio B	Son	M	Cha	11.0	S	Y	Y	Y	Guam	Unknown	Unknown	Y	None
	22	26	Gogue, Saturnina B	Daughter	F	Cha	3.0	S				Guam	Unknown	Unknown		None
	22	26	Mendiola, Candelaria B	Grand-daughter	F	Cha	1.0	S				Guam	Unknown	Unknown		None
San Juan De Letran Street	23	27	Huertas, Tomas	Head	M	Fil	17.0	S	N	Y	Y	Philippine Islands	Philippine Islands	Philippine Islands	Y	Servant
	24	28	Hong, Lam	Head	M	Chin	53.0	M		Y	N	China	China	China	N	Cook
	25	29	Rosario, Joaquin F	Head	M	Cha	38.0	S	N	Y	Y	Guam	Guam	Guam	Y	None
	26	30	Rojas, Maria R	Head	F	Cha	16.0	S	N	N	N	Guam	Unknown	Guam	Y	Servant
	26	31	Bautista, Aquilino	Head	M	Fil	18.0	S	N	Y	Y	Philippine Islands	Philippine Islands	Philippine Islands	Y	Laborer
	26	32	Austria, Emeterio	Head	M	Fil	18.0	S	N	Y	Y	Philippine Islands	Philippine Islands	Philippine Islands	Y	Laborer
	26	33	Cepeda, Andrea Q	Head	F	Cha	25.0	M		N	N	Guam	Unknown	Unknown	N	Laundress
	26	34	San Nicolas, Paula SN	Head	F	Cha	40.0	S		N	N	Guam	Unknown	Unknown	N	Laundress
	26	35	Vasco, Rita C	Head	F	Fil	26.0	S		Y	N	Guam	Philippine Islands	Guam	N	Laundress
	26	36	Fantas, Antonina A	Head	F	Cha	22.0	M		Y	N	Guam	Guam	Guam	Y	Laundress

18

(CHAMORRO ROOTS GENEALOGY PROJECT ™ TRANSCRIPTION)
(COMPILED/TRANSCRIBED BY BERNARD T. PUNZALAN / HTTP://WWW.CHAMORROROOTS.COM)

FOURTEENTH CENSUS OF THE UNITED STATES: 1920-POPULATION

ISLAND OF GUAM

ENUMERATED BY ME ON THE 30th DAY OF March, 1920

Joaquin Torres ENUMERATOR

DISTRICT **1**

NAME OF PLACE **Agana City**

[Proper name and, also, name of class, name of class, as city, town, village, barrio, etc]

	PLACE OF ABODE				NAME	RELATION	PERSONAL DESCRIPTION				EDUCATION			NATIVITY				OCCUPATION
Street, avenue, road, etc.	Number of dwelling house in order of visitation	Number of family in order of visitation			Name of each person	Relation to head of family	Sex	Color or race	Age at last birthday	Single, married, widowed or divorced	Attended school any time since Sept. 1, 1919	Whether able to read	Whether able to write	Place of birth of this person	Place of birth of father	Place of birth of mother	Whether able to speak English	Occupation
1	2	3		4		5	6	7	8	9	10	11	12	13	14	15	16	17
31st St	26	36		Fantas, Antonio A		Son	M	Fil	7.0	S	Y			Guam	Philippine Islands	Guam		None
	26	36		Fantas, Isabel A		Daughter	F	Fil	4.0	S				Guam	Philippine Islands	Guam		None
	27	37		Cruz, Jesus C		Head	M	Cha	48.0	M		Y	Y	Guam	Guam	Guam	N	Farmer
	27	37		Cruz, Gertrudes T		Wife	F	Cha	35.0	M		Y	N	Guam	Guam	Guam	N	None
	27	37		Cruz, Maria T		Daughter	F	Cha	11.0	S	Y	Y	N	Guam	Guam	Guam	N	None
	27	37		Cruz, Ignacio T		Son	M	Cha	8.0	S	Y	Y		Guam	Guam	Guam		None
	27	37		Cruz, Jesus T		Son	M	Cha	5.0	S	N			Guam	Guam	Guam		None
Isabela la Catolica Street	27	37		Cruz, Atanasio T		Son	M	Cha	3.0	S				Guam	Guam	Guam		None
	27	37		Cruz, Ana T		Daughter	F	Cha	1.0	S				Guam	Guam	Guam		None
	27	37		Torres, Ignacia T		Mother-in-law	F	Cha	78.0	Wd		N	N	Guam	Guam	Guam	N	None
	28	38		Franquez, Jose I		Head	M	Cha	35.0	M		Y	Y	Guam	Guam	Guam	N	Carpenter
	28	38		Franquez, Maria T		Wife	F	Cha	34.0	M		Y	Y	Guam	Guam	Guam	Y	None
	28	38		Franquez, Jesus T		Son	M	Cha	12.0	S	Y	Y	Y	Guam	Guam	Guam	N	None
	28	38		Franquez, Maria T		Daughter	F	Cha	9.0	S	Y			Guam	Guam	Guam	Y	None
	28	38		Franquez, Pedro T		Son	M	Cha	7.0	S	Y			Guam	Guam	Guam		None
	28	38		Franquez, Ana T		Daughter	F	Cha	5.0	S	N			Guam	Guam	Guam		None
	28	38		Franquez, Jose T		Son	M	Cha	4.0	S				Guam	Guam	Guam		None
	28	38		Franquez, Manuel T		Son	M	Cha	2.0	S				Guam	Guam	Guam		None
	28	38		Acosta, Jose C		Farm laborer	M	Cha	58.0	S		N	N	Guam	Guam	Guam	Y	Farm laborer
	29	39		Castro, Vicenta S		Head	F	Cha	47.0	S		N	N	Guam	Guam	Guam	N	None
	29	39		Castro, Juan S		Son	M	Cha	24.0	S		Y	Y	Guam	Unknown	Guam	Y	Servant
	29	39		Castro, Maria S		Daughter	F	Cha	21.0	S	N	Y	Y	Guam	Unknown	Guam	N	Laundress
	29	39		Castro, Ramon S		Son	M	Cha	18.0	S	N	Y	Y	Guam	Unknown	Guam	Y	Laborer
	29	39		Castro, Josefa S		Daughter	F	Cha	15.0	S	N	Y	Y	Guam	Unknown	Guam	N	None
	30	40		Borja, Ignacia R		Head	F	Cha	50.0	S		Y	Y	Guam	Guam	Guam	N	None

(CHAMORRO ROOTS GENEALOGY PROJECT ™ TRANSCRIPTION)
(COMPILED/TRANSCRIBED BY BERNARD T. PUNZALAN / HTTP://WWW.CHAMORROROOTS.COM)

FOURTEENTH CENSUS OF THE UNITED STATES: 1920-POPULATION

ISLAND OF GUAM

ENUMERATED BY ME ON THE 31st DAY OF March, 1920

Joaquin Torres ENUMERATOR

DISTRICT 1

NAME OF PLACE Agana City

[Proper name and, also, name of class, as city, town, village, barrio, etc]

	Dwelling	Family	NAME	RELATION	Sex	Color or race	Age	Single, married, widowed or divorced	Attended school since Sept. 1, 1919	Read	Write	Birthplace of person	Birthplace of father	Birthplace of mother	Speak English	OCCUPATION
26	30	40	Borja, Jose B	Son	M	Cha	22.0	S		Y	Y	Guam	Unknown	Guam	Y	None
27	30	40	Borja, Maria B	Daughter	F	Cha	19.0	S	N	Y	Y	Guam	Unknown	Guam	Y	Laundress
28	30	40	Borja, Pedro B	Son	M	Cha	15.0	S	N	Y	N	Guam	Unknown	Guam	N	Farm laborer home
29	30	40	Borja, Jesus B	Nephew	M	Cha	19.0	S	N	Y	Y	Guam	Unknown	Guam	Y	Laborer
30	31	41	San Miguel, Jose M	Head	M	Fil	48.0	M		Y	Y	Guam	Philippine Islands	Guam	N	Farmer
31	31	41	San Miguel, Vicenta R	Wife	F	Cha	46.0	M		Y	Y	Guam	Guam	Guam	N	None
32	31	41	Peredo, Jesus B	Lodger	M	Cha	22.0	S		Y	Y	Guam	Guam	Guam	Y	Laborer
33	31	41	Chargualaf, Rosa SN	Lodger	F	Cha	49.0	Wd		N	N	Guam	Guam	Guam	N	Weaver
34	31	41	Chargualaf, Dolores SN	Lodger	F	Cha	17.0	S	N	Y	Y	Guam	Guam	Guam	Y	None
35	31	41	Chargualaf, Manuel SN	Lodger	M	Cha	15.0	S	N	Y	Y	Guam	Guam	Guam	Y	Laborer
36	31	42	Borja, Maria B	Head	F	Cha	37.0	S		Y	Y	Guam	Unknown	Guam	N	Laundress
37	31	42	Borja, Manuel B	Son	M	Cha	16.0	S	N	Y	Y	Guam	Unknown	Guam	Y	Farm laborer home
38	31	42	Borja, Francisco B	Son	M	Cha	14.0	S	N	Y	Y	Guam	Unknown	Guam	Y	Servant
39	31	42	Borja, Antonio B	Son	M	Cha	12.0	S	Y	Y	Y	Guam	Unknown	Guam	Y	None
40	31	42	Borja, Jose B	Son	M	Cha	8.0	S	Y			Guam	Unknown	Guam		None
41	31	42	Borja, Juan B	Son	M	Cha	2.0	S				Guam	Unknown	Guam		None
42	31	42	Borja, Maria B	Daughter	F	Cha	1.0	S				Guam	Unknown	Guam		None
43	32	43	Un-Pingco, Maria U	Head	F	Cha	32.0	M		Y	Y	Guam	Unknown	Guam	N	Tailoress
44	32	43	Rivera, Asuncion U	Daughter	F	Cha	6.0	S	N			Guam	Guam	Guam		None
45	32	43	Rivera, Francisco U	Son	M	Cha	1.0	S				Guam	Guam	Guam		None
46	32	43	Rivera, Vicente U	Son	M	Cha	0.3	S				Guam	Guam	Guam		None
47	33	44	Leon Guerrero, Juan S	Head	M	Cha	26.0	M		Y	Y	Guam	Guam	Guam	Y	Farmer
48	33	44	Leon Guerrero, Concepcion B	Wife	F	Cha	24.0	M		Y	N	Guam	Guam	Guam	N	None
49	33	44	Leon Guerrero, Maria B	Daughter	F	Cha	4.0	S				Guam	Guam	Guam		None
50	33	45	Borja, Susana Q	Head	F	Cha	48.0	Wd		Y	N	Guam	Guam	Guam	N	Laundress

Street: Isabela la Catolica Street

20

(CHAMORRO ROOTS GENEALOGY PROJECT ™ TRANSCRIPTION)
(COMPILED/TRANSCRIBED BY BERNARD T. PUNZALAN / HTTP://WWW.CHAMORROROOTS.COM)

FOURTEENTH CENSUS OF THE UNITED STATES: 1920-POPULATION
ISLAND OF GUAM

DISTRICT 1
NAME OF PLACE Agana City

ENUMERATED BY ME ON THE 31st DAY OF March, 1920

Joaquin Torres ENUMERATOR

1	2	3	4 NAME	5 RELATION	6 Sex	7 Color or race	8 Age at last birthday	9 Single, married, widowed or divorced	10 Attended school since Sept. 1, 1919	11 Whether able to read	12 Whether able to write	13	14	15	16 Whether able to speak English	17 OCCUPATION
	33	45	Borja, Antonio Q	Son	M	Cha	22.0	S		Y	Y	Guam	Guam	Guam	N	Farm laborer home farm
	33	45	Borja, Ana Q	Daughter	F	Cha	20.0	S	N	N	N	Guam	Guam	Guam	N	Laundress
Isabela la Catolica Street	33	45	Borja, Ignacio Q	Son	M	Cha	15.0	S	N	Y	Y	Guam	Guam	Guam	Y	Farm laborer home farm
	33	45	Borja, Felicidad Q	Daughter	F	Cha	13.0	S	N	Y	Y	Guam	Guam	Guam	N	None
	33	45	Borja, Crecensia Q	Daughter	F	Cha	9.0	S	N			Guam	Guam	Guam		None
	33	45	Borja, Ejinio Q	Grand-son	M	Cha	0.9	S				Guam	Unkown			None
	34	46	San Nicolas, Vicente LG	Head	M	Cha	62.0	M		N	N	Guam	Guam	Guam	N	None
	34	46	San Nicolas, Martina C	Wife	F	Cha	60.0	M		N	N	Guam	Guam	Guam	N	None
	34	46	San Nicolas, Dolores C	Daughter	F	Cha	31.0	S		Y	Y	Guam	Guam	Guam	N	None
	35	47	Garrido, Ignacio L	Head	M	Cha	49.0	M		Y	Y	Guam	Guam	Guam	N	Farmer
	35	47	Garrido, Magdalena P	Wife	F	Cha	53.0	M		Y	Y	Guam	Guam	Guam	N	None
	35	47	Garrido, Rita P	Daughter	F	Cha	22.0	S		Y	Y	Guam	Guam	Guam	Y	Nurse
	35	47	Garrido, Elena P	Daughter	F	Cha	16.0	S		Y	Y	Guam	Guam	Guam	Y	None
	35	47	Garrido, Vicente P	Son	M	Cha	12.0	S	Y	Y	Y	Guam	Guam	Guam	Y	Laborer
	36	48	Garrido, Jose P	Head	M	Cha	23.0	M		Y	Y	Guam	Guam	Guam	Y	Laborer
	36	48	Garrido, Agueda A	Wife	F	Cha	20.0	M	N	N	N	Guam	Guam	Guam	N	None
	36	48	Garrido, Lotirde A	Daughter	F	Cha	2.0	S				Guam	Guam	Guam		None
	36	48	Garrido, Magdalena A	Daughter	F	Cha	0.8	S				Guam	Guam	Guam		None
	37	49	Flores, Carmen S	Head	F	Cha	33.0	Wd		Y	Y	Guam	Guam	Guam	N	Laundress
	37	49	Flores, Mariano S	Son	M	Cha	10.0	S	Y	Y	Y	Guam	Guam	Guam	N	None
	37	49	Flores, Jose S	Son	M	Cha	9.0	S	Y			Guam	Guam	Guam		None
	38	50	Blanco, Felipe P	Head	M	Cha	28.0	M		Y	Y	Guam	Guam	Guam	Y	Enlisted man USN
	38	50	Blanco, Joaquina F	Wife	F	Cha	27.0	M		Y	Y	Guam	Guam	Guam	Y	None
	38	50	Blanco, Consolacion F	Daughter	F	Cha	4.0	S				Guam	Guam	Guam		None
	38	50	Blanco, Delfina F	Daughter	F	Cha	2.0	S				Guam	Guam	Guam		None

(CHAMORRO ROOTS GENEALOGY PROJECT ™ TRANSCRIPTION)
(COMPILED/TRANSCRIBED BY BERNARD T. PUNZALAN / HTTP://WWW.CHAMORROROOTS.COM)
FOURTEENTH CENSUS OF THE UNITED STATES: 1920–POPULATION
ISLAND OF GUAM

DISTRICT 1
NAME OF PLACE Agana City

ENUMERATED BY ME ON THE 1st DAY OF April, 1920

Joaquin Torres ENUMERATOR

#	Street	Dwelling	Family	NAME	RELATION	Sex	Color or race	Age	Single, married, widowed or divorced	Attended school since Sept. 1, 1919	Able to read	Able to write	Place of birth of this person	Place of birth of father	Place of birth of mother	Able to speak English	OCCUPATION
		1	2	3	4	5	6	7	8	9	10	11	12	13	14	15	16	17
26		39	51	Rosario, Juan F	Head	M	Cha	68.0	M		Y	Y	Guam	Guam	Guam	N	None
27		39	51	Rosario, Luisa LG	Wife	F	Cha	54.0	M		Y	Y	Guam	Guam	Guam	N	None
28		39	51	Rosario, Ana LG	Daughter	F	Cha	37.0	S		Y	Y	Guam	Guam	Guam	N	None
29		39	51	Rosario, Vicente LG	Son	M	Cha	35.0	S		Y	Y	Guam	Guam	Guam	N	Farm laborer home
30		39	51	Rosario, Concepcion LG	Daughter	F	Cha	24.0	S		Y	Y	Guam	Guam	Guam	Y	None
31		39	51	Rosario, Francisca LG	Daughter	F	Cha	20.0	S	N	Y	Y	Guam	Guam	Guam	Y	None
32		40	52	Flores, Jose A	Head	M	Cha	53.0	M		Y	Y	Guam	Guam	Guam	N	Farmer
33		40	52	Flores, Ana C	Wife	F	Cha	50.0	M		Y	Y	Guam	Guam	Guam	N	None
34	Isabela la Catolica Street	40	52	Flores, Jose C	Son	M	Cha	16.0	S	N	Y	Y	Guam	Guam	Guam	Y	Farm laborer home
35		40	52	Flores, Ana C	Daughter	F	Cha	13.0	S	N	Y	Y	Guam	Guam	Guam	Y	None
36		40	52	Flores, Jesus C	Son	M	Cha	12.0	S	Y	Y	Y	Guam	Guam	Guam	Y	None
37		40	52	Flores, Magdalena B C	Daughter	F	Cha	7.0	S	Y	Y	Y	Guam	Guam	Guam	Y	None
38		40	52	Castro, Maria F	Daughter	F	Cha	18.0	M	N	Y	Y	Guam	Guam	Guam	Y	None
39		41	53	Borja, Maria F	Head	F	Cha	39.0	S		Y	N	Guam	Guam	Guam	N	None
40		42	54	Naputi, Elerio F	Head	M	Cha	21.0	S	N	Y	Y	Guam	Guam	Guam	Y	Shoemaker
41		42	54	Naputi, Joaquin F	Brother	M	Cha	18.0	S	N	Y	Y	Guam	Guam	Guam	Y	Shoemaker
42		43	55	Torres, Jose A	Head	M	Cha	32.0	M		Y	Y	Guam	Guam	Guam	Y	Enlisted man USN
43		43	55	Torres, Rosa F	Wife	F	Cha	30.0	M		Y	Y	Guam	Guam	Guam	N	None
44		43	55	Torres, Antonio F	Boarder	M	Cha	11.0	S	Y	Y	Y	Guam	Unknown	Unknown	N	None
45		43	55	Torres, Amanda F	Boarder	F	Cha	7.0	S	Y	Y	Y	Guam	Unknown	Unknown	N	None
46		43	55	Bargas, Maria U	Boarder	F	Cha	89.0	Wd		Y	Y	Guam	Guam	Guam	N	None
47		43	55	Flores, Francisca G	Boarder	F	Cha	3.0	S				Guam	Unknown	Guam		None
48		43	55	Flores, Rosa G	Cook	F	Cha	36.0	S		Y	N	Guam	Guam	Guam	N	Cook
49		44	56	Camacho, Rosa C	Head	F	Cha	65.0	Wd		Y	N	Rota	Guam	Guam	N	None
50		44	56	Camacho, Luis C	Son	M	Cha	17.0	S	N	Y	Y	Guam	Guam	Guam	Y	Blacksmith

22

(CHAMORRO ROOTS GENEALOGY PROJECT ™ TRANSCRIPTION)
(COMPILED/TRANSCRIBED BY BERNARD T. PUNZALAN / HTTP://WWW.CHAMORROROOTS.COM)
FOURTEENTH CENSUS OF THE UNITED STATES: 1920—POPULATION
ISLAND OF GUAM

DISTRICT 1
NAME OF PLACE Agana City
[Proper name and, also, name of class, as city, town, village, barrio, etc]

ENUMERATED BY ME ON THE 1st DAY OF April, 1920

Joaquin Torres ENUMERATOR

#	Street, avenue, road, etc.	No. dwelling	No. family	NAME	RELATION	Sex	Color or race	Age at last birthday	Single, married, widowed or divorced	Attended school since Sept. 1, 1919	Able to read	Able to write	Place of birth of this person	Place of birth of father	Place of birth of mother	Able to speak English	OCCUPATION
		2	3	4	5	6	7	8	9	10	11	12	13	14	15	16	17
1		45	57	Perez, Atanacio T	Head	M	Cha	45.0	M		Y	Y	China	Guam	Guam	Y	Chief Clerk to GMG
2		45	57	Perez, Carmen D	Wife	F	Cha	47.0	M		Y	Y	Guam	Guam	Guam	N	None
3		45	57	Perez, Maria T	Daughter	F	Cha	18.0	S	N	Y	Y	Guam	China	Guam	Y	Teacher
4		45	57	Perez, Isabel T	Daughter	F	Cha	16.0	S	N	Y	Y	Guam	China	Guam	Y	Teacher
5		45	57	Perez, Eliza T	Daughter	F	Cha	14.0	S	N	Y	Y	Guam	China	Guam	Y	None
6		45	57	Perez, Biatris T	Daughter	F	Cha	12.0	S	Y	Y	Y	Guam	China	Guam	Y	None
7		45	57	Perez, Ursula T	Daughter	F	Cha	11.0	S	Y	Y	Y	Guam	China	Guam		None
8		45	57	Perez, Brigida T	Daughter	F	Cha	8.0	S	Y			Guam	China	Guam		None
9	Isabela la Catolica Street	45	57	Perez, Francisco T	Son	M	Cha	6.0	S	N			Guam	China	Guam		None
10		46	58	Ada, Regino M	Head	M	Cha	39.0	M		Y	Y	Guam	Guam	Guam	N	Blacksmith
11		46	58	Ada, Rita C	Wife	F	Cha	28.0	M		Y	Y	Guam	Guam	Guam	Y	Tailoress
12		46	58	Ada, Antonio C	Son	M	Cha	5.0	S	N			Guam	Guam	Guam		None
13		46	58	Ada, Jose C	Son	M	Cha	2.0	S				Guam	Guam	Guam		None
14		46	58	Ada, Ana C	Daughter	F	Cha	0.1	S				Guam	Guam	Guam		None
15		47	59	Flores, Manuel T	Head	M	Cha	59.0	Wd		Y	Y	Guam	Guam	Guam		None
16		47	59	Flores, Maria M	Daughter	F	Cha	22.0	S		Y	Y	Guam	Guam	Guam	N	None
17		47	59	Flores, Juan M	Son	M	Cha	19.0	S	N	Y	Y	Guam	Guam	Guam	Y	Farm laborer home
18		47	59	Flores, Francisco M	Son	M	Cha	14.0	S	N	Y	Y	Guam	Guam	Guam	Y	Farm laborer home
19		47	59	Flores, Jose M	Son	M	Cha	10.0	S	Y	Y	Y	Guam	Guam	Guam	N	None
20		47	59	Flores, Rita M	Daughter	F	Cha	9.0	S	Y	Y	Y	Guam	Guam	Guam		None
21		47	59	Flores, Jesus M	Son	M	Cha	7.0	S	Y			Guam	Guam	Guam		None
22		47	59	Flores, Manuel M	Son	M	Cha	5.0	S	N			Guam	Guam	Guam		None
23		48	60	Torres, Luis E	Head	M	Cha	44.0	M		Y	Y	Guam	Guam	Guam	N	Farmer
24		48	60	Torres, Consolacion N	Wife	F	Cha	38.0	S		N	N	Guam	Unknown	Guam		None
25		48	60	Torres, Jesus N	Son	M	Cha	19.0	S	N	Y	Y	Guam	Guam	Guam	Y	Farm laborer home

(CHAMORRO ROOTS GENEALOGY PROJECT ™ TRANSCRIPTION)
(COMPILED/TRANSCRIBED BY BERNARD T. PUNZALAN / HTTP://WWW.CHAMORROROOTS.COM)

FOURTEENTH CENSUS OF THE UNITED STATES: 1920—POPULATION

ISLAND OF GUAM

ENUMERATED BY ME ON THE 1st DAY OF April, 1920

Joaquin Torres ENUMERATOR

DISTRICT 1

NAME OF PLACE Agana City

[Proper name and, also, name of class, as city, town, village, barrio, etc]

	Dwelling	Family	NAME	RELATION	Sex	Color or race	Age	Single/married/widowed/divorced	Attended school since Sept. 1, 1919	Able to read	Able to write	Birthplace of person	Birthplace of father	Birthplace of mother	Able to speak English	OCCUPATION
26	48	60	Torres, Maria N	Daughter	F	Cha	17.0	S	N	Y	Y	Guam	Guam	Guam	Y	None
27	48	60	Torres, Jose N	Son	M	Cha	16.0	S	N	Y	Y	Guam	Guam	Guam	Y	Farm laborer hom
28	48	60	Torres, Ana N	Daughter	F	Cha	14.0	S	N	Y	Y	Guam	Guam	Guam	Y	None
29	48	60	Torres, Joaquin N	Son	M	Cha	12.0	S	Y	Y	Y	Guam	Guam	Guam	Y	None
30	48	60	Torres, Remedios N	Daughter	F	Cha	11.0	S	Y	Y	Y	Guam	Guam	Guam	Y	None
31	48	60	Torres, Tomas N	Son	M	Cha	9.0	S	Y			Guam	Guam	Guam		None
32	48	60	Torres, Luis N	Son	M	Cha	3.0	S				Guam	Guam	Guam		None
33	49	61	Mendiola, Benigno C	Head	M	Cha	47.0	M		Y	Y	Guam	Guam	Guam	N	Farmer
34	49	61	Mendiola, Consolacion F	Wife	F	Cha	45.0	M		Y	Y	Guam	Guam	Guam	N	None
35	49	61	Mendiola, Vicente F	Son	M	Cha	16.0	S	N	Y	Y	Guam	Guam	Guam	Y	Messenger
36	49	61	Mendiola, Jose F	Son	M	Cha	15.0	S	N	Y	Y	Guam	Guam	Guam	Y	Servant
37	49	61	Mendiola, Maria F	Daughter	F	Cha	11.0	S	Y	Y	Y	Guam	Guam	Guam	Y	None
38	49	61	Mendiola, Rosa F	Daughter	F	Cha	5.0	S	N			Guam	Guam	Guam		None
39	49	61	Franquez, Josefa L	Sister-in-law	F	Cha	66.0	S		Y	Y	Guam	Unknown	Unknown		None
40	50	62	Rosario, Maria S	Head	F	Cha	32.0	S		Y	Y	Guam	Unknown	Guam	Y	Tailoress
41	50	62	Rosario, Carmen S	Sister	F	Cha	28.0	S		Y	Y	Guam	Guam	Guam	N	None
42	50	62	Rivera, Isabel R	Niece	F	Cha	14.0	S	N	Y	Y	Guam	Guam	Guam	Y	None
43	50	62	Rivera, Jesus R	Nephew	M	Cha	12.0	S	Y	Y	Y	Guam	Guam	Guam	Y	None
44	50	62	Rivera, Gregorio R	Nephew	M	Cha	4.0	S				Guam	Guam	Guam		None
45	51	63	Aflague, Vicente T	Head	M	Cha	22.0	M		Y	Y	Guam	Guam	Guam	Y	Silversmith
46	51	63	Aflague, Ana C	Wife	F	W	24.0	M		Y	Y	Rota	Philippine Islands	Guam	Y	None
47	52	64	Franquez, Pedro I	Head	M	Cha	32.0	M		Y	Y	Guam	Guam	Guam	Y	Plumber
48	52	64	Franquez, Ana C	Wife	F	Cha	28.0	M		Y	Y	Guam	Guam	Guam	N	None
49	52	64	Franquez, Pedro C	Son	M	Cha	9.0	S	Y	Y	Y	Guam	Guam	Guam	Y	None
50	52	64	Franquez, Rita C	Daughter	F	Cha	6.0	S	N			Guam	Guam	Guam	N	None

Street, avenue, road, etc.: Isabela la Catolica Street

(CHAMORRO ROOTS GENEALOGY PROJECT ™ TRANSCRIPTION)
(COMPILED/TRANSCRIBED BY BERNARD T. PUNZALAN / HTTP://WWW.CHAMORROROOTS.COM)

7

SHEET NO. 38A

FOURTEENTH CENSUS OF THE UNITED STATES: 1920—POPULATION
ISLAND OF GUAM

DISTRICT **1**
NAME OF PLACE **Agana City**

ENUMERATED BY ME ON THE 2nd DAY OF April, 1920

Joaquin Torres ENUMERATOR

1 Street	2 Dwelling	3 Family	4 NAME	5 RELATION	6 Sex	7 Color/race	8 Age	9 Marital	10 School since Sept 1, 1919	11 Read	12 Write	13 Birth of person	14 Birth of father	15 Birth of mother	16 Speak English	17 OCCUPATION
	52	64	Franquez, Maria C	Daughter	F	Cha	4.0	S				Guam	Guam	Guam		None
	52	64	Franquez, Isabel C	Daughter	F	Cha	1.0	S				Guam	Guam	Guam		None
	52	64	Franquez, Jesus I	Brother	M	Cha	22.0	S		Y	Y	Guam	Guam	Guam	Y	Enlisted man USN
	52	64	Franquez, Joaquin I	Brother	M	Cha	21.0	S	N	Y	Y	Guam	Guam	Guam	Y	Clerk
	52	64	Franquez, Ana I	Sister	F	Cha	18.0	S	N	Y	Y	Guam	Guam	Guam	Y	None
	52	64	Franquez, Remedios I	Sister	F	Cha	17.0	S	N	Y	Y	Guam	Guam	Guam	Y	None
	52	64	Ada, Pedro T	Farm laborer	M	Cha	26.0	S	N	Y	Y	Guam	Guam	Guam	Y	Farm laborer
	52	64	Susuico, Maria S	Servant	F	Cha	13.0	S	N	N	N	Guam	Unknown	Guam	N	Servant
Isabela la Catolica Street	53	65	Duenas, Dometila A	Head	F	Fil	63.0	Wd		Y	Y	Guam	Philippine Islands	Guam	N	None
	53	65	Duenas, Maria A	Daughter	F	Cha	45.0	S		Y	Y	Guam	Guam	Guam	N	None
	53	65	Arriola, Francisco D	Grand-son	M	Cha	19.0	S	N	Y	Y	Guam	Unknown	Guam	Y	Enlisted man USN
	53	65	Duenas, Maria A	Grand-daughter	F	Cha	7.0	S	Y			Guam	Unknown	Guam		None
	54	66	Duenas, Gregorio A	Head	M	Cha	26.0	M		Y	Y	Guam	Guam	Guam	Y	Silversmith
	54	66	Duenas, Manuela F	Wife	F	Cha	26.0	M		Y	Y	Guam	Guam	Guam	Y	None
	54	66	Duenas, Enrique F	Son	M	Cha	3.0	S				Guam	Guam	Guam		None
	54	66	Duenas, Joaquin F	Son	M	Cha	1.0	S				Guam	Guam	Guam		None
	54	66	Duenas, Antonio F	Son	M	Cha	0.0	S				Guam	Guam	Guam		None
	55	67	Duenas, Vicente A	Head	M	Cha	31.0	M		Y	Y	Guam	Guam	Guam	N	Farmer
	55	67	Duenas, Ana B	Wife	F	Cha	27.0	M		Y	Y	Guam	Unknown	Guam	N	None
	55	67	Duenas, Juan B	Son	M	Cha	8.0	S	Y			Guam	Guam	Guam		None
	55	67	Duenas, Joaquin B	Son	M	Cha	6.0	S	N			Guam	Guam	Guam		None
	55	67	Duenas, Catalina B	Daughter	F	Cha	2.0	S				Guam	Guam	Guam		None
	56	68	Peredo, Antonio S	Head	M	Cha	43.0	M		Y	Y	Guam	Guam	Guam	Y	Oiler
	56	68	Peredo, Ramona LG	Wife	F	Cha	33.0	M		Y	Y	Guam	Guam	Guam	N	None
	56	68	Peredo, Juan LG	Son	M	Cha	9.0	S	Y	Y	Y	Guam	Guam	Guam	Y	None

25

(CHAMORRO ROOTS GENEALOGY PROJECT ™ TRANSCRIPTION)
(COMPILED/TRANSCRIBED BY BERNARD T. PUNZALAN / HTTP://WWW.CHAMORROROOTS.COM)

FOURTEENTH CENSUS OF THE UNITED STATES: 1920-POPULATION
ISLAND OF GUAM

ENUMERATED BY ME ON THE 2nd DAY OF April, 1920

Joaquin Torres ENUMERATOR

DISTRICT 1
NAME OF PLACE Agana City

[Proper name and, also, name of class, as city, town, village, barrio, etc]

	Street, avenue, road, etc.	No. of dwelling house	No. of family	NAME	RELATION	Sex	Color or race	Age at last birthday	Single, married, widowed or divorced	Attended school since Sept. 1, 1919	Able to read	Able to write	Birthplace of person	Birthplace of father	Birthplace of mother	Able to speak English	OCCUPATION
1		2	3	4	5	6	7	8	9	10	11	12	13	14	15	16	17
26	Isabela la Catolica Street	56	68	Peredo, Concepcion LG	Daughter	F	Cha	7.0	S	N			Guam	Guam	Guam		None
27		56	68	Peredo, Joaquin LG	Son	M	Cha	4.0	S				Guam	Guam	Guam		None
28		56	69	Leon Guerrero, Ramon B	Head	M	Cha	71.0	Wd		Y	Y	Guam	Guam	Guam	N	Farmer
29		56	69	Leon Guerrero, Dolores A	Daughter	F	Cha	17.0	S	N	Y	Y	Guam	Guam	Guam	Y	None
30		56	69	Leon Guerrero, Rufina A	Daughter	F	Cha	14.0	S	N	Y	Y	Guam	Guam	Guam	Y	None
31		57	70	Siguenza, Dolores S	Head	F	Cha	57.0	S		Y	Y	Guam	Guam	Guam	N	None
32		57	70	Siguenza, Maria S	Daughter	F	Cha	24.0	S		Y	Y	Guam	Guam	Guam	Y	Cook
33		57	70	Siguenza, Jesus S	Son	M	Cha	18.0	S	N	Y	Y	Guam	Unknown	Unknown	Y	Enlisted man USN
34		57	70	Siguenza, Joaquin S	Grand-son	M	Cha	4.0	S				Guam	Unknown	Unknown		None
35		57	71	Siguenza, Maria C	Head	F	Cha	28.0	S		Y	Y	Guam	Guam	Guam	Y	Cook
36		57	71	Siguenza, Francisco C	Son	M	Cha	3.0	S				Guam	Unknown	Guam		None
37		58	72	Herrero, Francisco LG	Head	M	Cha	26.0	M		Y	Y	Guam	Guam	Guam	Y	Chauffeur
38		58	72	Herrero, Josefa SN	Wife	F	Cha	23.0	M		Y	Y	Guam	Guam	Guam	N	None
39		58	72	Herrero, Soledad SN	Daughter	F	Cha	3.0	S				Guam	Guam	Guam		None
40		58	72	Herrero, Jose SN	Son	M	Cha	1.0	S				Guam	Guam	Guam		None
41		58	73	San Nicolas, Joaquin P	Head	M	Cha	58.0	M		Y	Y	Guam	Guam	Guam	N	Farmer
42		58	73	San Nicolas, Felicitas L	Wife	F	Cha	56.0	M		N	N	Guam	Guam	Guam	N	None
43		59	74	Cepeda, Rita C	Head	F	Cha	67.0	S		Y	Y	Guam	Guam	Guam	N	None
44		59	74	Cepeda, Ana C	Daughter	F	Cha	47.0	S		Y	Y	Guam	Unknown	Unknown	N	Tailoress
45		60	75	Rosario, Francisco F	Head	M	Cha	65.0	Wd		Y	Y	Guam	Guam	Guam	N	None
46		61	76	Leon Guerrero, Carmen S	Head	F	Cha	53.0	Wd		Y	Y	Guam	Unknown	Guam	N	None
47		61	76	Leon Guerrero, Rosa S	Daughter	F	Cha	17.0	S	N	Y	Y	Guam	Guam	Guam	N	Laundress
48		61	76	Leon Guerrero, Angelina S	Daughter	F	Cha	15.0	S	N	N	N	Guam	Guam	Guam	Y	None
49		62	77	Atoigue, Jose R	Head	M	Cha	39.0	M		N	Y	Guam	Guam	Guam	N	Laborer
50		62	77	Atoigue, Rita T	Wife	F	Cha	39.0	M		Y	Y	Guam	Guam	Guam	N	None

26

(CHAMORRO ROOTS GENEALOGY PROJECT ™ TRANSCRIPTION)
(COMPILED/TRANSCRIBED BY BERNARD T. PUNZALAN / HTTP://WWW.CHAMORROROOTS.COM)

FOURTEENTH CENSUS OF THE UNITED STATES: 1920—POPULATION
ISLAND OF GUAM

DISTRICT 1
NAME OF PLACE **Agana City**

ENUMERATED BY ME ON THE 3rd DAY OF April, 1920

Joaquin Torres ENUMERATOR

Street	Dwelling	Family	NAME	RELATION	Sex	Color or race	Age	S/M/W/D	Attended school	Read	Write	Birthplace of person	Birthplace of father	Birthplace of mother	Speak English	OCCUPATION
	62	77	Atoigue, Francisco T	Son	M	Cha	18.0	S	N	Y	Y	Guam	Guam	Guam	Y	Farm laborer home
	62	77	Atoigue, Asuncion T	Daughter	F	Cha	14.0	S	N	Y	Y	Guam	Guam	Guam	N	None
Isabela la Catolica Street	62	77	Atoigue, Antonio T	Son	M	Cha	9.0	S	Y			Guam	Guam	Guam		None
	62	77	Atoigue, Joaquina T	Daughter	F	Cha	7.0	S	Y			Guam	Guam	Guam		None
	62	77	Atoigue, Antonia T	Daughter	F	Cha	5.0	S	N			Guam	Guam	Guam		None
	62	77	Atoigue, Teresa T	Daughter	F	Cha	1.0	S				Guam	Guam	Guam		None
	63	78	Fejarang, Josefa G	Head	F	Cha	50.0	S		N	N	Guam	Guam	Guam	N	Laundress
	63	78	Fejarang, Catalina G	Daughter	F	Cha	23.0	S		Y	Y	Guam	Unknown	Guam	N	Laundress
	63	78	Fejarang, Maria G	Grand-daughter	F	Cha	2.0	S				Guam	Unknown	Guam		None
	63	78	Fejarang, Pedro G	Grand-son	M	Cha	0.3	S				Guam	Unknown	Guam		None
	64	79	Cruz, Jose	Head	M	Cha	27.0	M		Y	Y	Guam	Guam	Guam	Y	Enlisted man USN
	64	79	Cruz, Maria A	Wife	F	Cha	24.0	M		Y	Y	Guam	Guam	Guam	Y	None
	64	79	Cruz, Maria A	Daughter	F	Cha	0.1	S				Guam	Guam	Guam		None
	64	79	Cruz, Josefa Q	Sister	F	Cha	16.0	S	N	Y	Y	Guam	Guam	Guam		None
	65	80	Aguigui, Santos A	Head	M	Cha	28.0	S		Y	Y	Guam	Unknown	Guam	N	Laborer
	65	80	Acfalle, Jose A	Brother	M	Cha	16.0	S	N	Y	N	Guam	Guam	Guam	N	Laborer
	66	81	Salas, Jose C	Head	M	Cha	36.0	M		Y	Y	Guam	Guam	Guam	N	Farmer
	66	81	Salas, Manuela SN	Wife	F	Cha	37.0	M		Y	N	Guam	Guam	Guam	N	None
Calle Magallanes	66	81	Salas, Mariano SN	Son	M	Cha	18.0	S	N	Y	Y	Guam	Guam	Guam	Y	Farm laborer home
	66	81	Salas, Jose SN	Son	M	Cha	16.0	S	N	Y	N	Guam	Guam	Guam	Y	Farm laborer home
	66	81	Salas, Antonio SN	Son	M	Cha	10.0	S	Y	Y	Y	Guam	Guam	Guam	Y	None
	66	81	Salas, Bartola SN	Daughter	F	Cha	8.0	S	Y	Y	Y	Guam	Guam	Guam		None
	66	81	Salas, Jesus SN	Son	M	Cha	4.0	S				Guam	Guam	Guam		None
	66	81	Salas, Teresa SN	Daughter	F	Cha	2.0	S				Guam	Guam	Guam		None
	66	81	Salas, Ana SN	Daughter	F	Cha	0.8	S				Guam	Guam	Guam		None

(CHAMORRO ROOTS GENEALOGY PROJECT ™ TRANSCRIPTION)
(COMPILED/TRANSCRIBED BY BERNARD T. PUNZALAN / HTTP://WWW.CHAMORROROOTS.COM)

FOURTEENTH CENSUS OF THE UNITED STATES: 1920—POPULATION

ISLAND OF GUAM

DISTRICT 1
NAME OF PLACE Agana City

[Proper name and, also, name of class, as city, town, village, barrio, etc]

ENUMERATED BY ME ON THE 3rd DAY OF April, 1920

Joaquin Torres ENUMERATOR

	Street	Dwelling No.	Family No.	NAME	RELATION	Sex	Color/race	Age	Marital	Attended school	Read	Write	Place of birth	Father birthplace	Mother birthplace	Speak English	OCCUPATION
	1	2	3	4	5	6	7	8	9	10	11	12	13	14	15	16	17
26		66	81	San Nicolas, Maria SN	Niece-in-law	F	Cha	24.0	S		Y	Y	Guam	Unknown	Guam	Y	None
27		66	82	Cabrera, Concepcion C	Head	F	Cha	27.0	S		Y	Y	Guam	Unknown	Guam	Y	Servant
28		66	82	Cabrera, Francisco C	Son	M	Cha	4.0	S				Guam	Unknown	Guam		None
29		66	82	Cabrera, Vicente C	Son	M	Cha	1.0	S				Guam	Unknown	Guam	N	None
30		67	83	Garcia, Gertrudes J	Head	F	Cha	50.0	Wd		N	N	Guam	Guam	Guam	Y	None
31		67	83	Garcia, Rosa J	Daughter	F	Cha	23.0	S		Y	Y	Guam	Guam	Guam	Y	Laundress
32		67	83	Garcia, Juan J	Son	M	Cha	18.0	S	N	Y	Y	Guam	Guam	Guam	Y	Farm laborer home
33		67	83	Garcia, Vicenta J	Daughter	F	Cha	12.0	S	N	Y	Y	Guam	Guam	Guam	N	None
34	Calle Magallanes	68	84	Siguenza, Jose P	Head	M	Cha	45.0	M		Y	N	Guam	Guam	Guam	N	Farmer
35		68	84	Siguenza, Maria C	Wife	F	Cha	34.0	M		N	N	Guam	Guam	Guam	N	None
36		68	84	Siguenza, Joaquin T	Son	M	Cha	22.0	S		Y	Y	Guam	Guam	Guam	Y	Farm laborer home
37		68	84	Siguenza, Maria T	Daughter	F	Cha	20.0	S	N	Y	Y	Guam	Guam	Guam	N	None
38		68	84	Siguenza, Jose T	Son	M	Cha	18.0	S	N	Y	Y	Guam	Guam	Guam	Y	Farm laborer home
39		68	84	Siguenza, Felipe T	Son	M	Cha	14.0	S	Y	Y	Y	Guam	Guam	Guam	Y	None
40		68	84	Siguenza, Juan C	Son	M	Cha	0.9	S				Guam	Guam	Guam		None
41		68	84	Taitinfong, Joaquina T	Mother-in-law	F	Cha	74.0	Wd		Y	N	Guam	Guam	Guam	N	None
42		69	85	San Nicolas, Vicente S	Head	M	Cha	30.0	M		Y	Y	Guam	Guam	Guam	Y	Electrician
43		69	85	San Nicolas, Remedios T	Wife	F	Cha	28.0	M		Y	N	Guam	Guam	Guam	N	None
44		69	85	San Nicolas, Maria T	Daughter	F	Cha	5.0	S	N			Guam	Guam	Guam		None
45		69	85	San Nicolas, Guadalupe T	Daughter	F	Cha	3.0	S				Guam	Guam	Guam		None
46		69	85	San Nicolas, Manuela T	Daughter	F	Cha	2.0	S				Guam	Guam	Guam		None
47		69	85	Toves, Maria S	Mother-in-law	F	Cha	62.0	Wd		Y	N	Guam	Guam	Guam	N	None
48		70	86	Reyes, Jose R	Head	M	Cha	48.0	M		Y	Y	Guam	Unknown	Guam	N	Farmer
49		70	86	Reyes, Rita Q	Wife	F	Cha	34.0	M		Y	Y	Guam	Guam	Guam	N	None
50		71	87	Cabrera, Enrique V	Head	M	Cha	30.0	M		Y	Y	Guam	Guam	Guam	Y	Store mason

(CHAMORRO ROOTS GENEALOGY PROJECT ™ TRANSCRIPTION)
(COMPILED/TRANSCRIBED BY BERNARD T. PUNZALAN / HTTP://WWW.CHAMORROROOTS.COM)

FOURTEENTH CENSUS OF THE UNITED STATES: 1920–POPULATION

ISLAND OF GUAM

DISTRICT 1
NAME OF PLACE Agana City
[Proper name and, also, name of class, as city, town, village, barrio, etc]

ENUMERATED BY ME ON THE 5th DAY OF April, 1920

Joaquin Torres ENUMERATOR

	Number of dwelling house in order of visitation	Number of family in order of visitation	NAME	RELATION	Sex	Color or race	Age at last birthday	Single, married, widowed or divorced	Attended school any time since Sept. 1, 1919	Whether able to read	Whether able to write	Place of birth of this person.	Place of birth of father of this person.	Place of birth of mother of this person.	Whether able to speak English.	OCCUPATION
1	2	3	4	5	6	7	8	9	10	11	12	13	14	15	16	17
1	71	87	Cabrera, Dolores SN	Wife	F	Cha	28.0	M		N	N	Guam	Unknown	Guam	N	None
2	71	87	Cabrera, Ana SN	Daughter	F	Cha	4.0	S				Guam	Guam	Guam		None
3	71	87	Cabrera, Rosalia SN	Daughter	F	Cha	2.0	S				Guam	Guam	Guam		None
4	72	88	Camacho, Juan S	Head	M	Cha	37.0	M		Y	Y	Guam	Guam	Guam	N	Farmer
5	72	88	Camacho, Joaquina C	Wife	F	Cha	35.0	M		Y	Y	Guam	Guam	Guam	N	None
6	72	88	Camacho, Gregorio C	Son	M	Cha	12.0	S		Y	Y	Guam	Guam	Guam	Y	None
7	72	88	Camacho, Manuela C	Daughter	F	Cha	6.0	S	Y	Y	Y	Guam	Guam	Guam	Y	None
8	72	88	Camacho, Vicenta C	Daughter	F	Cha	4.0	S	N			Guam	Guam	Guam		None
9	72	88	Camacho, Rosario C	Daughter	F	Cha	2.0	S				Guam	Guam	Guam		None
10	72	88	Camacho, Carmen C	Daughter	F	Cha	0.0	S				Guam	Guam	Guam		None
11	73	89	Camacho, Francisco S	Head	M	Cha	43.0	M		Y	Y	Guam	Guam	Guam	N	Farmer
12	73	89	Camacho, Rosa S	Wife	F	Cha	42.0	M		Y	Y	Guam	Guam	Guam	N	None
13	73	89	Camacho, Maria S	Daughter	F	Cha	17.0	S	N	Y	Y	Guam	Guam	Guam	Y	None
14	73	89	Camacho, Manuela S	Daughter	F	Cha	16.0	S	N	Y	Y	Guam	Guam	Guam	Y	None
15	73	89	Camacho, Maria S S	Daughter	F	Cha	14.0	S	N	Y	Y	Guam	Guam	Guam	Y	None
16	73	89	Camacho, Ana S	Daughter	F	Cha	13.0	S	N	Y	Y	Guam	Guam	Guam	Y	None
17	73	89	Camacho, Gregorio S	Son	M	Cha	11.0	S	Y	Y	Y	Guam	Guam	Guam	Y	None
18	73	89	Camacho, Jose S	Son	M	Cha	8.0	S	Y			Guam	Guam	Guam	Y	None
19	73	89	Camacho, Concepcion S	Daughter	F	Cha	5.0	S	N			Guam	Guam	Guam		None
20	73	89	Camacho, Jesus S	Son	M	Cha	2.0	S				Guam	Guam	Guam		None
21	73	89	Camacho, Rosario S	Daughter	F	Cha	0.2	S				Guam	Guam	Guam		None
22	74	90	Castro, Ramon C	Head	M	Cha	54.0	M		Y	Y	Guam	Guam	Guam	N	Farmer
23	74	90	Castro, Maria C	Wife	F	Cha	52.0	M		Y	Y	Guam	Guam	Guam	N	None
24	74	90	Castro, Mariano C	Son	M	Cha	29.0	S		Y	Y	Guam	Guam	Guam	Y	Farm laborer home
25	74	90	Castro, Jesus C	Son	M	Cha	21.0	S	N	Y	Y	Guam	Guam	Guam	Y	Farm laborer home

Calle Magallanes

29

(CHAMORRO ROOTS GENEALOGY PROJECT ™ TRANSCRIPTION)
(COMPILED/TRANSCRIBED BY BERNARD T. PUNZALAN / HTTP://WWW.CHAMORROROOTS.COM)

FOURTEENTH CENSUS OF THE UNITED STATES: 1920—POPULATION

ISLAND OF GUAM

ENUMERATED BY ME ON THE 5th DAY OF April, 1920

Joaquin Torres ENUMERATOR

DISTRICT 1
NAME OF PLACE Agana City

[Proper name and, also, name of class, as city, town, village, barrio, etc]

	Dwelling No.	Family No.	NAME	RELATION	Sex	Color or race	Age	Marital	School	Read	Write	Birthplace	Father birthplace	Mother birthplace	English	OCCUPATION
	2	3	4	5	6	7	8	9	10	11	12	13	14	15	16	17
26	74	90	Castro, Trinidad C	Daughter	F	Cha	19.0	S	N	Y	Y	Guam	Guam	Guam	Y	None
27	74	90	Castro, Juan C	Son	M	Cha	14.0	S	Y	Y	Y	Guam	Guam	Guam	Y	None
28	74	90	Castro, Vicente C	Son	M	Cha	10.0	S	Y	Y	Y	Guam	Guam	Guam	N	None
29	75	91	Castro, Jose C	Head	M	Cha	31.0	M		Y	Y	Guam	Guam	Guam	Y	Farmer
30	75	91	Castro, Ana S	Wife	F	Cha	29.0	M		Y	Y	Guam	Guam	Guam	Y	Midwife
31	75	91	Castro, Delfina S	Daughter	F	Cha	2.0	S				Guam	Guam	Guam		None
32	75	91	Castro, Pilar S	Daughter	F	Cha	0.2	S				Guam	Guam	Guam		None
33	76	92	Blas, Antonio C	Head	M	Cha	31.0	M		Y	Y	Guam	Guam	Guam	Y	Farmer
34	76	92	Blas, Angelina E	Wife	F	Cha	23.0	M		Y	Y	Guam	Guam	Guam	Y	None
35	76	92	Blas, Jesus E	Son	M	Cha	2.0	S				Guam	Guam	Guam		None
36	76	92	Blas, Jose E	Son	M	Cha	0.3	S				Guam	Guam	Guam		None
37	76	92	Eustaquio, Cornelio P	Father-in-law	M	Cha	55.0	Wd				Guam	Guam	Guam		Fireman
38	77	93	Baza, Maria A	Head	F	Cha	62.0	S		Y	Y	Guam	Guam	Guam	N	Weaver
39	77	93	Baza, Ignacia B	Daughter	F	Cha	36.0	S		Y	Y	Guam	Unknown	Guam	N	Laundress
40	77	93	Baza, Juan B	Grand-son	M	Cha	10.0	S	Y	Y	Y	Guam	Unknown	Guam	N	None
41	77	93	Baza, Maria B	Grand-daughter	F	Cha	8.0	S	Y			Guam	Unknown	Guam		None
42	77	93	Baza, Maria B	Boarder	F	Cha	14.0	S	N	Y	Y	Guam	Unknown	Guam	Y	None
43	78	94	Baza, Manuel B	Head	M	Cha	34.0	M		Y	Y	Guam	Unknown	Guam	Y	Painter
44	78	94	Baza, Ana M P	Wife	F	Cha	55.0	M		Y	Y	Guam	Guam	Guam	Y	None
45	78	94	Baza, Maria C	Daughter	F	Cha	8.0	S	Y			Guam	Guam	Guam	N	None
46	78	94	Baza, Jose H D	Son	M	Cha	4.0	S				Guam	Guam	Guam		None
47	79	95	Farfan, Vicente C	Head	M	Cha	40.0	M		Y	Y	Guam	Guam	Guam	N	Farmer
48	79	95	Farfan, Joaquina C	Wife	F	Cha	39.0	M		Y	Y	Guam	Guam	Guam	N	None
49	79	95	Farfan, Jose C	Son	M	Cha	7.0	S	Y			Guam	Guam	Guam	N	None
50	79	95	Farfan, Jesus C	Son	M	Cha	5.0	S	N			Guam	Guam	Guam		None

Street, avenue, road, etc.: Calle Magallanes

(CHAMORRO ROOTS GENEALOGY PROJECT ™ TRANSCRIPTION)
(COMPILED/TRANSCRIBED BY BERNARD T. PUNZALAN / HTTP://WWW.CHAMORROROOTS.COM)
FOURTEENTH CENSUS OF THE UNITED STATES: 1920-POPULATION
ISLAND OF GUAM

DISTRICT **1**
NAME OF PLACE **Agana City**
[Proper name and, also, name of class, as city, town, village, barrio, etc]

ENUMERATED BY ME ON THE 5th DAY OF April, 1920

Joaquin Torres ENUMERATOR

Street, avenue, road, etc.	Number of dwelling house in order of visitation	Number of family in order of visitation	NAME	RELATION	Sex	Color or race	Age at last birthday	Single, married, widowed or divorced	Attended school any time since Sept. 1, 1919	Whether able to read	Whether able to write	Place of birth of this person	Place of birth of father of this person	Place of birth of mother of this person	Whether able to speak English	OCCUPATION
1	2	3	4	5	6	7	8	9	10	11	12	13	14	15	16	17
	79	95	Farfan, Rosa C	Daughter	F	Cha	3.0	S				Guam	Guam	Guam		None
Calle Magallanes	79	95	Farfan, Francisca C	Daughter	F	Cha	2.0	S				Guam	Guam	Guam		None
	80	96	Finona, Joaquin F	Head	M	Cha	35.0	M		Y	Y	Guam	Guam	Guam	Y	Farmer
	80	96	Finona, Antonia R	Wife	F	Cha	28.0	M		Y	Y	Guam	Unknown	Guam	N	None
	80	96	Finona, Estela R	Daughter	F	Cha	2.0	S				Guam	Guam	Guam		None
	80	96	Finona, Maria R	Daughter	F	Cha	0.3	S				Guam	Guam	Guam		None
	81	97	Leon Guerrero, Vicente LG	Head	M	Cha	28.0	M		N	N	Guam	Unknown	Guam	N	Farmer
	81	97	Leon Guerrero, Dolores F	Wife	F	Cha	30.0	M		N	N	Guam	Guam	Guam	N	None
	81	97	Leon Guerrero, Maria F	Daughter	F	Cha	0.3	S				Guam	Guam	Guam		None
	82	98	Blas, Atanasio	Head	M	Cha	28.0	M		Y	Y	Guam	Guam	Guam	Y	Enlisted man USN
	82	98	Blas, Joaquina R	Wife	F	Cha	33.0	M		Y	Y	Guam	Unknown	Guam	N	None
	82	98	Blas, Biatris E	Daughter	F	Cha	4.0	S				Guam	Guam	Guam		None
	82	98	Blas, Rosalia E	Daughter	F	Cha	2.0	S				Guam	Guam	Guam		None
	82	98	Blas, Thomas E A	Son	M	Cha	0.2	S				Guam	Guam	Guam		None
	82	99	Reyes, Jesus LG	Head	M	Cha	40.0	S		Y	Y	Guam	Unknown	Guam	N	Farmer
Dr. Hessler Street	82	99	Reyes, Ana LG	Sister	F	Cha	38.0	S		Y	N	Guam	Unknown	Guam	N	None
	83	100	Pangelinan, Jose R	Head	M	Cha	37.0	S		Y	Y	Guam	Guam	Guam	N	Farmer
	83	100	Diaz, Francisca P	Sister	F	Cha	43.0	Wd		Y	Y	Guam	Guam	Guam	N	None
	83	100	Pangelinan, Ana R	Sister	F	Cha	39.0	S		Y	Y	Guam	Guam	Guam	N	None
	83	100	Pangelinan, Juana R	Sister	F	Cha	35.0	S		Y	Y	Guam	Guam	Guam	N	None
	83	100	Pangelinan, Joaquina R	Sister	F	Cha	30.0	S		Y	Y	Guam	Guam	Guam	N	None
	84	101	Deza, Josefa B	Head	F	W	48.0	S		N	N	Guam	Spain	Guam	N	None
	84	102	Camacho, Maria D	Head	F	W	21.0	M	N	N	Y	Guam	Unknown	Guam	N	None
	84	102	Camacho, Juan D	Son	M	Cha	0.7	S				Guam	Guam	Guam		None
	85	103	Blas, Juan C	Head	M	Cha	31.0	M		Y	Y	Guam	Guam	Guam	N	Farmer

31

(CHAMORRO ROOTS GENEALOGY PROJECT ™ TRANSCRIPTION)
(COMPILED/TRANSCRIBED BY BERNARD T. PUNZALAN / HTTP://WWW.CHAMORROROOTS.COM)
FOURTEENTH CENSUS OF THE UNITED STATES: 1920-POPULATION
ISLAND OF GUAM

DISTRICT 1
NAME OF PLACE Agana City
[Proper name and, also, name of class, as city, town, village, barrio, etc]

ENUMERATED BY ME ON THE 6th DAY OF April, 1920

Joaquin Torres ENUMERATOR

	Dwelling	Family	NAME	RELATION	Sex	Color or race	Age	Marital	School	Read	Write	Birth person	Birth father	Birth mother	Eng.	OCCUPATION
26	85	103	Blas, Dolores C	Wife	F	Cha	26.0	M		Y	Y	Guam	Guam	Guam	Y	None
27	85	103	Blas, Esperanza C	Daughter	F	Cha	7.0	S	Y			Guam	Guam	Guam		None
28	85	103	Blas, Francisca C	Daughter	F	Cha	5.0	S	N			Guam	Guam	Guam		None
29	85	103	Blas, Teresa C	Daughter	F	Cha	2.0	S				Guam	Guam	Guam		None
30	86	104	Villagomez, Jose C	Head	M	Cha	38.0	M		Y	Y	Guam	Guam	Guam	N	Farmer
31	86	104	Villagomez, Maria P	Wife	F	Cha	39.0	M		Y	Y	Guam	Guam	Guam	N	None
32	86	104	Villagomez, Soledad P	Daughter	F	Cha	10.0	S	Y	Y	Y	Guam	Guam	Guam	N	None
33	86	104	Villagomez, Jesus P	Son	M	Cha	9.0	S	Y	Y	Y	Guam	Guam	Guam		None
34	86	104	Villagomez, Jose P	Son	M	Cha	7.0	S	Y	Y	Y	Guam	Guam	Guam		None
35	86	104	Villagomez, Pedro P	Son	M	Cha	6.0	S	N			Guam	Guam	Guam		None
36	86	104	Villagomez, Maria P	Daughter	F	Cha	5.0	S	N			Guam	Guam	Guam		None
37	86	104	Villagomez, Francisco P	Son	M	Cha	3.0	S				Guam	Guam	Guam		None
38	87	105	Rosario, Vicente F	Head	M	Cha	62.0	M		Y	Y	Guam	Guam	Guam	N	Farmer
39	87	105	Rosario, Gertrudes C	Wife	F	Cha	54.0	M		Y	N	Guam	Guam	Guam	N	None
40	87	105	Rosario, Francisco C	Son	M	Cha	23.0	S		Y	Y	Guam	Guam	Guam	Y	Farm Laborer home
41	87	105	Camacho, Saturnina F	Mother-in-law	F	Cha	75.0	Wd		Y	N	Guam	Guam	Guam	N	None
42	88	106	Blas, Rebeca C	Head	F	Cha	62.0	Wd		N	N	Guam	Guam	Guam	N	None
43	88	106	Blaz, Vicente C	Son	M	Cha	18.0	S	N	Y	Y	Guam	Guam	Guam	Y	Enlisted man USN
44	88	106	Camacho, Carmen P	Sister-in-law	F	Cha	75.0	S		Y	N	Guam	Guam	Guam	N	None
45	89	107	Torres, Vicente A	Head	M	Cha	65.0	M		Y	Y	Guam	Guam	Guam	Y	Farmer
46	89	107	Torres, Dolores H	Wife	F	Cha	51.0	M		Y	Y	Guam	Guam	Guam	N	None
47	89	107	Torres, Jose H	Son	M	Cha	27.0	S		Y	Y	Guam	Guam	Guam	Y	Laborer
48	89	107	Torres, Felix H	Son	M	Cha	21.0	S	N	Y	Y	Guam	Guam	Guam	Y	Farm Laborer home
49	89	107	Torres, Concepcion H	Daughter	F	Cha	20.0	S	N	Y	Y	Guam	Guam	Guam	Y	None
50	89	107	Torres, Maria H	Daughter	F	Cha	18.0	S	N	Y	Y	Guam	Guam	Guam	Y	None

Street: Dr. Hessler Street

(CHAMORRO ROOTS GENEALOGY PROJECT ™ TRANSCRIPTION)
(COMPILED/TRANSCRIBED BY BERNARD T. PUNZALAN / HTTP://WWW.CHAMORROROOTS.COM)
FOURTEENTH CENSUS OF THE UNITED STATES: 1920—POPULATION
ISLAND OF GUAM

DISTRICT 1
NAME OF PLACE Agana City

ENUMERATED BY ME ON THE 6th DAY OF April, 1920

Joaquin Torres ENUMERATOR

[Proper name and, also, name of class, as city, town, village, barrio, etc]

	PLACE OF ABODE			NAME	RELATION	PERSONAL DESCRIPTION				EDUCATION			NATIVITY				OCCUPATION
Street, avenue, road, etc.	Number of dwelling house in order of visitation	Number of family in order of visitation		of each person whose place of abode on January 1, 1920, was in the family. Enter surname, firs, then given name and middle initial. If any. Include every person living on January 1, 1920. Omit children born since January 1, 1920.	Relationship of this person to the head of the family.	Sex	Color or race	Age at last birthday	Single, married, widowed or divorced	Attended school any time since Sept. 1, 1919	Whether able to read.	Whether able to write.	Place of birth of this person.	Place of birth of father of this person.	Place of birth of mother of this person.	Whether able to speak English.	Trade, profession, or particular kind of work done, as salesman, laborer, clerk, cook, merchant, washerwoman, etc.
1	2	3	4		5	6	7	8	9	10	11	12	13	14	15	16	17
	89	107	Torres, Josefina H	Daughter		F	Cha	16.0	S	N	Y	Y	Guam	Guam	Guam	Y	None
	89	107	Torres, Dolores H	Daughter		F	Cha	14.0	S	N	Y	Y	Guam	Guam	Guam	Y	None
	89	107	Torres, Jesus H	Son		M	Cha	11.0	S	Y	Y	Y	Guam	Guam	Guam	Y	None
	89	107	Torres, Maria A	Mother		F	Cha	82.0	D		Y	Y	Guam	Guam	Guam	N	None
	90	108	Saccomani, Remedio	Head		F	Cha	37.0	Wd		Y	Y	Guam	Guam	Guam	N	None
	90	108	Saccomani, Amelia	Daughter		F	W	16.0	S	Y	Y	Y	Guam	Italy	Guam	Y	None
	90	108	Saccomani, Elbira	Daughter		F	W	15.0	S	Y	Y	Y	Guam	Italy	Guam	Y	None
	90	108	Saccomani, Ida	Daughter		F	W	12.0	S	Y	Y	Y	Guam	Italy	Guam	Y	None
	90	108	Saccomani, Erculi	Daughter		F	W	9.0	S	Y			Guam	Italy	Guam		None
	90	108	Saccomani, Seserina	Daughter		F	W	7.0	S	Y			Guam	Italy	Guam		None
Dr. Hessler Street	90	108	Cruz, Maria C	Mother		F	Cha	82.0	Wd				Guam	Guam	Guam	N	None
	91	109	Camacho, Vicente P	Head		M	Cha	39.0	M		Y	Y	Guam	Guam	Guam	Y	Judge
	91	109	Camacho, Trinidad C	Wife		F	Cha	34.0	M		Y	Y	Guam	Guam	Guam	Y	None
	91	109	Camacho, Jesus P	Son		M	Cha	15.0	S	N	N	Y	Guam	Guam	Guam	Y	Clerk
	91	109	Camacho, Juana P	Sister		F	Cha	42.0	S		Y	Y	Guam	Guam	Guam	Y	None
	91	109	Manibusan, Francisco B	Boarder		M	Cha	4.0	S				Guam	Guam	Guam		None
	92	110	Manibusan, Juan R	Head		M	Cha	55.0	M		Y	Y	Guam	Guam	Guam	N	Farmer
	92	110	Manibusan, Ana C	Wife		F	Cha	49.0	M		Y	Y	Guam	Guam	Guam	N	None
	92	110	Manibusan, Jose C	Son		M	Cha	23.0	S		Y	Y	Guam	Guam	Guam	Y	Clerk
	92	110	Manibusan, Maria C	Daughter		F	Cha	15.0	S	N	Y	Y	Guam	Guam	Guam	Y	None
	92	110	Manibusan, Isabel C	Daughter		F	Cha	11.0	S	Y	Y	Y	Guam	Guam	Guam	Y	None
	92	110	Duenas, Ana M	Daughter		F	Cha	30.0	M		Y	Y	Guam	Guam	Guam	N	Tailoress
	93	111	Sablan, Vicente R	Head		M	Cha	51.0	M		Y	Y	Guam	Guam	Guam	N	Carpenter
	93	111	Sablan, Ana G	Wife		F	Cha	42.0	M		Y	Y	Guam	Guam	Guam	N	None
	93	111	Pangelinan, Maria S	Sister		F	Cha	44.0	Wd		Y	Y	Guam	Guam	Guam	N	None

(CHAMORRO ROOTS GENEALOGY PROJECT ™ TRANSCRIPTION)
(COMPILED/TRANSCRIBED BY BERNARD T. PUNZALAN / HTTP://WWW.CHAMORROROOTS.COM)

FOURTEENTH CENSUS OF THE UNITED STATES: 1920-POPULATION
ISLAND OF GUAM

ENUMERATED BY ME ON THE 7th DAY OF April, 1920

Joaquin Torres ENUMERATOR

DISTRICT 1
NAME OF PLACE Agana City
[Proper name and, also, name of class, as city, town, village, barrio, etc]

	Dwelling (2)	Family (3)	NAME (4)	RELATION (5)	Sex (6)	Color or race (7)	Age (8)	Marital (9)	School since Sept 1, 1919 (10)	Read (11)	Write (12)	Birthplace (13)	Father birthplace (14)	Mother birthplace (15)	Speak English (16)	OCCUPATION (17)
26	94	112	Manibusan, Vicente T	Head	M	Cha	44.0	M		Y	Y	Guam	Guam	Guam	N	Farmer
27	94	112	Manibusan, Ana M	Wife	F	Cha	45.0	M		Y	Y	Guam	Guam	Guam	N	None
28	94	112	Manibusan, Isabel M	Daughter	F	Cha	19.0	S		Y	Y	Guam	Guam	Guam	Y	None
29	94	112	Manibusan, Joaquin M	Son	M	Cha	17.0	S	N	Y	Y	Guam	Guam	Guam	Y	Farm laborer home
30	94	112	Manibusan, Jesus M	Son	M	Cha	16.0	S	N	Y	Y	Guam	Guam	Guam	Y	Servant
31	94	112	Manibusan, Dolores M	Daughter	F	Cha	11.0	S	Y	Y	Y	Guam	Guam	Guam	Y	None
32	94	112	Manibusan, Juan M	Son	M	Cha	9.0	S	Y	Y	Y	Guam	Guam	Guam	Y	None
33	94	112	Manibusan, Maria M	Daughter	F	Cha	6.0	S	N			Guam	Guam	Guam		None
34	94	112	Manibusan, Trinidad M	Daughter	F	Cha	3.0	S				Guam	Guam	Guam		None
35	95	113	Ada, Vicente B	Head	M	Cha	65.0	M		Y	Y	Guam	Guam	Guam	N	Stone mason
36	95	113	Ada, Maria M	Wife	F	Cha	64.0	M		Y	Y	Guam	Guam	Guam	N	None
37	96	114	Manibusan, Lorenzo M	Head	M	Cha	34.0	M		Y	Y	Guam	Guam	Guam	Y	Farmer
38	96	114	Manibusan, Regina A	Wife	F	Cha	35.0	M		Y	Y	Guam	Guam	Guam	N	None
39	96	114	Manibusan, Jose A	Son	M	Cha	5.0	S	N			Guam	Guam	Guam		None
40	96	114	Manibusan, Lorenzo A	Son	M	Cha	4.0	S				Guam	Guam	Guam		None
41	96	114	Manibusan, Juan A	Son	M	Cha	2.0	S				Guam	Guam	Guam		None
42	96	114	Manibusan, Vicente A	Son	M	Cha	0.0	S				Guam	Guam	Guam		None
43	97	115	Ada, Ramon M	Head	M	Cha	33.0	M		Y	Y	Guam	Guam	Guam	Y	Farmer
44	97	115	Ada, Joaquina M	Wife	F	Cha	33.0	M		Y	N	Guam	Unknown	Guam	N	None
45	97	115	Ada, Maria M	Daughter	F	Cha	5.0	S	N			Guam	Guam	Guam		None
46	97	115	Ada, Rosa M	Daughter	F	Cha	3.0	S				Guam	Guam	Guam		None
47	97	115	Ada, Jesus M	Son	M	Cha	0.7	S				Guam	Guam	Guam		None
48	98	116	Leon Guerrero, Vicenta de	Head	F	Cha	58.0	Wd		Y	Y	Guam	Guam	Guam	N	None
49	98	116	Guerrero, Jose DL	Son	M	Cha	31.0	S		Y	Y	Guam	Guam	Guam	Y	Enlisted man USN
50	98	116	Leon Guerrero, Maria de	Daughter	F	Cha	26.0	S		Y	Y	Guam	Guam	Guam	Y	None

Street: Dr. Hessler Street

(CHAMORRO ROOTS GENEALOGY PROJECT ™ TRANSCRIPTION)

(COMPILED/TRANSCRIBED BY BERNARD T. PUNZALAN / HTTP://WWW.CHAMORROROOTS.COM)

FOURTEENTH CENSUS OF THE UNITED STATES: 1920—POPULATION

ISLAND OF GUAM

DISTRICT 1

NAME OF PLACE Agana City

[Proper name and, also, name of class, as city, town, village, barrio, etc]

ENUMERATED BY ME ON THE 7th DAY OF April, 1920

Joaquin Torres ENUMERATOR

	Street, avenue, road, etc.	Number of dwelling house in order of visitation	Number of family in order of visitation	NAME	RELATION	Sex	Color or race	Age at last birthday	Single, married, widowed or divorced	Attended school any time since Sept. 1, 1919	Whether able to read	Whether able to write	Place of birth of this person	Place of birth of father of this person	Place of birth of mother of this person	Whether able to speak English	OCCUPATION
	1	2	3	4	5	6	7	8	9	10	11	12	13	14	15	16	17
1		98	116	Leon Guerrero, Ana de	Daughter	F	Cha	23.0	S		Y	Y	Guam	Guam	Guam	Y	None
2		98	116	Castro, Rosa LG	Sister	F	Cha	44.0	Wd		Y	Y	Guam	Guam	Guam	N	None
3		98	116	Castro, Maria LG	Niece	F	Cha	18.0	S	N	Y	Y	Guam	Guam	Guam	N	None
4		98	116	Leon Guerrero, Trinidad S	Niece	F	Cha	18.0	S	N	Y	Y	Guam	Guam	Guam	Y	None
5		98	116	Castro, Catalina LG	Niece	F	Cha	12.0	S	N	Y	Y	Guam	Guam	Guam	N	None
6		98	116	Castro, Jesus LG	Nephew	M	Cha	10.0	S	Y	Y	Y	Guam	Guam	Guam	N	None
7		99	117	Leon Guerrero, Ana S	Head	F	Cha	49.0	Wd		Y	N	Guam	Guam	Guam	N	Laundress
8		99	117	Leon Guerrero, Carmen S	Daughter	F	Cha	20.0	S	N	Y	Y	Guam	Guam	Guam	Y	
9	Dr. Hessler Street	99	117	Leon Guerrero, Vicente S	Son	M	Cha	19.0	S	N	Y	Y	Guam	Guam	Guam	Y	Farm laborer home
10		99	117	Leon Guerrero, Ignacio S	Son	M	Cha	17.0	S	N	Y	Y	Guam	Guam	Guam	Y	Laborer
11		99	117	Leon Guerrero, Juana S	Daughter	F	Cha	15.0	S	N	Y	Y	Guam	Guam	Guam	N	None
12		99	117	Leon Guerrero, Ana S	Daughter	F	Cha	13.0	S	N	Y	Y	Guam	Guam	Guam	Y	None
13		99	117	Leon Guerrero, Jose S	Son	M	Cha	10.0	S	Y	Y	Y	Guam	Guam	Guam	Y	None
14		99	117	Leon Guerrero, Vicenta S	Daughter	F	Cha	6.0	S	N	Y	Y	Guam	Guam	Guam	N	None
15		100	118	Taitano, Juan M	Head	M	Cha	51.0	M		Y	Y	Guam	Unknown	Guam	N	Painter
16		100	118	Taitano, Catalina C	Wife	F	Cha	56.0	M		Y	N	Guam	Guam	Guam	N	None
17		100	118	Taitano, Ana C	Daughter	F	Cha	22.0	S		Y	Y	Guam	Guam	Guam	Y	None
18		100	118	Taitano, Juan C	Son	M	Cha	17.0	S	N	Y	Y	Guam	Guam	Guam	Y	Messenger
19		100	118	Taitano, Maria C	Daughter	F	Cha	15.0	S	N	Y	Y	Guam	Guam	Guam	Y	None
20		100	119	Santos, Jose T	Head	M	Cha	36.0	M		Y	Y	Guam	Guam	Guam	Y	Farmer
21		100	119	Santos, Milagros C	Wife	F	Cha	31.0	M		Y	N	Guam	Guam	Guam	N	None
22		100	119	Santos, Miguel C	Son	M	Cha	11.0	S	N	Y	Y	Guam	Guam	Guam	Y	None
23		100	119	Santos, Gregorio C	Son	M	Cha	7.0	S	N	Y	Y	Guam	Guam	Guam		None
24		100	119	Santos, Jesus C	Son	M	Cha	1.0	S				Guam	Guam	Guam		None
25		100	119	Santos, Francisco C	Son	M	Cha	0.2	S				Guam	Guam	Guam		None

(CHAMORRO ROOTS GENEALOGY PROJECT ™ TRANSCRIPTION)
(COMPILED/TRANSCRIBED BY BERNARD T. PUNZALAN / HTTP://WWW.CHAMORROROOTS.COM)

FOURTEENTH CENSUS OF THE UNITED STATES: 1920–POPULATION

ISLAND OF GUAM

DISTRICT **1**

NAME OF PLACE **Agana City**

[Proper name and, also, name of class, as city, town, village, barrio, etc]

ENUMERATED BY ME ON THE 7th DAY OF April, 1920

Joaquin Torres ENUMERATOR

	Street, avenue, road, etc.	Dwelling house no.	Family no.	NAME	RELATION	Sex	Color or race	Age	Single, married, widowed, divorced	Attended school since Sept 1, 1919	Read	Write	Birthplace	Father	Mother	Speak English	OCCUPATION
26		101	120	Altero, Pascual S	Head	M	W	44.0	M		Y	Y	Spain	Spain	Spain	N	Farmer
27		101	120	Altero, Asuncion C	Wife	F	Cha	45.0	M		Y	Y	Guam	Guam	Guam	N	None
28		101	120	Altero, Jesus C	Son	M	W	16.0	S	N	Y	Y	Guam	Spain	Guam	Y	Farm laborer home
29		101	120	Altero, Antonio C	Son	M	W	14.0	S	N	Y	Y	Guam	Spain	Guam	Y	Farm laborer home
30		101	120	Altero, Isabel C	Daughter	F	W	12.0	S	Y	Y	Y	Guam	Spain	Guam	Y	None
31		101	120	Altero, Maria C	Daughter	F	W	10.0	S	Y	Y	Y	Guam	Spain	Guam	Y	None
32		101	120	Altero, Consuelo C	Daughter	F	W	8.0	S	Y			Guam	Spain	Guam	Y	None
33		101	120	Altero, Pascual C	Son	M	W	6.0	S	Y			Guam	Spain	Guam		None
34		101	120	Altero, Jose C	Son	M	W	4.0	S				Guam	Spain	Guam		None
35	Dr. Hessler Street	102	121	Perez, Felix F	Head	M	Cha	49.0	M		Y	Y	Guam	Guam	Guam	Y	Farmer
36		102	121	Perez, Josefa D	Wife	F	Cha	37.0	M		Y	Y	Guam	Guam	Guam	N	None
37		102	121	Perez, Juan D	Son	M	Cha	21.0	S	N	Y	Y	Guam	Guam	Guam	Y	Cable operator
38		102	121	Perez, Maria D	Daughter	F	Cha	20.0	S	N	Y	Y	Guam	Guam	Guam	Y	None
39		102	121	Perez, Antonio D	Son	M	Cha	18.0	S	N	Y	Y	Guam	Guam	Guam	Y	Cable operator
40		102	121	Perez, Gregorio D	Son	M	Cha	17.0	S	N	Y	Y	Guam	Guam	Guam	Y	Cable operator
41		102	121	Perez, Jose D	Son	M	Cha	15.0	S	Y	Y	Y	Guam	Guam	Guam	Y	None
42		102	121	Perez, Joaquin D	Son	M	Cha	13.0	S	Y	Y	Y	Guam	Guam	Guam	Y	None
43		102	121	Perez, Dolores D	Daughter	F	Cha	11.0	S	Y	Y	Y	Guam	Guam	Guam	Y	None
44		102	121	Perez, Josefina D	Daughter	F	Cha	10.0	S	Y	Y	Y	Guam	Guam	Guam	Y	None
45		102	121	Perez, Amelia D	Daughter	F	Cha	10.0	S	Y	Y	Y	Guam	Guam	Guam	Y	None
46		102	121	Perez, Pedro D	Son	M	Cha	8.0	S	Y			Guam	Guam	Guam		None
47		102	121	Perez, Francisca D	Daughter	F	Cha	6.0	S	N			Guam	Guam	Guam		None
48		102	121	Perez, Manuel D	Son	M	Cha	4.0	S				Guam	Guam	Guam		None
49		103	122	Rosario, Josefa C	Head	F	Cha	46.0	Wd		Y	N	Guam	Guam	Guam	N	None
50		103	122	Rosario, Teresa C	Daughter	F	Cha	24.0	S		Y	Y	Guam	Guam	Guam	N	None

36

(CHAMORRO ROOTS GENEALOGY PROJECT ™ TRANSCRIPTION)
(COMPILED/TRANSCRIBED BY BERNARD T. PUNZALAN / HTTP://WWW.CHAMORROROOTS.COM)
FOURTEENTH CENSUS OF THE UNITED STATES: 1920-POPULATION
ISLAND OF GUAM

SHEET NO. 44A

DISTRICT 1
NAME OF PLACE **Agana City**

[Proper name and, also, name of class, as city, town, village, barrio, etc]

ENUMERATED BY ME ON THE 8th DAY OF April, 1920

Joaquin Torres ENUMERATOR

	Street, avenue, road, etc.	Number of dwelling house in order of visitation	Number of family in order of visitation	NAME	RELATION	Sex	Color or race	Age at last birthday	Single, married, widowed or divorced	Attended school any time since Sept. 1, 1919	Whether able to read.	Whether able to write.	Place of birth of this person.	Place of birth of father of this person.	Place of birth of mother of this person.	Whether able to speak English.	OCCUPATION
	1	2	3	4	5	6	7	8	9	10	11	12	13	14	15	16	17
1		103	122	Rosario, Pedro C	Son	M	Cha	21.0	S	N	Y	Y	Guam	Guam	Guam	Y	Farm laborer home
2		103	122	Rosario, Maria C	Daughter	F	Cha	18.0	S	N	Y	Y	Guam	Guam	Guam	Y	None
3		103	122	Rosario, Vicenta C	Daughter	F	Cha	16.0	S	N	Y	Y	Guam	Guam	Guam	Y	None
4		103	122	Rosario, Concepcion C	Daughter	F	Cha	14.0	S	N	Y	Y	Guam	Guam	Guam	Y	None
5		103	122	Rosario, Jesus C	Son	M	Cha	11.0	S	Y	Y	Y	Guam	Guam	Guam	Y	None
6		103	122	Rosario, Domingo C	Son	M	Cha	10.0	S	Y	Y	Y	Guam	Guam	Guam	Y	None
7		103	122	Rosario, Remedios C	Daughter	F	Cha	7.0	S	Y			Guam	Guam	Guam		None
8		103	122	Rosario, Magdalena C	Daughter	F	Cha	5.0	S	N			Guam	Guam	Guam		None
9		104	123	Sablan, Manuel E	Head	M	Cha	52.0	M				Guam	Guam	Guam	Y	Island Attorney
10		104	123	Sablan, Rita T	Wife	F	Cha	42.0	M				Guam	Guam	Guam	N	None
11		104	123	Sablan, Jose T	Son	M	Cha	25.0	S		Y	Y	Guam	Guam	Guam	Y	Enlisted man USN
12		104	123	Sablan, Ramon T	Son	M	Cha	22.0	S		Y	Y	Guam	Guam	Guam	Y	Storekeeper
13		104	123	Sablan, Guadalupe T	Daughter	F	Cha	18.0	S	N	Y	Y	Guam	Guam	Guam	Y	None
14		104	123	Sablan, Manuel T	Son	M	Cha	12.0	S	Y	Y	Y	Guam	Guam	Guam	Y	None
15		104	123	Sablan, Ejinio T	Son	M	Cha	10.0	S	Y	Y	Y	Guam	Guam	Guam	Y	None
16		104	123	Sablan, Rosario T	Daughter	F	Cha	7.0	S	Y			Guam	Guam	Guam		None
17		104	123	Sablan, Fidel T	Son	M	Cha	1.0	S				Guam	Guam	Guam		None
18		104	123	Sablan, Maria T	Boarder	F	Cha	13.0	S	N	Y	Y	Guam	Unknown	Unknown	Y	None
19	Dr. Hessler Street	104	123	Sablan, Virginia T	Boarder	F	Cha	3.0	S				Guam	Unknown	Unknown		None
20		105	124	Sablan, Pedro R	Head	M	Cha	45.0	M		Y	Y	Guam	Guam	Guam	N	Farmer
21		105	124	Sablan, Concepcion M	Wife	F	Cha	39.0	M		Y	Y	Guam	Guam	Guam	N	None
22		105	124	Sablan, Maria M	Daughter	F	Cha	19.0	S		Y	Y	Guam	Guam	Guam	Y	None
23		105	124	Sablan, Ramon M	Son	M	Cha	18.0	S	N	Y	Y	Guam	Guam	Guam	Y	None
24		105	124	Sablan, Jose M	Son	M	Cha	15.0	S	Y	Y	Y	Guam	Guam	Guam	Y	None
25		106	125	Taitano, Manuel B	Head	M	Cha	42.0	M		Y	Y	Guam	Guam	Guam	N	Farmer

37

(CHAMORRO ROOTS GENEALOGY PROJECT ™ TRANSCRIPTION)
(COMPILED/TRANSCRIBED BY BERNARD T. PUNZALAN / HTTP://WWW.CHAMORROROOTS.COM)
FOURTEENTH CENSUS OF THE UNITED STATES: 1920-POPULATION
ISLAND OF GUAM

ENUMERATED BY ME ON THE 8th DAY OF April, 1920

Joaquin Torres ENUMERATOR

DISTRICT 1
NAME OF PLACE Agana City

[Proper name and, also, name of class, name of class, as city, town, village, barrio, etc]

	Street, avenue, road, etc.	Number of dwelling house is order of visitation	Number of family in order of visitation	NAME of each person whose place of abode on January 1, 1920, was in the family.	RELATION Relationship of this Person to the head of the family.	Sex	Color or race	Age at last birthday	Single, married, widowed or divorced	Attended school any time since Sept. 1, 1919	Whether able to read.	Whether able to write.	Place of birth of this person.	Place of birth of father of this person.	Place of birth of mother of this person.	Whether able to speak English.	OCCUPATION
	1	2	3	4	5	6	7	8	9	10	11	12	13	14	15	16	17
26		106	125	Taitano, Maria R	Wife	F	Cha	57.0	M		Y	Y	Guam	Unknown	Guam	N	None
27		106	125	Taitano, Joaquin R	Son	M	Cha	21.0	S	N	Y	Y	Guam	Guam	Guam	Y	Laborer
28		106	125	Taitano, Vicente R	Son	M	Cha	19.0	S	N	Y	Y	Guam	Guam	Guam	Y	Enlisted man USN
29		106	125	Taitano, Jesus R	Son	M	Cha	14.0	S	N	Y	Y	Guam	Guam	Guam	Y	Farm laborer home
30		106	125	Taitano, Concepcion R	Daughter	F	Cha	10.0	S	Y	Y	Y	Guam	Guam	Guam	Y	None
31		106	125	Taitano, Jose R	Son	M	Cha	8.0	S	Y	Y	Y	Guam	Guam	Guam		None
32		106	125	Taitano, Angel R	Son	M	Cha	6.0	S	N			Guam	Guam	Guam		None
33		106	125	Taitano, Antonio R	Son	M	Cha	2.0	S				Guam	Guam	Guam		None
34		106	125	Taitano, Ramon R	Son	M	Cha	1.0	S				Guam	Guam	Guam		None
35		107	126	Aguon, Joaquin LG	Head	M	Cha	48.0	M		Y	Y	Guam	Guam	Guam	N	Farmer
36		107	126	Aguon, Soledad O	Wife	F	Cha	41.0	M		Y	N	Guam	Guam	Guam	N	None
37		107	126	Aguon, Maria O	Daughter	F	Cha	20.0	S		Y	Y	Guam	Guam	Guam	N	None
38		107	126	Aguon, Isabel O	Daughter	F	Cha	17.0	S	N	Y	Y	Guam	Guam	Guam	N	None
39		107	126	Aguon, Concepcion O	Daughter	F	Cha	14.0	S	Y	Y	Y	Guam	Guam	Guam	Y	None
40		107	126	Aguon, Ignacio O	Son	M	Cha	9.0	S	Y	Y	Y	Guam	Guam	Guam	Y	None
41		107	126	Aguon, Ramon O	Son	M	Cha	3.0	S				Guam	Guam	Guam		None
42		107	126	Rosa, Ana de la	Step mother	F	Cha	60.0	Wd		N	N	Guam	Guam	Guam	N	None
43		107	126	Camacho, Maria C	Sister-in-law	F	Cha	31.0	S		Y	Y	Guam	Guam	Guam	N	None
44	Dr. Hessler Street	108	127	Camacho, Jose SN	Head	M	Cha	37.0	M		Y	Y	Guam	Guam	Guam	N	Farmer
45		108	127	Camacho, Carmen C	Wife	F	Cha	39.0	M		Y	Y	Guam	Guam	Guam	N	None
46		108	127	Camacho, Trinidad C	Daughter	F	Cha	15.0	S	N	Y	Y	Guam	Guam	Guam	N	Farm laborer home
47		108	127	Camacho, Vicente C	Son	M	Cha	14.0	S	N	Y	Y	Guam	Guam	Guam	Y	None
48		108	127	Camacho, Jesus C	Son	M	Cha	5.0	S	N			Guam	Guam	Guam		None
49		108	127	Camacho, Beatris C	Daughter	F	Cha	2.0	S				Guam	Guam	Guam		None
50		108	127	Camacho, Maria C	Daughter	F	Cha	0.2	S				Guam	Guam	Guam		None

38

(CHAMORRO ROOTS GENEALOGY PROJECT ™ TRANSCRIPTION)
(COMPILED/TRANSCRIBED BY BERNARD T. PUNZALAN / HTTP://WWW.CHAMORROROOTS.COM)

FOURTEENTH CENSUS OF THE UNITED STATES: 1920-POPULATION
ISLAND OF GUAM

DISTRICT 1
NAME OF PLACE **Agana City**
[Proper name and, also, name of class, as city, town, village, barrio, etc]

ENUMERATED BY ME ON THE 9th DAY OF April, 1920

Joaquin Torres ENUMERATOR

	Street, avenue, road, etc.	Number of dwelling house in order of visitation	Number of family in order of visitation	NAME	RELATION	Sex	Color or race	Age at last birthday	Single, married, widowed or divorced	Attended school any time since Sept. 1, 1919	Whether able to read.	Whether able to write.	Place of birth of this person.	Place of birth of father of this person.	Place of birth of mother of this person.	Whether able to speak English.	OCCUPATION
	1	2	3	4	5	6	7	8	9	10	11	12	13	14	15	16	17
1		108	128	Cruz, Vicente L	Head	M	Cha	65.0	Wd		Y	Y	Guam	Guam	Guam	N	None
2		109	129	Torres, Juan E	Head	M	Cha	47.0	M		Y	Y	Guam	Guam	Guam	N	Farmer
3	Dr. Hessler Street	109	129	Torres, Dolores P	Wife	F	Cha	48.0	M		Y	Y	Guam	Guam	Guam	N	None
4		109	129	Torres, Rosa P	Daughter	F	Cha	18.0	S	N	Y	Y	Guam	Guam	Guam	Y	None
5		109	129	Torres, Carlos P	Son	M	Cha	13.0	S	Y	Y	Y	Guam	Guam	Guam	Y	None
6		109	129	Torres, Gregorio P	Son	M	Cha	11.0	S	Y	Y	Y	Guam	Guam	Guam		None
7		109	129	Torres, Joaquina P	Daughter	F	Cha	9.0	S	Y			Guam	Guam	Guam		None
8		109	129	Torres, Antonio P	Son	M	Cha	4.0	S				Guam	Guam	Guam		None
9		109	129	Torres, Jose P	Son	M	Cha	2.0	S				Guam	Guam	Guam		None
10		110	130	Cruz, Juan S	Head	M	Cha	42.0	M		Y	Y	Guam	Guam	Guam	N	Farmer
11		110	130	Cruz, Ana R	Wife	F	Cha	21.0	M	N	Y	Y	Guam	Guam	Guam	N	None
12		110	130	Cruz, Jose F	Son	M	Cha	18.0	S	N	Y	Y	Guam	Guam	Guam	Y	Farm laborer home
13		110	130	Cruz, Concepcion F	Daughter	F	Cha	15.0	S	N	Y	Y	Guam	Guam	Guam		None
14		111	131	Camacho, Manuel SN	Head	M	Cha	35.0	M		Y	Y	Guam	Guam	Guam	N	Farmer
15		111	131	Camacho, Ana M	Wife	F	Cha	33.0	M		Y	Y	Guam	Guam	Guam	N	None
16		111	131	Camacho, Candelaria M	Daughter	F	Cha	11.0	S	Y	Y	Y	Guam	Guam	Guam	Y	None
17	Gerona Street	111	131	Camacho, Manuel M	Son	M	Cha	8.0	S	Y			Guam	Guam	Guam		None
18		111	131	Camacho, Alfonso M	Son	M	Cha	6.0	S	N			Guam	Guam	Guam		None
19		111	131	Camacho, Francisco M	Son	M	Cha	5.0	S	N			Guam	Guam	Guam		None
20		111	131	Fejarang, Pedela M	Sister-in-law	F	Cha	25.0	Wd		Y	Y	Guam	Guam	Guam	N	None
21		111	131	Fejarang, Maria M	Niece-in-law	F	Cha	3.0	S				Guam	Guam	Guam		None
22		112	132	Quitugua, Francisco B	Head	M	Cha	40.0	M		Y	Y	Guam	Guam	Guam	Y	Farmer
23		112	132	Quitugua, Ana L	Wife	F	Cha	22.0	M		Y	Y	Guam	Guam	Guam	N	None
24		112	132	Quitugua, Joaquin R	Son	M	Cha	15.0	S	N	Y	Y	Guam	Guam	Guam	N	Farm laborer home
25		112	132	Quitugua, Jose L	Son	M	Cha	0.1	S				Guam	Guam	Guam		None

(CHAMORRO ROOTS GENEALOGY PROJECT ™ TRANSCRIPTION)
(COMPILED/TRANSCRIBED BY BERNARD T. PUNZALAN / HTTP://WWW.CHAMORROROOTS.COM)
FOURTEENTH CENSUS OF THE UNITED STATES: 1920—POPULATION
ISLAND OF GUAM

DISTRICT 1
NAME OF PLACE Agana City
[Proper name and, also, name of class, as city, town, village, barrio, etc]

ENUMERATED BY ME ON THE 9th DAY OF April, 1920

Joaquin Torres ENUMERATOR

	PLACE OF ABODE			NAME	RELATION	PERSONAL DESCRIPTION				EDUCATION			NATIVITY				OCCUPATION
Street, avenue, road, etc.	Number of dwelling house is order of visitation	Number of family in order of visitation		Name of each person whose place of abode on January 1, 1920, was in this family.	Relationship of this Person to the head of the family.	Sex	Color or race	Age at last birthday	Single, married, widowed or divorced	Attended school any time since Sept. 1, 1919	Whether able to read.	Whether able to write.	Place of birth of this person.	Place of birth of father of this person.	Place of birth of mother of this person.	Whether able to speak English.	Trade, profession, or particular kind of work done, as salesman, laborer, clerk, cook, merchant, washerwoman, etc.
1	2	3	4		5	6	7	8	9	10	11	12	13	14	15	16	17
	112	132	Lujan, Maria SN	Step-daughter		F	Cha	4.0	S				Guam	Unknown	Guam		None
	112	132	Aguon, Ana S	Cook		F	Cha	24.0	S		N	N	Guam	Guam	Guam	N	Cook
	112	132	Aguon, Pedro S	Boarder		M	Cha	1.0	S				Guam	Unknown	Guam		None
	113	133	Aguon, Ramon T	Head		M	Cha	79.0	Wd		Y	Y	Guam	Guam	Guam	N	None
	113	133	Aguon, Juan T	Son		M	Cha	32.0	S		Y	Y	Guam	Guam	Guam	Y	Teamster
	113	133	Aguon, Ramon S	Grand-son		M	Cha	12.0	S	Y	Y	Y	Guam	Guam	Guam	Y	None
	114	134	Taitano, Mariano B	Head		M	Cha	34.0	M		Y	Y	Guam	Guam	Guam	N	Farmer
	114	134	Taitano, Trinidad C	Wife		F	Cha	40.0	M		Y	Y	Guam	Guam	Guam	N	None
Gerona Street	114	134	Taitano, Maria C	Daughter		F	Cha	7.0	S	Y			Guam	Guam	Guam		None
	114	134	Taitano, Antonio C	Son		M	Cha	6.0	S	N			Guam	Guam	Guam		None
	114	134	Taitano, Jose C	Son		M	Cha	5.0	S	N			Guam	Guam	Guam		None
	114	134	Taitano, Faustina C	Daughter		F	Cha	1.0	S				Guam	Guam	Guam		None
	115	135	Camacho, Jose D	Head		M	Cha	54.0	M		Y	Y	Guam	Guam	Guam	N	Farmer
	115	135	Camacho, Isabel D	Wife		F	Cha	52.0	M		Y	N	Guam	Spain	Guam	N	None
	115	135	Camacho, Vicente D	Son		M	Cha	19.0	S	N	Y	Y	Guam	Guam	Guam	Y	Blacksmith
	115	135	Camacho, Maria D	Daughter		F	Cha	15.0	S	N	Y	Y	Guam	Guam	Guam	Y	None
	116	136	Meza, Jose S	Head		M	Cha	61.0	M		Y	Y	Guam	Guam	Guam	N	Farmer
	116	136	Meza, Juliana B	Wife		F	Cha	66.0	M		Y	N	Guam	Guam	Guam	N	None
	116	136	Meza, Vicente B	Son		M	Cha	31.0	S		Y	Y	Guam	Guam	Guam	Y	Farm laborer home
	117	137	Camacho, Francisco F	Head		M	Cha	37.0	M		Y	Y	Guam	Guam	Guam	Y	Farmer
	117	137	Camacho, Maria M	Wife		F	Cha	33.0	M		Y	Y	Guam	Guam	Guam	Y	None
	117	137	Camacho, Maria M	Daughter		F	Cha	10.0	S	Y	Y	Y	Guam	Guam	Guam	Y	None
	117	137	Camacho, Jose M	Son		M	Cha	8.0	S	Y			Guam	Guam	Guam		None
	117	137	Camacho, Ana M	Daughter		F	Cha	4.0	S				Guam	Guam	Guam		None
	117	137	Camacho, Pedro M	Son		M	Cha	1.0	S				Guam	Guam	Guam		None

Row numbers: 26, 27, 28, 29, 30, 31, 32, 33, 34, 35, 36, 37, 38, 39, 40, 41, 42, 43, 44, 45, 46, 47, 48, 49, 50

(CHAMORRO ROOTS GENEALOGY PROJECT ™ TRANSCRIPTION)
(COMPILED/TRANSCRIBED BY BERNARD T. PUNZALAN / HTTP://WWW.CHAMORROROOTS.COM)

FOURTEENTH CENSUS OF THE UNITED STATES: 1920—POPULATION
ISLAND OF GUAM

ENUMERATED BY ME ON THE 10th DAY OF April, 1920

Joaquin Torres ENUMERATOR

DISTRICT **1**
NAME OF PLACE **Agana City**
[Proper name and, also, name of class, as city, town, village, barrio, etc]

Street, avenue, road, etc.	Number of dwelling house in order of visitation	Number of family in order of visitation	NAME of each person whose place of abode on January 1, 1920, was in the family.	RELATION Relationship of this Person to the head of the family.	Sex	Color or race	Age at last birthday	Single, married, widowed or divorced	Attended school any time since Sept. 1, 1919	Whether able to read.	Whether able to write.	Place of birth of this person.	Place of birth of father of this person.	Place of birth of mother of this person.	Whether able to speak English.	OCCUPATION Trade, profession, or particular kind of work done, as salesman, laborer, clerk, cook, merchant, washerwoman, etc.
1	2	3	4	5	6	7	8	9	10	11	12	13	14	15	16	17
	117	137	Camacho, Vicente M	Son	M	Cha	0.3	S				Guam	Guam	Guam		None
	118	138	Migofna, Antonio A	Head	M	Cha	25.0	S		Y	Y	Guam	Guam	Guam	Y	Laborer
	118	138	Migofna, Carmen A	Sister	F	Cha	19.0	S	N	Y	Y	Guam	Guam	Guam	Y	None
	118	138	Santos, Rosa C	Cook	F	Cha	31.0	S		Y	Y	Guam	Guam	Guam	N	Cook
	119	139	Lujan, Dolores T	Head	F	Cha	53.0	S		Y	Y	Guam	Guam	Guam	N	Tailoress
	119	139	Lujan, Vicenta T	Sister	F	Cha	62.0	S		Y	Y	Guam	Guam	Guam	N	None
	119	139	Lujan, Irene T	Niece	F	Cha	32.0	S		Y	Y	Guam	Unknown	Guam	N	Tailoress
	120	140	Manibusan, Josefa A	Head	F	Cha	46.0	Wd		Y	Y	Guam	Guam	Guam	N	Laundress
	120	140	Manibusan, Rosa A	Daughter	F	Cha	13.0	S	N	Y	Y	Guam	Guam	Guam	Y	None
	120	140	Manibusan, Jose A	Son	M	Cha	10.0	S	Y	Y	Y	Guam	Guam	Guam	N	None
Gerona Street	121	141	Perez, Jose M	Head	M	Cha	30.0	M		Y	Y	Guam	Guam	Guam	Y	Butcher
	121	141	Perez, Dolores F	Wife	F	Cha	27.0	M	Y	Y	Y	Guam	Guam	Guam	N	None
	121	141	Perez, Jesus F	Son	M	Cha	7.0	S	N			Guam	Guam	Guam		None
	121	141	Perez, Jose F	Son	M	Cha	6.0	S				Guam	Guam	Guam		None
	121	141	Perez, Emiliana F	Daughter	F	Cha	4.0	S				Guam	Guam	Guam		None
	121	141	Perez, Juan F	Son	M	Cha	1.0	S				Guam	Guam	Guam		None
	121	141	Francisco, Joaquin C	Brother-in-law	M	Cha	14.0	S	Y	Y	Y	Guam	Guam	Guam		None
	122	142	Aquiningoc, Maria F	Head	F	Cha	20.0	M	N	Y	Y	Guam	Guam	Guam	Y	None
	122	142	Aquiningoc, Josefa F	Daughter	F	Cha	0.2	S				Guam	Guam	Guam		None
	123	143	Calvo, Gregorio LG	Head	M	W	34.0	M		Y	Y	Guam	Philippine Islands	Guam		Shoemaker
	123	143	Calvo, Maria A	Wife	F	Cha	34.0	M		Y	Y	Guam	Unknown	Guam	N	None
	123	143	Calvo, Pedro A	Son	M	Cha	8.0	S	Y			Guam	Guam	Guam	N	None
	123	143	Calvo, Rita A	Daughter	F	Cha	6.0	S	N			Guam	Guam	Guam		None
	123	143	Calvo, Manuel A	Son	M	Cha	4.0	S				Guam	Guam	Guam		None
	123	143	Calvo, Maria A	Daughter	F	Cha	0.2	S				Guam	Guam	Guam		None

(CHAMORRO ROOTS GENEALOGY PROJECT ™ TRANSCRIPTION)
(COMPILED/TRANSCRIBED BY BERNARD T. PUNZALAN / HTTP://WWW.CHAMORROROOTS.COM)
FOURTEENTH CENSUS OF THE UNITED STATES: 1920-POPULATION
ISLAND OF GUAM

DISTRICT 1
NAME OF PLACE Agana City
[Proper name and, also, name of class, as city, town, village, barrio, etc]

ENUMERATED BY ME ON THE 10th DAY OF April, 1920

Joaquin Torres ENUMERATOR

	Street	No. dwelling	No. family	NAME	RELATION	Sex	Color or race	Age	Condition	School	Read	Write	Birthplace person	Birthplace father	Birthplace mother	English	OCCUPATION
26	Ger. St.	123	143	Borja, Vicenta S	Grand-mother	F	Cha	84.0	Wd		Y		Guam	Guam	Guam		None
27		124	144	Tokeymiya, Kichiro	Head	M	Jp	41.0	S		Y	Y	Japan	Japan	Japan	N	Candy maker
28		125	145	Stone, Charles H	Head	M	W	59.0	M		Y	Y	Michigan	Michigan	Michigan	Y	Accountant
29		126	146	Ynguillo, Crispulo R	Head	M	Fil	38.0	M		Y	Y	Philippine Islands	Philippine Islands	Philippine Islands	Y	Cook
30		126	146	Ynguillo, Trinidad LG	Wife	F	Cha	19.0	M	N	Y	Y	Guam	Unknown	Guam	Y	None
31		126	146	Ynguillo, Carlos LG	Son	M	Fil	2.0	S				Guam	Philippine Islands	Guam		None
32		126	146	Ynguillo, Martin LG	Son	M	Fil	0.1	S				Guam	Philippine Islands	Guam		None
33	General Terrero Street	127	147	Kamminga, Joaquina H	Head	F	Cha	63.0	Wd		Y	Y	Guam	Guam	Guam	Y	None
34		127	147	Kamminga, Joaquina H	Daughter	F	W	27.0	S		N	N	Guam	Holland	Guam	Y	None
35		128	148	Gillespic, Jack M	Head	M	W	34.0	M		Y	Y	California	Pennsylvania	Pennsylvania	Y	General Merchant Business Manager
36		128	148	Gillespic, Elma E	Wife	F	W	34.0	M		Y	Y	California	California	California	Y	None
37		129	149	Eclavea, Lucio Q	Head	M	Fil	56.0	M		Y	Y	Philippine Islands	Philippine Islands	Philippine Islands	N	Farmer
38		129	149	Eclavea, Tomasa R	Wife	F	Cha	49.0	M		Y	N	Guam	Guam	Guam	N	None
39		129	149	Eclavea, Jose R	Son	M	Fil	17.0	S	N	Y	Y	Guam	Philippine Islands	Guam	Y	Enlisted man USN
40		129	149	Eclavea, Virginia R	Daughter	F	Fil	14.0	S	Y	Y	Y	Guam	Philippine Islands	Guam	Y	None
41		129	149	Eclavea, Enrique R	Son	M	Fil	12.0	S	Y	Y	Y	Guam	Philippine Islands	Guam	Y	None
42		129	149	Eclavea, Gonzalo R	Son	M	Fil	10.0	S	Y	Y	Y	Guam	Philippine Islands	Guam	Y	None
43		129	149	Eclavea, Antonio R	Son	M	Fil	8.0	S				Guam	Philippine Islands	Guam		None
44		130	150	Esteban, Pedro P	Head	M	Cha	37.0	M		Y	Y	Guam	Guam	Guam	N	Farmer
45		130	150	Esteban, Maria E	Wife	F	Fil	29.0	M		Y	Y	Guam	Philippine Islands	Guam	N	None
46		130	150	Esteban, Jesus E	Son	M	Cha	10.0	S	Y	Y	Y	Guam	Guam	Guam	N	None
47		130	150	Esteban, Maria E	Daughter	F	Cha	8.0	S	Y	Y	Y	Guam	Guam	Guam		None
48		130	150	Esteban, Felipe E	Son	M	Cha	6.0	S	N			Guam	Guam	Guam		None
49		130	150	Esteban, Carmen E	Daughter	F	Cha	5.0	S	N			Guam	Guam	Guam		None
50		130	150	Esteban, Lagrimas E	Daughter	F	Cha	2.0	S				Guam	Guam	Guam		None

(CHAMORRO ROOTS GENEALOGY PROJECT ™ TRANSCRIPTION)
(COMPILED/TRANSCRIBED BY BERNARD T. PUNZALAN / HTTP://WWW.CHAMORROROOTS.COM)

FOURTEENTH CENSUS OF THE UNITED STATES: 1920—POPULATION
ISLAND OF GUAM

DISTRICT 1
NAME OF PLACE Agana City

[Proper name and, also, name of class, as city, town, village, barrio, etc]

SHEET NO. 47A

ENUMERATED BY ME ON THE 10th DAY OF April, 1920

Joaquin Torres ENUMERATOR

Street, avenue, road, etc.	Number of dwelling house in order of visitation	Number of family in order of visitation	NAME	RELATION	Sex	Color or race	Age at last birthday	Single, married, widowed or divorced	Attended school any time since Sept. 1, 1919	Whether able to read	Whether able to write	Place of birth of this person	Place of birth of father of this person	Place of birth of mother of this person	Whether able to speak English	OCCUPATION
	1	2	3	4	5	6	7	8	9	10	11	12	13	14	15	16	17
	130	150	Esteban, Natividad E	Daughter	F	Cha	0.0	S				Guam	Guam	Guam		None
	131	151	Camacho, Francisco L	Head	M	Cha	45.0	M		Y	Y	Guam	Guam	Guam	N	Farmer
	131	151	Camacho, Vicenta R	Wife	F	Cha	50.0	M		Y	N	Guam	Guam	Guam	N	None
	131	151	Camacho, Maria R	Daughter	F	Cha	12.0	S	Y	Y	Y	Guam	Guam	Guam		None
	131	151	Camacho, Lucia R	Daughter	F	Cha	9.0	S	Y	Y	Y	Guam	Guam	Guam		None
General Terrero Street	131	151	Camacho, Mariano R	Son	M	Cha	8.0	S	Y			Guam	Guam	Guam		None
	132	152	Santos, Jesus R	Head	M	Cha	26.0	M		Y	Y	Guam	Guam	Guam	Y	Cook
	132	152	Santos, Ignacia M	Wife	F	Cha	19.0	M	N	Y	Y	Guam	Guam	Guam	Y	None
	132	152	Santos, Rosa M	Daughter	F	Cha	3.0	S				Guam	Guam	Guam		None
	132	152	Santos, Clotide M	Daughter	F	Cha	2.0	S				Guam	Guam	Guam		None
	132	152	Santos, Maria M	Daughter	F	Cha	0.0	S				Guam	Guam	Guam		None
	133	153	Guerrero, Ana G	Head	F	Cha	29.0	Wd		N	N	Guam	Guam	Guam	N	None
	133	153	Guerrero, Juan G	Son	M	Cha	2.0	S				Guam	Guam	Guam		None
	133	153	Guerrero, Luis G	Son	M	Cha	1.0	S				Guam	Guam	Guam		None
	133	153	Lujan, Nieves SN	Aunt	F	Cha	61.0	Wd		Y	Y	Guam	Guam	Guam	N	None
	133	153	Lujan, Carmen SN	Cousin	F	Cha	26.0	S		Y	Y	Guam	Guam	Guam	N	None
	133	153	Lujan, Jesus SN	Cousin	M	Cha	19.0	S	N	Y	Y	Guam	Guam	Guam	N	Laborer
	133	153	Lujan, Joaquin SN	Cousin	M	Cha	18.0	S	N	Y	Y	Guam	Guam	Guam	N	Chauffeur
	134	154	Santos, Felomena Q	Head	F	Cha	43.0	Wd		Y	Y	Guam	Guam	Guam	N	None
	134	154	Santos, Jose Q	Son	M	Cha	15.0	S	Y	Y	Y	Guam	Guam	Guam	Y	None
	134	154	Santos, Ignacio Q	Son	M	Cha	8.0	S	Y			Guam	Guam	Guam		None
	134	154	Santos, Francisco Q	Son	M	Cha	4.0	S				Guam	Guam	Guam		None
	135	135	San Nicolas, Jesus S	Head	M	Cha	33.0	M		Y	Y	Guam	Guam	Guam	Y	Farmer
	135	135	San Nicolas, Rosario S	Wife	F	Cha	22.0	M	N	Y	Y	Guam	Guam	Guam	N	None
	136	156	San Nicolas, Gregorio C	Head	M	Cha	56.0	M		Y	Y	Guam	Guam	Guam	N	Shoemaker

(CHAMORRO ROOTS GENEALOGY PROJECT ™ TRANSCRIPTION)
(COMPILED/TRANSCRIBED BY BERNARD T. PUNZALAN / HTTP://WWW.CHAMORROROOTS.COM)
FOURTEENTH CENSUS OF THE UNITED STATES: 1920–POPULATION
ISLAND OF GUAM

DISTRICT **1**
NAME OF PLACE **Agana City**
[Proper name and, also, name of class, as city, town, village, barrio, etc]

ENUMERATED BY ME ON THE 10th DAY OF April, 1920
Joaquin Torres ENUMERATOR

	Street	Dwelling No.	Family No.	NAME	RELATION	Sex	Color/race	Age	Marital	School since Sept 1,1919	Read	Write	Birthplace person	Birthplace father	Birthplace mother	Speak English	OCCUPATION
26	General Terrero Street	136	156	San Nicolas, Maria C	Wife	F	Cha	62.0	M		Y	Y	Guam	Guam	Guam	N	None
27		136	156	San Nicolas, Joaquina C	Daughter	F	Cha	25.0	S		Y	Y	Guam	Guam	Guam	N	None
28		136	157	Baza, Jose B	Head	M	Cha	55.0	M		Y	Y	Guam	Guam	Guam	N	Farmer
29		136	157	Baza, Ramona C	Wife	F	Cha	56.0	M		Y	Y	Guam	Guam	Guam	N	None
30		136	157	Camacho, Ana M	Boarder	F	Cha	8.0	S	Y			Guam	Guam	Guam	N	None
31		137	158	Salas, Lucas S	Head	M	Cha	59.0	M		Y	Y	Guam	Guam	Guam	N	Farmer
32		137	158	Salas, Juana D	Wife	F	Cha	59.0	M		Y	N	Guam	Guam	Guam	N	None
33		137	158	Leon Guerrero, Ana M	Boarder	F	Cha	7.0	S				Guam	Guam	Guam	N	None
34		138	159	Sablan, Manuel C	Head	M	Cha	54.0	Wd		Y	Y	Guam	Guam	Guam	N	Farmer
35		138	159	Sablan, Antonia P	Daughter	F	Cha	24.0	S		Y	Y	Guam	Guam	Guam	N	None
36		138	159	Sablan, Jesus P	Son	M	Cha	22.0	S		Y	Y	Guam	Guam	Guam	Y	Enlisted man USN
37		138	159	Sablan, Jose P	Son	M	Cha	20.0	S	N	Y	Y	Guam	Guam	Guam	Y	Enlisted man USN
38		138	159	Sablan, Teresa P	Daughter	F	Cha	18.0	S	N	Y	Y	Guam	Guam	Guam	Y	None
39		139	160	Pangelinan, Vicente T	Head	M	Cha	55.0	M	N	Y	Y	Guam	Guam	Guam	N	Farmer
40		139	160	Pangelinan, Ignacia G	Wife	F	Cha	40.0	M		Y	Y	Guam	Guam	Guam	N	None
41		139	160	Pangelinan, Francisco G	Son	M	Cha	20.0	S	N	Y	Y	Guam	Guam	Guam	Y	Farm laborer home
42		139	160	Pangelinan, Jose G	Son	M	Cha	18.0	S	N	Y	Y	Guam	Guam	Guam	Y	Plumber
43		139	160	Pangelinan, Regina G	Daughter	F	Cha	12.0	S		Y	Y	Guam	Guam	Guam	Y	None
44		139	160	Pangelinan, Jesus G	Boarder	M	Cha	9.0	S				Guam	Unknown	Unknown	N	None
45		140	161	Manibusan, Joaquin P	Head	M	Cha	18.0	S	N	Y	Y	Guam	Guam	Guam	Y	Farm laborer
46		141	162	Blas, Gregorio B	Head	M	Cha	54.0	M		Y	Y	Guam	Unknown	Unknown	Y	Cook
47		141	162	Blas, Maria A	Wife	F	Cha	56.0	M		Y	Y	Guam	Guam	Guam	N	None
48		141	162	Blas, Juan A	Son	M	Cha	23.0	S	N	Y	Y	Caroline Islands	Guam	Guam	Y	Farm laborer home
49		141	162	Blas, Jose A	Son	M	Cha	19.0	S	N	Y	Y	Caroline Islands	Guam	Guam	Y	Electrician
50		141	162	Blas, Juliana A	Daughter	F	Cha	18.0	S	N	N	N	Caroline Islands	Guam	Guam	Y	None

44

(CHAMORRO ROOTS GENEALOGY PROJECT ™ TRANSCRIPTION)
(COMPILED/TRANSCRIBED BY BERNARD T. PUNZALAN / HTTP://WWW.CHAMORROROOTS.COM)

FOURTEENTH CENSUS OF THE UNITED STATES: 1920—POPULATION

ISLAND OF GUAM

DISTRICT 1
NAME OF PLACE Agana City

[Proper name and, also, name of class, as city, town, village, barrio, etc]

ENUMERATED BY ME ON THE 12th DAY OF April, 1920

Joaquin Torres ENUMERATOR

	PLACE OF ABODE		NAME	RELATION	PERSONAL DESCRIPTION				EDUCATION			NATIVITY				OCCUPATION
Street, avenue, road, etc.	Number of dwelling house in order of visitation	Number of family in order of visitation	of each person whose place of abode on January 1, 1920, was in the family.	Relationship of this Person to the head of the family.	Sex	Color or race	Age at last birthday	Single, married, widowed or divorced	Attended school any time since Sept. 1, 1919	Whether able to read.	Whether able to write.	Place of birth of this person.	Place of birth of father of this person.	Place of birth of mother of this person.	Whether able to speak English.	Trade, profession, or particular kind of work done
1	2	3	4	5	6	7	8	9	10	11	12	13	14	15	16	17
	141	162	Blas, Vicente A	Son	M	Cha	15.0	S	Y	Y	Y	Caroline Islands	Guam	Guam	Y	None
	141	162	Blas, Alice A	Daughter	F	Cha	12.0	S	Y	Y	Y	Caroline Islands	Guam	Guam	N	None
	141	162	Ada, Nicolasa B	Aunt	F	Cha	75.0	Wd		Y	N	Caroline Islands	Guam	Guam	N	None
	142	163	Camacho, Manuel F	Head	M	Cha	41.0	M		Y	Y	Guam	Guam	Guam	N	Farmer
	142	163	Camacho, Maria G	Wife	F	Cha	41.0	M		Y	Y	Guam	Guam	Guam	N	None
	142	163	Camacho, Vicente G	Son	M	Cha	21.0	S	N	N	N	Guam	Guam	Guam	N	Farm laborer home
	142	163	Camacho, Juan G	Son	M	Cha	18.0	S	N	Y	Y	Guam	Guam	Guam	N	Laborer
	142	163	Camacho, Isabel G	Daughter	F	Cha	13.0	S	Y	Y	Y	Guam	Guam	Guam		None
	142	163	Camacho, Felicitas G	Daughter	F	Cha	10.0	S	Y	Y	Y	Guam	Guam	Guam	Y	None
	142	163	Camacho, Jesus G	Son	M	Cha	8.0	S	Y	Y	Y	Guam	Guam	Guam	Y	None
	142	163	Camacho, Mercedes G	Daughter	F	Cha	5.0	S	N			Guam	Guam	Guam		None
	142	163	Camacho, Natividad G	Daughter	F	Cha	0.1	S				Guam	Guam	Guam		None
	143	164	Pangelinan, Jose T	Head	M	Cha	46.0	M		Y	Y	Guam	Guam	Guam	N	Farmer
	143	164	Pangelinan, Rosa LG	Wife	F	Cha	46.0	M		Y	N	Guam	Guam	Guam	N	None
	143	164	Pangelinan, Enrique G	Son	M	Cha	12.0	S	Y	Y	Y	Guam	Guam	Guam	Y	None
	143	164	Pangelinan, Genoveva G	Daughter	F	Cha	11.0	S	Y	Y	Y	Guam	Guam	Guam	Y	None
	144	165	Cruz, Susana L	Head	F	Cha	55.0	S		N	N	Guam	Guam	Guam	N	Laundress
	144	165	Cruz, Concepcion L	Daughter	F	Cha	19.0	S	N	Y	Y	Guam	Unknown	Guam	Y	Cook
	144	165	Cruz, Rosario L	Grand-daughter	F	Cha	2.0	S				Guam	Unknown	Guam		None
	145	166	Duenas, Jose C	Head	M	Cha	34.0	M		Y	Y	Guam	Guam	Guam	Y	Examiner of Titles
	145	166	Duenas, Concepcion C	Wife	F	Cha	30.0	M		Y	Y	Guam	Guam	Guam	N	None
	145	166	Duenas, Jesus C	Son	M	Cha	10.0	S	Y	Y	Y	Guam	Guam	Guam	Y	None
	145	166	Duenas, Jose C	Son	M	Cha	8.0	S	Y			Guam	Guam	Guam		None
	145	166	Duenas, Eduardo C	Son	M	Cha	6.0	S	N			Guam	Guam	Guam		None
	145	166	Duenas, Alfredo C	Son	M	Cha	3.0	S				Guam	Guam	Guam		None

Street: General Terrero Street

(CHAMORRO ROOTS GENEALOGY PROJECT ™ TRANSCRIPTION)
(COMPILED/TRANSCRIBED BY BERNARD T. PUNZALAN / HTTP://WWW.CHAMORROROOTS.COM)

FOURTEENTH CENSUS OF THE UNITED STATES: 1920—POPULATION
ISLAND OF GUAM

DISTRICT 1
NAME OF PLACE Agana City
[Proper name and, also, name of class, as city, town, village, barrio, etc]

ENUMERATED BY ME ON THE 12th DAY OF April, 1920

Joaquin Torres ENUMERATOR

	PLACE OF ABODE			NAME	RELATION	PERSONAL DESCRIPTION				EDUCATION			NATIVITY				OCCUPATION
Street, avenue, road, etc.	No. of dwelling house	No. of family			Sex	Color or race	Age at last birthday	Single, married, widowed or divorced	Attended school any time since Sept. 1, 1919	Whether able to read	Whether able to write	Place of birth of this person	Place of birth of father	Place of birth of mother	Whether able to speak English	Trade, profession
1	2	3	4	5	6	7	8	9	10	11	12	13	14	15	16	17
	145	166	Duenas, Carmen C	Daughter	F	Cha	1.0	S				Guam	Guam	Guam		None
	145	166	Aguon, Soledad P	Cook	F	Cha	15.0	S	N	Y	Y	Guam	Guam	Guam	N	Cook
	146	167	Leon Guerrero, Juan	Head	M	Cha	27.0	M		Y	Y	Guam	Guam	Philippine Islands	Y	Enlisted man USN
	146	167	Leon Guerrero, Joaquina S	Wife	F	Cha	20.0	M	N			Guam	Guam	Guam	Y	None
	146	167	Leon Guerrero, Josefina	Daughter	F	Cha	0.8	S				Guam	Guam	Guam		None
	146	167	Deza, Moses B	Cook	M	W	62.0	S		Y	Y	Guam	Spain	Guam	Y	Cook
General Terrero Street	147	168	Ito, Genyo	Head	M	Jp	41.0	M		Y	Y	Japan	Japan	Japan	N	Tailor
	147	168	Ito, Amalia S	Wife	F	Cha	28.0	M		Y	Y	Guam	Unknown	Guam	Y	Tailoress
	148	169	Aguon, Jesus C	Head	M	Cha	32.0	M		Y	Y	Guam	Guam	Guam	N	Farmer
	148	169	Aguon, Maria L	Wife	F	Cha	29.0	M	Y	Y	Y	Guam	Guam	Guam	N	None
	148	169	Aguon, Josefa L	Daughter	F	Cha	8.0	S	Y			Guam	Guam	Guam		None
	148	169	Aguon, Vicente L	Son	M	Cha	5.0	S	N			Guam	Guam	Guam		None
	148	169	Aguon, Juan L	Son	M	Cha	3.0	S				Guam	Guam	Guam		None
	148	169	Aguon, Maria L	Daughter	F	Cha	1.0	S				Guam	Guam	Guam		None
	149	170	Francisco, Jose P	Head	M	W	57.0	M		Y	Y	Guam	Portugal	Guam	N	Farmer
	149	170	Francisco, Rita F	Wife	F	Cha	39.0	M		N	N	Guam	Guam	Guam	N	None
	149	170	Francisco, Jose F	Son	M	Cha	2.0	S				Guam	Guam	Guam		None
	149	170	Francisco, Ignacio F	Son	M	Cha	0.3	S				Guam	Guam	Guam		None
	149	170	Flores, Josefa C	Sister-in-law	F	Cha	59.0	Wd		Y	Y	Guam	Guam	Guam	N	None
	149	171	Flores, Jose C	Head	M	Cha	52.0	S		Y	Y	Guam	Guam	Guam	N	Farmer
	149	171	Flores, Maria C	Daughter	F	Cha	20.0	S	N	Y	Y	Guam	Guam	Guam	N	None
	149	171	Flores, Ana C	Daughter	F	Cha	19.0	S	N	Y	Y	Guam	Guam	Guam	N	None
	149	171	Flores, Jose C	Son	M	Cha	14.0	S	N	Y	Y	Guam	Guam	Guam	N	Farm laborer home
	149	171	Flores, Juan C	Son	M	Cha	12.0	S	N	N	N	Guam	Guam	Guam	N	None
	149	171	Flores, Rosa C	Daughter	F	Cha	9.0	S	Y			Guam	Guam	Guam		None

(CHAMORRO ROOTS GENEALOGY PROJECT ™ TRANSCRIPTION)
(COMPILED/TRANSCRIBED BY BERNARD T. PUNZALAN / HTTP://WWW.CHAMORROROOTS.COM)

FOURTEENTH CENSUS OF THE UNITED STATES: 1920—POPULATION

ISLAND OF GUAM

SHEET NO. 49A

DISTRICT 1
NAME OF PLACE Agana City

ENUMERATED BY ME ON THE 13th DAY OF April, 1920

Joaquin Torres ENUMERATOR

#	Street	Dwelling No.	Family No.	NAME	RELATION	Sex	Color or race	Age	Single, married, widowed or divorced	Attended school	Able to read	Able to write	Place of birth	Father's birthplace	Mother's birthplace	Able to speak English	OCCUPATION
1		149	171	Flores, Carmen C	Daughter	F	Cha	3.0	S	N			Guam	Guam	Guam		None
2		150	172	Palacios, Francisco M	Head	M	Cha	62.0	M		Y	Y	Guam	Guam	Guam	N	Farmer
3		150	172	Palacios, Maria T	Wife	F	Cha	66.0	M		Y	Y	Guam	Unknown	Guam	N	None
4		150	172	Palacios, Juan T	Son	M	Cha	37.0	M		Y	Y	Guam	Unknown	Guam	N	Farm laborer home
5		150	172	Tenorio, Rita I	Sister-in-law	F	Cha	48.0	S	N	N	N	Guam	Unknown	Guam	N	None
6		150	172	Perez, Dolores M	Boarder	F	Cha	18.0	S		Y	Y	Guam	Guam	Guam	Y	None
7		150	172	Tenorio, Ignacio T	Boarder	M	Cha	4.0	S				Guam	Unknown	Guam		None
8		150	172	Santos, Jose S	Farm laborer	M	Cha	38.0	S		N	N	Guam	Unknown	Guam	N	Farm laborer
9		150	173	Palacios, Jose T	Head	M	Cha	36.0	M		Y	Y	Guam	Guam	Guam	Y	Farmer
10		150	173	Palacios, Maria C	Wife	F	Cha	31.0	M		Y	Y	Guam	Guam	Guam	N	None
11		150	173	Palacios, Francisco C	Son	M	Cha	9.0	S	Y	Y	Y	Guam	Guam	Guam		None
12	General Terrero Street	150	173	Palacios, Jose C	Son	M	Cha	8.0	S	Y	Y	Y	Guam	Guam	Guam		None
13		150	173	Palacios, Josefina C	Daughter	F	Cha	6.0	S	N			Guam	Guam	Guam		None
14		150	173	Palacios, Maria C	Daughter	F	Cha	5.0	S				Guam	Guam	Guam		None
15		150	173	Palacios, Francisca C	Daughter	F	Cha	3.0	S				Guam	Guam	Guam		None
16		150	173	Fejarang, Ramon C	Nephew-in-law	M	Cha	19.0	S	N	N	Y	Guam	Guam	Guam	Y	Farm laborer home
17		150	173	Aguon, Nicolasa C	Niece-in-law	F	Cha	16.0	S	N	Y	Y	Guam	Guam	Guam	Y	None
18		150	173	Aguon, Nieves C	Niece-in-law	F	Cha	12.0	S	Y	Y	Y	Guam	Guam	Guam	Y	None
19		150	173	Aguon, Carlos C	Nephew-in-law	M	Cha	10.0	S	Y	Y	Y	Guam	Guam	Guam	N	None
20		151	174	San Nicolas, Jose C	Head	M	Cha	50.0	M		Y	Y	Guam	Guam	Guam	N	Farmer
21		151	174	San Nicolas, Maria P	Wife	F	Cha	42.0	M		Y	Y	Guam	Guam	Guam	N	None
22		151	174	San Nicolas, Maria P	Daughter	F	Cha	23.0	S		Y	Y	Guam	Guam	Guam	Y	None
23		151	174	San Nicolas, Joaquin P	Son	M	Cha	16.0	S	N	N	N	Guam	Guam	Guam	Y	Laborer
24		151	174	San Nicolas, Ana P	Daughter	F	Cha	14.0	S	N	Y	Y	Guam	Guam	Guam	Y	None
25		151	174	San Nicolas, Juan P	Son	M	Cha	12.0	S	Y	Y	Y	Guam	Guam	Guam	Y	None

(CHAMORRO ROOTS GENEALOGY PROJECT ™ TRANSCRIPTION)
(COMPILED/TRANSCRIBED BY BERNARD T. PUNZALAN / HTTP://WWW.CHAMORROROOTS.COM)
FOURTEENTH CENSUS OF THE UNITED STATES: 1920—POPULATION
ISLAND OF GUAM

ENUMERATED BY ME ON THE 13th DAY OF April, 1920

Joaquin Torres ENUMERATOR

DISTRICT 1
NAME OF PLACE Agana City

[Proper name and, also, name of class, as city, town, village, barrio, etc]

Street	Dwelling No.	Family No.	NAME	RELATION	Sex	Color or race	Age	Marital	Attended school	Read	Write	Birthplace (person)	Birthplace (father)	Birthplace (mother)	Speak English	OCCUPATION
	151	174	San Nicolas, Trinidad P	Daughter	F	Cha	9.0	S	Y			Guam	Guam	Guam		None
	151	174	San Nicolas, Rosa P	Daughter	F	Cha	7.0	S	Y			Guam	Guam	Guam		None
	151	174	San Nicolas, Isabel P	Daughter	F	Cha	4.0	S				Guam	Guam	Guam		None
	151	174	San Nicolas, Mariano P	Son	M	Cha	1.0	S				Guam	Guam	Guam		None
	151	174	Pangelinan, Ana G	Sister-in-law	F	Cha	36.0	M		Y	Y	Guam	Guam	Guam	N	None
	152	175	Guerrero, Juan F	Head	M	Cha	44.0	M		Y	Y	Guam	Guam	Guam	N	Farmer
	152	175	Guerrero, Ana LG	Wife	F	Cha	46.0	M		Y	N	Guam	Guam	Guam	N	None
	152	175	Guerrero, Pedro LG	Son	M	Cha	9.0	S	Y			Guam	Guam	Guam		None
	152	175	Guerrero, Antonia LG	Daughter	F	Cha	8.0	S	Y	Y	Y	Guam	Guam	Guam		None
	152	175	Guerrero, Juan LG	Son	M	Cha	6.0	S	N			Guam	Guam	Guam		None
	152	175	Guerrero, Francisca LG	Daughter	F	Cha	3.0	S	N			Guam	Guam	Guam		None
General Terrero Street	152	175	Leon Guerrero, Francisca T	Mother-in-law	F	Cha	71.0	Wd				Guam	Guam	Guam	N	None
	153	176	Leon Guerrero, Manuel T	Head	M	Cha	42.0	M		Y	Y	Guam	Guam	Guam	N	Farmer
	153	176	Leon Guerrero, Luisa U	Wife	F	Cha	29.0	M		Y	N	Guam	Guam	Guam	N	None
	153	176	Leon Guerrero, Dolores U	Daughter	F	Cha	5.0	S	N			Guam	Guam	Guam		None
	153	176	Leon Guerrero, Maria U	Daughter	F	Cha	1.0	S				Guam	Guam	Guam		None
	154	177	Camacho, Jose D	Head	M	Cha	29.0	M		Y	Y	Guam	Guam	Guam	Y	Farmer
	154	177	Camacho, Ana SN	Wife	F	Cha	29.0	M		Y	Y	Guam	Guam	Guam	N	None
	154	177	Camacho, Gregorio SN	Son	M	Cha	9.0	S	Y			Guam	Guam	Guam		None
	154	177	Camacho, Jose SN	Son	M	Cha	7.0	S	Y	Y	Y	Guam	Guam	Guam		None
	154	177	Camacho, Pedro SN	Son	M	Cha	5.0	S	N			Guam	Guam	Guam		None
	154	177	Camacho, Vicente SN	Son	M	Cha	3.0	S				Guam	Guam	Guam		None
	154	177	Camacho, Jesus SN	Son	M	Cha	1.0	S				Guam	Guam	Guam		None
	155	178	Delgado, Vicenta M	Head	F	Cha	64.0	Wd		Y	Y	Guam	Guam	Guam	N	None
	155	178	Delgado, Jose M	Son	M	Cha	27.0	S		Y	Y	Guam	Guam	Guam	Y	Laborer

(CHAMORRO ROOTS GENEALOGY PROJECT ™ TRANSCRIPTION)
(COMPILED/TRANSCRIBED BY BERNARD T. PUNZALAN / HTTP://WWW.CHAMORROROOTS.COM)
FOURTEENTH CENSUS OF THE UNITED STATES: 1920-POPULATION
ISLAND OF GUAM

DISTRICT 1
NAME OF PLACE **Agana City**

ENUMERATED BY ME ON THE 14th DAY OF April, 1920

Joaquin Torres ENUMERATOR

[Proper name and, also, name of class, name of city, town, village, barrio, etc]

Street, avenue, road, etc.	Number of dwelling house	Number of family	NAME	RELATION	Sex	Color or race	Age at last birthday	Single, married, widowed or divorced	Attended school any time since Sept. 1, 1919	Whether able to read	Whether able to write	Place of birth of this person	Place of birth of father of this person	Place of birth of mother of this person	Whether able to speak English	OCCUPATION
	1	2	3	4	5	6	7	8	9	10	11	12	13	14	15	16	17
	155	178	Delgado, Maria M	Daughter	F	Cha	25.0	S		Y	Y	Guam	Guam	Guam	Y	None
General Terrero Street	156	179	Losongco, Antonio M	Head	M	Chin	52.0	M		Y	Y	Guam	China	Guam	Y	Watchman
	156	179	Losongco, Rosa D	Wife	F	Cha	45.0	M		Y	N	Guam	Guam	Guam	·	None
	156	179	Losongco, Joaquin D	Son	M	Cha	13.0	S	Y	Y	Y	Guam	Guam	Guam	N	None
	156	179	Losongco, Antonio D	Son	M	Cha	11.0	S	Y	Y	Y	Guam	Guam	Guam	Y	None
	156	179	Losongco, Ana D	Daughter	F	Cha	5.0	S	N			Guam	Guam	Guam		None
	156	179	Losongco, Dolores D	Daughter	F	Cha	3.0	S				Guam	Guam	Guam		None
	156	179	Losongco, Luis D	Son	M	Cha	1.0	S				Guam	Guam	Guam		None
	157	180	Santos, Ana M	Head	F	Cha	42.0	Wd		Y	Y	Guam	Guam	Guam	N	Laundress
	157	180	Muna, Maria M	Daughter	F	Cha	18.0	S	N	Y	Y	Guam	Guam	Guam	Y	Laundress
	157	180	Santos, Pedro M	Son	M	Cha	8.0	S	Y			Guam	Guam	Guam		None
	157	180	Santos, Rosa M	Daughter	F	Cha	5.0	S	N			Guam	Guam	Guam		None
	157	180	Santos, Juana M	Daughter	F	Cha	3.0	S				Guam	Guam	Guam		None
	157	180	Santos, Juan M	Son	M	Cha	1.0	S				Guam	Guam	Guam		None
	157	180	Santos, Juan T	Cousin-in-law	M	Cha	60.0	Wd		Y	Y	Guam	Guam	Guam		None
Hernan Cortez Street	158	181	Flores, Ignacio C	Head	M	Cha	55.0	M		Y	N	Guam	Guam	Guam	N	Farmer
	158	181	Flores, Rita C	Wife	F	Cha	46.0	M		Y	N	Guam	Guam	Guam	N	None
	158	181	Flores, Nicolasa C	Daughter	F	Cha	22.0	S	N	Y	Y	Guam	Guam	Guam	N	Farm laborer home
	158	181	Flores, Ana C	Daughter	F	Cha	19.0	S	N	Y	Y	Guam	Guam	Guam	Y	None
	158	181	Flores, Juan C	Son	M	Cha	17.0	S	N	Y	Y	Guam	Guam	Guam	Y	None
	158	181	Flores, Josefa C	Daughter	F	Cha	15.0	S	N	Y	Y	Guam	Guam	Guam	Y	None
	158	181	Flores, Vicente C	Son	M	Cha	12.0	S	Y	Y	Y	Guam	Guam	Guam	Y	None
	158	181	Flores, Josefa C	Daughter	F	Cha	10.0	S	Y	Y	Y	Guam	Guam	Guam	Y	None
	158	181	Flores, Joaquina C	Daughter	F	Cha	6.0	S	N			Guam	Unknown	Guam		None
	158	181	Flores, Oliva C	Grand-daughter	F	Cha	5.0	S	N			Guam	Guam	Guam		None

(CHAMORRO ROOTS GENEALOGY PROJECT ™ TRANSCRIPTION)
(COMPILED/TRANSCRIBED BY BERNARD T. PUNZALAN / HTTP://WWW.CHAMORROROOTS.COM)

FOURTEENTH CENSUS OF THE UNITED STATES: 1920-POPULATION
ISLAND OF GUAM

19b

ENUMERATED BY ME ON THE 14th DAY OF April, 1920

Joaquin Torres ENUMERATOR

DISTRICT 1
NAME OF PLACE **Agana City**

[Proper name and, also, name of class, as city, town, village, barrio, etc]

	PLACE OF ABODE			NAME	RELATION	PERSONAL DESCRIPTION					EDUCATION			NATIVITY				OCCUPATION
Street, avenue, road, etc.	Number of dwelling house in order of visitation	Number of family in order of visitation				Sex	Color or race	Age at last birthday	Single, married, widowed or divorced	Attended school any time since Sept. 1, 1919	Whether able to read	Whether able to write	Place of birth of this person	Place of birth of father of this person	Place of birth of mother of this person	Whether able to speak English	
1	2	3		4	5	6	7	8	9	10	11	12	13	14	15	16	17
	159	182	26	Meza, Vicente S	Head	M	Cha	49.0	M		Y	Y	Guam	Guam	Guam	N	Farmer
	159	182	27	Meza, Dolores R	Wife	F	Cha	56.0	M		Y	N	Guam	Guam	Guam	N	None
	159	182	28	Meza, Jose M	Son	M	Cha	26.0	S		Y	Y	Guam	Guam	Guam	Y	Farm laborer home
	159	182	29	Meza, Maria M	Daughter	F	Cha	24.0	S		Y	Y	Guam	Guam	Guam	Y	None
	159	182	30	Meza, Maria R	Daughter	F	Cha	17.0	S	N	Y	Y	Guam	Guam	Guam	Y	None
	159	182	31	Meza, Manuel R	Son	M	Cha	15.0	S	N	Y	Y	Guam	Guam	Guam	Y	Farm laborer home
	160	183	32	Tagae, Arayo	Head	M	Jp	40.0	M		Y	Y	Japan	Japan	Japan	N	Farm ??
	161	184	33	Blas, Maria A	Head	F	Cha	36.0	Wd		Y	Y	Guam	Guam	Guam	N	None
	161	184	34	Blas, Vicente A	Son	M	Cha	16.0	S	N	Y	Y	Guam	Guam	Guam	N	Cook
	161	184	35	Blas, Manuel A	Son	M	Cha	14.0	S	N	Y	Y	Guam	Guam	Guam	Y	Servant
	161	184	36	Aquiningoc, Ana A	Daughter	F	Cha	4.0	S				Guam	Guam	Guam		None
	161	184	37	Aquiningoc, Macrina A	Daughter	F	Cha	0.7	S				Guam	Guam	Guam		None
	161	184	38	Ada, Maria A	Niece	F	Cha	9.0	S				Guam	Guam	Guam		None
	162	185	39	Guerrero, Francisco G	Head	M	Cha	28.0	M		Y	Y	Guam	Guam	Guam	Y	Farmer
	162	185	40	Guerrero, Maria R	Wife	F	Cha	24.0	M		Y	Y	Guam	Guam	Guam	Y	None
	162	185	41	Guerrero, Rosalia R	Daughter	F	Cha	4.0	S				Guam	Guam	Guam		None
	162	185	42	Guerrero, Joaquin R	Son	M	Cha	3.0	S				Guam	Guam	Guam		None
	162	185	43	Guerrero, Ana R	Daughter	F	Cha	0.8	S				Guam	Guam	Guam		None
	162	185	44	San Nicolas, Joaquin G	Brother	M	Cha	40.0	S		Y	N	Guam	Guam	Guam		Farm laborer working out
	162	185	45	Rivera, Mariano G	Brother-in-law	M	Cha	21.0	S	N	Y	Y	Guam	Guam	Guam		Farm laborer home
	162	185	46	Rivera, Juan G	Brother-in-law	M	Cha	20.0	S	N	Y	Y	Guam	Guam	Guam		Laborer
	162	185	47	Rivera, Andrea G	Sister-in-law	F	Cha	18.0	S	N	Y	N	Guam	Guam	Guam		None
	162	185	48	Rivera, Ana LG	Grand mother-in-law	F	Cha	81.0	Wd		Y	Y	Guam	Guam	Guam		None
	163	186	49	San Nicolas, Miguel C	Head	M	Cha	44.0	M		Y	Y	Guam	Guam	Guam	N	Farmer
	163	186	50	San Nicolas, Margarita C	Wife	F	Cha	45.0	M		Y	Y	Guam	Guam	Guam	N	None

Hernan Cortez Street

50

(CHAMORRO ROOTS GENEALOGY PROJECT ™ TRANSCRIPTION)
(COMPILED/TRANSCRIBED BY BERNARD T. PUNZALAN / HTTP://WWW.CHAMORROROOTS.COM)

FOURTEENTH CENSUS OF THE UNITED STATES: 1920-POPULATION

ISLAND OF GUAM

20

SHEET NO. 51A

DISTRICT 1
NAME OF PLACE **Agana City**

[Proper name and, also, name of class, as city, town, village, barrio, etc]

ENUMERATED BY ME ON THE 14th DAY OF April, 1920

Joaquin Torres ENUMERATOR

	PLACE OF ABODE		NAME	RELATION	PERSONAL DESCRIPTION				EDUCATION			NATIVITY				OCCUPATION
Street, avenue, road, etc.	Number of dwelling house in order of visitation	Number of family in order of visitation	of each person whose place of abode on January 1, 1920, was in the family. Enter surname, first, then given name and middle initial. If any. Include every person living on January 1, 1920. Omit children born since January 1, 1920.	Relationship of this Person to the head of the family.	Sex	Color or race	Age at last birthday	Single, married, widowed or divorced	Attended school any time since Sept. 1, 1919	Whether able to read.	Whether able to write.	Place of birth of this person.	Place of birth of father of this person.	Place of birth of mother of this person.	Whether able to speak English.	Trade, profession, or particular kind of work done, as salesman, laborer, clerk, cook, merchant, washerwoman, etc.
1	2	3	4	5	6	7	8	9	10	11	12	13	14	15	16	17
	163	186	San Nicolas, Ignacio C	Son	M	Cha	20.0	S	N	Y	Y	Guam	Guam	Guam	Y	Plumber
	163	186	San Nicolas, Maria C	Daughter	F	Cha	18.0	S	N	Y	Y	Guam	Guam	Guam	Y	None
	163	186	San Nicolas, Vicenta C	Daughter	F	Cha	13.0	S	N	Y	Y	Guam	Guam	Guam	Y	None
	164	187	Santos, Vicente S	Head	M	Cha	64.0	M		N	N	Guam	Guam	Guam	N	Farmer
	164	187	Santos, Antonia R	Wife	F	Cha	57.0	M		N	N	Guam	Guam	Guam	N	None
	164	187	Santos, Natividad R	Daughter	F	Cha	41.0	S		Y	Y	Guam	Guam	Guam	N	None
	164	187	Santos, Ana R	Daughter	F	Cha	33.0	S		Y	Y	Guam	Guam	Guam	N	None
Hernan Cortez Street	164	187	Santos, Joaquina R	Daughter	F	Cha	25.0	S		Y	Y	Guam	Guam	Guam	N	None
	164	187	Santos, Rosa R	Daughter	F	Cha	23.0	S		Y	Y	Guam	Guam	Guam	N	None
	164	187	Santos, Jose R	Son	M	Cha	18.0	S	N	Y	Y	Guam	Guam	Guam	Y	Servant
	164	187	Santos, Antonia S	Grand-daughter	F	Cha	15.0	S	N	Y	Y	Guam	Unknown	Guam	N	None
	164	187	Santos, Amparo S	Grand-daughter	F	Cha	12.0	S	Y	Y	Y	Guam	Unknown	Guam	N	None
	164	187	Santos, Juan S	Grand-son	M	Cha	8.0	S	Y			Guam	Unknown	Guam		None
	164	187	Santos, Nicolas S	Grand-son	M	Cha	6.0	S	N			Guam	Unknown	Guam		None
	164	187	Santos, Francisco S	Grand-son	M	Cha	2.0	S				Guam	Unknown	Guam		None
	165	188	Santos, Geronimo P	Head	M	Fil	28.0	M		Y	Y	Philippine Islands	Philippine Islands	Philippine Islands	Y	Barber
	165	188	Santos, Rita T	Wife	F	Cha	22.0	M		Y	Y	Guam	Guam	Guam	N	None
	165	188	Santos, Feliciana T	Daughter	F	Fil	3.0	S				Philippine Islands	Philippine Islands	Guam		None
	165	188	Santos, Dolores T	Daughter	F	Fil	1.0	S				Philippine Islands	Philippine Islands	Guam		None
	165	188	Santos, Roque T	Son	M	Fil	0.0	S				Guam	Philippine Islands	Guam		None
	165	188	Santos, Apolenar P	Brother	M	Fil	22.0	S		Y	Y	Philippine Islands	Philippine Islands	Philippine Islands	Y	Barber
	166	189	Torres, Jose M	Head	M	Cha	38.0	M		Y	Y	Guam	Philippine Islands	Guam	Y	Retail merchant
	166	189	Torres, Maria C	Wife	F	W	31.0	M		Y	Y	Philippine Islands	Philippine Islands	Guam	N	None
	166	189	Torres, Francisco C	Son	M	Cha	12.0	S	Y	Y	Y	Guam	Guam	Guam	Y	None
	166	189	Torres, Concepcion C	Daughter	F	Cha	11.0	S	Y	Y	Y	Guam	Guam	Guam	Y	None

51

(CHAMORRO ROOTS GENEALOGY PROJECT ™ TRANSCRIPTION)
(COMPILED/TRANSCRIBED BY BERNARD T. PUNZALAN / HTTP://WWW.CHAMORROROOTS.COM)

FOURTEENTH CENSUS OF THE UNITED STATES: 1920-POPULATION
ISLAND OF GUAM

DISTRICT 1
NAME OF PLACE **Agana City**
[Proper name and, also, name of class, as city, town, village, barrio, etc]

ENUMERATED BY ME ON THE 15th DAY OF April, 1920

Joaquin Torres ENUMERATOR

	Street, avenue, road, etc.	Number of dwelling house	Number of family	NAME	RELATION	Sex	Color or race	Age at last birthday	Single, married, widowed or divorced	Attended school since Sept. 1, 1919	Whether able to read	Whether able to write	Place of birth of this person	Place of birth of father	Place of birth of mother	Whether able to speak English	OCCUPATION
	1	2	3	4	5	6	7	8	9	10	11	12	13	14	15	16	17
26		166	189	Torres, Jose C	Son	M	Cha	9.0	S	Y			Guam	Guam	Guam		None
27		166	189	Torres, Felix C	Son	M	Cha	8.0	S	Y			Guam	Guam	Guam		None
28		166	189	Torres, Maria C	Daughter	F	Cha	6.0	S	N			Guam	Guam	Guam		None
29		166	189	Torres, Pilar C	Daughter	F	Cha	4.0	S				Guam	Guam	Guam		None
30		166	189	San Nicolas, Pedro SN	Farm laborer	M	Cha	35.0	S		N	N	Guam	Unknown	Guam		Farm laborer
31		167	190	Flores, Rita B	Head	F	Cha	55.0	Wd		Y	Y	Guam	Guam	Guam	N	None
32		167	190	Flores, Manuel B	Son	M	Cha	35.0	S		Y	Y	Guam	Guam	Guam	N	Farm laborer
33		167	190	Flores, Jose B	Son	M	Cha	19.0	S	N	Y	Y	Guam	Guam	Guam	Y	Farm laborer
34		167	190	Flores, Joaquin B	Son	M	Cha	15.0	S	Y	Y	Y	Guam	Guam	Guam	Y	None
35		167	190	Castro, Dolores C	Cousin	F	Cha	64.0	S		Y	Y	Guam	Guam	Guam	N	None
36		167	191	Sturzaeta, Felomeno G	Head	M	Fil	24.0	M	Y	Y	Y	Philippine Islands	Spain	Philippine Islands	Y	Storekeeper
37		167	191	Sturzaeta, Melisia F	Wife	F	Fil	19.0	M	N	Y	Y	Philippine Islands	Philippine Islands	Philippine Islands	Y	None
38	Hernan Cortez Street	168	192	Veneziana, Ana G	Head	F	Cha	36.0	Wd		Y	Y	Guam	Unknown	Guam	Y	None
39		168	192	Veneziana, Rosa G	Daughter	F	W	16.0	S	Y	Y	Y	Guam	Greece	Greece	Y	None
40		168	192	Veneziana, Espiro G	Son	M	W	14.0	S	Y	Y	Y	Guam	Greece	Greece	Y	None
41		168	192	Veneziana, George G	Son	M	W	12.0	S	Y	Y	Y	Guam	Greece	Greece	Y	None
42		168	192	Veneziana, Enrique G	Son	M	W	9.0	S	N	Y	Y	Guam	Greece	Greece		None
43		168	192	Veneziana, Patrick G	Son	M	W	6.0	S	N			Guam	Greece	Greece		None
44		168	192	Veneziana, Elizabeth R	Mother-in-law	F	W	75.0	Wd		Y	Y	Greece	Greece	Greece	N	None
45		168	192	Toves, Jesus C	Chauffeur	M	Cha	26.0	S		Y	Y	Guam	Guam	Guam	Y	Chauffeur
46		168	192	Borja, Gregorio C	Chauffeur	M	Cha	19.0	S	N	Y	Y	Guam	Guam	Guam	Y	Chauffeur
47		168	192	Fegurgur, Concepcion SN	Servant	F	Cha	13.0	S	N	Y	Y	Guam	Guam	Guam	Y	Servant
48		169	193	Manibusan, Felomena G	Head	T	Cha	52.0	S		Y	Y	Guam	Guam	Guam	N	Laundress
49		169	193	Manibusan, Rosa G	Sister	T	Cha	36.0	S		Y	Y	Guam	Guam	Guam	N	Laundress
50		170	194	Cruz, Jose C	Head	M	Cha	44.0	M		Y	Y	Guam	Unknown	Guam	N	Farmer

(CHAMORRO ROOTS GENEALOGY PROJECT ™ TRANSCRIPTION)
(COMPILED/TRANSCRIBED BY BERNARD T. PUNZALAN / HTTP://WWW.CHAMORROROOTS.COM)

FOURTEENTH CENSUS OF THE UNITED STATES: 1920—POPULATION

ISLAND OF GUAM

DISTRICT 1
NAME OF PLACE Agana City
[Proper name and, also, name of class, as city, town, village, barrio, etc]

ENUMERATED BY ME ON THE 15th DAY OF April, 1920

Joaquin Torres ENUMERATOR

	1	2	3	4 NAME	5 RELATION	6 Sex	7 Color or race	8 Age at last birthday	9 Single, married, widowed or divorced	10 Attended school any time since Sept. 1, 1919	11 Whether able to read	12 Whether able to write	13 Place of birth of this person	14 Place of birth of father of this person	15 Place of birth of mother of this person	16 Whether able to speak English	17 OCCUPATION
1		170	194	Cruz, Ana R	Wife	F	Cha	41.0	M		Y	Y	Guam	Guam	Guam	N	None
2		170	195	Flores, Juan A	Head	M	Cha	21.0	M	N	Y	Y	Guam	Unknown	Guam	Y	Chauffeur
3		170	195	Flores, Rosa C	Wife	F	Cha	19.0	M	N	Y	Y	Guam	Guam	Guam	Y	None
4		170	195	Rosario, Jose L	Boarder	M	Cha	11.0	S	Y	Y	Y	Guam	Guam	Guam	Y	None
5		171	196	Blas, Joaquin T	Head	M	Cha	52.0	M		Y	Y	Guam	Guam	Guam	N	Farmer
6		171	196	Blas, Maria C	Wife	F	Cha	51.0	M		Y	Y	Guam	Guam	Guam	N	None
7		171	196	Blas, Maria C	Daughter	F	Cha	19.0	S		Y	Y	Guam	Guam	Guam	Y	None
8		171	196	Blas, Encarnacion C	Daughter	F	Cha	15.0	S	N	Y	Y	Guam	Guam	Guam	Y	None
9		171	196	Blas, Jesus C	Son	M	Cha	10.0	S	Y	Y	Y	Guam	Guam	Guam	Y	None
10		171	196	Blas, Pedro C	Son	M	Cha	6.0	S	N			Guam	Guam	Guam		None
11		171	197	Calvo, Felix P	Head	M	W	27.0	M		Y	Y	Guam	Philippine Islands	Guam	Y	Storekeeper
12	Castillo Street	171	197	Calvo, Antonia B	Wife	F	Cha	22.0	M		Y	Y	Guam	Guam	Guam	Y	None
13		171	197	Calvo, Fedela B	Daughter	F	Cha	2.0	S				Guam	Guam	Guam		None
14		172	198	Blas, Jose C	Head	M	Cha	31.0	M		Y	Y	Guam	Guam	Guam	N	Farmer
15		172	198	Blas, Ana G	Wife	F	Cha	26.0	M		Y	Y	Guam	Guam	Guam	N	None
16		172	198	Blas, Joaquin G	Son	M	Cha	8.0	S	Y			Guam	Guam	Guam		None
17		172	198	Blas, Pedro G	Son	M	Cha	7.0	S	Y			Guam	Guam	Guam		None
18		172	198	Blas, Antonia G	Daughter	F	Cha	5.0	S	N			Guam	Guam	Guam		None
19		172	198	Blas, Francisco G	Son	M	Cha	1.0	S				Guam	Guam	Guam		None
20		172	198	Blas, Isabel G	Daughter	F	Cha	0.5	S				Guam	Guam	Guam		None
21		173	199	Blas, Manuel C	Head	M	Cha	29.0	M		Y	Y	Guam	Guam	Guam	Y	Plumber
22		173	199	Blas, Ana C	Wife	F	Cha	26.0	M		Y	Y	Guam	Guam	Guam	N	None
23		173	199	Blas, Ana C	Daughter	F	Cha	6.0	S	N			Guam	Guam	Guam		None
24		173	199	Blas, Joaquin C	Son	M	Cha	4.0	S				Guam	Guam	Guam		None
25		173	199	Blas, Vicente C	Son	M	Cha	2.0	S				Guam	Guam	Guam		None

(CHAMORRO ROOTS GENEALOGY PROJECT ™ TRANSCRIPTION)
(COMPILED/TRANSCRIBED BY BERNARD T. PUNZALAN / HTTP://WWW.CHAMORROROOTS.COM)

FOURTEENTH CENSUS OF THE UNITED STATES: 1920–POPULATION
ISLAND OF GUAM

ENUMERATED BY ME ON THE 16th DAY OF April, 1920

Joaquin Torres ENUMERATOR

DISTRICT 1
NAME OF PLACE Agana City

Street	No. dwelling house	No. family	NAME	RELATION	Sex	Color or race	Age	Single, married, widowed or divorced	Attended school since Sept. 1, 1919	Able to read	Able to write	Place of birth of this person	Place of birth of father	Place of birth of mother	Able to speak English	OCCUPATION
	1	2	3	4	5	6	7	8	9	10	11	12	13	14	15	16	17
	174	200	Untalan, Rita B	Head	F	Cha	59.0	Wd		Y	Y	Guam	Guam	Guam	N	None
	174	200	Untalan, Joaquina B	Daughter	F	Cha	28.0	S		Y	Y	Guam	Guam	Guam	Y	Teacher
	174	200	Untalan, Ana B	Daughter	F	Cha	28.0	S		Y	Y	Guam	Guam	Guam	Y	None
	174	200	Untalan, Antonia B	Daughter	F	Cha	25.0	S		Y	Y	Guam	Guam	Guam	Y	Midwife
	174	200	Untalan, Concepcion B	Daughter	F	Cha	20.0	S	N	Y	Y	Guam	Guam	Guam	Y	Storekeeper
	174	200	Untalan, Maria B	Daughter	F	Cha	18.0	S	N	Y	Y	Guam	Guam	Guam	Y	Teacher
	174	200	Untalan, Rosa B	Daughter	F	Cha	13.0	S	Y	Y	Y	Guam	Guam	Guam	Y	None
	174	201	Untalan, Luis B	Head	M	Cha	36.0	M		Y	Y	Guam	Guam	Guam	Y	Farmer
	174	201	Untalan, Ignacia M	Wife	F	Cha	32.0	M	N	Y	Y	Guam	Guam	Guam	N	None
Castillo Street	174	201	Untalan, Juan M	Son	M	Cha	7.0	S	Y			Guam	Guam	Guam		None
	174	201	Untalan, Jose M	Son	M	Cha	4.0	S				Guam	Guam	Guam		None
	174	201	Untalan, Jesus M	Son	M	Cha	2.0	S				Guam	Guam	Guam		None
	174	201	Untalan, Maria M	Daughter	F	Cha	0.2	S				Guam	Guam	Guam		None
	175	202	Guzman, Jose M	Head	M	Cha	33.0	M		Y	Y	Guam	Guam	Guam	Y	Enlisted man USN
	175	202	Guzman, Dolores LG	Wife	F	Cha	28.0	M		Y	Y	Guam	Guam	Guam	N	None
	175	202	Guzman, Antonio LG	Son	M	Cha	9.0	S	Y			Guam	Guam	Guam		None
	175	202	Guzman, Jose LG	Son	M	Cha	7.0	S	Y	Y	Y	Guam	Guam	Guam		None
	175	202	Guzman, Juan LG	Son	M	Cha	4.0	S				Guam	Guam	Guam		None
	175	202	Guzman, Jesusa LG	Daughter	F	Cha	2.0	S				Guam	Guam	Guam		None
	175	202	Guzman, Vicente LG	Son	M	Cha	0.0	S				Guam	Guam	Guam		None
	176	203	Arriola, Vicente F	Head	M	Fil	63.0	Wd		Y	Y	Guam	Philippine Islands	Guam	N	Farmer
	177	204	Perez, Jesus F	Head	M	Cha	35.0	M		Y	Y	Guam	Guam	Guam	Y	Farmer
	177	204	Perez, Margarita D	Wife	F	Cha	29.0	M		Y	Y	Guam	Unknown	Guam		None
	177	204	Perez, Maria D	Daughter	F	Cha	8.0	S	Y	Y	Y	Guam	Guam	Guam		None
	177	204	Perez, Francisco D	Son	M	Cha	6.0	S	N			Guam	Guam	Guam		None

(CHAMORRO ROOTS GENEALOGY PROJECT ™ TRANSCRIPTION)
(COMPILED/TRANSCRIBED BY BERNARD T. PUNZALAN / HTTP://WWW.CHAMORROROOTS.COM)

FOURTEENTH CENSUS OF THE UNITED STATES: 1920-POPULATION

ISLAND OF GUAM

DISTRICT 1
NAME OF PLACE Agana City

[Proper name and, also, name of class, as city, town, village, barrio, etc]

ENUMERATED BY ME ON THE 16th DAY OF April, 1920

Joaquin Torres ENUMERATOR

	PLACE OF ABODE		NAME	RELATION	PERSONAL DESCRIPTION					EDUCATION			NATIVITY				OCCUPATION
Street, avenue, road, etc.	Number of dwelling house in order of visitation	Number of family in order of visitation	of each person whose place of abode on January 1, 1920, was in the family. Enter surname, firs, then given name and middle initial. If any. Include every person living on January 1, 1920. Omit children born since January 1, 1920.	Relationship of this Person to the head of the family.	Sex	Color or race	Age at last birthday	Single, married, widowed or divorced	Attended any school since Sept. 1, 1919	Whether able to read.	Whether able to write.	Place of birth of this person.	Place of birth of father of this person.	Place of birth of mother of this person.	Whether able to speak English.	Trade, profession, or particular kind of work done, as salesman, laborer, clerk, cook, merchant, washerwoman, etc.
1	2	3	4	5	6	7	8	9	10	11	12	13	14	15	16	17
	177	204	Perez, Consuelo D	Daughter	F	Cha	3.0	S				Guam	Guam	Guam		None
	177	204	Perez, Enrique D	Son	M	Cha	1.0	S				Guam	Guam	Guam		None
	178	205	Santos, Jesus B	Head	M	Cha	42.0	M		Y	Y	Guam	Guam	Guam		Teamster
	178	205	Santos, Dolores C	Wife	F	Cha	36.0	M		Y	Y	Guam	Guam	Guam	N	None
	178	205	Santos, Remedios C	Daughter	F	Cha	6.0	S	N			Guam	Guam	Guam		None
	178	205	Santos, Juan C	Son	M	Cha	0.1	S				Guam	Guam	Guam		None
	179	206	Rojas, Pedro A	Head	M	Cha	28.0	M		Y	Y	Guam	Guam	Guam	Y	Watchman
	179	206	Rojas, Nieves C	Wife	F	Cha	25.0	M		Y	Y	Guam	Guam	Guam	N	None
Castillo Street	179	206	Rojas, Concepcion C	Daughter	F	Cha	7.0	S	N			Guam	Guam	Guam		None
	179	206	Rojas, Rosa C	Daughter	F	Cha	2.0	S				Guam	Guam	Guam		None
	179	206	Rojas, Maria C	Daughter	F	Cha	0.6	S				Guam	Guam	Guam		None
	180	207	Evangelista, Apolonio E	Head	M	Cha	34.0	M		Y	Y	Guam	Unknown	Guam	N	Farmer
	180	207	Evangelista, Josefa M	Wife	F	Cha	36.0	M		Y	Y	Guam	Guam	Guam	N	None
	180	207	Evangelista, Jose M	Son	M	Cha	14.0	S	Y	Y	Y	Guam	Guam	Guam	Y	None
	180	207	Evangelista, Maria M	Daughter	F	Cha	12.0	S	Y	Y	Y	Guam	Guam	Guam	Y	None
	180	207	Evangelista, Jesus M	Son	M	Cha	9.0	S	Y			Guam	Guam	Guam		None
	180	207	Evangelista, Ana M	Daughter	F	Cha	6.0	S	N			Guam	Guam	Guam		None
	180	207	Evangelista, Vicente M	Son	M	Cha	4.0	S				Guam	Guam	Guam		None
	180	207	Mendiola, Consolacion B	Mother-in-law	F	Cha	60.0	Wd		Y	Y	Guam	Guam	Guam	N	None
	180	208	Mendiola, Joaquin B	Head	M	Cha	31.0	M		Y	Y	Guam	Guam	Guam	Y	Laborer
	180	208	Mendiola, Maria P	Wife	F	Cha	24.0	M		Y	Y	Guam	Unknown	Guam	N	None
	180	208	Mendiola, Pedro P	Son	M	Cha	4.0	S				Guam	Guam	Guam		None
	180	208	Mendiola, Antonio P	Son	M	Cha	2.0	S				Guam	Guam	Guam		None
	180	208	Mendiola, Soledad P	Daughter	F	Cha	0.0	S				Guam	Guam	Guam		None
	181	209	Mendiola, Filomena U	Head	F	Fil	38.0	Wd		Y	Y	Guam	Philippine Islands	Guam	N	None

(CHAMORRO ROOTS GENEALOGY PROJECT ™ TRANSCRIPTION)
(COMPILED/TRANSCRIBED BY BERNARD T. PUNZALAN / HTTP://WWW.CHAMORROROOTS.COM)

FOURTEENTH CENSUS OF THE UNITED STATES: 1920—POPULATION

ISLAND OF GUAM

ENUMERATED BY ME ON THE 17th DAY OF April, 1920

Joaquin Torres ENUMERATOR

DISTRICT 1
NAME OF PLACE Agana City

[Proper name and, also, name of class, as city, town, village, barrio, etc]

Street	Dwelling	Family	NAME	RELATION	Sex	Color or race	Age	Single/married/widowed/divorced	Attended school since Sept. 1, 1919	Able to read	Able to write	Birthplace of person	Birthplace of father	Birthplace of mother	Able to speak English	OCCUPATION
1	2	3	4	5	6	7	8	9	10	11	12	13	14	15	16	17
	181	209	Mendiola, Joaquina U	Daughter	F	Cha	14.0	S	N	Y	Y	Guam	Guam	Guam	Y	None
	181	209	Untalan, Jose C	Nephew	M	Cha	26.0	S		Y	Y	Guam	Guam	Guam	Y	Laborer
	181	209	Untalan, Luis P	Nephew	M	Cha	12.0	S	Y	Y	Y	Guam	Guam	Guam	Y	None
	182	210	Aguon, Vicente S	Head	M	Cha	34.0	M		Y	Y	Guam	Guam	Guam	Y	Blacksmith
	182	210	Aguon, Remedios S	Wife	F	Cha	33.0	M		Y	Y	Guam	Guam	Guam	N	Midwife
	182	210	Aguon, Manuel S	Son	M	Cha	10.0	S	Y	Y	Y	Guam	Guam	Guam	Y	None
	182	210	Aguon, Maria S	Daughter	F	Cha	6.0	S				Guam	Guam	Guam		None
	182	210	Aguon, Francisco S	Son	M	Cha	4.0	S				Guam	Guam	Guam		None
	182	210	Aguon, Rosa S	Sister	F	Cha	15.0	S	N	Y	Y	Guam	Guam	Guam	N	None
Castillo Street	182	210	Peredo, Francisco P	Brother-in-law	M	Cha	50.0	Wd		Y	N	Guam	Unknown	Guam	N	Laborer
	183	211	Ichijara, Jose	Head	M	Jp	35.0	M		Y	Y	Japan	Japan	Japan	N	Carpenter
	183	211	Ichijara, Dolores SM	Wife	F	Cha	34.0	M		Y	N	Saipan	Guam	Guam	Y	None
	183	211	Ichijara, Jose SM	Son	M	Jp	7.0	S	Y			Saipan	Japan	Saipan		None
	183	211	Ichijara, Joaquin SM	Son	M	Jp	4.0	S				Guam	Japan	Saipan		None
	183	211	Ichijara, Francisco SM	Son	M	Jp	2.0	S				Guam	Japan	Saipan		None
	183	211	Ichijara, Rita SM	Daughter	F	Jp	1.0	S				Guam	Japan	Saipan		None
	184	212	Tanaka, Rosa S	Head	F	Cha	33.0	Wd		Y	N	Guam	Unknown	Guam	N	Baker
	184	212	Tanaka, Maria S	Daughter	F	Jp	11.0	S	Y	Y	Y	Guam	Japan	Guam	N	None
	184	212	Tanaka, Biatris S	Daughter	F	Jp	9.0	S	Y	Y	Y	Guam	Japan	Guam		None
	184	212	Tanaka, Rosario S	Daughter	F	Jp	8.0	S	Y	Y	Y	Guam	Japan	Guam		None
	184	212	Tanaka, Carmen S	Daughter	F	Jp	7.0	S	Y			Guam	Japan	Guam		None
	184	212	Tanaka, Emeterio S	Son	M	Jp	5.0	S	N			Guam	Japan	Guam		None
	184	212	Tanaka, Tomas S	Son	M	Jp	4.0	S				Guam	Japan	Guam		None
	184	212	Tanaka, Asuncion S	Daughter	F	Jp	2.0	S				Guam	Japan	Guam		None
	184	212	Tanaka, Remedios S	Daughter	F	Jp	1.0	S				Guam	Japan	Guam		None

(CHAMORRO ROOTS GENEALOGY PROJECT ™ TRANSCRIPTION)
(COMPILED/TRANSCRIBED BY BERNARD T. PUNZALAN / HTTP://WWW.CHAMORROROOTS.COM)

FOURTEENTH CENSUS OF THE UNITED STATES: 1920–POPULATION
ISLAND OF GUAM

DISTRICT 1
NAME OF PLACE Agana City
[Proper name and, also, name of class, as city, town, village, barrio, etc]

ENUMERATED BY ME ON THE 17th DAY OF April, 1920

Joaquin Torres ENUMERATOR

Street, avenue, road, etc.	Dwelling No.	Family No.	NAME	RELATION	Sex	Color or race	Age at last birthday	Single, married, widowed or divorced	Attended school since Sept. 1, 1919	Able to read	Able to write	Birthplace of person	Birthplace of father	Birthplace of mother	Able to speak English	OCCUPATION
	184	212	Tanaka, Jesus S	Son	M	Jp	0.0					Guam	Japan	Guam		None
	185	213	Gogue, Agustin SL	Head	M	Cha	24.0	M		Y	Y	Guam	Guam	Guam	N	Laborer
	185	213	Gogue, Antonia S	Wife	F	Cha	24.0	M		Y	Y	Guam	Guam	Guam	N	None
	185	213	Gogue, Jose S	Son	M	Cha	3.0	S				Guam	Guam	Guam		None
	185	213	Gogue, Tomas S	Son	M	Cha	2.0	S				Guam	Guam	Guam		None
	185	213	Gogue, Maria S	Daughter	F	Cha	0.1	S				Guam	Guam	Guam		None
	185	213	Asuncion, Andres SL	Brother	M	Fil	9.0	S	Y			Guam	Philippine Islands	Guam		None
	186	214	Santos, Antonio L	Head	M	Cha	58.0	M		N	N	Guam	Guam	Guam	Y	Farmer
Castillo Street	186	214	Santos, Maria S	Wife	F	Cha	61.0	M		Y	Y	Guam	Guam	Guam	N	None
	186	214	Santos, Tomasa S	Daughter	F	Cha	18.0	S	N	Y	Y	Guam	Guam	Guam	Y	None
	187	215	Sablan, Gregorio S	Head	M	Cha	26.0	M		Y	Y	Guam	Guam	Guam	Y	Carpenter
	187	215	Sablan, Rosa F	Wife	F	Cha	26.0	M		Y	Y	Guam	Guam	Guam	N	None
	187	215	Sablan, Maria F	Daughter	F	Cha	5.0	S	N			Guam	Guam	Guam		None
	187	215	Sablan, Segundo F	Son	M	Cha	3.0	S				Guam	Guam	Guam		None
	187	215	Sablan, Augusto F	Son	M	Cha	2.0	S				Guam	Guam	Guam		None
	187	215	Sablan, Francisco F	Son	M	Cha	0.9	S				Guam	Guam	Guam		None
	188	216	Sablan, Pedro P	Head	M	Cha	51.0	M		Y	Y	Guam	Guam	Guam	N	Carpenter
	188	216	Sablan, Ana S	Wife	F	Cha	48.0	M		Y	Y	Guam	Guam	Guam	N	None
	188	216	Sablan, Vicenta S	Daughter	F	Cha	18.0	S	N	Y	Y	Guam	Guam	Guam	Y	None
	188	216	Sablan, Felix S	Son	M	Cha	12.0	S	Y	Y	Y	Guam	Guam	Guam	Y	None
	188	216	Sablan, Ana S	Daughter	F	Cha	11.0	S	N	Y	Y	Guam	Guam	Guam	N	None
	188	216	Sablan, Juan S	Son	M	Cha	7.0	S	Y	Y	Y	Guam	Guam	Guam		None
	188	216	Leon Guerrero, Maria S	Daughter	F	Cha	24.0	Wd		Y	Y	Guam	Guam	Guam	Y	None
	188	216	Leon Guerrero, Rosalia S	Grand-daughter	F	Cha	6.0	S	N		N	Guam	Guam	Guam		None
	188	216	Leon Guerrero, Gregorio S	Grand-son	M	Cha	5.0	S	N		N	Guam	Guam	Guam		None

(CHAMORRO ROOTS GENEALOGY PROJECT ™ TRANSCRIPTION)
(COMPILED/TRANSCRIBED BY BERNARD T. PUNZALAN / HTTP://WWW.CHAMORROROOTS.COM)

FOURTEENTH CENSUS OF THE UNITED STATES: 1920—POPULATION

ISLAND OF GUAM

DISTRICT **1**

NAME OF PLACE **Agana City**

[Proper name and, also, name of class, as city, town, village, barrio, etc]

ENUMERATED BY ME ON THE 18ᵗʰ DAY OF April, 1920.

Joaquin Torres ENUMERATOR

	Street, avenue, road, etc.	Number of dwelling house is in order of visitation	Number of family in order of visitation	NAME	RELATION	Sex	Color or race	Age at last birthday	Single, married, widowed or divorced	Attended school any time since Sept. 1, 1919	Whether able to read.	Whether able to write.	Place of birth of this person.	Place of birth of father of this person.	Place of birth of mother of this person.	Whether able to speak English.	OCCUPATION
	1	2	3	4	5	6	7	8	9	10	11	12	13	14	15	16	17
26		188	216	Leon Guerrero, Maria S	Grand-daughter	F	Cha	4.0	S				Guam	Guam	Guam		None
27		188	216	Leon Guerrero, Brijida S	Grand-daughter	F	Cha	1.0	S				Guam	Guam	Guam		None
28		189	217	Rojas, Antonio D	Head	M	Cha	55.0	M		Y	Y	Guam	Guam	Guam	N	Farmer
29		189	217	Rojas, Ana A	Wife	F	Cha	55.0	M		Y	Y	Guam	Guam	Guam	N	None
30		190	218	Cruz, Vicente LG	Head	M	Cha	20.0	S	N	Y	Y	Guam	Guam	Guam	Y	Laborer
31		190	219	Aguigui, Leon A	Head	M	Cha	24.0	S		N	N	Guam	Unknown	Guam	N	Laborer
32		190	220	Cruz, Ignacio T	Head	M	Cha	44.0	M		Y	Y	Guam	Guam	Guam	N	Laborer
33		190	220	Cruz, Susana P	Wife	F	Cha	26.0	M		Y	N	Guam	Guam	Guam	N	Laundress
34		190	220	Cruz, Vicente P	Son	M	Cha	12.0	S	Y	Y	Y	Guam	Guam	Guam	Y	None
35	Castillo Street	190	220	Cruz, Josefa P	Daughter	F	Cha	11.0	S	Y	Y	Y	Guam	Guam	Guam	N	None
36		191	221	Lujan, Jose SN	Head	M	Cha	34.0	M		Y	Y	Guam	Guam	Guam	Y	Farmer
37		191	221	Lujan, Dominga B	Wife	F	Cha	26.0	M		Y	Y	Guam	Guam	Guam	N	None
38		191	221	Lujan, Jesus B	Son	M	Cha	5.0	S	N			Guam	Guam	Guam		None
39		192	222	Lujan, Vicente R	Head	M	Cha	43.0	Wd		Y	Y	Guam	Guam	Guam	N	Farmer
40		192	222	Lujan, Lorenzo N	Son	M	Cha	15.0	S	N	Y	Y	Guam	Guam	Guam	Y	None
41		192	222	Lujan, Manuel N	Son	M	Cha	10.0	S	Y	Y	Y	Guam	Guam	Guam	N	None
42		192	222	Lujan, Vicente N	Son	M	Cha	8.0	S	Y	Y	Y	Guam	Guam	Guam	N	None
43				Here ends the enumeration of San Nicolas, Agana City													
44																	
45																	
46																	
47																	
48																	
49																	
50																	

(CHAMORRO ROOTS GENEALOGY PROJECT ™ TRANSCRIPTION)
(COMPILED/TRANSCRIBED BY BERNARD T. PUNZALAN / HTTP://WWW.CHAMORROROOTS.COM)
FOURTEENTH CENSUS OF THE UNITED STATES: 1920-POPULATION
ISLAND OF GUAM

DISTRICT 1
NAME OF PLACE **Agana City**
[Proper name and, also, name of class, as city, town, village, barrio, etc]

ENUMERATED BY ME ON THE 9th DAY OF April, 1920

Albert P. Manley ENUMERATOR

Street, avenue, road, etc.	Number of dwelling house in order of visitation	Number of family in order of visitation	NAME of each person whose place of abode on January 1, 1920, was in the family.	RELATION Relationship of this Person to the head of the family.	Sex	Color or race	Age at last birthday	Single, married, widowed or divorced	Attended school any time since Sept. 1, 1919	Whether able to read.	Whether able to write.	Place of birth of this person.	Place of birth of father of this person.	Place of birth of mother of this person.	Whether able to speak English.	OCCUPATION Trade, profession, or particular kind of work done, as salesman, laborer, clerk, cook, merchant, washerwoman, etc.
1	2	3	4	5	6	7	8	9	10	11	12	13	14	15	16	17
	1	1	Oliaz, Joaquin	Head	M	W	48.0	S		Y	Y	Spain	Spain	Spain	Y	?
	1	1	Torribio, Iraicoe	Missionary	M	W	50.0	S		Y	Y	Spain	Spain	Spain	N	Missionary
	1	1	Quintanilla, Ignacio M	Servant	M	Cha	17.0	S	N	Y	Y	Guam	Guam	Guam	Y	Servant
	2	2	Hugolino, Gainca	Head	M	W	38.0	S				Spain	Spain	Spain	N	Missionary
	2	2	Vera, Ramon	Missionary	M	W	42.0	S		Y	Y	Spain	Spain	Spain	Y	Missionary
	2	2	Acosta, Luis	Missionary	M	W	28.0	S		Y	Y	Spain	Spain	Spain	Y	Missionary
	2	2	Imbuluqueta, Crispin	Missionary	M	W	42.0	S		Y	Y	Spain	Spain	Spain	N	Missionary
	2	2	Rivera, Francisco R	Servant	M	Cha	65.0	Wd		Y	Y	Guam	Guam	Guam	N	Servant
	2	2	Benavente, Filipe C	Servant	M	Cha	20.0	S	N	Y	Y	Guam	Guam	Guam	Y	Servant
	2	2	Aquinigoc, Enrique C	Servant	M	Cha	15.0	S	Y	Y	Y	Guam	Guam	Guam	Y	Servant
	2	2	Charfauros, Andres C	Servant	M	Cha	14.0	S	Y	Y	Y	Guam	Guam	Guam	Y	Servant
	2	2	Delgado, Enrique SN	Servant	M	Cha	14.0	S	Y	Y	Y	Guam	Guam	Guam	Y	Servant
	3	3	Leon Guerrero, Antonia B	Head	F	Cha	57.0	Wd		Y	Y	Guam	Guam	Guam	N	None
	3	3	Leon Guerrero, Ana B	Daughter	F	Cha	37.0	S		Y	Y	Guam	Guam	Guam	Y	None
	3	3	Leon Guerrero, Maria B	Daughter	F	Cha	36.0	S		Y	Y	Guam	Guam	Guam	N	None
	3	3	Leon Guerrero, Carlos B	Son	M	Cha	31.0	S		Y	Y	Guam	Guam	Guam	Y	Farmer
	3	3	Leon Guerrero, Experancia B	Daughter	F	Cha	29.0	S		Y	Y	Guam	Guam	Guam	Y	None
	3	4	Leon Guerrero, Gonzalo B	Head	M	Cha	27.0	M		Y	Y	Guam	Guam	Guam	Y	Book-keeper
	3	4	Leon Guerrero, Maria A	Wife	F	Cha	26.0	M		Y	Y	Guam	Guam	Guam	N	None
	3	4	Leon Guerrero, Gonzalo A	Son	M	Cha	4.0	S				Guam	Guam	Guam	Y	None
	3	4	Leon Guerrero, Linia A	Daughter	F	Cha	2.0	S				Guam	Guam	Guam	Y	None
	3	4	Leon Guerrero, Caridad A	Daughter	F	Cha	0.1	S				Guam	Guam	Guam		None
	3	5	Leon Guerrero, Silvestre B	Head	M	Cha	34.0	Wd		Y	Y	Guam	Guam	Guam	Y	Musician USN
	3	5	Leon Guerrero, Vicente C	Son	M	Cha	9.0	S	Y			Guam	Guam	Guam		None
	3	5	Leon Guerrero, Joaquin C	Son	M	Cha	8.0	S	Y			Guam	Guam	Guam		None

Calle de San Ramon

(CHAMORRO ROOTS GENEALOGY PROJECT ™ TRANSCRIPTION)
(COMPILED/TRANSCRIBED BY BERNARD T. PUNZALAN / HTTP://WWW.CHAMORROROOTS.COM)
FOURTEENTH CENSUS OF THE UNITED STATES: 1920–POPULATION
ISLAND OF GUAM

DISTRICT **1**
NAME OF PLACE **Agana City**
[Proper name and, also, name of class, as city, town, village, barrio, etc]

ENUMERATED BY ME ON THE 9th DAY OF April, 1920

Albert P. Manley ENUMERATOR

	PLACE OF ABODE		NAME	RELATION	PERSONAL DESCRIPTION				EDUCATION			NATIVITY				OCCUPATION
Street, avenue, road, etc.	Number of dwelling house	Number of family	of each person whose place of abode on January 1, 1920, was in the family.	Relationship of this person to the head of the family.	Sex	Color or race	Age at last birthday	Single, married, widowed or divorced	Attended school any time since Sept. 1, 1919	Whether able to read.	Whether able to write.	Place of birth of this person.	Place of birth of father of this person.	Place of birth of mother of this person.	Whether able to speak English.	Trade, profession, or particular kind of work done, as salesman, laborer, clerk, cook, merchant, washerwoman, etc.
1	2	3	4	5	6	7	8	9	10	11	12	13	14	15	16	17
	3	5	Leon Guerrero, Juan C	Son	M	Cha	6.0	S	N			Guam	Guam	Guam		None
	3	5	Leon Guerrero, Silvestre C	Son	M	Cha	5.0	S	N			Guam	Guam	Guam		None
	3	5	Leon Guerrero, Ana C	Daughter	F	Cha	3.0	S				Guam	Guam	Guam		None
	3	5	Leon Guerrero, Remedios C	Daughter	F	Cha	2.0	S				Guam	Guam	Guam		None
	3	6	Leon Guerrero, Joaquin B	Head	M	Cha	26.0	M		Y	Y	Guam	Guam	Guam	Y	Storekeeper
	3	6	Leon Guerrero, Ana R	Wife	F	Cha	24.0	M		Y	Y	Guam	Guam	Guam	N	None
	3	6	Leon Guerrero, Ested R	Daughter	F	Cha	3.0	S				Guam	Guam	Guam		None
	4	7	Flores, Joaquin L	Head	M	W	22.0	M		Y	Y	Manila	Spain	Guam	Y	Seaman USN
	4	7	Flores, Dolores R	Wife	F	Cha	19.0	M	N	Y	Y	Guam	Guam	Guam	Y	None
	4	7	De Leon, Juana B	Great Grandmother	F	Cha	80.0	Wd		N	N	Guam	Guam	Guam	N	None
Calle de San Ramon	4	7	Aguon, Josefina C	Servant	F	Cha	11.0	S	Y	Y	Y	Guam	Guam	Guam	Y	Servant
	5	8	Torres, Luis LG	Head	M	Cha	22.0	M		Y	Y	Guam	Guam	Guam	Y	Silversmith
	5	8	Torres, Conception E	Wife	F	Cha	22.0	M		Y	Y	Guam	Guam	Guam	Y	None
	5	8	Torres, Leon Guerrero Rita	Aunt	F	Cha	60.0	S		N	N	Guam	Guam	Guam	Y	None
	5	8	Aguon, Luisa T	Cousin	F	Cha	53.0	S		Y	Y	Guam	Guam	Guam	Y	None
	5	8	Camacho, Josefina G	Servant	F	Cha	20.0	S	N	Y	Y	Guam	Guam	Guam	N	Servant
	5	8	Camacho, Rosa S	Servant	F	Cha	14.0	S	Y	Y	Y	Guam	Guam	Guam	Y	Servant
	5	8	Camacho, Jose S	Servant	M	Cha	7.0	S	N			Guam	Guam	Guam	Y	Servant
	5	8	Tenorio, Rita G	Servant	F	Cha	12.0	S	Y	Y	Y	Guam	Guam	Guam	Y	Servant
	6	9	Miner, Jose P	Head	M		55.0	M		Y	Y	Guam	America	Guam	Y	Carpenter
	6	9	Miner, Joaquina A	Wife	F	Cha	32.0	M	N	Y	Y	Guam	Guam	Guam	N	None
	6	9	Miner, Clara A	Daughter	F	Cha	16.0	S	N	Y	Y	Guam	Guam	Guam	Y	None
	6	9	Miner, Benectde A	Daughter	F	Cha	12.0	S	Y	Y	Y	Guam	Guam	Guam	Y	None
	6	9	Miner, Juan A	Son	M	Cha	10.0	S	Y	Y	Y	Guam	Guam	Guam	Y	None
	6	9	Charsagua, Ramona A	Niece	F	Cha	20.0	S	N	Y	Y	Guam	Guam	Guam	Y	None

Row numbers (left margin): 26, 27, 28, 29, 30, 31, 32, 33, 34, 35, 36, 37, 38, 39, 40, 41, 42, 43, 44, 45, 46, 47, 48, 49, 50

(CHAMORRO ROOTS GENEALOGY PROJECT ™ TRANSCRIPTION)
(COMPILED/TRANSCRIBED BY BERNARD T. PUNZALAN / HTTP://WWW.CHAMORROROOTS.COM)

FOURTEENTH CENSUS OF THE UNITED STATES: 1920—POPULATION
ISLAND OF GUAM

DISTRICT 1
NAME OF PLACE Agana City
[Proper name and, also, name of class, as city, town, village, barrio, etc]

ENUMERATED BY ME ON THE 9th DAY OF April, 1920

Albert P. Manley ENUMERATOR

	PLACE OF ABODE		NAME	RELATION	PERSONAL DESCRIPTION				EDUCATION			NATIVITY				OCCUPATION
Street, avenue, road, etc.	Number of dwelling house in order of visitation	Number of family in order of visitation	of each person whose place of abode on January 1, 1920, was in the family. Enter surname, first, then given name and middle initial. If any. Include every person living on January 1, 1920. Omit children born since January 1, 1920.	Relationship of this Person to the head of the family.	Sex	Color or race	Age at last birthday	Single, married, widowed or divorced	Attended school any time since Sept. 1, 1919	Whether able to read.	Whether able to write.	Place of birth of this person.	Place of birth of father of this person.	Place of birth of mother of this person.	Whether able to speak English.	Trade, profession, or particular kind of work done, as salesman, laborer, clerk, cook, merchant, washerwoman, etc.
1	2	3	4	5	6	7	8	9	10	11	12	13	14	15	16	17
Calle de San Ramon	6	9	Cruz, Manuel M	Servant	M	Cha	38.0	S		Y	Y	Guam	Guam	Guam	N	Servant
	6	10	Flores, Manuel P	Head	M	Cha	30.0	M		Y	Y	Guam	Guam	Guam	Y	Storekeeper
	6	10	Flores, Trinidad A	Wife	F	Cha	29.0	M		Y	Y	Guam	Guam	Guam	N	None
	6	10	Flores, Bergnes A	Daughter	F	Cha	2.0	S				Guam	Guam	Guam		None
	6	10	Flores, Rosa A	Daughter	F	Cha	1.0	S				Guam	Guam	Guam		None
	7	11	Torres, Maria A	Head	F	Cha	76.0	S		Y	Y	Guam	Guam	Guam	N	None
	7	11	Mendiola, Luis A	Nephew	M	Cha	55.0	S		Y	Y	Guam	Guam	Guam	Y	Laborer
	8	12	Fulgencio, Garcia T	Head	M	W	55.0	S		Y	Y	Spain	Spain	Spain	N	Retail Merchant dry goods
	8	13	Mariano, Soledad Q	Head	F	Cha	16.0	S	Y	Y	Y	Guam	Guam	Guam	Y	None
	8	13	Fernandez, Rosario L	Servant	F	Cha	15.0	S	Y	Y	Y	Guam	Guam	Guam	Y	Servant
	9	14	Martinez, Angel W	Head	M	Cha	34.0	M		Y	Y	Guam	Guam	Guam	Y	Silversmith
	9	14	Martinez, Emelia K	Wife	F	W	31.0	M		Y	Y	Guam	Holland	Guam	Y	None
	9	14	Martinez, Antonio K	Son	M	Cha	2.0	S				Guam	Guam	Guam	N	None
Esperansa Street	10	15	Herrero, Jose C	Head	M	Cha	49.0	S		Y	Y	Guam	Guam	Guam	N	Farmer
	10	15	Herrero, Josefa C	Sister	F	Cha	62.0	S		Y	Y	Guam	Guam	Guam	N	None
	10	15	Herrero, Maria C	Sister	F	Cha	59.0	S		Y	Y	Guam	Guam	Guam	N	None
	10	15	Herrero, Caridad C	Sister	F	Cha	52.0	S		Y	Y	Guam	Guam	Guam	N	None
	10	15	Herrero, Consuelo C	Sister	F	Cha	43.0	S		Y	Y	Guam	Guam	Guam	N	None
	10	15	Herrero, Francisco C	Brother	M	Cha	37.0	S		Y	Y	Guam	Guam	Guam	N	Farm laborer home farm
	10	15	Rosendo, Manuel H	Nephew	M	Cha	31.0	S		Y	Y	Guam	Guam	Guam	N	Farm laborer home farm
	10	15	Herrero, Enrique M	Nephew	M	Cha	25.0	S		Y	Y	Guam	Unknown	Guam	Y	Laborer
	11	16	Herrero, Tomas C	Head	M	Cha	47.0	M		Y	Y	Guam	Guam	Guam	N	Farmer
	11	16	Herrero, Maria C	Wife	F	Cha	37.0	M	N	Y	Y	Guam	Guam	Guam	N	None
	11	16	Herrero, Francisco C	Son	M	Cha	16.0	S	Y	Y	Y	Guam	Guam	Guam	Y	Blacksmith
	11	16	Herrero, Josefina C	Daughter	F	Cha	14.0	S	Y	Y	Y	Guam	Guam	Guam	Y	None

(CHAMORRO ROOTS GENEALOGY PROJECT ™ TRANSCRIPTION)
(COMPILED/TRANSCRIBED BY BERNARD T. PUNZALAN / HTTP://WWW.CHAMORROROOTS.COM)

FOURTEENTH CENSUS OF THE UNITED STATES: 1920-POPULATION

ISLAND OF GUAM

25b

DISTRICT 1
NAME OF PLACE Agana City
[Proper name and, also, name of class, as city, town, village, barrio, etc]

ENUMERATED BY ME ON THE 10th DAY OF April, 1920

Albert P. Manley ENUMERATOR

	Street	Dwelling house no.	Family no.	NAME	RELATION	Sex	Color or race	Age at last birthday	Single, married, widowed or divorced	Attended school since Sept. 1, 1919	Able to read	Able to write	Place of birth of this person	Place of birth of father	Place of birth of mother	Able to speak English	OCCUPATION
	1	2	3	4	5	6	7	8	9	10	11	12	13	14	15	16	17
26		11	16	Herrero, Lola C	Daughter	F	Cha	13.0	S	Y	Y	Y	Guam	Guam	Guam	Y	None
27		11	16	Herrero, Julia C	Daughter	F	Cha	9.0	S	Y	Y	Y	Guam	Guam	Guam		None
28		11	16	Herrero, Angel C	Son	M	Cha	8.0	S	Y			Guam	Guam	Guam		None
29		11	16	Herrero, Alfredo C	Son	M	Cha	5.0	S	N			Guam	Guam	Guam		None
30		11	16	Herrero, Edwardo C	Son	M	Cha	2.0	S				Guam	Guam	Guam		None
31		12	17	Englacias, Luis C	Head	M	Cha	39.0	M		Y	Y	Guam	Guam	Guam	N	Farmer
32		12	17	Englacias, Maria C	Wife	F	Cha	37.0	M		Y	Y	Guam	Guam	Guam	N	None
33		12	17	Englacias, Manuel C	Son	M	Cha	15.0	S	Y	Y	Y	Guam	Guam	Guam	N	Laborer
34		12	17	Englacias, Maria C	Daughter	F	Cha	1.0	S				Guam	Guam	Guam		None
35	Esperansa Street	13	18	San Nicolas, Jose T	Head	M	Cha	30.0	M		Y	Y	Guam	Guam	Guam	N	Laborer
36		13	18	San Nicolas, Maria S	Wife	F	Cha	36.0	M		Y	Y	Guam	Guam	Guam	N	None
37		13	18	San Nicolas, Joaquin S	Son	M	Cha	10.0	S	Y	Y	Y	Guam	Guam	Guam	Y	None
38		13	18	San Nicolas, Jose S	Son	M	Cha	9.0	S	Y	Y	Y	Guam	Guam	Guam	Y	None
39		14	19	Mendiola, Jose C	Head	M	Cha	40.0	M		Y	Y	Guam	Guam	Guam	N	Farmer
40		14	19	Mendiola, Josefa S	Wife	F	Cha	42.0	M		Y	Y	Guam	Guam	Guam	N	None
41		14	19	Mendiola, Vicente S	Son	M	Cha	25.0	S		Y	Y	Guam	Guam	Guam	N	Farmer
42		14	19	Mendiola, Pedro S	Son	M	Cha	24.0	S		Y	Y	Guam	Guam	Guam	N	Farm laborer home farm
43		14	19	Mendiola, Jesus S	Son	M	Cha	14.0	S	Y	Y	Y	Guam	Guam	Guam	Y	Farm laborer home farm
44		14	19	Mendiola, Ana S	Daughter	F	Cha	11.0	S	Y	Y	Y	Guam	Guam	Guam	Y	None
45		14	19	Mendiola, Manuel S	Brother	M	Cha	30.0	S		Y	Y	Guam	Guam	Guam	N	Farm laborer home farm
46		14	19	Mendiola, Soledad S	Sister	F	Cha	35.0	S		Y	Y	Guam	Guam	Guam	N	None
47		15	20	Quichocho, Jesus Q	Head	M	Cha	36.0	M		N	N	Guam	Unknown	Guam	N	Farmer
48		15	20	Quichocho, Joaquina Q	Wife	F	Cha	38.0	M		N	N	Guam	Guam	Guam	N	None
49		15	20	Quichocho, Julia C	Daughter	F	Cha	7.0	S	N			Guam	Guam	Guam		None
50		15	20	Quichocho, Antonio C	Son	M	Cha	4.0	S				Guam	Guam	Guam		None

(CHAMORRO ROOTS GENEALOGY PROJECT ™ TRANSCRIPTION)
(COMPILED/TRANSCRIBED BY BERNARD T. PUNZALAN / HTTP://WWW.CHAMORROROOTS.COM)

FOURTEENTH CENSUS OF THE UNITED STATES: 1920—POPULATION

ISLAND OF GUAM

DISTRICT 1
NAME OF PLACE Agana City

[Proper name and, also, name of class, as city, town, village, barrio, etc]

ENUMERATED BY ME ON THE 10th DAY OF April, 1920

Albert P. Manley ENUMERATOR

Street, avenue, road, etc.	Number of dwelling house in order of visitation	Number of family in order of visitation	NAME	RELATION	Sex	Color or race	Age at last birthday	Single, married, widowed or divorced	Attended school any time since Sept. 1, 1919	Whether able to read	Whether able to write	Place of birth of this person	Place of birth of father of this person	Place of birth of mother of this person	Whether able to speak English	OCCUPATION
	2	3	4	5	6	7	8	9	10	11	12	13	14	15	16	17
	15	20	Quichocho, Jesus C	Son	M	Cha	0.5	S				Guam	Unknown	Guam		None
	15	20	Quichocho, Nicolasa Q	Mother-in-law	F	Cha	58.0	S		N	N	Guam	Unknown	Guam	N	None
	15	21	Castro, Jose M	Head	M	Cha	36.0	M		Y	Y	Guam	Guam	Guam	N	Farmer
	15	21	Castro, Rosa S	Wife	F	Cha	27.0	M		Y	Y	Guam	Guam	Guam	Y	None
	15	21	Castro, Josefa S	Daughter	F	Cha	8.0	S				Guam	Guam	Guam		None
	15	21	Castro, Marcas A	Father	M	Cha	65.0	Wd		N	N	Guam	Guam	Guam	N	None
	16	22	Quichocho, Tomas Q	Head	M	Cha	58.0	M		Y	Y	Guam	Guam	Guam	Y	Farmer
	16	22	Quichocho, Francisca N	Wife	F	Cha	55.0	M		N	N	Guam	Unknown	Guam	N	None
	16	23	Quichocho, Vicente Q	Head	M	Cha	25.0	M		Y	Y	Guam	Guam	Guam	N	Farmer
	16	23	Quichocho, Carmela N	Wife	F	Cha	24.0	M		Y	Y	Guam	Unknown	Guam	N	None
	16	23	Quichocho, Pedro N	Son	M	Cha	6.0	S	N			Guam	Guam	Guam		None
	16	23	Quichocho, Jose N	Son	M	Cha	2.0	S				Guam	Guam	Guam		None
Esperansa Street	17	24	Tenorio, Manuel T	Head	M	Cha	36.0	M		Y	Y	Guam	Guam	Guam	N	Laborer
	17	24	Tenorio, Natividad N	Wife	F	Cha	41.0	M		Y	Y	Guam	Guam	Guam	N	None
	17	24	Tenorio, Manuel N	Son	M	Cha	20.0	S	N	Y	Y	Guam	Guam	Guam	Y	Farmer
	17	24	Tenorio, Rita N	Daughter	F	Cha	17.0	S	N	Y	Y	Guam	Guam	Guam	Y	None
	17	24	Tenorio, Jesus N	Son	M	Cha	15.0	S	Y	Y	Y	Guam	Guam	Guam	Y	Farm laborter home farm
	17	24	Tenorio, Remedio N	Daughter	F	Cha	10.0	S	Y	Y	Y	Guam	Guam	Guam	Y	None
	17	24	Tenorio, Teresa N	Daughter	F	Cha	6.0	S	N			Guam	Guam	Guam		None
	17	24	Tenorio, Mercedes N	Daughter	F	Cha	1.0	S				Guam	Guam	Guam		None
	18	25	San Nicolas, Mariano C	Head	M	Cha	76.0	M		Y	Y	Guam	Guam	Guam	N	None
	18	25	San Nicolas, Marcela C	Wife	F	Cha	34.0	M		Y	Y	Guam	Unknown	Guam	N	None
	18	25	San Nicolas, Maria C	Daughter	F	Cha	21.0	S	N	Y	Y	Guam	Guam	Guam	N	None
	18	25	San Nicolas, Dominarja C	Daughter	F	Cha	21.0	S	N	Y	Y	Guam	Guam	Guam	N	None
	18	25	San Nicolas, Catalina C	Daughter	F	Cha	20.0	S	N	Y	Y	Guam	Guam	Guam	N	None

(CHAMORRO ROOTS GENEALOGY PROJECT ™ TRANSCRIPTION)
(COMPILED/TRANSCRIBED BY BERNARD T. PUNZALAN / HTTP://WWW.CHAMORROROOTS.COM)

FOURTEENTH CENSUS OF THE UNITED STATES: 1920–POPULATION

ISLAND OF GUAM

DISTRICT **1**
NAME OF PLACE **Agana City**

ENUMERATED BY ME ON THE 12th DAY OF April, 1920

Albert P. Manley ENUMERATOR

	Street	Dwelling No.	Family No.	NAME	RELATION	Sex	Color or race	Age at last birthday	Single, married, widowed or divorced	Attended school since Sept. 1, 1919	Able to read	Able to write	Place of birth of this person	Place of birth of father	Place of birth of mother	Able to speak English	OCCUPATION
	1	2	3	4	5	6	7	8	9	10	11	12	13	14	15	16	17
26		18	25	San Nicolas, Ana C	Daughter	F	Cha	16.0	S	Y	Y	Y	Guam	Guam	Guam	Y	None
27		18	25	San Nicolas, Francisco C	Son	M	Cha	13.0	S	Y	Y	Y	Guam	Guam	Guam	Y	Farm laborer home farm
28		18	25	San Nicolas, Teresa C	Daughter	F	Cha	10.0	S	Y	Y	Y	Guam	Guam	Guam	Y	None
29		18	25	San Nicolas, Jose C	Son	M	Cha	5.0	S	Y			Guam	Guam	Guam	Y	None
30		19	26	Delgado, Jose M	Head	M	Cha	33.0	M		Y	Y	Guam	Guam	Guam	Y	Laborer
31		19	26	Delgado, Maria C	Wife	F	Cha	28.0	M		Y	Y	Guam	Guam	Guam	N	None
32		19	26	Delgado, Jesus C	Son	M	Cha	5.0	S	N			Guam	Guam	Guam		None
33		19	26	Delgado, Maria C	Daughter	F	Cha	4.0	S				Guam	Guam	Guam		None
34		19	26	Delgado, Jose C	Son	M	Cha	2.0	S				Guam	Guam	Guam		None
35		19	26	Delgado, Ana C	Daughter	F	Cha	0.9	S				Guam	Guam	Guam		None
36	peransa Street	20	27	Camacho, Ramon D	Head	M	Cha	50.0	M		Y	Y	Guam	Guam	Guam	Y	Carpenter
37		20	27	Camacho, Josefa A	Wife	F	Cha	51.0	M		Y	Y	Guam	Guam	Guam	N	None
38		20	27	Camacho, Ignacia A	Daughter	F	Cha	27.0	Wd		Y	Y	Guam	Guam	Guam	N	None
39		20	27	Camacho, Josefa A	Daughter	F	Cha	25.0	S	N	Y	Y	Guam	Guam	Guam	N	None
40		20	27	Camacho, Maria A	Daughter	F	Cha	18.0	S		Y	Y	Guam	Guam	Guam	N	None
41		20	27	Camacho, Dolores A	Daughter	F	Cha	14.0	S	Y	Y	Y	Guam	Guam	Guam	Y	None
42		20	27	Camacho, Felix A	Son	M	Cha	12.0	S	Y	Y	Y	Guam	Guam	Guam	Y	None
43		20	27	Camacho, Antonia A	Daughter	F	Cha	9.0	S	Y	Y	Y	Guam	Guam	Guam	Y	None
44		20	28	Camacho, Jose A	Head	M	Cha	20.0	M	N	Y	Y	Guam	Guam	Guam	Y	Blacksmith
45		20	28	Camacho, Maria SN	Wife	F	Cha	18.0	M	N	Y	Y	Guam	Guam	Guam	N	None
46		21	29	Namauleg, Joaquin N	Head	M	Cha	33.0	M		Y	Y	Guam	Unknown	Guam	N	Farmer
47		21	29	Namauleg, Rosa E	Wife	F	Cha	25.0	M		Y	Y	Guam	Guam	Guam	N	None
48		21	29	Namauleg, Jose E	Son	M	Cha	10.0	S	Y	Y	Y	Guam	Guam	Guam	Y	None
49		21	29	Namauleg, Jesus E	Son	M	Cha	3.0	S				Guam	Guam	Guam		None
50		21	29	Namauleg, Maria E	Daughter	F	Cha	2.0	S				Guam	Guam	Guam		None

(CHAMORRO ROOTS GENEALOGY PROJECT ™ TRANSCRIPTION)
(COMPILED/TRANSCRIBED BY BERNARD T. PUNZALAN / HTTP://WWW.CHAMORROROOTS.COM)

SHEET NO. 41A

FOURTEENTH CENSUS OF THE UNITED STATES: 1920—POPULATION
ISLAND OF GUAM

DISTRICT 1
NAME OF PLACE Agana City
[Proper name and, also, name of class, as city, town, village, barrio, etc]

ENUMERATED BY ME ON THE 12th DAY OF April, 1920

Albert P. Manley ENUMERATOR

	PLACE OF ABODE		NAME	RELATION	PERSONAL DESCRIPTION				EDUCATION			NATIVITY				OCCUPATION
Street, avenue, road, etc.	Number of dwelling house in order of visitation	Number of family in order of visitation	of each person whose place of abode on January 1, 1920, was in the family. Enter surname, firs, then given name and middle initial. If any. Include every person living on January 1, 1920. Omit children born since January 1, 1920.	Relationship of this Person to the head of the family.	Sex	Color or race	Age at last birthday	Single, married, widowed or divorced	Attended school any time since Sept. 1, 1919	Whether able to read.	Whether able to write.	Place of birth of this person.	Place of birth of father of this person.	Place of birth of mother of this person.	Whether able to speak English.	Trade, profession, or particular kind of work done, as salesman, laborer, clerk, cook, merchant, washerwoman, etc.
1	2	3	4	5	6	7	8	9	10	11	12	13	14	15	16	17
	21	29	Espinosa, Carmen E	Mother in law	F	Cha	64.0	Wd		Y	Y	Guam	Guam	Guam	N	None
	22	30	Charfauros, Joaquin C	Head	M	Cha	21.0	S	N	Y	Y	Guam	Guam	Guam	Y	Machinist
	23	31	Aguon, Maria M	Head	F	Cha	42.0	Wd		Y	Y	Guam	Guam	Guam	N	Laundress
	23	31	Aguon, Mariana M	Daughter	F	Cha	15.0	S	Y	Y	Y	Guam	Guam	Guam	Y	Laundress
	23	31	Aguon, Catalina M	Daughter	F	Cha	13.0	S	Y	Y	Y	Guam	Guam	Guam	Y	None
	23	31	Aguon, Josefina M	Daughter	F	Cha	10.0	S	Y	Y	Y	Guam	Guam	Guam	Y	None
	23	31	Aguon, Nicolas M	Son	M	Cha	7.0	S	N			Guam	Guam	Guam		None
	23	31	Aguon, Simon M	Son	M	Cha	4.0	S				Guam	Guam	Guam		None
	23	31	Aguon, Juan M	Son	M	Cha	1.0	S				Guam	Guam	Guam		None
Esperansa Street	23	32	Mendiola, Jose B	Head	M	Cha	27.0	M		Y	Y	Guam	Guam	Guam	Y	Farmer
	23	32	Mendiola, Joaquina M	Wife	F	Cha	18.0	M	N	Y	Y	Guam	Guam	Guam	N	None
	24	33	Gogo, Venancio G	Head	M	Cha	29.0	M		Y	Y	Guam	Unknown	Guam	N	Laborer
	24	33	Gogo, Maria C	Wife	F	Cha	24.0	M		N	N	Guam	Guam	Guam	N	None
	24	33	Gogo, Margarita C	Daughter	F	Cha	3.0	S				Guam	Guam	Guam		None
	24	33	Gogo, Rosario C	Daughter	F	Cha	2.0	S				Guam	Guam	Guam		None
	24	33	Gogo, Rosalia C	Daughter	F	Cha	0.2	S				Guam	Guam	Guam		None
	25	34	Castro, Ramon S	Head	M	Cha	29.0	M		Y	Y	Guam	Guam	Guam	N	Farmer
	25	34	Castro, Ana SN	Wife	F	Cha	38.0	M	N	Y	Y	Guam	Guam	Guam	N	None
	25	34	Castro, Dolores SN	Daughter	F	Cha	7.0	S				Guam	Guam	Guam		None
	25	34	Castro, Antonio SN	Son	M	Cha	4.0	S				Guam	Guam	Guam		None
	25	34	Castro, Maria SN	Daughter	F	Cha	3.0	S				Guam	Guam	Guam		None
	25	34	Castro, Baronica SN	Daughter	F	Cha	2.0	S				Guam	Guam	Guam		None
	26	35	Sablan, Maria C	Head	F	Cha	46.0	D		N	N	Guam	Guam	Guam	N	None
	26	35	Sablan, Jose C	Son	M	Cha	28.0	S		Y	Y	Guam	Guam	Guam	Y	Machinist
	26	35	Sablan, Carmen C	Daughter	F	Cha	22.0	S		Y	Y	Guam	Guam	Guam	Y	None

(CHAMORRO ROOTS GENEALOGY PROJECT ™ TRANSCRIPTION)
(COMPILED/TRANSCRIBED BY BERNARD T. PUNZALAN / HTTP://WWW.CHAMORROROOTS.COM)

27b

FOURTEENTH CENSUS OF THE UNITED STATES: 1920-POPULATION

ISLAND OF GUAM

DISTRICT **1**
NAME OF PLACE **Agana City**

[Proper name and, also, name of class, as city, town, village, barrio, etc]

ENUMERATED BY ME ON THE 12th DAY OF April, 1920

Albert P. Manley ENUMERATOR

	Dwelling	Family	NAME	RELATION	Sex	Color or race	Age	Single, married, widowed or divorced	Attended school since Sept. 1, 1919	Read	Write	Place of birth of this person	Place of birth of father	Place of birth of mother	English	OCCUPATION
1	2	3	4	5	6	7	8	9	10	11	12	13	14	15	16	17
	26	35	Sablan, Antonio C	Son	M	Cha	21.0	S	N	Y	Y	Guam	Guam	Guam	Y	Seaman USN
	27	36	Espinosa, Dolores F	Head	F	Cha	57.0	Wd		Y	Y	Guam	Guam	Guam	N	None
	27	36	Espinosa, Ana F	Daughter	F	Cha	17.0	S	N	Y	Y	Guam	Guam	Guam	Y	Laundress
	27	36	Espinosa, Consuelo F	Daughter	F	Cha	12.0	S	Y	Y	Y	Guam	Guam	Guam	N	None
	28	37	Camacho, Serlala M	Head	F	Cha	59.0	Wd		N	N	Guam	Guam	Guam	N	None
	28	37	Camacho, Maria M	Sister	F	Cha	58.0	S		N	N	Guam	Guam	Guam	N	None
	28	37	Camacho, Rosa M	Sister	F	Cha	50.0	S		N	N	Guam	Guam	Guam	N	None
Esperansa Street	28	37	Mendiola, Jose M	Nephew	M	Cha	25.0	S		Y	Y	Guam	Unknown	Guam	Y	Laborer
	28	38	Gogo, Jose C	Head	M	Cha	24.0	S		Y	Y	Guam	Guam	Guam	Y	Herder
	28	38	Gogo, Ana M	Wife	F	Cha	23.0	M		Y	Y	Guam	Guam	Guam	N	None
	28	38	Gogo, Isabel M	Daughter	F	Cha	1.0	S				Guam	Guam	Guam		None
	29	39	Delgado, Rufina M	Head	F	Cha	60.0	Wd		N	N	Guam	Guam	Guam	N	None
	29	39	Delgado, Maria M	Daughter	F	Cha	38.0	S		Y	Y	Guam	Guam	Guam	N	Laundress
	29	39	Delgado, Alfonso M	Son	M	Cha	29.0	S		Y	Y	Guam	Guam	Guam	Y	Laborer
	29	39	Delgado, Jesus M	Son	M	Cha	25.0	S		Y	Y	Guam	Guam	Guam	Y	Farmer
	29	39	Delgado, Rosa M	Daughter	F	Cha	21.0	S		Y	Y	Guam	Guam	Guam	N	None
	29	39	Mendiola, Rufina M	Granddaughter	F	Cha	6.0	S	N			Guam	Guam	Guam		None
	30	40	Castro, Miguel S	Head	M	Cha	23.0	M	N	Y	Y	Guam	Guam	Guam	Y	Farmer
	30	40	Castro, Rita M	Wife	F	Cha	26.0	M		Y	Y	Guam	Guam	Guam	Y	None
	30	40	Castro, Maria M	Daughter	F	Cha	1.0	S				Guam	Guam	Guam		None
	31	41	Quidagua, Juan S	Head	M	Cha	25.0	M		Y	Y	Guam	Guam	Guam	N	Farmer
	31	41	Quidagua, Ignacia C	Wife	F	Cha	30.0	M		N	N	Guam	Guam	Guam	N	None
	31	41	Espinosa, Francisco C	Stepson	M	Cha	4.0	S				Guam	Guam	Guam		None
	31	41	Quidagua, Maria C	Daughter	F	Cha	3.0	S				Guam	Guam	Guam		None
	31	41	Quidagua, Ana C	Daughter	F	Cha	0.3	S				Guam	Guam	Guam		None

(CHAMORRO ROOTS GENEALOGY PROJECT ™ TRANSCRIPTION)
(COMPILED/TRANSCRIBED BY BERNARD T. PUNZALAN / HTTP://WWW.CHAMORROROOTS.COM)

FOURTEENTH CENSUS OF THE UNITED STATES: 1920-POPULATION

ISLAND OF GUAM

DISTRICT 1

NAME OF PLACE Agana City

ENUMERATED BY ME ON THE 12th DAY OF April, 1920

Albert P. Manley ENUMERATOR

1 Street	2 Dwelling	3 Family	4 NAME	5 RELATION	6 Sex	7 Race	8 Age	9 Marital	10 School	11 Read	12 Write	13 Birthplace	14 Father	15 Mother	16 English	17 OCCUPATION
	31	42	Castro, Jose A	Head	M	Cha	61.0	M		Y	Y	Guam	Guam	Guam	N	Farmer
	31	42	Castro, Felisa L	Wife	F	Cha	55.0	M		Y	Y	Guam	Guam	Guam	N	None
	31	42	Castro, Ascemcion L	Daughter	F	Cha	24.0	S		Y	Y	Guam	Guam	Guam	Y	Laundress
	31	42	Castro, Josefa L	Daughter	F	Cha	18.0	S	N	Y	Y	Guam	Guam	Guam	Y	Laundress
	31	42	Castro, Joaquina L	Daughter	F	Cha	16.0	S	Y	Y	Y	Guam	Guam	Guam	Y	Laundress
	31	42	Castro, Jose L	Son	M	Cha	10.0	S	Y	Y	Y	Guam	Guam	Guam	Y	None
	31	42	Espinosa, Jose C	Grandson	M	Cha	11.0	S	Y	Y	Y	Guam	Guam	Guam	Y	None
	31	42	Espinosa, Maria C	Granddaughter	F	Cha	6.0	S	N			Guam	Guam	Guam		None
Esperansa Street	32	43	Aguigui, Miguel SN	Head	M	Cha	45.0	M		Y	Y	Guam	Guam	Guam	N	Farmer
	32	43	Aguigui, Antonia C	Wife	F	Cha	48.0	M		Y	N	Guam	Guam	Guam	N	None
	32	43	Aguigui, Joaquin C	Son	M	Cha	15.0	S	Y	Y	Y	Guam	Guam	Guam	Y	Farm laborer home farm
	32	43	Aguigui, Juan C	Son	M	Cha	8.0	S	Y	Y	Y	Guam	Guam	Guam	Y	None
	33	44	Camacho, Jose S	Head	M	Cha	50.0	M		Y	Y	Guam	Guam	Guam	N	Farmer
	33	44	Camacho, Ana C	Wife	F	Cha	52.0	M		Y	Y	Guam	Guam	Guam	N	None
	33	44	Camacho, Francisco C	Son	M	Cha	18.0	S	N	Y	Y	Guam	Guam	Guam	Y	Farm laborer home farm
	33	44	Camacho, Pedro C	Son	M	Cha	15.0	S	Y	Y	Y	Guam	Guam	Guam	Y	Carpenter
	33	44	Camacho, Maria C	Daughter	F	Cha	14.0	S	Y	Y	Y	Guam	Guam	Guam	Y	None
	34	45	Camacho, Ignacio N	Head	M	Cha	36.0	M		Y	Y	Guam	Guam	Guam	Y	Laborer
	34	45	Camacho, Maria D	Wife	F	Cha	34.0	M		Y	Y	Guam	Guam	Guam	N	None
	34	45	Camacho, Ana D	Daughter	F	Cha	5.0	S	N			Guam	Guam	Guam		None
	34	45	Camacho, Gregorio D	Son	M	Cha	4.0	S				Guam	Guam	Guam		None
	34	45	Camacho, Amable D	Daughter	F	Cha	2.0	S				Guam	Guam	Guam		None
	34	45	Camacho, Ignacio D	Son	M	Cha	0.3	S				Guam	Guam	Guam		None
	35	46	Gogo, Juan S	Head	M	Cha	52.0	M		Y	Y	Guam	Guam	Guam	N	Farmer
	35	46	Gogo, Consolacion N	Wife	F	Cha	50.0	M		Y	Y	Guam	Guam	Guam	N	None

(CHAMORRO ROOTS GENEALOGY PROJECT ™ TRANSCRIPTION)
(COMPILED/TRANSCRIBED BY BERNARD T. PUNZALAN / HTTP://WWW.CHAMORROROOTS.COM)
FOURTEENTH CENSUS OF THE UNITED STATES: 1920–POPULATION
ISLAND OF GUAM

DISTRICT 1
NAME OF PLACE Agana City
[Proper name and, also, name of class, as city, town, village, barrio, etc]

ENUMERATED BY ME ON THE 13th DAY OF April, 1920

Albert P. Manley ENUMERATOR

	Street	Dwelling # (2)	Family # (3)	NAME (4)	RELATION (5)	Sex (6)	Color or race (7)	Age (8)	Marital (9)	School (10)	Read (11)	Write (12)	Birthplace person (13)	Birthplace father (14)	Birthplace mother (15)	Speak English (16)	OCCUPATION (17)
26		35	46	Gogo, Jesus N	Son	M	Cha	18.0	S	N	Y	Y	Guam	Guam	Guam	Y	Laborer
27		35	46	Gogo, Ana N	Daughter	F	Cha	16.0	S	N	Y	Y	Guam	Guam	Guam	Y	None
28		35	46	Gogo, Joaquina N	Daughter	F	Cha	14.0	S	Y	Y	Y	Guam	Guam	Guam	Y	None
29		35	46	Gogo, Rosa N	Daughter	F	Cha	12.0	S	Y	Y	Y	Guam	Guam	Guam	Y	None
30		35	46	Gogo, Francisco N	Son	M	Cha	7.0	S	N			Guam	Guam	Guam		None
31		35	46	Gogo, Enrique N	Son	M	Cha	5.0	S	N			Guam	Guam	Guam		None
32		36	47	Guerrero, Vicente S	Head	M	Cha	29.0	M		N	N	Guam	Guam	Guam	N	Farmer
33		36	47	Guerrero, Dolores G	Wife	F	Cha	28.0	M		Y	Y	Guam	Guam	Guam	N	None
34		36	47	Guerrero, Felicidad G	Daughter	F	Cha	4.0	S				Guam	Guam	Guam		None
35		36	47	Guerrero, Lucio G	Son	M	Cha	2.0	S				Guam	Guam	Guam		None
36		37	48	Nego, Trudes D	Head	F	Cha	39.0	Wd		N	N	Guam	Guam	Guam	N	None
37	Esperansa Street	37	48	Nego, Jose D	Son	M	Cha	15.0	S	Y	Y	Y	Guam	Guam	Guam	Y	Farm laborer working out
38		37	48	Nego, Rosa D	Daughter	F	Cha	9.0	S	Y			Guam	Guam	Guam		None
39		37	48	Nego, Vicente D	Son	M	Cha	7.0	S	N			Guam	Guam	Guam		None
40		37	48	Camacho, Maria D	Daughter	F	Cha	3.0	S				Guam	Unknown	Guam		None
41		38	49	Castro, Vicente M	Head	M	Cha	39.0	M		Y	Y	Guam	Guam	Guam	N	Laborer
42		38	49	Castro, Trudes M	Wife	F	Cha	38.0	M		N	N	Guam	Guam	Guam	N	None
43		38	49	Castro, Jesus M	Brother	M	Cha	24.0	S		Y	Y	Guam	Guam	Guam	Y	Laborer
44		39	50	Santos, Manuel L	Head	M	Cha	42.0	M		Y	Y	Guam	Guam	Guam	N	Farmer
45		39	50	Santos, Concepcion C	Wife	F	Cha	44.0	M		Y	N	Guam	Guam	Guam	N	None
46		39	50	Santos, Maria C	Daughter	F	Cha	18.0	S	N	Y	Y	Guam	Guam	Guam	N	Laundress
47		39	50	Santos, Vicente C	Son	M	Cha	17.0	S	N	Y	Y	Guam	Guam	Guam	Y	Farm laborer home farm
48		39	50	Santos, Jose C	Son	M	Cha	14.0	S	Y	Y	Y	Guam	Guam	Guam	Y	Farm laborer home farm
49		39	50	Santos, Joaquin C	Son	M	Cha	12.0	S	Y	Y	Y	Guam	Guam	Guam	Y	Farm laborer home farm
50		39	50	Santos, Rita C	Daughter	F	Cha	8.0	S	Y	Y	Y	Guam	Guam	Guam	Y	None

(CHAMORRO ROOTS GENEALOGY PROJECT ™ TRANSCRIPTION)
(COMPILED/TRANSCRIBED BY BERNARD T. PUNZALAN / HTTP://WWW.CHAMORROROOTS.COM)
FOURTEENTH CENSUS OF THE UNITED STATES: 1920-POPULATION
ISLAND OF GUAM

DISTRICT 1
NAME OF PLACE **Agana City**
[Proper name and, also, name of class, as city, town, village, barrio, etc]

ENUMERATED BY ME ON THE 13th DAY OF April, 1920

Albert P. Manley ENUMERATOR

	PLACE OF ABODE			NAME	RELATION	PERSONAL DESCRIPTION					EDUCATION			NATIVITY				OCCUPATION
	Street, avenue, road, etc.	Number of dwelling house is order of visitation	Number of family in order of visitation	of each person whose place of abode on January 1, 1920, was in the family. Enter surname, firs, then given name and middle initial. If any. Include every person living on January 1, 1920. Omit children born since January 1, 1920.	Relationship of this person to the head of the family.	Sex	Color or race	Age at last birthday	Single, married, widowed or divorced	Attended any school since Sept. 1, 1919	Whether able to read.	Whether able to write.	Place of birth of this person.	Place of birth of father of this person.	Place of birth of mother of this person.	Whether able to speak English.	Trade, profession, or particular kind of work done, as salesman, laborer, clerk, cook, merchant, washerwoman, etc.
	1	2	3	4	5	6	7	8	9	10	11	12	13	14	15	16	17
1	Esperansa Street	39	50	Santos, Antonio C	Son	M	Cha	5.0	S	N			Guam	Guam	Guam		None
2		40	51	Lujan, Marcela G	Head	F	Cha	36.0	Wd		Y	Y	Guam	Guam	Guam	N	None
3		40	51	Gogue, Manuel G	Son	M	Cha	11.0	S	N	Y	Y	Guam	Unknown	Guam	Y	Farmer
4		40	52	Crisostomo, Ana G	Head	F	Cha	31.0	S		Y	Y	Guam	Guam	Guam	N	None
5		40	52	Crisostomo, Lucia G	Daughter	F	Cha	3.0	S				Guam	Unknown	Guam		None
6		41	53	Guevara, Antonio C	Head	M	Fil	46.0	Wd		Y	Y	Guam	Manila Philippines	Guam	N	Laborer
7		41	53	Guevara, Maria C	Sister	F	Fil	49.0	M		Y	Y	Guam	Manila Philippines	Guam	N	Seamstress
8		41	53	Guevara, Juan C	Son	M	Cha	14.0	S	Y	Y	Y	Guam	Guam	Guam	Y	Farm laborer home farm
9		41	53	Guevara, Gregorio D	Son	M	Cha	13.0	S	Y	Y	Y	Guam	Guam	Guam	Y	None
10		41	53	Guevara, Fralon D	Son	M	Cha	12.0	S	Y	Y	Y	Guam	Guam	Guam	Y	None
11		41	53	Guevara, Macario D	Son	M	Cha	11.0	S	Y	Y	Y	Guam	Guam	Guam	Y	None
12		41	53	Guevara, Juliana D	Daughter	F	Cha	6.0	S	N			Guam	Guam	Guam		None
13		41	53	Guevara, Aularia D	Daughter	F	Cha	4.0	S				Guam	Guam	Guam		None
14		41	53	Guevara, Maria D	Daughter	F	Cha	3.0	S				Guam	Guam	Guam		None
15	Paz Street	42	54	Guevara, Cecilio C	Head	M	Fil	58.0	M		Y	Y	Guam	Manila Philippines	Guam	N	Farmer
16		42	54	Guevara, Rosa C	Wife	F	Cha	45.0	M		Y	Y	Guam	Guam	Guam	N	None
17		42	55	Guevara, Fernando C	Head	M	Cha	28.0	M		Y	Y	Guam	Guam	Guam	N	Carpenter
18		42	55	Guevara, Isabel C	Wife	F	Cha	24.0	M		Y	Y	Guam	Guam	Guam	N	None
19		42	55	Guevara, Maria C	Daughter	F	Cha	3.0	S				Guam	Guam	Guam		None
20		42	55	Guevara, Enriqueta C	Daughter	F	Cha	2.0	S				Guam	Guam	Guam		None
21		43	56	Mendiola, Pedro D	Head	M	Cha	33.0	M		Y	Y	Guam	Guam	Guam	Y	Farm laborer working out
22		43	56	Mendiola, Maria S	Wife	F	Cha	48.0	M		Y	Y	Guam	Guam	Guam	Y	None
23		43	56	Atoigue, Remedio A	Servant	M	Cha	15.0	S	Y	Y	Y	Guam	Guam	Guam	N	Servant
24		43	56	Gogue, Pedro S	Servant	M	Cha	10.0	S	Y	Y	Y	Guam	Guam	Guam	Y	Servant
25		44	57	Reyes, Ignacio G	Head	M	Cha	29.0	M		Y	Y	Guam	Guam	Guam	Y	Farmer

(CHAMORRO ROOTS GENEALOGY PROJECT ™ TRANSCRIPTION)
(COMPILED/TRANSCRIBED BY BERNARD T. PUNZALAN / HTTP://WWW.CHAMORROROOTS.COM)
FOURTEENTH CENSUS OF THE UNITED STATES: 1920—POPULATION
ISLAND OF GUAM

DISTRICT 1
NAME OF PLACE Agana City
[Proper name and, also, name of class, as city, town, village, barrio, etc]

ENUMERATED BY ME ON THE 14th DAY OF April, 1920
Albert P. Manley ENUMERATOR

#	Street	Dwelling	Family	NAME	RELATION	Sex	Race	Age	Marital	School	Read	Write	Birthplace person	Birthplace father	Birthplace mother	English	OCCUPATION
26		44	57	Reyes, Maria R	Wife	F	Cha	29.0	M		Y	Y	Guam	Guam	Guam	Y	None
27		44	57	Reyes, Juan R	Son	M	Cha	3.0	S				Guam	Guam	Guam		None
28		44	57	Reyes, Fermin R	Son	M	Cha	0.1	S				Guam	Guam	Guam		None
29		44	57	Rosario, Silvestre C	Brother-in-law	M	Cha	14.0	S	Y	Y	Y	Guam	Guam	Guam		None
30		45	58	Reyes, Fermin A	Head	M	Cha	56.0	M		N	N	Guam	Guam	Guam	N	None
31		45	58	Reyes, Benita G	Wife	F	Cha	54.0	M		Y	Y	Guam	Guam	Guam	N	None
32		45	58	Reyes, Jose G	Son	M	Cha	27.0	Wd		Y	Y	Guam	Guam	Guam	Y	Laborer
33		45	58	Reyes, Juan G	Son	M	Cha	24.0	S		Y	Y	Guam	Guam	Guam	Y	?
34		45	58	Reyes, Vicente G	Son	M	Cha	22.0	S		Y	Y	Guam	Guam	Guam	Y	Farmer
35		45	58	Reyes, Elisa G	Daughter	F	Cha	17.0	S	N	Y	Y	Guam	Guam	Guam	Y	None
36	Paz Street	45	58	Reyes, Francisco G	Son	M	Cha	16.0	S	Y	Y	Y	Guam	Guam	Guam	Y	Laborer
37		45	58	Reyes, Mariano G	Son	M	Cha	15.0	S	Y	Y	Y	Guam	Guam	Guam	Y	Farm laborer home farm
38		45	58	Reyes, Jesus G	Son	M	Cha	12.0	S	Y	Y	Y	Guam	Guam	Guam	Y	None
39		45	59	Guevara, Teodora C	Head	F	Fil	28.0	Wd		Y	Y	Manila Philippines	Manila Philippines	Manila Philippines	N	Laundress
40		45	59	Guevara, Enriqueta C	Daughter	F	Fil	15.0	S	Y	Y	Y	Manila Philippines	Manila Philippines	Manila Philippines	Y	None
41		45	59	Guevara, Simion C	Son	M	Fil	4.0	S		Y	Y	Guam	Manila Philippines	Manila Philippines	Y	None
42		46	60	Aflague, Justo R	Head	M	Cha	20.0	M	N	Y	Y	Guam	Guam	Guam	Y	Bookkeeper
43		46	60	Aflague, Francisca G	Wife	F	Cha	18.0	M	N	Y	Y	Guam	Guam	Guam	Y	None
44		46	60	Aflague, Manuel G	Son	M	Cha	1.0	S				Guam	Guam	Guam		None
45		47	61	Aguon, Vicente C	Head	M	Cha	38.0	M		Y	Y	Guam	Guam	Guam	N	Laborer
46		47	61	Aguon, Ana T	Wife	F	Cha	38.0	M		Y	Y	Guam	Guam	Guam	N	None
47		47	61	Aguon, Maria T	Daughter	F	Cha	15.0	S	Y	Y	Y	Guam	Guam	Guam	Y	None
48		47	61	Gogue, Maria C	Niece	F	Cha	24.0	Wd		Y	Y	Guam	Guam	Guam	N	Laundress
49		48	62	Mesa, Vicente C	Head	M	Cha	50.0	M		Y	Y	Guam	Guam	Guam	Y	Farmer
50		48	62	Mesa, Felisa A	Wife	F	Cha	40.0	M		Y	Y	Guam	Guam	Guam	N	None

(CHAMORRO ROOTS GENEALOGY PROJECT ™ TRANSCRIPTION)
(COMPILED/TRANSCRIBED BY BERNARD T. PUNZALAN / HTTP://WWW.CHAMORROROOTS.COM)

FOURTEENTH CENSUS OF THE UNITED STATES: 1920—POPULATION

ISLAND OF GUAM

DISTRICT 1
NAME OF PLACE Agana City

ENUMERATED BY ME ON THE 14th DAY OF April, 1920

Albert P. Manley ENUMERATOR

	PLACE OF ABODE			NAME	RELATION	PERSONAL DESCRIPTION					EDUCATION			NATIVITY				OCCUPATION
Street, avenue, road, etc.	Number of dwelling house is order of visitation	Number of family in order of visitation		of each person whose place of abode on January 1, 1920, was in the family. Enter surname, first, then given name and middle initial. If any. Include every person living on January 1, 1920. Omit children born since January 1, 1920.	Relationship of this Person to the head of the family.	Sex	Color or race	Age at last birthday	Single, married, widowed or divorced	Attended school any time since Sept. 1, 1919	Whether able to read.	Whether able to write.	Place of birth of this person.	Place of birth of father of this person.	Place of birth of mother of this person.	Whether able to speak English.	Trade, profession, or particular kind of work done, as salesman, laborer, clerk, cook, merchant, washerwoman, etc.
1	2	3	4		5	6	7	8	9	10	11	12	13	14	15	16	17
Paz Street	48	62	1	Mesa, Antonio A	Son	M	Cha	13.0	S	Y	Y	Y	Guam	Guam	Guam	Y	Farm laborer home farm
	48	62	2	Mesa, Ignacio A	Son	M	Cha	10.0	S	Y	Y	Y	Guam	Guam	Guam	Y	None
	48	62	3	Mesa, Dolores A	Daughter	F	Cha	7.0	S	N			Guam	Guam	Guam		None
	48	62	4	Mesa, Juan A	Son	M	Cha	6.0	S	N			Guam	Guam	Guam		None
	48	62	5	Mesa, Vicente A	Son	M	Cha	2.0	S				Guam	Guam	Guam		None
	48	62	6	Mesa, Manuel A	Son	M	Cha	0.1	S				Guam	Guam	Guam		None
	48	62	7	Aguon, Ignacia C	Niece	F	Cha	26.0	S		Y	Y	Guam	Guam	Guam		None
	49	63	8	Santos, Juan A	Head	M	Cha	19.0	M	N	Y	Y	Guam	Guam	Guam	Y	Seaman USN
	49	63	9	Santos, Isabel P	Wife	F	Cha	18.0	M	N	Y	Y	Guam	Guam	Guam	Y	None
	49	63	10	Aflague, Frouctaso SN	Nephew	M	Cha	7.0	S	N			Guam	Guam	Guam		None
Calle de Madrid Street	50	64	11	Gogue, Vicente SL	Head	M	Cha	27.0	M		Y	Y	Guam	Guam	Guam	Y	Laborer
	50	64	12	Gogue, Rita A	Wife	F	Cha	29.0	M		Y	Y	Guam	Guam	Guam	N	None
	50	64	13	Gogue, Geronimo A	Son	M	Cha	6.0	S				Guam	Guam	Guam		None
	50	64	14	Gogue, Josefina A	Daughter	F	Cha	5.0	S				Guam	Guam	Guam		None
	50	64	15	Gogue, Maria A	Daughter	F	Cha	0.9	S				Guam	Guam	Guam		None
	51	65	16	Cruz, Jesus R	Head	M	Cha	23.0	M		Y	Y	Guam	Guam	Guam	Y	Laborer
	51	65	17	Cruz, Ana S	Wife	F	Cha	20.0	M	N	Y	Y	Guam	Guam	Guam	Y	None
	52	66	18	Rosario, Ignacio P	Head	M	Cha	53.0	M		Y	Y	Guam	Guam	Guam	N	Farmer
	52	66	19	Rosario, Nicolasa L	Wife	F	Cha	40.0	M		Y	Y	Guam	Guam	Guam	N	None
	52	66	20	Rosario, Joaquin C	Son	M	Cha	18.0	S	N	Y	Y	Guam	Guam	Guam	Y	Farm laborer home farm
	52	66	21	Rosario, Silvestre C	Son	M	Cha	14.0	S	Y	Y	Y	Guam	Guam	Guam	Y	None
	52	66	22	Rosario, Angelina L	Daughter	F	Cha	12.0	S	Y	Y	Y	Guam	Guam	Guam	Y	None
	52	66	23	Rosario, Ignacio L	Son	M	Cha	9.0	S	Y	Y	Y	Guam	Guam	Guam	Y	None
	52	66	24	Rosario, Milagros L	Daughter	F	Cha	8.0	S	Y	Y	Y	Guam	Guam	Guam	Y	None
	52	66	25	Rosario, Manuel L	Son	M	Cha	7.0	S	Y	Y	Y	Guam	Guam	Guam	Y	None

71

(CHAMORRO ROOTS GENEALOGY PROJECT ™ TRANSCRIPTION)
(COMPILED/TRANSCRIBED BY BERNARD T. PUNZALAN / HTTP://WWW.CHAMORROROOTS.COM)
FOURTEENTH CENSUS OF THE UNITED STATES: 1920-POPULATION
ISLAND OF GUAM

DISTRICT 1
NAME OF PLACE Agana City
[Proper name and, also, name of class, as city, town, village, barrio, etc]

ENUMERATED BY ME ON THE 15th DAY OF April, 1920

Albert P. Manley ENUMERATOR

	PLACE OF ABODE			NAME	RELATION	PERSONAL DESCRIPTION					EDUCATION			NATIVITY			OCCUPATION
Street, avenue, road, etc.	Number of dwelling house is in order of visitation	Number of family in order of visitation		of each person whose place of abode on January 1, 1920, was in the family. Enter surname, firs, then given name and middle initial. If any. Include every person living on January 1, 1920. Omit children born since January 1, 1920.	Relationship of this person to the head of the family.	Sex	Color or race	Age at last birthday	Single, married, widowed or divorced	Attended school any time since Sept. 1, 1919	Whether able to read.	Whether able to write.	Place of birth of this person.	Place of birth of father of this person.	Place of birth of mother of this person.	Whether able to speak English.	Trade, profession, or particular kind of work done, as salesman, laborer, clerk, cook, merchant, washerwoman, etc.
1	2	3		4	5	6	7	8	9	10	11	12	13	14	15	16	17
	52	66	26	Rosario, Rosa L	Daughter	F	Cha	6.0	S	N			Guam	Guam	Guam		None
	52	66	27	Rosario, Enrique L	Son	M	Cha	4.0	S				Guam	Guam	Guam		None
	52	66	28	Rosario, Jose L	Son	M	Cha	2.0	S				Guam	Guam	Guam		None
	53	67	29	Lalae, Florentino	Head	M	Cha	86.0	M		N	N	Guam	Guam	Guam	N	None
	53	67	30	Lalae, Martina LG	Wife	F	Cha	83.0	M		N	N	Guam	Guam	Guam	N	None
	54	68	31	Guevara, Vicente C	Head	M	Ot	40.0	M		Y	Y	Guam	Manila Philippines	Guam	Y	Shoemaker
	54	68	32	Guevara, Maria A	Wife	F	Cha	34.0	M		Y	Y	Guam	Guam	Guam	N	None
	54	68	33	Guevara, Vicente A	Son	M	Cha	10.0	S	Y	Y	Y	Guam	Guam	Guam	Y	None
	54	68	34	Guevara, Jose A	Son	M	Cha	5.0	S	N			Guam	Guam	Guam		None
	54	68	35	Guevara, Edwardo A	Son	M	Cha	1.0	S				Guam	Guam	Guam		None
	55	69	36	Lalae, Manuel U	Head	M	Cha	36.0	M		Y	Y	Guam	Guam	Guam	N	Farmer
	55	69	37	Lalae, Terasa G	Wife	F	Cha	40.0	M		Y	Y	Guam	Guam	Guam	N	None
	56	70	38	Taitano, Baldomero B	Head	M	Cha	49.0	M		Y	Y	Guam	Guam	Guam	N	Farmer
	56	70	39	Taitano, Rita C	Wife	F	Cha	48.0	M		Y	Y	Guam	Guam	Guam	N	None
	56	70	40	Taitano, Maria C	Daughter	F	Cha	20.0	S	N	Y	Y	Guam	Guam	Guam	N	None
	56	70	41	Taitano, Conception C	Daughter	F	Cha	19.0	S	N	Y	Y	Guam	Guam	Guam	N	None
	56	70	42	Taitano, Francisca C	Daughter	F	Cha	16.0	S	N	Y	Y	Guam	Guam	Guam	N	None
	56	70	43	Taitano, Isabel C	Daughter	F	Cha	14.0	S	Y	Y	Y	Guam	Guam	Guam	Y	None
	56	70	44	Taitano, Miguel C	Son	M	Cha	12.0	S	Y	Y	Y	Guam	Guam	Guam	Y	None
	56	70	45	Taitano, Jose C	Son	M	Cha	8.0	S	Y	Y	Y	Guam	Guam	Guam		None
	56	70	46	Taitano, Antonio C	Son	M	Cha	6.0	S				Guam	Guam	Guam		None
	56	70	47	Taitano, Rosario A	Granddaughter	F	Cha	2.0	S				Guam	Guam	Guam		None
	56	70	48	Taitano, Francisco C	Grandson	M	Cha	2.0	S				Guam	Guam	Guam		None
	57	71	49	Camacho, Vicente T	Head	M	Cha	44.0	S		Y	Y	Guam	Guam	Guam	N	Silversmith
	58	72	50	Paulino, Jose C	Head	M	Cha	23.0	S		Y	Y	Guam	Guam	Guam	Y	Policeman

Calle de Madrid Street

72

(CHAMORRO ROOTS GENEALOGY PROJECT ™ TRANSCRIPTION)
(COMPILED/TRANSCRIBED BY BERNARD T. PUNZALAN / HTTP://WWW.CHAMORROROOTS.COM)
FOURTEENTH CENSUS OF THE UNITED STATES: 1920-POPULATION
ISLAND OF GUAM

DISTRICT 1
NAME OF PLACE Agana City
[Proper name and, also, name of class, as city, town, village, barrio, etc]

SHEET NO. 45A

ENUMERATED BY ME ON THE 15th DAY OF April, 1920

Albert P. Manley ENUMERATOR

Street, avenue, road, etc.	Number of dwelling house in order of visitation	Number of family in order of visitation	NAME	RELATION	Sex	Color or race	Age at last birthday	Single, married, widowed or divorced	Attended school any time since Sept. 1, 1919	Whether able to read	Whether able to write	Place of birth of this person	Place of birth of father of this person	Place of birth of mother of this person	Whether able to speak English	OCCUPATION
1	2	3	4	5	6	7	8	9	10	11	12	13	14	15	16	17
Calle de Madrid Street	59	73	San Nicolas, Augustin T	Head	M	Cha	21.0	S	N	Y	Y	Guam	Guam	Guam	N	None
	60	74	Mendiola, Jose B	Head	M	Cha	54.0	M		Y	Y	Guam	Guam	Guam	N	Farmer
	60	74	Mendiola, Rosa C	Wife	F	Cha	36.0	M		Y	Y	Guam	Guam	Guam	N	None
	60	74	Mendiola, Jesus C	Son	M	Cha	17.0	S	N	Y	Y	Guam	Guam	Guam	Y	Laborer
	60	74	Mendiola, Vicenta C	Daughter	F	Cha	15.0	S	Y	Y	Y	Guam	Guam	Guam	Y	None
	60	74	Mendiola, Carlos C	Son	M	Cha	14.0	S	Y	Y	Y	Guam	Guam	Guam	Y	None
	61	75	Jackson, Dolores K	Head	F	W	39.0	D		Y	Y	Guam	Holland	Guam	Y	None
	61	75	Kamminga, Jose K	Son	M	Cha	15.0	S	N	Y	Y	Guam	Unknown	Guam	Y	Seaman USN
	61	75	Jackson, Frank K	Son	M	W	13.0	S	Y	Y	Y	Guam	New York	Guam	Y	None
	61	75	Jackson, Lilian K	Daughter	F	W	11.0	S	Y	Y	Y	Guam	New York	Guam	Y	None
	61	75	Jackson, Altura C	Son	M	W	5.0	S	N			Guam	New York	Guam		None
	61	75	Jackson, Enrique C	Son	M	W	3.0	S				Guam	New York	Guam		None

Here ends the enumeration of the San Ramon, Agana City

(CHAMORRO ROOTS GENEALOGY PROJECT ™ TRANSCRIPTION)
(COMPILED/TRANSCRIBED BY BERNARD T. PUNZALAN / HTTP://WWW.CHAMORROROOTS.COM)

FOURTEENTH CENSUS OF THE UNITED STATES: 1920-POPULATION
ISLAND OF GUAM

ENUMERATED BY ME ON THE 24th DAY OF February, 1920

Jose Kamminga ENUMERATOR

DISTRICT 1
NAME OF PLACE Dededo Barrio

[Proper name and, also, name of class, as city, town, village, barrio, etc]

1	2	3	4	5	6	7	8	9	10	11	12	13	14	15	16	17
Street, avenue, road, etc.	Number of dwelling house	Number of family	NAME	RELATION	Sex	Color or race	Age at last birthday	Single, married, widowed or divorced	Attended school since Sept. 1, 1919	Whether able to read	Whether able to write	Place of birth of this person	Place of birth of father of this person	Place of birth of mother of this person	Whether able to speak English	OCCUPATION
Dededo Barrio	1	1	Tenorio, Jose B	Head	M	Cha	25.0	M		Y	Y	Guam	Guam	Guam	N	Farmer
	1	1	Tenorio, Antonia S	Wife	F	Cha	23.0	M		Y	Y	Guam	Guam	Guam	N	None
	1	1	Tenorio, Gregorio S	Son	M	Cha	5.0	S	N			Guam	Guam	Guam		None
	1	1	Tenorio, Juan S	Son	M	Cha	4.0	S				Guam	Guam	Guam		None
	1	1	Tenorio, Antonio S	Son	M	Cha	1.0	S				Guam	Guam	Guam		None
	2	2	Santos, Ignacio A	Head	M	Cha	49.0	M		N	N	Guam	Guam	Guam	Y	Farmer
	2	2	Santos, Angela S	Wife	F	Cha	49.0	M		Y	N	Guam	Unknown	Guam	N	None
	2	2	Santos, Ana S	Daughter	F	Cha	18.0	S	N	Y	Y	Guam	Guam	Guam	Y	None
	2	2	Santos, Pedro S	Son	M	Cha	14.0	S	Y	Y	Y	Guam	Guam	Guam	Y	None
	2	2	Santos, Maria S	Daughter	F	Cha	12.0	S	Y	Y	Y	Guam	Guam	Guam	Y	None
	2	2	Santos, Jesus S	Son	M	Cha	9.0	S	Y	Y	N	Guam	Guam	Guam		None
	2	2	Santos, Rosario S	Daughter	F	Cha	7.0	S	Y			Guam	Guam	Guam		None
	2	2	Santos, Paz S	Mother-in-law	F	Cha	76.0	Wd				Guam	Guam	Guam		None
	2	2	Cruz, Domingo J	Servant	M	Cha	56.0	Wd		N	N	Rota Island	Guam	Rota Island	N	Servant
	2	2	Cruz, Vicente B	Servant	M	Cha	15.0	S	N	Y	Y	Guam	Rota Island	Guam	Y	Servant
	3	3	Tenorio, Vicente B	Head	M	Cha	31.0	M		N	N	Guam	Guam	Guam	N	Farmer
	3	3	Tenorio, Tomasa SN	Wife	F	Cha	30.0	M		Y		Guam	Unknown	Guam	N	None
	3	3	Tenorio, Francisco SN	Son	M	Cha	9.0	S	Y			Guam	Guam	Guam		None
	3	3	Tenorio, Dolores SN	Daughter	F	Cha	7.0	S	N			Guam	Guam	Guam		None
	3	3	Tenorio, Luis SN	Son	M	Cha	4.0	S				Guam	Guam	Guam		None
	3	3	Tenorio, Roberto SN	Son	M	Cha	2.0	S				Guam	Guam	Guam		None
	4	4	Benavente, Antonio M	Head	M	Cha	44.0	M		N	N	Guam	Guam	Guam	N	Farmer
	4	4	Benavente, Maria Q	Wife	F	Cha	46.0	M		Y	N	Guam	Guam	Guam	N	None
	4	4	Benavente, Cecilia Q	Daughter	F	Cha	14.0	S	N	Y	Y	Guam	Guam	Guam	Y	None
	4	4	Benavente, Ana	Daughter	F	Cha	7.0	S	N	N	N	Guam	Guam	Guam		None

(CHAMORRO ROOTS GENEALOGY PROJECT ™ TRANSCRIPTION)
(COMPILED/TRANSCRIBED BY BERNARD T. PUNZALAN / HTTP://WWW.CHAMORROROOTS.COM)

FOURTEENTH CENSUS OF THE UNITED STATES: 1920-POPULATION
ISLAND OF GUAM

DISTRICT 1
NAME OF PLACE Dededo Barrio

ENUMERATED BY ME ON THE 24th DAY OF February, 1920

Jose Kamminga ENUMERATOR

[Proper name and, also, name of class, name of class, as city, town, village, barrio, etc]

			NAME	RELATION	Sex	Color or race	Age at last birthday	Single, married, widowed or divorced	Attended any school since Sept. 1, 1919	Whether able to read	Whether able to write	Place of birth of this person	Place of birth of father of this person	Place of birth of mother of this person	Whether able to speak English	OCCUPATION
1	2	3	4	5	6	7	8	9	10	11	12	13	14	15	16	17
	4	4	Benavente, Rita Q	Daughter	F	Cha	6.0	S	N			Guam	Guam	Guam		None
	5	5	Lujan, Jesus S	Head	M	Cha	42.0	M		Y	Y	Guam	Guam	Guam	N	Farmer
	5	5	Lujan, Dolores G	Wife	F	Cha	44.0	M		N	N	Guam	Guam	Guam	N	None
	5	5	Lujan, Maria G	Daughter	F	Cha	21.0	S	N	Y	Y	Guam	Guam	Guam	Y	None
	5	5	Lujan, Engracia G	Daughter	F	Cha	19.0	S	N	Y	Y	Guam	Guam	Guam	Y	None
	5	5	Lujan, Jose G	Son	M	Cha	17.0	S	N	Y	Y	Guam	Guam	Guam	Y	Farm laborer home farm
	5	5	Lujan, Francisco G	Son	M	Cha	15.0	S	N	Y	Y	Guam	Guam	Guam	Y	Teacher
	5	5	Lujan, Maria G Jr.	Daughter	F	Cha	13.0	S	N	Y	Y	Guam	Guam	Guam	Y	None
	5	5	Lujan, Juan G	Son	M	Cha	11.0	S	Y	Y	Y	Guam	Guam	Guam	Y	None
	5	5	Lujan, Rosa G	Daughter	F	Cha	8.0	S	Y	Y		Guam	Guam	Guam		None
	5	5	Lujan, Joaquin G	Son	M	Cha	5.0	S	N	N		Guam	Guam	Guam		None
	6	6	Benavente, Manuel T	Head	M	Cha	37.0	M		N	N	Guam	Unknown	Guam	N	Farmer
	6	6	Benavente, Teresa Q	Wife	F	Cha	31.0	M		N	N	Guam	Unknown	Guam	N	None
	6	6	Benavente, Jose Q	Son	M	Cha	11.0	S	Y	Y	Y	Guam	Guam	Guam	Y	None
	6	6	Benavente, Tomas Q	Son	M	Cha	7.0	S	N	N		Guam	Guam	Guam		None
	6	6	Benavente, Manuel Q	Son	M	Cha	6.0	S	N			Guam	Guam	Guam		None
	6	6	Benavente, Eloi Q	Son	M	Cha	5.0	S				Guam	Guam	Guam		None
	6	6	Benavente, Antonia Q	Daughter	F	Cha	1.0	S				Guam	Guam	Guam		None
	7	7	San Agustin, Jose E	Head	M	Cha	37.0	M		N	N	Guam	Guam	Guam	N	Farmer
	7	7	San Agustin, Caridad R	Wife	F	Cha	25.0	M		N	N	Guam	Guam	Guam	N	None
	7	7	San Agustin, Juan R	Son	M	Cha	9.0	S	Y			Guam	Guam	Guam		None
	7	7	San Agustin, Isabel R	Daughter	F	Cha	6.0	S	N			Guam	Guam	Guam		None
	7	7	San Agustin, Manuel R	Son	M	Cha	4.0	S				Guam	Guam	Guam		None
	7	7	San Agustin, Francisco R	Son	M	Cha	1.0	S				Guam	Guam	Guam		None
	7	7	Cepeda, Juan S	Cousin	M	Cha	37.0	S		N	N	Guam	Guam	Guam	N	Farm laborer

Street, avenue, road: Dededo Barrio

(CHAMORRO ROOTS GENEALOGY PROJECT ™ TRANSCRIPTION)
(COMPILED/TRANSCRIBED BY BERNARD T. PUNZALAN / HTTP://WWW.CHAMORROROOTS.COM)

FOURTEENTH CENSUS OF THE UNITED STATES: 1920—POPULATION

ISLAND OF GUAM

DISTRICT 1

NAME OF PLACE Dededo Barrio

ENUMERATED BY ME ON THE 25th DAY OF February, 1920

Jose Kamminga ENUMERATOR

1 Street	2 Dwelling	3 Family	4 NAME	5 RELATION	6 Sex	7 Color or race	8 Age	9 Marital	10 Attended school	11 Read	12 Write	13 Birthplace	14 Father birthplace	15 Mother birthplace	16 English	17 OCCUPATION
	8	8	Fernandez, Jose Q	Head	M	W	44.0	M		Y	Y	Guam	Spain	Guam	N	Farmer
	8	8	Fernandez, Joaquina L	Wife	F	Cha	38.0	M		Y	N	Guam	Guam	Guam	N	None
	8	8	Fernandez, Jose L	Son	M	Mix	19.0	S	N	Y	Y	Guam	Guam	Guam	Y	Farm laborer home farm
	8	8	Fernandez, Juan L	Son	M	Mix	17.0	S	N	Y	Y	Guam	Guam	Guam	Y	Farm laborer home farm
	8	8	Fernandez, Juan L jr.	Son	M	Mix	15.0	S	N	Y	Y	Guam	Guam	Guam	Y	None
	8	8	Fernandez, Maria L	Daughter	F	Mix	13.0	S	N	Y	Y	Guam	Guam	Guam	Y	None
	8	8	Fernandez, Jesus L	Son	M	Mix	11.0	S	N	Y	Y	Guam	Guam	Guam	Y	None
	8	8	Fernandez, Jose L jr.	Son	M	Mix	10.0	S	Y	Y	Y	Guam	Guam	Guam	Y	None
Dededo Barrio	8	8	Fernandez, Maria L jr.	Daughter	F	Mix	9.0	S	Y	Y	Y	Guam	Guam	Guam	Y	None
	8	8	Fernandez, Jesus L jr.	Son	M	Mix	8.0	S	Y	Y	Y	Guam	Guam	Guam	Y	None
	8	8	Fernandez, Vicente L	Son	M	Mix	6.0	S	Y	Y	Y	Guam	Guam	Guam		None
	8	8	Fernandez, Gonzalo L	Son	M	Mix	4.0	S	N			Guam	Guam	Guam		None
	8	8	Fernandez, Paz L	Daughter	F	Mix	3.0	S				Guam	Guam	Guam		None
	9	9	Duenas, Jose M	Head	M	Cha	62.0	M		N	N	Guam	Guam	Guam	N	Farmer
	9	9	Duenas, Juana E	Wife	F	Cha	57.0	M		N	N	Guam	Unknown	Guam	N	None
	9	9	Duenas, Concepcion E	Daughter	F	Cha	31.0	S		N	N	Guam	Guam	Guam	Y	None
	9	9	Duenas, Ramon C	Grand-son	M	Cha	12.0	S	Y	Y	N	Guam	Unknown	Guam	N	None
	10	10	Rosario, Jose B	Head	M	Cha	36.0	M		Y	Y	Guam	Guam	Guam	Y	Farmer
	10	10	Rosario, Ana P	Wife	F	Fil	25.0	M		Y	Y	Guam	Philippine Islands	Guam	N	None
	10	10	Rosario, Jesus P	Son	M	Cha	7.0	S				Guam	Guam	Guam		None
	10	10	Rosario, Lourdes P	Daughter	F	Cha	6.0	S				Guam	Guam	Guam		None
	10	10	Rosario, Jose P	Son	M	Cha	4.0	S				Guam	Guam	Guam		None
	10	10	Rosario, Gregorio P	Son	M	Cha	0.5	S				Guam	Guam	Guam		None
	11	11	Duenas, Jesus E	Head	M	Cha	29.0	M		N	N	Guam	Guam	Guam	N	Farmer
	11	11	Duenas, Maria S	Wife	F	Cha	32.0	M		Y	Y	Guam	Guam	Guam	N	None

76

33b

(CHAMORRO ROOTS GENEALOGY PROJECT ™ TRANSCRIPTION)
(COMPILED/TRANSCRIBED BY BERNARD T. PUNZALAN / HTTP://WWW.CHAMORROROOTS.COM)
FOURTEENTH CENSUS OF THE UNITED STATES: 1920-POPULATION
ISLAND OF GUAM

DISTRICT **1**

NAME OF PLACE **Dededo Barrio**

[Proper name and, also, name of class, as city, town, village, barrio, etc]

ENUMERATED BY ME ON THE 26th DAY OF February, 1920

Jose Kamminga ENUMERATOR

		NAME	RELATION	Sex	Color or race	Age at last birthday	Single, married, widowed or divorced	Attended school any time since Sept. 1, 1919	Whether able to read.	Whether able to write.	Place of birth of this person.	Place of birth of father of this person.	Place of birth of mother of this person.	Whether able to speak English.	OCCUPATION
		4	5	6	7	8	9	10	11	12	13	14	15	16	17
26	11	Duenas, Isabel B	Daughter	F	Cha	6.0	S	N			Guam	Guam	Guam		None
27	11	Duenas, Maria B	Daughter	F	Cha	5.0	S	N			Guam	Guam	Guam		None
28	11	Duenas, Manuel B	Son	M	Cha	4.0	S				Guam	Guam	Guam		None
29	11	Cepeda, Joaquin C	Cousin	M	Cha	29.0	M		N	N	Guam	Unknown	Guam	N	Farm laborer
30	12	Duenas, Maria B	Head	F	Cha	38.0	Wd		Y	N	Guam	Guam	Guam	N	None
31	12	Duenas, Juan B	Son	M	Cha	15.0	S	N	Y	Y	Guam	Guam	Guam	Y	Farm laborer home farm
32	12	Duenas, Rosa B	Daughter	F	Cha	13.0	S	N	Y	Y	Guam	Guam	Guam	Y	None
33	12	Duenas, Ana B	Daughter	F	Cha	9.0	S	Y	Y		Guam	Guam	Guam		None
34	12	Duenas, Rita B	Daughter	F	Cha	7.0	S	Y			Guam	Guam	Guam		None
35	12	Duenas, Jose B	Son	M	Cha	5.0	S	N			Guam	Guam	Guam		None
36	12	Duenas, Remedios B	Daughter	F	Cha	3.0	S				Guam	Guam	Guam		None
37	12	Duenas, Jesus B	Son	M	Cha	2.0	S				Guam	Guam	Guam		None
38	12	Duenas, Josefa B	Daughter	F	Cha	0.8	S				Guam	Guam	Guam		None
39	12	Benavente, Pedro M	Son	M	Cha	20.0	S	N	N	N	Guam	Unknown	Guam	?	Farmer
40	13	Rosario, Juan B	Head	M	Cha	26.0	M		N	N	Guam	Guam	Guam	?	Farmer
41	13	Rosario, Maria C	Wife	F	Cha	35.0	M				Guam	Unknown	Guam	?	None
42	13	Rosario, Maria C jr.	Daughter	F	Cha	4.0	S				Guam	Guam	Guam		None
43	13	Rosario, Antonio C	Son	M	Cha	3.0	S				Guam	Guam	Guam		None
44	13	Rosario, Vicente C	Son	M	Cha	1.0	S				Guam	Guam	Guam		None
45															
46															
47															
48															
49															
50															

Street, avenue, road, etc. — Dededo Barrio

(Lines 45 - 50 were left blank by the Enumerator.)

(CHAMORRO ROOTS GENEALOGY PROJECT ™ TRANSCRIPTION)
(COMPILED/TRANSCRIBED BY BERNARD T. PUNZALAN / HTTP://WWW.CHAMORROROOTS.COM)
FOURTEENTH CENSUS OF THE UNITED STATES: 1920—POPULATION
ISLAND OF GUAM

DISTRICT 1
NAME OF PLACE Dededo Barrio
[Proper name and, also, name of class, as city, town, village, barrio, etc]

ENUMERATED BY ME ON THE 27th DAY OF February, 1920

Jose Kamminga ENUMERATOR

Street	No. dwelling house (2)	No. of family (3)	NAME (4)	RELATION (5)	Sex (6)	Color or race (7)	Age (8)	Single, married, widowed or divorced (9)	Attended school since Sept. 1, 1919 (10)	Able to read (11)	Able to write (12)	Place of birth of this person (13)	Place of birth of father (14)	Place of birth of mother (15)	Able to speak English (16)	OCCUPATION (17)
	14	14	Santos, Vicente M	Head	M	Cha	33.0	M		Y	Y	Guam	Unknown	Guam	?	Farmer
	14	14	Santos, Maria S	Wife	F	Fil	28.0	M		Y	N	Guam	Guam	Guam	?	None
	14	14	Santos, Pedro S	Son	M	Cha	8.0	S	Y			Guam	Guam	Guam		None
	14	14	Santos, Juan S	Son	M	Cha	7.0	S	N			Guam	Guam	Guam		None
	14	14	Santos, Ana S	Daughter	F	Cha	6.0	S	N			Guam	Guam	Guam		None
	14	14	Santos, Regina S	Daughter	F	Cha	4.0	S				Guam	Guam	Guam		None
	14	14	Santos, Jose S	Son	M	Cha	1.0	S				Guam	Guam	Guam		None
Dededo Barrio	15	15	Benavente, Vicente B	Head	M	Cha	35.0	M		Y	Y	Guam	Guam	Guam	N	Farmer
	15	15	Benavente, Maria G	Wife	F	Cha	30.0	M		Y	Y	Guam	Guam	Guam	N	None
	15	15	Benavente, Jose G	Son	M	Cha	10.0	S	Y	Y	Y	Guam	Guam	Guam	Y	None
	15	15	Benavente, Ignacia G	Daughter	F	Cha	8.0	S	Y	Y	Y	Guam	Guam	Guam		None
	15	15	Benavente, Mariano G	Son	M	Cha	7.0	S	Y			Guam	Guam	Guam		None
	15	15	Benavente, Joaquin G	Son	M	Cha	6.0	S	N			Guam	Guam	Guam		None
	15	15	Benavente, Manuela G	Daughter	F	Cha	5.0	S	N			Guam	Guam	Guam		None
	15	15	Benavente, Isabel G	Daughter	F	Cha	4.0	S				Guam	Guam	Guam		None
	15	15	Benavente, Ines G	Daughter	F	Cha	0.7	S				Guam	Guam	Guam		None
	16	16	Santos, Francisco P	Head	M	Cha	54.0	M		Y	Y	Guam	Guam	Guam	N	Farmer
	16	16	Santos, Rosa V	Wife	F	Cha	50.0	M		Y	N	Guam	Unknown	Guam	N	None
	16	16	Santos, Ana V	Daughter	F	Cha	21.0	S	N	Y	Y	Guam	Guam	Guam	Y	None
	16	16	Santos, Jose V	Son	M	Cha	19.0	S	N	Y	Y	Guam	Guam	Guam	Y	Farm laborer home farm
	16	16	Santos, Jesus V	Son	M	Cha	17.0	S	Y	Y	Y	Guam	Guam	Guam	Y	None
	16	16	Santos, Francisco V	Son	M	Cha	14.0	S	Y	Y	Y	Guam	Guam	Guam	Y	None
	16	16	Santos, Maria V	Daughter	F	Cha	11.0	S	Y	Y	Y	Guam	Guam	Guam	N	None
	17	17	Santos, Juan C	Head	M	Cha	56.0	Wd		N	N	Guam	Guam	Guam	N	Farmer
	17	17	Santos, Juliana C	Daughter	F	Cha	27.0	S		N	N	Guam	Guam	Guam	N	None

(CHAMORRO ROOTS GENEALOGY PROJECT ™ TRANSCRIPTION)
(COMPILED/TRANSCRIBED BY BERNARD T. PUNZALAN / HTTP://WWW.CHAMORROROOTS.COM)

FOURTEENTH CENSUS OF THE UNITED STATES: 1920-POPULATION

ISLAND OF GUAM

DISTRICT 1
NAME OF PLACE Dededo Barrio
[Proper name and, also, name of class, as city, town, village, barrio, etc]

ENUMERATED BY ME ON THE 27th DAY OF February, 1920

Jose Kamminga ENUMERATOR

	Dwelling (2)	Family (3)	NAME (4)	RELATION (5)	Sex (6)	Race (7)	Age (8)	Marital (9)	School (10)	Read (11)	Write (12)	Birth person (13)	Birth father (14)	Birth mother (15)	English (16)	OCCUPATION (17)
26	17	17	Santos, Ramon C	Son	M	Cha	21.0	S	N	Y	Y	Guam	Guam	Guam	N	Storekeeper
27	17	17	Santos, Joaquin C	Son	M	Cha	16.0	S	N	Y	Y	Guam	Guam	Guam	Y	Farm laborer home farm
28	17	17	Santos, Mercedes C	Daughter	F	Cha	15.0	S	N	Y	Y	Guam	Guam	Guam	Y	None
29	18	18	Sahagon, Rebelato C	Head	M	Fil	50.0	M		Y	N	Guam	Philippine Islands	Guam	N	None
30	18	18	Sahagon, Maria Q	Wife	F	Cha	46.0	M		N	N	Guam	Guam	Guam	N	None
31	18	18	Sahagon, Magdalena Q	Daughter	F	Fil	25.0	S		Y	Y	Guam	Guam	Guam	N	Cook
32	18	18	Sahagon, Jose Q	Son	M	Fil	22.0	S		Y	Y	Guam	Guam	Guam	Y	Farmer
33	18	18	Sahagon, Francisco Q	Son	M	Fil	19.0	S	N	Y	Y	Guam	Guam	Guam	Y	Farm laborer home farm
34	18	18	Sahagon, Ignacia Q	Daughter	F	Fil	17.0	S	N	Y	Y	Guam	Guam	Guam	Y	None
35	18	18	Sahagon, Enrique Q	Son	M	Fil	14.0	S	N	N	N	Guam	Guam	Guam	N	Farm laborer home farm
36	18	18	Sahagon, Trinidad Q	Daughter	F	Fil	12.0	S	Y	Y	Y	Guam	Guam	Guam	N	None
37	19	19	San Agustin, Jose C	Head	M	Cha	27.0	M		Y	N	Guam	Guam	Guam	N	Farmer
38	19	19	San Agustin, Maria C	Wife	F	Cha	26.0	M		N	N	Guam	Guam	Guam	N	None
39	19	19	San Agustin, Manuel C	Son	M	Cha	7.0	S	N			Guam	Guam	Guam		None
40	19	19	San Agustin, Gonzalo C	Son	M	Cha	5.0	S	N			Guam	Guam	Guam		None
41	19	19	San Agustin, Francisco C	Son	M	Cha	4.0	S				Guam	Guam	Guam		None
42	19	19	San Agustin, Jose C	Son	M	Cha	1.0	S				Guam	Guam	Guam		None
43	20	20	Taijeron, Geronimo C	Head	M	Cha	27.0	M		N	N	Guam	Guam	Guam	N	Farmer
44	20	20	Taijeron, Maria S	Wife	F	Cha	29.0	M		Y	Y	Guam	Guam	Guam	N	None
45	20	20	Taijeron, Isidro S	Son	M	Cha	0.7	S				Guam	Guam	Guam		None
46	21	21	Cruz, Juan A	Head	M	Cha	29.0	M		Y	Y	Guam	Guam	Guam	Y	Farmer
47	21	21	Cruz, Lucia T	Wife	F	Cha	25.0	M		N	Y	Guam	Guam	Guam	N	None
48	21	21	Cruz, Juan T	Son	M	Cha	1.0	S				Guam	Guam	Guam		None
49																
50																

Street, avenue, road, etc. (Column 1): Dededo Barrio

(Lines 49 and 50 were left blank by the Enumerator.)

(CHAMORRO ROOTS GENEALOGY PROJECT ™ TRANSCRIPTION)
(COMPILED/TRANSCRIBED BY BERNARD T. PUNZALAN / HTTP://WWW.CHAMORROROOTS.COM)

FOURTEENTH CENSUS OF THE UNITED STATES: 1920—POPULATION

ISLAND OF GUAM

SHEET NO. 4A

DISTRICT **1**
NAME OF PLACE **Dededo Barrio**
[Proper name and, also, name of class, as city, town, village, barrio, etc]

ENUMERATED BY ME ON THE 28th DAY OF February, 1920

Jose Kamminga ENUMERATOR

	PLACE OF ABODE		NAME	RELATION	PERSONAL DESCRIPTION				EDUCATION			NATIVITY				OCCUPATION
Street, avenue, road, etc.	Number of dwelling house is order of visitation	Number of family in order of visitation	of each person whose place of abode on January 1, 1920, was in the family. Enter surname, firs, then given name and middle initial. If any. Include every person living on January 1, 1920. Omit children born since January 1, 1920.	Relationship of this Person to the head of the family.	Sex	Color or race	Age at last birthday	Single, married, widowed or divorced	Attended school any time since Sept. 1, 1919	Whether able to read.	Whether able to write.	Place of birth of this person.	Place of birth of father of this person.	Place of birth of mother of this person.	Whether able to speak English.	Trade, profession, or particular kind of work done, as salesman, laborer, clerk, cook, merchant, washerwoman, etc.
1	2	3	4	5	6	7	8	9	10	11	12	13	14	15	16	17
	22	22	Lujan, Maria S	Head	F	Cha	38.0	S		Y	Y	Guam	Guam	Guam	N	None
	22	22	Lujan, Manuel M	Son	M	Cha	20.0	S	N	Y	Y	Guam	Unknown	Guam	Y	Chauffeur
	22	22	Lujan, Isabel M	Daughter	F	Cha	16.0	S	N	Y	Y	Guam	Unknown	Guam	Y	None
	22	22	Lujan, Enrique M	Son	M	Cha	13.0	S	Y	Y	Y	Guam	Unknown	Guam	N	None
	22	22	Lujan, Paz M	Daughter	F	Cha	11.0	S	Y	Y	Y	Guam	Unknown	Guam	N	None
	22	22	Lujan, Joaquin M	Son	M	Cha	4.0	S				Guam	Unknown	Guam		None
	22	22	Lujan, Juan M	Son	M	Cha	2.0	S				Guam	Unknown	Guam		None
Dededo Barrio	23	23	Cruz, Jesus F	Head	M	Cha	64.0	M		Y	Y	Guam	Guam	Guam	N	Farmer
	23	23	Cruz, Rosario A	Wife	F	Cha	63.0	M		Y	N	Guam	Guam	Guam	N	None
	23	23	Cruz, Jose A	Son	M	Cha	35.0	S		Y	Y	Guam	Guam	Guam	Y	Farm laborer home farm
	23	23	Cruz, Enrique A	Son	M	Cha	24.0	S	N	Y	Y	Guam	Guam	Guam	Y	Farm laborer home farm
	23	23	Cruz, Maria Ana	Grand daughter	F	Cha	16.0	S	N	Y	Y	Guam	Unknown	Guam	Y	None
	23	23	Cruz, Asuncion Ana	Grand daughter	F	Cha	7.0	S				Guam	Unknown	Guam		None
	24	24	Santos, Emilio V	Head	M	Cha	29.0	M	N	Y	Y	Guam	Guam	Guam	N	Farmer
	24	24	Santos, Dolores S	Wife	F	Cha	20.0	M		Y	Y	Guam	Guam	Guam	Y	None
	24	24	Santos, Francisca S	Daughter	F	Cha	3.0	S				Guam	Guam	Guam		None
	24	24	Santos, Joaquin S	Son	M	Cha	2.0	S				Guam	Guam	Guam		None
	25	25	San Nicolas, Jose G	Head	M	Cha	35.0	M		Y	Y	Guam	Guam	Guam	N	Farmer
	25	25	San Nicolas, Francisca C	Wife	F	Cha	28.0	M		Y	N	Guam	Guam	Guam	N	None
	25	25	San Nicolas, Remedios Q	Niece	F	Cha	4.0	S				Guam	Guam	Guam		None
	26	26	Cruz, Mariano R	Head	M	Cha	60.0	M	N	Y	Y	Guam	Guam	Guam	N	Farmer
	26	26	Cruz, Josefa S	Wife	F	Cha	57.0	M	N	Y	Y	Guam	Guam	Guam	N	None
	26	26	Cruz, Pedro S	Son	M	Cha	19.0	S	N	Y	Y	Guam	Guam	Guam	Y	Laborer
	26	26	Cruz, Maria S	Daughter	F	Cha	17.0	S	N	Y	Y	Guam	Guam	Guam	Y	None
	27	27	Camacho, Ignacio C	Head	M	Cha	43.0	M		Y	Y	Guam	Unknown	Guam	N	Farmer

80

(CHAMORRO ROOTS GENEALOGY PROJECT ™ TRANSCRIPTION)
(COMPILED/TRANSCRIBED BY BERNARD T. PUNZALAN / HTTP://WWW.CHAMORROROOTS.COM)

FOURTEENTH CENSUS OF THE UNITED STATES: 1920—POPULATION

ISLAND OF GUAM

DISTRICT **1**

NAME OF PLACE **Dededo Barrio**

[Proper name and, also, name of class, as city, town, village, barrio, etc]

ENUMERATED BY ME ON THE 28th DAY OF February, 1920

Jose Kamminga ENUMERATOR

	1	2	3	4	5	6	7	8	9	10	11	12	13	14	15	16	17
	Street, avenue, road, etc.	Number of dwelling house	Number of family	NAME	RELATION	Sex	Color or race	Age at last birthday	Single, married, widowed or divorced	Attended school since Sept. 1, 1919	Whether able to read	Whether able to write	Place of birth of this person	Place of birth of father	Place of birth of mother	Whether able to speak English	OCCUPATION
26		27	27	Camacho, Encarnacion R	Wife	F	Cha	49.0	M		Y	N	Guam	Guam	Guam	N	None
27			27	Camacho, Vicente R	Son	M	Cha	20.0	S	N	Y	Y	Guam	Guam	Guam	Y	None
28			27	Camacho, Emilia R	Daughter	F	Cha	15.0	S	N	Y	Y	Guam	Guam	Guam	Y	None
29			27	Camacho, Ignacio A	Son	M	Cha	13.0	S	Y	Y	Y	Guam	Guam	Guam	Y	None
30			27	Santos, Lorenzo C	Uncle	M	Cha	67.0	S		N	N	Guam	Guam	Guam	N	None
31		28	28	Cepeda, Vicente S	Head	M	Cha	44.0	M		N	N	Guam	Guam	Guam	N	Farmer
32			28	Cepeda, Joaquina B	Wife	F	Cha	51.0	M		N	N	Guam	Guam	Guam	N	None
33		29	29	Babauta, Fortunato J	Head	M	Cha	24.0	M		Y	Y	Guam	Unknown	Guam	Y	Farmer
34			29	Babauta, Ana S	Wife	F	Fil	27.0	M		Y	N	Guam	Guam	Guam	N	None
35		30	30	Delgado, Juan F	Head	M	Cha	43.0	M		Y	Y	Guam	Guam	Guam	Y	Farmer
36			30	Delgado, Rita M	Wife	F	Cha	42.0	M		Y	N	Guam	Guam	Guam	N	None
37			30	Delgado, Jesus M	Son	M	Cha	18.0	S	N	Y	Y	Guam	Guam	Guam	Y	Farm laborer home farm
38			30	Delgado, Elvina M	Daughter	F	Cha	17.0	S	N	Y	Y	Guam	Guam	Guam	N	None
39			30	Delgado, Pedro M	Son	M	Cha	15.0	S	Y	Y	Y	Guam	Guam	Guam	Y	None
40			30	Delgado, Ana M	Daughter	F	Cha	13.0	S	N	N	N	Guam	Guam	Guam	N	None
41			30	Delgado, Jose Maria	Nephew	M	Cha	21.0	S	N	Y	Y	Guam	Guam	Guam	Y	Laborer
42			30	Delgado, Rosa Maria	Niece	F	Cha	9.0	S	N	Y	Y	Guam	Guam	Guam	N	None
43		31	31	Benavente, Jose R	Head	M	Cha	35.0	M		N	N	Guam	Guam	Guam	N	Farmer
44			31	Benavente, Candelaria C	Wife	F	Cha	33.0	M		N	N	Guam	Guam	Guam	N	None
45			31	Benavente, Francisco C	Son	M	Cha	8.0	S	Y			Guam	Guam	Guam		None
46			31	Benavente, Maria C	Daughter	F	Cha	7.0	S	N			Guam	Guam	Guam		None
47			31	Benavente, Ana C	Daughter	F	Cha	6.0	S	N			Guam	Guam	Guam		None
48			31	Benavente, Concepcion C	Daughter	F	Cha	1.0	S				Guam	Guam	Guam		None
49		32	32	Taitano, Juan C	Head	M	Chin	44.0	M		Y	N	Guam	China	Guam	N	Farmer

Dededo Barrio

(Line 50 was left blank by the Enumerator.)

81

(CHAMORRO ROOTS GENEALOGY PROJECT ™ TRANSCRIPTION)
(COMPILED/TRANSCRIBED BY BERNARD T. PUNZALAN / HTTP://WWW.CHAMORROROOTS.COM)
FOURTEENTH CENSUS OF THE UNITED STATES: 1920-POPULATION
ISLAND OF GUAM

DISTRICT **1**
NAME OF PLACE **Dededo Barrio**
[Proper name and, also, name of class, as city, town, village, barrio, etc]

ENUMERATED BY ME ON THE 1ˢᵗ DAY OF March, 1920

Jose Kamminga ENUMERATOR

	PLACE OF ABODE		NAME	RELATION	PERSONAL DESCRIPTION				EDUCATION			NATIVITY				OCCUPATION
Street, avenue, road, etc.	Number of dwelling house in order of visitation	Number of family in order of visitation	of each person whose place of abode on January 1, 1920, was in the family. Enter surname first, then given name and middle initial. If any. Include every person living on January 1, 1920. Omit children born since January 1, 1920.	Relationship of this Person to the head of the family.	Sex	Color or race	Age at last birthday	Single, married, widowed or divorced	Attended school any time since Sept. 1, 1919	Whether able to read.	Whether able to write.	Place of birth of this person.	Place of birth of father of this person.	Place of birth of mother of this person.	Whether able to speak English.	Trade, profession, or particular kind of work done, as salesman, laborer, clerk, cook, merchant, washerwoman, etc.
1	2	3	4	5	6	7	8	9	10	11	12	13	14	15	16	17
1	33	33	Leon Guerrero, Francisco R	Head	M	Cha	48.0	M		Y	Y	Guam	Guam	Guam	N	Farmer
2	33	33	Leon Guerrero, Ignacia S	Wife	F	Cha	42.0	M		N	N	Guam	Unknown	Guam	N	None
3	33	33	Leon Guerrero, Antonia S	Daughter	F	Cha	16.0	S	N	Y	Y	Guam	Guam	Guam	N	None
4	33	33	Leon Guerrero, Vicente S	Son	M	Cha	12.0	S	N	Y	Y	Guam	Guam	Guam	Y	Servant
5	33	33	Leon Guerrero, Jose S	Son	M	Cha	10.0	S	Y	Y	Y	Guam	Guam	Guam	N	None
6	33	33	Leon Guerrero, Maria S	Daughter	F	Cha	8.0	S	Y			Guam	Guam	Guam		None
7	33	33	Leon Guerrero, Ana S	Daughter	F	Cha	6.0	S	N			Guam	Guam	Guam		None
8	33	33	Leon Guerrero, Maria R	Sister	F	Cha	52.0	Wd				Guam	Guam	Guam	N	None
9	34	34	Benavente, Joaquin M	Head	M	Cha	30.0	M		N	N	Guam	Guam	Guam	N	Farmer
10	34	34	Benavente, Rita S	Wife	F	Cha	25.0	M		Y	Y	Guam	Guam	Guam	Y	None
11	34	34	Benavente, Joaquin S	Son	M	Cha	3.0	S				Guam	Guam	Guam		None
12	34	34	Benavente, Agripina S	Daughter	F	Cha	0.9	S				Guam	Guam	Guam		None
13	35	35	Francisco, Vicente T	Head	M	Fil	47.0	M		Y	Y	Guam	Philippine Islands	Guam	Y	Farmer
14	35	35	Francisco, Ignacia S	Wife	F	Fil	50.0	M		Y	N	Guam	Unknown	Guam	N	None
15	35	35	Francisco, Vicente S	Son	M	Fil	13.0	S	N	Y	Y	Guam	Guam	Guam	Y	None
16	35	35	Francisco, Rosario S	Daughter	F	Fil	11.0	S	N	Y	N	Guam	Guam	Guam	N	None
17	35	35	Francisco, Josefa S	Daughter	F	Fil	3.0	S				Guam	Guam	Guam		None
18	36	36	Cruz, Nicolas G	Head	M	Cha	36.0	M		Y	Y	Guam	Guam	Guam	N	Farmer
19	36	36	Cruz, Antonia B	Wife	F	Cha	34.0	M		Y	Y	Guam	Guam	Guam	N	None
20	36	36	Cruz, Jose B	Son	M	Cha	10.0	S	N	N	N	Guam	Guam	Guam	Y	None
21	36	36	Cruz, Francisca B	Daughter	F	Cha	7.0	S	N			Guam	Guam	Guam		None
22	36	36	Cruz, Pilar B	Daughter	F	Cha	4.0	S				Guam	Guam	Guam		None
23	36	36	Cruz, Juan B	Son	M	Cha	2.0	S				Guam	Guam	Guam		None
24	37	37	San Agustin, Vicente D	Head	M	Cha	28.0	M		N	N	Guam	Guam	Guam	N	Farmer
25	37	37	San Agustin, Josefa P	Wife	F	Cha	24.0	M		N	N	Guam	Unknown	Guam	N	None

Dededo Barrio

(CHAMORRO ROOTS GENEALOGY PROJECT ™ TRANSCRIPTION)
(COMPILED/TRANSCRIBED BY BERNARD T. PUNZALAN / HTTP://WWW.CHAMORROROOTS.COM)
FOURTEENTH CENSUS OF THE UNITED STATES: 1920–POPULATION
ISLAND OF GUAM

DISTRICT **1**
NAME OF PLACE **Dededo Barrio**

[Proper name and, also, name of class, as city, town, village, barrio, etc]

ENUMERATED BY ME ON THE 2nd DAY OF March, 1920

Jose Kamminga ENUMERATOR

	Number of dwelling house	Number of family	NAME	RELATION	Sex	Color or race	Age at last birthday	Single, married, widowed or divorced	Attended school since Sept. 1, 1919	Whether able to read	Whether able to write	Place of birth of this person	Place of birth of father	Place of birth of mother	Whether able to speak English	OCCUPATION
	2	3	4	5	6	7	8	9	10	11	12	13	14	15	16	17
26	38	38	Camacho, Vicente C	Head	M	Cha	29.0	M		Y	Y	Guam	Unknown	Guam	N	Farmer
27	38	38	Camacho, Juana Q	Wife	F	Cha	26.0	M		Y	Y	Guam	Guam	Guam	N	None
28	38	38	Camacho, Juan T	Son	M	Cha	0.0	S				Guam	Guam	Guam		None
29	39	39	Iriarte, Jose R	Head	M	Cha	54.0	Wd		Y	Y	Guam	Unknown	Guam	N	Farmer
30	39	39	Quidachay, Joaquina	Servant	F	Cha	44.0	M		Y	Y	Guam	Guam	Guam	Y	None
31	40	40	Chiguina, Marcelo C	Head	M	Cha	43.0	M		N	N	Guam	Guam	Guam	N	Farm laborer
32	40	40	Chiguina, Maria T	Wife	F	Cha	46.0	M		N	N	Guam	Guam	Guam	N	None
33	40	40	Chiguina, Carmen T	Daughter	F	Cha	10.0	S	N	N	N	Guam	Guam	Guam		None
34	40	40	Chiguina, Juan T	Son	M	Cha	8.0	S	Y			Guam	Guam	Guam		None
35	40	40	Chiguina, Jose T	Son	M	Cha	6.0	S	N			Guam	Guam	Guam		None
36	40	40	Chiguina, Manuela T	Daughter	F	Cha	3.0	S				Guam	Guam	Guam		None
37	41	41	Garrido, Vicente B	Head	M	Cha	39.0	M		Y	Y	Guam	Guam	Guam	N	Farmer
38	41	41	Garrido, Maria C	Wife	F	Cha	37.0	M		Y	Y	Guam	Unknown	Guam	N	None
39	41	41	Garrido, Maria C jr.	Daughter	F	Cha	15.0	S	N	Y	Y	Guam	Guam	Guam	N	None
40	41	41	Garrido, Jesus C	Son	M	Cha	13.0	S	Y	Y	Y	Guam	Guam	Guam	Y	None
41	41	41	Garrido, Asuncion C	Daughter	F	Cha	10.0	S	N	Y	Y	Guam	Guam	Guam	N	None
42	42	42	Benavente, Felix R	Head	M	Cha	40.0	M		N	N	Guam	Guam	Guam	N	Farmer
43	42	42	Benavente, Maria SA	Wife	F	Cha	35.0	M		Y	Y	Guam	Guam	Guam	N	None
44	42	42	Benavente, Pedro SA	Son	M	Cha	10.0	S	Y	Y	Y	Guam	Guam	Guam	Y	None
45	42	42	Benavente, Vicente SA	Son	M	Cha	6.0	S	N			Guam	Guam	Guam		None
46	42	42	Benavente, Eufrasia SA	Daughter	F	Cha	4.0	S				Guam	Guam	Guam		None
47	42	42	Benavente, Francisca SA	Daughter	F	Cha	2.0	S				Guam	Guam	Guam		None
48	42	42	Benavente, Jesus SA	Son	M	Cha	0.2	S				Guam	Guam	Guam		None
49																
50																

Dededo Barrio

(Lines 49 and 50 were left blank by the Enumerator.)

(CHAMORRO ROOTS GENEALOGY PROJECT ™ TRANSCRIPTION)
(COMPILED/TRANSCRIBED BY BERNARD T. PUNZALAN / HTTP://WWW.CHAMORROROOTS.COM)

FOURTEENTH CENSUS OF THE UNITED STATES: 1920—POPULATION
ISLAND OF GUAM

DISTRICT 1
NAME OF PLACE Dededo Barrio
[Proper name and, also, name of class, as city, town, village, barrio, etc]

ENUMERATED BY ME ON THE 3rd DAY OF March, 1920

Jose Kamminga ENUMERATOR

	Number of dwelling house in order of visitation	Number of family in order of visitation	NAME	RELATION	Sex	Color or race	Age at last birthday	Single, married, widowed or divorced	Attended school any time since Sept. 1, 1919	Whether able to read.	Whether able to write.	Place of birth of this person.	Place of birth of father of this person.	Place of birth of mother of this person.	Whether able to speak English.	OCCUPATION
1	2	3	4	5	6	7	8	9	10	11	12	13	14	15	16	17
	43	43	San Agustin, Juan C	Head	M	Cha	33.0	M		Y	Y	Guam	Guam	Guam	N	Farmer
	43	43	San Agustin, Concepcion G	Wife	F	Cha	32.0	M		Y	N	Guam	Guam	Guam	N	None
	43	43	San Agustin, Vicente G	Son	M	Cha	5.0	S	N			Guam	Guam	Guam		None
	43	43	San Agustin, Doroteo G	Son	M	Cha	4.0	S				Guam	Guam	Guam		None
	43	43	San Agustin, Francisco G	Son	M	Cha	2.0	S				Guam	Guam	Guam		None
	44	44	San Agustin, Francisco E	Head	M	Cha	58.0	M		N	N	Guam	Guam	Guam	N	Farmer
	44	44	San Agustin, Antonia C	Wife	F	Cha	54.0	M		N	N	Guam	Guam	Guam	N	None
	44	44	San Agustin, Maria C	Daughter	F	Cha	26.0	S		Y	Y	Guam	Guam	Guam		Cook
	44	44	San Agustin, Jose C	Son	M	Cha	24.0	S		Y	Y	Guam	Guam	Guam		Policeman
	44	44	San Agustin, Mariano C	Son	M	Cha	19.0	S	N	Y	Y	Guam	Guam	Guam		Farm laborer home farm
	44	44	San Agustin, Ana C	Daughter	F	Cha	16.0	S	N	Y	Y	Guam	Guam	Guam		None
	44	44	San Agustin, Ana C	Daughter	F	Cha	3.0	S				Guam	Unknown	Guam		None
	44	44	Cepeda, Rose Concepcion	Grand daughter	F	Cha	15.0	S	N	N	N	Guam	Unknown	Guam	N	?
	45	45	Blas, Antonio L	Head	M	Cha	45.0	M		Y	Y	Guam	Guam	Guam	N	Farmer
	45	45	Perez, Tomasa E	Servant	F	Cha	52.0	Wd		Y	Y	Guam	Guam	Guam	N	None
	46	46	Millenchamp, Henry T	Head	M	Cha	75.0	Wd		Y	Y	Bonin Island	England	Taihiti	Y	None
	46	46	Mendosa, Ana M	Daughter	F	W	48.0	Wd		Y	Y	Guam	Boni Island	Guam	N	Dress maker
	47	47	Garrido, Joaquin G	Head	M	Cha	53.0	M		Y	N	Guam	Unknown	Guam	N	Farmer
	47	47	Garrido, Dolores R	Wife	F	Cha	55.0	M		Y	N	Guam	Guam	Guam	N	None
	48	48	Gumataotao, Antonio L	Head	M	Cha	34.0	M		Y	Y	Guam	Guam	Guam	Y	Farmer
	48	48	Gumataotao, Rita L	Wife	F	Cha	33.0	M		Y	N	Guam	Guam	Guam	N	None
	48	48	Gumataotao, Juan L	Son	M	Cha	9.0	S	Y			Guam	Guam	Guam		None
	48	48	Gumataotao, Emilia L	Daughter	F	Cha	4.0	S				Guam	Guam	Guam		None
	48	48	Gumataotao, Ana L	Daughter	F	Cha	2.0	S				Guam	Guam	Guam		None
	48	48	Gumataotao, Rafael L	Son	M	Cha	0.0	S				Guam	Guam	Guam		None

Dededo Barrio

(CHAMORRO ROOTS GENEALOGY PROJECT ™ TRANSCRIPTION)
(COMPILED/TRANSCRIBED BY BERNARD T. PUNZALAN / HTTP://WWW.CHAMORROROOTS.COM)
FOURTEENTH CENSUS OF THE UNITED STATES: 1920-POPULATION
ISLAND OF GUAM

DISTRICT 1
NAME OF PLACE **Dededo Barrio**

[Proper name and, also, name of class, of class, name of city, town, village, barrio, etc]

ENUMERATED BY ME ON THE 3rd DAY OF March, 1920

Jose Kamminga ENUMERATOR

	PLACE OF ABODE			NAME	RELATION	PERSONAL DESCRIPTION					EDUCATION			NATIVITY				OCCUPATION
Street, avenue, road, etc.	Number of dwelling house in order of visitation	Number of family in order of visitation		of each person whose place of abode on January 1, 1920, was in the family. Enter surname, first, then given name and middle initial. If any. Include every person living on January 1, 1920. Omit children born since January 1, 1920.	Relationship of this Person to the head of the family.	Sex	Color or race	Age at last birthday	Single, married, widowed or divorced	Attended school any time since Sept. 1, 1919	Whether able to read.	Whether able to write.	Place of birth of this person.	Place of birth of father of this person.	Place of birth of mother of this person.	Whether able to speak English.	Trade, profession, or particular kind of work done, as salesman, laborer, clerk, cook, merchant, washerwoman, etc.
1	2	3	4		5	6	7	8	9	10	11	12	13	14	15	16	17
26	49	49	Lujan, Jose G		Head	M	Cha	34.0	M		Y	Y	Guam	Guam	Guam	Y	Farmer
27	49	49	Lujan, Concepcion C		Wife	F	Cha	27.0	M		Y	Y	Guam	Unknown	Guam	N	None
28	49	49	Lujan, Maria C		Daughter	F	Cha	7.0	S	N			Guam	Guam	Guam		None
29	49	49	Lujan, Catalina C		Daughter	F	Cha	6.0	S	N			Guam	Guam	Guam		None
30	49	49	Lujan, Concepcion C jr.		Daughter	F	Cha	5.0	S	N			Guam	Guam	Guam		None
31	49	49	Lujan, Florencia C		Daughter	F	Cha	4.0	S				Guam	Guam	Guam		None
32	49	49	Lujan, Isabel C		Daughter	F	Cha	2.0	S				Guam	Guam	Guam		None
33	50	50	Matanane, Juan M		Head	M	Cha	65.0	Wd		Y	Y	Guam	Unknown	Guam	Y	Fisherman
34	50	50	Matanane, Jose C		Son	M	Cha	21.0	S	N	Y	Y	Guam	Guam	Guam	Y	Fisherman
35	50	50	Matanane, Jesus C		Son	M	Cha	17.0	S	N	Y	Y	Guam	Guam	Guam	Y	Fisherman
36	50	50	Matanane, Juan C		Son	M	Cha	14.0	S	N	Y	N	Guam	Guam	Guam	Y	Fisherman
37	50	50	Matanane, Ana C		Daughter	F	Cha	13.0	S	N	N	N	Guam	Guam	Guam	Y	None
38	51	51	Cruz, Felipe A		Head	M	Cha	45.0	M		Y	Y	Guam	Guam	Guam	N	Farmer
39	51	51	Cruz, Vicenta LG		Wife	F	Cha	44.0	M		Y	N	Guam	Guam	Guam	N	None
40	51	51	Cruz, Jose LG		Son	M	Cha	18.0	S	N	Y	Y	Guam	Guam	Guam	Y	Farm laborer home farm
41	51	51	Cruz, Antonia LG		Daughter	F	Cha	16.0	S	N	Y	Y	Guam	Guam	Guam	Y	None
42	51	51	Cruz, Juliana LG		Daughter	F	Cha	15.0	S	N	Y	Y	Guam	Guam	Guam	Y	None
43	51	51	Cruz, Pedro LG		Son	M	Cha	13.0	S	N	Y	Y	Guam	Guam	Guam	Y	None
44	51	51	Cruz, Isabel LG		Daughter	F	Cha	11.0	S	Y	Y	Y	Guam	Guam	Guam	Y	None
45	51	51	Cruz, Rosa LG		Daughter	F	Cha	5.0	S	N			Guam	Guam	Guam		None
46	51	51	Cruz, Adela LG		Daughter	F	Cha	3.0	S				Guam	Guam	Guam		None
47	52	52	Borja, Jose T		Head	M	Cha	49.0	M		N	N	Guam	Guam	Guam	N	Farmer
48	52	52	Borja, Maria SN		Wife	F	Cha	46.0	M		N	N	Saipan	Guam	Saipan	N	None
49	52	52	Borja, Rosa SN		Daughter	F	Cha	19.0	S	N	Y	Y	Guam	Guam	Guam	N	None
50																	

Dededo Barrio

(Line 50 was left blank by the Enumerator.)

85

(CHAMORRO ROOTS GENEALOGY PROJECT ™ TRANSCRIPTION)
(COMPILED/TRANSCRIBED BY BERNARD T. PUNZALAN / HTTP://WWW.CHAMORROROOTS.COM)

FOURTEENTH CENSUS OF THE UNITED STATES: 1920–POPULATION

ISLAND OF GUAM

ENUMERATED BY ME ON THE 4th DAY OF March, 1920

Jose Kamminga ENUMERATOR

DISTRICT 1
NAME OF PLACE Dededo Barrio
[Proper name and, also, name of class, as city, town, village, barrio, etc]

	PLACE OF ABODE		NAME	RELATION	PERSONAL DESCRIPTION				EDUCATION			NATIVITY				OCCUPATION
Street, avenue, road, etc.	Number of dwelling house in order of visitation	Number of family in order of visitation	of each person whose place of abode on January 1, 1920, was in the family. Enter surname first, then given name and middle initial. If any. Include every person living on January 1, 1920. Omit children born since January 1, 1920.	Relationship of this Person to the head of the family.	Sex	Color or race	Age at last birthday	Single, married, widowed or divorced	Attended school any time since Sept. 1, 1919	Whether able to read.	Whether able to write.	Place of birth of this person.	Place of birth of father of this person.	Place of birth of mother of this person.	Whether able to speak English.	Trade, profession, or particular kind of work done, as salesman, laborer, clerk, cook, merchant, washerwoman, etc.
	2	3	4	5	6	7	8	9	10	11	12	13	14	15	16	17
Dededo Barrio	53	53	Perez, Manuel T	Head	M	Cha	34.0	M		N	N	Guam	Guam	Guam	N	Fisherman
	53	53	Perez, Carmen C	Wife	F	Cha	26.0	M		N	N	Guam	Guam	Guam	N	None
	54	54	San Agustin, Joaquin C	Head	M	Cha	56.0	S		N	N	Guam	Guam	Guam	N	Fisherman
	54	54	Liizama, Feliza	Boarder	F	Cha	43.0	S		N	N	Guam	Unknown	Guam	Y	None
	54	54	Liizama, Juan L	Boarder	M	Cha	15.0	S	N	Y	Y	Guam	Unknown	Guam	Y	None
	54	54	Liizama, Rosa L	Boarder	F	Cha	12.0	S	N	Y	Y	Guam	Unknown	Guam	Y	None
	54	54	Liizama, Jose L	Boarder	M	Cha	7.0	S	Y			Guam	Unknown	Guam	Y	None
	55	55	Benavente, Vicente M	Head	M	Cha	44.0	M		Y	Y	Guam	Guam	Guam	N	Laborer
	55	55	Benavente, Vicenta G	Wife	F	Cha	37.0	M		Y	Y	Guam	Guam	Guam	N	None
	55	55	Benavente, Jose G	Son	M	Cha	7.0	S				Guam	Guam	Guam		None
	55	55	Benavente, Maria G	Daughter	F	Cha	6.0	S	N			Guam	Guam	Guam		None
	55	55	Benavente, Jesus G	Son	M	Cha	4.0	S				Guam	Guam	Guam		None
	55	55	Benavente, Joaquin G	Son	M	Cha	4.0	S				Guam	Guam	Guam		None
	55	55	Benavente, Ana G	Daughter	F	Cha	2.0	S				Guam	Guam	Guam		None
	56	56	Cruz, Joaquin A	Head	M	Cha	42.0	M		Y	Y	Guam	Guam	Guam	N	Farmer
	57	57	Evaristo, Jose E	Head	M	Cha	24.0	M		Y	Y	Guam	Unknown	Guam	Y	Laborer
	57	57	Evaristo, Maria L	Wife	F	Cha	16.0	M	N	Y	Y	Guam	Guam	Guam	N	None
	57	57	Evaristo, Pedro L	Son	M	Cha	0.1	S		N	N	Guam	Guam	Guam		None
	57	58	Cruz, Francisco S	Head	M	Cha	46.0	M		N	N	Guam	Guam	Guam	N	Fisherman
	57	58	Cruz, Dolores E	Wife	F	Cha	46.0	M		N	N	Guam	Unknown	Guam	N	None
	57	58	Cruz, Jesus E	Son	M	Cha	12.0	S	N	Y	N	Guam	Guam	Guam	Y	None
	58	59	Cruz, Rita C	Head	F	Cha	58.0	M		Y	N	Guam	Guam	Guam	N	None
	58	59	Taijeron, Elena C	Daughter	F	Cha	24.0	S		Y	Y	Guam	Guam	Guam		None
	58	59	Taijeron, Isabel E	Grand-daughter	F	Cha	4.0	S				Guam	Unknown	Unknown		None
	58	59	Taijeron, Maria E	Grand-daughter	F	Cha	1.0	S				Guam	Unknown	Unknown		None

38b

(CHAMORRO ROOTS GENEALOGY PROJECT ™ TRANSCRIPTION)
(COMPILED/TRANSCRIBED BY BERNARD T. PUNZALAN / HTTP://WWW.CHAMORROROOTS.COM)

FOURTEENTH CENSUS OF THE UNITED STATES: 1920-POPULATION

ISLAND OF GUAM

DISTRICT 1
NAME OF PLACE Dededo Barrio
[Proper name and, also, name of class, as city, town, village, barrio, etc]

ENUMERATED BY ME ON THE 5th DAY OF March, 1920

Jose Kamminga ENUMERATOR

	PLACE OF ABODE			NAME	RELATION	PERSONAL DESCRIPTION					EDUCATION			NATIVITY				OCCUPATION
Street, avenue, road, etc.	Number of dwelling house in order of visitation	Number of family in order of visitation	Name	Relationship of this Person to the head of the family.	Sex	Color or race	Age at last birthday	Single, married, widowed or divorced	Attended any school since Sept. 1, 1919	Whether able to read.	Whether able to write.	Place of birth of this person.	Place of birth of father of this person.	Place of birth of mother of this person.	Whether able to speak English.	Trade, profession, or particular kind of work done, as salesman, laborer, clerk, cook, merchant, washerwoman, etc.
1	2	3	4	5	6	7	8	9	10	11	12	13	14	15	16	17
	59	60	Flores, Juan G	Head	M	Cha	24.0	M		Y	Y	Guam	Guam	Guam	Y	Farmer
	59	60	Flores, Nicolasa C	Wife	F	Cha	21.0	M	N	Y	Y	Guam	Guam	Guam	N	None
	59	60	Flores, Rufina C	Daughter	F	Cha	3.0	S				Guam	Guam	Guam		None
	59	60	Flores, Juan C	Son	M	Cha	2.0	S				Guam	Guam	Guam		None
	59	60	Flores, Ana C	Daughter	F	Cha	0.4	S				Guam	Guam	Guam		None
	60	61	Flores, Ignacio G	Head	M	Cha	25.0	M		Y	Y	Guam	Guam	Guam	Y	Farmer
	60	61	Flores, Susana G	Wife	F	Cha	22.0	M		Y	Y	Guam	Guam	Guam	N	None
	60	61	Flores, Joaquin G	Son	M	Cha	1.0	S				Guam	Guam	Guam		None
Dededo Barrio	61	62	Santos, Antonio C	Head	M	Cha	38.0	S		Y	Y	Guam	Guam	Guam	N	Laborer
	62	63	Kukuri, Manuel L	Head	M	Jp	44.0	Wd		Y	Y	Japan	Japan	Japan	N	Farm laborer
	63	64	Benavente, Joaquin A	Head	M	Cha	29.0	M		N	N	Guam	Unknown	Guam	Y	Laborer
	63	64	Benavente, Ana L	Wife	F	Cha	22.0	M		Y	Y	Guam	Guam	Guam	Y	None
	63	64	Benavente, Nieves L	Daughter	F	Cha	0.3	S				Guam	Guam	Guam		None
	64	65	Babauta, Candelario C	Head	M	Cha	27.0	M		Y	N	Guam	Guam	Guam	N	Farm laborer
	64	65	Babauta, Luisa C	Wife	F	Cha	27.0	M		Y	N	Guam	Guam	Guam	N	None
	64	65	Babauta, Angelina C	Daughter	F	Cha	0.8	S				Guam	Guam	Guam		None
	65	66	Lujan, Jose S	Head	M	Cha	47.0	M		Y	N	Guam	Guam	Guam	Y	Deputy Commissioner
	65	66	Lujan, Nieves SA	Wife	F	Cha	57.0	M		N	N	Guam	Guam	Guam	N	None
	66	67	Tudela, Jose R	Head	M	Cha	51.0	Wd		Y	Y	Guam	Guam	Guam	N	Farm laborer
	66	67	Tudela, Ignacia R	Daughter	F	Cha	21.0	S	N	Y	Y	Guam	Guam	Guam	N	Cook
	66	67	Tudela, Jose R	Son	M	Cha	17.0	S	N	N	N	Guam	Guam	Guam	N	Farm laborer
	66	67	Tudela, Manuel R	Son	M	Cha	15.0	S	N	N	N	Guam	Guam	Guam	N	Farm laborer
	66	67	Tudela, Francisca R	Daughter	F	Cha	12.0	S	N	Y	Y	Guam	Guam	Guam	N	Servant

(Lines 49 and 50 were left blank by the Enumerator.)

(CHAMORRO ROOTS GENEALOGY PROJECT ™ TRANSCRIPTION)
(COMPILED/TRANSCRIBED BY BERNARD T. PUNZALAN / HTTP://WWW.CHAMORROROOTS.COM)
FOURTEENTH CENSUS OF THE UNITED STATES: 1920-POPULATION
ISLAND OF GUAM

DISTRICT 1
NAME OF PLACE Dededo Barrio
[Proper name and, also, name of class, as city, town, village, barrio, etc]

ENUMERATED BY ME ON THE 6th DAY OF March, 1920

Jose Kamminga ENUMERATOR

Street, avenue, road, etc.	Number of dwelling house in order of visitation	Number of family in order of visitation	NAME of each person whose place of abode on January 1, 1920, was in the family.	RELATION Relationship of this Person to the head of the family.	Sex	Color or race	Age at last birthday	Single, married, widowed or divorced	Attended school any time since Sept. 1, 1919	Whether able to read.	Whether able to write.	Place of birth of this person.	Place of birth of father of this person.	Place of birth of mother of this person.	Whether able to speak English.	OCCUPATION Trade, profession, or particular kind of work done
1	2	3	4	5	6	7	8	9	10	11	12	13	14	15	16	17
	67	68	Rosario, Bruno M	Head	M	Cha	60.0	M		N	N	Guam	Guam	Guam	N	Farmer
	68	69	Palomo, Juan P	Head	M	Cha	38.0	Wd		Y	Y	Guam	Unknown	Guam	N	Farmer
	68	69	Palomo, Francisco D	Son	M	Cha	16.0	S	N	Y	Y	Guam	Guam	Guam	Y	Farm laborer home farm
	68	69	Palomo, Vicente D	Son	M	Cha	12.0	S	Y	Y	Y	Guam	Guam	Guam	Y	None
	68	69	Palomo, Rita D	Daughter	F	Cha	10.0	S	Y	Y	Y	Guam	Guam	Guam	N	None
	68	69	Palomo, Juan D	Son	M	Cha	6.0	S	N		N	Guam	Guam	Guam		None
	69	70	Palomo, Vicente A	Head	M	Cha	47.0	M		Y	Y	Guam	Unknown	Guam	N	Farmer
	69	70	Palomo, Ana R	Wife	F	W	47.0	M		Y	N	Guam	England	Guam	N	None
Dededo Barrio	69	70	Palomo, Maria R	Daughter	F	Mix	18.0	S	N	Y	Y	Guam	Guam	Guam	Y	None
	69	70	Palomo, Jesus R	Son	M	Mix	12.0	S	Y	Y	Y	Guam	Guam	Guam	N	None
	69	70	Palomo, Vicente R	Son	M	Mix	5.0	S	N		N	Guam	Guam	Guam		None
	70	71	Kamminga, Jose	Head	M	W	29.0	M		Y	Y	Guam	Holland	Guam	Y	Teacher
	70	71	Kamminga, Maria F	Wife	F	Cha	28.0	M		Y	Y	Guam	Guam	Guam	N	None
	70	71	Kamminga, Magdalena F	Daughter	F	Mix	8.0	S	Y			Guam	Guam	Guam		None
	70	71	Kamminga, Gale F	Son	M	Mix	7.0	S	N			Guam	Guam	Guam		None
	70	71	Kamminga, Joaquina F	Daughter	F	Mix	5.0	S	N			Guam	Guam	Guam		None
	70	71	Kamminga, Maria F jr.	Daughter	F	Mix	4.0	S				Guam	Guam	Guam		None
	70	71	Kamminga, Jose F	Son	M	Mix	2.0	S				Guam	Guam	Guam		None
	70	71	Kamminga, Lorenzo F	Son	M	Mix	0.2	S				Guam	Guam	Guam		None
	70	71	Kamminga, Rita	Daughter	F	Mix	0.2	S				Guam	Guam	Guam		None
	71	72	Castro, Juan R	Head	M	Cha	45.0	S		Y	Y	Guam	Guam	Guam	N	Farmer
	72	73	Camacho, Vicente L	Head	M	Cha	50.0	S		Y	N	Guam	Guam	Guam	N	None
	73	74	Fergurgur, Remedios Q	Head	F	Cha	33.0	S		N	N	Guam	Guam	Guam	Y	Cook
	74	75	Perez, Juan	Head	M	Cha	45.0	M		Y	Y	Guam	Unknown	Guam	N	Farm laborer
	75	76	Taitano, John	Head	M	Cha	34.0	M		Y	Y	Guam	Guam	Guam	Y	Foreman

(CHAMORRO ROOTS GENEALOGY PROJECT ™ TRANSCRIPTION)
(COMPILED/TRANSCRIBED BY BERNARD T. PUNZALAN / HTTP://WWW.CHAMORROROOTS.COM)
FOURTEENTH CENSUS OF THE UNITED STATES: 1920—POPULATION
ISLAND OF GUAM

DISTRICT 1
NAME OF PLACE Dededo Barrio

ENUMERATED BY ME ON THE 6th DAY OF March, 1920

Jose Kamminga ENUMERATOR

[Proper name and, also, name of class, as city, town, village, barrio, etc]

Street, avenue, road, etc.	Number of dwelling house in order of visitation	Number of family in order of visitation	NAME	RELATION	Sex	Color or race	Age at last birthday	Single, married, widowed or divorced	Attended school any time since Sept. 1, 1919	Whether able to read.	Whether able to write.	Place of birth of this person.	Place of birth of father of this person.	Place of birth of mother of this person.	Whether able to speak English.	OCCUPATION
	2	3	4	5	6	7	8	9	10	11	12	13	14	15	16	17
Dededo Barrio	75	76	Taitano, Rosario F	Wife	F	Cha	30.0	M		Y	Y	Guam	Guam	Guam	Y	None
	75	76	Taitano, Rosario F	Daughter	F	Cha	13.0	S	Y	Y	Y	Guam	Guam	Guam	Y	None
	75	76	Taitano, Isabel F	Daughter	F	Cha	12.0	S	Y	Y	Y	Guam	Guam	Guam	Y	None
	75	76	Taitano, Carlos F	Son	M	Cha	10.0	S	Y	Y	Y	Guam	Guam	Guam	Y	None
	75	76	Taitano, Esther F	Daughter	F	Cha	8.0	S	N			Guam	Guam	Guam		None
	75	76	Taitano, Catalina F	Daughter	F	Cha	6.0	S	N			Guam	Guam	Guam		None
	75	76	Taitano, John F	Son	M	Cha	3.0	S				Guam	Guam	Guam		
	75	76	Pablo, Jose P	Boarder	M	Cha	57.0	Wd				Guam	Unknown	Guam		

Here ends the enumeration of Dededo Barrio

89

(CHAMORRO ROOTS GENEALOGY PROJECT ™ TRANSCRIPTION)
(COMPILED/TRANSCRIBED BY BERNARD T. PUNZALAN / HTTP://WWW.CHAMORROROOTS.COM)
FOURTEENTH CENSUS OF THE UNITED STATES: 1920-POPULATION
ISLAND OF GUAM

ENUMERATED BY ME ON THE 8th DAY OF March, 1920

Jose Kamminga ENUMERATOR

DISTRICT 1
NAME OF PLACE Barrigada Barrio

#	Dwelling	Family	NAME	RELATION	Sex	Color	Age	Marital	School	Read	Write	Birthplace	Father	Mother	English	OCCUPATION
1	1	1	Mesa, Juan D	Head	M	Cha	22.0	M		Y	Y	Rota	Rota	Guam	N	Farmer
2	1	1	Mesa, Rosa	Wife	F	Cha	22.0	M		Y	Y	Guam	Guam	Guam	N	None
3	1	1	Chiguina, Maria M	Sister in law	F	Cha	5.0	S	N			Guam	Guam	Guam		None
4	2	2	Rosario, Joaquin C	Head	M	Cha	28.0	M		Y	Y	Guam	Guam	Guam	N	Farmer
5	2	2	Rosario, Magdalena A	Wife	F	Cha	56.0	M		Y	Y	Guam	Guam	Guam	N	None
6	2	2	Rosario, Jose A	Son	M	Cha	1.0	S				Guam	Guam	Guam		None
7	2	2	Rosario, Vicente A	Son	M	Cha	0.2	S				Guam	Guam	Guam		None
8	3	3	Manibusan, Jose P	Head	M	Cha	22.0	M	N	N	N	Guam	Guam	Guam	Y	Farmer
9	3	3	Manibusan, Ignacia A	Wife	F	Cha	22.0	M		Y	Y	Guam	Guam	Guam	Y	None
10	3	3	Manibusan, Filomena A	Daughter	F	Cha	1.0	S				Guam	Guam	Guam		None
11	3	3	Manibusan, Maria	Daughter	F	Cha	0.1	S				Guam	Guam	Guam		None
12	4	4	Pangelinan, Vicente C	Head	M	Cha	35.0	M		N	N	Guam	Guam	Guam	Y	Farm laborer
13	5	5	Pablo, Jose C	Head	M	Cha	24.0	M		Y	Y	Guam	Guam	Guam	Y	Farmer
14	5	5	Pablo, Maria P	Wife	F	Cha	20.0	M	N	Y	Y	Guam	Guam	Guam	N	None
15	5	5	Pablo, Juan P	Son	M	Cha	1.0	S				Guam	Guam	Guam		None
16	6	6	Pereda, Juan S	Head	M	Cha	38.0	M		Y	Y	Guam	Guam	Guam	N	Farmer
17	6	6	Pereda, Josefa B	Wife	F	Cha	40.0	M		Y	N	Guam	Guam	Guam	N	None
18	6	6	Pereda, Susana B	Daughter	F	Cha	17.0	S	N	Y	Y	Guam	Guam	Guam	N	None
19	6	6	Pereda, Josefa B jr.	Daughter	F	Cha	10.0	S	N	Y	Y	Guam	Guam	Guam	N	None
20	6	6	Pereda, Jose B	Son	M	Cha	6.0	S	N			Guam	Guam	Guam	N	None
21	7	7	Perez, Jose P	Head	M	Cha	39.0	M		N	N	Guam	Unknown	Guam	N	Farmer
22	7	7	Perez, Ana C	Wife	F	Cha	41.0	M		N	N	Guam	Guam	Guam	N	None
23	7	7	Perez, Pedro C	Son	M	Cha	14.0	S	N	Y	Y	Guam	Guam	Guam	Y	None
24	7	7	Perez, Jose C	Son	M	Cha	13.0	S	N	Y	Y	Guam	Guam	Guam		None
25	7	7	Perez, Magdalena C	Daughter	F	Cha	9.0	S	N			Guam	Guam	Guam		None

(CHAMORRO ROOTS GENEALOGY PROJECT ™ TRANSCRIPTION)
(COMPILED/TRANSCRIBED BY BERNARD T. PUNZALAN / HTTP://WWW.CHAMORROROOTS.COM)
FOURTEENTH CENSUS OF THE UNITED STATES: 1920–POPULATION
ISLAND OF GUAM

DISTRICT 1
NAME OF PLACE Barrigada Barrio
[Proper name and, also, name of class, as city, town, village, barrio, etc]

ENUMERATED BY ME ON THE 8th DAY OF March, 1920

Jose Kamminga ENUMERATOR

	PLACE OF ABODE			NAME	RELATION	PERSONAL DESCRIPTION				EDUCATION			NATIVITY				OCCUPATION
Street, avenue, road, etc.	Number of dwelling house in order of visitation	Number of family in order of visitation		Name of each person whose place of abode on January 1, 1920, was in the family.	Relationship of this Person to the head of the family.	Sex	Color or race	Age at last birthday	Single, married, widowed or divorced	Attended school any time since Sept. 1, 1919	Whether able to read.	Whether able to write.	Place of birth of this person.	Place of birth of father of this person.	Place of birth of mother of this person.	Whether able to speak English.	Trade, profession, or particular kind of work done, as salesman, laborer, clerk, cook, merchant, washerwoman, etc.
1	2	3		4	5	6	7	8	9	10	11	12	13	14	15	16	17
Barrigada Barrio	7	7	26	Perez, Asuncion C	Daughter	F	Cha	8.0	S	N			Guam	Guam	Guam		None
	7	7	27	Perez, Ana C jr.	Daughter	F	Cha	6.0	S	N			Guam	Guam	Guam		None
	7	7	28	Perez, Antonio C	Son	M	Cha	5.0	S	N			Guam	Guam	Guam		None
	7	7	29	Perez, Rosario C	Daughter	F	Cha	3.0	S				Guam	Guam	Guam		None
	7	7	30	Perez, Felipe C	Son	M	Cha	0.6	S				Guam	Guam	Guam		None
	8	8	31	Blas, Jose T	Head	M	Cha	28.0	Wd		Y	Y	Guam	Guam	Guam	N	Farmer
	8	8	32	Blas, Maria F	Daughter	F	Cha	19.0	S	N	Y	Y	Guam	Guam	Guam	Y	None
	8	8	33	Blas, Guido F	Son	M	Cha	16.0	S	N	N	N	Guam	Guam	Guam	N	None
	8	8	34	Blas, Jose F	Son	M	Cha	13.0	S	Y	Y	Y	Guam	Guam	Guam	Y	Farm laborer
	9	9	35	Torres, Jose C	Head	M	Cha	46.0	M	Y	Y	Y	Guam	Guam	Guam	N	Farm laborer
	9	9	36	Torres, Trinidad P	Wife	F	Cha	44.0	M	N	Y	Y	Guam	Guam	Guam	N	None
	10	10	37	Rabon, Joaquin C	Head	M	Fil	21.0	M		Y	Y	Guam	Philippine Islands	Guam	Y	Farmer
	10	10	38	Rabon, Luisa LG	Wife	F	Cha	35.0	M		Y	Y	Guam	Guam	Guam	Y	None
	10	10	39	Rabon, Nicolasa C	Mother	F	Cha	75.0	M		N	N	Guam	Guam	Guam	N	None
	11	11	40	La Rosa, Joaquin R	Head	M	Cha	44.0	M	N	N	N	Guam	Guam	Guam	N	Farm laborer
	11	11	41	La Rosa, Teodora T	Wife	F	Cha	42.0	M		N	N	Guam	Guam	Guam	N	Laundress
	12	12	42	Rojas, Francisco A	Head	M	Cha	24.0	M	N	Y	Y	Guam	Guam	Guam	Y	Farmer
	12	12	43	Rojas, Antonia LG	Wife	F	Cha	20.0	M		Y	Y	Guam	Guam	Guam	Y	None
	13	13	44	Blas, Antonio B	Head	M	Cha	24.0	M		Y	Y	Guam	Guam	Guam	Y	Farmer
	13	13	45	Blas, Maria F	Wife	F	Cha	20.0	M	N	Y	Y	Guam	Guam	Guam	N	None
	13	13	46	Blas, Julia F	Daughter	F	Cha	2.0	S				Guam	Guam	Guam		None
	13	13	47	Blas, Francisco F	Son	M	Cha	1.0	S				Guam	Guam	Guam		None
	14	14	48	Blas, Leonardo A	Head	M	Cha	24.0	M		Y	Y	Yap	Guam	Guam	N	Farmer
	14	14	49	Blas, Juana C	Wife	F	Cha	31.0	M		Y	Y	Guam	Guam	Guam	N	None
	14	14	50	Blas, Teresa C	Daughter	F	Cha	1.0	S				Guam	Yap	Guam		None

(CHAMORRO ROOTS GENEALOGY PROJECT ™ TRANSCRIPTION)
(COMPILED/TRANSCRIBED BY BERNARD T. PUNZALAN / HTTP://WWW.CHAMORROROOTS.COM)

FOURTEENTH CENSUS OF THE UNITED STATES: 1920—POPULATION
ISLAND OF GUAM

DISTRICT **1**
NAME OF PLACE **Barrigada Barrio**
[Proper name and, also, name of class, as city, town, village, barrio, etc]

ENUMERATED BY ME ON THE 9th DAY OF March, 1920

Jose Kamminga ENUMERATOR

	PLACE OF ABODE		NAME	RELATION	PERSONAL DESCRIPTION				EDUCATION			NATIVITY				OCCUPATION
Street, avenue, road, etc.	Number of dwelling house is in order of visitation	Number of family in order of visitation	of each person whose place of abode on January 1, 1920, was in the family.	Relationship of this person to the head of the family.	Sex	Color or race	Age at last birthday	Single, married, widowed or divorced	Attended school any time since Sept. 1, 1919	Whether able to read.	Whether able to write.	Place of birth of this person.	Place of birth of father of this person.	Place of birth of mother of this person.	Whether able to speak English.	Trade, profession, or particular kind of work done, as salesman, laborer, clerk, cook, merchant, washerwoman, etc.
1	2	3	4	5	6	7	8	9	10	11	12	13	14	15	16	17
	15	15	Blas, Juan S	Head	M	Cha	27.0	M		Y	Y	Guam	Guam	Guam	Y	Farmer
	15	15	Blas, Antonia F	Wife	F	Cha	25.0	M		Y	Y	Guam	Guam	Guam	N	None
	15	15	Blas, Jose F	Son	M	Cha	0.9	S				Guam	Guam	Guam		None
	16	16	Jesus, Luis F	Head	M	Cha	32.0	M		Y	N	Guam	Guam	Guam	Y	Farmer
	16	16	Jesus, Angela C	Wife	F	Cha	44.0	M		N	N	Guam	Guam	Guam	N	None
Barrigada Barrio	16	16	Jesus, Concepcion C	Daughter	F	Cha	18.0	S	N	Y	Y	Guam	Guam	Guam	Y	Servant
	16	16	Jesus, Ana C	Daughter	F	Cha	16.0	S	N	Y	Y	Guam	Guam	Guam	Y	Servant
	17	17	Manibusan, Jose T	Head	M	Cha	36.0	M		N	N	Guam	Guam	Guam	N	Farmer
	17	17	Manibusan, Dolores B	Wife	F	Cha	46.0	M		N	N	Guam	Guam	Guam	N	None
	18	18	Fausto, Agualia Y	Head	M	Fil	44.0	M		N	N	Guam	Philippine Islands	Guam	N	Farm laborer
	18	18	Fausto, Antonia M	Wife	F	Cha	42.0	M		N	N	Guam	Guam	Guam	N	None
	18	18	Martinez, Manuela R	Mother-in-law	F	Cha	85.0	Wd		N	N	Guam	Guam	Guam	N	None
	18	18	Fausto, Francisco SN	Boarder	M	Cha	6.0	S	N			Guam	Unknown	Guam		None
	18	18	Martinez, Manuel M	Nephew	M	Cha	16.0	S	N	Y	Y	Guam	Unknown	Guam	Y	Farm laborer
	19	19	San Nicolas, Antonio SN	Head	M	Cha	40.0	M		Y	N	Guam	Guam	Guam	Y	Farmer
	19	19	San Nicolas, Nicolasa C	Wife	F	Cha	30.0	M		Y	N	Guam	Guam	Guam	N	None
	19	19	San Nicolas, Ana C	Daughter	F	Cha	14.0	S	N	N	N	Guam	Guam	Guam	N	None
	19	19	San Nicolas, Susana C	Daughter	F	Cha	10.0	S	N	Y	Y	Guam	Guam	Guam	N	None
	19	19	San Nicolas, Rosa C	Daughter	F	Cha	5.0	S	N			Guam	Guam	Guam		None
	19	19	San Nicolas, Maria C	Daughter	F	Cha	4.0	S				Guam	Guam	Guam		None
	19	19	San Nicolas, Beatris C	Daughter	F	Cha	0.1	S				Guam	Guam	Guam		
	20	20	Borja, Manuel S	Head	M	Cha	37.0	M		Y	Y	Guam	Guam	Guam	N	Shoemaker
	20	20	Borja, Dolores F	Wife	F	Cha	34.0	M		Y	Y	Guam	Guam	Guam	N	None
	20	20	Borja, Jose F	Son	M	Cha	0.3	S				Guam	Guam	Guam		None

(Line 25 was left blank by the Enumerator.)

(CHAMORRO ROOTS GENEALOGY PROJECT ™ TRANSCRIPTION)
(COMPILED/TRANSCRIBED BY BERNARD T. PUNZALAN / HTTP://WWW.CHAMORROROOTS.COM)

FOURTEENTH CENSUS OF THE UNITED STATES: 1920-POPULATION

ISLAND OF GUAM

ENUMERATED BY ME ON THE 10th DAY OF March, 1920

Jose Kamminga ENUMERATOR

DISTRICT 1
NAME OF PLACE Barrigada Barrio

[Proper name and, also, name of class, as city, town, village, barrio, etc]

Line	Street	Dwelling No.	Family No.	NAME	RELATION	Sex	Color or race	Age	Single, married, widowed or divorced	Attended school since Sept. 1, 1919	Read	Write	Birthplace person	Birthplace father	Birthplace mother	English	OCCUPATION
		2	3	4	5	6	7	8	9	10	11	12	13	14	15	16	17
26		21	21	Meno, Vicente M	Head	M	Cha	38.0	M		N	N	Guam	Guam	Guam	N	Farmer
27		21	21	Meno, Vicenta P	Wife	F	Cha	39.0	M		Y	Y	Guam	Guam	Guam	N	None
28		21	21	Meno, Jose P	Son	M	Cha	7.0	S	N			Guam	Guam	Guam		None
29		21	21	Meno, Jesus P	Son	M	Cha	4.0	S				Guam	Guam	Guam		None
30		21	21	Meno, Felix P	Son	M	Cha	1.0	S								None
31		22	22	Quichocho, Vicente Q	Head	M	Cha	30.0	M		Y	Y	Guam	Unknown	Guam	N	Farmer
32		22	22	Quichocho, Joaquina T	Wife	F	Cha	25.0	M		Y	N	Guam	Guam	Guam	N	None
33		22	22	Quichocho, Rosario T	Daughter	F	Cha	7.0	S	N			Guam	Guam	Guam		None
34		22	22	Quichocho, Maria T	Daughter	F	Cha	6.0	S	N			Guam	Guam	Guam		None
35		22	22	Quichocho, Jesus T	Son	M	Cha	3.0	S				Guam	Guam	Guam		None
36	Barrigada Barrio	22	22	Quichocho, Rosa T	Daughter	F	Cha	1.0	S				Guam	Guam	Guam		None
37		23	23	Meno, Juan M	Head	M	Cha	32.0	M		N	N	Guam	Unknown	Guam	N	Farmer
38		23	23	Meno, Maria P	Wife	F	Cha	29.0	M		N	N	Guam	Guam	Guam	N	None
39		23	23	Meno, Francisco P	Son	M	Cha	13.0	S	N	Y	Y	Guam	Guam	Guam	Y	None
40		23	23	Meno, Dolores P	Daughter	F	Cha	11.0	S	N	Y	Y	Guam	Guam	Guam	Y	None
41		23	23	Meno, Jesus P	Son	M	Cha	8.0	S	N			Guam	Guam	Guam		None
42		23	23	Meno, Justa P	Daughter	F	Cha	5.0	S	N			Guam	Guam	Guam		None
43		23	23	Meno, Asuncion P	Daughter	F	Cha	2.0	S				Guam	Guam	Guam		None
44		23	23	Meno, Antonio P	Son	M	Cha	0.5	S				Guam	Guam	Guam		None
45		24	24	Quichocho, Nicolas LG	Head	M	Cha	46.0	M		Y	Y	Guam	Guam	Guam	N	Farmer
46		24	24	Quichocho, Rosa Q	Wife	F	Cha	57.0	M		Y	N	Guam	Guam	Guam	N	None
47		24	24	Quichocho, Maria Q	Daughter	F	Cha	21.0	S	N	Y	Y	Guam	Guam	Guam	Y	None
48		24	24	Quichocho, Jesus Q	Son	M	Cha	18.0	S	N	Y	Y	Guam	Guam	Guam	Y	Farm laborer home farm
49		24	24	Quichocho, Jose Q	Son	M	Cha	15.0	S	N	Y	Y	Guam	Guam	Guam	Y	Farm laborer home farm
50																	

(Line 50 was intentionally left blank by the Enumerator.)

(CHAMORRO ROOTS GENEALOGY PROJECT ™ TRANSCRIPTION)
(COMPILED/TRANSCRIBED BY BERNARD T. PUNZALAN / HTTP://WWW.CHAMORROROOTS.COM)

FOURTEENTH CENSUS OF THE UNITED STATES: 1920—POPULATION

ISLAND OF GUAM

DISTRICT **1**
NAME OF PLACE **Barrigada Barrio**
[Proper name and, also, name of class, as city, town, village, barrio, etc]

ENUMERATED BY ME ON THE 11th DAY OF March, 1920

Jose Kamminga ENUMERATOR

	PLACE OF ABODE			NAME	RELATION	PERSONAL DESCRIPTION					EDUCATION			NATIVITY				OCCUPATION
Street, avenue, road, etc.	Number of dwelling house is order of visitation	Number of family in order of visitation		of each person whose place of abode on January 1, 1920, was in the family. Enter surname, first, then given name and middle initial. If any. Include every person living on January 1, 1920. Omit children born since January 1, 1920.	Relationship of this person to the head of the family.	Sex	Color or race	Age at last birthday	Single, married, widowed or divorced.	Attended school any time since Sept. 1, 1919	Whether able to read.	Whether able to write.	Place of birth of this person.	Place of birth of father of this person.	Place of birth of mother of this person.	Whether able to speak English.	Trade, profession, or particular kind of work done, as salesman, laborer, clerk, cook, merchant, washerwoman, etc.
1	2	3	4		5	6	7	8	9	10	11	12	13	14	15	16	17
	25	25	Quichocho, Jesus Q		Head	M	Cha	23.0	M		Y	Y	Guam	Unknown	Guam	N	Farmer
	25	25	Quichocho, Paula C		Wife	F	Cha	51.0	M		Y	Y	Guam	Guam	Guam	N	None
	26	26	Cepeda, Vicente F		Head	M	Cha	62.0	M		N	N	Guam	Guam	Guam	N	Farm laborer
	26	26	Cepeda, Natividad M		Wife	F	Cha	55.0	M		Y	N	Guam	Unknown	Guam	N	None
	26	26	Cepeda, Pancrasio M		Son	M	Cha	15.0	S	N	N	N	Guam	Guam	Guam	N	Farm laborer
	26	26	Cepeda, Antonia M		Daughter	F	Cha	12.0	S	N	N	N	Guam	Guam	Guam	N	None
	26	26	Cepeda, Antonio M		Son	M	Cha	10.0	S	N	N	N	Guam	Guam	Guam	N	None
	26	26	Cepeda, Vicente M		Son	M	Cha	5.0	S	N			Guam	Guam	Guam		None
	26	26	Cepeda, Concepcion M		Daughter	F	Cha	3.0	S				Guam	Guam	Guam		None
	26	26	Cepeda, Leon M		Son	M	Cha	2.0	S				Guam	Guam	Guam		None
	27	27	Santos, Soledad S		Head	F	Cha	43.0	S		Y	Y	Guam	Unknown	Guam	N	Farmer
	27	27	Santos, Vicenta S		Mother	F	Cha	70.0	Wd		Y	N	Guam	Guam	Guam	N	None
	27	27	Manibusan, Nicolasa S		Niece	F	Cha	15.0	S	N	Y	Y	Guam	Guam	Guam	N	None
	28	28	Quichocho, Nicolasa Q		Head	F	Cha	57.0	S		Y	N	Guam	Unknown	Guam	N	Farmer
	28	28	Quichocho, Maria Q		Daughter	F	Cha	29.0	S		Y	N	Guam	Unknown	Guam	N	None
	28	28	Quichocho, Rosa Q		Daughter	F	Cha	10.0	S		Y	N	Guam	Unknown	Guam	N	None
	28	28	Quichocho, Nicolas Q		Nephew	M	Cha	5.0	S	N	Y	Y	Guam	Unknown	Guam	N	None
	28	28	Quichocho, Jose Q		Nephew	M	Cha	0.3	S				Guam	Unknown	Guam		None
	29	29	Quichocho, Ana T		Head	F	Cha	27.0	Wd	N	Y	Y	Guam	Unknown	Guam	Y	Farmer
	29	29	Quichocho, Juan T		Son	M	Cha	7.0	S	N	Y	N	Guam	Guam	Guam		None
	29	29	Quichocho, Rosa T		Daughter	F	Cha	4.0	S				Guam	Guam	Guam		None
	29	29	Quichocho, Maria T		Daughter	F	Cha	2.0	S				Guam	Guam	Guam		None
	30	31	Villagomes, Juan C		Head	M	Cha	33.0	M		Y	Y	Guam	Guam	Guam	N	Farmer
	30	31	Villagomes, Josefa La T		Wife	F	Cha	24.0	M		Y	Y	Guam	Guam	Guam	N	None
	30	31	Villagomes, Rosabeda La T		Daughter	F	Cha	5.0	S	N			Guam	Guam	Guam		None

Barrigada Barrio

(CHAMORRO ROOTS GENEALOGY PROJECT ™ TRANSCRIPTION)

(COMPILED/TRANSCRIBED BY BERNARD T. PUNZALAN / HTTP://WWW.CHAMORROROOTS.COM)

FOURTEENTH CENSUS OF THE UNITED STATES: 1920-POPULATION
ISLAND OF GUAM

42b

DISTRICT **1**

NAME OF PLACE **Barrigada Barrio**

[Proper name and, also, name of class, as city, town, village, barrio, etc]

ENUMERATED BY ME ON THE 11th DAY OF March, 1920

Jose Kamminga ENUMERATOR

	PLACE OF ABODE			NAME	RELATION	PERSONAL DESCRIPTION				EDUCATION			NATIVITY				OCCUPATION
Street, avenue, road, etc.	No. of dwelling house	No. of family	Name of each person	Relationship	Sex	Color or race	Age at last birthday	Single, married, widowed or divorced	Attended school since Sept. 1, 1919	Whether able to read	Whether able to write	Place of birth of this person	Place of birth of father	Place of birth of mother	Whether able to speak English	Occupation
1	2	3	4	5	6	7	8	9	10	11	12	13	14	15	16	17
	30	30	Villagomes, Francisco La T	Son	M	Cha	3.0	S				Guam	Guam	Guam		None
	30	30	Villagomes, Gregorio La T	Son	M	Cha	1.0	S				Guam	Guam	Guam		None
	31	31	Crisostomo, Mariano B	Head	M	Cha	40.0	M		Y	N	Guam	Guam	Guam	N	Farmer
	31	31	Crisostomo, Juana S	Wife	F	Cha	42.0	M		N	N	Guam	Guam	Guam	N	None
	31	31	Crisostomo, Ignacio S	Son	M	Cha	16.0	S	N	N	N	Guam	Guam	Guam	N	Farm laborer home farm
	31	31	Crisostomo, Juana S	Daughter	F	Cha	6.0	S	N			Guam	Guam	Guam		None
	31	31	Crisostomo, Lourdes S	Daughter	F	Cha	4.0	S				Guam	Guam	Guam		None
Barrigada Barrio	32	32	Cruz, Joaquin S	Head	M	Cha	24.0	M		Y	Y	Guam	Guam	Guam	Y	Farmer
	32	32	Cruz, Maria C	Wife	F	Cha	21.0	M	N	Y	Y	Guam	Unknown	Guam	Y	None
	32	32	Cruz, Jose C	Son	M	Cha	1.0	S				Guam	Guam	Guam		None
	33	33	Borja, Juan M	Head	M	Cha	33.0	M		Y	Y	Guam	Guam	Guam	N	Farmer
	33	33	Borja, Ignacia R	Wife	F	Cha	19.0	M	N	Y	Y	Guam	Guam	Guam	Y	None
	33	33	Borja, Maria R	Daughter	F	Cha	3.0	S				Guam	Guam	Guam		None
	33	33	Borja, Jose R	Son	M	Cha	0.2	S				Guam	Guam	Guam		None
	34	34	Leon Guerrero, Jose P	Head	M	Cha	31.0	M		Y	Y	Guam	Guam	Guam	Y	Farmer
	34	34	Leon Guerrero, Trinidad P	Wife	F	Cha	32.0	M		Y	N	Guam	Guam	Guam	N	None
	34	34	Leon Guerrero, Enrique P	Son	M	Cha	16.0	S	N			Guam	Guam	Guam		None
	34	34	Leon Guerrero, Francisco P	Son	M	Cha	12.0	S				Guam	Guam	Guam		None
	35	35	Leon Guerrero, Joaquin P	Head	M	Cha	36.0	M		Y	Y	Guam	Guam	Guam	N	Farmer
	35	35	Leon Guerrero, Vicenta C	Wife	F	Cha	27.0	M		Y	Y	Guam	Guam	Guam	N	None
	35	35	Leon Guerrero, Vicente C	Son	M	Cha	8.0	S	Y			Guam	Guam	Guam		None
	35	35	Leon Guerrero, Ana C	Daughter	F	Cha	6.0	S	N			Guam	Guam	Guam		None
	35	35	Leon Guerrero, Rosario C	Daughter	F	Cha	4.0	S				Guam	Guam	Guam		None
	35	35	Leon Guerrero, Maria C	Daughter	F	Cha	2.0	S				Guam	Guam	Guam		None
	35	35	Cruz, Rosario M	Mother-in-law	F	Cha	61.0	Wd		Y	N	Guam	Guam	Guam	N	None

(CHAMORRO ROOTS GENEALOGY PROJECT ™ TRANSCRIPTION)
(COMPILED/TRANSCRIBED BY BERNARD T. PUNZALAN / HTTP://WWW.CHAMORROROOTS.COM)

FOURTEENTH CENSUS OF THE UNITED STATES: 1920-POPULATION

ISLAND OF GUAM

ENUMERATED BY ME ON THE 13th DAY OF March, 1920

Jose Kamminga ENUMERATOR

DISTRICT 1

NAME OF PLACE **Barrigada Barrio**

[Proper name and, also, name of class, as city, town, village, barrio, etc]

	Dwelling (2)	Family (3)	NAME (4)	RELATION (5)	Sex (6)	Color or race (7)	Age (8)	Single, married, widowed or divorced (9)	Attended school since Sept. 1, 1919 (10)	Able to read (11)	Able to write (12)	Place of birth of this person (13)	Place of birth of father (14)	Place of birth of mother (15)	Able to speak English (16)	OCCUPATION (17)
1	36	36	Rabon, Mariano C	Head	M	Fil	74.0	M		N	N	Philippine Islands	Philippine Islands	Philippine Islands	N	Ranchman
2	37	37	Cruz, Pedro M	Head	M	Cha	50.0	M		N	N	Guam	Guam	Guam	N	Farmer
3	37	37	Cruz, Felecita S	Wife	F	Cha	41.0	M		Y	Y	Guam	Guam	Guam	N	None
4	37	37	Salas, Tomasa S	Step daughter	F	Cha	16.0	S	N	Y	Y	Guam	Unknown	Guam	N	None
5	37	37	Cruz, Agustin S	Nephew	M	Cha	26.0	S		Y	Y	Guam	Guam	Guam	N	Farm laborer home farm
6	37	37	Cruz, Pedro M	Nephew	M	Cha	6.0	S				Guam	Unknown	Guam		None
7	38	38	Baza, Joaquin C	Head	M	Cha	31.0	M		Y	Y	Guam	Guam	Guam	N	Farmer
8	38	38	Baza, Josefa D	Wife	F	Cha	32.0	M		Y	Y	Guam	Guam	Guam	N	None
9	39	39	Quichocho, Manuel Q	Head	M	Cha	20.0	S		Y	Y	Guam	Unknown	Guam	Y	Farmer
10	39	39	Quichocho, Ana B	Mother	F	Cha	40.0	S		N	N	Guam	Unknown	Guam	N	None
11	39	39	Quichocho, Catalina Q	Niece	F	Cha	15.0	S	N	Y	Y	Guam	Unknown	Guam	Y	None
12	40	40	Camacho, Jose G	Head	M	Cha	23.0	M		Y	Y	Guam	Guam	Guam	N	Farmer
13	40	40	Camacho, Ana M	Wife	F	Cha	20.0	M		N	N	Guam	Guam	Guam	N	None
14	40	40	Camacho, Josefina M	Daughter	F	Cha	0.1	S				Guam	Guam	Guam		None
15	41	41	Mendiola, Jesus P	Head	M	Cha	22.0	M		Y	Y	Guam	Guam	Guam	Y	Farmer
16	41	41	Mendiola, Maria P	Wife	F	Cha	21.0	M	N	Y	Y	Guam	Guam	Guam	Y	None
17	42	42	Salas, Ramon C	Head	M	Cha	48.0	Wd		Y	Y	Guam	Guam	Guam	Y	Farmer
18	42	42	Salas, Antonio LG	Son	M	Cha	20.0	S	N	Y	Y	Guam	Guam	Guam	Y	Laborer
19	42	42	Salas, Mercedes LG	Daughter	F	Cha	18.0	S	N	Y	Y	Guam	Guam	Guam	N	None
20	43	43	Manibusan, Juan P	Head	M	Cha	26.0	M		Y	Y	Guam	Guam	Guam	Y	Farmer
21	43	43	Manibusan, Juana M	Wife	F	Cha	25.0	M		Y	Y	Guam	Unknown	Unknown	N	None
22	43	43	Materne, Francisco M	Mother-in-law	F	Cha	55.0	S		Y	Y	Guam	Guam	Guam	N	None
23	44	44	Manibusan, Jose C	Head	M	Cha	61.0	M		N	N	Guam	Guam	Guam	N	Farmer
24	44	44	Manibusan, Maria P	Wife	F	Cha	46.0	M		N	N	Guam	Guam	Guam	N	None
25	44	44	Manibusan, Ramon P	Son	M	Cha	28.0	S		Y	Y	Guam	Guam	Guam	Y	Farm laborer home farm

Street: Barrigada Barrio

(CHAMORRO ROOTS GENEALOGY PROJECT ™ TRANSCRIPTION)
(COMPILED/TRANSCRIBED BY BERNARD T. PUNZALAN / HTTP://WWW.CHAMORROROOTS.COM)

FOURTEENTH CENSUS OF THE UNITED STATES: 1920—POPULATION
ISLAND OF GUAM

DISTRICT **1**
NAME OF PLACE **Barrigada Barrio**
[Proper name and, also, name of class, as city, town, village, barrio, etc]

ENUMERATED BY ME ON THE 13th DAY OF March, 1920

Jose Kamminga ENUMERATOR

	PLACE OF ABODE			NAME	RELATION	PERSONAL DESCRIPTION				EDUCATION			NATIVITY				OCCUPATION
Street, avenue, road, etc.	Number of dwelling house is order of visitation	Number of family in order of visitation		of each person whose place of abode on January 1, 1920, was in the family. Enter surname, firs, then given name and middle initial. If any. Include every person living on January 1, 1920. Omit children born since January 1, 1920.	Relationship of this Person to the head of the family.	Sex	Color or race	Age at last birthday	Single, married, widowed or divorced	Attended school any time since sept. 1, 1919	Whether able to read.	Whether able to write.	Place of birth of this person.	Place of birth of father of this person.	Place of birth of mother of this person.	Whether able to speak English.	Trade, profession, or particular kind of work done, as salesman, laborer, clerk, cook, merchant, washerwoman, etc.
1	2	3		4	5	6	7	8	9	10	11	12	13	14	15	16	17
Barrigada Barrio	44	44		Manibusan, Luis P	Son	M	Cha	24.0	S		Y	Y	Guam	Guam	Guam		Farm laborer home farm
	44	44		Manibusan, Ana P	Daughter	F	Cha	16.0	S	N	Y	Y	Guam	Guam	Guam		None
	44	44		Manibusan, Maria P jr.	Daughter	F	Cha	14.0	S	N	Y	Y	Guam	Guam	Guam		None
	44	44		Manibusan, Vicente P	Son	M	Cha	10.0	S	Y	Y	Y	Guam	Guam	Guam		None
	44	44		Manibusan, Matias P	Son	M	Cha	8.0	S	N			Guam	Guam	Guam		None
	44	44		Manibusan, Antonio P	Son	M	Cha	6.0	S	N			Guam	Guam	Guam		None
	45	45		Gomez, Vicente S	Head	M	B	19.0	S	N	Y	Y	Guam	United States	Guam	Y	Storekeeper

Here ends the enumeration of Barrigada Barrio

97

Sheets 44, 44b, 45, 45b, & 46, consisted of 111 people and were too illegible to transcribe.

(CHAMORRO ROOTS GENEALOGY PROJECT ™ TRANSCRIPTION)
(COMPILED/TRANSCRIBED BY BERNARD T. PUNZALAN / HTTP://WWW.CHAMORROROOTS.COM)

FOURTEENTH CENSUS OF THE UNITED STATES: 1920—POPULATION
ISLAND OF GUAM

ENUMERATED BY ME ON THE 19th DAY OF March, 1920

Jose Kamminga ENUMERATOR

DISTRICT 1
NAME OF PLACE Sinajana Barrio
[Proper name and, also, name of class, as city, town, village, barrio, etc]

Street, avenue, road, etc.	Number of dwelling house in order of visitation	Number of family in order of visitation	NAME	RELATION	Sex	Color or race	Age at last birthday	Single, married, widowed or divorced	Attended school any time since Sept. 1, 1919	Whether able to read	Whether able to write	Place of birth of this person	Place of birth of father of this person	Place of birth of mother of this person	Whether able to speak English	OCCUPATION
1	2	3	4	5	6	7	8	9	10	11	12	13	14	15	16	17
	1	1	Cruz, Antonio Q	Head	M	Cha	25.0	M		Y	Y	Guam	Guam	Guam	Y	Farmer
	1	1	Cruz, Ana G	Wife	F	Cha	22.0	M		Y	Y	Guam	Guam	Guam	N	None
	1	1	Cruz, Pedro G	Son	M	Cha	2.0	S				Guam	Guam	Guam		None
	1	1	Cruz, Rosa G	Daughter	F	Cha	0.3	S				Guam	Guam	Guam		None
	2	2	Navaro, Maria M	Head	F	Cha	55.0	Wd		Y	N	Guam	Unknown	Guam	Y	None
	2	2	Navaro, Donisio M	Son	M	Fil	34.0	S		Y	Y	Guam	Philippine Islands	Guam	Y	Laborer
	2	2	Navaro, Mariano M	Son	M	Fil	26.0	S		Y	Y	Guam	Philippine Islands	Guam	Y	Laborer
	2	2	Navaro, Juan M	Son	M	Fil	22.0	S		Y	Y	Guam	Philippine Islands	Guam	Y	Farm laborer home farm
Sinajana Barrio	2	2	Navaro, Crispina M	Daughter	F	Fil	18.0	S	N	Y	Y	Guam	Philippine Islands	Guam	Y	None
	3	3	Mafnas, Joaquin F	Head	M	Cha	54.0	M		Y	N	Guam	Guam	Guam	N	Farmer
	3	3	Mafnas, Elena A	Wife	F	Cha	52.0	M		Y	N	Guam	Guam	Guam	N	None
	3	3	Atoigue, Trinidad A	Niece	F	Cha	24.0	S		Y	Y	Guam	Unknown	Guam	N	None
	3	3	Atoigue, Maria L	Niece	F	Cha	14.0	S	N	Y	Y	Guam	Guam	Guam	Y	None
	3	3	Atoigue, Ana L	Niece	F	Cha	11.0	S	Y	Y	Y	Guam	Guam	Guam	Y	None
	4	4	Gogo, Juan G	Head	M	Cha	30.0	M		N	N	Guam	Unknown	Guam	N	Farm laborer
	4	4	Gogo, Ana C	Wife	F	Cha	43.0	M		N	N	Guam	Guam	Guam	N	None
	4	4	Gogo, Pedro C	Son	M	Cha	4.0	S				Guam	Guam	Guam		None
	4	4	Gogo, Jose C	Son	M	Cha	1.0	S				Guam	Guam	Guam		None
	4	4	Gogo, Maria C	Daughter	F	Cha	14.0	S	N	N	N	Guam	Guam	Guam	N	None
	5	5	Gogue, Juan A	Head	M	Cha	23.0	M		Y	Y	Guam	Guam	Guam	N	Farmer
	5	5	Gogue, Ana Q	Wife	F	Cha	27.0	M		Y	Y	Guam	Guam	Guam	Y	None
	5	5	Gogue, Juan Q	Son	M	Cha	1.0	S				Guam	Guam	Guam		None
	5	5	Gogue, Jose Q	Son	M	Cha	0.3	S				Guam	Guam	Guam		None
	6	6	Achaigua, Dolores C	Head	F	Cha	45.0	Wd		N	N	Guam	Guam	Guam	N	Farmer
	6	6	Achaigua, Regina C	Daughter	F	Cha	16.0	S	N	Y	Y	Guam	Guam	Guam	Y	None

47b

(CHAMORRO ROOTS GENEALOGY PROJECT ™ TRANSCRIPTION)
(COMPILED/TRANSCRIBED BY BERNARD T. PUNZALAN / HTTP://WWW.CHAMORROROOTS.COM)
FOURTEENTH CENSUS OF THE UNITED STATES: 1920-POPULATION
ISLAND OF GUAM

DISTRICT 1
NAME OF PLACE Sinajana Barrio
[Proper name and, also, name of class, as city, town, village, barrio, etc]

ENUMERATED BY ME ON THE 19th DAY OF March, 1920

Jose Kamminga ENUMERATOR

1 Street	2 Dwelling	3 Family	4 Name	5 Relation	6 Sex	7 Color	8 Age	9 Cond.	10 School	11 Read	12 Write	13 Birth person	14 Birth father	15 Birth mother	16 Eng.	17 Occupation
	6	6	Achaigua, Jose C	Son	M	Cha	13.0	S	N	Y	Y	Guam	Guam	Guam	Y	None
	6	6	Achaigua, Juan C	Son	M	Cha	12.0	S	N	N	N	Guam	Guam	Guam	N	None
	6	6	Achaigua, Angel C	Son	M	Cha	9.0	S	N			Guam	Guam	Guam		None
	6	6	Achaigua, Enecasio C	Son	M	Cha	4.0	S				Guam	Guam	Guam		None
	7	7	San Nicolas, Vicente A	Head	M	Cha	29.0	M		N	N	Guam	Guam	Guam	N	Farmer
	7	7	San Nicolas, Magdalena G	Wife	F	Cha	30.0	M		N	N	Guam	Unknown	Guam	N	None
	7	7	San Nicolas, Vicente G	Son	M	Cha	12.0	S		N	N	Guam	Guam	Guam	N	None
	7	7	San Nicolas, Soledad G	Daughter	F	Cha	8.0	S	N			Guam	Guam	Guam		None
	7	7	San Nicolas, Ignacio G	Son	M	Cha	7.0	S	N			Guam	Guam	Guam		None
	7	7	San Nicolas, Jose G	Son	M	Cha	5.0	S	N			Guam	Guam	Guam		None
	7	7	San Nicolas, Maria G	Daughter	F	Cha	4.0	S				Guam	Guam	Guam		None
	8	8	Gogue, Jose A	Head	M	Cha	33.0	M		Y	Y	Guam	Guam	Guam	Y	Farmer
	8	8	Gogue, Joaquina G	Wife	F	Cha	28.0	M		Y	Y	Guam	Unknown	Guam	N	None
	8	8	Gogue, Juan G	Son	M	Cha	5.0	S	N			Guam	Guam	Guam		None
	8	8	Gogo, Carmela Q	Mother-in-law	F	Cha	65.0	S		Y	Y	Guam	Unknown	Guam	N	None
	8	8	Gogo, Teofera Q	Sister-in-law	F	Cha	35.0	S		Y	N	Guam	Unknown	Guam	N	None
	8	8	Gogo, Maria	Niece	F	Cha	9.0	S	Y			Guam	Unknown	Guam		None
	8	8	Gogo, Felecita	Niece	F	Cha	7.0	S	Y			Guam	Unknown	Guam		None
	8	8	Gogo, Jose	Nephew	M	Cha	6.0	S	N			Guam	Unknown	Guam		None
	8	8	Gogo, Adela	Niece	F	Cha	2.0	S				Guam	Unknown	Guam		None
Sinajana Barrio	9	9	Crisostomo, Felix C	Head	M	Cha	25.0	M		Y	Y	Guam	Unknown	Guam	Y	Farmer
	9	9	Crisostomo, Ana SN	Wife	F	Cha	20.0	S	N	N	Y	Guam	Guam	Guam	Y	None
	9	9	Crisostomo, Delfina SN	Daughter	F	Cha	2.0	S				Guam	Guam	Guam		None
	9	9	Crisostomo, Teodoro SN	Son	M	Cha	0.1	S				Guam	Guam	Guam		None

(*Line 50 was left blank by the Enumerator.)

(CHAMORRO ROOTS GENEALOGY PROJECT ™ TRANSCRIPTION)
(COMPILED/TRANSCRIBED BY BERNARD T. PUNZALAN / HTTP://WWW.CHAMORROROOTS.COM)

FOURTEENTH CENSUS OF THE UNITED STATES: 1920—POPULATION

ISLAND OF GUAM

DISTRICT **1**
NAME OF PLACE **Sinajana Barrio**
[Proper name and, also, name of class, as city, town, village, barrio, etc]

ENUMERATED BY ME ON THE 20th DAY OF March, 1920

Jose Kamminga ENUMERATOR

			NAME	RELATION				PERSONAL DESCRIPTION		EDUCATION			NATIVITY				OCCUPATION
Street, avenue, road, etc.	Number of dwelling house is order of visitation	Number of family in order of visitation	of each person whose place of abode on January 1, 1920, was in the family. Enter surname, firs, then given name and middle initial, if any. Include every person living on January 1, 1920. Omit children born since January 1, 1920.	Relationship of this Person to the head of the family.	Sex	Color or race	Age at last birthday	Single, married, widowed or divorced	Attended school any time since Sept. 1, 1919	Whether able to read.	Whether able to write.	Place of birth of this person.	Place of birth of father of this person.	Place of birth of mother of this person.	Whether able to speak English.	Trade, profession, or particular kind of work done, as salesman, laborer, clerk, cook, merchant, washerwoman, etc.
1	2	3	4	5	6	7	8	9	10	11	12	13	14	15	16	17
	10	10	Aguajlo, Miguel M	Head	M	Cha	44.0	M		Y	Y	Guam	Guam	Guam	N	Farmer
	10	10	Aguajlo, Ana M	Mother	F	Cha	80.0	Wd		N	N	Guam	Guam	Guam	N	None
	10	10	Aguajlo, Rita M	Sister	F	Cha	47.0	S		N	N	Guam	Guam	Guam	N	None
	10	10	Aguajlo, Carmen	Niece	F	Cha	20.0	S	N	Y	Y	Guam	Unknown	Guam	Y	None
	10	10	Aguajlo, Angelina	Niece	F	Cha	18.0	S	N	Y	Y	Guam	Unknown	Guam	Y	None
	10	10	Aguajlo, Vicente	Nephew	M	Cha	16.0	S	N	Y	Y	Guam	Unknown	Guam	Y	Farm laborer home farm
	11	11	Gogue, Maria A	Head	F	Cha	54.0	Wd		N	N	Guam	Guam	Guam	N	None
	11	11	Gogue, Rita A	Daughter	F	Cha	18.0	S	N	Y	Y	Guam	Guam	Guam	Y	None
	11	11	Gogue, Jesus A	Son	M	Cha	16.0	S	N	Y	Y	Guam	Guam	Guam	Y	Farm laborer home farm
	11	11	Gogue, Carmen A	Daughter	F	Cha	14.0	S	N	Y	Y	Guam	Guam	Guam	Y	None
	11	11	Divera, Vicenta G	Daughter	F	Cha	30.0	M	N	N	N	Guam	Guam	Guam	N	None
	11	11	Divera, Mercedes G	Grand daughter	F	Cha	6.0	S				Guam	Guam	Guam		None
	11	11	Divera, Ramon G	Grand son	M	Cha	3.0	S				Guam	Guam	Guam		None
	11	11	Divera, Lutilde G	Grand daughter	F	Cha	2.0	S				Guam	Guam	Guam		None
	11	11	Gogue, Jose	Grand son	M	Cha	9.0	S	N			Guam	Guam	Guam		None
	12	12	Atoigue, Jesus	Head	M	Cha	31.0	M		Y	Y	Guam	Unknown	Guam	N	Farmer
	12	12	Atoigue, Ana Q	Wife	F	Cha	41.0	M		N	N	Guam	Guam	Guam	N	None
	12	12	Atoigue, Francisco Q	Son	M	Cha	7.0	S	Y			Guam	Guam	Guam		None
	12	12	Atoigue, Vicente Q	Son	M	Cha	6.0	S	N			Guam	Guam	Guam		None
	12	12	Atoigue, Carlos Q	Son	M	Cha	2.0	S				Guam	Guam	Guam		None
	12	12	Atoigue, Jesus Q	Son	M	Cha	16.0	S	N	Y	Y	Guam	Guam	Guam	Y	Farm laborer home farm
	12	12	Atoigue, Pablo	Brother	M	Cha	29.0	S		Y	Y	Guam	Unknown	Guam	N	Farm laborer home farm
	12	12	Quichocho, Rita G	Sister-in-law	F	Cha	39.0	S	N	N	N	Guam	Guam	Guam	N	None
	12	12	Quichocho, Prodencio	Nephew	M	Cha	6.0	S				Guam	Unknown	Guam	N	None
	13	13	Tenorio, Jose G	Head	M	Cha	22.0	S		Y	Y	Guam	Guam	Guam	Y	Farmer

Sinajana Barrio

(CHAMORRO ROOTS GENEALOGY PROJECT ™ TRANSCRIPTION)
(COMPILED/TRANSCRIBED BY BERNARD T. PUNZALAN / HTTP://WWW.CHAMORROROOTS.COM)

FOURTEENTH CENSUS OF THE UNITED STATES: 1920—POPULATION
ISLAND OF GUAM

48b

ENUMERATED BY ME ON THE 20th DAY OF March, 1920

Jose Kamminga ENUMERATOR

DISTRICT 1
NAME OF PLACE Sinajana Barrio

[Proper name and, also, name of class, as city, town, village, barrio, etc]

	Dwelling No.	Family No.	NAME	RELATION	Sex	Color or race	Age	Condition	Attended school since Sept. 1, 1919	Able to read	Able to write	Place of birth of person	Place of birth of father	Place of birth of mother	Able to speak English	OCCUPATION
26	13	13	Tenorio, Francisco Y	Father	M	Cha	48.0	Wd		N	N	Guam	Guam	Guam	N	None
27	13	13	Tenorio, Maria Y	Sister	F	Cha	23.0	S		Y	Y	Guam	Guam	Guam	N	None
28	13	13	Tenorio, Enrique Y	Brother	M	Cha	18.0	S	N	Y	Y	Guam	Guam	Guam	Y	Farm laborer home farm
29	13	13	Tenorio, Vicente Y	Brother	M	Cha	17.0	S	N	Y	Y	Guam	Guam	Guam	Y	Farm laborer home farm
30	13	13	Tenorio, Ana Y	Sister	F	Cha	12.0	S	N	Y	Y	Guam	Guam	Guam	N	None
31	13	13	Tenorio, Oliva G	Sister	F	Cha	10.0	S	Y	Y	Y	Guam	Guam	Guam	N	None
32	13	13	Tenorio, Gregorio G	Nephew	M	Cha	4.0	S				Guam	Unknown	Guam		None
33	13	13	Tenorio, Delfina G	Niece	F	Cha	3.0	S				Guam	Unknown	Guam		None
34	14	14	Tertaotao, Gregorio T	Head	M	Cha	46.0	Wd		Y	Y	Guam	Unknown	Guam	N	Farmer
35	14	14	Afaisen, Susana T	Cousin	F	Cha	48.0	S		Y	N	Guam	Unknown	Guam	N	None
36	14	14	Tertaotao, Manuel	Nephew	M	Cha	32.0	S		Y	N	Guam	Unknown	Guam	N	Ranchero
37	14	14	Tertaotao, Marcelina	Niece	F	Cha	20.0	S	N	N	N	Guam	Unknown	Guam	N	None
38	15	15	Gogo, Juan G	Head	M	Cha	44.0	M		N	N	Guam	Unknown	Guam	N	Farmer
39	15	15	Gogo, Filomena A	Wife	F	Cha	47.0	M		Y	N	Guam	Guam	Guam	N	None
40	15	15	Atoigue, Juliana SN	Mother-in-law	F	Cha	81.0	Wd		N	N	Guam	Guam	Guam	N	None
41	15	15	Qiudachay, Jesus A	Nephew	M	Cha	7.0	S	N			Guam	Guam	Guam		None
42	16	16	Atoigue, Jose T	Head	M	Cha	44.0	M		Y	Y	Guam	Guam	Guam	N	Farmer
43	16	16	Atoigue, Dolores A	Wife	F	Cha	45.0	M		Y	N	Guam	Guam	Guam	N	None
44	16	16	Atoigue, Manuel A	Son	M	Cha	19.0	S	N	Y	Y	Guam	Guam	Guam	Y	Farm laborer home farm
45	16	16	Atoigue, Ana A	Daughter	F	Cha	16.0	S	N	Y	Y	Guam	Guam	Guam	Y	None
46	16	16	Atoigue, Bernadino A	Son	M	Cha	10.0	S	N	Y	Y	Guam	Guam	Guam	N	None
47	16	16	Atoigue, Maria A	Daughter	F	Cha	5.0	S	N			Guam	Guam	Guam		None
48	16	16	Atoigue, Vicente	Father	M	Cha	89.0	Wd		N	N	Guam	Guam	Guam	N	None
49																
50																

Street, avenue, road, etc: Sinajana Barrio

(Lines 49 and 50 were left blank by the Enumerator)

(CHAMORRO ROOTS GENEALOGY PROJECT ™ TRANSCRIPTION)
(COMPILED/TRANSCRIBED BY BERNARD T. PUNZALAN / HTTP://WWW.CHAMORROROOTS.COM)

FOURTEENTH CENSUS OF THE UNITED STATES: 1920—POPULATION

ISLAND OF GUAM

ENUMERATED BY ME ON THE 22nd DAY OF March, 1920

Jose Kamminga ENUMERATOR

DISTRICT 1
NAME OF PLACE Sinajana Barrio

[Proper name and, also, name of class, as city, town, village, barrio, etc]

	PLACE OF ABODE		NAME	RELATION	PERSONAL DESCRIPTION				EDUCATION			NATIVITY				OCCUPATION
Street, avenue, road, etc.	Number of dwelling house in order of visitation	Number of family in order of visitation	of each person whose place of abode on January 1, 1920, was in the family. Enter surname, first, then given name and middle initial. If any. Include every person living on January 1, 1920. Omit children born since January 1, 1920.	Relationship of this Person to the head of the family.	Sex	Color or race	Age at last birthday	Single, married, widowed or divorced	Attended school any time since Sept. 1, 1919	Whether able to read.	Whether able to write.	Place of birth of this person.	Place of birth of father of this person.	Place of birth of mother of this person.	Whether able to speak English.	Trade, profession, or particular kind of work done, as salesman, laborer, clerk, cook, merchant, washerwoman, etc.
1	2	3	4	5	6	7	8	9	10	11	12	13	14	15	16	17
	17	17	Gogo, Jose G	Head	M	Cha	24.0	M		Y	Y	Guam	Unknown	Guam	Y	Farmer
	17	17	Gogo, Felicita C	Wife	F	Cha	23.0	M		Y	Y	Guam	Guam	Guam	Y	None
	17	17	Gogo, Bernadita	Daughter	F	Cha	1.0	S				Guam	Guam	Guam		None
	18	18	Atoigue, Joaquina C	Head	F	Cha	40.0	Wd		Y	N	Guam	Guam	Guam	N	Farmer
	18	18	Atoigue, Antonia C	Daughter	F	Cha	22.0	S		Y	Y	Guam	Guam	Guam	N	None
Sinajana Barrio	18	18	Atoigue, Natividad C	Daughter	F	Cha	5.0	S	N	N		Guam	Guam	Guam	N	None
	18	18	Atoigue, Rosario C	Grand daughter	F	Cha	2.0	S				Guam	Unknown	Guam		None
	19	19	Quidachay, Ana A	Head	F	Cha	53.0	Wd		Y	N	Guam	Guam	Guam	N	Farmer
	20	20	Atoigue, Juan M	Head	M	Cha	30.0	M		Y	Y	Guam	Guam	Guam	N	Farmer
	20	20	Atoigue, Carmen T	Wife	F	Cha	27.0	M		Y	N	Guam	Guam	Guam	N	None
	20	20	Atoigue, Magdalena T	Daughter	F	Cha	5.0	S				Guam	Guam	Guam		None
	20	20	Atoigue, Jose T	Son	M	Cha	1.0	S	N			Guam	Guam	Guam		None
	20	20	Atoigue, Felipe M	Brother	M	Cha	16.0	S	N	Y	Y	Guam	Guam	Guam	Y	Laborer
	20	20	Siguenza, Rosalia A	Sister	F	Cha	25.0	Wd		Y	Y	Guam	Guam	Guam	Y	None
	20	20	Atoigue, Joaquin	Nephew	M	Cha	2.0	S				Guam	Unknown	Guam		None
	21	21	Atoigue, Juan SN	Head	M	Cha	37.0	M		Y	N	Guam	Guam	Guam	N	Farmer
	22	22	Gogo, Vicente G	Head	M	Cha	27.0	M		Y	Y	Guam	Unknown	Guam	Y	Enlisted man USN
	22	22	Gogo, Amparo A	Wife	F	Cha	21.0	M	N	Y	Y	Guam	Unknown	Guam	N	None
	22	22	Gogo, Ignacio A	Son	M	Cha	3.0	S				Guam	Guam	Guam		None
	22	22	Gogo, Marcela A	Daughter	F	Cha	0.3	S				Guam	Guam	Guam		None
	22	22	Gogo, Daniel G	Brother	M	Cha	25.0	S		Y	Y	Guam	Unknown	Guam	N	Farm laborer home farm
	22	22	Gogo, Maria G	Sister	F	Cha	21.0	S	N	Y	N	Guam	Unknown	Guam	N	None
	22	22	Gogo, Ramon G	Brother	M	Cha	8.0	S	N	Y	Y	Guam	Unknown	Guam	N	Farm laborer home farm
	22	22	Aguajlo, Pedro C	Nephew	M	Cha	9.0	S	Y			Guam	Guam	Guam		None
	22	22	Gogo, Ignacio C	Aunt	F	Cha	28.0	S		Y	Y	Guam	Guam	Guam	Y	None

(CHAMORRO ROOTS GENEALOGY PROJECT ™ TRANSCRIPTION)
(COMPILED/TRANSCRIBED BY BERNARD T. PUNZALAN / HTTP://WWW.CHAMORROROOTS.COM)
FOURTEENTH CENSUS OF THE UNITED STATES: 1920-POPULATION
ISLAND OF GUAM

DISTRICT 1
NAME OF PLACE Sinajana Barrio
[Proper name and, also, name of class, as city, town, village, barrio, etc]

ENUMERATED BY ME ON THE 22ⁿᵈ DAY OF March, 1920

Jose Kamminga ENUMERATOR

	PLACE OF ABODE			NAME	RELATION	PERSONAL DESCRIPTION				EDUCATION			NATIVITY				OCCUPATION
Street, avenue, road, etc.	Number of dwelling house is order of visitation	Number of family in order of visitation			Relationship of this person to the head of the family.	Sex	Color or race	Age at last birthday	Single, married, widowed or divorced	Attended school any time since sept. 1, 1919	Whether able to read.	Whether able to write.	Place of birth of this person.	Place of birth of father of this person.	Place of birth of mother of this person.	Whether able to speak English.	Trade, profession, or particular kind of work done, as salesman, laborer, clerk, cook, merchant, washerwoman, etc.
1	2	3	4		5	6	7	8	9	10	11	12	13	14	15	16	17
	23	23	Perez, Josefa G		Head	F	Cha	59.0	Wd		N	N	Guam	Guam	Guam		Farmer
	23	23	Perez, Joaquina G		Daughter	F	Cha	18.0	S	N	Y	Y	Guam	Guam	Guam		None
	24	24	Aguailo, Joaquina C		Head	F	Cha	34.0	Wd		Y	Y	Guam	Guam	Guam	N	None
	24	24	Aguailo, Jose C		Son	M	Cha	12.0	S	N	Y	N	Guam	Guam	Guam	N	None
	24	24	Aguailo, Jesus C		Son	M	Cha	6.0	S	N	Y	N	Guam	Guam	Guam	N	None
	24	24	Aguailo, Serefina C		Daughter	F	Cha	0.0	S				Guam	Guam	Guam		None
	25	25	Taisague, Jose La Rosa		Head	M	Cha	52.0	M		Y	Y	Guam	Guam	Guam	N	Farmer
	25	25	Taisague, Guadalupe C		Wife	F	Cha	51.0	M		Y	N	Guam	Guam	Guam	N	None
	26	26	Quidachay, Antonio G		Head	M	Cha	53.0	M		N	N	Guam	Guam	Guam	N	Farmer
	26	26	Quidachay, Ana V		Wife	F	Cha	49.0	M		N	N	Guam	Guam	Guam	N	None
	26	26	Quidachay, Jesus V		Son	M	Cha	20.0	S	N	Y	Y	Guam	Guam	Guam	Y	Farm laborer home farm
	26	26	Quidachay, Maria V		Daughter	F	Cha	16.0	S	N	Y	Y	Guam	Guam	Guam	Y	None
	26	26	Quidachay, Caridad V		Daughter	F	Cha	14.0	S	N	N	N	Guam	Guam	Guam	N	None
	26	26	Quidachay, Manuela V		Daughter	F	Cha	12.0	S	N	N	N	Guam	Guam	Guam	N	None
	26	26	Quidachay, Jose V		Son	M	Cha	10.0	S	N	N	N	Guam	Guam	Guam	N	None
	27	27	Quidachay, Baldovino A		Head	M	Cha	28.0	M	N	Y	Y	Guam	Guam	Guam	Y	Farmer
	27	27	Quidachay, Maria A		Wife	F	Cha	23.0	M	Y	Y	N	Guam	Guam	Guam	N	None
	27	27	Quidachay, Jesus A		Son	M	Cha	1.0	S				Guam	Guam	Guam		None
	28	28	Taimanglo, Juan F		Head	M	Cha	48.0	M		N	N	Guam	Guam	Guam	N	Farmer
	28	28	Taimanglo, Maria Q		Wife	F	Cha	46.0	M		N	N	Guam	Guam	Guam	N	None
	28	28	Taimanglo, Felix Q		Son	M	Cha	9.0	S	Y			Guam	Guam	Guam		None
	28	28	Taimanglo, Engracia Q		Daughter	F	Cha	6.0	S	N			Guam	Guam	Guam		None
	28	28	Taimanglo, Trinidad Q		Daughter	F	Cha	5.0	S				Guam	Guam	Guam		None
	28	28	Taimanglo, Gregorio Q		Son	M	Cha	2.0	S				Guam	Guam	Guam		None
	28	28	Taimanglo, Joaquin Q		Son	M	Cha	0.3	S				Guam	Guam	Guam		None

Sinajana Barrio

26
27
28
29
30
31
32
33
34
35
36
37
38
39
40
41
42
43
44
45
46
47
48
49
50

(CHAMORRO ROOTS GENEALOGY PROJECT ™ TRANSCRIPTION)
(COMPILED/TRANSCRIBED BY BERNARD T. PUNZALAN / HTTP://WWW.CHAMORROROOTS.COM)

FOURTEENTH CENSUS OF THE UNITED STATES: 1920–POPULATION

ISLAND OF GUAM

DISTRICT **1**

NAME OF PLACE **Sinajana Barrio**

[Proper name and, also, name of class, as city, town, village, barrio, etc]

ENUMERATED BY ME ON THE 23rd DAY OF March, 1920

Jose Kamminga ENUMERATOR

	Number of dwelling house in order of visitation	Number of family in order of visitation	NAME	RELATION	Sex	Color or race	Age at last birthday	Single, married, widowed or divorced	Attended school any time since Sept. 1, 1919	Whether able to read	Whether able to write	Place of birth of this person	Place of birth of father of this person	Place of birth of mother of this person	Whether able to speak English	OCCUPATION
1	2	3	4	5	6	7	8	9	10	11	12	13	14	15	16	17
	29	29	Gogue, Juana T	Head	F	Cha	53.0	Wd		Y	N	Guam	Guam	Guam	N	None
	29	29	Gogue, Vicente T	Son	M	Cha	16.0	S	N	Y	Y	Guam	Guam	Guam	Y	Farm laborer home farm
	29	29	Gogue, Dolores T	Daughter	F	Cha	13.0	S	N	Y	Y	Guam	Guam	Guam	Y	Servant
	29	29	Gogue, Amalia T	Daughter	F	Cha	9.0	S	N			Guam	Guam	Guam		None
	29	29	Fegurgur, Enrique F	Cousin	M	Cha	33.0	S		Y	Y	Guam	Unknown	Guam	Y	Farm laborer home farm
	29	29	Fegurgur, Maria SN	Sister-in-law	F	Cha	18.0	S		Y	N	Guam	Guam	Guam	N	None
	29	29	Taimanglo, Teresa Q	Niece	F	Cha	2.0	S				Guam	Guam	Guam	N	None
	30	30	Tertaotao, Salvador T	Head	M	Cha	43.0	M		Y	Y	Guam	Unknown	Guam	Y	Farmer
	30	30	Tertaotao, Rosa G	Wife	F	Cha	41.0	M		Y	Y	Guam	Guam	Guam	N	None
	30	30	Tertaotao, Lucas G	Son	M	Cha	14.0	S	N	Y	Y	Guam	Guam	Guam	Y	None
	30	30	Tertaotao, Jesus G	Son	M	Cha	5.0	S	N			Guam	Guam	Guam	Y	None
	30	30	Tertaotao, Antonio G	Son	M	Cha	2.0	S				Guam	Guam	Guam		None
	31	31	Rosa, Felix La Rosa	Head	M	Cha	36.0	M		Y	Y	Guam	Unknown	Guam	Y	Deputy Commissioner
	31	31	Rosa, Josefa G	Wife	F	Cha	35.0	M		Y	Y	Guam	Unknown	Guam	N	None
	31	31	Rosa, Lucas La Rosa	Brother	M	Cha	45.0	S		N	N	Guam	Unknown	Guam	N	Farm laborer home farm
	31	31	Rosa, Teresa G	Niece	F	Cha	26.0	S		Y	Y	Guam	Guam	Guam	Y	None
	31	31	Rosa, Maria G	Niece	F	Cha	25.0	S		Y	Y	Guam	Guam	Guam	Y	None
	31	31	Rosa, Emilio	Nephew	M	Cha	24.0	S		Y	Y	Guam	Guam	Guam	Y	Farm laborer home farm
	31	31	Gogo, Emilio G	Boarder	M	Cha	4.0	S				Guam	Unknown	Guam		None
	32	32	Perez, Jose G	Head	M	Cha	22.0	M		Y	Y	Guam	Guam	Guam	N	Farmer
	32	32	Perez, Maria A	Wife	F	Cha	22.0	M		Y	Y	Guam	Guam	Guam	N	None
	33	33	Chiguina, Vicente C	Head	M	Cha	43.0	M		Y	Y	Guam	Unknown	Guam	N	Farmer
	33	33	Chiguina, Marcela M	Wife	F	Cha	47.0	M		N	N	Guam	Guam	Guam	N	None
	33	33	Chiguina, Candelaria M	Daughter	F	Cha	19.0	S	N	N	N	Guam	Guam	Guam	N	None
	33	33	Chiguina, Enrique M	Son	M	Cha	18.0	S	N	N	N	Guam	Guam	Guam	N	Farm laborer home farm

(Street, avenue, road, etc. — column 1: Sinajana Barrio)

(CHAMORRO ROOTS GENEALOGY PROJECT ™ TRANSCRIPTION)
(COMPILED/TRANSCRIBED BY BERNARD T. PUNZALAN / HTTP://WWW.CHAMORROROOTS.COM)

FOURTEENTH CENSUS OF THE UNITED STATES: 1920-POPULATION

ISLAND OF GUAM

DISTRICT **1**

NAME OF PLACE **Sinajana Barrio**

[Proper name and, also, name of class, as city, town, village, barrio, etc]

ENUMERATED BY ME ON THE 23rd DAY OF March, 1920

Jose Kamminga ENUMERATOR

	PLACE OF ABODE		NAME	RELATION	PERSONAL DESCRIPTION				EDUCATION			NATIVITY				OCCUPATION
Street, avenue, road, etc.	Number of dwelling house is order of visitation	Number of family in order of visitation	of each person whose place of abode on January 1, 1920, was in the family. Enter surname, first, then given name and middle initial. If any. Include every person living on January 1, 1920. Omit children born since January 1, 1920.	Relationship of this Person to the head of the family.	Sex	Color or race	Age at last birthday	Single, married, widowed or divorced	Attended school any time since Sept. 1, 1919	Whether able to read.	Whether able to write.	Place of birth of this person.	Place of birth of father of this person.	Place of birth of mother of this person.	Whether able to speak English.	Trade, profession, or particular kind of work done, as salesman, laborer, clerk, cook, merchant, washerwoman, etc.
1	2	3	4	5	6	7	8	9	10	11	12	13	14	15	16	17
26	33	33	Chiquina, Antonio M	Son	M	Cha	9.0	S	Y			Guam	Guam	Guam		None
27	33	33	Chiquina, Jesus M	Son	M	Cha	3.0	S				Guam	Guam	Guam		None
28	34	34	Lizama, Juan C	Head	M	Cha	79.0	M		Y	Y	Guam	Guam	Guam	N	Farmer
29	34	34	Lizama, Luisa G	Wife	F	Cha	70.0	M		Y	N	Guam	Guam	Guam		None
30	34	34	Gogue, Jesus G	Nephew	M	Cha	15.0	S	N	Y	Y	Guam	Unknown	Guam	Y	Farm laborer home farm
31	35	35	San Miguel, Jose E	Head	M	Fil	28.0	S		N	N	Guam	Philippine Islands	Guam	N	Farm laborer
32	36	36	Rojas, Vicente T	Head	M	Cha	30.0	M		N	N	Guam	Guam	Guam	N	Farmer
33	36	36	Rojas, Francisca C	Wife	F	Cha	56.0	M		N	N	Guam	Guam	Guam	N	None
34	36	36	Cruz, Jose	Step-son	M	Cha	16.0	S	N	Y	Y	Guam	Unknown	Guam	N	Farm laborer home farm
35	36	36	Cruz, Jose	Step-son	M	Cha	13.0	S	Y	Y	Y	Guam	Unknown	Guam	Y	None
36	37	37	Bautista, Antonio C	Head	M	Fil	39.0	M		N	N	Guam	Philippine Islands	Guam	N	Farmer
37	37	37	Bautista, Rosa L	Wife	F	Cha	37.0	M		Y	Y	Guam	Guam	Guam	N	None
38	37	37	Bautista, Encarnacion L	Daughter	F	Fil	17.0	S	N	Y	Y	Guam	Guam	Guam	N	None
39	37	37	Bautista, Pedro L	Son	M	Fil	12.0	S	N	Y	Y	Guam	Guam	Guam	Y	None
40	37	37	Bautista, Matias L	Son	M	Fil	10.0	S	N	N	N	Guam	Guam	Guam	N	None
41	37	37	Bautista, Antonio L	Son	M	Fil	7.0	S				Guam	Guam	Guam		None
42	37	37	Bautista, Jesus L	Son	M	Fil	4.0	S				Guam	Guam	Guam		None
43	38	38	Pangelinan, Vicente P	Head	M	Cha	31.0	M		Y	Y	Guam	Unknown	Guam	N	Farmer
44	38	38	Pangelinan, Maria G	Wife	F	Cha	20.0	M	N	N	N	Guam	Guam	Guam	Y	None
45	38	38	Pangelinan, Dolores G	Daughter	F	Cha	1.0	S				Guam	Guam	Guam		None
46	39	39	Quichocho, Concepcion A	Head	F	Cha	32.0	Wd	N	N	N	Guam	Guam	Guam	Y	Farm laborer home farm
47	39	39	Quichocho, Felipe A	Son	M	Cha	17.0	S	N	Y	Y	Guam	Guam	Guam	N	None
48	39	39	Quichocho, Preciosa A	Daughter	F	Cha	14.0	S	N	Y	Y	Guam	Guam	Guam		None
49	39	39	Quichocho, Joaquin A	Son	M	Cha	9.0	S	Y	Y	Y	Guam	Guam	Guam		None
50	39	39	Quichocho, Soledad A	Daughter	F	Cha	4.0	S				Guam	Guam	Guam		None

Sinajana Barrio

(CHAMORRO ROOTS GENEALOGY PROJECT ™ TRANSCRIPTION)
(COMPILED/TRANSCRIBED BY BERNARD T. PUNZALAN / HTTP://WWW.CHAMORROROOTS.COM)

FOURTEENTH CENSUS OF THE UNITED STATES: 1920-POPULATION

ISLAND OF GUAM

DISTRICT 1

NAME OF PLACE Sinajana Barrio

[Proper name and, also, name of class, as city, town, village, barrio, etc]

ENUMERATED BY ME ON THE 24th DAY OF March, 1920

Jose Kamminga ENUMERATOR

	PLACE OF ABODE			NAME	RELATION	PERSONAL DESCRIPTION					EDUCATION			NATIVITY				OCCUPATION
	Street, avenue, road, etc.	Number of dwelling house is order of visitation	Number of family in order of visitation	of each person whose place of abode on January 1, 1920, was in the family. Enter surname, firs, then given name and middle initial. If any. Include every person living on January 1, 1920. Omit children born since January 1, 1920.	Relationship of this Person to the head of the family.	Sex	Color or race	Age at last birthday	Single, married, widowed or divorced	Attended school any time since Sept. 1, 1919	Whether able to read.	Whether able to write.	Place of birth of this person.	Place of birth of father of this person.	Place of birth of mother of this person.	Whether able to speak English.	Trade, profession, or particular kind of work done, as salesman, laborer, clerk, cook, merchant, washerwoman, etc.
	1	2	3	4	5	6	7	8	9	10	11	12	13	14	15	16	17
1	Sinajana Barrio	40	40	Quichocho, Luisa SA	Head	F	Cha	50.0	Wd		Y	N	Guam	Guam	Guam	N	None
2		40	40	Quichocho, Vicente SA	Son	M	Cha	25.0	S		Y	Y	Guam	Guam	Guam	N	Farm laborer home farm
3		40	40	Quichocho, Juan SA	Son	M	Cha	22.0	S		Y	Y	Guam	Guam	Guam	Y	Farm laborer home farm
4		40	40	Quichocho, Manuel SA	Son	M	Cha	20.0	S	N	Y	Y	Guam	Guam	Guam	Y	Farm laborer home farm
5		40	40	Quichocho, Jose SA	Son	M	Cha	19.0	S	N	Y	Y	Guam	Guam	Guam	Y	Farm laborer home farm
6		40	40	San Agustin, Juana	Niece	F	Cha	35.0	S		Y	N	Guam	Unknown	Guam	N	None
7		40	40	San Agustin, Jesus	Grand nephew	M	Cha	6.0	S	N			Guam	Unknown	Guam		None
8				Here ends the enumeration of Sinajana Barrio													
9																	
10																	
11																	
12																	
13																	
14																	
15																	
16																	
17																	
18																	
19																	
20																	
21																	
22																	
23																	
24																	
25																	

(CHAMORRO ROOTS GENEALOGY PROJECT ™ TRANSCRIPTION)
(COMPILED/TRANSCRIBED BY BERNARD T. PUNZALAN / HTTP://WWW.CHAMORROROOTS.COM)
FOURTEENTH CENSUS OF THE UNITED STATES: 1920–POPULATION
ISLAND OF GUAM

DISTRICT 1
NAME OF PLACE Machanao Barrio
[Proper name and, also, name of class, as city, town, village, barrio, etc]

ENUMERATED BY ME ON THE 25th DAY OF March, 1920

Jose Kamminga ENUMERATOR

	PLACE OF ABODE		NAME	RELATION	PERSONAL DESCRIPTION				EDUCATION			NATIVITY				OCCUPATION
Street, avenue, road, etc.	Number of dwelling house in order of visitation	Number of family in order of visitation	of each person whose place of abode on January 1, 1920, was in the family.	Relationship of this Person to the head of the family.	Sex	Color or race	Age at last birthday	Single, married, widowed or divorced	Attended school any time since Sept. 1, 1919	Whether able to read.	Whether able to write.	Place of birth of this person.	Place of birth of father of this person.	Place of birth of mother of this person.	Whether able to speak English.	Trade, profession, or particular kind of work done, as salesman, laborer, clerk, cook, merchant, washerwoman, etc.
1	2	3	4	5	6	7	8	9	10	11	12	13	14	15	16	17
	1	1	Santos, Nicolas S	Head	M	Cha	68.0	M		N	N	Guam	Unknown	Guam	N	Farmer
	1	1	Santos, Ana C	Wife	F	Cha	58.0	M		Y	Y	Guam	Guam	Guam	N	None
	2	2	Manibusan, Jose G	Head	M	Cha	29.0	M		N	N	Guam	Guam	Guam	N	Farmer
	2	2	Manibusan, Juana L	Wife	F	Cha	27.0	M		Y	Y	Guam	Guam	Guam	N	None
	2	2	Manibusan, Veronica L	Daughter	F	Cha	2.0	S				Guam	Guam	Guam		None
	2	2	Manibusan, Jesus L	Son	M	Cha	0.3	S				Guam	Guam	Guam		None
	2	2	Manibusan, Manuel G	Brother	M	Cha	27.0	S		N	N	Guam	Guam	Guam	N	Farm laborer home farm
	3	3	Mendiola, Francisco G	Head	M	Cha	36.0	S		N	N	Guam	Guam	Guam	N	Farmer
	3	3	Blas, Luis C	Servant	M	Cha	20.0	S	N	Y	Y	Guam	Guam	Guam	Y	Farm laborer home farm
	4	4	Camacho, Miguel B	Head	M	Cha	42.0	Wd		N	Y	Guam	Guam	Guam	N	Laborer
	4	4	Camacho, Vicenta B	Daughter	F	Cha	16.0	S	N	Y	Y	Guam	Guam	Guam	Y	None
	4	4	Camacho, Carmen B	Daughter	F	Cha	10.0	S	Y	Y	Y	Guam	Guam	Guam	Y	None
	5	5	Quichocho, Joaquin M	Head	M	Cha	44.0	M		N	Y	Guam	Unknown	Guam	N	Laborer
	6	6	Pablo, Ana V	Head	F	Cha	49.0	Wd		Y	Y	Guam	Unknown	Guam	N	None
	6	6	Pablo, Juan V	Son	M	Cha	25.0	S		Y	Y	Guam	Guam	Guam	Y	Laborer
Machanao Barrio	6	6	Pablo, Maria V	Daughter	F	Cha	22.0	S		Y	Y	Guam	Guam	Guam	Y	Servant
	6	6	Pablo, Dolores V	Daughter	F	Cha	20.0	S	N	Y	Y	Guam	Guam	Guam	N	None
	6	6	Pablo, Antonia V	Daughter	F	Cha	16.0	S	N	Y	Y	Guam	Guam	Guam	N	None
	6	6	Pablo, Natividad V	Daughter	F	Cha	14.0	S	N	Y	Y	Guam	Guam	Guam	N	None
	6	6	Pablo, Concepcion V	Daughter	F	Cha	11.0	S	N	N	N	Guam	Guam	Guam	N	None
	6	6	Pablo, Joaquin V	Son	M	Cha	8.0	S				Guam	Guam	Guam		None
	7	7	Flores, Manuel T	Head	M	Cha	23.0	M		Y	Y	Guam	Guam	Guam	Y	Farmer
	7	7	Flores, Juana A	Wife	F	Cha	21.0	M		Y	Y	Guam	Guam	Guam	Y	None
	7	7	Flores, Vicente A	Son	M	Cha	3.0	S				Guam	Guam	Guam		None
	7	7	Flores, Manuel A	Son	M	Cha	2.0	S				Guam	Guam	Guam		None

(CHAMORRO ROOTS GENEALOGY PROJECT ™ TRANSCRIPTION)
(COMPILED/TRANSCRIBED BY BERNARD T. PUNZALAN / HTTP://WWW.CHAMORROROOTS.COM)

FOURTEENTH CENSUS OF THE UNITED STATES: 1920-POPULATION

ISLAND OF GUAM

DISTRICT **1**

NAME OF PLACE **Machanao Barrio**

[Proper name and, also, name of class, as city, town, village, barrio, etc]

ENUMERATED BY ME ON THE 25th DAY OF <u>March</u>, 1920

Jose Kamminga ENUMERATOR

	PLACE OF ABODE		NAME	RELATION	PERSONAL DESCRIPTION					EDUCATION			NATIVITY				OCCUPATION
Street, avenue, road, etc.	Number of dwelling house is in order of visitation	Number of family in order of visitation	of each person whose place of abode on January 1, 1920, was in the family. Enter surname, firs, then given name and middle initial. If any. Include every person living on January 1, 1920. Omit children born since January 1, 1920.	Relationship of this Person to the head of the family.	Sex	Color or race	Age at last birthday	Single, married, widowed or divorced	Attended school any time since Sept. 1, 1919	Whether able to read.	Whether able to write.	Place of birth of this person.	Place of birth of father of this person.	Place of birth of mother of this person.	Whether able to speak English.	Trade, profession, or particular kind of work done, as salesman, laborer, clerk, cook, merchant, washerwoman, etc.
1	2	3	4	5	6	7	8	9	10	11	12	13	14	15	16	17
26	6	7	Flores, Luis A	Son	M	Cha	0.2	S				Guam	Guam	Guam		None
27	7	8	Camacho, Jose A	Head	M	Cha	30.0	S		N	N	Guam	Guam	Guam	N	Farm laborer
28	8	9	Castro, Fernando A	Head	M	Cha	48.0	M		N	N	Guam	Guam	Guam	N	Farmer
			Here ends the enumeration of Machanao Barrio													
30																
31																
32																
33																
34																
35																
36																
37																
38																
39																
40																
41																
42																
43																
44																
45																
46																
47																
48																
49																
50																

(CHAMORRO ROOTS GENEALOGY PROJECT ™ TRANSCRIPTION)
(COMPILED/TRANSCRIBED BY BERNARD T. PUNZALAN / HTTP://WWW.CHAMORROROOTS.COM)

FOURTEENTH CENSUS OF THE UNITED STATES: 1920-POPULATION

ISLAND OF GUAM

ENUMERATED BY ME ON THE 24th DAY OF March, 1920

Jose Kamminga ENUMERATOR

DISTRICT 1
NAME OF PLACE Agana City

[Proper name and, also, name of class, as city, town, village, barrio, etc]

	PLACE OF ABODE			NAME	RELATION	PERSONAL DESCRIPTION					EDUCATION			NATIVITY				OCCUPATION
Street, avenue, road, etc.	Number of dwelling house is order of visitation	Number of family in order of visitation		of each person whose place of abode on January 1, 1920, was in the family. Enter surname, firs, then given name and middle initial. If any. Include every person living on January 1, 1920. Omit children born since January 1, 1920.	Relationship of this Person to the head of the family.	Sex	Color or race	Age at last birthday	Single, married, widowed or divorced	Attended school any time since Sept. 1, 1919	Whether able to read.	Whether able to write.	Place of birth of this person.	Place of birth of father of this person.	Place of birth of mother of this person.	Whether able to speak English.	Trade, profession, or particular kind of work done, as salesman, laborer, clerk, cook, merchant, washerwoman, etc.
	2	3	4		5	6	7	8	9	10	11	12	13	14	15	16	17
1	1	1		Crisostomo, Joaquin M	Head	M	Cha	45.0	M		Y	Y	Guam	Guam	Guam	Y	Farmer
2	1	1		Crisostomo, Dolores A	Wife	F	Cha	36.0	M		Y	Y	Guam	Guam	Guam	N	None
3	1	1		Crisostomo, Jesus A	Son	M	Cha	14.0	S	Y	Y	Y	Guam	Guam	Guam	Y	None
4	1	1		Crisostomo, Joaquin A	Son	M	Cha	8.0	S	Y			Guam	Guam	Guam		None
5	1	1		Crisostomo, Ana A	Daughter	F	Cha	5.0	S	Y			Guam	Guam	Guam		None
6	1	1		Crisostomo, Catalina A	Daughter	F	Cha	2.0	S	N			Guam	Guam	Guam		None
7	1	1		Aguajlo, Dominga T	Mother-in-law	F	Cha	59.0	S		Y	Y	Guam	Guam	Guam	N	None
8	1	1		Aguajlo, Juan A	Brother-in-law	M	Cha	21.0	S	N	Y	Y	Guam	Unknown	Guam	N	Laborer
9	2	2		Martinez, Jose C	Head	M	Cha	28.0	M		Y	Y	Guam	Guam	Guam	Y	Blacksmith
10	2	2		Martinez, Ana M	Wife	F	Cha	25.0	M		Y	Y	Guam	Guam	Guam	N	None
11	2	2		Martinez, Dolores M	Daughter	F	Cha	7.0	S	N			Guam	Guam	Guam		None
12	2	2		Martinez, Vicente M	Son	M	Cha	6.0	S	N			Guam	Guam	Guam		None
13	2	2		Martinez, Oliva M	Daughter	F	Cha	0.2	S				Guam	Guam	Guam		None
14	2	2		Mendiola, Nieves R	Aunt	F	Cha	46.0	S		Y	N	Guam	Guam	Guam	N	None
15	3	3		Quintanilla, Ramon T	Head	M	Cha	39.0	M		Y	Y	Guam	Guam	Guam	Y	Farmer
16	3	3		Quintanilla, Maria C	Wife	F	Cha	38.0	M		Y	N	Guam	Guam	Guam	N	None
17	3	3		Quintanilla, Juan C	Son	M	Cha	16.0	S	N	Y	Y	Guam	Guam	Guam	N	Farm laborer home farm
18	3	3		Quintanilla, Rosa C	Daughter	F	Cha	13.0	S	Y	Y	Y	Guam	Guam	Guam		None
19	3	3		Quintanilla, Vicente C	Son	M	Cha	11.0	S	Y	Y	Y	Guam	Guam	Guam		None
20	3	3		Quintanilla, Maria C	Daughter	F	Cha	10.0	S	Y	Y	Y	Guam	Guam	Guam		None
21	3	3		Quintanilla, Carlos C	Son	M	Cha	8.0	S	Y	Y	Y	Guam	Guam	Guam		None
22	3	3		Quintanilla, Antonia C	Daughter	F	Cha	6.0	S	N			Guam	Guam	Guam		None
23	3	3		Quintanilla, Carmen C	Daughter	F	Cha	5.0	S	N			Guam	Guam	Guam		None
24	3	3		Quintanilla, Jose C	Son	M	Cha	2.0	S				Guam	Guam	Guam		None
25	3	3		Quintanilla, Emilia C	Daughter	F	Cha	1.0	S				Guam	Guam	Guam		None

Street, avenue, road: Trafalgar Street

(CHAMORRO ROOTS GENEALOGY PROJECT ™ TRANSCRIPTION)
(COMPILED/TRANSCRIBED BY BERNARD T. PUNZALAN / HTTP://WWW.CHAMORROROOTS.COM)
FOURTEENTH CENSUS OF THE UNITED STATES: 1920–POPULATION
ISLAND OF GUAM

ENUMERATED BY ME ON THE 24ᵗʰ DAY OF March, 1920

Jose Kamminga ENUMERATOR

DISTRICT 1
NAME OF PLACE Agana City

[Proper name and, also, name of class, name of city, town, village, barrio, etc]

	Dwelling No. (2)	Family No. (3)	NAME (4)	RELATION (5)	Sex (6)	Color or race (7)	Age (8)	Single, married, widowed or divorced (9)	Attended school since Sept. 1, 1919 (10)	Read (11)	Write (12)	Place of birth of this person (13)	Place of birth of father (14)	Place of birth of mother (15)	Speak English (16)	OCCUPATION (17)
26	4	4	Pangelinan, Vicente S	Head	M	Cha	35.0	S		Y	Y	Guam	Guam	Guam	N	Farmer
27	4	4	Pangelinan, Juan S	Brother	M	Cha	26.0	S		N	N	Guam	Guam	Guam	N	Farm laborer home farm
28	5	5	Quintanilla, Francisco T	Head	M	Cha	26.0	M		Y	Y	Guam	Guam	Guam	Y	Farmer
29	5	5	Quintanilla, Maria M	Wife	F	Cha	21.0	M	N	Y	Y	Guam	Guam	Guam	N	None
30	5	5	Guerrero, Maria B	Grandmother	F	Cha	75.0	Wd		Y	N	Guam	Guam	Guam	N	None
31	6	6	Palomo, Ignacio C	Head	M	Cha	23.0	M		Y	Y	Guam	Guam	Guam	Y	Foreman
32	6	6	Palomo, Maria SM	Wife	F	Cha	24.0	M		Y	Y	Guam	Guam	Guam	Y	None
33	6	6	San Miguel, Ana Q	Sister-in-law	F	Cha	15.0	S	N	Y	Y	Guam	Guam	Guam	Y	None
34	6	6	San Miguel, Manuel Q	Brother-in-law	M	Cha	18.0	S	N	Y	Y	Guam	Guam	Guam	Y	Tiler?
35	6	6	San Miguel, Juan Q	Brother-in-law	M	Cha	16.0	S	N	Y	Y	Guam	Guam	Guam	Y	None
36	6	6	San Miguel, Trinidad Q	Sister-in-law	F	Cha	8.0	S	Y	Y	Y	Guam	Guam	Guam		None
37	7	7	Ascension, Juana B	Head	F	Cha	28.0	Wd		Y	N	Guam	Guam	Guam	N	None
38	8	8	Rosario, Antonio T	Head	M	Cha	20.0	M	N	Y	Y	Guam	Unknown	Guam	Y	Enlisted man USN
39	8	8	Rosario, Soledad SA	Wife	F	Cha	20.0	M	N	Y	Y	Guam	Guam	Guam	N	None
40	8	8	Rosario, Crisy SA	Daughter	F	Cha	0.1	S				Guam	Guam	Guam		None
41	9	9	Garrido, Jose B	Head	M	Cha	41.0	M		Y	Y	Guam	Guam	Guam	N	Carpenter
42	9	9	Garrido, Vicenta T	Wife	F	Cha	44.0	M		Y	Y	Guam	Guam	Guam	N	None
43	9	9	Garrido, Manuel T	Son	M	Cha	18.0	S	N	Y	Y	Guam	Guam	Guam	Y	Laborer
44	9	9	Garrido, Ana T	Daughter	F	Cha	14.0	S	N	Y	Y	Guam	Guam	Guam	N	None
45	9	9	Garrido, Jose T	Son	M	Cha	11.0	S	Y	Y	Y	Guam	Guam	Guam	N	None
46	9	9	Garrido, Jesus T	Son	M	Cha	6.0	S	N			Guam	Guam	Guam		None
47	9	9	Garrido, Maria T	Daughter	F	Cha	3.0	S				Guam	Guam	Guam		None
48	10	10	Santos, Jose S	Head	M	Cha	26.0	M		N	N	Guam	Unknown	Guam	N	Laborer
49	10	10	Santos, Maria B	Wife	F	Cha	24.0	M		Y	Y	Guam	Guam	Guam	Y	None
50	10	10	Santos, Jesus B	Son	M	Cha	1.0	S				Guam	Guam	Guam		None

Street: Trafalgar Street (column 1)

111

(CHAMORRO ROOTS GENEALOGY PROJECT ™ TRANSCRIPTION)
(COMPILED/TRANSCRIBED BY BERNARD T. PUNZALAN / HTTP://WWW.CHAMORROROOTS.COM)

FOURTEENTH CENSUS OF THE UNITED STATES: 1920—POPULATION

ISLAND OF GUAM

54

DISTRICT **1**
NAME OF PLACE **Agana City**
[Proper name and, also, name of class, as city, town, village, barrio, etc]

ENUMERATED BY ME ON THE 26th DAY OF March, 1920

Jose Kamminga ENUMERATOR

	PLACE OF ABODE			NAME	RELATION	PERSONAL DESCRIPTION				EDUCATION			NATIVITY				OCCUPATION
Street, avenue, road, etc.	Number of dwelling house is order of visitation	Number of family in order of visitation		of each person whose place of abode on January 1, 1920, was in the family. Enter surname, firs, then given name and middle initial, if any. Include every person living on January 1, 1920. Omit children born since January 1, 1920.	Relationship of this person to the head of the family.	Sex	Color or race	Age at last birthday	Single, married, widowed or divorced	Attended school any time since Sept. 1, 1919	Whether able to read.	Whether able to write.	Place of birth of this person.	Place of birth of father of this person.	Place of birth of mother of this person.	Whether able to speak English.	Trade, profession, or particular kind of work done, as salesman, laborer, clerk, cook, merchant, washerwoman, etc.
1	2	3		4	5	6	7	8	9	10	11	12	13	14	15	16	17
	11	11	1	Acosta, Pedro A	Head	M	Cha	36.0	M		Y	Y	Guam	Unknown	Guam	N	Farmer
	11	11	2	Acosta, Concepcion R	Wife	F	Cha	40.0	M		Y	Y	Guam	Guam	Philippine Islands	N	None
	12	12	3	Peredo, Jose B	Head	M	Cha	78.0	M		Y	Y	Guam	Guam	Guam	N	None
	12	12	4	Peredo, Dominga T	Wife	F	Cha	43.0	M		Y	Y	Guam	Guam	Guam	N	None
	12	12	5	Peredo, Baldemero T	Son	M	Cha	23.0	S		Y	Y	Guam	Guam	Guam	Y	Laborer
	12	12	6	Peredo, Juana T	Daughter	F	Cha	14.0	S	N	Y	Y	Guam	Guam	Guam	N	None
	12	12	7	Peredo, Jose T	Son	M	Cha	11.0	S	Y	Y	Y	Guam	Guam	Guam	N	None
	12	12	8	Taitinfong, Juana	Mother-in-law	F	Cha	79.0	S		N	N	Guam	Unknown	Guam	N	None
Trafalgar Street	13	13	9	Mendiola, Vicente B	Head	M	Cha	55.0	M		Y	Y	Guam	Guam	Guam	Y	Constable
	13	13	10	Cruz, Maria B	Lodger	F	Cha	52.0	Wd		N	N	Guam	Guam	Guam	N	None
	13	13	11	Cruz, Simon B	Lodger	M	Cha	29.0	Wd		Y	Y	Guam	Guam	Guam	Y	Laborer
	13	13	12	Cruz, Tomas B	Lodger	M	Cha	30.0	S		Y	Y	Guam	Guam	Guam	Y	Farm laborer
	14	14	13	Pinaula, Jose P	Head	M	Cha	40.0	M		Y	Y	Guam	Unknown	Guam	N	Laborer
	14	14	14	Pinaula, Feliciana C	Wife	F	Cha	54.0	M		N	N	Guam	Guam	Guam	N	None
	14	14	15	Cruz, Jose C	Step son	M	Cha	24.0	S		Y	Y	Guam	Unknown	Guam	Y	Laborer
	14	14	16	Cruz, Francisca C	Step daughter	F	Cha	22.0	S		Y	Y	Guam	Unknown	Guam	Y	None
	14	14	17	Cruz, Felix C	Step son	M	Cha	21.0	S	N	Y	Y	Guam	Unknown	Guam	Y	Laborer
	14	14	18	Cruz, Joaquina C	Step daughter	F	Cha	18.0	S	N	Y	Y	Guam	Unknown	Guam	Y	None
	14	14	19	Cruz, Maria C	Step daughter	F	Cha	16.0	S	N	Y	Y	Guam	Unknown	Guam	Y	None
	14	14	20	Pinaula, Antonio C	Son	M	Cha	7.0	S	N			Guam	Guam	Guam	Y	None
	15	15	21	Flores, Pedro G	Head	M	Cha	32.0	M		Y	Y	Guam	Guam	Guam	Y	Farmer
	15	15	22	Flores, Ana B	Wife	F	Cha	33.0	M		Y	Y	Guam	Guam	Guam	N	None
	15	15	23	Flores, Gregorio B	Son	M	Cha	2.0	S				Guam	Guam	Guam		None
	15	15	24	Flores, Francisca B	Daughter	F	Cha	0.2	S				Guam	Guam	Guam		None
	16	16	25	Santos, Felix J	Head	M	Cha	24.0	S		Y	Y	Guam	Guam	Guam	N	Laborer

(CHAMORRO ROOTS GENEALOGY PROJECT ™ TRANSCRIPTION)
(COMPILED/TRANSCRIBED BY BERNARD T. PUNZALAN / HTTP://WWW.CHAMORROROOTS.COM)

FOURTEENTH CENSUS OF THE UNITED STATES: 1920-POPULATION
ISLAND OF GUAM

DISTRICT 1
NAME OF PLACE Agana City

[Proper name and, also, name of class, as city, town, village, barrio, etc]

ENUMERATED BY ME ON THE 26th DAY OF March, 1920

Jose Kamminga ENUMERATOR

	Dwelling No. (2)	Family No. (3)	NAME (4)	RELATION (5)	Sex (6)	Color or race (7)	Age (8)	Marital (9)	School (10)	Read (11)	Write (12)	Birthplace (13)	Father birthplace (14)	Mother birthplace (15)	English (16)	OCCUPATION (17)
26	17	17	Arriola, Ana C	Head	F	Cha	46.0	S				Guam	Unknown	Guam		None
27	18	18	Bautista, Juan C	Head	M	Fil	57.0	M		N	N	Guam	Philippine Islands	Guam	N	None
28	18	18	Bautista, Dolores S	Wife	F	Cha	48.0	M		N	N	Guam	Guam	Guam	N	None
29	18	18	Bautista, Juan S	Son	M	Fil	19.0	S	N	Y	Y	Guam	Guam	Guam	Y	Farm laborer home farm
30	18	18	Bautista, Manuel S	Son	M	Fil	18.0	S	N	Y	Y	Guam	Guam	Guam	Y	Laborer
31	18	18	Bautista, Jose S	Son	M	Fil	15.0	S	N	Y	Y	Guam	Guam	Guam	N	Farm laborer home farm
32	18	18	Bautista, Vicente S	Son	M	Fil	12.0	S	N	Y	Y	Guam	Guam	Guam	N	None
33	18	18	Bautista, Maria S	Daughter	F	Fil	11.0	S	N	Y	N	Guam	Guam	Guam	N	None
34	18	18	Bautista, Andres S	Son	M	Fil	8.0	S	N			Guam	Guam	Guam		None
35	18	18	Bautista, Juan D	Nephew	M	Fil	20.0	S	N	Y	Y	Guam	Guam	Guam	N	Farm laborer
36	19	19	San Agustin, Miguel E	Head	M	Cha	41.0	M		Y	Y	Guam	Guam	Guam	N	Farm laborer
37	19	19	San Agustin, Maria S	Wife	F	Cha	36.0	M		Y	Y	Guam	Unknown	Guam	N	None
38	19	19	San Agustin, Francisco S	Son	M	Cha	19.0	S	N	Y	Y	Guam	Guam	Guam	Y	Mess attendant
39	19	19	San Agustin, Maria S	Daughter	F	Cha	16.0	S	N	Y	Y	Guam	Guam	Guam	N	Laundress
40	19	19	San Agustin, Ramunda S	Daughter	F	Cha	15.0	S	Y	Y	Y	Guam	Guam	Guam	Y	Laundress
41	19	19	San Agustin, Rosa S	Daughter	F	Cha	12.0	S	Y	Y	Y	Guam	Guam	Guam	N	None
42	19	19	San Agustin, Nita S	Daughter	F	Cha	9.0	S	N			Guam	Guam	Guam		None
43	19	19	San Agustin, Isabel S	Daughter	F	Cha	5.0	S				Guam	Guam	Guam		None
44	19	19	San Agustin, Miguel S	Son	M	Cha	1.0	S				Guam	Guam	Guam		None
45	19	19	Salas, Ramunda F	Mother-in-law	F	Cha	60.0	Wd				Guam	Guam	Guam	N	None
46	20	20	Salas, Jose	Head	M	Cha	23.0	M		Y	Y	Guam	Guam	Guam	Y	Draftsman
47	20	20	Salas, Clotilde S	Wife	F	Cha	23.0	M		Y	Y	Guam	Guam	Guam	Y	None
48	20	20	Salas, Elpidia S	Daughter	F	Cha	2.0	S				Guam	Guam	Guam		None
49	20	20	Salas, Concepcion C	Daughter	F	Cha	0.0	S				Guam	Guam	Guam		None
50	20	20	San Nicolas, Maria S	Sister-in-law	F	Cha	19.0	S	N	Y	Y	Guam	Unknown	Guam	Y	None

Street, avenue, road, etc. (column 1): Trafalgar Street

(CHAMORRO ROOTS GENEALOGY PROJECT ™ TRANSCRIPTION)
(COMPILED/TRANSCRIBED BY BERNARD T. PUNZALAN / HTTP://WWW.CHAMORROROOTS.COM)

FOURTEENTH CENSUS OF THE UNITED STATES: 1920—POPULATION

ISLAND OF GUAM

ENUMERATED BY ME ON THE 27th DAY OF March, 1920

Jose Kamminga ENUMERATOR

DISTRICT 1
NAME OF PLACE Agana City
[Proper name and, also, name of class, as city, town, village, barrio, etc]

1	2	3	4 NAME	5 RELATION	6 Sex	7 Color or race	8 Age	9	10	11	12	13	14	15	16 English	17 OCCUPATION
	20	20	San Nicolas, Francisco S	Brother-in-law	M	Cha	12.0	S	Y	Y	Y	Guam	Unknown	Guam	Y	None
	21	21	Gomez, Jesus A	Head	M	Neg ro	27.0	M		Y	Y	Guam	United States	Guam	Y	Farmer
	21	21	Gomez, Maria C	Wife	F	Cha	30.0	M	Y	Y	N	Guam	Guam	Guam	N	None
	21	21	Gomez, Artemio C	Son	M	Neg ro	5.0	S	N			Guam	Guam	Guam		None
	22	22	Pangelinan, Jose G	Head	M	Cha	54.0	M		N	N	Guam	Unknown	Guam	N	Farmer
	22	22	Pangelinan, Dolores Q	Wife	F	Cha	53.0	M		Y	Y	Guam	Unknown	Guam	Y	None
	22	22	Pangelinan, Manuel Q	Son	M	Cha	26.0	S		Y	Y	Guam	Guam	Guam	Y	Laborer
	22	22	Pangelinan, Rita Q	Daughter	F	Cha	22.0	S		Y	Y	Guam	Guam	Guam	N	None
	22	22	Pangelinan, Juan Q	Son	M	Cha	20.0	S	N	Y	Y	Guam	Guam	Guam	Y	Laborer
Trafalgar Street	23	23	Gomez, Silvestre	Head	M	B	65.0	M		Y	Y	United States	United States	United States	Y	None
	23	23	Gomez, Emeteria P	Wife	F	Cha	60.0	M		N	N	Rota Island	Guam	Rota Island	N	None
	23	23	Gomez, Jose S	Son	M	B	20.0	S	N	N	N	Guam	United States	Guam	Y	Farm laborer home farm
	24	24	Ulloa, Mariano C	Head	M	Cha	23.0	M	N	Y	Y	Guam	United States	Guam	Y	Farmer
	24	24	Ulloa, Joaquina C	Wife	F	Cha	20.0	M		Y	Y	Guam	Guam	Guam	Y	None
	24	24	Ulloa, Maria C	Daughter	F	Cha	2.0	S				Guam	Guam	Guam		None
	24	24	Siguenza, Concepcion	Step-mother	F	Cha	57.0	Wd		Y	Y	Guam	Guam	Guam	N	None
	24	24	Tainatongo, Juana	Grandmother	F	Cha	82.0	Wd		Y	N	Guam	Guam	Guam	N	None
	25	25	Santos, Joaquin B	Head	M	Cha	44.0	M		Y	Y	Guam	Guam	Guam	N	Farmer
	25	25	Santos, Ana SN	Wife	F	Cha	55.0	M		Y	N	Guam	Guam	Guam	N	None
	25	25	Benavente, Maria SN	Step daughter	F	Cha	22.0	S		Y	Y	Guam	Guam	Guam	Y	None
	26	26	Rosario, Maria	Head	F	Cha	72.0	Wd		N	N	Guam	Unknown	Guam	N	None
	27	27	Blas, Dolores C	Daughter	F	Cha	38.0	S	N	Y	Y	Guam	Guam	Guam	N	None
	27	27	Blas, Ana C	Daughter	F	Cha	16.0	S	N	N	N	Guam	Guam	Guam	N	None
	27	27	Blas, Francisco C	Son	M	Cha	14.0	S	N	N	N	Guam	Guam	Guam	Y	Farm laborer home farm
	27	27	Blas, Maria	Daughter	F	Cha	10.0	S	N	Y	Y	Guam	Guam	Guam	Y	None

(COMPILED/TRANSCRIBED BY BERNARD T. PUNZALAN / HTTP://WWW.CHAMORROROOTS.COM)
(CHAMORRO ROOTS GENEALOGY PROJECT ™ TRANSCRIPTION)

FOURTEENTH CENSUS OF THE UNITED STATES: 1920-POPULATION
ISLAND OF GUAM

ENUMERATED BY ME ON THE 27th DAY OF March, 1920

Jose Kamminga ENUMERATOR

DISTRICT 1
NAME OF PLACE Agana City
[Proper name and, also, name of class, as city, town, village, barrio, etc]

	PLACE OF ABODE		NAME	RELATION	PERSONAL DESCRIPTION				EDUCATION			NATIVITY				OCCUPATION
Street, avenue, road, etc.	Number of dwelling house in order of visitation	Number of family in order of visitation	of each person whose place of abode on January 1, 1920, was in the family.	Relationship of this Person to the head of the family.	Sex	Color or race	Age at last birthday	Single, married, widowed or divorced	Attended school any time since Sept. 1, 1919	Whether able to read.	Whether able to write.	Place of birth of this person.	Place of birth of father of this person.	Place of birth of mother of this person.	Whether able to speak English.	Trade, profession, or particular kind of work done, as salesman, laborer, clerk, cook, merchant, washerwoman, etc.
1	2	3	4	5	6	7	8	9	10	11	12	13	14	15	16	17
	27	27	Blas, Rita C	Daughter	F	Cha	9.0	S	N			Guam	Guam	Guam		None
	27	27	Blas, Jose C	Son	M	Cha	7.0	S	N			Guam	Guam	Guam		None
	27	27	Blas, Jesus C	Son	M	Cha	5.0	S	N			Guam	Guam	Guam		None
	27	27	Blas, Concepcion C	Daughter	F	Cha	3.0	S				Guam	Guam	Guam		None
	27	27	Blas, Antonio C	Son	M	Cha	1.0	S				Guam	Guam	Guam		None
	28	28	Pablo, Antonio P	Head	M	Cha	38.0	M		Y	Y	Guam	Unknown	Guam	N	Farmer
	28	28	Pablo, Gertrudes B	Wife	F	Cha	35.0	M		N	N	Guam	Guam	Guam	N	None
Trafalgar Street	28	28	Pablo, Jose B	Son	M	Cha	12.0	S	Y	Y	Y	Guam	Guam	Guam	N	None
	28	28	Pablo, Jesus B	Son	M	Cha	10.0	S	Y	N	N	Guam	Guam	Guam		None
	28	28	Pablo, Magdalena B	Daughter	F	Cha	6.0	S	N			Guam	Guam	Guam		None
	28	28	Pablo, Concepcion B	Daughter	F	Cha	2.0	S				Guam	Guam	Guam		None
	29	29	Guerrero, Ignacio C	Head	M	Cha	59.0	M		Y	Y	Guam	Guam	Guam	N	Farmer
	29	29	Guerrero, Maria C	Wife	F	Cha	76.0	M		N	N	Guam	Guam	Guam	N	None
	29	29	Mafnas, Antonia C	Step daughter	F	Cha	49.0	S		Y	N	Guam	Unknown	Guam	N	Laundress
	29	29	Mafnas, Vicente C	Grandson	M	Cha	12.0	S	Y	Y	Y	Guam	Unknown	Rota	Y	None
	30	30	Pablo, Maria	Head	F	Cha	23.0	S		Y	N	Guam	Unknown	Guam	N	None
	30	30	Pablo, Remedios	Daughter	F	Cha	4.0	S				Guam	Unknown	Guam		None
	30	30	Pablo, Maria	Daughter	F	Cha	2.0	S				Guam	Unknown	Guam		None
	31	31	Castro, Santiago C	Head	M	Cha	43.0	M		Y	Y	Guam	Unknown	Guam	Y	None
	31	31	Castro, Dolores M	Wife	F	Cha	43.0	M		Y	Y	Guam	Guam	Guam	N	None
La Corte Street	31	31	Castro, Juan M	Son	M	Cha	14.0	S	N	Y	Y	Guam	Guam	Guam		None
	31	31	Castro, Felecita M	Daughter	F	Cha	11.0	S	N	Y	Y	Guam	Guam	Guam		None
	31	31	Castro, Librada M	Daughter	F	Cha	4.0	S				Guam	Guam	Guam		None
	31	31	Castro, Jose M	Son	M	Cha	2.0	S				Guam	Guam	Guam		None
	31	31	Castro, Maria O	Mother	F	Cha	69.0	S		Y	Y	Guam	Guam	Guam	N	None

(CHAMORRO ROOTS GENEALOGY PROJECT ™ TRANSCRIPTION)
(COMPILED/TRANSCRIBED BY BERNARD T. PUNZALAN / HTTP://WWW.CHAMORROROOTS.COM)

FOURTEENTH CENSUS OF THE UNITED STATES: 1920-POPULATION
ISLAND OF GUAM

DISTRICT **1**
NAME OF PLACE **Agana City**
[Proper name and, also, name of class, as city, town, village, barrio, etc]

ENUMERATED BY ME ON THE 29th DAY OF March, 1920

Jose Kamminga ENUMERATOR

	Street, avenue, road, etc.	Number of dwelling house is order of visitation	Number of family in order of visitation	NAME	RELATION	Sex	Color or race	Age at last birthday	Single, married, widowed or divorced	Attended school any time since Sept. 1, 1919	Whether able to read	Whether able to write	Place of birth of this person	Place of birth of father of this person	Place of birth of mother of this person	Whether able to speak English	OCCUPATION
		2	3	4	5	6	7	8	9	10	11	12	13	14	15	16	17
1		31	31	Cruz, Maria C	Aunt	F	Cha	80.0	Wd		N	N	Guam	Guam	Guam	N	None
2		32	32	Aguajlo, Vicente A	Head	M	Cha	39.0	M		Y	Y	Guam	Unknown	Guam	N	None
3		32	32	Aguajlo, Antonia S	Wife	F	Cha	45.0	M		Y	N	Guam	Guam	Guam	N	None
4		32	32	Aguajlo, Luis S	Son	M	Cha	25.0	S		Y	Y	Guam	Guam	Guam	Y	Chauffeur
5		32	32	Aguajlo, Ana S	Daughter	F	Cha	20.0	S	N	Y	Y	Guam	Guam	Guam	Y	None
6		32	32	Aguajlo, Juan S	Son	M	Cha	15.0	S	N	Y	Y	Guam	Guam	Guam	Y	Laborer
7		32	32	Santos, Isabel	Grand daughter	F	Cha	2.0	S				Guam	Unknown	Guam		None
8		33	33	Bautista, Pablo C	Head	M	Fil	46.0	M		N	N	Guam	Philippine Islands	Guam	N	Ranchero
9		33	33	Bautista, Rosa C	Wife	F	Cha	33.0	M		Y	N	Guam	Unknown	Guam	N	None
10		33	33	Bautista, Ignacio C	Son	M	Fil	14.0	S	N	Y	Y	Guam	Guam	Guam	N	None
11		33	33	Bautista, Maria C	Daughter	F	Fil	9.0	S	N			Guam	Guam	Guam		None
12		33	33	Bautista, Concepcion C	Daughter	F	Fil	7.0	S	N			Guam	Guam	Guam		None
13		33	33	Bautista, Isabel C	Daughter	F	Fil	5.0	S	N			Guam	Guam	Guam		None
14		33	33	Bautista, Enrique C	Son	M	Fil	4.0	S				Guam	Guam	Guam		None
15		33	33	Bautista, Jose C	Son	M	Fil	3.0	S				Guam	Guam	Guam		None
16	La Corte Street	33	33	Bautista, Francisca C	Daughter	F	Fil	1.0	S				Guam	Guam	Guam		None
17		34	34	Concepcion, Ignacia	Head	F	Cha	53.0	Wd		N	N	Guam	Unknown	Guam	N	None
18		34	34	Cruz, Concepcion C	Daughter	F	Cha	25.0	S		Y	Y	Guam	Guam	Guam	N	None
19		34	34	Cruz, Soledad C	Daughter	F	Cha	22.0	S		N	N	Guam	Guam	Guam	N	None
20		34	34	Cruz, Dolores C	Daughter	F	Cha	15.0	S	N	N	N	Guam	Guam	Guam	N	None
21		35	35	Rosario, Pedro A	Head	M	Cha	35.0	M		Y	Y	Guam	Guam	Guam	Y	Policeman
22		35	35	Rosario, Ana T	Wife	F	Cha	47.0	M		Y	Y	Guam	Guam	Guam	N	None
23		35	35	Rosario, Maria T	Daughter	F	Cha	10.0	S	Y	Y	Y	Guam	Guam	Guam	N	None
24		35	35	Rosario, Antonia T	Daughter	F	Cha	9.0	S				Guam	Guam	Guam		None
25		35	35	Rosario, Manuel T	Son	M	Cha	6.0	S				Guam	Guam	Guam		None

(CHAMORRO ROOTS GENEALOGY PROJECT ™ TRANSCRIPTION)
(COMPILED/TRANSCRIBED BY BERNARD T. PUNZALAN / HTTP://WWW.CHAMORROROOTS.COM)
FOURTEENTH CENSUS OF THE UNITED STATES: 1920-POPULATION
ISLAND OF GUAM

DISTRICT 1
NAME OF PLACE Agana City
[Proper name and, also, name of class, as city, town, village, barrio, etc]

ENUMERATED BY ME ON THE 29th DAY OF March, 1920

Jose Kamminga ENUMERATOR

	1	2	3	4	5	6	7	8	9	10	11	12	13	14	15	16	17
	Street, avenue, road, etc.	Number of dwelling house in order of visitation	Number of family in order of visitation	NAME	RELATION	Sex	Color or race	Age at last birthday	Single, married, widowed or divorced	Attended school any time since Sept. 1, 1919	Whether able to read.	Whether able to write.	Place of birth of this person.	Place of birth of father of this person.	Place of birth of mother of this person.	Whether able to speak English.	OCCUPATION
26		35	35	Rosario, Ana T	Daughter	F	Cha	4.0	S				Guam	Guam	Guam		None
27		35	35	Rosario, Rufina T	Daughter	F	Cha	3.0	S				Guam	Guam	Guam		None
28		35	35	Taitinfong, Felix S	Step son	M	Cha	20.0	S	N	N	N	Guam	Unknown	Guam	N	Farm laborer home farm
29		35	35	Taitinfong, Jose S	Step son	M	Cha	17.0	S	N	N	N	Guam	Unknown	Guam	N	Farm laborer home farm
30		35	35	Taitinfong, Joaquin S	Step son	M	Cha	13.0	S	N	N	N	Guam	Guam	Guam	N	Farm laborer home farm
31		36	36	Salas, Consolacion F	Head	F	Cha	35.0	S		N	N	Guam	Guam	Guam	N	None
32		36	36	Fegurgur, Enrique	Son	M	Cha	19.0	S	N	Y	Y	Guam	Unknown	Guam	Y	Farm laborer home farm
33		36	36	Fegurgur, Jose	Son	M	Cha	16.0	S	N	Y	Y	Guam	Unknown	Guam	Y	Laborer
34		36	36	Fegurgur, Teresa	Daughter	F	Cha	8.0	S	N			Guam	Unknown	Guam		None
35		36	36	Fegurgur, Maria	Daughter	F	Cha	5.0	S	N			Guam	Unknown	Guam		None
36	La Corte Street	37	37	Guerrero, Antonia S	Head	F	Cha	54.0	Wd		Y	N	Guam	Unknown	Guam	Y	None
37		37	37	Guerrero, Juan S	Son	M	Cha	31.0	Wd		Y	Y	Guam	Unknown	Guam	Y	Carpenter
38		38	38	Salas, Javier D	Head	M	Cha	45.0	M		Y	Y	Guam	Guam	Guam		Carpenter
39		38	38	Salas, Josefa B	Wife	F	Cha	53.0	M		Y	N	Guam	Unknown	Guam		None
40		38	38	Salas, Maria B	Daughter	F	Cha	20.0	S	N	Y	Y	Guam	Unknown	Guam		None
41		38	38	Salas, Felix B	Son	M	Cha	17.0	S	N	Y	Y	Guam	Guam	Guam		Farm laborer home farm
42		38	38	Salas, Tomasa B	Daughter	F	Cha	15.0	S	N	Y	Y	Guam	Guam	Guam		None
43		38	38	Salas, Ana B	Daughter	F	Cha	11.0	S	N	Y	Y	Guam	Guam	Guam		None
44		39	39	Taitingfong, Teresa T	Head	F	Cha	45.0	S		Y	N	Guam	Guam	Guam	N	Farmer
45		39	39	Taitingfong, Juan T	Son	M	Cha	15.0	S	N	Y	Y	Guam	Guam	Guam	N	Servant
46		39	39	Taitingfong, Pulfiria T	Daughter	F	Cha	7.0	S	Y	Y	Y	Guam	Guam	Guam	Y	None
47		40	40	Quidachay, Vicente A	Head	M	Cha	19.0	S	N	Y	Y	Guam	Guam	Guam	Y	Laborer
48		40	40	Quidachay, Ana A	Sister	F	Cha	16.0	S	N	Y	Y	Guam	Guam	Guam		None
49		40	40	Quidachay, Jesus A	Brother	M	Cha	8.0	S	N			Guam	Guam	Guam		None
50		40	40	Quidachay, Joaquin A	Uncle	M	Cha	40.0	M		N	N	Guam	Guam	Guam	N	Farm laborer

(CHAMORRO ROOTS GENEALOGY PROJECT ™ TRANSCRIPTION)
(COMPILED/TRANSCRIBED BY BERNARD T. PUNZALAN / HTTP://WWW.CHAMORROROOTS.COM)

FOURTEENTH CENSUS OF THE UNITED STATES: 1920-POPULATION
ISLAND OF GUAM

DISTRICT **1**
NAME OF PLACE **Agana City**
[Proper name and, also, name of class, as city, town, village, barrio, etc]

ENUMERATED BY ME ON THE 30th DAY OF March, 1920

Jose Kamminga ENUMERATOR

	Street	Dwelling No. (2)	Family No. (3)	NAME (4)	RELATION (5)	Sex (6)	Color or race (7)	Age (8)	Single, married, widowed or divorced (9)	Attended school since Sept. 1, 1919 (10)	Able to read (11)	Able to write (12)	Birthplace of person (13)	Birthplace of father (14)	Birthplace of mother (15)	Able to speak English (16)	OCCUPATION (17)
1		41	41	Iglesias, Francisco A	Head	M	Cha	45.0	M		Y	N	Guam	Guam	Guam	N	Farmer
2		41	41	Iglesias, Ferina G	Wife	F	Cha	46.0	M		Y	N	Guam	Guam	Guam	N	None
3		41	41	Iglesias, Joaquina G	Daughter	F	Cha	19.0	S	N	Y	Y	Guam	Guam	Guam	N	None
4		41	41	Iglesias, Maria G	Daughter	F	Cha	18.0	S	N	Y	N	Guam	Guam	Guam	N	None
5		41	41	Iglesias, Jose G	Son	M	Cha	14.0	S	N	Y	N	Guam	Guam	Guam	N	None
6		42	42	Rosario, Juan R	Head	M	Cha	32.0	M		Y	Y	Guam	Unknown	Guam	Y	Laborer
7		42	42	Rosario, Ana A	Wife	F	Cha	40.0	M		Y	N	Guam	Unknown	Guam	N	None
8	La Corte Street	43	43	Flores, Ignacio T	Head	M	Cha	34	M		Y	Y	Guam	Guam	Guam	Y	Carpenter
9		43	43	Flores, Rita LG	Wife	F	Cha	35	M		Y	N	Guam	Guam	Guam	N	None
10		43	43	Flores, Benigno LG	Son	M	Cha	9	S	Y			Guam	Guam	Guam		None
11		43	43	Flores, Jose LG	Son	M	Cha	7	S	Y			Guam	Guam	Guam		None
12		43	43	Flores, Vicente LG	Son	M	Cha	5	S	N			Guam	Guam	Guam		None
13		43	43	Flores, Mercedes LG	Daughter	F	Cha	3	S				Guam	Guam	Guam		None
14		43	43	Flores, Filomena LG	Daughter	F	Cha	0.1	S				Guam	Guam	Guam		None
15		44	44	Cruz, Pedro C	Head	M	Cha	48.0	S		Y	Y	Guam	Guam	Guam	N	Farmer
16		44	44	Cruz, Natividad C	Sister	F	Cha	52.0	S		N	N	Guam	Guam	Guam	N	None
17		45	45	Manibusan, Benigno C	Head	M	Cha	29.0	M		Y	Y	Guam	Guam	Guam	Y	Blacksmith
18		45	45	Manibusan, Joaquina B	Wife	F	Cha	24.0	M		Y	N	Guam	Guam	Guam	N	None
19		45	45	Manibusan, Jesus B	Son	M	Cha	3.0	S				Guam	Guam	Guam		None
20		45	45	Manibusan, Juan B	Son	M	Cha	0.0	S				Guam	Guam	Guam		None
21		46	46	Manibusan, Joaquin T	Head	M	Cha	48.0	Wd		Y	Y	Guam	Guam	Guam	N	Farmer
22		46	46	Manibusan, Manuel M	Son	M	Cha	23.0	S		Y	Y	Guam	Guam	Guam	Y	Farm laborer home farm
23		46	46	Manibusan, Jose M	Son	M	Cha	16.0	S	N	Y	Y	Guam	Guam	Guam	Y	Farm laborer home farm
24		46	46	Manibusan, Juan M	Son	M	Cha	15.0	S	N	Y	Y	Guam	Guam	Guam	Y	Farm laborer home farm
25		46	46	Manibusan, Antonio M	Son	M	Cha	13.0	S	Y	Y	Y	Guam	Guam	Guam	Y	Farm laborer home farm

(CHAMORRO ROOTS GENEALOGY PROJECT ™ TRANSCRIPTION)

(COMPILED/TRANSCRIBED BY BERNARD T. PUNZALAN / HTTP://WWW.CHAMORROROOTS.COM)

FOURTEENTH CENSUS OF THE UNITED STATES: 1920—POPULATION

ISLAND OF GUAM

57b

ENUMERATED BY ME ON THE 30th DAY OF March, 1920

Jose Kamminga ENUMERATOR

DISTRICT **1**

NAME OF PLACE **Agana City**

[Proper name and, also, name of class, as city, town, village, barrio, etc]

	Street, avenue, road, etc.	Number of dwelling house in order of visitation	Number of family in order of visitation	NAME	RELATION	Sex	Color or race	Age at last birthday	Single, married, widowed or divorced	Attended school any time since Sept. 1, 1919	Whether able to read	Whether able to write	Place of birth of this person	Place of birth of father of this person	Place of birth of mother of this person	Whether able to speak English	OCCUPATION
	1	2	3	4	5	6	7	8	9	10	11	12	13	14	15	16	17
26		45	46	Manibusan, Maria M	Daughter	F	Cha	12.0	S	N	Y	Y	Guam	Guam	Guam	Y	None
27		45	46	Salas, Juan S	Lodger	M	Cha	25.0	S		Y	Y	Guam	Guam	Guam	Y	Laborer
28		45	46	Salas, Jesus S	Lodger	M	Cha	6.0	S	N			Guam	Guam	Guam		None
29		46	47	Borja, Jose T	Head	M	Cha	39.0	S		Y	Y	Guam	Guam	Guam	N	Shoemaker
30		46	47	Bamba, Carmen B	Boarder	F	Cha	51.0	M		N	N	Saipan	Unknown	Guam	N	None
31		46	47	Bamba, Maria S	Boarder	F	Cha	70.0	Wd		N	N	Guam	Guam	Guam	N	None
32		46	47	Cruz, Gertrudes C	Servant	F	Cha	16.0	S	N	N	N	Guam	Unknown	Guam	N	Servant
33		47	48	San Agustin, Vicente T	Head	M	Cha	61	M		Y	N	Guam	Unknown	Guam	N	None
34		47	48	San Agustin, Juana C	Wife	F	Cha	53	M		Y	N	Guam	Unknown	Guam	N	None
35		47	48	San Agustin, Rosa C	Daughter	F	Cha	31	S		Y	Y	Guam	Guam	Guam	N	None
36		47	48	San Agustin, Ignacio C	Son	M	Cha	20	S	N	Y	Y	Guam	Guam	Guam	Y	Laborer
37		47	48	San Agustin, Joaquin C	Son	M	Cha	17	S	N	Y	Y	Guam	Guam	Guam	Y	Farm laborer home farm
38		47	48	San Agustin, Nicolasa C	Daughter	F	Cha	12	S	N	Y	N	Guam	Guam	Guam	N	None
39		47	48	San Agustin, Jose	Grandson	M	Cha	5.0	S				Guam	Unknown	Guam		None
40	La Corte Street	47	48	San Agustin, Agueda	Grand daughter	F	Cha	1.0	S				Guam	Unknown	Guam		None
41		48	49	Guerrero, Vicente LG	Head	M	Cha	48.0	M		Y	Y	Guam	Guam	Guam	N	Carpenter
42		48	49	Guerrero, Maria C	Wife	F	Cha	33.0	M		Y	Y	Guam	Guam	Guam	N	None
43		48	49	Guerrero, Joaquin C	Son	M	Cha	21.0	S				Guam	Guam	Guam		None
44		48	49	Guerrero, Francisco C	Son	M	Cha	19.0	S				Guam	Guam	Guam		None
45		48	49	Guerrero, Jose B	Son	M	Cha	17.0	S	Y	Y	Y	Guam	Guam	Guam	Y	None
46		48	49	Guerrero, Pedro B	Son	M	Cha	13.0	S	N	Y	Y	Guam	Guam	Guam	N	None
47		48	49	Guerrero, Rosa B	Daughter	F	Cha	11.0	S	Y	Y	Y	Guam	Guam	Guam	N	None
48		48	49	Guerrero, Juan B	Son	M	Cha	8.0	S	Y	N	N	Guam	Guam	Guam	N	None
49		49	50	Cruz, Josefa P	Head	F	Cha	48.0	Wd		N	N	Guam	Guam	Guam	N	None
50		49	50	Cruz, Gertrudes P	Daughter	F	Cha	19.0	S	N	Y	Y	Guam	Guam	Guam	Y	None

119

(CHAMORRO ROOTS GENEALOGY PROJECT ™ TRANSCRIPTION)
(COMPILED/TRANSCRIBED BY BERNARD T. PUNZALAN / HTTP://WWW.CHAMORROROOTS.COM)

FOURTEENTH CENSUS OF THE UNITED STATES: 1920-POPULATION
ISLAND OF GUAM

58

ENUMERATED BY ME ON THE 30th DAY OF March, 1920

Jose Kamminga ENUMERATOR

DISTRICT 1
NAME OF PLACE Agana City

	Dwelling #	Family #	NAME	RELATION	Sex	Color/race	Age	Marital	Attended school since Sept 1, 1919	Able to read	Able to write	Birthplace of person	Birthplace of father	Birthplace of mother	Able to speak English	OCCUPATION
1	49	50	Cruz, Paterno P	Son	M	Cha	18.0	S	N	Y	Y	Guam	Guam	Guam	Y	Laborer
2	49	50	Cruz, Concepcion P	Daughter	F	Cha	14.0	S	N	Y	Y	Guam	Guam	Guam	N	None
3	50	51	Martinez, Teodora V	Head	F	Cha	56.0	Wd		Y	N	Guam	Guam	Guam	N	None
4	50	51	Martinez, Jose V	Son	M	Cha	26.0	S		Y	Y	Guam	Guam	Guam	Y	Farm laborer home farm
5	50	51	Martinez, Dolores V	Daughter	F	Cha	14.0	S	N	Y	Y	Guam	Guam	Guam	Y	None
6	51	52	Benavente, Justo B	Head	M	Cha	46.0	M		Y	N	Guam	Unknown	Unknown	N	Laborer
7	51	52	Benavente, Dolores D	Wife	F	Cha	46.0	M		Y	N	Guam	Guam	Guam	N	None
8	51	52	Benavente, Josefa D	Daughter	F	Cha	3	S				Guam	Guam	Guam		None
9	51	52	San Agustin, Maria D	Step daughter	F	Cha	26	S		Y	Y	Guam	Guam	Guam	N	None
10	51	52	San Agustin, Jesus D	Step son	M	Cha	23	S		Y	Y	Guam	Guam	Guam	Y	Laborer
11	51	52	San Agustin, Jose D	Step son	M	Cha	21	S	N	Y	Y	Guam	Guam	Guam	Y	Farm laborer home farm
12	51	52	San Agustin, Dolores D	Step daughter	F	Cha	13	S	N	Y	Y	Guam	Guam	Guam	N	None
13	51	52	San Agustin, Rosalia D	Step daughter	F	Cha	11	S	Y	Y	Y	Guam	Guam	Guam	N	None
14	51	52	San Agustin, Joaquina D	Grand daughter	F	Cha	4.0	S				Guam	Unknown	Unknown		None
15	51	52	San Agustin, Rosario D	Grand daughter	F	Cha	1.0	S				Guam	Unknown	Unknown		None
16	51	52	San Agustin, Asuncion D	Grand daughter	F	Cha	0.6	S				Guam	Unknown	Unknown		None
17	52	53	Benavente, Ignacio G	Head	M	Cha	46.0	M		Y	N	Guam	Guam	Guam	N	Farmer
18	52	53	Benavente, Carmen L	Wife	F	Fil	43.0	M		Y	Y	Guam	Philippine Islands	Guam	N	None
19	52	53	Benavente, Ana L	Daughter	F	Cha	24.0	S		Y	Y	Guam	Guam	Guam	Y	None
20	52	53	Benavente, Juan L	Son	M	Cha	19.0	S	N	Y	Y	Guam	Guam	Guam	Y	Enlisted man USN
21	52	53	Benavente, Josefa L	Daughter	F	Cha	18.0	S	N	Y	Y	Guam	Guam	Guam	Y	None
22	52	53	Benavente, Jose L	Son	M	Cha	14.0	S	Y	Y	Y	Guam	Guam	Guam	Y	None
23	52	53	Benavente, Jose L jr	Son	M	Cha	11.0	S	Y	Y	Y	Guam	Guam	Guam	Y	None
24	52	53	Benavente, Maria L	Daughter	F	Cha	10.0	S	Y	Y	Y	Guam	Guam	Guam	N	None
25	52	53	Benavente, Carmen G	Sister	F	Cha	50.0	S		N	N	Guam	Guam	Guam	N	Laundress

Street: La Corte Street

(CHAMORRO ROOTS GENEALOGY PROJECT ™ TRANSCRIPTION)
(COMPILED/TRANSCRIBED BY BERNARD T. PUNZALAN / HTTP://WWW.CHAMORROROOTS.COM)

58b

FOURTEENTH CENSUS OF THE UNITED STATES: 1920—POPULATION

ISLAND OF GUAM

DISTRICT 1
NAME OF PLACE Agana City

ENUMERATED BY ME ON THE 31st DAY OF March, 1920

Jose Kamminga ENUMERATOR

	Street	No. dwelling house (2)	No. family (3)	NAME (4)	RELATION (5)	Sex (6)	Color or race (7)	Age (8)	Marital (9)	School (10)	Read (11)	Write (12)	Birthplace person (13)	Birthplace father (14)	Birthplace mother (15)	English (16)	OCCUPATION (17)
26		53	54	Cruz, Juan M	Head	M	Cha	57.0	M		Y	Y	Guam	Guam	Guam	N	Farmer
27		53	54	Cruz, Filomena G	Wife	F	Cha	40.0	M		Y	Y	Guam	Guam	Guam	N	None
28		53	54	Cruz, Jose M	Son	M	Cha	26.0	S		Y	Y	Guam	Guam	Guam	Y	Farm laborer home farm
29		53	54	Cruz, Francisca M	Daughter	F	Cha	15.0	S	N	Y	Y	Guam	Guam	Guam	N	None
30		53	54	Cruz, Vicente M	Son	M	Cha	12.0	S	Y	Y	Y	Guam	Guam	Guam	Y	None
31		54	55	Uson, Ramon	Head	M	Fil	23.0	M		Y	Y	Guam	Philippine Islands	Guam	Y	Harness maker
32		54	55	Uson, Maria A	Wife	F	Cha	26.0	M		Y	Y	Guam	Guam	Guam	Y	Midwife
33		54	55	Uson, Jose A	Son	M	Fil	5.0	S	N			Guam	Guam	Guam	Y	None
34		54	55	Uson, Juan A	Son	M	Fil	0.7	S				Guam	Guam	Guam		None
35	La Corte Street	54	55	Quidachay, Veronica	Servant	F	Cha	23.0	S		Y	N	Guam	Unknown	Guam	Y	Servant
36		54	55	Quidachay, Ramon	Boarder	M	Cha	1.0	S				Guam	Unknown	Guam		None
37		55	56	La Torre, Gregorio A	Head	M	Fil	52.0	M		Y	Y	Guam	Philippine Islands	Guam	N	Farmer
38		55	56	La Torre, Maria C	Wife	F	Cha	55.0	M		Y	N	Guam	Guam	Guam	N	None
39		55	56	La Torre, Jose C	Son	M	Fil	23.0	S	N	Y	Y	Guam	Guam	Guam	Y	Farm laborer home farm
40		55	56	La Torre, Jesus C	Son	M	Fil	21.0	S	N	Y	Y	Guam	Guam	Guam	Y	Enlisted man USN
41		55	56	La Torre, Joaquina C	Daughter	F	Fil	19.0	S	N	Y	Y	Guam	Guam	Guam	Y	None
42		55	56	La Torre, Maria C	Daughter	F	Fil	17.0	S	N	Y	Y	Guam	Guam	Guam	Y	None
43		55	56	La Torre, Consolasion C	Daughter	F	Fil	16.0	S	Y	Y	Y	Guam	Guam	Guam	Y	None
44		55	56	La Torre, Francisco C	Son	M	Cha	10.0	S	Y	Y	Y	Guam	Guam	Guam	N	None
45		55	56	Castro, Ana A	Sister-in-law	F	Cha	57.0	S		Y	N	Guam	Guam	Guam	N	None
46		56	57	Quichocho, Jose Q	Head	M	Cha	40.0	M		Y	Y	Guam	Unknown	Guam	Y	Farmer
47		56	57	Quichocho, Rosa P	Wife	F	Cha	41.0	M		Y	N	Guam	Guam	Guam	N	None
48		56	57	Quichocho, Maria P	Daughter	F	Cha	16.0	S	N	Y	N	Guam	Guam	Guam	Y	None
49		56	57	Nego, Isabel P	Niece	F	Cha	5.0	S	N			Guam	Guam	Guam	Y	None
50		57	58	Sanchez, Pablo A	Head	M	Fil	30.0	M		Y	Y	Guam	Philippine Islands	Philippine Islands	Y	Enlisted man USN

(CHAMORRO ROOTS GENEALOGY PROJECT ™ TRANSCRIPTION)
(COMPILED/TRANSCRIBED BY BERNARD T. PUNZALAN / HTTP://WWW.CHAMORROROOTS.COM)
FOURTEENTH CENSUS OF THE UNITED STATES: 1920-POPULATION
ISLAND OF GUAM

ENUMERATED BY ME ON THE 31st DAY OF March, 1920

Jose Kamminga ENUMERATOR

DISTRICT 1
NAME OF PLACE Agana City

	1	2	3	4 NAME	5 RELATION	6 Sex	7 Color or race	8 Age	9 Marital	10 School	11 Read	12 Write	13 Birthplace	14 Father	15 Mother	16 English	17 OCCUPATION
1		57	58	Sanchez, Ana C	Wife	F	Cha	28.0	M		N	N	Guam	Guam	Guam	N	None
2		57	58	Sanchez, Rosario C	Daughter	F	Fil	10.0	S	Y	Y	Y	Guam	Guam	Guam	Y	None
3		57	58	Sanchez, Micerecordia C	Daughter	F	Fil	8.0	S	Y	Y	Y	Guam	Guam	Guam		None
4		57	58	Sanchez, Engracia C	Daughter	F	Fil	7.0	S	Y			Guam	Guam	Guam		None
5		57	58	Sanchez, Isabel C	Daughter	F	Fil	6.0	S	N			Guam	Guam	Guam		None
6		57	58	Sanchez, Segundo C	Son	M	Fil	1.0	S				Guam	Guam	Guam		None
7		58	59	Iglay, Candido S	Head	M	Fil	60.0	M		Y	Y	Philippine Islands	Philippine Islands	Philippine Islands	Y	Farmer
8		58	59	Sanchez, Eleuteria A	Wife	F	Fil	58.0	M		Y	N	Philippine Islands	Philippine Islands	Philippine Islands	N	None
9		58	59	Sanchez, Josefa A	Daughter	F	Fil	26.0	S		Y	Y	Guam	Philippine Islands	Philippine Islands	Y	Teacher
10		58	60	Sanchez, Simon A	Head	M	Fil	24.0	M		Y	Y	Guam	Philippine Islands	Philippine Islands	Y	Teacher
11		58	60	Sanchez, Antonia C	Wife	F	Fil	20.0	M	N	Y	Y	Guam	Guam	Guam	Y	None
12	La Corte Street	58	60	Sanchez, Julia C	Daughter	F	Fil	2.0	S		Y	Y	Guam	Guam	Guam		None
13		58	60	Sanchez, Adriano C	Son	M	Fil	0.3	S				Guam	Guam	Guam		None
14		58	60	Cruz, Jose G	Cousin	M	Cha	13.0	S	Y	Y	Y	Guam	Guam	Guam	Y	None
15		59	61	San Agustin, Juan C	Head	M	Cha	37.0	M		N	N	Guam	Guam	Guam	Y	Laborer
16		59	61	San Agustin, Maria S	Wife	F	Fil	32.0	M		Y	Y	Guam	Philippine Islands	Philippine Islands	N	None
17		59	61	San Agustin, Vicenta S	Daughter	F	Cha	17.0	S	Y	Y	Y	Guam	Guam	Guam	Y	None
18		59	61	San Agustin, Ramon S	Son	M	Cha	14.0	S	Y	Y	Y	Guam	Guam	Guam	Y	None
19		59	61	San Agustin, Candido S	Son	M	Cha	12.0	S	Y	Y	Y	Guam	Guam	Guam	Y	None
20		59	61	San Agustin, Veronica S	Daughter	F	Cha	10.0	S	Y	Y	Y	Guam	Guam	Guam	Y	None
21		59	61	San Agustin, George S	Son	M	Cha	3.0	S				Guam	Guam	Guam		None
22		60	62	Rosario, Vicente G	Head	M	Cha	44.0	M		Y	Y	Guam	Guam	Guam	N	Farmer
23		60	62	Rosario, Vicenta C	Wife	F	Cha	51.0	M		Y	N	Guam	Guam	Guam	N	None
24		61	63	Camacho, Maria R	Head	F	Cha	53.0	Wd				Guam	Unknown	Guam	N	None
25		61	63	Camacho, Jose R	Son	M	Cha	25.0	S		Y	Y	Guam	Guam	Guam	Y	Farm laborer home farm

122

(CHAMORRO ROOTS GENEALOGY PROJECT ™ TRANSCRIPTION)
(COMPILED/TRANSCRIBED BY BERNARD T. PUNZALAN / HTTP://WWW.CHAMORROROOTS.COM)

FOURTEENTH CENSUS OF THE UNITED STATES: 1920-POPULATION
ISLAND OF GUAM

DISTRICT 1
NAME OF PLACE Agana City

[Proper name and, also, name of class, name of class, as city, town, village, barrio, etc]

ENUMERATED BY ME ON THE 31st DAY OF March, 1920

Jose Kamminga ENUMERATOR

	Street, avenue, road, etc.	Number of dwelling house in order of visitation	Number of family in order of visitation	NAME	RELATION	Sex	Color or race	Age at last birthday	Single, married, widowed or divorced	Attended school any time since Sept. 1, 1919	Whether able to read	Whether able to write	Place of birth of this person	Place of birth of father of this person	Place of birth of mother of this person	Whether able to speak English	OCCUPATION
	1	2	3	4	5	6	7	8	9	10	11	12	13	14	15	16	17
26		61	63	Camacho, Ana R	Daughter	F	Cha	23.0	S		Y	Y	Guam	Guam	Guam	Y	None
27		61	63	Camacho, Juan R	Son	M	Cha	21.0	S	N	Y	Y	Guam	Guam	Guam	Y	Enlisted man USN
28		61	63	Camacho, Pedro R	Son	M	Cha	19.0	S	N	Y	Y	Guam	Guam	Guam	Y	Storekeeper
29		61	63	Camacho, Candelaria R	Daughter	F	Cha	17.0	S	N	Y	Y	Guam	Guam	Guam	Y	None
30		61	64	Guerrero, Jose M	Head	M	Cha	33.0	M		Y	Y	Guam	Guam	Guam	N	Farmer
31		61	64	Guerrero, Antonia R	Wife	F	Cha	30.0	M		Y	Y	Guam	Unknown	Guam	N	None
32		61	64	Guerrero, Dolores R	Daughter	F	Cha	5.0	S	N			Guam	Guam	Guam		None
33		61	64	Guerrero, Maria R	Daughter	F	Cha	4.0	S				Guam	Guam	Guam		None
34	La Corte Street	61	64	Guerrero, Concepcion R	Daughter	F	Cha	1.0	S				Guam	Guam	Guam		None
35		62	65	Quitonguico, Amparo T	Head	F	Cha	32.0	S		Y	N	Guam	Guam	Guam	N	Laundress
36		62	65	Quitonguico, Antonio	Son	M	Cha	14.0	S	N	Y	Y	Guam	Unknown	Guam	Y	Servant
37		62	65	Quitonguico, Concepcion	Daughter	F	Cha	5.0	S	N			Guam	Unknown	Guam		None
38		62	65	Quitonguico, Engracia	Daughter	F	Cha	2.0	S				Guam	Unknown	Guam		None
39		62	65	Quitonguico, Joaquin	Son	M	Cha	0.3	S				Guam	Unknown	Guam		None
40		63	66	Martinez, Vicente C	Head	M	Cha	58.0	M		Y	Y	Guam	Guam	Guam	N	Farmer
41		63	66	Martinez, Carmen V	Wife	F	Cha	40.0	M		Y	Y	Guam	Guam	Guam	N	None
42		63	66	Martinez, Ignacia C	Daughter	F	Cha	26.0	S		Y	Y	Guam	Guam	Guam	Y	None
43		63	66	Martinez, Joaquina C	Daughter	F	Cha	24.0	S		Y	Y	Guam	Guam	Guam	Y	None
44		63	66	Martinez, Carmen C	Daughter	F	Cha	22.0	S		Y	Y	Guam	Guam	Guam	Y	None
45		63	66	Martinez, Mariano C	Son	M	Cha	20.0	S	N	Y	Y	Guam	Guam	Guam	Y	Farm laborer home farm
46		63	66	Martinez, Maria V	Daughter	F	Cha	12.0	S	N	Y	Y	Guam	Guam	Guam	Y	None
47		63	66	Martinez, Rosa V	Daughter	F	Cha	11.0	S	Y	Y	Y	Guam	Guam	Guam	Y	None
48		63	66	Martinez, Isabel V	Daughter	F	Cha	9.0	S	Y	Y	Y	Guam	Guam	Guam	N	None
49		63	66	Martinez, Vicente V	Son	M	Cha	4.0	S				Guam	Guam	Guam		None
50		63	66	Martinez, Francisco V	Son	M	Cha	2.0	S				Guam	Guam	Guam		None

(CHAMORRO ROOTS GENEALOGY PROJECT ™ TRANSCRIPTION)
(COMPILED/TRANSCRIBED BY BERNARD T. PUNZALAN / HTTP://WWW.CHAMORROROOTS.COM)

FOURTEENTH CENSUS OF THE UNITED STATES: 1920–POPULATION

ISLAND OF GUAM

ENUMERATED BY ME ON THE 1st DAY OF April, 1920

Jose Kamminga ENUMERATOR

DISTRICT 1
NAME OF PLACE **Agana City**
[Proper name and, also, name of class, as city, town, village, barrio, etc]

	1	2	3	4 NAME	5 RELATION	6 Sex	7 Color or race	8 Age at last birthday	9 Single, married, widowed or divorced	10 Attended school since Sept. 1, 1919	11 Whether able to read	12 Whether able to write	13 Place of birth of this person	14 Place of birth of father	15 Place of birth of mother	16 Whether able to speak English	17 OCCUPATION
1		63	66	Martinez, Juan V	Son	M	Cha	0.1	S				Guam	Guam	Guam		None
2		63	66	Martinez, Jesus	Grandson	M	Cha	2.0	S				Guam	Guam	Guam		None
3		63	66	Martinez, Marcus C	Brother	M	Cha	44.0	S				Guam	Guam	Guam	N	Farm laborer home farm
4		64	67	Martinez, Jose C	Head	M	Cha	28.0	M		Y	Y	Guam	Guam	Guam	N	Farmer
5		64	67	Martinez, Isabel SA	Wife	F	Cha	22.0	M		Y	Y	Guam	Guam	Guam	N	None
6		64	67	Martinez, Jesus SA	Son	M	Cha	0.8	S				Guam	Guam	Guam		None
7		65	68	Cruz, Juan SA	Head	M	Cha	49.0	M		Y	Y	Guam	Guam	Guam	N	Fisherman
8		65	68	Cruz, Ana G	Wife	F	Cha	48.0	M		Y	N	Guam	Guam	Guam	N	None
9		65	68	Cruz, Ignacio G	Son	M	Cha	20.0	S	N	Y	Y	Guam	Guam	Guam	Y	Farm laborer home farm
10		65	68	Cruz, Pedro G	Son	M	Cha	17.0	S	N	Y	Y	Guam	Guam	Guam	Y	Farm laborer home farm
11		65	68	Cruz, Andrea G	Daughter	F	Cha	14.0	S	N	Y	Y	Guam	Guam	Guam	N	None
12		65	68	Cruz, Juan G	Son	M	Cha	13.0	S	N	Y	Y	Guam	Guam	Guam	N	None
13		65	68	Cruz, Manuel G	Son	M	Cha	11.0	S	Y	Y	Y	Guam	Guam	Guam	N	None
14		65	68	Cruz, Antonio G	Son	M	Cha	6.0	S	N			Guam	Guam	Guam	N	None
15		66	69	Guerrero, Maria B	Head	F	Cha	28.0	S		Y	N	Guam	Guam	Guam	N	None
16		66	69	Bae, Aguida	Daughter	F	Cha	8.0	S	Y			Guam	Unknown	Guam		None
17	La Corte Street	66	69	Torres, Juan LG	Boarder	M	Cha	34.0	S		N	N	Guam	Guam	Guam	N	Farmer
18		67	70	Guerrero, Domingo B	Head	M	Cha	71.0	M		Y	Y	Guam	Guam	Guam	N	Farmer
19		67	70	Guerrero, Nieves LG	Wife	F	Cha	50.0	M		Y	N	Guam	Guam	Guam	N	None
20		67	70	Guerrero, Soledad B	Daughter	F	Cha	45.0	Wd		N	N	Guam	Guam	Guam	N	Laundress
21		67	70	Guerrero, Nicolas B	Son	M	Cha	32.0	D		Y	Y	Guam	Guam	Guam	Y	Farm laborer home farm
22		67	70	Guerrero, Francisco B	Son	M	Cha	26.0	S		Y	Y	Guam	Guam	Guam	Y	Farm laborer home farm
23		67	70	Guerrero, Domingo B	Son	M	Cha	20.0	S	N	Y	Y	Guam	Guam	Guam	Y	Laborer
24		67	70	Guerrero, Maria R	Grand daughter	F	Cha	7.0	S	Y			Guam	Guam	Guam		None
25		67	70	Guerrero, Silvestre R	Grand son	M	Cha	5.0	S	N			Guam	Guam	Guam		None

(CHAMORRO ROOTS GENEALOGY PROJECT ™ TRANSCRIPTION)
(COMPILED/TRANSCRIBED BY BERNARD T. PUNZALAN / HTTP://WWW.CHAMORROROOTS.COM)

FOURTEENTH CENSUS OF THE UNITED STATES: 1920—POPULATION

ISLAND OF GUAM

DISTRICT 1
NAME OF PLACE Agana City
[Proper name and, also, name of class, as city, town, village, barrio, etc]

ENUMERATED BY ME ON THE 1st DAY OF April, 1920

Jose Kamminga ENUMERATOR

	PLACE OF ABODE		NAME	RELATION	PERSONAL DESCRIPTION				EDUCATION			NATIVITY				OCCUPATION
Street, avenue, road, etc.	Number of dwelling house in order of visitation	Number of family in order of visitation	Name of each person	Relationship of this person to the head of the family	Sex	Color or race	Age at last birthday	Single, married, widowed or divorced	Attended any school since Sept. 1, 1919	Whether able to read	Whether able to write	Place of birth of this person	Place of birth of father of this person	Place of birth of mother of this person	Whether able to speak English	Trade, profession, etc.
1	2	3	4	5	6	7	8	9	10	11	12	13	14	15	16	17
	68	71	Rosario, Jose S	Head	M	Cha	58.0	M		Y	Y	Guam	Guam	Guam	Y	Cook
	68	71	Rosario, Dolores A	Wife	F	Cha	52.0	M		Y	N	Guam	Guam	Guam	N	None
	68	71	Rosario, Consuelo A	Daughter	F	Cha	21.0	S	N	Y	Y	Guam	Guam	Guam	Y	None
	68	71	Rosario, Josefina	Daughter	F	Cha	19.0	S	N	Y	Y	Guam	Guam	Guam	Y	None
	68	71	Quitugua, Carmen A	Niece	F	Cha	25.0	S		Y	Y	Guam	Guam	Guam	Y	None
	69	72	Rosario, Dolores M	Head	F	Cha	26.0	Wd			Y	Guam	Unknown	Guam	Y	Dressmaker
	69	72	Rosario, Rosa M	Daughter	F	Cha	5.0	S	N			Guam	Guam	Guam		None
	69	72	Mendiola, Filomena C	Mother	F	Cha	50.0	S		Y	Y	Guam	Guam	Guam	N	Servant
La Corte Street	70	73	Quitugua, Jose Q	Head	M	Cha	36.0	M		Y	N	Guam	Unknown	Guam	Y	Farmer
	70	73	Quitugua, Magdalena I	Wife	F	Cha	34.0	M		Y	Y	Guam	Guam	Guam	Y	None
	70	73	Quitugua, Maria I	Daughter	F	Cha	7.0	S	N	Y		Guam	Guam	Guam		None
	71	74	Rivera, Manuel U	Head	M	Cha	48.0	M		Y	Y	Guam	Guam	Guam	Y	Fireman
	71	74	Rivera, Magdalena B	Wife	F	Cha	45.0	M		Y	N	Guam	Guam	Guam	N	None
	72	75	Ogo, Ramona O	Head	F	Cha	40.0	S		Y	Y	Guam	Unknown	Unknown	Y	Servant
	72	75	Ogo, Dominga O	Daughter	F	Cha	19.0	S	N	Y	Y	Guam	Unknown	Unknown	Y	Nurse
	72	75	Toves, Ana S	Boarder	F	Cha	27.0	S		Y	Y	Guam	Guam	Guam	Y	Laundress
	72	75	Blas, Vicente D	Boarder	M	Cha	44.0	M		Y	Y	Guam	Guam	Guam	N	Laborer
	73	76	Mendiola, Juliana G	Head	F	Cha	59.0	Wd		Y	Y	Guam	Guam	Guam	N	None
	73	76	Mendiola, Jose G	Son	M	Cha	33.0	Wd		Y	Y	Guam	Guam	Guam	Y	Laborer
	73	76	Mendiola, Vicente G	Son	M	Cha	24.0	S		Y	Y	Guam	Guam	Guam	Y	Chauffeur
	73	76	Mendiola, Vicente M	Grandson	M	Cha	8.0	S	Y	Y	Y	Guam	Guam	Guam	Y	None
	73	76	Mendiola, Francisco M	Grandson	M	Cha	3.0	S				Guam	Guam	Guam		None
	73	77	Nenete, Jose C	Head	M	Cha	28.0	M		Y	Y	Guam	Guam	Guam	Y	Farmer
	73	77	Nenete, Grillerma M	Wife	F	Cha	27.0	M		Y	N	Guam	Guam	Guam	Y	None
	73	77	Nenete, Ignacio M	Son	M	Cha	7.0	S	N	Y		Guam	Guam	Guam	N	None

(CHAMORRO ROOTS GENEALOGY PROJECT ™ TRANSCRIPTION)

(COMPILED/TRANSCRIBED BY BERNARD T. PUNZALAN / HTTP://WWW.CHAMORROROOTS.COM)

FOURTEENTH CENSUS OF THE UNITED STATES: 1920-POPULATION

ISLAND OF GUAM

DISTRICT **1**

NAME OF PLACE **Agana City**

[Proper name and, also, name of class, as city, town, village, barrio, etc]

ENUMERATED BY ME ON THE 1st DAY OF April, 1920

Jose Kamminga ENUMERATOR

SHEET NO.
30A

	Street, avenue, road, etc.	Number of dwelling house in order of visitation	Number of family in order of visitation	NAME	RELATION	Sex	Color or race	Age at last birthday	Single, married, widowed or divorced	Attended school any time since Sept. 1, 1919	Whether able to read.	Whether able to write.	Place of birth of this person.	Place of birth of father of this person.	Place of birth of mother of this person.	Whether able to speak English.	OCCUPATION
	1	2	3	4	5	6	7	8	9	10	11	12	13	14	15	16	17
1		73	77	Nenete, Maria M	Daughter	F	Cha	4.0	S				Guam	Guam	Guam		None
2		73	77	Nenete, Rosario M	Daughter	F	Cha	3.0	S				Guam	Guam	Guam		None
3		73	77	Nenete, Jesus M	Son	M	Cha	0.7	S				Guam	Guam	Guam		None
4		74	78	Hernandez, Ignacio E	Head	M	Cha	36.0	M		N	N	Guam	Guam	Guam	N	Farmer
5		74	78	Hernandez, Joaquina B	Wife	F	Cha	49.0	M		Y	Y	Guam	Guam	Guam	N	None
6		74	78	Leon Guerrero, Antonia B	Step daughter	F	Cha	19.0	S	N	Y	Y	Guam	Guam	Guam	Y	Landress
7		74	78	Leon Guerrero, Maria B	Step daughter	F	Cha	15.0	S	N	Y	Y	Guam	Guam	Guam	Y	Servant
8		74	78	Hernandez, Jose B	Son	M	Cha	9.0	S	N	Y	Y	Guam	Guam	Guam		None
9		74	78	Hernandez, Jesus B	Son	M	Cha	7.0	S	N	Y	Y	Guam	Guam	Guam		None
10		74	79	Leon Guerrero, Vicente B	Head	M	Cha	21.0	M	N	Y	Y	Guam	Guam	Guam	Y	Laborer
11		74	79	Leon Guerrero, Maria C	Wife	F	Cha	17.0	M	N	Y	Y	Guam	Guam	Guam	N	None
12		75	80	Torres, Eduviges E	Head	F	Cha	45.0	D		Y	Y	Guam	Guam	Guam	N	None
13		75	80	Cruz, Josefa A	Servant	F	Cha	41.0	S		N	N	Guam	Guam	Guam	N	Servant
14		76	81	Rivera, Jose U	Head	M	Cha	38.0	M		Y	Y	Guam	Guam	Guam	Y	Fireman
15		76	81	Rivera, Carmen A	Wife	F	Cha	34.0	M		Y	Y	Guam	Unknown	Guam	N	None
16		76	81	Rivera, Maria A	Daughter	F	Cha	12.0	S	N	Y	Y	Guam	Guam	Guam	N	None
17		76	81	Rivera, Asuncion A	Daughter	F	Cha	7.0	S	N			Guam	Guam	Guam	N	None
18		76	81	Rivera, Juana A	Daughter	F	Cha	3.0	S				Guam	Guam	Guam		None
19		76	81	Rivera, Luisa A	Daughter	F	Cha	3.0	S				Guam	Guam	Guam		None
20		76	81	Rivera, Josefa A	Daughter	F	Cha	1.0	S				Guam	Guam	Guam		None
21		77	82	Cruz, Jose G	Head	M	Cha	31.0	M		Y	Y	Guam	Guam	Guam	Y	Farmer
22		77	82	Cruz, Maria C	Wife	F	Cha	28.0	M		Y	Y	Guam	Unknown	Guam	N	None
23		77	82	Cruz, Jose C	Son	M	Cha	9.0	S	Y			Guam	Guam	Guam		None
24		77	82	Cruz, Fermina C	Daughter	F	Cha	7.0	S	Y			Guam	Guam	Guam		None
25		77	82	Cruz, Jesus	Son	M	Cha	5.0	S	N			Guam	Guam	Guam		None

(Street column, left margin: La Corte Street)

(CHAMORRO ROOTS GENEALOGY PROJECT ™ TRANSCRIPTION)
(COMPILED/TRANSCRIBED BY BERNARD T. PUNZALAN / HTTP://WWW.CHAMORROROOTS.COM)

FOURTEENTH CENSUS OF THE UNITED STATES: 1920-POPULATION

ISLAND OF GUAM

DISTRICT 1
NAME OF PLACE **Agana City**

[Proper name and, also, name of class, as city, town, village, barrio, etc]

ENUMERATED BY ME ON THE 2nd DAY OF April, 1920

Jose Kamminga ENUMERATOR

SHEET NO. 30B

	Street, avenue, road, etc.	Number of dwelling house in order of visitation	Number of family in order of visitation	NAME	RELATION	Sex	Color or race	Age at last birthday	Single, married, widowed or divorced	Attended school any time since Sept. 1, 1919	Whether able to read.	Whether able to write.	Place of birth of this person.	Place of birth of father of this person.	Place of birth of mother of this person.	Whether able to speak English.	OCCUPATION
	1	2	3	4	5	6	7	8	9	10	11	12	13	14	15	16	17
26		77	82	Cruz, Francisco C	Son	M	Cha	3.0	S				Guam	Guam	Guam		None
27		77	82	Cruz, Maria C	Daughter	F	Cha	1.0	S				Guam	Guam	Guam		None
28		78	83	Cruz, Antonio G	Head	M	Cha	29.0	M		Y	N	Guam	Guam	Guam	N	Farmer
29		78	83	Cruz, Ana B	Wife	F	Cha	26.0	M		Y	N	Guam	Unknown	Guam	N	None
30		78	83	Cruz, Antonio B	Son	M	Cha	6.0	S	N			Guam	Guam	Guam		None
31		78	83	Cruz, Maria B	Daughter	F	Cha	5.0	S	N			Guam	Guam	Guam		None
32		78	83	Cruz, Jose B	Son	M	Cha	3.0	S				Guam	Guam	Guam		None
33		78	83	Cruz, Feliciana B	Daughter	F	Cha	1.0	S				Guam	Guam	Guam		None
34		78	83	Bautista, Francisco B	Brother-in-law	M	Cha	27.0	S		Y	N	Guam	Unknown	Guam	N	Farm laborer home farm
35		79	84	Guerrero, Manuel C	Head	M	Cha	55.0	M		Y	N	Guam	Guam	Guam	N	Farmer
36		79	84	Guerrero, Dolores M	Wife	F	Cha	53.0	M		Y	N	Guam	Guam	Guam	N	None
37		79	84	Guerrero, Maria M	Daughter	F	Cha	29.0	S		Y	Y	Guam	Guam	Guam	N	Laundress
38		79	84	Guerrero, Josefa M	Daughter	F	Cha	22.0	S		Y	Y	Guam	Guam	Guam	N	Laundress
39		79	84	Guerrero, Soledad M	Daughter	F	Cha	21.0	S	N	Y	Y	Guam	Guam	Guam	N	Laundress
40		79	84	Guerrero, Ana M	Daughter	F	Cha	16.0	S	N	Y	Y	Guam	Guam	Guam	Y	None
41		79	84	Guerrero, Jesus M	Son	M	Cha	11.0	S	Y	Y	Y	Guam	Guam	Guam	Y	None
42	La Corte Street	79	84	Guerrero, Nicolas M	Son	M	Cha	26.0	S		Y	Y	Guam	Guam	Guam	Y	Farm laborer home farm
43		80	85	Borja, Vicente I	Head	M	Cha	47.0	Wd		Y	Y	Guam	Guam	Guam	Y	Farmer
44		80	85	Borja, Joaquina C	Daughter	F	Cha	13.0	S	N	Y	Y	Guam	Guam	Guam	N	None
45		80	85	Borja, Juan C	Son	M	Cha	11.0	S	N	N	N	Guam	Guam	Guam	N	None
46		80	85	Borja, Paulina C	Daughter	F	Cha	9.0	S	Y			Guam	Guam	Guam		None
47		80	85	Borja, Pedro C	Son	M	Cha	7.0	S	Y			Guam	Guam	Guam		None
48		80	85	Borja, Maria C	Daughter	F	Cha	5.0	S	N			Guam	Guam	Guam		None
49		81	86	Sablan, Vicente G	Head	M	Cha	78.0	M		Y	Y	Guam	Guam	Guam	N	None
50		81	86	Sablan, Vicenta D	Wife	F	Cha	73.0	M		Y	Y	Guam	Guam	Guam	N	None

(CHAMORRO ROOTS GENEALOGY PROJECT ™ TRANSCRIPTION)
(COMPILED/TRANSCRIBED BY BERNARD T. PUNZALAN / HTTP://WWW.CHAMORROROOTS.COM)
FOURTEENTH CENSUS OF THE UNITED STATES: 1920-POPULATION
ISLAND OF GUAM

ENUMERATED BY ME ON THE 2nd DAY OF April, 1920

Jose Kamminga ENUMERATOR

DISTRICT 1
NAME OF PLACE Agana City
[Proper name and, also, name of class, as city, town, village, barrio, etc]

	Street	Dwelling No. (2)	Family No. (3)	NAME (4)	RELATION (5)	Sex (6)	Color or race (7)	Age (8)	Single, married, widowed or divorced (9)	Attended school since Sept. 1, 1919 (10)	Able to read (11)	Able to write (12)	Birthplace of person (13)	Birthplace of father (14)	Birthplace of mother (15)	Speak English (16)	OCCUPATION (17)
1		81	86	Sablan, Josefa D	Daughter	F	Cha	51.0	S		Y	Y	Guam	Guam	Guam	N	None
2		81	86	Sablan, Feliza D	Daughter	F	Cha	47.0	S		Y	Y	Guam	Guam	Guam	N	Laundress
3		81	86	Sablan, Dolores D	Daughter	F	Cha	44.0	S		Y	Y	Guam	Guam	Guam	N	None
4		82	87	Pablo, Joaquin P	Head	M	Cha	32.0	M		N	N	Guam	Unknown	Guam	Y	Laborer
5		82	87	Pablo, Antonia C	Wife	F	Cha	37.0	M		N	N	Guam	Guam	Guam	N	None
6		82	87	Pablo, Maria C	Daughter	F	Cha	9.0	S	Y			Guam	Guam	Guam	N	None
7		82	87	Pablo, Juan C	Son	M	Cha	6.0	S	N			Guam	Guam	Guam	N	None
8		82	87	Cruz, Manuela C	Step daughter	F	Cha	17.0	S	N	Y	Y	Guam	Unknown	Guam	Y	None
9		83	88	Duenas, Julian M	Head	M	Cha	56.0	Wd		N	Y	Guam	Guam	Guam	N	Chauffeur
10		83	88	Duenas, Manuel Q	Son	M	Cha	29.0	S		Y	Y	Guam	Guam	Guam	Y	Farm laborer home farm
11	La Corte Street	83	88	Duenas, Ramon Q	Son	M	Cha	28.0	S		Y	Y	Guam	Guam	Guam	Y	Farm laborer home farm
12		83	88	Duenas, Florencio Q	Son	M	Cha	26.0	S		Y	Y	Guam	Guam	Guam	Y	None
13		83	88	Duenas, Magdalena Q	Daughter	F	Cha	25.0	S		Y	Y	Guam	Guam	Guam	Y	Farm laborer home farm
14		83	88	Duenas, Juan Q	Son	M	Cha	23.0	S		Y	Y	Guam	Guam	Guam	Y	Farm laborer home farm
15		83	88	Duenas, Jose Q	Son	M	Cha	21.0	S	N	Y	Y	Guam	Guam	Guam	Y	None
16		83	88	Duenas, Maria Q	Daughter	F	Cha	20.0	S	N	Y	Y	Guam	Guam	Guam	Y	None
17		83	88	Duenas, Jesus Q	Son	M	Cha	17.0	S	N	Y	Y	Guam	Guam	Guam	Y	None
18		83	88	Duenas, Joaquin Q	Son	M	Cha	16.0	S	N	Y	Y	Guam	Guam	Guam	Y	None
19		83	88	Duenas, Ana Q	Daughter	F	Cha	13.0	S	N	Y	Y	Guam	Guam	Guam	Y	None
20		83	88	Duenas, Francisco Q	Son	M	Cha	12.0	S	N	Y	Y	Guam	Guam	Guam	Y	None
21		83	88	Duenas, Manuel L	Son	M	Cha	40.0	S		N	N	Guam	Guam	Guam	N	None
22		84	89	Rosario, Juliana B	Head	F	Cha	57.0	M		Y	N	Guam	Guam	Guam	N	None
23		84	89	Rosario, Vicente B	Son	M	Cha	18.0	S	N	Y	Y	Guam	Guam	Guam	Y	Machinist
24		84	89	Rosario, Ignacia B	Cousin	F	Cha	85.0	Wd		N	N	Guam	Guam	Guam	N	None
25		85	90	Acosta, Justo U	Head	M	Cha	65.0	M		Y	Y	Guam	Guam	Guam	N	Farmer

62b

(CHAMORRO ROOTS GENEALOGY PROJECT™ TRANSCRIPTION)
(COMPILED/TRANSCRIBED BY BERNARD T. PUNZALAN / HTTP://WWW.CHAMORROROOTS.COM)

FOURTEENTH CENSUS OF THE UNITED STATES: 1920—POPULATION
ISLAND OF GUAM

DISTRICT 1
NAME OF PLACE Agana City

[Proper name and, also, name of class, as city, town, village, barrio, etc]

ENUMERATED BY ME ON THE 3rd DAY OF April, 1920

Jose Kamminga ENUMERATOR

Street	Dwelling No.	Family No.	NAME	RELATION	Sex	Color or race	Age	Marital	Attended school since Sept. 1, 1919	Read	Write	Birthplace of person	Birthplace of father	Birthplace of mother	English	OCCUPATION
	85	90	Acosta, Antonia R	Wife	F	Cha	70.0	M		Y	Y	Guam	Guam	Guam	N	Teacher parochial school
	86	91	Benavente, Ana R	Head	F	Cha	60.0	Wd		N	N	Guam	Guam	Guam	N	None
	86	91	Benavente, Juan R	Son	M	Cha	26.0	S		N	N	Guam	Guam	Guam	N	Farm laborer home farm
	86	91	Benavente, Enrique R	Son	M	Cha	20.0	S	N	Y	Y	Guam	Guam	Guam	N	Laborer
	87	92	Carlos, Vicente M	Head	M	Fil	70.0	M		Y	Y	Philippine Islands	Philippine Islands	Philippine Islands	N	Farmer
	87	92	Carlos, Maria P	Wife	F	Cha	56.0	M		N	N	Guam	Guam	Guam	N	None
	87	93	Delgado, Francisco M	Head	M	Cha	24.0	S		Y	Y	Guam	Unknown	Guam	N	Laborer
	87	93	Taitano, Trinidad F	Boarder	F	Cha	25.0	M		Y	N	Guam	Guam	Guam	N	None
	87	93	Delgado, Inacensio M	Son	M	Cha	0.2	S				Guam	Guam	Guam		None
La Corte Street	87	93	San Nicolas, Adela F	Boarder	F	Cha	5.0	S	N			Guam	Guam	Guam		None
	88	94	Flores, Francisca G	Head	F	Cha	37.0	S		Y	Y	Guam	Guam	Guam	N	Laundress
	88	94	Flores, Antonia G	Sister	F	Cha	25.0	S		Y	Y	Guam	Guam	Guam	Y	None
	89	95	Payne, Ana A	Head	F	Cha	41.0	M		Y	Y	Guam	Guam	Guam	Y	Laundress
	89	95	Payne, Patrick A	Son	M	Cha	16.0	S	N	Y	Y	Guam	Guam	Guam	Y	None
	90	96	Taijito, Mamerto	Head	M	Cha	38.0	M		Y	Y	Guam	Unknown	Guam	N	Farmer
	90	96	Taijito, Ana B	Wife	F	Cha	32.0	M		Y	Y	Guam	Guam	Guam	N	None
	90	96	Taijito, Selistina B	Daughter	F	Cha	3.0	S				Guam	Guam	Guam		None
	90	96	Taijito, Maria B	Daughter	F	Cha	2.0	S				Guam	Guam	Guam		None
	90	96	Benavente, Maria M	Sister-in-law	F	Cha	27.0	S		Y	Y	Guam	Guam	Guam	N	None
	90	96	Benavente, Gabriela M	Sister-in-law	F	Cha	39.0	Wd		Y	N	Guam	Guam	Guam	N	None
	91	97	Perez, Mariano T	Head	M	Cha	40.0	M		Y	Y	Guam	Guam	Guam	N	Farmer
	91	97	Perez, Maria S	Wife	F	Cha	53.0	M		N	Y	Guam	Guam	Guam	N	None
	91	97	Quidachay, Antonia S	Boarder	F	Cha	5.0	S	N			Guam	Guam	Guam		None
	92	98	Tainatongo, Vicente	Head	M	Cha	42.0	M		Y	Y	Guam	Unknown	Guam	N	Farmer
	92	98	Tainatongo, Maria D	Wife	F	Cha	45.0	M		Y	Y	Guam	Guam	Guam	N	None

(CHAMORRO ROOTS GENEALOGY PROJECT ™ TRANSCRIPTION)
(COMPILED/TRANSCRIBED BY BERNARD T. PUNZALAN / HTTP://WWW.CHAMORROROOTS.COM)

FOURTEENTH CENSUS OF THE UNITED STATES: 1920-POPULATION

ISLAND OF GUAM

63

SHEET NO. 32A

DISTRICT 1

NAME OF PLACE Agana City

[Proper name and, also, name of class, as city, town, village, barrio, etc]

ENUMERATED BY ME ON THE 3rd DAY OF April, 1920

Jose Kamminga ENUMERATOR

Street, avenue, road, etc.	Number of dwelling house	Number of family in order of visitation	NAME	RELATION	Sex	Color or race	Age at last birthday	Single, married, widowed or divorced	Attended school any time since Sept. 1, 1919	Whether able to read	Whether able to write	Place of birth of this person	Place of birth of father of this person	Place of birth of mother of this person	Whether able to speak English	OCCUPATION
1	2	3	4	5	6	7	8	9	10	11	12	13	14	15	16	17
	92	98	Dydasco, Vicenta	Step daughter	F	Cha	18.0	S	N	Y	Y	Guam	Unknown	Guam	Y	None
	93	99	Perez, Vicente B	Head	M	Cha	66.0	M		Y	Y	Guam	Guam	Guam	N	None
	93	99	Perez, Josefa S	Wife	F	Cha	72.0	M		Y	Y	Guam	Guam	Guam	N	None
	93	99	Camacho, Concepcion C	Boarder	F	Cha	7.0	S	Y	Y	Y	Guam	Unknown	Guam	N	None
	93	100	Asuncion, Vicente B	Head	M	Cha	64.0	M		Y	Y	Guam	Guam	Guam	N	Farmer
	93	100	Perez, Nieves B	Wife	F	Cha	70.0	M		Y	N	Guam	Guam	Guam	N	None
	93	100	Chargualaf, Josefa S	Servant	F	Cha	13.0	S	N	Y	Y	Guam	Guam	Guam	N	None
	94	101	Jesus, Lucas F	Head	M	Cha	36.0	M		Y	N	Guam	Guam	Guam	Y	Farmer
	94	101	Jesus, Maria C	Wife	F	Cha	51.0	M		Y	N	Guam	Guam	Guam	N	None
La Corte Street	94	101	Cruz, Manuel V	Father-in-law	M	Cha	78.0	Wd		Y	Y	Guam	Guam	Guam	N	None
	94	101	Cruz, Juan V	Aunt	F	Cha	73.0	Wd		Y	N	Guam	Guam	Guam	N	None
	94	101	Cruz, Teresa	Niece	F	Cha	3.0	S				Guam	Unknown	Guam	N	None
	94	102	Cruz, Redosindo A	Head	M	Cha	43.0	M	N	N	N	Guam	Guam	Guam	N	Farm laborer
	94	102	Cruz, Ana L	Wife	F	Cha	45.0	M		N	N	Guam	Guam	Guam	N	None
	94	102	Cruz, Antonia L	Daughter	F	Cha	15.0	S	N	Y	Y	Guam	Guam	Guam	N	None
	94	102	Cruz, Juan L	Son	M	Cha	14.0	S	N	Y	Y	Guam	Guam	Guam	Y	Servant
	94	103	Cruz, Jose A	Head	M	Cha	37.0	M		Y	Y	Guam	Guam	Guam	N	Farm laborer
	94	103	Cruz, Ana A	Wife	F	Cha	25.0	M		Y	Y	Guam	Unknown	Guam	N	None
	94	103	Cruz, Vicente A	Son	M	Cha	2.0	S				Guam	Guam	Guam		None
	94	103	Cruz, Francisco A	Son	M	Cha	1.0	S				Guam	Guam	Guam		None
	95	104	Cruz, Pedro G	Head	M	Cha	39.0	M		Y	Y	Guam	Guam	Guam	N	Farmer
	95	104	Cruz, Maria H	Wife	F	Cha	37.0	M		Y	Y	Guam	Guam	Guam	N	None
	95	104	Cruz, Maria H	Daughter	F	Cha	17.0	S	N	Y	Y	Guam	Guam	Guam	Y	None
	95	104	Cruz, Elena H	Daughter	F	Cha	14.0	S	N	Y	Y	Guam	Guam	Guam	Y	None
	95	104	Cruz, Rosario H	Daughter	F	Cha	8.0	S	Y	Y	Y	Guam	Guam	Guam		None

(CHAMORRO ROOTS GENEALOGY PROJECT ™ TRANSCRIPTION)
(COMPILED/TRANSCRIBED BY BERNARD T. PUNZALAN / HTTP://WWW.CHAMORROROOTS.COM)

FOURTEENTH CENSUS OF THE UNITED STATES: 1920–POPULATION
ISLAND OF GUAM

DISTRICT **1**
NAME OF PLACE **Agana City**
[Proper name and, also, name of class, as city, town, village, barrio, etc]

ENUMERATED BY ME ON THE 3rd DAY OF April, 1920

Jose Kamminga ENUMERATOR

	Street, avenue, road, etc.	Number of dwelling house in order of visitation	Number of family in order of visitation	NAME	RELATION	Sex	Color or race	Age at last birthday	Single, married, widowed or divorced	Attended school any time since sept. 1, 1919	Whether able to read.	Whether able to write.	Place of birth of this person.	Place of birth of father of this person.	Place of birth of mother of this person.	Whether able to speak English.	OCCUPATION
	1	2	3	4	5	6	7	8	9	10	11	12	13	14	15	16	17
26	Str.	95	104	Cruz, Pedro H	Son	M	Cha	2.0	S				Guam	Guam	Guam		None
27		95	104	Cruz, Ignacia H	Daughter	F	Cha	0.5	S				Guam	Guam	Guam		None
28		96	105	Camacho, Antonia B	Head	F	Cha	56.0	Wd		Y	Y	Guam	Guam	Guam	N	None
29		96	105	Camacho, Teresa B	Daughter	F	Cha	31.0	D		Y	N	Guam	Guam	Guam	N	Laundress
30		96	105	Camacho, Juan B	Son	M	Cha	30.0	S		Y	Y	Guam	Guam	Guam	N	Laborer
31		96	105	Camacho, Cristina B	Daughter	F	Cha	24.0	S		Y	Y	Guam	Guam	Guam	Y	None
32		96	105	Camacho, Jesus	Grandson	M	Cha	6.0	S	N			Guam	Unknown	Unknown		None
33		96	105	Camacho, Geronimo	Grandson	M	Cha	2.0	S				Guam	Unknown	Unknown		None
34		96	105	Camacho, Silvestre	Grandson	M	Cha	0.0	S				Guam	Unknown	Guam		None
35		96	105	Concepcion, Maria C	Grand daughter	F	Cha	7.0	S	N			Guam	Guam	Guam		None
36		96	105	San Nicolas, Lusiano C	Boarder	M	Cha	24.0	S		N	N	Guam	Guam	Guam	N	Laborer
37		97	106	Rivera, Ignacio U	Head	M	Cha	43.0	M		Y	Y	Guam	Guam	Guam	Y	Machinist
38		97	106	Rivera, Maria SN	Wife	F	Cha	39.0	M		Y	Y	Guam	Unknown	Guam	N	None
39		97	106	Rivera, Manuel SN	Son	M	Cha	17.0	S	N	Y	Y	Guam	Guam	Guam	Y	Farm laborer home farm
40		97	106	Rivera, Juan SN	Son	M	Cha	13.0	S	N	Y	Y	Guam	Guam	Guam	Y	Farm laborer home farm
41		97	106	Rivera, Joaquin SN	Son	M	Cha	10.0	S	Y			Guam	Guam	Guam		None
42		97	106	Rivera, Maria SN	Daughter	F	Cha	8.0	S	N			Guam	Guam	Guam		None
43		97	106	Rivera, Ignacio SN	Son	M	Cha	6.0	S				Guam	Guam	Guam		None
44		97	106	Rivera, Gonzalo SN	Son	M	Cha	3.0	S				Guam	Guam	Guam		None
45		97	106	Rivera, Miguel SN	Son	M	Cha	0.0	S				Guam	Guam	Guam		None
46		97	106	San Nicolas, Benita B	Mother-in-law	F	Cha	54.0	S		Y	Y	Guam	Guam	Guam	N	None
47		98	107	Castro, Vicente I	Head	M	Cha	52.0	M		Y	Y	Guam	Guam	Guam	Y	Laborer
48		98	107	Castro, Maria F	Wife	F	Cha	48.0	M		Y	N	Guam	Guam	Guam	N	None
49		98	107	Castro, Francisco F	Son	M	Cha	22.0	S		Y	Y	Guam	Guam	Guam	Y	Servant
50		98	107	Castro, Soledad F	Daughter	F	Cha	13.0	S	N	Y	Y	Guam	Guam	Guam	N	None

San Victores Street

131

(CHAMORRO ROOTS GENEALOGY PROJECT ™ TRANSCRIPTION)
(COMPILED/TRANSCRIBED BY BERNARD T. PUNZALAN / HTTP://WWW.CHAMORROROOTS.COM)
FOURTEENTH CENSUS OF THE UNITED STATES: 1920—POPULATION
ISLAND OF GUAM

DISTRICT 1
NAME OF PLACE Agana City

ENUMERATED BY ME ON THE 5th DAY OF April, 1920

Jose Kamminga ENUMERATOR

1	2	3	4 NAME	5 RELATION	6 Sex	7 Color or race	8 Age at last birthday	9 Single, married, widowed or divorced	10 Attended school any time since Sept. 1, 1919	11 Whether able to read	12 Whether able to write	13 Place of birth of this person	14 Place of birth of father of this person	15 Place of birth of mother of this person	16 Whether able to speak English	17 OCCUPATION
1	99	108	Yamasaki, Bonsuro	Head	M	Jp	37.0	M		Y	Y	Japan	Japan	Japan	N	Farm laborer
2	99	108	Yamasaki, Pilar T	Wife	F	Cha	24.0	M		Y	Y	Guam	Unknown	Guam	N	None
3	99	108	Yamasaki, Maria T	Daughter	F	Jp	6.0	S	N			Guam	Japan	Guam		None
4	99	108	Yamasaki, Vicente T	Son	M	Jp	2.0	S				Guam	Japan	Guam	N	None
5	99	108	Taitinfong, Francisca	Mother-in-law	F	Cha	70.0	S		N	N	Guam	Guam	Guam	N	None
6	100	109	San Nicolas, Elario B	Head	M	Cha	62.0	M		N	N	Guam	Guam	Guam	N	Farmer
7	100	109	San Nicolas, Maria G	Wife	F	Cha	57.0	M		Y	N	Guam	Guam	Guam	N	None
8	100	109	San Nicolas, Dolores	Daughter	F	Cha	29.0	S		N	N	Guam	Guam	Guam	N	None
9	100	109	San Nicolas, Vicente	Son	M	Cha	28.0	S		Y	Y	Guam	Guam	Guam	N	Farm laborer home farm
10	100	109	San Nicolas, Joaquin	Son	M	Cha	26.0	S		Y	Y	Guam	Guam	Guam	N	Farm laborer home farm
11	100	109	San Nicolas, Juan	Son	M	Cha	18.0	S	N	Y	Y	Guam	Guam	Guam	N	Farm laborer home farm
12	100	109	San Nicolas, Antonio	Son	M	Cha	16.0	S	N	Y	Y	Guam	Guam	Guam	Y	Farm laborer home farm
13	100	109	San Nicolas, Concepcion Q	Grand daughter	F	Cha	6.0	S	N			Guam	Guam	Guam	Y	None
14	100	109	San Nicolas, Jose Q	Grandson	M	Cha	3.0	S				Guam	Guam	Guam		None
15	100	109	San Nicolas, Juan	Grandson	M	Cha		S				Guam	Unknown	Guam	N	None
16	100	110	Quichocho, Jose Q	Head	M	Cha	22.0	M		Y	N	Guam	Guam	Guam	N	Laborer
17	100	110	Quichocho, Josefa SN	Wife	F	Cha	24.0	M		Y	Y	Guam	Guam	Guam	N	None
18	100	110	Quichocho, Lourdes SN	Daughter	F	Cha	1.0	S				Guam	Guam	Guam	N	None
19	100	110	Quichocho, Jose SN	Son	M	Cha	0.0	S				Guam	Guam	Guam		None
20	101	111	Castro, Juan I	Head	M	Cha	42.0	M		Y	Y	Guam	Guam	Guam	N	Farmer
21	101	111	Castro, Feliciana R	Wife	F	Cha	35.0	M		N	N	Guam	Unknown	Guam	N	None
22	101	111	Castro, Jose R	Son	M	Cha	18.0	S	N	Y	Y	Guam	Guam	Guam	Y	Cook
23	101	111	Castro, Lucas R	Son	M	Cha	16.0	S	N	Y	Y	Guam	Guam	Guam	Y	Farm laborer home farm
24	101	111	Castro, Francisca R	Daughter	F	Cha	12.0	S	Y	Y	Y	Guam	Guam	Guam	N	None
25	101	111	Castro, Joaquin R	Son	M	Cha	10.0	S	Y	N	N	Guam	Guam	Guam	N	None

Street: San Victores Street

132

(CHAMORRO ROOTS GENEALOGY PROJECT ™ TRANSCRIPTION)
(COMPILED/TRANSCRIBED BY BERNARD T. PUNZALAN / HTTP://WWW.CHAMORROROOTS.COM)

FOURTEENTH CENSUS OF THE UNITED STATES: 1920-POPULATION
ISLAND OF GUAM

DISTRICT 1
NAME OF PLACE Agana City
[Proper name and, also, name of class, as city, town, village, barrio, etc]

ENUMERATED BY ME ON THE 5th DAY OF April, 1920

Jose Kamminga ENUMERATOR

	Street	Dwelling No.	Family No.	NAME	RELATION	Sex	Color or race	Age	Single, married, widowed or divorced	Attended school since Sept. 1, 1919	Able to read	Able to write	Birthplace of this person	Birthplace of father	Birthplace of mother	Able to speak English	OCCUPATION
		1	2	3	4	5	6	7	8	9	10	11	12	13	14	15	16	17
26		101	111	Castro, Margarita R	Daughter	F	Cha	8.0	S	Y			Guam	Guam	Guam		None
27		101	111	Castro, Jesus R	Son	M	Cha	5.0	S	N			Guam	Guam	Guam		None
28		101	111	Castro, Maria R	Daughter	F	Cha	4.0	S				Guam	Guam	Guam		None
29		101	111	Castro, Ana R	Daughter	F	Cha	2.0	S				Guam	Guam	Guam		None
30		101	111	Castro, Geronimo R	Son	M	Cha	0.3	S				Guam	Guam	Guam		None
31	San Victores Street	102	112	Mendiola, Jose G	Head	M	Cha	39.0	M		N	N	Guam	Guam	Guam	Y	Policeman
32		102	112	Mendiola, Maria S	Wife	F	Cha	41.0	M		N	N	Guam	Guam	Guam	N	None
33		102	112	Mendiola, Rosario S	Daughter	F	Cha	13.0	S		Y	Y	Guam	Guam	Guam	N	None
34		102	112	Mendiola, Juan S	Son	M	Cha	10.0	S	Y	Y	Y	Guam	Guam	Guam	N	None
35		102	112	Mendiola, Concepcion S	Daughter	F	Cha	6.0	S				Guam	Guam	Guam		None
36		102	112	Mendiola, Ignacio S	Son	M	Cha	3.0	S				Guam	Guam	Guam		None
37		102	112	Salas, Antonia D	Step daughter	F	Cha	21.0	S	N	Y	Y	Guam	Guam	Guam	Y	None
38		102	112	Salas, Rafael	Grandson	M	Cha	3.0	S				Guam	Guam	Guam		None
39		103	113	Salas, Maria D	Head	F	Cha	54.0	S	N	Y	Y	Guam	Guam	Guam	Y	None
40		103	113	Salas, Ana D	Sister	F	Cha	47.0	S		Y	Y	Guam	Guam	Guam	N	None
41		103	113	Salas, Regina	Niece	F	Cha	9.0	S	Y			Guam	Guam	Guam		None
42		103	114	Salas, Jose D	Head	M	Cha	24.0	M		Y	Y	Guam	Unknown	Unknown	Y	Harnessmaker
43		103	114	Salas, Josefa F	Wife	F	Cha	23.0	M		Y	Y	Guam	Guam	Guam	Y	None
44		104	115	Morcilla, Vicenta D	Head	F	Cha	35.0	Wd		Y	N	Guam	Unknown	Guam	N	None
45		104	115	Morcilla, Jesus D	S	M	Fil	17.0	S	N	Y	Y	Guam	Philippine Islands	Guam	Y	Laborer
46		104	115	Cruz, Feliciano D	S	M	Cha	20.0	S	N	Y	Y	Guam	Unknown	Guam	Y	Laborer
47		104	115	Rosario, Juan A	Boarder	M	Cha	50.0	S		Y	Y	Guam	Guam	Guam	Y	Farmer
48		105	116	Acosta, Carmen U	Head	F	Cha	28.0	S	N	Y	N	Guam	Guam	Guam	Y	Laundress
49		105	116	Acosta, Rosario U	Daughter	F	Cha	5.0	S	N			Guam	Unknown	Guam	Y	None
50		105	116	Acosta, Antonia U	Daughter	F	Cha	3.0	S				Guam	Unknown	Guam		None

(CHAMORRO ROOTS GENEALOGY PROJECT ™ TRANSCRIPTION)
(COMPILED/TRANSCRIBED BY BERNARD T. PUNZALAN / HTTP://WWW.CHAMORROROOTS.COM)

FOURTEENTH CENSUS OF THE UNITED STATES: 1920-POPULATION
ISLAND OF GUAM

SHEET NO. __34A__

ENUMERATED BY ME ON THE __5th__ DAY OF __April__, 1920

Jose Kamminga ENUMERATOR

DISTRICT __1__
NAME OF PLACE __Agana City__

[Proper name and, also, name of class, as city, town, village, barrio, etc]

	Dwelling No. (2)	Family No. (3)	NAME (4)	RELATION (5)	Sex (6)	Color or race (7)	Age (8)	Single, married, widowed or divorced (9)	Attended school since Sept. 1, 1919 (10)	Able to read (11)	Able to write (12)	Place of birth of this person (13)	Place of birth of father (14)	Place of birth of mother (15)	Able to speak English (16)	OCCUPATION (17)
1	105	116	Acosta, Juan U	Son	M	Cha		S				Guam	Unknown	Guam		None
2	105	116	Ulloa, Rosa N	Mother	F	Cha	68.0	Wd		Y	N	Guam	Guam	Guam		None
3	106	117	Santos, Jesus T	Head	M	Cha	34.0	M		Y	N	Guam	Guam	Guam	N	Farmer
4	106	117	Santos, Dolores T	Wife	F	Cha	35.0	M		Y	N	Guam	Guam	Guam	N	None
5	106	117	Santos, Maria T	Daughter	F	Cha	9.0	S	Y			Guam	Guam	Guam		None
6	106	117	Santos, Matilde T	Daughter	F	Cha	7.0	S	Y			Guam	Guam	Guam		None
7	106	117	Santos, Jose T	Son	M	Cha	5.0	S	N			Guam	Guam	Guam		None
8	106	117	Santos, Joaquin T	Son	M	Cha	3.0	S				Guam	Guam	Guam		None
9	106	117	Santos, Cresanta T	Daughter	F	Cha	0.3	S				Guam	Guam	Guam		None
10	106	117	Toves, Nicolas C	Nephew	M	Cha	14.0	S	N	Y	Y	Guam	Guam	Guam	N	None
11	107	118	Acosta, Miguel C	Head	M	Cha	48.0	M		Y	Y	Guam	Guam	Guam	N	Farmer
12	107	118	Acosta, Vicenta S	Wife	F	Cha	50.0	M		Y	Y	Guam	Guam	Guam	N	None
13	107	118	Acosta, Joaquina S	Daughter	F	Cha	27.0	S		Y	Y	Guam	Guam	Guam	N	None
14	107	118	Acosta, Ramon S	Son	M	Cha	25.0	S		Y	Y	Guam	Guam	Guam	Y	Machinist
15	107	118	Acosta, Jose S	Son	M	Cha	23.0	S		Y	Y	Guam	Guam	Guam	Y	Farm laborer home farm
16	107	118	Acosta, Felisa S	Daughter	F	Cha	21.0	S		Y	Y	Guam	Guam	Guam	Y	None
17	107	118	Acosta, Felix S	Son	M	Cha	18.0	S	N	Y	Y	Guam	Guam	Guam	Y	Farm laborer home farm
18	107	118	Acosta, Dolores S	Daughter	F	Cha	14.0	S	N	Y	Y	Guam	Guam	Guam	Y	None
19	107	118	Acosta, Rosa S	Daughter	F	Cha	12.0	S	Y	Y	Y	Guam	Guam	Guam	Y	None
20	107	118	Acosta, Manuel S	Son	M	Cha	9.0	S	N	Y	N	Guam	Guam	Guam	Y	None
21	107	118	Acosta, Concepcion S	Daughter	F	Cha	7.0	S	N			Guam	Guam	Guam		None
22	108	119	Cruz, Carla P	Head	F	Cha	46.0	S		N	N	Guam	Guam	Guam	N	Laundress
23	108	119	Cruz, Felisita	Daughter	F	Cha	20.0	S		Y	N	Guam	Unknown	Guam	N	Laundress
24	108	119	Cruz, Rosa	Daughter	F	Cha	16.0	S	N	Y	N	Guam	Unknown	Guam	N	Laundress
25	108	120	Cruz, Maria P	Head	F	Cha	44.0	S		Y	Y	Guam	Guam	Guam	N	Laundress

Street, avenue, road, etc. (1): San Victores Street

(CHAMORRO ROOTS GENEALOGY PROJECT ™ TRANSCRIPTION)
(COMPILED/TRANSCRIBED BY BERNARD T. PUNZALAN / HTTP://WWW.CHAMORROROOTS.COM)
FOURTEENTH CENSUS OF THE UNITED STATES: 1920-POPULATION
ISLAND OF GUAM

DISTRICT 1
NAME OF PLACE Agana City

ENUMERATED BY ME ON THE 6th DAY OF April, 1920

Jose Kamminga ENUMERATOR

[Proper name and, also, name of class, name of class, as city, town, village, barrio, etc]

	Street, avenue, road, etc.	Number of dwelling house in order of visitation	Number of family in order of visitation	NAME	RELATION	Sex	Color or race	Age at last birthday	Single, married, widowed or divorced	Attended school any time since Sept. 1, 1919	Whether able to read.	Whether able to write.	Place of birth of this person.	Place of birth of father of this person.	Place of birth of mother of this person.	Whether able to speak English.	OCCUPATION
		1	2	3	4	5	6	7	8	9	10	11	12	13	14	15	16	17
26	San Victores Street	108	120	Cruz, Mariano	Son	M	Cha	15.0	S	Y	Y		Guam	Unknown	Guam	Y	Farm laborer home farm
27		108	120	Cruz, Manuel	Son	M	Cha	7.0	S				Guam	Unknown	Guam		None
28		108	120	Cruz, Santiago	Son	M	Cha	3.0	S				Guam	Unknown	Guam		None
29		109	121	Duenas, Dolores C	Head	F	Cha	37.0	Wd		Y	N	Guam	Guam	Guam	N	Farmer
30		109	121	Duenas, Amalia C	Daughter	F	Cha	13.0	S	N	Y	N	Guam	Guam	Guam	N	None
31		109	121	Duenas, Francisco C	Son	M	Cha	11.0	S	N	Y	Y	Guam	Guam	Guam		None
32		109	121	Duenas, Antonio C	Son	M	Cha	8.0	S	Y	Y	Y	Guam	Guam	Guam		None
33		109	121	Duenas, Maria C	Daughter	F	Cha	6.0	S	N			Guam	Guam	Guam		None
34		109	121	Duenas, Rosalia C	Daughter	F	Cha	4.0	S				Guam	Guam	Guam		None
35		109	121	Duenas, Ignacio C	Son	M	Cha	1.0	S				Guam	Guam	Guam		None
36		110	122	Flores, Jose D	Head	M	Cha	56.0	M		Y	Y	Guam	Guam	Guam	N	Farmer
37		110	122	Flores, Dolores SN	Wife	F	Cha	48.0	M		Y	N	Guam	Guam	Guam	N	None
38		110	122	Flores, Ana SN	Daughter	F	Cha	9.0	S	Y			Guam	Guam	Guam		None
39		110	122	Flores, Jose SN	Son	M	Cha	7.0	S	N			Guam	Guam	Guam		None
40		110	122	Flores, Joaquin	Son	M	Cha	3.0	S				Guam	Guam	Guam		None
41		111	123	Palomo, Asuncion A	Head	F	Cha	46.0	Wd		Y	N	Guam	Guam	Guam	N	None
42		111	123	Palomo, Manuel A	Son	M	Cha	12.0	S	Y	Y	Y	Guam	Guam	Guam	Y	None
43		111	123	Palomo, Gabina A	Daughter	F	Cha	9.0	S	Y			Guam	Guam	Guam	N	None
44		111	123	Muna, Gabina A	Mother	F	Cha	79.0	Wd				Guam	Guam	Guam	N	None
45		111	123	Iglesias, Jose A	Cousin	M	Cha	36.0	S		Y	N	Guam	Guam	Guam	N	Farm laborer home farm
46		112	124	Santos, Vicente M	Head	M	Cha	39.0	M		Y	Y	Guam	Guam	Guam	N	Farmer
47		112	124	Santos, Rosa P	Wife	F	Cha	37.0	M		Y	Y	Guam	Unknown	Guam	N	None
48		112	124	Santos, Ana P	Daughter	F	Cha	18.0	S	N	N	Y	Guam	Guam	Guam	N	None
49		112	124	Santos, Jose P	Son	M	Cha	16.0	S	N	Y	Y	Guam	Guam	Guam	Y	Farm laborer home farm
50		112	124	Santos, Jesus P	Son	M	Cha	12.0	S	N	Y	Y	Guam	Guam	Guam	Y	None

135

(CHAMORRO ROOTS GENEALOGY PROJECT ™ TRANSCRIPTION)
(COMPILED/TRANSCRIBED BY BERNARD T. PUNZALAN / HTTP://WWW.CHAMORROROOTS.COM)
FOURTEENTH CENSUS OF THE UNITED STATES: 1920—POPULATION
ISLAND OF GUAM

ENUMERATED BY ME ON THE 7th DAY OF April, 1920

Jose Kamminga ENUMERATOR

DISTRICT **1**
NAME OF PLACE **Agana City**
[Proper name and, also, name of class, as city, town, village, barrio, etc]

Street, avenue, road, etc.	Number of dwelling house is order of visitation	Number of family in order of visitation	NAME of each person whose place of abode on January 1, 1920, was in the family. Enter surname, firs, then given name and middle initial. If any. Include every person living on January 1, 1920. Omit children born since January 1, 1920.	RELATION Relationship of this person to the head of the family.	Sex	Color or race	Age at last birthday	Single, married, widowed or divorced	Attended school any time since Sept. 1, 1919	Whether able to read.	Whether able to write.	Place of birth of this person.	Place of birth of father of this person.	Place of birth of mother of this person.	Whether able to speak English.	OCCUPATION Trade, profession, or particular kind of work done, as salesman, laborer, clerk, cook, merchant, washerwoman, etc.
	2	3	4	5	6	7	8	9	10	11	12	13	14	15	16	17
	112	124	Santos, Rosario P	Daughter	F	Cha	6.0	S	N	Y	Y	Guam	Guam	Guam	Y	None
	112	124	Santos, Juan P	Son	M	Cha	5.0	S	N			Guam	Guam	Guam		None
	112	124	Santos, Francisco P	Son	M	Cha	2.0	S				Guam	Guam	Guam		None
	113	125	Leon Guerrero, Juan D?	Head	M	Cha	58.0	M		Y	Y	Guam	Guam	Guam	N	Farmer
	113	125	Leon Guerrero, Ana P	Wife	F	Cha	57.0	M		Y	N	Guam	Guam	Guam	N	None
	113	126	Leon Guerrero, Vicente P	Head	M	Cha	33.0	M		Y	Y	Guam	Guam	Guam	N	Laborer
	113	126	Leon Guerrero, Manuela S	Wife	F	Cha	32.0	M		Y	Y	Guam	Guam	Guam	N	None
	113	126	Leon Guerrero, Maria S	Daughter	F	Cha	7.0	S	N			Guam	Guam	Guam		None
	113	126	Leon Guerrero, Juan S	Son	M	Cha	6.0	S	N			Guam	Guam	Guam		None
	113	126	Leon Guerrero, Francisco S	Son	M	Cha	1.0	S				Guam	Guam	Guam		None
	114	127	Borja, Jesus Q	Head	M	Cha	36.0	M		Y	Y	Guam	Guam	Guam	N	Blacksmith
	114	127	Borja, Emeliana L	Wife	F	Cha	30.0	M		Y	Y	Guam	Guam	Guam	N	None
	114	127	Borja, Jose L	Son	M	Cha	10.0	S	Y	Y	Y	Guam	Guam	Guam	Y	None
	114	127	Borja, Gabriela L	Daughter	F	Cha	9.0	S	Y	Y	Y	Guam	Guam	Guam		None
	114	127	Taitano, Ana S	Niece	F	Cha	4.0	S				Guam	Guam	Guam		None
	114	127	Fernandez, Francisco L	Boarder	M	Cha	22.0	S		Y	Y	Guam	Guam	Guam	Y	Enlisted man USN
	115	128	Borja, Antonio G	Head	M	Cha	63.0	M		Y	Y	Guam	Guam	Guam	N	Farmer
	115	128	Borja, Gabriela T	Wife	F	Cha	60.0	M		Y	N	Guam	Guam	Guam	N	None
	115	128	Borja, Maria T	Daughter	F	Cha	37.0	S		Y	N	Guam	Guam	Guam	N	Laundress
	115	128	Borja, Ana T	Daughter	F	Cha	34.0	S		Y	N	Guam	Guam	Guam	N	Laundress
	115	128	Borja, Joaquin T	Son	M	Cha	21.0	S	N	Y	Y	Guam	Guam	Guam	Y	Storekeeper
	115	128	Borja, Antonio T	Son	M	Cha	18.0	S	N	Y	Y	Guam	Guam	Guam	Y	Carpenter
	115	128	Borja, Josefa T	Daughter	F	Cha	16.0	S	N	Y	Y	Guam	Guam	Guam	N	Laundress
	115	128	Toves, Maria M	Niece	F	Cha	17.0	S	N	Y	Y	Guam	Guam	Guam	N	None
	115	128	Borja, Bernadita S	Granddaughter	F	Cha	3.0	S				Guam	Guam	Guam		None

San Victores Street

(CHAMORRO ROOTS GENEALOGY PROJECT ™ TRANSCRIPTION)
(COMPILED/TRANSCRIBED BY BERNARD T. PUNZALAN / HTTP://WWW.CHAMORROROOTS.COM)

FOURTEENTH CENSUS OF THE UNITED STATES: 1920—POPULATION

ISLAND OF GUAM

ENUMERATED BY ME ON THE 7th DAY OF April, 1920

Jose Kamminga ENUMERATOR

DISTRICT **1**
NAME OF PLACE **Agana City**
[Proper name, also, name of class, as city, town, village, barrio, etc]

	PLACE OF ABODE		NAME	RELATION	PERSONAL DESCRIPTION				EDUCATION			NATIVITY				OCCUPATION
Street, avenue, road, etc.	No. of dwelling house	No. of family	Name of each person	Relationship to head of family	Sex	Color or race	Age at last birthday	Single, married, widowed or divorced	Attended school since Sept. 1, 1919	Whether able to read	Whether able to write	Place of birth of this person	Place of birth of father	Place of birth of mother	Whether able to speak English	Occupation
1	2	3	4	5	6	7	8	9	10	11	12	13	14	15	16	17
	115	128	Borja, Juan S	Grandson	M	Cha	1.0	S				Guam	Guam	Guam		None
	116	129	Acosta, Joaquin A	Head	M	Cha	59.0	M		N	N	Guam	Guam	Guam	N	Farmer
	116	129	Acosta, Maria D	Wife	F	Cha	44.0	M		Y	N	Guam	Guam	Guam	N	None
	116	129	Acosta, Ana D	Daughter	F	Cha	15.0	S	N	Y	Y	Guam	Guam	Guam	Y	None
	116	129	Acosta, Joaquin D	Son	M	Cha	13.0	S	N	Y	Y	Guam	Guam	Guam	Y	None
	116	129	Crisostomo, Josefa D	Step daughter	F	Cha	25.0	S		Y	Y	Guam	Guam	Guam	N	Laundress
	116	129	Crisostomo, Jesus D	Step-son	M	Cha	23.0	S		Y	Y	Guam	Guam	Guam	Y	Chauffeur
	116	129	Crisostomo, Jose D	Step son	M	Cha	19.0	S	N	Y	Y	Guam	Guam	Guam	Y	Farm laborer
	116	129	Crisostomo, Antonio D	Grandson	M	Cha	4.0	S				Guam	Unknown	Guam		None
	116	129	Crisostomo, Tomas D	Grandson	M	Cha	1.0	S				Guam	Unknown	Guam		None
	116	129	Camacho, Natividad B	Mother-in-law	F	Cha	65.0	Wd		N	N	Guam	Guam	Guam	N	None
San Victores Street	117	130	Blas, Gregorio F	Head	M	Cha	39.0	M		Y	Y	Guam	Guam	Guam	Y	Farmer
	117	130	Blas, Rosa R	Wife	F	Cha	28.0	M		Y	Y	Guam	Unknown	Guam	N	None
	117	130	Blas, Lagrimas R	Daughter	F	Cha	9.0	S	Y			Guam	Guam	Guam		None
	117	130	Blas, Francisco R	Son	M	Cha	7.0	S	Y			Guam	Guam	Guam		None
	117	130	Blas, Josefa R	Daughter	F	Cha	5.0	S	N			Guam	Guam	Guam		None
	117	130	Blas, Rosario R	Daughter	F	Cha	3.0	S				Guam	Guam	Guam		None
	117	130	Blas, Mariano R	Son	M	Cha	2.0	S				Guam	Guam	Guam		None
	117	130	Blas, Regina R	Daughter	F	Cha	0.2	S				Guam	Guam	Guam		None
	117	130	Blas, Jose A	Head	M	Cha	67.0	M		Y	Y	Guam	Guam	Guam	N	Shoemaker
	117	130	Blas, Dolores C	Wife	F	Cha	59.0	M		Y	N	Guam	Guam	Guam	N	None
	117	130	Babauta, Francisco SN	Servant	M	Cha	12.0	S	Y	Y	Y	Guam	Guam	Guam	Y	None
	118	132	Miner, Baldomero P	Head	M	Wh	48.0	Wd		Y	Y	Guam	United States	Guam	Y	Carpenter
	118	132	Miner, Ana U	Daughter	F	Wh	18.0	S	N	Y	Y	Guam	Guam	Guam	Y	None
	118	132	Miner, Jose U	Son	M	Wh	16.0	S	N	Y	Y	Guam	Guam	Guam	Y	Carpenter

137

(CHAMORRO ROOTS GENEALOGY PROJECT ™ TRANSCRIPTION)
(COMPILED/TRANSCRIBED BY BERNARD T. PUNZALAN / HTTP://WWW.CHAMORROROOTS.COM)

FOURTEENTH CENSUS OF THE UNITED STATES: 1920-POPULATION

ISLAND OF GUAM

SHEET NO. 36A

DISTRICT 1
NAME OF PLACE Agana City

ENUMERATED BY ME ON THE 7th DAY OF April, 1920

Jose Kamminga ENUMERATOR

Street	No. of dwelling house	No. of family	NAME	RELATION	Sex	Color or race	Age at last birthday	Single, married, widowed or divorced	Attended school since Sept. 1, 1919	Whether able to read	Whether able to write	Place of birth of this person	Place of birth of father	Place of birth of mother	Whether able to speak English	OCCUPATION
1	2	3	4	5	6	7	8	9	10	11	12	13	14	15	16	17
	118	133	Ulloa, Marcelo	Head	M	Cha	29.0	M		Y	Y	Guam	Unknown	Guam	Y	Carpenter
	118	133	Ulloa, Julia A	Wife	F	Cha	27.0	M		Y	Y	Guam	Guam	Guam	Y	None
	118	133	Ulloa, Maria A	Daughter	F	Cha	5.0	S				Guam	Guam	Guam		None
	118	133	Ulloa, Rosalia A	Daughter	F	Cha	3.0	S	N			Guam	Guam	Guam		None
	118	133	Ulloa, Beatris A	Daughter	F	Cha	0.7	S				Guam	Guam	Guam		None
	119	134	Mafnas, Luis C	Head	M	Cha	42.0	M		Y	Y	Guam	Guam	Guam	N	Farmer
	119	134	Mafnas, Ana F	Wife	F	Cha	43.0	M		Y	Y	Guam	Guam	Guam	N	None
San Victores Street	119	134	Mafnas, Jose F	Son	M	Cha	14.0	S	N	Y	Y	Guam	Guam	Guam	Y	None
	119	134	Mafnas, Andres F	Son	M	Cha	5.0	S	N			Guam	Guam	Guam		None
	120	135	Reyes, Mariano R	Head	M	Cha	47.0	M		Y	N	Guam	Unknown	Guam	N	Laborer
	120	135	Reyes, Nicolasa SA	Wife	F	Cha	33.0	M		N	N	Guam	Guam	Guam	N	None
	120	135	Reyes, Jose SA	Son	M	Cha	12.0	S	Y	Y	Y	Guam	Guam	Guam	N	None
	120	135	Reyes, Joaquin SA	Son	M	Cha	10.0	S	Y	N	N	Guam	Guam	Guam	N	None
	120	135	Reyes, Ana SA	Daughter	F	Cha	7.0	S	Y			Guam	Guam	Guam		None
	120	135	Reyes, Oliva SA	Daughter	F	Cha	0.8	S				Guam	Guam	Guam		None
	120	135	Reyes, Apolonia	Mother	F	Cha	68.0	S		N	N	Guam	Guam	Guam	N	None
	120	135	Reyes, Natividad R	Sister	F	Cha	24.0	S		N	N	Guam	Guam	Guam	N	None
	121	136	Asuncion, Manuel B	Head	M	Cha	69.0	Wd		Y	Y	Guam	Unknown	Guam	Y	Farmer
	122	137	Isezaki, Vicente Y	Head	M	Jp	39.0	M		Y	Y	Japan	Japan	Japan	N	Laborer
	122	137	Isezaki, Marcelina P	Wife	F	Cha	28.0	M		Y	Y	Guam	Guam	Guam	N	None
	122	137	Isezaki, Jesus P	Son	M	Jp	6.0	S	N			Guam	Japan	Guam		None
	122	137	Isezaki, Vicente P	Son	M	Jp	5.0	S	N			Guam	Japan	Guam		None
	122	137	Isezaki, Jose P	Son	M	Jp	3.0	S				Guam	Japan	Guam		None
	122	137	Isezaki, Maria P	Daughter	F	Cha	0.8	S				Guam	Japan	Guam		None
	122	137	Pinaula, Feliciana	Niece	F	Cha	11.0	S	Y	Y	Y	Guam	Unknown	Guam	N	None

(CHAMORRO ROOTS GENEALOGY PROJECT ™ TRANSCRIPTION)
(COMPILED/TRANSCRIBED BY BERNARD T. PUNZALAN / HTTP://WWW.CHAMORROROOTS.COM)

FOURTEENTH CENSUS OF THE UNITED STATES: 1920—POPULATION
ISLAND OF GUAM

ENUMERATED BY ME ON THE 8th DAY OF April, 1920

Jose Kamminga ENUMERATOR

DISTRICT 1
NAME OF PLACE Agana City
[Proper name and, also, name of class, as city, town, village, barrio, etc]

Street	Dwelling	Family	NAME	RELATION	Sex	Color or race	Age	Marital	Attended school	Read	Write	Birthplace	Father birthplace	Mother birthplace	English	OCCUPATION
1	2	3	4	5	6	7	8	9	10	11	12	13	14	15	16	17
	123	138	Pangelinan, Dominga P	Head	F	Cha	38.0	M		N	N	Guam	Unknown	Guam		None
	123	138	Pangelinan, Enrique	Son	M	Cha	15.0	S	N	Y	Y	Guam	Unknown	Guam	Y	Servant
	123	138	Pangelinan, Jesus	Son	M	Cha	8.0	S	Y			Guam	Unknown	Guam		None
	123	138	Pangelinan, Francisco	Son	M	Cha	6.0	S	N			Guam	Unknown	Guam		None
	123	138	Cruz, Jose P	Son	M	Fil	13.0	S		Y	Y	Guam	Philippine Islands	Guam	N	None
	124	139	Blas, Vicente F	Head	M	Cha	53.0	M		Y	Y	Guam	Guam	Guam	N	Farmer
	124	139	Blas, Maria A	Wife	F	Cha	47.0	M				Guam	Guam	Guam	N	None
San Victores Street	124	139	Blas, Manuel A	Son	M	Cha	24.0	S		Y	Y	Guam	Guam	Guam	Y	Farm laborer home farm
	124	139	Blas, Josefa A	Daughter	F	Cha	23.0	S		Y	Y	Guam	Guam	Guam	Y	None
	124	139	Blas, Maria A	Daughter	F	Cha	20.0	S	N	Y	Y	Guam	Guam	Guam	Y	None
	124	139	Blas, Jose A	Son	M	Cha	18.0	S	N	Y	Y	Guam	Guam	Guam	Y	Farm laborer home farm
	124	139	Blas, Jesus A	Son	M	Cha	16.0	S	Y	Y	Y	Guam	Guam	Guam	Y	None
	124	139	Blas, Ana A	Daughter	F	Cha	14.0	S	N	Y	Y	Guam	Guam	Guam	Y	None
	124	139	Blas, Joaquin A	Son	M	Cha	10.0	S	Y	Y	Y	Guam	Guam	Guam	Y	None
	124	139	Blas, Rosa	Daughter	F	Cha	8.0	S	Y			Guam	Guam	Guam	N	None
	124	139	Villagomez, Rosa	Mother-in-law	F	Cha	66.0	Wd		Y	N	Guam	Unknown	Guam	N	None
	125	140	Hongyee, Alejandro	Head	M	Chi	42.0	M		Y	Y	China	China	China	Y	Cook
	125	140	Hongyee, Nieves P	Wife	F	Cha	24.0	M		Y	Y	Guam	China	Guam	Y	None
	125	140	Hongyee, Jose P	Son	M	Chi	8.0	S	Y			Guam	China	Guam		None
	125	140	Hongyee, Joaquin P	Son	M	Chi	6.0	S	N			Guam	China	Guam		None
	125	140	Hongyee, Isabel P	Daughter	F	Chi	5.0	S	N			Guam	China	Guam		None
	125	140	Hongyee, Jesus P	Son	M	Chi	2.0	S				Guam	China	Guam		None
	125	140	Hongyee, Juan R	Son	M	Chi	15.0	S	N	Y	Y	Guam	China	Guam	Y	Cook
	125	140	Hongyee, Vicente R	Son	M	Chi	13.0	S	N	Y	Y	Guam	China	Guam	N	None
	126	141	Camacho, Jose C	Head	M	Cha	26.0	M		N	N	Guam	Unknown	Guam	N	Farmer

139

(CHAMORRO ROOTS GENEALOGY PROJECT ™ TRANSCRIPTION)
(COMPILED/TRANSCRIBED BY BERNARD T. PUNZALAN / HTTP://WWW.CHAMORROROOTS.COM)

FOURTEENTH CENSUS OF THE UNITED STATES: 1920—POPULATION

ISLAND OF GUAM

68

ENUMERATED BY ME ON THE 8th DAY OF April, 1920

Jose Kamminga ENUMERATOR

DISTRICT **1**

NAME OF PLACE **Agana City**

[Proper name and, also, name of class, as city, town, village, barrio, etc]

	Street, avenue, road, etc.	Number of dwelling house in order of visitation	Number of family in order of visitation	NAME	RELATION	Sex	Color or race	Age at last birthday	Single, married, widowed or divorced	Attended school any time since Sept. 1, 1919	Whether able to read.	Whether able to write.	Place of birth of this person.	Place of birth of father of this person.	Place of birth of mother of this person.	Whether able to speak English.	OCCUPATION
	1	2	3	4	5	6	7	8	9	10	11	12	13	14	15	16	17
1		126	141	Camacho, Rita C	Wife	F	Cha	36.0	M		Y	Y	Guam	Guam	Guam	N	None
2		126	141	Camacho, Concepcion C	Daughter	F	Cha	2.0	M				Guam	Guam	Guam	N	None
3		126	141	Camacho, Antonio C	Son	M	Cha	1.0	S				Guam	Guam	Guam		None
4		126	141	Cruz, Elena G	Mother-in-law	F	Cha	60.0	Wd		Y	Y	Guam	Guam	Guam	N	None
5		127	142	Pangelinan, Joaquin T	Head	M	Cha	58.0	M		Y	Y	Guam	Guam	Guam	N	Farmer
6		127	142	Pangelinan, Maria U	Wife	F	Chin	50.0	M		Y	Y	Guam	China	Guam	Y	None
7		127	142	Pangelinan, Antonio U	Son	M	Cha	28.0	S		Y	Y	Guam	Guam	Guam	N	Farm laborer home farm
8		127	142	Pangelinan, Felix U	Son	M	Cha	18.0	S	N	Y	Y	Guam	Guam	Guam	N	Farm laborer home farm
9		127	142	Pangelinan, Venancio U	Son	M	Cha	14.0	S	N	Y	Y	Guam	Guam	Guam	Y	None
10	San Victores Street	127	142	Pangelinan, Vicente U	Son	M	Cha	9.0	S	Y			Guam	Guam	Guam	N	None
11		128	143	Leon Guerrero, Joaquin LG	Head	M	Cha	40.0	M		N	N	Guam	Unknown	Guam	N	Farmer
12		128	143	Leon Guerrero, Maria LG	Wife	F	Cha	38.0	M		N	Y	Guam	Unknown	Guam	N	None
13		128	143	Cruz, Feliza P	Boarder	F	Cha	16.0	S	N	Y	Y	Guam	Guam	Guam	Y	None
14		128	143	Flores, Josefa B	Mother-in-law	F	Cha	66.0	Wd		Y	Y	Guam	Guam	Guam	Y	None
15		128	143	Flores, Ana B	Sister-in-law	F	Cha	36.0	S	N	Y	Y	Guam	Unknown	Guam	N	None
16		128	143	Flores, Maria F	Niece	F	Cha	12.0	S	Y	Y	Y	Guam	Unknown	Guam	Y	None
17		128	143	Flores, Antonio F	Nephew	M	Cha	8.0	S	Y			Guam	Unknown	Guam		None
18		128	143	Flores, Jose F	Nephew	M	Cha	5.0	S	N			Guam	Unknown	Guam		None
19		128	143	Flores, Joaquin F	Nephew	M	Cha	1.0	S				Guam	Unknown	Guam		None
20		129	144	Tenorio, Antonio R	Head	M	Cha	38.0	M		Y	Y	Guam	Guam	Guam	N	Farmer
21		129	144	Tenorio, Dolores LT	Wife	F	Cha	37.0	M		Y	Y	Guam	Guam	Guam	N	None
22		129	144	Tenorio, Maria LT	Daughter	F	Cha	5.0	S				Guam	Guam	Guam		None
23		129	144	Tenorio, Jesus LT	Son	M	Cha	3.0	S				Guam	Guam	Guam		None
24		129	144	Tenorio, Concepcion LT	Daughter	F	Cha	1.0	S				Guam	Guam	Guam		None
25		129	145	La Torre, Juan A	Head	M	Fil	60.0	M		Y	Y	Guam	Philippine Islands	Guam	N	Farmer

(*CHAMORRO ROOTS GENEALOGY PROJECT ™ TRANSCRIPTION*)
(COMPILED/TRANSCRIBED BY BERNARD T. PUNZALAN / HTTP://WWW.CHAMORROROOTS.COM)

FOURTEENTH CENSUS OF THE UNITED STATES: 1920-POPULATION
ISLAND OF GUAM

SHEET NO. 37B

DISTRICT 1
NAME OF PLACE **Agana City**
[Proper name and, also, name of class, as city, town, village, barrio, etc]

ENUMERATED BY ME ON THE 8th DAY OF April, 1920
Jose Kamminga ENUMERATOR

	PLACE OF ABODE			NAME	RELATION	PERSONAL DESCRIPTION				EDUCATION			NATIVITY				OCCUPATION
	Street, avenue, road, etc.	Number of dwelling house is order of visitation	Number of family in order of visitation	of each person whose place of abode on January 1, 1920, was in the family. Enter surname, firs, then given name and middle initial. If any. Include every person living on January 1, 1920. Omit children born since January 1, 1920.	Relationship of this Person to the head of the family.	Sex	Color or race	Age at last birthday	Single, married, widowed or divorced	Attended school any time since Sept. 1, 1919	Whether able to read.	Whether able to write.	Place of birth of each person and parents of each person enumerated. If born in the United States, give the state or territory. If of foreign birth, give country of birth. Place of birth of this person.	Place of birth of father of this person.	Place of birth of mother of this person.	Whether able to speak English.	Trade, profession, or particular kind of work done, as salesman, laborer, clerk, cook, merchant, washerwoman, etc.
	1	2	3	4	5	6	7	8	9	10	11	12	13	14	15	16	17
26	San Victores Street	129	145	La Torre, Apolonia A	Wife	F	Cha	55.0	M		Y	N	Guam	Unknown	Guam		None
27		129	145	La Torre, Josefa A	Daughter	F	Fil	34.0	S		Y	Y	Guam	Guam	Guam		None
28		129	145	La Torre, Soledad A	Daughter	F	Fil	22.0	S		Y	Y	Guam	Guam	Guam		None
29		129	145	La Torre, Vicenta A	Daughter	F	Fil	20.0	S	N	Y	Y	Guam	Guam	Guam		None
30		129	145	La Torre, Juan A	Son	M	Fil	18.0	S	N	Y	Y	Guam	Guam	Guam	Y	Farm laborer home farm
31		129	145	La Torre, Felicita A	Daughter	F	Fil	16.0	S	N	Y	Y	Guam	Guam	Guam	Y	None
32		130	146	Santos, Jesus V	Head	M	Cha	24.0	M		Y	Y	Guam	Guam	Guam	Y	Machinist
33		130	146	Santos, Maria LG	Wife	F	Cha	22.0	M		Y	Y	Guam	Guam	Guam	Y	None
34		130	146	Santos, Juan LG	Son	M	Cha	1.0	S				Guam	Guam	Guam		None
35		130	146	Santos, Jose V	Brother	M	Cha	20.0	S	N	Y	Y	Guam	Guam	Guam	Y	Enlisted man USN
36		131	147	Perez, Pedro G	Head	M	Cha	32.0	M		Y	Y	Guam	Guam	Guam	Y	Carpenter
37		131	147	Perez, Ana A	Wife	F	Cha	29.0	M		Y	Y	Guam	Guam	Guam	N	None
38		131	147	Perez, Rosa A	Daughter	F	Cha	5.0	S	N			Guam	Guam	Guam		None
39		131	147	Perez, Joaquin A	Son	M	Cha	3.0	S				Guam	Guam	Guam		None
40		131	147	Perez, Maria A	Daughter	F	Cha	1.0	S				Guam	Guam	Guam		None
41		131	147	Perez, Francisco A	Son	M	Cha	0.1	S				Guam	Guam	Guam		None
42		132	148	Rivera, Jose C	Head	M	Cha	23.0	M		Y	Y	Guam	Guam	Guam	Y	Enlisted man USN
43		132	148	Rivera, Jesusa S	Wife	F	Cha	24.0	M		Y	Y	Guam	Guam	Guam	N	None
44		132	148	Rivera, Jesus S	Son	M	Cha	2.0	S				Guam	Guam	Guam		None
45		132	148	Rivera, Vicente	Son	M	Cha	0.0	S				Guam	Guam	Guam		None
46		133	149	Materne, Pedro D	Head	M	Cha	46.0	M		Y	Y	Guam	Guam	Guam	N	Farmer
47		133	149	Materne, Nieves D	Wife	F	Cha	41.0	M		Y	N	Guam	Guam	Guam	N	None
48		133	149	Materne, Francisco D	Son	M	Cha	14.0	S	N	Y	Y	Guam	Guam	Guam	Y	Farm laborer home farm
49		133	149	Materne, Manuel D	Son	M	Cha	10.0	S	N	Y	Y	Guam	Guam	Guam	N	None
50		133	149	Materne, Dolores D	Daughter	F	Cha	8.0	S	N			Guam	Guam	Guam		None

(CHAMORRO ROOTS GENEALOGY PROJECT ™ TRANSCRIPTION)
(COMPILED/TRANSCRIBED BY BERNARD T. PUNZALAN / HTTP://WWW.CHAMORROROOTS.COM)
FOURTEENTH CENSUS OF THE UNITED STATES: 1920-POPULATION
ISLAND OF GUAM

DISTRICT 1
NAME OF PLACE Agana City

[Proper name and, also, name of class, as city, town, village, barrio, etc]

ENUMERATED BY ME ON THE 9th DAY OF April, 1920

Jose Kamminga ENUMERATOR

Street, avenue, road, etc.	Number of dwelling house in order of visitation	Number of family in order of visitation	NAME	RELATION	Sex	Color or race	Age at last birthday	Single, married, widowed or divorced	Attended school any time since Sept. 1, 1919	Whether able to read	Whether able to write	Place of birth of this person	Place of birth of father of this person	Place of birth of mother of this person	Whether able to speak English	OCCUPATION
1	2	3	4	5	6	7	8	9	10	11	12	13	14	15	16	17
	134	150	Martinez, Ramon C	Head	M	Cha	49.0	M		Y	Y	Guam	Guam	Guam	N	Farmer
	134	150	Martinez, Antonia F	Wife	F	Cha	52.0	M		Y	Y	Guam	Guam	Guam	N	None
San Victores Street	134	150	Martinez, Jose F	Son	M	Cha	19.0	S	N	Y	Y	Guam	Guam	Guam	Y	Farm laborer home farm
	134	150	Martinez, Maria F	Daughter	F	Cha	17.0	S	N	Y	Y	Guam	Guam	Guam	Y	None
	135	151	Torres, Jose LG	Head	M	Cha	51.0	M		Y	Y	Guam	Guam	Guam	N	Carpenter
	135	151	Torres, Felecitas P	Wife	F	Cha	60.0	M		N	N	Guam	Guam	Guam	N	None
	135	151	Torres, Vicente P	Son	M	Cha	12.0	S	N	Y	Y	Guam	Guam	Guam	Y	None
	135	151	Torres, Ana P	Daughter	F	Cha	10.0	S	N	N	N	Guam	Guam	Guam	N	None
	135	151	Torres, Dolores P	Daughter	F	Cha	7.0	S	N	N	N	Guam	Guam	Guam		None
	135	152	Unpingco, Rita A	Head	F	Cha	47.0	Wd		Y	Y	Guam	Guam	Guam	N	None
	135	152	Unpingco, Jose A	Son	M	Cha	18.0	S	N	Y	Y	Guam	Guam	Guam	Y	Enlisted man USN
	135	152	Unpingco, Jesus A	Son	M	Cha	14.0	S	Y	Y	Y	Guam	Guam	Guam	Y	None
	135	152	Unpingco, Felipe A	Son	M	Cha	9.0	S	Y	Y	Y	Guam	Guam	Guam	Y	None
	136	153	Untalan, Pedro P	Head	M	Cha	25.0	M		Y	Y	Guam	Guam	Guam	Y	Enlisted man USN
	136	153	Untalan, Emiliana D	Wife	F	Cha	24.0	M		N	N	Guam	Guam	Guam	N	None
	137	154	Castro, Vicente P	Head	M	Cha	35.0	M		Y	Y	Guam	Guam	Guam	N	Farmer
	137	154	Castro, Concepcion C	Wife	F	Cha	34.0	M		N	N	Guam	Guam	Guam	Y	None
	137	154	Palomo, Joaquin B	Brother	M	Cha	18.0	S	N	Y	Y	Guam	Guam	Guam	Y	Farm laborer home farm
	138	155	Sholing, Rita P	Head	F	Cha	30.0	Wd		N	N	Guam	Guam	Guam	Y	None
	138	155	Sholing, Juan P	Son	M	Chin	10.0	S	Y	Y	Y	Guam	China	Guam	N	None
Santiago St	138	155	Sholing, Magdalena P	Daughter	F	Chin	8.0	S	Y	Y	Y	Guam	China	Guam	Y	None
	139	156	Migofna, Anatasio	Head	M	Cha	39.0	M		Y	Y	Guam	Unknown	Guam	Y	Shoemaker
	139	156	Migofna, Ana A	Wife	F	Cha	35.0	M		Y	Y	Guam	Guam	Guam	N	None
	139	156	Migofna, Felicidad A	Daughter	F	Cha	13.0	S	N	Y	Y	Guam	Guam	Guam	Y	None
	139	156	Migofna, Jose A	Son	M	Cha	12.0	S	N	Y	Y	Guam	Guam	Guam	Y	None

(CHAMORRO ROOTS GENEALOGY PROJECT ™ TRANSCRIPTION)
(COMPILED/TRANSCRIBED BY BERNARD T. PUNZALAN / HTTP://WWW.CHAMORROROOTS.COM)

FOURTEENTH CENSUS OF THE UNITED STATES: 1920—POPULATION

ISLAND OF GUAM

ENUMERATED BY ME ON THE 9th DAY OF April, 1920

Jose Kamminga ENUMERATOR

DISTRICT 1
NAME OF PLACE Agana City
[Proper name and, also, name of class, as city, town, village, barrio, etc]

Street, avenue, road, etc.	Number of dwelling house in order of visitation	Number of family in order of visitation	NAME	RELATION	Sex	Color or race	Age at last birthday	Single, married, widowed or divorced	Attended school any time since Sept. 1, 1919	Whether able to read.	Whether able to write.	Place of birth of this person.	Place of birth of father of this person.	Place of birth of mother of this person.	Whether able to speak English.	OCCUPATION
	1	2	3	4	5	6	7	8	9	10	11	12	13	14	15	16	17
	139	156	Migofna, Vicente A	Son	M	Cha	9.0	S	Y			Guam	Guam	Guam		None
	139	156	Migofna, Juan A	Son	M	Cha	6.0	S	N			Guam	Guam	Guam		None
	139	156	Migofna, Ignacio A	Son	M	Cha	4.0	S				Guam	Guam	Guam		None
	139	156	Migofna, Pedro A	Son	M	Cha	1.0	S				Guam	Guam	Guam		None
	140	157	Santos, Vicenta S	Head	F	Cha	62.0	Wd		Y	N	Guam	Guam	Guam	N	None
	140	157	Borja, Vicente S	Son	M	Cha	32.0	S		Y	Y	Guam	Guam	Guam	N	Farm laborer home farm
	140	157	Borja, Ana S	Daughter	F	Cha	27.0	S		Y	Y	Guam	Guam	Guam	Y	None
	140	157	Borja, Joaquin S	Son	M	Cha	22.0	S		Y	Y	Guam	Guam	Guam	Y	Farm laborer home farm
Santiago Street	140	157	Santos, Ignacio	Boarder	M	Cha	20.0	S	N	Y	Y	Guam	Unknown	Guam	Y	Farm laborer home farm
	140	157	Tenorio, Jesus B	Grandson	M	Cha	17.0	S	N	Y	Y	Guam	Guam	Guam	Y	Farm laborer home farm
	140	157	Tenorio, Jose B	Grandson	M	Cha	15.0	S	Y	Y	Y	Guam	Guam	Guam	Y	None
	140	157	Santos, Tomasa	Boarder	F	Cha	3.0	S				Guam	Unknown	Guam		None
	141	158	Borja, Vicente D	Head	M	Cha	37.0	M		Y	Y	Guam	Guam	Guam	N	Laborer
	141	158	Borja, Agustina S	Wife	F	Cha	35.0	M		Y	N	Guam	Guam	Guam	N	None
	141	158	Borja, Francisco S	Son	M	Cha	8.0	S	Y			Guam	Guam	Guam		None
	141	158	Borja, Jesus S	Son	M	Cha	6.0	S	N			Guam	Guam	Guam		None
	141	158	Borja, Vicente S	Son	M	Cha	5.0	S	N			Guam	Guam	Guam		None
	141	158	Borja, Josefa S	Daughter	F	Cha	3.0	S				Guam	Guam	Guam		None
	141	158	Borja, Jose S	Son	M	Cha	0.0	S				Guam	Guam	Guam		None
	142	159	Flores, Maria G	Head	F	Cha	42.0	S		Y	Y	Guam	Guam	Guam	N	None
	142	159	Flores, Ana G	Sister	F	Cha	40.0	S		Y	Y	Guam	Guam	Guam	N	None
	142	159	Flores, Jose G	Brother	M	Cha	23.0	S		Y	Y	Guam	Guam	Guam	Y	Farm laborer home farm
	142	159	Flores, Kelly LG	Niece	F	Cha	4.0	S				Guam	Guam	Guam		None
	143	160	Hernandez, Ramon E	Head	M	Cha	34.0	M		N	N	Guam	Guam	Guam	N	Farmer
	143	160	Hernandez, Maria B	Wife	F	Cha	35.0	M		Y	N	Guam	Guam	Guam	N	None

(CHAMORRO ROOTS GENEALOGY PROJECT ™ TRANSCRIPTION)
(COMPILED/TRANSCRIBED BY BERNARD T. PUNZALAN / HTTP://WWW.CHAMORROROOTS.COM)

FOURTEENTH CENSUS OF THE UNITED STATES: 1920-POPULATION
ISLAND OF GUAM

DISTRICT 1
NAME OF PLACE **Agana City**

[Proper name and, also, name of class, as city, town, village, barrio, etc]

ENUMERATED BY ME ON THE 9th DAY OF April, 1920

Jose Kamminga ENUMERATOR

Line	Street	Dwelling (2)	Family (3)	NAME (4)	RELATION (5)	Sex (6)	Color or race (7)	Age (8)	Marital (9)	School (10)	Read (11)	Write (12)	Birth person (13)	Birth father (14)	Birth mother (15)	English (16)	OCCUPATION (17)
1		143	160	Hernandez, Jose B	Son	M	Cha	11.0	S	Y	Y	N	Guam	Guam	Guam	N	None
2		143	160	Hernandez, Yunin B	Daughter	F	Cha	5.0	S	N			Guam	Guam	Guam	N	None
3		143	160	Hernandez, Francisco B	Son	M	Cha	3.0	S				Guam	Guam	Guam		None
4		143	160	Hernandez, Antonio B	Son	M	Cha	1.0	S				Guam	Guam	Guam		None
5		143	160	Benavente, Vicente A	Brother-in-law	M	Cha	25.0	S		Y	Y	Guam	Guam	Guam	Y	Laborer
6		143	160	Baza, Ana I	Boarder	F	Cha	40.0	Wd		N	N	Guam	Unknown	Guam	N	None
7		144	161	Benavente, Ignacio T	Head	M	Cha	68.0	M		Y	Y	Guam	Guam	Guam	N	Farmer
8		144	161	Benavente, Manuela D	Wife	F	Cha	69.0	M		Y	N	Guam	Guam	Guam	N	None
9		144	161	Ogo, Maria	Boarder	F	Cha	6.0	S	N			Guam	Unknown	Guam		None
10	Santiago Street	145	162	Hernandez, Ana F	Head	F	Cha	58.0	Wd		N	N	Guam	Guam	Guam	N	None
11		145	162	Hernandez, Joaquin F	Son	M	Cha	29.0	S	Y	Y	Y	Guam	Guam	Guam	Y	Farm laborer home farm
12		145	162	Hernandez, Jose F	Son	M	Cha	27.0	S	Y	Y	Y	Guam	Guam	Guam	Y	Farm laborer home farm
13		145	162	Hernandez, Ana F	Daughter	F	Cha	22.0	S	Y	Y	Y	Guam	Guam	Guam	Y	Laundress
14		145	162	Hernandez, Asuncion F	Daughter	F	Cha	19.0	S	N	Y	Y	Guam	Guam	Guam	Y	None
15		145	163	Hernandez, Pedro T	Head	M	Cha	60.0	Wd		N	N	Guam	Guam	Guam	N	Farmer
16		145	163	Hernandez, Manuel P	Son	M	Cha	14.0	S	N	Y	Y	Guam	Guam	Guam	Y	None
17		145	163	Hernandez, Precedes P	Daughter	F	Cha	12.0	S	N	Y	N	Guam	Guam	Guam	N	None
18		146	164	Quitugua, Vicente A	Head	M	Cha	44.0	M		Y	Y	Guam	Guam	Guam	Y	Farmer
19		146	164	Quitugua, Maria D	Wife	F	Cha	55.0	M		Y	Y	Guam	Guam	Guam	N	None
20		146	164	Tichaira, Josefa D	Step daughter	F	Wh	22.0	S		Y	Y	Guam	Portugal	Guam	N	None
21		146	165	Tichaira, Manuel D	Head	M	Wh	27.0	M		Y	Y	Guam	Portugal	Guam	Y	Farmer
22		146	165	Tichaira, Maria LG	Wife	F	Cha	23.0	M		Y	Y	Guam	Guam	Guam	N	None
23		146	165	Tichaira, Remedios LG	Daughter	F	Mix	5.0	S	N			Guam	Guam	Guam		None
24		146	165	Tichaira, Maria LG	Daughter	F	Mix	3.0	S				Guam	Guam	Guam		None
25		146	165	Tichaira, Erminia LG	Daughter	F	Mix	0.0	S				Guam	Guam	Guam		None

(CHAMORRO ROOTS GENEALOGY PROJECT ™ TRANSCRIPTION)
(COMPILED/TRANSCRIBED BY BERNARD T. PUNZALAN / HTTP://WWW.CHAMORROROOTS.COM)
FOURTEENTH CENSUS OF THE UNITED STATES: 1920–POPULATION
ISLAND OF GUAM

DISTRICT **1**
NAME OF PLACE **Agana City**
[Proper name and, also, name of class, as city, town, village, barrio, etc]

ENUMERATED BY ME ON THE 9th DAY OF April, 1920

Jose Kamminga ENUMERATOR

	Street	Dwelling no.	Family no.	NAME	RELATION	Sex	Color or race	Age	Single/married/widowed/divorced	Attended school since Sept. 1, 1919	Able to read	Able to write	Birthplace of person	Birthplace of father	Birthplace of mother	Able to speak English	OCCUPATION
		1	2	3	4	5	6	7	8	9	10	11	12	13	14	15	16	17
26	Santiago Street	147	166	Ibasco, Catalina	Head	F	Fil	23.0	S		N	N	Guam	Philippines	Guam	Y	None
27		147	166	Ibasco, Maria	Daughter	F	Fil	4.0	S				Guam	Unknown	Guam		None
28		147	166	Ibasco, Charlie	Son	M	Fil	0.1	S				Guam	Unknown	Guam		None
29		147	166	Ibasco, Santiago	Father	M	Fil	64.0	Wd		Y	N	Philippines	Philippines	Philippines	N	None
30		147	166	Ibasco, Josefa	Sister	F	Fil	33.0	S		Y	Y	Guam	Philippines	Guam	Y	None
31		147	166	Ibasco, Ana	Sister	F	Fil	26.0	S		Y	N	Guam	Philippines	Guam	Y	Cook
32		148	167	Santos, Enrique S	Head	M	Cha	33.0	M		Y	Y	Guam	Guam	Guam	Y	Laborer
33		148	167	Santos, Gertrudes T	Wife	F	Cha	30.0	M		Y	Y	Guam	Guam	Rota Island	Y	None
34		148	167	Santos, Maria T	Daughter	F	Cha	11.0	S	Y	Y	Y	Guam	Guam	Guam	Y	None
35		148	167	Santos, Jesus T	Son	M	Cha	10.0	S	Y	Y	Y	Guam	Guam	Guam	N	None
36		148	167	Santos, Vicente T	Son	M	Cha	5.0	S	N			Guam	Guam	Guam		None
37		148	167	Santos, Jose T	Son	M	Cha	3.0	S				Guam	Guam	Guam		None
38		148	167	Santos, Ana T	Daughter	F	Cha	1.0	S				Guam	Guam	Guam		None
39		149	168	Santos, Juan V	Head	M	Cha	30.0	M		Y	Y	Guam	Guam	Guam	Y	Laborer
40		149	168	Santos, Ampara D	Wife	F	Cha	38.0	M		Y	Y	Guam	Guam	Guam	N	None
41		149	168	Santos, Leonila D	Daughter	F	Cha	2.0	S				Guam	Guam	Guam		None
42		149	168	Santos, Jose D	Son	M	Cha	0.1	S				Guam	Guam	Guam		None
43		150	169	Rosario, Domingo R	Head	M	Fil	60.0	Wd		N	N	Philippines	Philippines	Philippines	N	None
44	(no street)	151	170	Flores, Francisco G	Head	M	Cha	36.0	M		Y	Y	Guam	Guam	Guam	Y	Farmer
45		151	170	Flores, Joaquina LG	Wife	F	Cha	29.0	M		Y	Y	Guam	Unknown	Unknown	Y	None
46		151	170	Flores, Angel LG	Son	M	Cha	10.0	S	Y	Y	Y	Guam	Guam	Guam	Y	None
47		151	170	Flores, Aurora LG	Daughter	F	Cha	9.0	S	Y	Y	Y	Guam	Guam	Guam	Y	None
48		151	170	Flores, Jesus LG	Son	M	Cha	6.0	S	N			Guam	Guam	Guam		None
49		151	170	Flores, Natividad LG	Daughter	F	Cha	3.0	S				Guam	Guam	Guam		None
50		151	170	Flores, Pedro LG	Son	M	Cha	0.5	S				Guam	Guam	Guam		None

(CHAMORRO ROOTS GENEALOGY PROJECT ™ TRANSCRIPTION)
(COMPILED/TRANSCRIBED BY BERNARD T. PUNZALAN / HTTP://WWW.CHAMORROROOTS.COM)

FOURTEENTH CENSUS OF THE UNITED STATES: 1920-POPULATION

ISLAND OF GUAM

DISTRICT 1
NAME OF PLACE Agana City

ENUMERATED BY ME ON THE 10th DAY OF April, 1920

Jose Kamminga ENUMERATOR

	PLACE OF ABODE			NAME	RELATION	PERSONAL DESCRIPTION					EDUCATION			NATIVITY				OCCUPATION
Street, avenue, road, etc.	No. dwelling house	No. of family		of each person whose place of abode on January 1, 1920, was in the family.	Relationship of this Person to the head of the family.	Sex	Color or race	Age at last birthday	Single, married, widowed, or divorced	Attended school any time since Sept. 1, 1919	Whether able to read.	Whether able to write.	Place of birth of this person.	Place of birth of father of this person.	Place of birth of mother of this person.	Whether able to speak English.	Trade, profession, or particular kind of work done
1	2	3	4		5	6	7	8	9	10	11	12	13	14	15	16	17
	151	170		Leon Guerrero, Joaquin A	Brother-in-law	M	Cha	25.0	S		Y	Y	Guam	Unknown	Guam	Y	Laborer
	152	171		Toves, Jose B	Head	M	Cha	55.0	M		Y	Y	Guam	Guam	Guam	N	Farmer
	152	171		Toves, Josefa H	Wife	F	Cha	49.0	M		N	N	Guam	Guam	Guam	N	None
[no street]	152	171		Toves, Candelaria H	Daughter	F	Cha	5.0	S	N			Guam	Guam	Guam	N	None
	152	171		Toves, Maria B	Daughter	F	Cha	22.0	S		Y	Y	Guam	Guam	Guam	Y	None
	152	171		Toves, Gabriela B	Daughter	F	Cha	19.0	S	N	Y	Y	Guam	Guam	Guam	N	None
	152	171		Toves, Rita B	Daughter	F	Cha	17.0	S	N	Y	Y	Guam	Guam	Guam	N	None
	152	171		Hernandez, Juan	Stepson	M	Cha	18.0	S	N	Y	Y	Guam	Unknown	Guam	N	Laborer
	152	171		Hernandez, Jesus	Stepson	M	Cha	14.0	S	N	Y	Y	Guam	Unknown	Guam	N	None
	152	171		Quichocho, Juan	Boarder	M	Cha	28.0	S		N	N	Guam	Unknown	Guam	N	Farm laborer working out
	152	172		Toves, Jesus B	Head	M	Cha	28.0	M		N	N	Guam	Guam	Guam	N	Farmer
	152	172		Toves, Manuela Q	Wife	F	Cha	27.0	M		Y	N	Guam	Unknown	Guam	N	None
	152	172		Toves, Maria Q	Daughter	F	Cha	4.0	S		N	N	Guam	Guam	Guam	N	None
	152	172		Toves, Jose Q	Son	M	Cha	1.0	S				Guam	Guam	Guam		None
	153	173		Ulloa, Juan LG	Head	M	Cha	51.0	M		Y	Y	Guam	Unknown	Guam	N	Mason
	153	173		Ulloa, Ana C	Wife	F	Cha	41.0	M		Y	Y	Guam	Guam	Guam	N	None
	153	173		Ulloa, Juan C	Son	M	Cha	16.0	S	N	Y	Y	Guam	Guam	Guam	Y	Laborer
Cerenola Street	153	173		Ulloa, Maria C	Daughter	F	Cha	14.0	S	N	Y	Y	Guam	Guam	Guam	Y	None
	153	174		Atoigue, Joaquina C	Head	F	Cha	28.0	M		Y	Y	Guam	Guam	Guam	N	Cook
	153	174		Atoigue, Jose C	Son	M	Cha	12.0	S	Y	Y	Y	Guam	Guam	Guam	N	None
	153	174		Atoigue, Eufracia C	Daughter	F	Cha	10.0	S	Y	Y	Y	Guam	Guam	Guam	N	None
	154	175		Rivera, Juan LG	Head	M	Cha	53.0	M		Y	Y	Guam	Guam	Guam	Y	Farmer
	154	175		Rivera, Manuel U	Son	M	Cha	8.0	S	Y			Guam	Guam	Guam		None
	154	175		Rivera, Juan U	Son	M	Cha	7.0	S	N			Guam	Guam	Guam		None
	154	175		Rivera, Leocardo U	Son	M	Cha	3.0	S				Guam	Guam	Guam		None

(CHAMORRO ROOTS GENEALOGY PROJECT ™ TRANSCRIPTION)
(COMPILED/TRANSCRIBED BY BERNARD T. PUNZALAN / HTTP://WWW.CHAMORROROOTS.COM)
FOURTEENTH CENSUS OF THE UNITED STATES: 1920—POPULATION
ISLAND OF GUAM

DISTRICT 1
NAME OF PLACE Agana City

ENUMERATED BY ME ON THE 10th DAY OF April, 1920

Jose Kamminga ENUMERATOR

[Proper name and, also, name of class, as city, town, village, barrio, etc]

	PLACE OF ABODE		NAME	RELATION	PERSONAL DESCRIPTION				EDUCATION			NATIVITY				OCCUPATION
Street, avenue, road, etc.	Number of dwelling house in order of visitation	Number of family in order of visitation	of each person whose place of abode on January 1, 1920, was in the family.	Relationship of this Person to the head of the family.	Sex	Color or race	Age at last birthday	Single, married, widowed or divorced	Attended school any time since sept. 1, 1919	Whether able to read.	Whether able to write.	Place of birth of this person.	Place of birth of father of this person.	Place of birth of mother of this person.	Whether able to speak English.	Trade, profession, or particular kind of work done, as salesman, laborer, clerk, cook, merchant, washerwoman, etc.
1	2	3	4	5	6	7	8	9	10	11	12	13	14	15	16	17
	154	175	Rivera, Benigno LG	Brother	M	Cha	46.0	S		Y	Y	Guam	Guam	Guam	N	Farm laborer home farm
	155	176	Castro, Jesus C	Head	M	Cha	32.0	M		Y	Y	Guam	Unknown	Guam	Y	Farmer
	155	176	Castro, Maria B	Wife	F	Cha	30.0	M		Y	Y	Guam	Guam	Guam	N	None
Gerenola Street	155	176	Castro, Jose B	Son	M	Cha	4.0	S				Guam	Guam	Guam		None
	155	176	Castro, Francisco B	Son	M	Cha	3.0	S				Guam	Guam	Guam		None
	155	176	Castro, Antonia B	Daughter	F	Cha	1.0	S				Guam	Guam	Guam		None
	156	178	Sablan, Lino A	Head	M	Cha	29.0	M		Y	Y	Guam	Guam	Guam	Y	Manager Soda work?
	156	178	Sablan, Antonia LG	Wife	F	Cha	25.0	M		Y	Y	Guam	Guam	Rota Island	Y	None
	156	178	Sablan, Antonio LG	Son	M	Cha	7.0	S	Y			Guam	Guam	Guam		None
	156	178	Sablan, Cristobal LG	Son	M	Cha	6.0	S	N			Guam	Guam	Guam		None
	156	178	Sablan, Dolores LG	Daughter	F	Cha	3.0	S				Guam	Guam	Guam		None
	156	178	Sablan, Vicente LG	Son	M	Cha	1.0	S				Guam	Guam	Guam		None
	157	179	Toves, Pedro	Head	M	Cha	35.0	M		Y	Y	Guam	Unknown	Guam	Y	Janitor
	157	179	Toves, Dolores S	Wife	F	Cha	31.0	M		Y	Y	Guam	Guam	Guam	N	None
	157	179	Toves, Elena S	Daughter	F	Cha	14.0	S	N	Y	Y	Guam	Guam	Guam	Y	None
Luchana Street	157	179	Toves, Agustin S	Son	M	Cha	10.0	S	Y	Y	Y	Guam	Guam	Guam	Y	None
	157	179	Toves, Jose S	Son	M	Cha	3.0	S				Guam	Guam	Guam		None
	157	179	Toves, Patricio S	Son	M	Cha	1.0	S				Guam	Guam	Guam		None
	157	179	Santos, Nieves T	Mother-in-law	F	Cha	58.0	Wd				Guam	Guam	Guam		None
	158	180	Acosta, Joaquin C	Head	M	Cha	48.0	Wd		N	N	Guam	Guam	Guam	N	Laborer
	158	180	Acosta, Antonio A	Son	M	Cha	16.0	S	N	N	N	Guam	Guam	Guam	N	Laborer
	158	180	Acosta, Maria A	Daughter	F	Cha	14.0	S	N	N	N	Guam	Guam	Guam	N	Laundress
	158	180	Acosta, Isabel A	Daughter	F	Cha	8.0	S	N			Guam	Guam	Guam		None
	158	180	Acosta, Dolores C	Sister	F	Cha	56.0	S		N	N	Guam	Guam	Guam	N	None
	159	181	Castro, Carmen C	Head	F	Cha	44.0	Wd		Y	Y	Guam	Guam	Guam	N	None

## 72

SHEET NO.
41A

(CHAMORRO ROOTS GENEALOGY PROJECT ™ TRANSCRIPTION)
(COMPILED/TRANSCRIBED BY BERNARD T. PUNZALAN / HTTP://WWW.CHAMORROROOTS.COM)

FOURTEENTH CENSUS OF THE UNITED STATES: 1920—POPULATION
ISLAND OF GUAM

DISTRICT 1
NAME OF PLACE Agana City

[Proper name and, also, name of class, as city, town, village, barrio, etc]

ENUMERATED BY ME ON THE 10th DAY OF April, 1920

Jose Kamminga ENUMERATOR

	PLACE OF ABODE		NAME	RELATION	PERSONAL DESCRIPTION				EDUCATION			NATIVITY				OCCUPATION
Street, avenue, road, etc.	Number of dwelling house in order of visitation	Number of family in order of visitation	Name of each person whose place of abode on January 1, 1920, was in the family. Enter surname, firs, then given name and middle initial if any. Include every person living on January 1, 1920. Omit children born since January 1, 1920.	Relationship of this person to the head of the family.	Sex	Color or race	Age at last birthday	Single, married, widowed or divorced	Attended school any time since Sept. 1, 1919	Whether able to read.	Whether able to write.	Place of birth of this person.	Place of birth of father of this person.	Place of birth of mother of this person.	Whether able to speak English.	Trade, profession, or particular kind of work done, as salesman, laborer, clerk, cook, merchant, washerwoman, etc.
1	2	3	4	5	6	7	8	9	10	11	12	13	14	15	16	17
	159	181	Castro, Juan C	Son	M	Cha	16.0	S	N	Y	Y	Guam	Guam	Guam	Y	Farm laborer home farm
	159	181	Castro, Jose C	Son	M	Cha	13.0	S	Y	Y	Y	Guam	Guam	Guam	N	None
	159	181	Castro, Miguel C	Son	M	Cha	9.0	S	Y			Guam	Guam	Guam		None
	159	182	Leon Guerrero, Rita A	Head	F	Cha	47.0	Wd		Y	N	Guam	Guam	Guam	N	None
	159	182	Palomo, Jesus LG	Son	M	Cha	30.0	S		Y	Y	Guam	Guam	Guam	N	Tinsmith
	159	182	Palomo, Tita LG	Daughter	F	Cha	26.0	S		Y	Y	Guam	Guam	Guam	N	None
	160	183	Leon Guerrero, Jesus P	Head	M	Cha	33.0	M		Y	Y	Guam	Guam	Guam	N	Farmer
	160	183	Leon Guerrero, Asuncion I	Wife	F	Cha	42.0	M		Y	N	Guam	Guam	Guam	N	None
	160	183	Leon Guerrero, Mariano I	Son	M	Cha	8.0	S	Y	Y		Guam	Guam	Guam	N	None
	160	183	Leon Guerrero, Joaquina I	Daughter	F	Cha	6.0	S	N			Guam	Guam	Guam		None
	160	183	Leon Guerrero, Maria I	Daughter	F	Cha	4.0	S				Guam	Guam	Guam		None
Luchana Street	161	184	Leon Guerrero, Jose P	Head	M	Cha	27.0	S		Y	Y	Guam	Guam	Guam	Y	Farmer
	161	184	Leon Guerrero, Maria P	Mother	F	Cha	55.0	Wd		Y	N	Guam	Guam	Guam	N	None
	161	184	Leon Guerrero, Vicente P	Brother	M	Cha	21.0	S	N	Y	N	Guam	Guam	Guam	N	Farm laborer home farm
	161	184	Leon Guerrero, Rosa P	Sister	F	Cha	17.0	S	N	Y	Y	Guam	Guam	Guam	N	None
	161	184	Leon Guerrero, Magdalena P	Sister	F	Cha	13.0	S	N	Y	Y	Guam	Guam	Guam	N	None
	161	184	Leon Guerrero, Luis P	Brother	M	Cha	10.0	S	N	Y	Y	Guam	Guam	Guam	N	None
	162	185	Perez, Luis C	Head	M	Cha	34.0	M		Y	Y	Guam	Guam	Guam	N	Farmer
	162	185	Perez, Maria P	Wife	F	Cha	36.0	M		Y	N	Guam	Guam	Guam	N	None
	162	185	Perez, Luis P	Son	M	Cha	13.0	S	Y	Y	Y	Guam	Guam	Guam	Y	None
	162	185	Perez, Soledad P	Daughter	F	Cha	12.0	S	N	N	N	Guam	Guam	Guam	N	None
	162	185	Perez, Vicente P	Son	M	Cha	10.0	S	Y	Y	Y	Guam	Guam	Guam	N	None
	162	185	Perez, Maria P jr	Daughter	F	Cha	7.0	S	N	Y	N	Guam	Guam	Guam	N	None
	162	185	Perez, Jose P	Son	M	Cha	6.0	S	N			Guam	Guam	Guam	N	None
	162	185	Perez, Juan P	Son	M	Cha	4.0	S				Guam	Guam	Guam		None

148

(CHAMORRO ROOTS GENEALOGY PROJECT ™ TRANSCRIPTION)
(COMPILED/TRANSCRIBED BY BERNARD T. PUNZALAN / HTTP://WWW.CHAMORROROOTS.COM)

FOURTEENTH CENSUS OF THE UNITED STATES: 1920—POPULATION

ISLAND OF GUAM

DISTRICT 1
NAME OF PLACE Agana City

[Proper name and, also, name of class, as city, town, village, barrio, etc]

ENUMERATED BY ME ON THE 12th DAY OF April, 1920

Jose Kamminga ENUMERATOR

	Street, avenue, road, etc.	Number of dwelling house in order of visitation	Number of family in order of visitation	NAME of each person whose place of abode on January 1, 1920, was in the family.	RELATION Relationship of this Person to the head of the family.	Sex	Color or race	Age at last birthday	Single, married, widowed or divorced	Attended school any time since Sept. 1, 1919	Whether able to read.	Whether able to write.	Place of birth of this person.	Place of birth of father of this person.	Place of birth of mother of this person.	Whether able to speak English.	OCCUPATION Trade, profession, or particular kind of work done
	1	2	3	4	5	6	7	8	9	10	11	12	13	14	15	16	17
26		162	185	Perez, Jesus P	Son	M	Cha	1.0	S				Guam	Guam	Guam		None
27		163	186	Mendiola, Venancio P	Head	M	Cha	41.0	M		Y	Y	Guam	Guam	Guam	N	Farmer
28		163	186	Mendiola, Vicenta B	Wife	F	Cha	35.0	M		Y	Y	Guam	Guam	Guam	N	None
29		163	186	Mendiola, Jose B	Son	M	Cha	12.0	S	Y	Y	Y	Guam	Guam	Guam	Y	None
30		163	186	Mendiola, Juan B	Son	M	Cha	11.0	S	Y	Y	Y	Guam	Guam	Guam	N	None
31		163	186	Mendiola, Maria B	Daughter	F	Cha	8.0	S	Y	Y	Y	Guam	Guam	Guam		None
32		163	186	Mendiola, Jesus B	Son	M	Cha	7.0	S	Y	Y	Y	Guam	Guam	Guam		None
33		164	187	Arriola, Francisco R	Head	M	Fil	42.0	M		Y	Y	Guam	Philippine Islands	Guam	N	Painter
34		164	187	Arriola, Ana C	Wife	F	Cha	41.0	M		Y	Y	Guam	Guam	Guam	N	None
35		164	187	Arriola, Dolores C	Daughter	F	Fil	20.0	S	N	Y	Y	Guam	Guam	Guam	Y	None
36		164	187	Arriola, Juan C	Son	M	Fil	16.0	S	N	Y	Y	Guam	Guam	Guam	Y	Farm laborer home farm
37		164	187	Arriola, Maria C	Daughter	F	Fil	13.0	S	N	Y	Y	Guam	Guam	Guam	N	None
38		164	187	Arriola, Josefa C	Daughter	F	Fil	7.0	S	Y			Guam	Guam	Guam		None
39		164	187	Arriola, Consolacion C	Daughter	F	Fil	4.0	S				Guam	Guam	Guam		None
40		164	187	Arriola, Filomena C	Daughter	F	Fil	2.0	S				Guam	Guam	Guam		None
41		165	188	Castro, Santiago O	Head	M	Cha	64.0	M		Y	Y	Guam	Guam	Guam	N	None
42		165	188	Castro, Nieves R	Wife	F	Cha	56.0	M		Y	Y	Guam	Guam	Guam	N	None
43		165	188	Castro, Joaquina R	Daughter	F	Cha	29.0	S		Y	Y	Guam	Guam	Guam	N	None
44		165	188	Castro, Juan R	Son	M	Cha	27.0	S		Y	Y	Guam	Guam	Guam	Y	Farm laborer home farm
45		165	188	Castro, Maria R	Daughter	F	Cha	20.0	S	N	Y	Y	Guam	Guam	Guam	Y	None
46		165	188	Castro, Manuel R	Son	M	Cha	16.0	S	N	Y	Y	Guam	Guam	Guam	Y	Farm laborer home farm
47		165	188	Palomo, Joaquin LG	Servant	M	Cha	22.0	S		Y	Y	Guam	Guam	Guam	Y	Servant
48	Luchana Street	166	189	Castro, Joaquin O	Head	M	Cha	53.0	M		Y	Y	Guam	Guam	Guam	N	Farmer
49		166	189	Castro, Maria C	Wife	F	Cha	52.0	M		Y	N	Guam	Guam	Guam	N	None
50		166	189	Mendiola, Manuel B	Boarder	M	Cha	13.0	S	Y	Y	Y	Guam	Guam	Guam	Y	None

149

## 73

SHEET NO.
42A

(CHAMORRO ROOTS GENEALOGY PROJECT ™ TRANSCRIPTION)
(COMPILED/TRANSCRIBED BY BERNARD T. PUNZALAN / HTTP://WWW.CHAMORROROOTS.COM)
FOURTEENTH CENSUS OF THE UNITED STATES: 1920-POPULATION
ISLAND OF GUAM

DISTRICT 1
NAME OF PLACE Agana City
[Proper name and, also, name of class, name of class, as city, town, village, barrio, etc]

ENUMERATED BY ME ON THE 12th DAY OF April, 1920

Jose Kamminga ENUMERATOR

Street, avenue, road, etc.	Number of dwelling house is order of visitation	Number of family in order of visitation	NAME	RELATION	Sex	Color or race	Age at last birthday	Single, married, widowed or divorced	Attended any school since sept. 1, 1919	Whether able to read.	Whether able to write.	Place of birth of this person.	Place of birth of father of this person.	Place of birth of mother of this person.	Whether able to speak English.	OCCUPATION
1	2	3	4	5	6	7	8	9	10	11	12	13	14	15	16	17
	167	190	Sablan, Ignacio C	Head	M	Cha	43.0	M		Y	Y	Guam	Guam	Guam	Y	Deputy Commissioner
	167	190	Sablan, Vicenta C	Wife	F	Cha	48.0	M		Y	Y	Guam	Guam	Guam	N	None
	167	190	Castro, Susana O	Sister-in-law	F	Cha	51.0	S		Y	Y	Guam	Guam	Guam	N	None
	168	191	Leon Guerrero, Filomena A	Head	F	Fil	61.0	Wd		Y	Y	Rota Island	Philippine Island	Guam	N	None
	168	191	Leon Guerrero, Jose A	Son	M	Fil	31.0	Wd	N	Y	N	Guam	Guam	Rota Island	N	Farm laborer home farm
Luchana Street	168	191	Leon Guerrero, Vicente A	Son	M	Fil	20.0	S		Y	Y	Guam	Guam	Rota Island	Y	Laborer
	168	192	Castro, Francisco R	Head	M	Cha	33.0	M		Y	Y	Guam	Guam	Guam	Y	Deputy Commissioner
	168	192	Castro, Ana LG	Wife	F	Cha	23.0	M		Y	Y	Guam	Rota Island	Rota Island	Y	None
	168	192	Castro, Tomas LG	Son	M	Cha	4.0	S				Guam	Guam	Guam		None
	168	192	Castro, Engracia LG	Daughter	F	Cha	2.0	S				Guam	Guam	Guam		None
	169	193	Acosta, Juan B	Head	M	Cha	45.0	M		Y	Y	Guam	Unknown	Guam	N	Farmer
	169	193	Acosta, Maria B	Wife	F	Cha	42.0	M		N	N	Guam	Guam	Guam	N	None
	169	193	Acosta, Rosa B	Daughter	F	Cha	24.0	S		N	N	Guam	Guam	Guam	Y	None
	169	193	Acosta, Amalia B	Daughter	F	Cha	15.0	S	N	N	N	Guam	Guam	Guam	Y	None
	169	193	Acosta, Jose B	Son	M	Cha	13.0	S	N	N	N	Guam	Guam	Guam	N	None
	169	193	Acosta, Juan B jr	Son	M	Cha	11.0	S	Y	Y	N	Guam	Guam	Guam	N	None
	169	193	Acosta, Francisco B	Son	M	Cha	7.0	S	Y			Guam	Guam	Guam	N	None
	170	194	Sypingco, Ignacia L	Head	M	Cha	42.0	M		Y	N	Guam	Unknown	Unknown	N	Laundress
	170	194	Sypingco, Maria L	Wife	M	Chi n	16.0	S	N	Y	Y	Guam	Guam	Guam	Y	None
San Nicolas Street	171	195	Flores, Jose P	Head	M	Cha	36.0	M		Y	Y	Guam	Guam	Guam	Y	Carpenter
	171	195	Flores, Dolores C	Wife	F	Cha	30.0	M		Y	Y	Guam	Guam	Guam	Y	None
	171	195	Flores, Maria C	Daughter	F	Cha	4.0	S				Guam	Guam	Guam		None
	171	195	Flores, Josefina C	Daughter	F	Cha	3.0	S				Guam	Guam	Guam		None
	171	195	Flores, Jose C	Son	M	Cha	1.0	S				Guam	Guam	Guam		None
	171	195	Flores, Jesus C	Son	M	Cha	0.2	S				Guam	Guam	Guam		None

(CHAMORRO ROOTS GENEALOGY PROJECT ™ TRANSCRIPTION)
(COMPILED/TRANSCRIBED BY BERNARD T. PUNZALAN / HTTP://WWW.CHAMORROROOTS.COM)

FOURTEENTH CENSUS OF THE UNITED STATES: 1920-POPULATION
ISLAND OF GUAM

DISTRICT 1
NAME OF PLACE **Agana City**
[Proper name and, also, name of class, as city, town, village, barrio, etc]

ENUMERATED BY ME ON THE 13th DAY OF April, 1920

Jose Kamminga ENUMERATOR

	2	3	4 NAME	5 RELATION	6 Sex	7 Color or race	8 Age	9	10	11	12	13	14	15	16	17 OCCUPATION
26	172	196	Flores, Josefa P	Head	F	Cha	61.0	Wd		Y	Y	Guam	Guam	Guam	N	None
27	172	196	Flores, Jesus P	Son	M	Cha	34.0	S		Y	Y	Guam	Guam	Guam	Y	Carpenter
28	172	196	Flores, Joaquin P	Son	M	Cha	31.0	S		Y	Y	Guam	Guam	Guam	Y	Carpenter
29	172	196	Flores, Ana P	Daughter	F	Cha	26.0	S		Y	Y	Guam	Guam	Guam	Y	None
30	172	196	Flores, Mercedez P	Daughter	F	Cha	20.0	S	N	Y	Y	Guam	Guam	Guam	Y	None
31	172	196	Flores, Jose	Boarder	M	Cha	6.0	S	N			Guam	Unknown	Guam		None
32	173	197	Torres, Rosa T	Head	F	Cha	54.0	Wd		Y	N	Guam	Guam	Guam	N	None
33	173	197	Torres, Jesus T	Son	M	Cha	29.0	S		Y	Y	Guam	Guam	Guam	Y	Farm laborer home farm
34	173	197	Torres, Maria T	Daughter	F	Cha	28.0	S		Y	Y	Guam	Guam	Guam	Y	Cook
35	173	197	Torres, Ancermo T	Son	M	Cha	26.0	S		Y	Y	Guam	Guam	Guam	Y	None
36	173	197	Torres, Mariano T	Son	M	Cha	22.0	S		Y	Y	Guam	Guam	Guam	Y	Farm laborer home farm
37	173	197	Torres, Josefa T	Daughter	F	Cha	19.0	S	N	Y	Y	Guam	Guam	Guam	Y	None
38	173	197	Torres, Ana T	Daughter	F	Cha	17.0	S	N	Y	Y	Guam	Guam	Guam	Y	None
39	173	197	Torres, Juana T	Daughter	F	Cha	7.0	S	N	Y	Y	Guam	Guam	Guam	Y	None
40	174	198	Perez, Matias LG	Head	M	Cha	33.0	M		Y	Y	Guam	Guam	Guam	Y	Carpenter
41	174	198	Perez, Josefa P	Wife	F	Cha	24.0	M		Y	Y	Guam	Guam	Guam	Y	None
42	174	198	Palomo, Antonio R	Brother-in-law	M	Cha	19.0	S	N	Y	Y	Guam	Guam	Guam	Y	Enlisted man USN
43	175	199	Palomo, Rita	Head	F	Cha	39.0	Wd	N	Y	N	Guam	Unknown	Guam	N	Laundress
44	175	199	Mendiola, Juan P	Son	M	Cha	16.0	S	N	Y	Y	Guam	Guam	Guam	Y	Storekeeper
45	175	199	Mendiola, Dolores P	Daughter	F	Cha	15.0	S	Y	Y	Y	Guam	Guam	Guam	Y	None
46	175	199	Mendiola, Francisco P	Son	M	Cha	12.0	S	Y	Y	Y	Guam	Guam	Guam	Y	None
47	175	199	Mendiola, Maria P	Daughter	F	Cha	11.0	S	Y	Y	Y	Guam	Guam	Guam	N	None
48	175	199	Mendiola, Asuncion P	Daughter	F	Cha	10.0	S	Y	Y	Y	Guam	Guam	Guam	N	None
49	175	199	Mendiola, Antonia P	Daughter	F	Cha	7.0	S	Y	Y	Y	Guam	Guam	Guam		None
50	175	199	Mendiola, Nicolasa P	Daughter	F	Cha	6.0	S	N			Guam	Guam	Guam		None

Street: San Nicolas Street

(CHAMORRO ROOTS GENEALOGY PROJECT ™ TRANSCRIPTION)
(COMPILED/TRANSCRIBED BY BERNARD T. PUNZALAN / HTTP://WWW.CHAMORROROOTS.COM)

FOURTEENTH CENSUS OF THE UNITED STATES: 1920-POPULATION

ISLAND OF GUAM

ENUMERATED BY ME ON THE 13th DAY OF April, 1920

Jose Kamminga ENUMERATOR

DISTRICT 1
NAME OF PLACE Agana City

[Proper name and, also, name of class, as city, town, village, barrio, etc]

	Street	Dwelling No.	Family No.	NAME	RELATION	Sex	Color or race	Age	Marital	Attended school since Sept. 1, 1919	Able to read	Able to write	Birthplace of person	Birthplace of father	Birthplace of mother	Able to speak English	OCCUPATION
		2	3	4	5	6	7	8	9	10	11	12	13	14	15	16	17
1		176	200	Baza, Luis M	Head	M	Cha	44.0	M		Y	Y	Guam	Guam	Guam	Y	Retail merchant
2		176	200	Baza, Rosa C	Wife	F	Cha	43.0	M		Y	Y	Guam	Guam	Guam	N	None
3		176	200	Baza, Antonio C	Son	M	Cha	13.0	S	N	Y	Y	Guam	Guam	Guam	Y	None
4		176	200	Baza, Feliza C	Daughter	F	Cha	11.0	S	Y	Y	Y	Guam	Guam	Guam	Y	None
5		176	200	Baza, Luis C	Son	M	Cha	9.0	S	Y			Guam	Guam	Guam		None
6		176	200	Baza, Maria C	Daughter	F	Cha	7.0	S	N			Guam	Guam	Guam		None
7		176	200	Baza, Jose C	Son	M	Cha	4.0	S				Guam	Guam	Guam		None
8		177	201	Castro, Mariano C	Head	M	Cha	47.0	M		Y	Y	Guam	Guam	Guam	N	Farmer
9		177	201	Castro, Ana B	Wife	F	Cha	47.0	M		Y	Y	Guam	Guam	Guam	N	None
10	San Nicolas Street	177	201	Castro, Rita B	Daughter	F	Cha	13.0	S	Y	Y	Y	Guam	Guam	Guam	Y	None
11		177	201	Castro, Concepcion B	Daughter	F	Cha	8.0	S	Y	Y	Y	Guam	Guam	Guam		None
12		177	201	Castro, Jose B	Son	M	Cha	3.0	S				Guam	Guam	Guam		None
13		177	201	Atoigue, Joaquina L	Servant	F	Cha	21.0	S	N	Y	Y	Guam	Guam	Guam	Y	Servant
14		177	201	Atoigue, Jesus L	Servant	M	Cha	17.0	S	N	Y	Y	Guam	Guam	Guam	Y	Servant
15		177	201	Cruz, Ana	Servant	F	Cha	19.0	S	N	Y	Y	Guam	Guam	Guam	N	Servant
16		178	202	Duenas, Luis P	Head	M	Cha	56.0	M		Y	Y	Guam	Guam	Guam	N	Farmer
17		178	202	Duenas, Josefa B	Wife	F	Cha	49.0	M		Y	Y	Guam	Guam	Guam	N	None
18		178	202	Duenas, Jesus B	Son	M	Cha	8.0	S	Y	Y	Y	Guam	Guam	Guam	N	None
19		178	202	Duenas, Pedro B	Son	M	Cha	5.0	S	N			Guam	Guam	Guam		None
20		178	202	Evaristo, Maria	Servant	F	Cha	17.0	S	N	Y	Y	Guam	Unknown	Guam	N	Servant
21		179	203	Leon Guerrero, Justa B	Head	F	Cha	52.0	Wd		Y	Y	Guam	Guam	Guam	N	None
22		179	203	Leon Guerrero, Francisco B	Son	M	Cha	21.0	S	N	Y	Y	Guam	Guam	Guam	Y	Poultry rancher
23		179	203	Leon Guerrero, Pedro B	Son	M	Cha	10.0	S	Y	Y	Y	Guam	Guam	Guam	Y	None
24		179	204	Camacho, Enrique M	Head	M	Cha	28.0	M		Y	Y	Guam	Guam	Guam	Y	Farmer
25		179	204	Camacho, Emeteria	Wife	F	Cha	24.0	M		Y	Y	Guam	Guam	Guam	Y	None

(CHAMORRO ROOTS GENEALOGY PROJECT ™ TRANSCRIPTION)
(COMPILED/TRANSCRIBED BY BERNARD T. PUNZALAN / HTTP://WWW.CHAMORROROOTS.COM)

FOURTEENTH CENSUS OF THE UNITED STATES: 1920-POPULATION

ISLAND OF GUAM

DISTRICT 1
NAME OF PLACE Agana City

[Proper name and, also, name of class, as city, town, village, barrio, etc]

ENUMERATED BY ME ON THE 13th DAY OF April, 1920

Jose Kamminga ENUMERATOR

	PLACE OF ABODE			NAME	RELATION	PERSONAL DESCRIPTION				EDUCATION			NATIVITY				OCCUPATION
Street, avenue, road, etc.	Number of dwelling house is order of visitation	Number of family in order of visitation		Name of each person whose place of abode on January 1, 1920, was in the family.	Relationship of this Person to the head of the family.	Sex	Color or race	Age at last birthday	Single, married, widowed or divorced	Attended school any time since Sept. 1, 1919	Whether able to read.	Whether able to write.	Place of birth of this person.	Place of birth of father of this person.	Place of birth of mother of this person.	Whether able to speak English.	Trade, profession, or particular kind of work done, as salesman, laborer, clerk, cook, merchant, washerwoman, etc.
1	2	3	4		5	6	7	8	9	10	11	12	13	14	15	16	17
26	179	204		Camacho, Antonia LG	Daughter	F	Cha	3.0	S				Guam	Guam	Guam		None
27	179	204		Camacho, Maria LG	Daughter	F	Cha	2.0	S				Guam	Guam	Guam		None
28	179	204		Camacho, Zuilo LG	Son	M	Cha	0.1	S				Guam	Guam	Guam		None
29	180	205		Leon Guerrero, Lorenzo M	Head	M	Cha	65.0	M		Y	Y	Guam	Guam	Guam	Y	Retail merchant
30	180	205		Leon Guerrero, Joaquina B	Wife	F	Cha	59.0	M		Y	Y	Guam	Guam	Guam	N	None
31	180	205		Leon Guerrero, Joaquin B	Son	M	Cha	25.0	S	N	Y	Y	Guam	Guam	Guam	Y	Storekeeper
32	180	205		Leon Guerrero, Rosario B	Daughter	F	Cha	21.0	S	N	Y	Y	Guam	Guam	Guam	Y	None
33	180	205		Borja, Lorenso R	Boarder	M	Cha	6.0	S				Guam	Guam	Guam		None
34	180	205		Quichocho, Rosa G	Servant	F	Cha	40.0	S		Y	Y	Guam	Guam	Guam	N	Servant
35	180	205		Quichocho, Tomasa	Servant	F	Cha	14.0	S	N	Y	Y	Guam	Unknown	Guam	N	Servant
36	180	205		Perez, Gregorio G	Servant	M	Cha	19.0	S	N	Y	Y	Guam	Unknown	Guam	Y	Servant
37	180	206		Leon Guerrero, Francisco B	Head	M	Cha	23.0	M		Y	Y	Guam	Guam	Guam	Y	Storekeeper
38	180	206		Leon Guerrero, Maria C	Wife	F	Cha	24.0	M		Y	Y	Guam	Guam	Guam	Y	None
39	180	206		Leon Guerrero, Emilia C	Daughter	F	Cha	3.0	S				Guam	Guam	Guam		None
40	180	206		Leon Guerrero, Enrique C	Son	M	Cha	2.0	S				Guam	Guam	Guam		None
41	180	206		Leon Guerrero, Victoria C	Daughter	F	Cha	1.0	S				Guam	Guam	Guam		None
42	181	207		Lujan, Juan R	Head	M	Cha	35.0	M		Y	Y	Guam	Guam	Guam	Y	Janitor
43	181	207		Lujan, Dolores C	Wife	F	Cha	21.0	M	N	Y	Y	Guam	Guam	Guam	Y	None
44	181	207		Lujan, Ana C	Daughter	F	Cha	1.0	S				Guam	Guam	Guam		None
45	181	208		Cruz, Rita S	Head	F	Cha	47.0	Wd		Y	N	Guam	Guam	Guam	N	None
46	181	208		Cruz, Vicente S	Son	M	Cha	28.0	S		Y	Y	Guam	Guam	Guam	Y	Farm laborer home farm
47	181	208		Cruz, Joaquina S	Daughter	F	Cha	19.0	S	N	Y	Y	Guam	Guam	Guam	Y	None
48	181	208		Cruz, Josefa S	Daughter	F	Cha	16.0	S		Y	Y	Guam	Guam	Guam	Y	None
49	182	209		Gogue, Josefa M	Head	M	Cha	33.0	M		Y	Y	Guam	Guam	Guam	N	Farmer
50	182	209		Gogue, Ana LG	Wife	F	Cha	26.0	M		Y	Y	Guam	Guam	Guam	N	None

San Nicolas Street

153

(CHAMORRO ROOTS GENEALOGY PROJECT ™ TRANSCRIPTION)

(COMPILED/TRANSCRIBED BY BERNARD T. PUNZALAN / HTTP://WWW.CHAMORROROOTS.COM)

FOURTEENTH CENSUS OF THE UNITED STATES: 1920–POPULATION
ISLAND OF GUAM

ENUMERATED BY ME ON THE 13th DAY OF April, 1920

Jose Kamminga ENUMERATOR

DISTRICT 1
NAME OF PLACE Agana City
[Proper name and, also, name of class, as city, town, village, barrio, etc]

	Dwelling No. (2)	Family No. (3)	NAME (4)	RELATION (5)	Sex (6)	Color or race (7)	Age (8)	Marital (9)	School (10)	Read (11)	Write (12)	Birthplace (13)	Father (14)	Mother (15)	English (16)	OCCUPATION (17)
1	182	209	Gogue, Jesus LG	Son	M	Cha	9.0	S	Y			Guam	Guam	Guam		None
2	182	209	Gogue, Justo LG	Son	M	Cha	6.0	S	N			Guam	Guam	Guam		None
3	182	209	Gogue, Jose LG	Son	M	Cha	1.0	S				Guam	Guam	Guam		None
4	183	210	Cruz, Jose S	Head	M	Cha	48.0	M		N	N	Guam	Guam	Guam	Y	Farmer
5	183	210	Meno, Amparo B	Wife	F	Cha	39.0	M		Y	Y	Guam	Guam	Guam	N	None
6	183	210	Meno, Josefa B	Step-daughter	F	Cha	20.0	S	N	Y	Y	Guam	Guam	Guam	Y	None
7	183	210	Meno, Ana B	Step-daughter	F	Cha	16.0	S	N	Y	Y	Guam	Guam	Guam	Y	Servant
8	183	210	Meno, Jose B	Step son	M	Cha	14.0	S	N	Y	N	Guam	Guam	Guam	N	Farm laborer home farm
9	183	210	Meno, Rosa B	Step-daughter	F	Cha	8.0	S	Y			Guam	Guam	Guam		None
10	183	210	Meno, Joaquin B	Step son	M	Cha	6.0	S	N			Guam	Guam	Guam		None
11	183	210	Meno, Maria B	Step-daughter	F	Cha	3.0	S				Guam	Guam	Guam		None
12	184	211	White, William P	Head	M	B	58.0	M		Y	Y	Guam	United States	Guam	Y	Farmer
13	184	211	White, Maria F	Wife	F	Cha	60.0	M		N	N	Guam	Guam	Guam	N	None
14	184	211	White, Magdalena F	Daughter	F	B	25.0	S		Y	Y	Guam	Guam	Guam	Y	None
15	184	211	White, Tomasa F	Daughter	F	B	21.0	S	N	Y	Y	Guam	Guam	Guam	Y	None
16	185	212	White, Juan F	Head	M	B	35.0	M		Y	Y	Guam	Guam	Guam	Y	Fireman
17	185	212	White, Antonia C	Wife	F	Cha	26.0	M		Y	Y	Guam	Guam	Guam	Y	None
18	185	212	White, Maria C	Daughter	F	B	7.0	S	N			Guam	Guam	Guam		None
19	185	212	White, Juan C	Son	M	B	5.0	S				Guam	Guam	Guam		None
20	185	212	White, Dolores C	Daughter	F	B	3.0	S				Guam	Guam	Guam		None
21	186	213	Untalan, Jesus B	Head	M	Cha	40.0	M		Y	Y	Guam	Guam	Guam	N	Farmer
22	186	213	Untalan, Ana F	Wife	F	Cha	29.0	M		Y	N	Guam	Guam	Guam	N	None
23	186	213	Untalan, Tomas F	Son	M	Cha	8.0	S	Y			Guam	Guam	Guam		None
24	186	213	Untalan, Josefina F	Daughter	F	Cha	6.0	S	Y			Guam	Guam	Guam		None
25	186	213	Untalan, Carlota F	Daughter	F	Cha	5.0	S	Y			Guam	Guam	Guam		None

Street: San Nicolas Street

(CHAMORRO ROOTS GENEALOGY PROJECT ™ TRANSCRIPTION)
(COMPILED/TRANSCRIBED BY BERNARD T. PUNZALAN / HTTP://WWW.CHAMORROROOTS.COM)
FOURTEENTH CENSUS OF THE UNITED STATES: 1920-POPULATION
ISLAND OF GUAM

DISTRICT 1
NAME OF PLACE Agana City

[Proper name and, also, name of class, as city, town, village, barrio, etc]

ENUMERATED BY ME ON THE 14th DAY OF April, 1920

Jose Kamminga ENUMERATOR

	Street, avenue, road, etc.	Number of dwelling house	Number of family	NAME	RELATION	Sex	Color or race	Age at last birthday	Single, married, widowed or divorced	Attended school since Sept. 1, 1919	Whether able to read	Whether able to write	Place of birth of this person	Place of birth of father	Place of birth of mother	Whether able to speak English	OCCUPATION
	1	2	3	4	5	6	7	8	9	10	11	12	13	14	15	16	17
26		186	213	Untalan, Maria F	Daughter	F	Cha	3.0	S				Guam	Guam	Guam		None
27		187	214	Sablan, Joaquin R	Head	M	Cha	48.0	M		Y	Y	Guam	Guam	Guam	N	Farmer
28		187	214	Sablan, Maria C	Wife	F	Cha	40.0	M				Guam	Guam	Guam	N	None
29		187	214	Sablan, Maria C jr	Daughter	F	Cha	15.0	S		Y	Y	Guam	Guam	Guam	Y	None
30		187	214	Sablan, Natividad C	Daughter	F	Cha	9.0	S	Y			Guam	Guam	Guam		None
31		187	214	Sablan, Mariano C	Son	M	Cha	7.0	S	Y			Guam	Guam	Guam		None
32		187	214	Sablan, Jose C	Son	M	Cha	4.0	S				Guam	Guam	Guam		None
33		187	214	Sablan, Ana C	Daughter	F	Cha	2.0	S				Guam	Guam	Guam		None
34		188	215	Aguon, Rosauro U	Head	M	Cha	40.0	M		Y	Y	Guam	Guam	Guam	N	Farmer
35		188	215	Aguon, Andrea S	Wife	F	Cha	43.0	M		Y	Y	Guam	Guam	Guam	N	None
36		188	215	Aguon, Jose S	Son	M	Cha	18.0	S	N	Y	Y	Guam	Guam	Guam	Y	Enlisted man USN
37		188	215	Aguon, Juan S	Son	M	Cha	16.0	S	N	Y	Y	Guam	Guam	Guam	Y	Storekeeper
38		188	215	Aguon, Ana S	Daughter	F	Cha	12.0	S	N	Y	Y	Guam	Guam	Guam	Y	None
39		188	215	Aguon, Joaquin S	Son	M	Cha	10.0	S	Y	Y	Y	Guam	Guam	Guam	Y	None
40		188	215	Aguon, Rosa S	Daughter	F	Cha	9.0	S	Y	Y	Y	Guam	Guam	Guam	Y	None
41	San Nicolas Street	188	215	Aguon, Francisco S	Son	M	Cha	7.0	S	Y			Guam	Guam	Guam		None
42		188	215	Aguon, Francis S	Son	M	Cha	5.0	S	N			Guam	Guam	Guam		None
43		188	215	Aguon, Magdalena S	Daughter	F	Cha	4.0	S				Guam	Guam	Guam		None
44		188	215	Aguon, Blandina S	Daughter	F	Cha	1.0	S				Guam	Guam	Guam		None
45		188	215	Aguon, Pedro S	Son	M	Cha	0.0	S				Guam	Guam	Guam		None
46		189	216	Francisco, Nicolas P	Head	M	Wh	55.0	M		Y	N	Guam	Portugal	Guam	Y	Farmer
47		189	216	Francisco, Ignacia C	Wife	F	Cha	43.0	M		Y	N	Guam	Guam	Guam	N	None
48		189	216	Francisco, Vicente C	Son	M	Mix	22.0	S		Y	Y	Guam	Guam	Guam	Y	Farm laborer home farm
49		189	216	Francisco, Jose C	Son	M	Mix	19.0	S	N	N	Y	Guam	Guam	Guam	Y	Farm laborer home farm
50		189	216	Francisco, Maria C	Daughter	F	Mix	17.0	S	N	Y	Y	Guam	Guam	Guam	Y	None

(CHAMORRO ROOTS GENEALOGY PROJECT ™ TRANSCRIPTION)
(COMPILED/TRANSCRIBED BY BERNARD T. PUNZALAN / HTTP://WWW.CHAMORROROOTS.COM)
FOURTEENTH CENSUS OF THE UNITED STATES: 1920—POPULATION
ISLAND OF GUAM

ENUMERATED BY ME ON THE 14th DAY OF April, 1920

Jose Kamminga ENUMERATOR

DISTRICT 1
NAME OF PLACE Agana City
[Proper name and, also, name of class, as city, town, village, barrio, etc]

	Street	Dwelling No.	Family No.	NAME	RELATION	Sex	Color or race	Age	Single/married/wid/div	Attended school since Sept. 1, 1919	Able to read	Able to write	Place of birth of this person	Place of birth of father	Place of birth of mother	Able to speak English	OCCUPATION
		2	3	4	5	6	7	8	9	10	11	12	13	14	15	16	17
1		189	216	Francisco, Pedro C	Son	M	Mix	16.0	S	N	Y	Y	Guam	Guam	Guam	Y	Farm laborer home farm
2		189	216	Francisco, Joaquin C	Son	M	Mix	14.0	S	N	Y	Y	Guam	Guam	Guam	Y	Farm laborer home farm
3		189	216	Francisco, Carmen C	Daughter	F	Mix	10.0	S	N	Y	N	Guam	Guam	Guam	N	None
4		189	216	Francisco, Juan C	Son	M	Mix	8.0	S	N			Guam	Guam	Guam		None
5		189	216	Francisco, Dolores C	Daughter	F	Mix	7.0	S	Y			Guam	Guam	Guam		None
6		189	216	Francisco, Antonio C	Son	M	Mix	5.0	S	N			Guam	Guam	Guam		None
7		190	217	Cabrera, Rosa M	Head	F	Cha	33.0	Wd		Y	Y	Guam	Guam	Guam	N	Laundress
8		190	217	Cabrera, Ignacio M	Son	M	Cha	14.0	S	N	Y	Y	Guam	Guam	Guam	Y	Farm laborer home farm
9		190	217	Cabrera, Juan M	Son	M	Cha	9.0	S	Y	Y	Y	Guam	Guam	Guam		None
10		190	217	Cabrera, Maria M	Daughter	F	Cha	7.0	S	Y	Y	Y	Guam	Guam	Guam		None
11		190	217	Cabrera, Rosario M	Daughter	F	Cha	3.0	S				Guam	Guam	Guam		None
12	San Nicolas Street	190	217	Cabrera, Concepcion M	Daughter	F	Cha	1.0	S				Guam	Guam	Guam		None
13		190	217	Palomo, Rosa P	Aunt	F	Cha	81.0	Wd		N	N	Guam	Guam	Guam	N	None
14		190	217	Cabrera, Maria T	Cousin	F	Cha	33.0	S		Y	Y	Saipan Island	Guam	Guam	N	Laundress
15		190	217	Cabrera, Ignacia	Niece	F	Cha	9.0	S	N			Saipan Island	Unknown	Saipan Island		None
16		191	218	Leon Guerrero, Francisco LG	Head	M	Cha	36.0	M		Y	Y	Guam	Guam	Guam	Y	Electrician
17		191	218	Leon Guerrero, Isabel D	Wife	F	Cha	32.0	M		Y	Y	Guam	Guam	Guam	N	None
18		191	218	Leon Guerrero, Concepcion D	Daughter	F	Cha	10.0	S	Y	Y	Y	Guam	Guam	Guam	Y	None
19		191	218	Leon Guerrero, Juan D	Son	M	Cha	8.0	S	Y	Y	Y	Guam	Guam	Guam		None
20		191	218	Leon Guerrero, Balbino D	Son	M	Cha	4.0	S				Guam	Guam	Guam		None
21		192	219	Castro, Vicente R	Head	M	Cha	59.0	S		Y	Y	Guam	Guam	Guam	N	Farmer
22		192	219	Castro, Luis R	Brother	M	Cha	44.0	S		Y	Y	Guam	Guam	Guam	N	Farm laborer home farm
23		192	219	Castro, Joaquina R	Sister	F	Cha	53.0	Wd		Y	Y	Guam	Guam	Guam	N	None
24		192	219	Castro, Juan C	Nephew	M	Cha	16.0	S	N	Y	Y	Guam	Guam	Guam	N	None
25		192	219	Castro, Concepcion C	Niece	F	Cha	15.0	S	N	Y	Y	Guam	Guam	Guam	Y	None

(CHAMORRO ROOTS GENEALOGY PROJECT ™ TRANSCRIPTION)
(COMPILED/TRANSCRIBED BY BERNARD T. PUNZALAN / HTTP://WWW.CHAMORROROOTS.COM)

FOURTEENTH CENSUS OF THE UNITED STATES: 1920–POPULATION
ISLAND OF GUAM

DISTRICT 1
NAME OF PLACE **Agana City**
[Proper name and, also, name of class, as city, town, village, barrio, etc]

ENUMERATED BY ME ON THE 15th DAY OF April, 1920

Jose Kamminga ENUMERATOR

	1	2	3	4 NAME	5 RELATION	6 Sex	7 Color or race	8 Age	9	10	11 Read	12 Write	13 Birthplace person	14 Birthplace father	15 Birthplace mother	16 Eng.	17 OCCUPATION
26		193	220	Arriola, Juana A	Head	M	Cha	50.0	Wd		N	N	Guam	Guam	Guam	N	None
27		193	220	Arriola, Concepcion A	Daughter	F	Cha	33.0	S		N	N	Guam	Guam	Guam	N	None
28		193	220	Arriola, Rufina A	Daughter	F	Cha	19.0	S	N	Y	Y	Guam	Guam	Guam	Y	None
29		193	220	Arriola, Vicente A	Son	M	Cha	16.0	S	N	Y	Y	Guam	Guam	Guam	Y	Carpenter
30		193	220	Arriola, Jose	Grandson	M	Cha	3.0	S				Guam	Unknown	Guam		None
31		193	220	Arriola, Jose	Grandson	M	Cha	1.0	S				Guam	Unknown	Guam		None
32		193	220	Alvarez, Dolores M	Cousin	F	Cha	69.0	Wd		N	N	Guam	Guam	Guam	N	None
33		193	220	Hernandez, Eugenio P	Boarder	M	Cha	10.0	S	N	N	N	Guam	Guam	Guam	N	None
34		194	221	Quichocho, Juan B	Head	M	Cha	50.0	M		N	N	Guam	Guam	Guam	N	Farmer
35	San Nicolas Street	194	221	Quichocho, Maria R	Wife	F	Cha	48.0	M		Y	Y	Guam	Guam	Guam	N	None
36		194	222	Quichocho, Jose R	Head	M	Cha	26.0	M		Y	Y	Guam	Guam	Guam	Y	Policeman
37		194	222	Quichocho, Rufina L	Wife	F	Cha	28.0	M		Y	N	Guam	Guam	Guam	Y	None
38		194	222	Quichocho, Maria L	Daughter	F	Cha	5.0	S				Guam	Guam	Guam		None
39		194	222	Quichocho, Jesus L	Son	M	Cha	2.0	S				Guam	Guam	Guam		None
40		195	223	Untalan, Ana P	Head	F	Cha	53.0	Wd		Y	Y	Guam	Guam	Guam	N	None
41		195	223	Untalan, Maria P	Daughter	F	Cha	30.0	S		Y	Y	Guam	Guam	Guam	N	None
42		195	223	Untalan, Joaquina P	Daughter	F	Cha	21.0	S	N	Y	Y	Guam	Guam	Guam	Y	None
43		195	223	Untalan, Vicente P	Son	M	Cha	19.0	S	N	Y	Y	Guam	Guam	Guam	Y	Farm laborer home farm
44		195	223	Untalan, Jesus P	Son	M	Cha	17.0	S	N	Y	Y	Guam	Guam	Guam	Y	Farm laborer home farm
45		195	223	Untalan, Joaquin P	Son	M	Cha	15.0	S	N	Y	Y	Guam	Guam	Guam	Y	None
46		196	224	Kamikabya, K	Head	M	Jp	42.0	M		Y	Y	Japan	Japan	Japan	Y	Retail merchant
47		196	224	Kamikabya, Lai	Wife	F	Jp	35.0	M		Y	Y	Japan	Japan	Japan	N	None
48		197	225	Palomo, Jose C	Head	M	Cha	58.0	M		Y	Y	Guam	Guam	Guam	N	Farmer
49		197	225	Palomo, Ana C	Wife	F	Cha	54.0	M		Y	Y	Guam	Guam	Guam	N	None
50		197	225	Palomo, Jose C	Son	M	Cha	21.0	S	N	Y	Y	Guam	Guam	Guam	Y	Laborer

(CHAMORRO ROOTS GENEALOGY PROJECT ™ TRANSCRIPTION)
(COMPILED/TRANSCRIBED BY BERNARD T. PUNZALAN / HTTP://WWW.CHAMORROROOTS.COM)

FOURTEENTH CENSUS OF THE UNITED STATES: 1920-POPULATION

ISLAND OF GUAM

SHEET NO. 46A

ENUMERATED BY ME ON THE 15th DAY OF April, 1920

Jose Kamminga ENUMERATOR

DISTRICT 1
NAME OF PLACE Agana City

[Proper name and, also, name of class, as city, town, village, barrio, etc]

	PLACE OF ABODE			NAME	RELATION	PERSONAL DESCRIPTION					EDUCATION			NATIVITY				OCCUPATION
Street, avenue, road, etc.	Number of dwelling house in order of visitation	Number of family in order of visitation		Name of each person whose place of abode on January 1, 1920, was in the family.	Relationship of this Person to the head of the family.	Sex	Color or race	Age at last birthday	Single, married, widowed or divorced	Attended any school since Sept. 1, 1919	Whether able to read.	Whether able to write.	Place of birth of this person.	Place of birth of father of this person.	Place of birth of mother of this person.	Whether able to speak English.	Trade, profession, or particular kind of work done, as salesman, laborer, clerk, cook, merchant, washerwoman, etc.
	2	3		4	5	6	7	8	9	10	11	12	13	14	15	16	17
	197	225		Palomo, Maria C	Daughter	F	Cha	16.0	S	N	Y	Y	Guam	Guam	Guam	N	None
	197	225		Palomo, Vicente C	Son	M	Cha	12.0	S	N	Y	Y	Guam	Guam	Guam	N	None
	197	226		Ojeda, Consolacion P	Head	F	Cha	37.0	Wd		Y	Y	Guam	Guam	Guam		None
	197	226		Ojeda, Carmen P	Daughter	F	Cha	4.0	S				Guam	Guam	Guam		None
	197	226		Ojeda, Maria P	Daughter	F	Cha	3.0	S				Guam	Guam	Guam		None
	197	226		Ojeda, Ana P	Daughter	F	Cha	2.0	S				Guam	Guam	Guam		None
	197	227		Palomo, Ramon C	Head	M	Cha	29.0	M		Y	Y	Guam	Guam	Guam		Farmer
	197	227		Palomo, Teresa N	Wife	F	Cha	25.0	M		Y	Y	Guam	Guam	Guam	N	None
	197	227		Palomo, Jesus N	Son	M	Cha	3.0	S				Guam	Guam	Guam	N	None
San Nicolas Street	197	227		Palomo, Jose N	Son	M	Cha	1.0	S				Guam	Guam	Guam		None
	198	228		Blas, Josefa F	Head	F	Cha	53.0	Wd	N	Y	N	Guam	Guam	Guam	N	None
	198	228		Blas, Ramon F	Son	M	Cha	20.0	S	N	Y	Y	Guam	Guam	Guam	Y	Enlisted man USN
	198	228		Blas, Ana M	Daughter	F	Cha	8.0	S	Y			Guam	Guam	Guam		None
	198	228		Mafnas, Rosa R	Servant	F	Cha	13.0	S	N	N	N	Guam	Guam	Guam	N	Servant
	198	228		Castro, Felix R	Boarder	M	Cha	51.0	S		Y	Y	Guam	Guam	Guam	N	Carpenter
	198	229		Blas, Joaquin F	Head	M	Cha	22.0	M		Y	Y	Guam	Guam	Guam	Y	Cook
	198	229		Blas, Asuncion R	Wife	F	Cha	20.0	M	N	Y	N	Guam	Guam	Guam	N	None
	199	230		Duenas, Jose F	Head	M	Cha	52.0	M		Y	Y	Guam	Guam	Guam	Y	Carpenter
	199	230		Duenas, Antonia C	Wife	F	Cha	44.0	M		Y	Y	Guam	Guam	Guam	Y	None
	199	230		Duenas, Manuela C	Daughter	F	Cha	20.0	S	N	Y	Y	Guam	Guam	Guam	Y	None
	199	230		Duenas, Ramon C	Son	M	Cha	18.0	S	N	Y	Y	Guam	Guam	Guam	Y	Farm laborer home farm
	199	230		Duenas, Clemente C	Son	M	Cha	15.0	S	N	Y	Y	Guam	Guam	Guam	Y	Farm laborer home farm
	199	230		Duenas, Jose C	Son	M	Cha	12.0	S	N	Y	Y	Guam	Guam	Guam	Y	None
	199	230		Duenas, Francisco C	Son	M	Cha	5.0	S				Guam	Guam	Guam		None
	199	230		Duenas, Ana C	Daughter	F	Cha	3.0	S				Guam	Guam	Guam		None

158

(CHAMORRO ROOTS GENEALOGY PROJECT ™ TRANSCRIPTION)
(COMPILED/TRANSCRIBED BY BERNARD T. PUNZALAN / HTTP://WWW.CHAMORROROOTS.COM)
FOURTEENTH CENSUS OF THE UNITED STATES: 1920-POPULATION
ISLAND OF GUAM

ENUMERATED BY ME ON THE 15th DAY OF April, 1920

Jose Kamminga ENUMERATOR

DISTRICT 1
NAME OF PLACE Agana City
[Proper name and, also, name of class, as city, town, village, barrio, etc]

	PLACE OF ABODE				NAME	RELATION	PERSONAL DESCRIPTION				EDUCATION			NATIVITY				OCCUPATION
Street, avenue, road, etc.	Number of dwelling house is order of visitation	Number of family in order of visitation			Name	Relationship of this Person to the head of the family.	Sex	Color or race	Age at last birthday	Single, married, widowed or divorced	Attended school any time since sept. 1, 1919	Whether able to read.	Whether able to write.	Place of birth of this person.	Place of birth of father of this person.	Place of birth of mother of this person.	Whether able to speak English.	Trade, profession, or particular kind of work done, as salesman, laborer, clerk, cook, merchant, washerwoman, etc.
1	2	3		4		5	6	7	8	9	10	11	12	13	14	15	16	17
			26	Cruz, Maria Q		Sister-in-law	F	Cha	50.0	S		Y	Y	Guam	Guam	Guam	N	None
	199	230	27	Perez, Manuel F		Head	M	Cha	42.0	M		Y	Y	Guam	Guam	Guam	Y	Farmer
	200	231	28	Perez, Ana T		Wife	F	Cha	36.0	M		Y	Y	Guam	Guam	Guam	N	None
	200	231	29	Perez, Isabel T		Daughter	F	Cha	14.0	S	N	Y	Y	Guam	Guam	Guam	Y	None
	200	231	30	Perez, Gregorio T		Son	M	Cha	10.0	S	Y	Y	Y	Guam	Guam	Guam	Y	None
	200	231	31	Perez, Jose T		Son	M	Cha	9.0	S	Y			Guam	Guam	Guam		None
	200	231	32	Perez, Clotilde T		Daughter	F	Cha	7.0	S	Y			Guam	Guam	Guam		None
	200	231	33	Perez, Francisco T		Son	M	Cha	6.0	S	N			Guam	Guam	Guam		None
	200	231	34	Perez, Emilia T		Daughter	F	Cha	4.0	S				Guam	Guam	Guam		None
	200	231	35	Perez, Vicente T		Son	M	Cha	3.0	S				Guam	Guam	Guam		None
	200	231	36	Perez, Juan T		Son	M	Cha	1.0	S				Guam	Guam	Guam		None
	201	232	37	Matanane, Dolores B		Head	F	Cha	44.0	Wd		Y	N	Guam	Guam	Guam	N	None
	201	232	38	Matanane, Vicente B		Son	M	Cha	15.0	S	N	Y	Y	Guam	Guam	Guam	Y	Farm laborer home farm
	201	232	39	Matanane, Ana B		Daughter	F	Cha	9.0	S	Y			Guam	Guam	Guam		None
	201	232	40	Matanane, Dolores B jr		Daughter	F	Cha	6.0	S	N			Guam	Guam	Guam		None
	201	232	41	Matanane, Engracia B		Daughter	F	Cha	4.0	S				Guam	Guam	Guam		None
	201	232	42	Bae, Angela LG		Aunt	F	Cha	70.0	S				Guam	Guam	Guam		None
	201	233	43	Atoigue, Jose U		Head	M	Cha	19.0	M		Y	Y	Guam	Guam	Guam	Y	Enlisted man USN
	201	233	44	Atoigue, Maria M		Wife	F	Cha	19.0	M		Y	Y	Guam	Guam	Guam	Y	None
	201	233	45	Atoigue, Alejandrina M		Daughter	F	Cha	0.1	S				Guam	Guam	Guam		None
	202	234	46	Quitugua, Ramon Q		Head	M	Cha	57.0	Wd		Y	N	Guam	Guam	Guam	N	Farmer
	202	234	47	Quitugua, Manuel C		Son	M	Cha	25.0	S		Y	Y	Guam	Guam	Guam	Y	Farm laborer home farm
	202	234	48	Quitugua, Ana C		Daughter	F	Cha	17.0	S	N	Y	Y	Guam	Guam	Guam	Y	None
	202	234	49	Quitugua, Maria C		Daughter	F	Cha	13.0	S	N	Y	Y	Guam	Guam	Guam	Y	None
San Nicolas Street	202	235	50	Camacho, Ana S		Head	F	Cha	49.0	S		N	N	Guam	Guam	Guam	N	Laundress

SHEET NO.
47A

(CHAMORRO ROOTS GENEALOGY PROJECT ™ TRANSCRIPTION)
(COMPILED/TRANSCRIBED BY BERNARD T. PUNZALAN / HTTP://WWW.CHAMORROROOTS.COM)
FOURTEENTH CENSUS OF THE UNITED STATES: 1920-POPULATION
ISLAND OF GUAM

ENUMERATED BY ME ON THE 16th DAY OF April, 1920

Jose Kamminga ENUMERATOR

DISTRICT 1
NAME OF PLACE Agana City
[Proper name and, also, name of class, as city, town, village, barrio, etc]

	PLACE OF ABODE			NAME	RELATION	PERSONAL DESCRIPTION				EDUCATION			NATIVITY					OCCUPATION
Street, avenue, road, etc.	Number of dwelling house in order of visitation	Number of family in order of visitation		of each person whose place of abode on January 1, 1920, was in the family. Enter surname, firs, then given name and middle initial. If any. Include every person living on January 1, 1920. Omit children born since January 1, 1920.	Relationship of this Person to the head of the family.	Sex	Color or race	Age at last birthday	Single, married, widowed or divorced	Attended school any time since Sept. 1, 1919	Whether able to read.	Whether able to write.	Place of birth of this person.	Place of birth of father of this person.	Place of birth of mother of this person.	Whether able to speak English.	Trade, profession, or particular kind of work done, as salesman, laborer, clerk, cook, merchant, washerwoman, etc.
1	2	3		4	5	6	7	8	9	10	11	12	13	14	15	16	17
1		202	235	Camacho, Josefa	Daughter	F	Cha	21.0	S	N	Y	Y	Guam	Unknown	Guam	Y	Laundress
2		202	235	Camacho, Jose	Son	M	Cha	18.0	S	N	Y	Y	Guam	Unknown	Guam	Y	Laborer
3		202	235	Camacho, Juan B	Nephew	M	Cha	22.0	S		Y	Y	Yap Island	Guam	Guam	Y	Farm laborer
4		203	236	Suzuki, F	Head	M	Jp	26.0	M		Y	Y	Japan	Japan	Japan	Y	Tailor
5		203	236	Suzuki, Shigeno	Wife	F	Jp	21.0	M	N	Y	Y	Japan	Japan	Japan	Y	Storekeeper
6		203	236	Suzuki, Yoshido	Daughter	F	Jp	2.0	S				Guam	Japan	Japan		None
7		204	237	San Nicolas, Ana A	Head	F	Cha	46.0	Wd		N	N	Guam	Guam	Guam	N	None
8		204	237	San Nicolas, Rosa A	Daughter	F	Cha	25.0	S		Y	Y	Guam	Guam	Guam	Y	Midwife
9		204	237	Alvarez, J SN	Son	M	Cha	23.0	S		Y	Y	Guam	Guam	Guam	Y	Enlisted man USN
10		204	238	Ibanez, Taitano SN	Head	M	Fil	28.0	M		Y	Y	Philippine Islands	Philippine Islands	Philippine Islands	Y	Cook
11		204	238	Ibanez, Candelaria SN	Wife	F	Cha	21.0	M	N	Y	Y	Guam	Guam	Guam	Y	None
12		204	238	Ibanez, Jose SN	Son	M	Fil	1.0	S				Philippine Islands	Philippine Islands	Guam		None
13		204	238	Ibanez, Pedro SN	Son	M	Fil	0.5	S				Guam	Philippine Islands	Guam		None
14		205	239	Alvarez, Jose G	Head	M	Cha	49.0	Wd		N	N	Guam	Guam	Guam	N	Fisherman
15		205	239	Alvarez, Ana SA	Daughter	F	Cha	26.0	S		Y	Y	Guam	Guam	Guam	N	None
16		205	239	Alvarez, Juan SA	Son	M	Cha	22.0	S		Y	Y	Guam	Guam	Guam	Y	Chauffeur
17		205	239	Alvarez, Dolores SA	Daughter	F	Cha	19.0	S	N	Y	N	Guam	Guam	Guam	N	None
18		205	239	Alvarez, Rufina SA	Daughter	F	Cha	17.0	S	N	Y	Y	Guam	Guam	Guam	N	None
19		205	240	San Agustin, Mariano T	Head	M	Cha	70.0	Wd		Y	Y	Guam	Guam	Guam	N	None
20		205	240	San Agustin, Dolores E	Daughter	F	Cha	45.0	S		Y	Y	Guam	Guam	Guam	N	None
21		205	240	San Agustin, Mariano	Grandson	M	Cha	15.0	S	N	Y	Y	Guam	Unknown	Guam	N	None
22		205	240	San Agustin, Jose	Grandson	M	Cha	12.0	S	N	N	N	Guam	Unknown	Guam	N	None
San Nicolas Street 23		205	241	Baza, Vicente U	Head	M	Cha	29.0	Wd		Y	Y	Guam	Guam	Guam	Y	Carpenter
24		205	241	Baza, Isabel A	Daughter	F	Cha	5.0	S	N			Guam	Guam	Guam		None
25		205	241	Baza, Prebiterio A	Son	M	Cha	3.0	S				Guam	Guam	Guam		None

160

(CHAMORRO ROOTS GENEALOGY PROJECT ™ TRANSCRIPTION)
(COMPILED/TRANSCRIBED BY BERNARD T. PUNZALAN / HTTP://WWW.CHAMORROROOTS.COM)
FOURTEENTH CENSUS OF THE UNITED STATES: 1920-POPULATION
ISLAND OF GUAM

DISTRICT 1
NAME OF PLACE Agana City
[Proper name and, also, name of class, as city, town, village, barrio, etc]

ENUMERATED BY ME ON THE 16th DAY OF April, 1920

Jose Kamminga ENUMERATOR

	Street	Dwelling (2)	Family (3)	NAME (4)	RELATION (5)	Sex (6)	Race (7)	Age (8)	Marital (9)	School (10)	Read (11)	Write (12)	Birth (13)	Father (14)	Mother (15)	English (16)	OCCUPATION (17)
26	San Nicolas Street	206	242	Quitugua, Vicente D	Head	M	Cha	23.0	S		Y	Y	Guam	Guam	Guam	N	Laborer
27		206	242	Quitugua, Maria D	Sister	F	Cha	25.0	S		Y	Y	Guam	Guam	Guam	Y	None
28		206	242	Quitugua, Jose D	Brother	M	Cha	21.0	S	N	Y	Y	Guam	Guam	Guam	Y	Farm laborer home farm
29		206	243	Quitugua, Joaquin Q	Head	M	Cha	58.0	Wd		N	N	Guam	Guam	Guam	N	Farmer
30		206	243	Quitugua, Vicenta C	Daughter	F	Cha	27.0	S		Y	N	Guam	Guam	Guam	N	None
31		206	243	Quitugua, Joaquina C	Daughter	F	Cha	22.0	S		Y	Y	Guam	Guam	Guam	Y	None
32		206	243	Camacho, Maria	Grand daughter	F	Cha	0.1					Guam	Unknown	Guam		None
33		207	244	Toves, Juan B	Head	M	Cha	46.0	M		Y	N	Guam	Guam	Guam	N	None
34		207	244	Toves, Ana H	Wife	F	Cha	50.0	M		N	N	Guam	Guam	Guam	N	None
35		207	244	Hernandez, Joaquin	Nephew	M	Cha	25.0	S	N	Y	Y	Guam	Unknown	Guam	Y	Farm laborer home farm
36		207	244	Hernandez, Vicente	Nephew	M	Cha	22.0	S	N	Y	Y	Guam	Unknown	Guam	Y	Farm laborer home farm
37		207	244	Hernandez, Jose	Nephew	M	Cha	15.0	S	N	Y	Y	Guam	Unknown	Guam	Y	Farm laborer home farm
38		207	244	Hernandez, Antonio	Nephew	M	Cha	12.0	S	N	N	N	Guam	Unknown	Guam	N	None
39		207	244	Aguero, Juan	Nephew	M	Cha	15.0	S	N	Y	Y	Guam	Unknown	Guam	Y	Farm laborer home farm
40		207	244	Aguero, Jose	Nephew	M	Cha	11.0	S	N	Y	N	Guam	Unknown	Guam	N	None
41		207	244	Aguero, Ana	Niece	F	Cha	13.0	S	N	Y	N	Guam	Unknown	Guam	N	None
42		207	244	Aguero, Rita	Niece	F	Cha	29.0	S		Y	N	Guam	Unknown	Guam	N	None
43		207	244	Hernandez, Maria	Sister-in-law	F	Cha	54.0	S		Y	N	Guam	Guam	Guam	N	Laundress
44		208	245	Ogo, Ana O	Head	F	Cha	30.0	Wd		N	N	Guam	Unknown	Guam	N	None
45		208	245	Ogo, Juan	Son	M	Cha	9.0	S	Y			Guam	Unknown	Guam	N	None
46		208	245	Ogo, Francisco	Son	M	Cha	3.0	S				Guam	Unknown	Guam		None
47		208	245	Ogo, Juan	Son	M	Cha	1.0	S				Guam	Unknown	Guam		None
48		209	246	Martinez, Ignacio C	Head	M	Cha	55.0	M		Y	Y	Guam	Guam	Guam	N	Farmer
49		209	246	Martinez, Francisca M	Wife	F	Cha	54.0	M		Y	Y	Guam	Guam	Guam	N	None
50		209	246	Martinez, Rosa M	Daughter	F	Cha	16.0	S	N	Y	Y	Guam	Guam	Guam	Y	None

(CHAMORRO ROOTS GENEALOGY PROJECT ™ TRANSCRIPTION)
(COMPILED/TRANSCRIBED BY BERNARD T. PUNZALAN / HTTP://WWW.CHAMORROROOTS.COM)

FOURTEENTH CENSUS OF THE UNITED STATES: 1920-POPULATION

ISLAND OF GUAM

SHEET NO. 48A

ENUMERATED BY ME ON THE 16th DAY OF April, 1920

Jose Kamminga ENUMERATOR

DISTRICT 1

NAME OF PLACE Agana City

	Number of dwelling house in order of visitation	Number of family in order of visitation	NAME of each person whose place of abode on January 1, 1920, was in the family.	RELATION Relationship of this Person to the head of the family.	Sex	Color or race	Age at last birthday	Single, married, widowed or divorced	Attended school any time since Sept. 1, 1919	Whether able to read.	Whether able to write.	Place of birth of this person.	Place of birth of father of this person.	Place of birth of mother of this person.	Whether able to speak English.	OCCUPATION Trade, profession, or particular kind of work done, as salesman, laborer, clerk, cook, merchant, washerwoman, etc.
	2	3	4	5	6	7	8	9	10	11	12	13	14	15	16	17
1	209	246	Martinez, Rosalia M	Daughter	F	Cha	13.0	S				Guam	Guam	Guam	Y	None
2	209	246	Martinez, Jesus M	Son	M	Cha	12.0	S				Guam	Guam	Guam	Y	None
3	209	246	Leon Guerrero, Ana M	Step daughter	F	Cha	25.0	S				Guam	Guam	Guam	Y	None
4	209	246	Leon Guerrero, Concepcion M	Step daughter	F	Cha	24.0	S				Guam	Guam	Guam	Y	Midwife
5	209	246	Leon Guerrero, Joaquin M	Stepson	M	Cha	20.0	S				Guam	Guam	Guam	Y	Laborer
6	209	246	Manglona, Ana M	Mother-in-law	F	Cha	76.0	Wd				Guam	Guam	Guam	N	None
7	210	247	Borja, Jose L	Head	M	Cha	64.0	M		Y	Y	Guam	Guam	Guam	N	None
8	210	247	Borja, Maria R	Wife	F	Cha	55.0	M		Y	Y	Guam	Guam	Guam	N	None
9	210	247	Borja, Rita R	Daughter	F	Cha	30.0	S		Y	Y	Guam	Guam	Guam	N	None
10	210	247	Borja, Mariano R	Son	M	Cha	20.0	S	N	Y	Y	Guam	Guam	Guam	N	Farm laborer home farm
11	210	247	Rosario, Joaquina B	Daughter	F	Cha	26.0	Wd		Y	Y	Guam	Guam	Guam	N	None
12	210	247	Duenas, Joaquin B	Grandson	M	Cha	2.0	S				Guam	Guam	Guam		None
13	210	248	Duenas, Vicente C	Head	M	Cha	34.0	M		Y	Y	Guam	Guam	Guam	Y	Carpenter
14	210	248	Duenas, Rosa B	Wife	F	Cha	22.0	M		Y	N	Guam	Guam	Guam	N	None
15	210	248	Duenas, Jesus B	Son	M	Cha	4.0	S				Guam	Guam	Guam		None
16	210	248	Duenas, Jose B	Son	M	Cha	2.0	S				Guam	Guam	Guam		None
17	210	248	Duenas, Juan B	Son	M	Cha	1.0	S				Guam	Guam	Guam		None
18	211	249	San Agustin, Juan E	Head	M	Cha	48.0	M		Y	Y	Guam	Guam	Guam	N	Carpenter
19	211	249	San Agustin, Dolores L	Wife	F	Cha	47.0	M		Y	N	Guam	Guam	Guam	N	None
20	211	249	San Agustin, Maria L	Daughter	F	Cha	23.0	S		Y	Y	Guam	Guam	Guam	Y	Laundress
21	211	249	San Agustin, Amalia L	Daughter	F	Cha	16.0	S	N	Y	Y	Guam	Guam	Guam	Y	Laundress
22	211	249	San Agustin, Rosa L	Daughter	F	Cha	12.0	S	N	Y	Y	Guam	Guam	Guam	N	None
23	212	250	Cruz, Paula G	Head	F	Cha	55.0	Wd		N	N	Guam	Guam	Guam	N	Laundress
24	212	250	Cruz, Rosa G	Daughter	F	Cha	19.0	S	N	Y	Y	Guam	Guam	Guam	N	Laundress
25	212	250	Cruz, Paulino G	Son	M	Cha	8.0	S	Y			Guam	Guam	Guam		None

Street, avenue, road, etc.: San Nicolas Street

(CHAMORRO ROOTS GENEALOGY PROJECT ™ TRANSCRIPTION)
(COMPILED/TRANSCRIBED BY BERNARD T. PUNZALAN / HTTP://WWW.CHAMORROROOTS.COM)

FOURTEENTH CENSUS OF THE UNITED STATES: 1920–POPULATION
ISLAND OF GUAM

ENUMERATED BY ME ON THE 17th DAY OF April, 1920

Jose Kamminga ENUMERATOR

DISTRICT 1
NAME OF PLACE Agana City

	Number of dwelling house	Number of family	NAME	RELATION	Sex	Color or race	Age at last birthday	Single, married, widowed or divorced	Attended school any time since Sept. 1, 1919	Whether able to read	Whether able to write	Place of birth of this person	Place of birth of father of this person	Place of birth of mother of this person	Whether able to speak English	OCCUPATION
26	213	251	Alecto, Agustin D	Head	M	Fil	52.0	M		Y	N	Philippine Islands	Philippine Islands	Philippine Islands	N	Laborer
27	213	251	Alecto, Natividad C	Wife	F	Fil	40.0	M		Y	Y	Guam	Philippine Islands	Guam	N	None
28	213	251	Alecto, Merchot C	Son	M	Fil	6.0	S	N			Guam	Philippine Islands	Guam		None
29	213	251	Alecto, Pedro C	Son	M	Fil	4.0	S				Guam	Philippine Islands	Guam		None
30	213	251	Alecto, Felix C	Son	M	Fil	2.0	S				Guam	Philippine Islands	Guam		None
31	213	251	Crusar, Antonia	Step daughter	F	Cha	11.0	S	Y	Y	Y	Guam	Unknown	Guam	Y	None
32	213	251	Migofna, Antonio G	Brother-in-law	M	Cha	24.0	S		Y	N	Guam	Guam	Guam	Y	Farm laborer home farm
33	213	251	Migofna, Dolores G	Sister-in-law	F	Cha	23.0	S		Y	N	Guam	Guam	Guam	N	None
34	214	252	Santos, Vicente SN	Head	M	Cha	19.0	S	N	Y	Y	Guam	Unknown	Guam	Y	Laborer
35	215	253	Borja, Jose D	Head	M	Cha	41.0	M		Y	Y	Guam	Guam	Guam	N	None
36	215	253	Borja, Filomena Q	Wife	F	Cha	49.0	M		Y	N	Guam	Guam	Guam	N	None
37	215	253	Borja, Luis Q	Son	M	Cha	18.0	S	N	Y	Y	Guam	Guam	Guam	Y	Laborer
38	215	253	Borja, Juan Q	Son	M	Cha	15.0	S	N	Y	Y	Guam	Guam	Guam	Y	None
39	215	253	Borja, Pedro Q	Son	M	Cha	13.0	S	N	Y	Y	Guam	Guam	Guam	Y	None
40	215	253	Duenas, Luisa B	Mother	F	Cha	52.0	Wd		N	N	Guam	Guam	Guam	N	None
41	215	254	Quitugua, Vicente	Head	M	Cha	24.0	M		Y	Y	Guam	Unknown	Guam	Y	Laborer
42	215	254	Quitugua, Ana T	Wife	F	Cha	19.0	M	N	Y	Y	Guam	Guam	Guam	Y	None
43	216	255	Meno, Isidro M	Head	M	Cha	41.0	M		Y	Y	Guam	Guam	Guam	N	Farmer
44	216	255	Meno, Carmen C	Wife	F	Cha	36.0	M		Y	N	Guam	Guam	Guam	N	None
45	216	255	Meno, Ana C	Daughter	F	Cha	12.0	S	Y	Y	Y	Guam	Guam	Guam	Y	None
46	217	256	Manalisay, Manuel LG	Head	M	Cha	67.0	M		Y	Y	Guam	Guam	Guam	N	Retail Merchant
47	217	256	Manalisay, Antonia S	Wife	F	Cha	64.0	M		Y	Y	Guam	Guam	Guam	N	None
48	217	256	Manalisay, Jesus S	Son	M	Cha	16.0	S	N	Y	Y	Guam	Guam	Guam	Y	Messenger
49	218	257	Leon Guerrero, Joaquin R	Head	M	Cha	49.0	M		Y	Y	Guam	Guam	Guam	N	Farmer
50	218	257	Leon Guerrero, Ana R	Wife	F	Cha	43.0	M		Y	N	Guam	Guam	Guam	N	None

Street: San Nicolas Street

(CHAMORRO ROOTS GENEALOGY PROJECT ™ TRANSCRIPTION)
(COMPILED/TRANSCRIBED BY BERNARD T. PUNZALAN / HTTP://WWW.CHAMORROROOTS.COM)

FOURTEENTH CENSUS OF THE UNITED STATES: 1920-POPULATION
ISLAND OF GUAM

ENUMERATED BY ME ON THE 17th DAY OF April, 1920

Jose Kamminga ENUMERATOR

DISTRICT 1
NAME OF PLACE **Agana City**
[Proper name and, also, name of class, as city, town, village, barrio, etc]

Street	Dwelling house	Family number	NAME	RELATION	Sex	Color or race	Age	Single, married, widowed or divorced	Attended school	Able to read	Able to write	Birthplace of person	Birthplace of father	Birthplace of mother	Able to speak English	OCCUPATION
1	2	3	4	5	6	7	8	9	10	11	12	13	14	15	16	17
	218	257	Leon Guerrero, Ascension R	Daughter	F	Cha	20.0	S	N	Y	Y	Guam	Guam	Guam	Y	Laundress
	218	257	Leon Guerrero, Ana R	Daughter	F	Cha	19.0	S	N	Y	Y	Guam	Guam	Guam	Y	Laundress
	218	257	Leon Guerrero, Manuel R	Son	M	Cha	17.0	S	N	Y	Y	Guam	Guam	Guam	Y	Farm laborer home farm
	218	257	Leon Guerrero, Joaquin R	Son	M	Cha	15.0	S	N	N	N	Guam	Guam	Guam	Y	Farm laborer home farm
	218	257	Leon Guerrero, Jose R	Son	M	Cha	13.0	S	N	Y	Y	Guam	Guam	Guam	Y	None
	218	257	Leon Guerrero, Ignacio R	Son	M	Cha	11.0	S	Y	Y	Y	Guam	Guam	Guam	Y	None
	218	257	Leon Guerrero, Maria R	Daughter	F	Cha	9.0	S	Y	Y	Y	Guam	Guam	Guam		None
	218	257	Leon Guerrero, Jesus R	Son	M	Cha	6.0	S	N			Guam	Guam	Guam		None
	218	257	Leon Guerrero, Juan R	Son	M	Cha	1.0	S				Guam	Guam	Guam		None
San Nicolas Street	219	258	Pangelinan, Carmelo P	Head	M	Cha	46.0	M		Y	N	Guam	Unknown	Guam	N	Laborer
	219	258	Pangelinan, Ramona R	Wife	F	Cha	40.0	M		Y	N	Guam	Guam	Guam	N	None
	219	258	Pangelinan, Francisco R	Son	M	Cha	14.0	S	N	Y	Y	Guam	Guam	Guam	Y	None
	219	258	Pangelinan, Ignacio R	Son	M	Cha	6.0	S	N			Guam	Guam	Guam		None
	219	258	Pangelinan, Maria R	Daughter	F	Cha	4.0	S				Guam	Guam	Guam		None
	219	258	Pangelinan, Vicente R	Son	M	Cha	1.0	S				Guam	Guam	Guam		None
	219	258	Rosario, Dolores A	Sister-in-law	F	Cha	38.0	S		Y	Y	Guam	Guam	Guam	N	Cook
	219	258	Rosario, Beatris	Niece	F	Cha	12.0	S	Y	Y	Y	Guam	Unknown	Guam	N	None
	219	258	Rosario, Amanda	Niece	F	Cha	10.0	S	Y	Y	Y	Guam	Unknown	Guam	N	None
	220	259	Taitinfong, Vicente L	Head	M	Cha	56.0	M	N	Y	N	Guam	Guam	Guam	N	Farmer
	220	259	Taitinfong, Ana B	Wife	F	Cha	45.0	M	N	Y	N	Guam	Guam	Guam	N	None
	220	259	Taitinfong, Jose B	Son	M	Cha	19.0	S	N	Y	Y	Guam	Guam	Guam	Y	Farm laborer home farm
	220	259	Taitinfong, Jesus B	Son	M	Cha	16.0	S	Y	Y	Y	Guam	Guam	Guam	Y	None
	220	259	Taitinfong, Joaquin B	Son	M	Cha	15.0	S	N	Y	N	Guam	Guam	Guam	Y	None
	220	259	Taitinfong, Maria B	Daughter	F	Cha	13.0	S	Y	Y	N	Guam	Guam	Guam	N	None
	220	259	Taitinfong, Vicente B	Son	M	Cha	11.0	S	Y	Y	Y	Guam	Guam	Guam	Y	None

(CHAMORRO ROOTS GENEALOGY PROJECT ™ TRANSCRIPTION)
(COMPILED/TRANSCRIBED BY BERNARD T. PUNZALAN / HTTP://WWW.CHAMORROROOTS.COM)

FOURTEENTH CENSUS OF THE UNITED STATES: 1920–POPULATION
ISLAND OF GUAM

DISTRICT 1
NAME OF PLACE Agana City
[Proper name and, also, name of class, as city, town, village, barrio, etc]

ENUMERATED BY ME ON THE 17th DAY OF April, 1920

Jose Kamminga ENUMERATOR

	Street	Dwelling No.	Family No.	NAME	RELATION	Sex	Color or race	Age	Single, married, widowed or divorced	Attended school since Sept. 1, 1919	Able to read	Able to write	Place of birth of person	Place of birth of father	Place of birth of mother	Able to speak English	OCCUPATION
	1	2	3	4	5	6	7	8	9	10	11	12	13	14	15	16	17
26		220	259	Taitinfong, Ignacio B	Son	M	Cha	7.0	S	Y			Guam	Guam	Guam		None
27		220	259	Taitinfong, Mariano B	Son	M	Cha	6.0	S	N			Guam	Guam	Guam		None
28		220	259	Taitinfong, Barbara B	Daughter	F	Cha	3.0	S				Guam	Guam	Guam		None
29		220	260	Taitinfong, Jose L	Head	M	Cha	50.0	M		Y	Y	Guam	Guam	Guam	N	Farmer
30		220	260	Taitinfong, Maria B	Daughter	F	Cha	49.0	M		Y	N	Guam	Guam	Guam	N	None
31		220	260	Taitinfong, Francisco B	Son	M	Cha	6.0	S	N	Y	Y	Guam	Guam	Guam	Y	Farm laborer home farm
32		221	261	Leon Guerrero, Luis T	Head	M	Cha	53.0	M		Y	Y	Guam	Guam	Guam	N	Farmer
33		221	261	Leon Guerrero, Isabel T	Wife	F	Cha	47.0	M		Y	Y	Guam	Unknown	Guam	N	None
34		222	262	Duenas, Bernadino F	Head	M	Cha	44.0	M		N	N	Guam	Guam	Guam	N	Farmer
35		222	262	Duenas, Antonia T	Wife	F	Cha	37.0	M		Y	Y	Guam	Guam	Guam	N	None
36	San Nicolas Street	222	262	Duenas, Juan T	Son	M	Cha	13.0	S	Y	Y	Y	Guam	Guam	Guam	Y	None
37		222	262	Duenas, Augustia T	Daughter	F	Cha	9.0	S	Y			Guam	Guam	Guam		None
38		222	262	Duenas, Vicente T	Son	M	Cha	6.0	S	N			Guam	Guam	Guam		None
39		222	262	Duenas, Joaquin T	Son	M	Cha	4.0	S				Guam	Guam	Guam		None
40		222	262	Duenas, Jose T	Son	M	Cha	2.0	S				Guam	Guam	Guam		None
41		222	262	Duenas, Rita T	Daughter	F	Cha	0.1	S				Guam	Guam	Guam		None
42		223	263	Ninaisan, Francisca	Head	F	Cha	54.0	S		N	N	Guam	Unknown	Unknown	N	None
43		223	263	Ninaisan, Ana	Daughter	F	Cha	34.0	S		N	N	Guam	Unknown	Unknown	N	None
44		223	263	Ninaisan, Jose	Grandson	M	Cha	15.0	S	N	Y	Y	Guam	Unknown	Unknown	Y	None
45		223	263	Ninaisan, Maria	Grand daughter	F	Cha	12.0	S	Y	Y	Y	Guam	Unknown	Unknown	N	None
46		223	263	Ninaisan, Juan	Grandson	M	Cha	6.0	S	N			Guam	Unknown	Unknown		None
47		223	263	Ninaisan, Ignacio	Grandson	M	Cha	5.0	S				Guam	Unknown	Unknown		None
48		223	263	Ninaisan, Rosa	Grand daughter	F	Cha	2.0	S				Guam	Unknown	Guam		None
49		223	263	Quichocho, Trinidad Q	Niece	F	Cha	25.0	S		N	N	Guam	Guam	Guam	N	None
50		224		Ito, Sanfiro	Head	M	Jp	37.0	M		Y	Y	Japan	Japan	Japan	N	Storekeeper

(CHAMORRO ROOTS GENEALOGY PROJECT ™ TRANSCRIPTION)
(COMPILED/TRANSCRIBED BY BERNARD T. PUNZALAN / HTTP://WWW.CHAMORROROOTS.COM)

FOURTEENTH CENSUS OF THE UNITED STATES: 1920-POPULATION

ISLAND OF GUAM

ENUMERATED BY ME ON THE 19th DAY OF April, 1920

Jose Kamminga ENUMERATOR

DISTRICT 1
NAME OF PLACE Agana City

[Proper name and, also, name of class, name of class, as city, town, village, barrio, etc]

	PLACE OF ABODE		NAME	RELATION	PERSONAL DESCRIPTION					EDUCATION			NATIVITY				OCCUPATION
Street, avenue, road, etc.	Number of dwelling house is order of visitation	Number of family in order of visitation	of each person whose place of abode on January 1, 1920, was in the family. Enter surname, first, then given name and middle initial. If any. Include every person living on January 1, 1920. Omit children born since January 1, 1920.	Relationship of this Person to the head of the family.	Sex	Color or race	Age at last birthday	Single, married, widowed or divorced	Attended school any time since Sept. 1, 1919	Whether able to read.	Whether able to write.	Place of birth of this person.	Place of birth of father of this person.	Place of birth of mother of this person.	Whether able to speak English.	Trade, profession, or particular kind of work done, as salesman, laborer, clerk, cook, merchant, washerwoman, etc.
1	2	3	4	5	6	7	8	9	10	11	12	13	14	15	16	17
	225	265	Francisco, Juan C	Head	M	Cha	29.0	M		Y	Y	Guam	Guam	Guam	N	Farmer
	225	265	Francisco, Consolacion C	Wife	F	Cha	27.0	M		Y	Y	Guam	Guam	Guam	N	None
	225	265	Francisco, Jose C	Son	M	Cha	1.0	S				Guam	Guam	Guam		None
	225	265	Susuico, Maria	Servant	F	Cha	10.0	S	Y	N	N	Guam	Unknown	Guam	N	Servant
	226	266	White, Jose F	Head	M	Cha	29.0	M		Y	Y	Guam	Guam	Guam	Y	Fireman
	226	266	White, Rosa A	Wife	F	Cha	24.0	M		Y	Y	Guam	Guam	Guam	N	None
	226	266	White, Asuncion A	Daughter	F	Cha	0.1	S				Guam	Guam	Guam		None
	227	267	Arima, T	Head	M	Jp	35.0	S		Y	Y	Japan	Japan	Japan	N	Retail merchant
San Nicolas Street	228	268	Yokoi, Jose T	Head	M	Jp	33.0	M		Y	Y	Japan	Japan	Japan	Y	Retail merchant
	228	268	Yokoi, Maria Q	Wife	F	Cha	23.0	M		Y	Y	Guam	Unknown	Guam	Y	None
	228	268	Yokoi, Gertrudes Q	Daughter	F	Jp	5.0	S	N			Guam	Japan	Guam		None
	228	268	Yokoi, Emilia Q	Daughter	F	Jp	1.0	S				Guam	Japan	Guam		None
	228	268	Quintanilla, Manuel	Brother-in-law	M	Cha	25.0	S				Guam	Unknown	Guam		Laborer
	229	269	San Nicolas, Vicenta D	Head	F	Chin	69.0	Wd		Y	Y	Guam	China	Guam	N	None
	229	269	San Nicolas, Maria D	Daughter	F	Cha	26.0	S		Y	Y	Guam	Guam	Guam	Y	Enlisted man USN
	229	269	San Nicolas, Antonio D	Son	M	Cha	23.0	S	N	Y	Y	Guam	Guam	Guam	Y	Farm laborer home farm
	229	269	San Nicolas, Jose D	Son	M	Cha	21.0	S	N	Y	Y	Guam	Guam	Guam	Y	None
	229	269	San Nicolas, Nieves D	Daughter	F	Cha	20.0	S	N	Y	Y	Guam	Guam	Guam	Y	None
	229	269	San Nicolas, Amparo D	Daughter	F	Cha	18.0	S	N	Y	Y	Guam	Guam	Guam	Y	None
	229	269	San Nicolas, Luis D	Son	M	Cha	13.0	S	Y	Y	Y	Guam	Guam	Guam	Y	None
	229	269	San Nicolas, Ana D	Daughter	F	Cha	10.0	S	Y	Y	Y	Guam	Guam	Guam	N	None
	229	269	San Nicolas, Regina D	Daughter	F	Cha	4.0	S				Guam	Guam	Guam		None
	229	269	San Nicolas, Soledad D	Daughter	F	Cha	2.0	S				Guam	Guam	Guam		None
	230	270	Taitano, Carmen G	Head	F	Cha	50.0	Wd		N	N	Guam	Guam	Guam	N	None
	230	270	Quichocho, Jose	Nephew	M	Cha	18.0	S	Y	Y	Y	Guam	Guam	Guam	Y	None

(CHAMORRO ROOTS GENEALOGY PROJECT ™ TRANSCRIPTION)

(COMPILED/TRANSCRIBED BY BERNARD T. PUNZALAN / HTTP://WWW.CHAMORROROOTS.COM)

FOURTEENTH CENSUS OF THE UNITED STATES: 1920-POPULATION

ISLAND OF GUAM

ENUMERATED BY ME ON THE 19th DAY OF April, 1920

Jose Kamminga ENUMERATOR

DISTRICT 1
NAME OF PLACE Agana City

[Proper name and, also, name of class, as city, town, village, barrio, etc]

| | PLACE OF ABODE | | NAME | RELATION | PERSONAL DESCRIPTION | | | | EDUCATION | | | NATIVITY | | | | OCCUPATION |
1	2	3	4	5	6	7	8	9	10	11	12	13	14	15	16	17
	231	271	Arriola, Juana F	Head	F	Cha	57.0	Wd		Y	Y	Guam	Guam	Guam	N	None
	231	271	Arriola, Vicente F	Son	M	Cha	24.0	S		Y	Y	Guam	Guam	Guam	Y	Assoc. Register of Land
	231	271	Arriola, Antonio F	Son	M	Cha	20.0	S	N	Y	Y	Guam	Guam	Guam	Y	Clerk
	232	272	Quintanilla, Juan P	Head	M	Cha	44.0	M		N	N	Guam	Guam	Guam	N	Farmer
	232	272	Quintanilla, Juana D	Wife	F	Cha	54.0	M		N	N	Guam	Guam	Guam	N	None
	232	272	Quintanilla, Ana D	Daughter	F	Cha	19.0	S	N	Y	Y	Guam	Guam	Guam	Y	None
	232	272	Quintanilla, Natividad D	Daughter	F	Cha	18.0	S	N	Y	Y	Guam	Guam	Guam	Y	None
	232	272	Quintanilla, Jesus D	Son	M	Cha	17.0	S	N	Y	Y	Guam	Guam	Guam	Y	Laborer
	232	272	Quintanilla, Regina D	Daughter	F	Cha	14.0	S	N	Y	Y	Guam	Guam	Guam	Y	None
	232	272	Quintanilla, Josefa D	Daughter	F	Cha	13.0	S	Y	Y	Y	Guam	Guam	Guam	N	None
	233	273	Matanane, Manuel M	Head	M	Cha	50.0	M		Y	Y	Guam	Unknown	Guam	N	Farmer
	233	273	Matanane, Ana Q	Wife	F	Cha	35.0	M		Y	Y	Guam	Guam	Guam	N	None
	233	273	Matanane, Maria Q	Daughter	F	Cha	2.0	S				Guam	Guam	Guam		None
	233	273	Matanane, Catalina Q	Daughter	F	Cha	0.1	S				Guam	Guam	Guam		None
San Nicolas Street	233	273	Santiago, Isabel G	Step daughter	F	Cha	12.0	S	N	Y	Y	Guam	Guam	Guam	N	None
	233	273	Santiago, Jose Q	Stepson	M	Cha	8.0	S	Y	Y	Y	Guam	Guam	Guam		None
	233	273	Santiago, Francisca Q	Step daughter	F	Cha	5.0	S	N			Guam	Guam	Guam		None
	233	273	Quintanilla, Nicolas	Father-in-law	M	Cha	70.0	Wd		Y	N	Guam	Guam	Guam		None
	233	273	Alufaq, Candida	Boarder	F	ot	58.0	S		Y	N	Caroline Islands	Caroline Islands	Caroline Islands	N	None
	233	273	Alufaq, Rita	Boarder	F	ot	34.0	S		Y	N	Guam	Guam	Guam	N	None
	234	274	Adriano, Juan	Head	M	Cha	52.0	M		N	N	Guam	Unknown	Guam	N	Farmer
	234	274	Adriano, Joaquina G	Wife	F	Cha	47.0	M		N	N	Guam	Unknown	Guam	N	None
	234	274	Adriano, Jose G	Son	M	Cha	17.0	S	N	Y	Y	Guam	Guam	Guam	Y	Laborer
	234	274	Adriano, Maria G	Daughter	F	Cha	11.0	S	Y	Y	Y	Guam	Guam	Guam	Y	None
	234	274	Blas, Jesus	Boarder	M	Cha	26.0	S	N	Y	N	Guam	Unknown	Guam	N	Laborer

167

(CHAMORRO ROOTS GENEALOGY PROJECT ™ TRANSCRIPTION)
(COMPILED/TRANSCRIBED BY BERNARD T. PUNZALAN / HTTP://WWW.CHAMORROROOTS.COM)
FOURTEENTH CENSUS OF THE UNITED STATES: 1920–POPULATION
ISLAND OF GUAM

SHEET NO. 51A

ENUMERATED BY ME ON THE 19th DAY OF April, 1920

Jose Kamminga ENUMERATOR

DISTRICT 1
NAME OF PLACE Agana City
[Proper name and, also, name of class, as city, town, village, barrio, etc]

Street	Dwelling	Family	NAME	RELATION	Sex	Color or race	Age	Marital	School	Read	Write	Birthplace person	Birthplace father	Birthplace mother	English	OCCUPATION
	235	275	Perez, Vicente P	Head	M	Cha	34.0	M		N	N	Guam	Unknown	Guam	N	Farmer
	235	275	Perez, Maria M	Wife	F	Cha	40.0	M		N	N	Guam	Guam	Guam	N	None
	235	275	Perez, Rosa M	Daughter	F	Cha	7.0	S	Y			Guam	Guam	Guam		None
	235	275	Perez, Jesus M	Son	M	Cha	11.0	S	N	N	N	Guam	Guam	Guam	N	None
	235	275	Perez, Merfida M	Daughter	F	Cha	4.0	S				Guam	Guam	Guam		None
	235	275	Perez, Jose M	Son	M	Cha	3.0	S				Guam	Guam	Guam		None
	236	276	Manibusan, Maria P	Head	F	Cha	43.0	Wd		Y	N	Guam	Guam	Guam	N	None
	236	276	Manibusan, Vicente P	Son	M	Cha	20.0	S	N	Y	Y	Guam	Guam	Guam	Y	Laborer
	236	276	Manibusan, Nicolasa P	Daughter	F	Cha	19.0	S	N	Y	Y	Guam	Guam	Guam	Y	None
	236	276	Manibusan, Maria P	Daughter	F	Cha	18.0	S	N	Y	Y	Guam	Guam	Guam		None
	236	276	Manibusan, Rosa P	Daughter	F	Cha	9.0	S	N			Guam	Guam	Guam		None
	236	276	Manibusan, Juan P	Grandson	M	Cha	1.0	S				Guam	Unknown	Guam		None
	237	277	Benavente, Maria I	Head	F	Cha	89.0	Wd		N	N	Guam	Guam	Guam	N	None
San Nicolas Street	238	278	Cruz, Pedro J	Head	M	Cha	31.0	M		Y	Y	Guam	Guam	Guam	N	Laborer
	238	278	Cruz, Maria B	Wife	F	Cha	31.0	M		Y	Y	Guam	Guam	Guam	N	None
	238	278	Cruz, Vicente B	Son	M	Cha	7.0	S	Y			Guam	Guam	Guam		None
	238	278	Cruz, Nicolasa B	Daughter	F	Cha	6.0	S	N			Guam	Guam	Guam		None
	238	278	Cruz, Josefina B	Daughter	F	Cha	4.0	S				Guam	Guam	Guam		None
	238	278	Cruz, Maria B	Daughter	F	Cha	1.0	S				Guam	Guam	Guam		None
	238	278	Cruz, Carlos J	Brother	M	Cha	28.0	S		Y	Y	Guam	Guam	Guam		Laborer
	238	278	Perez, Ignacio T	Boarder	M	Cha	28.0	M		N	N	Guam	Guam	Guam	N	None
	238	278	Perez, Francisca M	Boarder	F	Cha	70.0	M		N	N	Guam	Guam	Guam	N	None
	239	279	Castro, Luis P	Head	M	Cha	32.0	M		Y	Y	Guam	Guam	Guam	N	Farmer
	239	279	Castro, Concepcion B	Wife	F	Cha	31.0	M		Y	N	Guam	Guam	Guam	N	None
	239	279	Castro, Jesus B	Son	M	Cha	5.0	S	N			Guam	Guam	Guam		None

(CHAMORRO ROOTS GENEALOGY PROJECT ™ TRANSCRIPTION)
(COMPILED/TRANSCRIBED BY BERNARD T. PUNZALAN / HTTP://WWW.CHAMORROROOTS.COM)

FOURTEENTH CENSUS OF THE UNITED STATES: 1920—POPULATION
ISLAND OF GUAM

ENUMERATED BY ME ON THE 19th DAY OF April, 1920

Jose Kamminga ENUMERATOR

DISTRICT 1
NAME OF PLACE Agana City
[Proper name and, also, name of class, as city, town, village, barrio, etc]

	Street	Dwelling No.	Family No.	NAME	RELATION	Sex	Color or race	Age	Single, married, widowed or divorced	Attended school since Sept. 1, 1919	Able to read	Able to write	Birthplace of person	Birthplace of father	Birthplace of mother	Able to speak English	OCCUPATION
		1	2	3	4	5	6	7	8	9	10	11	12	13	14	15	16	17
26		239	279	Castro, Ana B	Daughter	F	Cha	3.0	S				Guam	Guam	Guam		None
27		239	279	Castro, Maria B	Daughter	F	Cha	1.0	S				Guam	Guam	Guam		None
28		239	279	Castro, Jose B	Son	M	Cha	0.5	S				Guam	Guam	Guam		None
29		239	279	Palomo, Gregorio P	Brother	M	Cha	20.0	S	N	Y	Y	Guam	Unknown	Guam	Y	Laborer
30		239	279	Lujan, Maria SN	Boarder	F	Cha	30.0	S		Y	N	Guam	Guam	Guam	N	None
31		240	280	Muna, Jose P	Head	M	Cha	30.0	M		Y	Y	Guam	Guam	Guam	N	Farmer
32		240	280	Muna, Josefa D	Wife	F	Chin	34.0	M		Y	Y	Guam	China	Guam	N	None
33		240	280	Muna, Gregorio D	Son	M	Cha	7.0	S	Y	Y	Y	Guam	Guam	Guam		None
34		240	280	Muna, Jose D	Son	M	Cha	6.0	S				Guam	Guam	Guam		None
35		240	280	Muna, Ignacio D	Son	M	Cha	4.0	S				Guam	Guam	Guam		None
36		240	280	Muna, Francisco D	Son	M	Cha	2.0	S				Guam	Guam	Guam		None
37		240	280	Muna, Felisitas D	Daughter	F	Cha	0.0	S				Guam	Guam	Guam		None
38		240	280	Dydasco, Vicente A	Brother-in-law	M	Chin	42.0	S		Y	N	Guam	China	Guam	N	Farm laborer
39		240	280	Dydasco, Joaquin A	Brother-in-law	M	Chin	32.0	S		Y	Y	Guam	China	Guam	Y	Carpenter
40	San Nicolas Street	241	281	Divera, Nicolas A	Head	M	Fil	30.0	M		Y	Y	Guam	Philippine Islands	Guam	N	Farmer
41		241	281	Divera, Carmen B	Wife	F	Cha	25.0	M		Y	N	Guam	Unknown	Unknown	N	None
42		241	281	Divera, Juan B	Son	M	Fil	5.0	S	N			Guam	Guam	Guam		None
43		241	281	Divera, Jacoba B	Daughter	F	Fil	3.0	S				Guam	Guam	Guam		None
44		241	281	Divera, Pablo B	Son	M	Fil	0.9	S				Guam	Guam	Guam		None
45		242	282	Borja, Ramon S	Head	M	Cha	36.0	M		Y	Y	Guam	Guam	Guam	N	Farmer
46		242	282	Borja, Isabel L	Wife	F	Cha	49.0	M		Y	Y	Guam	Guam	Guam	N	None
47		242	282	Borja, Maria L	Step daughter	F	Cha	31.0	S		Y	Y	Guam	Unknown	Guam	N	None
48		242	282	Guevara, Vicente R	Cousin	M	Fil	38.0	Wd		Y	Y	Guam	Philippine Islands	Guam	N	Farm laborer
49		242	282	Payne, Thomas SN	Boarder	M	W	60.0	M		Y	Y	Guam	United States	Guam	Y	None
50		243	283	Walters, Rita A	Head	M	Cha	38.0	Wd		Y	Y	Guam	Guam	Guam	Y	None

(CHAMORRO ROOTS GENEALOGY PROJECT ™ TRANSCRIPTION)
(COMPILED/TRANSCRIBED BY BERNARD T. PUNZALAN / HTTP://WWW.CHAMORROROOTS.COM)

FOURTEENTH CENSUS OF THE UNITED STATES: 1920—POPULATION

ISLAND OF GUAM

ENUMERATED BY ME ON THE 20th DAY OF April, 1920

Jose Kamminga ENUMERATOR

DISTRICT 1
NAME OF PLACE Agana City

[Proper name and, also, name of class, as city, town, village, barrio, etc]

Street	Dwelling house no.	Family no.	NAME	RELATION	Sex	Color or race	Age	Single, married, widowed or divorced	Attended school since Sept. 1, 1919	Able to read	Able to write	Place of birth of person	Place of birth of father	Place of birth of mother	Able to speak English	OCCUPATION
1	2	3	4	5	6	7	8	9	10	11	12	13	14	15	16	17
	243	283	Walters, Joe A	Son	M	W	15.0	S	Y	Y	Y	Guam	United States	Guam	Y	None
	243	283	Walters, Frank A	Son	M	W	0.4	S				Guam	United States	Guam		None
San Nicolas Street	244	284	Tass, Maria A	Head	F	Cha	35.0	M		Y	Y	Guam	Guam	Guam	Y	None
	244	284	Tass, Juan A	Son	M	W	10.0	S	N	N	N	Guam	United States	Guam	N	None
	244	284	Aguon, Ignacio U	Brother	M	Cha	37.0	S		Y	Y	Guam	Guam	Guam	Y	Farm laborer
	245	285	Perez, Francisco M	Head	M	Cha	32.0	M		Y	Y	Guam	Guam	Guam	Y	Storekeeper
	245	285	Perez, Rosa C	Wife	F	Cha	26.0	M		Y	Y	Guam	Guam	Guam	Y	None
	245	285	Perez, Honoria C	Daughter	F	Cha	9.0	S	Y			Guam	Guam	Guam		None
	245	285	Perez, Maria C	Daughter	F	Cha	5.0	S	N			Guam	Guam	Guam		None
	245	285	Perez, Joaquin C	Son	M	Cha	3.0	S				Guam	Guam	Guam		None
	245	285	Perez, Jesus C	Son	M	Cha	0.8	S				Guam	Guam	Guam		None
	245	285	Arriola, Luis M	Servant	M	Cha	36.0	S		N	N	Guam	Guam	Guam	N	Servant
	246	286	Naputi, Jesus N	Head	M	Cha	34.0	M	Y	Y	Y	Guam	Unknown	Guam	Y	Cook
	246	286	Naputi, Ana B	Wife	F	Cha	30.0	M		N	N	Guam	Guam	Guam	Y	None
	246	286	Naputi, Jose B	Son	M	Cha	10.0	S	Y	Y	Y	Guam	Guam	Guam	Y	None
	246	286	Naputi, Maria B	Daughter	F	Cha	7.0	S	Y	N	N	Guam	Guam	Guam		None
	246	286	Naputi, Rosa B	Daughter	F	Cha	4.0	S				Guam	Guam	Guam		None
	246	286	Naputi, Jesus B	Son	M	Cha	2.0	S				Guam	Guam	Guam		None
Ytgo Road	247	287	San Agustin, Alejandra C	Head	F	Cha	55.0	S		Y	Y	Guam	Guam	Guam	N	None
	247	287	San Agustin, Antonia	Daughter	F	Cha	17.0	S	N	Y	Y	Guam	Unknown	Guam	N	Laundress
	247	287	Hernandez, Jose SA	Grandson	M	Cha	5.0	S	N			Guam	Guam	Guam		None
	247	287	Taitinfong, Ignacio	Boarder	M	Cha	48.0	S		Y	Y	Guam	Guam	Guam	N	Laborer
	248	288	San Agustin, Faustino C	Head	M	Cha	31.0	M		Y	Y	Guam	Unknown	Guam	N	Farmer
	248	288	San Agustin, Josefa M	Wife	F	Cha	25.0	M				Guam	Guam	Guam	N	None
	248	288	San Agustin, Victor M	Son	M	Cha	4.0	S				Guam	Guam	Guam	N	None

(CHAMORRO ROOTS GENEALOGY PROJECT ™ TRANSCRIPTION)
(COMPILED/TRANSCRIBED BY BERNARD T. PUNZALAN / HTTP://WWW.CHAMORROROOTS.COM)
FOURTEENTH CENSUS OF THE UNITED STATES: 1920-POPULATION
ISLAND OF GUAM

DISTRICT 1
NAME OF PLACE Agana City
[Proper name and, also, name of class, as city, town, village, barrio, etc]

ENUMERATED BY ME ON THE 20th DAY OF April, 1920
Jose Kamminga ENUMERATOR

	Street, avenue, road, etc.	Number of dwelling house	Number of family in order of visitation	NAME	RELATION	Sex	Color or race	Age at last birthday	Single, married, widowed or divorced	Attended school any time since Sept. 1, 1919	Whether able to read	Whether able to write	Place of birth of this person	Place of birth of father of this person	Place of birth of mother of this person	Whether able to speak English	OCCUPATION
	1	2	3	4	5	6	7	8	9	10	11	12	13	14	15	16	17
26		248	288	San Agustin, Pedro M	Son	M	Cha	0.9	S				Guam	Guam	Guam		None
27		248	288	Manibusan, Francisco Q	Brother-in-law	M	Cha	23.0	S				Guam	Guam	Guam	N	Laborer
28		249	289	Gumabon, Ariston G	Head	M	Fil	55.0	M		Y	Y	Philippine Islands	Philippine Islands	Philippine Islands	N	Shoemaker
29		249	289	Gumabon, Carmen N	Wife	F	Cha	44.0	M		N	N	Guam	Unknown	Guam	N	None
30		249	289	Gumabon, Jose N	Son	M	Fil	15.0	S	N	Y	Y	Guam	Philippine Islands	Guam	Y	Servant
31		249	289	Gumabon, Vicente N	Son	M	Fil	10.0	S	Y	Y	Y	Guam	Philippine Islands	Guam	N	None
32		250	290	Bamba, Dolores SA	Head	F	Cha	47.0	Wd		N	N	Guam	Guam	Guam	N	None
33		250	290	Bamba, Juan SA	Son	M	Cha	19.0	S	N	Y	Y	Guam	Guam	Guam	Y	Laborer
34	Yigo Road	251	291	Bamba, Vicente SA	Head	M	Cha	23.0	M		Y	Y	Guam	Guam	Guam	Y	Laborer
35		251	291	Bamba, Concepcion C	Wife	F	Cha	22.0	M		Y	Y	Guam	Guam	Guam	N	None
36		251	291	Bamba, Maria C	Daughter	F	Cha	1.0	S				Guam	Guam	Guam		None
37		251	291	Bamba, Amalia C	Daughter	F	Cha	0.9	S				Guam	Guam	Guam		None
38		252	292	Marron, Rita B	Head	F	Cha	36.0	Wd		Y	Y	Guam	Guam	Guam	Y	Laborer
39		252	292	Marron, Geronimo B	Son	M	W	15.0	S	N	Y	Y	Guam	Mississippi	Mississippi	Y	None
40		252	292	Marron, Eduardo B	Son	M	W	14.0	S	N	Y	Y	Guam	Mississippi	Mississippi	Y	None
41		252	292	Marron, Lorenso B	Son	M	W	12.0	S	Y	Y	Y	Guam	Mississippi	Mississippi	Y	None
42		252	292	Benavente, Candelaria	Daughter	F	Cha	7.0	S	Y			Guam	Unknown	Guam		None
43		252	292	Benavente, Ana	Daughter	F	Cha	5.0	S	N			Guam	Unknown	Guam		None
44		252	292	Benavente, Victoria	Daughter	F	Cha	2.0	S				Guam	Unknown	Guam		None
45		251	292	Perez, Antonio	Boarder	M	Cha	37.0	S		Y	Y	Guam	Unknown	Guam	Y	Laborer
46		252	293	Sablan, Joaquin D	Head	M	Cha	32.0	M		Y	Y	Guam	Guam	Guam	Y	Carpenter
47		252	293	Sablan, Amalia R	Wife	F	Cha	30.0	M		Y	Y	Guam	Guam	Guam	N	None
48		252	293	Sablan, Ramon R	Son	M	Cha	10.0	S	Y	Y	Y	Guam	Guam	Guam	N	None
49		252	293	Sablan, Margarita R	Daughter	F	Cha	7.0	S	Y			Guam	Guam	Guam		None
50		252	293	Sablan, Rosalia R	Daughter	F	Cha	5.0	S	N			Guam	Guam	Guam		None

(CHAMORRO ROOTS GENEALOGY PROJECT ™ TRANSCRIPTION)
(COMPILED/TRANSCRIBED BY BERNARD T. PUNZALAN / HTTP://WWW.CHAMORROROOTS.COM)

FOURTEENTH CENSUS OF THE UNITED STATES: 1920-POPULATION
ISLAND OF GUAM

ENUMERATED BY ME ON THE 20th DAY OF April, 1920

Jose Kamminga ENUMERATOR

DISTRICT 1
NAME OF PLACE **Agana City**
[Proper name and, also, name of class, as city, town, village, barrio, etc]

	PLACE OF ABODE			NAME	RELATION	PERSONAL DESCRIPTION				EDUCATION			NATIVITY				OCCUPATION
Street, avenue, road, etc.	Number of dwelling house is order of visitation	Number of family in order of visitation		Name of each person whose place of abode on January 1, 1920, was in the family.	Relationship of this person to the head of the family.	Sex	Color or race	Age at last birthday	Single, married, widowed or divorced	Attended school any time since Sept. 1, 1919	Whether able to read.	Whether able to write.	Place of birth of this person.	Place of birth of father of this person.	Place of birth of mother of this person.	Whether able to speak English.	Trade, profession, or particular kind of work done, as salesman, laborer, clerk, cook, merchant, washerwoman, etc.
1	2	3		4	5	6	7	8	9	10	11	12	13	14	15	16	17
	252	293		Sablan, Antonio R	Son	M	Cha	3.0	S				Guam	Guam	Guam		None
	252	293		Sablan, Isabel R	Daughter	F	Cha	1.0	S				Guam	Guam	Guam		None
	253	294		Sablan, Jesus D	Head	M	Cha	36.0	M		Y	Y	Guam	Guam	Guam	N	Farmer
	253	294		Sablan, Josefa B	Wife	F	Cha	28.0	M		N	N	Guam	Guam	Guam	N	None
	253	294		Sablan, Francisco B	Son	M	Cha	12.0	S	Y	Y	Y	Guam	Guam	Guam	N	None
	253	294		Sablan, Manuela B	Daughter	F	Cha	9.0	S	Y			Guam	Guam	Guam		None
	253	294		Sablan, Maria B	Daughter	F	Cha	7.0	S	Y			Guam	Guam	Guam		None
	253	294		Sablan, Enrique B	Son	M	Cha	5.0	S	N			Guam	Guam	Guam		None
	253	294		Sablan, Jose B	Son	M	Cha	2.0	S				Guam	Guam	Guam		None
	253	294		Sablan, Vicenta B	Daughter	F	Cha	0.9	S				Guam	Guam	Guam		None
	254	295		Sablan, Antonio D	Head	M	Cha	43.0	M		Y	Y	Guam	Guam	Guam	N	Farmer
	254	295		Sablan, Ana B	Wife	F	Cha	33.0	M		Y	Y	Guam	Guam	Guam	N	None
Ytgo Road	254	295		Sablan, Pedro B	Son	M	Cha	18.0	S	N	Y	Y	Guam	Guam	Guam	Y	Farm laborer home farm
	254	295		Sablan, Jose B	Son	M	Cha	16.0	S	N	Y	Y	Guam	Guam	Guam	Y	Laborer
	254	295		Sablan, Dolores B	Daughter	F	Cha	13.0	S	N	Y	Y	Guam	Guam	Guam	Y	None
	254	295		Sablan, Amalia B	Daughter	F	Cha	11.0	S	N	Y	Y	Guam	Guam	Guam	N	None
	254	295		Sablan, Nicolas B	Son	M	Cha	8.0	S	Y			Guam	Guam	Guam		None
	254	295		Sablan, Vicente B	Son	M	Cha	6.0	S	N			Guam	Guam	Guam		None
	254	295		Sablan, Cristina B	Daughter	F	Cha	3.0	S				Guam	Guam	Guam		None
	254	295		Sablan, Maria B	Daughter	F	Cha	0.5	S				Guam	Guam	Guam		None
	255	296		Duenas, Jose S	Head	M	Cha	46.0	M		Y	N	Guam	Guam	Guam	N	Mason
	255	296		Duenas, Ana S	Wife	F	Cha	40.0	M		Y	Y	Guam	Guam	Guam	Y	None
	256	297		Duenas, Ramon S	Head	M	Cha	25.0	M		Y	Y	Guam	Guam	Guam	Y	Carpenter
	256	297		Duenas, Dolores S	Wife	F	Cha	21.0	M	N	Y	Y	Guam	Guam	Guam	Y	None
	256	297		Duenas, Jose S	Son	M	Cha	0.3	S				Guam	Guam	Guam		None

(CHAMORRO ROOTS GENEALOGY PROJECT ™ TRANSCRIPTION)
(COMPILED/TRANSCRIBED BY BERNARD T. PUNZALAN / HTTP://WWW.CHAMORROROOTS.COM)
FOURTEENTH CENSUS OF THE UNITED STATES: 1920–POPULATION
ISLAND OF GUAM

DISTRICT **1**
NAME OF PLACE **Agana City**

ENUMERATED BY ME ON THE 21st DAY OF April, 1920

Jose Kamminga ENUMERATOR

[Proper name and, also, name of class, as city, town, village, barrio, etc]

Street, avenue, road, etc.	Number of dwelling house in order of visitation	Number of family in order of visitation	NAME of each person whose place of abode on January 1, 1920, was in the family.	RELATION Relationship of this person to the head of the family.	Sex	Color or race	Age at last birthday	Single, married, widowed or divorced	Attended school any time since Sept. 1, 1919	Whether able to read.	Whether able to write.	Place of birth of this person.	Place of birth of father of this person.	Place of birth of mother of this person.	Whether able to speak English.	OCCUPATION Trade, profession, or particular kind of work done, as salesman, laborer, clerk, cook, merchant, washerwoman, etc.
1	2	3	4	5	6	7	8	9	10	11	12	13	14	15	16	17
	256	298	Mesa, Tomas S	Head	M	Cha	54.0	M		Y	Y	Guam	Guam	Guam	N	Mason
	256	298	Mesa, Dolores C	Wife	F	Cha	51.0	M		Y	Y	Guam	Guam	Guam	N	None
	256	298	Mesa, Luis C	Son	M	Cha	30.0	S		Y	Y	Guam	Guam	Guam	N	Laborer
	256	298	Mesa, Jose C	Son	M	Cha	18.0	S	N	Y	Y	Guam	Guam	Guam	Y	Farm laborer home farm
	256	298	Mesa, Jesus C	Son	M	Cha	16.0	S	N	Y	Y	Guam	Guam	Guam	Y	Farm laborer home farm
	256	298	Mesa, Jose C jr	Son	M	Cha	10.0	S	Y	Y	Y	Guam	Guam	Guam	N	None
	256	298	Mesa, Joaquin C	Son	M	Cha	5.0	S	N			Guam	Guam	Guam		None
	256	298	Cruz, Juan M	Son	M	Cha	21.0	S	N	Y	Y	Guam	Guam	Guam	Y	Enlisted man USN
Ylgo Road	257	299	Blas, Lorenso L	Head	M	Cha	39.0	M		Y	Y	Guam	Guam	Guam	N	Farmer
	257	299	Blas, Maria M	Wife	F	Cha	25.0	M		Y	Y	Guam	Guam	Guam	Y	None
	257	299	Blas, Maria M	Daughter	F	Cha	6.0	S	N			Guam	Guam	Guam	N	None
	257	299	Blas, Consuelo M	Daughter	F	Cha	2.0	S				Guam	Guam	Guam	N	None
	257	299	Blas, Asuncion M	Daughter	F	Cha	0.5	S				Guam	Guam	Guam	N	None
	258	300	Mesa, Manuela M	Head	F	Cha	58.0	Wd		Y	N	Guam	Guam	Guam	N	Salt maker
	259	301	Cruz, Juan M	Head	M	Cha	55.0	M		Y	Y	Guam	Guam	Guam	N	Fisherman
	259	301	Camacho, Ana	Boarder	F	Cha	31.0	S		Y	N	Guam	Unknown	Guam	N	None
	259	301	Camacho, Feliciana	Boarder	F	Cha	13.0	S	N	Y	Y	Guam	Unknown	Guam	N	None
	259	301	Camacho, Jesus	Boarder	M	Cha	11.0	S	N	Y	Y	Guam	Unknown	Guam	N	None
	259	301	Camacho, Maria	Boarder	F	Cha	6.0	S	N			Guam	Unknown	Guam	N	None
	259	301	Camacho, Engracia	Boarder	F	Cha	5.0	S	N			Guam	Unknown	Guam	N	None
	259	301	Camacho, Jose	Boarder	M	Cha	3.0	S	N			Guam	Unknown	Guam	N	None
Barrigada Road	260	302	Cruz, Francisco J	Head	M	Cha	33.0	M		Y	Y	Guam	Guam	Guam	Y	Policeman
	260	302	Cruz, Rosa B	Wife	F	Cha	34.0	M		Y	N	Guam	Guam	Guam	N	None
	260	302	Cruz, Rita B	Daughter	F	Cha	10.0	S	Y	Y	Y	Guam	Guam	Guam	Y	None
	260	302	Jesus, Maria H	Niece	F	Cha	3.0	S				Guam	Guam	Guam	N	None

26
27
28
29
30
31
32
33
34
35
36
37
38
39
40
41
42
43
44
45
46
47
48
49
50

173

(CHAMORRO ROOTS GENEALOGY PROJECT ™ TRANSCRIPTION)
(COMPILED/TRANSCRIBED BY BERNARD T. PUNZALAN / HTTP://WWW.CHAMORROROOTS.COM)
FOURTEENTH CENSUS OF THE UNITED STATES: 1920-POPULATION
ISLAND OF GUAM

DISTRICT 1
NAME OF PLACE Agana City

[Proper name and, also, name of class, as city, town, village, barrio, etc]

ENUMERATED BY ME ON THE 21st DAY OF April, 1920

Jose Kamminga ENUMERATOR

Street, avenue, road, etc.	Number of dwelling house is in order of visitation	Number of family in order of visitation	NAME	RELATION	Sex	Color or race	Age at last birthday	Single, married, widowed or divorced	Attended school any time since Sept. 1, 1919	Whether able to read.	Whether able to write.	Place of birth of this person.	Place of birth of father of this person.	Place of birth of mother of this person.	Whether able to speak English.	OCCUPATION
1	2	3	4	5	6	7	8	9	10	11	12	13	14	15	16	17
	260	302	Santos, Joaquin J	Cousin	M	Cha	27.0	S		Y	Y	Guam	Guam	Guam	N	Laborer
	261	303	Perez, Jose P	Head	M	Cha	33.0	M		Y	Y	Guam	Unknown	Guam	Y	Laborer
	261	303	Perez, Rita B	Wife	F	Cha	34.0	M		N	N	Guam	Unknown	Guam	N	None
	261	303	Perez, Jose B	Son	M	Cha	14.0	S	Y	Y	Y	Guam	Guam	Guam	Y	None
	261	303	Perez, Juana B	Daughter	F	Cha	12.0	S	Y	Y	Y	Guam	Guam	Guam	N	None
	261	303	Perez, Manuel B	Son	M	Cha	9.0	S	Y			Guam	Guam	Guam		None
	261	303	Perez, Josefina B	Daughter	F	Cha	0.1	S				Guam	Guam	Guam		None
	262	304	Chupaco, Luisa A	Head	F	Cha	23.0	S		Y	Y	Guam	Guam	Guam	Y	Cook
	262	304	Chupaco, Alfonso	Son	M	Cha	5.0	S	N			Guam	Unknown	Guam		None
	262	304	Adriano, Maria	Grandmother	F	Cha	65.0	S		N	N	Guam	Guam	Guam	N	None
	263	305	Talabera, Manuel M	Head	M	Fil	49.0	M		Y	Y	Guam	Philippine Islands	Guam	N	Farmer
	263	305	Talabera, Maria Q	Wife	F	Cha	51.0	M		Y	Y	Guam	Guam	Guam	N	None
	263	305	Talabera, Jose Q	Son	M	Fil	18.0	S	N	Y	Y	Guam	Guam	Guam	Y	Farm laborer home farm
	263	305	Talabera, Antonia Q	Daughter	F	Fil	16.0	S	N	Y	Y	Guam	Guam	Guam	N	None
	263	305	Talabera, Trinidad Q	Daughter	F	Fil	14.0	S	N	Y	Y	Guam	Guam	Guam	N	None
	263	305	Talabera, Antonio Q	Son	M	Fil	12.0	S	Y	Y	Y	Guam	Guam	Guam	Y	None
	263	305	Talabera, Felisitas Q	Daughter	F	Fil	10.0	S	N	Y	Y	Guam	Guam	Guam	N	None
	263	305	Talabera, Consuelo Q	Daughter	F	Fil	8.0	S	N			Guam	Guam	Guam	N	None
	263	305	Quichocho, Jose	Nephew	M	Cha	20.0	S	N	Y	Y	Guam	Unknown	Guam	N	Farm laborer home farm
	263	305	Quichocho, Rafael	Nephew	M	Cha	18.0	S	N	N	N	Guam	Unknown	Guam	N	Farm laborer home farm
	264	306	Quichocho, Rosa LG	Head	F	Cha	45.0	S		N	N	Guam	Guam	Guam	N	None
	264	306	Quichocho, Vicenta LG	Sister	F	Cha	47.0	S		N	N	Guam	Guam	Guam	N	None
	264	306	Quichocho, Maria T	Niece	F	Cha	22.0	S	Y	Y	Y	Guam	Guam	Guam	N	None
	264	306	Quichocho, Manuel T	Nephew	M	Cha	16.0	S	N	N	N	Guam	Guam	Guam	N	Farm laborer home farm
	264	306	Quichocho, Teodoro	Son	M	Cha	10.0	S	Y	N	N	Guam	Unknown	Guam	N	None

Barrigada Road

174

(CHAMORRO ROOTS GENEALOGY PROJECT ™ TRANSCRIPTION)
(COMPILED/TRANSCRIBED BY BERNARD T. PUNZALAN / HTTP://WWW.CHAMORROROOTS.COM)

FOURTEENTH CENSUS OF THE UNITED STATES: 1920-POPULATION

ISLAND OF GUAM

85b

DISTRICT 1
NAME OF PLACE Agana City

ENUMERATED BY ME ON THE 22nd DAY OF April, 1920

Jose Kamminga ENUMERATOR

Street	Dwelling No.	Family No.	NAME	RELATION	Sex	Color or race	Age	Single/married/widowed/divorced	Attended school since Sept 1, 1919	Able to read	Able to write	Birthplace of person	Birthplace of father	Birthplace of mother	Speak English	OCCUPATION
	264	306	Quichocho, Josefa	Niece	F	Cha	8.0	S	Y			Guam	Unknown	Guam		None
	265	307	Arceo, Vicente A	Head	M	Cha	54.0	Wd		Y	Y	Guam	Guam	Guam	N	Farmer
	265	307	Arceo, Gregoria C	Daughter	F	Cha	20.0	S	Y	Y	Y	Guam	Guam	Guam	Y	None
	265	307	Arceo, Francisco C	Son	M	Cha	17.0	S	N	Y	Y	Guam	Guam	Guam	Y	None
	265	307	Arceo, Jose C	Son	M	Cha	15.0	S	Y	Y	Y	Guam	Guam	Guam	Y	None
	265	307	Arceo, Vicente C	Son	M	Cha	9.0	S	Y			Guam	Guam	Guam		None
Barrigada Road	265	307	Arceo, Lydia C	Daughter	F	Cha	6.0	S	N			Guam	Guam	Guam		None
	265	308	Cruz, Ana A	Head	F	Cha	33.0	S		Y	Y	Guam	Guam	Guam	N	None
	265	308	Cruz, Jesus	Son	M	Cha	4.0	S				Guam	Unknown	Guam		None
	265	308	Cruz, Juan	Son	M	Cha	1.0	S				Guam	Unknown	Guam		None
	266	309	Cruz, Antonio M	Head	M	Cha	43.0	M		Y	N	Guam	Guam	Guam	N	Farmer
	266	309	Pangelinan, Dolores M	Wife	F	Cha	47.0	M		Y	N	Guam	Guam	Guam	N	None
	266	309	Pangelinan, Concepcion M	Step daughter	F	Cha	20.0	S	N	Y	Y	Guam	Guam	Guam	Y	None
	266	309	Pangelinan, Matias M	Step son	M	Cha	15.0	S	N	Y	Y	Guam	Guam	Guam	Y	Farm laborer home farm
	266	309	Pangelinan, Jose M	Step son	M	Cha	7.0	S	Y	Y	Y	Guam	Guam	Guam	Y	None
	266	309	Cruz, Vicente S	Son	M	Cha	16.0	S	N	Y	Y	Guam	Guam	Guam	Y	Laborer
	266	309	Cruz, Antonio S	Son	M	Cha	14.0	S	N	Y	Y	Guam	Guam	Guam	Y	None
	266	309	Cruz, Jose S	Son	M	Cha	12.0	S	Y	Y	Y	Guam	Guam	Guam	Y	None
	266	309	Cruz, Domingo S	Son	M	Cha	10.0	S	Y	Y	Y	Guam	Guam	Guam	Y	None
	266	309	Cruz, Juan S	Son	M	Cha	19.0	S	N	Y	Y	Guam	Guam	Guam	Y	Laborer
	266	310	Cruz, Anacleto M	Head	M	Cha	30.0	M	N	Y	Y	Guam	Guam	Guam	N	Farmer
	266	310	Cruz, Rita P	Wife	F	Cha	19.0	M		N	N	Guam	Guam	Guam	N	None
MongMong Road	267	311	Ojeda, Juan A	Head	M	Cha	61.0	M	N	Y	N	Guam	Guam	Guam	N	Farmer
MongMong Road	267	311	Ojeda, Rosa M	Wife	F	Cha	60.0	M				Guam	Guam	Guam	N	None
	267	311	Ojeda, Francisco M	Son	M	Cha	34.0	S		Y	Y	Guam	Guam	Guam	Y	Carpenter

(CHAMORRO ROOTS GENEALOGY PROJECT ™ TRANSCRIPTION)
(COMPILED/TRANSCRIBED BY BERNARD T. PUNZALAN / HTTP://WWW.CHAMORROROOTS.COM)
FOURTEENTH CENSUS OF THE UNITED STATES: 1920—POPULATION
ISLAND OF GUAM

DISTRICT 1
NAME OF PLACE Agana City

[Proper name and, also, name of class, as city, town, village, barrio, etc]

ENUMERATED BY ME ON THE 22nd DAY OF April, 1920

Jose Kamminga ENUMERATOR

	PLACE OF ABODE		NAME	RELATION	PERSONAL DESCRIPTION				EDUCATION			NATIVITY				OCCUPATION
Street, avenue, road, etc.	Number of dwelling house in order of visitation	Number of family in order of visitation	Name of each person whose place of abode on January 1, 1920, was in the family.	Relationship of this Person to the head of the family.	Sex	Color or race	Age at last birthday	Single, married, widowed or divorced	Attended school any time since Sept. 1, 1919	Whether able to read.	Whether able to write.	Place of birth of this person.	Place of birth of father of this person.	Place of birth of mother of this person.	Whether able to speak English.	Trade, profession, or particular kind of work done, as salesman, laborer, clerk, cook, merchant, washerwoman, etc.
1	2	3	4	5	6	7	8	9	10	11	12	13	14	15	16	17
	267	311	Ojeda, Juan M	Son	M	Cha	20.0	S	N	Y	Y	Guam	Guam	Guam	Y	Storekeeper
	268	312	Cruz, Manuel P	Head	M	Cha	50.0	M		Y	Y	Guam	Guam	Guam	N	Farerm
	268	312	Cruz, Dolores C	Wife	F	Cha	50.0	M		Y	Y	Guam	Guam	Guam	N	None
	268	312	Cruz, Francisco C	Son	M	Cha	16.0	S	N	Y	Y	Guam	Guam	Guam	Y	Farm laborer home farm
	268	312	Cruz, Manuel C	Son	M	Cha	15.0	S	N	Y	Y	Guam	Guam	Guam	Y	Laborer
	268	312	Cruz, Engracia C	Daughter	F	Cha	13.0	S	Y	Y	Y	Guam	Guam	Guam	Y	None
	268	312	Cruz, Maria C	Daughter	F	Cha	10.0	S	Y	Y	Y	Guam	Guam	Guam	N	None
Mongmong Road	269	313	Francisco, Domingo P	Head	M	Wh	57.0	M		Y	N	Guam	Portugal	Guam	N	Farmer
	269	313	Francisco, Carmen C	Wife	F	Mix	44.0	M		Y	Y	Guam	Guam	Guam	N	None
	269	313	Francisco, Rosa C	Daughter	F	Mix	26.0	S		Y	Y	Guam	Guam	Guam	N	Laundress
	269	313	Francisco, Ignacia C	Daughter	F	Mix	23.0	S		Y	Y	Guam	Guam	Guam	N	Laundress
	269	313	Francisco, Jesus C	Son	M	Mix	16.0	S	N	Y	Y	Guam	Guam	Guam	Y	Farm laborer home farm
	269	313	Francisco, Saturnina C	Daughter	F	Mix	14.0	S	N	Y	Y	Guam	Guam	Guam	N	None
	269	313	Francisco, Joaquina C	Daughter	F	Mix	12.0	S	N	Y	Y	Guam	Guam	Guam	N	None
	269	313	Francisco, Joaquin C	Son	M	Mix	10.0	S	Y	Y	Y	Guam	Guam	Guam	N	None
	269	313	Francisco, Antonio C	Son	M	Mix	5.0	S	N			Guam	Guam	Guam		None
	269	313	Francisco, Jose S	Son	M	Mix	0.8	S				Guam	Guam	Guam		None
	270	314	Mesa, Joaquin	Head	M	Cha	40.0	M		Y	Y	Guam	Unknown	Guam	N	Farmer
	270	314	Mesa, Rita M	Wife	F	Cha	34.0	M		Y	N	Guam	Guam	Guam	N	None
	270	314	Mesa, Maria M	Daughter	F	Cha	11.0	S	Y	Y	Y	Guam	Guam	Guam	N	None
	270	314	Mesa, Tomasa M	Daughter	F	Cha	9.0	S	N			Guam	Guam	Guam		None
	270	314	Mesa, Jose M	Son	M	Cha	6.0	S	N			Guam	Guam	Guam		None
	270	314	Mesa, Hester M	Daughter	F	Cha	5.0	S				Guam	Guam	Guam		None
	271	315	Leon Guerrero, Juan LG	Head	M	Cha	33.0	M		Y	Y	Guam	Guam	Guam	N	Carpenter
	271	315	Leon Guerrero, Maria C	Wife	F	Cha	25.0	M		Y	Y	Guam	Guam	Guam	N	None

(CHAMORRO ROOTS GENEALOGY PROJECT ™ TRANSCRIPTION)
(COMPILED/TRANSCRIBED BY BERNARD T. PUNZALAN / HTTP://WWW.CHAMORROROOTS.COM)

FOURTEENTH CENSUS OF THE UNITED STATES: 1920–POPULATION

ISLAND OF GUAM

DISTRICT **1**
NAME OF PLACE **Agana City**

[Proper name and, also, name of class, as city, town, village, barrio, etc]

ENUMERATED BY ME ON THE **22**nd DAY OF **April**, 1920

Jose Kamminga ENUMERATOR

Street, avenue, road, etc.	Number of dwelling house in order of visitation	Number of family in order of visitation	NAME	RELATION	Sex	Color or race	Age at last birthday	Single, married, widowed or divorced	Attended any school any time since Sept. 1, 1919	Whether able to read.	Whether able to write.	Place of birth of this person.	Place of birth of father of this person.	Place of birth of mother of this person.	Whether able to speak English.	OCCUPATION
1	2	3	4	5	6	7	8	9	10	11	12	13	14	15	16	17
	271	315	Leon Guerrero, Maria C	Daughter	F	Cha	7.0	S	Y			Guam	Guam	Guam		None
	271	315	Leon Guerrero, Rosa C	Daughter	F	Cha	4.0	S				Guam	Guam	Guam		None
	271	315	Leon Guerrero, Juan C	Son	M	Cha	2.0	S				Guam	Guam	Guam		None
	271	315	Leon Guerrero, Pedro C	Son	M	Cha	1.0	S				Guam	Guam	Guam		None
	272	316	Perez, Vicente F	Head	M	Cha	28.0	M		Y	Y	Guam	Guam	Guam	Y	Farmer
	272	316	Perez, Josefa S	Wife	F	Cha	17.0	M	N	Y	Y	Guam	Guam	Guam	N	None
	272	316	Perez, Luis S	Son	M	Cha	2.0	S				Guam	Guam	Guam		None
	272	316	Perez, Gregorio S	Son	M	Cha	1.0	S				Guam	Guam	Guam		None
	272	316	Borja, Maria G	Mother-in-law	F	Cha	35.0	Wd		Y	Y	Guam	Guam	Guam		None
	273	317	Taijeron, Juana	Head	F	Cha	60.0	Wd		N	N	Guam	Guam	Guam	N	None
Mongmong Road	273	317	Taijeron, Enrique	Son	M	Cha	40.0	S		Y	Y	Guam	Unknown	Guam	Y	Laborer
	274	318	Camacho, Vicente C	Head	M	Cha	22.0	S	N	Y	Y	Guam	Guam	Guam	Y	Laborer
	274	318	Guerrero, Josefa G	Servant	F	Cha	21.0	S		Y	Y	Guam	Unknown	Guam	N	None
	274	318	Guerrero, Maria	Servant	F	Cha	2.0	S				Guam	Unknown	Guam		None
	274	318	Guerrero, Juana	Servant	F	Cha	0.6	S				Guam	Unknown	Guam		None
	275	319	Untalan, Jose P	Head	M	Cha	28.0	M		Y	Y	Guam	Guam	Guam	Y	Carpenter
	275	319	Untalan, Trinidad R	Wife	F	Cha	24.0	M		Y	Y	Guam	Unknown	Guam	Y	None
	275	319	Untalan, Juan R	Son	M	Cha	4.0	S				Guam	Guam	Guam		None
	275	319	Untalan, Julita R	Daughter	F	Cha	3.0	S				Guam	Guam	Guam		None
	275	319	Untalan, Oliva R	Daughter	F	Cha	1.0	S				Guam	Guam	Guam		None
	276	320	Ignacio, Pedro A	Head	M	Cha	35.0	M		Y	Y	Guam	Guam	Guam		Farmer
	276	320	Ignacio, Marcela N	Wife	F	Cha	26.0	M		Y	Y	Guam	Unknown	Guam	N	None
	276	320	Ignacio, Francisco N	Son	M	Cha	7.0	S	N			Guam	Guam	Guam		None
	276	320	Ignacio, Jesus N	Son	M	Cha	5.0	S	N			Guam	Guam	Guam		None
	276	320	Ignacio, Maria N	Daughter	F	Cha	3.0	S				Guam	Guam	Guam		None

177

(CHAMORRO ROOTS GENEALOGY PROJECT ™ TRANSCRIPTION)
(COMPILED/TRANSCRIBED BY BERNARD T. PUNZALAN / HTTP://WWW.CHAMORROROOTS.COM)
FOURTEENTH CENSUS OF THE UNITED STATES: 1920—POPULATION
ISLAND OF GUAM

87

DISTRICT 1
NAME OF PLACE Agana City

[Proper name and, also, name of class, as city, town, village, barrio, etc]

ENUMERATED BY ME ON THE 23rd DAY OF April, 1920

Jose Kamminga ENUMERATOR

1 Street, avenue, road, etc.	2 Number of dwelling house in order of visitation	3 Number of family in order of visitation	4 NAME	5 RELATION	6 Sex	7 Color or race	8 Age at last birthday	9 Single, married, widowed or divorced	10 Attended school any time since Sept. 1, 1919	11 Whether able to read	12 Whether able to write	13 Place of birth of this person	14 Place of birth of father	15 Place of birth of mother	16 Whether able to speak English	17 OCCUPATION
	276	320	Ignacio, Jose N	Son	M	Cha	2.0	S				Guam	Guam	Guam		None
	276	320	Ignacio, Preciosa N	Daughter	F	Cha	1.0	S				Guam	Guam	Guam		None
	277	321	Susuico, Dominga	Head	F	Chin	43.0	S		N	N	Guam	China	Guam	N	None
	277	321	Susuico, Ignacio	Son	M	Chin	20.0	S	N	Y	Y	Guam	Unknown	Guam	Y	Laborer
	277	321	Susuico, Jose	Son	M	Chin	16.0	S	N	Y	N	Guam	Unknown	Guam	Y	Farm laborer home farm
	277	321	Susuico, Jesus	Son	M	Chin	3.0	S				Guam	Unknown	Guam		None
	277	321	Susuico, Carpio	Son	M	Chin	1.0	S				Guam	Unknown	Guam		None
	278	322	Nankawa, H	Head	M	Jp	40.0	M		Y	Y	Japan	Japan	Japan	Y	Carpenter
	278	322	Nankawa, Catalina D	Wife	F	Cha	31.0	M		Y	Y	Guam	Guam	Guam	Y	None
	278	322	Nankawa, Rufina D	Daughter	F	Jp	4.0	S				Guam	Japan	Guam		None
	278	322	Nankawa, Pedro D	Son	M	Jp	2.0	S				Guam	Japan	Guam		None
	279	323	Divera, Antonia A	Head	F	Cha	62.0	Wd		Y	Y	Guam	Guam	Guam	N	None
	279	323	Divera, Marcus A	Son	M	Fil	37.0	M		Y	Y	Guam	Philippine Islands	Guam	Y	Laborer
	279	323	Divera, Rogelio B	Grandson	M	Fil	2.0	S				Guam	Guam	Guam		None
Mongmong Road	280	324	White, Ana P	Head	F	Cha	54.0	S		Y	N	Guam	United States	Guam	N	None
	280	324	White, Rafaela P	Sister	F	Cha	48.0	S		Y	N	Guam	United States	Guam	N	Laundress
	280	324	White, Dolores P	Sister	F	Cha	53.0	Wd		Y	N	Guam	United States	Guam	N	Laundress
	280	324	Gogue, Ramona W	Sister	F	Cha	57.0	Wd		Y	N	Guam	United States	Guam	N	None
	280	324	Gogue, Vicenta W	Niece	F	Cha	34.0	S		Y	Y	Guam	Guam	Guam	N	None
	280	324	Gogue, Maria W	Niece	F	Cha	23.0	S		Y	Y	Guam	Guam	Guam	Y	Laundress
	280	324	Gogue, Enrique W	Nephew	M	Cha	21.0	S		Y	Y	Guam	Guam	Guam	Y	Farm laborer home farm
	280	324	Cruz, Antonia W	Niece	F	Cha	15.0	S		Y	Y	Guam	Guam	Guam	Y	Laundress
	280	324	Cruz, Dolores W	Niece	F	Cha	12.0	S		Y	Y	Guam	Guam	Guam	Y	None
	280	324	Cruz, Vicente W	Nephew	M	Cha	10.0	S	Y	Y	Y	Guam	Guam	Guam	Y	None
	280	324	Mesa, Gonzalo P	Boarder	M	Cha	9.0	S	N			Guam	Guam	Guam	N	None

178

(CHAMORRO ROOTS GENEALOGY PROJECT ™ TRANSCRIPTION)
(COMPILED/TRANSCRIBED BY BERNARD T. PUNZALAN / HTTP://WWW.CHAMORROROOTS.COM)

FOURTEENTH CENSUS OF THE UNITED STATES: 1920-POPULATION

ISLAND OF GUAM

ENUMERATED BY ME ON THE 23rd DAY OF April, 1920

Jose Kamminga ENUMERATOR

DISTRICT 1

NAME OF PLACE Agana City

[Proper name and, also, name of class, as city, town, village, barrio, etc]

	Street	Dwelling No.	Family No.	NAME	RELATION	Sex	Color or race	Age	Marital	Attended school	Read	Write	Birthplace	Father birthplace	Mother birthplace	Speak English	OCCUPATION
26		280	324	Mesa, Antonia P	Boarder	F	Cha	7.0	S	Y			Guam	Guam	Guam		None
27		281	325	Perez, Juan C	Head	M	Cha	28.0	M		Y	Y	Guam	Guam	Guam	Y	Carpenter
28		281	325	Perez, Carmen L	Wife	F	Cha	30.0	M		Y	Y	Guam	Guam	Guam	N	None
29	Monmong Road	281	325	Perez, Ignacio L	Son	M	Cha	5.0	S	N			Guam	Guam	Guam		None
30		281	325	Perez, Juan L	Son	M	Cha	4.0	S				Guam	Guam	Guam		None
31		281	325	Perez, Maria L	Daughter	F	Cha	3.0	S				Guam	Guam	Guam		None
32		282	326	Toves, Antonio LG	Head	M	Cha	49.0	M		N	N	Guam	Guam	Guam	N	Farmer
33		282	326	Toves, Ana Q	Wife	F	Cha	47.0	M		N	N	Guam	Guam	Guam	N	None
34		282	326	Toves, Francisco Q	Son	M	Cha	19.0	S	N	Y	Y	Guam	Guam	Guam	Y	Farm laborer home farm
35		282	326	Toves, Maria Q	Daughter	F	Cha	16.0	S	N	N	N	Guam	Guam	Guam	N	None
36		282	326	Toves, Juan Q	Son	M	Cha	13.0	S	N	N	N	Guam	Guam	Guam	N	None
37		282	326	Toves, Ana Q	Daughter	F	Cha	12.0	S	N	N	N	Guam	Guam	Guam	N	None
38		282	326	Toves, Rita Q	Daughter	F	Cha	8.0	S	N			Guam	Guam	Guam		None
39		282	326	Toves, Jose Q	Son	M	Cha	5.0	S	N			Guam	Guam	Guam		None
40		283	327	Pangelinan, Josefa B	Head	F	Cha	48.0	Wd		Y	Y	Guam	Guam	Guam	N	None
41		283	327	Pangelinan, Jose B	Step son	M	Cha	29.0	S		Y	Y	Guam	Guam	Guam	Y	Farm laborer home farm
42		283	327	Pangelinan, Magdalena B	Step daughter	F	Cha	24.0	S		Y	Y	Guam	Guam	Guam	Y	None
43	Soledad Street	283	327	Pangelinan, Manuel B	Step son	M	Cha	20.0	S	N	Y	Y	Guam	Guam	Guam	Y	Tailor
44		283	327	Pangelinan, Guido B	Son	M	Cha	16.0	S	N	Y	Y	Guam	Guam	Guam	Y	Laborer
45		283	327	Pangelinan, Joaquin B	Son	M	Cha	11.0	S	Y	Y	Y	Guam	Guam	Guam	Y	None
46		283	327	Blas, Apolonia T	Sister	F	Cha	57.0	S		Y	Y	Guam	Guam	Guam	N	None
47		283	327	Flores, Ana T	Cousin	F	Cha	51.0	S		N	N	Guam	Guam	Guam	N	None
48		284	328	Crisostomo, Juan B	Head	M	Cha	49.0	M		N	N	Guam	Guam	Guam	N	Laborer
49		284	328	Crisostomo, Maria C	Wife	F	Cha	65.0	M		N	N	Guam	Guam	Guam	N	None
50		284	328	Crisostomo, Maria C	Daughter	F	Cha	20.0	S	N	Y	Y	Guam	Guam	Guam	Y	None

(COMPILED/TRANSCRIBED BY BERNARD T. PUNZALAN / HTTP://WWW.CHAMORROROOTS.COM)
(CHAMORRO ROOTS GENEALOGY PROJECT ™ TRANSCRIPTION)
FOURTEENTH CENSUS OF THE UNITED STATES: 1920-POPULATION
ISLAND OF GUAM

SHEET NO. _57A_

ENUMERATED BY ME ON THE 23rd DAY OF April, 1920

Jose Kamminga ENUMERATOR

DISTRICT 1
NAME OF PLACE **Agana City**
[Proper name and, also, name of class, as city, town, village, barrio, etc]

	PLACE OF ABODE			NAME	RELATION	PERSONAL DESCRIPTION				EDUCATION			NATIVITY				OCCUPATION
Street, avenue, road, etc.	Number of dwelling house is in order of visitation	Number of family in order of visitation	of each person whose place of abode on January 1, 1920, was in the family. Enter surname, first, then given name and middle initial. If any. Include every person living on January 1, 1920. Omit children born since January 1, 1920.	Relationship of this person to the head of the family.	Sex	Color or race	Age at last birthday	Single, married, widowed or divorced	Attended school any time since Sept. 1, 1919	Whether able to read.	Whether able to write.	Place of birth of this person.	Place of birth of father of this person.	Place of birth of mother of this person.	Whether able to speak English.	Trade, profession, or particular kind of work done, as salesman, laborer, clerk, cook, merchant, washerwoman, etc.
1	2	3	4	5	6	7	8	9	10	11	12	13	14	15	16	17
	284	328	Crisostomo, Felisitas C	Daughter	F	Cha	15.0	S	N	Y	Y	Guam	Guam	Guam	Y	None
	284	328	Crisostomo, Ana C	Daughter	F	Cha	12.0	S	Y	Y	Y	Guam	Guam	Guam	Y	None
	284	329	San Agustin, Jose C	Head	M	Cha	25.0	M		Y	Y	Guam	Unknown	Guam	Y	Farmer
	284	329	San Agustin, Maria C	Wife	F	Cha	20.0	M	N	Y	Y	Guam	Guam	Guam	Y	None
Soledad Street	284	329	San Agustin, Juan C	Son	M	Cha	1.0	S				Guam	Guam	Guam		None
	284	329	San Agustin, Juana C	Daughter	F	Cha	0.2	S				Guam	Guam	Guam		None
	285	330	Crisostomo, Caila C	Head	F	Cha	40.0	Wd		Y	N	Rota Island	Guam	Guam	N	Laundress
	285	330	Crisostomo, Vicenta C	Daughter	F	Cha	18.0	S	N	Y	Y	Guam	Guam	Rota Island	Y	Laundress
	285	330	Crisostomo, Pedro C	Son	M	Cha	14.0	N	Y	Y	Guam	Guam	Rota Island	Y	Servant
	285	330	Crisostomo, Vicente C	Son	M	Cha	8.0	S	Y			Guam	Guam	Rota Island		None
	285	330	Crisostomo, Maria	Grand daughter	F	Cha	1.0	S				Guam	Guam	Guam		None
	285	330	Cruz, Jose	Brother	M	Cha	43.0	S		Y	N	Rota Island	Guam	Guam	N	None
	285	330	Jota, Toyoki	Head	M	Jp	38.0	S		Y	Y	Japan	Japan	Japan	Y	Manager soda? Work

Here ends the enumeration of San Antonio - Agana City

180

(CHAMORRO ROOTS GENEALOGY PROJECT ™ TRANSCRIPTION)
(COMPILED/TRANSCRIBED BY BERNARD T. PUNZALAN / HTTP://WWW.CHAMORROROOTS.COM)
FOURTEENTH CENSUS OF THE UNITED STATES: 1920—POPULATION
ISLAND OF GUAM

DISTRICT 1 Pago - Sinajana
NAME OF PLACE Pago - Sinajana
[Proper name and, also, name of class, as city, town, village, barrio, etc]

ENUMERATED BY ME ON THE 24th DAY OF April, 1920

Arthur W. Jackson ENUMERATOR

Street, avenue, road, etc.	Number of dwelling house is order of visitation	Number of family in order of visitation	NAME	RELATION	Sex	Color or race	Age at last birthday	Single, married, widowed or divorced	Attended school any time since Sept. 1, 1919	Whether able to read.	Whether able to write.	Place of birth of this person.	Place of birth of father of this person.	Place of birth of mother of this person.	Whether able to speak English.	OCCUPATION
1	2	3	4	5	6	7	8	9	10	11	12	13	14	15	16	17
	1	1	Santos, Justo N	Head	M	Fil	33.0	S		Y	Y	Guam	Philippine Islands	Guam	N	Farmer
	1	1	Ibasco, Magdalena C	Servant	F	Fil	43.0	S		Y	Y	Guam	Philippine Islands	Guam	N	None
	1	1	Ibasco, Enrique	Servant	M	Fil	15.0	S	N	Y	Y	Guam	Philippine Islands	Guam	N	None
	2	2	Santos, Juan N	Head	M	Fil	42.0	Wd		Y	Y	Guam	Philippine Islands	Guam	Y	Farmer
	2	2	Santos, Jesus SN	Son	M	Fil	15.0	S	N	N	N	Guam	Guam	Guam	N	None
	2	2	Santos, Soledad SN	Daughter	F	Fil	14.0	S		Y	Y	Guam	Guam	Guam	N	None
	3	3	Santos, Maria N	Head	F	Fil	44.0	S		Y	Y	Guam	Philippine Islands	Guam	N	Farmer
	3	3	Chiguina, Joaquina N	Servant	F	Cha	11.0	S	N	N	N	Guam	Guam	Guam	N	None
	4	4	Cariaga, Felix S	Head	M	Fil	25.0	S		Y	Y	Guam	Philippine Islands	Guam	Y	Farmer
	4	4	Cariaga, Carmen P	Wife	F	Cha	20.0	M		Y	Y	Guam	Guam	Guam	Y	None
	4	4	Cariaga, Juan P	Son	M	Mix	0.0	S				Guam	Guam	Guam		
	5	5	Borja, Francisco S	Head	M	Cha	51.0	M		Y	Y	Guam	Guam	Guam	N	Farmer
	5	5	Borja, Nicolasa S	Wife	F	Fil	52.0	M		N	N	Guam	Philippine Islands	Guam	N	None
	5	5	Ibasco, Ines S	Niece	F	Fil	11.0	S	N	Y	Y	Guam	Guam	Guam	N	None
	5	5	Quichocho, Josefa Q	Boarder	F	Cha	30.0	S		N	N	Guam	Guam	Guam	N	None
	6	6	Perez, Ana B	Head	F	Cha	55.0	M		Y	Y	Guam	Guam	Guam	N	None
	6	6	Perez, Maria B	Daughter	F	Cha	25.0	M		N	N	Guam	Guam	Guam	N	None
	6	6	Perez, Rita B	Daughter	F	Cha	18.0	S	N	Y	Y	Guam	Guam	Guam	Y	None
	6	6	Perez, Vicente B	Son	M	Cha	13.0	S	Y	Y	Y	Guam	Guam	Guam	Y	None
	7	7	Castro, Juan B	Head	M	Cha	49.0	M		Y	Y	Guam	Guam	Guam	Y	Farmer
	7	7	Castro, Maria B	Wife	F	Cha	51.0	M		Y	Y	Guam	Guam	Guam	N	None
	7	7	Castro, Josefa B	Daughter	F	Cha	16.0	S	Y	Y	Y	Guam	Guam	Guam	Y	None
	7	7	Castro, Sebastian B	Son	M	Cha	13.0	S	Y	Y	Y	Guam	Guam	Guam	Y	None
	8	8	Manibusan, Joaquin R	Head	M	Cha	52.0	M		N	N	Guam	Guam	Guam	N	Farmer
	8	8	Manibusan, Dolores S	Wife	F	Fil	36.0	M		Y	N	Guam	Philippine Islands	Guam	N	None

Pago - Sinajana Barrio

(CHAMORRO ROOTS GENEALOGY PROJECT ™ TRANSCRIPTION)

(COMPILED/TRANSCRIBED BY BERNARD T. PUNZALAN / HTTP://WWW.CHAMORROROOTS.COM)

89b

FOURTEENTH CENSUS OF THE UNITED STATES: 1920-POPULATION

ISLAND OF GUAM

DISTRICT 1
NAME OF PLACE Pago - Sinajana

[Proper name and, also, name of class, as city, town, village, barrio, etc]

ENUMERATED BY ME ON THE 24th DAY OF April, 1920

Arthur W. Jackson ENUMERATOR

Street, avenue, road, etc.	Number of dwelling house is order of visitation	Number of family in order of visitation	NAME of each person whose place of abode on January 1, 1920, was in the family. Enter surname, firs, then given name and middle initial. If any. Include every person living on January 1, 1920. Omit children born since January 1, 1920.	RELATION Relationship of this Person to the head of the family.	Sex	Color or race	Age at last birthday	Single, married, widowed or divorced	Attended school any time since Sept. 1, 1919	Whether able to read.	Whether able to write.	Place of birth of this person.	Place of birth of father of this person.	Place of birth of mother of this person.	Whether able to speak English.	OCCUPATION Trade, profession, or particular kind of work done, as salesman, laborer, clerk, cook, merchant, washerwoman, etc.
	2	3	4	5	6	7	8	9	10	11	12	13	14	15	16	17
26	8	8	Ibasco, Maria S	Step daughter	F	Cha	15.0	S	N	Y	Y	Guam	Guam	Guam	Y	None
27	8	8	Ibasco, Mercedes S	Step daughter	F	Cha	2.0	S				Guam	Guam	Guam		None
28	8	8	Quichocho, Ignacio	Nephew	M	Cha	14.0	S	N	Y	Y	Guam	Unknown	Guam	N	None
29	8	8	Manibusan, Rosario S	Daughter	F	Cha	1.0	S				Guam	Guam	Guam		None
30	9	9	Cepeda, Jose T	Head	M	Cha	22.0	S		Y	N	Guam	Unknown	Guam	N	Laborer
31			Here ends the enumeration of Pago - Sinajana Barrio.													
32																
33																
34																
35																
36																
37																
38																
39																
40																
41																
42																
43																
44																
45																
46																
47																
48																
49																
50																

Pago - Sinajana Barrio

182

District 2

(CHAMORRO ROOTS GENEALOGY PROJECT ™ TRANSCRIPTION)
(COMPILED/TRANSCRIBED BY BERNARD T. PUNZALAN / HTTP://WWW.CHAMORROROOTS.COM)

FOURTEENTH CENSUS OF THE UNITED STATES: 1920-POPULATION
ISLAND OF GUAM

SHEET NO. 38A

DISTRICT 2
NAME OF PLACE **Anigua - Agana City**
[Proper name and, also, name of class, as city, town, village, barrio, etc]

ENUMERATED BY ME ON THE 10th DAY OF April, 1920
Vicente Tydingco ENUMERATOR

	PLACE OF ABODE			NAME	RELATION	PERSONAL DESCRIPTION				EDUCATION			NATIVITY				OCCUPATION
	Street, avenue, road, etc.	Number of dwelling house is order of visitation	Number of family in order of visitation	of each person whose place of abode on January 1, 1920, was in the family. Enter surname, firs, then given name and middle initial. If any. Include every person living on January 1, 1920. Omit children born since January 1, 1920.	Relationship of this Person to the head of the family.	Sex	Color or race	Age at last birthday	Single, married, widowed or divorced	Attended school any time since Sept. 1, 1919	Whether able to read.	Whether able to write.	Place of birth of each person and parents of each person enumerated. If born in the United States, give the state or territory. If of foreign birth, give country of birth. Place of birth of this person.	Place of birth of father of this person.	Place of birth of mother of this person.	Whether able to speak English.	Trade, profession, or particular kind of work done, as salesman, laborer, clerk, cook, merchant, washerwoman, etc.
	1	2	3	4	5	6	7	8	9	10	11	12	13	14	15	16	17
1		1	1	Leon Guerrero, Francisco B	Head	M	Cha	46.0	M		Y	Y	Guam	Guam	Guam	N	Silversmith
2		1	1	Leon Guerrero, Mariana P	Wife	F	Cha	46.0	M		Y	Y	Guam	Portugal	Guam	N	None
3		1	1	Leon Guerrero, Maria P	Daughter	F	Cha	19.0	S	Y	Y	Y	Guam	Guam	Guam	Y	School teacher
4		1	1	Leon Guerrero, Remedios P	Daughter	F	Cha	17.0	S	Y	Y	Y	Guam	Guam	Guam	Y	School teacher
5		1	1	Leon Guerrero, Concepcion P	Daughter	F	Cha	16.0	S	Y	Y	Y	Guam	Guam	Guam	Y	School teacher
6		1	1	Leon Guerrero, Segundo P	Son	M	Cha	14.0	S	Y	Y	Y	Guam	Guam	Guam	Y	Messenger
7		1	1	Leon Guerrero, Eliza P	Daughter	F	Cha	12.0	S	Y	Y	Y	Guam	Guam	Guam	Y	None
8		1	1	Leon Guerrero, Tomasa P	Daughter	F	Cha	10.0	S	Y	Y	Y	Guam	Guam	Guam	Y	None
9		1	1	Leon Guerrero, Lagrimas P	Daughter	F	Cha	9.0	S	Y			Guam	Guam	Guam		None
10		1	1	Leon Guerrero, Francisco P	Son	M	Cha	4.0	S				Guam	Guam	Guam		None
11		1	1	Leon Guerrero, Tomasa C	Mother	F	Cha	74.0	Wd		Y	Y	Guam	Guam	Guam	N	None
12		1	1	Leon Guerrero, Antonio C	Uncle	M	Cha	65.0	D		Y	Y	Guam	Guam	Guam	N	None
13	Legaspi Street	1	1	Cruz, Jose C	Nephew	M	Cha	20.0	S	N	Y	Y	Guam	Unknown	Guam	Y	Silversmith
14		2	2	Uncanco, Jose G	Head	M	Cha	33.0	M		Y	Y	Guam	Guam	Guam	N	Farmer
15		2	2	Uncanco, Isabel S	Wife	F	Cha	33.0	M		Y	Y	Guam	Guam	Guam	N	None
16		2	2	Uncanco, Gregorio S	Son	M	Cha	2.0	S				Guam	Guam	Guam		None
17		2	2	Uncanco, Pricila S	Daughter	F	Cha	1.0	S				Guam	Guam	Guam		None
18		2	2	Uncanco, Vicente G	Brother	M	Cha	14.0	S	N	Y	Y	Guam	Guam	Guam	N	Home farm laborer
19		2	2	Mendiola, Maria	Niece	F	Cha	24.0	S		Y	Y	Guam	Guam	Guam	Y	None
20		2	2	Garrido, Jesus S	Brother-in-law	M	Cha	19.0	S	N			Guam	Guam	Guam	Y	Carpenter
21		3	3	Blas, Manuel A	Head	M	Cha	51.0	M		Y	Y	Guam	Guam	Guam	N	Farmer
22		3	3	Blas, Nicolasa S	Wife	F	Cha	54.0	M		Y	Y	Guam	Unknown	Guam	N	None
23		3	3	Blas, Juan S	Son	M	Cha	25.0	S		Y	Y	Guam	Guam	Guam	Y	Farmer
24		3	3	Blas, Rosa S	Daughter	F	Cha	18.0	S	N	Y	Y	Guam	Guam	Guam	Y	None
25		3	3	Santos, Maria S	Sister-in-law	F	Cha	40.0	S		N	N	Guam	Guam	Guam	N	None

(CHAMORRO ROOTS GENEALOGY PROJECT ™ TRANSCRIPTION)
(COMPILED/TRANSCRIBED BY BERNARD T. PUNZALAN / HTTP://WWW.CHAMORROROOTS.COM)

FOURTEENTH CENSUS OF THE UNITED STATES: 1920—POPULATION

ISLAND OF GUAM

ENUMERATED BY ME ON THE 10th DAY OF April, 1920

Vicente Tydingco ENUMERATOR

DISTRICT 2
NAME OF PLACE Anigua – Agana City
[Proper name and, also, name of class, as city, town, village, barrio, etc]

	Street	Dwelling No.	Family No.	NAME	RELATION	Sex	Color or race	Age	Marital	Attended school	Able to read	Able to write	Birthplace	Father birthplace	Mother birthplace	Speak English	OCCUPATION
	1	2	3	4	5	6	7	8	9	10	11	12	13	14	15	16	17
26		3	3	Santos, Jose S	Nephew	M	Cha	6.0	S	N			Guam	Unknown	Guam		None
27		3	3	Santos, Rosa S	Niece	F	Cha	4.0	S				Guam	Guam	Guam		None
28		4	4	Blas, Ramon T	Head	M	Cha	56.0	M		Y	Y	Guam	Guam	Guam	N	Farmer
29		4	4	Blas, Rosa B	Wife	F	Cha	57.0	M		N	N	Guam	Guam	Guam	N	None
30		4	4	Blas, Jesus B	Son	M	Cha	17.0	S	N	Y	Y	Guam	Guam	Guam	Y	Farm laborer
31		4	4	Blas, Trinidad B	Daughter	F	Cha	29.0	D		Y	Y	Guam	Guam	Guam	Y	None
32		4	4	Blas, Ramon	Grandson	M	Cha	8.0	S	Y	Y	Y	Guam	Unknown	Guam		None
33		4	4	Blas, Rosa	Grand daughter	F	Cha	6.0	S	N			Guam	Unknown	Guam		None
34	Legaspi Street	4	4	Blas, Carlos	Grandson	M	Cha	4.0	S				Guam	Unknown	Guam		None
35		4	5	Blas, Jose B	Head	M	Cha	27.0	M		Y	Y	Guam	Guam	Guam	Y	Laborer
36		4	5	Blas, Nicolasa B	Wife	F	Cha	24.0	M		Y	Y	Guam	Guam	Guam	N	None
37		4	5	Blas, Brigida B	Daughter	F	Cha	4.0	S				Guam	Guam	Guam		None
38		4	5	Blas, Maria B	Daughter	F	Cha	2.0	S				Guam	Guam	Guam		None
39		4	5	Blas, Juan A	Uncle	M	Cha	75.0	S		Y	Y	Guam	Guam	Guam	N	None
40		4	5	Blas, Francisco A	Uncle	M	Cha	70.0	Wd		Y	Y	Guam	Guam	Guam	N	Farm laborer home farm
41		5	6	Perez, Maria B	Head	F	Cha	24.0	S		Y	Y	Guam	Guam	Guam	Y	Laundress
42		5	6	Perez, Vicente B	Brother	M	Cha	13.0	S	N	Y	Y	Guam	Guam	Guam	Y	None
43		6	7	Salas, Juan S	Head	M	Cha	60.0	M		Y	Y	Guam	Unknown	Guam	N	Farmer
44		6	7	Salas, Carmen T	Wife	F	Cha	58.0	M		Y	Y	Guam	Guam	Guam	N	None
45		6	7	Quituqua, Magdalena P	Niece	F	Cha	15.0	S	N	Y	Y	Guam	Guam	Guam	Y	None
46		6	7	Pangelinan, Pedro P	Nephew	M	Cha	3.0	S				Guam	Unknown	Guam		None
47		7	8	Flores, Leon	Head	M	Fil	45.0	M		Y	Y	Luzon	Luzon	Luzon	Y	Civil Registrar
48		7	8	Flores, Ana C	Wife	F	Cha	23.0	S		Y	Y	Guam	Guam	Guam	Y	None
49		7	8	Flores, Leon D jr	Son	M	Fil	12.0	S	Y	Y	Y	Guam	Luzon	Luzon	Y	None
50		7	8	Flores, Sergio D	Son	M	Fil	8.0	S	Y	Y	Y	Guam	Luzon	Luzon	Y	None

(CHAMORRO ROOTS GENEALOGY PROJECT ™ TRANSCRIPTION)
(COMPILED/TRANSCRIBED BY BERNARD T. PUNZALAN / HTTP://WWW.CHAMORROROOTS.COM)
FOURTEENTH CENSUS OF THE UNITED STATES: 1920-POPULATION
ISLAND OF GUAM

DISTRICT 2
NAME OF PLACE Anigua – Agana City
[Proper name and, also, name of class, as city, town, village, barrio, etc]

ENUMERATED BY ME ON THE 10th DAY OF April, 1920

Vicente Tydingco ENUMERATOR

Street, avenue, road, etc.	Number of dwelling house is order of visitation	Number of family in order of visitation	NAME	RELATION	Sex	Color or race	Age at last birthday	Single, married, widowed or divorced	Attended school any time since Sept. 1, 1919	Whether able to read.	Whether able to write.	Place of birth of this person.	Place of birth of father of this person.	Place of birth of mother of this person.	Whether able to speak English.	OCCUPATION
	2	3	4	5	6	7	8	9	10	11	12	13	14	15	16	17
	7	9	Flores, Pedro C	Head	M	Fil	27.0	M		Y	Y	Luzon	Luzon	Luzon	Y	Architect
	7	9	Flores, Rosima S	Wife	F	Fil	24.0	M		Y	Y	Luzon	Luzon	Luzon	Y	None
	7	9	Flores, Magdalena S	Daughter	F	Fil	2.0	S				Luzon	Luzon	Luzon		None
	7	9	Salas, Joaquina T	Servant	F	Cha	36.0	Wd		Y	Y	Guam	Guam	Guam	N	Servant
	8	10	Mesa, Jose M	Head	M	Cha	36.0	M		Y	Y	Guam	Unkwown	Guam	Y	Farmer
	8	10	Mesa, Carmen M	Wife	F	Cha	23.0	M		Y	Y	Guam	Guam	Guam	N	None
	8	10	Mesa, Ana M	Daughter	F	Cha	1.0	S				Guam	Guam	Guam		None
	9	11	Cruz, Juan I	Head	M	Cha	48.0	M		Y	Y	Guam	Guam	Guam	N	Farmer
	9	11	Cruz, Maria M	Wife	F	Cha	49.0	M		N	N	Guam	Guam	Guam	N	None
	9	11	Cruz, Ignacio M	Son	M	Cha	19.0	S	N	Y	Y	Guam	Guam	Guam	Y	Laborer
Legaspi Street	9	11	Cruz, Josefa M	Daughter	F	Cha	16.0	S	N	Y	Y	Guam	Guam	Guam	Y	None
	9	11	Cruz, Paterno M	Son	M	Cha	12.0	S	Y	Y	Y	Guam	Guam	Guam	Y	None
	9	11	Cruz, Vicenta M	Niece	F	Cha	30.0	S		N	N	Guam	Guam	Guam	N	None
	9	11	Cruz, Jesus M	Nephew	M	Cha	9.0	S	Y			Guam	Guam	Guam		None
	10	12	Herrero, Vicente R	Head	M	Cha	63.0	M		Y	Y	Guam	Guam	Guam	Y	Retail merchant
	10	12	Herrero, Rosa SN	Wife	F	Cha	22.0	M		Y	Y	Guam	Guam	Guam	Y	None
	10	12	Herrero, Edward P	Son	M	Cha	17.0	S	N	Y	Y	Guam	Guam	Guam	Y	office boy
	10	12	Herrero, Fernando P	Son	M	Cha	14.0	S	Y	Y	Y	Guam	Guam	Guam	Y	None
	11	13	Duenas, Juan T	Head	M	Cha	41.0	M		Y	Y	Guam	Guam	Guam	N	Farmer
	11	13	Duenas, Ignacia LG	Wife	F	Cha	42.0	M		N	N	Guam	Guam	Guam	N	None
	11	13	Duenas, Pedro LG	Son	M	Cha	20.0	S	N	Y	Y	Guam	Guam	Guam	N	None
	11	13	Duenas, Maria LG	Daughter	F	Cha	17.0	S	N	N	N	Guam	Guam	Guam	Y	None
	11	13	Duenas, Rosa LG	Daughter	F	Cha	15.0	S	N	Y	Y	Guam	Guam	Guam	Y	None
	11	13	Duenas, Teresa LG	Daughter	F	Cha	14.0	S	Y	Y	Y	Guam	Guam	Guam	Y	None
	11	13	Duenas, Jose LG	Son	M	Cha	12.0	S	Y	Y	Y	Guam	Guam	Guam	Y	None

(CHAMORRO ROOTS GENEALOGY PROJECT ™ TRANSCRIPTION)
(COMPILED/TRANSCRIBED BY BERNARD T. PUNZALAN / HTTP://WWW.CHAMORROROOTS.COM)
FOURTEENTH CENSUS OF THE UNITED STATES: 1920-POPULATION
ISLAND OF GUAM

DISTRICT 2
NAME OF PLACE Anigua – Agana City
[Proper name and, also, name of class, name of class, as city, town, village, barrio, etc]

ENUMERATED BY ME ON THE 12th DAY OF April, 1920

Vicente Tydingco ENUMERATOR

	PLACE OF ABODE		NAME	RELATION	PERSONAL DESCRIPTION					EDUCATION			NATIVITY				OCCUPATION
Street, avenue, road, etc.	Number of dwelling house in order of visitation	Number of family in order of visitation	of each person whose place of abode on January 1, 1920, was in the family.	Relationship of this Person to the head of the family.	Sex	Color or race	Age at last birthday	Single, married, widowed or divorced	Attended school any time since Sept. 1, 1919	Whether able to read.	Whether able to write.	Place of birth of this person.	Place of birth of father of this person.	Place of birth of mother of this person.	Whether able to speak English.	Trade, profession, or particular kind of work done, as salesman, laborer, clerk, cook, merchant, washerwoman, etc.
1	2	3	4	5	6	7	8	9	10	11	12	13	14	15	16	17
	11	13	Duenas, Isabel LG	Daughter	F	Cha	9.0	S	Y			Guam	Guam	Guam		None
	11	13	Duenas, Guadalupe LG	Daughter	F	Cha	7.0	S	Y			Guam	Guam	Guam		None
	11	13	Duenas, Catalina LG	Daughter	F	Cha	5.0	S	N			Guam	Guam	Guam		None
	11	13	Duenas, Dolores LG	Daughter	F	Cha	1.0	S				Guam	Guam	Guam		None
	12	14	Leon Guerrero, Dolores I	Head	F	Cha	39.0	Wd		Y	Y	Guam	Guam	Guam	N	None
	12	14	Leon Guerrero, Jesus I	Son	M	Cha	19.0	S	N	Y	Y	Guam	Guam	Guam	Y	Policeman
	12	14	Leon Guerrero, Maria I	Daughter	F	Cha	16.0	S	N	Y	Y	Guam	Guam	Guam	Y	None
	12	14	Leon Guerrero, Concepcion I	Daughter	F	Cha	13.0	S	Y	Y	Y	Guam	Guam	Guam	Y	None
	12	14	Leon Guerrero, Juan I	Son	M	Cha	11.0	S	Y	Y	Y	Guam	Guam	Guam	Y	None
	12	14	Leon Guerrero, Susana I	Daughter	F	Cha	6.0	S	N	N	Y	Guam	Guam	Guam		None
	12	14	Leon Guerrero, Jose I	Son	M	Cha	5.0	S	N			Guam	Guam	Guam		None
Legaspi Street	12	14	Leon Guerrero, Joaquin I	Son	M	Cha	3.0	S				Guam	Guam	Guam		None
	12	15	Topasna, Paterno	Head	M	Cha	24.0	M		Y	Y	Guam	Unknown	Guam	Y	Machinist
	12	15	Topasna, Ana LG	Wife	F	Cha	17.0	M	N	Y	Y	Guam	Guam	Guam	Y	None
	13	16	Reyes, Francisco L	Head	M	Cha	40.0	M		Y	Y	Guam	Guam	Guam	N	Farmer
	13	16	Reyes, Josefa M	Wife	F	Cha	52.0	M		Y	Y	Guam	Guam	Guam	N	None
	13	16	Reyes, Juana M	Daughter	F	Cha	15.0	S	N	Y	Y	Guam	Guam	Guam	Y	None
	13	16	Reyes, Jose M	Son	M	Cha	14.0	S	N	Y	Y	Guam	Guam	Guam	Y	Home farm
	13	16	Reyes, Manuel M	Son	M	Cha	12.0	S	N	Y	Y	Guam	Guam	·Guam	Y	Home farm
	13	16	Reyes, Ignacio M	Son	M	Cha	10.0	S	Y	Y	Y	Guam	Guam	Guam	Y	None
	13	16	Reyes, Nicolasa M	Daughter	F	Cha	8.0	S	Y			Guam	Guam	Guam	N	None
	14	17	Lizama, Vicente L	Head	M	Cha	45.0	M		Y	Y	Guam	Unknown	Guam	N	Farm laborer
	14	17	Lizama, Rita N	Wife	F	Cha	43.0	M		Y	Y	Guam	Guam	Guam	N	None
	15	18	Mendiola, Paula L	Head	F	Cha	67.0	Wd		N	N	Guam	Guam	Guam	N	None
	15	18	Mendiola, Vicente L	Son	M	Cha	27.0	S		N	N	Guam	Guam	Guam	N	Farm laborer

| 26 |
| 27 |
| 28 |
| 29 |
| 30 |
| 31 |
| 32 |
| 33 |
| 34 |
| 35 |
| 36 |
| 37 |
| 38 |
| 39 |
| 40 |
| 41 |
| 42 |
| 43 |
| 44 |
| 45 |
| 46 |
| 47 |
| 48 |
| 49 |
| 50 |

(CHAMORRO ROOTS GENEALOGY PROJECT ™ TRANSCRIPTION)
(COMPILED/TRANSCRIBED BY BERNARD T. PUNZALAN / HTTP://WWW.CHAMORROROOTS.COM)

FOURTEENTH CENSUS OF THE UNITED STATES: 1920-POPULATION

ISLAND OF GUAM

DISTRICT 2

NAME OF PLACE Anigua - Agana City

[Proper name and, also, name of class, as city, town, village, barrio, etc]

ENUMERATED BY ME ON THE 12th DAY OF April, 1920

Vicente Tydingco ENUMERATOR

	PLACE OF ABODE			NAME	RELATION	PERSONAL DESCRIPTION					EDUCATION			NATIVITY				OCCUPATION
Street, avenue, road, etc.	Number of dwelling house is order of visitation	Number of family in order of visitation		of each person whose place of abode on January 1, 1920, was in the family. Enter surname, firs, then given name and middle initial. If any. Include every person living on January 1, 1920. Omit children born since January 1, 1920.	Relationship of this person to the head of the family.	Sex	Color or race	Age at last birthday	Single, married, widowed or divorced	Attended school any time since Sept. 1, 1919	Whether able to read.	Whether able to write.	Place of birth of this person.	Place of birth of father of this person.	Place of birth of mother of this person.	Whether able to speak English.	Trade, profession, or particular kind of work done, as salesman, laborer, clerk, cook, merchant, washerwoman, etc.
1	2	3		4	5	6	7	8	9	10	11	12	13	14	15	16	17
	15	19	1	Pangelinan, Joaquin P	Head	M	Cha	42.0	M		Y	Y	Guam	Unknown	Guam	Y	Farmer
	15	19	2	Pangelinan, Ramona M	Wife	F	Cha	36.0	M		Y	Y	Guam	Guam	Guam	N	None
	15	19	3	Pangelinan, Joaquin M	Son	M	Cha	14.0	S	Y	Y	Y	Guam	Guam	Guam	Y	None
	15	19	4	Pangelinan, Rosalia M	Daughter	F	Cha	11.0	S	Y	Y	Y	Guam	Guam	Guam	Y	None
	15	19	5	Pangelinan, Tomas M	Son	M	Cha	8.0	S	Y			Guam	Guam	Guam		None
	15	19	6	Pangelinan, Maria M	Daughter	F	Cha	6.0	S	N			Guam	Guam	Guam		None
	15	19	7	Pangelinan, Matilde M	Daughter	F	Cha	2.0	S				Guam	Guam	Guam		None
	16	20	8	Mendiola, Joaquin L	Head	M	Cha	43.0	Wd		Y	Y	Guam	Guam	Guam	N	Barber
	16	20	9	Mendiola, Manuel S	Son	M	Cha	18.0	S	N	Y	Y	Guam	Guam	Guam	Y	Farmer
	16	20	10	Mendiola, Jose S	Son	M	Cha	17.0	S	N	Y	Y	Guam	Guam	Guam	Y	None
	16	20	11	Mendiola, Isabel S	Daughter	F	Cha	15.0	S	N	Y	Y	Guam	Guam	Guam	Y	None
	16	20	12	Mendiola, Carmen S	Daughter	F	Cha	12.0	S	Y	Y	Y	Guam	Guam	Guam	Y	None
	17	21	13	Mendiola, Jose L	Head	M	Cha	32.0	M		Y	Y	Guam	Guam	Guam	N	Farmer
	17	21	14	Mendiola, Rita Q	Wife	F	Cha	36.0	M		N	N	Guam	Guam	Guam	N	None
	17	21	15	Quidachay, Enrique	Stepson	M	Cha	11.0	S	Y	Y	Y	Guam	Unknown	Guam	N	None
	18	22	16	Taisague, Joaquin C	Head	M	Cha	43.0	M		Y	Y	Guam	Guam	Guam	N	Farmer
	18	22	17	Taisague, Maria S	Wife	F	Cha	48.0	M		Y	Y	Guam	Unknown	Guam	N	None
	18	22	18	Taisague, Vicente S	Son	M	Cha	14.0	S	N	N	N	Guam	Guam	Guam	Y	None
	18	22	19	Taisague, Juan S	Son	M	Cha	12.0	S	Y	Y	Y	Guam	Guam	Guam	Y	None
	18	22	20	Taisague, Antonia S	Daughter	F	Cha	9.0	S	Y			Guam	Guam	Guam		None
	18	22	21	Taisague, Isabel S	Daughter	F	Cha	7.0	S	Y			Guam	Guam	Guam		None
	18	22	22	Taisague, Rosa S	Daughter	F	Cha	4.0	S				Guam	Guam	Guam		None
	18	22	23	Cruz, Vicente S	Nephew	M	Cha	20.0	S				Guam	Guam	Guam	Y	Laborer
	19	23	24	Laguana, Joaquin P	Head	M	Cha	62.0	Wd		N	N	Guam	Guam	Guam	N	None
	19	23	25	Laguana, Rosa P	Daughter	F	Cha	37.0	S		Y	Y	Guam	Guam	Guam	Y	None

Legaspi Street

(CHAMORRO ROOTS GENEALOGY PROJECT ™ TRANSCRIPTION)
(COMPILED/TRANSCRIBED BY BERNARD T. PUNZALAN / HTTP://WWW.CHAMORROROOTS.COM)

FOURTEENTH CENSUS OF THE UNITED STATES: 1920—POPULATION
ISLAND OF GUAM

DISTRICT 2
NAME OF PLACE Anigua - Agana City
[Proper name and, also, name of class, as city, town, village, barrio, etc]

ENUMERATED BY ME ON THE 12th DAY OF April, 1920

Vicente Tydingco ENUMERATOR

	PLACE OF ABODE		NAME	RELATION	PERSONAL DESCRIPTION				EDUCATION			NATIVITY				OCCUPATION
Street, avenue, road, etc.	Number of dwelling house in order of visitation	Number of family in order of visitation	Name	Relationship of this person to the head of the family.	Sex	Color or race	Age at last birthday	Single, married, widowed or divorced	Attended any school since Sept. 1, 1919	Whether able to read.	Whether able to write.	Place of birth of this person.	Place of birth of father of this person.	Place of birth of mother of this person.	Whether able to speak English.	Trade, profession, or particular kind of work done, as salesman, laborer, clerk, cook, merchant, washerwoman, etc.
1	2	3	4	5	6	7	8	9	10	11	12	13	14	15	16	17
	19	23	Laguana, Ignacia P	Daughter	F	Cha	33.0	S		Y	Y	Guam	Guam	Guam	N	Laundress
	19	23	Laguana, Soledad P	Daughter	F	Cha	28.0	S		Y	Y	Guam	Guam	Guam	N	None
	19	23	Laguana, Natividad P	Daughter	F	Cha	27.0	S		Y	Y	Guam	Guam	Guam	N	Laundress
	19	23	Laguana, Felicidad P	Daughter	F	Cha	23.0	S		Y	Y	Guam	Guam	Guam	Y	Laundress
	19	23	Laguana, Jose P	Son	M	Cha	20.0	S	N	Y	Y	Guam	Guam	Guam	Y	Farmer
	20	24	Martinez, Vicente B	Head	M	Cha	36.0	M		Y	Y	Guam	Guam	Guam	Y	Collector of Customs
	20	24	Martinez, Rita C	Wife	F	Cha	37.0	M		Y	Y	Guam	Guam	Guam	N	None
	20	24	Martinez, Grace J	Daughter	F	Cha	6.0	S	N			Guam	Guam	Guam		None
	20	24	Martinez, Lucy R	Daughter	F	Cha	5.0	S	N			Guam	Guam	Guam		None
	20	24	Martinez, Glen D	Son	M	Cha	4.0	S				Guam	Guam	Guam		None
	20	24	Martinez, Mary R	Daughter	F	Cha	1.0	S					Guam	Guam		None
	20	24	Camacho, Maria C	Servant	F	Cha	22.0	S		Y	Y	Guam	Guam	Guam	Y	Servant
Legaspi Street	21	25	Calvo, Antonio B	Head	M	Cha	47.0	M		Y	Y	Guam	Luzon	Guam	Y	Retail merchant
	21	25	Calvo, Rufina T	Wife	F	Cha	39.0	M		Y	Y	Guam	Guam	Guam	N	None
	21	25	Calvo, Guadalupe M	Daughter	F	Cha	21.0	S		Y	Y	Guam	Guam	Guam	Y	None
	21	25	Calvo, Felix V	Son	M	Cha	18.0	S	N	Y	Y	Guam	Guam	Guam	Y	Messenger
	21	25	Calvo, Pilar M	Daughter	F	Cha	15.0	S	N	Y	Y	Guam	Guam	Guam	Y	None
	21	25	Millenchamp, Maria B	Niece	F	Cha	18.0	S	N	Y	Y	Guam	Guam	Guam	Y	None
	21	25	Millenchamp, Enrique T	Nephew	M	Cha	13.0	S		Y	Y	Guam	Guam	Guam	Y	None
	22	26	Cruz, Bruno F	Head	M	Cha	71.0	M		Y	Y	Guam	Guam	Guam	N	Farmer home farm
	22	26	Cruz, Maria P	Wife	F	Cha	71.0	M		N	N	Guam	Guam	Guam	N	None
	22	26	Cruz, Serafin P	Son	M	Cha	35.0	S		Y	Y	Guam	Guam	Guam	N	Laborer
	22	27	Fejeran, Vicente C	Head	M	Cha	37.0	M		Y	Y	Guam	Guam	Guam	N	Butcher
	22	27	Fejeran, Francisca C	Wife	F	Cha	31.0	M		Y	Y	Guam	Guam	Guam	N	None
	23	28	Sablan, Guillermo D	Head	M	Cha	48.0	M		Y	Y	Guam	Guam	Guam	Y	Farmer

Row numbers: 26, 27, 28, 29, 30, 31, 32, 33, 34, 35, 36, 37, 38, 39, 40, 41, 42, 43, 44, 45, 46, 47, 48, 49, 50

(CHAMORRO ROOTS GENEALOGY PROJECT ™ TRANSCRIPTION)
(COMPILED/TRANSCRIBED BY BERNARD T. PUNZALAN / HTTP://WWW.CHAMORROROOTS.COM)
FOURTEENTH CENSUS OF THE UNITED STATES: 1920-POPULATION
ISLAND OF GUAM

SHEET NO. 41A

DISTRICT 2
NAME OF PLACE Anigua - Agana City
[Proper name and, also, name of class, as city, town, village, barrio, etc]

ENUMERATED BY ME ON THE 13th DAY OF April, 1920

Vicente Tydingco ENUMERATOR

	PLACE OF ABODE			NAME	RELATION	PERSONAL DESCRIPTION					EDUCATION			NATIVITY				OCCUPATION
Street, avenue, road, etc.	Number of dwelling house in order of visitation	Number of family in order of visitation		of each person whose place of abode on January 1, 1920, was in the family. Enter surname, first, then given name and middle initial, if any. Include every person living on January 1, 1920. Omit children born since January 1, 1920.	Relationship of this Person to the head of the family.	Sex	Color or race	Age at last birthday	Single, married, widowed or divorced	Attended school any time since Sept. 1, 1919	Whether able to read.	Whether able to write.	Place of birth of this person.	Place of birth of father of this person.	Place of birth of mother of this person.	Whether able to speak English.	Trade, profession, or particular kind of work done, as salesman, laborer, clerk, cook, merchant, washerwoman, etc.
1	2	3	4		5	6	7	8	9	10	11	12	13	14	15	16	17
	23	28	Sablan, Ana C		Wife	F	Cha	35.0	M		Y	Y	Guam	Guam	Guam	N	None
	23	28	Sablan, Ana P		Daughter	F	Cha	25.0	S		N	N	Guam	Guam	Guam	N	None
	23	28	Sablan, Jose P		Son	M	Cha	22.0	S		Y	Y	Guam	Guam	Guam	N	Farmer
	23	28	Sablan, Maria C		Daughter	F	Cha	14.0	S	N	Y	Y	Guam	Guam	Guam	Y	None
	23	28	Sablan, Enrique C		Son	M	Cha	12.0	S	Y	Y	Y	Guam	Guam	Guam	Y	None
	23	28	Sablan, Antonio C		Son	M	Cha	10.0	S	Y	Y	Y	Guam	Guam	Guam	Y	None
	23	28	Sablan, Carmen C		Daughter	F	Cha	6.0	S	N	Y	Y	Guam	Guam	Guam		None
	23	28	Sablan, Candelaria C		Daughter	F	Cha	4.0	S		Y	Y	Guam	Guam	Guam		None
	23	28	Sablan, Emilia C		Daughter	F	Cha	1.0	S		Y	Y	Guam	Guam	Guam		None
	23	28	Sablan, Rosario C		Daughter	F	Cha	0.3	S				Guam	Guam	Guam		None
	24	29	Duenas, Juana T		Head	F	Cha	60.0	Wd		N	N	Guam	Guam	Guam	N	None
	24	29	Duenas, Antonia T		Daughter	F	Cha	46.0	S		N	N	Guam	Guam	Guam	N	None
	24	29	Duenas, Ignacio T		Son	M	Cha	20.0	S	N	Y	Y	Guam	Guam	Guam	Y	Farm laborer
	24	30	Duenas, Antonio T		Head	M	Cha	29.0	M		Y	Y	Guam	Guam	Guam	N	Farmer
	24	30	Duenas, Rosa F		Wife	F	Cha	25.0	M		Y	Y	Guam	Guam	Guam	N	None
	24	31	Cruz, Vicente M		Head	M	Cha	29.0	M		Y	Y	Guam	Unknown	Guam	Y	Laborer
	24	31	Cruz, Ramona D		Wife	F	Cha	33.0	M		Y	Y	Guam	Guam	Guam	N	None
	24	31	Cruz, Maria D		Daughter	F	Cha	1.0	S				Guam	Guam	Guam		None
	25	32	Haniu, Jose H		Head	M	Jp	39.0	M		Y	Y	Japan	Japan	Japan	Y	Retail merchant
	25	32	Haniu, Maria B		Wife	F	Cha	39.0	M		Y	Y	Guam	Guam	Guam	N	None
	25	32	Haniu, Josefina B		Daughter	F	Jp	17.0	S	N	Y	Y	Guam	Japan	Guam	Y	None
	25	32	Haniu, Pilar B		Daughter	F	Jp	15.0	S	N	Y	Y	Guam	Japan	Guam	Y	None
	25	32	Haniu, Jesus B		Son	M	Jp	14.0	S	N	Y	Y	Guam	Japan	Guam	Y	Messenger
	25	32	Haniu, Asuncion B		Daughter	F	Jp	13.0	S	Y	Y	Y	Guam	Japan	Guam	Y	None
	25	32	Haniu, Atanasio B		Son	M	Jp	11.0	S	Y	Y	Y	Guam	Japan	Guam	Y	None

Legaspi Street

(CHAMORRO ROOTS GENEALOGY PROJECT ™ TRANSCRIPTION)
(COMPILED/TRANSCRIBED BY BERNARD T. PUNZALAN / HTTP://WWW.CHAMORROROOTS.COM)

FOURTEENTH CENSUS OF THE UNITED STATES: 1920—POPULATION
ISLAND OF GUAM

DISTRICT 2
NAME OF PLACE **Anigua – Agana City**
[Proper name and, also, name of class, as city, town, village, barrio, etc]

ENUMERATED BY ME ON THE 13th DAY OF April, 1920

Vicente Tydingco ENUMERATOR

	Street, avenue, road, etc.	No. of dwelling house	No. of family	NAME	RELATION	Sex	Color or race	Age	Single, married, widowed or divorced	Attended school since Sept. 1, 1919	Read	Write	Place of birth of this person	Place of birth of father	Place of birth of mother	English	OCCUPATION
	1	2	3	4	5	6	7	8	9	10	11	12	13	14	15	16	17
26		25	32	Haniu, Jose B	Son	M	Jp	6.0	S	N			Guam	Japan	Guam		None
27		25	32	Haniu, Juan B	Son	M	Jp	4.0	S				Guam	Japan	Guam		None
28		25	32	Haniu, Serafina B	Daughter	F	Jp	1.0	S				Guam	Japan	Guam		None
29		25	32	Desa, Nieves	Mother in law	F	Cha	65.0	Wd				Guam	Guam	Guam	N	None
30		26	33	Cruz, Francisco LG	Head	M	Cha	43.0	M		Y	Y	Guam	Guam	Guam	N	Teacher
31		26	33	Cruz, Rosario LG	Wife	F	Cha	36.0	M		Y	Y	Guam	Guam	Guam	N	Teacher
32		27	34	Ozone, Fudesaburo	Head	M	Jp	29.0	S		Y	Y	Japan	Japan	Japan	Y	Retail merchant
33		28	35	Manibusan, Juan P	Head	M	Cha	56.0	M		Y	Y	Guam	Guam	Guam	Y	Farmer
34		28	35	Manibusan, Mary D	Wife	F	W	51.0	M		Y	Y	Ireland	Ireland	Ireland	Y	None
35	Legaspi Street	28	35	Manibusan, Joe	Son	M	Cha	21.0	S	N	Y	Y	England	Guam	Ireland	Y	None
36		28	35	Manibusan, Maria	Daughter	F	Cha	18.0	S	N	Y	Y	England	Guam	Ireland	Y	None
37		28	36	Manibusan, Felix M	Head	M	Cha	45.0	M		Y	Y	Guam	Unknown	Guam	N	Farmer
38		28	36	Manibusan, Dolores L	Wife	F	Cha	38.0	M	N	N	N	Guam	Guam	Guam	N	None
39		28	36	Manibusan, Ana L	Daughter	F	Cha	21.0	S	N	Y	Y	Guam	Guam	Guam	N	None
40		28	36	Manibusan, Joaquin L	Son	M	Cha	19.0	S	N	Y	Y	Guam	Guam	Guam	Y	Laborer
41		28	36	Manibusan, Maria L	Daughter	F	Cha	18.0	S	N	Y	Y	Guam	Guam	Guam	N	None
42		28	36	Manibusan, Maria L jr	Daughter	F	Cha	15.0	S	N	Y	Y	Guam	Guam	Guam	N	None
43		28	36	Manibusan, Rosario L	Daughter	F	Cha	6.0	S	N			Guam	Guam	Guam		None
44		28	36	Manibusan, Regina L	Daughter	F	Cha	5.0	S				Guam	Guam	Guam		None
45		28	36	Manibusan, Oscarl L	Son	M	Cha	3.0	S				Guam	Guam	Guam	N	None
46		28	36	Manibusan, Manuel M	Cousin	M	Cha	27.0	S				Guam	Guam	Guam	N	Farm laborer
47		29	37	Bayona, Antonio I	Head	M	Fil	60.0	M		Y	Y	Luzon	Luzon	Luzon	N	Farmer
48		29	37	Bayona, Rosa G	Wife	F	Cha	56.0	M		N	N	Guam	Guam	Guam	N	None
49		29	37	Bayona, Juan I	Son	M	Fil	22.0	S		Y	Y	Guam	Luzon	Luzon	Y	Farm laborer
50		29	37	Bayona, Maria I	Daughter	F	Fil	16.0	S	N	Y	Y	Guam	Luzon	Luzon	Y	None

(CHAMORRO ROOTS GENEALOGY PROJECT ™ TRANSCRIPTION)
(COMPILED/TRANSCRIBED BY BERNARD T. PUNZALAN / HTTP://WWW.CHAMORROROOTS.COM)

FOURTEENTH CENSUS OF THE UNITED STATES: 1920–POPULATION

ISLAND OF GUAM

ENUMERATED BY ME ON THE 13th DAY OF April, 1920

Vicente Tydingco ENUMERATOR

DISTRICT 2

NAME OF PLACE Anigua – Agana City

[Proper name and, also, name of class, as city, town, village, barrio, etc]

Street	Dwelling no.	Family no.	NAME	RELATION	Sex	Color or race	Age	Single, married, widowed or divorced	Attended school since Sept. 1, 1919	Able to read	Able to write	Birthplace of person	Birthplace of father	Birthplace of mother	Able to speak English	OCCUPATION
	29	37	Bayona, Catalina I	Daughter	F	Fil	15.0	S	N	Y	Y	Guam	Luzon	Guam	N	None
	29	37	Bayona, Jose G	Son	M	Fil	8.0	S	Y			Guam	Luzon	Guam	N	None
	30	38	Lizama, Jose B	Head	M	Cha	58.0	Wd		N	N	Guam	Guam	Guam	N	Farmer
	31	39	Quitugua, Josefa C	Head	F	Cha	44.0	Wd		N	N	Guam	Guam	Guam	N	None
	31	39	Quitugua, Jose C	Son	M	Cha	13.0	S	N	Y	Y	Guam	Guam	Guam	Y	None
	31	39	Quitugua, Vicenta C	Daughter	F	Cha	9.0	S	Y			Guam	Guam	Guam		None
	31	39	Quitugua, Vicente C	Son	M	Cha	6.0	S	N			Guam	Guam	Guam		None
	32	40	Quitugua, Soledad G	Head	F	Cha	45.0	Wd		N	N	Guam	Guam	Guam	N	Laundress
	32	40	Quitugua, Juan S	Son	M	Cha	22.0	S		Y	Y	Guam	Guam	Guam	Y	Farmer
	32	40	Quitugua, Dolores G	Daughter	F	Cha	18.0	S	N	Y	Y	Guam	Guam	Guam	N	Servant
	32	40	Quitugua, Joaquin G	Son	M	Cha	16.0	S	N	Y	Y	Guam	Guam	Guam	N	Farm laborer home farm
	33	41	Guzman, Joaquin C	Head	M	Cha	35.0	M		Y	Y	Guam	Guam	Guam	N	Farmer
	33	41	Guzman, Ana M	Wife	F	Cha	28.0	M		Y	Y	Guam	Guam	Guam		None
	33	41	Guzman, Gonzalo M	Son	M	Cha	6.0	S	N			Guam	Guam	Guam		None
	33	41	Guzman, Jose M	Son	M	Cha	5.0	S	N			Guam	Guam	Guam		None
	33	41	Guzman, Julio S	Son	M	Cha	3.0	S				Guam	Guam	Guam		None
	33	41	Guzman, Fidela M	Daughter	F	Cha	0.3	S				Guam	Guam	Guam		None
	33	42	Crisostomo, Pedro	Head	M	Cha	60.0	M		N	N	Guam	Guam	Guam	N	Farmer
	33	42	Crisostomo, Dolores C	Wife	F	Cha	64.0	M		N	N	Guam	Guam	Guam	N	None
Legaspi Street	34	43	Mendiola, Antonio Q	Head	M	Cha	23.0	S		Y	Y	Guam	Guam	Guam	Y	Seaman USN
	34	43	Mendiola, Concepcion Q	Sister	F	Cha	24.0	S	N	Y	Y	Guam	Guam	Guam	Y	None
	34	43	Mendiola, Ana Q	Sister	F	Cha	18.0	S	N	Y	Y	Guam	Guam	Guam	Y	None
	34	43	Mendiola, Jesus Q	Brother	M	Cha	17.0	S	Y	Y	Y	Guam	Guam	Guam	Y	Farmer
	34	43	Mendiola, Purification Q	Sister	F	Cha	10.0	S	Y	Y	Y	Guam	Guam	Guam	N	None
	34	43	Quitugua, Juana S	Aunt	F	Cha	40.0	S		N	N	Guam	Guam	Guam	N	None

(CHAMORRO ROOTS GENEALOGY PROJECT ™ TRANSCRIPTION)
(COMPILED/TRANSCRIBED BY BERNARD T. PUNZALAN / HTTP://WWW.CHAMORROROOTS.COM)

FOURTEENTH CENSUS OF THE UNITED STATES: 1920-POPULATION

ISLAND OF GUAM

94b

DISTRICT 2
NAME OF PLACE Anigua - Agana City

[Proper name and, also, name of class, as city, town, village, barrio, etc]

ENUMERATED BY ME ON THE 13th DAY OF April, 1920

Vicente Tydingco ENUMERATOR

	PLACE OF ABODE		NAME	RELATION	PERSONAL DESCRIPTION				EDUCATION			NATIVITY				OCCUPATION
Street, avenue, road, etc.	Number of dwelling house is order of visitation	Number of family in order of visitation	of each person whose place of abode on January 1, 1920, was in the family. Enter surname, firs, then given name and middle initial. If any. Include every person living on January 1, 1920. Omit children born since January 1, 1920.	Relationship of this Person to the head of the family.	Sex	Color or race	Age at last birthday	Single, married, widowed or divorced	Attended school any time since Sept. 1, 1919	Whether able to read.	Whether able to write.	Place of birth of this person.	Place of birth of father of this person.	Place of birth of mother of this person.	Whether able to speak English.	Trade, profession, or particular kind of work done, as salesman, laborer, clerk, cook, merchant, washerwoman, etc.
1	2	3	4	5	6	7	8	9	10	11	12	13	14	15	16	17
	34	43	Quitugua, Fermina R	Aunt	F	Cha	68.0	Wd		N	N	Guam	Guam	Guam	N	None
	35	44	Toves, Juan C	Head	M	Cha	29.0	M		Y	Y	Guam	Guam	Guam	N	Farmer
	35	44	Toves, Maria M	Wife	F	Cha	28.0	M		Y	Y	Guam	Guam	Guam	N	None
	35	44	Toves, Ines M	Daughter	F	Cha	7.0	S	N			Guam	Guam	Guam		None
	35	44	Toves, Teodoro M	Son	M	Cha	5.0	S	N			Guam	Guam	Guam		None
	35	44	Toves, Rosario M	Daughter	F	Cha	4.0	S				Guam	Guam	Guam		None
	35	44	Toves, Julia M	Daughter	F	Cha	1.0	S				Guam	Guam	Guam		None
Legaspi Street	36	45	Sablan, Maria A	Head	F	Cha	41.0	Wd		Y	Y	Guam	Guam	Guam	N	Laundress
	36	45	Sablan, Agueda A	Daughter	F	Cha	18.0	S	N	Y	Y	Guam	Guam	Guam	Y	None
	36	45	Sablan, Honorato A	Son	M	Cha	17.0	S	N	Y	Y	Guam	Guam	Guam	Y	Carpenter
	36	45	Sablan, Angel A	Son	M	Cha	14.0	S	Y	Y	Y	Guam	Guam	Guam	Y	None
	36	45	Sablan, Iluminada A	Daughter	F	Cha	11.0	S	Y	Y	Y	Guam	Guam	Guam	Y	None
	36	45	Sablan, Marcial A	Son	M	Cha	9.0	S	Y	Y	Y	Guam	Guam	Guam	Y	None
	36	45	Sablan, Lourdes A	Daughter	F	Cha	7.0	S	Y			Guam	Guam	Guam		None
	36	45	Sablan, Emerenciana A	Daughter	F	Cha	4.0	S				Guam	Guam	Guam		None
	37	46	Akiyama, Jose S	Head	M	Jp	32.0	S		Y	Y	Japan	Japan	Japan	Y	Salesman
	38	47	Cabo, Antonio D	Head	M	Cha	51.0	M		Y	Y	Guam	Luzon	Guam	N	Carpenter
	38	47	Cabo, Nicolasa D	Wife	F	Cha	55.0	M		N	N	Guam	Guam	Guam	N	Laundress
	39	48	Reyes, Ana Q	Head	F	Cha	30.0	Wd		N	N	Guam	Guam	Guam	N	Laundress
	39	48	Reyes, Dolores Q	Daughter	F	Cha	18.0	S	N	Y	Y	Guam	Guam	Guam	Y	Laundress
	39	48	Reyes, Maria Q	Daughter	F	Cha	16.0	S	N	Y	Y	Guam	Guam	Guam	Y	None
	39	48	Reyes, Vicente Q	Son	M	Cha	10.0	S	Y	Y	Y	Guam	Guam	Guam	Y	None
	39	48	Reyes, Anunciacion Q	Daughter	F	Cha	9.0	S	Y	Y	Y	Guam	Guam	Guam	Y	None
	39	48	Reyes, Jose Q	Son	M	Cha	6.0	S	N			Guam	Guam	Guam		None
	39	48	Reyes, Jesus Q	Son	M	Cha	3.0	S				Guam	Guam	Guam		None

(CHAMORRO ROOTS GENEALOGY PROJECT ™ TRANSCRIPTION)
(COMPILED/TRANSCRIBED BY BERNARD T. PUNZALAN / HTTP://WWW.CHAMORROROOTS.COM)

SHEET NO. 43A

FOURTEENTH CENSUS OF THE UNITED STATES: 1920—POPULATION
ISLAND OF GUAM

DISTRICT 2
NAME OF PLACE Anigua - Agana City
[Proper name and, also, name of class, as city, town, village, barrio, etc]

ENUMERATED BY ME ON THE 14th DAY OF April, 1920

Vicente Tydingco ENUMERATOR

Street, avenue, road, etc.	Number of dwelling house in order of visitation	Number of family in order of visitation	NAME	RELATION	Sex	Color or race	Age at last birthday	Single, married, widowed or divorced	Attended school any time since sept. 1, 1919	Whether able to read	Whether able to write	Place of birth of this person	Place of birth of father of this person	Place of birth of mother of this person	Whether able to speak English	OCCUPATION
1	2	3	4	5	6	7	8	9	10	11	12	13	14	15	16	17
	39	48	Reyes, Juan Q	Son	M	Cha	2.0	S				Guam	Guam	Guam		None
	40	49	Terlaje, Francisco T	Head	M	Cha	58.0	M		Y	Y	Guam	Guam	Guam	N	Farmer
	40	49	Terlaje, Saturnina S	Wife	F	Cha	52.0	M		Y	Y	Guam	Guam	Guam	N	None
	40	49	Terlaje, Teresa S	Daughter	F	Cha	12.0	S	Y	Y	Y	Guam	Guam	Guam	Y	None
	40	49	Salas, Jose S	Brother in law	M	Cha	48.0	S		Y	Y	Guam	Guam	Guam	N	Farm laborer
	41	50	Terlaje, Maria G	Head	F	Cha	43.0	Wd		N	N	Guam	Guam	Guam	N	Farmer home farm
	41	50	Terlaje, Rosa G	Daughter	F	Cha	24.0	S		Y	Y	Guam	Guam	Guam	Y	None
	41	50	Terlaje, Antonia G	Daughter	F	Cha	23.0	S		Y	Y	Guam	Guam	Guam	Y	Laundress
Legaspi Street	42	51	Lucero, Maria C	Head	F	Cha	30.0	M		N	N	Guam	Guam	Guam	N	Laundress
	42	51	Lucero, Fidela C	Daughter	F	Cha	1.0	S				Guam	Guam	Guam		None
	43	52	Leon Guerrero, Pedro P	Head	M	Cha	44.0	M		Y	Y	Guam	Guam	Guam	N	Farmer
	43	52	Leon Guerrero, Juana C	Wife	F	Cha	48.0	M		Y	Y	Guam	Guam	Guam	N	None
	43	52	Leon Guerrero, Agueda C	Daughter	F	Cha	24.0	S		Y	Y	Guam	Guam	Guam	Y	Laundress
	43	52	Leon Guerrero, Ana C	Daughter	F	Cha	21.0	S	N	Y	Y	Guam	Guam	Guam	Y	Laundress
	43	52	Leon Guerrero, Francisco C	Son	M	Cha	19.0	S	N	Y	Y	Guam	Guam	Guam	Y	Farm laborer
	43	52	Leon Guerrero, Rosalia C	Daughter	F	Cha	18.0	S	N	Y	Y	Guam	Guam	Guam	Y	None
	43	52	Leon Guerrero, Jose C	Son	M	Cha	17.0	S	N	Y	Y	Guam	Guam	Guam	Y	Laborer
	43	52	Leon Guerrero, Rita C	Daughter	F	Cha	15.0	S	N	Y	Y	Guam	Guam	Guam	Y	None
	43	52	Leon Guerrero, Rosario C	Daughter	F	Cha	9.0	S	Y	Y	Y	Guam	Guam	Guam	Y	None
	43	52	Leon Guerrero, Pedro C	Son	M	Cha	8.0	S	Y	Y	Y	Guam	Guam	Guam	Y	None
	43	52	Leon Guerrero, Roberto C	Son	M	Cha	6.0	S	N			Guam	Guam	Guam	Y	None
	44	53	Toves, Rita G	Head	F	Cha	42.0	S		N	N	Guam	Unknown	Unknown	N	Laundress
	44	53	Toves, Vicente G	Son	M	Cha	15.0	S	N	Y	Y	Guam	Unknown	Unknown	Y	None
	44	53	Toves, Agueda G	Daughter	F	Cha	8.0	S	Y			Guam	Unknown	Unknown	Y	None
	44	53	Toves, Jose G	Son	M	Cha	4.0	S				Guam	Unknown	Unknown	Y	None

(CHAMORRO ROOTS GENEALOGY PROJECT ™ TRANSCRIPTION)

(COMPILED/TRANSCRIBED BY BERNARD T. PUNZALAN / HTTP://WWW.CHAMORROROOTS.COM)

FOURTEENTH CENSUS OF THE UNITED STATES: 1920—POPULATION

ISLAND OF GUAM

95b

DISTRICT 2

NAME OF PLACE Anigua – Agana City

ENUMERATED BY ME ON THE 14th DAY OF April, 1920

Vicente Tydingco ENUMERATOR

	PLACE OF ABODE		NAME	RELATION	PERSONAL DESCRIPTION				EDUCATION			NATIVITY				OCCUPATION
Street, avenue, road, etc.	Number of dwelling house in order of visitation	Number of family in order of visitation	of each person whose place of abode on January 1, 1920, was in the family.	Relationship of this person to the head of the family.	Sex	Color or race	Age at last birthday	Single, married, widowed or divorced	Attended school any time since Sept. 1, 1919	Whether able to read.	Whether able to write.	Place of birth of this person.	Place of birth of father of this person.	Place of birth of mother of this person.	Whether able to speak English.	Trade, profession, or particular kind of work done, as salesman, laborer, clerk, cook, merchant, washerwoman, etc.
1	2	3	4	5	6	7	8	9	10	11	12	13	14	15	16	17
	45	54	Sablan, Jose L	Head	M	Cha	38.0	M		N	N	Guam	Guam	Guam	N	Laborer
	45	54	Sablan, Maria T	Wife	F	Cha	22.0	M		Y	Y	Guam	Guam	Guam	N	None
	45	54	Sablan, Rosalia T	Daughter	F	Cha	6.0	S	N			Guam	Guam	Guam		None
	45	54	Sablan, Soledad T	Daughter	F	Cha	5.0	S	N			Guam	Guam	Guam		None
	45	54	Sablan, Carlos T	Son	M	Cha	1.0	S				Guam	Guam	Guam		None
	46	55	Aguon, Vicente T	Head	M	Cha	40.0	M		Y	Y	Guam	Guam	Guam	Y	Laborer
	46	55	Aguon, Rosa M	Wife	F	Cha	45.0	M		N	N	Guam	Guam	Guam	N	None
	46	55	Aguon, Vicenta M	Daughter	F	Cha	12.0	S	Y	Y	Y	Guam	Guam	Guam	Y	None
Legaspi Street	46	55	Aguon, Concepcion M	Daughter	F	Cha	5.0	S	Y			Guam	Guam	Guam		None
	46	55	Aguon, Joaquin M	Son	M	Cha	4.0	S				Guam	Guam	Guam		None
	46	55	Aguon, Jose M	Son	M	Cha	1.0	S				Guam	Guam	Guam		None
	46	55	Manglona, Vicente S	Brother-in-law	M	Cha	30.0	S		Y	Y	Guam	Guam	Guam		None
	47	56	Pangelinan, Jose C	Head	M	Cha	44.0	M		N	N	Guam	Guam	Guam	N	Farmer
	47	56	Pangelinan, Ignacia M	Wife	F	Cha	43.0	M		N	N	Guam	Guam	Guam	N	None
	47	56	Pangelinan, Carmen M	Daughter	F	Cha	14.0	S	N	Y	Y	Guam	Guam	Guam	N	None
	47	56	Pangelinan, Antonio M	Son	M	Cha	12.0	S	Y	Y	Y	Guam	Guam	Guam	Y	None
	47	56	Pangelinan, Jose M	Son	M	Cha	8.0	S	Y			Guam	Guam	Guam		None
	47	56	Pangelinan, Juan M	Son	M	Cha	6.0	S	N			Guam	Guam	Guam		None
	47	56	Pangelinan, Margarita M	Daughter	F	Cha	4.0	S				Guam	Guam	Guam		None
	47	56	Pangelinan, Rosa M	Daughter	F	Cha	3.0	S				Guam	Guam	Guam		None
	47	56	Pangelinan, Vicente M	Son	M	Cha	1.0	S				Guam	Guam	Guam		None
	47	56	Mafnas, Manuel R	Boarder	M	Cha	57.0	S		N	N	Guam	Guam	Guam	N	Farm laborer
	48	57	Nededog, Concepcion A	Head	F	Cha	24.0	S		Y	Y	Guam	Guam	Guam	Y	Laundress
	48	57	Nededog, Beatris A	Daughter	F	Cha	6.0	S	N			Guam	Unknown	Guam		None
	49	58	Guerrero, Vicente S	Head	M	Cha	40.0	M		Y	Y	Guam	Guam	Guam	N	Farmer

(CHAMORRO ROOTS GENEALOGY PROJECT ™ TRANSCRIPTION)
(COMPILED/TRANSCRIBED BY BERNARD T. PUNZALAN / HTTP://WWW.CHAMORROROOTS.COM)

FOURTEENTH CENSUS OF THE UNITED STATES: 1920-POPULATION

ISLAND OF GUAM

ENUMERATED BY ME ON THE 14th DAY OF April, 1920

Vicente Tydingco ENUMERATOR

DISTRICT 2
NAME OF PLACE **Anigua - Agana City**
[Proper name and, also, name of class, as city, town, village, barrio, etc]

	Street	Dwelling No.	Family No.	NAME	RELATION	Sex	Color or race	Age	Single, married, widowed or divorced	Attended school since Sept. 1, 1919	Able to read	Able to write	Birthplace of person	Birthplace of father	Birthplace of mother	Able to speak English	OCCUPATION
	1	2	3	4	5	6	7	8	9	10	11	12	13	14	15	16	17
1		49	58	Guerrero, Caridad M	Wife	F	Cha	39.0	M		Y	Y	Guam	Guam	Guam	N	None
2		49	58	Guerrero, Maria M	Daughter	F	Cha	16.0	S		Y	Y	Guam	Guam	Guam	N	None
3		49	58	Guerrero, Dolores M	Daughter	F	Cha	14.0	S	N	Y	Y	Guam	Guam	Guam	N	None
4		49	58	Guerrero, Jesus M	Son	M	Cha	12.0	S	N	Y	Y	Guam	Guam	Guam	Y	None
5		49	58	Guerrero, Jose M	Son	M	Cha	9.0	S	Y	Y	Y	Guam	Guam	Guam		None
6		49	58	Guerrero, Julian M	Son	M	Cha	5.0	S	N			Guam	Guam	Guam		None
7		49	58	Guerrero, Manuel M	Son	M	Cha	0.1	S				Guam	Guam	Guam		None
8		49	58	Merfalen, Juan P	Brother-in-law	M	Cha	33.0	S		Y	Y	Guam	Guam	Guam	N	Farm laborer
9		50	59	Cruz, Enrique C	Head	M	Cha	27.0	M		Y	Y	Guam	Guam	Guam	Y	Laborer
10		50	59	Cruz, Josefa M	Wife	F	Cha	23.0	M		N	N	Guam	Guam	Guam	N	None
11		50	59	Cruz, Maria M	Daughter	F	Cha	2.0	S				Guam	Guam	Guam		None
12		50	59	Cruz, Antonia M	Daughter	F	Cha	1.0	S				Guam	Guam	Guam		None
13		51	60	Cruz, Jose F	Head	M	Cha	32.0	M		Y	Y	Guam	Guam	Guam	Y	Laborer
14		51	60	Cruz, Maria O	Wife	F	Cha	28.0	M		Y	Y	Guam	Guam	Guam	N	None
15		51	60	Cruz, Dolores O	Daughter	F	Cha	3.0	S				Guam	Guam	Guam		None
16	Legaspi Street	51	60	Ogo, Manuel G	Brother-in-law	M	Cha	19.0	S	N	Y	Y	Guam	Guam	Guam	Y	Cook
17		51	60	Ogo, Francisco A	Father-in-law	M	Cha	58.0	Wd		Y	Y	Guam	Guam	Guam	N	Net maker
18		52	61	Mendiola, Antonina M	Head	F	Cha	23.0	S	N	Y	Y	Guam	Guam	Guam	Y	None
19		52	61	Mendiola, Pedro M	Brother	M	Cha	20.0	S	N	Y	Y	Guam	Guam	Guam	Y	Laborer
20		52	61	Mendiola, Margarita M	Sister	F	Cha	14.0	S	N	Y	Y	Guam	Guam	Guam	N	Servant
21		52	61	Mendiola, Maria M	Sister	F	Cha	9.0	S	Y			Guam	Guam	Guam		None
22		52	61	Mendiola, Ana M	Daughter	F	Cha	0.3	S				Guam	Unknown	Guam		None
23		53	62	Yamaguchi, Juan	Head	M	Jp	36.0	M		Y	Y	Japan	Japan	Japan	N	Carpenter
24		53	62	Yamaguchi, Ana A	Wife	F	Cha	25.0	M		Y	Y	Guam	Guam	Guam	Y	None
25		53	62	Yamaguchi, Manuel A	Son	M	Jp	8.0	S	Y			Guam	Japan	Guam		None

(CHAMORRO ROOTS GENEALOGY PROJECT ™ TRANSCRIPTION)
(COMPILED/TRANSCRIBED BY BERNARD T. PUNZALAN / HTTP://WWW.CHAMORROROOTS.COM)
FOURTEENTH CENSUS OF THE UNITED STATES: 1920-POPULATION
ISLAND OF GUAM

DISTRICT 2
NAME OF PLACE Anigua - Agana City
[Proper name and, also, name of class, as city, town, village, barrio, etc]

ENUMERATED BY ME ON THE 15th DAY OF April, 1920

Vicente Tydingco ENUMERATOR

	PLACE OF ABODE			NAME	RELATION	PERSONAL DESCRIPTION					EDUCATION			NATIVITY				OCCUPATION
Street, avenue, road, etc.	Number of dwelling house is order of visitation	Number of family in order of visitation				Sex	Color or race	Age at last birthday	Single, married, widowed or divorced	Attended school any time since Sept. 1, 1919	Whether able to read.	Whether able to write.	Place of birth of this person.	Place of birth of father of this person.	Place of birth of mother of this person.	Whether able to speak English.	
1	2	3	4	5	6	7	8	9	10	11	12	13	14	15	16	17
26	53	62	Yamaguchi, Josefina A	Daughter	F	Jp	5.0	S	N			Guam	Japan	Guam		None
27	53	62	Yamaguchi, Visitacion A	Daughter	F	Jp	4.0	S				Guam	Japan	Guam		None
28	53	62	Yamaguchi, Maria A	Daughter	F	Jp	2.0	S				Guam	Japan	Guam		None
29	54	63	Mesa, Ignacio M	Head	M	Cha	45.0	M		Y	Y	Guam	Guam	Guam	Y	Farmer
30	54	63	Mesa, Rosa T	Wife	F	Cha	34.0	M		N	N	Guam	Guam	Guam	N	None
31	54	63	Mesa, Ana T	Daughter	F	Cha	21.0	S	N	Y	Y	Guam	Guam	Guam	Y	None
32	54	63	Mesa, Joaquin T	Son	M	Cha	15.0	S	Y	Y	Y	Guam	Guam	Guam	Y	None
33	54	63	Taienao, Amparo M	Niece	F	Cha	20.0	S	N	Y	Y	Guam	Guam	Guam	Y	Servant
34	55	64	Muna, Manuel C	Head	M	Cha	56.0	Wd		Y	Y	Guam	Guam	Guam	N	None
35	56	65	Angoco, Pedro A	Head	M	Cha	32.0	M		Y	Y	Guam	Guam	Guam	Y	Seaman USN
36	56	65	Angoco, Manuela M	Wife	F	Cha	32.0	M		Y	Y	Guam	Guam	Guam		None
37	56	65	Angoco, Francisco M	Son	M	Cha	0.4	S				Guam	Guam	Guam		None
38	57	66	Cleofas, Sixto C	Head	M	Fil	68.0	M		N	N	Luzon	Luzon	Luzon	N	None
39	57	66	Cleofas, Maria C	Wife	F	Cha	46.0	M		N	N	Guam	Guam	Guam	N	None
40	57	66	Cleofas, Joaquin C	Son	M	Fil	19.0	S	N	Y	Y	Guam	Luzon	Guam	Y	Farm laborer
41	57	66	Cleofas, Ana C	Daughter	F	Fil	18.0	S	N	Y	Y	Guam	Luzon	Guam	N	None
42	57	66	Cleofas, Felecita C	Daughter	F	Fil	7.0	S	N	Y	Y	Guam	Luzon	Guam		None
43	57	66	Cruz, Tomas C	Grandson	M	Cha	3.0	S				Guam	Unknown	Guam		None
44	57	66	Cruz, Ana C	Servant	F	Cha	48.0	S		N	N	Guam	Guam	Guam	N	Servant
45	58	67	Torres, Vicente LG	Head	M	Cha	44.0	M		Y	Y	Guam	Guam	Guam	Y	Farmer
46	58	67	Torres, Ana C	Wife	F	Cha	40.0	M		Y	Y	Guam	Guam	Guam	N	None
47	58	67	Torres, Dolores C	Daughter	F	Cha	20.0	S	N	Y	Y	Guam	Guam	Guam	N	None
48	58	67	Torres, Maria C	Daughter	F	Cha	18.0	S	N	Y	Y	Guam	Guam	Guam	Y	None
49	58	67	Torres, Ana C jr	Daughter	F	Cha	16.0	S	N	Y	Y	Guam	Guam	Guam	Y	None
50	58	67	Torres, Concepcion C	Daughter	F	Cha	12.0	S	Y	Y	Y	Guam	Guam	Guam	Y	None

Legaspi Street

(CHAMORRO ROOTS GENEALOGY PROJECT ™ TRANSCRIPTION)
(COMPILED/TRANSCRIBED BY BERNARD T. PUNZALAN / HTTP://WWW.CHAMORROROOTS.COM)

FOURTEENTH CENSUS OF THE UNITED STATES: 1920-POPULATION

ISLAND OF GUAM

SHEET NO. 45A

DISTRICT 2
NAME OF PLACE Anigua – Agana City
[Proper name and, also, name of class, as city, town, village, barrio, etc]

ENUMERATED BY ME ON THE 15th DAY OF April, 1920

Vicente Tydingco ENUMERATOR

1 Street	2 Dwelling	3 Family	4 NAME	5 RELATION	6 Sex	7 Race	8 Age	9 Marital	10 School	11 Read	12 Write	13 Birth person	14 Birth father	15 Birth mother	16 English	17 OCCUPATION
	58	67	Torres, Vicente C	Son	M	Cha	7.0	S	N			Guam	Guam	Guam		None
	58	67	Torres, Josefina C	Daughter	F	Cha	6.0	S	N			Guam	Guam	Guam		None
	58	67	Torres, Francisco C	Son	M	Cha	4.0	S				Guam	Guam	Guam		None
	58	67	Torres, Ignacia C	Daughter	F	Cha	3.0	S				Guam	Guam	Guam		None
	58	67	Torres, Tomas C	Son	M	Cha	0.2	S				Guam	Guam	Guam		None
	58	68	Torres, Juan C	Head	M	Cha	22.0	M		Y	Y	Guam	Guam	Guam	Y	Seaman USN
	58	68	Torres, Maria B	Wife	F	Cha	18.0	M	N	Y	Y	Guam	Unknown	Guam	Y	None
	59	69	Concepcion, Juan	Head	M	Cha	36.0	M		Y	Y	Guam	Guam	Guam	Y	Seaman USN
	59	69	Concepcion, Dolores B	Wife	F	Cha	43.0	M		Y	Y	Guam	Guam	Guam	N	None
	59	69	Concepcion, Francisco A	Nephew	M	Cha	20.0	S	N	Y	Y	Guam	Guam	Guam	Y	Laborer
Agana Pitt Road	59	69	S. Nicolas, Geronimo C	Nephew	M	Cha	20.0	S	N	Y	Y	Guam	Guam	Guam	Y	Seaman USN
	60	70	Lazaro, Nicolas R	Head	M	Fil	59.0	M		Y	Y	Luzon	Luzon	Luzon	N	Farmer
	60	70	Lazaro, Josefa U	Wife	F	Fil	47.0	M		Y	Y	Guam	Luzon	Guam	N	None
	60	70	Lazaro, Juan U	Son	M	Fil	13.0	S	Y	Y	Y	Guam	Luzon	Guam	Y	None
	60	70	Lazaro, Antonia U	Daughter	F	Fil	12.0	S	Y	Y	Y	Guam	Luzon	Guam	Y	None
	60	70	Lazaro, Ernesto U	Son	M	Cha	5.0	S	N			Guam	Luzon	Guam		None
	61	71	Velasco, Sebastian	Head	M	Fil	40.0	S		Y	Y	Luzon	Luzon	Luzon	Y	Musician USN
	61	71	Aguon, Antonia C	Cook	F	Cha	38.0	S		Y	Y	Guam	Guam	Guam	N	Cook
	61	71	Santos, Carmelo SN	Servant	M	Cha	25.0	S		Y	Y	Guam	Guam	Guam	N	Servant
	61	71	Toves, Carmen A	Servant	F	Fil	12.0	S		Y	Y	Guam	Guam	Guam	N	Servant
	61	71	Salas, Jose A	Lodger	M	Cha	6.0	S	Y			Guam	Guam	Guam		None
	62	72	Untalan, Francisco C	Head	M	Fil	38.0	M		Y	Y	Guam	Luzon	Guam	Y	Farmer
	62	72	Untalan, Juana C	Wife	F	Cha	35.0	M		Y	Y	Guam	Guam	Guam	N	None
	62	72	Untalan, Eginio C	Son	M	Cha	11.0	S	Y	Y	Y	Guam	Guam	Guam	Y	None
	62	72	Untalan, Antonia C	Daughter	F	Cha	9.0	S	Y	Y	Y	Guam	Guam	Guam	Y	None

(CHAMORRO ROOTS GENEALOGY PROJECT ™ TRANSCRIPTION)
(COMPILED/TRANSCRIBED BY BERNARD T. PUNZALAN / HTTP://WWW.CHAMORROROOTS.COM)

FOURTEENTH CENSUS OF THE UNITED STATES: 1920-POPULATION

ISLAND OF GUAM

97b

ENUMERATED BY ME ON THE 16th DAY OF April, 1920

Vicente Tydingco ENUMERATOR

DISTRICT 2

NAME OF PLACE Anigua – Agana City

[Proper name and, also, name of class, as city, town, village, barrio, etc]

Street	Dwelling No.	Family No.	NAME	RELATION	Sex	Color or race	Age	Marital	Attended school	Read	Write	Birthplace	Father birthplace	Mother birthplace	English	OCCUPATION
	62	72	Sotomayor, Nicolas	Boarder	M	Ot	87.0	M		N	N	Luzon	Luzon	Luzon	N	None
	63	73	Untalan, Antonia C	Head	F	Cha	82.0	Wd		Y	Y	Guam	Guam	Guam	N	None
	64	74	Day, John E	Head	M	W	63.0	M		Y	Y	Massachusettes	Massachusettes	Massachusettes	Y	None
	64	74	Day, Petronila U	Wife	F	Cha	47.0	M		Y	Y	Guam	Luzon	Guam	Y	None
	64	74	Day, Josefina U	Adopted daughter	F	Cha	15.0	S	N	Y	Y	Guam	Guam	Guam	Y	None
	65	75	Camacho, Jose M	Head	M	Cha	45.0	M		Y	Y	Guam	Unknown	Guam	N	Farmer
	65	75	Camacho, Cristina C	Wife	F	Cha	20.0	M	N	Y	Y	Guam	Guam	Guam	Y	None
	65	75	Camacho, Barbara C	Daughter	F	Cha	4.0	S				Guam	Guam	Guam		None
Agana Pitt Road	65	75	Camacho, Maria C	Daughter	F	Cha	3.0	S				Guam	Guam	Guam		None
	65	75	Camacho, Jesus C	Son	M	Cha	0.1	S				Guam	Guam	Guam		None
	65	75	Cruz, Ignacia L	Mother in law	F	Cha	51.0	S		N	N	Guam	Guam	Guam	N	None
	66	76	S. Nicolas, Jose T	Head	M	Cha	52.0	M		Y	Y	Guam	Guam	Guam	N	Laundress
	66	76	S. Nicolas, Dolores C	Wife	F	Cha	49.0	M		N	N	Guam	Guam	Guam	N	Laborer
	66	76	S. Nicolas, Maria C	Daughter	F	Cha	17.0	S	N	Y	Y	Guam	Guam	Guam	Y	None
	66	76	S. Nicolas, Pedro C	Son	M	Cha	16.0	S	N	Y	Y	Guam	Guam	Guam	N	Farm laborer home farm
	66	76	S. Nicolas, Vicente C	Son	M	Cha	11.0	S	Y	Y	Y	Guam	Guam	Guam	N	None
	66	76	S. Nicolas, Juan C	Son	M	Cha	9.0	S	Y	Y	Y	Guam	Guam	Guam	N	None
	67	77	Alam, Carmen D	Head	F	Chi	30.0	M		Y	Y	Guam	China	Guam	N	Laundress
	67	77	Alam, Leon D	Daughter	F	Chin	10.0	S	Y	Y	Y	Guam	China	Guam	Y	None
	67	77	Alam, Pilar D	Daughter	F	Chin	1.0	S				Guam	China	Guam		None
	67	77	Diaz, Maria T	Mother	F	Cha	70.0	Wd		N	N	Guam	Guam	Guam	N	None
	68	78	Bautista, Vicente C	Head	M	Cha	48.0	M	N	N	N	Guam	Guam	Guam	N	Herder
	68	78	Bautista, Manuela A	Wife	F	Cha	40.0	M		N	N	Guam	Guam	Guam	N	None
	68	78	Bautista, Maria P	Daughter	F	Cha	17.0	S	N	Y	Y	Guam	Guam	Guam	Y	None
	68	78	Bautista, Luis P	Son	M	Cha	14.0	S	Y	Y	Y	Guam	Guam	Guam	Y	None

(CHAMORRO ROOTS GENEALOGY PROJECT ™ TRANSCRIPTION)
(COMPILED/TRANSCRIBED BY BERNARD T. PUNZALAN / HTTP://WWW.CHAMORROROOTS.COM)

FOURTEENTH CENSUS OF THE UNITED STATES: 1920-POPULATION
ISLAND OF GUAM

SHEET NO. 46A

ENUMERATED BY ME ON THE 16th DAY OF April, 1920

Vicente Tydingco ENUMERATOR

DISTRICT 2
NAME OF PLACE Anigua - Agana City
[Proper name and, also, name of class, as city, town, village, barrio, etc]

1 Street	2 House	3 Family	4 NAME	5 RELATION	6 Sex	7 Color or race	8 Age	9 S/M/Wd/D	10 School	11 Read	12 Write	13 Birth person	14 Birth father	15 Birth mother	16 English	17 OCCUPATION
	68	78	Bautista, Vicente P	Son	M	Cha	3.0	S				Guam	Guam	Guam		None
	68	78	Pablo, Rosa B	Niece	F	Cha	15.0	S	Y	Y	Y	Guam	Guam	Guam	Y	None
	68	78	Pablo, Juan B	Nephew	M	Cha	13.0	S	Y	Y	Y	Guam	Guam	Guam	Y	None
	68	78	Pablo, Maria B	Niece	F	Cha	11.0	S	Y	Y	Y	Guam	Guam	Guam	N	None
	68	78	Pablo, Jacinto A	Brother in law	M	Cha	45.0	Wd		Y	Y	Guam	Guam	Guam	N	Herder
	69	79	Materne, Mariano M	Head	M	Cha	68.0	M		Y	Y	Guam	Guam	Guam	N	Laborer
	69	79	Materne, Mariana P	Wife	F	Cha	41.0	M		Y	Y	Guam	Guam	Guam	N	None
	69	79	Materne, Maria P	Daughter	F	Cha	13.0	S	N	N	N	Guam	Guam	Guam	Y	None
	69	79	Materne, Joaquin P	Son	M	Cha	3.0	S				Guam	Guam	Guam		None
Agana Pitt Road	69	79	Materne, Ana P	Daughter	F	Cha	0.1	S				Guam	Guam	Guam		None
	69	79	Pablo, Jose P	Stepson	M	Cha	22.0	S	Y	Y	Y	Guam	Unknown	Guam	Y	Farmer
	70	80	Demapan, Mariano A	Head	M	Cha	43.0	M		Y	Y	Guam	Guam	Guam	Y	Laborer
	70	80	Demapan, Maria M	Wife	F	Cha	45.0	M		N	N	Guam	Unknown	Guam	N	None
	70	80	Demapan, Agueda M	Daughter	F	Cha	18.0	S	N	Y	Y	Guam	Guam	Guam	Y	None
	70	80	Demapan, Ana M	Daughter	F	Cha	17.0	S	N	Y	Y	Guam	Guam	Guam	N	Servant
	70	80	Demapan, Ignacio M	Son	M	Cha	6.0	S	N			Guam	Guam	Guam	Y	None
	70	80	Demapan, Mercedes M	Daughter	F	Cha	2.0	S				Guam	Guam	Guam		None
	71	81	Pablo, Jose A	Head	M	Cha	18.0	M	N	Y	Y	Guam	Guam	Guam	Y	Laborer
	71	81	Pablo, Josefa B	Wife	F	Cha	20.0	M	N	Y	Y	Guam	Guam	Guam	Y	None
	71	81	Pablo, Maria A	Daughter	F	Cha	0.6	S				Guam	Guam	Guam		None
	72	82	Cruz, Manuel P	Head	M	Cha	48.0	M		Y	Y	Guam	Guam	Guam	Y	Farmer
	72	82	Cruz, Rita D	Wife	F	Cha	47.0	M		Y	Y	Guam	Guam	Guam	N	None
	72	82	Cruz, Jose D	Son	M	Cha	16.0	S	Y	Y	Y	Guam	Guam	Guam	Y	Farm laborer home farm
	72	82	Cruz, Joaquin D	Son	M	Cha	10.0	S	Y	Y	Y	Guam	Guam	Guam	Y	None
	73	83	Aflague, Alfonso C	Head	M	Cha	38.0	M		Y	Y	Guam	Guam	Guam	N	Laborer

(CHAMORRO ROOTS GENEALOGY PROJECT ™ TRANSCRIPTION)
(COMPILED/TRANSCRIBED BY BERNARD T. PUNZALAN / HTTP://WWW.CHAMORROROOTS.COM)
FOURTEENTH CENSUS OF THE UNITED STATES: 1920-POPULATION
ISLAND OF GUAM

DISTRICT 2
NAME OF PLACE Anigua - Agana City

[Proper name and, also, name of class, as city, town, village, barrio, etc]

ENUMERATED BY ME ON THE 16th DAY OF April, 1920

Vicente Tydingco ENUMERATOR

Street, avenue, road, etc.	No. of dwelling house	No. of family	NAME	RELATION	Sex	Color or race	Age	Condition	School	Read	Write	Birthplace of person	Birthplace of father	Birthplace of mother	English	OCCUPATION
	1	2/3	4	5	6	7	8	9	10	11	12	13	14	15	16	17
	73	83	Aflague, Ana C	Wife	F	Cha	35.0	M		N	N	Guam	Unknown	Guam	N	None
	73	83	Aflague, Francisco C	Son	M	Cha	8.0	S	Y			Guam	Guam	Guam		None
	73	83	Aflague, Gregorio C	Son	M	Cha	0.1	S				Guam	Guam	Guam		None
	73	83	Aflague, Joaquin C	Son	M	Cha	0.1	S				Guam	Guam	Guam		None
	74	84	Torres, Vicente C	Head	M	Cha	35.0	M		Y	Y	Guam	Unknown	Guam	Y	Farmer
	74	84	Torres, Juana M	Wife	F	Cha	35.0	M		N	N	Guam	Guam	Guam	N	None
	74	84	Torres, Rosa M	Daughter	F	Cha	10.0	S	Y	Y	Y	Guam	Guam	Guam	N	None
	74	84	Torres, Delfina M	Daughter	F	Cha	5.0	S	N	Y	Y	Guam	Guam	Guam		None
	74	84	Torres, Juan M	Son	M	Cha	2.0	S				Guam	Guam	Guam		None
Agana Pitt Road	74	84	Torres, Jose M	Son	M	Cha	1.0	S				Guam	Guam	Guam		None
	75	85	Cruz, Mariano A	Head	M	Cha	30.0	M		Y	Y	Guam	Guam	Guam	N	Farmer
	75	85	Cruz, Luisa T	Wife	F	Cha	26.0	M		Y	Y	Guam	Guam	Guam	N	None
	75	85	Cruz, Tomas T	Son	M	Cha	6.0	S	N			Guam	Guam	Guam		None
	75	85	Cruz, Ignacio T	Son	M	Cha	1.0	S				Guam	Guam	Guam		None
	76	86	Gumataotao, Manuela G	Head	F	Fil	47.0	Wd		Y	Y	Guam	Luzon	Guam	N	None
	76	86	Gumataotao, Teresa G	Daughter	F	Cha	20.0	S	N	Y	Y	Guam	Guam	Guam	Y	None
	76	86	Gumataotao, Francisco G	Son	M	Cha	18.0	S	N	Y	Y	Guam	Guam	Guam	Y	Laborer
	76	86	Gumataotao, Eulogio G	Son	M	Cha	17.0	S	N	Y	Y	Guam	Guam	Guam	Y	Messenger
	76	86	Gumataotao, Paciano G	Son	M	Cha	16.0	S	Y	Y	Y	Guam	Guam	Guam	Y	None
	76	86	Gumataotao, Fermin G	Son	M	Cha	12.0	S	Y	Y	Y	Guam	Guam	Guam	Y	None
	77	87	Quituqua, Vicente Q	Head	M	Cha	35.0	M		Y	Y	Guam	Unknown	Guam	Y	Tanner
	77	87	Quituqua, Natividad C	Wife	F	Cha	43.0	M		Y	Y	Guam	Guam	Guam	N	None
	77	87	Quituqua, Juan C	Son	M	Cha	16.0	S	N	Y	Y	Guam	Guam	Guam	Y	Servant
	77	87	Quituqua, Consuelo C	Daughter	F	Cha	6.0	S	N			Guam	Guam	Guam		None
	77	87	Quituqua, Adela C	Daughter	F	Cha	3.0	S				Guam	Guam	Guam		None

(CHAMORRO ROOTS GENEALOGY PROJECT ™ TRANSCRIPTION)
(COMPILED/TRANSCRIBED BY BERNARD T. PUNZALAN / HTTP://WWW.CHAMORROROOTS.COM)

FOURTEENTH CENSUS OF THE UNITED STATES: 1920-POPULATION

ISLAND OF GUAM

SHEET NO. 47A

99

DISTRICT 2
NAME OF PLACE Anigua - Agana City

ENUMERATED BY ME ON THE 16th DAY OF April, 1920

Vicente Tydingco ENUMERATOR

Street	Dwelling No.	Family No.	NAME	RELATION	Sex	Color or race	Age	Single, married, widowed or divorced	Attended school since Sept. 1, 1919	Able to read	Able to write	Birthplace of this person	Birthplace of father	Birthplace of mother	Able to speak English	OCCUPATION
	77	87	Quitugua, Francisco C	Son	M	Cha	0.3	S				Guam	Guam	Guam		None
	78	88	Cruz, Tomas C	Head	M	Cha	46.0	M		Y	Y	Guam	Guam	Guam	N	Farmer
	78	88	Cruz, Clarita J	Wife	F	Cha	60.0	M		N	N	Guam	Guam	Guam	N	None
	78	88	Cruz, Jose C	Brother	M	Cha	40.0	S		N	N	Guam	Guam	Guam	N	Farm laborer
	79	89	Cruz, Vicente S	Head	M	Cha	56.0	M		Y	Y	Guam	Guam	Guam	N	Deputy Commissioner
	79	89	Cruz, Josefa U	Wife	F	Fil	55.0	M		Y	Y	Guam	Luzon	Guam	N	None
	79	89	Nauta, Rosa T	Servant	F	Cha	50.0	Wd		N	N	Guam	Guam	Guam	N	Servant
	79	89	Nauta, Juan T	Boarder	M	Cha	29.0	S		Y	Y	Guam	Guam	Guam	Y	Seaman USM
	79	89	Nauta, Antonio T	Boarder	M	Cha	17.0	S	N	Y	Y	Guam	Guam	Guam	Y	Farm laborer home farm
	79	89	Nauta, Eugenia T	Boarder	F	Cha	16.0	S	N	Y	Y	Guam	Guam	Guam	N	Servant
Agana Pitt Road	79	89	Concepcion, Juan	Servant	M	Cha	19.0	S	N	Y	Y	Guam	Unknown	Guam	Y	Servant
	80	90	Angoco, Ramona D	Head	F	Cha	46.0	Wd	N	N	N	Guam	Unknown	Guam	N	None
	80	90	Angoco, Vicente D	Son	M	Cha	18.0	S	N	Y	Y	Guam	Guam	Guam	N	Laborer
	80	90	Angoco, Manuel D	Son	M	Cha	17.0	S	N	Y	Y	Guam	Guam	Guam	Y	Farmer
	80	90	Angoco, Dolores D	Daughter	F	Cha	12.0	S	Y	Y	Y	Guam	Guam	Guam	N	None
	80	90	Angoco, Vicenta D	Daughter	F	Cha	10.0	S	Y	Y	Y	Guam	Guam	Guam	Y	None
	80	90	Angoco, Santiago D	Son	M	Cha	7.0	S				Guam	Guam	Guam	N	None
	80	90	Angoco, Jesus D	Son	M	Cha	6.0	S				Guam	Guam	Guam		None
	80	90	Diaz, Doroteo D	Son	M	Cha	22.0	S		Y	Y	Guam	Unknown	Guam	Y	Farm laborer
	80	90	Diaz, Jose D	Brother	M	Cha	36.0	S		N	N	Guam	Unknown	Guam	N	Farmer
	81	91	Angoco, Joaquin T	Head	M	Cha	30.0	M		Y	Y	Guam	Guam	Guam	N	Farmer
	81	91	Angoco, Rosa T	Wife	F	Cha	40.0	M		N	N	Guam	Unknown	Guam	N	None
	81	91	Angoco, Juan T	Son	M	Cha	14.0	S	Y	Y	Y	Guam	Guam	Guam	Y	None
	81	91	Chargualaf, Engracia SN	Niece	F	Cha	18.0	S	N	Y	N	Guam	Guam	Guam	Y	Servant
	81	91	Chargualaf, Jose C	Nephew	M	Cha	4.0	S				Guam	Unkpown	Guam		None

(CHAMORRO ROOTS GENEALOGY PROJECT ™ TRANSCRIPTION)
(COMPILED/TRANSCRIBED BY BERNARD T. PUNZALAN / HTTP://WWW.CHAMORROROOTS.COM)

FOURTEENTH CENSUS OF THE UNITED STATES: 1920-POPULATION

ISLAND OF GUAM

99b

ENUMERATED BY ME ON THE 17th DAY OF April, 1920

Vicente Tydingco ENUMERATOR

DISTRICT 2

NAME OF PLACE Anigua – Agana City

[Proper name and, also, name of class, as city, town, village, barrio, etc]

	Dwelling	Family	NAME	RELATION	Sex	Color or race	Age	Cond.	Attended school	Read	Write	Birthplace	Father	Mother	English	OCCUPATION
1	2	3	4	5	6	7	8	9	10	11	12	13	14	15	16	17
	82	92	Concepcion, Jesus G	Head	M	Cha	28.0	M		Y	Y	Guam	Guam	Guam	Y	Farmer
	82	92	Concepcion, Dominga A	Wife	F	Cha	26.0	M		Y	Y	Guam	Unknown	Guam	N	None
	82	92	Concepcion, Susana A	Daughter	F	Cha	2.0	S				Guam	Guam	Guam	N	None
	82	92	Concepcion, Dolores A	Daughter	F	Cha	0.3	S				Guam	Guam	Guam	N	None
	83	93	Cruz, Andres LG	Head	M	Cha	43.0	Wd		Y	Y	Guam	Guam	Guam	N	Fisherman
	83	93	Cruz, Maria B	Daughter	F	Cha	14.0	S	N	Y	Y	Guam	Guam	Guam	Y	None
	83	93	Cruz, Vicente B	Son	M	Cha	10.0	S	N	N	N	Guam	Guam	Guam	N	None
	83	93	Cruz, Gregorio B	Son	M	Cha	4.0	S				Guam	Guam	Guam	N	None
	84	94	Angoco, Pedro T	Head	M	Cha	53.0	M		Y	Y	Guam	Guam	Guam	N	Farmer
	84	94	Angoco, Ana G	Wife	F	Cha	52.0	M		Y	Y	Guam	Guam	Guam	N	None
	84	94	Angoco, Mariano	Nephew	M	Cha	39.0	S		N	N	Guam	Unknown	Guam	N	Farm laborer
	85	95	Mendiola, Jose Q	Head	M	Cha	30.0	M		Y	Y	Guam	Guam	Guam	Y	Carpenter
	85	95	Mendiola, Candelaria P	Wife	F	Cha	29.0	M		Y	Y	Guam	Guam	Guam	N	None
	85	95	Mendiola, Jose P	Son	M	Cha	11.0	S	Y	Y	Y	Guam	Guam	Guam	Y	None
	85	95	Mendiola, Demetrio P	Son	M	Cha	8.0	S	N			Guam	Guam	Guam	N	None
	85	95	Mendiola, Celia P	Daughter	F	Cha	2.0	S				Guam	Guam	Guam	N	None
	86	96	Lizama, Caridad	Head	F	Cha	38.0	S		N	N	Guam	Unknown	Unknown	N	Laundress
	86	96	Lizama, Vicente	Son	M	Cha	17.0	S	N	Y	Y	Guam	Unknown	Guam	Y	Laborer
	86	96	Lizama, Emilia	Daughter	F	Cha	5.0	S	N			Guam	Unknown	Guam	N	None
	87	97	Tenorio, Rosa G	Head	F	Cha	31.0	Wd		N	N	Guam	Unknown	Guam	N	Farmer
	87	97	Tenorio, Encarnacion G	Daughter	F	Cha	10.0	S	Y	Y	Y	Guam	Guam	Guam	N	None
	87	97	Tenorio, Jose G	Son	M	Cha	8.0	S	Y	Y	Y	Guam	Guam	Guam	N	None
	87	97	Tenorio, Juan G	Son	M	Cha	3.0	S				Guam	Guam	Guam	N	None
	87	97	Lizama, Maria M	Boarder	F	Cha	60.0	S		N	N	Guam	Guam	Guam	N	None
	88	98	Taimanglo, Vicenta M	Head	F	Cha	47.0	Wd		N	N	Guam	Guam	Guam	N	Laundress

Street: Agana Pitt Road

(CHAMORRO ROOTS GENEALOGY PROJECT ™ TRANSCRIPTION)
(COMPILED/TRANSCRIBED BY BERNARD T. PUNZALAN / HTTP://WWW.CHAMORROROOTS.COM)

FOURTEENTH CENSUS OF THE UNITED STATES: 1920-POPULATION

ISLAND OF GUAM

ENUMERATED BY ME ON THE 17th DAY OF April, 1920

Vicente Tydingco ENUMERATOR

DISTRICT 2
NAME OF PLACE Anigua - Agana City

	Dwelling house No.	Family No.	NAME	RELATION	Sex	Color or race	Age	Single, married, widowed or divorced	Attended school since Sept. 1, 1919	Able to read	Able to write	Place of birth of this person	Place of birth of father	Place of birth of mother	Able to speak English	OCCUPATION
	2	3	4	5	6	7	8	9	10	11	12	13	14	15	16	17
1	88	98	Taimanglo, Beatris M	Daughter	F	Cha	11.0	S	Y	Y	Y	Guam	Guam	Guam	N	None
2	88	98	Taimanglo, Ana M	Daughter	F	Cha	10.0	S	Y	Y	Y	Guam	Guam	Guam	N	None
3	88	98	Taimanglo, Vicente M	Son	M	Cha	5.0	S	N			Guam	Guam	Guam		None
4	88	98	Taimanglo, Jose M	Son	M	Cha	4.0	S				Guam	Guam	Guam		None
5	88	98	Taimanglo, Juan M	Son	M	Cha	1.0	S				Guam	Guam	Guam		None
6	89	99	Gonzalo, Pedro G	Head	M	Fil	24.0	M		Y	Y	Luzon	Luzon	Luzon	Y	Laborer
7	89	99	Gonzalo, Antonia T	Wife	F	Fil	20.0	M	N	Y	Y	Guam	Luzon	Guam	Y	None
8	89	99	Gonzalo, Josefina T	Daughter	F	Fil	2.0	S				Guam	Luzon	Guam		None
9	90	100	Tuncap, Joaquin N	Head	M	Fil	28.0	M		Y	Y	Guam	Luzon	Guam	Y	Farmer
10	90	100	Tuncap, Caridad P	Wife	F	Cha	31.0	M		Y	Y	Guam	Guam	Guam	Y	None
11	90	100	Tuncap, Jose P	Son	M	Fil	7.0	S	Y			Guam	Guam	Guam		None
12	90	100	Tuncap, Gonzalo P	Son	M	Fil	4.0	S				Guam	Guam	Guam		None
13	90	100	Tuncap, Manuel P	Son	M	Fil	3.0	S				Guam	Guam	Guam		None
14	90	100	Tuncap, Maria P	Daughter	F	Fil	2.0	S				Guam	Guam	Guam		None
15	91	101	Flores, Julian L	Head	M	Cha	36.0	M		Y	Y	Guam	Guam	Guam	N	Farmer
16	91	101	Flores, Rita T	Wife	F	Cha	26.0	M		Y	Y	Guam	Unknown	Guam	N	None
17	91	101	Flores, Gregorio T	Son	M	Cha	8.0	S	Y			Guam	Guam	Guam		None
18	91	101	Flores, Maria T	Daughter	F	Cha	6.0	S	N			Guam	Guam	Guam		None
19	91	101	Flores, Jesus T	Son	M	Cha	5.0	S	N			Guam	Guam	Guam		None
20	91	101	Flores, Jose T	Son	M	Cha	3.0	S				Guam	Guam	Guam		None
21	91	101	Flores, Joaquin T	Son	M	Cha	0.6	S				Guam	Guam	Guam		None
22	92	102	Gutierez, Luis M	Head	M	Fil	50.0	M		Y	Y	Guam	Luzon	Guam	N	Farmer
23	92	102	Gutierez, Filomena D	Wife	F	Cha	33.0	M	N	N	N	Guam	Guam	Guam	N	Laundress
24	92	102	Gutierez, Juan D	Son	M	Cha	17.0	S	N	Y	Y	Guam	Guam	Guam	Y	Servant
25	92	102	Gutierez, Rosa D	Daughter	F	Cha	15.0	S	N	Y	Y	Guam	Guam	Guam	Y	None

Street: Agana Piti Road

(CHAMORRO ROOTS GENEALOGY PROJECT ™ TRANSCRIPTION)
(COMPILED/TRANSCRIBED BY BERNARD T. PUNZALAN / HTTP://WWW.CHAMORROROOTS.COM)

FOURTEENTH CENSUS OF THE UNITED STATES: 1920–POPULATION
ISLAND OF GUAM

DISTRICT 2
NAME OF PLACE Anigua – Agana City
[Proper name and, also, name of class, as city, town, village, barrio, etc]

ENUMERATED BY ME ON THE 17th DAY OF April, 1920

Vicente Tydingco ENUMERATOR

	Street	No. dwelling	No. family	NAME	RELATION	Sex	Color or race	Age	Single, married, widowed or divorced	Attended school	Able to read	Able to write	Birthplace person	Birthplace father	Birthplace mother	Able to speak English	OCCUPATION
	1	2	3	4	5	6	7	8	9	10	11	12	13	14	15	16	17
26		92	102	Gutierrez, Tomasa D	Daughter	F	Cha	13.0	S	N	Y	Y	Guam	Guam	Guam	Y	None
27		92	102	Gutierrez, Maria D	Daughter	F	Cha	10.0	S	Y	Y	Y	Guam	Guam	Guam		None
28		92	102	Gutierrez, Ana D	Daughter	F	Cha	4.0	S				Guam	Guam	Guam		None
29		92	102	Gutierrez, Felecita D	Daughter	F	Cha	3.0	S				Guam	Guam	Guam		None
30		92	102	Gutierrez, Jose D	Son	M	Cha	2.0	S				Guam	Guam	Guam		None
31		93	103	Diaz, Antonio SN	Head	M	Cha	38.0	M		Y	Y	Guam	Guam	Guam	N	Farmer
32		93	103	Diaz, Ana G	Wife	F	Cha	31.0	M		Y	Y	Guam	Guam	Guam	N	None
33		93	103	Diaz, Maria G	Daughter	F	Cha	9.0	S	Y			Guam	Guam	Guam		None
34	Agana Pitt Road	93	103	Diaz, Julia G	Daughter	F	Cha	1.0	S				Guam	Guam	Guam		None
35		94	104	Tuncap, Rita D	Head	F	Cha	32.0	D		N	N	Guam	Unknown	Unknown	N	Laundress
36		94	104	Tuncap, Francisca D	Daughter	F	Cha	11.0	S	Y	Y	Y	Guam	Guam	Guam	Y	None
37		94	104	Tuncap, Felicita D	Daughter	F	Cha	6.0	S	N			Guam	Guam	Guam		None
38		95	105	Gutierrez, Domingo N	Head	M	Fil	43.0	M		Y	Y	Guam	Luzon	Guam	N	Farmer
39		95	105	Gutierrez, Rosa D	Wife	F	Cha	41.0	M		N	N	Guam	Unknown	Unknown	N	None
40		95	105	Gutierrez, Jose D	Son	M	Fil	18.0	S	N	Y	Y	Guam	Guam	Guam	Y	None
41		95	105	Gutierrez, Soledad D	Daughter	F	Cha	8.0	S	Y			Guam	Guam	Guam		None
42		95	105	Gutierrez, Leonila D	Daughter	F	Cha	5.0	S	N			Guam	Guam	Guam		None
43		96	106	Oracion, Maria C	Head	F	Cha	60.0	Wd				Guam	Guam	Guam	N	None
44		96	106	Cruz, Antonio C	Son	M	Cha	23.0	S		Y	Y	Guam	Unknown	Unknown	Y	Seaman USN
45		97	107	Flores, Ana L	Head	F	Cha	59.0	Wd		Y	Y	Guam	Guam	Guam	N	None
46		97	107	Flores, Maria L	Daughter	F	Cha	30.0	S		Y	Y	Guam	Guam	Guam	N	None
47		97	107	Flores, Concepcion L	Daughter	F	Cha	22.0	S		Y	Y	Guam	Guam	Guam	Y	None
48		97	107	Flores, Jesus L	Son	M	Cha	20.0	S	N	Y	Y	Guam	Guam	Guam	Y	Seaman USN
49		97	107	Flores, Jose L	Son	M	Cha	17.0	S	N	Y	Y	Guam	Guam	Guam	Y	Laborer
50		97	107	Flores, Manuel F	Grandson	M	Cha	5.0	S	N			Guam	Unknown	Guam		None

(CHAMORRO ROOTS GENEALOGY PROJECT ™ TRANSCRIPTION)
(COMPILED/TRANSCRIBED BY BERNARD T. PUNZALAN / HTTP://WWW.CHAMORROROOTS.COM)

FOURTEENTH CENSUS OF THE UNITED STATES: 1920—POPULATION

ISLAND OF GUAM

DISTRICT 2

NAME OF PLACE Anigua – Agana City

[Proper name and, also, name of class, as city, town, village, barrio, etc]

ENUMERATED BY ME ON THE 19th DAY OF April, 1920

Vicente Tydingco ENUMERATOR

	PLACE OF ABODE			NAME	RELATION	PERSONAL DESCRIPTION					EDUCATION			NATIVITY				OCCUPATION
Street, avenue, road, etc.	Number of dwelling house is order of visitation	Number of family in order of visitation		of each person whose place of abode on January 1, 1920, was in the family. Enter surname, firs, then given name and middle initial. If any. Include every person living on January 1, 1920. Omit children born since January 1, 1920.	Relationship of this Person to the head of the family.	Sex	Color or race	Age at last birthday	Single, married, widowed or divorced	Attended school any time since Sept. 1, 1919	Whether able to read.	Whether able to write.	Place of birth of this person.	Place of birth of father of this person.	Place of birth of mother of this person.	Whether able to speak English.	Trade, profession, or particular kind of work done, as salesman, laborer, clerk, cook, merchant, washerwoman, etc.
1	2	3	4		5	6	7	8	9	10	11	12	13	14	15	16	17
	98	108	1	Lujan, Mariano LG	Head	M	Cha	28.0	M		Y	Y	Guam	Guam	Guam	Y	Blacksmith
	98	108	2	Lujan, Ana F	Wife	F	Cha	27.0	M		Y	Y	Guam	Guam	Guam	Y	None
	99	109	3	Salas, Agapito N	Head	M	Cha	34.0	M		Y	Y	Guam	Guam	Guam	Y	Seaman USN
	99	109	4	Salas, Soledad A	Wife	F	Cha	35.0	M		N	N	Guam	Guam	Guam	N	None
	99	109	5	Salas, Vicente A	Son	M	Cha	13.0	S	Y	Y	Y	Guam	Guam	Guam	Y	None
	99	109	6	Salas, Juan A	Son	M	Cha	12.0	S	Y	Y	Y	Guam	Guam	Guam	N	None
	99	109	7	Salas, Jesus A	Son	M	Cha	8.0	S	Y			Guam	Guam	Guam	N	None
	99	109	8	Salas, Dolores A	Daughter	F	Cha	7.0	S				Guam	Guam	Guam	N	None
	99	109	9	Salas, Enrique A	Son	M	Cha	4.0	S				Guam	Guam	Guam	N	None
	99	109	10	Salas, Venancio A	Son	M	Cha	2.0	S				Guam	Guam	Guam	N	None
Agana Pitt Road	99	109	11	Salas, Ignacio N	Brother	M	Cha	25.0	S	N	Y	Y	Guam	Guam	Guam	Y	Seaman USN
	100	110	12	Gutierez, Esiquiel N	Head	M	Fil	45.0	M		Y	Y	Guam	Luzon	Guam	N	Farmer
	100	110	13	Gutierez, Maria T	Wife	F	Cha	44.0	M		Y	Y	Guam	Unknown	Guam	N	None
	100	110	14	Gutierez, Maria T jr	Daughter	F	Fil	17.0	S	N	Y	Y	Guam	Guam	Guam	Y	None
	100	110	15	Gutierez, Jesus T	Son	M	Fil	14.0	S	Y	Y	Y	Guam	Guam	Guam	Y	None
	100	110	16	Taijeron, Francisca	Mother in law	F	Cha	65.0	S		N	N	Guam	Unknown	Guam	N	None
	101	111	17	Salas, Vicente E	Head	M	Cha	59.0	M		N	N	Guam	Guam	Guam	N	Shoemaker
	101	111	18	Salas, Maria M	Wife	F	Cha	56.0	M		Y	Y	Guam	Guam	Guam	N	None
	101	112	19	Cruz, Joaquin M	Head	M	Cha	27.0	M		N	N	Guam	Guam	Guam	N	Laborer
	101	112	20	Cruz, Maria S	Wife	F	Cha	29.0	M		Y	Y	Guam	Guam	Guam	N	None
	101	112	21	Cruz, Joaquin S	Son	M	Cha	15.0	S	N	N	N	Guam	Guam	Guam	N	None
	101	112	22	Cruz, Regina S	Daughter	F	Cha	7.0	S	N			Guam	Guam	Guam	N	None
	101	112	23	Cruz, Antonia S	Daughter	F	Cha	4.0	S				Guam	Guam	Guam	N	None
	101	112	24	Cruz, Juan S	Son	M	Cha	1.0	S				Guam	Guam	Guam	N	None
	101	112	25	Lizama, Juan SN	Servant	M	Cha	20.0	S	N	Y	Y	Guam	Guam	Guam	Y	Servant

(CHAMORRO ROOTS GENEALOGY PROJECT ™ TRANSCRIPTION)
(COMPILED/TRANSCRIBED BY BERNARD T. PUNZALAN / HTTP://WWW.CHAMORROROOTS.COM)

FOURTEENTH CENSUS OF THE UNITED STATES: 1920—POPULATION

ISLAND OF GUAM

101b

DISTRICT 2

NAME OF PLACE Anigua – Agana City

ENUMERATED BY ME ON THE 19th DAY OF April, 1920

Vicente Tydingco ENUMERATOR

	Num- ber of dwell- ing house (2)	Num- ber of family (3)	NAME (4)	RELATION (5)	Sex (6)	Color or race (7)	Age (8)	Single, married, widowed or divorced (9)	Attended school since Sept. 1, 1919 (10)	Whether able to read (11)	Whether able to write (12)	Place of birth of this person (13)	Place of birth of father (14)	Place of birth of mother (15)	Whether able to speak English (16)	OCCUPATION (17)
26	102	113	Tuncap, Juan O	Head	M	Fil	67.0	M		N	N	Luzon	Luzon	Luzon	N	Farmer home farm
27	102	113	Tuncap, Escolastica N	Wife	F	Cha	58.0	M		N	N	Guam	Guam	Guam	N	None
28	102	113	Tuncap, Juan N	Son	M	Fil	37.0	D		Y	Y	Guam	Luzon	Guam	N	Fisherman
29	102	113	Tuncap, Dolores N	Daughter	F	Fil	28.0	S		Y	Y	Guam	Luzon	Guam	Y	None
30	102	113	Tuncap, Clemente N	Son	M	Fil	17.0	S	N	Y	Y	Guam	Luzon	Guam	Y	Farmer
31	102	113	Tuncap, Maria N	Daughter	F	Fil	14.0	S	N	Y	Y	Guam	Luzon	Guam	N	None
32	102	113	Tuncap, Concepcion N	Daughter	F	Fil	11.0	s	Y	Y	Y	Guam	Luzon	Guam	N	None
33	102	113	Tuncap, Delfina T	Grand daughter	F	Cha	4.0	S				Guam	Unknown	Guam		None
34	102	113	Tuncap, Jesus T	Grandson	M	Cha	0.6	S				Guam	Unknown	Guam		None
35	102	113	Fegurgur, Ana F	Servant	F	Cha	18.0	S	N	Y	Y	Guam	Unknown	Guam	Y	Servant
36	103	114	Cruz, Jose P	Head	M	Cha	22.0	M		Y	Y	Guam	Guam	Guam	Y	Seaman USN
37	103	114	Cruz, Concepcion A	Wife	F	Cha	18.0	M	N	Y	Y	Guam	Guam	Guam	Y	None
38	103	114	Angoco, Agustina C	Mother in law	F	Cha	36.0	Wd		Y	Y	Guam	Guam	Guam	Y	None
39	103	114	Angoco, Teodora C	Sister in law	F	Cha	16.0	S	N	Y	Y	Guam	Guam	Guam	N	None
40	104	115	Quitonguico, Pedro Q	Head	M	Cha	48.0	M		N	N	Guam	Guam	Guam	N	Farmer
41	104	115	Quitonguico, Simona F	Wife	F	Cha	58.0	M		N	N	Guam	Guam	Guam	N	None
42	104	115	Fegurgur, Victoriana F	Step daughter	F	Cha	26.0	S		N	N	Guam	Unknown	Guam	N	None
43	104	115	Fegurgur, Isabel F	Grand daughter	F	Cha	7.0	S	N			Guam	Unknown	Guam		None
44	104	115	Fegurgur, Francisco F	Grand son	M	Cha	4.0	S				Guam	Unknown	Guam		None
45	105	116	Namauleg, Maria T	Head	F	Cha	53.0	Wd		N	N	Guam	Guam	Guam	N	Farmer home farm
46	105	116	Namauleg, Eufracia Q	Daughter	F	Cha	12.0	S	Y	Y	Y	Guam	Guam	Guam	Y	None
47	106	117	Lizama, Felix	Head	M	Cha	30.0	M		Y	Y	Guam	Unknown	Guam	N	Farmer
48	106	117	Lizama, Maria A	Wife	F	Cha	30.0	M		N	N	Guam	Unknown	Guam	N	None
49	106	117	Lizama, Jose A	Son	M	Cha	3.0	S				Guam	Guam	Guam		None
50	106	117	Lizama, Francisco A	Son	M	Cha	0.1	S				Guam	Guam	Guam		None

Street: Agana Pitt Road

207

SHEET NO.
50A

(CHAMORRO ROOTS GENEALOGY PROJECT ™ TRANSCRIPTION)
(COMPILED/TRANSCRIBED BY BERNARD T. PUNZALAN / HTTP://WWW.CHAMORROROOTS.COM)
FOURTEENTH CENSUS OF THE UNITED STATES: 1920-POPULATION
ISLAND OF GUAM

ENUMERATED BY ME ON THE 19th DAY OF April, 1920

Vicente Tydingco ENUMERATOR

DISTRICT 2
NAME OF PLACE Anigua – Agana City
[Proper name and, also, name of class, as city, town, village, barrio, etc]

Street, avenue, road, etc.	Number of dwelling house is order of visitation	Number of family in order of visitation	NAME	RELATION	Sex	Color or race	Age at last birthday	Single, married, widowed or divorced	Attended school any time since Sept. 1, 1919	Whether able to read	Whether able to write	Place of birth of this person	Place of birth of father of this person	Place of birth of mother of this person	Whether able to speak English	OCCUPATION
1	2	3	4	5	6	7	8	9	10	11	12	13	14	15	16	17
	106	117	Lizama, Ignacio L	Cousin	M	Cha	31.0	S		Y	Y	Guam	Unknown	Guam	Yes	None
	107	118	Marcelo, Julian	Head	M	Fil	90.0	Wd		Y	Y	Luzon	Luzon	Luzon	N	Home farm
	107	118	Nauta, Maria N	Step daughter	F	Cha	50.0	S		N	N	Guam	Unknown	Guam	N	None
	107	118	Nauta, Magdalena N	Step daughter	F	Cha	25.0	S		Y	Y	Guam	Unknown	Guam	N	None
Agana Pitt Road	108	119	Nauta, Jesus N	Head	M	Cha	32.0	M		Y	Y	Guam	Unknown	Guam	N	Laborer
	108	119	Nauta, Francisca T	Wife	F	Cha	36.0	M		N	N	Guam	Unknown	Guam		None
	108	119	Nauta, Carmen T	Daughter	F	Cha	8.0	S				Guam	Guam	Guam		None
	108	119	Nauta, Pedro T	Son	M	Cha	4.0	S				Guam	Guam	Guam		None
	108	119	Nauta, Paulina T	Daughter	F	Cha	3.0	S				Guam	Guam	Guam		None
	109	120	Cruz, Domingo A	Head	M	Cha	24.0	M		Y	Y	Guam	Guam	Guam	N	Laborer
	109	120	Cruz, Carmen N	Wife	F	Cha	26.0	M		Y	Y	Guam	Unknown	Guam	N	None
	109	120	Cruz, Jose N	Son	M	Cha	3.0	S				Guam	Guam	Guam		None
	109	120	Cruz, Juan N	Son	M	Cha	2.0	S				Guam	Guam	Guam		None
	109	120	Cruz, Rita N	Daughter	F	Cha	0.8	S				Guam	Guam	Guam		None
	110	121	Materne, Juan	Head	M	Cha	27.0	M		Y	Y	Guam	Unknown	Guam	N	Farmer
	110	121	Materne, Potenciana C	Wife	F	Cha	23.0	S		Y	Y	Guam	Guam	Guam	Y	None
	110	121	Materne, Teresa C	Daughter	F	Cha	5.0	S	N			Guam	Guam	Guam		None
	110	121	Materne, Mercedes C	Daughter	F	Cha	3.0	S				Guam	Guam	Guam		None
	110	121	Materne, Domingo C	Son	M	Cha	1.0	S				Guam	Guam	Guam		None
	110	121	Materne, Francisca M	Mother	F	Cha	65.0	S		N	N	Guam	Unknown	Guam		None
	111	122	Mendiola, Ignacio B	Head	M	Cha	78.0	Wd		Y	Y	Guam	Guam	Guam	Y	Farmer home farm
	112	123	Concepcion, Ana C	Head	F	Cha	30.0	D		N	N	Guam	Guam	Guam	N	Laundress
	112	123	Concepcion, Candelaria C	Daughter	F	Cha	16.0	S	N	Y	Y	Guam	Guam	Guam	Y	Servant
	112	123	Concepcion, Asuncion C	Daughter	F	Cha	12.0	S	N	Y	Y	Guam	Guam	Guam	N	None
	112	123	Concepcion, Felecidad C	Daughter	F	Cha	10.0	S	Y	Y	Y	Guam	Guam	Guam	Y	None

208

(CHAMORRO ROOTS GENEALOGY PROJECT ™ TRANSCRIPTION)
(COMPILED/TRANSCRIBED BY BERNARD T. PUNZALAN / HTTP://WWW.CHAMORROROOTS.COM)
FOURTEENTH CENSUS OF THE UNITED STATES: 1920–POPULATION
ISLAND OF GUAM

DISTRICT 2
NAME OF PLACE Anigua – Agana City

ENUMERATED BY ME ON THE 20th DAY OF April, 1920

Vicente Tydingco ENUMERATOR

[Proper name and, also, name of class, as city, town, village, barrio, etc]

	2	3	4 NAME	5 RELATION	6 Sex	7 Color or race	8 Age at last birthday	9 Single, married, widowed or divorced	10 Attended school any time since Sept. 1, 1919	11 Whether able to read	12 Whether able to write	13 Place of birth of this person	14 Place of birth of father	15 Place of birth of mother	16 Whether able to speak English	17 OCCUPATION
26	112	123	Concepcion, Dolores C	Daughter	F	Cha	8.0	S	Y			Guam	Guam	Guam		None
27	112	123	Cruz, Maria A	Sister	F	Cha	29.0	S		N	N	Guam	Guam	Guam	N	Laundress
28	112	123	Cruz, Joaquina C	Niece	F	Cha	10.0	S	Y	Y	Y	Guam	Unknown	Guam	N	None
29	112	123	Cruz, Juan C	Nephew	M	Cha	3.0	S				Guam	Unknown	Guam		None
30	112	123	Cruz, Dolores C	Niece	F	Cha	0.3	S				Guam	Unknown	Guam		None
31	113	124	Mendiola, Juan B	Head	M	Cha	48.0	D		Y	Y	Guam	Unknown	Guam	N	Farm laborer
32	114	125	Guerrero, Jose C	Head	M	Cha	41.0	M		Y	Y	Guam	Guam	Guam	N	Farmer
33	114	125	Guerrero, Joaquina R	Wife	F	Cha	40.0	M		N	N	Guam	Guam	Guam	N	None
34	115	126	Reyes, Jesus R	Head	M	Cha	23.0	M		Y	Y	Guam	Unknown	Guam	Y	Laborer
35	115	126	Reyes, Maria SA	Wife	F	Cha	23.0	M		N	N	Guam	Unknown	Guam	N	None
36	115	126	Reyes, Francisco SA	Son	M	Cha	2.0	S				Guam	Guam	Guam		None
37	115	126	Reyes, Luis SA	Son	M	Cha	0.1	S				Guam	Guam	Guam		None
38	115	126	Reyes, Ramon R	Brother	M	Cha	15.0	S	N	N	N	Guam	Unknown	Guam	N	None
39	115	126	Babauta, Vicente R	Brother	M	Cha	7.0	S	N			Guam	Guam	Guam		None
40	115	126	Babauta, Manuel R	Brother	M	Cha	6.0	S	N			Guam	Guam	Guam		None
41	116	127	Ignacio, Francisco C	Head	M	Cha	27.0	M		N	N	Guam	Guam	Guam	N	Laborer
42	116	127	Ignacio, Trinidad R	Wife	F	Cha	26.0	M		N	N	Guam	Guam	Guam	N	None
43	117	128	Gumataotao, Joaquin M	Head	M	Cha	54.0	M		Y	Y	Guam	Guam	Guam	N	Farmer
44	117	128	Gumataotao, Ramona T	Wife	F	Cha	43.0	M		N	N	Guam	Guam	Guam	N	None
45	117	128	Gumataotao, Isabel T	Daughter	F	Cha	16.0	S	N	Y	Y	Guam	Guam	Guam	Y	None
46	117	128	Gumataotao, Atanasio T	Son	M	Cha	12.0	S	Y	Y	Y	Guam	Guam	Guam	Y	None
47	117	128	Gumataotao, Juan T	Son	M	Cha	7.0	S	Y			Guam	Guam	Guam		None
48	117	128	Gumataotao, Vicente T	Son	M	Cha	4.0	S				Guam	Guam	Guam		None
49	117	128	Gumataotao, Jose T	Son	M	Cha	2.0	S				Guam	Guam	Guam		None
50	117	128	S. Nicolas, Josefa	Niece	F	Cha	24.0	S		Y	Y	Guam	Unknown	Guam	Y	None

Column 1 (Street, avenue, road, etc.): Agana Pati Road

(CHAMORRO ROOTS GENEALOGY PROJECT ™ TRANSCRIPTION)
(COMPILED/TRANSCRIBED BY BERNARD T. PUNZALAN / HTTP://WWW.CHAMORROROOTS.COM)

FOURTEENTH CENSUS OF THE UNITED STATES: 1920-POPULATION

ISLAND OF GUAM

ENUMERATED BY ME ON THE 20th DAY OF April, 1920

Vicente Tydingco ENUMERATOR

DISTRICT 2

NAME OF PLACE Aniqua – Agana City

[Proper name and, also, name of class, as city, town, village, barrio, etc]

Street: Agana Pitt Road

#	Dwelling house no. (2)	Family no. (3)	NAME (4)	RELATION (5)	Sex (6)	Color or race (7)	Age (8)	Single, married, widowed or divorced (9)	Attended school since Sept. 1, 1919 (10)	Able to read (11)	Able to write (12)	Place of birth of this person (13)	Place of birth of father (14)	Place of birth of mother (15)	Able to speak English (16)	OCCUPATION (17)
1	117	128	Aguigui, Juan	Nephew	M	Cha	11.0	S	Y	Y	Y	Guam	Unknown	Guam	Y	None
2	117	128	Aguon, Jose C	Servant	M	Cha	26.0	S		N	N	Guam	Guam	Guam	N	Servant
3	118	129	Perez, Maria C	Head	F	Cha	44.0	Wd		N	N	Guam	Guam	Guam	N	None
4	118	129	Perez, Dolores C	Daughter	F	Cha	22.0	S		N	N	Guam	Guam	Guam	N	None
5	118	129	Perez, Maria P	Grand daughter	F	Cha	1.0	S				Guam	Unknown	Guam	N	None
6	119	130	Taimanglo, Mariano F	Head	M	Cha	51.0	M		Y	Y	Guam	Guam	Guam	N	Farmer
7	119	130	Taimanglo, Rita T	Wife	F	Cha	50.0	M		N	N	Guam	Guam	Guam	N	None
8	120	131	Terlaje, Vicente S	Head	M	Cha	48.0	M		Y	Y	Guam	Unknown	Guam	N	Farmer
9	120	131	Terlaje, Josefa S	Wife	F	Cha	48.0	M		N	N	Guam	Guam	Guam	N	None
10	120	131	Terlaje, Maria S	Daughter	F	Cha	19.0	S	N	Y	Y	Guam	Guam	Guam	Y	None
11	120	131	Terlaje, Vicenta S	Daughter	F	Cha	18.0	S	N	Y	Y	Guam	Guam	Guam	Y	None
12	120	131	Terlaje, Jesus S	Son	M	Cha	12.0	S	N	Y	Y	Guam	Guam	Guam	N	None
13	120	131	Terlaje, Rosalia S	Daughter	F	Cha	9.0	S	Y	Y	Y	Guam	Guam	Guam	N	None
14	120	131	Terlaje, Juan S	Son	M	Cha	8.0	S	Y			Guam	Guam	Guam	N	None
15	120	131	Laguana, Ignacia C	Aunt	F	Cha	70.0	Wd		N	N	Guam	Guam	Guam	N	None
16	121	132	Cruz, Antonio R	Head	M	Cha	48.0	M		Y	Y	Guam	Guam	Guam	N	Farmer
17	121	132	Cruz, Rosa I	Wife	F	Cha	46.0	M		Y	Y	Guam	Guam	Guam	N	None
18	121	132	Cruz, Antonio I	Son	M	Cha	15.0	S	Y	Y	Y	Guam	Guam	Guam	Y	None
19	121	132	Cruz, Manuel I	Son	M	Cha	14.0	S	Y	Y	Y	Guam	Guam	Guam	Y	None
20	121	132	Cruz, Maria I	Daughter	F	Cha	12.0	S	Y	Y	Y	Guam	Guam	Guam	Y	None
21	121	132	Cruz, Jose I	Son	M	Cha	5.0	S	N			Guam	Guam	Guam	N	None
22	122	133	Palomo, Getrudes T	Head	F	Cha	47.0	Wd		Y	Y	Guam	Guam	Guam	N	None
23	122	133	Palomo, Carmen T	Daughter	F	Cha	20.0	S	N	N	N	Guam	Guam	Guam	N	None
24	122	133	Palomo, Dominga T	Daughter	F	Cha	18.0	S	N	Y	Y	Guam	Guam	Guam	Y	None
25	122	133	Palomo, Jose T	Son	M	Cha	16.0	S	N	Y	Y	Guam	Guam	Guam	Y	Farmer

(CHAMORRO ROOTS GENEALOGY PROJECT ™ TRANSCRIPTION)
(COMPILED/TRANSCRIBED BY BERNARD T. PUNZALAN / HTTP://WWW.CHAMORROROOTS.COM)
FOURTEENTH CENSUS OF THE UNITED STATES: 1920-POPULATION
ISLAND OF GUAM

DISTRICT 2
NAME OF PLACE Anigua – Agana City

ENUMERATED BY ME ON THE 21st DAY OF April, 1920

Vicente Tydingco ENUMERATOR

[Proper name and, also, name of class, as city, town, village, barrio, etc]

	PLACE OF ABODE		NAME	RELATION	PERSONAL DESCRIPTION				EDUCATION			NATIVITY				OCCUPATION
Street, avenue, road, etc.	Number of dwelling house in order of visitation	Number of family in order of visitation			Sex	Color or race	Age at last birthday	Single, married, widowed or divorced	Attended any school since Sept. 1, 1919	Whether able to read.	Whether able to write.	Place of birth of this person.	Place of birth of father of this person.	Place of birth of mother of this person.	Whether able to speak English.	Trade, profession, or particular kind of work done, as salesman, laborer, clerk, cook, merchant, washerwoman, etc.
1	2	3	4	5	6	7	8	9	10	11	12	13	14	15	16	17
	122	133	Palomo, Ignacio T	Son	M	Cha	15.0	S	N	Y	Y	Guam	Guam	Guam	Y	Farm laborer home farm
	122	133	Palomo, Francisco P	Grandson	M	Cha	2.0	S				Guam	Unknown	Guam		None
	122	133	Palomo, Juan P	Grandson	M	Cha	2.0	S				Guam	Unknown	Guam		None
	122	133	Palomo, Rufina P	Grand daughter	F	Cha	0.2	S				Guam	Unknown	Guam		None
	123	134	Crisostomo, Pedro C	Head	M	Cha	37.0	M		Y	Y	Guam	Unknown	Guam	N	Farmer
	123	134	Crisostomo, Maria A	Wife	F	Cha	46.0	M		N	N	Guam	Guam	Guam	N	None
	123	134	Crisostomo, Jose A	Son	M	Cha	12.0	S	Y	Y	Y	Guam	Guam	Guam	Y	None
	123	134	Crisostomo, Josefa A	Daughter	F	Cha	6.0	S	N			Guam	Guam	Guam		None
Agana Piti Road	124	135	Ungacta, Domingo P	Head	M	Cha	42.0	M		Y	Y	Guam	Guam	Guam	N	Farmer
	124	135	Ungacta, Maria I	Wife	F	Cha	42.0	M		Y	Y	Guam	Guam	Guam	N	None
	124	135	Ungacta, Antonio I	Son	M	Cha	12.0	S	Y	Y	Y	Guam	Guam	Guam	Y	None
	124	135	Ungacta, Juan I	Son	M	Cha	10.0	S	Y	Y	Y	Guam	Guam	Guam	Y	None
	124	135	Ungacta, Maria I	Daughter	F	Cha	8.0	S	Y	Y	Y	Guam	Guam	Guam		None
	124	135	Ungacta, Servino I	Son	M	Cha	6.0	S	N			Guam	Guam	Guam		None
	124	135	Ungacta, Ana I	Daughter	F	Cha	4.0	S				Guam	Guam	Guam		None
	124	135	Ungacta, Trinidad I	Daughter	F	Cha	0.9	S				Guam	Guam	Guam		None
	125	136	Blas, Matias P	Head	M	Cha	55.0	Wd		N	N	Guam	Guam	Guam	Y	Farm laborer
	125	136	Alejandro, Martin	Boarder	M	Fil	28.0	S		Y	Y	Luzon	Luzon	Luzon	N	None
	126	137	Lorenzo, Estanislao SN	Head	M	Fil	33.0	M		N	N	Luzon	Luzon	Luzon	Y	Farmer
	126	137	Lorenzo, Rosa A	Wife	F	Cha	33.0	M		N	N	Guam	Guam	Guam	N	None
	126	137	Lorenzo, Cleotilde A	Daughter	F	Fil	10.0	S	Y	Y	Y	Guam	Luzon	Guam	Y	None
	126	137	Lorenzo, Gutierez A	Son	M	Fil	5.0	S	N			Guam	Luzon	Guam		None
	126	137	Lorenzo, Prudencia A	Daughter	F	Fil	1.0	S				Guam	Luzon	Guam		None
	127	138	Ignacio, Jesus R	Head	M	Cha	28.0	M		Y	Y	Guam	Guam	Guam	N	Farmer
	127	138	Ignacio, Consolacion M	Wife	F	Cha	20.0	M		Y	Y	Guam	Unknown	Guam	N	None

(Row numbers 26–50)

211

(CHAMORRO ROOTS GENEALOGY PROJECT ™ TRANSCRIPTION)
(COMPILED/TRANSCRIBED BY BERNARD T. PUNZALAN / HTTP://WWW.CHAMORROROOTS.COM)

FOURTEENTH CENSUS OF THE UNITED STATES: 1920—POPULATION
ISLAND OF GUAM

ENUMERATED BY ME ON THE 21st DAY OF April, 1920

Vicente Tydingco ENUMERATOR

DISTRICT 2
NAME OF PLACE Anigua – Agana City
[Proper name and, also, name of class, as city, town, village, barrio, etc]

	Dwelling (2)	Family (3)	NAME (4)	RELATION (5)	Sex (6)	Color or race (7)	Age (8)	Single, married, widowed, divorced (9)	Attended school (10)	Read (11)	Write (12)	Birthplace (13)	Father's birthplace (14)	Mother's birthplace (15)	Speak English (16)	OCCUPATION (17)
1	127	138	Ignacio, Enrique M	Son	M	Cha	5.0	S	N			Guam	Guam	Guam		None
2	127	138	Ignacio, Maria M	Daughter	F	Cha	3.0	S				Guam	Guam	Guam		None
3	127	138	Ignacio, Regina M	Daughter	F	Cha	2.0	S				Guam	Guam	Guam		None
4	127	138	Ignacio, Jose R	Brother	M	Cha	24.0	S		Y	Y	Guam	Guam	Guam		Farm laborer
5	127	138	Merfalen, Rosa Q	Mother in law	F	Cha	55.0	Wd		N	N	Guam	Guam	Guam		None
6	128	139	Cruz, Manuel A	Head	M	Cha	53.0	M		Y	Y	Guam	Guam	Guam		Farmer
7	128	139	Cruz, Ana M	Wife	F	Cha	55.0	M		N	N	Guam	Unknown	Guam	N	None
8	128	139	Cruz, Jose M	Son	M	Cha	24.0	S		Y	Y	Guam	Guam	Guam	N	None
9	128	139	Cruz, Maria M	Daughter	F	Cha	17.0	S	N	N	N	Guam	Guam	Guam	N	None
10	128	139	Cruz, Jesus M	Son	M	Cha	13.0	S	N	Y	Y	Guam	Guam	Guam	N	Farm laborer home farm
11	129	140	Hennicker, George C	Head	M	W	28.0	M		Y	Y	Ohio	Germany	Germany	Y	Labor foreman
12	129	140	Hennicker, Ignacia LG	Wife	F	Cha	24.0	M		Y	Y	Guam	Unknown	Guam	Y	None
13	129	140	Charfauros, Rosa B	Servant	F	Cha	20.0	S	N	Y	Y	Guam	Guam	Guam	Y	Servant
14	130	141	Nelson, Peter	Head	M	W	39.0	Wd		Y	Y	New York	Denmark	Denmark	Y	Clerk
15	130	141	Nelson, Henry	Son	M	W	14.0	S	Y	Y	Y	Guam	New York	Guam	Y	None
16	130	141	Nelson, Margaret	Daughter	F	W	13.0	S	Y	Y	Y	Guam	New York	Guam	Y	None
17	130	141	Nelson, Peter M	Son	M	W	11.0	S	Y	Y	Y	Guam	New York	Guam	Y	None
18	130	141	Nelson, Catherine C	Daughter	F	W	8.0	S	Y	Y	Y	Guam	New York	Guam	Y	None
19	130	141	Nelson, Florence	Daughter	F	W	7.0	S	Y			Guam	New York	Guam		None
20	130	141	Aguon, Ana F	Mother in law	F	Cha	63.0	Wd		Y	Y	Guam	Guam	Guam	N	None
21	130	141	Aguon, Maria F	Aunt	F	Cha	55.0	S		Y	Y	Guam	Guam	Guam	N	None

Street (column 1): Agana Pitt Road

Here ends the enumeration of Anigua – Agana City

(CHAMORRO ROOTS GENEALOGY PROJECT ™ TRANSCRIPTION)
(COMPILED/TRANSCRIBED BY BERNARD T. PUNZALAN / HTTP://WWW.CHAMORROROOTS.COM)

FOURTEENTH CENSUS OF THE UNITED STATES: 1920—POPULATION

ISLAND OF GUAM

DISTRICT **2**

NAME OF PLACE **Agana (City)**

[Proper name and, also, name of class, as city, town, village, barrio, etc]

ENUMERATED BY ME ON THE 24th DAY OF February, 1920

Arthur W. Jackson ENUMERATOR

	Street, avenue, road, etc.	Number of dwelling house in order of visitation	Number of family in order of visitation	NAME	RELATION	Sex	Color or race	Age at last birthday	Single, married, widowed or divorced	Attended school any time since Sept. 1, 1919	Whether able to read.	Whether able to write.	Place of birth of this person.	Place of birth of father of this person.	Place of birth of mother of this person.	Whether able to speak English.	OCCUPATION
	1	2	3	4	5	6	7	8	9	10	11	12	13	14	15	16	17
1		1	1	Guzman, Francisco H	Head	M	Cha	55.0	S		Y	Y	Guam	Guam	Guam	N	Farmer
2		1	1	Guzman, Emeliana P	Wife	F	Cha	46.0	S		Y	Y	Guam	Guam	Guam	N	None
3		1	1	Guzman, Jose P	Son	M	Cha	14.0	S	N	Y	Y	Guam	Guam	Guam	Y	Laborer
4		1	1	Guzman, Amalia P	Daughter	F	Cha	13.0	S	N	Y	Y	Guam	Guam	Guam	Y	None
5		1	1	Guzman, Agnes P	Daughter	F	Cha	13.0	S	N	Y	Y	Guam	Guam	Guam	Y	None
6		1	1	Guzman, Mercedes P	Daughter	F	Cha	11.0	S	Y	Y	Y	Guam	Guam	Guam	Y	None
7		1	1	Guzman, Pilar P	Daughter	F	Cha	9.0	S	Y			Guam	Guam	Guam		None
8		1	1	Guzman, Maria P	Daughter	F	Cha	7.0	S	Y			Guam	Guam	Guam		None
9		1	1	Guzman, Juan P	Son	M	Cha	4.0	S				Guam	Guam	Guam		None
10		1	2	Aflague, Concepcion L	Head	F	Cha	20.0	M	N	Y	Y	Guam	Guam	Guam	N	None
11	Soledad Street	1	2	Aflague, Fermin S	Son	M	Cha	0.2	S				Guam	Guam	Guam		None
12		2	3	Reyes, Macario B	Head	M	Fil	50.0	M		Y	Y	Philippine Islands	Philippine Islands	Philippine Islands	N	Farmer
13		2	3	Reyes, Josefa C	Wife	F	Cha	44.0	M		N	N	Guam	Guam	Guam	N	None
14		2	3	Reyes, Antonia B	Daughter	F	Fil	19.0	S	N	Y	Y	Guam	Philippine Islands	Guam	N	Laundress
15		2	3	Reyes, Juan B	Son	M	Fil	15.0	S	Y	Y	Y	Guam	Philippine Islands	Guam	Y	Farm laborer
16		2	3	Reyes, Regina B	Daughter	F	Cha	7.0	S	N	Y	Y	Guam	Philippine Islands	Guam		None
17		2	4	Pangelinan, Juana B	Head	F	Cha	20.0	M	N	Y	Y	Guam	Philippine Islands	Guam	N	Laundress
18		2	4	Pangelinan, Maria B	Daughter	F	Cha	4.0	S				Guam	Unknown	Guam		None
19		2	4	Pangelinan, Barsalisa B	Daughter	F	Cha	3.0	S				Guam	Unknown	Guam		None
20		3	5	Perez, Joaquin C	Head	M	Cha	28.0	M		Y	Y	Guam	Guam	Guam	Y	Carpenter
21		3	5	Perez, Ana B	Wife	F	Cha	26.0	M		Y	Y	Guam	Philippine Islands	Guam	N	None
22		3	5	Perez, Ignacio B	Son	M	Cha	8.0	S				Guam	Guam	Guam		None
23		3	5	Perez, Degadina B	Daughter	F	Cha	5.0	S				Guam	Guam	Guam		None
24		3	5	Perez, Francisco B	Son	M	Cha	4.0	S				Guam	Guam	Guam		None
25		3	5	Perez, Engracia B	Daughter	F	Cha	2.0	S				Guam	Guam	Guam		None

PERSONAL DESCRIPTION — **EDUCATION** — **NATIVITY**

Place of birth of each person and parents of each person enumerated. If born in the United States, give the state or territory. If of foreign birth, give country of birth.

OCCUPATION — Trade, profession, or particular kind of work done, as salesman, laborer, clerk, cook, merchant, washerwoman, etc.

(CHAMORRO ROOTS GENEALOGY PROJECT ™ TRANSCRIPTION)
(COMPILED/TRANSCRIBED BY BERNARD T. PUNZALAN / HTTP://WWW.CHAMORROROOTS.COM)

FOURTEENTH CENSUS OF THE UNITED STATES: 1920-POPULATION
ISLAND OF GUAM

ENUMERATED BY ME ON THE 24th DAY OF February, 1920

Arthur W. Jackson ENUMERATOR

DISTRICT 2
NAME OF PLACE Agana (City)

	1	2	3	4	5	6	7	8	9	10	11	12	13	14	15	16	17
	Street	Dwelling house no.	Family no.	NAME	RELATION	Sex	Color or race	Age at last birthday	Single, married, widowed or divorced	Attended school since Sept. 1, 1919	Whether able to read	Whether able to write	Place of birth of this person	Place of birth of father	Place of birth of mother	Whether able to speak English	OCCUPATION
26		3	5	Perez, Antonio B	Son	M	Cha	0.5	S				Guam	Guam	Guam		None
27		3	6	Castro, Lucia C	Head	F	Cha	29.0	S		N	N	Guam	Guam	Guam	Y	Laundress
28		3	6	Castro, Brigida C	Daughter	F	Cha	3.0	S				Guam	Unknown	Guam		None
29		3	6	Castro, Maria C	Daughter	F	Cha	1.0	S				Guam	Unknown	Guam		None
30		4	7	Franquez, Manuel I	Head	M	Cha	24.0	M		Y	Y	Guam	Guam	Guam	Y	Bookkeeper
31		4	7	Franquez, Rosalia P	Wife	F	Cha	17.0	M	Y	Y	Y	Guam	Guam	Guam	Y	Teacher
32		4	7	Franquez, George J	Son	M	Cha	1.0	S				Guam	Guam	Guam		None
33	Soledad Street	4	7	Pangelinan, Francisco	Brother-in-law	M	Cha	23.0	S	N	Y	Y	Guam	Guam	Guam		Musician US Navy
34		4	7	Mafnas, Jesus F	Servant	M	Cha	16.0	S		Y	Y	Guam	Guam	Guam		Servant
35		5	8	Reyes, Ignacia	Head	F	Cha	46.0	Wd		N	N	Guam	Guam	Guam	N	Laundress
36		6	9	Santos, Maria	Head	F	Cha	53.0	Wd		Y	Y	Guam	Guam	Guam	N	None
37		6	9	Santos, Ana LG	Daughter	F	Cha	25.0	S		Y	Y	Guam	Guam	Guam	N	Laundress
38		6	9	Santos, Juan LG	Son	M	Cha	20.0	S	N	Y	Y	Guam	Guam	Guam	N	Farmer
39		6	9	Leon Guerrero, Catalina	Granddaughter	F	Cha	0.6	S				Guam	Unknown	Guam		None
40		6	9	Pablo, Juana	Mother-in-law	F	Cha	80.0	Wd		N	N	Guam	Guam	Guam	N	None
41		6	10	Leon Guerrero, Soledad S	Head	F	Cha	35.0	M		Y	Y	Guam	Guam	Guam	Y	Seamstress
42		6	10	Leon Guerrero, Jose S	Son	M	Cha	15.0	S	Y	Y	Y	Guam	Unknown	Guam	Y	None
43		6	10	Leon Guerrero, Jesus S	Son	M	Cha	13.0	S	Y	Y	Y	Guam	Unknown	Guam	N	None
44		6	10	Leon Guerrero, Maria S	Daughter	F	Cha	6.0	S	Y	Y	Y	Guam	Unknown	Guam		None
45		6	10	Leon Guerrero, Mariano S	Son	M	Cha	2.0	S				Guam	Unknown	Guam		None
46		6	11	Anderson, Joaquin M	Head	M	Cha	31.0	M		Y	Y	Guam	Guam	Guam	Y	Farmer
47		6	11	Anderson, Tomasa LG	Wife	F	Cha	27.0	M		Y	Y	Guam	Guam	Guam	N	None
48		6	11	Anderson, Fidela LG	Daughter	F	Cha	6.0	S	N			Guam	Guam	Guam		None
49		6	11	Anderson, Antonio LG	Son	M	Cha	4.0	S				Guam	Guam	Guam		None
50		6	11	Anderson, Rosario LG	Daughter	F	Cha	3.0	S				Guam	Guam	Guam		None

(CHAMORRO ROOTS GENEALOGY PROJECT ™ TRANSCRIPTION)
(COMPILED/TRANSCRIBED BY BERNARD T. PUNZALAN / HTTP://WWW.CHAMORROROOTS.COM)
FOURTEENTH CENSUS OF THE UNITED STATES: 1920—POPULATION
ISLAND OF GUAM

DISTRICT 2
NAME OF PLACE Agana (City)
[Proper name and, also, name of class, as city, town, village, barrio, etc]

ENUMERATED BY ME ON THE 24th DAY OF February, 1920

Arthur W. Jackson ENUMERATOR

Street, avenue, road, etc.	Number of dwelling house in order of visitation	Number of family in order of visitation	NAME	RELATION	Sex	Color or race	Age at last birthday	Single, married, widowed or divorced	Attended school any time since Sept. 1, 1919	Whether able to read	Whether able to write	Place of birth of this person	Place of birth of father of this person	Place of birth of mother of this person	Whether able to speak English	OCCUPATION
	1	2	3	4	5	6	7	8	9	10	11	12	13	14	15	16	17
	6	11	Anderson, Josefina LG	Daughter	F	Cha	2.0	S				Guam	Guam	Guam		None
	7	12	Santos, Francisco B	Head	M	Cha	36.0	M		Y	Y	Guam	Guam	Guam	Y	Carpenter
	7	12	Santos, Dolores R	Wife	F	Cha	29.0	M		Y	Y	Guam	Guam	Guam	N	None
	7	12	Santos, Tomas R	Son	M	Cha	10.0	S	Y	Y	Y	Guam	Guam	Guam	Y	None
	7	12	Santos, Clementina R	Daughter	F	Cha	6.0	S	N			Guam	Guam	Guam		None
	7	12	Santos, Cristobal R	Son	M	Cha	4.0	S				Guam	Guam	Guam		None
	7	12	Santos, Requiel R	Daughter	F	Cha	0.3	S				Guam	Guam	Guam		None
	7	12	Leon Guerrero, Ana	Sister in law	F	Cha	16.0	S	N	Y	Y	Guam	Guam	Guam	N	Servant
	7	13	Santos, Jose B	Head	M	Cha	52.0	M		Y	Y	Guam	Guam	Guam	N	Farmer
	7	13	Santos, Ursula B	Wife	F	Cha	52.0	M		Y	Y	Guam	Guam	Guam	N	None
	8	14	Leon Guerrero, Manuel	Head	M	Cha	31.0	M		Y	Y	Guam	Guam	Guam	N	Laborer
	8	14	Leon Guerrero, Ana P	Wife	F	Cha	27.0	M		Y	Y	Guam	Guam	Guam	N	None
	8	14	Leon Guerrero, Vicenta P	Daughter	F	Cha	0.5	S				Guam	Guam	Guam		None
	8	14	Perez, Pedro I	Father in law	M	Cha	56.0	Wd		Y	Y	Guam	Guam	Guam	N	Farmer
Soledad Street	8	14	Camacho, Carmen C	Servant	F	Cha	12.0	S	Y	Y	Y	Guam	Guam	Guam	Y	Servant
	9	15	Lujan, Soledad G	Head	F	Cha	33.0	Wd		N	N	Guam	Guam	Guam	N	Laundress
	9	15	Lujan, Ana G	Daughter	F	Cha	10.0	S	Y	Y	Y	Guam	Guam	Guam	Y	None
	9	15	Lujan, Maria G	Daughter	F	Cha	8.0	S	Y	Y	Y	Guam	Guam	Guam		None
	9	15	Lujan, Victor G	Son	M	Cha	6.0	S	Y		Y	Guam	Guam	Guam		None
	9	15	Lujan, Juan G	Son	M	Cha	4.0	S				Guam	Guam	Guam		None
	9	15	Lujan, Carmen G	Daughter	F	Cha	1.0	S				Guam	Guam	Guam		None
	10	16	Cruz, Manuel S	Head	M	Cha	55.0	M		N	N	Guam	Guam	Guam	N	Farmer
	10	16	Cruz, Isabel SN	Wife	F	Cha	50.0	M		N	N	Guam	Guam	Guam	N	None
	10	16	San Nicolas, Carmen	Step daughter	F	Cha	30.0	S		N	N	Guam	Guam	Guam	N	None
	10	17	San Nicolas, Jose	Head	M	Cha	24.0	M		Y	Y	Guam	Unknown	Guam	Y	Enlisted man US Navy

(CHAMORRO ROOTS GENEALOGY PROJECT ™ TRANSCRIPTION)
(COMPILED/TRANSCRIBED BY BERNARD T. PUNZALAN / HTTP://WWW.CHAMORROROOTS.COM)

FOURTEENTH CENSUS OF THE UNITED STATES: 1920-POPULATION
ISLAND OF GUAM

SHEET NO. 2B

DISTRICT 2
NAME OF PLACE **Agana (City)**
[Proper name and, also, name of class, as city, town, village, barrio, etc]

ENUMERATED BY ME ON THE 24th DAY OF February, 1920
Arthur W. Jackson ENUMERATOR

	PLACE OF ABODE			NAME	RELATION	PERSONAL DESCRIPTION				EDUCATION			NATIVITY				OCCUPATION
	Street, avenue, road, etc.	Number of dwelling house is order of visitation	Number of family in order of visitation	of each person whose place of abode on January 1, 1920, was in the family. Enter surname, firs, then given name and middle initial. If any. Include every person living on January 1, 1920. Omit children born since January 1, 1920.	Relationship of this Person to the head of the family.	Sex	Color or race	Age at last birthday	Single, married, widowed or divorced	Attended school any time since Sept. 1, 1919	Whether able to read.	Whether able to write.	Place of birth of this person.	Place of birth of father of this person.	Place of birth of mother of this person.	Whether able to speak English.	Trade, profession, or particular kind of work done, as salesman, laborer, clerk, cook, merchant, washerwoman, etc.
	1	2	3	4	5	6	7	8	9	10	11	12	13	14	15	16	17
26	Soledad Street	10	17	San Nicolas, Rosalia P	Daughter	F	Cha	2.0	S				Guam	Guam	Guam		None
27		10	17	San Nicolas, Jesus P	Son	M	Cha	0.7	S				Guam	Guam	Guam		None
28		10	17	San Nicolas, Jose S	Nephew	M	Cha	6.0	S				Guam	Guam	Guam		None
29		11	18	Concepcion, Manuela R	Head	F	Cha	79.0	Wd		N	N	Guam	Guam	Guam	N	None
30		11	18	Concepcion, Concepcion M	Daughter	F	Cha	33.0	S		N	N	Guam	Guam	Guam	N	None
31		11	19	Guzman, Agustin F	Head	M	Cha	40.0	M		Y	Y	Guam	Guam	Guam	N	Farm laborer
32		11	19	Guzman, Antonia M	Wife	F	Cha	39.0	M		Y	Y	Guam	Guam	Guam	N	None
33		12	20	Mesa, Pedro	Head	M	Cha	58.0	M		N	N	Guam	Guam	Guam	N	Farmer
34		12	20	Mesa, Juana C	Wife	F	Cha	40.0	M		N	N	Guam	Guam	Guam	N	None
35		12	20	Mesa, Jesus C	Son	M	Cha	14.0	S	Y	Y	Y	Guam	Guam	Guam	Y	Farm laborer
36		13	21	Mesa, Rita P	Head	F	Cha	52.0	Wd		Y	Y	Guam	Guam	Guam	N	Laundress
37		13	21	Mesa, Maria P	Daughter	F	Cha	16.0	S	N	Y	Y	Guam	Guam	Guam	Y	None
38		13	21	Mesa, Ana P	Daughter	F	Cha	14.0	S	N	Y	Y	Guam	Guam	Guam	Y	None
39		13	21	Mesa, Remedios P	Daughter	F	Cha	11.0	S	Y	Y	Y	Guam	Guam	Guam	N	None
40		14	22	Castro, Felicita C	Head	F	Cha	27.0	M		N	N	Guam	Guam	Guam	N	Laundress
41		14	22	Castro, Jose C	Son	M	Cha	4.0	S				Guam	Unknown	Guam		None
42		14	22	Castro, Dolores C	Daughter	F	Cha	3.0	S				Guam	Unknown	Guam		None
43		14	22	Castro, Ernestina C	Daughter	F	Cha	0.8	S				Guam	Unknown	Guam		None
44		15	23	Mendiola, Juan C	Head	M	Cha	39.0	M		Y	Y	Guam	Guam	Guam	N	Farmer
45		15	23	Mendiola, Maria R	Wife	F	Cha	30.0	M		Y	Y	Guam	Guam	Guam	N	None
46		15	23	Mendiola, Ignacio R	Son	M	Cha	3.0	S				Guam	Guam	Guam		None
47		15	23	Mendiola, Andres R	Son	M	Cha	0.2	S				Guam	Guam	Guam		None
48		16	24	Oroso, Ana C	Head	F	Cha	49.0	Wd		N	N	Guam	Guam	Guam	N	None
49		16	24	Oroso, Enrique C	Son	M	Cha	17.0	S	N	Y	Y	Guam	Guam	Guam	Y	Farmer
50		16	24	Oroso, Emeliana C	Daughter	F	Cha	16.0	S	N	Y	Y	Guam	Guam	Guam	Y	None

(CHAMORRO ROOTS GENEALOGY PROJECT ™ TRANSCRIPTION)
(COMPILED/TRANSCRIBED BY BERNARD T. PUNZALAN / HTTP://WWW.CHAMORROROOTS.COM)

FOURTEENTH CENSUS OF THE UNITED STATES: 1920—POPULATION

ISLAND OF GUAM

SHEET NO. 3A

DISTRICT 2
NAME OF PLACE **Agana (City)**
[Proper name and, also, name of class, as city, town, village, barrio, etc]

ENUMERATED BY ME ON THE 25th DAY OF February, 1920

Arthur W. Jackson ENUMERATOR

	PLACE OF ABODE			NAME	RELATION	PERSONAL DESCRIPTION					EDUCATION			NATIVITY				OCCUPATION
Street, avenue, road, etc.	Number of dwelling house is order of visitation	Number of family in order of visitation		of each person whose place of abode on January 1, 1920, was in the family. Enter surname, firs, then given name and middle initial. If any. Include every person living on January 1, 1920. Omit children born since January 1, 1920.	Relationship of this Person to the head of the family.	Sex	Color or race	Age at last birthday	Single, married, widowed or divorced	Attended school any time since Sept. 1, 1919	Whether able to read.	Whether able to write.	Place of birth of this person.	Place of birth of father of this person.	Place of birth of mother of this person.	Whether able to speak English.	Trade, profession, or particular kind of work done, as salesman, laborer, clerk, cook, merchant, washerwoman, etc.
1	2	3	4		5	6	7	8	9	10	11	12	13	14	15	16	17
	16	24	Oroso, Maria C		Daughter	F	Cha	12.0	S	N	N	N	Guam	Guam	Guam	N	None
	17	25	Quidachay, Juan		Head	M	Cha	70.0	Wd		N	N	Guam	Guam	Guam	N	Farmer
	17	25	Quidachay, Vicente B		Son	M	Cha	23.0	S		Y	Y	Guam	Guam	Guam	Y	Laborer
	17	25	Quidachay, Jesus B		Son	M	Cha	16.0	S	N	Y	Y	Guam	Guam	Guam	Y	Servant
	17	25	Quidachay, Consolacion B		Daughter	F	Cha	14.0	S	N	Y	Y	Guam	Guam	Guam	Y	None
	17	25	Quidachay, Remedio B		Daughter	F	Cha	12.0	S	Y	Y	Y	Guam	Guam	Guam	Y	None
	17	25	Quidachay, Antonio B		Son	M	Cha	8.0	S	Y	Y	Y	Guam	Guam	Guam		None
	17	26	Cruz, Felix		Head	M	Cha	51.0	M		Y	Y	Guam	Guam	Guam	N	Farmer
	17	26	Cruz, Juana C		Wife	F	Cha	37.0	M	N	Y	Y	Guam	Guam	Guam	N	None
	17	26	Cruz, Asencion C		Daughter	F	Cha	20.0	S	N	Y	Y	Guam	Guam	Guam	Y	None
	17	26	Cruz, Maria C		Daughter	F	Cha	14.0	S	Y	Y	Y	Guam	Guam	Guam	Y	None
	17	26	Rosario, Jesus		Lodger	M	Cha	9.0	S	Y			Guam	Guam	Guam		None
	17	26	Rosario, Juan		Lodger	M	Cha	4.0	S				Guam	Guam	Guam		None
	18	27	Castro, Francisco A		Head	M	Cha	58.0	M		Y	Y	Guam	Guam	Guam	N	Farmer
	18	27	Castro, Josefa B		Wife	F	Cha	44.0	M	N	N	N	Guam	Guam	Guam	N	None
	18	27	Borja, Soledad		Step daughter	F	Cha	24.0	S	N	N	N	Guam	Guam	Guam	N	None
	18	27	Borja, Ignacia		Step daughter	F	Cha	21.0	S	N	Y	Y	Guam	Guam	Guam	N	None
	19	28	Villagomez, Jose		Head	M	Cha	24.0	M		Y	Y	Guam	Guam	Guam	Y	Carpenter
	19	28	Villagomez, Ana A		Wife	F	Cha	19.0	M	N	Y	Y	Guam	Guam	Guam	N	None
	19	28	Villagomez, Artemio A		Son	M	Cha	1.0	S				Guam	Guam	Guam		None
	19	29	Borja, Lorenzo L		Head	M	Cha	42.0	M		Y	Y	Guam	Guam	Guam	N	None
	19	29	Borja, Francisca C		Wife	F	Cha	27.0	M		Y	Y	Guam	Guam	Guam	N	None
	19	29	Borja, Joaquin C		Son	M	Cha	7.0	S	Y	Y	Y	Guam	Guam	Guam		None
	19	29	Borja, Francisca C		Daughter	F	Cha	1.0	S				Guam	Guam	Guam		None
	19	29	Pablo, Concepcion V		Servant	F	Cha	10.0	S	Y	Y	Y	Guam	Guam	Guam	N	Servant

Soledad Street

(CHAMORRO ROOTS GENEALOGY PROJECT ™ TRANSCRIPTION)
(COMPILED/TRANSCRIBED BY BERNARD T. PUNZALAN / HTTP://WWW.CHAMORROROOTS.COM)

FOURTEENTH CENSUS OF THE UNITED STATES: 1920-POPULATION

ISLAND OF GUAM

ENUMERATED BY ME ON THE 24th DAY OF February, 1920

Arthur W. Jackson ENUMERATOR

DISTRICT 2
NAME OF PLACE Agana (City)

	Street	No. dwelling house	No. of family	NAME	RELATION	Sex	Color or race	Age	Single/married/widowed/divorced	Attended school since Sept 1, 1919	Able to read	Able to write	Place of birth of this person	Place of birth of father	Place of birth of mother	Able to speak English	OCCUPATION
	1	2	3	4	5	6	7	8	9	10	11	12	13	14	15	16	17
26		20	30	Iriarte, Jesus C	Head	M	Cha	41.0	M		N	N	Guam	Guam	Guam	N	Farmer
27		20	30	Iriarte, Francisca J	Wife	F	Cha	42.0	M		Y	Y	Guam	Guam	Guam	N	None
28		20	30	toves, Pedro L	Servant	M	Cha	19.0	S	N	Y	Y	Guam	Guam	Guam	Y	Farm laborer
29		20	31	Leon Guerrero, Jose D	Head	M	Cha	28.0	M		Y	Y	Guam	Guam	Guam	Y	Blacksmith
30		20	31	Leon Guerrero, Josefa M	Wife	F	Cha	26.0	M		N	N	Guam	Guam	Guam	Y	None
31		20	31	Leon Guerrero, Ana M	Daughter	F	Cha	7.0	S	Y			Guam	Guam	Guam		None
32		20	31	Leon Guerrero, Lorenzo M	Son	M	Cha	5.0	S	N			Guam	Guam	Guam		None
33		20	31	Leon Guerrero, Josefina M	Daughter	F	Cha	2.0	S				Guam	Guam	Guam		None
34	Soledad Street	21	32	Sablan, Vicente P	Head	M	Cha	49.0	M		Y	Y	Guam	Guam	Guam	N	Carpenter
35		21	32	Sablan, Dolores A	Wife	F	Cha	43.0	M		Y	Y	Guam	Guam	Guam	N	None
36		21	32	Sablan, Jose A	Son	M	Cha	23.0	S		Y	Y	Guam	Guam	Guam	Y	Carpenter
37		21	32	Sablan, Francisco A	Son	M	Cha	16.0	S	Y	Y	Y	Guam	Guam	Guam	Y	Laborer
38		21	32	Sablan, Ana A	Daughter	F	Cha	11.0	S	Y	Y	Y	Guam	Guam	Guam	N	None
39		21	32	Sablan, Carmen A	Daughter	F	Cha	9.0	S	Y			Guam	Guam	Guam		None
40		22	33	Aparon, Ricardo S	Head	M	Fil	56.0	Wd		N	N	Philippine Islands	Philippine Islands	Philippine Islands	N	Laborer
41		22	33	Aparon, Manuel T	Son	M	Fil	15.0	S		Y	Y	Guam	Philippine Islands	Guam	Y	Laborer
42		22	33	Aparon, Alberta T	Daughter	F	Fil	13.0	S	N	Y	Y	Guam	Philippine Islands	Guam	Y	None
43		22	33	Aparon, Francisca T	Daughter	F	Fil	9.0	S	Y			Guam	Philippine Islands	Guam		None
44		22	33	Aparon, Simeon T	Son	M	Fil	6.0	S	Y			Guam	Philippine Islands	Guam		None
45		23	24	Cepeda, Jose S	Head	M	Cha	44.0	M		N	N	Guam	Guam	Guam	N	Farmer
46		23	24	Cepeda, Maria C	Wife	F	Cha	34.0	M		N	N	Guam	Guam	Guam	N	None
47		23	24	Cepeda, Jose C	Son	M	Cha	12.0	S	Y	Y	Y	Guam	Guam	Guam	Y	None
48		23	24	Cepeda, Amanda C	Daughter	F	Cha	10.0	S	Y	Y	Y	Guam	Guam	Guam	N	None
49		23	24	Cepeda, Ignacio C	Son	M	Cha	9.0	S	Y	Y	Y	Guam	Guam	Guam	N	None
50		23	24	Cepeda, Trinidad C	Son	M	Cha	6.0	S	N			Guam	Guam	Guam		None

(CHAMORRO ROOTS GENEALOGY PROJECT ™ TRANSCRIPTION)
(COMPILED/TRANSCRIBED BY BERNARD T. PUNZALAN / HTTP://WWW.CHAMORROROOTS.COM)

FOURTEENTH CENSUS OF THE UNITED STATES: 1920-POPULATION
ISLAND OF GUAM

DISTRICT 2
NAME OF PLACE Agana (City)
[Proper name and, also, name of class, as city, town, village, barrio, etc]

ENUMERATED BY ME ON THE 25th DAY OF February, 1920

Arthur W. Jackson ENUMERATOR

Dwelling No.	Family No.	NAME	RELATION	Sex	Color or race	Age	Single, married, widowed or divorced	Attended school since Sept. 1, 1919	Whether able to read	Whether able to write	Place of birth of this person	Place of birth of father	Place of birth of mother	Whether able to speak English	OCCUPATION
2	3	4	5	6	7	8	9	10	11	12	13	14	15	16	17
23	34	Cepeda, Maria C	Daughter	F	Cha	5.0	S	N			Guam	Guam	Guam		None
23	34	Cepeda, Jesus C	Son	M	Cha	2.0	S				Guam	Guam	Guam		None
23	34	Cepeda, Nicolasa M	Mother-in-law	F	Cha	55.0	M		N	N	Guam	Guam	Guam		None
23	34	Cepeda, Ana	Sister-in-law	F	Cha	28.0	S		N	N	Guam	Guam	Guam	N	None
23	34	Cepeda, Francisco	Nephew	M	Cha	6.0	S	N			Guam	Unknown	Guam	N	Cook
23	34	Cepeda, Nicolasa	Niece	F	Cha	1.0	S				Guam	Unknown	Guam		None
23	34	Cepeda, Jose	Brother-in-law	M	Cha	25.0	S		Y	Y	Guam	Unknown	Guam	Y	Laborer
23	34	Cepeda, Juan C	Nephew	M	Cha	1.0	S				Guam	Guam	Guam		None
24	35	Indalecio, Pedro	Head	M	Cha	49.0	M		N	N	Guam	Unknown	Guam	N	Farmer
24	35	Indalecio, Rufina C	Wife	F	Cha	43.0	M		N	N	Guam	Guam	Guam	N	None
24	35	Indalecio, Antonio C	Son	M	Cha	19.0	S	N	Y	Y	Guam	Guam	Guam	Y	Farm laborer
24	35	Indalecio, Rosalia C	Daughter	F	Cha	15.0	S	N	Y	Y	Guam	Guam	Guam	Y	None
24	35	Indalecio, Maria C	Daughter	F	Cha	13.0	S	Y	Y	Y	Guam	Guam	Guam	Y	None
24	35	Indalecio, Juan C	Son	M	Cha	11.0	S	Y	Y	Y	Guam	Guam	Guam	Y	None
24	35	Indalecio, Jose C	Son	M	Cha	9.0	S	Y			Guam	Guam	Guam		None
24	35	Indalecio, Catalina C	Daughter	F	Cha	6.0	S	N			Guam	Guam	Guam		None
25	36	Salas, Vicente S	Head	M	Cha	52.0	M		Y	Y	Guam	Guam	Guam	Y	Carpenter
25	36	Salas, Maria I	Wife	F	Cha	38.0	M		N	N	Guam	Guam	Guam	N	None
25	36	Salas, Maria I	Daughter	F	Cha	17.0	S	N	Y	Y	Guam	Guam	Guam	Y	None
25	36	Salas, Concepcion I	Daughter	F	Cha	13.0	S	Y	Y	Y	Guam	Guam	Guam	Y	None
25	36	Salas, Felix I	Son	M	Cha	11.0	S	Y	Y	Y	Guam	Guam	Guam	Y	None
25	36	Salas, Vicente I	Son	M	Cha	7.0	S	Y			Guam	Guam	Guam		None
25	36	Salas, Mercedes I	Daughter	F	Cha	5.0	S	N			Guam	Guam	Guam		None
25	36	Salas, Rosalia I	Daughter	F	Cha	3.0	S				Guam	Guam	Guam		None
25	36	Salas, Josefa I	Daughter	F	Cha	0.8	S				Guam	Guam	Guam		None

Street: Soledad Street

(CHAMORRO ROOTS GENEALOGY PROJECT ™ TRANSCRIPTION)
(COMPILED/TRANSCRIBED BY BERNARD T. PUNZALAN / HTTP://WWW.CHAMORROROOTS.COM)

FOURTEENTH CENSUS OF THE UNITED STATES: 1920-POPULATION
ISLAND OF GUAM

DISTRICT 2
NAME OF PLACE Agana (City)
[Proper name and, also, name of class, as city, town, village, barrio, etc]

ENUMERATED BY ME ON THE 25th DAY OF February, 1920.

Arthur W. Jackson ENUMERATOR

	Street	Dwelling house No.	Family No.	NAME	RELATION	Sex	Color or race	Age at last birthday	Single, married, widowed or divorced	Attended school since Sept. 1, 1919	Whether able to read	Whether able to write	Place of birth of this person	Place of birth of father	Place of birth of mother	Whether able to speak English	OCCUPATION
	1	2	3	4	5	6	7	8	9	10	11	12	13	14	15	16	17
26		26	37	Chargualaf, Francisco R	Head	M	Cha	22.0	M		Y	Y	Guam	Guam	Guam	Y	Farmer
27		26	37	Chargualaf, Maria C	Wife	F	Cha	24.0	M		Y	Y	Guam	Guam	Guam	N	None
28		26	37	Chargualaf, Julia C	Daughter	F	Cha	1.0	S				Guam	Guam	Guam		None
29		26	38	Fejarang, Ramon C	Head	M	Cha	63.0	M		N	N	Guam	Guam	Guam	N	Farmer
30		26	38	Fejarang, Juana C	Wife	F	Cha	55.0	M		N	N	Guam	Guam	Guam	N	None
31		26	38	Camacho, Juan	Step son	M	Cha	23.0	S		Y	Y	Guam	Unknown	Guam	Y	Farmer
32		27	39	Pangelinan, Concepcion	Head	F	Cha	57.0	S		N	N	Guam	Unknown	Guam	N	None
33		27	39	Pangelinan, Joaquin	Son	M	Cha	19.0	S	N	Y	Y	Guam	Unknown	Guam	N	Farmer
34		27	39	Pangelinan, Tomas	Son	M	Cha	17.0	S	N	Y	Y	Guam	Unknown	Guam	Y	None
35		27	39	Pangelinan, Vicente	Son	M	Cha	11.0	S	Y	Y	Y	Guam	Unknown	Guam	Y	None
36		27	39	Pangelinan, Artemio	Son	M	Cha	9.0	S	Y			Guam	Unknown	Guam		None
37		28	40	Iriarte, Juana C	Head	F	Cha	64.0	Wd		N	N	Guam	Guam	Guam	N	None
38		28	40	Iriarte, Pedro C	Son	M	Cha	28.0	S		Y	Y	Guam	Guam	Guam	N	Farmer
39	Soledad Street	28	40	Iriarte, Jose C	Son	M	Cha	19.0	S	N	Y	Y	Guam	Guam	Guam	Y	Farmer
40		29	41	Chargualaf, Eugenio R	Head	M	Cha	24.0	M		Y	Y	Guam	Guam	Guam	Y	Machinist
41		29	41	Chargualaf, Rosa C	Wife	F	Cha	27.0	M		Y	Y	Guam	Guam	Guam	N	None
42		29	41	Chargualaf, Elias C	Son	M	Cha	2.0	S				Guam	Guam	Guam		None
43		29	41	Castro, Jose S	Father-in-law	M	Cha	66.0	M		N	N	Guam	Guam	Guam	N	None
44		30	42	Blaz, Vicente S	Head	M	Cha	50.0	M		Y	Y	Guam	Guam	Guam	N	Farmer
45		30	42	Blaz, Maria C	Wife	F	Cha	68.0	M		N	N	Guam	Guam	Guam	N	None
46		31	43	Iriarte, Nicolas G	Head	M	Cha	51.0	M		Y	Y	Guam	Guam	Guam	N	Farmer
47		31	43	Iriarte, Agustina D	Wife	F	Cha	37.0	M		Y	Y	Guam	Guam	Guam	N	None
48		31	43	Iriarte, Juana D	Daughter	F	Cha	12.0	S	Y	Y	Y	Guam	Guam	Guam	Y	None
49		31	43	Iriarte, Natividad D	Daughter	F	Cha	11.0	S	Y	Y	Y	Guam	Guam	Guam	N	None
50		31	43	Iriarte, Monica D	Daughter	F	Cha	9.0	S	Y	Y	Y	Guam	Guam	Guam		None

(CHAMORRO ROOTS GENEALOGY PROJECT ™ TRANSCRIPTION)
(COMPILED/TRANSCRIBED BY BERNARD T. PUNZALAN / HTTP://WWW.CHAMORROROOTS.COM)

FOURTEENTH CENSUS OF THE UNITED STATES: 1920–POPULATION

ISLAND OF GUAM

ENUMERATED BY ME ON THE 26th DAY OF February, 1920

Arthur W. Jackson ENUMERATOR

DISTRICT 2
NAME OF PLACE **Agana (City)**

[Proper name and, also, name of class, as city, town, village, barrio, etc]

	Street, avenue, road, etc.	Number of dwelling house in order of visitation	Number of family in order of visitation	NAME	RELATION	Sex	Color or race	Age at last birthday	Single, married, widowed or divorced	Attended school any time since Sept. 1, 1919	Whether able to read	Whether able to write	Place of birth of this person.	Place of birth of father of this person.	Place of birth of mother of this person.	Whether able to speak English.	OCCUPATION
	1	2	3	4	5	6	7	8	9	10	11	12	13	14	15	16	17
1		31	43	Iriarte, Maria D	Daughter	F	Cha	8.0	S	Y			Guam	Guam	Guam		None
2		31	43	Iriarte, Tomas D	Son	M	Cha	6.0	S	N			Guam	Guam	Guam		None
3		31	43	Iriarte, Jesus D	Son	M	Cha	4.0	S				Guam	Guam	Guam		None
4		31	43	Iriarte, Dolores D	Daughter	F	Cha	2.0	S				Guam	Guam	Guam		None
5		32	44	Aguon, Felix D	Head	M	Cha	50.0	M		Y	Y	Guam	Guam	Guam	Y	Carpenter
6		32	44	Aguon, Genoveva I	Wife	F	Cha	40.0	M		N	N	Guam	Guam	Guam	N	None
7		32	44	Aguon, Pedro I	Son	M	Cha	7.0	S	N			Guam	Guam	Guam		None
8		32	44	Aguon, Rosa I	Daughter	F	Cha	6.0	S	N			Guam	Guam	Guam		None
9		32	44	Aguon, Josefa I	Daughter	F	Cha	4.0	S				Guam	Guam	Guam		None
10	Soledad Street	32	44	Aguon, Luis I	Son	M	Cha	2.0	S				Guam	Guam	Guam		None
11		33	45	Guerrero, Pedro F	Head	M	Cha	36.0	M		Y	Y	Guam	Guam	Guam	N	Farmer
12		33	45	Guerrero, Amparo C	Wife	F	Fil	33.0	M		Y	Y	Guam	Philippine Islands	Guam	N	None
13		33	45	Guerrero, Maria C	Daughter	F	Cha	12.0	S	Y	Y	Y	Guam	Guam	Guam	Y	None
14		33	45	Guerrero, Jose C	Son	M	Cha	10.0	S	Y	Y	Y	Guam	Guam	Guam	Y	None
15		33	45	Guerrero, Manuel C	Son	M	Cha	8.0	S	Y			Guam	Guam	Guam		None
16		33	45	Guerrero, Antonia C	Daughter	F	Cha	6.0	S	N			Guam	Guam	Guam		None
17		33	45	Guerrero, Pedro C	Son	M	Cha	1.0	S				Guam	Guam	Guam		None
18		34	46	San Nicolas, Eugenio V	Head	M	Cha	45.0	M		Y	Y	Guam	Guam	Guam	Y	Plumber
19		34	46	San Nicolas, Vicenta T	Wife	F	Cha	43.0	M		Y	Y	Guam	Guam	Guam	N	None
20		34	46	San Nicolas, Francisco T	Son	M	Cha	19.0	S	N	Y	Y	Guam	Guam	Guam	Y	Laborer
21		34	46	San Nicolas, Jose T	Son	M	Cha	17.0	S	Y	Y	Y	Guam	Guam	Guam	Y	None
22		34	46	San Nicolas, Ramona T	Daughter	F	Cha	14.0	S	N	Y	Y	Guam	Guam	Guam	Y	None
23		34	46	San Nicolas, Maria T	Daughter	F	Cha	12.0	S	N	Y	Y	Guam	Guam	Guam	Y	None
24		34	46	San Nicolas, Engracia T	Daughter	F	Cha	8.0	S	Y			Guam	Guam	Guam		None
25		34	46	San Nicolas, Olimpia T	Daughter	F	Cha	6.0	S	Y			Guam	Guam	Guam		None

(CHAMORRO ROOTS GENEALOGY PROJECT ™ TRANSCRIPTION)
(COMPILED/TRANSCRIBED BY BERNARD T. PUNZALAN / HTTP://WWW.CHAMORROROOTS.COM)
FOURTEENTH CENSUS OF THE UNITED STATES: 1920-POPULATION

ISLAND OF GUAM

DISTRICT 2
NAME OF PLACE Agana (City)
[Proper name and, also, name of class, as city, town, village, barrio, etc]

ENUMERATED BY ME ON THE 26th DAY OF February, 1920

Arthur W. Jackson ENUMERATOR

Street, avenue, road, etc.	No. of dwelling house	No. of family	NAME	RELATION	Sex	Color or race	Age at last birthday	Single, married, widowed or divorced	Attended school since sept. 1, 1919	Whether able to read	Whether able to write	Place of birth of this person	Place of birth of father	Place of birth of mother	Whether able to speak English	OCCUPATION
1	2	3	4	5	6	7	8	9	10	11	12	13	14	15	16	17
	34	36	San Nicolas, Eugenio T	Son	M	Cha	4.0	S				Guam	Guam	Guam		None
	34	47	San Nicolas, Vicente T	Head	M	Cha	22.0	M		Y	Y	Guam	Guam	Guam	Y	Plumber
	34	47	San Nicolas, Consolacion C	Wife	F	Cha	18.0	M	N	Y	Y	Guam	Guam	Guam	Y	None
	34	47	San Nicolas, Luis S	Son	M	Cha	2.0	S				Guam	Guam	Guam		None
	35	48	Calvo, Tomas A	Head	M	W	44.0	M		Y	Y	Philippine Islands	Spain	Guam	Y	Lawyer
	35	48	Calvo, Regina T	Wife	F	Cha	37.0	M		Y	Y	Guam	Guam	Guam	N	None
	35	48	Calvo, Adela T	Daughter	F	W	16.0	S	N	Y	Y	Guam	Philippine Islands	Guam	Y	None
Soledad Street	35	48	Calvo, Ismael T	Son	M	W	15.0	S	N	Y	Y	Guam	Philippine Islands	Guam	Y	Salesman
	35	48	Calvo, Trinidad T	Son	M	W	14.0	S	Y	Y	Y	Guam	Philippine Islands	Guam	Y	None
	35	48	Calvo, Hermina T	Daughter	F	W	12.0	S	Y	Y	Y	Guam	Philippine Islands	Guam	Y	None
	35	48	Calvo, Eduardo T	Son	M	W	10.0	S	Y	Y	Y	Guam	Philippine Islands	Guam	Y	None
	35	48	Calvo, Clotilde T	Daughter	F	W	8.0	S	Y	Y	Y	Guam	Philippine Islands	Guam	Y	None
	35	48	Calvo, Flora T	Daughter	F	W	7.0	S	Y	Y	Y	Guam	Philippine Islands	Guam		None
	35	48	Calvo, Ricardo T	Son	M	W	3.0	S				Guam	Philippine Islands	Guam		None
	35	48	Calvo, Carlos T	Son	M	W	0.2	S				Guam	Philippine Islands	Guam		None
	35	48	Calvo, Ana A	Mother	F	W	69.0	Wd		Y	Y	Guam	Philippine Islands	Guam	Y	None
	35	48	Calvo, Jacinto A	Brother	M	W	45.0	S		N	N	Philippine Islands	Spain	Guam	N	None
	35	48	Calvo, Angusto A	Brother	M	W	37.0	S		Y	Y	Philippine Islands	Spain	Guam	Y	Physician
	36	49	Taijiron, Jesus P	Head	M	Cha	30.0	M		Y	Y	Guam	Guam	Guam	Y	Laborer
	36	49	Taijiron, Antonia C	Wife	F	Cha	25.0	M		Y	Y	Guam	Guam	Guam	N	None
	36	49	Taijiron, Juan C	Son	M	Cha	2.0	S				Guam	Guam	Guam		None
	36	49	Cruz, Maricio C	Father-in-law	M	Cha	60.0	Wd		Y	Y	Guam	Guam	Guam	N	Farmer
	37	50	Castro, Maria C	Head	F	Cha	32.0	S		Y	Y	Guam	Guam	Guam	N	None
	37	50	Castro, Jose C	Son	M	Cha	5.0	S	N			Guam	Unknown	Guam		None
	37	50	Castro, Amalia C	Daughter	F	Cha	4.0	S				Guam	Unknown	Guam		None

Row numbers: 26, 27, 28, 29, 30, 31, 32, 33, 34, 35, 36, 37, 38, 39, 40, 41, 42, 43, 44, 45, 46, 47, 48, 49, 50

(CHAMORRO ROOTS GENEALOGY PROJECT ™ TRANSCRIPTION)
(COMPILED/TRANSCRIBED BY BERNARD T. PUNZALAN / HTTP://WWW.CHAMORROROOTS.COM)

110

SHEET NO. 6A

FOURTEENTH CENSUS OF THE UNITED STATES: 1920—POPULATION
ISLAND OF GUAM

ENUMERATED BY ME ON THE 26th DAY OF February, 1920

Arthur W. Jackson ENUMERATOR

DISTRICT 2
NAME OF PLACE Agana (City)
[Proper name and, also, name of class, as city, town, village, barrio, etc]

	PLACE OF ABODE			NAME	RELATION	PERSONAL DESCRIPTION				EDUCATION			NATIVITY				OCCUPATION
Street, avenue, road, etc.	Number of dwelling house is order of visitation	Number of family in order of visitation		of each person whose place of abode on January 1, 1920, was in the family. Enter surname, firs, then given name and middle initial. If any. Include every person living on January 1, 1920. Omit children born since January 1, 1920.	Relationship of this Person to the head of the family.	Sex	Color or race	Age at last birthday	Single, married, widowed or divorced	Attended school any time since Sept. 1, 1919	Whether able to read.	Whether able to write.	Place of birth of this person.	Place of birth of father of this person.	Place of birth of mother of this person.	Whether able to speak English.	Trade, profession, or particular kind of work done, as salesman, laborer, clerk, cook, merchant, washerwoman, etc.
1	2	3	4		5	6	7	8	9	10	11	12	13	14	15	16	17
	38	51	1	Santos, Antonio B	Head	M	Cha	47.0	M		Y	Y	Guam	Guam	Guam	N	Farmer
	38	51	2	Santos, Josefa G	Wife	F	Cha	54.0	M		N	N	Guam	Philippine Islands	Philippine Islands	N	None
	38	51	3	Santos, Tomasa G	Daughter	F	Cha	21.0	S	N	Y	Y	Guam	Guam	Guam	Y	None
	38	51	4	Santos, Jesus G	Son	M	Cha	15.0	S	N	Y	Y	Guam	Guam	Guam	Y	None
	38	51	5	Santos, Vicente G	Son	M	Cha	12.0	S	Y	Y	Y	Guam	Guam	Guam	Y	None
	38	51	6	Santos, Maria G	Daughter	F	Cha	10.0	S	Y	Y	Y	Guam	Guam	Guam	Y	None
	38	51	7	Cruz, Ana S	Lodger	F	Cha	85.0	Wd		N	N	Guam	Guam	Guam	N	None
	39	52	8	Castro, Vicente C	Head	M	Cha	34.0	M		Y	Y	Guam	Guam	Guam	Y	Carpenter
	39	52	9	Castro, Rosa B	Wife	F	Cha	25.0	M		Y	Y	Guam	Philippine Islands	Guam	N	None
	39	52	10	Castro, Regina B	Daughter	F	Cha	3.0	S				Guam	Guam	Guam		None
	39	52	11	Castro, Trinidad B	Daughter	F	Cha	1.0	S				Guam	Guam	Guam		None
	40	53	12	Perez, Joaquin T	Head	M	Cha	34.0	M		Y	Y	Guam	Guam	Guam	Y	Cook
	40	53	13	Perez, Maria L	Wife	F	Cha	34.0	M		N	N	Guam	Guam	Guam	N	None
	40	53	14	Perez, Francisco L	Son	M	Cha	10.0	S	Y	Y	Y	Guam	Guam	Guam	Y	None
	40	53	15	Perez, Vicente L	Son	M	Cha	9.0	S	Y	Y	Y	Guam	Guam	Guam		None
	40	53	16	Perez, Juan L	Son	M	Cha	8.0	S	Y			Guam	Guam	Guam		None
	40	53	17	Perez, Maria L	Daughter	F	Cha	4.0	S				Guam	Guam	Guam		None
	40	53	18	Perez, Henry L	Son	M	Cha	2.0	S				Guam	Guam	Guam		None
	40	53	19	Pangelinan, Pedro	Servant	M	Cha	13.0	S	N	N	N	Guam	Guam	Guam	N	Servant
	41	54	20	Cruz, Dolores B	Head	F	Cha	64.0	Wd		N	N	Guam	Guam	Guam	N	None
	41	54	21	Cruz, Saturnina B	Daughter	F	Cha	25.0	S		Y	Y	Guam	Guam	Guam	N	Laundress
	41	54	22	Cruz, Antonia B	Daughter	F	Cha	21.0	S	N	Y	Y	Guam	Guam	Guam	N	None
	41	54	23	Cruz, Pedro B	Son	M	Cha	20.0	S	N	Y	Y	Guam	Guam	Guam	Y	Laborer
	41	54	24	Cruz, Ana B	Daughter	F	Cha	17.0	S	N	Y	Y	Guam	Guam	Guam	Y	None
	41	54	25	Cruz, Teordoro B	Son	M	Cha	15.0	S	Y	Y	Y	Guam	Guam	Guam	Y	None

Soledad Street

223

(CHAMORRO ROOTS GENEALOGY PROJECT ™ TRANSCRIPTION)
(COMPILED/TRANSCRIBED BY BERNARD T. PUNZALAN / HTTP://WWW.CHAMORROROOTS.COM)

FOURTEENTH CENSUS OF THE UNITED STATES: 1920-POPULATION

ISLAND OF GUAM

ENUMERATED BY ME ON THE 26th DAY OF February, 1920

Arthur W. Jackson ENUMERATOR

DISTRICT 2
NAME OF PLACE Agana (City)

[Proper name and, also, name of class, as city, town, village, barrio, etc]

	Street	Dwelling No.	Family No.	NAME	RELATION	Sex	Color or race	Age	Single, married, widowed or divorced	Attended school since Sept. 1, 1919	Able to read	Able to write	Birthplace of person	Birthplace of father	Birthplace of mother	Able to speak English	OCCUPATION
	1	2	3	4	5	6	7	8	9	10	11	12	13	14	15	16	17
26		41	54	Cruz, Consolacion B	Daughter	F	Cha	28.0	Wd		Y	Y	Guam	Guam	Guam	N	None
27		41	54	Leon Guerrero, Dolores	Granddaughter	F	Cha	2.0	S				Guam	Guam	Guam		None
28		42	55	Aguon, Jose V	Head	M	Cha	25.0	M		Y	Y	Guam	Guam	Guam	N	Farmer
29		42	55	Aguon, Antonia B	Wife	F	Cha	26.0	M		Y	Y	Guam	Guam	Guam	N	None
30		42	55	Aguon, Vicente B	Son	M	Cha	4.0	S				Guam	Guam	Guam		None
31		42	55	Aguon, Dolores B	Daughter	F	Cha	2.0	S				Guam	Guam	Guam		None
32		43	56	Perez, Juan T	Head	M	Cha	24.0	M		Y	Y	Guam	Guam	Guam	Y	Enlisted USN
33		43	56	Perez, Josefa A	Wife	F	Cha	24.0	M		Y	Y	Guam	Guam	Guam	N	None
34	Soledad Street	44	57	Mendiola, Manuel P	Head	M	Cha	38.0	M		Y	Y	Guam	Guam	Guam	Y	Carpenter
35		44	57	Mendiola, Rufina P	Wife	F	Cha	26.0	M		Y	Y	Guam	Guam	Guam	N	None
36		44	57	Mendiola, Jose P	Son	M	Cha	3.0	S				Guam	Guam	Guam		None
37		44	57	Mendiola, Maria P	Daughter	F	Cha	0.3	S				Guam	Guam	Guam		None
38		44	57	Mendiola, Ana P	Mother	F	Cha	55.0	Wd		N	N	Guam	Guam	Guam		None
39		44	57	Mendiola, Joaquin P	Brother	M	Cha	28.0	S		Y	Y	Guam	Guam	Guam	Y	Farmer
40		45	58	Mendiola, Juan P	Head	M	Cha	36.0	M		Y	Y	Guam	Guam	Guam	Y	Carpenter
41		45	58	Mendiola, Teresa C	Wife	F	Cha	22.0	M		Y	Y	Guam	Guam	Guam	N	None
42		45	58	Mendiola, Jose C	Son	M	Cha	1.0	S				Guam	Guam	Guam		None
43		46	59	Manibusan, Jose C	Head	M	Cha	31.0	M		Y	Y	Guam	Guam	Guam	Y	Farmer
44		46	59	Manibusan, Ana C	Wife	F	Cha	30.0	M		Y	Y	Guam	Unknown	Guam	N	None
45		46	59	Manibusan, Ana C	Daughter	F	Cha	9.0	S	Y			Guam	Guam	Guam		None
46		46	59	Manibusan, Emeterio C	Son	M	Cha	5.0	S	N			Guam	Guam	Guam		None
47		46	59	Manibusan, Oscar C	Son	M	Cha	0.2	S		N	N	Guam	Guam	Guam		None
48		46	59	Blaz, Maria	Sister-in-law	F	Cha	47.0	S		N	N	Guam	Unknown	Guam	N	None
49		47	60	Cruz, Manuel C	Head	M	Cha	39.0	M		Y	Y	Guam	Guam	Guam	N	Cook
50		47	60	Cruz, Dolores P	Wife	F	Cha	29.0	M		Y	Y	Guam	Guam	Guam	N	None

(CHAMORRO ROOTS GENEALOGY PROJECT ™ TRANSCRIPTION)
(COMPILED/TRANSCRIBED BY BERNARD T. PUNZALAN / HTTP://WWW.CHAMORROROOTS.COM)

FOURTEENTH CENSUS OF THE UNITED STATES: 1920—POPULATION

ISLAND OF GUAM

DISTRICT **2**
NAME OF PLACE **Agana (City)**

[Proper name and, also, name of class, as city, town, village, barrio, etc]

ENUMERATED BY ME ON THE 27th DAY OF February, 1920

Arthur W. Jackson ENUMERATOR

	Street, avenue, road, etc.	Number of dwelling house in order of visitation	Number of family in order of visitation	NAME	RELATION	Sex	Color or race	Age at last birthday	Single, married, widowed or divorced	Attended school any time since Sept. 1, 1919	Whether able to read	Whether able to write	Place of birth of this person	Place of birth of father of this person	Place of birth of mother of this person	Whether able to speak English	OCCUPATION
	1	2	3	4	5	6	7	8	9	10	11	12	13	14	15	16	17
1		47	60	Cruz, Francisco P	Son	M	Cha	6.0	S	N			Guam	Guam	Guam		None
2		47	60	Cruz, Maria P	Daughter	F	Cha	3.0	S				Guam	Guam	Guam		None
3		47	60	Cruz, Pedro P	Son	M	Cha	0.2	S				Guam	Guam	Guam		None
4		47	60	Pangelinan, Luisa	Sister-in-law	F	Cha	31.0	S		Y	Y	Guam	Guam	Guam	N	None
5		47	60	Pangelinan, Jose	Nephew	M	Cha	3.0	S				Guam	Unknown	Guam		None
6		47	60	Pangelinan, Antonia	Niece	F	Cha	1.0	S				Guam	Unknown	Guam		None
7		48	61	Fejarang, Joaquin	Head	M	Cha	32.0	M		Y	Y	Guam	Guam	Guam	N	Laborer
8		48	61	Fejarang, Mercedes C	Wife	F	Cha	26.0	M		Y	Y	Guam	Guam	Guam	N	None
9		48	61	Fejarang, Gregorio C	Son	M	Cha	8.0	S	Y			Guam	Guam	Guam		None
10		48	61	Fejarang, Ana C	Daughter	F	Cha	5.0	S	N			Guam	Guam	Guam		None
11	Soledad Street	48	61	Fejarang, Jose C	Son	M	Cha	2.0	S				Guam	Guam	Guam		None
12		49	62	Reyes, Vicenta M	Head	F	Cha	82.0	Wd		N	N	Guam	Unknown	Guam	N	None
13		49	62	Torres, Maria R	Daughter	F	Cha	51.0	Wd		N	N	Guam	Guam	Guam	N	None
14		49	62	Torres, Ignacio R	Grandson	M	Cha	26.0	S		Y	Y	Guam	Guam	Guam	Y	Servant
15		49	63	Bondshu, Gregoria R	Head	F	Cha	20.0	M	N	Y	Y	Guam	Guam	Guam	Y	None
16		49	63	Bondshu, Frank R	Son	M	W	3.0	S				Guam	California	Guam		None
17		49	63	Bondshu, Theodore R	Son	M	W	1.0	S				Guam	California	Guam		None
18		49	63	Quinene, Ana	Servant	F	Cha	9.0	S	Y			Guam	Unknown	Unknown		Servant
19		50	64	Camacho, Jesus	Head	M	Cha	16.0	S	N	Y	Y	Guam	Unknown	Unknown	Y	Servant
20		51	65	Charsagua, Maria S	Head	F	Cha	47.0	Wd		N	N	Guam	Guam	Guam	N	Laundress
21		51	65	Duenas, Vicente M	Son-in-law	M	Cha	20.0	M	N	Y	Y	Guam	Guam	Guam	N	Farmer
22		51	65	Duenas, Rosa C	Daughter	F	Cha	21.0	M	N	Y	Y	Guam	Guam	Guam	N	None
23		51	65	Charsagua, Magdalena S	Daughter	F	Cha	13.0	S	Y	Y	Y	Guam	Guam	Guam	Y	None
24		51	65	Charsagua, Concepcion S	Daughter	F	Cha	11.0	S	Y	Y	Y	Guam	Guam	Guam	Y	None
25		52	66	Salas, Francisco P	Head	M	Cha	45.0	M		N	N	Guam	Guam	Guam	N	None

225

(CHAMORRO ROOTS GENEALOGY PROJECT ™ TRANSCRIPTION)
(COMPILED/TRANSCRIBED BY BERNARD T. PUNZALAN / HTTP://WWW.CHAMORROROOTS.COM)

FOURTEENTH CENSUS OF THE UNITED STATES: 1920—POPULATION
ISLAND OF GUAM

DISTRICT 2
NAME OF PLACE Agana (City)
[Proper name and, also, name of class, as city, town, village, barrio, etc]

ENUMERATED BY ME ON THE 27th DAY OF February, 1920

Arthur W. Jackson ENUMERATOR

	PLACE OF ABODE		NAME	RELATION	PERSONAL DESCRIPTION				EDUCATION			NATIVITY				OCCUPATION
Street, avenue, road, etc. (1)	Number of dwelling house in order of visitation (2)	Number of family in order of visitation (3)	of each person whose place of abode on January 1, 1920, was in the family. (4)	Relationship of this Person to the head of the family. (5)	Sex (6)	Color or race (7)	Age at last birthday (8)	Single, married, widowed or divorced (9)	Attended school any time since Sept. 1, 1919 (10)	Whether able to read. (11)	Whether able to write. (12)	Place of birth of this person. (13)	Place of birth of father of this person. (14)	Place of birth of mother of this person. (15)	Whether able to speak English. (16)	Trade, profession, or particular kind of work done, as salesman, laborer, clerk, cook, merchant, washerwoman, etc. (17)
	52	66	Salas, Maria C	Wife	F	Cha	40.0	M		N	N	Guam	Guam	Guam	N	None
	52	66	Salas, Joaquin C	Son	M	Cha	20.0	S	N	Y	Y	Guam	Guam	Guam	N	Farm laborer
	52	66	Salas, Jose C	Son	M	Cha	18.0	S	N	Y	Y	Guam	Guam	Guam	Y	Laborer
	52	66	Salas, Maria C	Daughter	F	Cha	17.0	S	N	Y	Y	Guam	Guam	Guam	Y	None
	52	66	Salas, Rosa C	Daughter	F	Cha	15.0	S	N	Y	Y	Guam	Guam	Guam	Y	None
	52	66	Salas, Ana C	Daughter	F	Cha	14.0	S	N	Y	Y	Guam	Guam	Guam	Y	None
	52	66	Salas, Vicente C	Son	M	Cha	9.0	S	Y	Y	Y	Guam	Guam	Guam		None
	53	67	Gumataotao, Juana D	Head	F	Cha	65.0	Wd		N	N	Guam	Guam	Guam	N	None
	54	68	Cruz, Jesus C	Head	M	Cha	25.0	M		Y	Y	Guam	Guam	Guam	N	Farmer
Soledad Street	54	68	Cruz, Maria S	Wife	F	Cha	24.0	M		Y	Y	Guam	Guam	Guam	N	None
	54	68	Cruz, Felix S	Son	M	Cha	2.0	S				Guam	Guam	Guam		None
	54	68	Cruz, Ana S	Daughter	F	Cha	0.5	S				Guam	Guam	Guam		None
	55	69	Santos, Joaquin U	Head	M	Cha	43.0	M		Y	Y	Guam	Guam	Guam	N	Farmer
	55	69	Santos, Ana R	Wife	F	Cha	42.0	M		N	N	Guam	Guam	Guam	N	None
	55	69	Santos, Rosario	Step daughter	F	Cha	17.0	S	N	Y	Y	Guam	Guam	Guam	Y	None
	56	70	Dungca, Jose S	Head	M	Fil	28.0	M		Y	Y	Guam	Philippine Islands	Philippine Islands	N	Peddler
	56	70	Dungca, Juana	Wife	F	Cha	48.0	M		N	N	Guam	Guam	Guam	N	None
	56	70	Dungca, Concepcion	Daughter	F	Fil	19.0	S	N	Y	Y	Guam	Guam	Guam	Y	None
	56	70	Dungca, Constancia	Daughter	F	Fil	7.0	S	Y			Guam	Guam	Guam		None
	56	70	Dungca, Dolores	Daughter	F	Fil	5.0	S	N			Guam	Guam	Guam		None
	57	71	Santos, Antonia	Head	F	Cha	43.0	S		Y	Y	Guam	Unknown	Guam	N	None
	57	71	Santos, Jose	Son	M	Cha	19.0	S	N	Y	Y	Guam	Unknown	Guam	N	None
	57	71	Santos, Joaquina	Daughter	F	Cha	12.0	S	Y	Y	Y	Guam	Unknown	Guam	Y	None
	57	71	Santos, Manuel	Son	M	Cha	10.0	S	Y	Y	Y	Guam	Unknown	Guam	N	None
	57	71	Santos, Ana	Daughter	F	Cha	8.0	S	Y	Y	Y	Guam	Unknown	Guam		None

226

(CHAMORRO ROOTS GENEALOGY PROJECT ™ TRANSCRIPTION)
(COMPILED/TRANSCRIBED BY BERNARD T. PUNZALAN / HTTP://WWW.CHAMORROROOTS.COM)

112

SHEET NO. 8A

FOURTEENTH CENSUS OF THE UNITED STATES: 1920-POPULATION

ISLAND OF GUAM

ENUMERATED BY ME ON THE 27th DAY OF February, 1920

Arthur W. Jackson ENUMERATOR

DISTRICT 2
NAME OF PLACE Agana (City)
[Proper name and, also, name of class, as city, town, village, barrio, etc]

	Street	Dwelling No.	Family No.	NAME	RELATION	Sex	Color or race	Age	Marital	School	Read	Write	Birthplace of person	Birthplace of father	Birthplace of mother	Speak English	OCCUPATION
1		57	71	Santos, Lourdes	Daughter	F	Cha	0.3	S				Guam	Unknown	Guam		None
2		58	72	Algarao, T	Head	M	Fil	62.0	M		Y	Y	Philippine Islands	Philippine Islands	Philippine Islands	N	Farmer
3		58	72	Algarao, Francisca C	Wife	F	Cha	52.0	M		N	N	Guam	Guam	Guam	N	None
4		58	72	Cruz, Milagro	Step daughter	F	Cha	12.0	S	Y	Y	Y	Guam	Unknown	Guam	Y	None
5		59	73	Rojas, Joaquin C	Head	M	Cha	40.0	M		Y	Y	Guam	Guam	Guam	Y	Laborer
6		59	73	Rojas, Maria S	Wife	F	Cha	27.0	M		Y	Y	Guam	Guam	Guam	N	None
7		59	73	Rojas, Francisco S	Son	M	Cha	6.0	S	N			Guam	Guam	Guam		None
8		59	73	Rojas, Margarita S	Daughter	F	Cha	4.0	S				Guam	Guam	Guam		None
9		59	73	Rojas, Pedro S	Son	M	Cha	2.0	S				Guam	Guam	Guam		None
10	Soledad Street	60	74	Santos, Josefa	Head	F	Cha	46.0	Wd		N	N	Guam	Guam	Guam	N	None
11		60	74	Santos, Jose P	Son	M	Cha	17.0	S	N	Y	Y	Guam	Guam	Guam	Y	Laborer
12		60	74	Santos, Rita P	Daughter	F	Cha	15.0	S	N	Y	Y	Guam	Guam	Guam	Y	None
13		60	74	Santos, Pedro P	Son	M	Cha	12.0	S	Y	Y	Y	Guam	Guam	Guam	Y	None
14		60	74	Santos, Juan P	Son	M	Cha	9.0	S	Y			Guam	Guam	Guam		None
15		61	75	Chargualaf, Ignacio M	Head	M	Cha	43.0	M		Y	Y	Guam	Guam	Guam	Y	Farmer
16		61	75	Chargualaf, Maria R	Wife	F	Cha	42.0	M		N	N	Guam	Guam	Guam	N	None
17		61	75	Chargualaf, Jose R	Son	M	Cha	20.0	S	N	Y	Y	Guam	Guam	Guam	Y	Laborer
18		61	75	Salas, Veronica	Step daughter	F	Cha	20.0	S	N	Y	Y	Guam	Unknown	Unknown	Y	None
19		61	75	Salas, Virginia	Step daughter	F	Cha	2.0	S				Guam	Unknown	Philippine Islands		None
20		61	76	Rojas, Mariano M	Head	M	Fil	80.0	Wd		N	N	Guam	Philippine Islands	Guam	N	None
21		61	76	Rojas, Jose S	Grandson	M	Cha	12.0	S	Y	Y	Y	Guam	Guam	Guam	Y	None
22		61	76	Rojas, Benita R	Granddaughter	F	Cha	7.0	S	N	N		Guam	Guam	Guam	N	None
23		61	76	Rojas, Maria R	Granddaughter	F	Cha	6.0	S	N			Guam	Guam	Guam		None
24		62	77	Rojas, Juan C	Head	M	Cha	31.0	M		N	N	Guam	Guam	Guam	N	Laborer
25		62	77	Rojas, Juana C	Wife	F	Cha	33.0	M		N	N	Guam	Guam	Guam	N	None

(CHAMORRO ROOTS GENEALOGY PROJECT ™ TRANSCRIPTION)
(COMPILED/TRANSCRIBED BY BERNARD T. PUNZALAN / HTTP://WWW.CHAMORROROOTS.COM)
FOURTEENTH CENSUS OF THE UNITED STATES: 1920-POPULATION
ISLAND OF GUAM

DISTRICT 2
NAME OF PLACE Agana (City)
[Proper name and, also, name of class, as city, town, village, barrio, etc]

ENUMERATED BY ME ON THE 27th DAY OF February, 1920

Arthur W. Jackson ENUMERATOR

	Street, avenue, road, etc.	Number of dwelling house in order of visitation	Number of family in order of visitation	NAME	RELATION	Sex	Color or race	Age at last birthday	Single, married, widowed or divorced	Attended school any time since Sept. 1, 1919	Whether able to read.	Whether able to write.	Place of birth of this person.	Place of birth of father of this person.	Place of birth of mother of this person.	Whether able to speak English.	OCCUPATION
	1	2	3	4	5	6	7	8	9	10	11	12	13	14	15	16	17
26		62	77	Rojas, Concepcion C	Daughter	F	Cha	6.0	S	N			Guam	Guam	Guam		None
27		62	77	Rojas, Tomas C	Son	M	Cha	5.0	S	N			Guam	Guam	Guam		None
28		62	77	Rojas, Natividad C	Daughter	F	Cha	2.0	S				Guam	Guam	Guam		None
29		63	78	Salas, Emeterio S	Head	M	Cha	44.0	M		Y	Y	Guam	Guam	Guam	N	Carpenter
30		63	78	Salas, Josefa M	Wife	F	Cha	47.0	M		Y	Y	Guam	Guam	Guam	N	None
31		63	78	Salas, Ignacia M	Daughter	F	Cha	12.0	S	Y	Y	Y	Guam	Guam	Guam	Y	None
32		63	78	Salas, Jose M	Son	M	Cha	10.0	S	Y	Y	Y	Guam	Guam	Guam	Y	None
33		63	78	Salas, Maria M	Daughter	F	Cha	6.0	S	N			Guam	Guam	Guam		None
34		63	78	Santos, Francisco M	Step son	M	Cha	19.0	S	Y	Y	Y	Guam	Guam	Guam	Y	Dentist's Asst
35		63	78	Santos, Vicenta M	Step daughter	F	Cha	17.0	S	N	Y	Y	Guam	Guam	Guam	Y	None
36	Soledad Street	63	78	Santos, Manuel M	Step son	M	Cha	15.0	S	N	Y	Y	Guam	Guam	Guam	Y	None
37		63	79	Okada, Shintoro J	Head	M	Jp	25.0	M		Y	Y	Japan	Japan	Japan	Y	Machinist
38		63	79	Okada, Joaquina S	Wife	F	Cha	23.0	M		Y	Y	Guam	Guam	Guam	Y	None
39		63	79	Okada, Juan S	Son	M	Jp	4.0	S				Guam	Japan	Guam		None
40		63	79	Okada, Carlos S	Son	M	Jp	2.0	S				Guam	Japan	Guam		None
41		63	79	Okada, Edward S	Son	M	Jp	1.0	S				Guam	Japan	Guam		None
42		64	80	Baza, Agustin U	Head	M	Cha	38.0	M		Y	Y	Guam	Guam	Guam	N	Laborer
43		64	80	Baza, Maria T	Wife	F	Cha	50.0	M		N	N	Guam	Guam	Guam	N	None
44		64	80	Baza, Pedro T	Son	M	Cha	14.0	S	Y	Y	Y	Guam	Guam	Guam	Y	None
45		64	80	Baza, Rita T	Daughter	F	Cha	12.0	S	Y	Y	Y	Guam	Guam	Guam	Y	None
46		65	81	Rios, Gregorio	Head	M	Cha	78.0	Wd		Y	Y	Guam	Guam	Guam	N	None
47		65	81	Rios, Trinidad G	Daughter	F	Cha	25.0	S		Y	Y	Guam	Guam	Guam	N	None
48		65	81	Rios, Manuel R	Grandson	M	Cha	11.0	S	Y	Y	Y	Guam	Unknown	Unknown	Y	None
49		65	81	Rios, Rosa R	Granddaughter	F	Cha	3.0	S				Guam	Unknown	Guam		None
50		65	82	Rosario, Luisa M	Head	F	Cha	65.0	Wd		Y	Y	Guam	Guam	Guam	N	None

228

(CHAMORRO ROOTS GENEALOGY PROJECT ™ TRANSCRIPTION)
(COMPILED/TRANSCRIBED BY BERNARD T. PUNZALAN / HTTP://WWW.CHAMORROROOTS.COM)
FOURTEENTH CENSUS OF THE UNITED STATES: 1920—POPULATION
ISLAND OF GUAM

DISTRICT 2
NAME OF PLACE **Agana (City)**
[Proper name and, also, name of class, as city, town, village, barrio, etc]

ENUMERATED BY ME ON THE 27th DAY OF February, 1920

Arthur W. Jackson ENUMERATOR

	Street	Dwelling No.	Family No.	NAME	RELATION	Sex	Color or race	Age	S/M/Wd/D	Attended school since Sept. 1, 1919	Able to read	Able to write	Birthplace of person	Birthplace of father	Birthplace of mother	Speak English	OCCUPATION
	1	2	3	4	5	6	7	8	9	10	11	12	13	14	15	16	17
1		65	82	Rosario, Domingo M	Son	M	Cha	30.0	S		Y	Y	Guam	Guam	Guam	N	Laborer
2		66	83	Concepcion, Jose E	Head	M	Cha	58.0	M		Y	Y	Guam	Guam	Guam	N	Farm laborer
3		66	83	Concepcion, Antonia M	Wife	F	Cha	55.0	M		N	N	Guam	Unknown	Guam	N	None
4		66	83	Concepcion, Maria M	Daughter	F	Cha	19.0	S	N	Y	Y	Guam	Guam	Guam	N	None
5		66	83	Concepcion, Jose M	Son	M	Cha	16.0	S	N	Y	Y	Guam	Guam	Guam	Y	None
6		66	83	Mendiola, Dolores	Servant	F	Cha	10.0	S	Y	Y	Y	Guam	Guam	Guam	Y	Servant
7		67	84	Reyes, Jesus T	Head	M	Cha	31.0	M		Y	Y	Guam	Guam	Guam	Y	Servant
8		67	84	Reyes, Dolores M	Wife	F	Cha	30.0	M		Y	Y	Guam	Guam	Guam	Y	None
9		67	84	Reyes, Henry M	Son	M	Cha	9.0	S	Y			Guam	Guam	Guam		None
10		67	84	Reyes, Carmen M	Daughter	F	Cha	8.0	S	Y			Guam	Guam	Guam		None
11		67	84	Reyes, Segundo M	Son	M	Cha	3.0	S				Guam	Guam	Guam		None
12	Soledad Street	68	85	Cruz, Juan G	Head	M	Cha	38.0	M		Y	Y	Guam	Guam	Guam	N	Farmer
13		68	85	Cruz, Isabel C	Wife	F	Cha	37.0	M		Y	Y	Guam	Guam	Guam	N	None
14		68	85	Cruz, Jose C	Son	M	Cha	14.0	S	Y	Y	Y	Guam	Guam	Guam	Y	None
15		68	85	Cruz, Maria C	Daughter	F	Cha	12.0	S	Y	Y	Y	Guam	Guam	Guam	Y	None
16		68	85	Cruz, Jesus C	Son	M	Cha	10.0	S	Y	Y	Y	Guam	Guam	Guam	N	None
17		68	85	Cruz, Juan C	Son	M	Cha	8.0	S	Y			Guam	Guam	Guam		None
18		68	85	Cruz, Ana C	Daughter	F	Cha	7.0	S	Y			Guam	Guam	Guam		None
19		68	85	Cruz, Concepcion C	Daughter	F	Cha	4.0	S				Guam	Guam	Guam		None
20		68	85	Cruz, Francisco C	Son	M	Cha	2.0	S				Guam	Guam	Guam		None
21		68	85	Cruz, Magdalena C	Daughter	F	Cha	1.0	S				Guam	Guam	Guam		None
22		69	86	Perez, Jesus S	Head	M	Cha	28.0	Wd		Y	Y	Guam	Guam	Guam	N	Carpenter
23		69	86	Perez, Pilar S	Daughter	F	Cha	8.0	S	Y			Guam	Guam	Guam		None
24		69	86	Perez, Candaleria S	Daughter	F	Cha	7.0	S	Y			Guam	Guam	Guam		None
25		69	86	Perez, Jose S	Son	M	Cha	5.0	S	N			Guam	Guam	Guam		None

(CHAMORRO ROOTS GENEALOGY PROJECT ™ TRANSCRIPTION)
(COMPILED/TRANSCRIBED BY BERNARD T. PUNZALAN / HTTP://WWW.CHAMORROROOTS.COM)
FOURTEENTH CENSUS OF THE UNITED STATES: 1920–POPULATION
ISLAND OF GUAM

DISTRICT 2
NAME OF PLACE Agana (City)

ENUMERATED BY ME ON THE 28th DAY OF February, 1920

Arthur W. Jackson ENUMERATOR

	Dwelling No.	Family No.	NAME	RELATION	Sex	Color or race	Age	Condition	School	Read	Write	Birthplace	Father	Mother	English	OCCUPATION
1	2	3	4	5	6	7	8	9	10	11	12	13	14	15	16	17
26	69	86	Perez, Concepcion S	Sister	F	Cha	20.0	S	N	Y	Y	Guam	Guam	Guam	N	None
27	70	87	Salas, Benigno D	Head	M	Cha	44.0	M		Y	Y	Guam	Guam	Guam	Y	Carpenter
28	70	87	Salas, Victoria S	Wife	F	Cha	45.0	M		Y	Y	Guam	Guam	Guam	N	None
29	71	88	Duenas, Jose T	Head	M	Cha	50.0	M		Y	Y	Guam	Guam	Guam	N	Farmer
30	71	88	Duenas, Luisa M	Wife	F	Cha	48.0	M		N	N	Guam	Guam	Guam	N	None
31	71	88	Duenas, Rosa M	Daughter	F	Cha	23.0	S		Y	Y	Guam	Guam	Guam	N	Laundress
32	71	88	Duenas, Manuel M	Son	M	Cha	10.0	S	Y	Y	Y	Guam	Guam	Guam	Y	None
33	71	88	Duenas, Irene M	Daughter	F	Cha	9.0	S	Y	Y	Y	Guam	Guam	Guam		None
34	71	89	Respecio, Antonio P	Head	M	Fil	21.0	M	N	Y	Y	Guam	Philippine Islands	Guam	Y	Enlisted US Navy
35	71	89	Respecio, Ana M	Wife	F	Cha	20.0	M	N	Y	Y	Guam	Guam	Guam	Y	None
36	71	89	Respecio, Roman M	Son	M	Fil	2.0	S				Guam	Guam	Guam		None
37	71	89	Respecio, Brigida M	Daughter	F	Fil	0.1	S				Guam	Guam	Guam		None
38	71	89	Duenas, Julia	Niece	F	Cha	4.0	S				Guam	Guam	Guam		None
39	72	90	Indalecio, Ana	Head	F	Cha	41.0	S	N	N	N	Guam	Unknown	Unknown	N	None
40	72	90	Indalecio, Vicente	Son	M	Cha	20.0	S	N	Y	Y	Guam	Unknown	Guam	Y	Laborer
41	72	90	Indalecio, Juan	Son	M	Cha	18.0	S	N	Y	Y	Guam	Unknown	Guam	Y	None
42	72	90	Indalecio, Jose	Son	M	Cha	15.0	S	N	Y	Y	Guam	Unknown	Guam	Y	None
43	72	90	Indalecio, Magdalena	Daughter	F	Cha	14.0	S	N	Y	Y	Guam	Unknown	Guam	Y	None
44	72	90	Indalecio, Dolores	Daughter	F	Cha	12.0	S	Y	Y	Y	Guam	Unknown	Guam	N	None
45	72	90	Indalecio, Rita	Daughter	F	Cha	10.0	S	Y	Y	Y	Guam	Unknown	Guam	N	None
46	73	91	Chargualaf, Felix	Head	M	Cha	28.0	M		Y	Y	Guam	Guam	Guam	N	Laborer
47	73	91	Chargualaf, Ignacia L	Wife	F	Cha	24.0	M		Y	Y	Guam	Guam	Guam	N	None
48	73	91	Chargualaf, Maria L	Daughter	F	Cha	3.0	S				Guam	Guam	Guam	N	None
49	73	91	Chargualaf, Rosario L	Daughter	F	Cha	0.2	S				Guam	Guam	Guam		None
50	74	92	Rojas, Manuel C	Head	M	Cha	35.0	Wd		Y	Y	Guam	Guam	Guam	Y	Janitor

Street, avenue, road, etc: Soledad Street

(CHAMORRO ROOTS GENEALOGY PROJECT ™ TRANSCRIPTION)
(COMPILED/TRANSCRIBED BY BERNARD T. PUNZALAN / HTTP://WWW.CHAMORROROOTS.COM)
FOURTEENTH CENSUS OF THE UNITED STATES: 1920-POPULATION
ISLAND OF GUAM

DISTRICT 2
NAME OF PLACE Agana (City)
[Proper name and, also, name of class, as city, town, village, barrio, etc]

ENUMERATED BY ME ON THE 28th DAY OF February, 1920
Arthur W. Jackson ENUMERATOR

Street, avenue, road, etc.	Number of dwelling house is in order of visitation	Number of family in order of visitation	NAME	RELATION	Sex	Color or race	Age at last birthday	Single, married, widowed or divorced	Attended school any time since Sept. 1, 1919	Whether able to read.	Whether able to write.	Place of birth of this person.	Place of birth of father of this person.	Place of birth of mother of this person.	Whether able to speak English.	OCCUPATION
1	2	3	4	5	6	7	8	9	10	11	12	13	14	15	16	17
	75	93	Mesa, Vicente S	Head	M	Cha	22.0	M		Y	Y	Guam	Guam	Guam	Y	Carpenter
	75	93	Mesa, Dolores C	Wife	F	Cha	21.0	M	N	Y	Y	Guam	Guam	Guam	N	None
	76	94	Perez, Jose S	Head	M	Cha	35.0	M		Y	Y	Guam	Guam	Guam	Y	Carpenter
	76	94	Perez, Concepcion C	Wife	F	Cha	33.0	M		Y	Y	Guam	Guam	Guam	N	None
	76	94	Perez, Josefina C	Daughter	F	Cha	10.0	S	Y	Y	Y	Guam	Guam	Guam	Y	None
	76	94	Perez, Jose C	Son	M	Cha	8.0	S	Y			Guam	Guam	Guam		None
	76	94	Perez, Elisa C	Daughter	F	Cha	6.0	S	N			Guam	Guam	Guam		None
	76	94	Perez, Juan C	Son	M	Cha	5.0	S	N			Guam	Guam	Guam		None
Soledad Street	76	94	Perez, Gregorio C	Son	M	Cha	3.0	S				Guam	Guam	Guam		None
	76	94	Perez, Manuel C	Son	M	Cha	2.0	S				Guam	Guam	Guam		None
	76	94	Perez, Maria C	Daughter	F	Cha	0.2	S				Guam	Guam	Guam		None
	76	94	Cruz, Maria B	Mother-in-law	F	Cha	64.0	Wd		N	N	Guam	Guam	Guam	N	None
	76	94	Iriarte, Ana	Servant	F	Cha	13.0	S	N	Y	Y	Guam	Guam	Guam	N	Servant
	77	95	Garrido, Vicente B	Head	M	Cha	27.0	M		Y	Y	Guam	Guam	Guam	Y	Enlisted US Navy
	77	95	Garrido, Vicenta L	Wife	F	Cha	24.0	M		Y	Y	Guam	Guam	Guam	Y	None
	77	95	Garrido, Dorotea L	Daughter	F	Cha	5.0	S	N			Guam	Guam	Guam		None
	77	95	Garrido, Carmen L	Daughter	F	Cha	4.0	S				Guam	Guam	Guam		None
	77	95	Garrido, Maria L	Daughter	F	Cha	3.0	S				Guam	Guam	Guam		None
	77	95	Garrido, Jesus L	Son	M	Cha	2.0	S				Guam	Guam	Guam		None
	77	95	Garrido, Vicente L	Son	M	Cha	0.6	S				Guam	Guam	Guam		None
	77	95	Lujan, Luisa G	Sister-in-law	F	Cha	27.0	S		Y	Y	Guam	Guam	Guam	N	None
	77	95	Pangelinan, Juana	Niece	F	Cha	13.0	S	N	Y	Y	Guam	Guam	Guam	Y	None
	78	96	Mafnas, Manuel P	Head	M	Cha	24.0	S	N	Y	Y	Guam	Guam	Guam	Y	Farmer
	78	96	Mafnas, Jose P	Brother	M	Cha	19.0	S	N	Y	Y	Guam	Guam	Guam	Y	Clerk
	78	96	Mafnas, Magdalena P	Sister	F	Cha	18.0	S	N	Y	Y	Guam	Guam	Guam	Y	None

(CHAMORRO ROOTS GENEALOGY PROJECT ™ TRANSCRIPTION)
(COMPILED/TRANSCRIBED BY BERNARD T. PUNZALAN / HTTP://WWW.CHAMORROROOTS.COM)

FOURTEENTH CENSUS OF THE UNITED STATES: 1920–POPULATION

ISLAND OF GUAM

DISTRICT 2
NAME OF PLACE Agana (City)

[Proper name and, also, name of class, as city, town, village, barrio, etc]

ENUMERATED BY ME ON THE 28th DAY OF February, 1920

Arthur W. Jackson ENUMERATOR

1	2	3	4	5	6	7	8	9	10	11	12	13	14	15	16	17
Street	Dwelling	Family	NAME	RELATION	Sex	Color or race	Age	Single/married/wid/div	Attended school since Sept 1, 1919	Read	Write	Birthplace of person	Birthplace of father	Birthplace of mother	Speak English	OCCUPATION
	78	96	Mafnas, Maria P	Sister	F	Cha	16.0	S	N	Y	Y	Guam	Guam	Guam	Y	Laundress
	78	96	San Nicolas, Dolores	Sister	F	Cha	36.0	M		N	N	Guam	Guam	Guam	N	Servant
	78	96	Mafnas, Maria P	Niece	F	Cha	12.0	S	Y	Y	Y	Guam	Unknown	Guam	Y	None
	79	97	Matanane, Jose	Head	M	Cha	30.0	M		Y	Y	Guam	Unknown	Guam	Y	Enlisted US Navy
	79	97	Matanane, Maria A	Wife	F	Cha	26.0	M		Y	Y	Guam	Guam	Guam	N	None
	80	98	Camacho, Tomasa P	Head	F	Cha	51.0	Wd		N	N	Guam	Guam	Guam	N	None
	80	98	Camacho, Luis P	Son	M	Cha	17.0	S	N	Y	Y	Guam	Guam	Guam	Y	Farmer
Soledad Street	81	99	Chargualaf, Juan R	Head	M	Cha	33.0	M		Y	Y	Guam	Guam	Guam	Y	Machinist
	81	99	Chargualaf, Ana R	Wife	F	Cha	30.0	M		Y	Y	Guam	Guam	Guam	Y	None
	81	99	Chargualaf, Juan R	Son	M	Cha	1.0	S				Guam	Guam	Guam		None
	82	100	Iriarte, Lorenzo	Head	M	Cha	42.0	M		Y	Y	Guam	Guam	Guam	N	Farmer
	82	100	Iriarte, Ana D	Wife	F	Cha	39.0	M		Y	Y	Guam	Guam	Guam	N	None
	82	100	Iriarte, Juan D	Son	M	Cha	17.0	S	N	Y	Y	Guam	Guam	Guam	Y	Laborer
	82	100	Iriarte, Vicente D	Son	M	Cha	16.0	S	N	Y	Y	Guam	Guam	Guam	Y	None
	82	100	Iriarte, Maria D	Daughter	F	Cha	15.0	S	N	Y	Y	Guam	Guam	Guam	Y	None
	82	100	Iriarte, Tomas D	Son	M	Cha	13.0	S	N	Y	Y	Guam	Guam	Guam	Y	None
	82	100	Iriarte, Ignacio D	Son	M	Cha	12.0	S	Y	Y	Y	Guam	Guam	Guam	Y	None
	82	100	Iriarte, Jose D	Son	M	Cha	11.0	S	Y	Y	Y	Guam	Guam	Guam	N	None
	82	100	Iriarte, Juan D	Son	M	Cha	10.0	S	Y	Y	Y	Guam	Guam	Guam	N	None
	82	100	Iriarte, Antonio D	Son	M	Cha	8.0	S	Y			Guam	Guam	Guam	N	None
	82	100	Iriarte, Ana D	Daughter	F	Cha	6.0	S	N			Guam	Guam	Guam		None
	82	100	Iriarte, Felisa D	Daughter	F	Cha	5.0	S	N			Guam	Guam	Guam		None
	82	100	Iriarte, Cristina D	Daughter	F	Cha	0.3	S				Guam	Guam	Guam		None
	83	101	Mafnas, Benancio C	Head	M	Cha	42.0	M		Y	Y	Guam	Guam	Guam	N	Farmer
	83	101	Mafnas, Juana T	Wife	F	Cha	44.0	M		Y	Y	Guam	Guam	Guam	N	None

(CHAMORRO ROOTS GENEALOGY PROJECT ™ TRANSCRIPTION)
(COMPILED/TRANSCRIBED BY BERNARD T. PUNZALAN / HTTP://WWW.CHAMORROROOTS.COM)
FOURTEENTH CENSUS OF THE UNITED STATES: 1920—POPULATION
ISLAND OF GUAM

ENUMERATED BY ME ON THE 1st DAY OF March, 1920

Arthur W. Jackson ENUMERATOR

DISTRICT 2
NAME OF PLACE Agana (City)
[Proper name and, also, name of class, as city, town, village, barrio, etc]

	PLACE OF ABODE		NAME	RELATION	PERSONAL DESCRIPTION					EDUCATION			NATIVITY				OCCUPATION
Street, avenue, road, etc.	Number of dwelling house in order of visitation	Number of family in order of visitation	Name of each person whose place of abode on January 1, 1920, was in the family.	Relationship of this person to the head of the family.	Sex	Color or race	Age at last birthday	Single, married, widowed or divorced	Attended school any time since Sept. 1, 1919	Whether able to read.	Whether able to write.	Place of birth of this person.	Place of birth of father of this person.	Place of birth of mother of this person.	Whether able to speak English.	Trade, profession, or particular kind of work done
1	2	3	4	5	6	7	8	9	10	11	12	13	14	15	16	17
	83	101	Mafnas, Rosa T	Daughter	F	Cha	18.0	S				Guam	Guam	Guam	Y	None
	84	102	Mendiola, Regino Q	Head	M	Cha	33.0	M	N	Y	Y	Guam	Guam	Guam	Y	Fireman
	84	102	Mendiola, Miguela V	Wife	F	Fil	29.0	M		Y	Y	Philippine Islands	Philippine Islands	Philippine Islands	Y	None
	84	102	Mendiola, Dolores P	Daughter	F	Cha	12.0	S	N	Y	Y	Guam	Guam	Guam	Y	None
	84	102	Mendiola, Antonia P	Daughter	F	Cha	11.0	S	Y	Y	Y	Guam	Unknown	Guam	Y	None
Soledad Street	85	103	Simoda, Juana C	Head	F	Cha	46.0	Wd		Y	Y	Guam	Japan	Guam	Y	None
	85	103	Simoda, Maria C	Daughter	F	Jp	25.0	S		Y	Y	Guam	Guam	Guam	Y	None
	85	103	Simoda, Encarnacion C	Granddaughter	F	Cha	6.0	S	N			Guam	Guam	Guam	N	None
	85	103	Simoda, Juana C	Granddaughter	F	Cha	2.0	S				Guam	Guam	Guam	Y	None
	86	104	Quichocho, Dolores C	Head	F	Cha	48.0	Wd		N	N	Guam	Guam	Guam	N	None
	86	104	Quichocho, Jesus C	Son	M	Cha	49.0	S	N	Y	Y	Guam	Guam	Guam	Y	Farm laborer
	86	104	Quichocho, Maria Q	Niece	F	Cha	21.0	S		Y	Y	Guam	Guam	Guam	N	None
	87	105	Anderson, Leon	Head	M	W	58.0	M		Y	Y	Guam	England	Guam	Y	Farmer
	87	105	Anderson, Antonia P	Wife	F	Cha	53.0	M		Y	Y	Guam	Guam	Guam	N	None
	87	105	Anderson, Engracia P	Daughter	F	W	21.0	S	N	Y	Y	Guam	Guam	Guam	Y	None
	87	105	Anderson, Vicente P	Son	M	W	19.0	S	N	Y	Y	Guam	Guam	Guam	Y	Cook
	87	105	Anderson, Jesusa P	Daughter	F	W	15.0	S	N	Y	Y	Guam	Guam	Guam	Y	None
Hernan Cortez Street	88	106	Perez, Antonio C	Head	M	Cha	75.0	Wd		Y	Y	Guam	Guam	Guam	N	None
	88	106	Perez, Ana LG	Daughter	F	Cha	32.0	S		Y	Y	Guam	Guam	Guam	Y	None
	88	107	Perez, Antonio LG	Head	M	Cha	29.0	M		Y	Y	Guam	Guam	Guam	Y	Blacksmith
	88	107	Perez, Nicolasa P	Wife	F	Cha	24.0	M		Y	Y	Guam	Guam	Guam	Y	None
	88	107	Perez, Cecilia P	Daughter	F	Cha	4.0	S				Guam	Guam	Guam		None
	88	107	Perez, Dortotea P	Daughter	F	Cha	3.0	S				Guam	Guam	Guam		None
	88	107	Perez, Clotilde P	Daughter	F	Cha	2.0	S				Guam	Guam	Guam		None
	88	107	Perez, Ernesto P	Son	M	Cha	1.0	S				Guam	Guam	Guam		None

(CHAMORRO ROOTS GENEALOGY PROJECT ™ TRANSCRIPTION)
(COMPILED/TRANSCRIBED BY BERNARD T. PUNZALAN / HTTP://WWW.CHAMORROROOTS.COM)
FOURTEENTH CENSUS OF THE UNITED STATES: 1920-POPULATION
ISLAND OF GUAM

DISTRICT 2
NAME OF PLACE Agana (City)
[Proper name and, also, name of class, as city, town, village, barrio, etc]

ENUMERATED BY ME ON THE 1st DAY OF March, 1920

Arthur W. Jackson ENUMERATOR

	Street	Dwelling	Family	NAME	RELATION	Sex	Color or race	Age	Marital	School	Read	Write	Birthplace person	Birthplace father	Birthplace mother	Eng.	OCCUPATION
26		88	108	Perez, Jose LG	Head	M	Cha	41.0	Wd		Y	Y	Guam	Guam	Guam	N	Blacksmith
27		88	108	Perez, Gregorio C	Son	M	Cha	3.0	S				Guam	Guam	Guam		None
28		88	108	Perez, Antonio C	Son	M	Cha	2.0	S				Guam	Guam	Guam		None
29		88	108	Rosa, Trinidad	Servant	F	Cha	21.0	S		Y	Y	Guam	Unknown	Guam	Y	Servant
30		88	108	Quintanilla, Jose	Servant	M	Cha	16.0	S	N	N	N	Guam	Unknown	Guam	N	Servant
31		89	109	Perez, Rosa F	Head	F	Cha	47.0	S		Y	Y	Guam	Guam	Guam	N	None
32		89	109	Perez, Emelia F	Sister	F	Cha	46.0	S				Guam	Guam	Guam	N	None
33		89	109	Perez, Joaquina F	Sister	F	Cha	37.0	S				Guam	Guam	Guam	N	None
34	Hernan Cortez Street	89	109	Perez, Joaquin F	Brother	M	Cha	34.0	S		Y	Y	Guam	Guam	Guam	Y	Carpenter
35		89	109	Torres, Ana P	Niece	F	Cha	17.0	S	N	Y	Y	Guam	Guam	Guam	Y	None
36		89	109	Torres, Maria P	Niece	F	Cha	15.0	S	N	Y	Y	Guam	Guam	Guam	Y	None
37		89	110	Perez, Jose F	Head	M	Cha	43.0	M		Y	Y	Guam	Guam	Guam	N	Farmer
38		89	110	Perez, Antonia M	Wife	F	Cha	32.0	M		Y	Y	Guam	Guam	Guam	Y	None
39		90	111	Custino, Joe K	Head	M	Cha	32.0	M		Y	Y	Terr. Hawaii	Guam	Terr. Hawaii	Y	Carpenter
40		90	111	Custino, Rosa T	Wife	F	Cha	39.0	M		Y	Y	Guam	Guam	Guam	Y	None
41		90	111	Custino, Helen T	Daughter	F	Cha	12.0	S	Y	Y	Y	Guam	Terr. Hawaii	Guam	Y	None
42		90	111	Custino, Annie T	Daughter	F	Cha	11.0	S	Y	Y	Y	Guam	Terr. Hawaii	Guam	Y	None
43		90	111	Custino, Ruth T	Daughter	F	Cha	9.0	S	Y			Guam	Terr. Hawaii	Guam		None
44		90	111	Custino, Joseph K T	Son	M	Cha	4.0	S				Guam	Terr. Hawaii	Guam		None
45		90	111	Custino, Edward T	Son	M	Cha	3.0	S				Guam	Terr. Hawaii	Guam		None
46		90	111	Custino, Charles T	Son	M	Cha	1.0	S				Guam	Terr. Hawaii	Guam		None
47		90	111	Custino, John E T	Son	M	Cha	0.2	S				Guam	Terr. Hawaii	Guam		None
48		91	112	Flores, Jose G	Head	M	Cha	32.0	M		Y	Y	Guam	Guam	Guam	Y	Plumber
49		91	112	Flores, Rita T	Wife	F	Cha	40.0	M		Y	Y	Guam	Guam	Guam	Y	None
50		91	112	Flores, Joaquin T	Son	M	Cha	12.0	S	Y	Y	Y	Guam	Guam	Guam	Y	None

(CHAMORRO ROOTS GENEALOGY PROJECT ™ TRANSCRIPTION)
(COMPILED/TRANSCRIBED BY BERNARD T. PUNZALAN / HTTP://WWW.CHAMORROROOTS.COM)

FOURTEENTH CENSUS OF THE UNITED STATES: 1920–POPULATION

ISLAND OF GUAM

DISTRICT 2
NAME OF PLACE Agana (City)
[Proper name and, also, name of class, as city, town, village, barrio, etc]

ENUMERATED BY ME ON THE 1st DAY OF March, 1920

Arthur W. Jackson ENUMERATOR

	PLACE OF ABODE		NAME	RELATION	PERSONAL DESCRIPTION				EDUCATION			NATIVITY				OCCUPATION
Street, avenue, road, etc.	Num-ber of dwell-ing house is order of visi-tation	Num-ber of family in order of visi-tation	of each person whose place of abode on January 1, 1920, was in the family.	Relationship of this Person to the head of the family.	Sex	Color or race	Age at last birthday	Single, married, widowed or divorced	Attended school any time since Sept. 1, 1919	Whether able to read.	Whether able to write.	Place of birth of this person.	Place of birth of father of this person.	Place of birth of mother of this person.	Whether able to speak English.	Trade, profession, or particular kind of work done, as salesman, laborer, clerk, cook, merchant, washerwoman, etc.
1	2	3	4	5	6	7	8	9	10	11	12	13	14	15	16	17
	91	112	Flores, Enrique T	Son	M	Cha	11.0	S	Y	Y	Y	Guam	Guam	Guam	Y	None
	91	112	Flores, Emelia T	Daughter	F	Cha	10.0	S	Y	Y	Y	Guam	Guam	Guam	Y	None
	91	112	Flores, Virginia T	Daughter	F	Cha	6.0	S	N			Guam	Guam	Guam		None
	91	112	Flores, Joseph T	Son	M	Cha	3.0	S				Guam	Guam	Guam		None
	92	113	Taitano, Jose M	Head	M	Cha	79.0	Wd		Y	Y	Guam	Guam	Guam	N	None
	92	114	Taitano, Francisco S	Head	M	Cha	29.0	M		Y	Y	Guam	Guam	Guam	Y	Clerk
	92	114	Taitano, Dolores S	Wife	F	Cha	26.0	M		Y	Y	Guam	Guam	Guam	Y	None
Hernan Cortez Street	92	114	Taitano, Rosa S	Daughter	F	Cha	9.0	S	Y			Guam	Guam	Guam		None
	92	114	Taitano, Loela S	Daughter	F	Cha	8.0	S	Y	Y	Y	Guam	Guam	Guam		None
	92	114	Taitano, Josefina S	Daughter	F	Cha	5.0	S	N			Guam	Guam	Guam		None
	92	114	Taitano, Francisco S	Son	M	Cha	3.0	S				Guam	Guam	Guam		None
	92	114	Taitano, Artemio S	Son	M	Cha	2.0	S				Guam	Guam	Guam		None
	92	114	Taitano, Juana S	Daughter	F	Cha	1.0	S				Guam	Guam	Guam		None
	93	115	Garcia, Juan SN	Head	M	Cha	32.0	M		Y	Y	Guam	Guam	Guam	Y	Carpenter
	93	115	Garcia, Rosa M	Wife	F	Cha	31.0	M		Y	Y	Guam	Guam	Guam	N	None
	93	115	Garcia, Jaime M	Son	M	Cha	10.0	S	Y			Guam	Guam	Guam	N	None
	93	115	Garcia, Francisco M	Son	M	Cha	9.0	S	Y	Y	Y	Guam	Guam	Guam		None
	93	115	Garcia, Josefina M	Daughter	F	Cha	5.0	S	Y			Guam	Guam	Guam		None
	93	115	Garcia, Jesus M	Son	M	Cha	2.0	S				Guam	Guam	Guam		None
	93	115	Garcia, Juan M	Son	M	Cha	0.4	S				Guam	Guam	Guam		None
	93	115	Mesa, Rufina S	Mother-in-law	F	Cha	57.0	Wd		Y	Y	Guam	Guam	Guam		None
	93	115	Mesa, Antonio	Brother-in-law	M	Cha	23.0	Wd		Y	Y	Guam	Guam	Guam	Y	Laborer
	93	115	Mesa, Ana	Sister-in-law	F	Cha	16.0	S	N	Y	Y	Guam	Guam	Guam	N	None
	93	115	Mesa, Trinidad	Sister-in-law	F	Cha	14.0	S	N	Y	Y	Guam	Guam	Guam	Y	None
	94	116	Cruz, Juan A	Head	M	Cha	45.0	M		Y	Y	Guam	Guam	Guam	Y	Farmer

116b

(CHAMORRO ROOTS GENEALOGY PROJECT ™ TRANSCRIPTION)
(COMPILED/TRANSCRIBED BY BERNARD T. PUNZALAN / HTTP://WWW.CHAMORROROOTS.COM)

FOURTEENTH CENSUS OF THE UNITED STATES: 1920-POPULATION
ISLAND OF GUAM

ENUMERATED BY ME ON THE 2nd DAY OF March, 1920

Arthur W. Jackson ENUMERATOR

DISTRICT 2
NAME OF PLACE Agana (City)
[Proper name and, also, name of class, as city, town, village, barrio, etc]

	PLACE OF ABODE		NAME	RELATION	PERSONAL DESCRIPTION				EDUCATION			NATIVITY				OCCUPATION
Street, avenue, road, etc.	Number of dwelling house in order of visitation	Number of family in order of visitation	Name	Relationship of this Person to the head of the family.	Sex	Color or race	Age at last birthday	Single, married, widowed or divorced	Attended school any time since Sept. 1, 1919	Whether able to read.	Whether able to write.	Place of birth of this person.	Place of birth of father of this person.	Place of birth of mother of this person.	Whether able to speak English.	Trade, profession, or particular kind of work done, as salesman, laborer, clerk, cook, merchant, washerwoman, etc.
1	2	3	4	5	6	7	8	9	10	11	12	13	14	15	16	17
	94	116	Cruz, Maria LG	Wife	F	Cha	43.0	M		Y	Y	Guam	Guam	Guam	N	None
	94	116	Cruz, Vicente LG	Son	M	Cha	21.0	S		Y	Y	Guam	Guam	Guam	N	Farmer
	94	116	Cruz, Josefa LG	Daughter	F	Cha	18.0	S	N	Y	Y	Guam	Guam	Guam	Y	None
	94	116	Cruz, Jesus LG	Son	M	Cha	16.0	S	N	Y	Y	Guam	Guam	Guam	Y	None
	94	116	Cruz, Jose LG	Son	M	Cha	14.0	S	N	Y	Y	Guam	Guam	Guam	Y	None
	94	116	Cruz, Juan LG	Son	M	Cha	12.0	S	Y	Y	Y	Guam	Guam	Guam	Y	None
	94	116	Cruz, Tomas LG	Son	M	Cha	11.0	S	Y	Y	Y	Guam	Guam	Guam	Y	None
	94	116	Cruz, Amparo LG	Daughter	F	Cha	7.0	S	Y			Guam	Guam	Guam		None
	94	116	Cruz, Mariano LG	Son	M	Cha	4.0	S				Guam	Guam	Guam		None
	94	116	Cruz, Maria LG	Daughter	F	Cha	3.0	S				Guam	Guam	Guam		None
	94	116	Cruz, Antonio LG	Son	M	Cha	0.6	S				Guam	Guam	Guam		None
	95	117	Garcia, Jose C	Head	M	Cha	30.0	M		Y	Y	Guam	Guam	Guam	Y	Carpenter
	95	117	Garcia, Magdalena A	Wife	F	Cha	27.0	M		Y	Y	Guam	Guam	Guam	N	None
	95	117	Garcia, Tomasa A	Daughter	F	Cha	7.0	S	Y			Guam	Guam	Guam		None
	95	117	Garcia, Jesus A	Son	M	Cha	5.0	S	N			Guam	Guam	Guam		None
	95	117	Garcia, Florencio A	Son	M	Cha	4.0	S				Guam	Guam	Guam		None
	95	117	Garcia, Francisco A	Son	M	Cha	2.0	S				Guam	Guam	Guam		None
	95	117	Garcia, Justo A	Son	M	Cha	0.2	S				Guam	Guam	Guam		None
	95	117	Garcia, Angela C	Mother	F	Cha	51.0	Wd		Y	Y	Guam	Unknown	Guam	N	None
	95	117	Garcia, Esparanca C	Sister	F	Cha	33.0	S		Y	Y	Guam	Guam	Guam	N	None
	96	118	Calvo, Leon P	Head	M	W	43.0	M		Y	Y	Guam	Spain	Guam	Y	Watchman
	96	118	Calvo, Maria LG	Wife	F	Cha	37.0	M		Y	Y	Guam	Guam	Guam	N	None
	96	118	Calvo, Jose LG	Son	M	W	10.0	M	Y	Y	Y	Guam	Guam	Guam	N	None
	96	118	Cruz, Susana P	Mother-in-law	F	Cha	68.0	Wd		Y	Y	Guam	Guam	Guam	N	None
	97	119	Perez, Juan LG	Head	M	Cha	39.0	M		Y	Y	Guam	Guam	Guam	Y	Carpenter

Street: Hernan Cortez Street

(CHAMORRO ROOTS GENEALOGY PROJECT ™ TRANSCRIPTION)
(COMPILED/TRANSCRIBED BY BERNARD T. PUNZALAN / HTTP://WWW.CHAMORROROOTS.COM)

FOURTEENTH CENSUS OF THE UNITED STATES: 1920–POPULATION
ISLAND OF GUAM

DISTRICT 2
NAME OF PLACE Agana (City)
[Proper name and, also, name of class, as city, town, village, barrio, etc]

ENUMERATED BY ME ON THE 2nd DAY OF March, 1920

Arthur W. Jackson ENUMERATOR

#	Street	Dwelling No.	Family No.	NAME	RELATION	Sex	Color or race	Age	Single, married, widowed or divorced	Attended school since Sept. 1, 1919	Read	Write	Birthplace of person	Birthplace of father	Birthplace of mother	Speak English	OCCUPATION
1		97	119	Perez, Ana C	Wife	F	Cha	31.0	M		Y	Y	Guam	Guam	Guam	N	None
2		97	119	Perez, Joaquin C	Son	M	Cha	9.0	S	Y			Guam	Guam	Guam		None
3		97	119	Perez, Josefina C	Daughter	F	Cha	3.0	S				Guam	Guam	Guam		None
4		97	119	Perez, Benancio C	Son	M	Cha	1.0	S				Guam	Guam	Guam		None
5		97	119	Perez, Alfreda C	Daughter	F	Cha	0.5	S				Guam	Guam	Guam		None
6		98	120	Perez, Jesus IG	Head	M	Cha	36.0	M		Y	Y	Guam	Guam	Guam	N	Farmer
7		98	120	Perez, Rosa M	Wife	F	Cha	33.0	M		Y	Y	Guam	Guam	Guam	N	None
8		98	120	Perez, Concepcion M	Daughter	F	Cha	13.0	S	N	Y	Y	Guam	Guam	Guam	Y	None
9	Hernan Cortez Street	98	120	Perez, Jesus M	Son	M	Cha	12.0	S	Y	Y	Y	Guam	Guam	Guam	Y	None
10		98	120	Perez, Maria M	Daughter	F	Cha	11.0	S	Y	Y	Y	Guam	Guam	Guam		None
11		98	120	Perez, Antonio M	Son	M	Cha	9.0	S	Y			Guam	Guam	Guam		None
12		98	120	Perez, Felisa M	Daughter	F	Cha	7.0	S	Y			Guam	Guam	Guam		None
13		98	120	Perez, Rosalia M	Daughter	F	Cha	6.0	S	N			Guam	Guam	Guam		None
14		98	120	Perez, Francisco M	Son	M	Cha	5.0	S	N			Guam	Guam	Guam		None
15		98	120	Perez, Jose M	Son	M	Cha	3.0	S				Guam	Guam	Guam		None
16		98	120	Perez, Josefa M	Daughter	F	Cha	0.6	S				Guam	Guam	Guam		None
17		99	121	Martinez, Pedro P	Head	M	Cha	27.0	M		Y	Y	Guam	Guam	Guam	Y	Clerk
18		99	121	Martinez, Maria T	Wife	F	Cha	24.0	M		Y	Y	Guam	Guam	Guam	Y	None
19		99	121	Martinez, Juan L	Son	M	Cha	3.0	S				Guam	Guam	Guam		None
20		99	121	Martinez, Ana L	Daughter	F	Cha	2.0	S				Guam	Guam	Guam		None
21		99	121	Martinez, Pedro M	Son	M	Cha	0.8	S				Guam	Guam	Guam		None
22		99	121	Torres, Rita LG	Sister-in-law	F	Cha	22.0	S		Y	Y	Guam	Guam	Guam		None
23		99	121	Torres, Josefa R	Aunt	F	Cha	52.0	S	N			Guam	Guam	Guam	N	None
24		99	121	Torres, Carmen LG	Sister-in-law	F	Cha	17.0	S	N	Y	Y	Guam	Guam	Guam	Y	None
25		99	121	Martinez, Antonia I	Sister	F	Cha	24.0	S		Y	Y	Guam	Guam	Guam	Y	Postal Clerk

(CHAMORRO ROOTS GENEALOGY PROJECT ™ TRANSCRIPTION)
(COMPILED/TRANSCRIBED BY BERNARD T. PUNZALAN / HTTP://WWW.CHAMORROROOTS.COM)

117b

FOURTEENTH CENSUS OF THE UNITED STATES: 1920—POPULATION

ISLAND OF GUAM

DISTRICT 2
NAME OF PLACE Agana (City)
[Proper name and, also, name of class, as city, town, village, barrio, etc]

ENUMERATED BY ME ON THE 3rd DAY OF March, 1920

Arthur W. Jackson ENUMERATOR

	Street, avenue, road, etc.	Number of dwelling house in order of visitation	Number of family in order of visitation	NAME of each person whose place of abode on January 1, 1920, was in the family.	RELATION Relationship of this Person to the head of the family.	Sex	Color or race	Age at last birthday	Single, married, widowed or divorced	Attended school any time since Sept. 1, 1919	Whether able to read.	Whether able to write.	Place of birth of this person.	Place of birth of father of this person.	Place of birth of mother of this person.	Whether able to speak English.	OCCUPATION Trade, profession, or particular kind of work done, as salesman, laborer, clerk, cook, merchant, washerwoman, etc.
	1	2	3	4	5	6	7	8	9	10	11	12	13	14	15	16	17
26		100	122	Leon Guerrero, Vicente M	Head	M	Cha	52.0	S		Y	Y	Guam	Guam	Guam	N	Blacksmith
27		100	122	Leon Guerrero, Maria R	Niece	F	Cha	31.0	S		Y	Y	Guam	Guam	Guam	N	None
28		100	123	Pangelinan, Genoveva	Head	F	Cha	8.0	S	Y			Guam	Guam	Guam		None
29		100	123	Pangelinan, Nieves	Sister	F	Cha	2.0	S				Guam	Guam	Guam		None
30		101	124	Lujan, Joaquin D	Head	M	Cha	59.0	M		Y	Y	Guam	Guam	Guam	N	None
31		101	124	Lujan, Ramona C	Wife	F	Cha	53.0	M		Y	Y	Guam	Guam	Guam	N	None
32		101	124	Lujan, Soledad C	Daughter	F	Cha	26.0	S		Y	Y	Guam	Guam	Guam	Y	None
33		102	125	Castro, Ana U	Head	F	Cha	51.0	S		Y	Y	Guam	Guam	Guam	N	None
34		102	125	Castro, Jesus	Son	M	Cha	24.0	S		Y	Y	Guam	Unknown	Guam	Y	Enlisted US Navy
35		103	126	Leon Guerrero, Juan T	Head	M	Cha	51.0	M		Y	Y	Guam	Guam	Guam	N	Shoemaker
36		103	126	Leon Guerrero, Soledad LG	Wife	F	Cha	32.0	M		Y	Y	Guam	Guam	Guam	N	None
37		103	126	Leon Guerrero, Jose LG	Son	M	Cha	8.0	S	Y	Y	Y	Guam	Guam	Guam		None
38		103	126	Leon Guerrero, Pedro LG	Son	M	Cha	5.0	S	N			Guam	Guam	Guam		None
39		103	126	Leon Guerrero, Ignacia LG	Daughter	F	Cha	1.0	S				Guam	Guam	Guam		None
40		104	127	Castro, Rita T	Head	F	Cha	47.0	S		Y	Y	Guam	Guam	Guam	N	Laundress
41		104	127	Castro, Isabel C	Daughter	F	Cha	20.0	S	N	Y	Y	Guam	Unknown	Guam	Y	None
42		104	127	Castro, Felix C	Son	M	Cha	16.0	S	N	Y	Y	Guam	Unknown	Guam	Y	Servant
43		104	127	Castro, Vicente T	Brother	M	Cha	36.0	S		N	N	Guam	Guam	Guam	N	Farmer
44		104	127	Yoshida, Ana C	Sister	F	Cha	35.0	Wd		N	N	Guam	Guam	Guam	N	None
45		105	128	Castro, Juan	Head	M	Cha	24.0	M		N	N	Guam	Guam	Guam	N	Farmer
46		105	128	Castro, Ana M	Wife	F	Cha	34.0	M		N	N	Guam	Guam	Guam	N	Laundress
47		106	129	Lujan, Jesus G	Head	M	Cha	36.0	M		Y	Y	Guam	Guam	Guam	N	Farmer
48		106	129	Lujan, Filomena C	Wife	F	Cha	40.0	M		Y	Y	Guam	Guam	Guam	N	None
49		106	129	Lujan, Magdalena C	Daughter	F	Cha	14.0	S	N	Y	Y	Guam	Guam	Guam	Y	None
50		106	129	Lujan, Pedro C	Son	M	Cha	12.0	S	Y	Y	Y	Guam	Guam	Guam	Y	None

Hernan Cortez Street

238

(CHAMORRO ROOTS GENEALOGY PROJECT ™ TRANSCRIPTION)
(COMPILED/TRANSCRIBED BY BERNARD T. PUNZALAN / HTTP://WWW.CHAMORROROOTS.COM)

FOURTEENTH CENSUS OF THE UNITED STATES: 1920—POPULATION

ISLAND OF GUAM

118

DISTRICT 2
NAME OF PLACE Agana (City)
[Proper name and, also, name of class, as city, town, village, barrio, etc]

ENUMERATED BY ME ON THE 3rd DAY OF March, 1920
Arthur W. Jackson ENUMERATOR

	Place of abode		Name	Relation	Personal Description				Education			Nativity			Eng.	Occupation
1	2	3	4	5	6	7	8	9	10	11	12	13	14	15	16	17
	106	129	Lujan, Trinidad C	Son	M	Cha	9.0	S	Y			Guam	Guam	Guam		None
	106	129	Lujan, Pepeto C	Son	M	Cha	7.0	S	Y			Guam	Guam	Guam		None
	106	129	Lujan, Margarita C	Daugther	F	Cha	6.0	S	N			Guam	Guam	Guam		None
	106	129	Lujan, Rufina C	Daugther	F	Cha	3.0	S				Guam	Guam	Guam		None
	106	129	Lujan, Maria C	Daugther	F	Cha	0.2	S				Guam	Guam	Guam		None
	106	129	Lujan, Nicolasa C	Daugther	F	Cha	0.2	S				Guam	Guam	Guam		None
	107	130	Wilson, Maria	Head	F	W	72.0	Wd		N	N	Guam	Guam	Guam	N	None
	107	130	Wilson, Dolores	Daugther	F	Cha	40.0	S		Y	Y	Guam	Guam	Guam	N	None
Hernan Cortez Street	107	130	Peterson, Rufina W	Daugther	F	Cha	30.0	M		Y	Y	Guam	Guam	Guam	Y	Teacher
	107	130	Peterson, Fred W	Grandson	M	W	11.0	S	Y	Y	Y	Guam	Kansas	Kansas	Y	None
	107	130	Peterson, Elmer W	Grandson	M	W	9.0	S	Y	Y	Y	Guam	Kansas	Kansas		None
	107	130	Peterson, Mabel W	Granddaughter	F	W	7.0	S	Y	Y	Y	Guam	Kansas	Kansas		None
	107	130	Peterson, Annie W	Granddaughter	F	W	5.0	S	Y	Y	Y	Guam	Kansas	Kansas		None
	108	131	Mesa, Jose dela R	Head	M	Cha	53.0	Wd		Y	Y	Guam	Guam	Guam	N	Farmer
	108	131	Mesa, Ana dela R	Sister	F	Cha	62.0	S		Y	Y	Guam	Guam	Guam	N	None
	108	131	Mesa, Nicolasa dela R	Sister	F	Cha	60.0	S		Y	Y	Guam	Guam	Guam	N	None
	108	131	Mesa, Rosalia dela R	Sister	F	Cha	58.0	S		Y	Y	Guam	Guam	Guam	N	None
	108	131	Mesa, Maria dela R	Sister	F	Cha	54.0	S		Y	Y	Guam	Guam	Guam	N	None
	108	131	Mesa, Sinmade dela R	Sister	F	Cha	18.0	S		Y	Y	Guam	Guam	Guam	N	None
	108	132	Iwatsu, Jose	Head	M	Jp	33.0	M		Y	Y	Japan	Japan	Japan	Y	Cook
	108	132	Iwatsu, Carmen S	Wife	F	Cha	29.0	M		Y	Y	Guam	Guam	Guam	N	None
	108	132	Iwatsu, Juana S	Daugther	F	Jp	3.0	S				Guam	Japan	Japan		None
	109	133	Taitinfong, Grabela C	Head	F	Cha	53.0	Wd		Y	Y	Guam	Guam	Guam	N	None
	109	133	Taitinfong, Carmen C	Daugther	F	Cha	28.0	S		Y	Y	Guam	Guam	Guam	N	None
	109	133	Taitinfong, Ignacio C	Son	M	Cha	26.0	S		Y	Y	Guam	Guam	Guam	N	Farmer

239

118b

(CHAMORRO ROOTS GENEALOGY PROJECT ™ TRANSCRIPTION)
(COMPILED/TRANSCRIBED BY BERNARD T. PUNZALAN / HTTP://WWW.CHAMORROROOTS.COM)
FOURTEENTH CENSUS OF THE UNITED STATES: 1920—POPULATION
ISLAND OF GUAM

ENUMERATED BY ME ON THE 3rd DAY OF March, 1920

Arthur W. Jackson ENUMERATOR

DISTRICT 2
NAME OF PLACE Agana (City)
[Proper name and, also, name of class, as city, town, village, barrio, etc]

	Street, avenue, road, etc.	Number of dwelling house in order of visitation	Number of family in order of visitation	NAME	RELATION	Sex	Color or race	Age at last birthday	Single, married, widowed or divorced	Attended school any time since Sept. 1, 1919	Whether able to read	Whether able to write	Place of birth of this person	Place of birth of father of this person	Place of birth of mother of this person	Whether able to speak English	OCCUPATION
	1	2	3	4	5	6	7	8	9	10	11	12	13	14	15	16	17
26		109	133	Taitinfong, Ramon C	Son	M	Cha	20.0	S	N	Y	Y	Guam	Guam	Guam	N	None
27		109	133	Taitinfong, Magdalena C	Daughter	F	Cha	18.0	S	N	Y	Y	Guam	Guam	Guam	Y	None
28		109	133	Taitinfong, Rita C	Daughter	F	Cha	12.0	S	Y	Y	Y	Guam	Guam	Guam	Y	None
29		109	133	Taitinfong, Jose C	Son	M	Cha	9.0	S	Y			Guam	Guam	Guam		None
30		110	134	Kurokawa, G	Head	M	Jp	38.0	S		Y	Y	Japan	Japan	Japan	Y	Tailor
31		111	135	Butler, Carl C	Head	M	W	35.0	M		Y	Y	Texas	Texas	Texas	Y	Merchant general merchandise
32		111	135	Butler, Ignacia B	Wife	F	W	22.0	M		Y	Y	Guam	Spain	Guam	Y	Teacher
33		111	135	Butler, James B	Son	M	W	3.0	S				Guam	Texas	Guam		None
34		111	135	Butler, Beatrice R	Daughter	F	W	2.0	S				Guam	Texas	Guam		None
35		111	135	Butler, Clara M	Daughter	F	W	1.0	S				Guam	Texas	Guam		None
36	Hernan Cortez Street	112	136	Aguon, Pedro	Head	M	Cha	27.0	M		Y	Y	Guam	Guam	Guam	N	Laborer
37		112	136	Aguon, Rosa S	Wife	F	Cha	29.0	M		N	N	Guam	Guam	Guam	N	None
38		112	136	Aguon, Remedios S	Daughter	F	Cha	4.0	S				Guam	Guam	Guam		None
39		112	136	Aguon, Rosario S	Daughter	F	Cha	0.2	S				Guam	Guam	Guam		None
40		113	137	Mafnas, Juan R	Head	M	Cha	30.0	M		Y	Y	Guam	Guam	Guam	N	Laborer
41		113	137	Mafnas, Maria C	Wife	F	Cha	28.0	M		N	N	Guam	Guam	Guam	N	None
42		113	137	Mafnas, Ana C	Daughter	F	Cha	4.0	S				Guam	Guam	Guam		None
43		113	137	Mafnas, Antonia C	Daughter	F	Cha	3.0	S				Guam	Guam	Guam		None
44		113	137	Mafnas, Placida C	Daughter	F	Cha	2.0	S				Guam	Guam	Guam		None
45		113	137	Mafnas, Joaquin C	Son	M	Cha	0.1	S				Guam	Guam	Guam		None
46		114	138	Mesa, Juan	Head	M	Cha	44.0	M		Y	Y	Guam	Unknown	Guam	N	Laborer
47		114	138	Mesa, Dolores A	Wife	F	Cha	49.0	M		N	N	Guam	Guam	Guam	N	None
48		114	138	Mesa, Enrique A	Son	M	Cha	13.0	S	Y	Y	Y	Guam	Guam	Guam	Y	None
49		114	138	Mesa, Francisco A	Son	M	Cha	9.0	S	Y	Y	Y	Guam	Guam	Guam		None
50		115	139	Cruz, Mariano M	Head	M	Cha	50.0	M		Y	Y	Guam	Guam	Guam	N	Farmer

240

(CHAMORRO ROOTS GENEALOGY PROJECT ™ TRANSCRIPTION)
(COMPILED/TRANSCRIBED BY BERNARD T. PUNZALAN / HTTP://WWW.CHAMORROROOTS.COM)

FOURTEENTH CENSUS OF THE UNITED STATES: 1920-POPULATION

ISLAND OF GUAM

DISTRICT 2
NAME OF PLACE Agana (City)

[Proper name and, also, name of class, as city, town, village, barrio, etc]

ENUMERATED BY ME ON THE 4th DAY OF March, 1920

Arthur W. Jackson ENUMERATOR

	PLACE OF ABODE		NAME	RELATION	PERSONAL DESCRIPTION				EDUCATION			NATIVITY				OCCUPATION
Street, avenue, road, etc.	No. of dwelling house	No. of family	of each person	Relationship	Sex	Color or race	Age at last birthday	Single, married, widowed or divorced	Attended school since Sept. 1, 1919	Whether able to read	Whether able to write	Place of birth of this person	Place of birth of father	Place of birth of mother	Whether able to speak English	Trade, profession
1	2	3	4	5	6	7	8	9	10	11	12	13	14	15	16	17
	115	139	Cruz, Luisa C	Wife	F	Cha	48.0	M		N	N	Guam	Guam	Guam	N	None
	115	139	Cruz, Vicente C	Son	M	Cha	21.0	S	N	Y	Y	Guam	Guam	Guam	Y	Laborer
	115	140	Cruz, Antonio C	Head	M	Cha	25.0	M		Y	Y	Guam	Guam	Guam	N	Farmer
	115	140	Cruz, Carmen A	Wife	F	Cha	25.0	M		Y	Y	Guam	Guam	Guam	N	None
	115	140	Cruz, Julia A	Daughter	F	Cha	2.0	S				Guam	Guam	Guam		None
	115	140	Cruz, Trinidad A	Daughter	F	Cha	0.5	S				Guam	Guam	Guam		None
	116	141	Mafnas, Vicenta C	Head	F	Cha	64.0	Wd		N	N	Guam	Guam	Guam	N	None
	116	141	Mafnas, Joaquin C	Son	M	Cha	26.0	S		N	N	Guam	Guam	Guam	N	Laborer
Hernan Cortez Street	117	142	Toves, Juan G	Head	M	Cha	36.0	M		Y	Y	Guam	Guam	Guam	Y	Laborer
	117	142	Toves, Maria A	Wife	F	Cha	33.0	M		N	N	Guam	Guam	Guam	N	None
	117	142	Toves, Jose A	Son	M	Cha	16.0	S	N	Y	Y	Guam	Guam	Guam	Y	None
	117	142	Toves, Juan A	Son	M	Cha	14.0	S	N	Y	Y	Guam	Guam	Guam	Y	None
	117	142	Toves, Ana A	Daughter	F	Cha	9.0	S	Y	Y	Y	Guam	Guam	Guam	Y	None
	117	142	Toves, Magdalena A	Daughter	F	Cha	6.0	S	N			Guam	Guam	Guam		None
	117	142	Toves, Francisco A	Son	M	Cha	3.0	S				Guam	Guam	Guam		None
	117	142	Toves, Concepcion A	Daughter	F	Cha	0.2	S				Guam	Guam	Guam		None
	118	143	Mafnas, Carmen C	Head	F	Cha	60.0	Wd		N	N	Guam	Guam	Guam	N	None
	119	144	Taitano, Francisco M	Head	M	Cha	32.0	M		Y	Y	Guam	Guam	Guam	Y	Farmer
	119	144	Taitano, Maria B	Wife	F	Cha	34.0	M		N	N	Guam	Guam	Guam	N	None
	119	144	Taitano, Maria B	Daughter	F	Cha	9.0	S	Y			Guam	Guam	Guam		None
	119	144	Taitano, Ana B	Daughter	F	Cha	7.0	S	Y			Guam	Guam	Guam		None
	119	144	Taitano, Josefina B	Daughter	F	Cha	5.0	S	N			Guam	Guam	Guam		None
	119	144	Taitano, Juan B	Son	M	Cha	3.0	S				Guam	Guam	Guam		None
	119	144	Taitano, Antonia B	Daughter	F	Cha	1.0	S				Guam	Guam	Guam		None
	120	145	Borja, Vicente M	Head	M	Cha	37.0	M		N	N	Guam	Guam	Guam	N	Farmer

(CHAMORRO ROOTS GENEALOGY PROJECT ™ TRANSCRIPTION)
(COMPILED/TRANSCRIBED BY BERNARD T. PUNZALAN / HTTP://WWW.CHAMORROROOTS.COM)

FOURTEENTH CENSUS OF THE UNITED STATES: 1920-POPULATION
ISLAND OF GUAM

119b

DISTRICT 2
NAME OF PLACE Agana (City)
[Proper name and, also, name of class, as city, town, village, barrio, etc]

ENUMERATED BY ME ON THE 4th DAY OF March, 1920

Arthur W. Jackson ENUMERATOR

	PLACE OF ABODE			NAME	RELATION	PERSONAL DESCRIPTION				EDUCATION			NATIVITY				OCCUPATION
Street, avenue, road, etc.	Number of dwelling house in order of visitation	Number of family in order of visitation		Name of each person whose place of abode on January 1, 1920, was in the family. Enter surname first, then given name and middle initial. If any. Include every person living on January 1, 1920. Omit children born since January 1, 1920.	Relationship of this Person to the head of the family.	Sex	Color or race	Age at last birthday	Single, married, widowed or divorced	Attended school any time since Sept. 1, 1919	Whether able to read.	Whether able to write.	Place of birth of this Person.	Place of birth of father of this person.	Place of birth of mother of this person.	Whether able to speak English.	Trade, profession, or particular kind of work done, as salesman, laborer, clerk, cook, merchant, washerwoman, etc.
1	2	3		4	5	6	7	8	9	10	11	12	13	14	15	16	17
	120	145	26	Borja, Joaquina S	Wife	F	Cha	34.0	M		N	N	Guam	Guam	Guam	N	None
	120	145	27	Borja, Juan S	Son	M	Cha	12.0	S	Y	Y	Y	Guam	Guam	Guam	Y	None
	120	145	28	Borja, Maria S	Daughter	F	Cha	11.0	S	Y	Y	Y	Guam	Guam	Guam	N	None
	120	145	29	Borja, Isabel S	Daughter	F	Cha	4.0	S			Y	Guam	Guam	Guam		None
	121	146	30	Rojas, Joaquin R	Head	M	Cha	48.0	M		N	N	Guam	Guam	Guam	N	Farmer
	121	146	31	Rojas, Maria M	Wife	F	Cha	62.0	M		N	N	Guam	Guam	Guam	N	None
	122	147	32	Mafnas, Joaquin R	Head	M	Cha	32.0	M		N	N	Guam	Guam	Guam	N	Farmer
	122	147	33	Mafnas, Maria C	Wife	F	Cha	31.0	M		N	N	Guam	Guam	Guam	N	None
	122	147	34	Mafnas, Antonio C	Son	M	Cha	8.0	S	Y			Guam	Guam	Guam		None
	122	147	35	Mafnas, Rosario C	Daughter	F	Cha	5.0	S	N			Guam	Guam	Guam		None
	122	147	36	Mafnas, Juan C	Son	M	Cha	3.0	S				Guam	Guam	Guam		None
	122	147	37	Mafnas, Francisco C	Son	M	Cha	1.0	S				Guam	Guam	Guam		None
	123	148	38	Castro, Francisco W	Head	M	Cha	51.0	M		Y	Y	Guam	Guam	Guam	N	Blacksmith
	123	148	39	Castro, Maria P	Wife	F	Cha	50.0	M		Y	Y	Guam	Guam	Guam	Y	None
	123	148	40	Castro, Francisco P	Son	M	Cha	20.0	S	N	Y	Y	Guam	Guam	Guam	Y	Chauffeur
	123	148	41	Castro, Felix P	Son	M	Cha	18.0	S	N	Y	Y	Guam	Guam	Guam	Y	App. Machinist
	123	148	42	Castro, Margarita P	Daughter	F	Cha	16.0	S	N	Y	Y	Guam	Guam	Guam	Y	None
	123	148	43	Castro, Vicente P	Son	M	Cha	15.0	S	N	Y	Y	Guam	Guam	Guam	Y	Farm laborer
	123	148	44	Castro, Maria P	Daughter	F	Cha	13.0	S	Y	Y	Y	Guam	Guam	Guam	Y	None
	123	148	45	Castro, Antonia P	Daughter	F	Cha	11.0	S	Y	Y	Y	Guam	Guam	Guam	Y	None
	123	148	46	Castro, Carmen P	Daughter	F	Cha	7.0	S	Y			Guam	Guam	Guam		None
	124	149	47	Camacho, Antonio P	Head	M	Cha	43.0	M		Y	Y	Guam	Guam	Guam	N	Farmer
	124	149	48	Camacho, Josefa R	Wife	F	Cha	40.0	M		N	N	Guam	Guam	Guam	N	None
	124	149	49	Camacho, Concepcion R	Daughter	F	Cha	20.0	S	N	Y	Y	Guam	Guam	Guam	Y	None
	124	149	50	Camacho, Jose R	Son	M	Cha	17.0	S	N	Y	Y	Guam	Guam	Guam	Y	None

Street, avenue, road, etc.: Hernan Cortez Street

(CHAMORRO ROOTS GENEALOGY PROJECT ™ TRANSCRIPTION)
(COMPILED/TRANSCRIBED BY BERNARD T. PUNZALAN / HTTP://WWW.CHAMORROROOTS.COM)

FOURTEENTH CENSUS OF THE UNITED STATES: 1920—POPULATION

ISLAND OF GUAM

DISTRICT 2
NAME OF PLACE Agana (City)

[Proper name and, also, name of class, as city, town, village, barrio, etc]

ENUMERATED BY ME ON THE 4th DAY OF March, 1920

Arthur W. Jackson ENUMERATOR

Street	Dwelling No.	Family No.	NAME	RELATION	Sex	Color or race	Age	Marital	Attended school	Read	Write	Birthplace	Father birthplace	Mother birthplace	English	OCCUPATION
	124	149	Camacho, Carmen R	Daughter	F	Cha	15.0	S	Y	Y	Y	Guam	Guam	Guam	Y	None
	124	149	Camacho, Nicolasa R	Daughter	F	Cha	13.0	S	Y	Y	Y	Guam	Guam	Guam	Y	None
	124	149	Camacho, Gregorio R	Son	M	Cha	11.0	S	Y	Y	Y	Guam	Guam	Guam	N	None
	124	149	Camacho, Rosa R	Daughter	F	Cha	9.0	S	Y	Y	Y	Guam	Guam	Guam		None
	124	149	Camacho, Vicente R	Son	M	Cha	5.0	S	N			Guam	Guam	Guam		None
	124	149	Camacho, Simeon R	Son	M	Cha	3.0	S				Guam	Guam	Guam		None
	124	149	Camacho, Atanasio R	Son	M	Cha	2.0	S				Guam	Guam	Guam		None
	125	150	Rivera, Maria G	Head	F	Cha	66.0	Wd		N	N	Guam	Guam	Guam	N	None
Hernan Cortez Street	126	151	Rosario, Jose B	Head	M	Cha	51.0	M		Y	Y	Guam	Guam	Guam	N	Farmer
	126	151	Rosario, Vicenta R	Wife	F	Cha	42.0	M		Y	Y	Guam	Guam	Guam	N	None
	126	151	Rosario, Maria R	Daughter	F	Cha	24.0	S		Y	Y	Guam	Guam	Guam	Y	Teacher
	126	151	Rosario, Rosa R	Daughter	F	Cha	22.0	S		Y	Y	Guam	Guam	Guam	Y	None
	126	151	Rosario, Juan R	Son	M	Cha	20.0	S		Y	Y	Guam	Guam	Guam	Y	None
	126	151	Rosario, Francisco R	Son	M	Cha	17.0	S		Y	Y	Guam	Guam	Guam	Y	None
	126	151	Rosario, Jose R	Son	M	Cha	14.0	S		Y	Y	Guam	Guam	Guam	Y	None
	126	151	Rosario, Miguel R	Son	M	Cha	12.0	S	Y	Y	Y	Guam	Guam	Guam	Y	None
	126	151	Rosario, Domingo R	Son	M	Cha	9.0	S	Y	Y	Y	Guam	Guam	Guam	Y	None
	126	151	Rosario, Carlos R	Son	M	Cha	6.0	S	N			Guam	Guam	Guam		None
	126	151	Rosario, Tomas R	Son	M	Cha	3.0	S				Guam	Guam	Guam		None
	127	152	Rios, Brigido A	Head	M	Cha	53.0	M		Y	Y	Guam	Guam	Philippine Islands	N	Farmer
	127	152	Rios, Josefa LG	Wife	F	Cha	51.0	M		N	N	Guam	Guam	Guam	N	None
	127	152	Rios, Jose LG	Son	M	Cha	21.0	S		Y	Y	Guam	Guam	Guam	Y	None
	127	152	Rios, Vicente LG	Son	M	Cha	20.0	S		Y	Y	Guam	Guam	Guam	Y	Messenger
	127	152	Rios, Enrique LG	Son	M	Cha	16.0	S	Y	Y	Y	Guam	Guam	Guam	Y	None
	127	152	Rios, Maria LG	Daughter	F	Cha	12.0	S	Y	Y	Y	Guam	Guam	Guam	Y	None

(CHAMORRO ROOTS GENEALOGY PROJECT ™ TRANSCRIPTION)
(COMPILED/TRANSCRIBED BY BERNARD T. PUNZALAN / HTTP://WWW.CHAMORROROOTS.COM)
FOURTEENTH CENSUS OF THE UNITED STATES: 1920-POPULATION
ISLAND OF GUAM

ENUMERATED BY ME ON THE 5th DAY OF March, 1920

Arthur W. Jackson ENUMERATOR

DISTRICT 2
NAME OF PLACE Agana (City)

[Proper name and, also, name of class, as city, town, village, barrio, etc]

	Street	Dwelling house No.	Family No.	NAME	RELATION	Sex	Color or race	Age	Marital	Attended school	Read	Write	Birthplace person	Birthplace father	Birthplace mother	Speak English	OCCUPATION
26		127	153	Cruz, Candalerio M	Head	M	Cha	30.0	M		Y	Y	Guam	Guam	Guam	N	Laborer
27		127	153	Cruz, Asencion R	Wife	F	Cha	21.0	M	N	Y	Y	Guam	Guam	Guam	Y	None
28		127	153	Cruz, Juan R	Son	M	Cha	4.0	S				Guam	Guam	Guam		None
29		127	153	Cruz, Estella R	Daughter	F	Cha	0.2	S				Guam	Guam	Guam		None
30		128	154	Taitano, Jose W	Head	M	Cha	33.0	M		Y	Y	Guam	Guam	Guam	Y	Farmer
31		128	154	Taitano, Maria P	Wife	F	Cha	30.0	M		Y	Y	Guam	Guam	Guam	N	None
32		128	154	Taitano, Florencio P	Son	M	Cha	10.0	S	Y	Y	Y	Guam	Guam	Guam	N	None
33		128	154	Taitano, Carmen P	Daughter	F	Cha	9.0	S	Y			Guam	Guam	Guam		None
34		128	154	Taitano, Marcelina P	Daughter	F	Cha	7.0	S	Y			Guam	Guam	Guam		None
35		128	154	Taitano, Concepcion P	Daughter	F	Cha	6.0	S	N			Guam	Guam	Guam		None
36		128	154	Taitano, Gregorio P	Son	M	Cha	1.0	S				Guam	Guam	Guam		None
37		128	154	Mendiola, Rosa C	Servant	F	Cha	16.0	S				Guam	Guam	Guam	Y	None
38		129	155	Perez, Monica M	Head	F	Cha	65.0	Wd		N	N	Guam	Guam	Guam	N	None
39		130	156	Sakakibara, S	Head	M	Jp	29.0	M		Y	Y	Japan	Japan	Japan	Y	Merchant general retail
40		130	156	Sakakibara, Concepcion P	Wife	F	Jp	22.0	M		Y	Y	Guam	Guam	Guam	Y	None
41		130	156	Sakakibara, Hana P	Daughter	F	Jp	2.0	S				Guam	Japan	Guam		None
42		130	156	Sakakibara, Florence P	Daughter	F	Jp	1.0	S				Guam	Japan	Guam		None
43		130	156	Sakakibara, Nogi P	Brother	M	Jp	20.0	S				Japan	Japan	Japan	Y	Salesman
44		131	157	Calvo, Juana P	Head	F	Cha	66.0	Wd		Y	Y	Guam	Guam	Guam	N	None
45		131	157	Calvo, Gregorio P	Son	M	W	44.0	S		Y	Y	Guam	Spain	Spain	Y	Silversmith
46		131	157	Calvo, Vicente P	Son	M	W	22.0	S		Y	Y	Guam	Spain	Spain	Y	Clerk
47		131	157	Cepeda, Ignacia M	Servant	F	Cha	16.0	S	N	Y	Y	Guam	Guam	Guam	Y	Servant
48		131	157	Afaron, Francisca T	Servant	F	Cha	8.0	S				Guam	Guam	Guam	Y	Servant
49		132	158	Torres, Gregorio M	Head	M	Cha	36.0	M		Y	Y	Guam	Guam	Guam	Y	Farmer
50		132	158	Torres, Josefa A	Wife	F	Cha	46.0	M		Y	Y	Guam	Guam	Guam	Y	None

Street: Hernan Cortez Street

(CHAMORRO ROOTS GENEALOGY PROJECT ™ TRANSCRIPTION)
(COMPILED/TRANSCRIBED BY BERNARD T. PUNZALAN / HTTP://WWW.CHAMORROROOTS.COM)

FOURTEENTH CENSUS OF THE UNITED STATES: 1920-POPULATION
ISLAND OF GUAM

ENUMERATED BY ME ON THE 5th DAY OF March, 1920

Arthur W. Jackson ENUMERATOR

DISTRICT 2
NAME OF PLACE Agana (City)

[Proper name and, also, name of class, as city, town, village, barrio, etc]

Street	Dwelling house no. (2)	Family no. (3)	NAME (4)	RELATION (5)	Sex (6)	Color or race (7)	Age (8)	Single, married, widowed or divorced (9)	Attended school (10)	Able to read (11)	Able to write (12)	Birthplace person (13)	Birthplace father (14)	Birthplace mother (15)	Speak English (16)	OCCUPATION (17)
	132	158	Torres, Pilar A	Daughter	F	Cha	14.0	S	N	Y	Y	Guam	Guam	Guam	Y	None
	132	158	Roberto, Juan A	Step son	M	Cha	20.0	S	N	Y	Y	Guam	Guam	Guam	Y	Clerk
	132	158	Roberto, Dolores A	Step daughter	F	Cha	19.0	S	N	Y	Y	Guam	Guam	Guam	Y	None
	132	158	Roberto, Concepcion A	Grand daughter	F	Cha	3.0	S				Guam	Guam	Guam		None
	133	159	Martinez, Francisco G	Head	M	Cha	43.0	M		Y	Y	Guam	Guam	Guam	N	Farmer
	133	159	Martinez, Juana P	Wife	F	Cha	42.0	M		Y	Y	Guam	Guam	Guam	N	None
	133	159	Martinez, Joaquin P	Son	M	Cha	18.0	S	N	Y	Y	Guam	Guam	Guam	Y	Cook
	133	159	Martinez, Vicente P	Son	M	Cha	15.0	S	N	Y	Y	Guam	Guam	Guam	Y	App. Machinist
	133	159	Martinez, Maria P	Daughter	F	Cha	13.0	S	N	Y	Y	Guam	Guam	Guam	Y	None
	133	159	Martinez, Manuel P	Son	M	Cha	7.0	S	Y			Guam	Guam	Guam		None
Hernan Cortez Street	133	159	Martinez, Rosa P	Daughter	F	Cha	5.0	S	N			Guam	Guam	Guam		None
	133	159	Martinez, Jesus P	Son	M	Cha	4.0	S				Guam	Guam	Guam		None
	133	159	Martinez, Francisco P	Son	M	Cha	0.1	S				Guam	Guam	Guam		None
	134	160	Martinez, Manuela J	Head	F	Cha	75.0	Wd		Y	Y	Guam	Guam	Guam	N	None
	134	161	Martinez, Juan P	Head	M	Cha	20.0	M	N	Y	Y	Guam	Guam	Guam	Y	Farmer
	134	161	Martinez, Dolores LG	Wife	F	Cha	19.0	M	N	Y	Y	Guam	Guam	Guam	Y	None
	135	162	Ochia, B	Head	M	Jp	34.0	M		Y	Y	Japan	Japan	Japan	Y	Merchant general retail
	135	162	Ochia, Soledad B	Wife	F	Cha	29.0	M		Y	Y	Guam	Guam	Guam	Y	None
	135	162	Ochia, Gonzalo B	Son	M	Jp	9.0	S	Y			Guam	Japan	Guam		None
	135	162	Ochia, Herman B	Son	M	Jp	7.0	S	Y			Guam	Japan	Guam		None
	135	162	Ochia, Jose B	Son	M	Jp	4.0	S				Guam	Japan	Guam		None
	135	162	Ochia, Maria B	Daughter	F	Jp	3.0	S				Guam	Japan	Guam		None
	135	162	Ochia, Alfredo B	Son	M	Jp	2.0	S				Guam	Japan	Guam		None
	135	162	Ochia, Artemio B	Son	M	Jp	0.3	S				Guam	Japan	Guam		None
	136	163	Noda, N	Head	M	Jp	25.0	S		Y	Y	Japan	Japan	Japan	Y	Restaurant keeper

121b

(CHAMORRO ROOTS GENEALOGY PROJECT ™ TRANSCRIPTION)
(COMPILED/TRANSCRIBED BY BERNARD T. PUNZALAN / HTTP://WWW.CHAMORROROOTS.COM)
FOURTEENTH CENSUS OF THE UNITED STATES: 1920-POPULATION
ISLAND OF GUAM

ENUMERATED BY ME ON THE 6th DAY OF March, 1920

Arthur W. Jackson ENUMERATOR

DISTRICT 2
NAME OF PLACE Agana (City)
[Proper name and, also, name of class, as city, town, village, barrio, etc]

	Number of dwelling house in order of visitation (2)	Number of family in order of visitation (3)	NAME (4)	RELATION (5)	Sex (6)	Color or race (7)	Age at last birthday (8)	Single, married, widowed or divorced (9)	Attended school any time since Sept. 1, 1919 (10)	Whether able to read (11)	Whether able to write (12)	Place of birth of this person (13)	Place of birth of father of this person (14)	Place of birth of mother of this person (15)	Whether able to speak English (16)	OCCUPATION (17)
26	137	164	Pangelinan, Juan P	Head	M	Cha	27.0	M		Y	Y	Guam	Guam	Guam	Y	Chauffeur
27	137	164	Pangelinan, Ana R	Wife	F	Cha	22.0	M		Y	Y	Guam	Unknown	Guam	Y	None
28	137	164	Pangelinan, Manuel P	Brother	M	Cha	19.0	S	N	Y	Y	Guam	Guam	Guam	Y	Farmer
29	137	164	Pangelinan, Maria P	Sister	F	Cha	18.0	S	N	Y	Y	Guam	Guam	Guam	Y	None
30	137	164	Pangelinan, Francisco P	Brother	M	Cha	13.0	S	Y	Y	Y	Guam	Guam	Guam	Y	None
31	137	164	Pangelinan, Ignacio P	Brother	M	Cha	9.0	S	Y			Guam	Guam	Guam		None
32	137	164	Pangelinan, Jose P	Brother	M	Cha	7.0	S	Y			Guam	Guam	Guam		None
33	138	165	Kochi, K	Head	M	Jp	53.0	M		Y	Y	Japan	Japan	Japan	Y	Barber
34	139	166	Dungca, Justo B	Head	M	Fil	70.0	M		Y	Y	Philippine Islands	Philippine Islands	Philippine Islands	N	Merchant general mdse.
35	139	166	Dungca, Marcela G	Wife	F	Fil	72.0	M		Y	Y	Philippine Islands	Philippine Islands	Philippine Islands	N	None
36	139	166	Dungca, Soledad G	Daughter	F	Fil	42.0	S		Y	Y	Philippine Islands	Philippine Islands	Philippine Islands	N	None
37	139	167	Palting, Pacracio R	Head	M	Fil	41.0	Wd		Y	Y	Guam	Philippine Islands	Philippine Islands	Y	Lawyer
38	139	167	Palting, Margarito D	Son	M	Fil	13.0	S	Y	Y	Y	Guam	Philippine Islands	Guam	Y	None
39	139	167	Palting, Florencia D	Daughter	F	Fil	8.0	S	Y			Guam	Philippine Islands	Guam		None
40	139	167	Corella, Aniceto P	Nephew	M	Fil	23.0	S		Y	Y	Philippine Islands	Philippine Islands	Philippine Islands	Y	Peddler
41	139	167	Cruz, Antonio	Servant	M	Cha	27.0	S		N	N	Guam	Unknown	Guam	N	Servant
42	139	167	Mendiola, Concepcion S	Servant	F	Cha	19.0	S	N	Y	Y	Guam	Guam	Guam	Y	Servant
43	139	168	Dungca, Teodoro G	Head	M	Fil	30.0	M		Y	Y	Guam	Philippine Islands	Philippine Islands	Y	Electrician
44	139	168	Dungca, Emelia Q	Wife	F	Cha	19.0	M	N	Y	Y	Guam	Guam	Guam	Y	None
45	139	168	Dungca, Felicita C	Niece	F	Fil	19.0	S	N	Y	Y	Guam	Guam	Guam	Y	None
46	139	168	Dungca, Jose	Nephew	M	Fil	12.0	S	Y	Y	Y	Guam	Guam	Guam	Y	None
47	139	168	Dungca, Francisco C	Nephew	M	Fil	11.0	S	Y	Y	Y	Guam	Guam	Guam	Y	None
48	140	169	Mendiola, Josefa C	Head	F	Cha	70.0	Wd		N	N	Guam	Guam	Guam	N	None
49	140	169	Mendiola, Martina C	Daughter	F	Cha	42.0	S				Guam	Guam	Guam	N	None
50	140	169	Mendiola, Ana C	Daughter	F	Cha	37.0	S		Y	Y	Guam	Guam	Guam	N	None

Hernan Cortez Street

(CHAMORRO ROOTS GENEALOGY PROJECT ™ TRANSCRIPTION)
(COMPILED/TRANSCRIBED BY BERNARD T. PUNZALAN / HTTP://WWW.CHAMORROROOTS.COM)
FOURTEENTH CENSUS OF THE UNITED STATES: 1920–POPULATION
ISLAND OF GUAM

DISTRICT 2
NAME OF PLACE Agana (City)

[Proper name and, also, name of class, as city, town, village, barrio, etc]

ENUMERATED BY ME ON THE 6th DAY OF March, 1920

Arthur W. Jackson ENUMERATOR

		PLACE OF ABODE		NAME	RELATION	PERSONAL DESCRIPTION				EDUCATION			NATIVITY				OCCUPATION
Street, avenue, road, etc.	Number of dwelling house in order of visitation	Number of family in order of visitation		of each person whose place of abode on January 1, 1920, was in the family. Enter surname, first, then given name and middle initial. If any. Include every person living on January 1, 1920. Omit children born since January 1, 1920.	Relationship of this Person to the head of the family.	Sex	Color or race	Age at last birthday	Single, married, widowed or divorced.	Attended school any time since Sept. 1, 1919	Whether able to read.	Whether able to write.	Place of birth of this person.	Place of birth of father of this person.	Place of birth of mother of this person.	Whether able to speak English.	Trade, profession, or particular kind of work done, as clerk, cook, merchant, salesman, laborer, washerwoman, etc.
1	2	3	4		5	6	7	8	9	10	11	12	13	14	15	16	17
	140	169	Mendiola, Rosa C	Daughter		F	Cha	30.0	S		Y	Y	Guam	Guam	Guam	N	None
	140	169	Mendiola, Rita C	Daughter		F	Cha	27.0	S		Y	Y	Guam	Guam	Guam	N	None
	141	170	Terlaje, Luis A	Head		M	Cha	48.0	M		Y	Y	Guam	Guam	Guam	N	Farmer
	141	170	Terlaje, Carmen F	Wife		F	Cha	46.0	M		N	N	Guam	Guam	Guam	N	None
	141	170	Terlaje, Maria F	Daughter		F	Cha	17.0	S	N	Y	Y	Guam	Guam	Guam	Y	None
	141	170	Terlaje, Consuelo F	Daughter		F	Cha	14.0	S	N	Y	Y	Guam	Guam	Guam	Y	None
	141	170	Terlaje, Jose F	Son		M	Cha	12.0	S	N	Y	Y	Guam	Guam	Guam	Y	None
	141	170	Terlaje, Pedro F	Son		M	Cha	10.0	S	Y	Y	Y	Guam	Guam	Guam	N	None
	141	170	Terlaje, Jesus F	Son		M	Cha	7.0	S	Y	Y	Y	Guam	Guam	Guam		None
	141	170	Terlaje, Rosario F	Daughter		F	Cha	6.0	S	N			Guam	Guam	Guam		None
	141	170	Terlaje, Vicente F	Son		M	Cha	2.0	S				Guam	Guam	Guam		None
	142	171	Cruz, Francisco M	Head		M	Cha	39.0	S		Y	Y	Guam	Guam	Guam	Y	Foreman
	142	171	Cruz, Asencion P	Wife		F	Cha	33.0	S		Y	Y	Guam	Guam	Guam	N	None
	142	171	Cruz, Agosto P	Son		M	Cha	9.0	S	Y			Guam	Guam	Guam		None
	142	171	Cruz, Cerafina P	Daughter		F	Cha	7.0	S	Y			Guam	Guam	Guam		None
	142	171	Cruz, Antonia P	Daughter		F	Cha	1.0	S				Guam	Guam	Guam		None
	143	172	Torres, Jesus P	Head		M	Cha	20.0	M	N	Y	Y	Guam	Guam	Guam	Y	Salesman
	143	172	Torres, Maria U	Wife		F	Cha	18.0	M	N	Y	Y	Guam	Guam	Guam	Y	None
	144	173	Castro, Lucia	Head		F	Cha	25.0	S		Y	Y	Guam	Unknown	Guam	Y	None
	144	173	Castro, Rosario	Daughter		F	Cha	3.0	S				Guam	Unknown	Guam		None
	145	174	Castro, Juan W	Head		M	Cha	48.0	M		Y	Y	Guam	Guam	Guam	N	Blacksmith
	145	174	Castro, Nicolasa M	Wife		F	Cha	48.0	M		Y	Y	Guam	Guam	Guam	N	None
	145	174	Castro, Regina M	Daughter		F	Cha	19.0	S	N	Y	Y	Guam	Guam	Guam	Y	None
	145	174	Castro, Ana M	Daughter		F	Cha	17.0	S	N	Y	Y	Guam	Guam	Guam	Y	None
	145	174	Castro, Concepcion M	Daughter		F	Cha	15.0	S	N	Y	Y	Guam	Guam	Guam	Y	None

Hernan Cortez Street

(CHAMORRO ROOTS GENEALOGY PROJECT ™ TRANSCRIPTION)
(COMPILED/TRANSCRIBED BY BERNARD T. PUNZALAN / HTTP://WWW.CHAMORROROOTS.COM)
FOURTEENTH CENSUS OF THE UNITED STATES: 1920-POPULATION
ISLAND OF GUAM

ENUMERATED BY ME ON THE 6th DAY OF March, 1920

Arthur W. Jackson ENUMERATOR

DISTRICT 2
NAME OF PLACE Agana (City)
[Proper name and, also, name of class, as city, town, village, barrio, etc]

	Place of Abode		Name	Relation	_	_	_	_	_	_	_	Nativity			_	Occupation
Street	Dwelling #	Family #			Sex	Color/race	Age	Marital	School	Read	Write	Birth of person	Birth of father	Birth of mother	English	
1	2	3	4	5	6	7	8	9	10	11	12	13	14	15	16	17
	145	174	Castro, Santiago M	Son	M	Cha	12.0	S	Y			Guam	Guam	Guam	Y	None
	145	174	Castro, Maria M	Daughter	F	Cha	8.0	S	Y			Guam	Guam	Guam		None
	145	175	Castro, Enrique M	Head	M	Cha	21.0	M	N	Y	Y	Guam	Guam	Guam	Y	Carpenter
	145	175	Castro, Ana S	Wife	F	Cha	18.0	M	N	Y	Y	Guam	Guam	Guam	Y	None
	145	175	Castro, Beatrice S	Daughter	F	Cha	0.5	S				Guam	Guam	Guam		None
	146	176	Sawada, K	Head	M	Jp	49.0	M		Y	Y	Japan	Japan	Japan	Y	Merchant general ret.
	146	176	Sawada, Nao	Wife	F	Jp	29.0	M		Y	Y	Japan	Japan	Guam	N	None
	147	177	Cepeda, Maria LG	Head	F	Cha	59.0	Wd		Y	Y	Guam	Guam	Guam	N	None
	147	177	Cepeda, Ana LG	Daughter	F	Cha	21.0	S	N	Y	Y	Guam	Guam	Guam	Y	Nurse
	148	178	Fabian, Braulio	Head	M	W	29.0	M		Y	Y	Spain	Spain	Spain	Y	Merchant general retail
	148	178	Fabian, Felisa G	Wife	F	W	21.0	M		Y	Y	Spain	Spain	Spain	N	None
	148	178	Fabian, Jesus G	Son	M	W	0.8	S				Manila	Spain	Spain		None
	148	178	Garcia, Fulencio	Brother-in-law	M	W	28.0	S		Y	Y	Spain	Spain	Spain		Merchant general retail
Hernan Cortez Street	149	179	Calvo, Ramon P	Head	M	W	29.0	M		Y	Y	Guam	Spain	Guam	Y	Plumber
	149	179	Calvo, Isabel L	Wife	F	Cha	26.0	M		Y	Y	Guam	Guam	Guam	Y	None
	149	179	Calvo, Oscar L	Son	M	W	4.0	S				Guam	Guam	Guam	Y	None
	149	179	Calvo, Tomas L	Son	M	W	3.0	S				Guam	Guam	Guam		None
	149	179	Calvo, Pilar L	Daughter	F	W	1.0	S				Guam	Guam	Guam		None
	150	180	Ignacio, Filomina C	Head	F	Cha	30.0	S		Y	Y	Guam	Guam	Guam	N	None
	150	180	Ignacio, Maria	Daughter	F	Cha	7.0	S	Y			Guam	Unknown	Guam		None
	150	180	Ignacio, Ana	Daughter	F	Cha	3.0	S				Guam	Unknown	Guam		None
	151	181	Tejada, Josefa C	Head	F	W	49.0	Wd		Y	Y	Philippine Islands	Philippine Islands	Philippine Islands	N	None
	151	181	Tejada, Jose F	Son	M	W	23.0	S		Y	Y	Philippine Islands	Spain	Philippine Islands	Y	Foreman
	151	181	Tejada, Pedro C	Son	M	W	21.0	S	N	Y	Y	Philippine Islands	Spain	Philippine Islands	Y	Laborer
	151	181	Tejada, Rosario M	Daughter	F	W	20.0	S	N	Y	Y	Philippine Islands	Spain	Philippine Islands	Y	None

248

(CHAMORRO ROOTS GENEALOGY PROJECT ™ TRANSCRIPTION)
(COMPILED/TRANSCRIBED BY BERNARD T. PUNZALAN / HTTP://WWW.CHAMORROROOTS.COM)

FOURTEENTH CENSUS OF THE UNITED STATES: 1920—POPULATION
ISLAND OF GUAM

DISTRICT 2
NAME OF PLACE **Agana (City)**
[Proper name and, also, name of class, as city, town, village, barrio, etc]

ENUMERATED BY ME ON THE 8th DAY OF March, 1920

Arthur W. Jackson ENUMERATOR

	Street, avenue, road, etc.	Number of dwelling house in order of visitation	Number of family in order of visitation	NAME	RELATION	Sex	Color or race	Age at last birthday	Single, married, widowed or divorced	Attended school any time since Sept. 1, 1919	Whether able to read.	Whether able to write.	Place of birth of this person.	Place of birth of father of this person.	Place of birth of mother of this person.	Whether able to speak English.	OCCUPATION
	1	2	3	4	5	6	7	8	9	10	11	12	13	14	15	16	17
1		151	181	Tejada, Dolores G	Daughter	F	W	19.0	S	N	Y	Y	China	Spain	Philippine Islands	Y	None
2		151	181	Tejada, Maria J	Daughter	F	W	15.0	S	N	Y	Y	Yap, Car Is.	Spain	Philippine Islands	Y	None
3		151	181	Tejada, Roberto	Son	M	W	14.0	S	Y	Y	Y	Yap, Car Is.	Spain	Philippine Islands	Y	None
4		151	181	Tejada, Rosa I	Daughter	F	W	8.0	S	Y			Saipan, MI	Spain	Philippine Islands	Y	None
5		151	181	Tejada, Estefania M	Daughter	F	W	5.0	S	N			Saipan, MI	Spain	Philippine Islands		None
6		151	181	Cepeda, Ana M	Servant	F	W	19.0	S		Y	Y	Guam	Guam	Guam	Y	Servant
7		152	182	Flores, Ana G	Head	F	Cha	50.0	Wd		Y	Y	Guam	Guam	Guam	N	None
8		152	182	Flores, Maria G	Daughter	F	Cha	28.0	S		Y	Y	Guam	Guam	Guam	N	None
9		152	182	Flores, Joaquin G	Son	M	Cha	19.0	S	N	Y	Y	Guam	Guam	Guam	Y	Farm laborer
10		152	182	Flores, Vicente G	Son	M	Cha	17.0	S	N	Y	Y	Guam	Guam	Guam	Y	App. Machinist
11		152	182	Flores, Francisco G	Son	M	Cha	15.0	S	N	Y	Y	Guam	Guam	Guam	Y	Messenger
12		152	182	Flores, Ramon G	Son	M	Cha	13.0	S	Y	Y	Y	Guam	Guam	Guam	Y	None
13	Hernan Cortez Street	152	182	Flores, Tomas G	Son	M	Cha	9.0	S	Y			Guam	Guam	Guam		None
14		153	183	Cruz, Jose P	Head	M	Cha	42.0	M		Y	Y	Guam	Guam	Guam	N	Farmer
15		153	183	Cruz, Maria M	Wife	F	Cha	33.0	M		Y	Y	Guam	Guam	Guam	N	None
16		153	183	Cruz, Enrique M	Son	M	Cha	20.0	S	N	Y	Y	Guam	Guam	Guam	Y	Laborer
17		153	183	Cruz, Dolores M	Daughter	F	Cha	17.0	S	N	Y	Y	Guam	Guam	Guam	Y	None
18		153	183	Cruz, Jose M	Son	M	Cha	15.0	S	N	Y	Y	Guam	Guam	Guam	Y	None
19		153	183	Cruz, Maria M	Daughter	F	Cha	13.0	S	Y	Y	Y	Guam	Guam	Guam	Y	None
20		153	184	Matanane, Victorina F	Head	F	Cha	22.0	S		Y	Y	Guam	Unknown	Guam	Y	None
21		153	184	Matanane, Ignacio M	Son	M	Cha	1.0	S				Guam	Unknown	Guam		None
22		154	185	Perez, Ramon A	Head	M	Cha	78.0	Wd		N	N	Guam	Unknown	Guam	N	None
23		154	185	Perez, Jose A	Grand son	M	Cha	19.0	S	N	Y	Y	Guam	Unknown	Guam	Y	Laborer
24		154	185	Perez, Dolores A	Grand daughter	F	Cha	17.0	S	N	Y	Y	Guam	Unknown	Guam	Y	None
25		155	186	Diaz, Vicente F	Head	M	Cha	65.0	M		Y	Y	Guam	Guam	Guam	N	Merchant general retail

(CHAMORRO ROOTS GENEALOGY PROJECT ™ TRANSCRIPTION)
(COMPILED/TRANSCRIBED BY BERNARD T. PUNZALAN / HTTP://WWW.CHAMORROROOTS.COM)
FOURTEENTH CENSUS OF THE UNITED STATES: 1920-POPULATION
ISLAND OF GUAM

DISTRICT 2
NAME OF PLACE **Agana (City)**
[Proper name and, also, name of class, as city, town, village, barrio, etc]

ENUMERATED BY ME ON THE 8th DAY OF March, 1920

Arthur W. Jackson ENUMERATOR

Street	Dwelling No.	Family No.	NAME	RELATION	Sex	Color or race	Age	Single, married, widowed or divorced	Attended school since Sept. 1, 1919	Able to read	Able to write	Place of birth of this person	Father	Mother	English	OCCUPATION
	155	186	Diaz, Amparo G	Wife	F	Cha	48.0	M		Y	Y	Guam	Guam	Spain	N	None
	155	186	Diaz, Josefa T	Daughter	F	Cha	27.0	S		Y	Y	Guam	Guam	Guam	N	None
	155	186	Diaz, Rita G	Daughter	F	Cha	24.0	S		Y	Y	Saipan, M.I.	Guam	Guam	N	None
	155	186	Diaz, Concepcion G	Daughter	F	Cha	22.0	S		Y	Y	Saipan, M.I.	Guam	Guam	Y	None
	155	186	Diaz, Josefina G	Daughter	F	Cha	15.0	S	Y	Y	Y	Saipan, M.I.	Guam	Guam	Y	None
	155	186	Diaz, Dolores G	Daughter	F	Cha	10.0	S	Y	Y	Y	Saipan, M.I.	Guam	Guam	Y	None
	155	186	Diaz, Rosa G	Daughter	F	Cha	8.0	S	Y			Saipan, M.I.	Guam	Guam		None
Hernan Cortez Street	155	186	Diaz, Francisco T	Nephew	M	Cha	17.0	S	N	Y	Y	Guam	Guam	Guam	Y	Tailor
	156	187	Cruz, Jose M	Head	M	Cha	58.0	M		N	N	Guam	Guam	Guam	N	Farmer
	156	187	Cruz, Rita LG	Wife	F	Cha	39.0	M		N	N	Guam	Guam	Guam	N	None
	156	187	Cruz, Juan LG	Son	M	Cha	13.0	S	N	Y	Y	Guam	Guam	Guam	Y	None
	156	187	Cruz, Antonio LG	Son	M	Cha	12.0	S	Y	Y	Y	Guam	Guam	Guam	Y	None
	156	187	Cruz, Francisco LG	Son	M	Cha	9.0	S	N			Guam	Guam	Guam		None
	157	188	Taitano, Jose SN	Head	M	Cha	44.0	M		Y	Y	Guam	Guam	Guam	Y	Watchman
	157	188	Taitano, Dolores P	Wife	F	Cha	42.0	M		N	N	Guam	Guam	Guam	N	None
	157	188	Taitano, Jose P	Son	M	Cha	19.0	S	N	Y	Y	Guam	Guam	Guam	Y	App. Plumber
	157	188	Taitano, Francisco P	Son	M	Cha	17.0	S	N	Y	Y	Guam	Guam	Guam	Y	Farm laborer
	157	188	Taitano, Ramon P	Son	M	Cha	15.0	S	N	Y	Y	Guam	Guam	Guam	Y	Servant
	157	188	Taitano, Juan P	Son	M	Cha	13.0	S	N	Y	Y	Guam	Guam	Guam	Y	Farm laborer
	157	188	Taitano, Maria P	Daughter	F	Cha	12.0	S	Y	Y	Y	Guam	Guam	Guam	Y	None
	157	188	Taitano, Ana P	Daughter	F	Cha	10.0	S	Y	Y	Y	Guam	Guam	Guam	Y	None
	157	188	Taitano, Enrique P	Son	M	Cha	9.0	S	Y	Y	Y	Guam	Guam	Guam	Y	None
	157	188	Taitano, Rafael P	Son	M	Cha	7.0	S	Y			Guam	Guam	Guam		None
	157	188	Taitano, Carlos P	Son	M	Cha	3.0	S				Guam	Guam	Guam		None
	158	189	Dimapan, Vicente A	Head	M	Cha	29.0	M		Y	Y	Guam	Guam	Guam	N	Laborer

(CHAMORRO ROOTS GENEALOGY PROJECT ™ TRANSCRIPTION)
(COMPILED/TRANSCRIBED BY BERNARD T. PUNZALAN / HTTP://WWW.CHAMORROROOTS.COM)

FOURTEENTH CENSUS OF THE UNITED STATES: 1920—POPULATION
ISLAND OF GUAM

DISTRICT 2
NAME OF PLACE Agana (City)

[Proper name and, also, name of class, as city, town, village, barrio, etc]

ENUMERATED BY ME ON THE 9th DAY OF March, 1920

Arthur W. Jackson ENUMERATOR

Street, avenue, road, etc.	Number of dwelling house in order of visitation	Number of family in order of visitation	NAME	RELATION	Sex	Color or race	Age at last birthday	Single, married, widowed or divorced	Attended school any time since Sept. 1, 1919	Whether able to read	Whether able to write	Place of birth of this person	Place of birth of father of this person	Place of birth of mother of this person	Whether able to speak English	OCCUPATION
	1	2	3	4	5	6	7	8	9	10	11	12	13	14	15	16	17
	158	189	Dimapan, Carmen C	Wife	F	Cha	35.0	M		N	N	Guam	Guam	Guam	N	None
	158	189	Dimapan, Jesus C	Son	M	Cha	16.0	S	N	Y	Y	Guam	Guam	Guam	Y	None
	158	189	Dimapan, Francisco C	Son	M	Cha	14.0	S	N	Y	Y	Guam	Guam	Guam	Y	None
	158	189	Dimapan, Rosa C	Daughter	F	Cha	3.0	S				Guam	Guam	Guam		None
	158	189	Dimapan, Jose C	Son	M	Cha	0.2	S				Guam	Guam	Guam		
	159	190	Cristobal, Adriano M	Head	M	Fil	32.0	M		Y	Y	Philippine Islands	Philippine Islands	Philippine Islands	Y	Clerk
	159	190	Cristobal, Carmen U	Wife	F	Cha	23.0	M		Y	Y	Guam	Guam	Guam	Y	None
	159	190	Cristobal, Fe G	Daughter	F	Fil	4.0	S				Guam	Philippine Islands	Guam		None
	159	190	Cristobal, Jorge E	Son	M	Fil	1.0	S				Guam	Philippine Islands	Guam		None
	159	191	de Leon, Maria I	Head	F	Cha	79.0	Wd		N	N	Guam	Guam	Guam	N	None
	159	192	Untalan, Dolores L	Head	F	Cha	43.0	Wd		Y	Y	Guam	Guam	Guam	N	None
	159	192	Untalan, Jose L	Son	M	Cha	22.0	S		Y	Y	Guam	Guam	Guam	Y	Clerk
	159	192	Untalan, Rosario L	Daughter	F	Cha	13.0	S	N	Y	Y	Guam	Guam	Guam	Y	None
	159	192	Untalan, Delfina L	Daughter	F	Cha	11.0	S	Y	Y	Y	Guam	Guam	Guam	Y	None
	159	192	Untalan, Antonia L	Daughter	F	Cha	7.0	S	Y			Guam	Guam	Guam		None
	160	193	Herrero, Vicente P	Head	M	W	37.0	M		Y	Y	Guam	Guam	Guam	Y	Supt. of markets
	160	193	Herrero, Alice L	Wife	F	W	34.0	M		Y	Y	Bonin Islands	Bonin Islands	Bonin Islands	Y	Teacher
	160	193	Herrero, Florence B	Daughter	F	W	13.0	S	Y	Y	Y	Guam	Guam	Bonin Islands	Y	None
	160	193	Herrero, Henry A	Son	M	W	11.0	S	Y	Y	Y	Guam	Guam	Bonin Islands	Y	None
	160	193	Herrero, Edward P	Son	M	W	10.0	S	Y	Y	Y	Guam	Guam	Bonin Islands	Y	None
	160	193	Herrero, Helen C	Daughter	F	W	6.0	S				Guam	Guam	Bonin Islands		None
	160	193	Herrero, Leillian J	Daughter	F	W	4.0	S				Guam	Guam	Bonin Islands		None
	160	193	Herrero, Ruth L	Daughter	F	W	3.0	S				Guam	Guam	Bonin Islands		None
	160	193	Asa, Ono	Servant	F	Jp	72.0	Wd		N	N	Japan	Japan	Japan	N	Servant
	161	194	Kitamura, Naoshi	Head	M	Jp	33.0	S		Y	Y	Japan	Japan	Japan	Y	Merchant general retail

Hernan Cortez Street

(CHAMORRO ROOTS GENEALOGY PROJECT ™ TRANSCRIPTION)
(COMPILED/TRANSCRIBED BY BERNARD T. PUNZALAN / HTTP://WWW.CHAMORROROOTS.COM)

FOURTEENTH CENSUS OF THE UNITED STATES: 1920-POPULATION

ISLAND OF GUAM

DISTRICT 2
NAME OF PLACE Agana (City)
[Proper name and, also, name of class, as city, town, village, barrio, etc]

ENUMERATED BY ME ON THE 9th DAY OF March, 1920

Arthur W. Jackson ENUMERATOR

	Dwelling No.	Family No.	NAME	RELATION	Sex	Color or race	Age	S/M/Wd	Attended school	Able to read	Able to write	Birthplace of person	Birthplace of father	Birthplace of mother	Speak English	OCCUPATION
26	162	195	Lujan, Rosa G	Head	F	Cha	38.0	Wd		Y	Y	Guam	Guam	Guam	N	Laundress
27	162	195	Lujan, Juliana G	Daughter	F	Cha	13.0	S	N	Y	Y	Guam	Unknown	Guam	Y	None
28	162	195	Rosario, Jose L	Son	M	Cha	11.0	S	Y	Y	Y	Guam	Guam	Guam	N	None
29	162	195	Rosario, Manuel L	Son	M	Cha	10.0	S	Y	Y	Y	Guam	Guam	Guam	N	None
30	162	195	Rosario, Maria L	Daughter	F	Cha	8.0	S	Y			Guam	Guam	Guam		None
31	162	195	Rosario, Pedro L	Son	M	Cha	4.0	S				Guam	Guam	Guam		None
32	162	195	Rosario, Rosalia L	Daughter	F	Cha	2.0	S				Guam	Guam	Guam		None
33	163	196	Mesa, Geronimo R	Head	M	Cha	58.0	M		Y	Y	Guam	Guam	Guam	N	Farmer
34	163	196	Mesa, Vicenta F	Wife	F	Cha	44.0	M		Y	Y	Guam	Guam	Guam	N	None
35	163	196	Mesa, Maria F	Daughter	F	Cha	25.0	S		Y	Y	Guam	Guam	Guam	N	Laundress
36	163	196	Mesa, Ana F	Daughter	F	Cha	23.0	S		Y	Y	Guam	Guam	Guam	N	Laundress
37	163	196	Mesa, Jose F	Son	M	Cha	19.0	S	N	Y	Y	Guam	Guam	Guam	Y	Machinist
38	163	196	Mesa, Soledad F	Daughter	F	Cha	16.0	S	N	Y	Y	Guam	Guam	Guam	Y	None
39	163	196	Mesa, Juan F	Son	M	Cha	14.0	S	N	Y	Y	Guam	Guam	Guam	Y	Farm laborer
40	163	196	Mesa, Rosa F	Daughter	F	Cha	13.0	S	Y	Y	Y	Guam	Guam	Guam	Y	None
41	163	196	Mesa, Vicente F	Son	M	Cha	10.0	S	Y	Y	Y	Guam	Guam	Guam	Y	None
42	163	196	Mesa, Carmen F	Daughter	F	Cha	7.0	S	Y			Guam	Guam	Guam		None
43	163	196	Mesa, Gloria F	Daughter	F	Cha	6.0	S				Guam	Guam	Guam		None
44	163	196	Mesa, Concepcion F	Daughter	F	Cha	4.0	S				Guam	Guam	Guam		None
45	164	197	Anderson, Arthur	Head	M	W	35.0	M		Y	Y	Scotland	Scotland	Scotland	Y	Electrician
46	164	197	Anderson, Rosa C	Wife	F	Cha	31.0	M		Y	Y	Guam	Guam	Guam	Y	None
47	164	197	Anderson, Arthur G	Son	M	W	7.0	S	Y			Guam	Scotland	Guam		None
48	164	197	Anderson, Henry C	Son	M	W	6.0	S	N			Guam	Scotland	Guam		None
49	164	197	Anderson, John C	Son	M	W	4.0	S				Guam	Scotland	Guam		None
50	164	197	Anderson, Lillian C	Daughter	F	W	3.0	S				Guam	Scotland	Guam		None

Street: Travesia de Gomez Street

(CHAMORRO ROOTS GENEALOGY PROJECT ™ TRANSCRIPTION)
(COMPILED/TRANSCRIBED BY BERNARD T. PUNZALAN / HTTP://WWW.CHAMORROROOTS.COM)
FOURTEENTH CENSUS OF THE UNITED STATES: 1920—POPULATION
ISLAND OF GUAM

DISTRICT 2
NAME OF PLACE Agana (City)
[Proper name and, also, name of class, as city, town, village, barrio, etc]

ENUMERATED BY ME ON THE 9th DAY OF March, 1920

Arthur W. Jackson ENUMERATOR

Street	Dwelling No. (2)	Family No. (3)	NAME (4)	RELATION (5)	Sex (6)	Color or race (7)	Age (8)	Single, married, widowed or divorced (9)	Attended school since Sept. 1, 1919 (10)	Read (11)	Write (12)	Place of birth of this person (13)	Place of birth of father (14)	Place of birth of mother (15)	Able to speak English (16)	OCCUPATION (17)
	164	197	Anderson, Joseph C	Son	M	W	0.5	S				Guam	Scotland	Guam		None
	165	198	Torres, Antonio M	Head	M	Cha	42.0	M		Y	Y	Guam	Guam	Guam	N	Merchant general retail
	165	198	Torres, Concepcion C	Wife	F	Cha	47.0	M		Y	Y	Guam	Guam	Guam	N	None
	165	198	Torres, Maria C	Daughter	F	Cha	17.0	S	N	Y	Y	Guam	Guam	Guam	Y	None
	165	198	Torres, Carmen C	Daughter	F	Cha	15.0	S	N	Y	Y	Guam	Guam	Guam	Y	None
	165	198	Torres, Concepcion C	Daughter	F	Cha	13.0	S	N	Y	Y	Guam	Guam	Guam	N	None
	165	198	Castro, Feliciana	Mother-in-law	F	Cha	80.0	Wd		N	N	Guam	Guam	Guam	N	None
	166	199	Camacho, Rita M	Head	F	Cha	47.0	S		N	N	Guam	Guam	Guam	N	None
	166	199	Camacho, Rosa C	Daughter	F	Cha	14.0	S	N	Y	Y	Guam	Unknown	Guam	Y	None
	166	199	Camacho, Filomena C	Daughter	F	Cha	12.0	S	N	Y	Y	Guam	Unknown	Guam	N	None
Travesia de Gomez Street	166	200	Cepeda, Jesus S	Head	M	Cha	34.0	M		N	N	Guam	Guam	Guam	N	Laborer
	166	200	Cepeda, Vicenta C	Wife	F	Cha	49.0	M		N	N	Guam	Guam	Guam	N	None
	166	200	Cepeda, Juan C	Son	M	Cha	15.0	S	N	Y	Y	Guam	Guam	Guam	Y	None
	166	200	Cepeda, Jose C	Son	M	Cha	13.0	S	N	Y	Y	Guam	Guam	Guam	Y	None
	166	200	Cepeda, Joaquin C	Son	M	Cha	11.0	S	Y	Y	Y	Guam	Guam	Guam	Y	None
	166	200	Cepeda, Lourdes C	Daughter	F	Cha	7.0	S	Y			Guam	Guam	Guam		None
	166	200	Camacho, Francisco C	Step son	M	Cha	24.0	S		Y	Y	Guam	Guam	Guam	N	Farmer
	166	200	Camacho, Josefa	Sister-in-law	F	Cha	52.0	S		N	N	Guam	Guam	Guam	N	None
	166	200	Camacho, Maria C	Niece	F	Cha	19.0	S		Y	Y	Guam	Unknown	Unknown	Y	None
	166	200	Camacho, Carmen C	Niece	F	Cha	15.0	S	N	Y	Y	Guam	Unknown	Unknown	Y	None
	167	201	Castro, Jose I	Head	M	Cha	50.0	M		Y	Y	Guam	Guam	Guam	Y	Painter
	167	201	Castro, Angela P	Wife	F	Cha	61.0	M		Y	Y	Guam	Guam	Guam	N	None
	167	201	Torres, Ana P	Step daughter	F	Cha	34.0	S		N	N	Guam	Guam	Guam	N	None
	167	201	Pablo, Juan	Step son	M	Cha	28.0	S		N	N	Guam	Guam	Guam	N	Laborer
	167	201	Torres, Francisco	Step son	M	Cha	39.0	Wd		N	N	Guam	Guam	Guam	N	Farmer

(CHAMORRO ROOTS GENEALOGY PROJECT ™ TRANSCRIPTION)
(COMPILED/TRANSCRIBED BY BERNARD T. PUNZALAN / HTTP://WWW.CHAMORROROOTS.COM)

FOURTEENTH CENSUS OF THE UNITED STATES: 1920-POPULATION

ISLAND OF GUAM

DISTRICT 2
NAME OF PLACE Agana (City)
[Proper name and, also, name of class, as city, town, village, barrio, etc]

ENUMERATED BY ME ON THE 10th DAY OF March, 1920

Arthur W. Jackson ENUMERATOR

	PLACE OF ABODE			NAME	RELATION	PERSONAL DESCRIPTION					EDUCATION			NATIVITY				OCCUPATION
Street, avenue, road, etc.	Number of dwelling house is order of visitation	Number of family in order of visitation		Name of each person whose place of abode on January 1, 1920, was in the family. Enter surname, firs, then given name and middle initial. If any. Include every person living on January 1, 1920. Omit children born since January 1, 1920.	Relationship of this Person to the head of the family.	Sex	Color or race	Age at last birthday	Single, married, widowed or divorced,	Attended school any time since Sept. 1, 1919	Whether able to read.	Whether able to write.	Place of birth of this person.	Place of birth of father of this person.	Place of birth of mother of this person.	Whether able to speak English.	Trade, profession, or particular kind of work done, as salesman, laborer, clerk, cook, merchant, washerwoman, etc.
	2	3		4	5	6	7	8	9	10	11	12	13	14	15	16	17
26	168	202		Ulloa, Jose SN	Head	M	Cha	48.0	M		Y	Y	Guam	Guam	Guam	N	Farmer
27	168	202		Ulloa, Nicolasa S	Wife	F	Cha	45.0	M		Y	Y	Guam	Guam	Guam	N	None
28	168	202		Ulloa, Josefa S	Daughter	F	Cha	20.0	S	N	Y	Y	Guam	Guam	Guam	Y	None
29	168	202		Ulloa, Maria S	Daughter	F	Cha	18.0	S	N	Y	Y	Guam	Guam	Guam	Y	None
30	168	202		Ulloa, Regina S	Daughter	F	Cha	12.0	S	Y	Y	Y	Guam	Guam	Guam	Y	None
31	168	202		Ulloa, Juan S	Son	M	Cha	10.0	S	Y	Y	Y	Guam	Guam	Guam	Y	None
32	168	202		Ulloa, Engracia S	Daughter	F	Cha	8.0	S	Y			Guam	Guam	Guam		None
33	168	202		Ulloa, Gregorio S	Son	M	Cha	6.0	S	N			Guam	Guam	Guam		None
34	168	202		Ulloa, Magdalena S	Daughter	F	Cha	4.0	S				Guam	Guam	Guam		None
35	168	202		Ulloa, Isabel S	Daughter	F	Cha	2.0	S				Guam	Guam	Guam		None
36	169	203	Saguato Street	Toves, Dolores L	Head	F	Cha	40.0	Wd		Y	Y	Guam	Guam	Guam	N	Farmer
37	169	203		Toves, Pedro L	Son	M	Cha	19.0	S	N	Y	Y	Guam	Guam	Guam	Y	Laborer
38	169	203		Toves, Jose L	Son	M	Cha	17.0	S	N	Y	Y	Guam	Guam	Guam	Y	None
39	169	203		Toves, Maria L	Daughter	F	Cha	16.0	S	N	Y	Y	Guam	Guam	Guam	Y	None
40	169	203		Toves, Ana L	Daughter	F	Cha	15.0	S	N	Y	Y	Guam	Guam	Guam	Y	None
41	169	203		Toves, Concepcion L	Daughter	F	Cha	13.0	S	N	Y	Y	Guam	Guam	Guam	Y	None
42	169	203		Lujan, Atanasio	Son	M	Cha	8.0	S	Y			Guam	Unknown	Unknown		None
43	169	203		Lujan, Rosalia	Daughter	F	Cha	6.0	S	N			Guam	Unknown	Unknown		None
44	169	203		Lujan, Guardalupe	Daughter	F	Cha	0.7	S				Guam	Unknown	Guam		None
45	170	204		Santos, Marcos U	Head	M	Cha	32.0	M	N	Y	Y	Guam	Guam	Guam	N	Farmer
46	170	204		Santos, Maria G	Wife	F	Cha	21.0	M		Y	Y	Guam	Guam	Guam		None
47	170	204		Santos, Romaldo G	Son	M	Cha	2.0	S				Guam	Guam	Guam		None
48	170	204		Santos, Maria U	Sister	F	Cha	41.0	S		N	N	Guam	Guam	Guam	N	None
49	171	205		Cruz, Josefa I	Head	F	Cha	50.0	Wd		Y	Y	Guam	Guam	Guam	N	None
50	171	205		Cruz, Pedro I	Son	M	Cha	26.0	S		Y	Y	Guam	Guam	Guam	N	None

(CHAMORRO ROOTS GENEALOGY PROJECT ™ TRANSCRIPTION)
(COMPILED/TRANSCRIBED BY BERNARD T. PUNZALAN / HTTP://WWW.CHAMORROROOTS.COM)

FOURTEENTH CENSUS OF THE UNITED STATES: 1920-POPULATION

ISLAND OF GUAM

DISTRICT **2**

NAME OF PLACE **Agana (City)**

[Proper name and, also, name of class, as city, town, village, barrio, etc]

ENUMERATED BY ME ON THE 10th DAY OF March, 1920

Arthur W. Jackson ENUMERATOR

	PLACE OF ABODE			NAME	RELATION	PERSONAL DESCRIPTION					EDUCATION			NATIVITY				OCCUPATION
Street, avenue, road, etc.	Number of dwelling house is order of visitation	Number of family in order of visitation		Name of each person whose place of abode on January 1, 1920, was in the family.	Relationship of this Person to the head of the family.	Sex	Color or race	Age at last birthday	Single, married, widowed or divorced	Attended school any time since Sept. 1, 1919	Whether able to read.	Whether able to write.	Place of birth of this person.	Place of birth of father of this person.	Place of birth of mother of this person.	Whether able to speak English.	Trade, profession, or particular kind of work done, as salesman, laborer, clerk, cook, merchant, washerwoman, etc.
1	2	3		4	5	6	7	8	9	10	11	12	13	14	15	16	17
1	171	205		Cruz, Jesus I	Son	M	Cha	16.0	S	N	Y	Y	Guam	Guam	Guam	N	Laborer
2	172	206		Santos, Izequiel	Head	M	Cha	38.0	M		Y	Y	Guam	Unknown	Guam	N	Laborer
3	172	206		Santos, Rosa C	Wife	F	Cha	43.0	M		Y	Y	Guam	Guam	Guam	N	None
4	173	207		Salas, Cecilio L	Head	M	Cha	29.0	M		Y	Y	Philippine Islands	Guam	Guam	Y	Carpenter
5	173	207		Salas, Trinidad G	Wife	F	Cha	21.0	M		Y	Y	Guam	Guam	Guam	Y	None
6	173	207		Salas, Emeterio G	Son	M	Cha	5.0	S	N			Guam	Philippine Islands	Guam		None
7	173	207		Salas, Aurea G	Daughter	F	Cha	2.0	S	N			Guam	Philippine Islands	Guam		None
8	173	207		Salas, Jose G	Son	M	Cha	0.8	S				Guam	Philippine Islands	Guam		None
9	173	207		Salas, Nicolasa L	Mother	F	Cha	58.0	Wd		Y	Y	Guam	Guam	Guam	N	None
10	174	208		Roberto, Mercedes B	Head	F	Cha	24.0	S		Y	Y	Guam	Guam	Guam	Y	Midwife
11	174	208		Roberto, Emma	Daughter	F	Cha	4.0	S				Guam	Unknown	Guam		None
12	174	208		Roberto, Hessel	Son	M	Cha	2.0	S				Guam	Unknown	Guam		None
13	174	208		Roberto, Wallace	Son	M	Cha	0.7	S				Guam	Unknown	Guam		None
14	175	209		Pereda, Gabriel S	Head	M	Cha	47.0	M		N	N	Guam	Guam	Guam	N	None
15	175	209		Pereda, Rosa C	Wife	F	Cha	56.0	M		Y	Y	Guam	Guam	Guam	N	None
16	175	209		Pereda, Maria C	Daughter	F	Cha	18.0	S	N	Y	Y	Guam	Guam	Guam	Y	None
17	175	209		Pereda, Isabel C	Daughter	F	Cha	16.0	S	N	Y	Y	Guam	Guam	Guam	Y	None
18	175	209		Pereda, Francisco C	Son	M	Cha	13.0	S	Y	Y	Y	Guam	Guam	Guam	N	None
19	175	209		Pereda, Ascension C	Daughter	F	Cha	11.0	S	Y	Y	Y	Guam	Guam	Guam		None
20	175	209		Pereda, Rosa C	Daughter	F	Cha	9.0	S	Y			Guam	Guam	Guam		None
21	175	209		Pereda, Fidela C	Daughter	F	Cha	6.0	S	N			Guam	Guam	Guam		None
22	175	209		Pereda, Natividad C	Daughter	F	Cha	4.0	S				Guam	Guam	Guam		None
23	175	209		Pereda, Margarita C	Daughter	F	Cha	2.0	S				Guam	Guam	Guam		None
24	201	201		Cruz, Jose	Head	M	Cha	21.0	M	N	Y	Y	Guam	Unknown	Unknown	Y	Carpenter
25	201	201		Cruz, Andrea M	Wife	F	Cha	17.0	M	N	Y	Y	Guam	Unknown	Guam	Y	None

Segunto Street

(CHAMORRO ROOTS GENEALOGY PROJECT ™ TRANSCRIPTION)
(COMPILED/TRANSCRIBED BY BERNARD T. PUNZALAN / HTTP://WWW.CHAMORROROOTS.COM)

FOURTEENTH CENSUS OF THE UNITED STATES: 1920-POPULATION

ISLAND OF GUAM

DISTRICT 2

NAME OF PLACE Agana (City)

[Proper name and, also, name of class, as city, town, village, barrio, etc]

ENUMERATED BY ME ON THE 11th DAY OF March, 1920

Arthur W. Jackson ENUMERATOR

	Street, avenue, road, etc.	Number of dwelling house in order of visitation	Number of family in order of visitation	NAME	RELATION	Sex	Color or race	Age at last birthday	Single, married, widowed or divorced	Attended school any time since Sept. 1, 1919	Whether able to read.	Whether able to write.	Place of birth of this person.	Place of birth of father of this person.	Place of birth of mother of this person.	Whether able to speak English.	OCCUPATION
	1	2	3	4	5	6	7	8	9	10	11	12	13	14	15	16	17
26		176	211	Mendiola, Maria G	Head	F	Cha	74.0	Wd		N	N	Guam	Guam	Guam	N	None
27		176	211	Mendiola, Vicente G	Son	M	Cha	50.0	S		N	N	Guam	Guam	Guam	N	Farmer
28		176	211	Mendiola, Joaquin G	Son	M	Cha	34.0	S		N	N	Guam	Guam	Guam	N	Laborer
29		176	211	Mendiola, Ana G	Daughter	F	Cha	33.0	S		N	N	Guam	Guam	Guam	N	None
30		177	212	Cepeda, Juan	Head	M	Cha	30.0	M		Y	Y	Guam	Guam	Guam	N	Farmer
31		177	212	Cepeda, Francisca Q	Wife	F	Cha	31.0	M		N	N	Guam	Guam	Guam	N	None
32		177	212	Cepeda, Jesus Q	Son	M	Cha	17.0	S	N	Y	Y	Guam	Guam	Guam	Y	None
33		177	212	Cepeda, Jose Q	Son	M	Cha	15.0	S	N	Y	Y	Guam	Guam	Guam	Y	None
34		177	212	Cepeda, Ana Q	Daughter	F	Cha	14.0	S	N	Y	Y	Guam	Guam	Guam	Y	None
35		177	212	Cepeda, Nicolasa Q	Daughter	F	Cha	13.0	S	Y	Y	Y	Guam	Guam	Guam	Y	None
36		177	212	Cepeda, Rita Q	Daughter	F	Cha	11.0	S	Y	Y	Y	Guam	Guam	Guam	Y	None
37		177	212	Cepeda, Juan Q	Son	M	Cha	8.0	S	Y			Guam	Guam	Guam		None
38		177	212	Cepeda, Trinidad Q	Daughter	F	Cha	6.0	S	N			Guam	Guam	Guam		None
39		177	212	Cepeda, Joaquin Q	Son	M	Cha	3.0	S				Guam	Guam	Guam		None
40		177	212	Cepeda, Rosa Q	Daughter	F	Cha	2.0	S				Guam	Guam	Guam		None
41	Sagunto Street	177	212	Cepeda, Antonio Q	Son	M	Cha	0.2	S				Guam	Guam	Guam		None
42		178	213	San Nicolas, Faustino	Head	M	Cha	28.0	M		Y	Y	Guam	Unknown	Guam	Y	Blacksmith
43		178	213	San Nicolas, Rita P	Wife	F	Cha	26.0	M		Y	Y	Guam	Guam	Guam	N	None
44		178	213	San Nicolas, Ignacio P	Son	M	Cha	1.0	S				Guam	Guam	Guam		None
45		178	213	San Nicolas, Francisco P	Son	M	Cha	0.1	S				Guam	Guam	Guam		None
46		179	214	Mendiola, Magdalena H	Head	M	W	55.0	Wd		Y	Y	Guam	England	Guam	N	Farmer
47		179	214	Mendiola, Juan H	Son	M	Cha	26.0	S		Y	Y	Guam	Guam	Guam	N	Farmer
48		179	214	Mendiola, Consolacion H	Daughter	F	Cha	13.0	S	N	Y	Y	Guam	Guam	Guam	Y	None
49		180	215	Martinez, Juan C	Head	M	Cha	42.0	M		Y	Y	Guam	Guam	Guam	N	Shoemaker
50		180	215	Martinez, Rita P	Wife	F	Cha	44.0	M		Y	Y	Guam	Guam	Guam	N	None

256

(CHAMORRO ROOTS GENEALOGY PROJECT ™ TRANSCRIPTION)
(COMPILED/TRANSCRIBED BY BERNARD T. PUNZALAN / HTTP://WWW.CHAMORROROOTS.COM)

FOURTEENTH CENSUS OF THE UNITED STATES: 1920–POPULATION

ISLAND OF GUAM

DISTRICT 2
NAME OF PLACE Agana (City)

[Proper name and, also, name of class, as city, town, village, barrio, etc]

ENUMERATED BY ME ON THE 11th DAY OF March, 1920

Arthur W. Jackson ENUMERATOR

Street	Dwelling house No.	Family No.	NAME	RELATION	Sex	Color or race	Age	Single, married, widowed or divorced	Attended school since Sept. 1, 1919	Able to read	Able to write	Place of birth of this person	Place of birth of father	Place of birth of mother	Able to speak English	OCCUPATION
1	2	3	4	5	6	7	8	9	10	11	12	13	14	15	16	17
	180	215	Martinez, Jose P	Son	M	Cha	13.0	S	Y	Y	Y	Guam	Guam	Guam	Y	None
	180	215	Martinez, Antonio P	Son	M	Cha	12.0	S	Y	Y	Y	Guam	Guam	Guam	Y	None
	180	215	Martinez, Juan P	Son	M	Cha	10.0	S	Y	Y	Y	Guam	Guam	Guam	N	None
	180	215	Martinez, Concepcion P	Daughter	F	Cha	8.0	S	Y	Y	Y	Guam	Guam	Guam		None
	180	215	Martinez, Eduvegis P	Daughter	F	Cha	5.0	S	N			Guam	Guam	Guam		None
	180	215	Martinez, Nieves P	Daughter	F	Cha	2.0	S				Guam	Guam	Guam		None
	180	215	Martinez, Eduvegis P	Mother	F	Cha	68.0	Wd		N	N	Guam	Guam	Guam	N	None
	181	216	Martinez, Manuel C	Head	M	Cha	26.0	M		Y	Y	Guam	Guam	Guam	N	Shoemaker
	181	216	Martinez, Remedios C	Wife	F	Cha	26.0	M		Y	Y	Guam	Guam	Guam	N	None
	181	216	Martinez, Angelina C	Daughter	F	Cha	3.0	S				Guam	Guam	Guam		None
Segundo Street	181	216	Martinez, Ana C	Daughter	F	Cha	1.0	S				Guam	Guam	Guam		None
	182	217	Fejarang, Josefa C	Head	F	Cha	43.0	Wd		Y	Y	Guam	Unknown	Guam	N	None
	182	217	Fejarang, Joaquin C	Son	M	Cha	25.0	S		Y	Y	Guam	Guam	Guam	N	Laborer
	182	217	Fejarang, Vicente C	Son	M	Cha	22.0	S	N	Y	Y	Guam	Guam	Guam	Y	Farmer
	182	217	Fejarang, Jose C	Son	M	Cha	14.0	S	Y	Y	Y	Guam	Guam	Guam	Y	None
	182	217	Fejarang, Rosa C	Daughter	F	Cha	11.0	S	Y	Y	Y	Guam	Guam	Guam	N	None
	182	217	Fejarang, Magdalena C	Daughter	F	Cha	9.0	S	Y			Guam	Guam	Guam		None
	182	217	Fejarang, Manuel C	Son	M	Cha	6.0	S	N			Guam	Guam	Guam		None
	182	217	Fejarang, Rosalia C	Daughter	F	Cha	3.0	S				Guam	Guam	Guam		None
	182	217	Perez, Dolores C	Mother	F	Cha	80.0	Wd		N	N	Guam	Guam	Guam	N	None
	183	218	Fejarang, Juan P	Head	M	Cha	38.0	M		Y	Y	Guam	Guam	Guam	N	Farmer
	183	218	Fejarang, Francisca C	Wife	F	Cha	33.0	M		N	N	Guam	Guam	Guam	N	None
	183	218	Fejarang, Jesus C	Son	M	Cha	13.0	S	Y	Y	Y	Guam	Guam	Guam	Y	None
	183	218	Fejarang, Jose C	Son	M	Cha	11.0	S	Y	Y	Y	Guam	Guam	Guam	N	None
	183	218	Fejarang, Luis C	Son	M	Cha	7.0	S	N			Guam	Guam	Guam	N	None

(CHAMORRO ROOTS GENEALOGY PROJECT ™ TRANSCRIPTION)
(COMPILED/TRANSCRIBED BY BERNARD T. PUNZALAN / HTTP://WWW.CHAMORROROOTS.COM)

FOURTEENTH CENSUS OF THE UNITED STATES: 1920-POPULATION

ISLAND OF GUAM

DISTRICT 2
NAME OF PLACE Agana (City)

[Proper name and, also, name of class, as city, town, village, barrio, etc]

ENUMERATED BY ME ON THE 11th DAY OF March, 1920

Arthur W. Jackson ENUMERATOR

	Street, avenue, road, etc.	PLACE OF ABODE — Number of dwelling house in order of visitation	PLACE OF ABODE — Number of family in order of visitation	NAME	RELATION	Sex	Color or race	Age at last birthday	Single, married, widowed or divorced	Attended school any time since Sept. 1, 1919	Whether able to read	Whether able to write	Place of birth of this person	Place of birth of father of this person	Place of birth of mother of this person	Whether able to speak English	OCCUPATION
	1	2	3	4	5	6	7	8	9	10	11	12	13	14	15	16	17
26		183	218	Fejarang, Francisco C	Son	M	Cha	5.0	S	N			Guam	Guam	Guam		None
27		183	218	Fejarang, Maria C	Daughter	F	Cha	3.0	S				Guam	Guam	Guam		None
28		183	218	Fejarang, Joaquin C	Son	M	Cha	1.0	S				Guam	Guam	Guam		None
29		184	219	Fejarang, Jose S	Head	M	Cha	70.0	M		N	N	Guam	Unknown	Guam	N	None
30		184	219	Fejarang, Vicenta P	Wife	F	Cha	57.0	M		N	N	Guam	Guam	Guam	N	None
31		184	219	Fejarang, Joaquin P	Son	M	Cha	33.0	S		N	N	Guam	Guam	Guam	Y	Farmer
32		184	220	Munoz, Joaquin I	Head	M	Cha	18.0	M	N	Y	Y	Guam	Guam	Guam	Y	App. Electrician
33		184	220	Munoz, Josefa F	Wife	F	Cha	17.0	M	N	Y	Y	Guam	Guam	Guam	Y	None
34		184	220	Munoz, Jesus F	Son	M	Cha	0.1	S				Guam	Guam	Guam		None
35	Saguato Street	185	221	Concepcion, Juan C	Head	M	Cha	54.0	M		Y	Y	Guam	Guam	Guam	N	Farmer
36		185	221	Concepcion, Magdalena C	Wife	F	Cha	45.0	M		Y	Y	Guam	Guam	Guam	N	None
37		185	221	Concepcion, Ana C	Daughter	F	Cha	18.0	S	N	Y	Y	Guam	Guam	Guam	Y	None
38		185	221	Concepcion, Juan C	Son	M	Cha	16.0	S	N	Y	Y	Guam	Guam	Guam	Y	Farm laborer
39		185	221	Concepcion, Joaquin C	Son	M	Cha	14.0	S	Y	Y	Y	Guam	Guam	Guam	Y	None
40		185	221	Concepcion, Rosario C	Daughter	F	Cha	13.0	S	Y	Y	Y	Guam	Guam	Guam	Y	None
41		185	221	Concepcion, Maria C	Daughter	F	Cha	4.0	S				Guam	Guam	Guam		None
42		186	222	Salas, Antonio D	Head	M	Cha	28.0	M		Y	Y	Guam	Guam	Guam	Y	Carpenter
43		186	222	Salas, Ana C	Wife	F	Cha	31.0	M		N	N	Guam	Guam	Guam	N	None
44		186	222	Salas, Jose C	Son	M	Cha	4.0	S				Guam	Guam	Guam		None
45		186	222	Salas, Rita C	Daughter	F	Cha	2.0	S				Guam	Guam	Guam		None
46		187	223	Pereda, Vicente S	Head	M	Cha	53.0	M	N	N	N	Guam	Guam	Guam	N	Farmer
47		187	223	Pereda, Asencion P	Wife	F	Cha	60.0	M	N	N	N	Guam	Guam	Guam	N	None
48		187	223	Pereda, Ignacio P	Son	M	Cha	20.0	S	N	N	N	Guam	Guam	Guam	N	Carpenter
49		187	223	Pangelinan, Ana P	Step daughter	F	Cha	26.0	M		Y	Y	Guam	Guam	Guam	N	None
50		188	224	Reyes, Vicente C	Head	M	Cha	45.0	M		Y	Y	Guam	Guam	Guam	N	Farmer

258

(CHAMORRO ROOTS GENEALOGY PROJECT ™ TRANSCRIPTION)
(COMPILED/TRANSCRIBED BY BERNARD T. PUNZALAN / HTTP://WWW.CHAMORROROOTS.COM)

FOURTEENTH CENSUS OF THE UNITED STATES: 1920—POPULATION
ISLAND OF GUAM

DISTRICT 2
NAME OF PLACE Agana (City)

ENUMERATED BY ME ON THE 12th DAY OF March, 1920

Arthur W. Jackson ENUMERATOR

[Proper name and, also, name of class, as city, town, village, barrio, etc]

Street, avenue, road, etc.	Number of dwelling house in order of visitation	Number of family in order of visitation	NAME	RELATION	Sex	Color or race	Age at last birthday	Single, married, widowed or divorced	Attended school any time since Sept. 1, 1919	Whether able to read.	Whether able to write.	Place of birth of this person.	Place of birth of father of this person.	Place of birth of mother of this person.	Whether able to speak English.	OCCUPATION
	1	2	3	4	5	6	7	8	9	10	11	12	13	14	15	16	17
	188	224	Reyes, Ana D	Wife	F	Cha	44.0	M		Y	Y	Guam	Philippine Islands	Guam		None
	189	225	Pereda, Jesus S	Head	M	Cha	45.0	M		Y	Y	Guam	Guam	Unknown	N	Farmer
	189	225	Pereda, Maria P	Wife	F	Cha	39.0	M		Y	Y	Guam	Guam	Guam	N	None
	189	225	Pereda, Juan P	Son	M	Cha	12.0	S	Y	Y	Y	Guam	Guam	Guam	Y	None
	189	225	Pereda, Jesus P	Son	M	Cha	11.0	S	Y	Y	Y	Guam	Guam	Guam	Y	None
	189	225	Pereda, Maria P	Daughter	F	Cha	7.0	S	Y			Guam	Guam	Guam		None
	189	225	Pereda, Antonio P	Son	M	Cha	3.0	S				Guam	Guam	Guam		None
	189	225	Pereda, Concepcion P	Daughter	F	Cha	0.6	S				Guam	Guam	Guam		None
	190	226	Castro, Manuel C	Head	M	Cha	61.0	M		Y	Y	Guam	Guam	Guam	N	Farmer
	190	226	Castro, Rita C	Wife	F	Cha	51.0	M		N	N	Guam	Guam	Guam	N	None
	190	226	Castro, Pedro C	Son	M	Cha	26.0	S		Y	Y	Guam	Guam	Guam	N	Farmer
	190	226	Castro, Nicolasa C	Daughter	F	Cha	24.0	S	N	Y	Y	Guam	Guam	Guam	N	None
	190	226	Castro, Ana C	Daughter	F	Cha	19.0	S	N	Y	Y	Guam	Guam	Guam	N	None
	190	226	Castro, Teresa C	Daughter	F	Cha	15.0	S		Y	Y	Guam	Guam	Guam	Y	None
	191	227	Perez, Caesario B	Head	M	Cha	55.0	Wd		Y	Y	Guam	Guam	Guam	N	Farmer
	191	227	Perez, Rosalia B	Daughter	F	Cha	31.0	S				Guam	Guam	Guam		None
	191	227	Perez, Tomasa B	Daughter	F	Cha	18.0	S	N	Y	Y	Guam	Guam	Guam	Y	None
	192	228	Perez, Jose F	Head	M	Cha	36.0	M				Guam	Guam	Guam		Farmer
	192	228	Perez, Maria L	Wife	F	Cha	31.0	M		N	N	Guam	Guam	Guam	N	None
	192	228	Perez, Rosario L	Daughter	F	Cha	4.0	S				Guam	Guam	Guam		None
	192	228	Perez, Amanda L	Daughter	F	Cha	1.0	S				Guam	Guam	Guam		None
Segundo Street	193	229	Taigiron, Ramona G	Head	F	Cha	42.0	Wd		Y	Y	Guam	Guam	Guam	N	Laundress
	193	229	Taigiron, Antonio G	Son	M	Cha	14.0	S	Y	Y	Y	Guam	Guam	Guam	Y	Servant
	193	229	Taigiron, Juliana G	Daughter	F	Cha	12.0	S	Y	Y	Y	Guam	Guam	Guam	N	None
	193	229	Taigiron, Mercedes G	Daughter	F	Cha	10.0	S	Y	Y	Y	Guam	Guam	Guam	N	None

(CHAMORRO ROOTS GENEALOGY PROJECT ™ TRANSCRIPTION)
(COMPILED/TRANSCRIBED BY BERNARD T. PUNZALAN / HTTP://WWW.CHAMORROROOTS.COM)

FOURTEENTH CENSUS OF THE UNITED STATES: 1920-POPULATION
ISLAND OF GUAM

ENUMERATED BY ME ON THE 12th DAY OF March, 1920

Arthur W. Jackson ENUMERATOR

DISTRICT 2
NAME OF PLACE Agana (City)

[Proper name and, also, name of class, as city, town, village, barrio, etc]

	Street	Dwelling No.	Family No.	NAME	RELATION	Sex	Color or race	Age	Single/married/widowed/divorced	Attended school since Sept. 1, 1919	Able to read	Able to write	Birthplace of person	Birthplace of father	Birthplace of mother	Able to speak English	OCCUPATION
	1	2	3	4	5	6	7	8	9	10	11	12	13	14	15	16	17
26		193	229	Taigiron, Jose G	Son	M	Cha	6.0	S	N			Guam	Guam	Guam		None
27		194	230	Un-Pingco, Pedro	Head	M	Cha	54.0	M		Y	Y	Guam	Guam	Guam	N	Farmer
28		194	230	Un-Pingco, Maria R	Wife	F	Cha	44.0	M		Y	Y	Guam	Guam	Guam	N	None
29		194	230	Un-Pingco, Ana R	Daughter	F	Cha	23.0	S		Y	Y	Guam	Guam	Guam	Y	None
30		194	230	Un-Pingco, Josefina R	Daughter	F	Cha	19.0	S	Y	Y	Y	Guam	Guam	Guam	Y	None
31		194	230	Un-Pingco, Juan R	Son	M	Cha	18.0	S	Y	Y	Y	Guam	Guam	Guam	Y	None
32		194	230	Un-Pingco, Magdalena R	Daughter	F	Cha	17.0	S	Y	Y	Y	Guam	Guam	Guam	Y	None
33		194	230	Un-Pingco, Rosario R	Daughter	F	Cha	13.0	S	Y	Y	Y	Guam	Guam	Guam	Y	None
34		194	230	Un-Pingco, Jose R	Son	M	Cha	12.0	S	Y	Y	Y	Guam	Guam	Guam	N	None
35		194	230	Un-Pingco, Jesus R	Son	M	Cha	7.0	S	Y	Y	Y	Guam	Guam	Guam		None
36		194	230	Un-Pingco, Consuelo R	Daughter	F	Cha	5.0	S	N			Guam	Guam	Guam		None
37		195	231	Taitano, Jose M	Head	M	Cha	49.0	M		Y	Y	Guam	Guam	Guam	N	Farmer
38	Segundo Street	195	231	Taitano, Andrea G	Wife	F	Cha	45.0	M		N	N	Guam	Guam	Guam	N	None
39		195	231	Taitano, Rosario G	Daughter	F	Cha	21.0	S	N	Y	Y	Guam	Guam	Guam	Y	None
40		195	231	Taitano, Manuel G	Son	M	Cha	17.0	S	N	Y	Y	Guam	Guam	Guam	Y	Farm laborer
41		195	231	Taitano, Maria G	Daughter	F	Cha	16.0	S	N	Y	Y	Guam	Guam	Guam	Y	None
42		195	231	Taitano, Rosa G	Daughter	F	Cha	14.0	S	Y	Y	Y	Guam	Guam	Guam	Y	None
43		195	231	Taitano, Liberato G	Son	M	Cha	12.0	S	Y	Y	Y	Guam	Guam	Guam	Y	None
44		195	231	Taitano, Francisco G	Son	M	Cha	9.0	S	Y			Guam	Guam	Guam		None
45		195	231	Taitano, Emelia G	Daughter	F	Cha	8.0	S	Y			Guam	Guam	Guam		None
46		195	231	Taitano, Ana G	Daughter	F	Cha	7.0	S	Y			Guam	Guam	Guam		None
47		195	231	Taitano, Mariano G	Son	M	Cha	4.0	S				Guam	Guam	Guam		None
48		195	231	Taitano, Rita G	Daughter	F	Cha	2.0	S				Guam	Guam	Guam		None
49		196	232	James, Joseph H	Head	M	W	51.0	M		Y	Y	Ireland	Ireland	Ireland	Y	Painter
50		196	232	James, Dolores F	Wife	F	Cha	38.0	M		Y	Y	Guam	Guam	Guam	Y	None

(CHAMORRO ROOTS GENEALOGY PROJECT ™ TRANSCRIPTION)
(COMPILED/TRANSCRIBED BY BERNARD T. PUNZALAN / HTTP://WWW.CHAMORROROOTS.COM)

FOURTEENTH CENSUS OF THE UNITED STATES: 1920—POPULATION
ISLAND OF GUAM

DISTRICT **2**
NAME OF PLACE **Agana (City)**

[Proper name and, also, name of class, as city, town, village, barrio, etc]

ENUMERATED BY ME ON THE 13th DAY OF March, 1920

Arthur W. Jackson ENUMERATOR

	PLACE OF ABODE		NAME	RELATION	PERSONAL DESCRIPTION				EDUCATION			NATIVITY				OCCUPATION
Street, avenue, road, etc.	Number of dwelling house in order of visitation	Number of family in order of visitation	of each person whose place of abode on January 1, 1920, was in this family.	Relationship of this Person to the head of the family.	Sex	Color or race	Age at last birthday	Single, married, widowed or divorced	Attended school any time since Sept. 1, 1919	Whether able to read.	Whether able to write.	Place of birth of this person.	Place of birth of father of this person.	Place of birth of mother of this person.	Whether able to speak English.	Trade, profession, or particular kind of work done, as salesman, laborer, clerk, cook, merchant, washerwoman, etc.
1	2	3	4	5	6	7	8	9	10	11	12	13	14	15	16	17
	196	232	James, Eugenia F	Daughter	F	W	19.0	S	Y	Y	Y	Island of Palau	Ireland	Guam	Y	None
	196	232	James, David W. R.	Son	M	W	18.0	S	N	Y	Y	Guam	Ireland	Guam	Y	Enlisted USN
	196	232	James, William F	Son	M	W	16.0	S	Y	Y	Y	Island of Palau	Ireland	Guam	Y	None
	196	232	James, Lily F	Daughter	F	W	15.0	S	Y	Y	Y	Island of Palau	Ireland	Guam	Y	None
	196	232	James, Joseph F	Son	M	W	13.0	S	Y	Y	Y	Guam	Ireland	Guam	Y	None
	196	232	James, Daisy F	Daughter	F	W	7.0	S	Y			Guam	Ireland	Guam		None
	196	232	James, Pedro F	Son	M	W	5.0	S				Guam	Ireland	Guam		None
	196	232	James, Woodrow F	Son	M	W	2.0	S	N			Guam	Ireland	Guam		None
	196	232	Flores, Felisa	Sister-in-law	F	Cha	66.0	Wd		Y	Y	Guam	Guam	Guam	N	None
Sagunto Street	197	233	Un-Pingco, Francisco	Head	M	Cha	23.0	M		Y	Y	Guam	Guam	Guam	Y	Clerk
	197	233	Un-Pingco, Rita M	Wife	F	Cha	15.0	M	N	Y	Y	Guam	Guam	Guam	Y	None
	198	234	Gumataotao, Ignacio S	Head	M	Cha	34.0	M		Y	Y	Guam	Guam	Guam	N	Farmer
	198	234	Gumataotao, Rita U	Wife	F	Cha	34.0	M				Guam	Guam	Guam	N	None
	198	234	Gumataotao, Virginia U	Daughter	F	Cha	9.0	S	Y	Y	Y	Guam	Guam	Guam	Y	None
	198	234	Gumataotao, Agustin U	Son	M	Cha	5.0	S	N			Guam	Guam	Guam		None
	198	234	Gumataotao, Francisco U	Son	M	Cha	3.0	S				Guam	Guam	Guam		None
	198	234	Leon Guerrero, Maria U	Niece	F	Cha	17.0	S	N	Y	Y	Guam	Guam	Guam	Y	None
	198	234	Leon Guerrero, Juan U	Nephew	M	Cha	19.0	S	N	Y	Y	Guam	Guam	Guam	Y	Farm laborer
	198	234	Leon Guerrero, Dolores U	Niece	F	Cha	15.0	S	N	Y	Y	Guam	Guam	Guam	Y	None
	198	234	Leon Guerrero, Jesus U	Nephew	M	Cha	11.0	S	Y	Y	Y	Guam	Guam	Guam	Y	None
	198	234	Ungacta, Rosa	Niece	F	Cha	27.0	S				Guam	Guam	Guam	Y	Midwife
	198	234	Ungacta, Felix	Nephew	M	Cha	9.0	S	Y	Y	Y	Guam	Guam	Guam		None
	198	234	Ungacta, Gregorio	Nephew	M	Cha	2.0	S				Guam	Guam	Guam		None
	199	235	Borja, Santiago M	Head	M	Cha	29.0	M	N	Y	Y	Guam	Guam	Guam	Y	Laborer
	199	235	Borja, Ana S	Wife	F	Cha	21.0	M	N		Y	Guam	Guam	Guam	N	None

(CHAMORRO ROOTS GENEALOGY PROJECT ™ TRANSCRIPTION)
(COMPILED/TRANSCRIBED BY BERNARD T. PUNZALAN / HTTP://WWW.CHAMORROROOTS.COM)
FOURTEENTH CENSUS OF THE UNITED STATES: 1920–POPULATION
ISLAND OF GUAM

DISTRICT 2
NAME OF PLACE Agana (City)
[Proper name and, also, name of class, as city, town, village, barrio, etc]

ENUMERATED BY ME ON THE 13th DAY OF March, 1920
Arthur W. Jackson ENUMERATOR

	PLACE OF ABODE		NAME	RELATION	PERSONAL DESCRIPTION				EDUCATION			NATIVITY				OCCUPATION
Street, avenue, road, etc.	Number of dwelling house in order of visitation	Number of family in order of visitation	Name of each person whose place of abode on January 1, 1920, was in the family.	Relationship of this Person to the head of the family.	Sex	Color or race	Age at last birthday	Single, married, widowed or divorced	Attended school any time since Sept. 1, 1919	Whether able to read.	Whether able to write.	Place of birth of this person.	Place of birth of father of this person.	Place of birth of mother of this person.	Whether able to speak English.	Trade, profession, or particular kind of work done, as salesman, laborer, clerk, cook, merchant, washerwoman, etc.
1	2	3	4	5	6	7	8	9	10	11	12	13	14	15	16	17
26		199	235	Borja, Merigilda S	Daughter	F	Cha	2.0	S				Guam	Guam	Guam		None
27		199	235	Borja, Maria S	Daughter	F	Cha	0.2	S				Guam	Guam	Guam		None
28		199	235	Ungacta, Nicolasa	Mother-in-law	F	Cha	56.0	Wd		N	N	Guam	Guam	Guam	N	None
29		200	236	Borja, Joaquin M	Head	M	Cha	36.0	M		Y	Y	Guam	Guam	Guam	Y	Fireman
30		200	236	Borja, Ana C	Wife	F	Cha	27.0	M		Y	Y	Guam	Guam	Guam	N	None
31		200	236	Borja, Engracia C	Daughter	F	Cha	10.0	S	Y	Y	Y	Guam	Guam	Guam	Y	None
32		200	236	Borja, Francisco C	Son	M	Cha	8.0	S	Y			Guam	Guam	Guam		None
33		200	236	Borja, Gregorio C	Son	M	Cha	6.0	S	N			Guam	Guam	Guam		None
34		200	236	Borja, Jose C	Son	M	Cha	3.0	S				Guam	Guam	Guam		None
35	Sagunto Street	200	236	Borja, Nicolasa C	Daughter	F	Cha	1.0	S				Guam	Guam	Guam		None
36		201	237	Cruz, Jose G	Father-in-law	M	Cha	58.0	Wd		Y	Y	Guam	Guam	Guam	N	Farmer
37		201	237	Cruz, Jose C	Brother-in-law	M	Cha	20.0	S	N	Y	Y	Guam	Guam	Guam	Y	Farmer
38		201	237	Cruz, Carmen C	Sister-in-law	F	Cha	17.0	S	N	Y	Y	Guam	Guam	Guam	Y	None
39		201	237	Camacho, Francisco S	Lodger	M	Cha	78.0	Wd		Y	Y	Guam	Guam	Guam	N	None
40		201	237	Camacho, Joaquina S	Lodger	F	Cha	42.0	S		N	N	Guam	Guam	Guam	N	None
41		202	238	Castro, Josefa S	Head	F	Cha	58.0	M		Y	Y	Guam	Guam	Guam	N	None
42		202	238	Castro, Dolores S	Daughter	F	Cha	29.0	S	N	Y	Y	Guam	Guam	Guam	N	None
43		202	238	Castro, Ana S	Daughter	F	Cha	19.0	S	N	Y	Y	Guam	Guam	Guam	Y	None
44		202	238	Ignacio, Josefa S	Niece	F	Cha	14.0	S	Y	Y	Y	Guam	Guam	Guam	Y	None
45		202	238	Ignacio, Jesus C	Nephew	M	Cha	9.0	S				Guam	Guam	Guam		None
46		202	238	Ignacio, Gregorio C	Nephew	M	Cha	7.0	S				Guam	Guam	Guam		None
47		203	239	Cruz, Manuel	Head	M	Cha	43.0	M		Y	Y	Guam	Unknown	Guam	N	Farmer
48		203	239	Cruz, Dolores P	Wife	F	Cha	49.0	M		Y	Y	Guam	Guam	Guam	N	None
49		203	239	Cruz, Jose P	Son	M	Cha	22.0	S		Y	Y	Guam	Guam	Guam	Y	Enlisted US Navy
50		203	239	Cruz, Jesus P	Son	M	Cha	19.0	S	N	Y	Y	Guam	Guam	Guam	Y	Carpenter

(CHAMORRO ROOTS GENEALOGY PROJECT ™ TRANSCRIPTION)
(COMPILED/TRANSCRIBED BY BERNARD T. PUNZALAN / HTTP://WWW.CHAMORROROOTS.COM)
FOURTEENTH CENSUS OF THE UNITED STATES: 1920—POPULATION
ISLAND OF GUAM

ENUMERATED BY ME ON THE 13th DAY OF March, 1920

Arthur W. Jackson ENUMERATOR

DISTRICT 2
NAME OF PLACE Agana (City)

[Proper name and, also, name of class, as city, town, village, barrio, etc]

	Number of dwelling house in order of visitation	Number of family in order of visitation	NAME	RELATION	Sex	Color or race	Age at last birthday	Single, married, widowed or divorced	Attended school any time since Sept. 1, 1919	Whether able to read	Whether able to write	Place of birth of this person	Place of birth of father of this person	Place of birth of mother of this person	Whether able to speak English	OCCUPATION
	2	3	4	5	6	7	8	9	10	11	12	13	14	15	16	17
1	203	239	Cruz, Ramon P	Son	M	Cha	17.0	S	N	Y	Y	Guam	Guam	Guam	Y	Farm laborer
2	203	239	Cruz, Francisco P	Son	M	Cha	14.0	S	N		Y	Guam	Guam	Guam	Y	None
3	203	239	Cruz, Trinidad P	Daughter	F	Cha	9.0	S	Y			Guam	Guam	Guam		None
4	203	239	Cruz, Antonio P	Son	M	Cha	3.0	S				Guam	Guam	Guam		None
5	204	240	Garrido, Juan C	Head	M	Cha	40.0	M		Y	Y	Guam	Guam	Guam	N	Laborer
6	204	240	Garrido, Ana B	Wife	F	Cha	28.0	M		Y	Y	Guam	Guam	Guam	N	None
7	204	240	Garrido, Enselmo B	Son	M	Cha	7.0	S	Y			Guam	Guam	Guam		None
8	204	240	Garrido, Facundo B	Son	M	Cha	4.0	S				Guam	Guam	Guam		None
9	204	240	Garrido, Felisa B	Daughter	F	Cha	3.0	S				Guam	Guam	Guam		None
10	204	240	Garrido, Simona B	Daughter	F	Cha	2.0	S				Guam	Guam	Guam		None
11	204	240	Garrido, Victorano J. B	Son	M	Cha	0.8	S				Guam	Guam	Guam		None
12	204	240	Garrido, Mariana C	Mother	F	Cha	71.0	Wd		N	N	Guam	Guam	Guam	N	None
13	205	241	Perez, Felipe C	Head	M	Cha	43.0	Wd		Y	Y	Guam	Guam	Guam	N	Laborer
14	205	241	Perez, Jose R	Son	M	Cha	17.0	S	N	Y	Y	Guam	Guam	Guam	N	None
15	205	241	Perez, Dolores R	Daughter	F	Cha	14.0	S	N	Y	Y	Guam	Guam	Guam	Y	None
16	205	241	Perez, Angel R	Son	M	Cha	11.0	S	N	Y	Y	Guam	Guam	Guam	Y	None
17	205	241	Perez, Manuel R	Son	M	Cha	3.0	S				Guam	Guam	Guam		None
18	206	242	dela Rosa, Rita M	Head	F	Cha	64.0	Wd		N	N	Guam	Guam	Guam	N	None
19	206	242	dela Rosa, Manuel M	Son	M	Cha	18.0	S	N	Y	Y	Guam	Guam	Guam	Y	Farm laborer
20	207	243	Juan, Camilo C	Head	M	Fil	66.0	M	N	Y	Y	Philippine Islands	Philippine Islands	Philippine Islands	N	Farmer
21	207	243	Juan, Isabel M	Wife	F	Cha	46.0	M		N	N	Guam	Guam	Guam	N	None
22	207	244	Santos, Joaquin T	Head	M	Cha	24.0	M		Y	Y	Guam	Guam	Guam	Y	Laborer
23	207	244	Santos, Mariana M	Wife	F	Cha	21.0	M	N	N	N	Guam	Guam	Guam	Y	None
24	207	244	Santos, Froilan T	Brother	M	Cha	19.0	S		Y	Y	Guam	Guam	Guam	Y	None
25	208	245	Mesa, Jose	Head	M	Cha	47.0	M	N	N	N	Guam	Unknown	Guam	N	Farmer

Street: Segundo Street

(CHAMORRO ROOTS GENEALOGY PROJECT ™ TRANSCRIPTION)
(COMPILED/TRANSCRIBED BY BERNARD T. PUNZALAN / HTTP://WWW.CHAMORROROOTS.COM)
FOURTEENTH CENSUS OF THE UNITED STATES: 1920-POPULATION
ISLAND OF GUAM

DISTRICT 2
NAME OF PLACE Agana (City)
[Proper name and, also, name of class, as city, town, village, barrio, etc]

ENUMERATED BY ME ON THE 15th DAY OF March, 1920

Arthur W. Jackson ENUMERATOR

	PLACE OF ABODE		NAME	RELATION	PERSONAL DESCRIPTION				EDUCATION			NATIVITY				OCCUPATION
Street, avenue, road, etc.	Number of dwelling house in order of visitation	Number of family in order of visitation	of each person whose place of abode on January 1, 1920, was in the family.	Relationship of this person to the head of the family.	Sex	Color or race	Age at last birthday	Single, married, widowed or divorced	Attended school any time since Sept. 1, 1919	Whether able to read.	Whether able to write.	Place of birth of this person.	Place of birth of father of this person.	Place of birth of mother of this person.	Whether able to speak English.	Trade, profession, or particular kind of work done, as salesman, laborer, clerk, cook, merchant, washerwoman, etc.
1	2	3	4	5	6	7	8	9	10	11	12	13	14	15	16	17
	208	245	Mesa, Antonia M	Wife	F	Cha	36.0	M		N	N	Guam	Guam	Guam	N	None
	208	245	Mesa, Vicente M	Son	M	Cha	10.0	S	Y	Y	Y	Guam	Guam	Guam	Y	None
	208	245	Mesa, Jose M	Son	M	Cha	2.0	S				Guam	Guam	Guam		None
	209	246	Chargualaf, Agustin M	Head	M	Cha	32.0	M		Y	Y	Guam	Guam	Guam	N	Farmer
	209	246	Chargualaf, Maria C	Wife	F	Cha	24.0	M		Y	Y	Guam	Guam	Guam	N	None
	209	246	Chargualaf, Justo C	Son	M	Cha	8.0	S	Y			Guam	Guam	Guam		None
	209	246	Chargualaf, Antonia C	Daughter	F	Cha	6.0	S	N			Guam	Guam	Guam		None
	209	246	Chargualaf, Vicente C	Son	M	Cha	3.0	S				Guam	Guam	Guam		None
Segunto Street	209	246	Chargualaf, Rita C	Daughter	F	Cha	0.2	S				Guam	Guam	Guam		None
	210	247	Cruz, Joaquin C	Head	M	Cha	37.0	M		Y	Y	Guam	Guam	Guam	N	Farmer
	210	247	Cruz, Magdalena C	Wife	F	Cha	38.0	M		Y	Y	Guam	Guam	Guam	N	None
	210	247	Cruz, Antonio C	Son	M	Cha	13.0	S	Y	Y	Y	Guam	Guam	Guam	Y	None
	210	247	Cruz, Tomasa C	Daughter	F	Cha	12.0	S	Y	Y	Y	Guam	Guam	Guam	N	None
	210	247	Cruz, Juan C	Son	M	Cha	8.0	S	Y			Guam	Guam	Guam		None
	210	247	Cruz, Vicente C	Son	M	Cha	6.0	S	N			Guam	Guam	Guam		None
	210	247	Cruz, Adela C	Daughter	F	Cha	1.0	S				Guam	Guam	Guam		None
	211	248	Respicio, Luisa P	Head	F	Cha	54.0	Wd		Y	Y	Guam	Guam	Guam	N	None
	211	248	Respicio, Carmen P	Daughter	F	Cha	26.0	S		Y	Y	Guam	Guam	Guam	N	None
	211	248	Respicio, Maria P	Daughter	F	Cha	17.0	S	N	Y	Y	Guam	Guam	Guam	Y	Laundress
	211	248	Perez, Nieves L.	Sister	F	Cha	53.0	S		N	N	Guam	Guam	Guam	N	None
	212	249	Salles, Jose I	Head	M	Fil	35.0	M		Y	Y	Guam	Philippine Islands	Guam	N	Laborer
	212	249	Salles, Nieves T	Wife	F	Cha	23.0	M		Y	Y	Guam	Guam	Guam	N	None
	212	249	Salles, Jose T	Son	M	Cha	0.6	S				Guam	Guam	Guam		None
	213	250	Salas, Pedro C	Head	M	Cha	61.0	M		Y	Y	Guam	Guam	Guam	N	Farmer
	213	250	Salas, Rosa C	Wife	F	Cha	60.0	M		Y	Y	Guam	Guam	Guam	N	None

264

SHEET NO. 27A

(CHAMORRO ROOTS GENEALOGY PROJECT ™ TRANSCRIPTION)
(COMPILED/TRANSCRIBED BY BERNARD T. PUNZALAN / HTTP://WWW.CHAMORROROOTS.COM)
FOURTEENTH CENSUS OF THE UNITED STATES: 1920-POPULATION
ISLAND OF GUAM

DISTRICT 2
NAME OF PLACE Agana (City)
[Proper name and, also, name of class, as city, town, village, barrio, etc]

ENUMERATED BY ME ON THE 15th DAY OF March, 1920

Arthur W. Jackson ENUMERATOR

	PLACE OF ABODE		NAME	RELATION	PERSONAL DESCRIPTION				EDUCATION			NATIVITY				OCCUPATION
Street, avenue, road, etc.	Number of dwelling house in order of visitation	Number of family in order of visitation	of each person whose place of abode on January 1, 1920, was in the family. Enter surname, firs, then given name and middle initial. If any. Include every person living on January 1, 1920. Omit children born since January 1, 1920.	Relationship of this Person to the head of the family.	Sex	Color or race	Age at last birthday	Single, married, widowed or divorced	Attended school any time since Sept. 1, 1919	Whether able to read.	Whether able to write.	Place of birth of this person.	Place of birth of father of this person.	Place of birth of mother of this person.	Whether able to speak English.	Trade, profession, or particular kind of work done, as salesman, laborer, clerk, cook, merchant, washerwoman, etc.
1	2	3	4	5	6	7	8	9	10	11	12	13	14	15	16	17
	213	250	Salas, Domingo C	Son	M	Cha	29.0	S		Y	Y	Guam	Guam	Guam	N	Farmer
	213	250	Salas, Francisco C	Son	M	Cha	27.0	S		Y	Y	Guam	Guam	Guam	N	Carpenter
	213	250	Salas, Pedro C	Son	M	Cha	22.0	S		Y	Y	Guam	Guam	Guam	Y	Enlisted US Navy
	213	250	Salas, Elisa C	Daughter	F	Cha	18.0	S	N	Y	Y	Guam	Guam	Guam	Y	None
	214	251	Valenzuela, Joaquin C	Head	M	Cha	30.0	M		Y	Y	Guam	Guam	Guam	N	Farmer
	214	251	Valenzuela, Antonia S	Wife	F	Cha	26.0	M		Y	Y	Guam	Guam	Guam	N	None
	214	251	Valenzuela, Francisco S	Son	M	Cha	5.0	S	N			Guam	Guam	Guam		None
	214	251	Valenzuela, Regina S	Daughter	F	Cha	3.0	S				Guam	Guam	Guam		None
	214	251	Valenzuela, Ignacio S	Son	M	Cha	2.0	S				Guam	Guam	Guam		None
	215	252	Ida, Yoki	Head	M	Jp	62.0	Wd		Y	Y	Japan	Japan	Japan	N	Merchant gen mdse.
	216	253	Idol, Fabian G	Head	M	Fil	62.0	M		Y	Y	Philippine Islands	Philippine Islands	Philippine Islands	N	Machinist
	216	253	Idol, Dolores P	Wife	F	Cha	44.0	M		Y	Y	Guam	Guam	Guam	Y	Cook
	216	253	Fejarang, Jose R	Servant	M	Cha	9.0	S	Y			Guam	Guam	Guam		Servant
	217	254	Pangelinan, Jesus G	Head	M	Cha	35.0	M		Y	Y	Guam	Guam	Guam	N	Farmer
	217	254	Pangelinan, Nicolasa P	Wife	F	Cha	34.0	M		N	N	Guam	Guam	Guam	N	None
	217	254	Pangelinan, Manuel P	Son	M	Cha	10.0	S	Y	Y	Y	Guam	Guam	Guam	N	None
	217	254	Pangelinan, Maria P	Daughter	F	Cha	8.0	S	Y			Guam	Guam	Guam	N	None
	217	254	Pangelinan, Pedro P	Son	M	Cha	3.0	S				Guam	Guam	Guam		None
	217	254	Guerrero, Maria P	Mother	F	Cha	54.0	Wd		Y	Y	Guam	Guam	Guam	N	None
	218	255	Perez, Ignacio V	Head	M	Cha	53.0	M		Y	Y	Guam	Guam	Guam	N	Farmer
	218	255	Perez, Ana G	Wife	F	Cha	53.0	M		N	N	Guam	Guam	Guam	N	None
	218	255	Perez, Consolacion G	Daughter	F	Cha	13.0	S	N	Y	Y	Guam	Guam	Guam	N	None
	218	255	Perez, Isabel G	Daughter	F	Cha	11.0	S	Y	Y	Y	Guam	Guam	Guam	Y	None
	218	255	Perez, Francisco G	Son	M	Cha	6.0	S	N			Guam	Guam	Guam	Y	None
	219	256	Espinosa, Dolores B	Head	F	Cha	60.0	Wd		Y	Y	Guam	Guam	Guam	N	None

Sagunto Street

(CHAMORRO ROOTS GENEALOGY PROJECT ™ TRANSCRIPTION)

(COMPILED/TRANSCRIBED BY BERNARD T. PUNZALAN / HTTP://WWW.CHAMORROROOTS.COM)

FOURTEENTH CENSUS OF THE UNITED STATES: 1920-POPULATION

ISLAND OF GUAM

DISTRICT 2
NAME OF PLACE Agana (City)
[Proper name and, also, name of class, as city, town, village, barrio, etc]

ENUMERATED BY ME ON THE 16th DAY OF March, 1920

Arthur W. Jackson ENUMERATOR

1	2	3	4	5	6	7	8	9	10	11	12	13	14	15	16	17
Street, avenue, road, etc.	Number of dwelling house in order of visitation	Number of family in order of visitation	NAME	RELATION	Sex	Color or race	Age at last birthday	Single, married, widowed or divorced	Attended school any time since sept. 1, 1919	Whether able to read.	Whether able to write.	Place of birth of this person.	Place of birth of father of this person.	Place of birth of mother of this person.	Whether able to speak English.	OCCUPATION
	219	256	Espinosa, Maria B	Daughter	F	Cha	20.0	S	N	Y	Y	Guam	Guam	Guam	Y	None
	219	256	Espinosa, Francisco B	Son	M	Cha	16.0	S	N	Y	Y	Guam	Guam	Guam	Y	App. Machinist
	219	256	Blas, Antonio LG	Brother	M	Cha	57.0	Wd		Y	Y	Guam	Guam	Guam	N	Farmer
	220	257	Rosario, Manuel B	Head	M	Cha	36.0	Wd		Y	Y	Guam	Guam	Guam	N	Laborer
	221	258	Nauta, Joaquin	Head	M	Cha	35.0	M		N	N	Guam	Unknown	Guam	N	Farmer
	221	258	Nauta, Antonia S	Wife	F	Cha	30.0	M		N	N	Guam	Guam	Guam	N	None
	221	258	Nauta, Juan S	Son	M	Cha	8.0	S	Y			Guam	Guam	Guam		None
	221	258	Nauta, Jose S	Son	M	Cha	7.0	S	Y			Guam	Guam	Guam		None
	221	258	Nauta, Maria S	Daughter	F	Cha	5.0	S	N			Guam	Guam	Guam		None
	221	258	Nauta, Emelia S	Daughter	F	Cha	3.0	S				Guam	Guam	Guam		None
	221	258	Nauta, Joaquin S	Son	M	Cha	1.0	S				Guam	Guam	Guam		None
	222	259	Pereda, Gabriel P	Head	M	Cha	30.0	M		N	N	Guam	Guam	Guam	N	None
	222	259	Pereda, Rosa C	Wife	F	Cha	26.0	M		N	N	Guam	Guam	Guam	N	None
	222	259	Pereda, Maria C	Daughter	F	Cha	8.0	S	Y			Guam	Guam	Guam		None
	222	259	Pereda, Juan C	Son	M	Cha	6.0	S	N			Guam	Guam	Guam		None
	222	259	Pereda, Ana C	Daughter	F	Cha	4.0	S				Guam	Guam	Guam		None
	222	259	Pereda, Catalina C	Daughter	F	Cha	2.0	S				Guam	Guam	Guam		None
	222	259	Pereda, Pedro C	Son	M	Cha	0.2	S				Guam	Guam	Guam		None
	222	259	Concepcion, Felix C	Father-in-law	M	Cha	53.0	M		N	N	Guam	Guam	Guam	N	Farmer
	222	259	Concepcion, Rosa G	Mother-in-law	F	Cha	58.0	M		N	N	Guam	Guam	Guam	N	None
	222	259	Concepcion, Ramon G	Brother-in-law	M	Cha	18.0	S	N	Y	Y	Guam	Guam	Guam	Y	None
	222	259	Concepcion, Antonia C	Cousin	F	Cha	5.0	S	N			Guam	Guam	Guam		None
	223	260	Bitanga, Anatalio A	Head	M	Fil	59.0	M		N	N	Philippine Islands	Philippine Islands	Philippine Islands	N	Farmer
	223	260	Bitanga, Maria G	Wife	F	Cha	52.0	M		N	N	Guam	Guam	Guam	N	None
	223	260	Bitanga, Jose G	Son	M	Fil	27.0	S		Y	Y	Guam	Philippine Islands	Guam	N	Asst. Land Judge

266

132

(CHAMORRO ROOTS GENEALOGY PROJECT ™ TRANSCRIPTION)
(COMPILED/TRANSCRIBED BY BERNARD T. PUNZALAN / HTTP://WWW.CHAMORROROOTS.COM)

FOURTEENTH CENSUS OF THE UNITED STATES: 1920—POPULATION
ISLAND OF GUAM

DISTRICT 2
NAME OF PLACE **Agana (City)**

[Proper name and, also, name of class, as city, town, village, barrio, etc]

ENUMERATED BY ME ON THE 16th DAY OF March, 1920

Arthur W. Jackson ENUMERATOR

	Street, avenue, road, etc.	Number of dwelling house in order of visitation	Number of family in order of visitation	NAME	RELATION	Sex	Color or race	Age at last birthday	Single, married, widowed or divorced	Attended school any time since Sept. 1, 1919	Whether able to read.	Whether able to write.	Place of birth of this person.	Place of birth of father of this person.	Place of birth of mother of this person.	Whether able to speak English.	OCCUPATION
	1	2	3	4	5	6	7	8	9	10	11	12	13	14	15	16	17
1		223	260	Bitanga, Maria G	Daughter	F	Fil	21.0	S	N	Y	Y	Guam	Philippine Islands	Guam	Y	None
2		223	260	Bitanga, Vicente G	Son	M	Fil	17.0	S	N	Y	Y	Guam	Philippine Islands	Guam	Y	None
3		223	260	Bitanga, Inocencio G	Son	M	Fil	15.0	S	N	Y	Y	Guam	Philippine Islands	Guam	Y	None
4		223	260	Bitanga, Francisca G	Daughter	F	Fil	11.0	S	Y	Y	Y	Guam	Philippine Islands	Guam	N	None
5		223	260	Bitanga, Firmin G	Son	M	Fil	7.0	S	Y			Guam	Philippine Islands	Guam		None
6		224	261	Guerrero, Vicente C	Head	M	Cha	42.0	M		Y	Y	Guam	Guam	Guam	N	Farmer
7		224	261	Guerrero, Rita T	Wife	F	Cha	42.0	M		Y	Y	Guam	Guam	Guam	Y	None
8		224	261	Guerrero, Benancio T	Son	M	Cha	14.0	S	N	Y	Y	Guam	Guam	Guam	Y	None
9		224	261	Guerrero, Jesus T	Son	M	Cha	12.0	S	Y	Y	Y	Guam	Guam	Guam	Y	None
10		224	261	Guerrero, Maria T	Daughter	F	Cha	10.0	S	Y	Y	Y	Guam	Guam	Guam	N	None
11		224	261	Guerrero, Juan T	Son	M	Cha	8.0	S	Y			Guam	Guam	Guam		None
12		224	261	Guerrero, Ana T	Daughter	F	Cha	6.0	S	N			Guam	Guam	Guam		None
13		224	261	Guerrero, Rita T	Daughter	F	Cha	5.0	S	N			Guam	Guam	Guam		None
14	Saguno Street	224	261	Guerrero, Jose T	Son	M	Cha	1.0	S				Guam	Guam	Guam		None
15		225	262	Roberto, Felix	Head	M	Cha	53.0	M		Y	Y	Guam	Guam	Guam	Y	Foreman
16		225	262	Roberto, Isabel B	Wife	F	Cha	56.0	M		Y	Y	Guam	Guam	Guam	N	None
17		225	262	Roberto, Luisa B	Daughter	F	Cha	28.0	S		Y	Y	Guam	Guam	Guam	Y	Laundress
18		225	262	Roberto, Cristina B	Daughter	F	Cha	25.0	S		Y	Y	Guam	Guam	Guam	Y	Laundress
19		225	262	Roberto, Ana B	Daughter	F	Cha	24.0	S		Y	Y	Guam	Guam	Guam	Y	Laundress
20		225	262	Roberto, Maria B	Daughter	F	Cha	18.0	S	N	Y	Y	Guam	Guam	Guam	Y	None
21		225	262	Roberto, Manuel B	Son	M	Cha	16.0	S	N	Y	Y	Guam	Guam	Guam	Y	Messenger
22		225	262	Roberto, Antonia B	Daughter	F	Cha	15.0	S	N	Y	Y	Guam	Guam	Guam	Y	None
23		225	262	Roberto, Enrique B	Son	M	Cha	14.0	S	N	Y	Y	Guam	Guam	Guam	Y	None
24		225	262	Roberto, Vicente	Grand son	M	Cha	4.0	S				Guam	Unknown	Guam		None
25		225	262	Roberto, Juan	Grand son	M	Cha	2.0	S				Guam	Unknown	Guam		None

(CHAMORRO ROOTS GENEALOGY PROJECT ™ TRANSCRIPTION)
(COMPILED/TRANSCRIBED BY BERNARD T. PUNZALAN / HTTP://WWW.CHAMORROROOTS.COM)

FOURTEENTH CENSUS OF THE UNITED STATES: 1920—POPULATION
ISLAND OF GUAM

132b

ENUMERATED BY ME ON THE 17th DAY OF March, 1920

Arthur W. Jackson ENUMERATOR

DISTRICT 2
NAME OF PLACE Agana (City)

[Proper name and, also, name of class, as city, town, village, barrio, etc]

	Dwelling No.	Family No.	NAME	RELATION	Sex	Color or race	Age	Single, married, widowed or divorced	Attended school since Sept. 1, 1919	Able to read	Able to write	Birthplace of person	Birthplace of father	Birthplace of mother	Able to speak English	OCCUPATION
26	226	263	Blaz, Jose	Head	M	Cha	57.0	M		Y	Y	Guam	Unknown	Guam	N	Farmer
27	226	263	Blaz, Josefa I	Wife	F	Cha	49.0	M		Y	Y	Guam	Guam	Guam	N	None
28	226	263	Blaz, Ana I	Daughter	F	Cha	24.0	S		Y	Y	Guam	Guam	Guam	N	None
29	226	263	Blaz, Maria I	Daughter	F	Cha	22.0	S		Y	Y	Guam	Guam	Guam	N	None
30	226	263	Blaz, Rosa I	Daughter	F	Cha	19.0	S	N	Y	Y	Guam	Guam	Guam	Y	None
31	226	263	Blaz, Jose I	Son	M	Cha	16.0	S	N	Y	Y	Guam	Guam	Guam	Y	None
32	226	263	Blaz, Felisa I	Daughter	F	Cha	15.0	S	N	Y	Y	Guam	Guam	Guam	Y	None
33	226	263	Blaz, Magdalena I	Daughter	F	Cha	10.0	S	Y	Y	Y	Guam	Guam	Guam	Y	None
34	226	263	Blaz, Tomasa I	Daughter	F	Cha	8.0	S	Y	Y	Y	Guam	Guam	Guam	Y	None
35	226	263	Blaz, Francisco I	Son	M	Cha	2.0	S				Guam	Guam	Guam		None
36	226	264	Blaz, Antonio I	Head	M	Cha	26.0	M		Y	Y	Guam	Guam	Guam	Y	Plumber
37	226	264	Blaz, Maria P	Wife	F	Cha	21.0	M	N	Y	Y	Guam	Guam	Guam	Y	None
38	227	265	Guerrero, Felipe G	Head	M	Cha	25.0	M		Y	Y	Guam	Guam	Guam	N	None
39	227	265	Guerrero, Maria C	Wife	F	Cha	19.0	M		Y	Y	Guam	Guam	Guam	Y	None
40	227	265	Guerrero, Juan C	Son	M	Cha	1.0	S	N			Guam	Guam	Guam	N	None
41	227	265	Castro, Concepcion	Mother-in-law	F	Cha	40.0	S		Y	Y	Guam	Guam	Guam	N	None
42	228	266	Estebes, Maria C	Head	F	Cha	37.0	M		Y	Y	Guam	Guam	Guam	N	Laundress
43	228	266	Cepeda, Tomas	Nephew	M	Cha	10.0	S	Y	Y	Y	Guam	Guam	Guam	N	None
44	229	267	Guerrero, Dolores C	Head	F	Cha	43.0	S		Y	Y	Guam	Guam	Guam	N	Farmer
45	229	267	Guerrero, Vicente C	Son	M	Cha	28.0	S		Y	Y	Guam	Guam	Guam	N	None
46	229	267	Guerrero, Maria C	Daughter	F	Cha	24.0	S		Y	Y	Guam	Guam	Guam	N	None
47	229	267	Guerrero, Rosa C	Daughter	F	Cha	16.0	S	N	Y	Y	Guam	Guam	Guam	Y	None
48	229	267	Guerrero, Jesus	Grand son	M	Cha	4.0	S				Guam	Unknown	Unknown		None
49	229	267	Guerrero, Manuel	Grand son	M	Cha	2.0	S				Guam	Unknown	Unknown		None
50	229	267	Guerrero, Beatrice	Grand daughter	F	Cha	1.0	S				Guam	Unknown	Unknown		None

Street: Segundo Street

(CHAMORRO ROOTS GENEALOGY PROJECT ™ TRANSCRIPTION)
(COMPILED/TRANSCRIBED BY BERNARD T. PUNZALAN / HTTP://WWW.CHAMORROROOTS.COM)
FOURTEENTH CENSUS OF THE UNITED STATES: 1920—POPULATION
ISLAND OF GUAM

DISTRICT 2
NAME OF PLACE **Agana (City)**

[Proper name and, also, name of class, as city, town, village, barrio, etc]

ENUMERATED BY ME ON THE 17th DAY OF March, 1920

Arthur W. Jackson ENUMERATOR

	PLACE OF ABODE			NAME	RELATION	PERSONAL DESCRIPTION					EDUCATION			NATIVITY				OCCUPATION
Street, avenue, road, etc.	Number of dwelling house in order of visitation	Number of family in order of visitation		of each person whose place of abode on January 1, 1920, was in the family.	Relationship of this person to the head of the family.	Sex	Color or race	Age at last birthday	Single, married, widowed or divorced	Attended school any time since Sept. 1, 1919	Whether able to read.	Whether able to write.	Place of birth of this person.	Place of birth of father of this person.	Place of birth of mother of this person.	Whether able to speak English.	Trade, profession, or particular kind of work done, as salesman, laborer, clerk, cook, merchant, washerwoman, etc.
1	2	3	4		5	6	7	8	9	10	11	12	13	14	15	16	17
1	230	268	Atoigue, Vicente C		Head	M	Cha	41.0	M		Y	Y	Guam	Guam	Guam	N	Farmer
2	230	268	Atoigue, Joaquina P		Wife	F	Cha	37.0	M		Y	Y	Guam	Guam	Guam	N	None
3	231	269	Cruz, Jose A		Head	M	Cha	46.0	M		Y	Y	Guam	Philippine Islands	Guam	N	None
4	231	269	Cruz, Candaleria T		Wife	F	Cha	48.0	M		Y	Y	Guam	Guam	Guam	N	None
5	231	269	Cruz, Maria T		Daughter	F	Cha	20.0	S	N	Y	Y	Guam	Guam	Guam	Y	None
6	231	269	Cruz, Rita T		Daughter	F	Cha	19.0	S	N	Y	Y	Guam	Guam	Guam	Y	None
7	231	269	Cruz, Ana T		Daughter	F	Cha	18.0	S	N	Y	Y	Guam	Guam	Guam	Y	None
8	231	269	Cruz, Ascencion T		Daughter	F	Cha	16.0	S	N	Y	Y	Guam	Guam	Guam	Y	None
9	231	269	Cruz, Beatrice T		Daughter	F	Cha	6.0	S	N			Guam	Guam	Guam		None
10	232	270	Mafnas, Jose C		Head	M	Cha	35.0	M		Y	Y	Guam	Guam	Guam	N	Farmer
11	232	270	Mafnas, Filomena R		Wife	F	Cha	32.0	M		Y	Y	Guam	Guam	Guam	N	None
12	232	270	Mafnas, Carmen R		Daughter	F	Cha	11.0	S	Y	Y	Y	Guam	Guam	Guam	N	None
13	232	270	Mafnas, Ignacia R		Daughter	F	Cha	7.0	S	Y	Y	Y	Guam	Guam	Guam		None
14	232	270	Mafnas, Jose R		Son	M	Cha	4.0	S				Guam	Guam	Guam		None
15	232	270	Mafnas, Maria R		Daughter	F	Cha	3.0	S				Guam	Guam	Guam		None
16	232	270	Mafnas, Joaquin R		Son	M	Cha	1.0	S				Guam	Guam	Guam		None
17	232	270	Mafnas, Ignacia C		Mother	F	Cha	80.0	Wd		N	N	Guam	Guam	Guam	N	None
18	233	271	Mafnas, Vicente P		Head	M	Cha	30.0	M		Y	Y	Guam	Guam	Guam	N	Farmer
19	233	271	Mafnas, Maria B		Wife	F	Cha	25.0	M		Y	Y	Guam	Guam	Guam	N	None
20	233	271	Mafnas, Antonio B		Son	M	Cha	2.0	S				Guam	Guam	Guam		None
21	233	271	Mafnas, Ana B		Daughter	F	Cha	1.0	S				Guam	Guam	Guam		None
22	234	272	Mafnas, Santiago C		Head	M	Cha	42.0	M		Y	Y	Guam	Guam	Guam	N	None
23	234	272	Mafnas, Remedios M		Wife	F	Cha	43.0	M		Y	Y	Guam	Guam	Guam	N	None
24	234	272	Mafnas, Jesus M		Son	M	Cha	15.0	S	N	Y	Y	Guam	Guam	Guam	Y	None
25	234	272	Mafnas, Ignacio M		Son	M	Cha	11.0	S	Y	Y	Y	Guam	Guam	Guam	N	None

Pizarro Street

269

(CHAMORRO ROOTS GENEALOGY PROJECT ™ TRANSCRIPTION)

(COMPILED/TRANSCRIBED BY BERNARD T. PUNZALAN / HTTP://WWW.CHAMORROROOTS.COM)

FOURTEENTH CENSUS OF THE UNITED STATES: 1920—POPULATION
ISLAND OF GUAM

DISTRICT 2
NAME OF PLACE Agana (City)
[Proper name and, also, name of class, as city, town, village, barrio, etc]

ENUMERATED BY ME ON THE 17th DAY OF March, 1920

Arthur W. Jackson ENUMERATOR

Street	Dwelling	Family	NAME	RELATION	Sex	Color or race	Age	Single/married/widowed/divorced	Attended school	Able to read	Able to write	Birthplace of person	Birthplace of father	Birthplace of mother	Able to speak English	OCCUPATION
	1	2	3	4	5	6	7	8	9	10	11	12	13	14	15	16	17
26	234	272	Mafnas, Magdalena M	Daughter	F	Cha	4.0	S				Guam	Guam	Guam		None
27	234	272	Mafnas, Felipe M	Son	M	Cha	2.0	S				Guam	Guam	Guam		None
28	235	273	Garrido, Jose C	Head	M	Cha	35.0	M		Y	Y	Guam	Guam	Guam	Y	Teamster
29	235	273	Garrido, Ana L	Wife	F	Cha	37.0	M		N	N	Guam	Guam	Guam	N	None
30	235	273	Garrido, Francisco L	Son	M	Cha	8.0	S	Y			Guam	Guam	Guam		None
31	235	273	Garrido, Vicente L	Son	M	Cha	6.0	S	N			Guam	Guam	Guam		None
32	235	273	Garrido, Rufina L	Daughter	F	Cha	3.0	S				Guam	Guam	Guam		None
33	235	273	Lizama, Rita P	Sister-in-law	F	Cha	38.0	S		Y	Y	Guam	Guam	Guam		Laundress
34	236	274	Manibusan, Joaquin F	Head	M	Cha	34.0	M		Y	Y	Guam	Guam	Guam	N	Farmer
35	236	274	Manibusan, Luisa LG	Wife	F	Cha	31.0	M		Y	Y	Guam	Guam	Guam	N	None
36	236	274	Manibusan, Jesus LG	Son	M	Cha	14.0	S	Y	Y	Y	Guam	Guam	Guam	Y	None
37	236	274	Manibusan, Maria LG	Daughter	F	Cha	11.0	S	Y	Y	Y	Guam	Guam	Guam	N	None
38	236	274	Manibusan, Ana LG	Daughter	F	Cha	9.0	S	Y	Y	Y	Guam	Guam	Guam		None
39	236	274	Manibusan, Josefina LG	Daughter	F	Cha	8.0	S	Y	Y	Y	Guam	Guam	Guam		None
40	236	274	Manibusan, Ascencion LG	Daughter	F	Cha	4.0	S				Guam	Guam	Guam		None
41	236	274	Manibusan, Jose LG	Son	M	Cha	3.0	S				Guam	Guam	Guam		None
42	237	275	Lizama, Jose P	Head	M	Cha	50.0	M		Y	Y	Guam	Guam	Guam	N	Farmer
43	237	275	Lizama, Maria S	Wife	F	Cha	50.0	M		N	N	Guam	Guam	Guam	N	None
44	237	275	Lizama, Ana S	Daughter	F	Cha	25.0	S	N	N	N	Guam	Guam	Guam	Y	Seamstress
45	237	275	Lizama, Rita S	Daughter	F	Cha	20.0	S	N	N	N	Guam	Guam	Guam	Y	None
46	237	275	Lizama, Vicente S	Son	M	Cha	16.0	S	N	Y	Y	Guam	Guam	Guam	Y	None
47	237	275	Lizama, Catalina S	Daughter	F	Cha	15.0	S	Y	Y	Y	Guam	Guam	Guam	Y	None
48	237	275	Lizama, Dolores S	Daughter	F	Cha	10.0	S	Y	Y	Y	Guam	Guam	Guam	N	None
49	238	276	Quinata, Jose V	Head	M	Cha	40.0	M		Y	Y	Guam	Guam	Guam	Y	Gardner
50	238	276	Quinata, Rosa C	Wife	F	Cha	42.0	M		Y	Y	Guam	Guam	Guam	N	None

Street: Pizarro Street

270

(CHAMORRO ROOTS GENEALOGY PROJECT ™ TRANSCRIPTION)
(COMPILED/TRANSCRIBED BY BERNARD T. PUNZALAN / HTTP://WWW.CHAMORROROOTS.COM)
FOURTEENTH CENSUS OF THE UNITED STATES: 1920-POPULATION
ISLAND OF GUAM

ENUMERATED BY ME ON THE 18th DAY OF March, 1920

Arthur W. Jackson ENUMERATOR

DISTRICT 2
NAME OF PLACE Agana (City)
[Proper name and, also, name of class, as city, town, village, barrio, etc]

	Place of Abode		Street	NAME	RELATION	Sex	Color or race	Age	Single, married, widowed or divorced	Attended school since Sept. 1, 1919	Able to read	Able to write	Place of birth of this person	Place of birth of father	Place of birth of mother	Able to speak English	OCCUPATION
	2	3	1	4	5	6	7	8	9	10	11	12	13	14	15	16	17
1	238	276		Quinata, Maria C	Daughter	F	Cha	14.0	S	Y	Y	Y	Guam	Guam	Guam	Y	None
2	238	276		Quinata, Dolores C	Daughter	F	Cha	13.0	S	Y	Y	Y	Guam	Guam	Guam	Y	None
3	238	276		Quinata, Trinidad C	Daughter	F	Cha	11.0	S	Y	Y	Y	Guam	Guam	Guam	Y	None
4	238	276		Quinata, Rita C	Daughter	F	Cha	9.0	S	Y	Y		Guam	Guam	Guam		None
5	238	276		Quinata, Jose C	Son	M	Cha	7.0	S	Y			Guam	Guam	Guam		None
6	238	276		Quinata, Joaquina C	Daughter	F	Cha	4.0	S				Guam	Guam	Guam		None
7	238	276		Quinata, Enrique C	Son	M	Cha	0.4	S				Guam	Guam	Guam		None
8	239	277		Rojas, Pedro R	Head	M	Cha	58.0	M		Y	Y	Guam	Guam	Guam	N	Farmer
9	239	277		Rojas, Ana M	Wife	F	Cha	59.0	M		N	N	Guam	Guam	Guam	N	None
10	240	278		Cruz, Maria V	Head	F	Cha	59.0	Wd		Y	Y	Guam	Guam	Guam	N	None
11	240	278		Cruz, Jose V	Son	M	Cha	29.0	S		Y	Y	Guam	Guam	Guam	Y	Clerk
12	240	278		Cruz, Maria V	Daughter	F	Cha	27.0	S		Y	Y	Guam	Guam	Guam	Y	None
13	240	278	Pizarro Street	Cruz, Juan V	Son	M	Cha	22.0	S		Y	Y	Guam	Guam	Guam	Y	Enlisted US Navy
14	240	278		Cruz, Eugenio V	Son	M	Cha	20.0	S	N	Y	Y	Guam	Guam	Guam	Y	Farmer
15	240	278		Cruz, Jesus V	Son	M	Cha	24.0	Wd		Y	Y	Guam	Guam	Guam	Y	Enlisted US Navy
16	241	279		Perez, Juan S	Head	M	Cha	51.0	M		N	N	Guam	Guam	Guam	N	Farmer
17	241	279		Perez, Maria A	Wife	F	Cha	53.0	M		N	N	Guam	Guam	Guam	N	None
18	241	279		Perez, Luis A	Son	M	Cha	16.0	S	N	Y	Y	Guam	Guam	Guam	Y	None
19	241	279		Perez, Ana A	Daughter	F	Cha	16.0	S	N	Y	Y	Guam	Guam	Guam	Y	None
20	241	279		Perez, Dolores A	Daughter	F	Cha	11.0	S	Y	Y	Y	Guam	Guam	Guam	N	None
21	242	280		Diaz, Francisco S	Head	M	Cha	56.0	M		Y	Y	Guam	Guam	Guam	N	Farmer
22	242	280		Diaz, Maria S	Wife	F	Cha	58.0	M		Y	Y	Guam	Guam	Guam	N	None
23	242	280		Diaz, Juan S	Son	M	Cha	31.0	S		Y	Y	Guam	Guam	Guam	N	Farm laborer
24	242	281		Diaz, Francisco S	Head	M	Cha	35.0	M		Y	Y	Guam	Guam	Guam	N	Farmer
25	242	281		Diaz, Ignacia F	Wife	F	Cha	30.0	M		Y	Y	Guam	Guam	Guam	N	None

(CHAMORRO ROOTS GENEALOGY PROJECT ™ TRANSCRIPTION)
(COMPILED/TRANSCRIBED BY BERNARD T. PUNZALAN / HTTP://WWW.CHAMORROROOTS.COM)

FOURTEENTH CENSUS OF THE UNITED STATES: 1920—POPULATION
ISLAND OF GUAM

134b

DISTRICT 2
NAME OF PLACE **Agana (City)**
[Proper name and, also, name of class, as city, town, village, barrio, etc]

ENUMERATED BY ME ON THE 18th DAY OF March, 1920

Joaquin Torres ENUMERATOR

Street	No. dwelling house (2)	No. family (3)	NAME (4)	RELATION (5)	Sex (6)	Color or race (7)	Age (8)	Single, married, widowed or divorced (9)	Attended school since Sept. 1, 1919 (10)	Able to read (11)	Able to write (12)	Place of birth of this person (13)	Place of birth of father (14)	Place of birth of mother (15)	Able to speak English (16)	OCCUPATION (17)
	242	281	Diaz, Jesus F	Son	M	Cha	8.0	S	Y			Guam	Guam	Guam		None
	242	281	Diaz, Joaquin F	Son	M	Cha	6.0	S	N			Guam	Guam	Guam		None
	242	281	Diaz, Ignacio F	Son	M	Cha	1.0	S				Guam	Guam	Guam		None
	242	281	Santos, Jesus	Servant	M	Cha	16.0	S				Guam	Guam	Guam	N	Farm laborer
	243	282	Cruz, Faustino LG	Head	M	Cha	40.0	M		Y	Y	Guam	Guam	Guam	N	Farmer
	243	282	Cruz, Maria C	Wife	F	Cha	43.0	M		N	N	Guam	Guam	Guam	N	None
	243	282	Cruz, Maria C	Daughter	F	Cha	19.0	S	N	Y	Y	Guam	Guam	Guam	Y	None
	243	282	Cruz, Juan C	Son	M	Cha	14.0	S	N	Y	Y	Guam	Guam	Guam	Y	None
Pizarro Street	243	282	Cruz, Rosa C	Daughter	F	Cha	11.0	S	Y	Y	Y	Guam	Guam	Guam	N	None
	243	282	Cruz, Ana C	Daughter	F	Cha	9.0	S	Y	Y	Y	Guam	Guam	Guam		None
	243	282	Cruz, Vicente C	Son	M	Cha	7.0	S	Y			Guam	Guam	Guam		None
	243	282	Cruz, Lourdes C	Daughter	F	Cha	4.0	S				Guam	Guam	Guam		None
	243	282	Cruz, Dolores C	Daughter	F	Cha	1.0	S				Guam	Guam	Guam		None
	244	283	Guerrero, Ignacia P	Head	F	Cha	47.0	S		N	N	Guam	Guam	Guam	N	None
	244	283	Guerrero, Ignacia	Grand daughter	F	Cha	8.0	S	Y			Guam	Guam	Guam		None
	245	284	Guerrero, Jose P	Head	M	Cha	35.0	Wd		Y	Y	Guam	Unknown	Guam	N	Farmer
	245	284	Guerrero, Francesca P	Daughter	F	Cha	14.0	S	Y	Y	Y	Guam	Guam	Guam	Y	None
	245	284	Guerrero, Jose P	Son	M	Cha	12.0	S	Y	Y	Y	Guam	Guam	Guam	Y	None
	245	284	Guerrero, Caesario P	Son	M	Cha	10.0	S	Y	Y	Y	Guam	Guam	Guam	Y	None
	245	284	Guerrero, Maria P	Daughter	F	Cha	8.0	S	Y	Y	Y	Guam	Guam	Guam	N	None
	245	284	Guerrero, Jesus P	Son	M	Cha	7.0	S	Y			Guam	Guam	Guam		None
	245	284	Guerrero, Enrique P	Son	M	Cha	5.0	S	N			Guam	Guam	Guam		None
	245	284	Guerrero, Josephina P	Daughter	F	Cha	3.0	S				Guam	Guam	Guam		None
	246	285	Guerrero, Juan P	Head	M	Cha	47.0	M		N	N	Guam	Guam	Guam	N	Farmer
	246	285	Guerrero, Ana C	Wife	F	Cha	40.0	M		N	N	Guam	Guam	Guam	N	None

(CHAMORRO ROOTS GENEALOGY PROJECT ™ TRANSCRIPTION)
(COMPILED/TRANSCRIBED BY BERNARD T. PUNZALAN / HTTP://WWW.CHAMORROROOTS.COM)
FOURTEENTH CENSUS OF THE UNITED STATES: 1920–POPULATION
ISLAND OF GUAM

DISTRICT 2
NAME OF PLACE **Agana (City)**
[Proper name and, also, name of class, as city, town, village, barrio, etc]

ENUMERATED BY ME ON THE 19th DAY OF March, 1920

Arthur W. Jackson ENUMERATOR

	Street	Dwelling house no.	Family no.	NAME	RELATION	Sex	Color or race	Age	Single, married, widowed or divorced	Attended school since Sept. 1, 1919	able to read	able to write	Place of birth of this person	Place of birth of father	Place of birth of mother	Whether able to speak English	OCCUPATION
	1	2	3	4	5	6	7	8	9	10	11	12	13	14	15	16	17
1		246	285	Guerrero, Maria C	Daughter	F	Cha	21.0	S	N	Y	Y	Guam	Guam	Guam	Y	None
2		246	285	Guerrero, Josefa C	Daughter	F	Cha	18.0	S	N	Y	Y	Guam	Guam	Guam	Y	None
3		246	285	Guerrero, Juan C	Son	M	Cha	12.0	S	Y	Y	Y	Guam	Guam	Guam	N	None
4		246	285	Guerrero, Ana	Step daughter	F	Cha	20.0	S	N	Y	Y	Guam	Unknown	Guam	N	None
5		246	285	Cruz, Josefa P	Sister	F	Cha	33.0	Wd		Y	Y	Guam	Guam	Guam	N	None
6		246	285	Santos, Juan P	Nephew	M	Cha	10.0	S	Y	Y	Y	Guam	Guam	Guam	N	None
7		246	285	Santos, Maria P	Niece	F	Cha	8.0	S	Y			Guam	Guam	Guam		None
8		247	286	Flores, Vicente C	Head	M	Cha	55.0	Wd		N	N	Guam	Guam	Guam	N	None
9		247	286	Flores, Andrea C	Daughter	F	Cha	34.0	S		N	N	Guam	Guam	Guam	N	None
10		247	286	Flores, Maria C	Daughter	F	Cha	26.0	S		Y	Y	Guam	Guam	Guam	N	None
11	Pizarro Street	247	286	Flores, Rita C	Daughter	F	Cha	18.0	S	N	Y	Y	Guam	Guam	Guam	Y	None
12		247	286	Flores, Rosario C	Daughter	F	Cha	12.0	S	Y	Y	Y	Guam	Guam	Guam	Y	None
13		247	286	Flores, Juan	Grand son	M	Cha	2.0	S				Guam	Unknown	Guam		None
14		247	287	Flores, Antonio C	Head	M	Cha	30.0	M		Y	Y	Guam	Unknown	Guam	Y	Farmer
15		247	287	Flores, Maria C	Wife	F	Cha	28.0	M		N	N	Guam	Guam	Guam	N	None
16		247	287	Flores, Maria C	Daughter	F	Cha	9.0	S	Y			Guam	Guam	Guam		None
17		247	287	Flores, Vicenta C	Daughter	F	Cha	7.0	S	Y			Guam	Guam	Guam		None
18		247	287	Flores, Dolores C	Daughter	F	Cha	4.0	S				Guam	Guam	Guam		None
19		247	287	Flores, Jose C	Son	M	Cha	2.0	S				Guam	Guam	Guam		None
20		247	287	Flores, Antonio C	Son	M	Cha	0.2	S				Guam	Guam	Guam		None
21		248	288	Ignacio, Ramon C	Head	M	Cha	79.0	M		Y	Y	Guam	Guam	Guam		Farmer
22		248	288	Ignacio, Tomasa A	Wife	F	Cha	64.0	M		Y	Y	Guam	Guam	Guam	N	None
23		248	289	Ignacio, Manuel A	Head	M	Cha	48.0	M		N	N	Guam	Guam	Guam	N	None
24		248	289	Ignacio, Rosa C	Wife	F	Cha	59.0	M		N	N	Guam	Guam	Guam	N	None
25		248	289	Ignacio, Placido C	Daughter	F	Cha	16.0	S	N	Y	Y	Guam	Guam	Guam	Y	None

(CHAMORRO ROOTS GENEALOGY PROJECT ™ TRANSCRIPTION)
(COMPILED/TRANSCRIBED BY BERNARD T. PUNZALAN / HTTP://WWW.CHAMORROROOTS.COM)

FOURTEENTH CENSUS OF THE UNITED STATES: 1920-POPULATION

ISLAND OF GUAM

135b

DISTRICT 2
NAME OF PLACE Agana (City)
[Proper name and, also, name of class, as city, town, village, barrio, etc]

ENUMERATED BY ME ON THE 19th DAY OF March, 1920

Arthur W. Jackson ENUMERATOR

Street	Dwelling No.	Family No.	NAME	RELATION	Sex	Color or race	Age	Marital	School	Read	Write	Birthplace person	Birthplace father	Birthplace mother	English	OCCUPATION
1	2	3	4	5	6	7	8	9	10	11	12	13	14	15	16	17
	249	290	Perez, Joaquin S	Head	M	Cha	33.0	M		Y	Y	Guam	Guam	Guam	Y	Carpenter
	249	290	Perez, Juana B	Wife	F	Cha	28.0	M		Y	Y	Guam	Guam	Guam	N	None
	249	290	Perez, Vicente B	Son	M	Cha	13.0	S	Y	Y	Y	Guam	Guam	Guam	Y	None
	249	290	Perez, Jesus B	Son	M	Cha	11.0	S	Y	Y	Y	Guam	Guam	Guam	N	None
	249	290	Perez, Segundo B	Son	M	Cha	9.0	S	Y	Y	Y	Guam	Guam	Guam		None
	249	290	Perez, Oliva B	Daughter	F	Cha	6.0	S	N			Guam	Guam	Guam		None
	249	290	Perez, Engracia B	Daughter	F	Cha	3.0	S				Guam	Guam	Guam		None
	249	290	Borja, Josefa LG	Mother-in-law	F	Cha	47.0	Wd		Y	Y	Guam	Guam	Guam	N	None
Pizarro Street	250	291	Castro, Antonio I	Head	M	Cha	38.0	M		Y	Y	Guam	Guam	Guam	N	Farmer
	250	291	Castro, Antonia T	Wife	F	Cha	36.0	M		N	N	Guam	Guam	Guam	N	None
	250	291	Castro, Josefa T	Daughter	F	Cha	11.0	S	Y	Y	Y	Guam	Guam	Guam	N	None
	250	291	Castro, Maria T	Daughter	F	Cha	8.0	S	Y	Y	Y	Guam	Guam	Guam		None
	250	291	Castro, Ana T	Daughter	F	Cha	4.0	S				Guam	Guam	Guam		None
	251	292	Guzman, Antonia C	Head	F	Cha	54.0	Wd		N	N	Guam	Guam	Guam	N	None
	251	292	Leon Guerrero, Emeliana B	Niece	F	Cha	23.0	S		Y	Y	Guam	Guam	Guam	N	None
	251	293	Ramirez, Jesus B	Head	M	Cha	34.0	M		Y	Y	Guam	Guam	Guam	N	None
	251	293	Ramirez, Maria T	Wife	F	Cha	28.0	M		Y	Y	Guam	Guam	Guam	N	None
	251	293	Ramirez, Juliana T	Daughter	F	Cha	10.0	S	Y	Y	Y	Guam	Guam	Guam	N	None
	251	293	Ramirez, Concepcion T	Daughter	F	Cha	9.0	S	Y	Y	Y	Guam	Guam	Guam		None
	251	293	Ramirez, Josefina T	Daughter	F	Cha	6.0	S	N			Guam	Guam	Guam		None
	251	293	Ramirez, Florencio T	Son	M	Cha	4.0	S				Guam	Guam	Guam		None
	251	293	Ramirez, Jose T	Son	M	Cha	3.0	S				Guam	Guam	Guam		None
	252	294	Perez, Manuela C	Head	F	Cha	38.0	Wd		Y	Y	Guam	Guam	Guam	N	None
	252	294	Perez, Ana C	Daughter	F	Cha	17.0	S	N	Y	Y	Guam	Guam	Guam	Y	None
	252	294	Perez, Emelia C	Daughter	F	Cha	15.0	S	N	Y	Y	Guam	Guam	Guam	Y	None

(CHAMORRO ROOTS GENEALOGY PROJECT ™ TRANSCRIPTION)
(COMPILED/TRANSCRIBED BY BERNARD T. PUNZALAN / HTTP://WWW.CHAMORROROOTS.COM)

FOURTEENTH CENSUS OF THE UNITED STATES: 1920-POPULATION

ISLAND OF GUAM

ENUMERATED BY ME ON THE 20th DAY OF March, 1920

Arthur W. Jackson ENUMERATOR

DISTRICT 2
NAME OF PLACE Agana (City)
[Proper name and, also, name of class, as city, town, village, barrio, etc]

#	Street	Dwelling No. (2)	Family No. (3)	NAME (4)	RELATION (5)	Sex (6)	Color or race (7)	Age (8)	Marital (9)	School (10)	Read (11)	Write (12)	Birthplace person (13)	Birthplace father (14)	Birthplace mother (15)	Speak English (16)	OCCUPATION (17)
1		252	294	Perez, Artemio C	Son	M	Cha	12.0	S	Y	Y	Y	Guam	Guam	Guam	N	None
2		252	294	Perez, Locario C	Son	M	Cha	9.0	S	Y			Guam	Guam	Guam		None
3		252	294	Perez, Jose C	Son	M	Cha	7.0	S	Y			Guam	Guam	Guam		None
4		252	294	Perez, Angelica C	Daughter	F	Cha	6.0	S	N			Guam	Guam	Guam		None
5		252	294	Perez, Joaquin C	Son	M	Cha	4.0	S				Guam	Guam	Guam		None
6		253	295	Leon Guerrero, Vicente A	Head	M	Cha	55.0	M		Y	Y	Guam	Guam	Guam	N	None
7		253	295	Leon Guerrero, Maria M	Wife	F	Cha	48.0	M		Y	Y	Guam	Guam	Guam	N	None
8		253	295	Leon Guerrero, Ana M	Daughter	F	Cha	15.0	S	N	Y	Y	Guam	Guam	Guam	Y	None
9		253	295	Leon Guerrero, Josefina M	Daughter	F	Cha	12.0	S	Y	Y	Y	Guam	Guam	Guam	Y	None
10		253	295	Leon Guerrero, Mariana M	Daughter	F	Cha	6.0	S	N			Guam	Guam	Guam		None
11	Pizarro Street	253	295	Leon Guerrero, Vicente M	Son	M	Cha	4.0	S				Guam	Guam	Guam		None
12		254	296	Leon Guerrero, Matias T	Head	M	Cha	40.0	M		Y	Y	Guam	Guam	Guam	Y	Electrician
13		254	296	Leon Guerrero, Rita C	Wife	F	Cha	35.0	M		Y	Y	Guam	Guam	Guam	N	None
14		254	296	Leon Guerrero, Ezeqiel C	Son	M	Cha	9.0	S	Y			Guam	Guam	Guam		None
15		254	296	Leon Guerrero, Antonio C	Son	M	Cha	8.0	S	Y			Guam	Guam	Guam		None
16		254	296	Leon Guerrero, Emogines C	Son	M	Cha	5.0	S	N			Guam	Guam	Guam		None
17		254	296	Leon Guerrero, Rosario C	Daughter	F	Cha	4.0	S				Guam	Guam	Guam		None
18		254	296	Leon Guerrero, Agapito C	Son	M	Cha	1.0	S				Guam	Guam	Guam		None
19		255	297	Hines, Fabian	Head	M	Mu	37.0	M		Y	Y	Porto Rico	Porto Rico	Virgin Islands	Y	Chauffeur
20		255	297	Hines, Maria C	Wife	F	Cha	38.0	M		Y	Y	Guam	Guam	Guam	N	None
21		255	297	Hines, Ascencion C	Daughter	F	Mu	16.0	S	N	Y	Y	Guam	Porto Rico	Guam	Y	None
22		255	297	Hines, Eloise C	Daughter	F	Mu	12.0	S	N	Y	Y	Guam	Porto Rico	Guam	N	None
23		255	297	Hines, Lagrimas C	Daughter	F	Mu	11.0	S	N	Y	Y	Guam	Porto Rico	Guam	N	None
24		255	297	Hines, Cristobal C	Son	M	Mu	9.0	S	N			Guam	Porto Rico	Guam	N	None
25		255	297	Hines, Adolofo C	Son	M	Mu	8.0	S	N			Guam	Porto Rico	Guam		None

(CHAMORRO ROOTS GENEALOGY PROJECT™ TRANSCRIPTION)
(COMPILED/TRANSCRIBED BY BERNARD T. PUNZALAN / HTTP://WWW.CHAMORROROOTS.COM)

FOURTEENTH CENSUS OF THE UNITED STATES: 1920-POPULATION
ISLAND OF GUAM

ENUMERATED BY ME ON THE 20th DAY OF March, 1920

Arthur W. Jackson ENUMERATOR

DISTRICT 2
NAME OF PLACE Agana (City)

[Proper name and, also, name of class, as city, town, village, barrio, etc]

	Street	Dwelling No.	Family No.	NAME	RELATION	Sex	Color or race	Age	Single/married/widowed/divorced	Attended school since Sept. 1, 1919	Able to read	Able to write	Place of birth of this person	Place of birth of father	Place of birth of mother	Able to speak English	OCCUPATION
	1	2	3	4	5	6	7	8	9	10	11	12	13	14	15	16	17
26		255	297	Hines, Arturo C	Son	M	Mu	7.0	S	N			Guam	Porto Rico	Guam		None
27		255	297	Hines, Viviana C	Daughter	F	Mu	4.0	S				Guam	Porto Rico	Guam		None
28		255	297	Camacho, Alejandra T	Mother-in-law	F	Cha	69.0	S		N	N	Guam	Guam	Guam	N	None
29		256	298	Salas, Juan S	Head	M	Cha	54.0	M		Y	Y	Guam	Guam	Guam	Y	Carpenter
30		256	298	Salas, Dolores S	Wife	F	Cha	48.0	M		Y	Y	Guam	Guam	Guam	N	None
31		256	298	Salas, Francisco S	Son	M	Cha	24.0	S		Y	Y	Guam	Guam	Guam	Y	None
32		256	298	Salas, Miguel S	Son	M	Cha	4.0	S				Guam	Guam	Guam		None
33		257	298	Borja, Manuel B	Head	M	Cha	24.0	M		Y	Y	Guam	Guam	Guam	Y	Carpenter
34		257	298	Borja, Concepcion G	Wife	F	Cha	25.0	M		Y	Y	Guam	Guam	Guam	N	None
35		257	298	Borja, Beatrice G	Daughter	F	Cha	4.0	S				Guam	Guam	Guam		None
36		257	298	Borja, Manuel G	Son	M	Cha	3.0	S				Guam	Guam	Guam		None
37		257	298	Borja, Josefina G	Daughter	F	Cha	1.0	S				Guam	Guam	Guam		None
38	Pizarro Street	258	300	Cepeda, Francisco F	Head	M	Cha	47.0	M		Y	Y	Guam	Guam	Guam	N	Carpenter
39		258	300	Cepeda, Ana F	Wife	F	Cha	45.0	M		Y	Y	Guam	Guam	Guam	N	None
40		258	300	Cepeda, Pedro F	Son	M	Cha	23.0	M		Y	Y	Guam	Guam	Guam	Y	Laborer
41		258	300	Cepeda, Ana C	Daughter-in-law	F	Cha	22.0	M		Y	Y	Guam	Guam	Guam	Y	None
42		258	300	Cepeda, Dolores C	Sister	F	Cha	22.0	S		Y	Y	Guam	Guam	Guam	N	Laundress
43		259	301	Blaz, Maria P	Head	F	Cha	35.0	M		Y	Y	Guam	Guam	Guam	N	Laundress
44		259	301	Blaz, Jose P	Son	M	Cha	14.0	S	N	Y	Y	Guam	Guam	Guam	Y	None
45		259	301	Blaz, Natividad P	Daughter	F	Cha	11.0	S	Y	Y	Y	Guam	Guam	Guam	N	None
46		259	301	Blaz, Vicenta P	Daughter	F	Cha	10.0	S	Y	Y	Y	Guam	Guam	Guam	N	None
47		259	301	Blaz, Josefa P	Daughter	F	Cha	6.0	S	N			Guam	Guam	Guam		None
48		259	301	Perez, Carmen P	Daughter	F	Cha	4.0	S				Guam	Unknown	Guam		None
49		260	302	Pangelinan, Francisco B	Head	M	Cha	55.0	M		Y	Y	Guam	Guam	Guam	N	Carpenter
50		260	302	Pangelinan, Josefa C	Wife	F	Cha	51.0	M		Y	Y	Guam	Guam	Guam	N	None

(COMPILED/TRANSCRIBED BY BERNARD T. PUNZALAN / HTTP://WWW.CHAMORROROOTS.COM)
(CHAMORRO ROOTS GENEALOGY PROJECT ™ TRANSCRIPTION)

FOURTEENTH CENSUS OF THE UNITED STATES: 1920–POPULATION
ISLAND OF GUAM

DISTRICT 2
NAME OF PLACE Agana (City)
[Proper name and, also, name of class, as city, town, village, barrio, etc]

ENUMERATED BY ME ON THE 20th DAY OF March, 1920

Arthur W. Jackson ENUMERATOR

	PLACE OF ABODE			NAME	RELATION	PERSONAL DESCRIPTION				EDUCATION			NATIVITY				OCCUPATION
Street, avenue, road, etc.	Number of dwelling house in order of visitation	Number of family in order of visitation		Name of each person whose place of abode on January 1, 1920, was in the family. Enter surname, first, then given name and middle initial. If any. Include every person living on January 1, 1920. Omit children born since January 1, 1920.	Relationship of this person to the head of the family.	Sex	Color or race	Age at last birthday	Single, married, widowed or divorced	Attended school any time since Sept. 1, 1919	Whether able to read.	Whether able to write.	Place of birth of this person.	Place of birth of father of this person.	Place of birth of mother of this person.	Whether able to speak English.	Trade, profession, or particular kind of work done, as salesman, laborer, clerk, cook, merchant, washerwoman, etc.
1	2	3	4		5	6	7	8	9	10	11	12	13	14	15	16	17
	260	302	Pangelinan, Eliza C	Daughter		F	Cha	19.0	S	N	Y	Y	Guam	Guam	Guam	Y	None
	260	302	Pangelinan, Rosa C	Daughter		F	Cha	15.0	S	N	Y	Y	Guam	Guam	Guam	Y	None
	261	303	Pangelinan, Vicente C	Head		M	Cha	27.0	M		Y	Y	Guam	Guam	Guam	Y	Carpenter
	261	303	Pangelinan, Joaquina C	Wife		F	Cha	23.0	M		Y	Y	Guam	Guam	Guam	Y	None
	261	303	Pangelinan, Julia C	Daughter		F	Cha	3.0	S				Guam	Guam	Guam		None
	261	303	Pangelinan, Jesus C	Son		M	Cha	2.0	S				Guam	Guam	Guam		None
	262	304	Guzman, Juan A	Head		M	Fil	46.0	M		Y	Y	Philippine Islands	Philippine Islands	Philippine Islands	N	Barber
	262	304	Guzman, Trinidad I	Wife		F	Cha	47.0	M		Y	Y	Guam	Guam	Guam	N	None
	262	304	Guzman, Rita I	Daughter		F	Fil	13.0	S	N	Y	Y	Guam	Philippine Islands	Guam	Y	None
	262	304	Guzman, Esperanza I	Daughter		F	Fil	12.0	S	Y	Y	Y	Guam	Philippine Islands	Guam	Y	None
	262	304	Guzman, Caridad I	Daughter		F	Fil	9.0	S	Y			Guam	Philippine Islands	Guam		None
	262	304	Ignacio, Maria	Mother-in-law		F	Cha	83.0	Wd		N	N	Guam	Guam	Guam	N	None
	262	304	Contrares, Miguel	Lodger		M	Fil	47.0	S		Y	Y	Philippine Islands	Philippine Islands	Philippine Islands	N	Laborer
	263	305	Aguon, Vicente T	Head		M	Cha	53.0	M		Y	Y	Guam	Guam	Guam	N	Laborer
	263	305	Aguon, Sabina I	Wife		F	Cha	53.0	M		N	N	Guam	Guam	Guam	N	None
	263	305	Aguon, Ignacio I	Son		M	Cha	22.0	S	N	Y	Y	Guam	Guam	Guam	N	Farmer
	263	305	Aguon, Antonio I	Son		M	Cha	13.0	S	Y	Y	Y	Guam	Guam	Guam	Y	None
	263	305	Aguon, Jesus I	Son		M	Cha	10.0	S	Y	Y	Y	Guam	Guam	Guam	Y	None
	264	306	Aquino, Carmen C	Head		F	Cha	63.0	Wd		Y	Y	Guam	Guam	Guam	N	None
	264	306	Aquino, Ignacia C	Daughter		F	Cha	24.0	S	N	Y	Y	Guam	Guam	Guam	Y	Servant
	264	306	Aquino, Nicolasa C	Daughter		F	Cha	20.0	S	N	Y	Y	Guam	Guam	Guam	Y	Servant
	264	306	Aquino, Jose C	Son		M	Cha	19.0	S	N	Y	Y	Guam	Guam	Guam	Y	Servant
	264	306	Aquino, Juan C	Son		M	Cha	17.0	S	N	Y	Y	Guam	Guam	Guam	Y	Farm laborer
	264	306	Aquino, Pedro C	Son		M	Cha	13.0	S	N	Y	Y	Guam	Guam	Guam	N	None
	264	306	Aquino, Barsalisa C	Grand daughter		F	Cha	4.0	S				Guam	Unknown	Guam		None

Pizarro Street

(CHAMORRO ROOTS GENEALOGY PROJECT ™ TRANSCRIPTION)
(COMPILED/TRANSCRIBED BY BERNARD T. PUNZALAN / HTTP://WWW.CHAMORROROOTS.COM)
FOURTEENTH CENSUS OF THE UNITED STATES: 1920-POPULATION
ISLAND OF GUAM

DISTRICT 2
NAME OF PLACE Agana (City)

ENUMERATED BY ME ON THE 22nd DAY OF March, 1920

Arthur W. Jackson ENUMERATOR

[Proper name and, also, name of class, as city, town, village, barrio, etc]

	Number of dwelling house is order of visitation (2)	Number of family in order of visitation (3)	NAME (4)	RELATION (5)	Sex (6)	Color or race (7)	Age at last birthday (8)	Single, married, widowed or divorced (9)	Attended school any time since Sept. 1, 1919 (10)	Whether able to read (11)	Whether able to write (12)	Place of birth of this person (13)	Place of birth of father of this person (14)	Place of birth of mother of this person (15)	Whether able to speak English (16)	OCCUPATION (17)
26	265	307	Portusach, Antonia M	Head	F	Cha	44.0	Wd		Y	Y	Guam	Guam	Guam	Y	None
27	265	307	Portusach, Beatrice M	Daughter	F	Cha	15.0	S	N	Y	Y	Guam	Guam	Guam	Y	None
28	265	307	Portusach, Emelia M	Daughter	F	Cha	10.0	S	Y	Y	Y	Guam	Guam	Guam	Y	None
29	265	307	Portusach, Magdalena M	Daughter	F	Cha	8.0	S	Y	Y	Y	Guam	Guam	Guam		None
30	265	307	Portusach, Maria M	Daughter	F	Cha	6.0	S	N			Guam	Guam	Guam		None
31	265	307	Benito, Pedro R	Lodger	M	Fil	25.0	S		Y	Y	Philippine Islands	Philippine Islands	Philippine Islands	Y	Salesman
32	266	308	Mendiola, Juliana P	Head	F	Cha	56.0	Wd		N	N	Guam	Guam	Guam	N	None
33	266	308	Mendiola, Ignacio P	Son	M	Cha	20.0	S	N	Y	Y	Guam	Guam	Guam	Y	Farmer
34	267	309	Siguenza, Jose	Head	M	Cha	29.0	M		Y	Y	Guam	Guam	Guam	Y	Enlisted US Navy
35	267	309	Siguenza, Consolacion C	Wife	F	Cha	24.0	M		Y	Y	Guam	Guam	Guam	N	None
36	267	309	Siguenza, Emelia C	Daughter	F	Cha	1.0	S				Guam	Guam	Guam		None
37	268	310	Liizama, Justo P	Head	M	Cha	43.0	M		N	N	Guam	Guam	Guam	N	Farmer
38	268	310	Liizama, Juliana P	Wife	F	Cha	30.0	M		N	N	Guam	Guam	Guam	N	None
39	268	310	Liizama, Francisco P	Son	M	Cha	9.0	S				Guam	Guam	Guam		None
40	268	310	Liizama, Catalina P	Daughter	F	Cha	2.0	S				Guam	Guam	Guam		None
41	269	311	Liizama, Juan P	Head	M	Cha	33.0	M		Y	Y	Guam	Guam	Guam	N	Farmer
42	269	311	Liizama, Ana S	Wife	F	Cha	36.0	M		Y	Y	Guam	Guam	Guam	N	None
43	269	311	Liizama, Jose S	Son	M	Cha	10.0	S	Y	Y	Y	Guam	Guam	Guam	N	None
44	269	311	Liizama, Rosa S	Daughter	F	Cha	8.0	S	Y			Guam	Guam	Guam		None
45	269	311	Liizama, Juan S	Son	M	Cha	6.0	S	N			Guam	Guam	Guam		None
46	269	311	Liizama, Carmen S	Daughter	F	Cha	4.0	S				Guam	Guam	Guam		None
47	269	311	Liizama, Maria S	Daughter	F	Cha	3.0	S				Guam	Guam	Guam		None
48	269	311	Liizama, Dolores S	Daughter	F	Cha	1.0	S				Guam	Guam	Guam		None
49	270	312	Camacho, Joaquin F	Head	M	Cha	39.0	M		Y	Y	Guam	Guam	Guam	N	Farmer
50	270	312	Camacho, Concepcion G	Wife	F	Cha	37.0	M		Y	Y	Guam	Guam	Guam	N	None

Pizarro Street

278

(CHAMORRO ROOTS GENEALOGY PROJECT ™ TRANSCRIPTION)
(COMPILED/TRANSCRIBED BY BERNARD T. PUNZALAN / HTTP://WWW.CHAMORROROOTS.COM)

FOURTEENTH CENSUS OF THE UNITED STATES: 1920—POPULATION
ISLAND OF GUAM

DISTRICT 2
NAME OF PLACE Agana (City)
[Proper name and, also, name of class, as city, town, village, barrio, etc]

ENUMERATED BY ME ON THE 22nd DAY OF March, 1920

Arthur W. Jackson ENUMERATOR

	PLACE OF ABODE			NAME	RELATION	PERSONAL DESCRIPTION					EDUCATION			NATIVITY				OCCUPATION
Street, avenue, road, etc.	Number of dwelling house in order of visitation	Number of family in order of visitation		Name of each person whose place of abode on January 1, 1920, was in the family. Enter surname, first, then given name and middle initial. If any. Include every person living on January 1, 1920. Omit children born since January 1, 1920.	Relationship of this Person to the head of the family.	Sex	Color or race	Age at last birthday	Single, married, widowed or divorced	Attended school any time since Sept. 1, 1919	Whether able to read.	Whether able to write.	Place of birth of this person.	Place of birth of father of this person.	Place of birth of mother of this person.	Whether able to speak English.	Trade, profession, or particular kind of work done, as salesman, laborer, clerk, cook, merchant, washerwoman, etc.
1	2	3		4	5	6	7	8	9	10	11	12	13	14	15	16	17
	270	312	1	Camacho, Cecilio G	Son	M	Cha	13.0	S	Y	Y	Y	Guam	Guam	Guam	Y	None
	270	312	2	Camacho, Ignacio G	Son	M	Cha	10.0	S	Y	Y	Y	Guam	Guam	Guam	N	None
	270	312	3	Camacho, Maria G	Daughter	F	Cha	7.0	S	Y			Guam	Guam	Guam		None
	270	312	4	Camacho, Felicita G	Daughter	F	Cha	5.0	S	N			Guam	Guam	Guam		None
	270	312	5	Camacho, Jose G	Son	M	Cha	4.0	S				Guam	Guam	Guam		None
	270	312	6	Camacho, Juan G	Son	M	Cha	3.0	S				Guam	Guam	Guam		None
	271	313	7	Guerrero, Felipe G	Head	M	Cha	33.0	Wd	Y	Y	Y	Guam	Guam	Guam	N	Farmer
	271	313	8	Guerrero, Jose R	Son	M	Cha	13.0	S	N	Y	Y	Guam	Guam	Guam	Y	None
	271	313	9	Guerrero, Tomas R	Son	M	Cha	11.0	S	N	Y	Y	Guam	Guam	Guam	N	None
	271	313	10	Guerrero, Delfina R	Daughter	F	Cha	8.0	S	Y			Guam	Guam	Guam		None
	271	313	11	Guerrero, Rosario R	Daughter	F	Cha	4.0	S				Guam	Guam	Guam		None
	271	313	12	Guerrero, Jose C	Nephew	M	Cha	16.0	S	N	Y	Y	Guam	Guam	Guam	Y	Laborer
Pizarro Street	272	314	13	Castro, Jose P	Head	M	Cha	27.0	M		Y	Y	Guam	Guam	Guam	Y	Clerk
	272	314	14	Castro, Rosa S	Wife	F	Cha	25.0	M		Y	Y	Guam	Guam	Guam	Y	None
	272	314	15	Castro, Enrique S	Son	M	Cha	5.0	S	N			Guam	Guam	Guam		None
	272	314	16	Castro, Jose S	Son	M	Cha	3.0	S				Guam	Guam	Guam		None
	273	315	17	Cruz, Vicente M	Head	M	Cha	60.0	M	N	N	N	Guam	Guam	Guam	N	Farmer
	273	315	18	Cruz, Josefa P	Wife	F	Cha	53.0	M	N	N	N	Guam	Guam	Guam	N	None
	273	315	19	Cruz, Manuel C	Nephew	M	Cha	4.0	S				Guam	Guam	Guam		None
	274	316	20	San Nicolas, Jose A	Head	M	Cha	21.0	M	N	Y	Y	Guam	Guam	Guam	Y	Farmer
	274	316	21	San Nicolas, Vicenta C	Wife	F	Cha	18.0	M	N	Y	Y	Guam	Guam	Guam	Y	None
	274	316	22	San Nicolas, Jose C	Son	M	Cha	1.0	S				Guam	Guam	Guam		None
	275	317	23	Cruz, Jose SN	Head	M	Cha	36.0	M	Y	Y	Y	Guam	Guam	Guam	N	Farmer
	275	317	24	Cruz, Vicenta R	Wife	F	Cha	36.0	M	Y	Y	Y	Guam	Guam	Guam	N	None
	275	317	25	Cruz, Raymundo R	Son	M	Cha	13.0	S	Y	Y	Y	Guam	Guam	Guam	Y	None

(CHAMORRO ROOTS GENEALOGY PROJECT ™ TRANSCRIPTION)
(COMPILED/TRANSCRIBED BY BERNARD T. PUNZALAN / HTTP://WWW.CHAMORROROOTS.COM)
FOURTEENTH CENSUS OF THE UNITED STATES: 1920–POPULATION
ISLAND OF GUAM

ENUMERATED BY ME ON THE 23rd DAY OF March, 1920

Arthur W. Jackson ENUMERATOR

DISTRICT 2
NAME OF PLACE Agana (City)
[Proper name and, also, name of class, as city, town, village, barrio, etc]

	Street, avenue, road, etc.	Number of dwelling house in order of visitation	Number of family in order of visitation	NAME	RELATION	Sex	Color or race	Age at last birthday	Single, married, widowed or divorced	Attended school any time since Sept. 1, 1919	Whether able to read	Whether able to write	Place of birth of this person	Place of birth of father of this person	Place of birth of mother of this person	Whether able to speak English	OCCUPATION
	1	2	3	4	5	6	7	8	9	10	11	12	13	14	15	16	17
26		275	317	Cruz, Felix R	Son	M	Cha	11.0	S	Y	Y	Y	Guam	Guam	Guam	N	None
27		275	317	Cruz, Dolores R	Daughter	F	Cha	8.0	S	Y			Guam	Guam	Guam		None
28		275	317	Cruz, Soledad R	Daughter	F	Cha	5.0	S	N			Guam	Guam	Guam		None
29		275	317	Cruz, Maria R	Daughter	F	Cha	2.0	S				Guam	Guam	Guam		None
30		275	317	Cruz, Nicolasa M	Aunt	F	Cha	39.0	S		N	N	Guam	Guam	Guam	N	None
31		275	317	Rojas, Cecilio	Father-in-law	M	Cha	84.0	Wd		N	N	Guam	Guam	Guam		None
32		276	318	Acosta, Jose V	Head	M	Cha	38.0	M		Y	Y	Guam	Guam	Guam	N	Farmer
33		276	318	Acosta, Rosa P	Wife	F	Cha	37.0	M		Y	Y	Guam	Guam	Guam	Y	None
34		276	318	Acosta, Maria P	Daughter	F	Cha	12.0	S	Y	Y	Y	Guam	Guam	Guam	Y	None
35		277	319	Mafnas, Antonio C	Head	M	Cha	51.0	M		Y	Y	Guam	Guam	Guam	N	Farmer
36		277	319	Mafnas, Lucia R	Wife	F	Cha	54.0	M		N	N	Guam	Guam	Guam	N	None
37		277	319	Mafnas, Ignacia R	Daughter	F	Cha	20.0	S	N	Y	Y	Guam	Guam	Guam	N	None
38		277	319	Mafnas, Tomasa R	Daughter	F	Cha	18.0	S	N	Y	Y	Guam	Guam	Guam	N	None
39		277	319	Mafnas, Rosa R	Daughter	F	Cha	16.0	S	N	Y	Y	Guam	Guam	Guam	Y	None
40	Pizarro Street	277	319	Mafnas, Vicente R	Son	M	Cha	11.0	S	Y	Y	Y	Guam	Guam	Guam	Y	None
41		278	320	Pangelinan, Alfonso C	Head	M	Cha	50.0	M		N	N	Guam	Guam	Guam	N	Farmer
42		278	320	Pangelinan, Maria C	Wife	F	Cha	45.0	M		N	N	Guam	Guam	Guam	N	None
43		278	320	Pangelinan, Manuel C	Son	M	Cha	19.0	S	N	Y	Y	Guam	Guam	Guam	Y	None
44		278	320	Pangelinan, Antonio C	Son	M	Cha	15.0	S	N	Y	Y	Guam	Guam	Guam	Y	None
45		278	320	Pangelinan, Ana C	Daughter	F	Cha	13.0	S	N	Y	Y	Guam	Guam	Guam	Y	None
46		278	320	Pangelinan, Manuela C	Daughter	F	Cha	12.0	S	Y	Y	Y	Guam	Guam	Guam	N	None
47		278	320	Pangelinan, Candaleria C	Daughter	F	Cha	9.0	S	Y	Y	Y	Guam	Guam	Guam		None
48		278	320	Pangelinan, Maria C	Daughter	F	Cha	7.0	S				Guam	Guam	Guam		None
49		278	320	Pangelinan, Rosario C	Daughter	F	Cha	4.0	S				Guam	Guam	Guam		None
50		278	320	Pangelinan, Vicente C	Son	M	Cha	2.0	S				Guam	Guam	Guam		None

(CHAMORRO ROOTS GENEALOGY PROJECT ™ TRANSCRIPTION)
(COMPILED/TRANSCRIBED BY BERNARD T. PUNZALAN / HTTP://WWW.CHAMORROROOTS.COM)

FOURTEENTH CENSUS OF THE UNITED STATES: 1920—POPULATION
ISLAND OF GUAM

DISTRICT 2
NAME OF PLACE **Agana (City)**
[Proper name and, also, name of class, as city, town, village, barrio, etc]

ENUMERATED BY ME ON THE 23rd DAY OF March, 1920

Arthur W. Jackson ENUMERATOR

Street, avenue, road, etc.	No. dwelling house	No. family	NAME	RELATION	Sex	Color or race	Age at last birthday	Single, married, widowed or divorced	Attended school since Sept. 1, 1919	Whether able to read	Whether able to write	Place of birth of this person	Place of birth of father	Place of birth of mother	Whether able to speak English	OCCUPATION
1	2	3	4	5	6	7	8	9	10	11	12	13	14	15	16	17
	279	321	Pangelinan, Juana	Head	F	Cha	25.0	M		Y	Y	Guam	Unknown	Guam	N	Seamstress
	280	322	Cruz, Tomas A	Head	M	Cha	49.0	M		Y	Y	Guam	Guam	Guam	N	Laborer
	280	322	Cruz, Ana LG	Wife	F	Cha	34.0	M		N	N	Guam	Guam	Guam	N	None
	280	322	Cruz, Josefa LG	Daughter	F	Cha	14.0	S	N	Y	Y	Guam	Guam	Guam	Y	None
	280	322	Cruz, Jose LG	Son	M	Cha	12.0	S	Y	Y	Y	Guam	Guam	Guam	Y	None
	280	322	Cruz, Maria LG	Daughter	F	Cha	9.0	S	Y			Guam	Guam	Guam		None
Pizarro Street	280	322	Cruz, Jesus LG	Son	M	Cha	6.0	S	N			Guam	Guam	Guam		None
	280	322	Cruz, Remedio LG	Daughter	F	Cha	4.0	S				Guam	Guam	Guam		None
	280	322	Cruz, Joaquin LG	Son	M	Cha	1.0	S				Guam	Guam	Guam		None
	280	322	Mafnas, Jose	Servant	M	Cha	20.0	S	N	Y	Y	Guam	Guam	Guam	Y	Servant
	281	323	Mafnas, Juan C	Head	M	Cha	61.0	Wd		Y	Y	Guam	Guam	Guam	N	Farmer
	281	323	Mafnas, Jose C	Son	M	Cha	21.0	S	N	Y	Y	Guam	Guam	Guam	Y	Laborer
	281	323	Mafnas, Rosa C	Daughter	F	Cha	19.0	S	N	Y	Y	Guam	Guam	Guam	Y	None
	281	323	Mafnas, Jose	Grandson	M	Cha	1.0	S				Guam	Guam	Guam		None
	282	324	Leon Guerrero, Jose P	Head	M	Cha	25.0	M		Y	Y	Guam	Guam	Guam	N	Farmer
	282	324	Leon Guerrero, Maria P	Wife	F	Cha	26.0	M		N	N	Guam	Guam	Guam	N	None
	282	324	Leon Guerrero, Jesus P	Son	M	Cha	7.0	S	Y			Guam	Guam	Guam		None
	282	324	Leon Guerrero, Pedro P	Son	M	Cha	6.0	S	N			Guam	Guam	Guam		None
	282	324	Leon Guerrero, Delfin P	Son	M	Cha	4.0	S				Guam	Guam	Guam		None
	282	324	Leon Guerrero, Felipe P	Son	M	Cha	3.0	S				Guam	Guam	Guam		None
	282	324	Leon Guerrero, Ana P	Daughter	F	Cha	0.3	S				Guam	Guam	Guam		None
General Terrero St	283	325	Asano, Yoshiro	Head	M	Jp	34.0	M		Y	Y	Japan	Japan	Japan	Y	Barber
	283	325	Asano, Maria F	Wife	F	Cha	26.0	M		Y	Y	Guam	Guam	Guam	N	None
	283	325	Asano, Isabel F	Daughter	F	Jp	0.1	S				Guam	Japan	Guam		None
	284	326	Muna, Vicente	Head	M	Cha	52.0	S	N	N	N	Guam	Guam	Guam	N	None

(CHAMORRO ROOTS GENEALOGY PROJECT ™ TRANSCRIPTION)
(COMPILED/TRANSCRIBED BY BERNARD T. PUNZALAN / HTTP://WWW.CHAMORROROOTS.COM)
FOURTEENTH CENSUS OF THE UNITED STATES: 1920-POPULATION
ISLAND OF GUAM

DISTRICT 2
NAME OF PLACE Agana (City)
[Proper name and, also, name of class, as city, town, village, barrio, etc]

ENUMERATED BY ME ON THE 23rd DAY OF March, 1920
Arthur W. Jackson ENUMERATOR

	Number of dwelling house in order of visitation	Number of family in order of visitation	NAME	RELATION	Sex	Color or race	Age at last birthday	Single, married, widowed or divorced	Attended school any time since Sept. 1, 1919	Whether able to read	Whether able to write	Place of birth of this person	Place of birth of father of this person	Place of birth of mother of this person	Whether able to speak English	OCCUPATION
	1	2	3	4	5	6	7	8	9	10	11	12	13	14	15	16	17
26	284	326	Muna, Juan	Son	M	Cha	20.0	S	N	Y	Y	Guam	Unknown	Guam	Y	Clerk
27	285	327	Guzman, Tomas	Head	M	Cha	28.0	M		Y	Y	Guam	Guam	Guam	Y	Enlisted US Navy
28	285	327	Guzman, Ana M	Wife	F	Cha	24.0	M		Y	Y	Guam	Unknown	Guam	N	None
29	285	327	Guzman, Gregorio M	Son	M	Cha	3.0	S				Guam	Guam	Guam		None
30	285	327	Guzman, Jesus M	Son	M	Cha	2.0	S				Guam	Guam	Guam		None
31	285	327	Guzman, Antonia M	Daughter	F	Cha	1.0	S				Guam	Guam	Guam		None
32	285	327	Duenas, Concepcion B	Niece	F	Cha	10.0	S	Y	Y	Y	Guam	Guam	Guam	N	None
33	286	328	Takahashi, Kikuzi	Head	M	Jp	47.0	S		Y	Y	Japan	Japan	Japan	N	Salesman
34	286	328	Yamanaka, Iwakichi	Lodger	M	Jp	35.0	S		Y	Y	Japan	Japan	Japan	N	Salesman
35	287	329	Torres, Juan M	Head	M	Cha	35.0	M		Y	Y	Guam	Guam	Guam	Y	Island Treasurer
36	287	329	Torres, Concepcion C	Wife	F	Cha	34.0	M		Y	Y	Guam	Guam	Guam	Y	None
37	287	329	Torres, Antonia C	Daughter	F	Cha	10.0	S	Y	Y	Y	Guam	Guam	Guam	Y	None
38	287	329	Torres, Jose C	Son	M	Cha	8.0	S	Y	Y	Y	Guam	Guam	Guam	Y	None
39	287	329	Torres, Lope C	Son	M	Cha	7.0	S	Y	Y	Y	Guam	Guam	Guam	Y	None
40	287	329	Torres, Ricardo C	Son	M	Cha	5.0	S	N			Guam	Guam	Guam	Y	None
41	287	329	Torres, Juan C	Son	M	Cha	3.0	S				Guam	Guam	Guam		None
42	287	329	Torres, Concepcion C	Daughter	F	Cha	2.0	S				Guam	Guam	Guam		None
43	288	330	Guzman, Juan D	Head	M	Cha	52.0	M		Y	Y	Guam	Guam	Guam	N	Farmer
44	288	330	Guzman, Dolores C	Wife	F	Cha	50.0	M		Y	Y	Guam	Guam	Guam	N	None
45	288	330	Guzman, Natividad C	Daughter	F	Cha	18.0	S	N	Y	Y	Guam	Guam	Guam	Y	None
46	288	330	Guzman, Josefa C	Daughter	F	Cha	15.0	S	N	Y	Y	Guam	Guam	Guam	Y	None
47	288	330	Guzman, Vicente C	Son	M	Cha	13.0	S	Y	Y	Y	Guam	Guam	Guam	Y	None
48	288	330	Guzman, Juan C	Son	M	Cha	12.0	S	Y	Y	Y	Guam	Guam	Guam	Y	None
49	288	330	Guzman, Francisco C	Son	M	Cha	11.0	S	Y	Y	Y	Guam	Guam	Guam	N	None
50	288	330	Guzman, Jesus C	Son	M	Cha	7.0	S	Y	Y	Y	Guam	Guam	Guam		None

Street: General Tereiro Street

(CHAMORRO ROOTS GENEALOGY PROJECT ™ TRANSCRIPTION)
(COMPILED/TRANSCRIBED BY BERNARD T. PUNZALAN / HTTP://WWW.CHAMORROROOTS.COM)
FOURTEENTH CENSUS OF THE UNITED STATES: 1920-POPULATION
ISLAND OF GUAM

DISTRICT 2
NAME OF PLACE Agana (City)
[Proper name and, also, name of class, as city, town, village, barrio, etc]

ENUMERATED BY ME ON THE 24th DAY OF March, 1920

Arthur W. Jackson ENUMERATOR

	PLACE OF ABODE		NAME	RELATION	PERSONAL DESCRIPTION				EDUCATION			NATIVITY				OCCUPATION
Street, avenue, road, etc.	No. of dwelling house	No. of family	Name	Relationship to head of family	Sex	Color or race	Age at last birthday	Single, married, widowed or divorced	Attended school since Sept. 1, 1919	Whether able to read	Whether able to write	Place of birth of this person	Place of birth of father	Place of birth of mother	Whether able to speak English	Occupation
1	2	3	4	5	6	7	8	9	10	11	12	13	14	15	16	17
	288	330	Perez, Mariano C	Step son	M	Cha	25.0	S		Y	Y	Guam	Guam	Guam	N	Laborer
	288	330	Castro, Feliciana G	Lodger	F	Cha	75.0	Wd		Y	Y	Guam	Guam	Guam	N	None
	289	331	Flores, Vicente S	Head	M	Cha	58.0	M		Y	Y	Guam	Guam	Guam	N	Stone mason
	289	331	Flores, Maria C	Wife	F	Cha	53.0	M		Y	Y	Guam	Guam	Guam	N	None
	289	331	Flores, Felix C	Son	M	Cha	9.0	S	Y			Guam	Guam	Guam		None
	290	332	Cruz, Ignacio M	Head	M	Cha	35.0	Wd		Y	Y	Guam	Guam	Guam	N	Carpenter
	290	332	Cruz, Regina F	Daughter	F	Cha	13.0	S	Y	Y	Y	Guam	Guam	Guam	Y	None
	290	332	Cruz, Jose F	Son	M	Cha	11.0	S	Y	Y	Y	Guam	Guam	Guam	N	None
General Terrero Street	290	332	Cruz, Vicente F	Son	M	Cha	7.0	S	Y	Y	Y	Guam	Guam	Guam		None
	290	332	Cruz, Rosario F	Daughter	F	Cha	6.0	S	N			Guam	Guam	Guam		None
	290	332	Cruz, Eugenio F	Son	M	Cha	4.0	S				Guam	Guam	Guam		None
	291	333	Cruz, Vicente C	Head	M	Cha	30.0	M		Y	Y	Guam	Guam	Guam	N	Farmer
	291	333	Cruz, Maria C	Wife	F	Cha	30.0	M		Y	Y	Guam	Guam	Guam	N	None
	292	334	Mendiola, Juan L	Head	M	Cha	37.0	M		Y	Y	Guam	Guam	Guam	N	Farmer
	292	334	Mendiola, Ursula A	Wife	F	Cha	39.0	M		Y	Y	Guam	Guam	Guam	N	None
	292	334	Mendiola, Jose A	Son	M	Cha	13.0	S	Y	Y	Y	Guam	Guam	Guam	Y	None
	292	334	Mendiola, Jesus A	Son	M	Cha	11.0	S	Y	Y	Y	Guam	Guam	Guam	Y	None
	292	334	Mendiola, Gonzalo A	Son	M	Cha	7.0	S	Y			Guam	Guam	Guam		None
	292	334	Mendiola, Juan A	Son	M	Cha	6.0	S	N			Guam	Guam	Guam		None
	292	334	Mendiola, Maria A	Daughter	F	Cha	4.0	S				Guam	Guam	Guam		None
	292	334	Mendiola, Ana A	Daughter	F	Cha	1.0	S				Guam	Guam	Guam		None
	293	335	Borja, Jose	Head	M	Cha	31.0	M		Y	Y	Guam	Unknown	Guam	N	Farmer
	293	335	Borja, Dolores O	Wife	F	Cha	32.0	M		Y	Y	Guam	Guam	Guam	N	None
	293	335	Borja, Maria O	Daughter	F	Cha	13.0	S	N	Y	Y	Guam	Guam	Guam	Y	None
	293	335	Borja, Jose O	Son	M	Cha	10.0	S	Y	Y	Y	Guam	Guam	Guam	N	None

(CHAMORRO ROOTS GENEALOGY PROJECT ™ TRANSCRIPTION)
(COMPILED/TRANSCRIBED BY BERNARD T. PUNZALAN / HTTP://WWW.CHAMORROROOTS.COM)

FOURTEENTH CENSUS OF THE UNITED STATES: 1920-POPULATION
ISLAND OF GUAM

ENUMERATED BY ME ON THE 24th DAY OF March, 1920

Arthur W. Jackson ENUMERATOR

DISTRICT 2
NAME OF PLACE **Agana (City)**
[Proper name and, also, name of class, as city, town, village, barrio, etc]

	PLACE OF ABODE			NAME	RELATION	PERSONAL DESCRIPTION					EDUCATION			NATIVITY				OCCUPATION
Street, avenue, road, etc.	Number of dwelling house in order of visitation	Number of family in order of visitation	Name of each person whose place of abode on January 1, 1920, was in the family. Enter surname, firs, then given name and middle initial. If any. Include every person living on January 1, 1920. Omit children born since January 1, 1920.	Relationship of this Person to the head of the family.	Sex	Color or race	Age at last birthday	Single, married, widowed or divorced	Attended school any time since Sept. 1, 1919	Whether able to read.	Whether able to write.	Place of birth of this person.	Place of birth of father of this person.	Place of birth of mother of this person.	Whether able to speak English.	Trade, profession, or particular kind of work done, as salesman, laborer, clerk, cook, merchant, washerwoman, etc.
1	2	3	4	5	6	7	8	9	10	11	12	13	14	15	16	17
26	293	335	Borja, Juan O	Son	M	Cha	7.0	S	Y			Guam	Guam	Guam		None
27	293	335	Borja, Delfina O	Daughter	F	Cha	5.0	S	N			Guam	Guam	Guam		None
28	293	335	Borja, Pilar O	Daughter	F	Cha	4.0	S				Guam	Guam	Guam		None
29	293	335	Borja, Eduvegis O	Daughter	F	Cha	1.0	S				Guam	Guam	Guam		None
30	293	335	delos Santos, Lucindo C	Lodger	M	Cha	87.0	M				Guam	Guam	Guam	N	None
31	293	335	delos Santos, Narcisa M	Lodger	F	Cha	75.0	M				Guam	Guam	Guam	N	None
32	294	336	Castro, Consolacion R	Head	F	Cha	44.0	Wd		Y	Y	Guam	Guam	Guam	N	None
33	294	336	Castro, Enrique R	Son	M	Cha	16.0	S	N	Y	Y	Guam	Guam	Guam	Y	Farm laborer
34	294	336	Castro, Emelia R	Daughter	F	Cha	14.0	S	N	Y	Y	Guam	Guam	Guam	Y	None
35	294	336	Castro, Josefina R	Daughter	F	Cha	12.0	S	Y	Y	Y	Guam	Guam	Guam	Y	None
36	294	336	Castro, Jose R	Son	M	Cha	7.0	S	Y			Guam	Guam	Guam		None
37	294	336	Castro, Joaquina R	Daughter	F	Cha	5.0	S	N			Guam	Guam	Guam		None
38	294	336	Castro, Felix R	Son	M	Cha	3.0	S				Guam	Guam	Guam		None
39	295	337	Duenas, Juan M	Head	M	Cha	40.0	Wd		Y	Y	Guam	Guam	Guam	N	Carpenter
40	295	337	Duenas, Pedro B	Son	M	Cha	12.0	S	Y	Y	Y	Guam	Guam	Guam	Y	None
41	295	337	Duenas, Francisco B	Son	M	Cha	9.0	S	Y	Y	Y	Guam	Guam	Guam		None
42	295	337	Duenas, Antonio B	Son	M	Cha	7.0	S	Y			Guam	Guam	Guam		None
43	295	337	Duenas, Ignacio B	Son	M	Cha	4.0	S	N			Guam	Guam	Guam		None
44	295	337	Concepcion, Dolores M	Sister-in-law	F	Cha	57.0	S		N	N	Guam	Guam	Guam		None
45	296	338	Mendiola, Mariano C	Head	M	Cha	45.0	M		Y	Y	Guam	Guam	Guam	N	Farmer
46	296	338	Mendiola, Francisca C	Wife	F	Cha	38.0	M		N	N	Guam	Guam	Guam	N	None
47	296	338	Mendiola, Juan C	Son	M	Cha	17.0	S	N	Y	Y	Guam	Guam	Guam	Y	Cook
48	296	338	Mendiola, Maria C	Daughter	F	Cha	15.0	S	N	Y	Y	Guam	Guam	Guam	Y	None
49	296	338	Mendiola, Ana C	Daughter	F	Cha	13.0	S	N	Y	Y	Guam	Guam	Guam	Y	None
50	296	338	Mendiola, Jose C	Son	M	Cha	12.0	S	Y	Y	Y	Guam	Guam	Guam	Y	None

General Terrero Street

284

(CHAMORRO ROOTS GENEALOGY PROJECT ™ TRANSCRIPTION)
(COMPILED/TRANSCRIBED BY BERNARD T. PUNZALAN / HTTP://WWW.CHAMORROROOTS.COM)
FOURTEENTH CENSUS OF THE UNITED STATES: 1920-POPULATION
ISLAND OF GUAM

DISTRICT 2
NAME OF PLACE Agana (City)

[Proper name and, also, name of class, as city, town, village, barrio, etc]

ENUMERATED BY ME ON THE 24th DAY OF March, 1920

Arthur W. Jackson ENUMERATOR

	Street, avenue, road, etc.	Number of dwelling house in order of visitation	Number of family in order of visitation	NAME	RELATION	Sex	Color or race	Age at last birthday	Single, married, widowed or divorced	Attended school any time since Sept. 1, 1919	Whether able to read	Whether able to write	Place of birth of this person.	Place of birth of father of this person.	Place of birth of mother of this person.	Whether able to speak English.	OCCUPATION
	1	2	3	4	5	6	7	8	9	10	11	12	13	14	15	16	17
1		296	338	Mendiola, Mariano C	Son	M	Cha	10.0	S	Y	Y	Y	Guam	Guam	Guam	N	None
2		296	338	Mendiola, Jesus C	Son	M	Cha	8.0	S	Y			Guam	Guam	Guam		None
3		296	338	Mendiola, Carmen C	Daughter	F	Cha	6.0	S	N			Guam	Guam	Guam		None
4		296	338	Mendiola, Enrique C	Son	M	Cha	4.0	S				Guam	Guam	Guam		None
5		296	338	Mendiola, Veronica C	Daughter	F	Cha	2.0	S				Guam	Guam	Guam		None
6	General Terrero Street	297	339	Pangelinan, Ignacio D	Head	M	Cha	47.0	M		Y	Y	Guam	Guam	Guam	N	Farmer
7		297	339	Pangelinan, Maria G	Wife	F	Cha	47.0	M		Y	Y	Guam	Guam	Guam	N	None
8		297	339	Pangelinan, Antonia G	Daughter	F	Cha	17.0	S	N	Y	Y	Guam	Guam	Guam	Y	None
9		297	339	Pangelinan, Rita G	Daughter	F	Cha	15.0	S	N	Y	Y	Guam	Guam	Guam	Y	None
10		297	339	Pangelinan, Jose G	Son	M	Cha	12.0	S	Y	Y	Y	Guam	Guam	Guam	N	None
11		297	339	Pangelinan, Maria G	Daughter	F	Cha	11.0	S	Y	Y	Y	Guam	Guam	Guam	N	None
12		297	339	Pangelinan, Ana G	Daughter	F	Cha	9.0	S	Y			Guam	Guam	Guam		None
13		297	339	Pangelinan, Joaquin G	Son	M	Cha	7.0	S	Y			Guam	Guam	Guam		None
14		297	339	Pangelinan, Vicente G	Son	M	Cha	6.0	S	N			Guam	Guam	Guam		None
15		297	339	Pangelinan, Magdalena G	Daughter	F	Cha	4.0	S	N			Guam	Guam	Guam		None
16		298	340	Watkin, Dolores	Head	F	Cha	38.0	S	Y	Y	Y	Guam	Unknown	Guam	Y	Seamstress
17		298	340	Watkin, Rosa	Daughter	F	Cha	16.0	S	N	Y	Y	Guam	Unknown	Guam	Y	None
18	San Ignacio Street	299	341	Peraira, Manuel D	Head	M	W	45.0	M		Y	Y	Guam	Portugal	Guam	N	Farmer
19		299	341	Peraira, Josefa C	Wife	F	Cha	40.0	M		Y	Y	Guam	Guam	Guam	N	None
20		299	341	Peraira, Ignacio C	Son	M	Cha	19.0	S	N	Y	Y	Guam	Guam	Guam	Y	None
21		299	341	Peraira, Juan C	Son	M	Cha	17.0	S	N	Y	Y	Guam	Guam	Guam	Y	None
22		299	341	Peraira, Pilar C	Daughter	F	Cha	15.0	S	N	Y	Y	Guam	Guam	Guam	Y	None
23		299	341	Peraira, Rita C	Daughter	F	Cha	13.0	S	Y	Y	Y	Guam	Guam	Guam	Y	None
24		299	341	Peraira, Francisco C	Son	M	Cha	11.0	S	Y	Y	Y	Guam	Guam	Guam	Y	None
25		299	341	Peraira, Maria B. C	Daughter	F	Cha	2.0	S				Guam	Guam	Guam	N	None

(CHAMORRO ROOTS GENEALOGY PROJECT ™ TRANSCRIPTION)
(COMPILED/TRANSCRIBED BY BERNARD T. PUNZALAN / HTTP://WWW.CHAMORROROOTS.COM)

FOURTEENTH CENSUS OF THE UNITED STATES: 1920—POPULATION
ISLAND OF GUAM

ENUMERATED BY ME ON THE 25th DAY OF March, 1920

Arthur W. Jackson ENUMERATOR

DISTRICT 2
NAME OF PLACE Agana (City)

	Dwelling No.	Family No.	NAME	RELATION	Sex	Color or race	Age at last birthday	Single, married, widowed or divorced	Attended school since Sept. 1, 1919	Able to read	Able to write	Place of birth of this person	Place of birth of father	Place of birth of mother	Able to speak English	OCCUPATION
	2	3	4	5	6	7	8	9	10	11	12	13	14	15	16	17
26	299	341	Peraira, Herman C	Son	M	Cha	1.0	S				Guam	Guam	Guam		None
27	300	342	dela Cruz, Eulogio C	Head	M	Fil	49.0	M		Y	Y	Philippine Islands	Philippine Islands	Philippine Islands	Y	Farmer
28	300	342	dela Cruz, Maria U	Wife	F	Fil	38.0	M		Y	Y	Guam	Philippine Islands	Guam	N	None
29	300	342	Zafra, Angusta E	Lodger	F	Fil	24.0	S		Y	Y	Guam	Philippine Islands	Guam	Y	None
30	300	342	Zafra, Vicente E	Lodger	M	Fil	17.0	S	N	Y	Y	Guam	Philippine Islands	Guam	Y	Messenger
31	300	342	Muna, Ana G	Servant	F	Cha	17.0	S	N	Y	Y	Guam	Guam	Guam	Y	Servant
32	301	343	dela Cruz, Francisco M	Head	M	Fil	24.0	S		Y	Y	Guam	Philippine Islands	Philippine Islands	Y	None
33	301	343	dela Cruz, Jose M	Brother	M	Fil	22.0	S		Y	Y	Guam	Philippine Islands	Philippine Islands	Y	None
34	302	344	Camacho, Jose M	Head	M	Cha	32.0	M		Y	Y	Guam	Guam	Guam	Y	Clerk
35	302	344	Camacho, Catalina E	Wife	F	Fil	24.0	M	Y	Y	Y	Guam	Philippine Islands	Guam	Y	Teacher
36	302	344	Camacho, Jose J	Son	M	Cha	8.0	S	Y			Guam	Guam	Guam		None
37	302	344	Camacho, Raimundo V	Son	M	Cha	7.0	S	Y			Guam	Guam	Guam		None
38	302	344	Camacho, Pedro G	Son	M	Cha	5.0	S	N			Guam	Guam	Guam		None
39	302	344	Camacho, Vicente L	Son	M	Cha	3.0	S				Guam	Guam	Guam		None
40	302	344	Camacho, Sigena M	Daughter	F	Cha	1.0	S				Guam	Guam	Guam		None
41	302	344	Camacho, Rita M	Sister	F	Cha	37.0	S		Y	Y	Guam	Guam	Guam	Y	None
42	303	345	Duenas, Antonia L	Head	F	Cha	44.0	Wd	N	Y	Y	Guam	Guam	Guam	N	None
43	303	345	Duenas, Juan L	Son	M	Cha	19.0	S	N	Y	Y	Guam	Guam	Guam	Y	Bank teller
44	303	345	Duenas, Maria L	Sister	F	Cha	14.0	S	Y	Y	Y	Guam	Guam	Guam	Y	None
45	303	345	Duenas, Rufina L	Sister	F	Cha	8.0	S	N	Y		Guam	Guam	Guam		None
46	303	345	Leon Guerrero, Pedro C	Servant	M	Cha	11.0	S	N	Y	Y	Guam	Guam	Guam	N	Servant
47	304	346	Castro, Nicolas M	Head	M	Cha	47.0	M		Y	Y	Guam	Guam	Guam	N	Farmer
48	304	346	Castro, Vicenta S	Wife	F	Cha	46.0	M		Y	Y	Guam	Guam	Guam	N	None
49	304	346	Santos, Maria P	Mother-in-law	F	Cha	70.0	Wd		Y	Y	Guam	Guam	Guam	N	None
50	304	346	Santos, Pedro V	Nephew	M	Cha	12.0	S	Y	Y	Y	Guam	Guam	Guam	Y	None

Street: San Ignacio Street

(CHAMORRO ROOTS GENEALOGY PROJECT ™ TRANSCRIPTION)
(COMPILED/TRANSCRIBED BY BERNARD T. PUNZALAN / HTTP://WWW.CHAMORROROOTS.COM)

FOURTEENTH CENSUS OF THE UNITED STATES: 1920-POPULATION

ISLAND OF GUAM

DISTRICT 2
NAME OF PLACE Agana (City)

ENUMERATED BY ME ON THE 25th DAY OF March, 1920

Arthur W. Jackson ENUMERATOR

[Proper name and, also, name of class, as city, town, village, barrio, etc]

Street, avenue, road, etc.	Number of dwelling house in order of visitation (2)	Number of family in order of visitation (3)	NAME (4)	RELATION (5)	Sex (6)	Color or race (7)	Age at last birthday (8)	Single, married, widowed or divorced (9)	Attended school any time since Sept. 1, 1919 (10)	Whether able to read. (11)	Whether able to write. (12)	Place of birth of this person. (13)	Place of birth of father of this person. (14)	Place of birth of mother of this person. (15)	Whether able to speak English. (16)	OCCUPATION (17)
San Ignacio Street	305	347	Scharff, George	Head	M	W	24.0	M		Y	Y	Germany	Germany	Germany	Y	Machinist
	305	347	Scharff, Antonia F	Wife	F	Cha	20.0	M	N	Y	Y	Guam	Guam	Guam	Y	None
	306	348	Borja, Ignacio S	Head	M	Cha	29.0	M		Y	Y	Guam	Guam	Guam	Y	Watchman
	306	348	Borja, Vicenta S	Wife	F	Cha	31.0	M		Y	Y	Guam	Guam	Guam	N	None
	306	348	Borja, Concepcion S	Daughter	F	Cha	7.0	S	Y			Guam	Guam	Guam		None
	306	348	Borja, Juan S	Son	M	Cha	6.0	S	N			Guam	Guam	Guam		None
	306	348	Borja, Dolores S	Daughter	F	Cha	3.0	S				Guam	Guam	Guam		None
	307	349	Cruz, Tomas L	Head	M	Cha	36.0	S		Y	Y	Guam	Guam	Guam	N	Tailor
	308	350	Salas, Rosa S	Head	F	Cha	36.0	Wd		Y	Y	Guam	Guam	Guam	N	None
	308	350	Salas, Juan S	Son	M	Cha	19.0	S	N	Y	Y	Guam	Guam	Guam	Y	Laborer
	308	350	Salas, Ana S	Daughter	F	Cha	18.0	S	N	Y	Y	Guam	Guam	Guam	N	None
	308	350	Salas, Ramon S	Son	M	Cha	16.0	S	N	Y	Y	Guam	Guam	Guam	Y	Laborer
	308	350	Salas, Engracia S	Daughter	F	Cha	14.0	S	N	Y	Y	Guam	Guam	Guam	Y	None
	308	350	Salas, Magdalena S	Daughter	F	Cha	13.0	S	Y	Y	Y	Guam	Guam	Guam	Y	None
	308	350	Salas, Enrique S	Son	M	Cha	11.0	S	N	Y	Y	Guam	Guam	Guam	N	None
	308	350	Salas, Esperanza S	Daughter	F	Cha	6.0	S				Guam	Guam	Guam		None
	308	350	Salas, Felix S	Son	M	Cha	5.0	S				Guam	Guam	Guam		None
	308	350	Salas, Patricio S	Son	M	Cha	2.0	S				Guam	Guam	Guam		None
	309	351	Blaz, Luis A	Head	M	Cha	26.0	M		Y	Y	Guam	Guam	Guam	Y	Carpenter
	309	351	Blaz, Francisca S	Wife	F	Cha	22.0	M		Y	Y	Guam	Guam	Guam	N	None
	309	351	Salas, Catalina	Step daughter	F	Cha	2.0	S				Guam	Guam	Guam		None
	310	352	Mesa, Vicente	Head	M	Cha	38.0	M	N	Y	Y	Guam	Guam	Guam	N	Farmer
	310	352	Mesa, Ana P	Wife	F	Cha	46.0	M		Y	Y	Guam	Guam	Guam	N	None
	310	352	Mesa, Josefa L	Daughter	F	Cha	20.0	S	N	Y	Y	Guam	Guam	Guam	Y	None
	310	352	Mesa, Ana L	Daughter	F	Cha	16.0	S	N	Y	Y	Guam	Guam	Guam	Y	None

(CHAMORRO ROOTS GENEALOGY PROJECT ™ TRANSCRIPTION)
(COMPILED/TRANSCRIBED BY BERNARD T. PUNZALAN / HTTP://WWW.CHAMORROROOTS.COM)

FOURTEENTH CENSUS OF THE UNITED STATES: 1920-POPULATION
ISLAND OF GUAM

DISTRICT 2
NAME OF PLACE **Agana (City)**
[Proper name and, also, name of class, as city, town, village, barrio, etc]

ENUMERATED BY ME ON THE 25th DAY OF March, 1920

Arthur W. Jackson ENUMERATOR

	Street	No. dwelling house (2)	No. family (3)	NAME (4)	RELATION (5)	Sex (6)	Color or race (7)	Age (8)	Single, married, widowed, divorced (9)	Attended school since Sept. 1, 1919 (10)	Whether able to read (11)	Whether able to write (12)	Place of birth of this person (13)	Place of birth of father (14)	Place of birth of mother (15)	Whether able to speak English (16)	OCCUPATION (17)
26		310	352	Mesa, Jose P	Son	M	Cha	12.0	S	Y	Y	Y	Guam	Guam	Guam	Y	None
27		310	352	Mesa, Felix P	Son	M	Cha	7.0	S	Y			Guam	Guam	Guam	Y	None
28		310	352	Mesa, Manuel P	Son	M	Cha	5.0	S	N			Guam	Guam	Guam	Y	None
29		310	352	Mesa, Maria P	Step daughter	F	Cha	22.0	S		Y	Y	Guam	Guam	Guam	Y	None
30		310	352	Mesa, Concepcion P	Step daughter	F	Cha	20.0	S	N	Y	Y	Guam	Guam	Guam	Y	None
31		310	352	Mesa, Francisco P	Step son	M	Cha	18.0	S	N	Y	Y	Guam	Guam	Guam	Y	App. Printer
32		310	352	Mesa, Joaquin P	Step son	M	Cha	16.0	S	N	Y	Y	Guam	Guam	Guam	Y	Farm laborer
33	San Ignacio Street	311	353	Untalan, Pedro C	Head	M	Fil	37.0	M		Y	Y	Guam	Philippine Islands	Guam	N	Tanner
34		311	353	Untalan, Rita LG	Wife	F	Cha	33.0	M		Y	Y	Guam	Guam	Guam	N	None
35		311	353	Untalan, Teodoro LG	Son	M	Fil	13.0	S	Y	Y	Y	Guam	Guam	Guam	Y	None
36		311	353	Untalan, Enrique LG	Son	M	Fil	12.0	S	Y	Y	Y	Guam	Guam	Guam	N	None
37		311	353	Untalan, Serafina LG	Daughter	F	Fil	10.0	S	Y	Y	Y	Guam	Guam	Guam	Y	None
38		311	353	Untalan, Oliva LG	Daughter	F	Fil	8.0	S	Y	Y		Guam	Guam	Guam	Y	None
39		311	353	Untalan, Guardalupe LG	Daughter	F	Fil	4.0	S				Guam	Guam	Guam		None
40		311	353	Untalan, Antonia LG	Daughter	F	Fil	2.0	S				Guam	Guam	Guam		None
41		311	353	Untalan, Jose LG	Son	M	Fil	0.2	S				Guam	Guam	Guam		None
42		312	354	Untalan, Rosa L	Head	F	Cha	45.0	Wd		Y	Y	Guam	Guam	Guam	N	None
43		312	354	Untalan, Joaquin L	Son	M	Fil	22.0	S		Y	Y	Guam	Philippine Islands	Guam	Y	Enlisted US Navy
44		312	354	Untalan, Agustin L	Son	M	Fil	19.0	S	N	Y	Y	Guam	Philippine Islands	Guam	Y	Carpenter
45		312	354	Untalan, Virginia L	Daughter	F	Fil	18.0	S	N	Y	Y	Guam	Philippine Islands	Guam	Y	None
46		312	354	Untalan, Antonio L	Son	M	Fil	15.0	S	N	Y	Y	Guam	Philippine Islands	Guam	Y	None
47		312	354	Untalan, Manuel L	Son	M	Fil	12.0	S	Y	Y	Y	Guam	Philippine Islands	Guam	Y	None
48		312	354	Untalan, Olimpia L	Daughter	F	Fil	10.0	S	Y	Y	Y	Guam	Philippine Islands	Guam	N	None
49		312	354	Untalan, Lourdes L	Daughter	F	Fil	8.0	S	Y	Y		Guam	Philippine Islands	Guam		None
50		312	354	Untalan, Modesta L	Daughter	F	Fil	6.0	S	N			Guam	Philippine Islands	Guam		None

288

(CHAMORRO ROOTS GENEALOGY PROJECT ™ TRANSCRIPTION)
(COMPILED/TRANSCRIBED BY BERNARD T. PUNZALAN / HTTP://WWW.CHAMORROROOTS.COM)

FOURTEENTH CENSUS OF THE UNITED STATES: 1920—POPULATION

ISLAND OF GUAM

DISTRICT 2
NAME OF PLACE **Agana (City)**
[Proper name and, also, name of class, as city, town, village, barrio, etc]

ENUMERATED BY ME ON THE 26th DAY OF March, 1920

Arthur W. Jackson ENUMERATOR

	PLACE OF ABODE		NAME	RELATION	PERSONAL DESCRIPTION				EDUCATION			NATIVITY				OCCUPATION
Street, avenue, road, etc.	Number of dwelling house in order of visitation	Number of family in order of visitation	Name of each person whose place of abode on January 1, 1920, was in the family.	Relationship of this person to the head of the family.	Sex	Color or race	Age at last birthday	Single, married, widowed or divorced	Attended school any time since Sept. 1, 1919	Whether able to read.	Whether able to write.	Place of birth of this person.	Place of birth of father of this person.	Place of birth of mother of this person.	Whether able to speak English.	Trade, profession, or particular kind of work done, as salesman, laborer, clerk, cook, merchant, washerwoman, etc.
1	2	3	4	5	6	7	8	9	10	11	12	13	14	15	16	17
	313	355	Bernardo, Guillermo C	Head	M	Fil	52.0	M		N	N	Philippine Islands	Philippine Islands	Philippine Islands	N	Stone mason
	313	355	Bernardo, Ana T	Wife	F	Cha	28.0	M		Y	Y	Guam	Guam	Guam	N	None
	313	355	Bernardo, Pedro C	Son	M	Fil	19.0	S	N	Y	Y	Guam	Philippine Islands	Guam	Y	Farm laborer
	313	355	Bernardo, Dominga C	Daughter	F	Fil	17.0	S	N	Y	Y	Guam	Philippine Islands	Guam	Y	None
	313	355	Bernardo, Joaquin C	Son	M	Fil	15.0	S	N	Y	Y	Guam	Philippine Islands	Guam	Y	None
	313	355	Bernardo, Andres C	Son	M	Fil	11.0	S	Y	Y	Y	Guam	Philippine Islands	Guam	N	None
	313	355	Bernardo, Artemio C	Son	M	Fil	4.0	S				Guam	Philippine Islands	Guam	N	None
	314	356	Leon Guerrero, Vicente F	Head	M	Cha	37.0	M		Y	Y	Guam	Guam	Guam	N	Laborer
	314	356	Leon Guerrero, Ana C	Wife	F	Cha	27.0	M		Y	Y	Guam	Guam	Guam	N	None
	314	356	Leon Guerrero, Rita C	Daughter	F	Cha	11.0	S	Y	Y	Y	Guam	Guam	Guam	N	None
San Ignacio Street	314	356	Leon Guerrero, Justo C	Son	M	Cha	3.0	S				Guam	Guam	Guam	N	None
	314	356	Leon Guerrero, Efrain C	Son	M	Cha	0.6	S				Guam	Guam	Guam	N	None
	315	357	Shinohara, Takekuma	Head	M	Jp	29.0	S		Y	Y	Japan	Japan	Japan	Y	Salesman
	316	358	de la Torre, Joaquin B	Head	M	Cha	32.0	M		Y	Y	Guam	Guam	Guam	N	Farmer
	316	358	de la Torre, Felisidad U	Wife	F	Cha	27.0	M		Y	Y	Guam	Guam	Guam	N	None
	316	358	de la Torre, Jose U	Son	M	Cha	3.0	S				Guam	Guam	Guam	N	None
	316	358	de la Torre, Vicente U	Son	M	Cha	1.0	S				Guam	Guam	Guam		None
	317	359	George, Felix P	Head	M	W	58.0	Wd		Y	Y	Guam	England	Guam	N	Farmer
	317	359	George, Zara M	Daughter	F	W	18.0	S	N	Y	Y	Guam	Guam	Guam	Y	None
	317	359	George, Josefa M	Daughter	F	W	16.0	S	N	Y	Y	Guam	Guam	Guam	Y	None
	317	359	George, Jose M	Son	M	W	12.0	S	Y	Y	Y	Guam	Guam	Guam	Y	None
	317	359	Quidachay, Jose M	Step son	M	Cha	22.0	S		Y	Y	Guam	Guam	Guam	Y	Enlisted US. Navy. Not an Am. Citizen
	318	360	Manibusan, Jose R	Head	M	Cha	59.0	M		N	N	Guam	Guam	Guam	N	Farmer
	318	360	Manibusan, Juana G	Wife	F	Cha	62.0	M		N	N	Guam	Guam	Guam	N	None
	318	360	Manibusan, Antonio F	Son	M	Cha	32.0	M		Y	Y	Guam	Guam	Guam	N	Farmer

(CHAMORRO ROOTS GENEALOGY PROJECT ™ TRANSCRIPTION)
(COMPILED/TRANSCRIBED BY BERNARD T. PUNZALAN / HTTP://WWW.CHAMORROROOTS.COM)

FOURTEENTH CENSUS OF THE UNITED STATES: 1920-POPULATION
ISLAND OF GUAM

ENUMERATED BY ME ON THE 26th DAY OF March, 1920

Arthur W. Jackson ENUMERATOR

DISTRICT 2
NAME OF PLACE Agana (City)
[Proper name and, also, name of class, as city, town, village, barrio, etc]

	Street	Dwelling	Family	NAME	RELATION	Sex	Color or race	Age	Single, married, widowed or divorced	Attended school since sept. 1, 1919	Able to read	Able to write	Birthplace of person	Birthplace of father	Birthplace of mother	Able to speak English	OCCUPATION
	1	2	3	4	5	6	7	8	9	10	11	12	13	14	15	16	17
26		318	360	Manibusan, Pedro F	Son	M	Cha	15.0	S	N	Y	Y	Guam	Guam	Guam	Y	Farm laborer
27		318	360	Manibusan, Antonia F	Daughter	F	Cha	14.0	S	N	Y	Y	Guam	Guam	Guam	Y	None
28		319	361	Santos, Carmelo A	Head	M	Cha	42.0	M		Y	Y	Guam	Guam	Guam	N	None
29		319	361	Santos, Faustina C	Wife	F	Cha	52.0	M		N	N	Guam	Guam	Guam	N	None
30		319	361	Taitano, Rosa L	Lodger	F	Cha	5.0	S	N			Guam	Guam	Guam		None
31		320	362	Taitano, Antonio M	Head	M	Cha	35.0	M		Y	Y	Guam	Guam	Guam	N	Farmer
32		320	362	Taitano, Manuela L	Wife	F	Cha	30.0	M		Y	Y	Guam	Guam	Guam	N	None
33	San Ignacio Street	320	362	Taitano, Ana L	Daughter	F	Cha	15.0	S	N	Y	Y	Guam	Guam	Guam	Y	None
34		320	362	Taitano, Felicita L	Daughter	F	Cha	12.0	S	Y	Y	Y	Guam	Guam	Guam	N	None
35		320	362	Taitano, Maria L	Daughter	F	Cha	9.0	S	Y	Y	Y	Guam	Guam	Guam		None
36		320	362	Taitano, Rosario L	Daughter	F	Cha	7.0	S	Y		Y	Guam	Guam	Guam		None
37		320	362	Taitano, Joaquin L	Son	M	Cha	4.0	S				Guam	Guam	Guam		None
38		320	362	Taitano, Concepcion L	Daughter	F	Cha	2.0	S				Guam	Guam	Guam		None
39		321	363	Terlaje, Jose S	Head	M	Cha	28.0	M		Y	Y	Guam	Guam	Guam	N	Farmer
40		321	363	Terlaje, Maria C	Wife	F	Cha	28.0	M		Y	Y	Guam	Guam	Guam	N	None
41		321	363	Terlaje, Francisco C	Son	M	Cha	2.0	S				Guam	Guam	Guam		None
42		322	364	Aguon, Jose T	Head	M	Cha	27.0	S		Y	Y	Guam	Guam	Guam	Y	Farmer
43		322	364	Aguon, Joaquin T	Brother	M	Cha	20.0	S	N	Y	Y	Guam	Guam	Guam	Y	Enlisted US Navy. Not an Am. Citizen
44		322	364	Aguon, Felicita T	Sister	F	Cha	19.0	S	N	Y	Y	Guam	Guam	Guam	Y	None
45		323	365	Santos, Ignacio A	Head	M	Cha	57.0	M		Y	Y	Guam	Guam	Guam	N	Farmer
46		323	365	Santos, Maria A	Wife	F	Cha	45.0	M		N	N	Guam	Guam	Guam	N	None
47		323	365	Santos, Magdalena A	Daughter	F	Cha	9.0	S	Y			Guam	Guam	Guam		None
48		323	365	Santos, Luisa A	Daughter	F	Cha	5.0	S	N			Guam	Guam	Guam		None
49		323	365	Santos, Antonio A	Son	M	Cha	2.0	S				Guam	Guam	Guam		None
50		323	365	Arriola, Jose	Step son	M	Cha	14.0	S	N	Y	Y	Guam	Unknown	Guam	N	None

(CHAMORRO ROOTS GENEALOGY PROJECT ™ TRANSCRIPTION)
(COMPILED/TRANSCRIBED BY BERNARD T. PUNZALAN / HTTP://WWW.CHAMORROROOTS.COM)

FOURTEENTH CENSUS OF THE UNITED STATES: 1920-POPULATION

ISLAND OF GUAM

DISTRICT 2
NAME OF PLACE Agana (City)
[Proper name and, also, name of class, as city, town, village, barrio, etc]

ENUMERATED BY ME ON THE 27th DAY OF March, 1920

Arthur W. Jackson ENUMERATOR

1	2	3	4 NAME	5 RELATION	6 Sex	7 Color or race	8 Age at last birthday	9 Single, married, widowed or divorced	10 Attended school any time since Sept. 1, 1919	11 Whether able to read	12 Whether able to write	13 Place of birth of this person	14 Place of birth of father of this person	15 Place of birth of mother of this person	16 Whether able to speak English	17 OCCUPATION
1	323	365	Arriola, Margarita	Step daughter	F	Cha	13.0	S	N	Y	Y	Guam	Unknown	Guam	Y	None
2	324	366	Castro, Mercedes L	Head	F	Cha	51.0	Wd		Y	Y	Guam	Guam	Guam	N	None
3	324	366	Castro, Luisa L	Daughter	F	Cha	22.0	S		Y	Y	Guam	Guam	Guam	Y	Weaver
4	324	366	Castro, Santiago L	Son	M	Cha	21.0	S	N	Y	Y	Guam	Guam	Guam	Y	Farmer
5	324	366	Castro, Juana L	Daughter	F	Cha	20.0	S	N	Y	Y	Guam	Guam	Guam	Y	None
6	325	367	Lujan, Maria T	Head	F	Cha	61.0	Wd		Y	Y	Guam	Guam	Guam	N	None
7	325	367	Lujan, Luis T	Son	M	Cha	40.0	S		Y	Y	Guam	Guam	Guam	N	Farmer
8	326	368	de la Cruz, Encarnacion P	Head	F	W	42.0	Wd		Y	Y	Guam	Portugal	Guam	N	None
9	326	368	de la Cruz, Carlos P	Son	M	Fil	10.0	S	Y	Y	Y	Guam	Philippine Islands	Guam	N	None
10	326	368	de la Cruz, Regina P	Daughter	F	Fil	7.0	S	Y			Guam	Philippine Islands	Guam		None
11	326	368	de la Cruz, Candaleria P	Daughter	F	Fil	6.0	S	N			Guam	Philippine Islands	Guam		None
12	326	368	de la Cruz, Alejandro P	Son	M	Cha	4.0	S				Guam	Philippine Islands	Guam		None
13	327	369	Cruz, Joaquin G	Head	M	Cha	43.0	M		Y	Y	Guam	Guam	Guam	N	Farmer
14	327	369	Cruz, Rita G	Wife	F	Cha	35.0	M		Y	Y	Guam	Unknown	Guam	N	None
15	327	369	Cruz, Maria G	Daughter	F	Cha	10.0	S	Y	Y	Y	Guam	Guam	Guam	Y	None
16	327	369	Cruz, Jesus G	Son	M	Cha	8.0	S	Y			Guam	Guam	Guam		None
17	327	369	Cruz, Pedro G	Son	M	Cha	6.0	S	N			Guam	Guam	Guam		None
18	327	369	Cruz, Tomasa G	Daughter	F	Cha	3.0	S				Guam	Guam	Guam		None
19	328	370	Atoigue, Antonio C	Head	M	Cha	48.0	M		Y	Y	Guam	Guam	Guam	N	Farmer
20	328	370	Atoigue, Maria U	Wife	F	Cha	47.0	M		Y	Y	Guam	Guam	Guam	N	None
21	328	370	Atoigue, Josefa U	Daughter	F	Cha	22.0	S		Y	Y	Guam	Guam	Guam	Y	None
22	328	370	Atoigue, Vicente U	Son	M	Cha	21.0	S	N	Y	Y	Guam	Guam	Guam	Y	Enlisted US Navy not an Am. Citizen
23	328	370	Guzman, Joaquin U	Nephew	M	Cha	13.0	S	Y	Y	Y	Guam	Guam	Guam	Y	None
24	329	371	Martinez, Joaquin C	Head	M	Cha	32.0	M		Y	Y	Guam	Guam	Guam	Y	Carpenter
25	329	371	Martinez, Soledad M	Wife	F	Cha	28.0	M		Y	Y	Guam	Guam	Guam	N	None

Street, avenue, road, etc.: San Ignacio Street

(CHAMORRO ROOTS GENEALOGY PROJECT ™ TRANSCRIPTION)
(COMPILED/TRANSCRIBED BY BERNARD T. PUNZALAN / HTTP://WWW.CHAMORROROOTS.COM)

FOURTEENTH CENSUS OF THE UNITED STATES: 1920-POPULATION
ISLAND OF GUAM

144b

DISTRICT 2
NAME OF PLACE Agana (City)
[Proper name and, also, name of class, as city, town, village, barrio, etc]

ENUMERATED BY ME ON THE 27th DAY OF MARCH, 1920

Arthur W. Jackson ENUMERATOR

	Dwelling No.	Family No.	NAME	RELATION	Sex	Color or race	Age	Single/married	Attended school	Read	Write	Birthplace	Father birthplace	Mother birthplace	Speak English	OCCUPATION
26	329	371	Martinez, Pilar M	Daughter	F	Cha	8.0	S	Y			Guam	Guam	Guam		None
27	329	371	Martinez, Concepcion M	Daughter	F	Cha	7.0	S	Y			Guam	Guam	Guam		None
28	329	371	Martinez, Manuel M	Son	M	Cha	5.0	S	N			Guam	Guam	Guam		None
29	329	371	Martinez, Rosario M	Daughter	F	Cha	3.0	S				Guam	Guam	Guam		None
30	329	371	Martinez, Ignacio M	Son	M	Cha	1.0	S				Guam	Guam	Guam		None
31	330	372	Camacho, Ignacio L	Head	M	Cha	57.0	M		Y	Y	Guam	Guam	Guam	N	Blacksmith
32	330	372	Camacho, Maria M	Wife	F	Cha	52.0	M		Y	Y	Guam	Guam	Guam	N	None
33	330	372	Camacho, Luis M	Son	M	Cha	25.0	S		Y	Y	Guam	Guam	Guam	Y	Carpenter
34	330	372	Camacho, Jose M	Son	M	Cha	21.0	S	N	Y	Y	Guam	Guam	Guam	Y	Electrician
35	330	372	Camacho, Pedro M	Son	M	Cha	19.0	S	N	Y	Y	Guam	Guam	Guam	Y	Clerk
36	330	372	Camacho, Jesus M	Son	M	Cha	13.0	S	Y	Y	Y	Guam	Guam	Guam	Y	None
37	330	372	Camacho, Francisco M	Son	M	Cha	11.0	S	Y	Y	Y	Guam	Guam	Guam	N	None
38	330	372	Camacho, Carlos M	Son	M	Cha	9.0	S	Y	Y	Y	Guam	Guam	Guam		None
39	331	373	Sablan, Lorenzo A	Head	M	Cha	32.0	M		Y	Y	Guam	Guam	Guam	Y	Cook
40	331	373	Sablan, Joaquina A	Wife	F	Cha	41.0	M		N	N	Guam	Guam	Guam	N	None
41	331	373	Sablan, Asencion A	Daughter	F	Cha	10.0	S	Y	Y	Y	Guam	Guam	Guam	N	None
42	331	373	Sablan, Jose A	Son	M	Cha	6.0	S	N			Guam	Guam	Guam		None
43	331	373	Aguon, Jose P	Servant	M	Cha	12.0	S	Y	Y	Y	Guam	Guam	Guam	N	Servant
44	332	374	Perez, Vicente M	Head	M	Cha	27.0	M		Y	Y	Guam	Guam	Guam	Y	Laborer
45	332	374	Perez, Soledad R	Wife	F	Cha	23.0	M		Y	Y	Guam	Guam	Guam	N	None
46	332	374	Perez, Emeliana R	Daughter	F	Cha	5.0	S	N			Guam	Guam	Guam		None
47	332	374	Perez, Rosa R	Daughter	F	Cha	3.0	S				Guam	Guam	Guam		None
48	332	374	Perez, Jose R	Son	M	Cha	0.3	S				Guam	Guam	Guam		None
49	333	375	Mesa, Antonio M	Head	M	Cha	52.0	M		Y	Y	Guam	Guam	Guam	N	Farmer
50	333	375	Mesa, Maria T	Wife	F	Cha	55.0	M		N	N	Guam	Guam	Guam	N	None

Street: San Ignacio Street

(CHAMORRO ROOTS GENEALOGY PROJECT ™ TRANSCRIPTION)
(COMPILED/TRANSCRIBED BY BERNARD T. PUNZALAN / HTTP://WWW.CHAMORROROOTS.COM)
FOURTEENTH CENSUS OF THE UNITED STATES: 1920—POPULATION
ISLAND OF GUAM

DISTRICT 2
NAME OF PLACE Agana (City)

ENUMERATED BY ME ON THE 27th DAY OF March, 1920

Arthur W. Jackson ENUMERATOR

[Proper name and, also, name of class, as city, town, village, barrio, etc]

	PLACE OF ABODE			NAME	RELATION	PERSONAL DESCRIPTION					EDUCATION			NATIVITY				OCCUPATION
Street, avenue, road, etc.	Number of dwelling house in order of visitation	Number of family in order of visitation		Name of each person whose place of abode on January 1, 1920, was in the family.	Relationship of this Person to the head of the family.	Sex	Color or race	Age at last birthday	Single, married, widowed or divorced	Attended school any time since Sept. 1, 1919	Whether able to read.	Whether able to write.	Place of birth of this person.	Place of birth of father of this person.	Place of birth of mother of this person.	Whether able to speak English.	Trade, profession, or particular kind of work done, as salesman, laborer, clerk, cook, merchant, washerwoman, etc.
1	2	3	4		5	6	7	8	9	10	11	12	13	14	15	16	17
	333	375	Mesa, Antonio T		Son	M	Cha	24.0	S		Y	Y	Guam	Guam	Guam	Y	Farm laborer
	333	375	Mesa, Jose T		Son	M	Cha	18.0	S	N	Y	Y	Guam	Guam	Guam	Y	Farm laborer
	334	376	Camacho, Vidal A		Head	M	Cha	38.0	Wd		Y	Y	Guam	Guam	Guam	N	Shoe maker
	334	376	Camacho, Vicente P		Son	M	Cha	12.0	S	Y	Y	Y	Guam	Guam	Guam	Y	None
	334	376	Camacho, Silvestre P		Son	M	Cha	11.0	S	Y	Y	Y	Guam	Guam	Guam	Y	None
	334	376	Camacho, Ignacia P		Daughter	F	Cha	6.0	S	N			Guam	Guam	Guam		None
	334	376	Camacho, Rita P		Daughter	F	Cha	2.0	S				Guam	Guam	Guam		None
	335	377	Cruz, Joaquin S		Head	M	Cha	54.0	M		Y	Y	Guam	Guam	Guam	N	Farmer
	335	377	Cruz, Maria A		Wife	F	Cha	55.0	M		N	N	Guam	Guam	Guam	N	None
	335	377	Ada, Joaquin S		Lodger	M	Cha	7.0	S				Guam	Guam	Guam		None
	336	378	Cabo, Jose D		Head	M	Fil	46.0	M		Y	Y	Guam	Phillippine Islands	Guam	Y	Chauffeur
	336	378	Cabo, Dolores C		Wife	F	Cha	45.0	M		Y	Y	Guam	Guam	Guam	N	None
	337	379	Toves, Ana I		Head	F	Cha	47.0	Wd		N	N	Guam	Guam	Guam	N	None
	337	379	Toves, Pedro I		Son	M	Cha	24.0	S		Y	Y	Guam	Guam	Guam	N	None
	337	379	Toves, Felisidad I		Daughter	F	Cha	21.0	S	N	Y	Y	Guam	Guam	Guam	N	None
	338	380	Aquino, Matias C		Head	M	Cha	42.0	Wd		Y	Y	Guam	Guam	Guam	N	Laborer
	338	380	Aquino, Vicenta M		Daughter	F	Cha	13.0	S	N	Y	Y	Guam	Guam	Guam	Y	None
	338	380	Aquino, Rosa M		Daughter	F	Cha	11.0	S	Y	Y	Y	Guam	Guam	Guam	N	None
	338	380	Aquino, Concepcion M		Daughter	F	Cha	10.0	S	Y	Y	Y	Guam	Guam	Guam	N	None
	338	380	Aquino, Ramon M		Son	M	Cha	7.0	S	Y			Guam	Guam	Guam		None
	338	380	Aquino, Rufina M		Daughter	F	Cha	5.0	S				Guam	Guam	Guam		None
	338	380	Manibusan, Vicenta R		Mother-in-law	F	Cha	52.0	Wd		N	N	Guam	Unknown	Guam	N	None
	338	380	Manibusan, Maria M		Sister-in-law	F	Cha	27.0	S				Guam	Guam	Guam	N	None
	339	381	Pangelinan, Joaquin C		Head	M	Cha	48.0	M		Y	Y	Guam	Guam	Guam	N	Farmer
	339	381	Pangelinan, Maria T		Wife	F	Cha	44.0	M		Y	Y	Guam	Guam	Guam	N	None

San Ignacio Street

(CHAMORRO ROOTS GENEALOGY PROJECT ™ TRANSCRIPTION)
(COMPILED/TRANSCRIBED BY BERNARD T. PUNZALAN / HTTP://WWW.CHAMORROROOTS.COM)

FOURTEENTH CENSUS OF THE UNITED STATES: 1920–POPULATION
ISLAND OF GUAM

DISTRICT 2
NAME OF PLACE Agana (City)
[Proper name and, also, name of class, as city, town, village, barrio, etc]

ENUMERATED BY ME ON THE 29th DAY OF March, 1920

Arthur W. Jackson ENUMERATOR

	Street	Dwelling No.	Family No.	NAME	RELATION	Sex	Color or race	Age	Marital	School	Read	Write	Birth this person	Birth father	Birth mother	English	OCCUPATION
	1	2	3	4	5	6	7	8	9	10	11	12	13	14	15	16	17
26	San Ignacio Street	339	381	Pangelinan, Joaquina T	Daughter	F	Cha	19.0	S	N	Y	Y	Guam	Guam	Guam	Y	None
27		339	381	Pangelinan, Lino T	Son	M	Cha	12.0	S	Y	Y	Y	Guam	Guam	Guam	Y	None
28		339	381	Pangelinan, Antonio T	Son	M	Cha	8.0	S	Y	Y		Guam	Guam	Guam	Y	None
29		340	382	Perez, Antonio F	Head	M	Cha	32.0	M		Y	Y	Guam	Guam	Guam	Y	Farmer
30		340	382	Perez, Ramona T	Wife	F	Cha	27.0	M		Y	Y	Guam	Guam	Guam	Y	None
31		340	382	Perez, Pilar T	Daughter	F	Cha	1.0	S				Guam	Guam	Guam	Y	None
32		341	383	Borja, Antonio P	Head	M	Cha	69.0	M		Y	Y	Guam	Guam	Guam	N	None
33		341	383	Borja, Ana M	Wife	F	Cha	44.0	M		N	N	Guam	Guam	Guam	N	None
34		341	383	Borja, Joaquin M	Son	M	Cha	19.0	S	N	Y	Y	Guam	Guam	Guam	Y	Farmer
35		341	383	Borja, Maria M	Daughter	F	Cha	17.0	S	N	Y	Y	Guam	Guam	Guam	Y	None
36		341	383	Borja, Rosa M	Daughter	F	Cha	13.0	S	N	Y	Y	Guam	Guam	Guam	Y	None
37		341	383	Borja, Pedro M	Son	M	Cha	9.0	S	Y	Y	Y	Guam	Guam	Guam	Y	None
38		341	383	Materne, Antonio M	Brother-in-law	M	Cha	33.0	S		Y	Y	Guam	Guam	Guam	N	Barber
39	Santa Cruz Street	342	384	Baza, Maria C	Head	F	Cha	45.0	Wd		Y	Y	Guam	Guam	Guam	N	None
40		342	384	Baza, Jesus C	Son	M	Cha	28.0	S		Y	Y	Guam	Guam	Guam	N	Farmer
41		342	384	Baza, Ana C	Daughter	F	Cha	18.0	S	N	Y	Y	Guam	Guam	Guam	Y	None
42		342	384	Baza, Juan C	Son	M	Cha	13.0	S	Y	Y	Y	Guam	Guam	Guam	Y	None
43		342	384	Baza, Vicente C	Son	M	Cha	11.0	S	Y	Y	Y	Guam	Guam	Guam	N	None
44		342	384	Baza, Ignacio C	Son	M	Cha	8.0	S	Y			Guam	Guam	Guam	N	None
45		343	385	Baza, Manuel C	Head	M	Cha	19.0	M	N	Y	Y	Guam	Guam	Guam	Y	Farmer
46		343	385	Baza, Maria LG	Wife	F	Cha	22.0	M		Y	Y	Guam	Guam	Guam	N	None
47		343	385	Baza, Jose LG	Son	M	Cha	0.1	S				Guam	Guam	Guam	N	None
48		344	386	Pangelinan, Silvino D	Head	M	Cha	44.0	M		Y	Y	Guam	Guam	Guam	N	Carpenter
49		344	386	Pangelinan, Maria P	Wife	F	Cha	45.0	M		Y	Y	Guam	Guam	Guam	N	None
50		345	387	Camacho, Juan F	Head	M	Cha	35.0	M		Y	Y	Guam	Guam	Guam	N	Farmer

(CHAMORRO ROOTS GENEALOGY PROJECT ™ TRANSCRIPTION)
(COMPILED/TRANSCRIBED BY BERNARD T. PUNZALAN / HTTP://WWW.CHAMORROROOTS.COM)
FOURTEENTH CENSUS OF THE UNITED STATES: 1920-POPULATION
ISLAND OF GUAM

DISTRICT 2
NAME OF PLACE **Agana** (City)

[Proper name and, also, name of class, as city, town, village, barrio, etc]

ENUMERATED BY ME ON THE 29th DAY OF March, 1920

Arthur W. Jackson ENUMERATOR

	PLACE OF ABODE				NAME	RELATION	PERSONAL DESCRIPTION					EDUCATION			NATIVITY				OCCUPATION
Street, avenue, road, etc.	Number of dwelling house is order of visitation	Number of family in order of visitation			of each person whose place of abode on January 1, 1920, was in the family. Enter surname, firs, then given name and middle initial. If any. Include every person living on January 1, 1920. Omit children born since January 1, 1920.	Relationship of this Person to the head of the family.	Sex	Color or race	Age at last birthday	Single, married, widowed or divorced	Attended school any time since Sept. 1, 1919	Whether able to read.	Whether able to write.	Place of birth of this person.	Place of birth of father of this person.	Place of birth of mother of this person.	Whether able to speak English.	Trade, profession, or particular kind of work done, as salesman, laborer, clerk, cook, merchant, washerwoman, etc.
1	2	3			4	5	6	7	8	9	10	11	12	13	14	15	16	17
	345	387			Camacho, Ana M	Wife	F	Cha	37.0	M	Y	Y		Guam	Unknown	Guam	N	None
	345	387			Camacho, Cecilio M	Son	M	Cha	7.0	S	Y			Guam	Guam	Guam		None
	345	387			Camacho, Joaquin M	Son	M	Cha	4.0	S				Guam	Guam	Guam		None
	345	387			Camacho, Maria M	Daughter	F	Cha	2.0	S				Guam	Guam	Guam		None
	345	387			Mesa, Ana F	Servant	F	Cha	19.0	S	N	Y	Y	Guam	Guam	Guam	Y	Servant
	345	387			Mesa, Nicolasa	Lodger	F	Cha	73.0	S		N	N	Guam	Unknown	Guam	N	None
	346	388			Ada, Felix B	Head	M	Cha	64.0	Wd		Y	Y	Guam	Guam	Guam	Y	Foreman
	346	388			Ada, Maria F	Daughter	F	Cha	30.0	S		Y	Y	Guam	Guam	Guam	N	None
	346	388			Ada, Carmen F	Daughter	F	Cha	27.0	S		Y	Y	Guam	Guam	Guam	N	None
	346	388			Ada, Antonio F	Son	M	Cha	26.0	S	N	Y	Y	Guam	Guam	Guam	N	None
	346	388			Ada, Ignacio F	Son	M	Cha	34.0	Wd		Y	Y	Guam	Guam	Guam	N	Farmer
	346	388			Ada, Rosa S	Grand daughter	F	Cha	13.0	S	N	Y	Y	Guam	Guam	Guam	Y	None
	346	388			Ada, Maria S	Grand daughter	F	Cha	11.0	S	Y	Y	Y	Guam	Guam	Guam	N	None
	346	388			Ada, Joaquin S	Grand son	M	Cha	7.0	S	Y			Guam	Guam	Guam		None
	346	388			Ada, Antonio S	Grand son	M	Cha	5.0	S	N			Guam	Guam	Guam		None
	346	388			Ada, Manuel S	Grand son	M	Cha	9.0	S	Y			Guam	Guam	Guam		None
Santa Cruz Street	347	389			Cruz, Herminihildo G	Head	M	Cha	40.0	M		Y	Y	Guam	Guam	Guam	N	Shoe maker
	347	389			Cruz, Ana A	Wife	F	Cha	33.0	M		Y	Y	Guam	Guam	Guam	N	None
	347	389			Cruz, Rosa A	Daughter	F	Cha	16.0	S	N	Y	Y	Guam	Guam	Guam	Y	None
	347	389			Cruz, Candaleria A	Daughter	F	Cha	14.0	S	N	Y	Y	Guam	Guam	Guam	Y	None
	347	389			Cruz, Vicente A	Son	M	Cha	13.0	S	Y	Y	Y	Guam	Guam	Guam	Y	None
	347	389			Cruz, Soledad A	Daughter	F	Cha	11.0	S	N	Y	Y	Guam	Guam	Guam	N	None
	347	389			Cruz, Maria A	Daughter	F	Cha	4.0	S				Guam	Guam	Guam		None
	347	389			Cruz, Jose A	Son	M	Cha	2.0	S				Guam	Guam	Guam		None
	348	390			Aguon, Vicente C	Head	M	Cha	60.0	M		Y	Y	Guam	Guam	Guam	N	Farmer

(CHAMORRO ROOTS GENEALOGY PROJECT ™ TRANSCRIPTION)
(COMPILED/TRANSCRIBED BY BERNARD T. PUNZALAN / HTTP://WWW.CHAMORROROOTS.COM)

146b

FOURTEENTH CENSUS OF THE UNITED STATES: 1920—POPULATION
ISLAND OF GUAM

ENUMERATED BY ME ON THE 30th DAY OF March, 1920

Arthur W. Jackson ENUMERATOR

DISTRICT 2
NAME OF PLACE Agana (City)

[Proper name and, also, name of class, as city, town, village, barrio, etc]

	Dwelling No.	Family No.	NAME	RELATION	Sex	Color or race	Age	Single, married, widowed, divorced	Attended school since Sept. 1, 1919	Able to read	Able to write	Birthplace of person	Birthplace of father	Birthplace of mother	Able to speak English	OCCUPATION
	1/2	3	4	5	6	7	8	9	10	11	12	13	14	15	16	17
26	348	390	Aguon, Rosa V	Wife	F	Cha	55.0	M		N	N	Guam	Guam	Guam	N	None
27	349	391	Cruz, Caridad S	Head	F	Cha	22.0	S		Y	Y	Guam	Guam	Guam	Y	None
28	349	391	Cruz, Pedro S	Brother	M	Cha	21.0	S	N	Y	Y	Guam	Guam	Guam	Y	Chauffeur
29	349	391	Cruz, Manuel S	Brother	M	Cha	19.0	S	N	Y	Y	Guam	Guam	Guam	Y	Laborer
30	349	391	Cruz, Rosa S	Sister	F	Cha	14.0	S	N	Y	Y	Guam	Guam	Guam	N	None
31	349	391	Cruz, Priciosa S	Sister	F	Cha	11.0	S	Y	Y	Y	Guam	Guam	Guam	N	None
32	349	391	Cruz, Potenciana S	Sister	F	Cha	9.0	S	Y			Guam	Guam	Guam		None
33	349	391	Cruz, Isabel S	Sister	F	Cha	8.0	S	Y			Guam	Guam	Guam		None
34	350	392	Manibusan, Nicolas C	Head	M	Cha	55.0	M		Y	Y	Guam	Guam	Guam	N	Carpenter
35	350	392	Manibusan, Maria M	Wife	F	Cha	54.0	M		N	N	Guam	Guam	Guam	N	None
36	350	392	Manibusan, Magdalena M	Daughter	F	Cha	19.0	S	N	Y	Y	Guam	Guam	Guam	Y	None
37	350	392	Manibusan, Felicita M	Daughter	F	Cha	18.0	S	N	Y	Y	Guam	Guam	Guam	Y	None
38	350	392	Manibusan, Antonio M	Son	M	Cha	16.0	S	N	Y	Y	Guam	Guam	Guam	Y	None
39	350	392	Manibusan, Jose M	Son	M	Cha	14.0	S	N	Y	Y	Guam	Guam	Guam	Y	None
40	351	393	Camacho, Jose G	Head	M	Cha	23.0	M		Y	Y	Guam	Guam	Guam	Y	Farmer
41	351	393	Camacho, Ana M	Wife	F	Cha	22.0	M		Y	Y	Guam	Guam	Guam	Y	None
42	351	393	Camacho, Josefina M	Daughter	F	Cha	0.2	S				Guam	Guam	Guam		None
43	351	393	Mendiola, Pedro B	Lodger	M	Cha	87.0	Wd		N	N	Guam	Guam	Guam	N	None
44	351	393	Guzman, Jose M	Lodger	M	Cha	25.0	S		Y	Y	Guam	Guam	Guam	Y	Blacksmith
45	352	394	Castro, Jose R	Head	M	Cha	58.0	Wd		Y	Y	Guam	Guam	Guam	N	Farmer
46	353	395	Flores, Vicente A	Head	M	Cha	52.0	D		Y	Y	Guam	Guam	Guam	Y	Chauffeur
47	353	395	Taitano, Ramon SN	Head	M	Cha	39.0	M		Y	Y	Guam	Guam	Guam	Y	Machinist
48	353	395	Taitano, Dolores F	Wife	F	Cha	30.0	M		Y	Y	Guam	Guam	Guam	Y	None
49	353	395	Taitano, Alfredo F	Son	M	Cha	10.0	S	Y	Y	Y	Guam	Guam	Guam	N	None
50	353	395	Taitano, Roberto F	Son	M	Cha	9.0	S	Y	Y	Y	Guam	Guam	Guam	Y	None

Street: Santa Cruz Street

(CHAMORRO ROOTS GENEALOGY PROJECT ™ TRANSCRIPTION)
(COMPILED/TRANSCRIBED BY BERNARD T. PUNZALAN / HTTP://WWW.CHAMORROROOTS.COM)

FOURTEENTH CENSUS OF THE UNITED STATES: 1920–POPULATION
ISLAND OF GUAM

DISTRICT 2
NAME OF PLACE Agana (City)
[Proper name and, also, name of class, as city, town, village, barrio, etc]

ENUMERATED BY ME ON THE 30th DAY OF March, 1920

Arthur W. Jackson ENUMERATOR

	PLACE OF ABODE		NAME	RELATION	PERSONAL DESCRIPTION				EDUCATION			NATIVITY				OCCUPATION
Street, avenue, road, etc.	Number of dwelling house in order of visitation	Number of family in order of visitation	Name of each person whose place of abode on January 1, 1920, was in the family.	Relationship of this person to the head of the family.	Sex	Color or race	Age at last birthday	Single, married, widowed or divorced	Attended school any time since Sept. 1, 1919	Whether able to read.	Whether able to write.	Place of birth of this person.	Place of birth of father of this person.	Place of birth of mother of this person.	Whether able to speak English.	Trade, profession, or particular kind of work done, as salesman, laborer, clerk, cook, merchant, washerwoman, etc.
1	2	3	4	5	6	7	8	9	10	11	12	13	14	15	16	17
	353	395	Taitano, Jorge F	Son	M	Cha	6.0	S	N			Guam	Guam	Guam		None
	353	395	Taitano, Delfina F	Daughter	F	Cha	4.0	S				Guam	Guam	Guam		None
	353	395	Taitano, Elminia F	Daughter	F	Cha	2.0	S				Guam	Guam	Guam		None
	353	395	Pablo, Dolores B	Servant	F	Cha	20.0	S	N	Y	Y	Guam	Guam	Guam	Y	None
	354	396	Tenorio, Joaquin S	Head	M	Cha	50.0	M		Y	Y	Guam	Guam	Guam	N	Farmer
	354	396	Tenorio, Maria Q	Wife	F	Cha	36.0	M		Y	Y	Guam	Guam	Guam	N	None
	354	396	Tenorio, Jose Q	Son	M	Cha	18.0	S	N	Y	Y	Guam	Guam	Guam	Y	None
	354	396	Tenorio, Maria Q	Daughter	F	Cha	17.0	S	N	Y	Y	Guam	Guam	Guam	Y	None
	354	396	Tenorio, Jesus Q	Son	M	Cha	14.0	S	N	Y	Y	Guam	Guam	Guam	Y	None
	354	396	Tenorio, Joaquin Q	Son	M	Cha	12.0	S	Y	Y	Y	Guam	Guam	Guam	Y	None
	354	396	Tenorio, Francisco Q	Son	M	Cha	10.0	S	Y	Y	Y	Guam	Guam	Guam	Y	None
	354	396	Tenorio, Ana B. Q	Daughter	F	Cha	7.0	S	Y			Guam	Guam	Guam		None
Santa Cruz Street	354	396	Tenorio, Ramon Q	Son	M	Cha	4.0	S				Guam	Guam	Guam		None
	354	396	Tenorio, Juan Q	Son	M	Cha	2.0	S				Guam	Guam	Guam		None
	354	396	Benavente, Josefa C	Aunt	F	Cha	70.0	S		N	N	Guam	Guam	Guam	N	None
	355	397	Sakai, Juan	Head	M	Jp	35.0	M		Y	Y	Japan	Japan	Japan	Y	Blacksmith
	355	397	Sakai, Rita F	Wife	F	Cha	24.0	M		Y	Y	Guam	Guam	Guam	N	None
	355	397	Sakai, Ana F	Daughter	F	Jp	1.0	S				Guam	Japan	Guam		None
	356	398	Garrido, Juan M	Head	M	Cha	54.0	M		Y	Y	Guam	Guam	Guam	N	Farmer
	356	398	Garrido, Dolores M	Wife	F	Cha	51.0	M		N	N	Guam	Guam	Guam	N	None
	356	398	Garrido, Jesus M	Son	M	Cha	24.0	S		Y	Y	Guam	Guam	Guam	Y	Laborer
	356	398	Garrido, Joaquin M	Son	M	Cha	22.0	S		Y	Y	Guam	Guam	Guam	Y	Farm laborer
	356	398	Garrido, Maria M	Daughter	F	Cha	20.0	S	N	Y	Y	Guam	Guam	Guam	N	None
	356	398	Garrido, Ana M	Daughter	F	Cha	17.0	S	N	Y	Y	Guam	Guam	Guam	Y	None
	357	399	Chargualaf, Getrudes R	Head	F	Cha	52.0	Wd		Y	Y	Guam	Guam	Guam	N	None

(CHAMORRO ROOTS GENEALOGY PROJECT ™ TRANSCRIPTION)
(COMPILED/TRANSCRIBED BY BERNARD T. PUNZALAN / HTTP://WWW.CHAMORROROOTS.COM)

FOURTEENTH CENSUS OF THE UNITED STATES: 1920–POPULATION

ISLAND OF GUAM

ENUMERATED BY ME ON THE 30th DAY OF March, 1920

Arthur W. Jackson ENUMERATOR

DISTRICT 2

NAME OF PLACE Agana (City)

[Proper name and, also, name of class, as city, town, village, barrio, etc]

	1 Street	2 Dwelling	3 Family	4 NAME	5 RELATION	6 Sex	7 Color or race	8 Age	9 Single, married	10 Attended school	11 Read	12 Write	13 Birth person	14 Birth father	15 Birth mother	16 Speak English	17 OCCUPATION
26		357	399	Chargualaf, Jose R	Son	M	Cha	20.0	S	N	Y	Y	Guam	Guam	Guam	Y	Oiler
27		357	399	Chargualaf, Vicente R	Son	M	Cha	16.0	S	N	Y	Y	Guam	Guam	Guam	Y	Farm laborer
28		357	400	Mesa, Juan G	Head	M	Cha	26.0	M		Y	Y	Guam	Guam	Guam	Y	Farmer
29		357	400	Mesa, Maria C	Wife	F	Cha	26.0	M		Y	Y	Guam	Guam	Guam	Y	None
30		357	400	Mesa, Juan C	Son	M	Cha	3.0	S				Guam	Guam	Guam		None
31		357	400	Mesa, Francisco C	Son	M	Cha	0.1	S				Guam	Guam	Guam		None
32		358	401	Un Cangco, Vicente T	Head	M	Cha	52.0	M		Y	Y	Guam	China	Guam	N	Farmer
33		358	401	Un Cangco, Rosa L	Wife	F	Cha	58.0	M		Y	Y	Guam	Guam	Guam	N	None
34		358	401	Un Cangco, Pedro L	Son	M	Cha	20.0	S	N	Y	Y	Guam	Guam	Guam	Y	Farm laborer
35		358	401	Un Cangco, Maria L	Daughter	F	Cha	16.0	S	N	Y	Y	Guam	Guam	Guam	Y	None
36		359	402	Garrido, Jose M	Head	M	Cha	27.0	M		N	N	Guam	Guam	Guam	N	Laborer
37		359	402	Garrido, Maria B	Wife	F	Cha	26.0	M		Y	N	Guam	Guam	Guam	N	None
38	Santa Cruz Street	359	402	Garrido, Enrique B	Son	M	Cha	4.0	S				Guam	Guam	Guam		None
39		359	402	Garrido, Jesus B	Son	M	Cha	2.0	S				Guam	Guam	Guam		None
40		359	402	Garrido, Antonia B	Daughter	F	Cha	1.0	S				Guam	Guam	Guam		None
41		360	403	Maanao, Dolores I	Head	F	Cha	42.0	Wd		Y	Y	Guam	Guam	Guam	N	None
42		360	403	Maanao, Jose I	Son	M	Cha	16.0	S	N	Y	Y	Guam	Guam	Guam	Y	Laborer
43		360	403	Maanao, Gregorio I	Son	M	Cha	14.0	S	N	Y	Y	Guam	Guam	Guam	Y	Farm laborer
44		360	403	Maanao, Maria I	Daughter	F	Cha	10.0	S	Y	Y	Y	Guam	Guam	Guam	N	None
45		360	403	Maanao, Rosalia I	Daughter	F	Cha	6.0	S	N			Guam	Guam	Guam		None
46		360	403	Maanao, Artemio I	Son	M	Cha	2.0	S				Guam	Guam	Guam		None
47		361	404	Taitano, Juan W	Head	M	Cha	29.0	M		Y	Y	Guam	Guam	Guam	Y	Foreman
48		361	404	Taitano, Maria T	Wife	F	Cha	28.0	M		Y	Y	Guam	Guam	Guam	N	None
49		361	404	Taitano, Julita T	Daughter	F	Cha	9.0	S	Y	Y	Y	Guam	Guam	Guam		None
50		361	404	Taitano, Rosario T	Daughter	F	Cha	6.0	S	N			Guam	Guam	Guam		None

(CHAMORRO ROOTS GENEALOGY PROJECT ™ TRANSCRIPTION)
(COMPILED/TRANSCRIBED BY BERNARD T. PUNZALAN / HTTP://WWW.CHAMORROROOTS.COM)

FOURTEENTH CENSUS OF THE UNITED STATES: 1920-POPULATION
ISLAND OF GUAM

SHEET NO. 44A

DISTRICT 2

NAME OF PLACE Agana (City)
[Proper name and, also, name of class, as city, town, village, barrio, etc]

ENUMERATED BY ME ON THE 31st DAY OF March, 1920

Arthur W. Jackson ENUMERATOR

	Dwelling	Family	NAME	RELATION	Sex	Color or race	Age	Single, married, widowed or divorced	Attended school since Sept. 1, 1919	Read	Write	Place of birth of this person	Place of birth of father	Place of birth of mother	Speak English	OCCUPATION
1	361	404	Taitano, Jorge T	Son	M	Cha	5.0	S	N			Guam	Guam	Guam		None
2	361	404	Taitano, Guillermo T	Son	M	Cha	3.0	S				Guam	Guam	Guam		None
3	361	404	Taitano, Rita W	Mother	F	Cha	55.0	Wd		Y	Y	Guam	Guam	Guam	N	None
4	361	404	Taitano, Francisco W	Brother	M	Cha	16.0	S	N	Y	Y	Guam	Guam	Guam	Y	Cook
5	361	404	Mendiola, Maria T	Sister	F	Cha	27.0	Wd		Y	Y	Guam	Guam	Guam	N	None
6	362	405	Borja, Juan S	Head	M	Cha	31.0	M		Y	Y	Guam	Guam	Guam	Y	Electrician
7	362	405	Borja, Dolores C	Wife	F	Cha	27.0	M		Y	Y	Guam	Guam	Guam	N	None
8	362	405	Borja, Francisco C	Son	M	Cha	5.0	S	N			Guam	Guam	Guam		None
9	362	405	Borja, Vicente C	Son	M	Cha	4.0	S				Guam	Guam	Guam		None
10	362	405	Borja, Delfina C	Daughter	F	Cha	3.0	S				Guam	Guam	Guam		None
11	362	405	Borja, Juan C	Son	M	Cha	2.0	S				Guam	Guam	Guam		None
12	363	406	de Leon Guerrero, Justo S	Head	M	Cha	75.0	Wd		Y	Y	Guam	Guam	Guam	N	None
13	363	406	de Leon Guerrero, Maria P	Head	F	Cha	36.0	Wd		Y	Y	Guam	Unknown	Guam	N	None
14	363	406	de Leon Guerrero, Maria P	Daughter	F	Cha	12.0	S	Y	Y	Y	Guam	Guam	Guam	Y	None
15	363	406	de Leon Guerrero, Jesus P	Son	M	Cha	12.0	S	Y	Y	Y	Guam	Guam	Guam	Y	None
16	363	406	de Leon Guerrero, Francisca P	Daughter	F	Cha	10.0	S	Y	Y	Y	Guam	Guam	Guam	N	None
17	363	406	de Leon Guerrero, Ana P	Daughter	F	Cha	8.0	S	Y			Guam	Guam	Guam		None
18	363	406	de Leon Guerrero, Jose P	Son	M	Cha	7.0	S	Y			Guam	Guam	Guam		None
19	363	406	de Leon Guerrero, Getrudes P	Daughter	F	Cha	3.0	S				Guam	Guam	Guam		None
20	363	406	de Leon Guerrero, Dolores P	Daughter	F	Cha	2.0	S				Guam	Guam	Guam		None
21	363	406	de Leon Guerrero, Joaquin P	Son	M	Cha	1.0	S				Guam	Guam	Guam		None
22	363	406	Perez, Francisco	Brother	M	Cha	39.0	S		Y	Y	Guam	Unknown	Unknown	N	Farmer
23	363	406	Perez, Concepcion	Sister	F	Cha	27.0	S		Y	Y	Guam	Unknown	Unknown	N	None
24	364	408	Mesa, Francisco G	Head	M	Cha	36.0	M		Y	Y	Guam	Guam	Guam	N	Shoe maker
25	364	408	Mesa, Rosario C	Wife	F	Cha	36.0	M		Y	Y	Guam	Guam	Guam	N	None

Street: Santa Cruz Street

(CHAMORRO ROOTS GENEALOGY PROJECT ™ TRANSCRIPTION)
(COMPILED/TRANSCRIBED BY BERNARD T. PUNZALAN / HTTP://WWW.CHAMORROROOTS.COM)

148b

SHEET NO. _44B_

FOURTEENTH CENSUS OF THE UNITED STATES: 1920-POPULATION

ISLAND OF GUAM

ENUMERATED BY ME ON THE 31st DAY OF March, 1920

Arthur W. Jackson ENUMERATOR

DISTRICT 2
NAME OF PLACE Agana (City)
[Proper name and, also, name of class, as city, town, village, barrio, etc]

	PLACE OF ABODE			NAME	RELATION	PERSONAL DESCRIPTION					EDUCATION			NATIVITY				OCCUPATION
Street, avenue, road, etc.	Number of dwelling house in order of visitation	Number of family in order of visitation		Name	Relationship of this Person to the head of the family.	Sex	Color or race	Age at last birthday	Single, married, widowed or divorced	Attended school any time since Sept. 1, 1919	Whether able to read.	Whether able to write.	Place of birth of this person.	Place of birth of father of this person.	Place of birth of mother of this person.	Whether able to speak English.	Trade, profession, or particular kind of work done, as salesman, laborer, clerk, cook, merchant, washerwoman, etc.
1	2	3	4		5	6	7	8	9	10	11	12	13	14	15	16	17
	364	408		Mesa, Eduardo C	Son	M	Cha	10.0	S	Y	Y		Guam	Guam	Guam	N	None
	364	408		Mesa, Vicente C	Son	M	Cha	9.0	S	Y	Y		Guam	Guam	Guam	N	None
	365	409		Soriano, Enrique	Head	M	Cha	27.0	M		Y	Y	Guam	Unknown	Guam	Y	Carpenter
	365	409		Soriano, Rita G	Wife	F	Cha	29.0	M		Y	Y	Guam	Guam	Guam	N	None
	365	409		Soriano, Lucia G	Daughter	F	Cha	4.0	S				Guam	Guam	Guam		None
	365	409		Soriano, Jose G	Son	M	Cha	3.0	S				Guam	Guam	Guam		None
	365	409		Soriano, Miguel G	Son	M	Cha	0.1	S				Guam	Guam	Guam		None
	366	410		Reyes, Dolores R	Head	F	Cha	47.0	M		N	N	Guam	Unknown	Guam	N	None
	366	410		Indalecio, Jose R	Nephew	M	Cha	11.0	S	N	Y	Y	Guam	Unknown	Guam	N	None
	366	410		Indalecio, Rita R	Niece	F	Cha	9.0	S	Y	Y	Y	Guam	Guam	Guam	Y	Carpenter
	367	411		Garcia, Antonio SN	Head	M	Cha	25.0	M	N	Y	Y	Guam	Guam	Guam	N	None
	367	411		Garcia, Ana F	Wife	F	Cha	20.0	M	N	Y	Y	Guam	Guam	Guam	N	None
	367	411		Garcia, Francisco F	Son	M	Cha	3.0	S				Guam	Guam	Guam		None
	367	411		Garcia, Maria F	Daughter	F	Cha	1.0	S				Guam	Guam	Guam		None
	367	411		Garcia, Demetro LG	Father	M	Cha	59.0	Wd		Y	Y	Guam	Guam	Guam	N	Farmer
	367	411		Garcia, Trinidad SN	Sister	F	Cha	20.0	S	N	Y	Y	Guam	Guam	Guam	Y	None
	367	412		Garrido, Maria G	Head	F	Cha	36.0	Wd		Y	Y	Guam	Guam	Guam	N	None
	367	412		Garrido, Isabel G	Daughter	F	Cha	12.0	S	Y	Y	Y	Guam	Guam	Guam	Y	None
	367	412		Garrido, Jose G	Son	M	Cha	10.0	S	Y	Y	Y	Guam	Guam	Guam	N	None
	367	412		Garrido, Maria G	Daughter	F	Cha	8.0	S	Y	Y	Y	Guam	Guam	Guam	N	None
	368	413		Charfauros, Bardovina D	Head	M	Cha	57.0	M		Y	Y	Guam	Guam	Guam	N	Stone mason
	368	413		Charfauros, Maria G	Wife	F	Cha	51.0	M		N	N	Guam	Guam	Guam	N	None
	369	414		Gutierrez, Tomas C	Head	M	W	42.0	M		Y	Y	Guam	Spain	Guam	N	Farmer
	369	414		Gutierrez, Maria T	Wife	F	Cha	42.0	M		Y	Y	Guam	Guam	Guam	N	None
	369	414		Gutierrez, Agueda T	Daughter	F	W	20.0	S		Y	Y	Guam	Guam	Guam	Y	Teacher

Santa Cruz Street

300

(CHAMORRO ROOTS GENEALOGY PROJECT ™ TRANSCRIPTION)
(COMPILED/TRANSCRIBED BY BERNARD T. PUNZALAN / HTTP://WWW.CHAMORROROOTS.COM)

FOURTEENTH CENSUS OF THE UNITED STATES: 1920-POPULATION
ISLAND OF GUAM

DISTRICT 2
NAME OF PLACE Agana (City)

[Proper name and, also, name of class, as city, town, village, barrio, etc]

ENUMERATED BY ME ON THE 31st DAY OF March, 1920

Arthur W. Jackson ENUMERATOR

	PLACE OF ABODE			NAME	RELATION	PERSONAL DESCRIPTION				EDUCATION			NATIVITY				OCCUPATION
Street, avenue, road, etc.	Number of dwelling house is in order of visitation	Number of family in order of visitation		Name of each person whose place of abode on January 1, 1920, was in the family. Enter surname, first, then given name and middle initial. If any. Include every person living on January 1, 1920. Omit children born since January 1, 1920.	Relationship of this Person to the head of the family.	Sex	Color or race	Age at last birthday	Single, married, widowed or divorced	Attended school any time since Sept. 1, 1919	Whether able to read.	Whether able to write.	Place of birth of this person.	Place of birth of father of this person.	Place of birth of mother of this person.	Whether able to speak English.	Trade, profession, or particular kind of work done, as salesman, laborer, clerk, cook, merchant, washerwoman, etc.
1	2	3		4	5	6	7	8	9	10	11	12	13	14	15	16	17
	369	414		Gutierrez, Maria T	Daughter	F	W	18.0	S	Y	Y	Y	Guam	Guam	Guam	Y	Teacher
	369	414		Gutierrez, Jane T	Daughter	F	W	16.0	S	Y	Y	Y	Guam	Guam	Guam	Y	None
	369	414		Gutierrez, Rosa T	Daughter	F	W	15.0	S	Y	Y	Y	Guam	Guam	Guam	Y	None
	369	414		Gutierrez, Ana T	Daughter	F	W	13.0	S	Y	Y	Y	Guam	Guam	Guam	Y	None
	369	414		Gutierrez, Frederico T	Son	M	W	12.0	S	Y	Y	Y	Guam	Guam	Guam	Y	None
	369	414		Gutierrez, Julia T	Daughter	F	W	11.0	S	Y	Y	Y	Guam	Guam	Guam	Y	None
	369	414		Gutierrez, Jose T	Son	M	W	9.0	S	Y	Y	Y	Guam	Guam	Guam		None
	369	414		Gutierrez, Antonia T	Daughter	F	W	8.0	S	Y			Guam	Guam	Guam		None
	369	414		Gutierrez, Tomas T	Son	M	W	7.0	S	Y			Guam	Guam	Guam		None
	369	414		Gutierrez, Angusta T	Daughter	F	W	5.0	S	N			Guam	Guam	Guam		None
	369	414		Gutierrez, Agosto T	Son	M	W	4.0	S				Guam	Guam	Guam		None
	369	414		Gutierrez, Carlos T	Son	M	W	3.0	S				Guam	Guam	Guam		None
	369	414		Gutierrez, Grace T	Daughter	F	W	2.0	S				Guam	Guam	Guam		None
	369	414		Aflague, Josefa P	Lodger	F	Cha	74.0	Wd		N	N	Guam	Guam	Guam	N	None
Santa Cruz Street	370	415		Leon Guerrero, Vicente P	Head	M	Cha	42.0	S		Y	Y	Guam	Guam	Guam	Y	Blacksmith
	370	415		Leon Guerrero, Maria P	Sister	F	Cha	29.0	S		Y	Y	Guam	Guam	Guam	Y	None
	370	415		Leon Guerrero, Jose P	Brother	M	Cha	26.0	S		Y	Y	Guam	Guam	Guam	Y	Blacksmith
	370	415		Santos, Jesus S	Servant	M	Cha	33.0	S		Y	Y	Guam	Guam	Guam	N	Servant
	370	415		Aquininog, Joaquina	Servant	F	Cha	20.0	S		N	N	Guam	Unknown	Guam	N	Servant
	371	416		Blaz, Rosa C	Head	F	Cha	28.0	M	N	N	N	Guam	Guam	Guam	N	None
	371	416		Blaz, Francisco B	Son	M	Cha	12.0	S	Y	Y	Y	Guam	Guam	Guam		None
	371	416		Blaz, Jose C	Son	M	Cha	10.0	S	Y	Y	Y	Guam	Guam	Guam		None
	371	416		Blaz, Josefa C	Daughter	F	Cha	8.0	S	Y	Y	Y	Guam	Guam	Guam		None
	371	416		Blaz, Lourdes C	Daughter	F	Cha	6.0	S	N			Guam	Guam	Guam		None
	371	416		Blaz, Domingo C	Son	M	Cha	1.0	S				Guam	Guam	Guam		None

(CHAMORRO ROOTS GENEALOGY PROJECT ™ TRANSCRIPTION)

(COMPILED/TRANSCRIBED BY BERNARD T. PUNZALAN / HTTP://WWW.CHAMORROROOTS.COM)

FOURTEENTH CENSUS OF THE UNITED STATES: 1920–POPULATION

ISLAND OF GUAM

DISTRICT 2
NAME OF PLACE Agana (City)
[Proper name and, also, name of class, as city, town, village, barrio, etc]

ENUMERATED BY ME ON THE 1st DAY OF April, 1920

Arthur W. Jackson ENUMERATOR

	PLACE OF ABODE			NAME	RELATION	PERSONAL DESCRIPTION					EDUCATION			NATIVITY				OCCUPATION
Street, avenue, road, etc.	Number of dwelling house is order of visitation	Number of family in order of visitation		of each person whose place of abode on January 1, 1920, was in the family. Enter surname, firs, then given name and middle initial. If any. Include every person living on January 1, 1920. Omit children born since January 1, 1920.	Relationship of this Person to the head of the family.	Sex	Color or race	Age at last birthday	single, married, widowed or divorced	Attended school any time since Sept. 1, 1919	Whether able to read.	Whether able to write.	Place of birth of this person.	Place of birth of father of this person.	Place of birth of mother of this person.	Whether able to speak English.	Trade, profession, or particular kind of work done, as salesman, laborer, clerk, cook, merchant, washerwoman, etc.
1	2	3		4	5	6	7	8	9	10	11	12	13	14	15	16	17
26	372	417		Arceo, Maria C	Head	F	Cha	52.0	Wd		N	N	Guam	Guam	Guam	N	None
27	372	417		Arceo, Nicolasa C	Daughter	F	Cha	32.0	S		Y	Y	Guam	Guam	Guam	N	Laundress
28	372	417		Arceo, Maria C	Daughter	F	Cha	28.0	S		Y	Y	Guam	Guam	Guam	N	None
29	372	417		Arceo, Rosalia C	Daughter	F	Cha	19.0	S		Y	Y	Guam	Guam	Guam	Y	None
30	372	417		Arceo, Ignacio C	Son	M	Cha	15.0	S	N	Y	Y	Guam	Guam	Guam	Y	Farm laborer
31	372	417		Arceo, Jose C	Son	M	Cha	9.0	S	N			Guam	Guam	Guam		None
32	372	418		Cruz, Antonio	Head	M	Cha	28.0	M	Y	Y	Y	Guam	Guam	Guam	N	Farmer
33	372	418		Cruz, Carmen A	Wife	F	Cha	22.0	M		Y	Y	Guam	Guam	Guam	Y	None
34	372	418		Cruz, Juan A	Son	M	Cha	3.0	S				Guam	Guam	Guam		None
35	372	418		Cruz, Segundo A	Son	M	Cha	1.0	S				Guam	Guam	Guam		None
36	372	418		Arceo, Rosario	Niece	F	Cha	5.0	S				Guam	Unknown	Guam		None
37	373	419		Dejima, T	Head	M	Jp	34.0	S		Y	Y	Japan	Japan	Japan	Y	Merchant general retail
38	374	420		Garcia, Antonio L	Head	M	Fil	52.0	M		Y	Y	Guam	Philippine Islands	Guam	N	Farmer
39	374	420		Garcia, Gertrudes C	Wife	F	Cha	42.0	M		N	N	Guam	Guam	Guam	N	None
40	374	420		Garcia, Jesus C	Son	M	Fil	20.0	S	N	Y	Y	Guam	Guam	Guam	Y	Laborer
41	374	420		Garcia, Juan C	Son	M	Fil	17.0	S	N	Y	Y	Guam	Philippine Islands	Guam	Y	Farm laborer
42	375	421		Dungca, Felix G	Head	M	Fil	35.0	M		Y	Y	Guam	Philippine Islands	Guam	Y	Machinist
43	375	421		Dungca, Maria T	Wife	F	Cha	26.0	M		Y	Y	Guam	Guam	Guam	Y	None
44	375	421		Dungca, Josefina T	Daughter	F	Fil	11.0	S	Y	Y	Y	Guam	Guam	Guam	N	None
45	375	421		Dungca, Adela T	Daughter	F	Fil	10.0	S	Y	Y	Y	Guam	Guam	Guam	N	None
46	375	421		Dungca, Felix T	Son	M	Fil	8.0	S	Y	Y	Y	Guam	Guam	Guam		None
47	375	421		Dungca, Justo T	Son	M	Fil	6.0	S	N			Guam	Guam	Guam		None
48	375	421		Dungca, Esparanca T	Daughter	F	Fil	3.0	S				Guam	Guam	Guam		None
49	375	421		Dungca, Felicita T	Daughter	F	Fil	1.0	S				Guam	Guam	Guam		None
50	376	422		Torres, Antonio C	Head	M	Cha	36.0	M		Y	Y	Guam	Guam	Guam	Y	Merchant general retail

Santa Cruz Street

302

(CHAMORRO ROOTS GENEALOGY PROJECT ™ TRANSCRIPTION)

(COMPILED/TRANSCRIBED BY BERNARD T. PUNZALAN / HTTP://WWW.CHAMORROROOTS.COM)

FOURTEENTH CENSUS OF THE UNITED STATES: 1920-POPULATION

ISLAND OF GUAM

150

DISTRICT 2

NAME OF PLACE Agana (City)

[Proper name and, also, name of class, as city, town, village, barrio, etc]

ENUMERATED BY ME ON THE 1ˢᵗ DAY OF April, 1920

Arthur W. Jackson ENUMERATOR

Street, avenue, road, etc.	Number of dwelling house in order of visitation	Number of family in order of visitation	NAME	RELATION	Sex	Color or race	Age at last birthday	Single, married, widowed or divorced	Attended school any time since Sept. 1, 1919	Whether able to read.	Whether able to write.	Place of birth of this person.	Place of birth of father of this person.	Place of birth of mother of this person.	Whether able to speak English.	OCCUPATION
1	2	3	4	5	6	7	8	9	10	11	12	13	14	15	16	17
	376	422	Torres, Josefa C	Wife	F	Cha	35.0	M		Y	Y	Guam	Guam	Guam	N	None
	377	423	Mesa, Juana G	Head	F	Cha	54.0	Wd		N	N	Guam	Guam	Guam	N	None
	377	423	Mesa, Maria G	Daughter	F	Cha	30.0	S		Y	Y	Guam	Guam	Guam	N	None
	377	423	Mesa, Jesus G	Son	M	Cha	19.0	S	N	Y	Y	Guam	Guam	Guam	Y	Chauffeur
	377	423	Mesa, Matilde	Grand daughter	F	Cha	8.0	S	Y			Guam	Unknown	Guam		None
	377	423	Rivera, Jesus	Servant	M	Cha	10.0	S	Y	Y	Y	Guam	Guam	Guam	Y	Servant
	378	424	Rivera, Joaquin U	Head	M	Cha	49.0	Wd		Y	Y	Guam	Guam	Guam	N	Farmer
	378	425	Taison, Ana T	Head	F	Cha	42.0	Wd		Y	Y	Guam	Guam	Guam	N	None
	378	425	Taison, Socoro T	Daughter	F	Cha	21.0	S	N	Y	Y	Guam	Guam	Guam	Y	None
	378	425	Taison, Rosa T	Daughter	F	Cha	11.0	S	Y	Y	Y	Guam	Guam	Guam	N	None
	378	425	Taison, Antonio T	Son	M	Cha	9.0	S	Y			Guam	Guam	Guam		None
	378	425	Taison, Maria T	Daughter	F	Cha	3.0	S				Guam	Guam	Guam		None
	378	425	Taison, Romana	Grand daughter	F	Cha	0.4	S				Guam	Unknown	Guam		None
	379	426	Rupley, Magdalena I	Head	F	Cha	34.0	M		Y	Y	Guam	Philippine Islands	Guam	Y	None
	379	426	Rupley, Juan I	Son	M	W	14.0	S	N	Y	Y	Guam	United States	Guam	Y	App. Carpenter
	380	427	Cruz, Josefa A	Head	F	Cha	70.0	Wd		Y	Y	Guam	Guam	Guam	N	None
	380	427	Cruz, Maria A	Daughter	F	Cha	47.0	S		Y	Y	Guam	Guam	Guam	N	Seamstress
	380	427	Cruz, Rosa A	Daughter	F	Cha	42.0	S		Y	Y	Guam	Guam	Guam	N	None
	380	427	Cruz, Jose A	Son	M	Cha	37.0	S		Y	Y	Guam	Guam	Guam	N	Farmer
	380	427	Santos, Maria	Servant	F	Cha	23.0	S		Y	Y	Guam	Unknown	Guam	Y	Servant
	381	428	Arceo, Gregorio C	Head	M	Cha	28.0	M		Y	Y	Guam	Guam	Guam	Y	Enlisted US Navy not an Am citizen
	381	428	Arceo, Joaquina T	Wife	F	Cha	27.0	M		Y	Y	Guam	Guam	Guam	N	None
	381	428	Arceo, Trinidad T	Daughter	F	Cha	0.5	S		Y	Y	Guam	Guam	Guam		None
Santa Cruz Street	382	429	Mesa, Vicente de la R	Head	M	Cha	50.0	M		Y	Y	Guam	Guam	Guam	N	Farmer
	382	429	Mesa, Dolores R	Wife	F	Cha	54.0	M		Y	Y	Guam	Guam	Philippine Islands	N	None

(CHAMORRO ROOTS GENEALOGY PROJECT ™ TRANSCRIPTION)
(COMPILED/TRANSCRIBED BY BERNARD T. PUNZALAN / HTTP://WWW.CHAMORROROOTS.COM)
FOURTEENTH CENSUS OF THE UNITED STATES: 1920-POPULATION
ISLAND OF GUAM

DISTRICT 2
NAME OF PLACE Agana (City)
[Proper name and, also, name of class, as city, town, village, barrio, etc]

ENUMERATED BY ME ON THE 1st DAY OF April, 1920

Arthur W. Jackson ENUMERATOR

	Dwelling (2)	Family (3)	NAME (4)	RELATION (5)	Sex (6)	Color (7)	Age (8)	Marital (9)	School (10)	Read (11)	Write (12)	Birthplace (13)	Father (14)	Mother (15)	English (16)	OCCUPATION (17)
26	382	479	Mesa, Ascencion R	Daughter	F	Cha	20.0	S	N	Y	Y	Guam	Guam	Guam	Y	None
27	382	479	Mesa, Josefina R	Daughter	F	Cha	16.0	S	N	Y	Y	Guam	Guam	Guam	Y	None
28	382	479	Mesa, Tomas R	Son	M	Cha	12.0	S	Y	Y	Y	Guam	Guam	Guam	Y	None
29	382	479	Mesa, Benigna R	Daughter	F	Cha	10.0	S	Y	Y	Y	Guam	Guam	Guam	N	None
30	382	479	Rios, Josefa	Servant	F	Cha	19.0	S	N	Y	Y	Guam	Guam	Guam	Y	Servant
31	383	430	Flores, Antonio M	Head	M	Cha	35.0	M		Y	Y	Guam	Guam	Guam	Y	Silversmith
32	383	430	Flores, Maria LG	Wife	F	Cha	35.0	M		Y	Y	Guam	Guam	Guam	N	None
33	383	430	Flores, Juana M	Sister	F	Cha	30.0	S		Y	Y	Guam	Guam	Guam	N	Saleswoman
34	384	431	de los Santos, Felix	Head	M	Cha	62.0	M		N	N	Guam	Guam	Guam	N	Farmer
35	384	431	de los Santos, Juana G	Wife	F	Cha	56.0	M		N	N	Guam	Guam	Guam	N	None
36	384	431	de los Santos, Ana G	Daughter	F	Cha	31.0	S		Y	Y	Guam	Guam	Guam	N	None
37	384	431	de los Santos, Jose G	Son	M	Cha	27.0	S		Y	Y	Guam	Guam	Guam	N	Farmer
38	384	431	de los Santos, Felicita G	Daughter	F	Cha	24.0	S		Y	Y	Guam	Guam	Guam	N	None
39	384	431	de los Santos, Felisidad G	Daughter	F	Cha	22.0	S		Y	Y	Guam	Guam	Guam	N	None
40	384	431	de los Santos, Joaquin G	Son	M	Cha	16.0	S	N	Y	Y	Guam	Guam	Guam	Y	Farm laborer
41	385	432	Cruz, Felix	Head	M	Cha	51.0	M		Y	Y	Guam	Guam	Guam	Y	Farmer
42	385	432	Cruz, Juana C	Wife	F	Cha	37.0	M		Y	Y	Guam	Guam	Guam	N	None
43	385	432	Cruz, Ascencion C	Daughter	F	Cha	20.0	S	N	Y	Y	Guam	Guam	Guam	Y	None
44	385	432	Cruz, Maria C	Daughter	F	Cha	14.0	S	N	Y	Y	Guam	Guam	Guam	Y	None
45	385	432	Rosario, Jesus C	Lodger	M	Cha	9.0	S	Y			Guam	Guam	Guam		None
46	385	432	Rosario, Juan C	Lodger	M	Cha	4.0	S				Guam	Guam	Guam		None
47	386	433	Arceo, Vicente C	Head	M	Cha	30.0	M		Y	Y	Guam	Guam	Guam	N	Farmer
48	386	433	Arceo, Josefa S	Wife	F	Cha	25.0	M		Y	Y	Guam	Guam	Guam	N	None
49	386	433	Arceo, Rosa S	Daughter	F	Cha	8.0	S	Y			Guam	Guam	Guam		None
50	386	433	Arceo, Ana S	Daughter	F	Cha	6.0	S	N			Guam	Guam	Guam	N	None

Street: Santa Cruz Street

(CHAMORRO ROOTS GENEALOGY PROJECT ™ TRANSCRIPTION)
(COMPILED/TRANSCRIBED BY BERNARD T. PUNZALAN / HTTP://WWW.CHAMORROROOTS.COM)

FOURTEENTH CENSUS OF THE UNITED STATES: 1920-POPULATION

ISLAND OF GUAM

151

DISTRICT 2
NAME OF PLACE Agana (City)
[Proper name and, also, name of class, as city, town, village, barrio, etc]

ENUMERATED BY ME ON THE 2nd DAY OF April, 1920

Arthur W. Jackson ENUMERATOR

	PLACE OF ABODE		NAME	RELATION	PERSONAL DESCRIPTION				EDUCATION			NATIVITY				OCCUPATION
Street	Number of dwelling house	Number of family	Name	Relation	Sex	Color or race	Age at last birthday	Single, married, widowed or divorced	Attended school since Sept. 1, 1919	Whether able to read	Whether able to write	Place of birth of this person	Place of birth of father	Place of birth of mother	Whether able to speak English	Occupation
1	2	3	4	5	6	7	8	9	10	11	12	13	14	15	16	17
	386	433	Arceo, Antonia S	Daughter	F	Cha	5.0	S	N			Guam	Guam	Guam		None
	386	433	Arceo, Lucia S	Daughter	F	Cha	4.0	S				Guam	Guam	Guam		None
	386	433	Arceo, Felicita S	Daughter	F	Cha	3.0	S				Guam	Guam	Guam		None
	386	433	Arceo, Maria S	Daughter	F	Cha	0.1	S				Guam	Guam	Guam		None
	387	434	Materne, Eduvegis M	Head	F	Cha	52.0	S		N	N	Guam	Guam	Guam	N	Farmer
	387	434	Materne, Dolores M	Daughter	F	Cha	19.0	S	N	Y	Y	Guam	Unknown	Guam	N	None
	387	435	Materne, Antonio	Head	M	Cha	18.0	M	N	Y	Y	Guam	Unknown	Guam	Y	Laborer
	387	435	Materne, Dolores	Wife	F	Cha	20.0	M	N	Y	Y	Guam	Unknown	Guam	Y	None
	388	436	Leon, Maria M	Head	F	Cha	65.0	Wd		N	N	Guam	Guam	Guam	N	None
	388	436	Fejarang, Enrique	Lodger	M	Cha	5.0	S	N			Guam	Guam	Guam	N	None
	388	437	Leon, Juan M	Head	M	Cha	25.0	M		Y	Y	Guam	Guam	Guam	N	None
	388	437	Leon, Ascencion P	Wife	F	Cha	29.0	M		N	N	Guam	Guam	Guam	N	Farmer
	388	437	Leon, Joaquin	Nephew	M	Cha	8.0	S	Y			Guam	Guam	Guam	N	None
	389	438	Cabo, Manuela D	Head	F	Cha	70.0	Wd		N	N	Guam	Guam	Guam	N	None
	389	438	Cabo, Angel D	Son	M	Cha	40.0	S		N	N	Guam	Guam	Guam	N	Farmer
	389	438	Cabo, Maria D	Daughter	F	Cha	42.0	Wd		N	N	Guam	Guam	Guam	N	None
Santa Cruz Street	389	438	Reyes, Ignacio C	Grand son	M	Cha	16.0	S	N	Y	Y	Guam	Guam	Guam	Y	Farm laborer
	389	438	Reyes, Francisco C	Grand son	M	Cha	12.0	S	Y	Y	Y	Guam	Guam	Guam	Y	None
	389	438	Duenas, Supriana	Sister	F	Cha	64.0	Wd		N	N	Guam	Guam	Guam	N	None
	390	439	Crisostomo, Juan P	Head	M	Cha	34.0	M		Y	Y	Guam	Guam	Guam	Y	Farmer
	390	439	Crisostomo, Concepcion C	Wife	F	Cha	26.0	M		N	N	Guam	Guam	Guam	N	None
	390	439	Crisostomo, Miguel C	Son	M	Cha	4.0	S				Guam	Guam	Guam	N	None
	390	439	Crisostomo, Francisco C	Son	M	Cha	2.0	S				Guam	Guam	Guam	N	None
	390	439	Pangelinan, Aniceto	Step brother	M	Cha	27.0	S		Y	Y	Guam	Unknown	Guam	N	Farmer
	391	440	Fejarang, Jose C	Head	M	Cha	57.0	S		N	N	Guam	Guam	Guam	N	None

(CHAMORRO ROOTS GENEALOGY PROJECT ™ TRANSCRIPTION)
(COMPILED/TRANSCRIBED BY BERNARD T. PUNZALAN / HTTP://WWW.CHAMORROROOTS.COM)

FOURTEENTH CENSUS OF THE UNITED STATES: 1920-POPULATION

ISLAND OF GUAM

DISTRICT 2
NAME OF PLACE Agana (City)
[Proper name and, also, name of class, as city, town, village, barrio, etc]

SHEET NO. 47B

ENUMERATED BY ME ON THE 2nd DAY OF April, 1920

Arthur W. Jackson ENUMERATOR

	Dwelling No.	Family No.	NAME	RELATION	Sex	Color or race	Age	Condition	Attended school	Able to read	Able to write	Birthplace	Father birthplace	Mother birthplace	Speak English	OCCUPATION
26	391	440	Taitano, Joaquin C	Nephew	M	Cha	17.0	S	N	Y	Y	Guam	Guam	Guam	Y	Farm laborer
27	391	440	Taitano, Rosa C	Niece	F	Cha	10.0	S	Y	Y	Y	Guam	Guam	Guam	N	None
28	392	441	Quenga, Francisco T	Head	M	Cha	22.0	M		Y	Y	Guam	Guam	Guam	Y	Farmer
29	392	441	Quenga, Ana M	Wife	F	Cha	20.0	M		Y	Y	Guam	Guam	Guam	Y	None
30	392	441	Quenga, Antonia M	Daughter	F	Cha	2.0	S				Guam	Guam	Guam		None
31	392	441	Quenga, Matilde M	Daughter	F	Cha	1.0	S				Guam	Guam	Guam		None
32	393	442	Guerrero, Joaquin	Head	M	Cha	27.0	S		Y	Y	Guam	Unknown	Guam	Y	Horticulturist
33	393	442	Guerrero, Emelia G	Mother	F	Cha	51.0	S		Y	Y	Guam	Guam	Guam	N	None
34	393	442	Guerrero, Jose G	Brother	M	Cha	13.0	S	Y	Y	Y	Guam	Unknown	Guam	Y	None
35	394	443	Semiya, Takeyoshi	Head	M	Jp	38.0	M		Y	Y	Japan	Japan	Japan	Y	Cook
36	394	443	Semiya, Antonia A	Wife	F	Cha	35.0	M		Y	Y	Guam	Guam	Guam	N	None
37	394	443	Semiya, Joaquin A	Son	M	Jp	15.0	S	N	Y	Y	Guam	Japan	Guam	Y	Servant
38	394	443	Semiya, Jose A	Son	M	Jp	13.0	S	Y	Y	Y	Guam	Japan	Guam	Y	None
39	394	443	Semiya, Juan A	Son	M	Jp	8.0	S	Y			Guam	Japan	Guam	Y	None
40	395	444	Quitugua, Felipe M	Head	M	Cha	41.0	Wd		Y	Y	Guam	Guam	Guam	N	Farmer
41	395	444	Quitugua, Juliana M	Mother	F	Cha	62.0	Wd		N	N	Guam	Guam	Guam	N	None
42	395	444	Mendiola, Rosa M	Step sister	F	Cha	22.0	S		Y	Y	Guam	Guam	Guam	N	None
43	395	444	Reyes, Maria Q	Niece	F	Cha	16.0	S	N	Y	Y	Guam	Guam	Guam	N	None
44	395	444	Reyes, Vicente Q	Nephew	M	Cha	11.0	S	Y	Y	Y	Guam	Guam	Guam	N	None
45	396	445	Leon Guerrero, Ana T	Head	F	Cha	44.0	Wd		N	N	Guam	Guam	Guam	N	Farmer
46	396	446	Aguon, Juan T	Head	M	Cha	25.0	M		Y	Y	Guam	Guam	Guam	Y	None
47	396	446	Aguon, Manuela LG	Wife	F	Cha	21.0	M	N	Y	Y	Guam	Guam	Guam	Y	None
48	396	446	Aguon, Julian LG	Son	M	Cha	2.0	S				Guam	Guam	Guam		None
49	396	446	Aguon, Maria LG	Daughter	F	Cha	0.6	S				Guam	Guam	Guam		None
50	396	446	Leon Guerrero, Miguel A	Brother-in-law	M	Cha	19.0	S	N	Y	Y	Guam	Guam	Guam	Y	Farmer

Street, avenue, road, etc.: Santa Cruz Street

(CHAMORRO ROOTS GENEALOGY PROJECT ™ TRANSCRIPTION)
(COMPILED/TRANSCRIBED BY BERNARD T. PUNZALAN / HTTP://WWW.CHAMORROROOTS.COM)

FOURTEENTH CENSUS OF THE UNITED STATES: 1920-POPULATION
ISLAND OF GUAM

ENUMERATED BY ME ON THE 2nd DAY OF April, 1920

Arthur W. Jackson ENUMERATOR

DISTRICT 2
NAME OF PLACE Agana (City)
[Proper name and, also, name of class, as city, town, village, barrio, etc]

	Num-ber of dwelling house	Num-ber of family	NAME	RELATION	Sex	Color or race	Age at last birthday	Single, married, widowed or divorced	Attended school since Sept. 1, 1919	Whether able to read	Whether able to write	Place of birth of this person	Place of birth of father	Place of birth of mother	Whether able to speak English	OCCUPATION
1	2	3	4	5	6	7	8	9	10	11	12	13	14	15	16	17
1	397	447	Cruz, Soledad T	Head	F	Cha	50.0	Wd		Y	Y	Guam	Guam	Guam	N	None
2	397	447	Cruz, Ana T	Daughter	F	Cha	18.0	S	N	Y	Y	Guam	Guam	Guam	Y	None
3	397	447	Cruz, Francisco T	Son	M	Cha	16.0	S	N	Y	Y	Guam	Guam	Guam	Y	None
4	397	447	Cruz, Concepcion T	Daughter	F	Cha	11.0	S	Y	Y	Y	Guam	Guam	Guam	N	None
5	398	448	Merfalen, Joaquin P	Head	M	Cha	29.0	M		Y	Y	Guam	Guam	Guam	Y	Farmer
6	398	448	Merfalen, Maria M	Wife	F	Cha	26.0	M		Y	Y	Guam	Guam	Guam	N	None
7	398	448	Merfalen, Antonio M	Son	M	Cha	10.0	S	Y	Y	Y	Guam	Guam	Guam	Y	None
8	398	448	Merfalen, Lourdes M	Daughter	F	Cha	4.0	S				Guam	Guam	Guam		None
9	398	448	Merfalen, Jose M	Son	M	Cha	3.0	S				Guam	Guam	Guam		None
10	398	448	Merfalen, Concepcion M	Daughter	F	Cha	0.2	S				Guam	Guam	Guam		None
11	399	449	Pablo, Jose A	Head	M	Cha	62.0	M		N	Y	Guam	Guam	Guam	N	None
12	399	449	Pablo, Rosa G	Wife	F	Cha	52.0	M		N	N	Guam	Guam	Guam	N	None
13	399	449	Pablo, Jose G	Son	M	Cha	30.0	S		Y	Y	Guam	Guam	Guam	N	Farmer
14	399	449	Pablo, Elena G	Daughter	F	Cha	23.0	S		Y	Y	Guam	Guam	Guam	N	None
15	399	449	Pablo, Nicolasa G	Daughter	F	Cha	20.0	S	N	Y	Y	Guam	Guam	Guam	Y	None
16	399	449	Pablo, Alfonso G	Son	M	Cha	15.0	S	N	Y	Y	Guam	Guam	Guam	Y	Farm laborer
17	399	449	Pablo, Ignacio	Grand son	M	Cha	1.0	S				Guam	Unknown	Guam		None
18	400	450	Cruz, Consolacion LG	Head	F	Cha	51.0	Wd		N	N	Guam	Guam	Guam	N	None
19	400	450	Cruz, Antonia LG	Daughter	F	Cha	27.0	S		Y	Y	Guam	Guam	Guam	N	None
20	400	450	Cruz, Felipe LG	Son	M	Cha	25.0	S		Y	Y	Guam	Guam	Guam	N	Laborer
21	400	450	Cruz, Jose LG	Son	M	Cha	22.0	S		Y	Y	Guam	Guam	Guam	Y	Farmer
22	400	450	Cruz, Vicente LG	Son	M	Cha	20.0	S	N	Y	Y	Guam	Guam	Guam	Y	None
23	400	450	Cruz, Ana LG	Daughter	F	Cha	17.0	S	N	Y	Y	Guam	Guam	Guam	Y	None
24	400	450	Cruz, Enrique LG	Son	M	Cha	14.0	S	N	Y	Y	Guam	Guam	Guam	Y	None
25	400	450	Cruz, Juan LG	Son	M	Cha	12.0	S	Y	Y	Y	Guam	Guam	Guam	Y	None

Street, avenue, road, etc.: Santa Cruz Street

(CHAMORRO ROOTS GENEALOGY PROJECT ™ TRANSCRIPTION)
(COMPILED/TRANSCRIBED BY BERNARD T. PUNZALAN / HTTP://WWW.CHAMORROROOTS.COM)

FOURTEENTH CENSUS OF THE UNITED STATES: 1920-POPULATION
ISLAND OF GUAM

DISTRICT 2
NAME OF PLACE Agana (City)
[Proper name and, also, name of class, as city, town, village, barrio, etc]

ENUMERATED BY ME ON THE 3rd DAY OF April, 1920

Arthur W. Jackson ENUMERATOR

	PLACE OF ABODE					PERSONAL DESCRIPTION				EDUCATION			NATIVITY				OCCUPATION
Street	Dwelling	Family	NAME	RELATION	Sex	Color or race	Age	Marital	School	Read	Write	Birthplace person	Father	Mother	English	Trade/profession
1	2	3	4	5	6	7	8	9	10	11	12	13	14	15	16	17
26		450	Cruz, Dolores LG	Daughter	F	Cha	4.0	S				Guam	Guam	Guam		None
27	401	451	Leon Guerrero, Ignacio P	Head	M	Cha	39.0	M		Y	Y	Guam	Guam	Guam	N	Farmer
28	401	451	Leon Guerrero, Carmen P	Wife	F	Cha	50.0	M		N	N	Guam	Guam	Guam	N	None
29	401	451	Leon Guerrero, Ana P	Daughter	F	Cha	20.0	S		Y	Y	Guam	Guam	Guam	Y	None
30	401	451	Leon Guerrero, Jose P	Son	M	Cha	18.0	S	N	Y	Y	Guam	Guam	Guam	Y	None
31	401	451	Leon Guerrero, Rosa P	Daughter	F	Cha	14.0	S	N	Y	Y	Guam	Guam	Guam	Y	None
32	401	451	Leon Guerrero, Dolores P	Daughter	F	Cha	11.0	S	N	Y	Y	Guam	Guam	Guam	N	None
33	401	451	Leon Guerrero, Jesus P	Son	M	Cha	10.0	S	Y	Y	Y	Guam	Guam	Guam	N	None
34	401	451	Leon Guerrero, Regina P	Daughter	F	Cha	9.0	S	Y	Y	Y	Guam	Guam	Guam		None
35	401	451	Leon Guerrero, Lourdes P	Daughter	F	Cha	7.0	S	Y			Guam	Guam	Guam		None
36	401	451	Leon Guerrero, Juan P	Son	M	Cha	4.0	S				Guam	Guam	Guam		None
37	402	452	Guerrero, Ramon P	Head	M	Cha	51.0	M		N	N	Guam	Guam	Guam	N	Farmer
38	402	452	Guerrero, Luisa A	Wife	F	Cha	43.0	M		N	N	Guam	Guam	Guam	N	None
39	402	452	Guerrero, Caridad A	Daughter	F	Cha	23.0	S		Y	Y	Guam	Guam	Guam	Y	None
40	403	453	Aguero, Concepcion Q	Head	F	Cha	26.0	M		Y	Y	Guam	Guam	Guam	N	None
41	403	453	Aguero, Felix Q	Son	M	Cha	4.0	S				Guam	Guam	Guam		None
42	403	453	Aguero, Emeliana Q	Daughter	F	Cha	2.0	S				Guam	Guam	Guam		None
43	404	454	Shimizu, Jose K	Head	M	Jp	48.0	Wd		Y	Y	Japan	Japan	Japan	Y	Merchant general merchandise retail
44	404	454	Shimizu, Ichiryo J	Son	M	Jp	20.0	S	N	Y	Y	Saipan MI	Japan	Saipan MI	Y	Clerk
45	404	454	Shimizu, Carmen T	Daughter	F	Jp	14.0	S	N	Y	Y	Guam	Japan	Guam	Y	None
46	404	454	Shimizu, Jesus T	Son	M	Jp	13.0	S	Y	Y	Y	Guam	Japan	Guam	Y	None
47	404	454	Shimizu, Joaquin T	Son	M	Jp	12.0	S	Y	Y	Y	Guam	Japan	Guam	Y	None
48	404	454	Torres, Joaquina M	Mother-in-law	F	Cha	59.0	Wd		Y	Y	Guam	Guam	Guam	N	None
49	404	454	Torres, Jesus F	Lodger	M	Cha	17.0	S	N	N	N	Guam	Guam	Guam	Y	None
50	405	455	Okiyama, Ginusuki F	Head	M	Jp	37.0	M		Y	Y	Japan	Japan	Japan	N	Carpenter

Street: Santa Cruz Street; Dr. Hesler Street

308

(CHAMORRO ROOTS GENEALOGY PROJECT ™ TRANSCRIPTION)
(COMPILED/TRANSCRIBED BY BERNARD T. PUNZALAN / HTTP://WWW.CHAMORROROOTS.COM)
FOURTEENTH CENSUS OF THE UNITED STATES: 1920-POPULATION
ISLAND OF GUAM

SHEET NO. 49A

DISTRICT 2
NAME OF PLACE Agana (City)
[Proper name and, also, name of class, as city, town, village, barrio, etc]

ENUMERATED BY ME ON THE 3rd DAY OF April, 1920

Arthur W. Jackson ENUMERATOR

Street, avenue, road, etc.	Number of dwelling house in order of visitation	Number of family in order of visitation	NAME	RELATION	Sex	Color or race	Age at last birthday	Single, married, widowed or divorced	Attended school any time since Sept. 1, 1919	Whether able to read	Whether able to write	Place of birth of this person	Place of birth of father of this person	Place of birth of mother of this person	Whether able to speak English	OCCUPATION
1	2	3	4	5	6	7	8	9	10	11	12	13	14	15	16	17
	405	455	Okiyama, Jacoba C	Wife	F	Cha	30.0	S		Y	Y	Guam	Guam	Guam	N	None
	405	455	Okiyama, Maria C	Daughter	F	Jp	6.0	S	N			Guam	Japan	Guam		None
	405	455	Okiyama, Ana C	Daughter	F	Jp	5.0	S	N			Guam	Japan	Guam		None
	405	455	Okiyama, Carmen C	Daughter	F	Jp	4.0	S				Guam	Japan	Guam		None
	406	456	Martinez, Antonia C	Head	F	Cha	73.0	Wd		Y	Y	Guam	Guam	Guam	N	Merchant Gen. retail
	406	456	Muna, Juana	Servant	F	Cha	27.0	S		Y	Y	Guam	Guam	Guam	Y	Servant
	406	456	Bamba, Maria B	Servant	F	Cha	10.0	S	Y	Y	Y	Guam	Guam	Guam	N	Servant
	406	456	Flores, Laurete C	Lodger	F	Cha	5.0	S	N			Guam	Guam	Guam		None
	407	457	Kitamura, Toyoye	Head	M	Jp	29.0	S		Y	Y	Japan	Japan	Japan	Y	Merchant Gen. retail
	408	458	Hirano, Moto	Head	M	Jp	41.0	M		Y	Y	Japan	Japan	Japan	Y	Merchant Gen. retail
	408	458	Hirano, Ai	Wife	F	Jp	35.0	M		Y	Y	Japan	Japan	Japan	N	None
Dr. Hesler Street	409	459	Martinez, Rita M	Head	F	W	47.0	Wd		Y	Y	Guam	Guam	Guam	Y	None
	409	459	Martinez, Julia M	Daughter	F	W	16.0	S	N	Y	Y	Guam	Guam	Guam	Y	None
	409	459	Mendiola, Ana M	Servant	F	Cha	14.0	S		Y	Y	Guam	Guam	Guam	Y	None
	410	460	San Nicolas, Juan V	Head	M	Cha	50.0	M		Y	Y	Guam	Guam	Guam	N	Farmer
	410	460	San Nicolas, Trinidad I	Wife	F	Cha	50.0	M		N	N	Guam	Guam	Guam	N	None
	411	461	Tenorio, Dolores S	Head	F	Cha	50.0	Wd		N	N	Guam	Guam	Guam	N	None
	411	461	Tenorio, Vicente S	Son	M	Cha	12.0	S	N	Y	Y	Guam	Guam	Guam	Y	None
	412	462	Diaz, Josefa B	Head	F	Cha	67.0	Wd		N	N	Guam	Guam	Guam	N	None
	412	462	Borja, Jose	Son	M	Cha	37.0	M		N	N	Guam	Unknown	Unknown	N	Farmer
	412	462	Borja, Consuelo M	Daughter	F	Cha	34.0	M		Y	Y	Guam	Unknown	Unknown	N	None
	413	463	Perez, Gregorio F	Head	M	Cha	32.0	M		Y	Y	Guam	Guam	Guam	N	Clerk
	413	463	Perez, Rosario E	Wife	F	Fil	27.0	M		Y	Y	Guam	Philippine Islands	Guam	Y	Teacher
	413	463	Perez, Edward E	Son	M	Cha	6.0	S	N	Y	Y	Guam	Guam	Guam	Y	None
	413	463	Perez, Tomas E	Son	M	Cha	4.0	S				Guam	Guam	Guam		None

(CHAMORRO ROOTS GENEALOGY PROJECT ™ TRANSCRIPTION)
(COMPILED/TRANSCRIBED BY BERNARD T. PUNZALAN / HTTP://WWW.CHAMORROROOTS.COM)

FOURTEENTH CENSUS OF THE UNITED STATES: 1920-POPULATION
ISLAND OF GUAM

ENUMERATED BY ME ON THE 3rd DAY OF April, 1920

Arthur W. Jackson ENUMERATOR

DISTRICT 2
NAME OF PLACE Agana (City)
[Proper name and, also, name of class, as city, town, village, barrio, etc]

Line	Dwelling	Family	NAME	RELATION	Sex	Race	Age	Marital	Sch.	Read	Write	Birth person	Birth father	Birth mother	English	OCCUPATION
26	413	463	Perez, Albert E	Son	M	Cha	3.0	S				Guam	Guam	Guam		None
27	413	463	Perez, Rosa E	Daughter	F	Cha	1.0	S				Guam	Guam	Guam		None
28	413	463	Torres, Ana	Lodger	F	Cha	70.0	Wd			N	Guam	Guam	Guam	N	None
29	414	464	Liizama, Juan P	Head	M	Cha	45.0	M		M	Y	Guam	Guam	Guam	N	Farmer
30	414	464	Liizama, Maria F	Wife	F	Cha	44.0	M		Y	Y	Guam	Guam	Guam	N	None
31	414	464	Liizama, Jose F	Son	M	Cha	25.0	S		Y	Y	Guam	Guam	Guam	N	Farmer
32	414	464	Liizama, Ignacio F	Son	M	Cha	24.0	S		Y	Y	Guam	Guam	Guam	N	Laborer
33	414	464	Liizama, Francisco F	Son	M	Cha	22.0	S		Y	Y	Guam	Guam	Guam	Y	Laborer
34	414	464	Liizama, Maria F	Daughter	F	Cha	20.0	S	N	Y	Y	Guam	Guam	Guam	N	None
35	414	464	Liizama, Ana F	Daughter	F	Cha	18.0	S	N	Y	Y	Guam	Guam	Guam	Y	None
36	414	464	Liizama, Felix F	Son	M	Cha	11.0	S	Y	Y	Y	Guam	Guam	Guam	N	None
37	414	464	Liizama, Juan F	Son	M	Cha	7.0	S	Y	Y	Y	Guam	Guam	Guam		None
38	414	464	Liizama, Simeon F	Son	M	Cha	5.0	S	N			Guam	Guam	Guam		None
39	415	465	Fujikawa, Masayoshi	Head	M	Jp	34.0	Wd		Y	Y	Japan	Japan	Japan	Y	Shoe maker
40	416	466	Torres, Vicente M	Head	M	Cha	45.0	M		Y	Y	Guam	Guam	Guam	Y	Silversmith
41	416	466	Torres, Tomasa C	Wife	F	Cha	39.0	M		Y	Y	Guam	Guam	Guam		None
42	416	466	Achaigma, Esperanza S	Servant	F	Cha	14.0	S	N	Y	Y	Guam	Guam	Guam	N	Servant
43	417	467	Tachira, Juan D	Head	M	W	24.0	M		Y	Y	Guam	Portugal	Guam	Y	Farmer
44	417	467	Tachira, Manuela C	Wife	F	Cha	20.0	M		Y	Y	Guam	Guam	Guam	N	None
45	417	467	Tachira, Mafada C	Daughter	F	W	2.0	S				Guam	Guam	Guam		None
46	417	467	Tachira, Dolores C	Daughter	F	W	0.8	S				Guam	Guam	Guam		None
47	418	468	de Torres, Rita C	Head	F	Cha	75.0	Wd		Y	Y	Guam	Guam	Guam	N	None
48	418	468	de Torres, Luis C	Son	M	Cha	53.0	S		Y	Y	Guam	Guam	Guam	N	Sock raiser
49	418	468	de Torres, Vicente C	Son	M	Cha	49.0	S		Y	Y	Guam	Guam	Guam	N	Farmer
50	418	468	de Torres, Caridad C	Daughter	F	Cha	44.0	S		Y	Y	Guam	Guam	Guam	N	None

Street (column 1): Dr. Hesler Street

(CHAMORRO ROOTS GENEALOGY PROJECT ™ TRANSCRIPTION)
(COMPILED/TRANSCRIBED BY BERNARD T. PUNZALAN / HTTP://WWW.CHAMORROROOTS.COM)

FOURTEENTH CENSUS OF THE UNITED STATES: 1920—POPULATION

ISLAND OF GUAM

DISTRICT 2
NAME OF PLACE Agana (City)

[Proper name and, also, name of class, as city, town, village, barrio, etc]

ENUMERATED BY ME ON THE 5th DAY OF April, 1920

Arthur W. Jackson ENUMERATOR

Street, avenue, road, etc.	Dwelling no.	Family no.	NAME	RELATION	Sex	Color or race	Age	S/M/W/D	Attended school	Read	Write	Birthplace of person	Birthplace of father	Birthplace of mother	Speak English	OCCUPATION
	418	468	de Torres, Concepcion C	Daughter	F	Cha	43.0	S		Y	Y	Guam	Guam	Guam	N	None
Dr. Hesler Street	419	469	Giles, Albert H	Head	M	W	42.0	M		Y	Y	England	England	England	Y	Asst Manager Gen Wholesal mdse
	419	469	Giles, Maud C	Wife	F	W	40.0	M		Y	Y	England	England	England	Y	None
	419	469	Giles, Frank C	Son	M	W	12.0	S	Y	Y	Y	England	England	England	Y	None
	419	469	Giles, Elizabeth V	Daughter	F	W	2.0	S				California	England	England		None
	419	469	Giles, Nancy M	Daughter	F	W	2.0	S				California	England	England		None
	420	470	Logan, Arthur U	head	M	W	35.0	M		Y	Y	Illinois	West Virginia	Ohio	Y	Missionary
	420	470	Logan, Edith C	Wife	F	W	41.0	M		Y	Y	Indiana	Kentucky	Indiana	Y	None
	420	470	Logan, William A	Son	M	W	7.0	S	Y			Guam	Illinois	Indiana		None
	420	470	Logan, David E	Son	M	W	5.0	S	N			Guam	Illinois	Indiana		None
	420	470	Logan, John P	Son	M	W	2.0	S				Guam	Illinois	Indiana		None
	420	470	Taitano, Magdalena C	Servant	F	Cha	17.0	S	Y	Y	Y	Guam	Guam	Guam		Servant
	421	461	San Nicolas, Vicente I	Head	M	Cha	26.0	M		Y	Y	Guam	Guam	Guam	Y	Farmer
	421	461	San Nicolas, Ana M	Wife	F	Cha	25.0	M		Y	Y	Guam	Guam	Guam	N	None
	421	461	San Nicolas, Trinidad M	Daughter	F	Cha	4.0	S				Guam	Guam	Guam		None
	421	461	San Nicolas, Beatrice M	Daughter	F	Cha	0.1	S				Guam	Guam	Guam		None
	422	472	Miasaki, Tomagoro	Head	M	Jp	35.0	S		Y	Y	Japan	Japan	Japan	Y	Cook
Numancia Street	423	473	Ocampo, Eliseo	Head	M	Fil	32.0	M		Y	Y	Philippine Islands	Philippine Islands	Philippine Islands	Y	Weaver
	423	473	Ocampo, Pemental	Wife	F	Fil	27.0	M		Y	Y	Philippine Islands	Philippine Islands	Philippine Islands	Y	Teacher of Donation Services
	423	473	Ocampo, Maria E	Daughter	F	Fil	5.0	S	N			Philippine Islands	Philippine Islands	Philippine Islands		None
	423	473	Ocampo, Jorge	Son	M	Fil	4.0	S				Philippine Islands	Philippine Islands	Philippine Islands		None
	423	473	Ocampo, Pacifica	Daughter	F	Fil	0.1	S				Guam	Philippine Islands	Philippine Islands		None
	423	473	Sarang, Satrunina	Servant	F	Fil	11.0	S	Y	Y	Y	Philippine Islands	Philippine Islands	Philippine Islands		Servant
Numancia Street	424	474	Cruz, Vicente M	Head	M	Cha	33.0	M		Y	Y	Guam	Guam	Guam	Y	Machinist
	424	474	Cruz, Dolores C	Wife	F	Cha	30.0	M		N	N	Guam	Guam	Guam	N	None

(CHAMORRO ROOTS GENEALOGY PROJECT ™ TRANSCRIPTION)
(COMPILED/TRANSCRIBED BY BERNARD T. FUNZALAN / HTTP://WWW.CHAMORROROOTS.COM)

FOURTEENTH CENSUS OF THE UNITED STATES: 1920-POPULATION
ISLAND OF GUAM

ENUMERATED BY ME ON THE 5th DAY OF April, 1920

Arthur W. Jackson ENUMERATOR

DISTRICT 2
NAME OF PLACE Agana (City)

	Dwelling (2)	Family (3)	NAME (4)	RELATION (5)	Sex (6)	Color or race (7)	Age (8)	Marital (9)	School (10)	Read (11)	Write (12)	Birthplace (13)	Father (14)	Mother (15)	English (16)	OCCUPATION (17)
26	424	474	Cruz, Vicente C	Son	M	Cha	9.0	S	Y			Guam	Guam	Guam		None
27	424	474	Cruz, Justo C	Son	M	Cha	5.0	S	N			Guam	Guam	Guam		None
28	425	475	Cruz, Jose M	Head	M	Cha	39.0	M		Y	Y	Guam	Guam	Guam	Y	Farmer
29	425	475	Cruz, Carmen C	Daughter	F	Cha	21.0	M	N	Y	Y	Guam	Guam	Guam	Y	None
30	425	475	Cruz, Jose C	Son	M	Cha	1.0	S				Guam	Guam	Guam		None
31	426	476	Munoz, Juan C	Head	M	W	32.0	M		Y	Y	Guam	Spain	Guam	Y	Machinist
32	426	476	Munoz, Regina F	Wife	F	Cha	38.0	M		Y	Y	Guam	Unknown	Guam	N	None
33	426	476	Munoz, Vicente F	Son	M	W	8.0	S	Y			Guam	Guam	Guam		None
34	426	476	Munoz, Adela F	Daughter	F	W	7.0	S	Y			Guam	Guam	Guam		None
35	426	476	Munoz, Jose F	Son	M	W	4.0	S				Guam	Guam	Guam		None
36	426	476	Munoz, Jesusa F	Daughter	F	W	1.0	S				Guam	Guam	Guam		None
37	427	477	Blaz, Jose B	Head	M	Cha	36.0	M		Y	Y	Guam	Guam	Guam	Y	Carpenter
38	427	477	Blaz, Rosa U	Wife	F	Cha	44.0	M		Y	Y	Guam	Guam	Guam	N	None
39	427	477	Blaz, Maria U	Daughter	F	Cha	15.0	S	N	Y	Y	Guam	Guam	Guam	Y	None
40	427	477	Blaz, Jose U	Son	M	Cha	14.0	S	N	Y	Y	Guam	Guam	Guam	Y	None
41	427	477	Blaz, Antonia U	Daughter	F	Cha	13.0	S	Y	Y	Y	Guam	Guam	Guam	Y	None
42	427	477	Blaz, Flora U	Daughter	F	Cha	9.0	S	Y	Y	Y	Guam	Guam	Guam	Y	None
43	427	477	Blaz, Demetro U	Son	M	Cha	7.0	S	Y			Guam	Guam	Guam		None
44	427	477	Blaz, Concepcion U	Daughter	F	Cha	6.0	S	N			Guam	Guam	Guam		None
45	427	477	Blaz, Dolores U	Daughter	F	Cha	4.0	S				Guam	Guam	Guam		None
46	427	477	Blaz, Rosa U	Daughter	F	Cha	1.0	S				Guam	Guam	Guam		None
47	428	478	Guzman, Francisco C	Head	M	Cha	23.0	M		Y	Y	Guam	Guam	Guam	Y	Laborer
48	428	478	Guzman, Carmen C	Wife	F	Cha	21.0	M	N	Y	N	Guam	Guam	Guam	N	None
49	428	478	Guzman, Gregorio C	Son	M	Cha	2.0	S				Guam	Guam	Guam		None
50	428	478	Guzman, Francisco	Son	M	Cha	0.7	S				Guam	Guam	Guam		None

Street (Column 1): Numancia Street

312

(CHAMORRO ROOTS GENEALOGY PROJECT ™ TRANSCRIPTION)
(COMPILED/TRANSCRIBED BY BERNARD T. PUNZALAN / HTTP://WWW.CHAMORROROOTS.COM)
FOURTEENTH CENSUS OF THE UNITED STATES: 1920-POPULATION
ISLAND OF GUAM

DISTRICT 2
NAME OF PLACE Agana (City)
[Proper name and, also, name of class, as city, town, village, barrio, etc]

ENUMERATED BY ME ON THE 6th DAY OF April, 1920

Arthur W. Jackson ENUMERATOR

Street, avenue, road, etc.	Number of dwelling house in order of visitation	Number of family in order of visitation	NAME	RELATION	Sex	Color or race	Age at last birthday	Single, married, widowed or divorced	Attended school any time since Sept. 1, 1919	Whether able to read.	Whether able to write.	Place of birth of this person.	Place of birth of father of this person.	Place of birth of mother of this person.	Whether able to speak English.	OCCUPATION
	2	3	4	5	6	7	8	9	10	11	12	13	14	15	16	17
	429	479	Duenas, Jose A	Head	M	Cha	41.0	M		Y	Y	Guam	Guam	Guam	Y	Carpenter
	429	479	Duenas, Maria SN	Wife	F	Cha	44.0	M		Y	Y	Guam	Guam	Guam	N	None
	429	479	Duenas, Eugenia SN	Daughter	F	Cha	11.0	S	Y	Y	Y	Guam	Guam	Guam	N	None
	429	479	Duenas, Jose SN	Son	M	Cha	9.0	S	Y			Guam	Guam	Guam		None
	429	479	Duenas, Agustin SN	Son	M	Cha	8.0	S	Y			Guam	Guam	Guam		None
	429	479	Duenas, Antonio SN	Son	M	Cha	6.0	S	N			Guam	Guam	Guam		None
	429	479	Duenas, Vicente SN	Son	M	Cha	4.0	S				Guam	Guam	Guam		None
	430	480	Indalecio, Rosa	Head	F	Cha	36.0	S		Y	Y	Guam	Guam	Guam	N	None
	430	480	Indalecio, Maria	Daughter	F	Cha	15.0	S	N	Y	Y	Guam	Unknown	Guam	Y	None
	430	480	Indalecio, Jose	Son	M	Cha	13.0	S	Y	Y	Y	Guam	Unknown	Guam	Y	None
	430	480	Indalecio, Ana	Daughter	F	Cha	10.0	S	Y	Y	Y	Guam	Unknown	Guam		None
	430	480	Indalecio, Dolores	Daughter	F	Cha	7.0	S	Y			Guam	Unknown	Guam		None
	430	480	Indalecio, Carmen	Daughter	F	Cha	4.0	S				Guam	Unknown	Guam		None
	430	480	Materne, Antonio	Lodger	M	Cha	28.0	S	Y	Y	Y	Guam	Guam	Guam	Y	Cook
	431	481	San Nicolas, Pedro S	Head	M	Cha	44.0	M		N	N	Guam	Guam	Guam	N	Farmer
	431	481	San Nicolas, Dominga A	Wife	F	Cha	38.0	M		Y	Y	Guam	Guam	Guam	N	None
	431	481	San Nicolas, Rita A	Daughter	F	Cha	20.0	S	N	Y	Y	Guam	Guam	Guam	Y	None
	431	481	San Nicolas, Ana A	Daughter	F	Cha	13.0	S	Y	Y	Y	Guam	Guam	Guam	Y	None
	431	481	San Nicolas, Jesus A	Son	M	Cha	8.0	S	Y			Guam	Guam	Guam		None
	431	481	San Nicolas, Joaquin A	Son	M	Cha	7.0	S	Y			Guam	Guam	Guam		None
	431	481	San Nicolas, Dolores A	Daughter	F	Cha	4.0	S				Guam	Guam	Guam		None
	431	481	San Nicolas, Juan A	Son	M	Cha	1.0	S				Guam	Guam	Guam		None
	432	482	Santos, Rita A	Head	F	Cha	75.0	M		N	N	Guam	Guam	Guam	N	None
	432	482	Cruz, Encarnasion	Lodger	F	Cha	65.0	Wd		N	N	Guam	Guam	Guam	N	None
Numancia Street	432	482	San Nicolas, Rita A	Lodger	F	Cha	15.0	S	N	Y	Y	Guam	Guam	Guam	Y	None

(CHAMORRO ROOTS GENEALOGY PROJECT ™ TRANSCRIPTION)
(COMPILED/TRANSCRIBED BY BERNARD T. PUNZALAN / HTTP://WWW.CHAMORROROOTS.COM)

FOURTEENTH CENSUS OF THE UNITED STATES: 1920-POPULATION
ISLAND OF GUAM

DISTRICT 2
NAME OF PLACE Agana (City)
[Proper name and, also, name of class, as city, town, village, barrio, etc]

ENUMERATED BY ME ON THE 6th DAY OF April, 1920

Arthur W. Jackson ENUMERATOR

	PLACE OF ABODE		NAME	RELATION	PERSONAL DESCRIPTION				EDUCATION			NATIVITY				OCCUPATION
Street, avenue, road, etc.	No. dwelling house	No. family	Name	Relationship to head of family	Sex	Color or race	Age at last birthday	Single, married, widowed or divorced	Attended school since Sept. 1, 1919	Able to read	Able to write	Place of birth of this person	Place of birth of father	Place of birth of mother	Able to speak English	Occupation
1	2	3	4	5	6	7	8	9	10	11	12	13	14	15	16	17
	433	483	Taisague, Vicente G	Head	M	Cha	26.0	S		Y	Y	Guam	Guam	Guam	N	Servant
	434	484	Mendiola, Antonio C	Head	M	Cha	52.0	M		Y	Y	Guam	Guam	Guam	N	Farmer
	434	484	Mendiola, Consolacion G	Wife	F	Cha	49.0	M		Y	Y	Guam	Guam	Guam	N	None
	434	484	Mendiola, Luisa G	Daughter	F	Cha	26.0	S		Y	Y	Guam	Guam	Guam	Y	None
	434	484	Mendiola, Jose G	Son	M	Cha	18.0	S	N	Y	Y	Guam	Guam	Guam	Y	None
	434	484	Mendiola, Isabel G	Daughter	F	Cha	11.0	S	Y	Y	Y	Guam	Guam	Guam	Y	None
	434	484	Mendiola, Francisco G	Son	M	Cha	7.0	S	Y			Guam	Guam	Guam	Y	None
San Juan de Letran Street	435	485	Perez, Joaquin C	Head	M	Cha	60.0	M		Y	Y	Guam	Guam	Guam	Y	Land Judge
	435	485	Perez, Felisa S	Wife	F	Cha	46.0	M		Y	Y	Guam	Guam	Guam	N	None
	435	485	Perez, Jose S	Son	M	Cha	3.0	S				Guam	Guam	Guam		None
	435	485	Salas, Juan I	Step son	M	Cha	17.0	S	N	Y	Y	Guam	Unknown	Guam	Y	Laborer
	435	485	Salas, Maria I	Step Daughter	F	Cha	12.0	S	N	Y	Y	Guam	Unknown	Guam	Y	None
	435	485	Salas, Jesus I	Step Son	M	Cha	10.0	S	Y	Y	Y	Guam	Unknown	Guam	N	None
	435	485	Salas, Genoveva I	Sister-in-law	F	Cha	42.0	S		Y	Y	Guam	Guam	Guam	N	None
	435	485	Pangelinan, Vicente P	Servant	M	Cha	18.0	S	N	Y	Y	Guam	Unknown	Guam	Y	Servant
	435	486	Terlaje, Francisco F	Head	M	Cha	21.0	M	N	Y	Y	Guam	Guam	Guam	Y	Enlisted US Navy
	435	486	Terlaje, Maria S	Wife	F	Cha	23.0	M		Y	Y	Guam	Guam	Guam	Y	None
	436	487	Aflague, Jose C	Head	M	Cha	60.0	M		Y	Y	Guam	Guam	Guam	N	Farmer
	436	487	Aflague, Vicenta S	Wife	F	Cha	58.0	M		Y	Y	Guam	Guam	Guam	N	None
	436	487	Aflague, Inocencio S	Son	M	Cha	26.0	S		Y	Y	Guam	Guam	Guam	Y	Machinist
	436	487	Aflague, Ana S	Daughter	F	Cha	16.0	S	N	Y	Y	Guam	Guam	Guam	Y	None
	436	487	Aflague, Jose S	Son	M	Cha	12.0	S	Y	Y	Y	Guam	Guam	Guam	Y	None
	436	488	Aflague, Francisco S	Head	M	Cha	30.0	M		Y	Y	Guam	Guam	Guam	N	Farmer
	436	488	Aflague, Rosa SM	Wife	F	Cha	29.0	M		Y	Y	Guam	Guam	Guam	N	None
	436	488	Aflague, Pilar SM	Daughter	F	Cha	9.0	S	Y	Y	Y	Guam	Guam	Guam		None

314

(CHAMORRO ROOTS GENEALOGY PROJECT ™ TRANSCRIPTION)
(COMPILED/TRANSCRIBED BY BERNARD T. PUNZALAN / HTTP://WWW.CHAMORROROOTS.COM)
FOURTEENTH CENSUS OF THE UNITED STATES: 1920—POPULATION
ISLAND OF GUAM

DISTRICT 2
NAME OF PLACE Agana (City)
[Proper name and, also, name of class, as city, town, village, barrio, etc]

ENUMERATED BY ME ON THE 6th DAY OF April, 1920

Arthur W. Jackson ENUMERATOR

	PLACE OF ABODE		NAME	RELATION	PERSONAL DESCRIPTION				EDUCATION			NATIVITY				OCCUPATION
Street, avenue, road, etc.	Number of dwelling house in order of visitation	Number of family in order of visitation	of each person whose place of abode on January 1, 1920, was in the family. Enter surname, first, then given name and middle initial. If any. Include every person living on January 1, 1920. Omit children born since January 1, 1920.	Relationship of this Person to the head of the family.	Sex	Color or race	Age at last birthday	Single, married, widowed or divorced	Attended school any time since Sept. 1, 1919	Whether able to read.	Whether able to write.	Place of birth of this person.	Place of birth of father of this person.	Place of birth of mother of this person.	Whether able to speak English.	Trade, profession, or particular kind of work done, as salesman, laborer, clerk, cook, merchant, washerwoman, etc.
1	2	3	4	5	6	7	8	9	10	11	12	13	14	15	16	17
	436	488	Aflague, Fructoso SM	Son	M	Cha	7.0	S	Y			Guam	Guam	Guam		None
	436	488	Aflague, Tomas SM	Son	M	Cha	6.0	S	N			Guam	Guam	Guam		None
	436	488	Aflague, Dolores SM	Daughter	F	Cha	4.0	S				Guam	Guam	Guam		None
	436	488	Aflague, Josefina SM	Daughter	F	Cha	2.0	S				Guam	Guam	Guam		None
	436	488	Aflague, Inocencio SM	Son	M	Cha	1.0	S				Guam	Guam	Guam		None
	437	489	Peredo, Jose C	Head	M	Cha	33.0	M		Y	Y	Guam	Guam	Guam		Blacksmith
	437	489	Peredo, Pedro M	Son	M	Cha	11.0	S	Y	Y	Y	Guam	Guam	Guam	N	None
	437	489	Peredo, Maria M	Daughter	F	Cha	9.0	S	Y	Y	Y	Guam	Guam	Guam	N	None
San Juan de Letran Street	437	489	Peredo, Remedios M	Daughter	F	Cha	7.0	S	Y			Guam	Guam	Guam		None
	437	489	Peredo, Carmen M	Daughter	F	Cha	5.0	S	N			Guam	Guam	Guam		None
	437	489	Peredo, Antonio M	Son	M	Cha	3.0	S				Guam	Guam	Guam		None
	437	489	Peredo, Mercedes M	Daughter	F	Cha	1.0	S				Guam	Guam	Guam		None
	437	490	Peredo, Fernando G	Head	M	Cha	61.0	M		Y	Y	Guam	Guam	Guam	N	Farmer
	437	490	Peredo, Ana C	Wife	F	Cha	60.0	M		Y	Y	Guam	Guam	Guam	N	None
	437	490	Peredo, Joaquina C	Daughter	F	Cha	39.0	S		Y	Y	Guam	Guam	Guam	N	None
	438	491	Achaigua, Ana S	Head	F	Cha	41.0	Wd		Y	Y	Guam	Guam	Guam	N	None
	438	491	Achaigua, Felisa S	Daughter	F	Cha	22.0	S		Y	Y	Guam	Guam	Guam	Y	None
	438	491	Achaigua, Maria S	Daughter	F	Cha	16.0	S	N	Y	Y	Guam	Guam	Guam	Y	None
	438	491	Achaigua, Pedro S	Son	M	Cha	11.0	S	Y	Y	Y	Guam	Guam	Guam	Y	None
	438	491	Achaigua, Concepcion S	Daughter	F	Cha	6.0	S	N			Guam	Guam	Guam		None
	438	491	Achaigua, Elisa S	Daughter	F	Cha	2.0	S				Guam	Guam	Guam		None
	439	492	Munoz, Manuel C	Head	M	W	22.0	S	N	Y	Y	Guam	Spain	Spain	Y	Farmer
	439	492	Munoz, Enrique C	Brother	M	W	17.0	S	N	Y	Y	Guam	Spain	Spain	Y	None
	439	492	Cruz, Carmen B	Lodger	F	Cha	19.0	S	N	Y	Y	Guam	Guam	Guam	Y	None
	439	492	Cruz, Dolores B	Lodger	F	Cha	17.0	S	N	Y	Y	Guam	Guam	Guam	Y	None

(CHAMORRO ROOTS GENEALOGY PROJECT ™ TRANSCRIPTION)
(COMPILED/TRANSCRIBED BY BERNARD T. PUNZALAN / HTTP://WWW.CHAMORROROOTS.COM)

FOURTEENTH CENSUS OF THE UNITED STATES: 1920–POPULATION
ISLAND OF GUAM

DISTRICT 2
NAME OF PLACE Agana (City)

ENUMERATED BY ME ON THE 7th DAY OF April, 1920

Arthur W. Jackson ENUMERATOR

	Dwelling no. (2)	Family no. (3)	NAME (4)	RELATION (5)	Sex (6)	Color or race (7)	Age (8)	Marital (9)	School (10)	Read (11)	Write (12)	Birth of person (13)	Birth of father (14)	Birth of mother (15)	English (16)	OCCUPATION (17)
26	439	492	Cruz, Pedro B	Lodger	M	Cha	13.0	S	Y	Y	Y	Guam	Guam	Guam	Y	None
27	439	492	Cruz, Rosario B	Lodger	F	Cha	8.0	S	Y			Guam	Guam	Guam		None
28	440	493	Bamba, Felisa	Head	F	Cha	44.0	S		Y	Y	Guam	Unknown	Guam	N	None
29	440	493	Bamba, Jesus	Son	M	Cha	26.0	S		Y	Y	Guam	Unknown	Guam	Y	Farmer
30	440	493	Bamba, Manuel	Son	M	Cha	12.0	S	Y	Y	Y	Guam	Unknown	Guam	N	None
31	440	493	Bamba, Josefa	Daughter	F	Cha	10.0	S	Y	Y	Y	Guam	Unknown	Guam	N	None
32	440	493	Bamba, Vicente	Son	M	Cha	5.0	S	N			Guam	Unknown	Guam		None
33	440	494	Bamba, Jose	Head	M	Cha	20.0	M	N	Y	Y	Guam	Unknown	Guam	Y	Stenographer
34	440	494	Bamba, Rita M	Wife	F	Cha	19.0	M	N	Y	Y	Guam	Guam	Guam	Y	None
35	440	494	Bamba, Maria S	Grandmother	F	Cha	67.0	Wd		N	N	Guam	Guam	Guam	N	None
36	441	495	Aguon, Juan T	Head	M	Cha	50.0	M		Y	Y	Guam	Guam	Guam	N	Farmer
37	441	495	Aguon, Manuela U	Wife	F	Chin	53.0	M		Y	Y	Guam	China	Guam	N	None
38	441	495	Aguon, Rita U	Daughter	F	Cha	27.0	S		Y	Y	Guam	Guam	Guam	Y	None
39	441	495	Aguon, Ana U	Daughter	F	Cha	18.0	S	N	Y	Y	Guam	Guam	Guam	Y	None
40	441	495	Aguon, Juan U	Son	M	Cha	14.0	S	Y	Y	Y	Guam	Guam	Guam	Y	None
41	442	496	San Nicolas, Jose C	Head	M	Cha	41.0	M		N	N	Guam	Guam	Guam	N	Farmer
42	442	496	San Nicolas, Carmen R	Wife	F	Cha	38.0	M		N	N	Guam	Guam	Guam	N	None
43	442	496	San Nicolas, Enrique R	Son	M	Cha	17.0	S	N	Y	Y	Guam	Guam	Guam	Y	Laborer
44	442	496	San Nicolas, Magdalena R	Daughter	F	Cha	14.0	S	N	Y	Y	Guam	Guam	Guam	Y	None
45	442	496	San Nicolas, Joaquina R	Daughter	F	Cha	13.0	S	Y	Y	Y	Guam	Guam	Guam	Y	None
46	442	496	San Nicolas, Pedro R	Son	M	Cha	12.0	S	Y	Y	Y	Guam	Guam	Guam	Y	None
47	442	496	San Nicolas, Olimpia R	Daughter	F	Cha	10.0	S	Y	Y	Y	Guam	Guam	Guam	Y	None
48	442	496	San Nicolas, Juana R	Daughter	F	Cha	8.0	S	Y	Y	Y	Guam	Guam	Guam	N	None
49	442	496	San Nicolas, Francisco R	Son	M	Cha	5.0	S	N			Guam	Guam	Guam		None
50	442	496	San Nicolas, Rosa R	Daughter	F	Cha	3.0	S				Guam	Guam	Guam		None

Street (column 1): San Juan de Letran Street

(CHAMORRO ROOTS GENEALOGY PROJECT ™ TRANSCRIPTION)
(COMPILED/TRANSCRIBED BY BERNARD T. PUNZALAN / HTTP://WWW.CHAMORROROOTS.COM)

FOURTEENTH CENSUS OF THE UNITED STATES: 1920-POPULATION

ISLAND OF GUAM

SHEET NO. 53A

ENUMERATED BY ME ON THE 7th DAY OF April, 1920

Arthur W. Jackson ENUMERATOR

DISTRICT 2
NAME OF PLACE Agana (City)

[Proper name and, also, name of class, as city, town, village, barrio, etc]

	PLACE OF ABODE			NAME	RELATION	PERSONAL DESCRIPTION				EDUCATION			NATIVITY				OCCUPATION
Street, avenue, road, etc.	Number of dwelling house is order of visitation	Number of family in order of visitation		Name of each person whose place of abode on January 1, 1920, was in the family. Enter surname, firs, then given name and middle initial. If any. Include every person living on January 1, 1920. Omit children born since January 1, 1920.	Relationship of this Person to the head of the family.	Sex	Color or race	Age at last birthday	Single, married, widowed or divorced	Attended school any time since Sept. 1, 1919	Whether able to read.	Whether able to write.	Place of birth of this person.	Place of birth of father of this person.	Place of birth of mother of this person.	Whether able to speak English.	Trade, profession, or particular kind of work done, as salesman, laborer, clerk, cook, merchant, washerwoman, etc.
1	2	3	4		5	6	7	8	9	10	11	12	13	14	15	16	17
1	442	496		San Nicolas, Maria R	Daughter	F	Cha	1.0	S				Guam	Guam	Guam		None
2	442	497		Finona, Maria M	Head	F	Cha	70.0	Wd		N	N	Guam	Guam	Guam	N	None
3	442	497		Mendiola, Carmen C	Niece	F	Cha	15.0	S	N	Y	Y	Guam	Guam	Guam	N	None
4	444	498		Camacho, Vicente P	Head	M	Cha	23.0	M		Y	Y	Guam	Guam	Guam	Y	Enlisted US Navy not an Am Citizen
5	444	498		Camacho, Nicolasa M	Wife	F	Cha	24.0	M		Y	Y	Guam	Guam	Guam	Y	None
6	445	499		Borja, Luis G	Head	M	Cha	44.0	M		Y	Y	Guam	Guam	Guam	N	Farmer
7	445	499		Borja, Paz C	Wife	F	Cha	45.0	M		Y	Y	Guam	Guam	Guam	N	None
8	445	499		Cruz, Francisca P	Lodger	F	Cha	15.0	S		Y	Y	Guam	Guam	Guam	Y	None
9	445	499		Cruz, Jose P	Lodger	M	Cha	12.0	S	Y	Y	Y	Guam	Guam	Guam	Y	None
10	446	500		Cruz, Jose P	Head	M	Cha	37.0	Wd		Y	Y	Guam	Unknown	Guam	Y	Clerk
11	446	500		Cruz, Cristobal F. P	Son	M	Cha	10.0	S	Y	Y	Y	Guam	Guam	Phillippine Islands	Y	None
12	447	501		Ulloa, Manuel	Head	M	Cha	27.0	M		Y	Y	Guam	Unknown	Guam	Y	Chauffeur
13	447	501		Ulloa, Maria A	Wife	F	Cha	21.0	M	Y	Y	Y	Guam	Guam	Guam	Y	Teacher
14	447	501		Ulloa, Lucy P. A	Daughter	F	Cha	1.0	S				Guam	Guam	Guam		None
15	448	502		Duenas, Maria F	Head	F	Cha	79.0	Wd				Guam	Guam	Guam	N	None
16	448	502		Duenas, Joaquin A	Grandson	M	Cha	13.0	S	Y	Y	Y	Guam	Guam	Guam	Y	None
17	448	502		Duenas, Gracie A	Grand daughter	F	Cha	12.0	S	Y	Y	Y	Guam	Guam	Guam	Y	None
18	448	502		Duenas, Francisco A	Grandson	M	Cha	10.0	S	Y	Y	Y	Guam	Guam	Guam	Y	None
19	448	502		Aguigui, Juan	Servant	M	Cha	12.0	S	N	Y	Y	Guam	Guam	Guam	N	Servant
20	449	503		San Nicolas, Ignacia A	Head	F	Cha	30.0	Wd		N	N	Guam	Guam	Guam	N	None
21	449	503		San Nicolas, Magdalena A	Daughter	F	Cha	10.0	S	Y	Y	Y	Guam	Guam	Guam	N	None
22	449	503		San Nicolas, Luis A	Son	M	Cha	7.0	S	Y	Y	Y	Guam	Guam	Guam		None
23	449	503		San Nicolas, Lorenzo A	Son	M	Cha	4.0	S				Guam	Guam	Guam		None
24	449	503		San Nicolas, Felipe A	Son	M	Cha	3.0	S				Guam	Guam	Guam		None
25	449	503		San Nicolas, Juan A	Son	M	Cha	2.0	S				Guam	Guam	Guam		None

San Juan de Letran Street

Saragosa Street

(CHAMORRO ROOTS GENEALOGY PROJECT ™ TRANSCRIPTION)
(COMPILED/TRANSCRIBED BY BERNARD T. PUNZALAN / HTTP://WWW.CHAMORROROOTS.COM)

FOURTEENTH CENSUS OF THE UNITED STATES: 1920-POPULATION
ISLAND OF GUAM

ENUMERATED BY ME ON THE 7th DAY OF April, 1920

Arthur W. Jackson ENUMERATOR

DISTRICT 2
NAME OF PLACE Agana (City)
[Proper name and, also, name of class, as city, town, village, barrio, etc]

	PLACE OF ABODE		NAME	RELATION	PERSONAL DESCRIPTION					EDUCATION			NATIVITY					OCCUPATION
Street, avenue, road, etc.	Number of dwelling house is in order of visitation	Number of family in order of visitation	of each person whose place of abode on January 1, 1920, was in the family.	Relationship of this Person to the head of the family.	Sex	Color or race	Age at last birthday	Single, married, widowed or divorced	Attended school any time since Sept. 1, 1919	Whether able to read.	Whether able to write.	Place of birth of this person.	Place of birth of father of this person.	Place of birth of mother of this person.	Whether able to speak English.	Trade, profession, or particular kind of work done, as salesman, laborer, clerk, cook, merchant, washerwoman, etc.
1	2	3	4	5	6	7	8	9	10	11	12	13	14	15	16	17
26	450	504	San Nicolas, Ramona U	Head	F	Cha	27.0	S		Y	Y	Guam	Guam	Guam	N	None
27	450	504	San Nicolas, Felipe U	Brother	M	Cha	23.0	S		Y	Y	Guam	Guam	Guam	Y	Laborer
28	451	505	O'Connor, Antonia U	Head	F	Cha	39.0	M		Y	Y	Guam	Guam	Guam	Y	Seamstress
29	451	505	O'Connor, Isabel U	Daughter	F	W	16.0	S	N	Y	Y	Guam	United States	Guam	Y	None
30	452	506	San Nicolas, Vicente U	Head	M	Cha	29.0	S		Y	Y	Guam	Guam	Guam	N	Farmer
31	453	507	Isidro, Dolores A	Head	F	Cha	69.0	Wd		N	N	Guam	Guam	Guam	N	None
32	453	507	Isidro, Victoria A	Daughter	F	Fil	39.0	S		Y	Y	Guam	Philippine Islands	Guam	Y	Laundress
33	453	507	Isidro, Ursula A	Daughter	F	Fil	35.0	S		Y	Y	Guam	Philippine Islands	Guam	Y	Laundress
34	454	508	Torres, Maria P	Head	F	Cha	45.0	S		N	N	Guam	Guam	Guam	N	None
35	454	508	Torres, Maria P	Daughter	F	Cha	21.0	S	N	Y	Y	Guam	Unknown	Guam	Y	Teacher
36	454	508	Torres, Rita P	Daughter	F	Cha	19.0	S	N	Y	Y	Guam	Unknown	Guam	Y	None
37	454	508	Torres, Ana P	Daughter	F	Cha	14.0	S	Y	Y	Y	Guam	Unknown	Guam	Y	None
38	454	508	Torres, Pedro P	Son	M	Cha	10.0	S	Y	Y	Y	Guam	Unknown	Guam	Y	None
39	454	508	Torres, Josefa P	Daughter	F	Cha	8.0	S	Y			Guam	Unknown	Guam		None
40	454	508	Torres, Ascension P	Daughter	F	Cha	3.0	S				Guam	Unknown	Guam		None
41	455	509	Cruz, Concepcion B	Head	F	Cha	54.0	S		Y	Y	Guam	Unknown	Guam	N	Enlisted US Navy not an Am citizen
42	455	509	Garrido, Vicente C	Son	M	Cha	24.0	S		Y	Y	Guam	Unknown	Guam	Y	Enlisted US Navy not an Am citizen
43	456	510	Leon Guerrero, Matias	Head	M	Cha	34.0	M		Y	Y	Guam	Guam	Guam	Y	None
44	456	510	Leon Guerrero, Maria P	Wife	F	Cha	25.0	M		Y	Y	Guam	Guam	Guam	Y	None
45	456	510	Leon Guerrero, Juan P	Son	M	Cha	6.0	S	N			Guam	Guam	Guam		None
46	456	510	Leon Guerrero, Margarita P	Daughter	F	Cha	4.0	S				Guam	Guam	Guam		None
47	456	510	Leon Guerrero, Jose P	Son	M	Cha	2.0	S				Guam	Guam	Guam		None
48	456	510	Leon Guerrero, Felix P	Son	M	Cha	0.2	S				Guam	Guam	Guam		None
49	457	511	Mendiola, Rosa C	Head	F	Cha	77.0	Wd		N	N	Guam	Guam	Guam	N	None
50	457	511	Mendiola, Rita C	Daughter	F	Cha	50.0	S		N	N	Guam	Guam	Guam	N	None

Saragosa Street

Maria Ana de Austria Street

318

(CHAMORRO ROOTS GENEALOGY PROJECT ™ TRANSCRIPTION)
(COMPILED/TRANSCRIBED BY BERNARD T. PUNZALAN / HTTP://WWW.CHAMORROROOTS.COM)
FOURTEENTH CENSUS OF THE UNITED STATES: 1920-POPULATION
ISLAND OF GUAM

DISTRICT 2
NAME OF PLACE Agana (City)
[Proper name and, also, name of class, as city, town, village, barrio, etc]

ENUMERATED BY ME ON THE 8th DAY OF April, 1920

Arthur W. Jackson ENUMERATOR

	PLACE OF ABODE			NAME	RELATION	PERSONAL DESCRIPTION					EDUCATION			NATIVITY				OCCUPATION
Street, avenue, road, etc.	Number of dwelling house in order of visitation	Number of family in order of visitation		of each person whose place of abode on January 1, 1920, was in the family. Enter surname, first, then given name and middle initial. If any. Include every person living on January 1, 1920. Omit children born since January 1, 1920.	Relationship of this Person to the head of the family.	Sex	Color or race	Age at last birthday	Single, married, widowed or divorced	Attended school any time since Sept. 1, 1919	Whether able to read.	Whether able to write.	Place of birth of this person.	Place of birth of father of this person.	Place of birth of mother of this person.	Whether able to speak English.	Trade, profession, or particular kind of work done, as salesman, laborer, clerk, cook, merchant, washerwoman, etc.
1	2	3	4		5	6	7	8	9	10	11	12	13	14	15	16	17
	457	511	Mendiola, Maria C		Daughter	F	Cha	39.0	S		Y	Y	Guam	Guam	Guam	Y	Laundress
	457	511	Mendiola, Juan		Grandson	M	Cha	5.0	S	N			Guam	Unknown	Guam		None
	457	512	Mendiola, Juan C		Head	M	Cha	42.0	M		Y	Y	Guam	Guam	Guam	Y	Farmer
	457	512	Mendiola, Rosa M		Wife	F	Cha	20.0	M	N	Y	Y	Guam	Guam	Guam	Y	None
	457	512	Mendiola, Ascencion M		Niece	F	Cha	14.0	S	N	Y	Y	Guam	Guam	Guam	Y	None
	458	513	Mendiola, Jose C		Head	M	Cha	38.0	M		Y	Y	Guam	Guam	Guam	Y	Farmer
	458	513	Mendiola, Francisca M		Wife	F	Cha	36.0	M		N	N	Guam	Guam	Guam	N	None
	458	513	Mendiola, Josefina M		Daughter	F	Cha	11.0	S	Y	Y	Y	Guam	Guam	Guam	N	None
	458	513	Mendiola, Jose M		Son	M	Cha	7.0	S	N			Guam	Guam	Guam		None
	458	513	Mendiola, Engracia M		Daughter	F	Cha	6.0	S	N	Y	Y	Guam	Guam	Guam	N	None
	458	513	Mendiola, Rosa M		Daughter	F	Cha	4.0	S		Y	Y	Guam	Guam	Guam	N	None
	458	513	Mendiola, Francisca M		Daughter	F	Cha	2.0	S		N	N	Guam	Guam	Guam	N	None
	458	513	Mendiola, Juan M		Son	M	Cha	1.0	S				Guam	Guam	Guam		None
	459	514	Cruz, Francisco B		Head	M	Cha	33.0	M		Y	Y	Guam	Guam	Guam	N	Laborer
	459	514	Cruz, Ana C		Wife	F	Cha	32.0	M		Y	Y	Guam	Guam	Guam	N	None
Maria Ana de Austria Street	460	515	Cruz, Maria P		Head	F	Cha	74.0	Wd		Y	Y	Guam	Guam	Guam	N	None
	460	515	Cruz, Iolala P		Daughter	F	Cha	59.0	S		N	N	Guam	Guam	Guam	N	None
	460	515	Cruz, Maria P		Daughter	F	Cha	41.0	S		N	N	Guam	Guam	Guam	N	None
	460	515	Cruz, Natividad		Grand daughter	F	Cha	11.0	S	Y	Y	Y	Guam	Unknown	Guam	Y	None
	460	515	Cruz, Antonio		Grandson	M	Cha	8.0	S	Y	Y	Y	Guam	Unknown	Guam	Y	None
	460	515	Cruz, Pedro		Grandson	M	Cha	3.0	S				Guam	Unknown	Guam		None
	460	515	Franquez, Rita C		Grand daughter	F	Cha	5.0	S	N			Guam	Guam	Guam		None
	461	516	Cepeda, Pedro L		Head	M	Cha	50.0	Wd		Y	Y	Guam	Guam	Guam	Y	Farmer
	461	516	Cepeda, Juan M		Son	M	Cha	22.0	S		Y	Y	Guam	Guam	Guam	Y	Printer
	461	516	Cepeda, Maria M		Daughter	F	Cha	19.0	S	N	Y	Y	Guam	Guam	Guam	Y	Telephone Operator

(CHAMORRO ROOTS GENEALOGY PROJECT ™ TRANSCRIPTION)
(COMPILED/TRANSCRIBED BY BERNARD T. PUNZALAN / HTTP://WWW.CHAMORROROOTS.COM)

FOURTEENTH CENSUS OF THE UNITED STATES: 1920-POPULATION
ISLAND OF GUAM

ENUMERATED BY ME ON THE 8th DAY OF April, 1920

Arthur W. Jackson ENUMERATOR

DISTRICT 2
NAME OF PLACE Agana (City)

[Proper name and, also, name of class, as city, town, village, barrio, etc]

	Dwelling No.	Family No.	NAME	RELATION	Sex	Color or race	Age	Single, married, widowed or divorced	Attended school since Sept. 1, 1919	Able to read	Able to write	Place of birth of this person	Place of birth of father	Place of birth of mother	Able to speak English	OCCUPATION
	2	3	4	5	6	7	8	9	10	11	12	13	14	15	16	17
26	461	516	Cepeda, Jesus M	Son	M	Cha	16.0	S	N	Y	Y	Guam	Guam	Guam	Y	Farm laborer
27	461	516	Cepeda, Jose M	Son	M	Cha	14.0	S	N	Y	Y	Guam	Guam	Guam	Y	None
28	461	516	Cepeda, Joaquina M	Daughter	F	Cha	10.0	S	Y			Guam	Guam	Guam	N	None
29	461	516	Cepeda, Vicente A	Son	M	Cha	8.0	S	Y			Guam	Guam	Guam		None
30	461	516	Cepeda, Alfredo M	Son	M	Cha	5.0	S	N			Guam	Guam	Guam		Enlisted US Navy not an Am citizen
31	461	517	Cepeda, Pedro M	Head	M	Cha	29.0	M		Y	Y	Guam	Guam	Guam	Y	None
32	461	517	Cepeda, Maria C	Wife	F	Cha	24.0	M		Y	Y	Guam	Guam	Guam	Y	None
33	461	517	Cepeda, Pedro C	Son	M	Cha	2.0	S				Guam	Guam	Guam		None
34	461	517	Cepeda, Juan C	Son	M	Cha	1.0	S				Guam	Guam	Guam		None
35	462	518	Castro, Jose G	Head	M	Cha	56.0	M		Y	Y	Guam	Guam	Guam	N	None
36	462	518	Castro, Antonia LG	Wife	F	Cha	47.0	M		Y	Y	Guam	Guam	Guam	N	None
37	462	518	Castro, Natividad LG	Daughter	F	Cha	15.0	S	N	Y	Y	Guam	Guam	Guam	Y	None
38	462	518	Castro, Rafael LG	Son	M	Cha	10.0	S	Y	Y	Y	Guam	Guam	Guam	N	None
39	462	518	Castro, Delfina LG	Daughter	F	Cha	9.0	S	Y	Y	Y	Guam	Guam	Guam		None
40	462	518	Castro, Ricardo LG	Son	M	Cha	6.0	S	N			Guam	Guam	Guam		None
41	463	519	Calvo, Magdalena A	Head	F	W	29.0	S		Y	Y	Philippine Islands	Spain	Guam	Y	None
42	463	519	Mendiola, Margarita M	Servant	F	Cha	14.0	S	N			Guam	Guam	Guam	N	None
43	464	520	Torres, Jose C	Head	M	Cha	54.0	M		Y	Y	Guam	Guam	Guam	Y	Farmer
44	464	520	Torres, Ana C	Wife	F	Cha	42.0	M		Y	Y	Guam	Guam	Guam	N	None
45	464	520	Tanigosh, Manuel C	Lodger	M	Jp	15.0	S	N	N	N	Guam	Japan	Guam	N	None
46	464	520	Sablan, Manuel C	Lodger	M	Cha	13.0	S	Y	Y	Y	Guam	Guam	Guam	Y	None
47	465	521	Anderson, Antonio Q	Head	M	W	58.0	M		Y	Y	Guam	Guam	Guam	Y	Farmer
48	465	521	Anderson, Joaquina M	Wife	F	W	58.0	M		Y	Y	Guam	Guam	Guam	N	None
49	465	521	Anderson, Rita M	Daughter	F	W	24.0	S		Y	Y	Guam	Guam	Guam	Y	None
50	465	521	Anderson, Pedro M	Son	M	W	23.0	S		Y	Y	Guam	Guam	Guam	Y	Farmer

Street (rows 41–50): Maria Ana de Austria Street

(CHAMORRO ROOTS GENEALOGY PROJECT ™ TRANSCRIPTION)
(COMPILED/TRANSCRIBED BY BERNARD T. PUNZALAN / HTTP://WWW.CHAMORROROOTS.COM)

FOURTEENTH CENSUS OF THE UNITED STATES: 1920–POPULATION
ISLAND OF GUAM

ENUMERATED BY ME ON THE 9th DAY OF April, 1920

Arthur W. Jackson ENUMERATOR

DISTRICT 2
NAME OF PLACE Agana (City)

Street: Maria Ana de Austria Street

#	Dwelling (2)	Family (3)	NAME (4)	RELATION (5)	Sex (6)	Color/race (7)	Age (8)	Marital (9)	Attended school (10)	Able to read (11)	Able to write (12)	Birthplace (13)	Father's birthplace (14)	Mother's birthplace (15)	English (16)	OCCUPATION (17)
1	465	521	Anderson, Ramona M	Daughter	F	W	21.0	S	N	Y	Y	Guam	Guam	Guam	Y	Servant
2	465	521	Anderson, Juan M	Son	M	W	17.0	S	N	Y	Y	Guam	Guam	Guam	Y	Farm laborer
3	465	521	Anderson, Maria M	Grand daughter	F	W	6.0	S	N			Guam	Unknown	Guam		None
4	465	521	Anderson, Emelia M	Grand daughter	F	W	4.0	S				Guam	Unknown	Guam		None
5	466	522	Torres, Juliana P	Head	F	Cha	58.0	Wd		Y	Y	Guam	Guam	Guam	N	None
6	466	522	Perez, Maria S	Sister	F	Cha	53.0	S		Y	Y	Guam	Guam	Guam	N	None
7	466	522	Torres, Rosa P	Sister	F	Cha	55.0	Wd		Y	Y	Guam	Guam	Guam	N	None
8	466	522	Ada, Herman T	Grandson	M	Cha	10.0	S	Y	Y	Y	Guam	Saipan MI	Guam	Y	None
9	466	522	Castro, Oliva LG	Lodger	F	Cha	13.0	S	Y	Y	Y	Guam	Guam	Guam	Y	None
10	467	523	Roberto, Andres A	Head	M	Cha	60.0	M		Y	Y	Guam	Guam	Guam	Y	Farmer
11	467	523	Roberto, Dolores T	Wife	F	Cha	52.0	M		Y	Y	Guam	Guam	Guam	N	None
12	467	523	Roberto, Jose	Son	M	Cha	31.0	S		Y	Y	Guam	Guam	Guam	Y	Clerk
13	467	524	Roberto, Ignacio T	Head	M	Cha	29.0	M		Y	Y	Guam	Guam	Guam	Y	Machinist
14	467	524	Roberto, Margarita P	Wife	F	Cha	24.0	M		Y	Y	Guam	Guam	Guam	Y	None
15	467	524	Roberto, William A	Son	M	Cha	1.0	S				Guam	Guam	Guam		None
16	467	525	Roberto, Maria A	Head	F	Cha	46.0	S		Y	Y	Guam	Guam	Guam	Y	Nurse
17	467	525	Roberto, Lorenza A	Adopted daughter	F	Cha	10.0	S	Y	Y	Y	Guam	Guam	Guam	Y	None
18	468	526	Aflague, Miguel S	Head	M	Cha	35.0	M	Y	Y	Y	Guam	Guam	Guam	Y	Stone mason
19	468	526	Aflague, Ana R	Wife	F	Cha	29.0	M		Y	Y	Guam	Guam	Guam	Y	None
20	468	526	Aflague, Rigoberto R	Son	M	Cha	5.0	S	N			Guam	Guam	Guam	N	None
21	468	526	Aflague, Simeon R	Son	M	Cha	4.0	S				Guam	Guam	Guam		None
22	468	526	Aflague, Concepcion R	Daughter	F	Cha	3.0	S				Guam	Guam	Guam		None
23	468	526	Aflague, Rosario R	Daughter	F	Cha	0.3	S				Guam	Guam	Guam		None
24	469	527	Aflague, Maria C	Head	F	Cha	58.0	S		Y	Y	Guam	Guam	Guam	N	Laundress
25	469	527	Aflague, Ana C	Sister	F	Cha	52.0	S		Y	Y	Guam	Guam	Guam	N	Laundress

(CHAMORRO ROOTS GENEALOGY PROJECT ™ TRANSCRIPTION)
(COMPILED/TRANSCRIBED BY BERNARD T. PUNZALAN / HTTP://WWW.CHAMORROROOTS.COM)

FOURTEENTH CENSUS OF THE UNITED STATES: 1920-POPULATION

ISLAND OF GUAM

DISTRICT 2
NAME OF PLACE Agana (City)
[Proper name and, also, name of class, as city, town, village, barrio, etc]

SHEET NO. _55B_

ENUMERATED BY ME ON THE 9th DAY OF April, 1920

Arthur W. Jackson ENUMERATOR

	PLACE OF ABODE			NAME	RELATION	PERSONAL DESCRIPTION					EDUCATION			NATIVITY				OCCUPATION
Street, avenue, road, etc.	Number of dwelling house is order of visitation	Number of family in order of visitation		of each person whose place of abode on January 1, 1920, was in the family. Enter surname, firs, then given name and middle initial. If any. Include every person living on January 1, 1920. Omit children born since January 1, 1920.	Relationship of this Person to the head of the family.	Sex	Color or race	Age at last birthday	Single, married, widowed or divorced	Attended school any time since Sept. 1, 1919	Whether able to read.	Whether able to write.	Place of birth of this person.	Place of birth of father of this person.	Place of birth of mother of this person.	Whether able to speak English.	Trade, profession, or particular kind of work done, as salesman, laborer, clerk, cook, merchant, washerwoman, etc.
1	2	3		4	5	6	7	8	9	10	11	12	13	14	15	16	17
26	469	527		Aflague, Vicenta C	Sister	F	Cha	44.0	S		N	N	Guam	Guam	Guam	N	Laundress
27	470	528		Quichocho, Antonia P	Head	F	Cha	42.0	Wd		N	N	Guam	Guam	Guam	N	None
28	470	528		Quichocho, Jose P	Son	M	Cha	23.0	S		Y	Y	Guam	Guam	Guam	Y	Machinist
29	470	528		Quichocho, Jesus P	Son	M	Cha	18.0	S	N	Y	Y	Guam	Guam	Guam	Y	Farm laborer
30	470	528		Quichocho, Manuel P	Son	M	Cha	14.0	S	N	Y	Y	Guam	Guam	Guam	Y	None
31	471	529		Delgado, Nicolasa D	Head	F	Cha	84.0	S		N	N	Guam	Guam	Guam	N	None
32	471	529		Delgado, Juana D	Sister	F	Cha	76.0	Wd		N	N	Guam	Guam	Guam	N	None
33	472	530		Camacho, Mariana P	Head	F	Cha	50.0	S		N	N	Guam	Guam	Guam	N	Laundress
34	472	530		Camacho, Maria P	Daughter	F	Cha	19.0	S	N	Y	Y	Guam	Guam	Guam	Y	Laundress
35	472	530		Camacho, Jesus P	Son	M	Cha	17.0	S	N	Y	Y	Guam	Guam	Guam	Y	App. Carpenter
36	472	530		Camacho, Felisidad P	Daughter	F	Cha	15.0	S	N	Y	Y	Guam	Guam	Guam	Y	None
37	472	530		Camacho, Joaquin P	Son	M	Cha	12.0	S	Y	Y	Y	Guam	Guam	Guam	Y	None
38	473	531		Guerrero, Ignacio G	Head	M	Cha	56.0	M		N	N	Guam	Guam	Guam	N	Farmer
39	473	531		Guerrero, Rosa T	Wife	F	Cha	43.0	M		Y	Y	Guam	Guam	Guam	Y	None
40	473	531		Guerrero, Maria R. T	Daughter	F	Cha	19.0	S	N	Y	Y	Guam	Guam	Guam	Y	Laundress
41	473	531		Guerrero, Rita J. T	Daughter	F	Cha	18.0	S	N	Y	Y	Guam	Guam	Guam	Y	Weaver
42	473	531		Guerrero, Joaquina T	Daughter	F	Cha	17.0	S	N	Y	Y	Guam	Guam	Guam	Y	None
43	473	531		Guerrero, Dolores T	Daughter	F	Cha	14.0	S	N	Y	Y	Guam	Guam	Guam	Y	None
44	473	531		Guerrero, Ignacio T	Son	M	Cha	13.0	S	N	Y	Y	Guam	Guam	Guam	N	None
45	473	531		Guerrero, Joaquin T	Son	M	Cha	11.0	S	Y	Y	Y	Guam	Guam	Guam	N	None
46	473	531		Guerrero, Santiago T	Son	M	Cha	9.0	S	Y			Guam	Guam	Guam		None
47	473	531		Guerrero, Maria E	Daughter	F	Cha	8.0	S	Y			Guam	Guam	Guam		None
48	473	531		Guerrero, Regina T	Daughter	F	Cha	7.0	S	Y			Guam	Guam	Guam		None
49	473	531		Guerrero, Virginia T	Daughter	F	Cha	4.0					Guam	Guam	Guam		None
50	473	531		Guerrero, Jesus T	Son	M	Cha	2.0	S				Guam	Guam	Guam		None

Payta Street

(CHAMORRO ROOTS GENEALOGY PROJECT ™ TRANSCRIPTION)
(COMPILED/TRANSCRIBED BY BERNARD T. PUNZALAN / HTTP://WWW.CHAMORROROOTS.COM)

FOURTEENTH CENSUS OF THE UNITED STATES: 1920-POPULATION
ISLAND OF GUAM

ENUMERATED BY ME ON THE 10th DAY OF April, 1920

Arthur W. Jackson ENUMERATOR

DISTRICT 2

NAME OF PLACE Agana (City)

[Proper name and, also, name of class, as city, town, village, barrio, etc]

	Street	No. dwelling house	No. family	NAME	RELATION	Sex	Color or race	Age at last birthday	Single, married, widowed or divorced	Attended school since Sept. 1, 1919	Whether able to read	Whether able to write	Place of birth of this person	Place of birth of father	Place of birth of mother	Whether able to speak English	OCCUPATION
	1	2	3	4	5	6	7	8	9	10	11	12	13	14	15	16	17
1		473	531	Guerrero, Higinio T	Son	M	Cha	1.0	S				Guam	Guam	Guam		None
2		474	532	de Leon, Joaquin I	Head	M	Cha	56.0	M		Y	Y	Guam	Guam	Guam	N	Farmer
3		474	532	de Leon, Antonia P	Wife	F	Cha	48.0	M		Y	Y	Guam	Guam	Guam	N	None
4		474	532	de Leon, Maria P	Daughter	F	Cha	26.0	S		Y	Y	Guam	Guam	Guam	Y	None
5		474	532	de Leon, Antonio P	Son	M	Cha	21.0	S	N	Y	Y	Guam	Guam	Guam	Y	None
6		474	532	de Leon, Dolores P	Daughter	F	Cha	19.0	S	N	Y	Y	Guam	Guam	Guam	Y	None
7		474	532	de Leon, Manuel P	Son	M	Cha	17.0	S	N	Y	Y	Guam	Guam	Guam	Y	App. Cable Operator
8		474	532	de Leon, Francisco P	Son	M	Cha	15.0	S	N	Y	Y	Guam	Guam	Guam	Y	App. Cable Operator
9		474	532	de Leon, Joaquin P	Son	M	Cha	13.0	S	Y	Y	Y	Guam	Guam	Guam	Y	None
10		474	532	de Leon, Julia P	Daughter	F	Cha	12.0	S	Y	Y	Y	Guam	Guam	Guam	Y	None
11		474	532	de Leon, Luisa P	Daughter	F	Cha	10.0	S	Y	Y	Y	Guam	Guam	Guam	N	None
12		474	532	de Leon, Adela P	Daughter	F	Cha	6.0	S	N			Guam	Guam	Guam	Y	None
13	Lekanto Street	475	533	Salas, Ignacio Q	Head	M	Cha	27.0	M		Y	Y	Guam	Guam	Guam	N	Farmer
14		475	533	Salas, Maria S	Wife	F	Cha	24.0	M		Y	Y	Guam	Guam	Guam	N	None
15		475	533	Salas, Francisco S	Son	M	Cha	4.0	S				Guam	Guam	Guam		None
16		475	533	Salas, Luisa S	Sister	F	Cha	22.0	S		Y	Y	Guam	Guam	Guam	Y	None
17		475	533	Singuenza, Juana T	Sister-in-law	F	Cha	18.0	S	N	Y	Y	Guam	Guam	Guam		None
18		475	533	Singuenza, Joaquina T	Sister-in-law	F	Cha	16.0	S	N	Y	Y	Guam	Guam	Guam		None
19		475	533	Singuenza, Rosa T	Sister-in-law	F	Cha	13.0	S	Y	Y	Y	Guam	Guam	Guam	Y	None
20		475	533	Singuenza, Ana T	Sister-in-law	F	Cha	12.0	S	Y	Y	Y	Guam	Guam	Guam	Y	None
21		475	533	Singuenza, Jose T	Brother-in-law	M	Cha	10.0	S	Y	Y	Y	Guam	Guam	Guam	Y	None
22		475	533	Singuenza, Concepcion T	Sister-in-law	F	Cha	8.0	S	Y	Y	Y	Guam	Guam	Guam		None
23		476	534	Aflague, Rosa A	Head	F	Cha	60.0	Wd		N	N	Guam	Guam	Guam	N	None
24		476	534	Aflague, Rita A	Daughter	F	Cha	19.0	S	N	Y	Y	Guam	Guam	Guam	N	Laundress
25		477	535	Javier, Dolores A	Head	F	Cha	41.0	M	Y	Y	Y	Guam	Guam	Guam	Y	None

(CHAMORRO ROOTS GENEALOGY PROJECT ™ TRANSCRIPTION)
(COMPILED/TRANSCRIBED BY BERNARD T. PUNZALAN / HTTP://WWW.CHAMORROROOTS.COM)

FOURTEENTH CENSUS OF THE UNITED STATES: 1920-POPULATION
ISLAND OF GUAM

160b

ENUMERATED BY ME ON THE 10th DAY OF April, 1920

Arthur W. Jackson ENUMERATOR

DISTRICT 2
NAME OF PLACE Agana (City)
[Proper name and, also, name of class, as city, town, village, barrio, etc]

Street	Dwelling No.	Family No.	NAME	RELATION	Sex	Color or race	Age	Single, married, widowed or divorced	Attended school since Sept. 1, 1919	Able to read	Able to write	Place of birth of this person	Place of birth of father	Place of birth of mother	Able to speak English	OCCUPATION
	1	2	3	4	5	6	7	8	9	10	11	12	13	14	15	16	17
26	477	535	Javier, Maria A	Daughter	F	Cha	10.0	S	Y	Y	Y	Guam	Guam	Guam	N	None
27	477	535	Javier, Isabel A	Daughter	F	Cha	4.0	S				Guam	Guam	Guam	N	None
28	478	536	Santos, Juan	Head	M	Cha	53.0	M		Y	Y	Guam	Unknown	Guam	N	Farmer
29	478	536	Santos, Luisa G	Wife	F	Cha	51.0	M		N	N	Guam	Guam	Guam	N	None
30	478	536	Santos, Luisa G	Daughter	F	Cha	14.0	S	Y	Y	Y	Guam	Guam	Guam	Y	Weaver
31	478	536	Santos, Angelina G	Daughter	F	Cha	13.0	S	Y	Y	Y	Guam	Guam	Guam	Y	None
32	479	537	Cruz, Lorenzo G	Head	M	Cha	30.0	M		Y	Y	Guam	Guam	Guam	Y	Laborer
33	479	537	Cruz, Natividad S	Wife	F	Cha	24.0	M		Y	Y	Guam	Guam	Guam	Y	None
34	479	537	Cruz, Juan S	Son	M	Cha	7.0	S	Y			Guam	Guam	Guam		None
35	479	537	Cruz, Jose S	Son	M	Cha	6.0	S	N			Guam	Guam	Guam		None
36	479	537	Cruz, Pedro S	Son	M	Cha	4.0	S				Guam	Guam	Guam		None
37	479	537	Cruz, Matilde S	Daughter	F	Cha	1.0	S				Guam	Guam	Guam		None
38	480	538	Eustaquio, Jose G	Head	M	Cha	38.0	M		Y	Y	Guam	Guam	Guam	Y	Carpenter
39	480	538	Eustaquio, Ana C	Wife	F	Cha	22.0	M		Y	Y	Guam	Guam	Guam	Y	None
40	480	538	Eustaquio, Maria B	Daughter	F	Cha	17.0	S	N	Y	Y	Guam	Guam	Guam	Y	None
41	480	538	Eustaquio, Gregorio B	Son	M	Cha	14.0	S	N	Y	Y	Guam	Guam	Guam	Y	None
42	480	538	Eustaquio, Antonio B	Son	M	Cha	12.0	S	Y	Y	Y	Guam	Guam	Guam	Y	None
43	480	538	Eustaquio, Angel B	Son	M	Cha	10.0	S	Y	Y	Y	Guam	Guam	Guam	Y	None
44	480	538	Eustaquio, Jose B	Son	M	Cha	7.0	S	Y			Guam	Guam	Guam		None
45	480	538	Eustaquio, Felix B	Son	M	Cha	6.0	S	N			Guam	Guam	Guam	N	None
46	480	538	Eustaquio, Elena B	Daughter	F	Cha	3.0	S				Guam	Guam	Guam		None
47	480	538	Eustaquio, Florencia B	Daughter	F	Cha	1.0	S				Guam	Guam	Guam		None
48	480	539	Salas, Maria E	Head	F	Cha	29.0	Wd		Y	Y	Guam	Guam	Guam	N	None
49	480	539	Salas, Clotilde E	Daughter	F	Cha	7.0	S	Y			Guam	Guam	Guam		None
50	480	539	Salas, Ricardo E	Son	M	Cha	6.0	S	N			Guam	Guam	Guam		None

Street: Lekanto Street

324

(CHAMORRO ROOTS GENEALOGY PROJECT ™ TRANSCRIPTION)
(COMPILED/TRANSCRIBED BY BERNARD T. PUNZALAN / HTTP://WWW.CHAMORROROOTS.COM)

FOURTEENTH CENSUS OF THE UNITED STATES: 1920-POPULATION

ISLAND OF GUAM

DISTRICT 2

NAME OF PLACE **Agana** (City)

[Proper name and, also, name of class, as city, town, village, barrio, etc]

161

ENUMERATED BY ME ON THE 12th DAY OF April, 1920

Arthur W. Jackson ENUMERATOR

	PLACE OF ABODE			NAME	RELATION	PERSONAL DESCRIPTION				EDUCATION			NATIVITY				OCCUPATION
Street, avenue, road, etc.	Number of dwelling house in order of visitation	Number of family in order of visitation		of each person whose place of abode on January 1, 1920, was in the family. Enter surname, first, then given name and middle initial, if any. Include every person living on January 1, 1920. Omit children born since January 1, 1920.	Relationship of this person to the head of the family.	Sex	Color or race	Age at last birthday	Single, married, widowed or divorced	Attended any school since Sept. 1, 1919	Whether able to read.	Whether able to write.	Place of birth of this person.	Place of birth of father of this person.	Place of birth of mother of this person.	Whether able to speak English.	Trade, profession, or particular kind of work done, as salesman, laborer, clerk, cook, merchant, washerwoman, etc.
1	2	3	4		5	6	7	8	9	10	11	12	13	14	15	16	17
	480	539	Eustaquio, Reducinda G		Mother	F	Cha	60.0	Wd		Y	Y	Guam	Guam	Guam	N	None
	481	540	Ojeda, Pedro C		Head	M	Cha	35.0	M		Y	Y	Guam	Guam	Guam	Y	Farmer
	481	540	Ojeda, Rosalia G		Wife	F	Cha	29.0	M		Y	Y	Guam	Unknown	Guam	Y	None
	481	540	Ojeda, Carmen G		Daughter	F	Cha	11.0	S	Y	Y	Y	Guam	Guam	Guam	Y	None
	481	540	Ojeda, Felisidad G		Daughter	F	Cha	10.0	S	Y	Y	Y	Guam	Guam	Guam	N	None
	481	540	Ojeda, Antonia G		Daughter	F	Cha	7.0	S	Y			Guam	Guam	Guam		None
	481	540	Ojeda, Eugenia G		Daughter	F	Cha	6.0	S	N			Guam	Guam	Guam		None
	481	540	Ojeda, Maria G		Daughter	F	Cha	4.0	S				Guam	Guam	Guam		None
	481	540	Ojeda, Eliso G		Son	M	Cha	1.0	S				Guam	Guam	Guam		None
	482	541	Sternberg, Carmen B		Head	F	Cha	53.0	Wd		Y	Y	Guam	Guam	Guam	N	None
	482	541	Garrido, Maria B		Daughter	F	Cha	20.0	S	N	Y	Y	Guam	Guam	Guam	Y	None
	482	541	Garrido, Rosa B		Daughter	F	Cha	18.0	S	N	Y	Y	Guam	Guam	Guam	Y	None
	482	541	Garrido, Salomon B		Son	M	Cha	14.0	S	N	Y	Y	Guam	Guam	Guam	Y	None
	482	541	Sternberg, Jose B		Son	M	W	11.0	S	Y	Y	Y	Guam	United States	Guam	Y	None
	482	541	Sternberg, John B		Son	M	W	10.0	S	Y	Y	Y	Guam	United States	Guam	Y	None
	482	541	Sternberg, George B		Son	M	W	3.0	S				Guam	United States	Guam		None
	483	542	Salas, Maria L		Head	F	Cha	40.0	Wd		Y	Y	Guam	Guam	Guam	N	None
	483	542	Salas, Pilar L		Daughter	F	Cha	20.0	S	N	Y	Y	Guam	Guam	Guam	Y	Teacher
	483	542	Salas, Jesus L		Son	M	Cha	19.0	S	N	Y	Y	Guam	Guam	Guam	Y	Clerk
	483	542	Salas, Galo G		Son	M	Cha	18.0	S	N	Y	Y	Guam	Guam	Guam	Y	App. Machinist
	483	542	Salas, Felix G		Son	M	Cha	16.0	S	Y	Y	Y	Guam	Guam	Guam	Y	None
	483	542	Salas, Jose L		Son	M	Cha	14.0	S	Y	Y	Y	Guam	Guam	Guam	Y	None
	483	542	Salas, Simplicia L		Daughter	F	Cha	12.0	S	Y	Y	Y	Guam	Guam	Guam	Y	None
	483	542	Salas, Matilde L		Daughter	F	Cha	11.0	S	Y	Y	Y	Guam	Guam	Guam	N	None
	483	542	Salas, Carlos L		Son	M	Cha	8.0	S	Y	Y	Y	Guam	Guam	Guam		None

Lekanto Street

(CHAMORRO ROOTS GENEALOGY PROJECT ™ TRANSCRIPTION)
(COMPILED/TRANSCRIBED BY BERNARD T. PUNZALAN / HTTP://WWW.CHAMORROROOTS.COM)

FOURTEENTH CENSUS OF THE UNITED STATES: 1920—POPULATION
ISLAND OF GUAM

ENUMERATED BY ME ON THE 12th DAY OF April, 1920

Arthur W. Jackson ENUMERATOR

DISTRICT 2
NAME OF PLACE Agana (City)

[Proper name and, also, name of class, as city, town, village, barrio, etc]

Street	Dwelling No.	Family No.	NAME	RELATION	Sex	Color or race	Age	Marital	Attended school	Read	Write	Birthplace of person	Birthplace of father	Birthplace of mother	Speak English	OCCUPATION
1	2	3	4	5	6	7	8	9	10	11	12	13	14	15	16	17
Lekanto Street	483	542	Salas, Rafaela L	Daughter	F	Cha	6.0	S	N			Guam	Guam	Guam		None
	483	542	Salas, Albina L	Daughter	F	Cha	5.0	S	N			Guam	Guam	Guam		None
	483	542	Salas, Salvador L	Son	M	Cha	3.0	S				Guam	Guam	Guam		None
	483	542	Salas, Providencia L	Daughter	F	Cha	1.0	S				Guam	Guam	Guam		None
	484	543	Suzuki, Suckichi	Head	M	Jp	46.0	M		Y	Y	Japan	Japan	Japan	N	Gardener
	485	544	Salas, Antonio Q	Head	M	Cha	35.0	M		Y	Y	Guam	Guam	Guam	N	Farmer
	485	544	Salas, Manuela C	Wife	F	Cha	34.0	M				Guam	Guam	Guam	N	None
	485	544	Salas, Ana C	Daughter	F	Cha	14.0	S	Y	Y	Y	Guam	Guam	Guam	Y	None
	485	544	Salas, Maria C	Daughter	F	Cha	13.0	S	Y	Y	Y	Guam	Guam	Guam	Y	None
	485	544	Salas, Rosario C	Daughter	F	Cha	11.0	S	Y	Y	Y	Guam	Guam	Guam	N	None
	485	544	Salas, Remedios C	Daughter	F	Cha	10.0	S	Y	Y	Y	Guam	Guam	Guam	N	None
	485	544	Salas, Regina C	Daughter	F	Cha	7.0	S	Y	Y	Y	Guam	Guam	Guam		None
	485	544	Salas, Superanca C	Daughter	F	Cha	6.0	S	N			Guam	Guam	Guam		None
	485	544	Salas, Joaquin C	Son	M	Cha	4.0	S				Guam	Guam	Guam		None
	485	544	Salas, Engracia C	Daughter	F	Cha	3.0	S				Guam	Guam	Guam		None
San Quintin Street	486	545	Mariano, Ana Q	Head	F	Cha	52.0	Wd		Y	Y	Guam	Guam	Guam	N	Farmer
	486	545	Mariano, Antonio Q	Son	M	Cha	36.0	S		Y	Y	Guam	Guam	Guam	N	None
	486	545	Mariano, Maria Q	Daughter	F	Cha	17.0	S	Y	Y	Y	Guam	Guam	Guam	Y	None
	487	546	Santos, Francisco F	Head	M	Fil	44.0	M		Y	Y	Philippine Islands	Philippine Islands	Philippine Islands	Y	Carpenter
	487	546	Santos, Antonia M	Wife	F	Cha	34.0	M		Y	Y	Guam	Guam	Guam	N	None
	487	546	Santos, Carlos M	Son	M	Fil	14.0	S	Y	Y	Y	Guam	Philippine Islands	Guam	Y	None
	487	546	Santos, Juan M	Son	M	Fil	12.0	S	Y	Y	Y	Guam	Philippine Islands	Guam	N	None
	487	546	Santos, Francisco M	Son	M	Fil	10.0	S	Y	Y	Y	Guam	Philippine Islands	Guam	N	None
	487	546	Santos, Fortoso M	Son	M	Fil	8.0	S	Y	Y	Y	Guam	Philippine Islands	Guam	N	None
	487	546	Santos, Leonida M	Daughter	F	Fil	6.0	S	N			Guam	Philippine Islands	Guam		None

(CHAMORRO ROOTS GENEALOGY PROJECT ™ TRANSCRIPTION)
(COMPILED/TRANSCRIBED BY BERNARD T. PUNZALAN / HTTP://WWW.CHAMORROROOTS.COM)

FOURTEENTH CENSUS OF THE UNITED STATES: 1920-POPULATION

ISLAND OF GUAM

DISTRICT **2**

NAME OF PLACE **Agana (City)**

[Proper name and, also, name of class, as city, town, village, barrio, etc]

ENUMERATED BY ME ON THE 12th DAY OF April, 1920

Arthur W. Jackson ENUMERATOR

	PLACE OF ABODE				NAME	RELATION	PERSONAL DESCRIPTION					EDUCATION			NATIVITY				OCCUPATION
Street, avenue, road, etc.	Number of dwelling house is order of visitation	Number of family in order of visitation			Name of each person whose place of abode on January 1, 1920, was in the family.	Relationship of this Person to the head of the family.	Sex	Color or race	Age at last birthday	Single, married, widowed or divorced	Attended school any time since Sept. 1, 1919	Whether able to read.	Whether able to write.	Place of birth of this person.	Place of birth of father of this person.	Place of birth of mother of this person.	Whether able to speak English.	Trade, profession, or particular kind of work done, as salesman, laborer, clerk, cook, merchant, washerwoman, etc.
1	2	3		4		5	6	7	8	9	10	11	12	13	14	15	16	17
1	487	546			Santos, Ignacio M	Son	M	Fil	4.0	S				Guam	Philippine Islands	Guam		None
2	487	546			Santos, Jesus M	Son	M	Fil	1.0	S				Guam	Philippine Islands	Guam		None
3	487	546			Santos, Nicolas F	Brother	M	Fil	33.0	S		N	N	Philippine Islands	Philippine Islands	Philippine Islands	N	None
4	488	547			Johnson, Ignacia P	Head	F	Cha	30.0	M		Y	Y	Guam	Guam	Guam	N	Laundress
5	488	547			Johnson, Andrew P	Son	M	W	12.0	S	Y	Y	Y	Guam	Michigan	Guam	Y	None
6	488	547			Johnson, Patrick P	Son	M	W	10.0	S	Y	Y	Y	Guam	Michigan	Guam	Y	None
7	488	547			Johnson, Olga P	Daughter	F	W	8.0	S	Y			Guam	Michigan	Guam		None
8	488	547			Perez, Juan P	Son	M	Cha	5.0	S	N			Guam	Unknown	Guam		None
9	488	547			Perez, Leonisa P	Daughter	F	Cha	4.0	S				Guam	Unknown	Guam		None
10	488	547			Perez, Aurelia P	Daughter	F	Cha	1.0	S				Guam	Unknown	Guam		None
11	489	548			Camacho, Victoriano P	Head	M	Cha	27.0	M		Y	Y	Guam	Guam	Guam	Y	Carpenter
12	489	548			Camacho, Concepcion C	Wife	F	Cha	26.0	M		N	N	Guam	Guam	Guam	N	None
13	489	548			Camacho, Rosalia C	Daughter	F	Cha	6.0	S	N			Guam	Guam	Guam		None
14	489	548			Camacho, Maria C	Daughter	F	Cha	3.0	S				Guam	Guam	Guam		None
15	489	548			Camacho, Pedro C	Son	M	Cha	1.0	S				Guam	Guam	Guam		None
16	490	549			Javier, Francisco G	Head	M	Cha	49.0	M		Y	Y	Guam	Guam	Guam	N	Farmer
17	490	549			Javier, Rosa P	Wife	F	Cha	39.0	M		N	N	Guam	Guam	Guam	N	None
18	490	549			Javier, Maria P	Daughter	F	Cha	19.0	S	N	Y	Y	Guam	Guam	Guam	Y	None
19	490	549			Javier, Jesus P	Son	M	Cha	15.0	S	N	Y	Y	Guam	Guam	Guam	Y	None
20	490	549			Javier, Josefa P	Daughter	F	Cha	9.0	S	Y			Guam	Guam	Guam		None
21	490	549			Javier, Jose P	Son	M	Cha	4.0	S				Guam	Guam	Guam		None
22	490	549			Javier, Julia P	Daughter	F	Cha	2.0	S				Guam	Guam	Guam		None
23	491	550			Salas, Nicolas Q	Head	M	Cha	33.0	M		N	N	Guam	Guam	Guam	N	Farmer
24	491	550			Salas, Maria F	Wife	F	Cha	28.0	M		Y	Y	Guam	Guam	Guam		None
25	492	551			Campos, Antonio C	Head	M	Cha	44.0	M		Y	Y	Guam	Unknown	Unknown	N	Farmer

San Quintin Street

(CHAMORRO ROOTS GENEALOGY PROJECT ™ TRANSCRIPTION)
(COMPILED/TRANSCRIBED BY BERNARD T. FUNZALAN / HTTP://WWW.CHAMORROROOTS.COM)

FOURTEENTH CENSUS OF THE UNITED STATES: 1920—POPULATION
ISLAND OF GUAM

ENUMERATED BY ME ON THE 13th DAY OF April, 1920

Arthur W. Jackson ENUMERATOR

DISTRICT 2
NAME OF PLACE Agana (City)
[Proper name and, also, name of class, as city, town, village, barrio, etc]

	Street	Dwelling (2)	Family (3)	NAME (4)	RELATION (5)	Sex (6)	Color or race (7)	Age (8)	Marital (9)	School (10)	Read (11)	Write (12)	Birth person (13)	Birth father (14)	Birth mother (15)	English (16)	OCCUPATION (17)
26		492	551	Campos, Antonia R	Wife	F	Cha	44.0	S		N	N	Guam	Guam	Guam	N	None
27		492	551	Campos, Ramon R	Son	M	Cha	12.0	S	Y	Y	Y	Guam	Guam	Guam	N	None
28		492	551	Campos, Juan R	Son	M	Cha	9.0	S	Y	Y		Guam	Guam	Guam		None
29		492	551	Campos, Luisa R	Daughter	F	Cha	6.0	S	N			Guam	Guam	Guam		None
30		492	551	Campos, Joaquin R	Son	M	Cha	4.0	S				Guam	Guam	Guam		None
31		493	552	Cruz, Juan C	Head	M	Cha	25.0	M		Y	Y	Guam	Guam	Guam	Y	Laborer
32		493	552	Cruz, Ascencion T	Wife	F	Cha	19.0	M	N	Y	Y	Guam	Guam	Guam	N	None
33		493	552	Cruz, Juan T	Son	M	Cha	0.5	S				Guam	Guam	Guam		None
34		494	553	Afaisen, Ramon SN	Head	M	Cha	27.0	M		Y	Y	Guam	Guam	Guam	Y	Laborer
35	San Quintin Street	494	553	Afaisen, Josefa A	Wife	F	Cha	23.0	M		Y	Y	Guam	Guam	Guam	N	None
36		494	553	Afaisen, Romana A	Daughter	F	Cha	3.0	S				Guam	Guam	Guam		none
37		494	554	Farrol, Maria A	Head	F	Cha	36.0	M		Y	Y	Guam	Guam	Guam	N	Servant
38		494	554	Farrol, Filomena A	Daughter	F	W	17.0	S	N	Y	Y	Guam	United States	Guam	Y	Servant
39		494	554	Aflague, Antonia	Daughter	F	Cha	2.0	S				Guam	Unknown	Guam		None
40		495	555	Mariano, Juan Q	Head	M	Cha	32.0	M		Y	Y	Guam	Guam	Guam	N	Farmer
41		495	555	Mariano, Candalaria F	Wife	F	Cha	34.0	M				Guam	Guam	Guam	N	None
42		495	555	Mariano, Ana F	Daughter	F	Cha	11.0	S	Y	Y	Y	Guam	Guam	Guam	N	None
43		495	555	Mariano, Vicente F	Son	M	Cha	9.0	S	Y	Y	Y	Guam	Guam	Guam	N	None
44		495	555	Mariano, Amalia F	Daughter	F	Cha	7.0	S	Y			Guam	Guam	Guam		None
45		496	556	Blaz, Carmen B	Head	F	Cha	38.0	S		Y	Y	Guam	Guam	Guam	Y	Seamstress
46		496	556	Blaz, Jesusa B	Daughter	F	Cha	17.0	S	N	Y	Y	Guam	Unknown	Guam	Y	Telephone operator
47		496	556	Blaz, Angustia B	Daughter	F	Cha	14.0	S	N	Y	Y	Guam	Unknown	Guam	Y	Servant
48		496	556	Blaz, Antonia B	Adopted daughter	F	Cha	14.0	S	N	Y	Y	Guam	Guam	Guam	Y	None
49		496	556	Blaz, Henry B	Grandson	M	Cha	4.0	M				Guam	Unknown	Guam		None
50		496	557	Blaz, Jose B	Head	M	Cha	19.0	M	N	Y	Y	Guam	Unknown	Guam	Y	Enlisted US Navy not an Am citizen

328

(CHAMORRO ROOTS GENEALOGY PROJECT ™ TRANSCRIPTION)
(COMPILED/TRANSCRIBED BY BERNARD T. PUNZALAN / HTTP://WWW.CHAMORROROOTS.COM)

FOURTEENTH CENSUS OF THE UNITED STATES: 1920-POPULATION

ISLAND OF GUAM

ENUMERATED BY ME ON THE 13th DAY OF April, 1920

Arthur W. Jackson ENUMERATOR

DISTRICT 2
NAME OF PLACE Agana (City)
[Proper name and, also, name of class, as city, town, village, barrio, etc]

SHEET NO. 59A

	PLACE OF ABODE			NAME	RELATION	PERSONAL DESCRIPTION					EDUCATION			NATIVITY				OCCUPATION
Street, avenue, road, etc.	Number of dwelling house in order of visitation	Number of family in order of visitation		Name of each person whose place of abode on January 1, 1920, was in this family.	Relationship of this person to the head of the family.	Sex	Color or race	Age at last birthday	Single, married, widowed or divorced	Attended any school since Sept. 1, 1919	Whether able to read.	Whether able to write.	Place of birth of this person.	Place of birth of father of this person.	Place of birth of mother of this person.	Whether able to speak English.	Trade, profession, or particular kind of work done, as salesman, laborer, clerk, cook, merchant, washerwoman, etc.
1	2	3		4	5	6	7	8	9	10	11	12	13	14	15	16	17
	496	557	1	Blaz, Rita L	Wife	F	Cha	19.0	M	N	Y	Y	Guam	Guam	Guam	Y	None
	496	557	2	Blaz, Nicolasa L	Daughter	F	Cha	0.1	S				Guam	Guam	Guam		None
	497	558	3	Salas, Jose Q	Head	M	Cha	44.0	M		Y	Y	Guam	Guam	Guam	N	Farmer
	497	558	4	Salas, Ramona LG	Wife	F	Cha	43.0	M		Y	Y	Guam	Unknown	Guam	N	None
	497	558	5	Salas, Miguel LG	Son	M	Cha	24.0	S		Y	Y	Guam	Guam	Guam	Y	Teacher
	497	558	6	Salas, Rita LG	Daughter	F	Cha	22.0	S		Y	Y	Guam	Guam	Guam	Y	None
	497	558	7	Salas, Jose LG	Son	M	Cha	19.0	S	N	Y	Y	Guam	Guam	Guam	Y	Farm laborer
	497	558	8	Salas, Francisco LG	Son	M	Cha	17.0	S	N	Y	Y	Guam	Guam	Guam	Y	Farm laborer
	497	558	9	Salas, Jesus LG	Son	M	Cha	15.0	S	N	Y	Y	Guam	Guam	Guam	Y	Servant
	497	558	10	Salas, Maria LG	Daughter	F	Cha	13.0	S	Y	Y	Y	Guam	Guam	Guam	Y	None
	497	558	11	Salas, Tomasa LG	Daughter	F	Cha	11.0	S	Y	Y	Y	Guam	Guam	Guam	Y	None
	497	558	12	Salas, Dionisio LG	Son	M	Cha	9.0	S	Y			Guam	Guam	Guam		None
	497	558	13	Salas, Ana LG	Daughter	F	Cha	7.0	S	Y			Guam	Guam	Guam		None
	497	558	14	Salas, Rosa LG	Daughter	F	Cha	6.0	S	N			Guam	Guam	Guam		None
	497	558	15	Salas, Joaquin LG	Son	M	Cha	5.0	S	N			Guam	Guam	Guam		None
	497	558	16	Salas, Atanasio LG	Son	M	Cha	2.0	S				Guam	Guam	Guam		None
	497	558	17	Leon Guerrero, Ana	Mother-in-law	F	Cha	73.0	Wd		N	N	Guam	Guam	Guam		None
	497	558	18	Torres, Josefa R	Lodger	F	Cha	84.0	S		N	N	Guam	Guam	Guam		None
	498	559	19	Peraira, Juan A	Head	M	Cha	32.0	S		Y	Y	Guam	Guam	Guam	Y	Rigger
	498	559	20	Peraira, Ana A	Sister	F	Cha	21.0	S	N	Y	Y	Guam	Guam	Guam	Y	None
	498	559	21	Peraira, Milagro A	Sister	F	Cha	19.0	S	N	Y	Y	Guam	Guam	Guam	Y	Teacher
	498	559	22	Cruz, Joaquina B	Lodger	F	Cha	77.0	D		Y	Y	Guam	Guam	Guam	N	None
	498	559	23	Quichocho, Jose R	Lodger	M	Cha	57.0	S				Guam	Guam	Guam		Farmer
San Quintin Street	498	559	24	Mariano, Nicolas F	Lodger	M	Cha	6.0	S	N			Guam	Guam	Guam	N	None
	498	559	25	Mariano, Antonia F	Lodger	F	Cha	0.5	S				Guam	Guam	Guam		None

(CHAMORRO ROOTS GENEALOGY PROJECT ™ TRANSCRIPTION)
(COMPILED/TRANSCRIBED BY BERNARD T. PUNZALAN / HTTP://WWW.CHAMORROROOTS.COM)

FOURTEENTH CENSUS OF THE UNITED STATES: 1920—POPULATION
ISLAND OF GUAM

163b

ENUMERATED BY ME ON THE 13th DAY OF April, 1920

Arthur W. Jackson ENUMERATOR

DISTRICT 2
NAME OF PLACE Agana (City)
[Proper name and, also, name of class, as city, town, village, barrio, etc]

	Street	Dwell. No.	Fam. No.	NAME	RELATION	Sex	Color or race	Age	Single, married, widowed, or divorced	Attended school since Sept. 1, 1919	Able to read	Able to write	Place of birth of this person	Place of birth of father	Place of birth of mother	Able to speak English	OCCUPATION
	1	2	3	4	5	6	7	8	9	10	11	12	13	14	15	16	17
26	San Quintin Street	499	560	Santos, Ines P	Head	F	Cha	33.0	S	N	N	N	Guam	Guam	Guam	N	Laundress
27		499	560	Santos, Ana P	Daughter	F	Cha	17.0	S	N	Y	Y	Guam	Unknown	Guam	Y	None
28		499	560	Santos, Juan P	Son	M	Cha	10.0	S	Y	Y	Y	Guam	Unknown	Guam	N	None
29		499	560	Santos, Maria P	Daughter	F	Cha	6.0	S	Y			Guam	Unknown	Guam		None
30		499	560	Santos, Jesus P	Son	M	Cha	4.0	S	N			Guam	Unknown	Guam		None
31		499	560	Santos, Cecilia P	Daughter	F	Cha	2.0	S				Guam	Unknown	Guam		None
32		500	561	Siguenza, Lorenzo T	Head	M	Cha	14.0	S	N	Y	Y	Guam	Guam	Guam	Y	Servant
33		501	562	Gogo, Vicenta C	Head	F	Cha	64.0	S		N	N	Guam	Guam	Guam	N	None
34		501	562	Gogo, Felix C	Son	M	Cha	36.0	S		Y	Y	Guam	Unknown	Guam	N	Shoe maker
35		502	563	Uncangco, Bardomero C	Head	M	Chn	59.0	M		N	N	Guam	China	Guam	N	Farmer
36		502	563	Uncangco, Ana S	Wife	F	Cha	57.0	M		N	N	Guam	Guam	Guam	N	None
37		502	563	Uncangco, Eduardo S	Son	M	Chn	13.0	S	Y	Y	Y	Guam	Guam	Guam	Y	None
38		502	563	Uncangco, Rita S	Daughter	F	Chn	12.0	S	Y	Y	Y	Guam	Guam	Guam	N	None
39		502	564	Uncangco, Jose B	Head	M	Cha	27.0	M		Y	Y	Guam	Guam	Guam	Y	Farmer
40		502	564	Uncangco, Magdalena S	Wife	F	Cha	18.0	M	N	Y	Y	Guam	Guam	Guam	Y	None
41		502	564	Uncangco, Concepcion S	Daughter	F	Chn	5.0	S	N			Guam	Guam	Guam	N	None
42	Cristobal Colon Street	503	565	Chamora, Juana C	Head	F	Cha	30.0	M		Y	Y	Guam	Unknown	Guam	N	None
43		503	565	Chamora, Doroteo C	Son	M	Fil	11.0	S	Y	Y	Y	Guam	Philippine Islands	Guam	N	None
44		503	565	Chamora, Ursula C	Daughter	F	Fil	8.0	S	Y	Y	Y	Guam	Philippine Islands	Guam		None
45		503	565	Chamora, Rosita C	Daughter	F	Fil	5.0	S	N			Guam	Philippine Islands	Guam		None
46		504	566	Santos, Jose R	Head	M	Cha	48.0	M		Y	Y	Guam	Guam	Guam	Y	Laborer
47		504	566	Santos, Maria C	Wife	F	Cha	40.0	M		N	N	Guam	Guam	Guam	N	None
48		504	566	Santos, Maria C	Daughter	F	Cha	4.0	S				Guam	Guam	Guam		None
49		504	566	Santos, Juan C	Son	M	Cha	3.0	S				Guam	Guam	Guam		None
50		504	566	Santos, Antonio C	Son	M	Cha	1.0	S				Guam	Guam	Guam		None

(CHAMORRO ROOTS GENEALOGY PROJECT ™ TRANSCRIPTION)
(COMPILED/TRANSCRIBED BY BERNARD T. PUNZALAN / HTTP://WWW.CHAMORROROOTS.COM)

FOURTEENTH CENSUS OF THE UNITED STATES: 1920–POPULATION
ISLAND OF GUAM

DISTRICT 2
NAME OF PLACE Agana (City)
[Proper name and, also, name of class, as city, town, village, barrio, etc]

ENUMERATED BY ME ON THE 14th DAY OF April, 1920
Arthur W. Jackson ENUMERATOR

	PLACE OF ABODE		NAME	RELATION	PERSONAL DESCRIPTION					EDUCATION			NATIVITY				OCCUPATION
Street, avenue, road, etc.	Number of dwelling house in order of visitation	Number of family in order of visitation	Name of each person...	Relationship of this Person to the head of the family.	Sex	Color or race	Age at last birthday	Single, married, widowed or divorced	Attended any school since Sept. 1, 1919	Whether able to read.	Whether able to write.	Place of birth of this person.	Place of birth of father of this person.	Place of birth of mother of this person.	Whether able to speak English.	Trade, profession, or particular kind of work done...
1	2	3	4	5	6	7	8	9	10	11	12	13	14	15	16	17
	505	567	Cruz, Vidal J	Head	M	Cha	35.0	M		Y	Y	Guam	Guam	Guam	N	Laborer
	505	567	Cruz, Rufina C	Wife	F	Cha	31.0	M		N	N	Guam	Guam	Guam	N	None
	505	567	Cruz, Ana C	Daughter	F	Cha	3.0	S				Guam	Guam	Guam		None
	506	568	Torres, Jose C	Head	M	Cha	24.0	M		Y	Y	Guam	Guam	Guam	Y	Farmer
	506	568	Torres, Maria S	Wife	F	Cha	19.0	M	N	Y	Y	Guam	Unknown	Guam	Y	None
	506	568	Torres, Jose S	Son	M	Cha	1.0	S				Guam	Guam	Guam		None
	507	569	Concepcion, Ana SN	Head	F	Cha	50.0	S		N	N	Guam	Guam	Guam	N	Laundress
	507	569	Concepcion, Maria SN	Daughter	F	Cha	13.0	S	N	Y	Y	Guam	Unknown	Guam	N	None
	507	569	Concepcion, Estefania SN	Daughter	F	Cha	12.0	S	N	Y	Y	Guam	Unknown	Guam	Y	Servant
	508	570	Concepcion, Jose C	Head	M	Cha	23.0	M	N	Y	Y	Guam	Guam	Guam	Y	Enlisted US Navy not an Am citizen
	508	570	Concepcion, Teresa A	Wife	F	Cha	20.0	M	N	N	N	Guam	Unknown	Guam	N	None
	508	570	Concepcion, Juan A	Son	M	Cha	2.0	S				Guam	Guam	Guam		None
	508	570	Concepcion, Joaquin A	Son	M	Cha	1.0	S				Guam	Guam	Guam		None
Cristobal Colon Street	509	571	Mafnas, Jose C	Head	M	Cha	21.0	M	N	Y	Y	Guam	Guam	Guam	N	Laborer
	509	571	Mafnas, Rosa L	Wife	F	Cha	29.0	M	N	Y	Y	Guam	Guam	Guam	N	None
	509	571	Mafnas, Regina L	Daughter	F	Cha	5.0	S				Guam	Guam	Guam		None
	509	571	Mafnas, Francisco L	Son	M	Cha	3.0	S				Guam	Guam	Guam		None
	509	571	Mafnas, Antonio L	Son	M	Cha	1.0	S				Guam	Guam	Guam		None
	510	572	Tolentino, Maximo L	Head	M	Fil	42.0	M		Y	Y	Philippine Islands	Philippine Islands	Philippine Islands	Y	Messenger
	510	572	Tolentino, Tomasa L	Wife	F	Fil	30.0	M		N	N	Guam	Philippine Islands	Guam	N	None
	510	572	Tolentino, Maria L	Daughter	F	Fil	11.0	S	Y	Y	Y	Guam	Philippine Islands	Guam	N	None
	510	572	Tolentino, Carmen L	Daughter	F	Fil	9.0	S	Y	Y	Y	Guam	Philippine Islands	Guam		None
	510	572	Tolentino, Vicente L	Son	M	Fil	6.0	S	Y	N	N	Guam	Philippine Islands	Guam		None
	510	572	Tolentino, Manuel L	Brother	M	Cha	37.0	S		Y	Y	Philippine Islands	Philippine Islands	Philippine Islands	N	Laborer
	510	573	Liizama, Vicente C	Head	M	Cha	70.0	M		N	N	Guam	Guam	Guam	N	None

(CHAMORRO ROOTS GENEALOGY PROJECT ™ TRANSCRIPTION)
(COMPILED/TRANSCRIBED BY BERNARD T. PUNZALAN / HTTP://WWW.CHAMORROROOTS.COM)

FOURTEENTH CENSUS OF THE UNITED STATES: 1920-POPULATION
ISLAND OF GUAM

DISTRICT 2
NAME OF PLACE Agana (City)
[Proper name and, also, name of class, as city, town, village, barrio, etc]

ENUMERATED BY ME ON THE 14th DAY OF April, 1920

Arthur W. Jackson ENUMERATOR

	PLACE OF ABODE			NAME	RELATION	PERSONAL DESCRIPTION				EDUCATION			NATIVITY				OCCUPATION
Street, avenue, road, etc.	Number of dwelling house is order of visitation	Number of family in order of visitation	of each person whose place of abode on January 1, 1920, was in the family. Enter surname, first, then given name and middle initial. If any. Include every person living on January 1, 1920. Omit children born since January 1, 1920.	Relationship of this Person to the head of the family.	Sex	Color or race	Age at last birthday	Single, married, widowed or divorced	Attended school any time since Sept. 1, 1919	Whether able to read.	Whether able to write.	Place of birth of this person.	Place of birth of father of this person.	Place of birth of mother of this person.	Whether able to speak English.	Trade, profession, or particular kind of work done, as salesman, laborer, clerk, cook, merchant, washerwoman, etc.
1	2	3	4	5	6	7	8	9	10	11	12	13	14	15	16	17
	510	573	Lizama, Dolores C	Wife	F	Cha	65.0	M		N	N	Guam	Guam	Guam	N	None
	511	574	Muna, Jose C	Head	M	Cha	44.0	M		Y	Y	Guam	Guam	Guam	N	Farmer
	511	574	Muna, Ana G	Wife	F	Cha	40.0	M		N	N	Guam	Guam	Guam	N	None
	511	574	Muna, Felipe G	Son	M	Cha	16.0	S	N	Y	Y	Guam	Guam	Guam	Y	None
	511	574	Muna, Tomasa G	Daughter	F	Cha	13.0	S	N	Y	Y	Guam	Guam	Guam	Y	None
	511	574	Muna, Saturnina G	Daughter	F	Cha	11.0	S	N	Y	Y	Guam	Guam	Guam	N	None
	511	574	Muna, Vicenta C	Sister	F	Cha	41.0	S		N	N	Guam	Guam	Guam	N	None
	511	574	Muna, Antonio C	Brother	M	Cha	45.0	M		Y	Y	Guam	Guam	Guam	N	Farmer
	511	574	Muna, Mother C	Mother	F	Cha	75.0	Wd		N	N	Guam	Guam	Guam	N	None
	512	575	Guzman, Maria F	Head	F	Cha	52.0	S		N	N	Guam	Guam	Guam	N	None
	512	575	Guzman, Potenciana F	Daughter	F	Cha	21.0	S	N	Y	Y	Guam	Unknown	Guam	Y	Servant
	512	575	Fejarang, Manuel	Grandson	M	Cha	2.0	S				Guam	Unknown	Guam		None
	513	576	Atoigue, Joaquina C	Head	F	Cha	44.0	S		Y	Y	Guam	Guam	Guam	N	None
	513	576	Cruz, Maria A	Niece	F	Cha	6.0	S	N			Guam	Guam	Guam		None
	513	576	Atoigue, Jesus C	Nephew	M	Cha	24.0	S		Y	Y	Guam	Guam	Guam	N	Farmer
	513	576	Atoigue, Joaquin C	Nephew	M	Cha	20.0	S	N	Y	Y	Guam	Guam	Guam	Y	None
	514	577	Pangelinan, Emelio	Head	M	Cha	30.0	M		N	N	Guam	Unknown	Guam	N	Farmer
	514	577	Pangelinan, Maria A	Wife	F	Cha	40.0	M		N	N	Guam	Guam	Guam	N	None
	514	577	Pangelinan, Maria A	Daughter	F	Cha	7.0	S	Y			Guam	Guam	Guam		None
	514	577	Pangelinan, Juan A	Son	M	Cha	3.0	S				Guam	Guam	Guam		None
	514	577	Pangelinan, Bartola A	Daughter	F	Cha	2.0	S				Guam	Guam	Guam		None
	515	578	Cruz, Jose M	Head	M	Cha	42.0	Wd		Y	Y	Guam	Guam	Guam		Farmer
	515	578	Cruz, Francisco R	Son	M	Cha	12.0	S	N	Y	Y	Guam	Guam	Guam	N	None
	515	578	Cruz, Rosa R	Daughter	F	Cha	10.0	S	Y	Y	Y	Guam	Guam	Guam	Y	None
	515	578	Cruz, Miguel R	Son	M	Cha	8.0	S	Y	Y	Y	Guam	Guam	Guam	N	None

Cristobal Colon Street

332

(CHAMORRO ROOTS GENEALOGY PROJECT ™ TRANSCRIPTION)
(COMPILED/TRANSCRIBED BY BERNARD T. PUNZALAN / HTTP://WWW.CHAMORROROOTS.COM)

FOURTEENTH CENSUS OF THE UNITED STATES: 1920-POPULATION
ISLAND OF GUAM

DISTRICT 2
NAME OF PLACE Agana (City)
[Proper name and, also, name of class, as city, town, village, barrio, etc]

ENUMERATED BY ME ON THE 15th DAY OF April, 1920

Arthur W. Jackson ENUMERATOR

	Dwelling	Family	NAME	RELATION	Sex	Color or race	Age	Single, married, widowed or divorced	Attended school	Read	Write	Birthplace of person	Birthplace of father	Birthplace of mother	English	OCCUPATION
1	515	578	Cruz, Agustin R	Son	M	Cha	4.0	S				Guam	Guam	Guam		None
2	516	579	Cruz, Ignacio M	Head	M	Cha	52.0	M		N	N	Guam	Guam	Guam	N	Farmer
3	516	579	Cruz, Ana P	Wife	F	Cha	51.0	M		N	N	Guam	Guam	Guam	N	None
4	516	579	Cruz, Jose P	Son	M	Cha	25.0	S		Y	Y	Guam	Guam	Guam	N	Farm laborer
5	516	579	Cruz, Dolores P	Daughter	F	Cha	22.0	S		Y	Y	Guam	Guam	Guam	N	None
6	516	579	Cruz, Vicente P	Son	M	Cha	20.0	S	N	Y	Y	Guam	Guam	Guam	Y	Farm laborer
7	516	579	Cruz, Tomasa P	Daughter	F	Cha	16.0	S	N	Y	Y	Guam	Guam	Guam	Y	None
8	516	579	Cruz, Juan P	Son	M	Cha	10.0	S	Y	Y	Y	Guam	Guam	Guam	Y	None
9	517	580	Warren, Frederick	Head	M	W	32.0	M		Y	Y	England	England	England	Y	Manager of general wholesale mdse.
10	517	580	Warren, Elenor	Wife	F	W	33.0	M		Y	Y	Maryland	New York	Maryland	Y	None
11	517	580	Warren, Ewart	Son	M	W	2.0	S				Guam	England	Maryland		None
12	518	581	Cruz, Silvestre C	Head	M	Cha	36.0	M		Y	Y	Guam	Guam	Guam	N	Farmer
13	518	581	Cruz, Maria L	Wife	F	Cha	35.0	M		Y	Y	Guam	Guam	Guam	N	None
14	518	581	Cruz, Rosario L	Daughter	F	Cha	15.0	S	N	Y	Y	Guam	Guam	Guam	Y	None
15	518	581	Cruz, Mariano L	Son	M	Cha	12.0	S	N	Y	Y	Guam	Guam	Guam	Y	None
16	518	581	Cruz, Consolacion L	Daughter	F	Cha	7.0	S	Y			Guam	Guam	Guam		None
17	518	581	Cruz, Jose L	Son	M	Cha	5.0	S	N			Guam	Guam	Guam		None
18	518	581	Cruz, Miguel L	Son	M	Cha	3.0	S				Guam	Guam	Guam		None
19	518	581	Cruz, Dolores L	Daughter	F	Cha	0.5	S				Guam	Guam	Guam		None
20	519	582	Pangelinan, Juan SN	Head	M	Cha	50.0	M		Y	Y	Guam	Unknown	Guam	N	Farmer
21	519	582	Pangelinan, Maria M	Wife	F	Cha	39.0	M		N	N	Guam	Unknown	Guam	N	None
22	519	582	Pangelinan, Pedro M	Son	M	Cha	6.0	S	N			Guam	Guam	Guam		None
23	519	582	Pangelinan, Concepcion M	Daughter	F	Cha	5.0	S				Guam	Guam	Guam		None
24	519	582	Pangelinan, Francisco M	Son	M	Cha	3.0	S				Guam	Guam	Guam		None
25	519	582	Pangelinan, Juan M	Son	M	Cha	1.0	S				Guam	Guam	Guam		None

Street: Cristobal Colon Street

(CHAMORRO ROOTS GENEALOGY PROJECT ™ TRANSCRIPTION)
(COMPILED/TRANSCRIBED BY BERNARD T. PUNZALAN / HTTP://WWW.CHAMORROROOTS.COM)
FOURTEENTH CENSUS OF THE UNITED STATES: 1920—POPULATION
ISLAND OF GUAM

ENUMERATED BY ME ON THE 15th DAY OF April, 1920

Arthur W. Jackson ENUMERATOR

DISTRICT 2
NAME OF PLACE Agana (City)
[Proper name and, also, name of class, as city, town, village, barrio, etc]

Street: Cristobal Colon Street

	Dwelling	Family	NAME	RELATION	Sex	Color or race	Age	Single, married, widowed or divorced	Attended school since Sept. 1, 1919	Able to read	Able to write	Place of birth of this person	Place of birth of father	Place of birth of mother	Able to speak English	OCCUPATION
	2	3	4	5	6	7	8	9	10	11	12	13	14	15	16	17
26	520	583	Lizama, Felipe A	Head	M	Cha	30.0	M		Y	Y	Guam	Guam	Guam	N	Farmer
27	520	583	Lizama, Saturnina A	Wife	F	Cha	31.0	M		N	N	Guam	Guam	Guam	N	None
28	520	583	Lizama, Cristobal A	Son	M	Cha	7.0	S	Y			Guam	Guam	Guam	N	None
29	520	583	Lizama, Carmen A	Daughter	F	Cha	5.0	S	N			Guam	Guam	Guam		None
30	520	583	Lizama, Magdalena	Niece	F	Cha	17.0	S	N	Y	Y	Guam	Unknown	Guam	Y	None
31	520	583	Lizama, Marcelino B	Father	M	Cha	62.0	Wd		N	N	Guam	Guam	Guam	N	Farmer
32	521	584	de la Rosa, Mariano R	Head	M	Cha	38.0	M		Y	Y	Guam	Guam	Guam	N	Farmer
33	521	584	de la Rosa, Antonia T	Wife	F	Cha	34.0	M		N	N	Guam	Guam	Guam	N	None
34	521	584	de la Rosa, Dolores T	Daughter	F	Cha	11.0	S	Y	Y	Y	Guam	Guam	Guam	N	None
35	521	584	de la Rosa, Maria T	Daughter	F	Cha	9.0	S	Y			Guam	Guam	Guam	N	None
36	521	584	de la Rosa, Agueda T	Daughter	F	Cha	5.0	S	N			Guam	Guam	Guam		None
37	521	584	de la Rosa, Francisco T	Son	M	Cha	2.0	S				Guam	Guam	Guam		None
38	522	585	San Nicolas, Joaquin T	Head	M	Cha	59.0	M		N	N	Guam	Guam	Guam	N	Farmer
39	522	585	San Nicolas, Manuela S	Wife	F	Cha	44.0	M		N	N	Guam	Guam	Guam	N	None
40	522	585	San Nicolas, Trinidad S	Daughter	F	Cha	15.0	S	N	Y	Y	Guam	Guam	Guam	Y	None
41	522	585	San Nicolas, Jesus S	Son	M	Cha	4.0	S				Guam	Guam	Guam		None
42	523	586	Crisostomo, Basilio	Head	M	Cha	34.0	M		Y	Y	Guam	Unknown	Guam	N	Farmer
43	523	586	Crisostomo, Soledad V	Wife	F	Cha	33.0	M		N	N	Guam	Guam	Guam	N	None
44	523	586	Crisostomo, Rita V	Daughter	F	Cha	13.0	S	N	Y	Y	Guam	Guam	Guam	Y	None
45	523	586	Crisostomo, Josefina V	Daughter	F	Cha	9.0	S	Y			Guam	Guam	Guam	N	None
46	523	586	Crisostomo, Purification V	Daughter	F	Cha	6.0	S	N			Guam	Guam	Guam		None
47	523	586	Crisostomo, Francisco V	Son	M	Cha	0.3	S				Guam	Guam	Guam		None
48	524	587	Manglona, Juan S	Head	M	Cha	20.0	M		N	Y	Guam	Guam	Guam	Y	Farmer
49	524	587	Manglona, Dolores C	Wife	F	Cha	24.0	M		Y	Y	Guam	Guam	Guam	Y	None
50	524	587	Manglona, Antonio C	Son	M	Cha	2.0	S				Guam	Guam	Guam		None

(CHAMORRO ROOTS GENEALOGY PROJECT ™ TRANSCRIPTION)
(COMPILED/TRANSCRIBED BY BERNARD T. PUNZALAN / HTTP://WWW.CHAMORROROOTS.COM)

FOURTEENTH CENSUS OF THE UNITED STATES: 1920—POPULATION

ISLAND OF GUAM

166

DISTRICT 2
NAME OF PLACE Agana (City)
[Proper name and, also, name of class, as city, town, village, barrio, etc]

ENUMERATED BY ME ON THE 15th DAY OF April, 1920
Arthur W. Jackson ENUMERATOR

Street	Dwelling house No.	Family No.	NAME	RELATION	Sex	Color or race	Age	Single, married, widowed, divorced	Attended school since Sept. 1, 1919	Able to read	Able to write	Place of birth of this person	Place of birth of father	Place of birth of mother	Able to speak English	OCCUPATION
	524	587	Manglona, Francisco C	Son	M	Cha	0.1	S				Guam	Guam	Guam		None
	525	588	Manglona, Felix C	Head	M	Cha	55.0	M		Y	Y	Guam	Guam	Guam	N	Farmer
	525	588	Manglona, Maria S	Wife	F	Cha	57.0	M		Y	Y	Guam	Guam	Guam	N	None
	525	588	Manglona, Ana S	Daughter	F	Cha	24.0	S		Y	Y	Guam	Guam	Guam	Y	Servant
	525	588	Manglona, Susana S	Daughter	F	Cha	22.0	S		Y	Y	Guam	Guam	Guam	Y	Servant
	525	588	Manglona, Isabel S	Daughter	F	Cha	11.0	S	Y	Y	Y	Guam	Guam	Guam	Y	None
	526	589	Manglona, Vicente S	Head	M	Cha	33.0	M		Y	Y	Guam	Guam	Guam	N	Farmer
	526	589	Manglona, Ana L	Wife	F	Cha	37.0	M		Y	Y	Guam	Guam	Guam		None
	526	589	Manglona, Carmen L	Daughter	F	Cha	14.0	S	N	Y	Y	Guam	Guam	Guam	Y	None
	526	589	Manglona, Gregorio L	Son	M	Cha	9.0	S	Y			Guam	Guam	Guam		None
	526	589	Manglona, Raimundo L	Son	M	Cha	7.0	S	Y			Guam	Guam	Guam		None
	526	589	Manglona, Maria L	Daughter	F	Cha	5.0	S	N			Guam	Guam	Guam		None
	526	589	Manglona, Virginia L	Daughter	F	Cha	3.0	S				Guam	Guam	Guam		None
	526	589	Manglona, Luisa L	Daughter	F	Cha	0.2	S				Guam	Guam	Guam		None
Cristobal Colon Street	527	590	Jesus, Rosalia C	Head	F	Chn	46.0	Wd		N	N	Guam	China	Guam	N	None
	527	590	Jesus, Antonio C	Son	M	Chn	24.0	S		Y	Y	Guam	Guam	Guam	Y	Laborer
	527	590	Jesus, Rita C	Daughter	F	Cha	21.0	S	N	Y	Y	Guam	Guam	Guam	Y	None
	527	590	Jesus, Caridad C	Daughter	F	Cha	17.0	S	N	Y	Y	Guam	Guam	Guam	Y	Servant
	527	590	Jesus, Francisco C	Son	M	Cha	13.0	S	N	Y	Y	Guam	Guam	Guam	Y	None
	527	590	Jesus, Jose C	Son	M	Cha	7.0	S	Y	Y	Y	Guam	Guam	Guam	Y	None
	527	590	Jesus, Josefa C	Daughter	F	Cha	6.0	S	N			Guam	Guam	Guam		None
	527	590	Jesus, Vicenta C	Daughter	F	Cha	3.0	S				Guam	Guam	Guam		None
	528	591	Damian, Justo	Head	M	Fil	39.0	M		Y	Y	Philippine Islands	Philippine Islands	Philippine Islands	Y	Enlisted US Navy not an Am citizen
	528	591	Damian, Petronila B	Wife	F	Ot	37.0	M		Y	Y	Singapore	Singapore	Singapore	Y	None
	528	591	Damian, Jose B	Son	M	Fil	21.0	S	N	Y	Y	Brit. North Borneo	Phillippine Islands	Singapore	Y	Typist

(CHAMORRO ROOTS GENEALOGY PROJECT ™ TRANSCRIPTION)
(COMPILED/TRANSCRIBED BY BERNARD T. PUNZALAN / HTTP://WWW.CHAMORROROOTS.COM)

FOURTEENTH CENSUS OF THE UNITED STATES: 1920—POPULATION
ISLAND OF GUAM

ENUMERATED BY ME ON THE 16th DAY OF April, 1920

Arthur W. Jackson ENUMERATOR

DISTRICT 2
NAME OF PLACE Agana (City)
[Proper name and, also, name of class, as city, town, village, barrio, etc]

	PLACE OF ABODE		NAME	RELATION	PERSONAL DESCRIPTION				EDUCATION			NATIVITY				OCCUPATION
Street, avenue, road, etc.	Number of dwelling house in order of visitation	Number of family in order of visitation	Name of each person	Relationship of this Person to the head of the family	Sex	Color or race	Age at last birthday	Single, married, widowed or divorced	Attended school any time since Sept. 1, 1919	Whether able to read	Whether able to write	Place of birth of this person	Place of birth of father	Place of birth of mother	Whether able to speak English	Occupation
1	2	3	4	5	6	7	8	9	10	11	12	13	14	15	16	17
	528	591	Damian, Gregoria B	Daughter	F	Fil	18.0	S		Y	Y	Brit. North Borneo	Philippine Islands	Singapore	Y	Nurse
	528	591	Damian, Damazo B	Son	M	Fil	13.0	S	N	Y	Y	Philippine Islands	Philippine Islands	Singapore	Y	Messenger
	528	591	Damian, Candido B	Son	M	Fil	10.0	S	Y	Y	Y	Guam	Philippine Islands	Singapore	Y	None
	528	591	Damian, Florentino B	Son	M	Fil	8.0	S	Y			Philippine Islands	Philippine Islands	Singapore		None
	528	591	Damian, Egracio B	Son	M	Fil	5.0	S	N			Guam	Philippine Islands	Singapore		None
	528	591	Damian, Priscila B	Daughter	F	Fil	3.0	S				Guam	Philippine Islands	Singapore		None
	528	591	Damian, Andres B	Son	M	Fil	2.0	S				Guam	Philippine Islands	Singapore		None
	529	592	Meno, Fabiana S	Head	F	Cha	24.0	S		Y	Y	Guam	Guam	Guam	N	None
	529	592	Meno, Teodora S	Daughter	F	Cha	2.0	S				Guam	Unknown	Guam		None
	530	593	Meno, Maria S	Head	F	Cha	27.0	S		Y	Y	Guam	Guam	Guam	N	None
Cristobal Colon Street	530	593	Meno, Baltazara	Daughter	F	Cha	8.0	S	Y			Guam	Unknown	Guam		None
	531	594	Sablan, Lino R	Head	M	Cha	69.0	M		N	N	Guam	Guam	Guam	N	Farmer
	531	594	Sablan, Nieves L	Wife	F	Cha	53.0	M		N	N	Guam	Guam	Guam	N	None
	531	594	Sablan, Magdalena L	Daughter	F	Cha	25.0	S		Y	Y	Guam	Guam	Guam	N	None
	531	594	Sablan, Manuel L	Son	M	Cha	22.0	S	N	Y	Y	Guam	Guam	Guam	Y	Laborer
	531	594	Sablan, Jesus L	Son	M	Cha	19.0	S	N	Y	Y	Guam	Guam	Guam	Y	Farm laborer
	531	594	Mendiola, Juan C	Lodger	M	Cha	19.0	S		Y	Y	Guam	Guam	Guam	Y	Laborer
	532	595	Guerrero, Rita F	Head	F	Cha	50.0	Wd		N	N	Guam	Guam	Guam	N	None
	532	595	Guerrero, Ignacio F	Son	M	Cha	22.0	S		Y	Y	Guam	Guam	Guam	Y	Farmer
	532	596	Santos, Jose A	Head	M	Cha	25.0	M		Y	Y	Guam	Guam	Guam	N	Laborer
	532	596	Santos, Maria G	Wife	F	Cha	28.0	M		Y	Y	Guam	Guam	Guam	N	None
	532	596	Santos, Concepcion G	Daughter	F	Cha	8.0	S	Y	Y	Y	Guam	Guam	Guam		None
	532	596	Santos, Rosario G	Daughter	F	Cha	6.0	S	N	N	N	Guam	Guam	Guam		None
	533	597	Fausto, Joaquina G	Head	F	Fil	58.0	S		N	N	Guam	Philippine Islands	Guam	N	None
	533	597	Fausto, Carmen	Daughter	F	Fil	16.0	S	N	Y	Y	Guam	Unknown	Guam	N	None

336

(CHAMORRO ROOTS GENEALOGY PROJECT ™ TRANSCRIPTION)
(COMPILED/TRANSCRIBED BY BERNARD T. PUNZALAN / HTTP://WWW.CHAMORROROOTS.COM)

FOURTEENTH CENSUS OF THE UNITED STATES: 1920—POPULATION
ISLAND OF GUAM

DISTRICT 2
NAME OF PLACE Agana (City)
[Proper name and, also, name of class, as city, town, village, barrio, etc]

ENUMERATED BY ME ON THE 16th DAY OF April, 1920

Arthur W. Jackson ENUMERATOR

Street	Dwelling No.	Family No.	NAME	RELATION	Sex	Color or race	Age	Marital	Attended school	Read	Write	Birthplace	Father birthplace	Mother birthplace	Speak English	OCCUPATION
			4	5	6	7	8	9	10	11	12	13	14	15	16	17
		533	597	Fausto, Maria	Daughter	F	Fil	12.0	S	Y	Y	Y	Guam	Unknown	Guam	Y	None
	534	598	Balajadia, Vicente L	Head	M	Cha	51.0	M		N	N	Guam	Guam	Guam	N	Farmer
	534	598	Balajadia, Ines LG	Wife	F	Cha	65.0	M		Y	Y	Guam	Guam	Guam	N	None
	534	598	Balajadia, Josefa LG	Daughter	F	Cha	23.0	S		Y	Y	Guam	Guam	Guam	N	None
	534	598	Leon Guerrero, Isabel	Step daughter	F	Cha	35.0	S		Y	Y	Guam	Unknown	Guam	N	None
	534	598	Leon Guerrero, Jose	Step son	M	Cha	31.0	S		Y	Y	Guam	Unknown	Guam	Y	None
	534	598	Leon Guerrero, Jesus	Lodger	M	Cha	15.0	S	N	Y	Y	Guam	Unknown	Guam	Y	Farm laborer
	534	598	Leon Guerrero, Juan	Lodger	M	Cha	12.0	S	Y	Y	Y	Guam	Unknown	Guam	Y	None
Cristobal Colon Street	534	598	Leon Guerrero, Gregorio	Lodger	M	Cha	8.0	S	Y	Y	Y	Guam	Unknown	Guam		None
	535	599	Mesa, Adriano C	Head	M	Cha	29.0	M		Y	Y	Guam	Guam	Guam	N	Machinist
	535	599	Mesa, Susana B	Wife	F	Cha	24.0	M		Y	Y	Guam	Guam	Guam	N	None
	536	600	Pangelinan, Jose	Head	M	Cha	61.0	M		N	N	Guam	Unknown	Guam	N	Farmer
	536	600	Pangelinan, Josefa C	Wife	F	Cha	48.0	M		N	N	Guam	Guam	Guam	N	None
	537	601	George, Vicente	Head	M	Cha	44.0	M		N	N	Guam	Unknown	Guam	Y	Watchman
	537	601	George, Luisa L	Wife	F	Cha	35.0	M		N	N	Guam	Guam	Guam	N	None
	537	601	George, Maria L	Daughter	F	Cha	18.0	S	N	Y	Y	Guam	Guam	Guam	Y	None
	537	601	George, Pilar L	Daughter	F	Cha	13.0	S	N	Y	Y	Guam	Guam	Guam	Y	None
	537	601	George, Rosario L	Daughter	F	Cha	7.0	S	Y	N	N	Guam	Guam	Guam	N	None
	537	601	George, Rosa L	Daughter	F	Cha	5.0	S	N			Guam	Guam	Guam		None
	537	601	George, Regina L	Daughter	F	Cha	4.0	S				Guam	Guam	Guam		None
	537	601	Balajadia, Francisco C	Lodger	M	Cha	31.0	S		Y	Y	Guam	Unknown	Guam	N	None
	538	602	Rojas, Juana D	Head	F	Cha	49.0	S		N	N	Guam	Unknown	Guam	N	None
	538	602	Rojas, Ana	Daughter	F	Cha	22.0	S		Y	Y	Guam	Unknown	Unknown	Y	None
	538	602	Rojas, Jose	Son	M	Cha	10.0	S	Y	Y	Y	Guam	Unknown	Unknown	N	None
	538	602	Rojas, Ignacio	Son	M	Cha	8.0	S	Y	Y	Y	Guam	Unknown	Guam	N	None

(CHAMORRO ROOTS GENEALOGY PROJECT ™ TRANSCRIPTION)
(COMPILED/TRANSCRIBED BY BERNARD T. PUNZALAN / HTTP://WWW.CHAMORROROOTS.COM)
FOURTEENTH CENSUS OF THE UNITED STATES: 1920—POPULATION
ISLAND OF GUAM

DISTRICT 2
NAME OF PLACE Agana (City)
[Proper name and, also, name of class, as city, town, village, barrio, etc]

ENUMERATED BY ME ON THE 16th DAY OF April, 1920

Arthur W. Jackson ENUMERATOR

	Street	Number of dwelling house	Number of family	NAME	RELATION	Sex	Color or race	Age at last birthday	Single, married, widowed or divorced	Attended school since Sept. 1, 1919	Whether able to read	Whether able to write	Place of birth of this person	Place of birth of father of this person	Place of birth of mother of this person	Whether able to speak English	OCCUPATION
	1	2	3	4	5	6	7	8	9	10	11	12	13	14	15	16	17
26		538	602	Rojas, Mariano	Grandson	M	Cha	1.0	S				Guam	Unknown	Guam		None
27		539	603	San Agustin, Pedro	Head	M	Cha	27.0	M		Y	Y	Guam	Unknown	Guam	N	Farmer
28		539	603	San Agustin, Josefa B	Wife	F	Cha	24.0	M		Y	Y	Guam	Guam	Guam	N	None
29		539	603	San Agustin, Ana B	Daughter	F	Cha	8.0	S	Y			Guam	Guam	Guam		None
30		539	603	San Agustin, Asencion G	Daughter	F	Cha	6.0	S	N			Guam	Guam	Guam		None
31		539	603	San Agustin, Vicente B	Son	M	Cha	5.0	S				Guam	Guam	Guam		None
32		539	603	San Agustin, Dolores B	Daughter	F	Cha	3.0	S				Guam	Guam	Guam		None
33		539	603	San Agustin, Remedios B	Daughter	F	Cha	2.0	S				Guam	Guam	Guam		None
34	Cristobal Colon Street	539	604	Borja, Maria L	Head	F	Cha	51.0	Wd		N	N	Guam	Guam	Guam	N	None
35		539	604	Borja, Magdalena L	Daughter	F	Cha	15.0	S	N	Y	Y	Guam	Guam	Guam	Y	None
36		539	605	Borja, Manuel L	Head	M	Cha	24.0	M		Y	Y	Guam	Guam	Guam	Y	Farmer
37		539	605	Borja, Maria M	Wife	F	Cha	30.0	M		N	N	Guam	Guam	Guam	N	None
38		539	605	Borja, Maria M	Daughter	F	Cha	1.0	S				Guam	Guam	Guam		None
39		540	606	Cruz, Ignacio M	Head	M	Cha	45.0	M		Y	Y	Guam	Guam	Guam	N	Farmer
40		540	606	Cruz, Nicolasa F	Wife	F	Cha	54.0	M		Y	Y	Guam	Guam	Guam	N	None
41		541	607	Pangelinan, Francisco C	Head	M	Cha	48.0	M		Y	Y	Guam	Guam	Guam	N	Farmer
42		541	607	Pangelinan, Maria D	Wife	F	Cha	40.0	M		N	N	Guam	Guam	Guam	N	None
43		541	607	Dimapan, Jose A	Brother-in-law	M	Cha	24.0	S		Y	Y	Guam	Guam	Guam	N	Farmer
44		542	608	Crisostomo, Vicente C	Head	M	Cha	52.0	M		Y	Y	Guam	Guam	Guam	N	Farmer
45		542	608	Crisostomo, Vicenta P	Wife	F	Cha	49.0	M		N	N	Guam	Guam	Guam	N	None
46		542	608	Crisostomo, Angel P	Son	M	Cha	15.0	S	N	Y	Y	Guam	Guam	Guam	Y	Farm laborer
47		542	608	Crisostomo, Juan P	Son	M	Cha	13.0	S	Y	Y	Y	Guam	Guam	Guam	Y	None
48		542	608	Crisostomo, Antonio P	Son	M	Cha	10.0	S	Y	N	N	Guam	Guam	Guam	N	None
49		542	608	Cruz, Maria R	Lodger	F	Cha	75.0	Wd		N	N	Guam	Guam	Guam	N	None
50		543	609	Lizama, Concepcion C	Head	F	Cha	43.0	M		N	N	Guam	Guam	Guam	N	None

(CHAMORRO ROOTS GENEALOGY PROJECT ™ TRANSCRIPTION)
(COMPILED/TRANSCRIBED BY BERNARD T. PUNZALAN / HTTP://WWW.CHAMORROROOTS.COM)

FOURTEENTH CENSUS OF THE UNITED STATES: 1920-POPULATION

ISLAND OF GUAM

ENUMERATED BY ME ON THE 17th DAY OF April, 1920

Arthur W. Jackson ENUMERATOR

DISTRICT 2
NAME OF PLACE Agana (City)
[Proper name and, also, name of class, as city, town, village, barrio, etc]

#	Street	Dwelling (2)	Family (3)	NAME (4)	RELATION (5)	Sex (6)	Color/race (7)	Age (8)	Marital (9)	School (10)	Read (11)	Write (12)	Birth person (13)	Birth father (14)	Birth mother (15)	English (16)	OCCUPATION (17)
1		543	609	Lizama, Remedios C	Daughter	F	Cha	16.0	S	N	Y	Y	Guam	Guam	Guam	Y	None
2		543	609	Lizama, Rosa C	Daughter	F	Cha	13.0	S	Y	Y	Y	Guam	Guam	Guam	Y	Servant
3		543	609	Lizama, Ana C	Daughter	F	Cha	10.0	S	Y	Y	Y	Guam	Guam	Guam	Y	Servant
4		543	609	Lizama, Florencia C	Daughter	F	Cha	9.0	S	Y			Guam	Guam	Guam		None
5		543	609	Lizama, Juan C	Son	M	Cha	7.0	S	Y			Guam	Guam	Guam		None
6		543	609	Lizama, Jose C	Son	M	Cha	6.0	S	N			Guam	Guam	Guam		None
7		543	609	Lizama, Joaquina C	Daughter	F	Cha	3.0	S				Guam	Guam	Guam		None
8		543	609	Crisostomo, Dolores C	Lodger	F	Cha	41.0	S		N	N	Guam	Guam	Guam	N	None
9		544	610	Lizama, Juan B	Head	M	Cha	45.0	M		Y	Y	Guam	Guam	Guam	Y	Farmer
10		544	610	Lizama, Rosa G	Wife	F	Cha	42.0	M		Y	N	Guam	Unknown	Guam	N	None
11		544	610	Lizama, Juan G	Son	M	Cha	15.0	S	N	Y	Y	Guam	Guam	Guam	Y	None
12		544	610	Lizama, Jose G	Son	M	Cha	13.0	S	N	Y	Y	Guam	Guam	Guam	Y	None
13		544	610	Lizama, Jesus G	Son	M	Cha	12.0	S	Y	Y	Y	Guam	Guam	Guam	Y	None
14		544	610	Lizama, Oliva G	Daughter	F	Cha	7.0	S	Y			Guam	Guam	Guam		None
15		544	610	Lizama, Joaquin G	Son	M	Cha	4.0	S				Guam	Guam	Guam		None
16		544	610	Lizama, Felicita G	Daughter	F	Cha	1.0	S				Guam	Guam	Guam		None
17		544	611	Manibusan, Juan M	Head	M	Cha	28.0	M		Y	Y	Guam	Guam	Guam	Y	Farmer
18		544	611	Manibusan, Soledad G	Wife	F	Cha	24.0	M		Y	Y	Guam	Guam	Guam	N	None
19		544	611	Manibusan, Francisco L	Son	M	Cha	2.0	S				Guam	Guam	Guam		None
20		545	612	Estrellas, Maria P	Head	F	Cha	52.0	Wd		N	N	Guam	Philippine Islands	Guam	N	None
21		546	613	Crisostomo, Jose T	Head	M	Cha	54.0	Wd		Y	Y	Guam	Guam	Guam	N	Farmer
22		546	613	Crisostomo, Joaquin T	Son	M	Cha	19.0	S	N	Y	Y	Guam	Guam	Guam	Y	Laborer
23		546	613	Crisostomo, Juan T	Son	M	Cha	17.0	S	N	Y	Y	Guam	Guam	Guam	Y	None
24		546	613	Crisostomo, Ana T	Daughter	F	Cha	16.0	S	N	Y	Y	Guam	Guam	Guam	Y	None
25		546	613	Crisostomo, Concepcion T	Daughter	F	Cha	13.0	S	Y	Y	Y	Guam	Guam	Guam	Y	None

Street: Cristobal Colon Street

(CHAMORRO ROOTS GENEALOGY PROJECT ™ TRANSCRIPTION)
(COMPILED/TRANSCRIBED BY BERNARD T. PUNZALAN / HTTP://WWW.CHAMORROROOTS.COM)

FOURTEENTH CENSUS OF THE UNITED STATES: 1920-POPULATION
ISLAND OF GUAM

ENUMERATED BY ME ON THE 17th DAY OF April, 1920

Arthur W. Jackson ENUMERATOR

DISTRICT 2
NAME OF PLACE Agana (City)
[Proper name and, also, name of class, as city, town, village, barrio, etc]

	PLACE OF ABODE		NAME	RELATION	PERSONAL DESCRIPTION				EDUCATION			NATIVITY				OCCUPATION
Street, avenue, road, etc.	Number of dwelling house in order of visitation	Number of family in order of visitation	of each person whose place of abode on January 1, 1920, was in the family. Enter surname, firs, then given name and middle initial. If any. Include every person living on January 1, 1920. Omit children born since January 1, 1920.	Relationship of this Person to the head of the family.	Sex	Color or race	Age at last birthday	single, married, widowed or divorced	Attended school any time since Sept. 1, 1919	Whether able to read.	Whether able to write.	Place of birth of this person.	Place of birth of father of this person.	Place of birth of mother of this person.	Whether able to speak English.	Trade, profession, or particular kind of work done, as salesman, laborer, clerk, cook, merchant, washerwoman, etc.
	2	3	4	5	6	7	8	9	10	11	12	13	14	15	16	17
	546	613	Crisostomo, Concepcion T	Sister	F	Cha	56.0	S		N	N	Guam	Guam	Guam	N	None
	547	614	Flores, Joaquin D	Head	M	Cha	48.0	M		Y	Y	Guam	Guam	Guam	Y	Farmer
	547	614	Flores, Maria C	Wife	F	Cha	44.0	M		N	N	Guam	Unknown	Guam	N	None
	547	614	Flores, Juan C	Son	M	Cha	12.0	S	Y	Y	Y	Guam	Guam	Guam	Y	None
	547	614	Flores, Joaquin C	Son	M	Cha	10.0	S	Y	Y	Y	Guam	Guam	Guam	N	None
	547	614	Flores, Dolores C	Daughter	F	Cha	8.0	S	Y			Guam	Guam	Guam		None
	547	614	Flores, Engracia C	Daughter	F	Cha	3.0	S				Guam	Guam	Guam		None
	547	614	Cruz, Josefa	Mother-in-law	F	Cha	80.0	S		N	N	Guam	Guam	Guam	N	None
Cristobal Colon Street	548	615	Gumataotao, Francisco	Head	M	Cha	62.0	Wd		Y	Y	Guam	Unknown	Guam	N	Farmer
	548	615	Gumataotao, Maria S	Daughter	F	Cha	32.0	S		Y	Y	Guam	Guam	Guam	N	None
	548	615	Gumataotao, Ana S	Daughter	F	Cha	30.0	S		Y	Y	Guam	Guam	Guam	N	None
	548	615	Gumataotao, Soledad S	Daughter	F	Cha	21.0	S	N	Y	Y	Guam	Guam	Guam	N	None
	548	616	Gumataotao, Jose S	Head	M	Cha	33.0	M		Y	Y	Guam	Guam	Guam	Y	Farmer
	548	616	Gumataotao, Maria T	Wife	F	Cha	24.0	M		N	N	Guam	Guam	Guam	N	None
	548	616	Gumataotao, Lorenzo T	Son	M	Cha	3.0	S				Guam	Guam	Guam		None
	548	616	Gumataotao, Rita T	Daughter	F	Cha	1.0	S				Guam	Guam	Guam		None
	548	616	Gumataotao, Antonio	Nephew	M	Cha	10.0	S	N	Y	Y	Guam	Unknown	Guam	N	None
	549	617	Cruz, Ignacio M	Head	M	Cha	40.0	M		N	N	Guam	Guam	Guam	N	Farmer
	549	617	Cruz, Nicolasa F	Wife	F	Cha	41.0	M		N	N	Guam	Guam	Guam	N	None
	549	617	Fausto, Juan	Step son	M	Cha	23.0	S		Y	Y	Guam	Unknown	Guam	Y	Laborer
	549	617	Fausto, Jose	Step son	M	Cha	21.0	S	N	Y	Y	Guam	Unknown	Guam	Y	Farm laborer
	549	617	Fausto, Vicenta	Step daughter	F	Cha	19.0	S	N	Y	Y	Guam	Unknown	Guam	Y	None
	549	617	Fausto, Felix	Step son	M	Cha	12.0	S	N	N	N	Guam	Unknown	Guam	N	None
	549	618	Fausto, Ignacia	Head	F	Cha	39.0	S		N	N	Guam	Unknown	Guam	N	None
	549	618	Fausto, Jose	Son	M	Cha	4.0	S				Guam	Unknown	Guam	N	None

(CHAMORRO ROOTS GENEALOGY PROJECT ™ TRANSCRIPTION)
(COMPILED/TRANSCRIBED BY BERNARD T. PUNZALAN / HTTP://WWW.CHAMORROROOTS.COM)

FOURTEENTH CENSUS OF THE UNITED STATES: 1920-POPULATION
ISLAND OF GUAM

DISTRICT 2
NAME OF PLACE Agana (City)
[Proper name and, also, name of class, as city, town, village, barrio, etc]

ENUMERATED BY ME ON THE 19th DAY OF April, 1920

Arthur W. Jackson ENUMERATOR

	Street, avenue, road, etc.	Number of dwelling house (2)	Number of family (3)	NAME (4)	RELATION (5)	Sex (6)	Color or race (7)	Age at last birthday (8)	Single, married, widowed or divorced (9)	Attended school since Sept. 1, 1919 (10)	Whether able to read (11)	Whether able to write (12)	Place of birth of this person (13)	Place of birth of father (14)	Place of birth of mother (15)	Whether able to speak English (16)	OCCUPATION (17)
1		549	618	Fausto, Jesus	Son	M	Cha	2.0	S				Guam	Unknown	Guam		None
2		550	619	Concepcion, Enrique S	Head	M	Cha	38.0	M		Y	Y	Guam	Guam	Guam	Y	Fireman
3		550	619	Concepcion, Juana P	Wife	F	Cha	38.0	M		Y	Y	Guam	Guam	Guam	N	None
4		550	619	Concepcion, Felisidad P	Daughter	F	Cha	11.0	S	N	Y	Y	Guam	Guam	Guam	Y	None
5		550	619	Concepcion, Enrique P	Son	M	Cha	8.0	S	Y			Guam	Guam	Guam		None
6		550	619	Concepcion, Catalina P	Daughter	F	Cha	4.0	S				Guam	Guam	Guam		None
7		550	619	Concepcion, Inocencio P	Son	M	Cha	2.0	S				Guam	Guam	Guam		None
8		551	620	Taitano, Joaquin G	Head	M	Cha	33.0	M		Y	Y	Guam	Guam	Guam	N	Farmer
9		551	620	Taitano, Maria C	Wife	F	Cha	29.0	M		Y	Y	Guam	Guam	Guam	N	None
10		551	620	Taitano, Juan C	Son	M	Cha	4.0	S				Guam	Guam	Guam		None
11		551	620	Taitano, Jose C	Son	M	Cha	2.0	S				Guam	Guam	Guam		None
12		552	621	Cruz, Jose C	Head	M	Cha	50.0	Wd		Y	Y	Guam	Guam	Guam	N	Farmer
13		552	621	Cruz, Ana Q	Daughter	F	Cha	17.0	S	N	Y	Y	Guam	Guam	Guam	Y	None
14		552	621	Cruz, Jose Q	Son	M	Cha	12.0	S	Y	Y	Y	Guam	Guam	Guam	Y	None
15		552	621	Cruz, Josefa Q	Daughter	F	Cha	10.0	S	Y	Y	Y	Guam	Guam	Guam	Y	None
16	Cristobal Colon Street	553	622	Borja, Paulino B	Head	M	Cha	41.0	M		N	N	Guam	Unknown	Guam	N	Barber
17		553	622	Borja, Maria C	Wife	F	Cha	39.0	M		N	N	Guam	Unknown	Guam	N	None
18		553	622	Borja, Jesus C	Son	M	Cha	17.0	S	Y	Y	Y	Guam	Guam	Guam	Y	Servant
19		553	622	Borja, Francisco C	Son	M	Cha	12.0	S	Y	Y	Y	Guam	Guam	Guam	Y	None
20		553	622	Borja, Luisa C	Daughter	F	Cha	8.0	S				Guam	Guam	Guam		None
21		553	622	Borja, Vicente C	Son	M	Cha	4.0	S				Guam	Guam	Guam		None
22		553	622	Borja, Catalina C	Daughter	F	Cha	3.0	S				Guam	Guam	Guam		None
23		553	622	Rivera, Camilo	Lodger	M	Fil	30.0	M		Y	Y	Philippine Islands	Philippine Islands	Philippine Islands	N	None
24		554	623	Crisostomo, Lorenzo B	Head	M	Cha	50.0	M		N	N	Guam	Guam	Guam	N	Barber
25		554	623	Crisostomo, Paula C	Wife	F	Cha	49.0	M		N	N	Guam	Guam	Guam	N	Farmer

(CHAMORRO ROOTS GENEALOGY PROJECT ™ TRANSCRIPTION)
(COMPILED/TRANSCRIBED BY BERNARD T. PUNZALAN / HTTP://WWW.CHAMORROROOTS.COM)

FOURTEENTH CENSUS OF THE UNITED STATES: 1920-POPULATION

ISLAND OF GUAM

ENUMERATED BY ME ON THE 19th DAY OF April, 1920

Arthur W. Jackson ENUMERATOR

DISTRICT 2

NAME OF PLACE Agana (City)

[Proper name and, also, name of class, as city, town, village, barrio, etc]

	Street	Dwelling No.	Family No.	NAME	RELATION	Sex	Color or race	Age	Single, married, widowed or divorced	Attended school since Sept. 1, 1919	Able to read	Able to write	Birth of this person	Birth of father	Birth of mother	Able to speak English	OCCUPATION
26		554	623	Crisostomo, Faustino C	Son	M	Cha	24.0	S		Y	Y	Guam	Guam	Guam	Y	Farmer
27		554	623	Crisostomo, Rosa C	Daughter	F	Cha	22.0	S		Y	Y	Guam	Guam	Guam	Y	None
28		554	623	Crisostomo, Jesus C	Son	M	Cha	16.0	S	N	Y	Y	Guam	Guam	Guam	Y	Laborer
29		554	623	Crisostomo, Remedios C	Daughter	F	Cha	13.0	S	N	Y	Y	Guam	Guam	Guam	Y	None
30		554	623	Crisostomo, Marcelo C	Son	M	Cha	9.0	S	Y			Guam	Guam	Guam	N	None
31		555	624	Crisostomo, Mariano C	Head	M	Cha	77.0	M		Y	Y	Guam	Guam	Guam	N	None
32		555	624	Crisostomo, Maria P	Wife	F	W	60.0	M		Y	Y	Guam	Portugal	Guam	N	None
33		555	624	Crisostomo, Josefa P	Daughter	F	Cha	33.0	S		Y	Y	Guam	Guam	Guam	N	None
34		555	624	Crisostomo, Maria P	Daughter	F	Cha	32.0	S		Y	Y	Guam	Guam	Guam	N	None
35		555	624	Crisostomo, Jesus P	Son	M	Cha	24.0	S		Y	Y	Guam	Guam	Guam	N	Silversmith
36		555	624	Crisostomo, Antonio P	Son	M	Cha	21.0	S	N	Y	Y	Guam	Guam	Guam	N	Farmer
37		555	624	Crisostomo, Vicente P	Son	M	Cha	19.0	S	N	Y	Y	Guam	Guam	Guam	Y	Blacksmith
38		555	624	Crisostomo, Ana P	Daughter	F	Cha	16.0	S	N	Y	Y	Guam	Guam	Guam	Y	None
39	Cristobal Colon Street	555	625	Aguon, Juan C	Head	M	Cha	31.0	M		Y	Y	Guam	Guam	Guam	N	Farmer
40		555	625	Aguon, Isabel C	Wife	F	Cha	30.0	M		Y	Y	Guam	Guam	Guam	N	None
41		555	625	Aguon, Engracia C	Daughter	F	Cha	4.0	S				Guam	Guam	Guam		None
42		555	625	Aguon, Joaquin C	Son	M	Cha	3.0	S				Guam	Guam	Guam		None
43		555	625	Aguon, Martina C	Daughter	F	Cha	2.0	S				Guam	Guam	Guam		None
44		555	625	Aguon, Segundo C	Son	M	Cha	0.2	S				Guam	Guam	Guam		None
45		556	626	Crisostomo, Francisco P	Head	M	Cha	22.0	M		Y	Y	Guam	Guam	Guam	Y	Farmer
46		556	626	Crisostomo, Dolores P	Wife	F	Cha	20.0	M	N	Y	Y	Guam	Guam	Guam	Y	None
47		556	626	Crisostomo, Felicita P	Daughter	F	Cha	2.0	S				Guam	Guam	Guam		None
48		556	626	Crisostomo, Jose P	Son	M	W	1.0	S				Guam	Guam	Guam		None
49		557	627	Pangelinan, Ana P	Head	F	Cha	53.0	Wd		Y	Y	Guam	Portugal	Portugal	Y	None
50		557	627	Pangelinan, Maria P	Daughter	F	Cha	33.0	S		Y	Y	Guam	Guam	Guam	N	None

342

(CHAMORRO ROOTS GENEALOGY PROJECT ™ TRANSCRIPTION)

(COMPILED/TRANSCRIBED BY BERNARD T. PUNZALAN / HTTP://WWW.CHAMORROROOTS.COM)

FOURTEENTH CENSUS OF THE UNITED STATES: 1920-POPULATION

ISLAND OF GUAM

170

DISTRICT 2

NAME OF PLACE Agana (City)

[Proper name and, also, name of class, as city, town, village, barrio, etc]

ENUMERATED BY ME ON THE 19th DAY OF April, 1920

Arthur W. Jackson ENUMERATOR

Street, avenue, road, etc.	Number of dwelling house in order of visitation	Number of family in order of visitation	NAME	RELATION	Sex	Color or race	Age at last birthday	Single, married, widowed or divorced	Attended school any time since Sept. 1, 1919	Whether able to read.	Whether able to write.	Place of birth of this person.	Place of birth of father of this person.	Place of birth of mother of this person.	Whether able to speak English.	OCCUPATION
1	2	3	4	5	6	7	8	9	10	11	12	13	14	15	16	17
	557	627	Pangelinan, Francisco P	Son	M	Cha	27.0	S		Y	Y	Guam	Guam	Guam	N	Farmer
	557	627	Pangelinan, Trinidad P	Daughter	F	Cha	25.0	S		Y	Y	Guam	Guam	Guam	N	None
	557	627	Pangelinan, Tomas P	Grand son	M	Cha	14.0	S	N	Y	Y	Guam	Unknown	Guam	Y	Messenger
	558	628	Pangelinan, Maria C	Head	F	Cha	69.0	Wd		N	N	Guam	Guam	Guam	N	None
	558	628	Pangelinan, Pedro C	Son	M	Cha	42.0	S		N	N	Guam	Guam	Guam	N	Farmer
	558	628	Pangelinan, Maria C	Daughter	F	Cha	37.0	S		N	N	Guam	Guam	Guam	N	None
	559	629	Sablan, Ana A	Head	F	Cha	62.0	Wd		N	N	Guam	Guam	Guam	N	None
	559	629	Sablan, Jose A	Son	M	Cha	24.0	S		Y	Y	Guam	Guam	Guam	Y	Laborer
	560	630	Aguon, Jose P	Head	M	Cha	27.0	M		N	N	Guam	Guam	Guam	N	Laborer
	560	630	Aguon, Catalina C	Wife	F	Cha	20.0	M	N	N	N	Guam	Guam	Guam	N	None
	560	630	Aguon, Luisa C	Daughter	F	Cha	3.0	S				Guam	Guam	Guam		None
	560	630	Aguon, Vicente C	Son	M	Cha	2.0	S				Guam	Guam	Guam		None
	561	631	Aguon, Candaleria P	Head	F	Cha	51.0	Wd		N	N	Guam	Guam	Guam	N	None
	561	631	Aguon, Juan P	Son	M	Cha	22.0	S		Y	Y	Guam	Guam	Guam	Y	Laborer
	561	631	Aguon, Maria P	Daughter	F	Cha	20.0	S	N	Y	Y	Guam	Guam	Guam	Y	None
	561	631	Aguon, Soledad P	Daughter	F	Cha	16.0	S	N	Y	Y	Guam	Guam	Guam	Y	None
	561	631	Aguon, Tomasa P	Daughter	F	Cha	14.0	S	N	Y	Y	Guam	Guam	Guam	Y	None
	562	632	Mafnas, Vicente	Head	M	Cha	25.0	M		Y	Y	Guam	Unknown	Guam	Y	Farmer
	562	632	Mafnas, Ana A	Wife	F	Cha	29.0	M		N	N	Guam	Guam	Guam	N	None
	562	632	Mafnas, Concepcion A	Daughter	F	Cha	6.0	S				Guam	Guam	Guam		None
	562	632	Mafnas, Antonio A	Son	M	Cha	4.0	S				Guam	Guam	Guam		None
	562	632	Mafnas, Antonia A	Daughter	F	Cha	2.0	S				Guam	Guam	Guam		None
	563	633	Toves, Jose C	Head	M	Cha	24.0	S		Y	Y	Guam	Guam	Guam	Y	Laborer
	563	633	Toves, Vicente C	Brother	M	Cha	22.0	S		Y	Y	Guam	Guam	Guam	Y	Enlisted US Navy not an Am citizen
	563	633	Toves, Ana C	Sister	F	Cha	19.0	S	N	Y	Y	Guam	Guam	Guam	Y	None

Cristobal Colon Street

343

(CHAMORRO ROOTS GENEALOGY PROJECT ™ TRANSCRIPTION)
(COMPILED/TRANSCRIBED BY BERNARD T. PUNZALAN / HTTP://WWW.CHAMORROROOTS.COM)
FOURTEENTH CENSUS OF THE UNITED STATES: 1920-POPULATION
ISLAND OF GUAM

DISTRICT 2
NAME OF PLACE Agana (City)
[Proper name and, also, name of class, as city, town, village, barrio, etc]

ENUMERATED BY ME ON THE 20th DAY OF April, 1920

Arthur W. Jackson ENUMERATOR

	PLACE OF ABODE		NAME	RELATION	PERSONAL DESCRIPTION				EDUCATION			NATIVITY				OCCUPATION
Street, avenue, road, etc.	No. of dwelling house	No. of family	of each person whose place of abode on January 1, 1920, was in the family.	Relationship of this Person to the head of the family.	Sex	Color or race	Age at last birthday	Single, married, widowed or divorced	Attended school any time since Sept. 1, 1919	Whether able to read.	Whether able to write.	Place of birth of this person.	Place of birth of father of this person.	Place of birth of mother of this person.	Whether able to speak English.	Trade, profession, or particular kind of work done
1	2	3	4	5	6	7	8	9	10	11	12	13	14	15	16	17
	563	633	Toves, Concepcion C	Sister	F	Cha	13.0	S	Y	Y	Y	Guam	Guam	Guam	Y	None
	564	634	Leon Guerrero, Jose R	Head	M	Cha	42.0	M		Y	Y	Guam	Guam	Guam	N	Farmer
	564	634	Leon Guerrero, Maria M	Wife	F	W	30.0	M		Y	Y	Guam	Spain	Guam	N	None
	564	634	Leon Guerrero, Rosario M	Daughter	F	Cha	5.0	S	N			Guam	Guam	Guam		None
	564	634	Leon Guerrero, Jose M	Son	M	Cha	3.0	S				Guam	Guam	Guam		None
	564	634	Leon Guerrero, Maria M	Daughter	F	Cha	0.1	S				Guam	Guam	Guam		None
	564	634	Toves, Ana P	Servant	F	Cha	12.0	S	Y	Y	Y	Guam	Guam	Guam	Y	Servant
	564	634	Santos, Sebastian J	Servant	M	Cha	25.0	S		N	N	Guam	Guam	Guam	N	Servant
Cristobal Colon Street	564	634	Cepeda, Teresa L	Lodger	F	Cha	52.0	S		N	N	Guam	Guam	Guam	N	None
	565	635	Munoz, Jose C	Head	M	W	25.0	M		Y	Y	Guam	Spain	Guam	Y	Policeman
	565	635	Munoz, Ana B	Wife	F	Cha	27.0	M		N	N	Guam	Guam	Guam	N	None
	566	636	Cruz, Gregorio Q	Head	M	Cha	31.0	M		Y	Y	Guam	Guam	Guam	N	Farmer
	566	636	Cruz, Marcela T	Wife	F	Cha	46.0	M		N	N	Guam	Guam	Guam	N	None
	566	636	Tenorio, Vicente	Stepson	M	Cha	11.0	S	Y	Y	Y	Guam	Guam	Guam	N	None
	566	637	Tenorio, Jose T	Head	M	Cha	26.0	M		Y	Y	Guam	Unknown	Guam	Y	Machinist
	566	637	Tenorio, Rosa G	Wife	F	Cha	29.0	M		N	Y	Guam	Guam	Guam		None
	566	637	Tenorio, Gonzalo G	Son	M	Cha	4.0	S				Guam	Guam	Guam		None
	566	637	Tenorio, Delfina G	Daughter	F	Cha	2.0	S				Guam	Guam	Guam		None
	567	638	Munoz, Jose C	Head	M	W	40.0	M		Y	Y	Guam	Spain	Guam	Y	Electrician
	567	638	Munoz, Rosa I	Wife	F	Cha	40.0	M		N	N	Guam	Guam	Guam	N	None
	567	638	Munoz, Rosa I	Daughter	F	W	16.0	S	N	Y	Y	Guam	Guam	Guam	Y	None
	567	638	Munoz, Jesus I	Son	M	W	14.0	S	N	Y	Y	Guam	Guam	Guam	Y	None
	567	638	Munoz, Jose I	Son	M	W	11.0	S	Y	Y	Y	Guam	Guam	Guam	N	None
	567	638	Munoz, Antonio I	Son	M	W	10.0	S	Y	Y	Y	Guam	Guam	Guam	N	None
	567	638	Munoz, Joaquina I	Daughter	F	W	8.0	S	Y	Y	Y	Guam	Guam	Guam	N	None

(CHAMORRO ROOTS GENEALOGY PROJECT ™ TRANSCRIPTION)
(COMPILED/TRANSCRIBED BY BERNARD T. PUNZALAN / HTTP://WWW.CHAMORROROOTS.COM)

FOURTEENTH CENSUS OF THE UNITED STATES: 1920-POPULATION

ISLAND OF GUAM

DISTRICT 2

NAME OF PLACE Agana (City)

[Proper name and, also, name of class, as city, town, village, barrio, etc]

ENUMERATED BY ME ON THE 20th DAY OF April, 1920

Arthur W. Jackson ENUMERATOR

Street, avenue, road, etc.	Number of dwelling house in order of visitation	Number of family in order of visitation	NAME of each person whose place of abode on January 1, 1920, was in the family. Enter surname, first, then given name and middle initial, if any. Include every person living on January 1, 1920. Omit children born since January 1, 1920.	RELATION Relationship of this Person to the head of the family.	Sex	Color or race	Age at last birthday	Single, married, widowed or divorced	Attended school any time since Sept. 1, 1919	Whether able to read.	Whether able to write.	Place of birth of this person.	Place of birth of father of this person.	Place of birth of mother of this person.	Whether able to speak English.	OCCUPATION Trade, profession, or particular kind of work done, as salesman, laborer, clerk, cook, merchant, washerwoman, etc.
1	2	3	4	5	6	7	8	9	10	11	12	13	14	15	16	17
	567	638	Munoz, Ramon I	Son	M	Cha	6.0	S	N			Guam	Guam	Guam		None
	567	638	Munoz, Isabel I	Daughter	F	Cha	4.0	S				Guam	Guam	Guam		None
	567	638	Munoz, Juan I	Son	M	Cha	2.0	S				Guam	Guam	Guam		None
	568	639	Quichocho, Vicente Q	Head	M	Cha	38.0	M		Y	Y	Guam	Guam	Guam	N	Laborer
	568	639	Quichocho, Maria P	Wife	F	Cha	35.0	M		Y	Y	Guam	Guam	Guam	Y	None
	568	639	Quichocho, Eufasia P	Daughter	F	Cha	14.0	S	N	Y	Y	Guam	Guam	Guam	N	None
	568	639	Quichocho, Jesus P	Son	M	Cha	10.0	S	Y	Y	Y	Guam	Guam	Guam	N	None
	568	639	Quichocho, Patrosino P	Son	M	Cha	8.0	S	Y			Guam	Guam	Guam		None
	568	639	Quichocho, Jose P	Son	M	Cha	4.0	S				Guam	Guam	Guam		None
Cristobal Colon Street	568	639	Quichocho, Ana P	Daughter	F	Cha	3.0	S				Guam	Guam	Guam		None
	568	639	Quichocho, Agatomia P	Daughter	F	Cha	2.0	S				Guam	Guam	Guam		None
	568	639	Perez, Juana C	Lodger	F	Cha	70.0	Wd		N	N	Guam	Guam	Guam	N	None
	569	640	Salas, Juan S	Head	M	Cha	50.0	M		Y	Y	Guam	Guam	Guam	Y	Fireman
	569	640	Salas, Susana Q	Wife	F	Cha	47.0	M		N	N	Guam	Guam	Guam	N	None
	569	640	Salas, Joaquin Q	Son	M	Cha	14.0	S	N	Y	Y	Guam	Guam	Guam	Y	None
	569	640	Salas, Juan Q	Son	M	Cha	12.0	S	Y	Y	Y	Guam	Guam	Guam	Y	None
	569	640	Salas, Rosario Q	Daughter	F	Cha	9.0	S	Y			Guam	Guam	Guam		None
	569	640	Salas, Andres Q	Son	M	Cha	6.0	S	N			Guam	Guam	Guam		None
	569	640	Quichocho, Nicolasa S	Mother-in-law	F	Cha	70.0	Wd		N	N	Guam	Guam	Guam	N	None
	570	641	Anderson, Francisco Q	Head	M	Cha	43.0	M		Y	Y	Guam	Guam	Guam	N	Farmer
	570	641	Anderson, Josefa B	Wife	F	Cha	33.0	M		N	N	Guam	Unknown	Guam	N	None
	570	641	Anderson, Francisco B	Son	M	Cha	16.0	S	N	Y	Y	Guam	Guam	Guam	Y	None
	570	641	Anderson, Ana B	Daughter	F	Cha	14.0	S	Y	Y	Y	Guam	Guam	Guam	Y	None
	570	641	Anderson, Jose B	Son	M	Cha	12.0	S	Y	Y	Y	Guam	Guam	Guam	Y	None
	570	641	Anderson, Ramon B	Son	M	Cha	11.0	S	Y	Y	Y	Guam	Guam	Guam	N	None

(CHAMORRO ROOTS GENEALOGY PROJECT ™ TRANSCRIPTION)
(COMPILED/TRANSCRIBED BY BERNARD T. PUNZALAN / HTTP://WWW.CHAMORROROOTS.COM)
FOURTEENTH CENSUS OF THE UNITED STATES: 1920-POPULATION
ISLAND OF GUAM

ENUMERATED BY ME ON THE 20th DAY OF April, 1920

Arthur W. Jackson ENUMERATOR

DISTRICT 2
NAME OF PLACE Agana (City)
[Proper name and, also, name of class, as city, town, village, barrio, etc]

Street	Dwelling No.	Family No.	NAME	RELATION	Sex	Color or race	Age	Marital	School	Read	Write	Birthplace	Father birthplace	Mother birthplace	English	OCCUPATION
1	2	3	4	5	6	7	8	9	10	11	12	13	14	15	16	17
	570	641	Anderson, Maria B	Daugther	F	Cha	8.0	S	Y			Guam	Guam	Guam		None
	570	641	Anderson, Tomas B	Son	M	Cha	6.0	S	N			Guam	Guam	Guam		None
	570	641	Anderson, Antonia B	Daugther	F	Cha	4.0	S				Guam	Guam	Guam		None
	570	641	Anderson, Dolores B	Daugther	F	Cha	2.0	S				Guam	Guam	Guam		None
	570	641	Benavente, Ana B	Mother-in-law	F	Cha	58.0	Wd		Y	Y	Guam	Guam	Guam	N	None
	571	642	de Leon, Antonio C	Head	M	Cha	33.0	Wd		Y	Y	Guam	Guam	Guam	N	Farmer
	571	642	de Leon, Juan M	Son	M	Cha	13.0	S	N	Y	Y	Guam	Guam	Guam	Y	None
	571	642	de Leon, Enrique M	Son	M	Cha	11.0	S	Y	Y	Y	Guam	Guam	Guam	N	None
	571	642	de Leon, Lourdes M	Daugther	F	Cha	5.0	S	N			Guam	Guam	Guam		None
	571	642	de Leon, Raimundo M	Son	M	Cha	3.0	S				Guam	Guam	Guam		None
Cristobal Colon Street	572	643	Pangelinan, Jose C	Head	M	Cha	40.0	M		Y	Y	Guam	Guam	Guam	N	Farmer
	572	643	Pangelinan, Rita L	Wife	F	Cha	42.0	M		N	N	Guam	Guam	Guam	N	None
	572	643	Pangelinan, Maria L	Daugther	F	Cha	19.0	S	N	Y	Y	Guam	Guam	Guam	Y	None
	572	643	Pangelinan, Juana L	Daugther	F	Cha	18.0	S	N	Y	Y	Guam	Guam	Guam	Y	None
	572	643	Pangelinan, Hilaria L	Daugther	F	Cha	16.0	S	N	Y	Y	Guam	Guam	Guam	Y	None
	572	643	Pangelinan, Concepcion L	Daugther	F	Cha	12.0	S	Y	Y	Y	Guam	Guam	Guam	N	None
	573	644	Leddy, Henry V	Head	M	W	40.0	Wd		Y	Y	New York	New York	New York	Y	Foreman
	573	644	Leddy, John B	Son	M	W	14.0	S	N	Y	Y	Guam	New York	Guam	Y	None
	573	644	Leddy, Lucy B	Daugther	F	W	11.0	S	Y	Y	Y	Guam	New York	Guam	Y	None
	573	644	Leddy, Daniel B	Son	M	W	8.0	S	Y	Y	Y	Guam	New York	Guam		None
	573	644	Leddy, Elsie B	Daugther	F	W	2.0	S				Guam	New York	Guam		None
	573	644	Pangelinan, Lorenzo L	Lodger	M	Cha	10.0	S	Y	Y	Y	Guam	Guam	Guam	N	None
	573	644	Pangelinan, Luisa L	Lodger	F	Cha	5.0	S	N			Guam	Guam	Guam		None
	573	644	Pangelinan, Rosario L	Lodger	F	Cha	3.0	S				Guam	Guam	Guam		None
	573	644	Pangelinan, Rosalia L	Lodger	F	Cha	1.0	S				Guam	Guam	Guam		None

Row numbers: 26–50

(CHAMORRO ROOTS GENEALOGY PROJECT ™ TRANSCRIPTION)
(COMPILED/TRANSCRIBED BY BERNARD T. PUNZALAN / HTTP://WWW.CHAMORROROOTS.COM)

FOURTEENTH CENSUS OF THE UNITED STATES: 1920-POPULATION

ISLAND OF GUAM

SHEET NO. _68A_

ENUMERATED BY ME ON THE 21th DAY OF April, 1920

Arthur W. Jackson ENUMERATOR

DISTRICT **2**

NAME OF PLACE **Agana (City)**

[Proper name and, also, name of class, as city, town, village, barrio, etc]

	Number of dwelling house is order of visitation	Number of family in order of visitation	NAME	RELATION	Sex	Color or race	Age at last birthday	Single, married, widowed or divorced	Attended school any time since Sept. 1, 1919	Whether able to read.	Whether able to write.	Place of birth of this person.	Place of birth of father of this person.	Place of birth of mother of this person.	Whether able to speak English.	OCCUPATION Trade, profession, or particular kind of work done, as salesman, laborer, clerk, cook, merchant, washerwoman, etc.
	2	3	4	5	6	7	8	9	10	11	12	13	14	15	16	17
1	574	645	Atoigue, Joaquin C	Head	M	Cha	60.0	M		Y	Y	Guam	Guam	Guam	N	Farmer
2	574	645	Atoigue, Dolores B	Wife	F	Cha	50.0	M		N	N	Guam	Guam	Guam	N	None
3	574	645	Atoigue, Juan B	Son	M	Cha	17.0	S	N	Y	Y	Guam	Guam	Guam	Y	Farm laborer
4	574	645	Atoigue, Jose B	Son	M	Cha	16.0	S	N	Y	Y	Guam	Guam	Guam	Y	None
5	574	645	Atoigue, Carmen B	Daughter	F	Cha	13.0	S	Y	Y	Y	Guam	Guam	Guam	Y	None
6	575	646	Fejarang, Jose P	Head	M	Cha	27.0	M		Y	Y	Guam	Guam	Guam	N	Farm laborer
7	575	646	Fejarang, Maria S	Wife	F	Cha	17.0	M	N	Y	Y	Guam	Guam	Guam	Y	None
8	576	647	Ignacio, Vicente A	Head	M	Cha	39.0	Wd		Y	Y	Guam	Guam	Guam	N	Herder
9	576	647	Ignacio, Ursula C	Daughter	F	Cha	13.0	S	Y	Y	Y	Guam	Guam	Guam	N	None
10	576	647	Ignacio, Maria C	Daughter	F	Cha	10.0	S	Y	Y	Y	Guam	Guam	Guam	N	None
11			Here ends the enumeration of Agana City District No 2.													
12																
13																
14																
15																
16																
17																
18																
19																
20																
21																
22																
23																
24																
25																

Street: Cristobal Colon Street

(CHAMORRO ROOTS GENEALOGY PROJECT ™ TRANSCRIPTION)
(COMPILED/TRANSCRIBED BY BERNARD T. PUNZALAN / HTTP://WWW.CHAMORROROOTS.COM)

FOURTEENTH CENSUS OF THE UNITED STATES: 1920-POPULATION

ISLAND OF GUAM

SHEET NO. 69A

DISTRICT 2

NAME OF PLACE Tutujan (sub-District)

[Proper name and, also, name of class, as city, town, village, barrio, etc]

ENUMERATED BY ME ON THE 21st DAY OF April, 1920

Arthur W. Jackson ENUMERATOR

	PLACE OF ABODE			NAME	RELATION	PERSONAL DESCRIPTION				EDUCATION			NATIVITY				OCCUPATION
Street, avenue, road, etc.	Number of dwelling house is order of visitation	Number of family in order of visitation		of each person whose place of abode on January 1, 1920, was in the family.	Relationship of this person to the head of the family.	Sex	Color or race	Age at last birthday	Single, married, widowed or divorced	Attended school any time since Sept. 1, 1919	Whether able to read.	Whether able to write.	Place of birth of this person.	Place of birth of father of this person.	Place of birth of mother of this person.	Whether able to speak English.	Trade, profession, or particular kind of work done, as salesman, laborer, clerk, cook, merchant, washerwoman, etc.
1	2	3	4		5	6	7	8	9	10	11	12	13	14	15	16	17
	577	648	Jackson, Arthur W	Head	M	W	40.0	D		Y	Y	New York	Canada	Canada	Y	Lawyer
	577	648	Campos, Jose R	Servant	M	Cha	10.0	S	Y	Y	Y	Guam	Guam	Guam	Y	Servant
	578	649	Ulloa, Potenciana	Head	F	Cha	65.0	Wd		Y	Y	Guam	Guam	Guam	N	None
	578	649	Ulloa, Ana C	Daughter	F	Cha	36.0	S		Y	Y	Guam	Guam	Guam	Y	Seamstress
	578	649	Pinaula, Jose	Lodger	M	Cha	4.0	S				Guam	Unknown	Unknown		None
	579	650	Toves, Felix U	Head	M	Cha	56.0	Wd		Y	Y	Guam	Guam	Guam	N	Farmer
	580	651	San Nicolas, Nicolasa	Head	F	Cha	47.0	S		N	N	Guam	Unknown	Unknown	N	Farmer
	581	652	Toves, Jose U	Head	M	Cha	46.0	Wd		N	N	Guam	Guam	Guam	N	Farmer
	581	652	Toves, Juan M	Son	M	Cha	14.0	S	N	Y	Y	Guam	Guam	Guam	Y	None
	581	652	Toves, Felix P	Son	M	Cha	6.0	S	N			Guam	Guam	Guam	N	None
	581	652	Cruz, Maria C	Servant	F	Cha	47.0	D		N	N	Guam	Guam	Guam	N	Servant
	582	653	Montales, Eduardo R	Head	M	Fil	69.0	Wd		N	N	Philippine Islands	Philippine Islands	Philippine Islands	N	None
	583	654	Bontugan, Antonio C	Head	M	Fil	30.0	M		Y	Y	Guam	Philippine Islands	Guam	N	Laborer
	583	654	Bontugan, Francisca F	Wife	F	Cha	23.0	M		N	N	Guam	Guam	Guam	N	None
	584	655	Santos, Alvasio I	Head	M	Cha	39.0	M		N	N	Guam	Guam	Guam	N	Farmer
	584	655	Santos, Dolores C	Wife	F	Cha	44.0	M		N	N	Guam	Guam	Guam	N	None
	584	655	Santos, Ana C	Daughter	F	Cha	22.0	S		N	N	Guam	Guam	Guam	N	None
	584	655	Santos, Rosa C	Daughter	F	Cha	14.0	S	N	Y	Y	Guam	Guam	Guam	Y	None
	584	655	Santos, Pedro C	Son	M	Cha	9.0	S	Y			Guam	Guam	Guam		None
	584	655	Santos, Rosario C	Daughter	F	Cha	6.0	S	N			Guam	Guam	Guam		None
	584	655	Santos, Manuel C	Son	M	Cha	4.0	S				Guam	Guam	Guam		None
	585	656	Atoigue, Ursula T	Head	F	Cha	23.0	S		Y	Y	Guam	Guam	Guam	Y	Servant
	586	657	Reyes, Jose T	Head	M	Cha	34.0	M		Y	Y	Guam	Guam	Guam	N	Farmer
	586	657	Reyes, Maria S	Wife	F	Cha	39.0	M		N	N	Guam	Guam	Guam	N	None
	586	657	Reyes, Ana S	Daughter	F	Cha	11.0	S	Y	Y	Y	Guam	Guam	Guam	Y	None

348

(CHAMORRO ROOTS GENEALOGY PROJECT ™ TRANSCRIPTION)
(COMPILED/TRANSCRIBED BY BERNARD T. PUNZALAN / HTTP://WWW.CHAMORROROOTS.COM)

FOURTEENTH CENSUS OF THE UNITED STATES: 1920-POPULATION
ISLAND OF GUAM

ENUMERATED BY ME ON THE 22nd DAY OF April, 1920

Arthur W. Jackson ENUMERATOR

DISTRICT 2
NAME OF PLACE Tutujan (sub-District)

[Proper name and, also, name of class, as city, town, village, barrio, etc]

	PLACE OF ABODE		NAME	RELATION	PERSONAL DESCRIPTION				EDUCATION			NATIVITY				OCCUPATION
Street, avenue, road, etc.	Number of dwelling house is order of visitation	Number of family in order of visitation	of each person whose place of abode on January 1, 1920, was in the family. Enter surname, firs, then given name and middle initial. If any. Include every person living on January 1, 1920. Omit children born since January 1, 1920.	Relationship of this Person to the head of the family.	Sex	Color or race	Age at last birthday	Single, married, widowed or divorced	Attended school any time since Sept. 1, 1919	Whether able to read.	Whether able to write.	Place of birth of this person.	Place of birth of father of this person.	Place of birth of mother of this person.	Whether able to speak English.	Trade, profession, or particular kind of work done, as salesman, laborer, clerk, cook, merchant, washerwoman, etc.
1	2	3	4	5	6	7	8	9	10	11	12	13	14	15	16	17
26	587	658	Ulloa, Joaquin	Head	M	Cha	39.0	M		Y	Y	Guam	Unknown	Guam	N	Farmer
27	587	658	Ulloa, Rosalie I	Wife	F	Cha	41.0	M		N	N	Guam	Guam	Guam	N	None
28	587	658	Ulloa, Francisco I	Son	M	Cha	12.0	S	N	Y	Y	Guam	Guam	Guam	Y	None
29	587	658	Ulloa, Juan I	Son	M	Cha	11.0	S	Y	Y	Y	Guam	Guam	Guam	Y	None
30	587	658	Ulloa, Joaquin I	Son	M	Cha	7.0	S	N			Guam	Guam	Guam		None
31	587	658	Ulloa, Maria I	Daughter	F	Cha	2.0	S				Guam	Guam	Guam		None
32	587	658	Reyes, Jose S	Lodger	M	Cha	7.0	S	Y			Guam	Guam	Guam		None
33	588	659	Sablan, Juan A	Head	M	Cha	38.0	M		Y	Y	Guam	Guam	Guam	Y	Laborer
34	588	659	Sablan, Isabel C	Wife	F	Cha	28.0	M		N	N	Guam	Guam	Guam	N	None
35	588	659	Sablan, Regina C	Daughter	F	Cha	10.0	S	Y	Y	Y	Guam	Guam	Guam	Y	None
36	588	659	Sablan, Rafael C	Son	M	Cha	9.0	S	Y	Y	Y	Guam	Guam	Guam		None
37	588	659	Sablan, Jose C	Son	M	Cha	7.0	S	Y	Y	Y	Guam	Guam	Guam		None
38	588	659	Sablan, Pedro C	Son	M	Cha	6.0	S	N			Guam	Guam	Guam		None
39	588	659	Sablan, Vicente C	Son	M	Cha	4.0	S				Guam	Guam	Guam		None
40	588	659	Sablan, Natividad C	Daughter	F	Cha	1.0	S				Guam	Guam	Guam		None
41	589	660	Cruz, Miguel M	Head	M	Cha	42.0	M		Y	Y	Guam	Guam	Guam	N	Farmer
42	589	660	Cruz, Maria C	Wife	F	Cha	40.0	M		N	N	Guam	Guam	Guam	N	None
43	589	660	Cruz, Jose C	Son	M	Cha	16.0	S	N	Y	Y	Guam	Guam	Guam	Y	Farm laborer
44	589	660	Cruz, Juan C	Son	M	Cha	14.0	S	N	Y	Y	Guam	Guam	Guam	Y	None
45	589	660	Cruz, Antonio C	Son	M	Cha	10.0	S	Y	Y	Y	Guam	Guam	Guam	Y	None
46	589	660	Cruz, Enrique C	Son	M	Cha	8.0	S	Y	Y	Y	Guam	Guam	Guam	N	None
47	589	660	Cruz, Jesus C	Son	M	Cha	6.0	S	N			Guam	Guam	Guam		None
48	589	660	Cruz, Carmen C	Daughter	F	Cha	4.0	S				Guam	Guam	Guam		None
49	589	660	Cruz, Felix C	Son	M	Cha	2.0	S				Guam	Guam	Guam		None
50	590	661	Taitano, Maria S	Head	F	Cha	39.0	M				Guam	Guam	Guam	N	Cook

(CHAMORRO ROOTS GENEALOGY PROJECT ™ TRANSCRIPTION)

(COMPILED/TRANSCRIBED BY BERNARD T. PUNZALAN / HTTP://WWW.CHAMORROROOTS.COM)

FOURTEENTH CENSUS OF THE UNITED STATES: 1920—POPULATION

ISLAND OF GUAM

ENUMERATED BY ME ON THE 23rd DAY OF April, 1920

Arthur W. Jackson ENUMERATOR

DISTRICT 2
NAME OF PLACE Tutujan (sub-District)
[Proper name and, also, name of class, as city, town, village, barrio, etc]

	PLACE OF ABODE			NAME	RELATION		PERSONAL DESCRIPTION				EDUCATION			NATIVITY				OCCUPATION
Street, avenue, road, etc.	Number of dwelling house is order of visitation	Number of family in order of visitation		of each person whose place of abode on January 1, 1920, was in the family. Enter surname, first, then given name and middle initial. If any. Include every person living on January 1, 1920. Omit children born since January 1, 1920.	Relationship of this Person to the head of the family.	Sex	Color or race	Age at last birthday	Single, married, widowed or divorced	Attended school any time since Sept. 1, 1919	Whether able to read.	Whether able to write.	Place of birth of this person.	Place of birth of father of this person.	Place of birth of mother of this person.	Whether able to speak English.	Trade, profession, or particular kind of work done, as salesman, laborer, clerk, cook, merchant, washerwoman, etc.
1	2	3		4	5	6	7	8	9	10	11	12	13	14	15	16	17
1	590	661		Mendiola, Juan S	Son	M	Cha	21.0	S	N	Y	Y	Guam	Guam	Guam	Y	Laborer
2	590	661		Mendiola, Ana S	Daughter	F	Cha	21.0	S	N	Y	Y	Guam	Guam	Guam	N	None
3	591	662		Ojeda, Jose M	Head	M	Cha	32.0	M		Y	Y	Guam	Guam	Guam	Y	Laborer
4	591	662		Ojeda, Ana T	Wife	F	Cha	34.0	M		Y	Y	Guam	Guam	Guam	N	None
5	591	662		Ojeda, Amalia T	Daughter	F	Cha	3.0	S				Guam	Guam	Guam		None
6	592	663		Manibusan, Francisco Q	Head	M	Cha	25.0	S		Y	Y	Guam	Guam	Guam	N	Farm laborer
7				Here ends the enumeration of Tutujan (sub-District) Agana.													
8																	
9																	
10																	
11																	
12																	
13																	
14																	
15																	
16																	
17																	
18																	
19																	
20																	
21																	
22																	
23																	
24																	
25																	

(CHAMORRO ROOTS GENEALOGY PROJECT ™ TRANSCRIPTION)
(COMPILED/TRANSCRIBED BY BERNARD T. PUNZALAN / HTTP://WWW.CHAMORROROOTS.COM)
FOURTEENTH CENSUS OF THE UNITED STATES: 1920–POPULATION
ISLAND OF GUAM

DISTRICT 2
NAME OF PLACE Maina (sub-District)

ENUMERATED BY ME ON THE 24th DAY OF April, 1920

Arthur W. Jackson ENUMERATOR

[Proper name and, also, name of class, name of class, town, village, barrio, etc]

	PLACE OF ABODE			NAME	RELATION	PERSONAL DESCRIPTION					EDUCATION			NATIVITY				OCCUPATION
Street, avenue, road, etc.	Number of dwelling house in order of visitation	Number of family in order of visitation		Name	Relationship of this Person to the head of the family.	Sex	Color or race	Age at last birthday	Single, married, widowed or divorced	Attended school any time since Sept. 1, 1919	Whether able to read.	Whether able to write.	Place of birth of this person.	Place of birth of father of this person.	Place of birth of mother of this person.	Whether able to speak English.	Trade, profession, or particular kind of work done, as salesman, laborer, clerk, cook, merchant, washerwoman, etc.
1	2	3		4	5	6	7	8	9	10	11	12	13	14	15	16	17
1	593	664		San Nicolas, Vicente I	Head	M	Cha	26.0	M		Y	Y	Guam	Guam	Guam	N	Farmer
2	593	664		San Nicolas, Ana M	Wife	F	Cha	25.0	M		N	N	Guam	Guam	Guam	N	None
3	593	664		San Nicolas, Trinidad M	Daughter	F	Cha	3.0	S						Guam		None
4	593	664		San Nicolas, Beatrice M	Daughter	F	Cha	0.3	S				Guam		Guam		None
5	594	665		Cruz, Jose P	Head	M	Cha	21.0	S	N	Y	Y	Guam	Guam	Guam	N	Enlisted US Navy not an Am citizen
6	595	666		Ninete, Joaquin C	Head	M	Cha	26.0	M		Y	Y	Guam	Guam	Guam	N	Farmer
7	595	666		Ninete, Rosalia P	Wife	F	Cha	29.0	M		Y	Y	Guam	Guam	Guam	N	None
8	595	666		Ninete, Pedro P	Son	M	Cha	2.0	S				Guam	Guam	Guam		None
9	595	666		Ninete, Vicente P	Son	M	Cha	1.0	S				Guam	Guam	Guam		None
10	596	667		Quitugua, Enrique	Head	M	Cha	23.0	S		Y	Y	Guam	Unknown	Guam	Y	Enlisted US Navy not an Am citizen
11	597	668		Ogo, Pedro A	Head	M	Cha	57.0	M		N	N	Guam	Guam	Guam	N	Farmer
12	597	668		Ogo, Rufina T	Wife	F	Cha	57.0	M		N	N	Guam	Guam	Guam	N	None
13	597	668		Ogo, Jose T	Son	M	Cha	24.0	S		Y	Y	Guam	Guam	Guam	Y	Laborer
14	597	668		Ogo, Maria T	Daughter	F	Cha	22.0	S		Y	Y	Guam	Guam	Guam	Y	None
15	598	669		Kamminga, Jose H	Head	M	W	19.0	S	Y	Y	Y	Guam	Unknown	Guam	Y	Enlisted US Navy not an Am citizen
16	599	670		Pascual, Jesus R	Head	M	Cha	19.0	S	Y	Y	Y	Guam	Guam	Guam	Y	Enlisted US Navy not an Am citizen
17	600	671		Pangelinan, Juan	Head	M	Cha	22.0	S		Y	Y	Guam	Guam	Guam	Y	Laborer
18	601	672		Crisostomo, Pedro C	Head	M	Cha	24.0	S		Y	Y	Guam	Guam	Guam	N	Laborer
19	602	673		Leon Guerrero, Vicente C	Head	M	Cha	14.0	S	N	Y	Y	Guam	Guam	Guam	Y	Servant
20	603	674		Borja, Pedro Q	Head	M	Cha	24.0	S		Y	Y	Guam	Guam	Guam	N	Laborer
21	604	675		Blaz, Ana M	Head	F	Cha	17.0	S	N	Y	Y	Guam	Guam	Guam	Y	Servant
22	605	676		Mizushima, Umikidi	Head	M	Jp	50.0	M		Y	Y	Japan	Japan	Japan	N	Laborer
23	605	676		Mafnas, Juan A	Lodger	M	Cha	24.0	S		N	N	Guam	Guam	Guam	N	None
24	605	676		Mendiola, Joaquin F	Lodger	M	Cha	27.0	M		Y	Y	Guam	Guam	Guam	N	None
25	605	676		Cabrera, Maria C	Lodger	F	Cha	8.0	S	N			Guam	Guam	Guam	N	None

(CHAMORRO ROOTS GENEALOGY PROJECT ™ TRANSCRIPTION)
(COMPILED/TRANSCRIBED BY BERNARD T. PUNZALAN / HTTP://WWW.CHAMORROROOTS.COM)

FOURTEENTH CENSUS OF THE UNITED STATES: 1920-POPULATION
ISLAND OF GUAM

ENUMERATED BY ME ON THE 24th DAY OF April, 1920

Arthur W. Jackson ENUMERATOR

DISTRICT 2
NAME OF PLACE Maina (sub-District)
[Proper name and, also, name of class, as city, town, village, barrio, etc]

	PLACE OF ABODE			NAME	RELATION	PERSONAL DESCRIPTION					EDUCATION			NATIVITY				OCCUPATION
	Street, avenue, road, etc.	Number of dwelling house is order of visitation	Number of family in order of visitation	of each person whose place of abode on January 1, 1920, was in the family. Enter surname, firs, then given name and middle initial. If any. Include every person living on January 1, 1920. Omit children born since January 1, 1920.	Relationship of this Person to the head of the family.	Sex	Color or race	Age at last birthday	Single, married, widowed or divorced	Attended school any time since Sept. 1, 1919	Whether able to read.	Whether able to write.	Place of birth of this person.	Place of birth of father of this person.	Place of birth of mother of this person.	Whether able to speak English.	Trade, profession, or particular kind of work done, as salesman, laborer, clerk, cook, merchant, washerwoman, etc.
	1	2	3	4	5	6	7	8	9	10	11	12	13	14	15	16	17
26		605	676	Arriola, Ana A	Lodger	F	Cha	49.0	Wd		N	N	Guam	Guam	Guam	N	None
27		605	676	Santos, Ana C	Lodger	F	Cha	34.0	M		Y	Y	Guam	Guam	Guam	N	None
28		605	676	Tajalle, Josefa C	Lodger	F	Cha	45.0	M		N	N	Guam	Guam	Guam	N	None
29				Here ends the enumeration of Maina (sub-District) Agana													
30																	
31																	
32																	
33																	
34																	
35																	
36																	
37																	
38																	
39																	
40																	
41																	
42																	
43																	
44																	
45																	
46																	
47																	
48																	
49																	
50																	

District 3

(CHAMORRO ROOTS GENEALOGY PROJECT ™ TRANSCRIPTION)
(COMPILED/TRANSCRIBED BY BERNARD T. PUNZALAN / HTTP://WWW.CHAMORROROOTS.COM)

FOURTEENTH CENSUS OF THE UNITED STATES: 1920–POPULATION

ISLAND OF GUAM

ENUMERATED BY ME ON THE 24th DAY OF February, 1920

Vicente Tydingco ENUMERATOR

DISTRICT 3
NAME OF PLACE Asan Barrio

[Proper name and, also, name of class, as city, town, village, barrio, etc]

Street, avenue, road, etc.	Number of dwelling house is in order of visitation	Number of family in order of visitation	NAME	RELATION	Sex	Color or race	Age at last birthday	Single, married, widowed or divorced	Attended school any time since Sept. 1, 1919	Whether able to read	Whether able to write	Place of birth of this person	Place of birth of father of this person	Place of birth of mother of this person	Whether able to speak English	OCCUPATION
1	2	3	4	5	6	7	8	9	10	11	12	13	14	15	16	17
	1	1	Taitano, Leocadio T	Head	M	Cha	42.0	M		Y	Y	Guam	Guam	Guam	N	Laborer
	1	1	Taitano, Dolores G	Wife	F	Cha	42.0	M		N	N	Guam	Guam	Guam	N	None
	1	1	Taitano, Felicita G	Daughter	F	Cha	15.0	S	N	Y	Y	Guam	Guam	Guam	Y	None
	1	1	Taitano, Carmen G	Daughter	F	Cha	14.0	S	N	N	N	Guam	Guam	Guam	N	None
	1	1	Taitano, Maria G	Daughter	F	Cha	8.0	S	Y			Guam	Guam	Guam		None
	1	1	Taitano, Manuela G	Daughter	F	Cha	5.0	S	N			Guam	Guam	Guam		None
	1	1	Taitano, Jesus G	Son	M	Cha	3.0	S				Guam	Guam	Guam		
	2	2	Aguon, Juan C	Head	M	Cha	39.0	Wd		Y	Y	Guam	Guam	Guam	Y	Electrician
	2	2	Aguon, Carmen M	Daughter	F	Cha	5.0	S	Y			Guam	Guam	Guam		None
	2	2	Maanao, Ramona M	Mother in law	F	Cha	55.0	Wd		N	N	Guam	Guam	Guam	N	Cook
Agana Piti Road	3	3	Taijito, Francisco T	Head	M	Cha	40.0	Wd		Y	Y	Guam	Guam	Guam	Y	Laborer
	3	3	Taijito, Vicente C	Son	M	Cha	9.0	S	Y			Guam	Guam	Guam	N	None
	3	3	Taijito, Hermina T	Mother	F	Cha	70.0	Wd		N	N	Guam	Guam	Guam	N	None
	4	4	Cruz, Vicenta T	Head	F	Cha	33.0	D		N	N	Guam	Guam	Guam	N	Laundress
	4	4	Cruz, Engracia T	Daughter	F	Cha	15.0	S	N	N	N	Guam	Guam	Guam	N	Laundress
	5	5	Taijito, Jose T	Head	M	Cha	43.0	M		Y	Y	Guam	Guam	Guam	N	S?erder?
	5	5	Taijito, Vicenta S	Wife	F	Cha	48.0	M		Y	Y	Guam	Guam	Guam	N	None
	5	5	Taijito, Magdalena S	Daughter	F	Cha	14.0	S	N	Y	Y	Guam	Guam	Guam	Y	Farm laborer home farm
	5	5	Taijito, Francisco S	Son	M	Cha	12.0	S	Y	Y	Y	Guam	Guam	Guam	Y	None
	5	5	Taijito, Soledad S	Daughter	F	Cha	8.0	S	N			Guam	Guam	Guam		None
	5	5	Taijito, Juan S	Son	M	Cha	6.0	S	N			Guam	Guam	Guam		None
	5	5	Taijito, Jose S	Son	M	Cha	4.0	S				Guam	Guam	Guam		None
	5	5	Taijito, Maria S	Daughter	F	Cha	1.0	S				Guam	Guam	Guam		None
	6	6	Aflleje, Jose T	Head	M	Cha	27.0	M		Y	Y	Guam	Guam	Guam	Y	Laborer
	6	6	Aflleje, Rosario C	Wife	F	Cha	24.0	M		Y	Y	Guam	Guam	Guam	Y	None

(CHAMORRO ROOTS GENEALOGY PROJECT ™ TRANSCRIPTION)
(COMPILED/TRANSCRIBED BY BERNARD T. PUNZALAN / HTTP://WWW.CHAMORROROOTS.COM)

FOURTEENTH CENSUS OF THE UNITED STATES: 1920-POPULATION

ISLAND OF GUAM

ENUMERATED BY ME ON THE 24th DAY OF February, 1920

Vicente Tydingco ENUMERATOR

DISTRICT 3

NAME OF PLACE Asan Barrio

[Proper name and, also, name of class, as city, town, village, barrio, etc]

	Dwelling No.	Family No.	NAME	RELATION	Sex	Color/race	Age	Marital	School	Read	Write	Birthplace	Father's birthplace	Mother's birthplace	English	OCCUPATION
26	6	6	Aflleje, Rosa C	Daughter	F	Cha	4.0	S				Guam	Guam	Guam		None
27	7	7	Ignacio, Enrique R	Head	M	Cha	22.0	M		Y	Y	Guam	Guam	Guam	Y	Salesman
28	7	7	Ignacio, Soledad J	Wife	F	Cha	25.0	M		Y	Y	Guam	Guam	Guam	N	None
29	7	7	Jesus, Concepcion L	Mother-in-law	F	Cha	52.0	Wd		N	N	Guam	Guam	Guam	N	None
30	7	7	Limtiaco, Ana T	Aunt	F	Cha	48.0	S		N	N	Guam	Guam	Guam	N	Laundress
31	8	8	Chargualaf, Justo Q	Head	M	Cha	46.0	M		Y	Y	Guam	Guam	Guam	N	Farmer
32	8	8	Chargualaf, Dolores T	Wife	F	Cha	38.0	M		Y	Y	Guam	Guam	Guam		None
33	8	8	Chargualaf, Maria T	Daughter	F	Cha	11.0	S		N	N	Guam	Guam	Guam		None
34	8	8	Chargualaf, Antonio T	Son	M	Cha	4.0	S	N			Guam	Guam	Guam		None
35	8	8	Chargualaf, Encarnacion T	Daughter	F	Cha	1.0	S				Guam	Guam	Guam		None
36	9	9	Liizama, Rodovico C	Head	M	Cha	39.0	M		Y	Y	Guam	Guam	Guam	N	Laborer
37	9	9	Liizama, Ana Q	Wife	F	Cha	35.0	M		N	N	Guam	Unknown	Guam	N	None
38	9	9	Liizama, Maria Q	Daughter	F	Cha	17.0	S	N	Y	Y	Guam	Guam	Guam	Y	None
39	9	9	Liizama, Filomena Q	Daughter	F	Cha	14.0	S	N	Y	Y	Guam	Guam	Guam	Y	None
40	9	9	Liizama, Milagro Q	Daughter	F	Cha	12.0	S	Y	Y	Y	Guam	Guam	Guam	Y	None
41	9	9	Liizama, Jose Q	Son	M	Cha	9.0	S	N			Guam	Guam	Guam		None
42	9	9	Liizama, Vicente Q	Son	M	Cha	4.0	S				Guam	Guam	Guam		None
43	9	9	Liizama, Josefina B	Daughter	F	Cha	2.0	S				Guam	Guam	Guam		None
44	10	10	Quitugua, Juan Q	Head	M	Cha	28.0	M		Y	Y	Guam	Unknown	Guam	Y	Electrician
45	10	10	Quitugua, Maria F	Wife	F	Cha	29.0	M		N	N	Guam	Guam	Guam	N	None
46	10	10	Quitugua, Eliza F	Daughter	F	Cha	9.0	S				Guam	Guam	Guam		None
47	10	10	Quitugua, Ana F	Daughter	F	Cha	4.0	S				Guam	Guam	Guam		None
48	11	11	Quitugua, Vicente Q	Head	M	Cha	22.0	S		Y	Y	Guam	Unknown	Guam		Laborer
49	11	11	Quitugua, Rita R	Aunt	F	Cha	60.0	S		N	N	Guam	Guam	Guam		None
50	11	11	Quitugua, Teburcio R	Uncle	M	Cha	48.0	S		N	N	Guam	Guam	Guam		Servant

Street (column 1): Agana Pitt Road

(CHAMORRO ROOTS GENEALOGY PROJECT ™ TRANSCRIPTION)
(COMPILED/TRANSCRIBED BY BERNARD T. PUNZALAN / HTTP://WWW.CHAMORROROOTS.COM)

FOURTEENTH CENSUS OF THE UNITED STATES: 1920-POPULATION

ISLAND OF GUAM

ENUMERATED BY ME ON THE 25th DAY OF February, 1920

Vicente Tydingco ENUMERATOR

DISTRICT 3

NAME OF PLACE Asan Barrio

Street	No. dwelling house	No. family	NAME	RELATION	Sex	Color or race	Age	S/M/Wd/D	Attended school	Able to read	Able to write	Birthplace of person	Birthplace of father	Birthplace of mother	Speak English	OCCUPATION
	11	11	Quitugua, Pedro R	Uncle	M	Cha	45.0	S		N	N	Guam	Guam	Guam	N	Farmer
	12	12	Tydingco, Vicente	Head	M	Cha	27.0	M		Y	Y	Guam	Guam	Guam	Y	Teacher
	12	12	Tydingco, Francisca L	Wife	F	Cha	24.0	M		Y	Y	Guam	Guam	Guam		None
	12	12	Tydingco, Carlos P	Son	M	Cha	4.0	S				Guam	Guam	Guam		None
	12	12	Tydingco, Helen C	Daughter	F	Cha	1.0	S				Guam	Guam	Guam		None
	12	12	Tydingco, Dolores C	Sister	F	Cha	21.0	S	N	Y	Y	Guam	Guam	Guam	Y	None
	12	12	Tydingco, Maria P	Sister	F	Cha	20.0	S	Y	Y	Y	Guam	Guam	Guam	Y	Teacher
	12	12	Tydingco, Jose C	Brother	M	Cha	18.0	S	N	Y	Y	Guam	Guam	Guam	Y	Chauffeur
	12	12	Tydingco, Consolacion C	Sister	F	Cha	15.0	S	Y	Y	Y	Guam	Guam	Guam	Y	None
	12	12	Tydingco, Antonio C	Brother	M	Cha	12.0	S	Y	Y	Y	Guam	Guam	Guam	Y	None
	12	12	Tydingco, Ana C	Sister	F	Cha	11.0	S	Y	Y	Y	Guam	Guam	Guam	Y	Laborer
	12	12	Cruz, Juan C	Uncle	M	Cha	40.0	Wd		N	N	Guam	Guam	Guam	N	None
	13	13	Cruz, Maria R	Cousin	F	Cha	3.0	S				Guam	Guam	Guam		
Agana Piti Road	13	13	Cruz, Joaquin S	Head	M	Cha	26.0	M		Y	Y	Guam	Guam	Guam	Y	Seaman USN
	13	13	Cruz, Cristina T	Wife	F	Cha	33.0	M		N	N	Guam	Guam	Guam	N	None
	13	13	Fejeran, Rosa T	Step-daughter	F	Cha	15.0	S	N	Y	Y	Guam	Guam	Guam	Y	None
	13	13	Balajadia, Rita T	Step-daughter	F	Cha	4.0	S				Guam	Guam	Guam		None
	14	14	Cruz, Vicente S	Head	M	Cha	28.0	M		Y	Y	Guam	Guam	Guam	Y	Seaman USN
	14	14	Cruz, Maria M	Wife	F	Cha	33.0	M		N	N	Guam	Guam	Guam	N	None
	15	15	Cruz, Nicolas G	Head	M	Cha	50.0	Wd		N	N	Guam	Guam	Guam	N	Farmer
	15	15	Cruz, Jose M	Son	M	Cha	14.0	S	N	N	N	Guam	Guam	Guam	N	None
	15	15	Cruz, Juana M	Daughter	F	Cha	11.0	S	Y	Y	Y	Guam	Guam	Guam	Y	None
	15	15	Cruz, Nicolas M	Son	M	Cha	6.0	S	N			Guam	Guam	Guam		None
	16	16	Taitano, Manuel B	Head	M	Cha	25.0	M		Y	Y	Guam	Unknown	Guam	Y	Laborer
	16	16	Taitano, Antonia F	Wife	F	Cha	28.0	M		Y	Y	Guam	Guam	Guam	Y	None

(CHAMORRO ROOTS GENEALOGY PROJECT ™ TRANSCRIPTION)
(COMPILED/TRANSCRIBED BY BERNARD T. PUNZALAN / HTTP://WWW.CHAMORROROOTS.COM)
FOURTEENTH CENSUS OF THE UNITED STATES: 1920-POPULATION
ISLAND OF GUAM

DISTRICT 3
NAME OF PLACE Asan Barrio
[Proper name and, also, name of class, as city, town, village, barrio, etc]

ENUMERATED BY ME ON THE 25th DAY OF February, 1920

Vicente Tydingco ENUMERATOR

1	2	3	4 NAME	5 RELATION	6 Sex	7 Color or race	8 Age at last birthday	9 Single, married, widowed or divorced	10 Attended school	11 able to read	12 able to write	13 Place of birth	14 Place of birth of father	15 Place of birth of mother	16 able to speak English	17 OCCUPATION
26	16	16	Taitano, Teodoro F	Son	M	Cha	4.0	S				Guam	Guam	Guam		None
27	16	16	Taitano, Delfina F	Daughter	F	Cha	3.0	S				Guam	Guam	Guam		None
28	16	16	Taitano, Dolores F	Cousin	F	Cha	16.0	S	N	Y	Y	Guam	Unknown	Guam		Laundress
29	16	16	Taitano, Emilia B	Mother	F	Cha	50.0	S		N	N	Guam	Guam	Guam		None
30	16	16	Taitano, Felipe B	Uncle	M	Cha	48.0	S		N	N	Guam	Guam	Guam		Farm laborer home farm
31	17	17	Aguon, Magdalena T	Head	F	Cha	50.0	Wd		Y	Y	Guam	Guam	Guam		None
32	17	17	Aguon, Jose T	Son	M	Cha	14.0	S	N	Y	Y	Guam	Guam	Guam		None
33	17	17	Aguon, Ingracia T	Daughter	F	Cha	13.0	S	N	Y	Y	Guam	Guam	Guam		None
34	17	17	Aguon, Mariano T	Son	M	Cha	10.0	S	Y	Y	Y	Guam	Guam	Guam		None
35	17	17	Aguon, Santiago T	Son	M	Cha	7.0	S	Y	Y	Y	Guam	Guam	Guam		None
36	18	18	Taitano, Carmen T	Head	F	Cha	59.0	Wd		N	N	Guam	Guam	Guam	N	Laundress
37	18	18	Taitano, Manuel T	Son	M	Cha	29.0	S		N	N	Guam	Guam	Guam	N	None
38	18	18	Teltras, Antonia T	Cousin	F	Cha	50.0	M		N	Y	Guam	France	Guam	N	Laundress
39	19	19	Quitugua, Jose Q	Head	M	Cha	30.0	M		Y	Y	Guam	Unknown	Unknown	N	Laborer
40	19	19	Quitugua, Rosa T	Wife	F	Cha	24.0	M		Y	Y	Guam	Guam	Guam	N	None
41	19	19	Quitugua, Jesus T	Son	M	Cha	10.0	S	Y	Y	Y	Guam	Guam	Guam		None
42	19	19	Quitugua, Enrique T	Son	M	Cha	8.0	S	Y		Y	Guam	Guam	Guam		None
43	19	19	Quitugua, Joaquin T	Son	M	Cha	5.0	S	N			Guam	Guam	Guam		None
44	19	19	Quitugua, Miguel T	Son	M	Cha	3.0	S				Guam	Guam	Guam		None
45	19	19	Quitugua, Demetrio T	Son	M	Cha	0.3	S				Guam	Guam	Guam		None
46	20	20	Barbour, James	Head	M	W	45.0	M		Y	Y	Minnesota	Scotland	Scotland	Y	Foreman
47	20	20	Barbour, Maria C	Wife	F	Cha	43.0	M		N	N	Guam	Guam	Guam	N	None
48	21	21	Terlaje, Jose C	Head	M	Cha	38.0	M		Y	Y	Guam	Guam	Guam	Y	Laborer
49	21	21	Terlaje, Josefa S	Wife	F	Cha	35.0	M		Y	Y	Guam	Guam	Guam	N	None
50	22	22	Fejeran, Juan S	Head	M	Cha	50.0	Wd		Y	Y	Guam	Guam	Guam	Y	Laborer

Street, avenue, road: Agana Pitt Road

(CHAMORRO ROOTS GENEALOGY PROJECT ™ TRANSCRIPTION)
(COMPILED/TRANSCRIBED BY BERNARD T. PUNZALAN / HTTP://WWW.CHAMORROROOTS.COM)

FOURTEENTH CENSUS OF THE UNITED STATES: 1920—POPULATION

ISLAND OF GUAM

DISTRICT 3
NAME OF PLACE Asan Barrio
[Proper name and, also, name of class, as city, town, village, barrio, etc]

ENUMERATED BY ME ON THE 25th DAY OF February, 1920

Vicente Tydingco ENUMERATOR

PLACE OF ABODE			NAME	RELATION	PERSONAL DESCRIPTION				EDUCATION			NATIVITY				OCCUPATION
Street, avenue, road, etc.	Number of dwelling house in order of visitation	Number of family in order of visitation	of each person whose place of abode on January 1, 1920, was in the family. Enter surname, first, then given name and middle initial. If any. Include every person living on January 1, 1920. Omit children born since January 1, 1920.	Relationship of this Person to the head of the family.	Sex	Color or race	Age at last birthday	Single, married, widowed or divorced	Attended school any time since Sept. 1, 1919	Whether able to read.	Whether able to write.	Place of birth of this person.	Place of birth of father of this person.	Place of birth of mother of this person.	Whether able to speak English.	Trade, profession, or particular kind of work done, as salesman, laborer, clerk, cook, merchant, washerwoman, etc.
1	2	3	4	5	6	7	8	9	10	11	12	13	14	15	16	17
	22	22	Fejeran, Cerilo A	Son	M	Cha	28.0	S		Y	Y	Guam	Guam	Guam	Y	None
	22	22	Fejeran, Jose A	Son	M	Cha	25.0	S		Y	Y	Guam	Guam	Guam	Y	Servant
	22	22	Fejeran, Luis A	Son	M	Cha	20.0	S	N	Y	Y	Guam	Guam	Guam	Y	Farmer
	22	22	Fejeran, Remedios A	Daughter	F	Cha	16.0	S	N	Y	Y	Guam	Guam	Guam	Y	None
	22	22	Fejeran, Pedro A	Son	M	Cha	14.0	S	N	Y	Y	Guam	Guam	Guam	Y	Farm laborer home farm
	22	22	Fejeran, Ignacio A	Son	M	Cha	9.0	S		Y		Guam	Guam	Guam		None
	23	23	Salas, Pedro E	Head	M	Cha	50.0	M		N	N	Guam	Guam	Guam	N	Farmer
	23	23	Salas, Maria J	Wife	F	Cha	28.0	M		N	N	Guam	Guam	Guam	N	Laundress
	23	23	Salas, Jose J	Son	M	Cha	15.0	S	N	Y	Y	Guam	Guam	Guam	Y	Farm laborer home farm
	23	23	Salas, Teresa J	Daughter	F	Cha	13.0	S	N	N	N	Guam	Guam	Guam		None
	23	23	Salas, Catalina J	Daughter	F	Cha	12.0	S	Y	Y	Y	Guam	Guam	Guam		None
	23	23	Salas, Nicolasa J	Daughter	F	Cha	8.0	S	Y	Y	Y	Guam	Guam	Guam		None
	23	23	Salas, Jesus J	Son	M	Cha	6.0	S	N			Guam	Guam	Guam		None
	23	23	Salas, Felisa J	Daughter	F	Cha	3.0	S				Guam	Guam	Guam		None
	23	23	Salas, Joaquin J	Son	M	Cha	2.0	S				Guam	Guam	Guam		None
	23	23	Salas, Manuel J	Son	M	Cha	0.0	S				Guam	Guam	Guam		None
	24	24	Cruz, Joaquin C	Head	M	Cha	37.0	M		Y	Y	Guam	Guam	Guam	N	Farmer
	24	24	Cruz, Rosa J	Wife	F	Cha	24.0	M		Y	Y	Guam	Guam	Guam		None
	24	24	Cruz, Consolacion J	Daughter	F	Cha	2.0	S				Guam	Guam	Guam		None
	24	24	Cruz, Maria J	Daughter	F	Cha	1.0	S				Guam	Guam	Guam		None
	25	25	Limtiaco, Jose L	Head	M	Cha	23.0	M		Y	Y	Guam	Unknown	Guam	Y	Farmer
	25	25	Limtiaco, Angela C	Wife	F	Cha	23.0	M		N	N	Guam	Unknown	Guam	N	None
	26	26	Terlaje, Magdalena A	Head	F	Cha	44.0	S		N	N	Guam	Guam	Guam	N	Laundress
	26	26	Terlaje, Joaquin T	Son	M	Cha	6.0	S	Y			Guam	Unknown	Guam		None
	26	26	Terlaje, Francisco T	Son	M	Cha	2.0	S				Guam	Unknown	Guam		None

Agana Pitt Road

(CHAMORRO ROOTS GENEALOGY PROJECT ™ TRANSCRIPTION)
(COMPILED/TRANSCRIBED BY BERNARD T. PUNZALAN / HTTP://WWW.CHAMORROROOTS.COM)
FOURTEENTH CENSUS OF THE UNITED STATES: 1920-POPULATION
ISLAND OF GUAM

DISTRICT 3
NAME OF PLACE **Asan Barrio**
[Proper name and, also, name of class, name of city, town, village, barrio, etc]

ENUMERATED BY ME ON THE 26th DAY OF February, 1920

Vicente Tydingco ENUMERATOR

Street	Dwelling No.	Family No.	NAME	RELATION	Sex	Color or race	Age	Marital	Attended school	Able to read	Able to write	Birthplace of person	Birthplace of father	Birthplace of mother	Able to speak English	OCCUPATION
26	27	27	Aflleje, Antonio T	Head	M	Cha	40.0	M		Y	Y	Guam	Guam	Guam	N	Laborer
27	27	27	Aflleje, Dolores G	Wife	F	Cha	43.0	M		Y	Y	Guam	Guam	Guam	N	None
28	27	27	Aflleje, Natividad G	Daughter	F	Cha	20.0	S	N	Y	Y	Guam	Guam	Guam	Y	Laundress
29	27	27	Aflleje, Maria G	Daughter	F	Cha	15.0	S	N	Y	Y	Guam	Guam	Guam	Y	None
30	27	27	Aflleje, Jose G	Son	M	Cha	9.0	S	Y			Guam	Guam	Guam		None
31	27	27	Aflleje, Teresa G	Daughter	F	Cha	1.0	S				Guam	Guam	Guam		None
32	27	27	Aflleje, Marcela T	Mother	F	Cha	59.0	Wd		Y	N	Guam	Guam	Guam	N	None
33	28	28	Maanao, Jose A	Head	M	Cha	40.0	Wd		Y	N	Guam	Guam	Guam	N	Laborer
34	28	28	Maanao, Vicente A	Son	M	Cha	18.0	S	N	Y	Y	Guam	Guam	Guam	Y	Farm laborer
35	28	28	Maanao, Manuel A	Son	M	Cha	12.0	S	N	Y	Y	Guam	Guam	Guam	Y	None
36	28	28	Maanao, Maria A	Daughter	F	Cha	10.0	S	Y	Y	Y	Guam	Guam	Guam	N	None
37	28	28	Maanao, Martina A	Daughter	F	Cha	7.0	S	Y			Guam	Guam	Guam		None
38	29	29	Teltras, Vicente T	Head	M	W	48.0	M		Y	Y	Guam	France	Guam	Y	Laborer
39	29	29	Teltras, Andrea A	Wife	F	Cha	44.0	M		N	N	Guam	Guam	Guam	N	None
40	29	29	Teltras, Jose A	Son	M	Cha	20.0	S	N	Y	Y	Guam	Guam	Guam	Y	Chauffeur
41	30	30	Tajalle, Bartola C	Head	M	Cha	33.0	Wd	N	N	N	Guam	Unknown	Guam	N	Laundress
42	30	30	Tajalle, Martina C	Daughter	F	Cha	16.0	S	N	Y	Y	Guam	Guam	Guam	Y	Servant
43	30	30	Tajalle, Antonia C	Daughter	F	Cha	8.0	S	Y	Y	Y	Guam	Guam	Guam	N	None
44	30	30	Tajalle, Andrea C	Daughter	F	Cha	5.0	S	N			Guam	Guam	Guam		None
45	31	31	Munoz, Alejandro Sta R	Head	M	Fil	57.0	M		N	N	Philippine Islands	Philippine Islands	Philippine Islands	N	Laborer
46	31	31	Munoz, Manuela C	Wife	F	Cha	28.0	M		Y	Y	Guam	Unknown	Guam	N	None
47	32	32	Acfalle, Juan N	Head	M	Cha	35.0	M		Y	Y	Guam	Guam	Guam	Y	Laborer
48	32	32	Acfalle, Genoveva C	Wife	F	Cha	47.0	S	N	N	N	Guam	Guam	Guam	N	None
49	32	32	Acfalle, Jose C	Son	M	Cha	9.0	S	Y	Y	Y	Guam	Guam	Guam	N	None
50	31	32	Taitano, Matias T	Head	M	Cha	40.0	M		Y	Y	Guam	Guam	Guam	N	Laborer

Agana Piti Road

359

(CHAMORRO ROOTS GENEALOGY PROJECT ™ TRANSCRIPTION)
(COMPILED/TRANSCRIBED BY BERNARD T. PUNZALAN / HTTP://WWW.CHAMORROROOTS.COM)
FOURTEENTH CENSUS OF THE UNITED STATES: 1920-POPULATION
ISLAND OF GUAM

DISTRICT 3
NAME OF PLACE **Asan Barrio**
[Proper name and, also, name of class, as city, town, village, barrio, etc]

SHEET NO. _4A_

ENUMERATED BY ME ON THE 26th DAY OF February, 1920

Vicente Tydingco ENUMERATOR

Street, avenue, road, etc.	Number of dwelling house in order of visitation	Number of family in order of visitation	NAME	RELATION	Sex	Color or race	Age at last birthday	Single, married, widowed or divorced	Attended school any time since Sept. 1, 1919	Whether able to read.	Whether able to write.	Place of birth of this person.	Place of birth of father of this person.	Place of birth of mother of this person.	Whether able to speak English.	OCCUPATION
	1	2	3	4	5	6	7	8	9	10	11	12	13	14	15	16	17
	31	32	Taitano, Ana G	Wife	F	Cha	30.0	M		N	N	Guam	Guam	Guam	Y	None
	31	32	Taitano, Justo G	Son	M	Cha	14.0	S	N	Y	Y	Guam	Guam	Guam	Y	Farm laborer home farm
	31	32	Taitano, Pedro G	Son	M	Cha	10.0	S	Y	Y	Y	Guam	Guam	Guam	Y	None
	31	32	Taitano, Francisco G	Son	M	Cha	4.0	S	N			Guam	Guam	Guam	N	None
	32	34	Limtiaco, Carlina A	Head	F	Cha	47.0	Wd		N	N	Guam	Guam	Guam	Y	Laundress
	32	34	Limtiaco, Jose A	Son	M	Cha	19.0	S	N	Y	Y	Guam	Guam	Guam	Y	Servant
	32	34	Limtiaco, Francisco A	Son	M	Cha	16.0	S	N	Y	Y	Guam	Guam	Guam	Y	Farm laborer home farm
	32	34	Limtiaco, Maria A	Daughter	F	Cha	14.0	S	Y	Y	Y	Guam	Guam	Guam	Y	None
	32	34	Limtiaco, Antonio A	Son	M	Cha	12.0	S	Y	Y	Y	Guam	Guam	Guam	Y	None
	32	34	Limtiaco, Joaquina A	Daughter	F	Cha	8.0	S	Y			Guam	Guam	Guam	N	None
	32	34	Quitugua, Rosa A	Niece	F	Cha	39.0	Wd		N	N	Guam	Guam	Guam	N	Laundress
	32	34	Aflague, Magdalena	Niece	F	Cha	8.0	S	Y			Guam	Unknown	Guam	N	None
	33	35	Aflleje, Nicolasa P	Head	F	Cha	49.0	Wd		N	N	Guam	Guam	Guam	N	Laundress
	33	35	Santos, Maria A	Step Mother	F	Cha	65.0	Wd		N	N	Guam	Guam	Guam	N	None
	34	36	Namauleg, Ana P	Head	F	Cha	38.0	S		Y	Y	Guam	Guam	Guam	Y	Laundress
	34	36	Namauleg, Maria P	Daughter	F	Cha	19.0	S	N	N	N	Guam	Guam	Guam	N	Laundress
	34	36	Namauleg, Lorenza P	Daughter	F	Cha	16.0	S	N	Y	Y	Guam	Guam	Guam	Y	None
	34	36	Namauleg, Ursia P	Daughter	F	Cha	12.0	S	Y	Y	Y	Guam	Guam	Guam	Y	None
	34	36	Namauleg, Magdalena P	Daughter	F	Cha	8.0	S	Y			Guam	Guam	Guam		None
	34	36	Namauleg, Catalina P	Daughter	F	Cha	3.0	S				Guam	Guam	Guam		None
	34	36	Namauleg, Joaquin N	Grandson	M	Cha	1.0	S				Guam	Unknown	Guam		None
Agana Piti Road	35	37	Chargualaf, Eugenio Q	Head	M	Cha	57.0	M		Y	Y	Guam	Guam	Guam	N	Farmer
	35	37	Chargualaf, Ana T	Wife	F	Cha	54.0	M		N	N	Guam	Guam	Guam	N	None
	35	37	Taijito, Mariano T	Nephew	M	Cha	23.0	S		Y	Y	Guam	Unknown	Unknown	Y	Laborer
	35	37	Taijito, Manuela T	Niece	F	Cha	11.0	S	Y	Y	Y	Guam	Unknown	Guam	Y	None

360

(CHAMORRO ROOTS GENEALOGY PROJECT ™ TRANSCRIPTION)
(COMPILED/TRANSCRIBED BY BERNARD T. PUNZALAN / HTTP://WWW.CHAMORROROOTS.COM)

FOURTEENTH CENSUS OF THE UNITED STATES: 1920—POPULATION

ISLAND OF GUAM

DISTRICT 3
NAME OF PLACE Asan Barrio

[Proper name and, also, name of class, as city, town, village, barrio, etc]

ENUMERATED BY ME ON THE 26th DAY OF February, 1920

Vicente Tydingco ENUMERATOR

	Street, avenue, road, etc.	Number of dwelling house	Number of family	NAME	RELATION	Sex	Color or race	Age at last birthday	Single, married, widowed or divorced	Attended school since Sept. 1, 1919	Whether able to read	Whether able to write	Place of birth of this person	Place of birth of father	Place of birth of mother	Whether able to speak English	OCCUPATION
	1	2	3	4	5	6	7	8	9	10	11	12	13	14	15	16	17
26		36	38	Chargualaf, Nicolas Q	Head	M	Cha	57.0	Wd		N	N	Guam	Guam	Guam	N	Farmer
27		36	38	Terlaje, Juan T	Nephew	M	Cha	16.0	S	N	Y	Y	Guam	Unknown	Guam	Y	Farm laborer home farm
28		37	39	Chargualaf, Francisco Q	Head	M	Cha	43.0	M		Y	Y	Guam	Guam	Guam	N	Herder
29		37	39	Chargualaf, Dolores S	Wife	F	Cha	30.0	M	N	Y	Y	Guam	Guam	Guam	N	None
30		37	39	Chargualaf, Carmela S	Daughter	F	Cha	16.0	S	N	Y	N	Guam	Guam	Guam	Y	None
31		37	39	Chargualaf, Joaquina S	Daughter	F	Cha	14.0	S	Y	Y	Y	Guam	Guam	Guam	N	None
32		37	39	Chargualaf, Jose S	Son	M	Cha	12.0	S	Y	Y	Y	Guam	Guam	Guam		None
33		37	39	Chargualaf, Antonio S	Son	M	Cha	9.0	S	N			Guam	Guam	Guam		None
34		37	39	Chargualaf, Preciosa S	Daughter	F	Cha	6.0	S				Guam	Guam	Guam		None
35		37	39	Chargualaf, Maria S	Daughter	F	Cha	3.0	S				Guam	Guam	Guam		None
36		38	40	Cruz, Joaquin P	Head	M	Cha	34.0	M		Y	Y	Guam	Unknown	Guam	Y	Chauffeur
37		38	40	Cruz, Teodora T	Wife	F	Cha	29.0	M		Y	Y	Guam	Guam	Guam	Y	None
38	Agana Pitt Road	38	40	Cruz, Joaquin T	Son	M	Cha	6.0	S	N			Guam	Guam	Guam		None
39		38	40	Cruz, Tomas T	Son	M	Cha	2.0	S				Guam	Guam	Guam		None
40		38	40	Cruz, Maria T	Daughter	F	Cha	0.2	S				Guam	Guam	Guam		None
41		38	40	Crisostomo, Juan T	Servant	M	Cha	23.0	S		N	N	Guam	Guam	Guam	Y	Servant
42		34	41	Castro, Juan C	Head	M	Cha	34.0	M		N	N	Guam	Unknown	Guam	N	Farm laborer home farm
43		34	41	Castro, Cristina T	Wife	F	Cha	32.0	M		Y	Y	Guam	Guam	Guam	N	None
44		34	41	Castro, Ignacio T	Son	M	Cha	14.0	S	N	N	N	Guam	Guam	Guam	N	None
45		34	41	Castro, Maria T	Daughter	F	Cha	12.0	S	N	N	N	Guam	Guam	Guam	N	None
46		34	41	Castro, Francisco T	Son	M	Cha	10.0	S	Y	Y	Y	Guam	Guam	Guam	N	None
47		34	41	Castro, Angelina T	Daughter	F	Cha	6.0	S	N			Guam	Guam	Guam		None
48		34	41	Castro, Jose T	Son	M	Cha	3.0	S				Guam	Guam	Guam		None
49		34	41	Castro, Anuncia T	Daughter	F	Cha	0.8	S				Guam	Guam	Guam		None
50		40	42	Fejeran, Joaquin P	Head	M	Cha	27.0	M		Y	Y	Guam	Guam	Guam	Y	Seaman USN

(CHAMORRO ROOTS GENEALOGY PROJECT ™ TRANSCRIPTION)

(COMPILED/TRANSCRIBED BY BERNARD T. PUNZALAN / HTTP://WWW.CHAMORROROOTS.COM)

FOURTEENTH CENSUS OF THE UNITED STATES: 1920—POPULATION

ISLAND OF GUAM

DISTRICT 3
NAME OF PLACE Asan Barrio
[Proper name and, also, name of class, as city, town, village, barrio, etc]

ENUMERATED BY ME ON THE 27th DAY OF February, 1920

Vicente Tydingco ENUMERATOR

#	Dwelling No.	Family No.	NAME	RELATION	Sex	Color or race	Age	Marital	School since Sept 1919	Read	Write	Birthplace	Father birthplace	Mother birthplace	Speak English	OCCUPATION
1	40	42	Fejeran, Rosa Q	Wife	F	Cha	26.0	M		Y	Y	Guam	Unknown	Guam	N	None
2	40	42	Fejeran, Hermenguido J	Son	M	Cha	0.7	S				Guam	Guam	Guam		None
3	41	43	Santos, Martin M	Head	M	Cha	59.0	M		Y	Y	Guam	Guam	Guam	N	Farmer
4	41	43	Santos, Maria A	Wife	F	Cha	57.0	M		Y	Y	Guam	Guam	Guam	N	None
5	41	43	Santos, Juan A	Son	M	Cha	34.0	S		Y	Y	Guam	Guam	Guam	Y	Seaman USN
6	41	43	Santos, Blas A	Son	M	Cha	32.0	S		Y	Y	Guam	Guam	Guam	Y	Seaman USN
7	41	43	Santos, Pedro A	Son	M	Cha	26.0	S		Y	Y	Guam	Guam	Guam	Y	Chauffeur
8	41	43	Santos, Maria A	Daughter	F	Cha	21.0	S	N	Y	Y	Guam	Guam	Guam	Y	Laundress
9		43	Santos, Jesus A	Son	M	Cha	20.0	S	N	Y	Y	Guam	Guam	Guam	Y	Chauffeur
10	41	43	Santos, Rita A	Daughter	F	Cha	16.0	S	N	Y	Y	Guam	Guam	Guam	Y	None
11	42	44	Gamboa, Vicente C	Head	M	Cha	28.0	M		Y	Y	Guam	Guam	Guam	N	Laborer
12	42	44	Gamboa, Isabel P	Wife	F	Cha	37.0	M		N	N	Guam	Guam	Guam	N	None
13	42	44	Gamboa, Lorenzo P	Son	M	Cha	7.0	S	Y			Guam	Guam	Guam		None
14	42	44	Gamboa, Julia P	Daughter	F	Cha	5.0	S	N			Guam	Guam	Guam		None
15	42	44	Gamboa, Antonio P	Son	M	Cha	4.0	S				Guam	Guam	Guam		None
16	42	44	Gamboa, Vicente P	Son	M	Cha	0.3	S				Guam	Guam	Guam		None
17	43	45	Rapolla, Francisca C	Head	F	Cha	59.0	Wd		N	N	Guam	Guam	Guam	N	None
18	43	45	Rapolla, Lorenzo C	Son	M	Cha	23.0	S		Y	Y	Guam	Guam	Guam	Y	Laborer
19	43	45	Rapolla, Enrique C	Son	M	Cha	20.0	S	N	Y	Y	Guam	Guam	Guam	Y	Laborer
20	44	46	Rapolla, Antonio C	Head	M	Cha	28.0	M		Y	Y	Guam	Guam	Guam	Y	Farmer
21	44	46	Rapolla, Carmela R	Wife	F	Cha	23.0	M		Y	Y	Guam	Guam	Guam	N	None
22	45	47	Rapolla, Juan C	Head	M	Cha	27.0	M		Y	Y	Guam	Guam	Guam	Y	Laborer
23	45	47	Rapolla, Vicenta T	Wife	F	Cha	28.0	M		Y	Y	Guam	Unknown	Guam	N	None
24	45	47	Rapolla, Natividad R	Daughter	F	Cha	7.0	S	Y	Y	Y	Guam	Guam	Guam	N	None
25	45	47	Rapolla, Francisco T	Son	M	Cha	6.0	S	N	N	N	Guam	Guam	Guam	N	None

Street: Agana Pitt Road

(CHAMORRO ROOTS GENEALOGY PROJECT ™ TRANSCRIPTION)
(COMPILED/TRANSCRIBED BY BERNARD T. PUNZALAN / HTTP://WWW.CHAMORROROOTS.COM)
FOURTEENTH CENSUS OF THE UNITED STATES: 1920—POPULATION
ISLAND OF GUAM

DISTRICT 3
NAME OF PLACE Asan Barrio

[Proper name and, also, name of class, as city, town, village, barrio, etc]

ENUMERATED BY ME ON THE 27th DAY OF February, 1920

Vicente Tydingco ENUMERATOR

Street, avenue, road, etc.	Number of dwelling house (order of visitation)	Number of family (order of visitation)	NAME	RELATION	Sex	Color or race	Age at last birthday	Single, married, widowed or divorced	Attended school any time since Sept. 1, 1919	Whether able to read	Whether able to write	Place of birth of this person	Place of birth of father	Place of birth of mother	Whether able to speak English	OCCUPATION
	1	2	3	4	5	6	7	8	9	10	11	12	13	14	15	16	17
	45	47	Rapolla, Maria T	Daughter	F	Cha	4.0	S				Guam	Guam	Guam		None
	45	47	Rapolla, Carmen T	Daughter	F	Cha	1.0	S				Guam	Guam	Guam		None
	46	48	S. Nicolas, Joaquin S	Head	M	Cha	27.0	D		Y	Y	Guam	Guam	Guam	N	Farmer
	46	48	S. Nicolas, Maria S	Mother	F	Cha	48.0	Wd		N	N	Guam	Guam	Guam	N	None
	46	48	S. Nicolas, Consolacion S	Sister	F	Cha	26.0	S		Y	Y	Guam	Guam	Guam	Y	Laundress
	46	48	S. Nicolas, Luis S	Brother	M	Cha	24.0	S		Y	Y	Guam	Guam	Guam	Y	Farm laborer home farm
	46	48	S. Nicolas, Carlina S	Sister	F	Cha	22.0	S		Y	Y	Guam	Guam	Guam	Y	None
	46	48	S. Nicolas, Antonia S	Sister	F	Cha	20.0	S	N	Y	Y	Guam	Guam	Guam	Y	Laundress
	46	48	S. Nicolas, Jose S	Brother	M	Cha	19.0	S	N	Y	Y	Guam	Guam	Guam	Y	Laborer
Agana Pitt Road	46	48	S. Nicolas, Juan S	Brother	M	Cha	16.0	S	N	Y	Y	Guam	Guam	Guam	Y	None
	46	48	S. Nicolas, Maria S	Sister	F	Cha	13.0	S	Y	Y	Y	Guam	Guam	Guam	Y	None
	46	48	S. Nicolas, Ignacia S	Sister	F	Cha	8.0	S	Y			Guam	Guam	Guam		None
	46	48	S. Nicolas, Ana S	Sister	F	Cha	6.0	S	N			Guam	Guam	Guam		None
	47	49	Santos, Vicente A	Head	M	Cha	31.0	M		Y	Y	Guam	Guam	Guam	Y	Laborer
	47	49	Santos, Josefa B	Wife	F	Cha	31.0	M		Y	Y	Guam	Guam	Guam	N	None
	47	49	Santos, Dolores B	Daughter	F	Cha	12.0	S	Y	Y	Y	Guam	Guam	Guam	Y	None
	47	49	Santos, Francisco B	Son	M	Cha	10.0	S	Y	Y	Y	Guam	Guam	Guam	Y	None
	47	49	Santos, Rosalia B	Daughter	F	Cha	7.0	S	N	N	N	Guam	Guam	Guam		None
	47	49	Santos, Regina B	Daughter	F	Cha	5.0	S				Guam	Guam	Guam		None
	47	49	Santos, Saturnina B	Daughter	F	Cha	2.0	S				Guam	Guam	Guam		None
	48	50	Limtiaco, Santiago A	Head	M	Cha	31.0	M		Y	Y	Guam	Guam	Guam	Y	Chauffeur
	48	50	Limtiaco, Ana SN	Wife	F	Cha	29.0	M		Y	Y	Guam	Guam	Guam	N	None
	48	50	Limtiaco, Matilde SN	Daughter	F	Cha	7.0	S	N			Guam	Guam	Guam		None
	48	50	Limtiaco, Josefina SN	Daughter	F	Cha	5.0	S	N			Guam	Guam	Guam		None
	49	51	Santos, Manuel A	Head	M	Cha	38.0	M		Y	Y	Guam	Guam	Guam	Y	Laborer

(CHAMORRO ROOTS GENEALOGY PROJECT ™ TRANSCRIPTION)
(COMPILED/TRANSCRIBED BY BERNARD T. PUNZALAN / HTTP://WWW.CHAMORROROOTS.COM)

FOURTEENTH CENSUS OF THE UNITED STATES: 1920—POPULATION
ISLAND OF GUAM

DISTRICT 3
NAME OF PLACE Asan Barrio

ENUMERATED BY ME ON THE 27th DAY OF February, 1920

Vicente Tydingco ENUMERATOR

Street, avenue, road, etc.	Number of dwelling house	Number of family	NAME	RELATION	Sex	Color or race	Age at last birthday	Single, married, widowed or divorced	Attended school since Sept. 1, 1919	Whether able to read	Whether able to write	Place of birth of this person	Place of birth of father	Place of birth of mother	Whether able to speak English	OCCUPATION
1	2	3	4	5	6	7	8	9	10	11	12	13	14	15	16	17
	49	51	Santos, Rita B	Wife	F	Cha	36.0	M		N	N	Guam	Unknown	Guam	N	None
	49	51	Santos, Maria B	Daughter	F	Cha	14.0	S	N	Y	Y	Guam	Guam	Guam	Y	None
	49	51	Santos, Getrudes B	Daughter	F	Cha	13.0	S	Y	Y	Y	Guam	Guam	Guam	Y	None
	49	51	Santos, Beatris B	Daughter	F	Cha	8.0	S	Y			Guam	Guam	Guam		None
	49	51	Santos, Enrique B	Son	M	Cha	6.0	S	N			Guam	Guam	Guam		None
	49	51	Santos, Ana B	Daughter	F	Cha	4.0	S				Guam	Guam	Guam		None
	49	51	Santos, Rosa B	Daughter	F	Cha	0.3	S				Guam	Guam	Guam		None
	50	52	Aflague, Jose C	Head	M	Cha	48.0	M		Y	Y	Guam	Guam	Guam		Laborer
	50	52	Aflague, Rosa N	Wife	F	Cha	36.0	M		N	N	Guam	Guam	Guam	N	None
	50	52	Aflague, Maria N	Daughter	F	Cha	6.0	S	Y			Guam	Guam	Guam		None
Agana Piti Road	51	53	Jesus, Joaquin L	Head	M	Cha	23.0	M		Y	Y	Guam	Guam	Guam	Y	Farmer
	51	53	Jesus, Josefa G	Wife	F	Cha	24.0	M		Y	Y	Guam	Guam	Guam	N	None
	51	53	Jesus, Eufemia G	Daughter	F	Cha	1.0	S				Guam	Guam	Guam		None
	52	54	Limtiaco, Antonio T	Head	M	Chin	52.0	M		Y	Y	Guam	China	Guam	N	Carpenter
	52	54	Limtiaco, Antonia A	Wife	F	Cha	50.0	M		N	N	Guam	Guam	Guam	N	None
	52	54	Limtiaco, Juan A	Son	M	Cha	29.0	S		Y	Y	Guam	Guam	Guam	Y	Farmer
	52	54	Limtiaco, Sebastian A	Son	M	Cha	24.0	S		Y	Y	Guam	Guam	Guam	Y	Chauffeur
	52	54	Limtiaco, Maria A	Daughter	F	Cha	19.0	S	N	Y	Y	Guam	Guam	Guam	Y	None
	52	54	Limtiaco, Joaquin A	Son	M	Cha	17.0	S	N	Y	Y	Guam	Guam	Guam	Y	Chauffeur
	52	54	Limtiaco, Rosa A	Daughter	F	Cha	15.0	S	N	Y	Y	Guam	Guam	Guam	Y	None
	52	54	Limtiaco, Adela A	Daughter	F	Cha	12.0	S	Y	Y	Y	Guam	Guam	Guam	Y	None
	52	54	Limtiaco, Ana A	Daughter	F	Cha	10.0	S	Y	Y	Y	Guam	Guam	Guam	Y	None
	52	54	Limtiaco, Vicente A	Son	M	Cha	6.0	S	Y			Guam	Guam	Guam		None
	53	55	Blas, Joaquin L	Head	M	Cha	30.0	M		Y	Y	Guam	Guam	Guam	N	None
	53	55	Blas, Lorenzo L	Son	M	Cha	3.0	S				Guam	Guam	Guam		None

(CHAMORRO ROOTS GENEALOGY PROJECT ™ TRANSCRIPTION)
(COMPILED/TRANSCRIBED BY BERNARD T. PUNZALAN / HTTP://WWW.CHAMORROROOTS.COM)

FOURTEENTH CENSUS OF THE UNITED STATES: 1920-POPULATION
ISLAND OF GUAM

DISTRICT 3
NAME OF PLACE **Asan Barrio**
[Proper name and, also, name of class, as city, town, village, barrio, etc]

ENUMERATED BY ME ON THE 28th DAY OF February, 1920

Vicente Tydingco ENUMERATOR

	PLACE OF ABODE		NAME	RELATION	PERSONAL DESCRIPTION				EDUCATION			NATIVITY				OCCUPATION
Street, avenue, road, etc.	Number of dwelling house in order of visitation	Number of family in order of visitation	Name of each person whose place of abode on January 1, 1920, was in the family.	Relationship of this Person to the head of the family.	Sex	Color or race	Age at last birthday	Single, married, widowed or divorced	Attended any school since Sept. 1, 1919	Whether able to read.	Whether able to write.	Place of birth of this person.	Place of birth of father of this person.	Place of birth of mother of this person.	Whether able to speak English.	Trade, profession, or particular kind of work done
1	2	3	4	5	6	7	8	9	10	11	12	13	14	15	16	17
	53	55	Blas, Juan L	Son	M	Cha	2.0	S				Guam	Guam	Guam		None
	53	55	Blas, Antonia L	Daughter	F	Cha	0.2	S				Guam	Guam	Guam		None
	54	56	Santos, Juan M	Head	M	Cha	59.0	M		N	N	Guam	Guam	Guam	N	Farmer
	54	56	Santos, Juana A	Wife	F	Cha	53.0	M		N	N	Guam	Guam	Guam	N	Laundress
	54	56	Santos, Catalina A	Daughter	F	Cha	22.0	S		Y	Y	Guam	Guam	Guam	Y	Laundress
	54	56	Aguahlo, Ignacio T	Servant	M	Cha	40.0	S		N	N	Guam	Guam	Guam	N	Servant
	55	57	Aflague, Ana S	Head	F	Cha	55.0	Wd		N	N	Guam	Guam	Guam	N	None
	55	57	Aflague, Antonio S	Son	M	Cha	37.0	S		Y	Y	Guam	Guam	Guam	Y	Seaman USN
Agana Piti Road	55	57	Aflague, Lorenzo S	Son	M	Cha	19.0	S	N	Y	Y	Guam	Guam	Guam	Y	Farmer
	55	57	Aflague, Concepcion S	Daughter	F	Cha	16.0	S	N	Y	Y	Guam	Guam	Guam	N	None
	55	57	Aflague, Francisco S	Son	M	Cha	13.0	S	Y	Y	Y	Guam	Guam	Guam	Y	None
	56	58	S. Nicolas, Vicente T	Head	M	Cha	40.0	M		Y	Y	Guam	Unknown	Guam	Y	Laborer
	56	58	S. Nicolas, Maria A	Wife	F	Cha	38.0	M		Y	N	Guam	Guam	Guam	N	None
	56	58	S. Nicolas, Francisco A	Son	M	Cha	18.0	S	N	Y	Y	Guam	Guam	Guam	Y	Farmer
	56	58	S. Nicolas, Florencio A	Son	M	Cha	14.0	S	Y	Y	Y	Guam	Guam	Guam	Y	Farm laborer home farm
	56	58	S. Nicolas, Gregorio A	Son	M	Cha	11.0	S	Y	Y	Y	Guam	Guam	Guam	Y	None
	56	58	S. Nicolas, Maria A jr.	Daughter	F	Cha	9.0	S	Y			Guam	Guam	Guam		None
	56	58	S. Nicolas, Rita A	Daughter	F	Cha	3.0	S				Guam	Guam	Guam		None
	56	58	Aguahlo, Santiago T	Servant	M	Cha	47.0	D		Y	Y	Guam	Guam	Guam	Y	Servant
	57	59	Fejeran, Consolacion	Head	F	Cha	47.0	Wd		N	N	Guam	Guam	Guam	N	Laundress
	57	59	Fejeran, Vicente SN	Son	M	Cha	19.0	S	N	Y	Y	Guam	Guam	Guam	Y	Laborer
	57	59	Fejeran, Antonia SN	Daughter	F	Cha	17.0	S	N	N	N	Guam	Guam	Guam	N	Servant
	57	59	Fejeran, Rosa SN	Daughter	F	Cha	8.0	S	Y			Guam	Guam	Guam		None
	58	60	Santos, Nicolas S	Head	M	Cha	50.0	S		Y	Y	Guam	Unknown	Guam	N	Farmer
	58	60	Santos, Rosa F	Wife	F	Cha	52.0	S		N	N	Guam	Guam	Guam	N	None

(CHAMORRO ROOTS GENEALOGY PROJECT ™ TRANSCRIPTION)
(COMPILED/TRANSCRIBED BY BERNARD T. PUNZALAN / HTTP://WWW.CHAMORROROOTS.COM)

FOURTEENTH CENSUS OF THE UNITED STATES: 1920-POPULATION

ISLAND OF GUAM

ENUMERATED BY ME ON THE 28th DAY OF February, 1920

Vicente Tydingco ENUMERATOR

DISTRICT 3

NAME OF PLACE Asan Barrio

Street, avenue, road, etc.	Dwelling No.	Family No.	NAME	RELATION	Sex	Color or race	Age at last birthday	Single, married, widowed or divorced	Attended school since Sept. 1, 1919	Whether able to read	Whether able to write	Place of birth of this person	Place of birth of father	Place of birth of mother	Whether able to speak English	OCCUPATION
	58	60	Santos, Manuel F	Son	M	Cha	22.0	S		Y	Y	Guam	Guam	Guam	Y	Laborer
	58	60	Santos, Carmen F	Daughter	F	Cha	16.0	S	N	Y	Y	Guam	Guam	Guam	N	Laundress
	59	61	Jesus, Joaquin SN	Head	M	Cha	27.0	M		Y	Y	Guam	Guam	Guam	Y	Laborer
	59	61	Jesus, Vicenta C	Wife	F	Cha	24.0	M		N	N	Guam	Guam	Guam	N	None
	60	62	S. Nicolas, Filomeno	Head	M	Cha	49.0	M		Y	Y	Guam	Unknown	Guam	N	Farmer
	60	62	S. Nicolas, Vicenta C	Wife	F	Cha	32.0	M		N	N	Guam	Guam	Guam	N	None
	60	62	S. Nicolas, Severa C	Daughter	F	Cha	13.0	S	Y	Y	Y	Guam	Guam	Guam	Y	None
	60	62	S. Nicolas, Grabiela C	Daughter	F	Cha	11.0	S	Y	Y	Y	Guam	Guam	Guam	Y	None
Agana Piti Road	60	62	S. Nicolas, Jose C	Son	M	Cha	7.0	S	Y			Guam	Guam	Guam		None
	60	62	S. Nicolas, Maria C	Daughter	F	Cha	5.0	S	N			Guam	Guam	Guam		None
	60	62	S. Nicolas, Consuelo C	Daughter	F	Cha	4.0	S				Guam	Guam	Guam		None
	60	62	S. Nicolas, Rosalia C	Daughter	F	Cha	1.0	S				Guam	Guam	Guam		None
	61	63	Aflleje, Juan P	Head	M	Cha	40.0	M		Y	Y	Guam	Guam	Guam	N	Farmer
	61	63	Aflleje, Rita T	Wife	F	Cha	35.0	M		N	N	Guam	Guam	Guam	N	None
	61	63	Aflleje, Jose T	Son	M	Cha	12.0	S	Y	Y	Y	Guam	Guam	Guam	Y	None
	61	63	Aflleje, Joaquina T	Daughter	F	Cha	8.0	S	Y			Guam	Guam	Guam		None
	61	63	Aflleje, Regina T	Daughter	F	Cha	5.0	S	N			Guam	Guam	Guam		None
	61	63	Aflleje, Ana T	Daughter	F	Cha	3.0	S				Guam	Guam	Guam		None
	61	63	Aflleje, Vicente T	Son	M	Cha	1.0	S				Guam	Guam	Guam		None
	61	63	Taitano, Remedios	Step-daughter	F	Cha	17.0	S	N	Y	Y	Guam	Unknown	Guam	Y	Laundress
	62	64	Fejeran, Jose SN	Head	M	Cha	51.0	Wd		N	N	Guam	Guam	Guam	N	Farmer
	62	64	Fejeran, Enrique P	Son	M	Cha	19.0	S	N	Y	Y	Guam	Guam	Guam	Y	Laborer
	62	64	Fejeran, Soledad P	Daughter	F	Cha	17.0	S	N	Y	Y	Guam	Guam	Guam	N	Laundress
	62	64	Fejeran, Amanda P	Daughter	F	Cha	14.0	S	Y	Y	Y	Guam	Guam	Guam	Y	None
	62	64	Fejeran, Florencio P	Son	M	Cha	10.0	S	Y	Y	Y	Guam	Guam	Guam	Y	None

(CHAMORRO ROOTS GENEALOGY PROJECT ™ TRANSCRIPTION)
(COMPILED/TRANSCRIBED BY BERNARD T. PUNZALAN / HTTP://WWW.CHAMORROROOTS.COM)

FOURTEENTH CENSUS OF THE UNITED STATES: 1920-POPULATION
ISLAND OF GUAM

ENUMERATED BY ME ON THE 28th DAY OF February, 1920

Vicente Tydingco ENUMERATOR

DISTRICT 3
NAME OF PLACE Asan Barrio

[Proper name and, also, name of class, as city, town, village, barrio, etc]

	PLACE OF ABODE			NAME	RELATION	PERSONAL DESCRIPTION					EDUCATION			NATIVITY				OCCUPATION
	Street, avenue, road, etc.	Number of dwelling house	Number of family	Name	Relation to head	Sex	Color or race	Age at last birthday	Single, married, widowed or divorced	Attended school since Sept. 1, 1919	Whether able to read	Whether able to write	Place of birth of this person	Place of birth of father	Place of birth of mother	Whether able to speak English	Occupation
	1	2	3	4	5	6	7	8	9	10	11	12	13	14	15	16	17
26		62	64	Fejeran, Jose P	Son	M	Cha	8.0	S	Y			Guam	Guam	Guam		None
27		63	65	Terlaje, Felix A	Head	M	Cha	49.0	M		N	N	Guam	Guam	Guam	N	Farmer
28		63	65	Terlaje, Dolores S	Wife	F	Cha	50.0	M		N	N	Guam	Guam	Guam	N	Laundress
29		64	66	Aflleje, Josefa P	Head	F	Cha	60.0	Wd		N	N	Guam	Guam	Guam	N	None
30		64	66	Aflleje, Joaquin P	Son	M	Cha	30.0	S	N	Y	Y	Guam	Guam	Guam	N	Seaman USN
31		64	66	Aflleje, Dolores P	Daughter	F	Cha	17.0	S		Y	Y	Guam	Guam	Guam	Y	None
32		65	67	Taitano, Rosa S	Head	F	Cha	36.0	Wd		N	N	Guam	Unknown	Guam	N	Laundress
33		65	67	Taitano, Vicente S	Son	M	Cha	19.0	S	N	Y	Y	Guam	Guam	Guam	Y	Laborer
34		65	67	Taitano, Jose S	Son	M	Cha	6.0	S	N			Guam	Guam	Guam		None
35		65	67	Taitano, Ana S	Daughter	F	Cha	4.0	S				Guam	Guam	Guam		None
36		65	67	Taitano, Balbina S	Daughter	F	Cha	3.0	S				Guam	Guam	Guam		None
37		66	68	Rojas, Juan R	Head	M	Cha	59.0	M		N	N	Guam	China	Guam	N	Carpenter
38	Agana Piti Road	66	68	Rojas, Ana S	Wife	F	Chi n	42.0	M		N	N	Guam	Guam	Guam	N	Laundress
39		66	68	Rojas, Manuel S	Son	M	Cha	19.0	S	N	Y	Y	Guam	Guam	Guam	Y	Laborer
40		66	68	Rojas, Magdalena S	Daughter	F	Cha	17.0	S	N	Y	Y	Guam	Guam	Guam	Y	None
41		66	68	Rojas, Pedro S	Son	M	Cha	14.0	S	Y	Y	Y	Guam	Guam	Guam	Y	Farm laborer home farm
42		66	68	Rojas, Ramon S	Son	M	Cha	8.0	S	Y			Guam	Guam	Guam		None
43		66	68	Rojas, Antonia S	Daughter	F	Cha	5.0	S	N			Guam	Guam	Guam		None
44		66	68	Rojas, Juan S	Son	M	Cha	3.0	S				Guam	Guam	Guam		None
45		66	68	Sococo, Manuel	Father-in-law	M	Chi n	97.0	Unk		Y	Y	China	China	China	N	None
46				Here ends the enumeration of Asan Barrio													
47																	
48																	
49																	
50																	

(CHAMORRO ROOTS GENEALOGY PROJECT ™ TRANSCRIPTION)
(COMPILED/TRANSCRIBED BY BERNARD T. PUNZALAN / HTTP://WWW.CHAMORROROOTS.COM)
FOURTEENTH CENSUS OF THE UNITED STATES: 1920—POPULATION
ISLAND OF GUAM

ENUMERATED BY ME ON THE 1st DAY OF March, 1920

Vicente Tydingco ENUMERATOR

DISTRICT 3
NAME OF PLACE Tepungan Barrio
[Proper name and, also, name of class, as city, town, village, barrio, etc]

	Street	Dwelling no.	Family no.	NAME	RELATION	Sex	Color or race	Age	Marital	School	Read	Write	Birthplace	Father	Mother	English	OCCUPATION
	1	2	3	4	5	6	7	8	9	10	11	12	13	14	15	16	17
1		67	69	Quenga, Sebastian C	Head	M	Chin	36.0	M		Y	Y	Guam	China	Guam	N	Farmer
2		67	69	Quenga, Milagro SN	Wife	F	Cha	39.0	M		Y	Y	Guam	Guam	Guam	N	None
3		67	69	Quenga, Juan SN	Son	M	Cha	15.0	S	Y	Y	Y	Guam	Guam	Guam	Y	Farm laborer home farm
4		67	69	Quenga, Vicente SN	Son	M	Cha	12.0	S	Y	Y	Y	Guam	Guam	Guam	Y	None
5		67	69	Quenga, Carolina SN	Daughter	F	Cha	9.0	S	Y			Guam	Guam	Guam		None
6		67	69	Quenga, Manuel SN	Son	M	Cha	6.0	S	N			Guam	Guam	Guam		None
7		67	69	Quenga, Joaquin SN	Son	M	Cha	3.0	S					Guam	Guam		
8		68	70	Quenga, Ana SN	Head	F	Cha	42.0	Wd		N	N	Guam	Guam	Guam	N	Laundress
9		68	70	Quenga, Jose SN	Son	M	Cha	21.0	S	N	Y	Y	Guam	Guam	Guam	Y	Farmer
10		68	70	Quenga, Angustia SN	Daughter	F	Cha	20.0	S	N	Y	Y	Guam	Guam	Guam	Y	Laundress
11		68	70	Quenga, Cristina SN	Daughter	F	Cha	17.0	S	N	Y	Y	Guam	Guam	Guam	Y	Laundress
12		68	70	Quenga, Manuel SN	Son	M	Cha	15.0	S	N	Y	Y	Guam	Guam	Guam	Y	Farm laborer home farm
13	Agana Piti Road	69	71	Quenga, Vicente C	Head	M	Chin	44.0	M		Y	N	Guam	China	Guam	N	Farmer
14		69	71	Quenga, Gabina C	Wife	F	Cha	40.0	M		N	N	Guam	Guam	Guam	N	None
15		69	71	Quenga, Antonia C	Daughter	F	Cha	21.0	S	N	Y	Y	Guam	Guam	Guam	Y	Laundress
16		69	71	Quenga, Severa C	Daughter	F	Cha	19.0	S	N	Y	Y	Guam	Guam	Guam	Y	Laundress
17		69	71	Quenga, Josefina C	Daughter	F	Cha	17.0	S	N	Y	Y	Guam	Guam	Guam	Y	Laundress
18		69	71	Quenga, Jose C	Son	M	Cha	15.0	S	N	Y	Y	Guam	Guam	Guam	Y	Farm laborer home farm
19		69	71	Quenga, Dolores C	Daughter	F	Cha	12.0	S	Y	Y	Y	Guam	Guam	Guam	Y	None
20		69	71	Quenga, Jesus S	Son	M	Cha	8.0	S	Y			Guam	Guam	Guam		None
21		69	71	Quenga, Rosalia C	Daughter	F	Cha	3.0	S				Guam	Guam	Guam		None
22		69	71	Abrera, Rosa C	Daughter	F	Cha	23.0	Wd		Y	Y	Guam	Guam	Guam	Y	Laundress
23		70	72	Quenga, Antonio C	Head	M	Chin	47.0	M		Y	Y	Guam	China	Guam	N	Farmer
24		70	72	Quenga, Natividad SN	Wife	F	Cha	48.0	M		Y	Y	Guam	Guam	Guam	N	None
25		70	72	Quenga, Joaquin SN	Son	M	Cha	18.0	S		Y	Y	Guam	Guam	Guam	Y	Chauffeur

(CHAMORRO ROOTS GENEALOGY PROJECT ™ TRANSCRIPTION)
(COMPILED/TRANSCRIBED BY BERNARD T. PUNZALAN / HTTP://WWW.CHAMORROROOTS.COM)

FOURTEENTH CENSUS OF THE UNITED STATES: 1920-POPULATION

ISLAND OF GUAM

183b

SHEET NO. 8B

DISTRICT 3

NAME OF PLACE **Tepungan Barrio**

[Proper name and, also, name of class, as city, town, village, barrio, etc]

ENUMERATED BY ME ON THE 1st DAY OF March, 1920

Vicente Tydingco ENUMERATOR

	PLACE OF ABODE			NAME	RELATION	PERSONAL DESCRIPTION					EDUCATION			NATIVITY				OCCUPATION
	Street, avenue, road, etc.	Number of dwelling house in order of visitation	Number of family in order of visitation		Relationship of this Person to the head of the family.	Sex	Color or race	Age at last birthday	Single, married, widowed or divorced	Attended school any time since Sept. 1, 1919	Whether able to read.	Whether able to write.	Place of birth of this person.	Place of birth of father of this person.	Place of birth of mother of this person.	Whether able to speak English.	Trade, profession, or particular kind of work done, as salesman, laborer, clerk, cook, merchant, washerwoman, etc.
	1	2	3	4	5	6	7	8	9	10	11	12	13	14	15	16	17
26		70	72	Quenga, Antonia SN	Daughter	F	Cha	17.0	S	N	Y	Y	Guam	Guam	Guam	Y	None
27		70	72	Quenga, Vicente SN	Son	M	Cha	15.0	S	N	Y	Y	Guam	Guam	Guam	Y	Farm laborer home farm
28		70	72	Quenga, Maria SN	Daughter	F	Cha	13.0	S	Y	Y	Y	Guam	Guam	Guam	Y	None
29		70	72	Quenga, Angelina SN	Daughter	F	Cha	12.0	S	Y	Y	Y	Guam	Guam	Guam	Y	None
30		70	72	Quenga, Teodoro SN	Son	M	Cha	10.0	S	Y	Y	Y	Guam	Guam	Guam	Y	None
31		70	72	Quenga, Lourdes SN	Daughter	F	Cha	6.0	S				Guam	Guam	Guam		None
32		70	72	Quenga, Carlos SN	Son	M	Cha	2.0	S				Guam	Guam	Guam		None
33		71	73	Quenga, Feix C	Head	M	Cha	48.0	M		Y	Y	Guam	China	Guam	N	Farmer
34		71	73	Quenga, Maria T	Wife	F	Cha	44.0	M		N	N	Guam	Guam	Guam	N	None
35	Agana Piti Road	71	73	Quenga, Barbara T	Daughter	F	Cha	25.0	S		Y	Y	Guam	Guam	Guam	Y	Laundres
36		71	73	Quenga, Maria T	Daughter	F	Cha	20.0	S	N	Y	Y	Guam	Guam	Guam	Y	Laundres
37		71	73	Quenga, Dolores T	Daughter	F	Cha	18.0	S	N	Y	Y	Guam	Guam	Guam	Y	Laundres
38		71	73	Quenga, Jose T	Son	M	Cha	12.0	S	Y	Y	Y	Guam	Guam	Guam	Y	None
39		71	73	Quenga, Lorenzo T	Son	M	Cha	10.0	S	Y	Y	Y	Guam	Guam	Guam	Y	None
40		71	73	Quenga, Vicenta T	Daughter	F	Cha	7.0	S	Y			Guam	Guam	Guam		None
41		71	73	Quenga, Manuel T	Son	M	Cha	6.0	S	N			Guam	Guam	Guam		None
42		71	73	Quenga, Servino T	Son	M	Cha	2.0	S				Guam	Guam	Guam		None
43		71	73	Taijeron, Dolores	Mother-in-law	F	Cha	70.0	Wd		N	N	Guam	Guam	Guam	N	None
44		72	74	Quenga, Maria B	Head	F	Cha	56.0	Wd		N	N	Guam	Guam	Guam	N	None
45		72	74	Quenga, Vicenta B	Daughter	F	Cha	20.0	S	N	Y	Y	Guam	Guam	Guam	N	None
46		72	74	Quenga, Maria B jr	Daughter	F	Cha	18.0	S	N	Y	Y	Guam	Guam	Guam	Y	Laundres
47		72	74	Quenga, Pedro B	Son	M	Cha	16.0	S	N	Y	Y	Guam	Guam	Guam	Y	Laundres
48		72	74	Quenga, Magdalena B	Daughter	F	Cha	14.0	S	Y	Y	Y	Guam	Guam	Guam	Y	Servant
49		72	74	Quenga, Juana B	Daughter	F	Cha	9.0	S	Y	Y	Y	Guam	Guam	Guam	Y	None
50		72	74	Quichocho, Mariana	Servant	F	Cha	13.0	S	N	Y	Y	Guam	Guam	Guam	N	Servant

(CHAMORRO ROOTS GENEALOGY PROJECT ™ TRANSCRIPTION)
(COMPILED/TRANSCRIBED BY BERNARD T. PUNZALAN / HTTP://WWW.CHAMORRROOTS.COM)

FOURTEENTH CENSUS OF THE UNITED STATES: 1920-POPULATION
ISLAND OF GUAM

DISTRICT 3
NAME OF PLACE Tepungan Barrio
[Proper name and, also, name of class, as city, town, village, barrio, etc]

ENUMERATED BY ME ON THE 3RD DAY OF March, 1920

Vicente Tydingco ENUMERATOR

	1	2	3	4 NAME	5 RELATION	6 Sex	7 Color or race	8 Age at last birthday	9 Single, married, widowed or divorced	10 Attended school since Sept. 1, 1919	11 Whether able to read	12 Whether able to write	13 Place of birth of this person	14 Place of birth of father	15 Place of birth of mother	16 Whether able to speak English	17 OCCUPATION
1		73	75	Aflleje, Vicente C	Head	M	Cha	77.0	Wd		N	N	Guam	Guam	Guam	N	None
2		73	75	Aflleje, Maria T	Daughter	F	Cha	39.0	S		N	N	Guam	Guam	Guam	N	Farmer
3		73	75	Aflleje, Mariano	Son	M	Cha	28.0	S		Y	Y	Guam	Guam	Guam	Y	Corpsman USN
4		73	75	Aflleje, Perpetua T	Daughter	F	Cha	36.0	S		N	N	Guam	Guam	Guam	N	None
5		73	75	Aflleje, Isabel	Grand daughter	F	Cha	10.0	S	Y	Y	Y	Guam	Unknown	Guam	Y	None
6		73	75	Aflleje, Juana	Grand daughter	F	Cha	5.0	S	N			Guam	Unknown	Guam		None
7		73	75	Aflleje, Rosa	Grand daughter	F	Cha	1.0	S				Guam	Unknown	Guam		None
8		73	75	Aflleje, Catalina	Grand daughter	F	Cha	14.0	S	Y	Y	Y	Guam	Unknown	Guam	Y	None
9		73	75	Aflleje, Magdalena	Grand daughter	F	Cha	2.0	S				Guam	Unknown	Guam		None
10	Agana Pitti Road	74	76	Cruz, Antonio S	Head	M	Cha	23.0	M		Y	Y	Guam	Guam	Guam	Y	Laborer
11		74	76	Cruz, Soledad Q	Wife	F	Cha	24.0	M		Y	Y	Guam	Guam	Guam	Y	None
12		75	77	Blas, Josefa A	Head	F	Cha	59.0	S		N	N	Guam	Guam	Guam	N	Laundress
13		75	77	Blas, Juana A	Mother	F	Cha	86.0	Wd		N	N	Guam	Guam	Guam	Y	Laundress
14		75	77	Blas, Soledad A	Daughter	F	Cha	24.0	S		Y	Y	Guam	Guam	Guam	Y	None
15		75	77	Blas, Francisco A	Son	M	Cha	21.0	S	N	Y	Y	Guam	Guam	Guam	Y	Laborer
16		76	78	Blas, Ignacio B	Head	M	Cha	26.0	M		Y	Y	Guam	Guam	Guam	Y	Laborer
17		76	78	Blas, Consolacion A	Wife	F	Cha	23.0	M		Y	Y	Guam	Guam	Guam	Y	None
18		76	78	Blas, Ana A	Daughter	F	Cha	5.0	S	N			Guam	Guam	Guam	Y	None
19		76	78	Blas, Ignacio A	Son	M	Cha	1.0	S				Guam	Guam	Guam		None
20		77	79	Santos, Jose B	Head	M	Cha	38.0	M		Y	Y	Guam	Guam	Guam	Y	Fireman USN
21		77	79	Santos, Teresa C	Wife	F	Cha	38.0	M		Y	Y	Guam	Unknown	Guam	N	None
22		77	79	Santos, Rosa C	Daughter	F	Cha	14.0	S	Y	Y	Y	Guam	Guam	Guam	Y	None
23		77	79	Santos, Pedro C	Son	M	Cha	11.0	S	Y	Y	Y	Guam	Guam	Guam	Y	None
24		77	79	Santos, Jose C	Son	M	Cha	8.0	S	Y	Y	Y	Guam	Guam	Guam	Y	None
25		77	79	Santos, Vicente C	Son	M	Cha	5.0	S	N			Guam	Guam	Guam		None

(CHAMORRO ROOTS GENEALOGY PROJECT ™ TRANSCRIPTION)
(COMPILED/TRANSCRIBED BY BERNARD T. PUNZALAN / HTTP://WWW.CHAMORROROOTS.COM)
FOURTEENTH CENSUS OF THE UNITED STATES: 1920-POPULATION
ISLAND OF GUAM

DISTRICT 3
NAME OF PLACE Tepungan Barrio
[Proper name and, also, name of class, as city, town, village, barrio, etc]

ENUMERATED BY ME ON THE 4th DAY OF March, 1920

Vicente Tydingco ENUMERATOR

	PLACE OF ABODE			NAME	RELATION	PERSONAL DESCRIPTION					EDUCATION			NATIVITY			OCCUPATION
Street, avenue, road, etc.	Number of dwelling house is order of visitation	Number of family in order of visitation		of each person whose place of abode on January 1, 1920, was in the family. Enter surname, first, then given name and middle initial. If any. Include every person living on January 1, 1920. Omit children born since January 1, 1920.	Relationship of this Person to the head of the family.	Sex	Color or race	Age at last birthday	Single, married, widowed or divorced	Attended school any time since Sept. 1, 1919	Whether able to read.	Whether able to write.	Place of birth of this person.	Place of birth of father of this person.	Place of birth of mother of this person.	Trade, profession, or particular kind of work done, as salesman, laborer, clerk, cook, merchant, washerwoman, etc.	Whether able to speak English.
1	2	3		4	5	6	7	8	9	10	11	12	13	14	15	17	16
	78	80	26	Manibusan, Manuel SN	Head	M	Cha	37.0	M		Y	Y	Guam	Guam	Guam	Farmer	Y
	78	80	27	Manibusan, Maria C	Wife	F	Cha	36.0	M		Y	Y	Guam	Unknown	Guam	None	Y
	78	80	28	Manibusan, Francisco C	Son	M	Cha	10.0	S	Y	Y	Y	Guam	Guam	Guam	None	Y
	78	80	29	Manibusan, Miguel C	Son	M	Cha	7.0	S	Y			Guam	Guam	Guam	None	
	78	80	30	Manibusan, Herminia C	Daughter	F	Cha	6.0	S	N			Guam	Guam	Guam	None	
	78	80	31	Manibusan, Vicente C	Son	M	Cha	1.0	S				Guam	Guam	Guam	None	
	79	81	32	Megofna, Carmen C	Head	F	Cha	49.0	Wd		N	N	Guam	Unknown	Guam	Laundress	N
	79	81	33	Megofna, Engracia C	Daughter	F	Cha	17.0	S	N	Y	Y	Guam	Guam	Guam	Laundress	N
	79	81	34	Megofna, Rita C	Daughter	F	Cha	14.0	S		Y	Y	Guam	Guam	Guam	None	Y
Agana Piti Road	80	82	35	Terlaje, Manuel T	Head	M	Cha	53.0	M		Y	Y	Guam	Unknown	Guam	Farmer	N
	80	82	36	Terlaje, Grabiela A	Wife	F	Cha	48.0	M		N	N	Guam	Guam	Guam	Laundress	N
	80	82	37	Terlaje, Mercedes A	Daughter	F	Cha	22.0	S		Y	Y	Guam	Guam	Guam	Laundress	Y
	80	82	38	Terlaje, Dolores A	Daughter	F	Cha	20.0	S	N	Y	Y	Guam	Guam	Guam	Laundress	Y
	80	82	39	Terlaje, Luis A	Son	M	Cha	17.0	S	N	Y	Y	Guam	Guam	Guam	Farm laborer home farm	Y
	80	82	40	Terlaje, Jesus A	Son	M	Cha	14.0	S	N	Y	Y	Guam	Guam	Guam	Farm laborer home farm	Y
	80	82	41	Terlaje, Miguel A	Son	M	Cha	7.0	S	N			Guam	Guam	Guam	None	
	80	82	42	Taitano, Maria A	Mother-in-law	F	Cha	70.0	Wd		N	N	Guam	Guam	Guam	None	N
	81	82	43	Nauta, Mariano N	Head	M	Cha	32.0	M		Y	Y	Guam	Guam	Guam	Laborer	N
	81	82	44	Nauta, Maria Q	Wife	F	Cha	30.0	M		Y	Y	Guam	Guam	Guam	None	N
	81	82	45	Nauta, Vicente Q	Son	M	Cha	13.0	S	Y	Y	Y	Guam	Guam	Guam	None	Y
	81	82	46	Nauta, Martina Q	Daughter	F	Cha	12.0	S	Y	Y	Y	Guam	Guam	Guam	None	Y
	81	82	47	Nauta, Lucia Q	Daughter	F	Cha	10.0	S	Y	Y	Y	Guam	Guam	Guam	None	N
	81	82	48	Nauta, Manuel Q	Son	M	Cha	8.0	S	Y			Guam	Guam	Guam	None	
	81	82	49	Nauta, Pedro Q	Son	M	Cha	6.0	S	N			Guam	Guam	Guam	None	
	81	82	50	Nauta, Joaquina Q	Daughter	F	Cha	4.0	S				Guam	Guam	Guam	None	

371

(CHAMORRO ROOTS GENEALOGY PROJECT ™ TRANSCRIPTION)
(COMPILED/TRANSCRIBED BY BERNARD T. PUNZALAN / HTTP://WWW.CHAMORROROOTS.COM)

FOURTEENTH CENSUS OF THE UNITED STATES: 1920—POPULATION

ISLAND OF GUAM

ENUMERATED BY ME ON THE 4th DAY OF March, 1920

Vicente Tydingco ENUMERATOR

DISTRICT 3
NAME OF PLACE **Tepungan Barrio**

	PLACE OF ABODE		NAME	RELATION	PERSONAL DESCRIPTION				EDUCATION			NATIVITY				OCCUPATION
Street, avenue, road, etc.	No. of dwelling house	No. of family		Relationship to head of family	Sex	Color or race	Age at last birthday	Single, married, widowed, divorced	Attended school	Able to read	Able to write	Place of birth of this person	Place of birth of father	Place of birth of mother	Whether able to speak English	Trade, profession, or particular kind of work
1	2	3	4	5	6	7	8	9	10	11	12	13	14	15	16	17
	81	82	Nauta, Jesus Q	Son	M	Cha	3.0	S				Guam	Guam	Guam		None
	81	82	Nauta, Ignacio Q	Son	M	Cha	1.0	S				Guam	Guam	Guam		None
	82	84	Chargualaf, Ana C	Head	F	Cha	31.0	S		Y	Y	Guam	Unknown	Guam	Y	Laundress
	82	84	Chargualaf, Esperanza C	Daughter	F	Cha	12.0	S	Y	Y	Y	Guam	Unknown	Guam	Y	None
	82	84	Chargualaf, Enrique C	Son	M	Cha	10.0	S	Y	Y	Y	Guam	Unknown	Guam	Y	None
	82	84	Chargualaf, Consolacion C	Daughter	F	Cha	4.0	S				Guam	Unknown	Guam		None
	82	84	Chargualaf, Juan C	Son	M	Cha	2.0	S				Guam	Unknown	Guam		None
	82	85	Mesa, Bartolome	Head	M	Cha	50.0	Wd		N	N	Guam	Guam	Guam	N	Laborer
	82	85	Mesa, Nicolasa C	Daughter	F	Cha	22.0	S		Y	Y	Guam	Guam	Guam	Y	Laundress
Agana Pitt Road	82	85	Mesa, Engracia C	Grand daughter	F	Cha	0.3	S				Guam	Unknown	Guam		None
	83	86	Nauta, Jose N	Head	M	Cha	35.0	M		N	N	Guam	Unknown	Guam	N	Laborer
	83	86	Nauta, Felicita T	Wife	F	Cha	34.0	M		N	N	Guam	Unknown	Guam	N	None
	83	86	Terlaje, Amalia T	Mother-in-law	F	Chi n	59.0	?		N	N	Guam	China	Guam	N	None
	84	87	Quenga, Dolores C	Head	F	Cha	38.0	S	N	Y	Y	Guam	Unknown	Guam	N	Laundress
	84	87	Quenga, Enrique C	Son	M	Cha	17.0	S	Y	Y	Y	Guam	Unknown	Guam	Y	Farm laborer
	84	87	Quenga, Felix C	Son	M	Cha	8.0	S	N			Guam	Unknown	Guam		None
	84	87	Quenga, Rufina C	Daughter	F	Cha	5.0	S				Guam	Unknown	Guam		None
	84	88	Atao, Ana M	Head	F	Cha	31.0	S		N	N	Guam	Unknown	Guam	N	Laundress
	84	88	Atao, Dolores M	Daughter	F	Cha	7.0	S	N			Guam	Unknown	Guam		None
	84	88	Atao, Juan M	Son	M	Cha	5.0	S	N			Guam	Unknown	Guam		None
	85	89	Chargualaf, Filiomena	Head	F	Cha	26.0	S		Y	Y	Guam	Unknown	Guam	Y	Modwifery
	86	90	Cruz, Juan P	Head	M	Cha	38.0	D		Y	Y	Guam	Guam	Guam	Y	Fireman USN
	87	91	Acfalle, Nieves C	Head	F	Cha	68.0	Wd		N	N	Guam	Guam	Guam	N	None
	87	91	Acfalle, Ignacio C	Son	M	Cha	26.0	S		Y	Y	Guam	Guam	Guam	Y	Laborer
	87	91	Acfalle, Jesus C	Son	M	Cha	24.0	S		Y	Y	Guam	Guam	Guam	Y	Seaman USN

(CHAMORRO ROOTS GENEALOGY PROJECT ™ TRANSCRIPTION)
(COMPILED/TRANSCRIBED BY BERNARD T. PUNZALAN / HTTP://WWW.CHAMORROROOTS.COM)

FOURTEENTH CENSUS OF THE UNITED STATES: 1920—POPULATION
ISLAND OF GUAM

DISTRICT 3
NAME OF PLACE Tepungan Barrio
[Proper name and, also, name of class, as city, town, village, barrio, etc]

ENUMERATED BY ME ON THE 6th DAY OF March, 1920

Vicente Tydingco ENUMERATOR

	Street	Dwelling No.	Family No.	NAME	RELATION	Sex	Color or race	Age	Marital status	School since Sept 1, 1919	Read	Write	Birthplace	Father birthplace	Mother birthplace	Speak English	OCCUPATION
	1	2	3	4	5	6	7	8	9	10	11	12	13	14	15	16	17
26		88	92	Aguahlo, Maria C	Head	F	Cha	29.0	D		N	N	Guam	Guam	Guam	N	Laundress
27		88	92	Aguahlo, Aleandro C	Son	M	Cha	11.0	S	Y	Y	Y	Guam	Guam	Guam	Y	None
28		88	92	Aguahlo, Jose C	Son	M	Cha	9.0	S	N	Y	Y	Guam	Guam	Guam	Y	None
29		88	92	Aguahlo, Miguel C	Son	M	Cha	4.0	S				Guam	Guam	Guam		None
30		89	93	Kamminga, John S	Head	M	W	79.0	M		Y	Y	Holland	Holland	Holland	Y	None
31		89	93	Kamminga, Juana R	Wife	F	Cha	63.0	M				Guam	Guam	Guam	Y	None
32		89	93	Kamminga, Guele R	Son	M	W	24.0	S		Y	Y	Guam	Holland	Guam	Y	Chauffeur
33		89	93	Kamminga, Frank R	Son	M	W	22.0	S		Y	Y	Guam	Holland	Guam	Y	Chauffeur
34	Agana Pitt Road	89	93	Sococo, Jose S	Lodger	M	Cha	24.0	S		Y	Y	Guam	Unknown	Guam	Y	Seaman USN
35		89	93	Sococo, Catalina S	Lodger	F	Cha	20.0	S	N	Y	Y	Guam	Unknown	Guam	Y	Servant
36		90	94	Rios, Felipe R	Head	M	Cha	48.0	M		N	N	Guam	Guam	Guam	N	Laborer
37		90	94	Rios, Antonia S	Wife	F	Cha	33.0	M		Y	Y	Guam	Guam	Guam	N	None
38		90	94	Rios, Ana S	Daughter	F	Cha	16.0	S	N	Y	Y	Guam	Guam	Guam	Y	Laundress
39		90	94	Rios, Jesus S	Son	M	Cha	13.0	S	Y	Y	Y	Guam	Guam	Guam	Y	None
40		90	94	Rios, Jose S	Son	M	Cha	10.0	S	Y	Y	Y	Guam	Guam	Guam	Y	None
41		90	94	Rios, Lagrimas S	Daughter	F	Cha	8.0	S	Y			Guam	Guam	Guam		None
42		90	94	Rios, Maria S	Daughter	F	Cha	5.0	S	N			Guam	Guam	Guam		None
43		90	94	Rios, Rita S	Daughter	F	Cha	3.0	S				Guam	Guam	Guam		None
44		90	94	Rios, Rosa S	Daughter	F	Cha	1.0	S				Guam	Guam	Guam		None
45		91	95	Kamminga, Felix R	Head	M	W	38.0	M		Y	Y	Guam	Holland	Guam	Y	Carpenter
46		91	95	Kamminga, Maria H	Wife	F	Cha	42.0	M		Y	Y	Guam	Guam	Guam	N	None
47		91	95	Kamminga, Lolkie H	Daughter	F	Cha	10.0	S	Y	Y	Y	Guam	Guam	Guam	Y	None
48		91	95	Kamminga, Simon	Head	M	W	39.0	M		Y	Y	Guam	Holland	Guam	Y	Seaman USN
49		91	95	Kamminga, Felicita SN	Wife	F	Cha	38.0	M		Y	Y	Guam	Guam	Guam	Y	None
50		91	95	Kamminga, Juana SN	Daughter	F	Cha	5.0	S	N			Guam	Guam	Guam	N	None

(CHAMORRO ROOTS GENEALOGY PROJECT ™ TRANSCRIPTION)
(COMPILED/TRANSCRIBED BY BERNARD T. PUNZALAN / HTTP://WWW.CHAMORROROOTS.COM)

FOURTEENTH CENSUS OF THE UNITED STATES: 1920—POPULATION

ISLAND OF GUAM

186

DISTRICT 3

NAME OF PLACE Tepungan Barrio

[Proper name and, also, name of class, as city, town, village, barrio, etc]

ENUMERATED BY ME ON THE 7th DAY OF March, 1920

Vicente Tydingco ENUMERATOR

Street	Dwelling house No.	Family No.	NAME	RELATION	Sex	Color or race	Age	S/M/Wd/D	Attended school since Sept. 1, 1919	Able to read	Able to write	Birthplace of person	Birthplace of father	Birthplace of mother	Speak English	OCCUPATION
	91	95	Kamminga, George SN	Daughter	F	Cha	4.0	S				Guam	Guam	Guam		None
	91	95	Kamminga, Pilar SN	Daughter	F	Cha	2.0	S				Guam	Guam	Guam		None
	93	97	Salas, Cecilio M	Head	M	Cha	55.0	M		Y	Y	Guam	Guam	Guam	Y	Laborer
	93	97	Salas, Rosa F	Wife	F	Cha	27.0	M		Y	Y	Guam	Guam	Guam	Y	None
	93	97	Salas, Antonia F	Daughter	F	Cha	6.0	S	N			Guam	Guam	Guam		None
	93	97	Salas, Joaquin F	Son	M	Cha	5.0	S	N			Guam	Guam	Guam		None
	94	98	Salas, Ana M	Head	F	Cha	70.0	Wd		N	N	Guam	Guam	Guam	N	None
	94	98	Salas, Vicente M	Son	M	Cha	26.0	S		Y	Y	Guam	Guam	Guam	Y	Corswain? USN
Agana Piti Road	95	99	Perez, Rita S	Head	F	Cha	34.0	M		N	N	Guam	Guam	Guam	N	Laundress
	95	99	Perez, Beatris S	Daughter	F	Cha	15.0	S	N	Y	Y	Guam	Guam	Guam	Y	None
	95	99	Perez, Jose S	Son	M	Cha	13.0	S	Y	Y	Y	Guam	Guam	Guam	Y	Farm laborer home farm
	95	99	Perez, Dinna S	Daughter	F	Cha	12.0	S	Y	Y	Y	Guam	Guam	Guam	Y	None
	95	99	Perez, Ana S	Daughter	F	Cha	10.0	S	Y	Y	Y	Guam	Guam	Guam	Y	None
	95	99	Perez, Juan S	Son	M	Cha	5.0	S				Guam	Guam	Guam		None
	95	99	Perez, Vicente S	Son	M	Cha	3.0	S				Guam	Guam	Guam		None
	95	99	Perez, Maria S	Daughter	F	Cha	0.2	S				Guam	Guam	Guam		None
	96	100	Certeza, Grabiel A	Head	M	Fil	25.0	M		Y	Y	Philippine Islands	Philippine Islands	Philippine Islands	Y	Machinist
	96	100	Certeza, Maria Q	Wife	F	Chn	20.0	M	N	Y	Y	Guam	China	Guam	Y	None
	97	101	Quenga, Vicenta Q	Head	F	Cha	51.0	Wd		N	N	Guam	Guam	Guam	N	Laundress
	97	101	Quenga, Marcela Q	Daughter	F	Chn	17.0	S	N			Guam	China	China	Y	Weaving of mats
	97	101	Quenga, Manuel Q	Son	M	Chn	11.0	S	Y	Y	Y	Guam	China	China	Y	None
	97	101	Terlaje, Maria M	Mother	F	Cha	76.0	Wd		N	N	Guam	Guam	Guam	N	None
	98	102	Salas, Jose M	Head	M	Cha	37.0	M		Y	Y	Guam	Guam	Guam	Y	Laborer
	98	102	Salas, Dolores I	Wife	F	Cha	38.0	M		N	N	Guam	Unknown	Guam	N	None
	98	102	Salas, Soledad I	Daughter	F	Cha	9.0	S	Y	Y	Y	Guam	Guam	Guam	N	None

(CHAMORRO ROOTS GENEALOGY PROJECT ™ TRANSCRIPTION)
(COMPILED/TRANSCRIBED BY BERNARD T. PUNZALAN / HTTP://WWW.CHAMORROROOTS.COM)
FOURTEENTH CENSUS OF THE UNITED STATES: 1920-POPULATION
ISLAND OF GUAM

ENUMERATED BY ME ON THE 8th DAY OF March, 1920

Vicente Tydingco ENUMERATOR

DISTRICT 3
NAME OF PLACE Tepungan Barrio
[Proper name and, also, name of class, as city, town, village, barrio, etc]

	Place of abode		NAME	RELATION	Sex	Color or race	Age at last birthday	Single, married, widowed or divorced	Attended school since Sept. 1, 1919	Whether able to read	Whether able to write	Place of birth of this person	Place of birth of father	Place of birth of mother	Whether able to speak English	OCCUPATION
1	2	3	4	5	6	7	8	9	10	11	12	13	14	15	16	17
26	98	102	Salas, Ana I	Daughter	F	Cha	7.0	S	Y			Guam	Guam	Guam		None
27	98	102	Salas, Maria I	Daughter	F	Cha	4.0	S				Guam	Guam	Guam		None
28	98	102	Salas, Jose I	Son	M	Cha	3.0	S				Guam	Guam	Guam		None
29	99	103	Salas, Antonio C	Head	M	Cha	42.0	M		Y	Y	Guam	Guam	Guam	Y	Corswain USN
30	99	103	Salas, Martina C	Wife	F	Cha	41.0	M		N	N	Guam	Unknown	Guam	N	None
31	99	103	Salas, Jesus S	Son	M	Cha	18.0	S	N	Y	Y	Guam	Guam	Guam	Y	Farm laborer home farm
32	99	103	Salas, Maria C	Daughter	F	Cha	18.0	S	N	Y	Y	Guam	Guam	Guam	Y	Laundress
33	99	103	Salas, Ana C	Daughter	F	Cha	16.0	S	N	Y	Y	Guam	Guam	Guam	Y	Laundress
34	99	103	Salas, Josefa C	Daughter	F	Cha	14.0	S	Y	Y	Y	Guam	Guam	Guam	Y	None
35	99	103	Salas, Jose C	Son	M	Cha	11.0	S	Y	Y	Y	Guam	Guam	Guam		None
36	99	103	Salas, Ignacio C	Son	M	Cha	9.0	S	Y			Guam	Guam	Guam		None
37	99	103	Salas, Juan C	Son	M	Cha	7.0	S	N			Guam	Guam	Guam		None
38	99	103	Salas, Marcela C	Daughter	F	Cha	4.0	S				Guam	Guam	Guam		None
39	99	103	Salas, Magdalena C	Daughter	F	Cha	0.5	S				Guam	Guam	Guam		None
40	100	104	Cruz, Juan M	Head	M	Cha	39.0	M		Y	Y	Guam	Unknown	Guam	N	Laborer
41	100	104	Cruz, Carmen C	Wife	F	Cha	39.0	M		N	N	Guam	Guam	Guam	N	None
42	100	104	Cruz, Antonia C	Daughter	F	Cha	12.0	S	Y	Y	Y	Guam	Guam	Guam	Y	None
43	100	104	Cruz, Manuela C	Daughter	F	Cha	10.0	S	Y	Y	Y	Guam	Guam	Guam	Y	None
44	100	104	Cruz, Ana C	Daughter	F	Cha	8.0	S	Y			Guam	Guam	Guam		None
45	100	104	Cruz, Ines C	Daughter	F	Cha	6.0	S	N			Guam	Guam	Guam		None
46	100	104	Cruz, Pedro C	Son	M	Cha	4.0	S				Guam	Guam	Guam		None
47	100	104	Cruz, Paz C	Daughter	F	Cha	2.0	S				Guam	Guam	Guam		None
48	101	105	Lizama, Vicente L	Head	M	Cha	37.0	M		Y	Y	Guam	Guam	Guam	Y	Machinist USN
49	101	105	Lizama, Vicenta Q	Wife	F	Cha	35.0	M		Y	N	Guam	Unknown	Guam	N	None
50	101	105	Lizama, Maria Q	Daughter	F	Cha	16.0	S	Y	Y	Y	Guam	Guam	Guam	Y	None

Street, avenue, road, etc: Agana Piti Road

(CHAMORRO ROOTS GENEALOGY PROJECT ™ TRANSCRIPTION)

(COMPILED/TRANSCRIBED BY BERNARD T. PUNZALAN / HTTP://WWW.CHAMORROROOTS.COM)

FOURTEENTH CENSUS OF THE UNITED STATES: 1920-POPULATION

ISLAND OF GUAM

DISTRICT 3

NAME OF PLACE **Tepungan Barrio**

[Proper name and, also, name of class, as city, town, village, barrio, etc]

ENUMERATED BY ME ON THE 9th DAY OF March, 1920

Vicente Tydingco ENUMERATOR

	PLACE OF ABODE			NAME	RELATION	\multicolumn{2}{c}{} PERSONAL DESCRIPTION			EDUCATION			NATIVITY				OCCUPATION
Street, avenue, road, etc.	Number of dwelling house in order of visitation	Number of family in order of visitation		of each person whose place of abode on January 1, 1920, was in the family.	Relationship of this Person to the head of the family.	Sex	Color or race	Age at last birthday	Single, married, widowed or divorced	Attended school any time since Sept. 1, 1919	Whether able to read.	Whether able to write.	Place of birth of this person.	Place of birth of father of this person.	Place of birth of mother of this person.	Whether able to speak English.	Trade, profession, or particular kind of work done, as salesman, laborer, clerk, cook, merchant, washerwoman, etc.
1	2	3	4	5	6	7	8	9	10	11	12	13	14	15	16	17
	101	105		Lizama, Jose Q	Son	M	Cha	13.0	S	Y	Y	Y	Guam	Guam	Guam	Y	None
	101	105		Lizama, Manuel Q	Son	M	Cha	11.0	S	Y	Y	Y	Guam	Guam	Guam	Y	None
	101	105		Lizama, Jesus Q	Son	M	Cha	9.0	S	Y			Guam	Guam	Guam		None
	101	105		Lizama, Joaquin Q	Son	M	Cha	6.0	S	N			Guam	Guam	Guam		None
	101	105		Lizama, Rosa Q	Daughter	F	Cha	2.0	S				Guam	Guam	Guam	N	None
	101	105		Quitugua, Maria	Mother-in-law	F	Cha	65.0	S		N	N	Guam	Unknown	Guam	N	None
	101	105		Quitugua, Dolores Q	Niece	F	Cha	12.0	S	Y	Y	Y	Guam	Unknown	Guam	Y	Fireman USN
	102	106		Aguigui, Juan	Head	M	Cha	37.0	M		Y	Y	Guam	Unknown	Guam	N	None
	102	106		Aguigui, Maria P	Wife	F	Cha	28.0	M		N	N	Guam	Guam	Guam	N	None
	102	106		Aguigui, Luis P	Son	M	Cha	5.0	S	N			Guam	Guam	Guam	Y	Seaman USN
	103	107		Quitugua, Antonio M	Head	M	Cha	22.0	M		Y	Y	Guam	Guam	Guam	Y	None
	103	107		Quitugua, Rosa S	Wife	F	Cha	26.0	M		Y	Y	Guam	Guam	Guam	N	None
	103	107		Quitugua, Ines S	Daughter	F	Cha	2.0	S				Guam	Guam	Guam	N	None
	104	108		Quitugua, Ana M	Head	F	Cha	65.0	Wd		N	N	Guam	Guam	Guam	N	Servant
	104	108		Ronqauillo, Micaila M	Sister-in-law	F	Cha	56.0	Wd		N	N	Guam	Unknown	Guam	Y	Fireman USN
	104	108		Cruz, Filomena C	Niece	F	Cha	11.0	S	N	Y	Y	Guam	Guam	Guam	N	None
	105	109		Cepeda, Manuel	Head	M	Cha	37.0	M		Y	Y	Guam	Guam	Guam	Y	None
	105	109		Cepeda, Rita S	Wife	F	Cha	35.0	M	Y	Y	Y	Guam	Guam	Guam		None
	105	109		Cepeda, Jose S	Son	M	Cha	11.0	S	Y			Guam	Guam	Guam		None
	105	109		Cepeda, Juan S	Son	M	Cha	9.0	S				Guam	Guam	Guam		None
	105	109		Cepeda, Francisco S	Son	M	Cha	3.0	S				Guam	Guam	Guam		None
	105	109		Cepeda, Margarita S	Daughter	F	Cha	1.0	S				Guam	Guam	Guam		None
	106	110		Edwards, Charles W	Head	M	W	36.0	M		Y	Y	Michigan	Michigan	Michigan	Y	Stock pair?
	106	110		Edwards, Frances D	Wife	F	W	27.0	M		Y	Y	Massachusetts	Massachusetts	Massachusetts	Y	None
	106	110		Edwards, Edwin E	Son	M	W	1.0	S				Guam	Michigan	Massachusetts		None

Agana Piti Road

(CHAMORRO ROOTS GENEALOGY PROJECT ™ TRANSCRIPTION)
(COMPILED/TRANSCRIBED BY BERNARD T. PUNZALAN / HTTP://WWW.CHAMORROROOTS.COM)

FOURTEENTH CENSUS OF THE UNITED STATES: 1920-POPULATION

ISLAND OF GUAM

DISTRICT 3
NAME OF PLACE Tepungan Barrio

[Proper name and, also, name of class, as city, town, village, barrio, etc]

ENUMERATED BY ME ON THE 9th DAY OF March, 1920

Vicente Tydingco ENUMERATOR

	PLACE OF ABODE			NAME	RELATION	PERSONAL DESCRIPTION				EDUCATION			NATIVITY				OCCUPATION
Street, avenue, road, etc.	No. of dwelling house	No. of family		Name	Relationship of this person to the head of the family.	Sex	Color or race	Age at last birthday	Single, married, widowed or divorced	Attended school any time since Sept. 1, 1919	Whether able to read.	Whether able to write.	Place of birth of this person.	Place of birth of father of this person.	Place of birth of mother of this person.	Whether able to speak English.	Trade, profession, or particular kind of work done, as salesman, laborer, clerk, cook, merchant, washerwoman, etc.
1	2	3		4	5	6	7	8	9	10	11	12	13	14	15	16	17
	106	110		Edwards, Richard H.	Son	M	W	0.3	S				Guam	Michigan	Massachusetts		None
	106	110		Mendiola, Maria C	Servant	F	Cha	45.0	S				Guam	Guam	Guam	N	Servant
	107	111		Concepcion, Joaquin P	Head	M	Cha	33.0	M		Y	Y	Guam	Guam	Guam	Y	Fireman USN
Agana Piti Road	107	111		Concepcion, Maria Q	Wife	F	Cha	26.0	M		Y	Y	Guam	Unknown	Guam	Y	None
	107	111		Concepcion, Jesus Q	Son	M	Cha	7.0	S	Y			Guam	Guam	Guam		None
	107	111		Concepcion, Jose Q	Son	M	Cha	5.0	S	N			Guam	Guam	Guam		None
	107	111		Concepcion, Ana Q	Daughter	F	Cha	3.0	S				Guam	Guam	Guam		None
	107	111		Concepcion, Vicente P	Brother	M	Cha	40.0	S		Y	Y	Guam	Guam	Guam	N	Farm laborer home farm
	107	111		Quitugua, Ramon Q	Brother-in-law	M	Cha	19.0	S	N	Y	Y	Guam	Unknown	Guam	Y	Farm laborer
	108	112		Santos, Manuel S	Head	M	Cha	47.0	M		Y	Y	Guam	Unknown	Guam	N	Farmer
	108	112		Santos, Magdalena Q	Wife	F	Cha	40.0	M		N	N	Guam	China	Guam	N	None
	108	112		Tyguiengco, Lorenzo B	Servant	M	Cha	23.0	S		Y	Y	Guam	Guam	Guam	Y	Servant
	108	112		Quichocho, Ignacio	Boarder	M	Cha	8.0	S	Y			Guam	Unknown	Guam		None
	108	112		Quichocho, Consolacion	Boarder	F	Cha	5.0	S	N			Guam	Unknown	Guam		None
	109	113		Babauta, Julian D	Head	M	Cha	27.0	S		Y	Y	Guam	Guam	Guam	Y	Laborer

Here ends the enumeration of Tepungan Barrio

(CHAMORRO ROOTS GENEALOGY PROJECT ™ TRANSCRIPTION)
(COMPILED/TRANSCRIBED BY BERNARD T. PUNZALAN / HTTP://WWW.CHAMORROROOTS.COM)

FOURTEENTH CENSUS OF THE UNITED STATES: 1920-POPULATION
ISLAND OF GUAM

ENUMERATED BY ME ON THE 10th DAY OF March, 1920

Vicente Tydingco ENUMERATOR

DISTRICT **3**
NAME OF PLACE **Piti Town**

[Proper name and, also, name of class, as city, town, village, barrio, etc]

Street, avenue, road, etc.	Number of dwelling house is in order of visitation	Number of family in order of visitation	NAME	RELATION	Sex	Color or race	Age at last birthday	Single, married, widowed or divorced	Attended any school since Sept. 1, 1919	Whether able to read.	Whether able to write.	Place of birth of this person.	Place of birth of father of this person.	Place of birth of mother of this person.	Whether able to speak English.	OCCUPATION
1	2	3	4	5	6	7	8	9	10	11	12	13	14	15	16	17
	1	1	Okazaki, Joaquin Q	Head	M	Jp	35.0	M		Y	Y	Japan	Japan	Japan	N	Machinist
	1	1	Okazaki, Carmen B	Wife	F	Cha	25.0	M		N	N	Guam	Guam	Guam	N	Laundress
	1	1	Okazaki, Joaquina B	Daughter	F	Jp	4.0	S				Guam	Japan	Guam		None
	1	1	Okazaki, Jesus B	Son	M	Jp	2.0	S				Guam	Japan	Guam		None
	1	1	Okazaki, Rita B	Daughter	F	Jp	0.3	S				Guam	Japan	Guam		None
	2	2	Naputi, Venancio	Head	M	Cha	22.0	M		Y	Y	Guam	Guam	Guam	Y	Seaman USN
	2	2	Naputi, Josefa R	Wife	F	Cha	24.0	M		Y	Y	Guam	Guam	Guam	N	None
	2	2	Meno, Ana N	Sister	F	Cha	12.0	S	Y	Y	Y	Guam	Guam	Guam	Y	None
	3	3	Yoshida, Jose	Head	M	Jp	40.0	M		Y	Y	Japan	Japan	Japan	N	Carpenter
	3	3	Yoshida, Dolores M	Wife	F	Cha	30.0	M		N	N	Guam	Unknown	Guam	N	None
	3	3	Yoshida, Juan A	Son	M	Jp	11.0	S	Y	Y	Y	Guam	Japan	Guam	Y	None
	3	3	Yoshida, Guadalupe A	Daughter	F	Jp	9.0	S	Y			Guam	Japan	Guam		None
	3	3	Yoshida, Concepcion A	Daughter	F	Jp	7.0	S	N			Guam	Japan	Guam		None
	3	3	Yoshida, Enrique A	Son	M	Jp	3.0	S				Guam	Japan	Guam		None
	4	4	Petros, Lorenzo M	Head	M	Cha	32.0	M		Y	Y	Guam	Guam	Guam		Farmer
	4	4	Petros, Ana L	Wife	F	Cha	26.0	M		Y	Y	Guam	Guam	Guam	N	None
	4	4	Petros, Jose L	Son	M	Cha	6.0	S	N			Guam	Guam	Guam		None
	4	4	Petros, Vicente L	Son	M	Cha	5.0	S	N			Guam	Guam	Guam		None
	4	4	Petros, Joaquin L	Son	M	Cha	4.0	S				Guam	Guam	Guam		None
	4	4	Petros, Pedro L	Son	M	Cha	2.0	S				Guam	Guam	Guam		None
	4	4	Petros, Magdalena L	Daughter	F	Cha	0.7	S				Guam	Guam	Guam		None
	5	5	Martinez, Susana B	Head	F	Cha	55.0	Wd		N	N	Guam	Guam	Guam	N	Farm laborer home farm
	5	5	Martinez, Jose B	Son	M	Cha	16.0	S	N	Y	Y	Guam	Guam	Guam	Y	Farm laborer home farm
	6	6	S. Nicolas, Manuel	Head	M	Cha	28.0	M		Y	Y	Guam	Unknown	Guam	Y	Farmer
	6	6	S. Nicolas, Consolacion C	Wife	F	Cha	31.0	M		Y	Y	Guam	Guam	Guam	N	None

Agana Piti Road

378

188b

(CHAMORRO ROOTS GENEALOGY PROJECT ™ TRANSCRIPTION)
(COMPILED/TRANSCRIBED BY BERNARD T. PUNZALAN / HTTP://WWW.CHAMORROROOTS.COM)
FOURTEENTH CENSUS OF THE UNITED STATES: 1920—POPULATION
ISLAND OF GUAM

DISTRICT **3**
NAME OF PLACE **Piti Town**
[Proper name and, also, name of class, as city, town, village, barrio, etc]

ENUMERATED BY ME ON THE 10th DAY OF March, 1920

Vicente Tydingco ENUMERATOR

	PLACE OF ABODE			NAME	RELATION	PERSONAL DESCRIPTION					EDUCATION			NATIVITY			Whether able to speak English	OCCUPATION
Street, avenue, road, etc.	Number of dwelling house in order of visitation	Number of family in order of visitation				Sex	Color or race	Age at last birthday	Single, married, widowed or divorced	Attended school any time since Sept. 1, 1919	Whether able to read.	Whether able to write.	Place of birth of this person.	Place of birth of father of this person.	Place of birth of mother of this person.		
1	2	3		4	5	6	7	8	9	10	11	12	13	14	15	16	17
26	6	6		S. Nicolas, Josefina C	Daughter	F	Cha	5.0	S	N			Guam	Guam	Guam		None
27	6	6		S. Nicolas, Jose C	Son	M	Cha	3.0	S				Guam	Guam	Guam		None
28	6	6		S. Nicolas, Jesus C	Son	M	Cha	0.7	S				Guam	Guam	Guam		None
29	7	7		Santos, Mariano C	Head	M	Cha	32.0	M		Y	Y	Guam	Unknown	Guam	N	Farmer
30	7	7		Santos, Ana SN	Wife	F	Cha	34.0	M		Y	Y	Guam	Guam	Guam	N	None
31	7	7		Santos, Jose SN	Son	M	Cha	12.0	S	Y	Y	Y	Guam	Guam	Guam	Y	None
32	7	7		Santos, Maria SN	Daughter	F	Cha	10.0	S	Y	Y	Y	Guam	Guam	Guam	N	None
33	7	7		Santos, Lagrimas SN	Daughter	F	Cha	4.0	S				Guam	Guam	Guam		None
34	8	8		Castro, Juan S	Head	M	Cha	23.0	M		Y	Y	Guam	Guam	Guam	Y	Seaman USN
35	8	8		Castro, Carmen S	Wife	F	Cha	24.0	M		Y	Y	Guam	Guam	Guam	N	Weaver mats
36	9	9		Salas, Vicente S	Head	M	Cha	21.0	M	N	Y	Y	Guam	Guam	Guam	Y	Seaman USN
37	9	9		Salas, Carmen A	Wife	F	Cha	19.0	M	N	Y	Y	Guam	Unknown	Guam	N	None
38	9	9		Salas, Ana A	Daughter	F	Cha	0.7	S				Guam	Guam	Guam		None
39	10	10		Uchida, Buenaventura S	Head	M	Jp	35.0	M		Y	Y	Japan	Japan	Japan	Y	Retail merchant
40	10	10		Uchida, Fumi	Wife	F	Jp	26.0	M		Y	Y	Japan	Japan	Japan	N	None
41	10	10		Uchida, Takeo	Son	M	Jp	1.0	S				Guam	Japan	Japan		None
42	10	10		Babauta, Ana D	Servant	F	Cha	18.0	S	N	Y	Y	Guam	Guam	Guam	Y	Servant
43	11	11		Cruz, Mariano G	Head	M	Cha	47.0	M		Y	N	Guam	Guam	Guam	N	Farmer
44	11	11		Cruz, Vicenta M	Wife	F	Cha	45.0	M		N	N	Guam	Guam	Guam	N	Laundress
45	11	11		Cruz, Regina A	Daughter	F	Cha	25.0	S		N	N	Guam	Guam	Guam	N	Laundress
46	11	11		Cruz, Grabiel S	Brother	M	Cha	28.0	S		Y	Y	Guam	Guam	Guam	Y	Laborer
47	12	12		Duenas, Mariano	Head	M	Cha	38.0	M		N	N	Guam	Unknown	Guam	N	Farmer
48	12	12		Duenas, Maria SN	Wife	F	Cha	50.0	M		N	N	Guam	Guam	Guam	N	Laundress
49	13	13		Santos, Vicente A	Head	M	Cha	53.0	M		Y	Y	Guam	Guam	Guam	N	Farmer
50	13	13		Santos, Dolores SN	Wife	F	Cha	27.0	M		Y	Y	Guam	Unknown	Guam	N	None

Agana Piti Road

379

(CHAMORRO ROOTS GENEALOGY PROJECT ™ TRANSCRIPTION)
(COMPILED/TRANSCRIBED BY BERNARD T. PUNZALAN / HTTP://WWW.CHAMORROROOTS.COM)

FOURTEENTH CENSUS OF THE UNITED STATES: 1920–POPULATION
ISLAND OF GUAM

DISTRICT 3
NAME OF PLACE Piti Town
[Proper name and, also, name of class, as city, town, village, barrio, etc]

ENUMERATED BY ME ON THE 11th DAY OF March, 1920
Vicente Tydingco ENUMERATOR

	Dwelling	Family	NAME	RELATION	Sex	Color or race	Age at last birthday	Single, married, widowed or divorced	Attended school since Sept. 1, 1919	Able to read	Able to write	Place of birth of person	Place of birth of father	Place of birth of mother	Able to speak English	OCCUPATION
1	13	13	Santos, Antonio	Son	M	Cha	26.0	S		Y	Y	Guam	Guam	Guam	Y	Farm laborer
2	13	13	Santos, Jose	Son	M	Cha	23.0	S		Y	Y	Guam	Guam	Guam	Y	Seaman USN
3	13	13	Santos, Juan	Son	M	Cha	20.0	S	N	Y	Y	Guam	Guam	Guam	Y	Laborer
4	13	13	Santos, Santiago	Son	M	Cha	18.0	S	N	Y	Y	Guam	Guam	Guam	Y	Laborer
5	13	13	Santos, Vicente	Son	M	Cha	15.0	S	N	Y	Y	Guam	Guam	Guam	Y	Farm laborer home farm
6	13	13	Santos, Manuel	Son	M	Cha	11.0	S	Y	Y	Y	Guam	Guam	Guam	Y	None
7	13	13	Santos, Maria SN	Daughter	F	Cha	4.0	S				Guam	Guam	Guam	Y	None
8	13	13	Santos, Rosalia SN	Daughter	F	Cha	2.0	S				Guam	Guam	Guam		None
9	14	14	Cruz, Lorenzo B	Head	M	Fil	60.0	Wd		Y	Y	Guam	Philippine Islands	Guam	N	Farmer
10	14	14	Cruz, Maria S	Daughter	F	Cha	25.0	S		Y	Y	Guam	Guam	Guam	Y	Laundress
11	14	14	Cruz, Jose S	Son	M	Cha	21.0	S	N	Y	Y	Guam	Guam	Guam	Y	Seaman USN
12	14	14	Cruz, Romana S	Daughter	F	Cha	18.0	S	N	Y	Y	Guam	Guam	Guam	Y	Laundress
13	14	14	Cruz, Josefina S	Daughter	F	Cha	14.0	S	N	Y	Y	Guam	Guam	Guam	N	None
14	15	15	Cruz, Vicente C	Head	M	Cha	32.0	Wd		Y	Y	Guam	Guam	Guam	N	Farmer
15	15	15	Cruz, Maria A	Daughter	F	Cha	11.0	S	Y	Y	Y	Guam	Guam	Guam	N	None
16	15	15	Cruz, Trinidad A	Daughter	F	Cha	9.0	S	Y	Y	Y	Guam	Guam	Guam		None
17	16	16	Santos, Jose S	Head	M	Cha	44.0	M		N	N	Guam	Unknown	Guam	N	Farmer
18	16	16	Santos, Barbara S	Wife	F	Cha	38.0	M		N	N	Guam	Unknown	Guam	N	Laundress
19	16	16	Santos, Joaquin S	Grandson	M	Cha	7.0	S	N			Guam	Unknown	Guam	N	None
20	16	16	Babauta, Andrea B	Sister-in-law	F	Cha	30.0	M		N	N	Guam	Unknown	Guam	N	Servant
21	17	17	Ignacio, Joaquin C	Head	M	Cha	51.0	M		N	N	Guam	Guam	Guam	N	Farmer
22	17	17	Ignacio, Juana C	Wife	F	Cha	47.0	M		N	N	Guam	Guam	Guam	N	None
23	17	17	Ignacio, Jose C	Son	M	Cha	20.0	S	N	Y	Y	Guam	Guam	Guam	Y	Seaman USN
24	17	17	Ignacio, Concepcion M	Daughter	F	Cha	18.0	S	N	Y	Y	Guam	Guam	Guam	N	None
25	17	17	Ignacio, Juan C	Son	M	Cha	16.0	S	N	Y	Y	Guam	Guam	Guam	Y	Farm laborer home farm

Street: Agana Piti Road

(CHAMORRO ROOTS GENEALOGY PROJECT ™ TRANSCRIPTION)
(COMPILED/TRANSCRIBED BY BERNARD T. PUNZALAN / HTTP://WWW.CHAMORROROOTS.COM)

FOURTEENTH CENSUS OF THE UNITED STATES: 1920-POPULATION

ISLAND OF GUAM

189b

DISTRICT 3
NAME OF PLACE Piti Town

[Proper name and, also, name of class, as city, town, village, barrio, etc]

ENUMERATED BY ME ON THE 12th DAY OF March, 1920

Vicente Tydingco ENUMERATOR

	Dwelling	Family	NAME	RELATION	Sex	Color or race	Age	Single/married	School since 1919	Read	Write	Birthplace	Father	Mother	English	OCCUPATION
	1	2	3	4	5	6	7	8	9	10	11	12	13	14	15	16	17
26		17	17	Ignacio, Manuel C	Son	M	Cha	14.0	S	Y	Y	Y	Guam	Guam	Guam	Y	Farm laborer home farm
27		17	17	Ignacio, Isabel C	Daughter	F	Cha	4.0	S				Guam	Guam	Guam		None
28		18	18	Ignacio, Antonio C	Head	M	Cha	27.0	M		Y	Y	Guam	Guam	Guam	N	Farmer
29		18	18	Ignacio, Josefina C	Wife	F	Cha	25.0	M		Y	Y	Guam	Unknown	Guam	N	None
30		18	18	Ignacio, Embertriz C	Daughter	F	Cha	1.0	S				Guam	Guam	Guam		None
31		19	19	Cruz, Josefa S	Head	F	Cha	42.0	Wd		Y	Y	Guam	Guam	Guam	N	None
32		19	19	Cruz, Rosa S	Daughter	F	Cha	25.0	S		Y	Y	Guam	Guam	Guam	Y	Servant
33		19	19	Cruz, Maria S	Daughter	F	Cha	24.0	S		Y	Y	Guam	Guam	Guam	Y	Servant
34		19	19	Cruz, Fecundo C	Son	M	Cha	22.0	S		Y	Y	Guam	Guam	Guam	Y	Seaman USN
35	Agana Piti Road	19	19	Cruz, Juan S	Son	M	Cha	19.0	S	N	Y	Y	Guam	Guam	Guam	Y	Farm laborer
36		19	19	Cruz, Ana S	Daughter	F	Cha	12.0	S	Y	Y	Y	Guam	Guam	Guam	Y	None
37		19	19	Cruz, Antonio S	Son	M	Cha	10.0	S	Y	Y	Y	Guam	Guam	Guam	Y	None
38		19	19	Cruz, Jose S	Son	M	Cha	9.0	S	Y	Y	Y	Guam	Guam	Guam	Y	None
39		19	19	Cruz, Vicente S	Son	M	Cha	8.0	S	Y	Y	Y	Guam	Guam	Guam	Y	None
40		19	19	Cruz, Francisco S	Son	M	Cha	6.0	S	N			Guam	Guam	Guam	Y	None
41		19	19	Cruz, Caridad S	Daughter	F	Cha	0.3	S				Guam	Guam	Guam		None
42		20	20	Aflleje, Juan T	Head	M	Cha	25.0	M		Y	Y	Guam	Guam	Guam	Y	Seaman USN
43		20	20	Aflleje, Cristina N	Wife	F	Cha	22.0	M		Y	Y	Guam	Guam	Guam	Y	None
44		20	20	Aflleje, Maria N	Daughter	F	Cha	0.4	S				Guam	Guam	Guam		None
45		21	21	Fejeran, Justo S	Head	M	Cha	37.0	M		Y	Y	Guam	Guam	Guam	Y	Labor foreman
46		21	21	Fejeran, Ana C	Wife	F	Cha	35.0	M		N	N	Guam	Guam	Guam	N	None
47		21	21	Fejeran, Joaquin C	Son	M	Cha	14.0	S	Y	Y	Y	Guam	Guam	Guam	Y	Farm laborer home farm
48		21	21	Fejeran, Carmela C	Daughter	F	Cha	12.0	S	Y	Y	Y	Guam	Guam	Guam	Y	None
49		21	21	Fejeran, Jesus C	Son	M	Cha	10.0	S	Y	Y	Y	Guam	Guam	Guam	Y	None
50		21	21	Fejeran, Regina C	Daughter	F	Cha	8.0	S	Y	Y	Y	Guam	Guam	Guam	Y	None

(CHAMORRO ROOTS GENEALOGY PROJECT ™ TRANSCRIPTION)
(COMPILED/TRANSCRIBED BY BERNARD T. PUNZALAN / HTTP://WWW.CHAMORROROOTS.COM)

FOURTEENTH CENSUS OF THE UNITED STATES: 1920-POPULATION

ISLAND OF GUAM

ENUMERATED BY ME ON THE 12th DAY OF March, 1920

Vicente Tydingco ENUMERATOR

DISTRICT 3
NAME OF PLACE Piti Town

Street	Dwelling No.	Family No.	NAME	RELATION	Sex	Color or race	Age	Single, married, widowed or divorced	Attended school since Sept. 1, 1919	Able to read	Able to write	Place of birth of this person	Place of birth of father	Place of birth of mother	Able to speak English	OCCUPATION
	1	2	3	4	5	6	7	8	9	10	11	12	13	14	15	16	17
	21	21	Fejeran, Jose C	Son	M	Cha	6.0	S	N			Guam	Guam	Guam		None
	21	21	Fejeran, Francisco C	Son	M	Cha	4.0	S				Guam	Guam	Guam		None
	21	21	Fejeran, Juan C	Son	M	Cha	0.3	S				Guam	Guam	Guam	N	None
	21	21	Rosa, Mariano M	Godfather	M	Cha	64.0	Wd		Y	Y	Guam	Guam	Guam	Y	Farmer
	22	22	Fejeran, Domingo SN	Head	M	Cha	42.0	M		Y	Y	Guam	Guam	Guam	Y	Farm laborer home farm
	22	22	Fejeran, Maria S	Wife	F	Cha	47.0	M	N	N	N	Guam	Guam	Guam	N	None
	22	22	Fejeran, Joaquin S	Son	M	Cha	16.0	S	N	Y	Y	Guam	Guam	Guam	Y	None
	22	22	Fejeran, Remedios S	Daughter	F	Cha	14.0	S	Y	Y	Y	Guam	Guam	Guam	Y	None
	22	22	Fejeran, Jesus S	Son	M	Cha	11.0	S	Y	Y	Y	Guam	Guam	Guam		None
	22	22	Fejeran, Juan S	Son	M	Cha	8.0	S	N			Guam	Guam	Guam		None
	22	22	Fejeran, Maria S jr.	Daughter	F	Cha	5.0	S	Y			Guam	Guam	Guam		None
	22	22	Fejeran, Dolores S	Daughter	F	Cha	5.0	S	N			Guam	Guam	Guam	Y	None
Agana Piti Road	23	23	Perez, Juan	Head	M	Cha	38.0	M	N	Y	Y	Guam	Guam	Guam	Y	Oiler USN
	23	23	Perez, Basilia C	Wife	F	Cha	28.0	M		Y	Y	Guam	Guam	Guam	N	None
	23	23	Perez, Joaquin S	Son	M	Cha	16.0	S	N	Y	Y	Guam	Guam	Guam	Y	Farm laborer home farm
	23	23	Perez, Vicente Q	Son	M	Cha	15.0	S	Y	Y	Y	Guam	Guam	Guam	Y	Farm laborer home farm
	23	23	Perez, Encarnacion	Daughter	F	Cha	3.0	S				Guam	Guam	Guam		None
	23	23	Cruz, Beatris C	Step daughter	F	Cha	7.0	S	Y			Guam	Guam	Guam		None
	23	23	Cruz, Joaquin C	Stepson	M	Cha	6.0	S	N			Guam	Guam	Guam		None
	23	23	Saluago, Cristina C	Sister-in-law	F	Cha	27.0	Wd				Guam	Guam	Guam	Y	Laundress
	24	24	Cruz, Manuel A	Head	M	Cha	36.0	M		Y	Y	Guam	Guam	Guam	Y	Seaman USN
	24	24	Cruz, Maria A	Wife	F	Cha	46.0	M		Y	Y	Guam	Unknown	Guam	Y	None
	24	24	Cruz, Ana A	Daughter	F	Cha	13.0	S	Y	Y	Y	Guam	Guam	Guam	Y	None
	24	24	Cruz, Jose S	Son	M	Cha	11.0	S	Y	Y	Y	Guam	Guam	Guam	Y	None
	24	24	Cruz, Dolores A	Daughter	F	Cha	9.0	S	Y	Y	Y	Guam	Guam	Guam	Y	None

(CHAMORRO ROOTS GENEALOGY PROJECT ™ TRANSCRIPTION)
(COMPILED/TRANSCRIBED BY BERNARD T. PUNZALAN / HTTP://WWW.CHAMORROROOTS.COM)

FOURTEENTH CENSUS OF THE UNITED STATES: 1920—POPULATION

ISLAND OF GUAM

DISTRICT 3
NAME OF PLACE Piti Town

[Proper name and, also, name of class, as city, town, village, barrio, etc]

ENUMERATED BY ME ON THE 13th DAY OF March, 1920

Vicente Tydingco ENUMERATOR

Street, avenue, road, etc.	Number of dwelling house	Number of family	NAME	RELATION	Sex	Color or race	Age at last birthday	Single, married, widowed or divorced	Attended school any time since Sept. 1, 1919	Whether able to read	Whether able to write	Place of birth of this person	Place of birth of father	Place of birth of mother	Whether able to speak English	OCCUPATION
1	2	3	4	5	6	7	8	9	10	11	12	13	14	15	16	17
	24	24	Cruz, Gregorio A	Son	M	Cha	7.0	S	Y			Guam	Guam	Guam		None
	24	24	Cruz, Marcela A	Daughter	F	Cha	4.0	S				Guam	Guam	Guam		None
	24	24	Aflague, Leola A	Step daughter	F	Cha	17.0	S	N	Y	Y	Guam	Unknown	Guam	Y	Laundress
	25	25	Cruz, Ramon M	Head	M	Cha	60.0	M		Y	Y	Guam	Guam	Guam	N	Farmer
	25	25	Cruz, Maria A	Wife	F	Cha	49.0	M		N	N	Guam	Guam	Guam	N	None
	25	25	Cruz, Soledad A	Daughter	F	Cha	15.0	S	Y	Y	Y	Guam	Guam	Guam	Y	None
	25	25	Cruz, Joaquin A	Son	M	Cha	14.0	S	Y	Y	Y	Guam	Guam	Guam	Y	Farm laborer home farm
	25	25	Cruz, Francisco A	Son	M	Cha	7.0	S				Guam	Guam	Guam		None
Agana Piti Road	26	26	Machignia, Rafael C	Head	M	Jp	39.0	M		Y	Y	Japan	Japan	Japan	N	Carpenter
	26	26	Machignia, Carmen M	Wife	F	Cha	35.0	M		Y	Y	Guam	Guam	Guam	N	None
	26	26	Machignia, Maria M	Daughter	F	Jp	6.0	S				Guam	Japan	Guam		None
	26	26	Machignia, Jesus M	Son	M	Jp	4.0	S				Guam	Japan	Guam		None
	26	26	Machignia, Josefina M	Daughter	F	Jp	3.0	S				Guam	Japan	Guam		None
	26	26	Machignia, Jose M	Son	M	Jp	2.0	S				Guam	Japan	Guam		None
	27	27	Inoye, Ana S	Head	F	Cha	33.0	M		Y	Y	Guam	Guam	Guam	Y	Laundress
	27	27	Inoye, Joaquin S	Son	M	Jp	8.0	S	Y			Guam	Japan	Guam		None
	27	27	Inoye, Maria S	Daughter	F	Jp	6.0	S	N			Guam	Japan	Guam		None
	27	27	Inoye, Benedicta S	Daughter	F	Jp	1.0	S				Guam	Japan	Guam		None
	28	28	Leon Guerrero, Bernada C	Head	F	Fil	67.0	Wd		Y	Y	Luzon	Luzon	Luzon	N	None
	28	28	Leon Guerrero, Carmen C	Daughter	F	Cha	30.0	S		Y	Y	Guam	Guam	Guam	N	Teacher
	29	29	Concepcion, Jose C	Head	M	Cha	22.0	M		Y	Y	Guam	Guam	Guam	Y	Seaman USN
	29	29	Concepcion, Rosa M	Wife	F	Cha	30.0	M		Y	Y	Guam	Guam	Guam	Y	None
	29	29	Delgado, Juan P	Servant	M	Cha	40.0	S		N	N	Guam	Guam	Guam	N	Servant
	29	29	Diaz, Antonia SN	Aunt	F	Cha	70.0	Wd		Y	Y	Guam	Guam	Guam	Y	None
	30	30	Aguon, Maria M	Head	F	Cha	47.0	Wd		N	N	Guam	Unknown	Guam	N	Laundress

(CHAMORRO ROOTS GENEALOGY PROJECT ™ TRANSCRIPTION)
(COMPILED/TRANSCRIBED BY BERNARD T. PUNZALAN / HTTP://WWW.CHAMORROROOTS.COM)
FOURTEENTH CENSUS OF THE UNITED STATES: 1920-POPULATION
ISLAND OF GUAM

ENUMERATED BY ME ON THE 13th DAY OF March, 1920

Vicente Tydingco ENUMERATOR

DISTRICT 3
NAME OF PLACE Piti Town

[Proper name and, also, name of class, as city, town, village, barrio, etc]

	Street, avenue, road, etc.	Number of dwelling house is order of visitation	Number of family in order of visitation	NAME	RELATION	Sex	Color or race	Age at last birthday	Single, married, widowed or divorced	Attended school any time since Sept. 1, 1919	Whether able to read.	Whether able to write.	Place of birth of this person.	Place of birth of father of this person.	Place of birth of mother of this person.	Whether able to speak English.	OCCUPATION
	1	2	3	4	5	6	7	8	9	10	11	12	13	14	15	16	17
1		30	30	Aguon, Francisco M	Son	M	Cha	29.0	S		Y	Y	Guam	Guam	Guam	Y	Farmer
2		30	30	Aguon, Vicente M	Son	M	Cha	10.0	S	Y	Y	Y	Guam	Guam	Guam	Y	None
3		30	30	Aguon, Trinidad M	Daughter	F	Cha	5.0	S	N			Guam	Guam	Guam		None
4		30	30	Cruz, Polonia T	Mother	F	Cha	68.0	Wd				Guam	Guam	Guam	N	None
5		31	31	Manibusan, Juan SN	Head	M	Cha	40.0	M		Y	Y	Guam	Guam	Guam	Y	Farmer
6		31	31	Manibusan, Ana F	Wife	F	Cha	47.0	M		Y	Y	Guam	Guam	Guam	N	None
7		31	31	Flores, Vicente F	Nephew	M	Cha	17.0	S	N	Y	Y	Guam	Unknown	Guam	Y	Farm laborer home farm
8		31	31	Flores, Ramona F	Niece	F	Cha	12.0	S	Y	Y	Y	Guam	Unknown	Guam	Y	None
9		31	31	Meno, Visitacion C	Servant	F	Cha	10.0	S	Y	Y	Y	Guam	Unknown	Guam	N	Servant
10		31	31	S. Nicolas, Marina S	Niece	F	Cha	22.0	S		Y	Y	Guam	Guam	Guam	Y	Cook
11		31	31	Meno, Maria G	Servant	F	Cha	11.0	S	Y	Y	Y	Guam	Unknown	Guam	Y	Servant
12		32	32	Suzuki, Ushimatiu	Head	M	Jp	55.0	Wd		Y	Y	Japan	Japan	Japan	N	Carpenter
13		33	33	Soleta, Mariano S	Head	M	Fil	33.0	M		Y	Y	Luzon	Luzon	Luzon	Y	Seaman USN
14		33	33	Soleta, Maria M	Wife	F	Fil	27.0	M	Y	Y	Y	Guam	Unknown	Guam	N	None
15		33	33	Soleta, Gregorio M	Son	M	Fil	8.0	S	Y	Y	Y	Guam	Luzon	Luzon		None
16		33	33	Soleta, Bernardo M	Son	M	Fil	4.0	S				Guam	Luzon	Luzon		None
17		33	33	Megofna, Maria C	Sister-in-law	F	Cha	22.0	S		Y	Y	Guam	Guam	Guam	Y	Laundress
18	Agana Piti Road	34	34	S. Nicolas, Juan P	Head	M	Cha	69.0	M		Y	Y	Guam	Guam	Guam	N	Farmer
19		34	34	S. Nicolas, Carlina F	Wife	F	Cha	67.0	M		Y	Y	Guam	Guam	Guam	N	None
20		34	34	S. Nicolas, Vicente F	Son	M	Cha	33.0	Wd		Y	Y	Guam	Guam	Guam	Y	Farmer
21		34	34	S. Nicolas, Guillermo F	Son	M	Cha	23.0	S		Y	Y	Guam	Guam	Guam	Y	Farm laborer
22		34	34	S. Nicolas, Jose F	Son	M	Cha	22.0	S		Y	Y	Guam	Guam	Guam	Y	Farm laborer
23		35	35	S. Nicolas, Antonio F	Head	M	Cha	43.0	M		Y	Y	Guam	Guam	Guam	Y	Retail merchant
24		35	35	S. Nicolas, Magdalena L	Wife	F	Cha	22.0	M		Y	Y	Guam	Guam	Guam	Y	None
25		35	35	S. Nicolas, Josefina W	Daughter	F	Cha	19.0	S	N	Y	Y	Guam	Guam	Guam	Y	None

(CHAMORRO ROOTS GENEALOGY PROJECT ™ TRANSCRIPTION)
(COMPILED/TRANSCRIBED BY BERNARD T. PUNZALAN / HTTP://WWW.CHAMORROROOTS.COM)

FOURTEENTH CENSUS OF THE UNITED STATES: 1920-POPULATION
ISLAND OF GUAM

DISTRICT 3
NAME OF PLACE Piti Town

ENUMERATED BY ME ON THE 15th DAY OF March, 1920

Vicente Tydingco ENUMERATOR

	Dwelling	Family	NAME	RELATION	Sex	Race	Age	S/M	School	Read	Write	Birthplace	Father birthplace	Mother birthplace	English	OCCUPATION
	1	2	3	4	5	6	7	8	9	10	11	12	13	14	15	16	17
26	35	35	Sypingco, Vicente S	Servant	M	Cha	18.0	S	N	Y	Y	Guam	Unknown	Guam	Y	Servant
27	36	36	Haller, Dolores C	Head	F	Cha	38.0	M		Y	Y	Guam	Guam	Guam	Y	None
28	36	36	Taisague, Ana G	Servant	F	Cha	23.0	S		Y	Y	Guam	Guam	Guam	Y	Servant
29	37	37	Yamanaka, Carmelo U	Head	M	Jp	31.0	M		Y	Y	Japan	Japan	Japan	N	Carpenter
30	37	37	Yamanaka, Paula B	Wife	F	Cha	26.0	M		Y	Y	Guam	Guam	Guam	N	None
31	37	37	Yamanaka, Maria B	Daughter	F	Jp	5.0	S				Guam	Japan	Guam		None
32	37	37	Yamanaka, Alfonsina B	Daughter	F	Jp	4.0	S				Guam	Japan	Guam		None
33	37	37	Yamanaka, Carmen B	Daughter	F	Jp	2.0	S				Guam	Japan	Guam		None
34	37	37	Yamanaka, Concepcion B	Daughter	F	Jp	0.8	S				Guam	Japan	Guam		None
35	38	38	Diaz, Jose F	Head	M	Cha	19.0	S	N	Y	Y	Guam	Guam	Guam	Y	Chauffeur
36	38	38	Diaz, Consolacion F	Sister	F	Cha	21.0	S	N	Y	Y	Guam	Guam	Guam	Y	None
37	38	38	Diaz, Joaquin F	Brother	M	Cha	18.0	S	N	Y	Y	Guam	Guam	Guam	Y	None
38	38	38	Diaz, Maria F	Sister	F	Cha	16.0	S		Y	Y	Guam	Guam	Guam	Y	None
39	38	38	Diaz, Ana F	Sister	F	Cha	14.0	S	Y	Y	Y	Guam	Guam	Guam	Y	None
40	38	38	Diaz, Antonia F	Sister	F	Cha	13.0	S	Y	Y	Y	Guam	Guam	Guam	Y	None
41	38	38	Diaz, Emilia F	Sister	F	Cha	10.0	S	Y	Y	Y	Guam	Guam	Guam	Y	None
42	38	38	Flores, Rita A	Sister	F	Cha	45.0	S		Y	Y	Guam	Guam	Guam	N	None
43	38	38	Acfalle, Joaquin A	Servant	M	Cha	18.0	S	N	Y	Y	Guam	Guam	Guam	Y	Servant
44	39	39	Taijeron, Vicente T	Head	M	Cha	36.0	M		Y	Y	Guam	Unknown	Guam	Y	Fireman USN
45	39	39	Taijeron, Dolores J	Wife	F	Cha	30.0	M		Y	Y	Guam	Guam	Guam	N	None
46	39	39	Taijeron, Barbara J	Daughter	F	Cha	11.0	S	Y	Y	Y	Guam	Guam	Guam	Y	None
47	39	39	Taijeron, Juan J	Son	M	Cha	10.0	S	Y	Y	Y	Guam	Guam	Guam	Y	None
48	39	39	Taijeron, Jose J	Son	M	Cha	8.0	S	Y	Y	Y	Guam	Guam	Guam	N	None
49	39	39	Taijeron, Maria J	Daughter	F	Cha	6.0	S	N			Guam	Guam	Guam		None
50	39	39	Taijeron, Rosario J	Daughter	F	Cha	4.0	S				Guam	Guam	Guam		None

Street: Agana Piti Road

(CHAMORRO ROOTS GENEALOGY PROJECT ™ TRANSCRIPTION)
(COMPILED/TRANSCRIBED BY BERNARD T. PUNZALAN / HTTP://WWW.CHAMORROROOTS.COM)
FOURTEENTH CENSUS OF THE UNITED STATES: 1920—POPULATION
ISLAND OF GUAM

ENUMERATED BY ME ON THE 16th DAY OF March, 1920

Vicente Tydingco ENUMERATOR

DISTRICT 3
NAME OF PLACE Piti Town

	PLACE OF ABODE		NAME	RELATION	PERSONAL DESCRIPTION				EDUCATION			NATIVITY				OCCUPATION
Street, avenue, road, etc.	No. of dwelling house	No. of family		Relationship to head	Sex	Color or race	Age at last birthday	Single, married, widowed or divorced	Attended school since Sept. 1, 1919	Able to read	Able to write	Place of birth of this person	Place of birth of father	Place of birth of mother	Able to speak English	Occupation
1	2	3	4	5	6	7	8	9	10	11	12	13	14	15	16	17
	39	39	Taijeron, Jesus J	Son	M	Cha	3.0	S				Guam	Guam	Guam		None
	39	39	Taijeron, Joaquin J	Son	M	Cha	0.2	S				Guam	Guam	Guam		None
	40	40	Cruz, Antonio M	Head	M	Cha	27.0	M		Y	Y	Guam	Guam	Guam	Y	Seaman USN
	40	40	Cruz, Rosa T	Wife	F	Cha	29.0	M		Y	Y	Guam	Guam	Guam	Y	None
	40	40	Blas, Consuelo M	Niece	F	Cha	2.0	S				Guam	Guam	Guam		None
	40	40	Santos, Consolacion T	Sister-in-law	F	Cha	24.0	S		Y	Y	Guam	Guam	Guam	Y	None
	40	40	Santos, Juan T	Nephew	M	Cha	2.0	S				Guam	Unknown	Guam		None
Agana Piti Road	41	41	Flores, Manuel G	Head	M	Cha	34.0	M		Y	Y	Guam	Guam	Guam	Y	Storeman
	41	41	Flores, Remedios D	Wife	F	Cha	30.0	M		Y	Y	Guam	Guam	Guam	N	None
	41	41	Flores, Helen D	Daughter	F	Cha	10.0	S	Y	Y	Y	Guam	Guam	Guam	Y	None
	41	41	Flores, Francisco D	Son	M	Cha	9.0	S	Y			Guam	Guam	Guam		None
	41	41	Flores, Enrique D	Son	M	Cha	6.0	S	N			Guam	Guam	Guam		None
	42	42	Quenga, Juan B	Head	M	Cha	29.0	M		Y	Y	Guam	Guam	Guam	Y	Chauffeur
	42	42	Quenga, Maria S	Wife	F	Cha	27.0	M		Y	Y	Guam	Guam	Guam	Y	None
	42	42	Quenga, Jose S	Son	M	Cha	9.0	S	Y			Guam	Guam	Guam		None
	42	42	Quenga, Magdalena S	Daughter	F	Cha	8.0	S	Y			Guam	Guam	Guam		None
	42	42	Quenga, Ana S	Daughter	F	Cha	6.0	S	N			Guam	Guam	Guam		None
	42	42	Quenga, Maria S jr.	Daughter	F	Cha	0.3	S				Guam	Guam	Guam		None
	43	43	Yaneyama, Hyojaro S	Head	M	Jp	29.0	M	Y	Y	Y	Guam	Guam	Guam	Y	Salesman
	44	44	Perez, Antonio C	Head	M	Cha	32.0	M		Y	Y	Guam	Guam	Guam	Y	Fireman USN
	44	44	Perez, Ana N	Wife	F	Cha	34.0	M		Y	Y	Guam	Guam	Guam	N	None
	44	44	Perez, Maria N	Daughter	F	Cha	9.0	S	Y	Y	Y	Guam	Guam	Guam		None
	44	44	Perez, Antonio N	Son	M	Cha	2.0	S				Guam	Guam	Guam		None
	44	44	Perez, Juan N	Son	M	Cha	0.2	S				Guam	Guam	Guam		None
	45	45	Tajalle, Feilx	Head	M	Cha	28.0	M		Y	Y	Guam	Guam	Guam	Y	Corswain USN

(CHAMORRO ROOTS GENEALOGY PROJECT ™ TRANSCRIPTION)
(COMPILED/TRANSCRIBED BY BERNARD T. PUNZALAN / HTTP://WWW.CHAMORROROOTS.COM)

192b

FOURTEENTH CENSUS OF THE UNITED STATES: 1920-POPULATION

ISLAND OF GUAM

SHEET NO. _17B_

ENUMERATED BY ME ON THE 17th DAY OF March, 1920

Vicente Tydingco ENUMERATOR

DISTRICT 3
NAME OF PLACE Piti Town

[Proper name and, also, name of class, as city, town, village, barrio, etc]

	PLACE OF ABODE			NAME	RELATION	PERSONAL DESCRIPTION					EDUCATION			NATIVITY				OCCUPATION
	Street, avenue, road, etc.	Number of dwelling house in order of visitation	Number of family in order of visitation	of each person whose place of abode on January 1, 1920, was in the family. Enter surname, firs, then given name and middle initial if any. Include every person living on January 1, 1920. Omit children born since January 1, 1920.	Relationship of this Person to the head of the family.	Sex	Color or race	Age at last birthday	Single, married, widowed or divorced	Attended school any time since Sept. 1, 1919	Whether able to read.	Whether able to write.	Place of birth of this person.	Place of birth of father of this person.	Place of birth of mother of this person.	Whether able to speak English.	Trade, profession, or particular kind of work done, as salesman, laborer, clerk, cook, merchant, washerwoman, etc.
	1	2	3	4	5	6	7	8	9	10	11	12	13	14	15	16	17
26		45	45	Tajalle, Soledad S	Wife	F	Cha	30.0	M		Y	Y	Guam	Guam	Guam	Y	None
27		45	45	Tajalle, Juan S	Son	M	Cha	0.2	S				Guam	Guam	Guam		None
28	Agana Piti Road	45	45	Tajalle, Justo C	Brother	M	Cha	16.0	S	N	Y	Y	Guam	Guam	Guam	Y	None
29		45	45	Tajalle, Joaquina C	Sister	F	Cha	14.0	S	N	Y	Y	Guam	Guam	Guam	Y	None
30		46	46	Torres, Luis H	Head	M	Cha	30.0	M		Y	Y	Guam	Guam	Guam	N	Chauffeur
31		46	46	Torres, Ana P	Wife	F	Cha	40.0	M		Y	Y	Guam	Guam	Guam	N	None
32		46	46	Torres, Maria P	Daughter	F	Cha	4.0	S		Y	Y	Guam	Guam	Guam		None
33		46	46	Torres, Josefina P	Daughter	F	Cha	2.0	S		Y	Y	Guam	Guam	Guam		None
34		46	46	Taijeron, Jose T	Servant	M	Cha	32.0	S		N	N	Guam	Unknown	Guam	N	Servant
35		47	47	Cruz, Antonio	Head	M	Cha	31.0	M		Y	Y	Guam	Guam	Guam	Y	Coswain USN
36		47	47	Cruz, Flora C	Wife	F	Cha	26.0	M		Y	Y	Guam	Guam	Guam	N	None
37		48	48	Mesa, Jose T	Head	M	Cha	20.0	M	N	Y	Y	Guam	Guam	Guam	Y	Seaman USN
38		48	48	Mesa, Dolores R	Wife	F	Cha	19.0	M	N	Y	Y	Guam	Guam	Guam	N	None
39		48	48	Mesa, Consolacion T	Sister	F	Cha	24.0	S		Y	Y	Guam	Guam	Guam	N	Laundress
40		48	48	Mesa, Vicente T	Brother	M	Cha	5.0	S	N			Guam	Guam	Guam		None
41	Piti Sumay Road	49	49	Santos, Felix A	Head	M	Cha	50.0	M		Y	Y	Guam	Guam	Guam	N	Laborer
42		49	49	Santos, Amparo C	Wife	F	Cha	50.0	M		N	N	Guam	Guam	Guam	N	None
43		49	49	Santos, Rufina I	Daughter	F	Cha	25.0	S		Y	Y	Guam	Guam	Guam	Y	None
44		49	49	Santos, Jose I	Son	M	Cha	21.0	S	N	Y	Y	Guam	Guam	Guam	Y	Laborer
45		49	49	Santos, Ana I	Daughter	F	Cha	14.0	S	N	Y	Y	Guam	Guam	Guam	Y	None
46		49	49	Santos, Gregorio C	Son	M	Cha	6.0	S	N			Guam	Guam	Guam		None
47		49	49	Santos, Ested S	Grand daughter	F	Cha	4.0	S				Guam	Unknown	Unknown		None
48		50	50	Cruz, Luis A	Head	M	Cha	23.0	M		Y	Y	Guam	Guam	Guam	Y	Farmer
49		50	50	Cruz, Rosario C	Wife	F	Cha	22.0	M		Y	Y	Guam	Guam	Guam	N	None
50		50	50	Cruz, Concepcion C	Daughter	F	Cha	1.0	S				Guam	Guam	Guam		None

387

(CHAMORRO ROOTS GENEALOGY PROJECT ™ TRANSCRIPTION)
(COMPILED/TRANSCRIBED BY BERNARD T. PUNZALAN / HTTP://WWW.CHAMORROROOTS.COM)

193

FOURTEENTH CENSUS OF THE UNITED STATES: 1920-POPULATION
ISLAND OF GUAM

ENUMERATED BY ME ON THE 19th DAY OF March, 1920

Vicente Tydingco ENUMERATOR

DISTRICT 3
NAME OF PLACE Piti Town

[Proper name and, also, name of class, as city, town, village, barrio, etc]

	Dwelling No. (2)	Family No. (3)	NAME (4)	RELATION (5)	Sex (6)	Color or race (7)	Age (8)	Single, married, widowed or divorced (9)	Attended school since Sept. 1, 1919 (10)	Read (11)	Write (12)	Birthplace (13)	Father's birthplace (14)	Mother's birthplace (15)	Speak English (16)	OCCUPATION (17)
1	51	51	Santos, Teburcio A	Head	M	Cha	56.0	Wd		N	N	Guam	Guam	Guam	N	Farmer
2	51	51	Santos, Regina C	Daughter	F	Cha	25.0	S		Y	Y	Guam	Guam	Guam	Y	None
3	51	51	Santos, Ana C	Daughter	F	Cha	21.0	S	N	Y	Y	Guam	Guam	Guam	Y	None
4	51	51	Santos, Maria C	Daughter	F	Cha	19.0	S	N	Y	Y	Guam	Guam	Guam	Y	None
5	51	51	Santos, Dolores C	Daughter	F	Cha	17.0	S	N	Y	Y	Guam	Guam	Guam	Y	None
6	51	51	Santos, Jesus C	Son	M	Cha	15.0	S	Y	Y	Y	Guam	Guam	Guam	Y	None
7	51	51	Santos, Nicolas C	Son	M	Cha	13.0	S	Y	Y	Y	Guam	Guam	Guam	Y	None
8	51	51	Santos, Natividad C	Daughter	F	Cha	11.0	S	Y	Y	Y	Guam	Guam	Guam	Y	None
9	51	51	Santos, Juan	Son	M	Cha	7.0	S	Y			Guam	Guam	Guam		None
10	51	51	Santos, Maria M	Daughter	F	Cha	5.0	S	N			Guam	Guam	Guam		None
11	52	52	Sablan, Enrique	Head	M	Cha	29.0	M		Y	Y	Guam	Guam	Guam	Y	Boatswainmate USN
12	52	52	Sablan, Nicolasa S	Wife	F	Cha	31.0	M		Y	Y	Guam	Guam	Guam	N	None
13	52	52	Sablan, Martina S	Daughter	F	Cha	4.0	S				Guam	Guam	Guam		None
14	52	52	Sablan, Vicente S	Son	M	Cha	3.0	S				Guam	Guam	Guam		None
15	52	52	Sablan, Maria S	Daughter	F	Cha	1.0	S				Guam	Guam	Guam		None
16	53	53	Santos, Jose C	Head	M	Cha	33.0	M		Y	Y	Guam	Guam	Guam	Y	Chauffeur
17	53	53	Santos, Antonia S	Wife	F	Cha	31.0	M		Y	Y	Guam	Guam	Guam	N	None
18	53	53	Santos, Martina S	Daughter	F	Cha	11.0	S	Y	Y	Y	Guam	Guam	Guam	Y	None
19	53	53	Santos, Virginia S	Daughter	F	Cha	8.0	S	Y	Y	Y	Guam	Guam	Guam		None
20	53	53	Santos, Ignacio S	Son	M	Cha	5.0	S	N			Guam	Guam	Guam		None
21	53	53	Santos, Nicolasa S	Daughter	F	Cha	0.3	S				Guam	Guam	Guam		None
22	54	54	Santos, Luis	Head	M	Cha	34.0	M		Y	Y	Guam	Unknown	Guam	N	Laborer
23	54	54	Santos, Magdalena C	Wife	F	Cha	34.0	M		N	N	Guam	Guam	Guam	N	None
24	54	54	Santos, Lorenzo C	Son	M	Cha	10.0	S	Y	Y	Y	Guam	Guam	Guam	Y	None
25	54	54	Santos, Antonia C	Daughter	F	Cha	8.0	S	Y	Y	Y	Guam	Guam	Guam		None

Street: Piti Sumay Road

(CHAMORRO ROOTS GENEALOGY PROJECT ™ TRANSCRIPTION)
(COMPILED/TRANSCRIBED BY BERNARD T. PUNZALAN / HTTP://WWW.CHAMORROROOTS.COM)

FOURTEENTH CENSUS OF THE UNITED STATES: 1920—POPULATION

ISLAND OF GUAM

193b

DISTRICT 3
NAME OF PLACE Piti Town
[Proper name and, also, name of class, as city, town, village, barrio, etc]

ENUMERATED BY ME ON THE 19th DAY OF March, 1920

Vicente Tydingco ENUMERATOR

	Dwelling	Family	NAME	RELATION	Sex	Color or race	Age at last birthday	Single, married, widowed or divorced	Attended school since Sept. 1, 1919	Whether able to read	Whether able to write	Place of birth of this person	Place of birth of father	Place of birth of mother	Whether able to speak English	OCCUPATION
	2	3	4	5	6	7	8	9	10	11	12	13	14	15	16	17
26	54	54	Santos, Catalina C	Daughter	F	Cha	6.0	S	N			Guam	Guam	Guam		None
27	54	54	Santos, Angelina C	Daughter	F	Cha	4.0	S				Guam	Guam	Guam		None
28	54	54	Santos, Ines C	Daughter	F	Cha	2.0	S				Guam	Guam	Guam		None
29	55	55	Cruz, Enrique	Head	M	Cha	27.0	Wd		Y	Y	Guam	Guam	Guam	Y	Seaman USN
30	55	55	Cruz, Lourdes C	Daughter	F	Cha	7.0	S	Y			Guam	Guam	Guam		None
31	55	55	Cruz, Balbina C	Daughter	F	Cha	5.0	S	N			Guam	Guam	Guam		None
32	55	55	Cruz, Josefa C	Daughter	F	Cha	4.0	S				Guam	Guam	Guam		None
33	55	55	Cruz, Veronica C	Daughter	F	Cha	1.0	S				Guam	Guam	Guam		None
34	56	56	Santos, Jesus F	Head	M	Cha	41.0	Wd		Y	Y	Guam	Guam	Guam	Y	Coswain USN
35	56	56	Fejeran, Antonia C	Daughter	F	Cha	19.0	S	N	Y	Y	Guam	Guam	Guam	Y	None
36	56	56	Fejeran, Sabina C	Daughter	F	Cha	17.0	S	N	Y	Y	Guam	Guam	Guam	Y	None
37	56	56	Fejeran, Jose C	Son	M	Cha	15.0	S	N	Y	Y	Guam	Guam	Guam	Y	Farm laborer home farm
38	56	56	Fejeran, Elena C	Daughter	F	Cha	13.0	S	N	Y	Y	Guam	Guam	Guam	Y	None
39	56	56	Fejeran, Joaquin T	Son	M	Cha	4.0	S				Guam	Guam	Guam		None
40	56	56	Fejeran, Francisca	Grand daughter	F	Cha	0.3	S				Guam	Unknown	Guam		None
41	57	57	Manibusan, Ignacio C	Head	M	Cha	36.0	M		Y	Y	Guam	Guam	Guam	Y	Coswain USN
42	57	57	Manibusan, Ana C	Wife	F	Cha	38.0	M		Y	Y	Guam	Guam	Guam	N	None
43	57	57	Manibusan, Vicente C	Son	M	Cha	13.0	S	Y	Y	Y	Guam	Guam	Guam	Y	None
44	57	57	Manibusan, Rufina C	Daughter	F	Cha	10.0	S	Y	Y	Y	Guam	Guam	Guam	Y	None
45	57	57	Manibusan, Adela C	Daughter	F	Cha	9.0	S	Y			Guam	Guam	Guam		None
46	57	57	Manibusan, Maria C	Daughter	F	Cha	6.0	S	N			Guam	Guam	Guam		None
47	57	57	Manibusan, Ana C jr.	Daughter	F	Cha	3.0	S				Guam	Guam	Guam		None
48	58	58	Santos, Francisco A	Head	M	Cha	48.0	M		N	N	Guam	Guam	Guam	N	Farmer
49	58	58	Santos, Delgadina Q	Wife	F	Cha	47.0	M		N	N	Guam	Unknown	Guam	N	None
50	58	58	Santos, Maria C	Daughter	F	Cha	26.0	S		Y	Y	Guam	Guam	Guam	N	None

Street, avenue, road, etc.: Piti Sumay Road

(CHAMORRO ROOTS GENEALOGY PROJECT ™ TRANSCRIPTION)
(COMPILED/TRANSCRIBED BY BERNARD T. PUNZALAN / HTTP://WWW.CHAMORROROOTS.COM)

FOURTEENTH CENSUS OF THE UNITED STATES: 1920-POPULATION

ISLAND OF GUAM

ENUMERATED BY ME ON THE 20th DAY OF March, 1920

Vicente Tydingco ENUMERATOR

DISTRICT 3
NAME OF PLACE Piti Town

	PLACE OF ABODE			NAME	RELATION	PERSONAL DESCRIPTION					EDUCATION			NATIVITY				OCCUPATION
Street, avenue, road, etc.	Number of dwelling house in order of visitation	Number of family in order of visitation		of each person whose place of abode on January 1, 1920, was in the family. Enter surname, firs, then given name and middle initial. If any. Include every person living on January 1, 1920. Omit children born since January 1, 1920.	Relationship of this Person to the head of the family.	Sex	Color or race	Age at last birthday	Single, married, widowed or divorced	Attended school any time since Sept. 1, 1919	Whether able to read.	Whether able to write.	Place of birth of this person.	Place of birth of father of this person.	Place of birth of mother of this person.	Whether able to speak English.	Trade, profession, or particular kind of work done, as salesman, laborer, clerk, cook, merchant, washerwoman, etc.
1	2	3	4		5	6	7	8	9	10	11	12	13	14	15	16	17
	58	58	Santos, Nicolasa Q	Daughter		F	Cha	25.0	S		Y	Y	Guam	Guam	Guam	Y	None
	58	58	Santos, Getrudes Q	Daughter		F	Cha	23.0	S		Y	Y	Guam	Guam	Guam	Y	None
	58	58	Santos, Joaquin Q	Son		M	Cha	21.0	S	N	Y	Y	Guam	Guam	Guam	Y	Laborer
	58	58	Santos, Angela Q	Daughter		F	Cha	18.0	S	N	Y	Y	Guam	Guam	Guam	Y	None
	58	58	Santos, Ignacio Q	Son		M	Cha	16.0	S	N	Y	Y	Guam	Guam	Guam	Y	Farm laborer home farm
	58	58	Santos, Jose Q	Son		M	Cha	14.0	S	N	Y	Y	Guam	Guam	Guam	Y	Farm laborer home farm
	58	58	Santos, Ana Q	Daughter		F	Cha	12.0	S	Y	Y	Y	Guam	Guam	Guam	Y	None
	58	58	Santos, Francisco Q	Son		M	Cha	10.0	S	Y	Y	Y	Guam	Guam	Guam	Y	None
	58	58	Santos, Antonio Q	Son		M	Cha	6.0	S	N			Guam	Guam	Guam		None
Piti Sumay Road	58	58	Santos, Antonina Q	Daughter		F	Cha	3.0	S				Guam	Guam	Guam		
	59	59	Fejeran, Lucas S	Head		M	Cha	55.0	M		N	N	Guam	Guam	Guam	N	Laborer
	59	59	Fejeran, Encarnacion S	Wife		F	Cha	43.0	M		N	N	Guam	Guam	Guam	N	None
	59	59	Fejeran, Antonio S	Son		M	Cha	23.0	S		Y	Y	Guam	Guam	Guam	Y	None
	59	59	Fejeran, Rosario S	Daughter		F	Cha	21.0	S	N	Y	Y	Guam	Guam	Guam	Y	None
	59	59	Fejeran, Felix S	Son		M	Cha	18.0	S	N	Y	Y	Guam	Guam	Guam	Y	Servant
	59	59	Fejeran, Jose S	Son		M	Cha	14.0	S	N	Y	Y	Guam	Guam	Guam	Y	Farm laborer home farm
	59	59	Fejeran, Domingo S	Son		M	Cha	13.0	S	N	Y	Y	Guam	Guam	Guam	Y	Farm laborer home farm
	59	59	Fejeran, Pilar S	Daughter		F	Cha	11.0	S	Y	Y	Y	Guam	Guam	Guam	Y	None
	59	59	Fejeran, Maria S	Daughter		F	Cha	8.0	S	Y	Y	Y	Guam	Guam	Guam		None
	59	59	Fejeran, Juana S	Daughter		F	Cha	6.0	S	N			Guam	Guam	Guam		None
	59	59	Fejeran, Manuel S	Son		M	Cha	4.0	S				Guam	Guam	Guam		None
	59	59	Fejeran, Ramona S	Daughter		F	Cha	2.0	S				Guam	Guam	Guam		None
	60	60	Concepcion, Juan C	Head		M	Cha	25.0	M		Y	Y	Guam	Guam	Guam	Y	Coswain USN
	60	60	Concepcion, Saturnina T	Wife		F	Cha	27.0	M		Y	Y	Guam	Guam	Guam	N	None
	60	60	Concepcion, Antonio T	Son		M	Cha	4.0	S				Guam	Guam	Guam		None

(CHAMORRO ROOTS GENEALOGY PROJECT ™ TRANSCRIPTION)
(COMPILED/TRANSCRIBED BY BERNARD T. PUNZALAN / HTTP://WWW.CHAMORROROOTS.COM)

194b

FOURTEENTH CENSUS OF THE UNITED STATES: 1920-POPULATION

ISLAND OF GUAM

ENUMERATED BY ME ON THE 20th DAY OF March, 1920

Vicente Tydingco ENUMERATOR

DISTRICT 3

NAME OF PLACE Piti Town

[Proper name and, also, name of class, as city, town, village, barrio, etc]

	1	2	3	4 NAME	5 RELATION	6 Sex	7 Color or race	8 Age at last birthday	9 Single, married, widowed or divorced	10 Attended school any time since Sept. 1, 1919	11 Whether able to read	12 Whether able to write	13 Place of birth of this person	14 Place of birth of father	15 Place of birth of mother	16 Whether able to speak English	17 OCCUPATION
26		60	60	Concepcion, Rosa T	Daughter	F	Cha	2.0	S				Guam	Guam	Guam		None
27		60	60	Mesa, Juan T	Brother-in-law	M	Cha	9.0	S	Y			Guam	Guam	Guam		None
28		61	61	Concepcion, Jose	Head	M	Cha	50.0	M		Y	Y	Guam	Unknown	Guam	Y	Laborer
29		61	61	Concepcion, Maria C	Wife	F	Cha	34.0	M		N	N	Guam	Guam	Guam	Y	None
30		61	61	Concepcion, Caridad C	Daughter	F	Cha	13.0	S	N	Y	Y	Guam	Guam	Guam	Y	Laundress
31		61	61	Concepcion, Jose C jr	Son	M	Cha	12.0	S	N	N	N	Guam	Guam	Guam	N	None
32		61	61	Concepcion, Beatris C	Daughter	F	Cha	10.0	S	N	N	N	Guam	Guam	Guam	N	None
33	Piti Sumay Road	61	61	Concepcion, Engracia C	Daughter	F	Cha	8.0	S	Y			Guam	Guam	Guam		None
34		61	61	Concepcion, Cristina C	Daughter	F	Cha	5.0	S	N			Guam	Guam	Guam		None
35		61	61	Concepcion, Jesus C	Son	M	Cha	3.0	S				Guam	Guam	Guam		None
36		61	61	Concepcion, Manuel C	Son	M	Cha	1.0	S				Guam	Guam	Guam		None
37		62	62	S. Nicolas, Francisco D	Head	M	Cha	27.0	M		Y	Y	Guam	Guam	Guam	Y	Laborer
38		62	62	S. Nicolas, Manuela S	Wife	F	Cha	33.0	M		N	N	Guam	Guam	Guam	N	None
39		62	62	S. Nicolas, Vicente S	Son	M	Cha	6.0	S	N			Guam	Guam	Guam		None
40		62	62	S. Nicolas, Jesus S	Son	M	Cha	1.0	S				Guam	Guam	Guam		None
41		62	62	S. Nicolas, Jose S	Son	M	Cha	0.3	S				Guam	Guam	Guam		None
42		62	62	Babauta, Antonio B	Servant	M	Cha	13.0	S	N	Y	Y	Guam	Unknown	Guam	Y	Servant
43		63	63	Finona, Rita SN	Head	F	Cha	68.0	Wd		N	N	Guam	Guam	Guam	N	None
44		63	63	Finona, Maria SN	Daughter	F	Cha	45.0	S		N	N	Guam	Guam	Guam	N	None
45		63	63	Santos, Ignacio	Boarder	M	Cha	41.0	S		N	N	Guam	Unknown	Guam	N	Laborer
46		63	63	Santos, Francisco	Nephew	M	Cha	12.0	S	Y	Y	Y	Guam	Unknown	Guam	Y	Farm laborer farm home
47		63	63	Santos, Ana C	Cousin	F	Cha	65.0	S		N	N	Guam	Guam	Guam	N	None
48		64	64	Tajalle, Juan C	Head	M	Cha	32.0	M		Y	Y	Guam	Guam	Guam	Y	Laborer
49		64	64	Tajalle, Dolores M	Wife	F	Cha	27.0	S		Y	Y	Guam	Guam	Guam	Y	Laborer
50		64	64	Tajalle, Maria M	Daughter	F	Cha	7.0	S	N			Guam	Guam	Guam	N	None

(CHAMORRO ROOTS GENEALOGY PROJECT ™ TRANSCRIPTION)
(COMPILED/TRANSCRIBED BY BERNARD T. PUNZALAN / HTTP://WWW.CHAMORROROOTS.COM)

FOURTEENTH CENSUS OF THE UNITED STATES: 1920-POPULATION
ISLAND OF GUAM

ENUMERATED BY ME ON THE 22nd DAY OF March, 1920

Vicente Tydingco ENUMERATOR

DISTRICT 3
NAME OF PLACE Piti Town

[Proper name and, also, name of class, as city, town, village, barrio, etc]

Street	Dwelling house no.	Family no.	NAME	RELATION	Sex	Color or race	Age at last birthday	Single, married, widowed or divorced	Attended school since Sept. 1, 1919	Whether able to read	Whether able to write	Place of birth of this person	Place of birth of father	Place of birth of mother	Whether able to speak English	OCCUPATION
1	2	3	4	5	6	7	8	9	10	11	12	13	14	15	16	17
Piti Sumay Road	64	64	Tajalle, Francisco M	Son	M	Cha	4.0	S				Guam	Guam	Guam		None
	64	64	Tajalle, Felix M	Son	M	Cha	2.0	S				Guam	Guam	Guam		None
	64	64	Tajalle, Manuel C	Brother	M	Cha	9.0	S	Y			Guam	Guam	Guam		None
	65	65	Finona, Jose SN	Head	M	Cha	42.0	M		Y	Y	Guam	Guam	Guam	N	Farmer
	65	65	Finona, Manuela C	Wife	F	Cha	42.0	M		N	N	Guam	Unknown	Guam	N	None
	65	65	Finona, Rita C	Daughter	F	Cha	12.0	S	N	Y	Y	Guam	Guam	Guam	Y	None
	65	65	Finona, Antonio C	Son	M	Cha	11.0	S	Y	Y	Y	Guam	Guam	Guam	Y	None
	65	65	Finona, Francisco C	Son	M	Cha	9.0	S	Y	Y	Y	Guam	Guam	Guam		None
	65	65	Finona, Regina C	Daughter	F	Cha	7.0	S	Y			Guam	Guam	Guam		None
	65	65	Finona, Manuel C	Son	M	Cha	5.0	S	N			Guam	Guam	Guam		None
	65	65	Finona, Joaquin C	Son	M	Cha	4.0	S				Guam	Guam	Guam		None
	66	66	Iglesias, Magdalena Q	Head	F	Cha	50.0	Wd		N	N	Guam	Guam	Guam	N	None
	66	66	Iglesias, Juan Q	Son	M	Cha	27.0	S		Y	Y	Guam	Guam	Guam	Y	Fireman USN
	66	66	Iglesias, Francisco Q	Son	M	Cha	20.0	S	N	Y	Y	Guam	Guam	Guam	Y	Farmer
	66	66	Iglesias, Jose Q	Son	M	Cha	9.0	S	Y			Guam	Guam	Guam		None
	67	67	Quitugua, Francisco Q	Head	M	Cha	27.0	M		Y	Y	Guam	Unknown	Guam	Y	Farmer
	67	67	Quitugua, Milagro A	Wife	F	Cha	25.0	M		Y	Y	Guam	Unknown	Guam	Y	None
	67	67	Quitugua, Antonia A	Daughter	F	Cha	4.0	S				Guam	Guam	Guam		None
	67	67	Quitugua, Maria A	Daughter	F	Cha	3.0	S				Guam	Guam	Guam		None
	67	67	Quitugua, Rosalia A	Daughter	F	Cha	2.0	S				Guam	Guam	Guam		None
	68	68	S. Nicolas, Pedro D	Head	M	Cha	30.0	M		N	N	Guam	Guam	Guam	N	Farmer
	68	68	S. Nicolas, Rosa A	Wife	F	Cha	27.0	M		N	N	Guam	Guam	Guam	N	Laundress
	68	68	S. Nicolas, Maria A	Daughter	F	Cha	2.0	S				Guam	Guam	Guam		None
	68	68	S. Nicolas, Jose A	Son	M	Cha	1.0	S				Guam	Guam	Guam		None
	68	68	Babauta, Antonio D	Brother	M	Cha	21.0	S	N	Y	Y	Guam	Guam	Guam	Y	None

(CHAMORRO ROOTS GENEALOGY PROJECT ™ TRANSCRIPTION)
(COMPILED/TRANSCRIBED BY BERNARD T. PUNZALAN / HTTP://WWW.CHAMORROROOTS.COM)

FOURTEENTH CENSUS OF THE UNITED STATES: 1920–POPULATION
ISLAND OF GUAM

DISTRICT 3
NAME OF PLACE Piti Town

ENUMERATED BY ME ON THE 22nd DAY OF March, 1920

Vicente Tydingco ENUMERATOR

[Proper name and, also, name of class, as city, town, village, barrio, etc]

	Dwelling No.	Family No.	NAME	RELATION	Sex	Color or race	Age	Cond.	School	Read	Write	Birthplace person	Birthplace father	Birthplace mother	Speak English	OCCUPATION
	1/2/3		4	5	6	7	8	9	10	11	12	13	14	15	16	17
26		68	Cruz, Consolacion	Servant	F	Cha	27.0	S		N	N	Guam	Unknown	Guam	N	Servant
27		68	Cruz, Maria C	Niece	F	Cha	7.0	S	Y			Guam	Unknown	Guam		None
28		68	Cruz, Jose C	Nephew	M	Cha	4.0	S				Guam	Unknown	Guam		None
29		68	Cruz, Agustina C	Niece	F	Cha	1.0	S				Guam	Unknown	Guam		None
30		69	Fejeran, Isidro S	Head	M	Cha	35.0	M		N	N	Guam	Guam	Guam	N	Farmer
31		69	Fejeran, Caridad R	Wife	F	Cha	29.0	M		N	N	Guam	Guam	Guam	N	None
32		69	Fejeran, Joaquina R	Daughter	F	Cha	14.0	S	N	Y	Y	Guam	Guam	Guam	Y	None
33		69	Fejeran, Tomas R	Son	M	Cha	4.0	S				Guam	Guam	Guam		None
34		69	Fejeran, Antonio R	Son	M	Cha	1.0	S				Guam	Guam	Guam		None
35		70	Unsiog, Francisca J	Head	F	Cha	26.0	S		Y	Y	Guam	Guam	Guam	N	None
36		70	Unsiog, Joaquin J	Brother	M	Cha	23.0	S		Y	Y	Guam	Guam	Guam	Y	Farmer
37		71	Muna, Rufina C	Head	F	Cha	52.0	M		N	N	Guam	Guam	Guam	N	Farm laborer home farm
38		71	Muna, Magdalena C	Daughter	F	Cha	25.0	S		Y	Y	Guam	Guam	Guam	N	Laundress
39		71	Muna, Maria C	Daughter	F	Cha	22.0	S	N			Guam	Guam	Guam	Y	None
40		71	Muna, Joaquin C	Grandson	M	Cha	6.0	S	N			Guam	Guam	Guam		None
41		71	Muna, Manuel C	Grandson	M	Cha	5.0	S				Guam	Guam	Guam		None
42		71	Muna, Clarita C	Grand daughter	F	Cha	3.0	S				Guam	Guam	Guam		None
43		71	Muna, Jose C	Grandson	M	Cha	0.1	S				Guam	Guam	Guam		None
44		72	Lizama, Jose L	Head	M	Cha	46.0	M		Y	Y	Guam	Guam	Guam	N	Farmer
45		72	Lizama, Soledad S	Wife	F	Cha	45.0	M		N	N	Guam	Guam	Guam	N	None
46		72	Santos, Dolores SN	Mother-in-law	F	Cha	62.0	Wd		N	N	Guam	Guam	Guam	N	None
47		72	Santos, Nieves S	Niece	F	Cha	8.0	S	N			Guam	Unknown	Guam		None
48		72	Santos, Francisco S	Nephew	M	Cha	5.0	S				Guam	Unknown	Guam		None
49		72	Santos, Lourdes M	Niece	F	Cha	1.0	S				Guam	Unknown	Guam		None
50		73	Quituqua, Jose C	Head	M	Cha	30.0	M		Y	Y	Guam	Guam	Guam	N	Farmer

Street, avenue, road (Column 1): Piti Sumay Road

(CHAMORRO ROOTS GENEALOGY PROJECT ™ TRANSCRIPTION)
(COMPILED/TRANSCRIBED BY BERNARD T. PUNZALAN / HTTP://WWW.CHAMORROROOTS.COM)

FOURTEENTH CENSUS OF THE UNITED STATES: 1920-POPULATION
ISLAND OF GUAM

SHEET NO. 21A

ENUMERATED BY ME ON THE 23rd DAY OF March, 1920

Vicente Tydingco ENUMERATOR

DISTRICT 3
NAME OF PLACE Piti Town

Street	No. dwelling	No. family	NAME	RELATION	Sex	Color or race	Age	Marital	Attended school since Sept 1, 1919	Able to read	Able to write	Place of birth of person	Place of birth of father	Place of birth of mother	Able to speak English	OCCUPATION
	73	73	Quitugua, Antonia C	Wife	F	Cha	38.0	M		N	N	Guam	Guam	Guam	N	None
	73	73	Quitugua, Juan C	Son	M	Cha	9.0	S	Y			Guam	Guam	Guam	N	None
	73	73	Quitugua, Dolores C	Daughter	F	Cha	6.0	S	N			Guam	Guam	Guam	N	None
	73	73	Quitugua, Vicente C	Son	M	Cha	0.4	S				Guam	Guam	Guam		None
	74	74	Santos, Toribio B	Head	M	Fil	62.0	Wd		Y	Y	Panay	Panay	Panay	N	Laborer
	74	74	Santos, Juan C	Son	M	Fil	18.0	S	N	Y	Y	Guam	Panay	Guam	Y	Farm laborer home farm
	74	74	Santos, Lucia C	Daughter	F	Fil	12.0	S	Y	Y	Y	Guam	Panay	Guam	Y	None
	75	75	Ignacio, Leonicio C	Head	M	Cha	40.0	M		Y	Y	Guam	Guam	Guam	N	Farmer
	75	75	Ignacio, Antonia C	Wife	F	Cha	41.0	M		Y	Y	Guam	Guam	Guam	Y	Laundress
	75	75	Ignacio, Jose C	Son	M	Cha	21.0	S	N	Y	Y	Guam	Guam	Guam	Y	Servant
	75	75	Ignacio, Maria C	Daughter	F	Cha	19.0	S	N	Y	Y	Guam	Guam	Guam	Y	None
	75	75	Ignacio, Luis C	Son	M	Cha	14.0	S	N	Y	Y	Guam	Guam	Guam	Y	None
	75	75	Ignacio, Jesus C	Son	M	Cha	12.0	S	Y	Y	Y	Guam	Guam	Guam	Y	None
	75	75	Ignacio, Carmen C	Daughter	F	Cha	10.0	S	N			Guam	Guam	Guam	Y	None
	75	75	Ignacio, Rosa C	Daughter	F	Cha	2.0	S				Guam	Guam	Guam		None
Piti Sumay Road	76	76	Ignacio, Rafael P	Head	M	Cha	43.0	M		N	N	Guam	Guam	Guam	N	Farmer
	76	76	Ignacio, Rita C	Wife	F	Cha	47.0	M		N	N	Guam	Guam	Guam	N	None
	76	76	Concepcion, Manuel C	Stepson	M	Cha	18.0	S	N	Y	Y	Guam	Guam	Guam	Y	Farm laborer
	76	76	Concepcion, Jesus C	Stepson	M	Cha	16.0	S	N	Y	Y	Guam	Guam	Guam	Y	Farm laborer home farm
	76	76	Concepcion, Ana C	Step daughter	F	Cha	12.0	S	Y	Y	Y	Guam	Guam	Guam	Y	None
	76	76	Concepcion, Concepcion C	Step daughter	F	Cha	8.0	S	Y			Guam	Guam	Guam	Y	None
	77	77	Ignacio, Manuel A	Head	M	Cha	54.0	M		N	N	Guam	Guam	Guam	N	Farmer
	77	77	Ignacio, Rosa C	Wife	F	Cha	50.0	M		N	N	Guam	Guam	Guam	N	None
	77	77	Ignacio, Placida C	Daughter	F	Cha	16.0	S	N	Y	Y	Guam	Guam	Guam	Y	None
	78	78	Fejeran, Juan	Head	M	Cha	36.0	Wd		Y	Y	Guam	Guam	Guam	Y	Coswain USN

(CHAMORRO ROOTS GENEALOGY PROJECT ™ TRANSCRIPTION)
(COMPILED/TRANSCRIBED BY BERNARD T. PUNZALAN / HTTP://WWW.CHAMORROROOTS.COM)

FOURTEENTH CENSUS OF THE UNITED STATES: 1920-POPULATION

ISLAND OF GUAM

ENUMERATED BY ME ON THE 23rd DAY OF March, 1920

Vicente Tydingco ENUMERATOR

DISTRICT 3
NAME OF PLACE Piti Town

[Proper name and, also, name of class, as city, town, village, barrio, etc]

Street, avenue, road, etc.	No. dwelling house	No. family	NAME	RELATION	Sex	Color or race	Age	Single/married	Attended school	Read	Write	Birthplace person	Birthplace father	Birthplace mother	Speak English	OCCUPATION
	1	2	3	4	5	6	7	8	9	10	11	12	13	14	15	16	17
26	78	78	Fejeran, Jose R	Son	M	Cha	8.0	S	Y			Guam	Guam	Guam		None
27	78	78	Fejeran, Magdalena R	Daughter	F	Cha	6.0	S	N			Guam	Guam	Guam		None
28	78	78	Fejeran, Pedro R	Son	M	Cha	5.0	S	N			Guam	Guam	Guam		None
29	78	78	Fejeran, Joaquin R	Son	M	Cha	3.0	S				Guam	Guam	Guam		None

Here ends the enumeration of Piti Town

Piti Sumay Road

(CHAMORRO ROOTS GENEALOGY PROJECT ™ TRANSCRIPTION)

(COMPILED/TRANSCRIBED BY BERNARD T. PUNZALAN / HTTP://WWW.CHAMORROROOTS.COM)

FOURTEENTH CENSUS OF THE UNITED STATES: 1920-POPULATION

ISLAND OF GUAM

ENUMERATED BY ME ON THE 24th DAY OF March, 1920

Vicente Tydingco ENUMERATOR

DISTRICT 3

NAME OF PLACE Sumay Town

	Dwelling	Family	NAME	RELATION	Sex	Color	Age	S/M/Wd	School	Read	Write	Birthplace	Father	Mother	English	Occupation
	2	3	4	5	6	7	8	9	10	11	12	13	14	15	16	17
1	1	1	Santos, Maria G	Head	F	Cha	69.0	Wd		Y	Y	Guam	Guam	Guam	N	None
2		1	Santos, Maria G jr	Daughter	F	Cha	35.0	S		Y	Y	Guam	Guam	Guam	N	Laundress
3		1	Santos, Jorge	Grandson	M	Cha	5.0	S	N			Guam	Unknown	Guam		None
4		2	Reyes, Juan B	Head	M	Cha	36.0	M		Y	Y	Guam	Guam	Guam	Y	Shoemaker
5		2	Reyes, Concepcion S	Wife	F	Cha	27.0	M		Y	Y	Guam	Guam	Guam	Y	None
6		2	Reyes, Maria S	Daughter	F	Cha	6.0	S	N			Guam	Guam	Guam		None
7		2	Reyes, Jose S	Son	M	Cha	4.0	S				Guam	Guam	Guam		None
8		2	Reyes, Jesus S	Son	M	Cha	2.0	S				Guam	Guam	Guam		None
9		3	Borja, Francisco S	Head	M	Cha	28.0	M		Y	Y	Guam	Guam	Guam	Y	Carpenter
10		3	Borja, Isabel M	Wife	F	Cha	20.0	M	N	Y	Y	Guam	Spain	Guam	Y	None
11		4	Borja, Rafael T	Head	M	Cha	56.0	M		Y	Y	Guam	Guam	Guam	Y	Farmer
12		4	Borja, Carmen N	Wife	F	Cha	38.0	M		Y	Y	Guam	Guam	Guam	N	None
13		4	Borja, Francisco N	Son	M	Cha	11.0	S	Y	Y	Y	Guam	Guam	Guam	Y	None
14		4	Borja, Rafael N	Son	M	Cha	6.0	S	N			Guam	Guam	Guam		None
15		4	Borja, Gregorio N	Son	M	Cha	1.0	S				Guam	Guam	Guam		None
16		4	Borja, Pedro N	Son	M	Cha	1.0	S				Guam	Guam	Guam		None
17		5	Santos, Jose	Head	M	Cha	55.0	M		Y	Y	Guam	Guam	Guam	Y	Seaman USN
18		5	Santos, Ana B	Wife	F	Cha	46.0	M	N	Y	Y	Guam	Guam	Guam	N	None
19		5	Babauta, Ana A	Servant	F	Cha	16.0	S	N	Y	Y	Guam	Guam	Guam	N	Servant
20		6	Wongpat, Ignacio	Head	M	Chin	47.0	M	N	Y	Y	China	China	China	Y	Retail merchant
21		6	Wongpat, Maria B	Wife	F	Cha	28.0	M		Y	Y	Guam	Guam	Guam	Y	None
22		6	Wongpat, Antonio B	Son	M	Chin	11.0	S	Y	Y	Y	Guam	China	Guam	Y	None
23		6	Wongpat, Ignacio B	Son	M	Chin	9.0	S	Y	Y	Y	Guam	China	Guam	Y	None
24		6	Wongpat, John B	Son	M	Chin	5.0	S	N			Guam	China	Guam		None
25		6	Wongpat, Vicente B	Son	M	Chin	1.0	S				Guam	China	Guam		None

Street, avenue, road, etc: Jose de los Calles Street

(CHAMORRO ROOTS GENEALOGY PROJECT ™ TRANSCRIPTION)
(COMPILED/TRANSCRIBED BY BERNARD T. PUNZALAN / HTTP://WWW.CHAMORROROOTS.COM)

FOURTEENTH CENSUS OF THE UNITED STATES: 1920-POPULATION
ISLAND OF GUAM

197b

DISTRICT 3
NAME OF PLACE **Sumay Town**
[Proper name and, also, name of class, as city, town, village, barrio, etc]

ENUMERATED BY ME ON THE 24th DAY OF March, 1920

Vicente Tydingco ENUMERATOR

	Dwelling	Family	NAME	RELATION	Sex	Color or race	Age	S/M/Wd	School	Read	Write	Birthplace	Father	Mother	English	OCCUPATION
	2	3	4	5	6	7	8	9	10	11	12	13	14	15	16	17
26	6	6	Wongpat, Francisco B	Son	M	Chn	0.3	S				Guam	China	Guam		None
27	6	6	Chiguina, Ingracia C	Servant	F	Cha	17.0	S	N	Y	Y	Guam	Guam	Guam	N	Servant
28	7		Toves, Manuela	Head	F	Cha	43.0	S		Y	Y	Guam	Unknown	Guam	N	None
29	7		Toves, Jose	Son	M	Cha	21.0	S	N	Y	Y	Guam	Unknown	Guam	Y	Cable operator
30	7		Toves, Juan	Son	M	Cha	19.0	S	N	Y	Y	Guam	Unknown	Guam	Y	Cable operator
31	7		Toves, Maria	Daughter	F	Cha	18.0	S	Y	Y	Y	Guam	Unknown	Guam	Y	None
32	7		Toves, Josefina	Daughter	F	Cha	15.0	S	N	Y	Y	Guam	Unknown	Guam	Y	None
33	7		Toves, Jesus	Son	M	Cha	12.0	S	Y	Y	Y	Guam	Unknown	Guam	Y	None
34	7		Toves, Pedro	Son	M	Cha	10.0	S	Y	Y	Y	Guam	Unknown	Guam	Y	None
35	7		Baliesta, Francisco B	Step-father	M	OF	97.0	Wd				Philippine Islands	Philippine Islands	Philippine Islands	N	Carpenter
36	8		Perez, Santiago T	Head	M	Cha	41.0	M		Y	Y	Guam	Guam	Guam	Y	Carpenter
37	8		Perez, Ana C	Wife	F	Cha	35.0	M		Y	Y	Guam	Guam	Guam	N	None
38	8		Perez, Mariano C	Son	M	Cha	17.0	S		Y	N	Guam	Guam	Guam	Y	Carpenter
39	8		Perez, Antonio C	Son	M	Cha	13.0	S	N	Y	Y	Guam	Guam	Guam	Y	None
40	8		Perez, Dolores C	Daughter	F	Cha	6.0	S	N	Y	Y	Guam	Guam	Guam	Y	None
41	8		Perez, Santiago C	Son	M	Cha	3.0	S	N			Guam	Guam	Guam		None
42	8		Perez, Jesus C	Son	M	Cha	1.0	S				Guam	Guam	Guam		None
43	9		Santos, Juan G	Head	M	Cha	48.0	M		Y	Y	Guam	Guam	Guam	N	Farmer
44	9		Santos, Maria B	Wife	F	Cha	45.0	M		Y	Y	Guam	Guam	Guam	Y	None
45	9		Freegord, Guadalupe	Daughter	F	Cha	27.0	M		Y	Y	Guam	Guam	Guam	Y	None
46	9		Cruz, Carmen C	Servant	F	Cha	16.0	S	N	Y	Y	Guam	Unknown	Guam	Y	Servant
47	9		Castro, Manuela C	Servant	F	Cha	22.0	S		Y	Y	Guam	Guam	Guam	Y	Servant
48	10		Santos, Antonio B	Head	M	Cha	25.0	M		Y	Y	Guam	Guam	Guam	Y	Chauffeur
49	10		Santos, Maria H	Wife	F	Cha	25.0	M		Y	Y	Guam	Guam	Guam	Y	None
50	10		Santos, Isabel H	Daughter	F	Cha	4.0	S				Guam	Guam	Guam	Y	None

Street, avenue, road, etc.: Jose de los Calles Street

(CHAMORRO ROOTS GENEALOGY PROJECT ™ TRANSCRIPTION)
(COMPILED/TRANSCRIBED BY BERNARD T. PUNZALAN / HTTP://WWW.CHAMORROROOTS.COM)

FOURTEENTH CENSUS OF THE UNITED STATES: 1920-POPULATION

ISLAND OF GUAM

ENUMERATED BY ME ON THE 25th DAY OF March, 1920

Vicente Tydingco ENUMERATOR

DISTRICT 3
NAME OF PLACE Sumay Town

[Proper name and, also, name of class, as city, town, village, barrio, etc]

Street	Dwelling No.	Family No.	NAME	RELATION	Sex	Color or race	Age at last birthday	Single, married, widowed or divorced	Attended school since Sept. 1, 1919	Whether able to read	Whether able to write	Place of birth of this person	Place of birth of father	Place of birth of mother	Whether able to speak English	OCCUPATION
1	2	3	4	5	6	7	8	9	10	11	12	13	14	15	16	17
Jose de los Calles Street	10	10	Santos, Aurelia H	Daughter	F	Cha	2.0	S				Guam	Guam	Guam		None
	11	11	Duenas, Santiago S	Head	M	Cha	27.0	M		Y	Y	Guam	Guam	Guam	Y	Seaman USN
	11	11	Duenas, Maria Q	Wife	F	Cha	24.0	M		Y	Y	Guam	Guam	Guam	N	Laundress
	11	11	Duenas, Pedro Q	Son	M	Cha	6.0	S	N			Guam	Guam	Guam		None
	11	11	Duenas, Catalina Q	Daughter	F	Cha	5.0	S	N			Guam	Guam	Guam		None
	11	11	Duenas, Felisa Q	Daughter	F	Cha	2.0	S				Guam	Guam	Guam		None
	11	11	Duenas, Pedro S	Brother	M	Cha	16.0	S	N	Y	Y	Guam	Guam	Guam	Y	Farm laborer home farm
	11	11	Cruz, Joaquin C	Servant	M	Cha	26.0	S		Y	Y	Guam	Guam	Guam	Y	Servant
	12	12	Ulloa, Gaspar	Head	M	Cha	27.0	M		Y	Y	Guam	Unknown	Guam	Y	Laborer
	12	12	Ulloa, Enoveva J	Wife	F	Cha	30.0	M		N	N	Guam	Guam	Guam	N	None
	12	12	Ulloa, Francisco J	Son	M	Cha	3.0	S				Guam	Guam	Guam		None
	12	12	Jesus, Natividad J	Step daughter	F	Cha	15.0	S	N	Y	Y	Guam	Unknown	Guam	Y	None
	12	12	Jesus, Jose J	Step son	M	Cha	11.0	S	Y	Y	Y	Guam	Unknown	Guam	Y	None
	12	12	Jesus, Felix J	Step son	M	Cha	9.0	S	Y	Y	Y	Guam	Unknown	Guam	Y	None
	13	13	Baleto, Vicente D	Head	M	Cha	51.0	M		Y	Y	Guam	Unknown	Guam	N	Farmer
	13	13	Baleto, Maria S	Wife	F	Cha	49.0	M		Y	Y	Guam	Guam	Guam	N	None
	13	13	Baleto, Remedios S	Daughter	F	Cha	25.0	S		Y	Y	Guam	Guam	Guam	Y	None
	13	13	Baleto, Jose S	Son	M	Cha	22.0	S		Y	Y	Guam	Guam	Guam	Y	Servant
	13	13	Baleto, Antonio S	Son	M	Cha	17.0	S	N	Y	Y	Guam	Guam	Guam	Y	Cook
	13	13	Baleto, Maria S	Daughter	F	Cha	14.0	S	Y	Y	Y	Guam	Guam	Guam	Y	None
	13	13	Baleto, Francisco S	Son	M	Cha	11.0	S	Y	Y	Y	Guam	Guam	Guam	Y	None
	13	13	Baleto, Jesus S	Son	M	Cha	8.0	S	Y			Guam	Guam	Guam	Y	None
	13	13	Baleto, Vicente S	Son	M	Cha	4.0	S				Guam	Guam	Guam	Y	None
	13	13	S. Nicolas, Asuncion	Servant	F	Cha	18.0	S	N	Y	Y	Guam	Guam	Guam	Y	None
	14	14	Demapan, Maria	Head	F	Cha	40.0	Wd		N	N	Guam	Guam	Guam	N	Laundress

(CHAMORRO ROOTS GENEALOGY PROJECT ™ TRANSCRIPTION)
(COMPILED/TRANSCRIBED BY BERNARD T. PUNZALAN / HTTP://WWW.CHAMORROROOTS.COM)

FOURTEENTH CENSUS OF THE UNITED STATES: 1920-POPULATION
ISLAND OF GUAM

198b

ENUMERATED BY ME ON THE 25th DAY OF March, 1920

Vicente Tydingco ENUMERATOR

DISTRICT 3
NAME OF PLACE **Sumay Town**

[Proper name and, also, name of class, as city, town, village, barrio, etc]

	Dwell (2)	Fam (3)	NAME (4)	RELATION (5)	Sex (6)	Color/race (7)	Age (8)	S/M/Wd (9)	School (10)	Read (11)	Write (12)	Birthplace (13)	Father (14)	Mother (15)	Eng (16)	OCCUPATION (17)
26	14	14	Demapan, Manuel	Son	M	Cha	23.0	S		Y	Y	Guam	Guam	Guam	Y	Laborer
27	14	14	Demapan, Pedro	Son	M	Cha	13.0	S	N	Y	Y	Guam	Guam	Guam	N	None
28	15	15	Concepcion, Juan S	Head	M	Cha	46.0	M		Y	Y	Guam	Guam	Guam	Y	Farmer
29	15	15	Concepcion, Josefa D	Wife	F	Cha	36.0	M		Y	Y	Guam	Guam	Guam	N	None
30	15	15	Concepcion, Rosalia T	Daughter	F	Cha	18.0	S	N	Y	Y	Guam	Guam	Guam	Y	Farm laborer home farm
31	15	15	Concepcion, Antonio T	Son	M	Cha	17.0	S	N	Y	Y	Guam	Guam	Guam	N	Farm laborer home farm
32	15	15	Concepcion, Jose T	Son	M	Cha	15.0	S	N	Y	Y	Guam	Guam	Guam	Y	None
33	15	15	Concepcion, Juan T	Son	M	Cha	12.0	S	Y	Y	Y	Guam	Guam	Guam	Y	None
34	15	15	Concepcion, Enrique T	Son	M	Cha	6.0	S	N			Guam	Guam	Guam	Y	None
35	15	15	Concepcion, Soledad T	Daughter	F	Cha	5.0	S				Guam	Guam	Guam		None
36	15	15	Concepcion, Balbino T	Son	M	Cha	3.0	S				Guam	Guam	Guam		None
37	16	16	Diaz, Jose C	Head	M	Cha	30.0	M		Y	Y	Guam	Guam	Guam	Y	Chauffeur
38	16	16	Diaz, Rosa C	Wife	F	Cha	28.0	M		Y	Y	Guam	Unknown	Guam	Y	None
39	16	16	Diaz, Pedro C	Son	M	Cha	8.0	S	Y			Guam	Guam	Guam	Y	None
40	16	16	Diaz, Guadalupe C	Daughter	F	Cha	6.0	S	N			Guam	Guam	Guam		None
41	16	16	Diaz, Lourdes C	Daughter	F	Cha	2.0	S				Guam	Guam	Guam		None
42	17	17	Brown, Frank	Head	M	W	33.0	M		Y	Y	New Jersey	Ireland	Ireland	Y	Foreman
43	17	17	Brown, Maria	Wife	F	Cha	58.0	M		N	N	Guam	Guam	Guam		None
44	17	17	Brown, Teodora	Step-daughter	F	Cha	20.0	S	N	Y	Y	Guam	Unknown	Guam	Y	None
45	18	18	Guerrero, Ignacio V	Head	M	Cha	33.0	M		Y	Y	Guam	Unknown	Guam	Y	Farmer
46	18	18	Guerrero, Maxima M	Wife	F	Cha	28.0	M		Y	Y	Guam	Guam	Guam	N	None
47	18	18	Guerrero, Maria M	Daughter	F	Cha	2.0	S				Guam	Guam	Guam		None
48	18	18	Guerrero, Jose M	Son	M	Cha	0.2	S				Guam	Guam	Guam		None
49	18	18	Guerrero, Victoriana V	Sister	F	Cha	28.0	S		Y	Y	Guam	Unknown	Unknown	Y	None
50	18	18	Guerrero, Enrique C	Brother	M	Cha	23.0	Unk		Y	Y	Guam	Unknown	Unknown	Y	Laborer

Street, avenue, road, etc. (column 1): Nuestra Senora de Guadalupe

(CHAMORRO ROOTS GENEALOGY PROJECT™ TRANSCRIPTION)
(COMPILED/TRANSCRIBED BY BERNARD T. PUNZALAN / HTTP://WWW.CHAMORROROOTS.COM)

FOURTEENTH CENSUS OF THE UNITED STATES: 1920—POPULATION
ISLAND OF GUAM

ENUMERATED BY ME ON THE 25th DAY OF March, 1920

Vicente Tydingco ENUMERATOR

DISTRICT 3
NAME OF PLACE Sumay Town

Street	Dwelling	Family	NAME	RELATION	Sex	Color or race	Age	Marital	Attended school since Sept. 1, 1919	Able to read	Able to write	Birthplace of person	Father	Mother	Speak English	OCCUPATION
1	2	3	4	5	6	7	8	9	10	11	12	13	14	15	16	17
	18	18	Guerrero, Juan V	Grandson	M	Cha	4.0	S				Guam	Unknown	Guam		None
	19	19	Guerrero, Carmelo G	Head	M	Cha	55.0	M		Y	Y	Guam	Guam	Guam	N	Farmer
	19	19	Guerrero, Maria P	Wife	F	Cha	53.0	M		Y	Y	Guam	Guam	Guam	N	None
	19	19	Guerrero, Dolores P	Daughter	F	Cha	24.0	S		Y	Y	Guam	Guam	Guam	Y	Laundress
	19	19	Guerrero, Francisca P	Daughter	F	Cha	23.0	S		Y	Y	Guam	Guam	Guam	Y	Laundress
	19	19	Guerrero, Joaquin P	Son	M	Cha	19.0	S	N	Y	Y	Guam	Guam	Guam	Y	Laborer
	19	19	Guerrero, Rufina P	Daughter	F	Cha	16.0	S	N	Y	Y	Guam	Guam	Guam	Y	Laundress
	19	19	Guerrero, Felecita P	Daughter	F	Cha	15.0	S	N	Y	Y	Guam	Guam	Guam	Y	None
	19	19	Guerrero, Carmen P	Daughter	F	Cha	13.0	S	Y	Y	Y	Guam	Guam	Guam	Y	None
	19	19	Guerrero, Juan P	Son	M	Cha	8.0	S	Y			Guam	Guam	Guam	Y	None
	19	19	Guerrero, Antonio P	Grandson	M	Cha	4.0	S				Guam	Unknown	Guam	Y	None
	20	20	Taitano, Margarita P	Head	F	Cha	25.0	M		Y	Y	Guam	Guam	Guam	Y	None
	20	20	Taitano, Rosario P	Daughter	F	Cha	0.1	S				Guam	Guam	Guam	Y	None
	21	21	Sablan, Tomas P	Head	M	Cha	30.0	S		Y	Y	Guam	Guam	Guam	Y	Carpenter
	22	22	Pangelinan, Pedro B	Head	M	Cha	36.0	M		Y	Y	Guam	Guam	Guam	Y	Chauffeur
	22	22	Pangelinan, Cristina S	Wife	F	Cha	35.0	M		Y	Y	Guam	Guam	Guam	N	None
	22	22	Pangelinan, Virginia S	Daughter	F	Cha	11.0	S	Y	Y	Y	Guam	Guam	Guam	Y	None
	22	22	Pangelinan, Emilia S	Daughter	F	Cha	10.0	S	Y	Y	Y	Guam	Guam	Guam	Y	None
	22	22	Pangelinan, Andrea S	Daughter	F	Cha	6.0	S	N			Guam	Guam	Guam		None
	22	22	Pangelinan, Laura S	Daughter	F	Cha	4.0	S				Guam	Guam	Guam		None
	22	22	Pangelinan, Benedicto S	Son	M	Cha	3.0	S				Guam	Guam	Guam		None
	22	22	Pangelinan, Francisco S	Son	M	Cha	0.1	S				Guam	Guam	Guam		None
	22	22	Aguon, Emilia C	Servant	F	Cha	26.0	S		N	N	Guam	Guam	Guam		Servant
	22	22	Taimanglo, Joaquin	Servant	M	Cha	21.0	S	N	Y	Y	Guam	Unknown	Guam		Servant
	23	23	Sablan, Vicente U	Head	M	Cha	62.0	M		Y	Y	Guam	Guam	Guam	Y	Farmer

Street, avenue, road, etc.: Nuestra Senora de Guadalupe

(CHAMORRO ROOTS GENEALOGY PROJECT ™ TRANSCRIPTION)
(COMPILED/TRANSCRIBED BY BERNARD T. PUNZALAN / HTTP://WWW.CHAMORROROOTS.COM)

FOURTEENTH CENSUS OF THE UNITED STATES: 1920—POPULATION

ISLAND OF GUAM

DISTRICT 3
NAME OF PLACE Sumay Town

ENUMERATED BY ME ON THE 26th DAY OF March, 1920

Vicente Tydingco ENUMERATOR

	PLACE OF ABODE			NAME	RELATION	PERSONAL DESCRIPTION				EDUCATION			NATIVITY				OCCUPATION
Street, avenue, road, etc.	Number of dwelling house in order of visitation	Number of family in order of visitation		of each person whose place of abode on January 1, 1920, was in the family. Enter surname, firs, then given name and middle initial. If any. Include every person living on January 1, 1920. Omit children born since January 1, 1920.	Relationship of this Person to the head of the family.	Sex	Color or race	Age at last birthday	Single, married, widowed or divorced	Attended school any time since Sept. 1, 1919	Whether able to read.	Whether able to write.	Place of birth of this person.	Place of birth of father of this person.	Place of birth of mother of this person.	Whether able to speak English.	Trade, profession, or particular kind of work done, as salesman, laborer, clerk, cook, merchant, washerwoman, etc.
1	2	3	4		5	6	7	8	9	10	11	12	13	14	15	16	17
	23	23	Sablan, Carmen S		Wife	F	Cha	60.0	M		Y	Y	Guam	Guam	Guam	Y	None
	23	23	Sablan, Ana S		Daughter	F	Cha	32.0	S		Y	Y	Guam	Guam	Guam	Y	Laundress
	23	23	Sablan, Vicente S		Son	M	Cha	20.0	S	N	Y	Y	Guam	Guam	Guam	Y	Servant
	23	23	Sablan, Jose S		Son	M	Cha	17.0	S	N	Y	Y	Guam	Guam	Guam	Y	Home farm
	23	23	Sablan, Juan S		Grandson	M	Cha	4.0	S				Guam	Guam	Guam		None
	24	24	Santos, Miguel G		Head	M	Cha	39.0	M		Y	Y	Guam	Guam	Guam	Y	Farmer
	24	24	Santos, Carmen S		Wife	F	Cha	37.0	M		Y	Y	Guam	Guam	Guam	N	None
	24	24	Santos, Maria S		Daughter	F	Cha	15.0	S	N	Y	Y	Guam	Guam	Guam	Y	None
	24	24	Santos, Vicente S		Son	M	Cha	11.0	S	Y	Y	Y	Guam	Guam	Guam	Y	None
	24	24	Santos, Antonio S		Son	M	Cha	9.0	S	Y			Guam	Guam	Guam		None
	24	24	Santos, Rosa S		Daughter	F	Cha	6.0	S	N			Guam	Guam	Guam		None
	24	24	Santos, Concepcion S		Daughter	F	Cha	4.0	S				Guam	Guam	Guam		None
	24	24	Santos, Delfina S		Daughter	F	Cha	1.0	S				Guam	Guam	Guam		None
	25	25	Sablan, Juan S		Head	M	Cha	37.0	M		Y	Y	Guam	Guam	Guam	Y	Laundry p?
	25	25	Sablan, Rosa A		Wife	F	Cha	28.0	M		Y	Y	Guam	Guam	Guam	Y	Tailoress
	25	25	Sablan, Joaquin A		Son	M	Cha	10.0	S	Y	Y	Y	Guam	Guam	Guam	Y	None
	25	25	Sablan, Vicente A		Son	M	Cha	8.0	S	Y	Y	Y	Guam	Guam	Guam		None
	25	25	Sablan, Silvestre A		Son	M	Cha	6.0	S	N			Guam	Guam	Guam		None
	26	26	Sablan, Dolores B		Head	F	Cha	60.0	Wd		Y	Y	Guam	Guam	Guam	N	Bank ..?
	26	26	Sablan, Maria B		Daughter	F	Cha	41.0	S		Y	Y	Guam	Guam	Guam	N	None
	26	26	Sablan, Joaquin B		Son	M	Cha	35.0	S		Y	Y	Guam	Guam	Guam	N	None
	27	27	Ishizaki, Francisco		Head	M	Jp	33.0	M		Y	Y	Japan	Japan	Japan	Y	Cook
	27	27	Ishizaki, Filomena P		Wife	F	Cha	28.0	M		Y	Y	Guam	Guam	Guam	N	None
	27	27	Ishizaki, Agueda P		Daughter	F	Jp	2.0	S				Guam	Japan	Guam		None
	27	27	Ishizaki, Joaquin P		Son	M	Jp	1.0	S				Guam	Japan	Guam		None

Nuestra Senora de Guadalupe

26 27 28 29 30 31 32 33 34 35 36 37 38 39 40 41 42 43 44 45 46 47 48 49 50

401

(CHAMORRO ROOTS GENEALOGY PROJECT ™ TRANSCRIPTION)
(COMPILED/TRANSCRIBED BY BERNARD T. PUNZALAN / HTTP://WWW.CHAMORROROOTS.COM)

FOURTEENTH CENSUS OF THE UNITED STATES: 1920—POPULATION
ISLAND OF GUAM

DISTRICT 3
NAME OF PLACE Sumay Town

[Proper name and, also, name of class, as city, town, village, barrio, etc]

ENUMERATED BY ME ON THE 27th DAY OF March, 1920

Vicente Tydingco ENUMERATOR

1 Street, avenue, road, etc.	2 Dwelling	3 Family	4 NAME	5 RELATION	6 Sex	7 Color or race	8 Age	9 Marital	10 School	11 Read	12 Write	13 Birthplace of person	14 Birthplace of father	15 Birthplace of mother	16 English	17 OCCUPATION
Nuestra Senora de Guadalupe	28	28	Perez, Vicente T	Head	M	Cha	40.0	Wd		Y	Y	Guam	Guam	Guam	N	Laborer
	28	28	Perez, Engracia C	Daughter	F	Cha	10.0	S	Y	Y	Y	Guam	Guam	Guam	Y	None
	28	28	Perez, Maria P	Niece	F	Cha	6.0	S	N	Y	Y	Guam	Guam	Guam	N	None
	28	28	Santos, Ana B	Aunt	F	Cha	62.0	S		N	N	Guam	Guam	Guam	N	None
	29	29	Guerrero, Nicolas G	Head	M	Cha	32.0	M		Y	Y	Guam	Guam	Guam	Y	Servant
	29	29	Guerrero, Consuelo P	Wife	F	Cha	26.0	M		Y	Y	Guam	Guam	Guam	Y	Laundress
	29	29	Camacho, Hazel P	Step daughter	F	Cha	6.0	S	N			Guam	Unknown	Guam	N	None
	29	29	Ventura, Maria B?	Mother	F	Cha	52.0	S		N	N	Guam	Guam	Guam	N	None
	30	30	S. Nicolas, Maria C	Head	F	Cha	42.0	S		N	N	Guam	Guam	Guam	N	Laundress
	30	30	S. Nicolas, Regina C	Daughter	F	Cha	1.0	S				Guam	Unknown	Guam	N	None
	31	31	Cruz, Froilan D	Head	M	Cha	59.0	M		Y	Y	Guam	Guam	Guam	N	Farmer
	31	31	Cruz, Magdalena M	Wife	F	Cha	59.0	M		N	N	Guam	Guam	Guam	N	None
	31	31	Cruz, Mariano M	Son	M	Cha	30.0	S		Y	Y	Guam	Guam	Guam	Y	Laborer
	31	31	Cruz, Consolacion M	Daughter	F	Cha	20.0	S	N	Y	Y	Guam	Guam	Guam	Y	Laundress
	31	31	Cruz, Magdalena M	Daughter	F	Cha	14.0	S	N	Y	Y	Guam	Guam	Guam	Y	Servant
	31	31	Cruz, Juan C	Grandson	M	Cha	1.0	S				Guam	Unknown	Guam		None
General Prince Street	32	32	Mendiola, Maria R	Head	F	Cha	68.0	Wd		Y	Y	Guam	Guam	Guam	N	None
	32	32	Mendiola, Nicolasa B	Daughter	F	Cha	30.0	S		Y	Y	Guam	Guam	Guam	Y	Laundress
	32	32	Mendiola, Caridad B	Grand daughter	F	Cha	10.0	S	Y	Y	Y	Guam	Unknown	Guam	Y	None
	32	32	Mendiola, Jesusa B	Grand daughter	F	Cha	2.0	S				Guam	Unknown	Guam		None
	33	33	Rice, John	Head	M	W	61.0	M		Y	Y	Massachusetts	Ireland	Scotland	Y	Seaman USN
	33	33	Rice, Ana M	Wife	F	Cha	35.0	M		Y	Y	Guam	Guam	Guam	Y	None
	33	33	Rice, Ana M jr	Daughter	F	W	11.0	S	Y	Y	Y	Guam	Massachusetts	Guam	Y	None
	33	33	Rice, John T	Son	M	W	8.0	S	Y	Y	Y	Guam	Massachusetts	Guam		None
	33	33	Rice, James H	Son	M	W	7.0	S	Y	Y	Y	Guam	Massachusetts	Guam		None

(CHAMORRO ROOTS GENEALOGY PROJECT ™ TRANSCRIPTION)
(COMPILED/TRANSCRIBED BY BERNARD T. PUNZALAN / HTTP://WWW.CHAMORROROOTS.COM)
FOURTEENTH CENSUS OF THE UNITED STATES: 1920—POPULATION
ISLAND OF GUAM

DISTRICT 3
NAME OF PLACE **Sumay Town**
[Proper name and, also, name of class, as city, town, village, barrio, etc]

ENUMERATED BY ME ON THE 27th DAY OF March, 1920

Vicente Tydingco ENUMERATOR

	Dwelling	Family	NAME	RELATION	Sex	Color or race	Age	Single/married/widowed/divorced	Attended school	able to read	able to write	Place of birth this person	Place of birth father	Place of birth mother	able to speak English	OCCUPATION
26	34	34	Mendiola, Mariano R	Head	M	Cha	48.0	M		Y	Y	Guam	Guam	Guam	N	Carpenter
27	34	34	Mendiola, Maria U	Wife	F	Cha	44.0	M		Y	Y	Guam	Guam	Guam	N	None
28	34	34	Mendiola, Josefa U	Daughter	F	Cha	22.0	S		Y	Y	Guam	Guam	Guam	Y	Laundress
29	34	34	Mendiola, Francisco U	Son	M	Cha	20.0	S	N	Y	Y	Guam	Guam	Guam	Y	Seaman USN
30	34	34	Mendiola, Cristina U	Daughter	F	Cha	17.0	S	N	Y	Y	Guam	Guam	Guam	Y	None
31	34	34	Mendiola, Juan U	Son	M	Cha	16.0	S	N	Y	Y	Guam	Guam	Guam	Y	Laborer
32	34	34	Mendiola, Francisco U jr	Son	M	Cha	14.0	S	N	Y	Y	Guam	Guam	Guam	Y	None
33	34	34	Mendiola, Concepcion U	Daughter	F	Cha	10.0	S	Y	Y	Y	Guam	Guam	Guam	N	None
34	34	34	Mendiola, Tomas U	Son	M	Cha	4.0	S				Guam	Guam	Guam		None
35	34	34	Ulloa, Vicente D	Brother-in-law	M	Cha	35.0	S		Y	Y	Guam	Guam	Guam	Y	Laborer
36	34	34	Ulloa, Juan D	Brother-in-law	M	Cha	34.0	S		Y	Y	Guam	Guam	Guam	Y	Farmer
37	35	35	Sarmiento, Maria P	Head	F	Cha	56.0	Wd		Y	Y	Guam	Guam	Guam	Y	None
38	35	35	Perez, Rosa C	Sister	F	Cha	48.0	D		Y	Y	Guam	Guam	Guam	N	Laundress
39	35	35	Perez, Ignacia C	Sister	F	Cha	40.0	S		Y	Y	Guam	Guam	Guam	N	Laundress
40	35	35	Perez, Inara C	Niece	F	Cha	12.0	S	Y	Y	Y	Guam	Unknown	Guam	Y	None
41	36	36	Sarmiento, Juan P	Head	M	Cha	27.0	M		Y	Y	Guam	Guam	Guam	Y	Seaman USN
42	36	36	Sarmiento, Soledad B	Wife	F	Cha	20.0	M	N	Y	Y	Guam	Guam	Guam	Y	None
43	36	36	Sarmiento, Basilisa B	Daughter	F	Cha	2.0	S				Guam	Guam	Guam		None
44	36	36	Sarmiento, Juan B	Son	M	Cha	0.3	S				Guam	Guam	Guam		None
45	37	37	Gumataotao, Antonio B	Head	M	Cha	49.0	M		Y	Y	Guam	Guam	Guam	N	Farmer
46	37	37	Gumataotao, Adela D	Wife	F	Cha	42.0	M		Y	Y	Guam	Guam	Guam	N	None
47	37	37	Gumataotao, Leon D	Son	M	Cha	23.0	S		Y	Y	Guam	Guam	Guam	Y	Cable operator
48	37	37	Gumataotao, Jose D	Son	M	Cha	22.0	S	N	Y	Y	Guam	Guam	Guam	Y	Laborer
49	37	37	Gumataotao, Maria D	Daughter	F	Cha	20.0	S	N	Y	Y	Guam	Guam	Guam	Y	None
50	37	37	Gumataotao, Joaquin D	Son	M	Cha	18.0	S	N	Y	Y	Guam	Guam	Guam	Y	Servant

Street, avenue, road, etc.: General Prince Street

403

(CHAMORRO ROOTS GENEALOGY PROJECT ™ TRANSCRIPTION)

(COMPILED/TRANSCRIBED BY BERNARD T. PUNZALAN / HTTP://WWW.CHAMORROROOTS.COM)

SHEET NO. _26A_

FOURTEENTH CENSUS OF THE UNITED STATES: 1920–POPULATION

ISLAND OF GUAM

ENUMERATED BY ME ON THE 27th DAY OF March, 1920

Vicente Tydingco ENUMERATOR

DISTRICT 3

NAME OF PLACE **Sumay Town**

[Proper name and, also, name of class, as city, town, village, barrio, etc]

1 Street, avenue, road, etc.	2 Number of dwelling house in order of visitation	3 Number of family in order of visitation	4 NAME	5 RELATION	6 Sex	7 Color or race	8 Age at last birthday	9 Single, married, widowed or divorced	10 Attended school any time since Sept. 1, 1919	11 Whether able to read.	12 Whether able to write.	13 Place of birth of this person.	14 Place of birth of father of this person.	15 Place of birth of mother of this person.	16 Whether able to speak English.	17 OCCUPATION
	37	37	Gumataotao, Rosa D	Daughter	F	Cha	15.0	S	Y	Y	Y	Guam	Guam	Guam	Y	None
	37	37	Gumataotao, Nicolas D	Son	M	Cha	12.0	S	Y	Y	Y	Guam	Guam	Guam	Y	None
	37	37	Gumataotao, Oscar D	Son	M	Cha	5.0	S	N			Guam	Guam	Guam	Y	None
	37	37	Gumataotao, Pedro D	Son	M	Cha	2.0	S				Guam	Guam	Guam		None
	38	38	Borja, Vicente T	Head	M	Cha	54.0	M		Y	Y	Guam	Guam	Guam	Y	Commissioner
	38	38	Borja, Ana S	Wife	F	Cha	43.0	M				Guam	Guam	Guam	N	None
	38	38	Borja, Amelia S	Daughter	F	Cha	22.0	S		Y	Y	Guam	Guam	Guam	Y	None
	38	38	Borja, Maria S	Daughter	F	Cha	19.0	S	N	Y	Y	Guam	Guam	Guam	Y	Saleswoman
	38	38	Borja, Gregorio S	Son	M	Cha	18.0	S	N	Y	Y	Guam	Guam	Guam	Y	Abstract clerk
	38	38	Borja, Rita S	Daughter	F	Cha	14.0	S	Y	Y	Y	Guam	Guam	Guam	Y	None
	38	38	Borja, Ana S	Daughter	F	Cha	12.0	S	Y	Y	Y	Guam	Guam	Guam	Y	None
	38	38	Borja, Vicente S	Son	M	Cha	11.0	S	Y	Y	Y	Guam	Guam	Guam	Y	None
	38	38	Torres, Dolores B	Daughter	F	Cha	24.0	Wd		Y	Y	Guam	Guam	Guam	Y	None
	38	38	Pegurgur, Guadalupe C	Servant	F	Cha	15.0	S	N			Guam	Guam	Guam	Y	Servant
	38	38	Chargualaf, Angelina	Lodger	F	Cha	4.0	S				Guam	Unknown	Guam		None
General Prince Street	39	39	Borja, Lucas T	Head	M	Cha	48.0	M		Y	Y	Guam	Guam	Guam	Y	Farmer
	39	39	Borja, Carmen M	Wife	F	Cha	46.0	M				Guam	Guam	Guam	N	None
	39	39	Borja, Juan M	Son	M	Cha	26.0	S		Y	Y	Guam	Guam	Guam	N	Seaman USN
	39	39	Borja, Ana M	Daughter	F	Cha	24.0	S		Y	Y	Guam	Guam	Guam	Y	Laundress
	39	39	Borja, Rosa M	Daughter	F	Cha	23.0	S		Y	Y	Guam	Guam	Guam	Y	Laundress
	39	39	Borja, Maria M	Daughter	F	Cha	21.0	S	N	Y	Y	Guam	Guam	Guam	Y	Laundress
	39	39	Borja, Jose M	Son	M	Cha	19.0	S	N	Y	Y	Guam	Guam	Guam	Y	Chauffeur
	39	39	Borja, Dolores M	Daughter	F	Cha	17.0	S	N	Y	Y	Guam	Guam	Guam	Y	None
	39	39	Borja, Gregorio M	Son	M	Cha	15.0	S	N	Y	Y	Guam	Guam	Guam	Y	Farm laborer home farm
	39	39	Borja, Concepcion M	Daughter	F	Cha	13.0	S	Y	Y	Y	Guam	Guam	Guam	Y	None

(CHAMORRO ROOTS GENEALOGY PROJECT ™ TRANSCRIPTION)
(COMPILED/TRANSCRIBED BY BERNARD T. PUNZALAN / HTTP://WWW.CHAMORROROOTS.COM)

201b

FOURTEENTH CENSUS OF THE UNITED STATES: 1920-POPULATION

ISLAND OF GUAM

DISTRICT 3

NAME OF PLACE **Sumay Town**

[Proper name and, also, name of class, as city, town, village, barrio, etc]

ENUMERATED BY ME ON THE 29th DAY OF March, 1920

Vicente Tydingco ENUMERATOR

	PLACE OF ABODE		NAME	RELATION	PERSONAL DESCRIPTION				EDUCATION			NATIVITY				OCCUPATION
Street, avenue, road, etc.	Number of dwelling house in order of visitation	Number of family in order of visitation	Name of each person whose place of abode on January 1, 1920, was in the family.	Relationship of this person to the head of the family.	Sex	Color or race	Age at last birthday	Single, married, widowed or divorced	Attended any school since Sept. 1, 1919	Whether able to read.	Whether able to write.	Place of birth of this person.	Place of birth of father of this person.	Place of birth of mother of this person.	Whether able to speak English.	Trade, profession, or particular kind of work done, as salesman, laborer, clerk, cook, merchant, washerwoman, etc.
1	2	3	4	5	6	7	8	9	10	11	12	13	14	15	16	17
	39	39	Borja, Guadalupe M	Daughter	F	Cha	11.0	S	Y	Y	Y	Guam	Guam	Guam	Y	None
	39	39	Borja, Ignacio M	Son	M	Cha	10.0	S	Y	Y	Y	Guam	Guam	Guam	Y	None
	39	39	Borja, Daniel M	Son	M	Cha	7.0	S	Y	Y	Y	Guam	Guam	Guam	Y	None
	40	40	Liizama, Esiquiel	Head	M	Cha	54.0	M		Y	Y	Guam	Guam	Guam	Y	Farmer
	40	40	Liizama, Candelaria C	Wife	F	Cha	42.0	M		Y	Y	Guam	Guam	Guam	N	Laundress
	40	40	Liizama, Rosa C	Daughter	F	Cha	25.0	S		Y	Y	Guam	Guam	Guam	Y	Laundress
	40	40	Liizama, Pedro C	Son	M	Cha	22.0	S		Y	Y	Guam	Guam	Guam	Y	Chauffeur
	40	40	Liizama, Juan C	Son	M	Cha	18.0	S	N	Y	Y	Guam	Guam	Guam	Y	Chauffeur
	40	40	Liizama, Soledad C	Daughter	F	Cha	11.0	S	Y	Y	Y	Guam	Guam	Guam	Y	None
	41	41	Borja, Vicenta C	Head	F	Cha	22.0	M		Y	Y	Guam	Guam	Guam	Y	None
	41	41	Borja, Antonio C	Son	M	Cha	1.0	S				Guam	Guam	Guam		None
General Prince Street	41	41	Borja, Lucas C	Son	M	Cha	0.2	S				Guam	Guam	Guam		
	41	41	Perez, Carmelo C	Uncle	M	Cha	46.0	Wd		Y	Y	Guam	Guam	Guam	N	Farmer
	41	41	Concepcion, Tomasa	Mother	F	Cha	32.0	Wd		Y	Y	Guam	Guam	Guam	N	Laundress
	42	42	Ooka, Takichi O	Head	M	Jp	41.0	M		Y	Y	Japan	Japan	Japan	Y	Salesman
	42	42	Ooka, Rita C	Wife	F	Cha	36.0	M		Y	Y	Guam	Guam	Guam	N	None
	42	42	Ooka, Antonio C	Son	M	Jp	8.0	S	Y	Y	Y	Guam	Japan	Guam	N	None
	42	42	Ooka, Tomas C	Son	M	Jp	6.0	S	N	Y	Y	Guam	Japan	Guam		None
	42	42	Ooka, Antolin C	Son	M	Jp	4.0	S				Guam	Japan	Guam		None
	42	42	Ooka, Jesus C	Son	M	Jp	2.0	S				Guam	Japan	Guam		None
	42	42	Ooka, Mateo C	Son	M	Jp	0.3	S				Guam	Japan	Guam		None
	42	42	Meno, Maria L. Grro	Servant	F	Cha	14.0	S	N	Y	Y	Guam	Guam	Guam	Y	Servant
	43	43	Guzman, Maria D	Head	F	Cha	55.0	Wd		Y	Y	Guam	Guam	Guam	N	None
	43	43	Guzman, Ana D	Daughter	F	Cha	27.0	S		Y	Y	Guam	Guam	Guam	Y	Laundress
	43	43	Guzman, Vicente D	Son	M	Cha	23.0	S		Y	Y	Guam	Guam	Guam	Y	Seaman USN

405

(CHAMORRO ROOTS GENEALOGY PROJECT ™ TRANSCRIPTION)
(COMPILED/TRANSCRIBED BY BERNARD T. PUNZALAN / HTTP://WWW.CHAMORROROOTS.COM)

FOURTEENTH CENSUS OF THE UNITED STATES: 1920-POPULATION
ISLAND OF GUAM

ENUMERATED BY ME ON THE 30th DAY OF March, 1920

Vicente Tydingco ENUMERATOR

DISTRICT 3
NAME OF PLACE Sumay Town
[Proper name and, also, name of class, as city, town, village, barrio, etc]

#	Street	Dwelling (2)	Family (3)	NAME (4)	RELATION (5)	Sex (6)	Color or race (7)	Age (8)	Marital (9)	School (10)	Read (11)	Write (12)	Birthplace (13)	Father birthplace (14)	Mother birthplace (15)	English (16)	OCCUPATION (17)
1		43	43	Guzman, Maria D	Daughter	F	Cha	17.0	S	N	Y	Y	Guam	Guam	Guam	Y	Laundress
2		43	43	Guzman, Juan D	Son	M	Cha	10.0	S	Y	Y	Y	Guam	Guam	Guam	Y	None
3		44	44	Cruz, Manuela U	Head	F	Cha	76.0	Wd		N	N	Guam	Guam	Guam	Y	None
4		44	44	Cruz, Vicente U	Son	M	Cha	39.0	S		Y	Y	Guam	Guam	Guam	Y	Farmer
5		44	44	Cruz, Jose U	Son	M	Cha	34.0	S		Y	Y	Guam	Guam	Guam	Y	Seaman USN
6		44	44	Borja, Rita U	Niece	F	Cha	39.0	S		N	N	Guam	Guam	Guam	N	Servant
7		45	45	Camacho, Jose C	Head	M	Cha	44.0	M		Y	Y	Guam	Unknown	Unknown	N	Farmer
8	General Prince Street	45	45	Camacho, Josefa S	Wife	F	Cha	38.0	M		Y	Y	Guam	Guam	Guam	N	None
9		45	45	Camacho, Julita S	Daughter	F	Cha	14.0	S	N	Y	Y	Guam	Guam	Guam	Y	None
10		45	45	Camacho, Antonia S	Daughter	F	Cha	13.0	S	Y	Y	Y	Guam	Guam	Guam	Y	None
11		45	45	Camacho, Ana S	Daughter	F	Cha	8.0	S	Y			Guam	Guam	Guam		None
12		45	45	Camacho, Francisco S	Son	M	Cha	6.0	S	N			Guam	Guam	Guam		None
13		45	45	Camacho, Maria S	Daughter	F	Cha	2.0	S				Guam	Guam	Guam		None
14		45	45	Camacho, Manuel C	Son	M	Cha	32.0	Wd		Y	Y	Guam	Unknown	Unknown	N	Laborer
15		46	46	Sablan, Joaquin P	Head	M	Cha	41.0	Wd		Y	Y	Guam	Guam	Guam	N	Farmer
16		47	47	Dumanal, Martin L	Head	M	ot	57.0	M		Y	Y	Philippine Islands	Philippine Islands	Philippine Islands	N	Farmer
17		47	47	Dumanal, Vicenta G	Wife	F	Cha	48.0	M		N	N	Guam	Guam	Guam	N	Laundress
18		47	47	Dumanal, Margarita G	Daughter	F	ot	27.0	S		Y	Y	Guam	Philippine Islands	Guam	N	Laborer
19		47	47	Dumanal, Maria G	Daughter	F	ot	22.0	S		Y	Y	Guam	Philippine Islands	Guam	Y	Laundress
20		47	47	Dumanal, Jose G	Son	M	ot	15.0	S	N	Y	Y	Guam	Philippine Islands	Guam	Y	Farm laborer home farm
21		47	47	Dumanal, Rosalia G	Daughter	F	ot	11.0	S	Y	Y	Y	Guam	Philippine Islands	Guam	Y	None
22		47	47	Dumanal, Candelaria G	Daughter	F	ot	9.0	S	Y			Guam	Philippine Islands	Guam	Y	None
23		48	48	Santos, Jose C	Head	M	Cha	45.0	M		Y	Y	Guam	Unknown	Unknown	Y	Farmer
24		48	48	Santos, Maria S	Wife	F	Cha	44.0	M		Y	Y	Guam	Guam	Guam	N	None
25		48	48	Santos, Maria S jr	Daughter	F	Cha	20.0	S	N	Y	Y	Guam	Guam	Guam	Y	None

(CHAMORRO ROOTS GENEALOGY PROJECT ™ TRANSCRIPTION)
(COMPILED/TRANSCRIBED BY BERNARD T. PUNZALAN / HTTP://WWW.CHAMORROROOTS.COM)

FOURTEENTH CENSUS OF THE UNITED STATES: 1920—POPULATION
ISLAND OF GUAM

DISTRICT 3
NAME OF PLACE Sumay Town

ENUMERATED BY ME ON THE 30th DAY OF March, 1920

Vicente Tydingco ENUMERATOR

[Proper name and, also, name of class, as city, town, village, barrio, etc]

Street, avenue, road, etc.	Number of dwelling house	Number of family	NAME	RELATION	Sex	Color or race	Age at last birthday	Single, married, widowed or divorced	Attended school since Sept. 1, 1919	Whether able to read.	Whether able to write.	Place of birth of this person.	Place of birth of father of this person.	Place of birth of mother of this person.	Whether able to speak English.	OCCUPATION
1	2	3	4	5	6	7	8	9	10	11	12	13	14	15	16	17
	48	48	Santos, Jesus S	Son	M	Cha	16.0	S	N	Y	Y	Guam	Guam	Guam	Y	Farm laborer home farm
	48	48	Santos, Amalia S	Daughter	F	Cha	12.0	S	Y			Guam	Guam	Guam	Y	None
	48	48	Santos, Feliciana S	Daughter	F	Cha	7.0	S	Y			Guam	Guam	Guam		None
	48	48	Santos, Rosalia S	Daughter	F	Cha	4.0	S				Guam	Guam	Guam		None
General Prince Street	49	49	Myers, Robert S	Head	M	B	64.0	M		N	N	Bermuda	Bermuda	Bermuda	Y	Laborer
	49	49	Myers, Guadalupe S	Wife	F	Cha	55.0	M		N	N	Guam	Guam	Guam	Y	None
	50	50	Sanchez, Ceriaco A	Head	M	Cha	29.0	M		Y	Y	Guam	Guam	Guam	Y	Carpenter
	50	50	Sanchez, Enriqueta S	Wife	F	Cha	23.0	M		Y	Y	Guam	Guam	Guam	Y	None
	50	50	Arceo, Maria M	Servant	F	Cha	62.0	Wd		Y	Y	Guam	Guam	Guam	N	Servant
	51	51	Cruz, Joaquin B	Head	M	Cha	40.0	M		Y	Y	Guam	Guam	Guam	Y	Farmer
	51	51	Cruz, Guadalupe S	Wife	F	Cha	39.0	M		Y	N	Guam	Guam	Guam	N	None
	51	51	Cruz, Tomas S	Son	M	Cha	3.0	S				Guam	Guam	Guam		None
	51	51	Cruz, Gregorio S	Son	M	Cha	2.0	S				Guam	Guam	Guam		None
	51	51	Santos, Vicente S	Stepson	M	Cha	14.0	S	Y	Y	Y	Guam	Guam	Guam	Y	None
	52	52	Guzman, Juan S	Head	M	Cha	52.0	M		Y	Y	Guam	Guam	Guam	N	Farmer
	52	52	Guzman, Agueda D	Wife	F	Cha	58.0	M		Y	Y	Guam	Guam	Guam	N	None
	52	52	Guzman, Maria S	Sister	F	Cha	32.0	Wd		N	N	Guam	Guam	Guam	N	None
Don Vicente Gomez Street	53	53	Anderson, Felix LG	Head	M	Cha	40.0	M		Y	Y	Guam	Guam	Guam	Y	Laborer
	53	53	Anderson, Isabel A	Wife	F	Cha	30.0	M		Y	Y	Guam	Guam	Guam	N	Laundress
	53	53	Anderson, Mariano A	Son	M	Cha	11.0	S	Y	Y	Y	Guam	Guam	Guam	Y	None
	53	53	Anderson, Jose A	Son	M	Cha	8.0	S	Y	Y		Guam	Guam	Guam		None
	53	53	Anderson, Fidela A	Daughter	F	Cha	4.0	S				Guam	Guam	Guam		None
	53	53	Anderson, Jesus A	Son	M	Cha	1.0	S				Guam	Guam	Guam		None
	53	53	Anderson, Vicenta	Mother	F	Cha	59.0	Wd				Guam	Guam	Guam	N	Midwifery
	53	53	Anderson, Francisco	Brother	M	Cha	22.0	S		Y	Y	Guam	Guam	Guam	Y	Cook

(CHAMORRO ROOTS GENEALOGY PROJECT ™ TRANSCRIPTION)

(COMPILED/TRANSCRIBED BY BERNARD T. PUNZALAN / HTTP://WWW.CHAMORROROOTS.COM)

FOURTEENTH CENSUS OF THE UNITED STATES: 1920-POPULATION

ISLAND OF GUAM

DISTRICT 3

NAME OF PLACE **Sumay Town**

[Proper name and, also, name of class, as city, town, village, barrio, etc]

SHEET NO. _28A_

ENUMERATED BY ME ON THE 30ᵗʰ DAY OF March, 1920

Vicente Tydingco ENUMERATOR

	PLACE OF ABODE			NAME	RELATION	PERSONAL DESCRIPTION					EDUCATION			NATIVITY				OCCUPATION
Street, avenue, road, etc.	Number of dwelling house is order of visitation	Number of family in order of visitation		of each person whose place of abode on January 1, 1920, was in the family. Enter surname, first, then given name and middle initial. If any. Include every person living on January 1, 1920. Omit children born since January 1, 1920.	Relationship of this Person to the head of the family.	Sex	Color or race	Age at last birthday	Single, married, widowed or divorced	Attended school any time since Sept. 1, 1919	Whether able to read.	Whether able to write.	Place of birth of this person.	Place of birth of father of this person.	Place of birth of mother of this person.	Whether able to speak English.	Trade, profession, or particular kind of work done, as salesman, laborer, clerk, cook, merchant, washerwoman, etc.
1	2	3		4	5	6	7	8	9	10	11	12	13	14	15	16	17
	54	54	1	Aguon, Lorenzo Q	Head	M	Cha	35.0	M		Y	Y	Guam	Guam	Guam	N	Farmer
	54	54	2	Aguon, Soledad M	Wife	F	Cha	30.0	M		N	N	Guam	Guam	Guam	N	None
	54	54	3	Aguon, Jose M	Son	M	Cha	5.0	S	N			Guam	Guam	Guam		None
	54	54	4	Aguon, Juan M	Son	M	Cha	3.0	S				Guam	Guam	Guam		None
	54	54	5	Aguon, Ignacio M	Son	M	Cha	0.1	S				Guam	Guam	Guam		None
	55	55	6	Agulto, Juan M	Head	M	Cha	46.0	M		Y	Y	Guam	Philippine Islands	Guam	Y	Farmer
	55	55	7	Agulto, Emilia C	Wife	F	Cha	35.0	M		N	N	Guam	Guam	Guam	N	None
	55	55	8	Agulto, Ana C	Daughter	F	Cha	21.0	S		Y	Y	Guam	Guam	Guam	Y	Laundress
	55	55	9	Agulto, Antonio C	Son	M	Cha	19.0	S	N	Y	Y	Guam	Guam	Guam	Y	Laborer
	55	55	10	Agulto, Pedro C	Son	M	Cha	14.0	S	N	Y	Y	Guam	Guam	Guam	Y	Farm laborer home farm
	55	55	11	Perez, Antonio B	Servant	M	Cha	38.0	S		N	N	Guam	Guam	Guam	N	Servant
	56	56	12	Gumataotao, Juan C	Head	M	Cha	69.0	M		Y	Y	Guam	Guam	Guam	N	None
	56	56	13	Gumataotao, Teresa B	Wife	F	Cha	69.0	M		Y	Y	Guam	Guam	Guam	N	None
	56	56	14	Gumataotao, Jose B	Son	M	Cha	37.0	S		Y	Y	Guam	Guam	Guam	Y	Farmer
	56	56	15	Gumataotao, Andres B	Son	M	Cha	33.0	S		Y	Y	Guam	Guam	Guam	Y	Farm laborer home farm
	57	57	16	Sablan, Juan D	Head	M	Cha	55.0	M		Y	Y	Guam	Guam	Guam	N	Farmer
	57	57	17	Sablan, Elena S	Wife	F	Cha	52.0	M		Y	Y	Guam	Guam	Guam	Y	None
	57	57	18	Sablan, Francisco S	Son	M	Cha	19.0	S	N	Y	Y	Guam	Guam	Guam	Y	Cable operator
	58	58	19	Munoz, Francisco C	Head	M	Cha	28.0	M		Y	Y	Guam	Guam	Guam	Y	Foreman
	58	58	20	Munoz, Dolores S	Wife	F	Cha	25.0	M		Y	Y	Guam	Guam	Guam	Y	None
	58	58	21	Munoz, Isabel S	Daughter	F	Cha	5.0	S	N			Guam	Guam	Guam		None
	58	58	22	Munoz, Juan S	Son	M	Cha	3.0	S				Guam	Guam	Guam		None
	59	59	23	Santos, Luis C	Head	M	Cha	48.0	M		Y	Y	Guam	Guam	Guam	N	Farmer
	59	59	24	Santos, Pilar T	Wife	F	Cha	60.0	M		N	N	Guam	Guam	Guam	N	None
	60	60	25	Salas, Jose N	Head	M	Cha	70.0	M		Y	Y	Guam	Guam	Guam	N	Farmer

Don Vicente Gomez Street

(CHAMORRO ROOTS GENEALOGY PROJECT ™ TRANSCRIPTION)
(COMPILED/TRANSCRIBED BY BERNARD T. PUNZALAN / HTTP://WWW.CHAMORROROOTS.COM)

FOURTEENTH CENSUS OF THE UNITED STATES: 1920-POPULATION

ISLAND OF GUAM

DISTRICT 3
NAME OF PLACE **Sumay Town**
[Proper name and, also, name of class, as city, town, village, barrio, etc]

ENUMERATED BY ME ON THE 31st DAY OF March, 1920

Vicente Tydingco ENUMERATOR

Street, avenue, road, etc.	Number of dwelling house in order of visitation	Number of family in order of visitation	NAME	RELATION	Sex	Color or race	Age at last birthday	Single, married, widowed or divorced	Attended school any time since Sept. 1, 1919	Whether able to read	Whether able to write	Place of birth of this person	Place of birth of father of this person	Place of birth of mother of this person	Whether able to speak English	OCCUPATION
	1	2	3	4	5	6	7	8	9	10	11	12	13	14	15	16	17
	60	60	Salas, Maria S	Wife	F	Cha	56.0	M		N	N	Guam	Guam	Guam	N	None
	60	60	Susuica, Dolores S	Granddaughter	F	Cha	27.0	S		Y	Y	Guam	Guam	Guam	N	Laundress
	60	60	Susuica, Antonio	Grandson	M	Cha	0.2	S				Guam	Unknown	Guam		None
	61	61	Castro, Marta S	Head	F	Cha	29.0	M		Y	Y	Guam	Guam	Guam	Y	None
	61	61	Castro, Concepcion S	Daughter	F	Cha	8.0	S	Y			Guam	Guam	Guam		None
	61	61	Castro, Atanasio S	Son	M	Cha	4.0	S				Guam	Guam	Guam		None
	61	61	Sanchez, Josefa S	Mother	F	Cha	65.0	Wd		N	N	Guam	Guam	Guam	N	None
	61	61	Sanchez, Juana S	Sister	F	Cha	25.0	S		Y	Y	Guam	Guam	Guam	Y	Laundress
	61	61	Sablan, Ana S	Niece	F	Cha	18.0	S	N	Y	Y	Guam	Unknown	Guam	Y	Servant
	61	61	Sablan, Vicente	Nephew	M	Cha	14.0	S	Y	Y	Y	Guam	Unknown	Guam	Y	None
	62	62	Sablan, Jose	Head	M	Cha	30.0	M		Y	Y	Guam	Guam	Guam	Y	Farmer
	62	62	Sablan, Macaila S	Wife	F	Cha	27.0	M		Y	Y	Guam	Guam	Guam	Y	None
	62	62	Sablan, Rosa S	Daughter	F	Cha	9.0	S	Y			Guam	Guam	Guam		None
	62	62	Sablan, Josefa S	Daughter	F	Cha	8.0	S				Guam	Guam	Guam		None
	62	62	Sablan, Lourdes S	Daughter	F	Cha	4.0	S				Guam	Guam	Guam		None
	62	62	Sablan, Manuel S	Son	M	Cha	2.0	S				Guam	Guam	Guam		None
	62	62	Sablan, Francisco S	Son	M	Cha	0.3	S				Guam	Guam	Guam		None
	63	63	Alcantara, Maria S	Head	F	Cha	38.0	Wd		Y	Y	Guam	Guam	Guam	N	Laundress
	63	63	Alcantara, Joaquin S	Son	M	Cha	16.0	S	N	Y	Y	Guam	Guam	Guam	Y	Servant
	63	63	Alcantara, Luis S	Son	M	Cha	11.0	S	Y	Y	Y	Guam	Guam	Guam	Y	None
	64	64	Duenas, Josefa L	Head	F	Cha	51.0	S		Y	Y	Guam	Guam	Guam	N	None
	64	64	Perez, Carmen C	Niece	F	Cha	39.0	S		Y	Y	Guam	Guam	Guam	N	None
	64	64	S. Nicolas, Juan S	Servant	M	Cha	19.0	S		Y	Y	Guam	Unknown	Guam	Y	Servant
	65	65	Ulloa, Mariano D	Head	M	Cha	43.0	M		Y	Y	Guam	Guam	Guam	Y	Farmer
	65	65	Ulloa, Rosa LG	Wife	F	Cha	42.0	M		Y	Y	Guam	Guam	Guam	N	Laundress

Don Vicente Gomez Street

(CHAMORRO ROOTS GENEALOGY PROJECT ™ TRANSCRIPTION)
(COMPILED/TRANSCRIBED BY BERNARD T. PUNZALAN / HTTP://WWW.CHAMORROROOTS.COM)

FOURTEENTH CENSUS OF THE UNITED STATES: 1920-POPULATION
ISLAND OF GUAM

ENUMERATED BY ME ON THE 31st DAY OF March, 1920

Vicente Tydingco ENUMERATOR

DISTRICT 3
NAME OF PLACE **Sumay Town**
[Proper name and, also, name of class, as city, town, village, barrio, etc]

Dwelling	Family	NAME	RELATION	Sex	Color or race	Age	Marital	Attended school since Sept 1, 1919	Read	Write	Birthplace of person	Birthplace of father	Birthplace of mother	Speak English	OCCUPATION
2	3	4	5	6	7	8	9	10	11	12	13	14	15	16	17
65	65	Ulloa, Maria LG	Daughter	F	Cha	13.0	S	N	Y	Y	Guam	Guam	Guam	Y	None
65	65	Ulloa, Joaquina LG	Daughter	F	Cha	6.0	S	N			Guam	Guam	Guam		None
65	65	Ulloa, Juan LG	Son	M	Cha	2.0	S				Guam	Guam	Guam		None
66	66	Olano, Angel U	Head	M	W	28.0	S		Y	Y	Spain	Spain	Spain	Y	Missonary
67	67	Perez, Ana T	Head	F	Cha	42.0	Wd		N	N	Guam	Guam	Guam	N	Laundress
67	67	Perez, Ana T jr	Daughter	F	Cha	10.0	S	Y	Y	Y	Guam	Guam	Guam	N	None
67	67	Perez, Beatris T	Daughter	F	Cha	4.0	S				Guam	Guam	Guam		None
67	68	Quintanilla, Joaquin R	Head	M	Cha	25.0	M	N	Y	Y	Guam	Guam	Guam	Y	Laborer
67	68	Quintanilla, Antonia P	Wife	F	Cha	20.0	M	N	N	N	Guam	Guam	Guam	N	None
67	68	Quintanilla, Lucy P	Daughter	F	Cha	2.0	S				Guam	Guam	Guam		None
68	69	Diaz, Juan M	Head	M	Cha	34.0	M		Y	Y	Guam	Guam	Guam	N	Farmer
68	69	Diaz, Ana P	Wife	F	Cha	32.0	M		Y	Y	Guam	Unknown	Guam	N	None
68	69	Diaz, Vicente P	Son	M	Cha	13.0	S	Y	Y	Y	Guam	Guam	Guam	Y	None
68	69	Diaz, Ana P jr	Daughter	F	Cha	6.0	S	N			Guam	Guam	Guam		None
68	69	Diaz, Juana P	Daughter	F	Cha	5.0	S	N			Guam	Guam	Guam		None
68	69	Diaz, Dolores P	Daughter	F	Cha	2.0	S				Guam	Guam	Guam		None
68	69	Diaz, Magdalena M	Mother	F	Cha	56.0	Wd		Y	Y	Guam	Guam	Guam	N	None
69	70	Aquiningoc, Antonio B	Head	M	Cha	57.0	M		Y	Y	Guam	Guam	Guam	Y	Farmer
69	70	Aquiningoc, Dolores P	Wife	F	Cha	49.0	M	N	N	N	Guam	Guam	Guam	N	None
69	70	Aquiningoc, Trinidad P	Daughter	F	Cha	28.0	S		Y	Y	Guam	Guam	Guam	Y	None
69	70	Aquiningoc, Susana P	Daughter	F	Cha	17.0	S	N	Y	N	Guam	Guam	Guam	Y	None
69	70	Aquiningoc, Amparo P	Daughter	F	Cha	11.0	S	Y	Y	Y	Guam	Guam	Guam	Y	None
69	70	Aquiningoc, Grabiel P	Grandson	M	Cha	4.0	S				Guam	Unknown	Guam		None
69	70	Aquiningoc, Santiago P	Grandson	M	Cha	1.0	S				Guam	Unknown	Unknown		None
70	71	Lizama, Benedicto F	Head	M	Cha	60.0	S		Y	Y	Guam	Guam	Guam	N	Farmer

Street: Don Vicente Gomez Street

(CHAMORRO ROOTS GENEALOGY PROJECT ™ TRANSCRIPTION)
(COMPILED/TRANSCRIBED BY BERNARD T. PUNZALAN / HTTP://WWW.CHAMORROROOTS.COM)

FOURTEENTH CENSUS OF THE UNITED STATES: 1920-POPULATION
ISLAND OF GUAM

204b

DISTRICT 3
NAME OF PLACE **Sumay Town**
[Proper name and, also, name of class, as city, town, village, barrio, etc]

ENUMERATED BY ME ON THE 31st DAY OF March, 1920

Vicente Tydingco ENUMERATOR

Street	Dwelling No.	Family No.	NAME	RELATION	Sex	Color or race	Age	Marital	Attended school since Sept. 1, 1919	Read	Write	Birthplace of person	Birthplace of father	Birthplace of mother	Speak English	OCCUPATION
					6	7	8	9	10	11	12	13	14	15	16	17
Don Vicente Gomez Street	71	72	Javier, Joaquina G	Head	F	Cha	49.0	S		Y	Y	Guam	Philippine Islands	Guam	Y	Servant
	72	73	Cruz, Ignacio M	Head	M	Cha	53.0	M		Y	Y	Guam	Guam	Guam	Y	Farmer
	72	73	Cruz, Maria A	Wife	F	Cha	52.0	M		Y	Y	Guam	Guam	Guam	N	None
	72	73	Cruz, Dolores A	Daughter	F	Cha	24.0	S		Y	Y	Guam	Guam	Guam	Y	Teach
	72	73	Cruz, Ana A	Daughter	F	Cha	22.0	S		Y	Y	Guam	Guam	Guam	Y	None
	72	73	Cruz, Josefina A	Daughter	F	Cha	19.0	S	N	Y	Y	Guam	Guam	Guam	Y	None
	72	73	Cruz, Maria A	Daughter	F	Cha	17.0	S	N	Y	Y	Guam	Guam	Guam	Y	None
	72	73	Cruz, Ignacio A	Son	M	Cha	15.0	S	N	Y	Y	Guam	Guam	Guam	Y	None
	73	74	Babauta, Felix C	Head	M	Cha	22.0	M		Y	Y	Guam	Guam	Guam	Y	Chauffeur
	73	74	Babauta, Rita C	Wife	F	Cha	21.0	M	N	Y	Y	Guam	Guam	Guam	Y	None
	73	74	Babauta, Carmen C	Mother	F	Cha	56.0	Wd		Y	Y	Guam	Guam	Guam	N	None
	73	74	Babauta, Juan C	Brother	M	Cha	17.0	S	N	Y	Y	Guam	Guam	Guam	Y	Servant
Velasco Street	74	75	Aquiningoc, Francisco	Head	M	Cha	41.0	M		Y	Y	Guam	Guam	Guam	Y	Farmer
	74	75	Aquiningoc, Maria C	Wife	F	Cha	39.0	M		N	N	Guam	Guam	Guam	N	None
	74	75	Aquiningoc, Rosalia C	Daughter	F	Cha	17.0	S	N	Y	Y	Guam	Guam	Guam	Y	None
	75	76	Concepcion, Jose B	Head	M	Cha	59.0	M		N	N	Guam	Guam	Guam	Y	None
	75	76	Concepcion, Ana L	Daughter	F	Cha	37.0	S	N	Y	Y	Guam	Guam	Guam	Y	None
	75	76	Concepcion, Juan C	Grandson	M	Cha	1.0	S				Guam	Unknown	Guam	N	None
	76	77	Charfauros, Juan B	Head	M	Cha	27.0	M		Y	Y	Guam	Guam	Guam	Y	Laborer
	76	77	Charfauros, Teordora F	Wife	F	Cha	24.0	M		Y	Y	Guam	Guam	Guam	Y	None
	76	77	Charfauros, Jose F	Son	M	Cha	1.0	S				Guam	Guam	Guam	N	None
	76	77	Feja, Candelaria S	Sister-in-law	F	Cha	18.0	S	N	Y	Y	Guam	Guam	Guam	Y	None
	77	78	Perez, Maria C	Head	F	Cha	54.0	Wd		Y	Y	Guam	Guam	Guam	N	None
	77	78	Mendiola, Maria P	Grand daughter	F	Cha	16.0	D	N	Y	Y	Guam	Guam	Guam	Y	None
	78	79	Sablan, Francisco S	Head	M	Cha	40.0	M		Y	Y	Guam	Guam	Guam	Y	Farmer

(CHAMORRO ROOTS GENEALOGY PROJECT ™ TRANSCRIPTION)
(COMPILED/TRANSCRIBED BY BERNARD T. PUNZALAN / HTTP://WWW.CHAMORROROOTS.COM)

FOURTEENTH CENSUS OF THE UNITED STATES: 1920-POPULATION
ISLAND OF GUAM

ENUMERATED BY ME ON THE 31st DAY OF March, 1920

Vicente Tydingco ENUMERATOR

DISTRICT 3
NAME OF PLACE Sumay Town

1	2	3	4 NAME	5 RELATION	6 Sex	7 Color or race	8 Age	9	10	11	12	13	14	15	16	17 OCCUPATION
	77	79	Sablan, Maria S	Wife	F	Cha	41.0	M		Y	Y	Guam	Guam	Guam	N	Laundress
	78	80	Cruz, Guadalupe M	Head	F	Cha	45.0	M		Y	Y	Guam	Guam	Guam	N	None
	78	80	Cruz, Juan M	Son	M	Cha	21.0	S	N	Y	Y	Guam	Guam	Guam	Y	Deputy Commissioner
	78	80	Cruz, Joaquin M	Son	M	Cha	13.0	S	Y	Y	Y	Guam	Guam	Guam	Y	Servant
	78	80	Cruz, Jose M	Son	M	Cha	11.0	S	Y	Y	Y	Guam	Guam	Guam	Y	None
	79	81	Duenas, Juan S	Head	M	Cha	43.0	M		Y	Y	Guam	Guam	Guam	Y	Laborer
	79	81	Duenas, Carmen A	Wife	F	Cha	33.0	M		Y	Y	Guam	Guam	Guam	N	None
	79	81	Duenas, Segundo A	Son	M	Cha	0.3	S				Guam	Guam	Guam		None
Velasco Street	79	81	Aguiningoc, Jesus C	Nephew	M	Cha	17.0	S	N	Y	Y	Guam	Guam	Guam		Farm laborer home farm
	80	82	Wisle, Ignacio T	Head	M	Cha	60.0	S		Y	Y	Guam	Guam	Guam	N	Farmer
	80	82	Wisle, Dolores T	Sister	F	Cha	53.0	S		N	N	Guam	Guam	Guam	N	None
	80	82	Wisle, Jose W	Nephew	M	Cha	26.0	S		Y	N	Guam	Unknown	Guam	Y	Cook
	81	83	Cruz, Nicolasa C	Head	M	Cha	50.0	M		Y	Y	Guam	Guam	Guam	Y	Farmer
	81	83	Cruz, Ignacia D	Wife	F	Cha	38.0	M		Y	Y	Guam	Guam	Guam	N	Laundress
	81	83	Duenas, Paz D	Step daughter	F	Cha	18.0	S	N	Y	Y	Guam	Unknown	Guam	Y	Laundress
	81	83	Duenas, Jesus D	Stepson	M	Cha	16.0	S	N	Y	Y	Guam	Unknown	Guam	Y	Servant
	81	83	Cruz, Nicolas A	Nephew	M	Cha	11.0	S	Y	Y	Y	Guam	Unknown	Guam	Y	None
	82	84	Lizama, Felix F	Head	M	Cha	56.0	M		N	N	Guam	Guam	Guam	N	Farmer
	82	84	Lizama, Rosa F	Wife	F	Cha	50.0	M		Y	Y	Guam	Guam	Guam	Y	None
	82	84	Lizama, Manuel D	Son	M	Cha	29.0	S		Y	Y	Guam	Guam	Guam	Y	Farmer
	82	84	Lizama, Maria D	Daughter	F	Cha	24.0	S		Y	Y	Guam	Guam	Guam	Y	None
	82	84	Lizama, Vicente D	Son	M	Cha	20.0	S	N	Y	Y	Guam	Guam	Guam	Y	Laborer
	82	84	Lizama, Francisco D	Son	M	Cha	12.0	S	Y	Y	Y	Guam	Guam	Guam	Y	None
	82	84	Duenas, Agueda S	Daughter-in-law	F	Cha	31.0	M		Y	Y	Guam	Guam	Guam	Y	None
	82	85	Diaz, Joaquin M	Head	M	Cha	28.0	M		Y	Y	Guam	Guam	Guam	Y	Chauffeur

(CHAMORRO ROOTS GENEALOGY PROJECT ™ TRANSCRIPTION)
(COMPILED/TRANSCRIBED BY BERNARD T. PUNZALAN / HTTP://WWW.CHAMORROROOTS.COM)

FOURTEENTH CENSUS OF THE UNITED STATES: 1920-POPULATION
ISLAND OF GUAM

DISTRICT 3
NAME OF PLACE **Sumay Town**

[Proper name and, also, name of class, as city, town, village, barrio, etc]

ENUMERATED BY ME ON THE 1st DAY OF April, 1920

Vicente Tydingco ENUMERATOR

Street, avenue, road, etc.	Number of dwelling house in order of visitation	Number of family in order of visitation	NAME	RELATION	Sex	Color or race	Age at last birthday	Single, married, widowed or divorced	Attended school any time since Sept. 1, 1919	Whether able to read	Whether able to write	Place of birth of this person	Place of birth of father of this person	Place of birth of mother of this person	Whether able to speak English	OCCUPATION
	1	2	3	4	5	6	7	8	9	10	11	12	13	14	15	16	17
	82	85	Diaz, Concepcion L	Wife	F	Cha	22.0	M		Y	Y	Guam	Guam	Guam	Y	None
	83	86	Guzman, Antonio S	Head	M	Cha	50.0	M		Y	Y	Guam	Guam	Guam	N	Fisherman
	83	86	Guzman, Dolores C	Wife	F	Cha	49.0	M		N	N	Guam	Unknown	Unknown	N	None
	83	86	Guzman, Guadalupe C	Daughter	F	Cha	24.0	S		Y	Y	Guam	Guam	Guam	Y	Laundress
	83	86	Guzman, Josefa C	Daughter	F	Cha	19.0	S	N	Y	Y	Guam	Guam	Guam	Y	None
	83	86	Guzman, Petronila G	Grand daughter	F	Cha	0.3	S				Guam	Unknown	Guam		None
	83	86	Guzman, Ernestina G	Grand daughter	F	Cha	0.2	S				Guam	Unknown	Guam		None
	84	87	Pangelinan, Ana T	Head	F	Cha	46.0	Wd		Y	Y	Guam	Guam	Guam	N	Retail merchant
	84	87	Pangelinan, Josefina T	Daughter	F	Cha	15.0	S	Y	Y	Y	Guam	Guam	Guam	Y	None
	84	87	Pangelinan, Gloria T	Daughter	F	Cha	11.0	S	Y	Y	Y	Guam	Guam	Guam	Y	None
	84	87	Pangelinan, Felix T jr	Son	M	Cha	9.0	S	Y	Y	Y	Guam	Guam	Guam		None
	84	87	Anderson, Antonia	Servant	F	Cha	16.0	S	N	Y	Y	Guam	Guam	Guam	Y	Servant
	85	88	Cruz, Ignacio B	Head	M	Cha	60.0	M		Y	Y	Guam	Guam	Guam	N	Farmer
	85	88	Cruz, Carmen A	Wife	F	Cha	40.0	M		Y	Y	Guam	Guam	Guam	N	None
	85	88	Cruz, Maria A	Daughter	F	Cha	11.0	S	Y	Y	Y	Guam	Guam	Guam	Y	None
	85	88	Cruz, Ignacio A	Son	M	Cha	9.0	S	Y			Guam	Guam	Guam		None
	85	88	Cruz, Ana A	Daughter	F	Cha	7.0	S	N			Guam	Guam	Guam		None
	86	89	Charfauros, Maria T	Head	F	Cha	56.0	Wd		Y	Y	Guam	Guam	Guam	N	None
	86	89	Charfauros, Ana T	Daughter	F	Cha	25.0	S		Y	Y	Guam	Guam	Guam	N	None
	86	89	Charfauros, Joaquin	Son	M	Cha	19.0	S	N	Y	Y	Guam	Guam	Guam	Y	Cable operator
	87	90	Mendiola, Nicolas C	Head	M	Cha	55.0	M		Y	Y	Guam	Guam	Guam	N	Farmer
	87	90	Mendiola, Ana S	Wife	F	Cha	53.0	M		Y	Y	Guam	Guam	Guam	N	None
	87	90	Mendiola, Luis S	Son	M	Cha	31.0	S		N	N	Guam	Guam	Guam	Y	Laborer
	87	90	Mendiola, Martina S	Daughter	F	Cha	29.0	S		Y	Y	Guam	Guam	Guam	Y	Retail merchant
	87	90	Mendiola, Consolacion S	Daughter	F	Cha	20.0	S	N	Y	Y	Guam	Guam	Guam	Y	Baker

Velasco Street

| 26 |
| 27 |
| 28 |
| 29 |
| 30 |
| 31 |
| 32 |
| 33 |
| 34 |
| 35 |
| 36 |
| 37 |
| 38 |
| 39 |
| 40 |
| 41 |
| 42 |
| 43 |
| 44 |
| 45 |
| 46 |
| 47 |
| 48 |
| 49 |
| 50 |

SHEET NO.
_31A_

(CHAMORRO ROOTS GENEALOGY PROJECT ™ TRANSCRIPTION)
(COMPILED/TRANSCRIBED BY BERNARD T. PUNZALAN / HTTP://WWW.CHAMORROROOTS.COM)

FOURTEENTH CENSUS OF THE UNITED STATES: 1920—POPULATION
ISLAND OF GUAM

ENUMERATED BY ME ON THE 1st DAY OF April, 1920

Vicente Tydingco ENUMERATOR

DISTRICT 3
NAME OF PLACE Sumay Town

[Proper name and, also, name of class, as city, town, village, barrio, etc]

Street, avenue, road, etc.	Number of dwelling house is order of visitation	Number of family in order of visitation	NAME	RELATION	Sex	Color or race	Age at last birthday	Single, married, widowed or divorced	Attended any school since Sept. 1, 1919	Whether able to read.	Whether able to write.	Place of birth of this person.	Place of birth of father of this person.	Place of birth of mother of this person.	Whether able to speak English.	OCCUPATION
1	2	3	4	5	6	7	8	9	10	11	12	13	14	15	16	17
	87	90	Mendiola, Dolores S	Daughter	F	Cha	17.0	S	N	Y	Y	Guam	Guam	Guam	Y	None
	87	90	Mendiola, Beatris S	Daughter	F	Cha	15.0	S	Y	Y	Y	Guam	Guam	Guam	Y	None
	87	90	Mendiola, Ignacio S	Son	M	Cha	12.0	S	Y	Y	Y	Guam	Guam	Guam	Y	None
	88	91	Perez, Ana M	Head	F	Cha	27.0	M		Y	Y	Guam	Guam	Guam	N	None
	88	91	Perez, Juan M	Son	M	Cha	4.0	S				Guam	Guam	Guam		None
	88	91	Perez, Jose M	Son	M	Cha	2.0	S				Guam	Guam	Guam		None
	89	92	Carbullido, Baltazar	Head	M	Cha	20.0	S	N	Y	Y	Guam	Guam	Guam	Y	Teacher
	90	93	Mendiola, Vicente Q	Head	M	Cha	44.0	S		Y	Y	Guam	Guam	Guam	N	Farmer
	90	93	Mendiola, Ignacio Q	Brother	M	Cha	40.0	S		Y	Y	Guam	Guam	Guam	Y	Laborer
	90	93	Mendiola, Maria Q	Sister	F	Cha	32.0	S		Y	Y	Guam	Guam	Guam	Y	Laundress
	91	94	Cruz, Jose B	Head	M	Cha	47.0	M		Y	Y	Guam	Guam	Guam	N	Farmer
	91	94	Cruz, Josefa C	Wife	F	Cha	43.0	M		Y	Y	Guam	Guam	Guam	N	None
	91	94	Cruz, Jesus C	Son	M	Cha	19.0	S	N	Y	Y	Guam	Guam	Guam	Y	Chauffeur
	91	94	Cruz, Rosa C	Daughter	F	Cha	13.0	S	Y	Y	Y	Guam	Guam	Guam	Y	None
	91	94	Cruz, Ana C	Daughter	F	Cha	11.0	S	Y	Y	Y	Guam	Guam	Guam	Y	None
	91	94	Cruz, Maria C	Daughter	F	Cha	9.0	S	Y	Y	Y	Guam	Guam	Guam	Y	None
	91	94	Cruz, Juan C	Son	M	Cha	4.0	S				Guam	Guam	Guam		None
	91	94	Cruz, Luis C	Son	M	Cha	2.0	S				Guam	Guam	Guam		None
	92	95	Cruz, Juan B	Head	M	Cha	45.0	M		Y	Y	Guam	Guam	Guam	Y	Carpenter
	92	95	Cruz, Caridad B	Wife	F	Cha	35.0	M		Y	Y	Guam	Unknown	Guam	Y	Laundress
	93	96	Cruz, Vicente B	Head	M	Cha	40.0	S		Y	Y	Guam	Guam	Guam	Y	Laborer
	93	96	Cruz, Rita B	Sister	F	Cha	49.0	S		Y	Y	Guam	Guam	Guam	N	Laundress
	93	96	Cruz, Maria B	Sister	F	Cha	44.0	S		Y	Y	Guam	Guam	Guam	N	Laundress
	93	96	Cruz, Ana B	Sister	F	Cha	38.0	S		Y	Y	Guam	Guam	Guam	N	Laundress
	93	96	Santos, Maria C	Servant	F	Cha	12.0	S	N	Y	Y	Guam	Guam	Guam	N	Servant

Velasco Street

(CHAMORRO ROOTS GENEALOGY PROJECT ™ TRANSCRIPTION)
(COMPILED/TRANSCRIBED BY BERNARD T. PUNZALAN / HTTP://WWW.CHAMORROROOTS.COM)

206b

FOURTEENTH CENSUS OF THE UNITED STATES: 1920-POPULATION

ISLAND OF GUAM

SHEET NO. _31B_

DISTRICT 3
NAME OF PLACE **Sumay Town**

[Proper name and, also, name of class, as city, town, village, barrio, etc]

ENUMERATED BY ME ON THE 2nd DAY OF April, 1920

Vicente Tydingco ENUMERATOR

	PLACE OF ABODE			NAME	RELATION	PERSONAL DESCRIPTION					EDUCATION			NATIVITY				OCCUPATION
Street, avenue, road, etc.	Number of dwelling house in order of visitation	Number of family in order of visitation		Name of each person whose place of abode on January 1, 1920, was in the family.	Relationship of this Person to the head of the family.	Sex	Color or race	Age at last birthday	Single, married, widowed or divorced	Attended school any time since Sept. 1, 1919	Whether able to read.	Whether able to write.	Place of birth of this person.	Place of birth of father of this person.	Place of birth of mother of this person.	Whether able to speak English.	Trade, profession, or particular kind of work done, as salesman, laborer, clerk, cook, merchant, washerwoman, etc.
1	2	3		4	5	6	7	8	9	10	11	12	13	14	15	16	17
26	94	97		Quintanilla, Felix V	Head	M	Cha	45.0	M		Y	Y	Guam	Guam	Guam	N	Farmer
27	94	97		Quintanilla, Soledad L	Wife	F	Cha	35.0	M		Y	Y	Guam	Guam	Guam	N	None
28	94	97		Quintanilla, Ana L	Daughter	F	Cha	13.0	S	Y	Y	Y	Guam	Guam	Guam	Y	None
29	94	97		Quintanilla, Carmen L	Daughter	F	Cha	4.0	S				Guam	Guam	Guam		None
30	94	97		Quintanilla, Jose L	Son	M	Cha	1.0	S				Guam	Guam	Guam		None
31	94	97		Manibusan, Antonia D	Aunt	F	Cha	57.0	S		N	N	Guam	Guam	Guam	N	None
32	95	98		Quintanilla, Jose C	Head	M	Cha	72.0	M		Y	Y	Guam	Guam	Guam	N	Farmer
33	95	98		Quintanilla, Manuela V	Wife	F	Cha	73.0	M		Y	N	Guam	Guam	Guam	N	None
34	95	98		Quintanilla, Ana V	Daughter	F	Cha	42.0	D		Y	Y	Guam	Guam	Guam	Y	None
35	95	98		Quintanilla, Carmen V	Daughter	F	Cha	40.0	S		N	N	Guam	Guam	Guam	N	Laundress
36	95	98		Quintanilla, Jose V	Son	M	Cha	33.0	S		Y	Y	Guam	Guam	Guam	Y	Laborer
37	95	98		Quintanilla, Pedro Q	Grandson	M	Cha	1.0	S				Guam	Guam	Guam		None
38	96	99		Quintanilla, Guillermo V	Head	M	Cha	44.0	M		Y	Y	Guam	Guam	Guam	Y	Laborer
39	96	99		Quintanilla, Carmen SN	Wife	F	Cha	33.0	M		N	N	Guam	Guam	Guam	N	None
40	96	99		Quintanilla, Antonio SN	Son	M	Cha	11.0	S	Y	Y	Y	Guam	Guam	Guam	N	None
41	96	99		Quintanilla, Lucio SN	Son	M	Cha	1.0	S				Guam	Guam	Guam		None
42	96	99		Quintanilla, Matias SN	Son	M	Cha	1.0	S				Guam	Guam	Guam		None
43	97	100		Cruz, Antonio B	Head	M	Cha	54.0	M		N	N	Guam	Guam	Guam	N	Laborer
44	97	100		Cruz, Maria Q	Wife	F	Cha	51.0	M		Y	Y	Guam	Guam	Guam	N	None
45	97	100		Cruz, Guadalupe C	Daughter	F	Cha	22.0	S		Y	Y	Guam	Guam	Guam	Y	None
46	97	100		Cruz, Jose C	Son	M	Cha	20.0	S	N	Y	Y	Guam	Guam	Guam	Y	Farmer
47	97	100		Cruz, Ana C	Daughter	F	Cha	18.0	S	N	Y	Y	Guam	Guam	Guam	Y	None
48	97	100		Cruz, Soledad C	Daughter	F	Cha	15.0	S	N	Y	Y	Guam	Guam	Guam	Y	None
49	97	100		Cruz, Vicente C	Son	M	Cha	12.0	S	Y	Y	Y	Guam	Guam	Guam	Y	None
50	98	101		Sablan, Joaquin C	Head	M	Cha	39.0	M		Y	Y	Guam	Guam	Guam	Y	Laborer

Velasco Street

415

(CHAMORRO ROOTS GENEALOGY PROJECT ™ TRANSCRIPTION)

(COMPILED/TRANSCRIBED BY BERNARD T. PUNZALAN / HTTP://WWW.CHAMORROROOTS.COM)

207

FOURTEENTH CENSUS OF THE UNITED STATES: 1920—POPULATION
ISLAND OF GUAM

ENUMERATED BY ME ON THE 2nd DAY OF April, 1920

Vicente Tydingco ENUMERATOR

DISTRICT 3
NAME OF PLACE Sumay Town
[Proper name and, also, name of class, as city, town, village, barrio, etc]

Street, avenue, road, etc.	Number of dwelling house in order of visitation	Number of family in order of visitation	NAME	RELATION	Sex	Color or race	Age at last birthday	Single, married, widowed or divorced	Attended school any time since Sept. 1, 1919	Whether able to read	Whether able to write	Place of birth of this person	Place of birth of father of this person	Place of birth of mother of this person	Whether able to speak English	OCCUPATION
1	2	3	4	5	6	7	8	9	10	11	12	13	14	15	16	17
Velasco Street	98	101	Sablan, Guadalupe P	Wife	F	Cha	31.0	M		Y	Y	Guam	Guam	Guam	Y	None
	98	101	Sablan, Tomasa P	Daughter	F	Cha	11.0	S	Y	Y	Y	Guam	Guam	Guam	N	None
	98	101	Sablan, Vicente P	Son	M	Cha	7.0	S	Y			Guam	Guam	Guam		None
	98	101	Sablan, Enrique P	Son	M	Cha	5.0	S	N			Guam	Guam	Guam		None
	98	101	Sablan, Jose P	Son	M	Cha	3.0	S				Guam	Guam	Guam		None
	98	101	Sablan, Jesusa P	Daughter	F	Cha	1.0	S				Guam	Guam	Guam		None
	98	101	Taijeron, Silvano	Servant	M	Cha	20.0	S	N	Y	Y	Guam	Unknown	Guam	Y	Servant
	99	102	Sablan, Juan C	Head	M	Cha	26.0	M		Y	Y	Guam	Guam	Guam	Y	Seaman USN
	99	102	Sablan, Rosa L	Wife	F	Cha	27.0	M		Y	Y	Guam	Guam	Guam	Y	None
	99	102	Limtiaco, Dolores M	Mother-in-law	F	Cha	54.0	Wd		Y	Y	Guam	Guam	Guam	N	None
	100	103	Cruz, Jesus C	Head	M	Cha	28.0	M		Y	Y	Guam	Guam	Guam	Y	Carpenter
	100	103	Cruz, Tomasa Q	Wife	F	Cha	35.0	M		N	N	Guam	Guam	Guam	N	None
	100	103	Cruz, Jose Q	Son	M	Cha	9.0	S	Y			Guam	Guam	Guam		None
	100	103	Cruz, Juan Q	Son	M	Cha	2.0	S				Guam	Guam	Guam		None
	100	103	Cruz, Jesus Q	Son	M	Cha	1.0	S				Guam	Guam	Guam		None
Gomez Quintero Street	101	104	Quintanilla, Felix C	Head	M	Cha	43.0	M		N	N	Guam	Guam	Guam	N	Farmer
	101	104	Quintanilla, Milagros P	Wife	F	Cha	33.0	M		N	N	Guam	Guam	Guam	N	None
	101	104	Quintanilla, Antonia P	Daughter	F	Cha	14.0	S	N	Y	Y	Guam	Guam	Guam	Y	None
	101	104	Quintanilla, Manuel P	Son	M	Cha	6.0	S	N			Guam	Guam	Guam		None
	101	104	Quintanilla, Ignacio P	Son	M	Cha	4.0	S				Guam	Guam	Guam		None
	101	104	Quintanilla, Maria P	Daughter	F	Cha	2.0	S				Guam	Guam	Guam		None
	102	105	Camacho, Ines C	Head	F	Cha	75.0	S		N	N	Guam	Unknown	Guam	N	None
	102	105	Camacho, Jose C	Son	M	Cha	36.0	S		Y	Y	Guam	Unknown	Guam	N	Laborer
	103	106	Camacho, Tomas S	Head	M	Cha	49.0	M		Y	Y	Guam	Guam	Guam	N	Farmer
	103	106	Camacho, Dolores M	Wife	F	Cha	47.0	M		N	N	Guam	Guam	Guam	N	None

(CHAMORRO ROOTS GENEALOGY PROJECT ™ TRANSCRIPTION)
(COMPILED/TRANSCRIBED BY BERNARD T. PUNZALAN / HTTP://WWW.CHAMORROROOTS.COM)

FOURTEENTH CENSUS OF THE UNITED STATES: 1920-POPULATION

ISLAND OF GUAM

DISTRICT 3
NAME OF PLACE **Sumay Town**
[Proper name and, also, name of class, as city, town, village, barrio, etc]

ENUMERATED BY ME ON THE 3rd DAY OF April, 1920

Vicente Tydingco ENUMERATOR

	PLACE OF ABODE			NAME	RELATION	PERSONAL DESCRIPTION				EDUCATION			NATIVITY				OCCUPATION
Street, avenue, road, etc.	Number of dwelling house in order of visitation	Number of family in order of visitation		of each person whose place of abode on January 1, 1920, was in the family.	Relationship of this person to the head of the family.	Sex	Color or race	Age at last birthday	Single, married, widowed or divorced	Attended school any time since Sept. 1, 1919	Whether able to read.	Whether able to write.	Place of birth of this person.	Place of birth of father of this person.	Place of birth of mother of this person.	Whether able to speak English.	Trade, profession, or particular kind of work done, as salesman, laborer, clerk, cook, merchant, washerwoman, etc.
	2	3	4		5	6	7	8	9	10	11	12	13	14	15	16	17
26	103	106		Camacho, Antonio M	Son	M	Cha	20.0	S	N	Y	Y	Guam	Guam	Guam	Y	Seaman USN
27	104	107		Quintanilla, Maria C	Head	F	Cha	54.0	Wd		Y	Y	Guam	Unknown	Guam	N	None
28	104	107		Quintanilla, Jose C	Son	M	Cha	20.0	S	N	Y	Y	Guam	Guam	Guam	Y	Laborer
29	105	108		Grey, Paul	Head	M	W	42.0	M		Y	Y	Germany	Germany	Germany	Y	Retail merchant
30	105	108		Grey, Rosario C	Wife	F	Cha	22.0	M		Y	Y	Guam	Guam	Guam	Y	Saleswoman
31	105	108		Grey, Wilhelmina	Daughter	F	W	1.0	S				Guam	Germany	Guam		None
32	105	108		Grey, Gustav	Son	M	W	0.1	S				Guam	Germany	Guam		None
33	105	108		Maekawa, Rosa T	Sister-in-law	F	Cha	14.0	S	N	Y	Y	Guam	Japan	Guam	Y	Laundress
34	105	108		Maekawa, Aurelia T	Sister-in-law	F	Jp	11.0	S	Y	Y	Y	Guam	Japan	Guam	Y	None
35	105	108		Duenas, Jose C	Grand father-in-law	M	Cha	68.0	Wd		Y	Y	Guam	Guam	Guam	N	None
36	106	109		Aquiningoc, Antonio D	Head	M	Cha	44.0	M		Y	Y	Guam	Guam	Guam	N	Laborer
37	106	109		Aquiningoc, Ana D	Wife	F	Cha	34.0	M		Y	Y	Guam	Guam	Guam	N	None
38	106	109		Aquiningoc, Vicente D	Son	M	Cha	16.0	S	N	Y	Y	Guam	Guam	Guam	Y	Laborer
39	106	109		Aquiningoc, Manuel C	Nephew	M	Cha	14.0	S	Y	Y	Y	Guam	Guam	Guam	Y	None
40	107	110		Mendiola, Catalino Q	Head	M	Cha	30.0	M		Y	Y	Guam	Guam	Guam	Y	Laborer
41	107	110	Gomez Quinteco Street	Mendiola, Preciosa G	Wife	F	Cha	30.0	M		Y	Y	Guam	Guam	Guam	N	None
42	107	110		Mendiola, Jose G	Son	M	Cha	1.0	S				Guam	Guam	Guam		None
43	107	110		Mendiola, Jesus G	Son	M	Cha	0.3	S				Guam	Guam	Guam		None
44	108	111		Mendiola, Antonio R	Head	M	Cha	56.0	M		Y	Y	Guam	Guam	Guam	N	Farmer
45	108	111		Mendiola, Ana Q	Wife	F	Cha	57.0	M		Y	Y	Guam	Guam	Guam	N	None
46	108	111		Mendiola, Rosa Q	Daughter	F	Cha	33.0	S		Y	Y	Guam	Guam	Guam	N	None
47	108	111		Mendiola, Juan Q	Son	M	Cha	32.0	S		Y	Y	Guam	Guam	Guam	Y	Farm laborer
48	108	111		Mendiola, Satrunino Q	Son	M	Cha	28.0	S		Y	Y	Guam	Guam	Guam	Y	Laborer
49	108	111		Mendiola, Manuel Q	Son	M	Cha	25.0	S		Y	Y	Guam	Guam	Guam	Y	Laborer
50	108	111		Mendiola, Dolores Q	Daughter	F	Cha	19.0	S	N	Y	Y	Guam	Guam	Guam	Y	None

417

(CHAMORRO ROOTS GENEALOGY PROJECT ™ TRANSCRIPTION)
(COMPILED/TRANSCRIBED BY BERNARD T. PUNZALAN / HTTP://WWW.CHAMORROROOTS.COM)

FOURTEENTH CENSUS OF THE UNITED STATES: 1920–POPULATION
ISLAND OF GUAM

ENUMERATED BY ME ON THE 3rd DAY OF April, 1920

Vicente Tydingco ENUMERATOR

DISTRICT 3
NAME OF PLACE Sumay Town

[Proper name and, also, name of class, as city, town, village, barrio, etc]

Street	Dwelling No.	Family No.	NAME	RELATION	Sex	Color or race	Age	Single/married/etc	School since Sept 1 1919	Read	Write	Birthplace person	Birthplace father	Birthplace mother	Speak English	OCCUPATION
1	2	3	4	5	6	7	8	9	10	11	12	13	14	15	16	17
	108	111	Mendiola, Ignacio Q	Son	M	Cha	17.0	S	N	Y	Y	Guam	Guam	Guam	Y	Servant
	108	111	Mendiola, Maria Q	Daughter	F	Cha	14.0	S	N	Y	Y	Guam	Guam	Guam	Y	None
	109	112	Sablan, Luis C	Head	M	Cha	32.0	M		Y	Y	Guam	Guam	Guam	Y	Farmer
	109	112	Sablan, Asuncion S	Wife	F	Cha	38.0	M		Y	Y	Guam	Unknown	Unknown	Y	None
	109	112	Sablan, Rosalia S	Step daughter	F	Cha	17.0	S	N	Y	Y	Guam	Unknown	Guam	Y	None
	110	113	Chin, Juan Q	Head	M	Chin	45.0	M				China	China	China	Y	Fisherman
	110	113	Chin, Engracia C	Wife	F	Cha	33.0	M		Y	Y	Guam	Guam	Guam	N	None
	110	113	Chin, Aleandro C	Son	M	Chin	12.0	S	Y	Y	Y	Guam	China	Guam	Y	None
	110	113	Chin, Gregorio C	Son	M	Chin	11.0	S	Y	Y	Y	Guam	China	Guam	Y	None
	110	113	Chin, Regina C	Daughter	F	Chin	6.0	S	N			Guam	China	Guam	Y	None
	110	113	Chin, Regino C	Son	M	Chin	4.0	S				Guam	China	Guam	Y	None
	110	113	Chin, Rosalia C	Daughter	F	Chin	3.0	S				Guam	China	Guam	Y	None
	110	113	Chin, Delfina C	Daughter	F	Chin	1.0	S				Guam	China	Guam	Y	None
	111	114	Aflleje, Ignacia P	Head	F	Cha	50.0	Wd	N	N	N	Guam	Guam	Guam	N	Farmer
	111	114	Aflleje, Ana P	Daughter	F	Cha	31.0	S	Y	Y	Y	Guam	Guam	Guam	Y	Laundress
	111	114	Aflleje, Vicenta P	Daughter	F	Cha	23.0	S	Y	Y	Y	Guam	Guam	Guam	Y	Laundress
	111	114	Aflleje, Encarnacion P	Daughter	F	Cha	16.0	S	N	Y	Y	Guam	Guam	Guam	Y	Farm laborer home farm
	111	114	Aflleje, Manuel P	Son	M	Cha	11.0	S	N	Y	Y	Guam	Guam	Guam	Y	None
	112	115	Crisostomo, Ramon J	Head	M	Cha	60.0	M		Y	Y	Guam	Guam	Guam	N	Farmer
	112	115	Crisostomo, Ignacia M	Wife	F	Cha	59.0	M		Y	Y	Guam	Guam	Guam	N	None
	112	115	Crisostomo, Hinaro M	Son	M	Cha	27.0	S		Y	Y	Guam	Guam	Guam	Y	Farm laborer
	112	115	Crisostomo, Concepcion M	Daughter	F	Cha	25.0	S		Y	Y	Guam	Guam	Guam	Y	None
	112	115	Crisostomo, Soledad M	Daughter	F	Cha	20.0	S	N	Y	Y	Guam	Guam	Guam	Y	None
	112	115	Crisostomo, Maria M	Daughter	F	Cha	19.0	S		Y	Y	Guam	Guam	Guam	Y	None
	113	116	Crisostomo, Francisco M	Head	M	Cha	29.0	M		Y	Y	Guam	Guam	Guam	Y	Laborer

Street: Gomez Quinteno Street

(CHAMORRO ROOTS GENEALOGY PROJECT ™ TRANSCRIPTION)
(COMPILED/TRANSCRIBED BY BERNARD T. PUNZALAN / HTTP://WWW.CHAMORROROOTS.COM)

FOURTEENTH CENSUS OF THE UNITED STATES: 1920-POPULATION

ISLAND OF GUAM

208b

DISTRICT 3
NAME OF PLACE Sumay Town

[Proper name and, also, name of class, as city, town, village, barrio, etc]

ENUMERATED BY ME ON THE 5th DAY OF April, 1920

Vicente Tydingco ENUMERATOR

	Dwelling house no.	Family no.	NAME	RELATION	Sex	Color or race	Age at last birthday	Single, married, widowed or divorced	Attended school since Sept. 1, 1919	Able to read	Able to write	Place of birth of this person	Place of birth of father	Place of birth of mother	Able to speak English	OCCUPATION
26	113	116	Crisostomo, Margarita M	Wife	F	Cha	30.0	M		Y	Y	Guam	Guam	Guam	N	None
27	113	116	Crisostomo, Concepcion M	Daughter	F	Cha	0.3	S				Guam	Guam	Guam		None
28	114	117	Lizama, Francisca Q	Head	F	Cha	88.0	Wd		N	N	Guam	Guam	Guam	N	None
29	115	118	Santos, Manuel C	Head	M	Cha	45.0	M		Y	Y	Guam	Guam	Guam	N	Farmer
30	115	118	Santos, Maria P	Wife	F	Cha	36.0	M		N	N	Guam	Guam	Guam	N	None
31	116	119	Guzman, Francisco S	Head	M	Cha	44.0	M		Y	Y	Guam	Guam	Guam	N	Farmer
32	116	119	Guzman, Maria C	Wife	F	Cha	50.0	M		N	N	Guam	Guam	Guam	N	None
33	116	119	Guzman, Juan C	Son	M	Cha	12.0	S	Y	Y	Y	Guam	Guam	Guam		None
34	116	119	Guzman, Jose C	Son	M	Cha	11.0	S	Y	Y	Y	Guam	Guam	Guam		None
35	116	119	Guzman, Joaquin C	Son	M	Cha	8.0	S	Y			Guam	Guam	Guam		None
36	116	119	Guzman, Jesus C	Son	M	Cha	6.0	S	N			Guam	Guam	Guam		None
37	116	119	Guzman, Carmen C	Daughter	F	Cha	3.0	S				Guam	Guam	Guam		None
38	116	119	Guzman, Antonia C	Daughter	F	Cha	1.0	S				Guam	Guam	Guam		None
39	116	120	Concepcion, Clara	Head	F	Cha	49.0	S		N	N	Guam	Guam	Guam	N	None
40	116	120	Concepcion, Vicenta C	Daughter	F	Cha	42.0	S		N	N	Guam	Unknown	Guam	N	None
41	116	120	Concepcion, Dolores C	Daughter	F	Cha	28.0	S		N	N	Guam	Unknown	Guam	N	Laundress
42	117	121	Quintanilla, Manuel	Head	M	Cha	42.0	M		Y	Y	Guam	Guam	Guam	Y	Coswain USN
43	117	121	Quintanilla, Ana	Wife	F	Cha	37.0	M		N	N	Guam	Guam	Guam	N	None
44	117	121	Quintanilla, Jose	Son	M	Cha	16.0	S	N	Y	Y	Guam	Guam	Guam	Y	None
45	117	121	Quintanilla, Andresina	Daughter	F	Cha	14.0	S	Y	Y	Y	Guam	Guam	Guam	Y	None
46	117	121	Quintanilla, Juan	Son	M	Cha	9.0	S	Y	Y	Y	Guam	Guam	Guam		None
47	117	121	Quintanilla, Vicente	Son	M	Cha	6.0	S	N	N	N	Guam	Guam	Guam		None
48	117	121	Quintanilla, Soledad	Daughter	F	Cha	3.0	S				Guam	Guam	Guam		None
49	118	122	Santos, Jose L	Head	M	Cha	60.0	M		Y	Y	Guam	Guam	Guam	N	Farmer
50	118	122	Santos, Alejandra S	Wife	F	Cha	33.0	M		N	N	Guam	Guam	Guam	N	None

Street: Gomez Quinteto Street

419

(CHAMORRO ROOTS GENEALOGY PROJECT ™ TRANSCRIPTION)
(COMPILED/TRANSCRIBED BY BERNARD T. PUNZALAN / HTTP://WWW.CHAMORROROOTS.COM)

FOURTEENTH CENSUS OF THE UNITED STATES: 1920-POPULATION
ISLAND OF GUAM

ENUMERATED BY ME ON THE 6th DAY OF April, 1920

Vicente Tydingco ENUMERATOR

DISTRICT 3
NAME OF PLACE Sumay Town

[Proper name and, also, name of class, as city, town, village, barrio, etc]

Street	Dwelling house no.	Family no.	NAME	RELATION	Sex	Color or race	Age at last birthday	Single, married, widowed or divorced	Attended school since Sept. 1, 1919	Able to read	Able to write	Place of birth of this person	Place of birth of father	Place of birth of mother	Able to speak English	OCCUPATION
	118	122	Santos, Maria S	Daughter	F	Cha	5.0	S	N			Guam	Guam	Guam		None
	118	122	Santos, Abraham S	Son	M	Cha	2.0	S				Guam	Guam	Guam		None
	118	122	Santos, Joaquin S	Son	M	Cha	0.1	S				Guam	Guam	Guam		None
	118	122	Quinata, Eugenio A	Servant	M	Cha	15.0	S	N	Y	Y	Guam	Guam	Guam		Servant
	118	122	Tajalle, Maria T	Servant	F	Cha	20.0	S		Y	Y	Guam	Guam	Guam		Servant
	119	123	Lizama, Jose D	Head	M	Cha	32.0	M		Y	Y	Guam	Guam	Guam	N	Laundress
	119	123	Lizama, Dolores Q	Wife	F	Cha	27.0	M		N	N	Guam	Guam	Guam	N	None
	119	123	Lizama, Daniel Q	Son	M	Cha	4.0	S				Guam	Guam	Guam		None
	119	123	Lizama, Cecilia Q	Daughter	F	Cha	2.0	S				Guam	Guam	Guam		None
	119	123	Quitugua, Ana Q	Step daughter	F	Cha	7.0	S	N			Guam	Unknown	Guam		None
	119	123	Quitugua, Antonia C	Mother-in-law	F	Cha	65.0	Wd		Y	Y	Guam	Guam	Guam	N	Laundress
Gomez Quintero Street	120	124	Camacho, Guillermo S	Head	M	Cha	60.0	M		Y	Y	Guam	Guam	Guam	N	Farmer
	120	124	Camacho, Rita T	Wife	F	Cha	58.0	M		N	N	Guam	Guam	Guam	N	None
	120	124	Camacho, Tomas T	Son	M	Cha	32.0	Wd		Y	Y	Guam	Guam	Guam	Y	Laborer
	120	124	Camacho, Maria T	Daughter	F	Cha	18.0	S		Y	Y	Guam	Guam	Guam	Y	Laundress
	120	124	Quintanilla, Jose C	Grandson	M	Cha	20.0	S	N	Y	Y	Guam	Guam	Guam	Y	Servant
	120	124	Quintanilla, Francisco C	Grandson	M	Cha	14.0	S	N	Y	Y	Guam	Guam	Guam	Y	Farm laborer home farm
	120	124	Quintanilla, Maria C	Grand daughter	F	Cha	12.0	S	Y	Y	Y	Guam	Guam	Guam	Y	None
	120	124	Quintanilla, Francisca C	Grand daughter	F	Cha	9.0	S	Y	Y	Y	Guam	Guam	Guam	Y	None
	121	125	Aquiningoc, Jose C	Head	M	Cha	21.0	M	N	Y	Y	Guam	Guam	Guam	Y	Farmer
	121	125	Aquiningoc, Rosario Q	Wife	F	Cha	36.0	M		N	N	Guam	Unknown	Guam	N	None
	121	125	Quintanilla, Francisca	Step daughter	F	Cha	9.0	S	Y			Guam	Guam	Guam		None
	121	125	Aquiningoc, Dolores A	Aunt	F	Cha	35.0	S	N	N	N	Guam	Guam	Guam	N	Laundress
	121	125	Aquiningoc, Francisco	Cousin	M	Cha	3.0	S				Guam	Guam	Guam		None
	122	126	Sanchez, Lorenzo Q	Head	M	Cha	27.0	M		Y	Y	Guam	Guam	Guam	N	Farmer

(CHAMORRO ROOTS GENEALOGY PROJECT ™ TRANSCRIPTION)
(COMPILED/TRANSCRIBED BY BERNARD T. PUNZALAN / HTTP://WWW.CHAMORROROOTS.COM)

FOURTEENTH CENSUS OF THE UNITED STATES: 1920—POPULATION
ISLAND OF GUAM

209b

DISTRICT 3
NAME OF PLACE **Sumay Town**
[Proper name and, also, name of class, as city, town, village, barrio, etc]

ENUMERATED BY ME ON THE 6th DAY OF April, 1920

Vicente Tydingco ENUMERATOR

	Dwelling (2)	Family (3)	NAME (4)	RELATION (5)	Sex (6)	Color/race (7)	Age (8)	S/M/Wd (9)	School (10)	Read (11)	Write (12)	Birth (13)	Father (14)	Mother (15)	Eng. (16)	OCCUPATION (17)
26	122	126	Sanchez, Amparo G	Wife	F	Cha	36.0	M		Y	Y	Guam	Guam	Guam	N	None
27	122	126	Aquiningoc, Mariano C	Nephew	M	Cha	11.0	S	Y	Y	Y	Guam	Guam	Guam	N	None
28	122	126	Quinata, Faustina	Servant	F	Cha	4.0	S				Guam	Guam	Guam	N	None
29	123	127	Aquiningoc, Vicente B	Head	M	Cha	42.0	M		Y	Y	Guam	Guam	Guam	N	Farmer
30	123	127	Aquiningoc, Magdalena W	Wife	F	Cha	45.0	M		N	N	Guam	Guam	Guam	N	None
31	123	127	Aquiningoc, Antonio W	Son	M	Cha	19.0	S	N	Y	Y	Guam	Guam	Guam	Y	None
32	123	127	Aquiningoc, Ana W	Daughter	F	Cha	8.0	S	Y	Y	Y	Guam	Guam	Guam	N	None
33	123	127	Aquiningoc, Joaquin W	Son	M	Cha	6.0	S	N			Guam	Guam	Guam	N	None
34	124	128	Pangelinan, Luis	Head	M	Cha	28.0	M		N	N	Guam	Guam	Guam	N	Laborer
35	124	128	Pangelinan, Rufina C	Wife	F	Cha	29.0	M		N	N	Guam	Guam	Guam	N	Laundress
36	124	128	Pangelinan, Jose C	Son	M	Cha	10.0	S	Y	Y	Y	Guam	Guam	Guam	N	None
37	125	129	Wisle, Supiano T	Head	M	Cha	55.0	Wd		N	N	Guam	Guam	Guam	N	Farmer
38	125	129	Wisle, Vicente D	Son	M	Cha	26.0	S		Y	Y	Guam	Guam	Guam	Y	Farmer
39	125	129	Wisle, Juan D	Son	M	Cha	18.0	S	N	Y	Y	Guam	Guam	Guam	Y	Servant
40	125	129	Wisle, Maria D	Daughter	F	Cha	16.0	S	N	Y	Y	Guam	Guam	Guam	Y	None
41	126	130	Santos, Pedro T	Head	M	Cha	39.0	M		Y	Y	Guam	Guam	Guam	N	Farmer
42	126	130	Santos, Maria L	Wife	F	Cha	32.0	M		Y	Y	Guam	Guam	Guam	N	Servant
43	126	130	Santos, Jose L	Son	M	Cha	10.0	S	Y	Y	Y	Guam	Guam	Guam	N	None
44	126	130	Santos, Concepcion L	Daughter	F	Cha	7.0	S	Y			Guam	Guam	Guam		None
45	126	130	Santos, Ana L	Daughter	F	Cha	3.0	S				Guam	Guam	Guam		None
46	126	130	Santos, Dolores L	Daughter	F	Cha	1.0	S				Guam	Guam	Guam		None
47	127	131	Fegurgur, Domingo C	Head	M	Cha	58.0	Wd		N	N	Guam	Guam	Guam	N	Farmer
48	127	131	Fegurgur, Jesus S	Son	M	Cha	12.0	S	Y	Y	Y	Guam	Guam	Guam	Y	None
49	127	131	Fegurgur, Joaquin S	Son	M	Cha	10.0	S	Y	Y	Y	Guam	Guam	Guam	N	None
50	127	131	Lizama, Victorina T	Mother-in-law	F	Cha	77.0	Wd		N	N	Guam	Guam	Guam	N	None

Street, avenue, road, etc. (column 1): Gomez Quintero Street

(CHAMORRO ROOTS GENEALOGY PROJECT ™ TRANSCRIPTION)
(COMPILED/TRANSCRIBED BY BERNARD T. PUNZALAN / HTTP://WWW.CHAMORROROOTS.COM)

FOURTEENTH CENSUS OF THE UNITED STATES: 1920—POPULATION
ISLAND OF GUAM

DISTRICT 3
NAME OF PLACE Sumay Town
[Proper name and, also, name of class, as city, town, village, barrio, etc]

ENUMERATED BY ME ON THE 7th DAY OF April, 1920

Vicente Tydingco ENUMERATOR

Street, avenue, road, etc.	Number of dwelling house in order of visitation	Number of family in order of visitation	NAME of each person whose place of abode on January 1, 1920, was in the family.	RELATION Relationship of this Person to the head of the family.	Sex	Color or race	Age at last birthday	Single, married, widowed or divorced	Attended school any time since Sept. 1, 1919	Whether able to read.	Whether able to write.	Place of birth of this person.	Place of birth of father of this person.	Place of birth of mother of this person.	Whether able to speak English.	OCCUPATION Trade, profession, or particular kind of work done
1	2	3	4	5	6	7	8	9	10	11	12	13	14	15	16	17
Gomez Quintero Street	128	132	Concepcion, Teodoro L	Head	M	Cha	26.0	M		Y	Y	Guam	Guam	Guam	Y	Laborer
	128	132	Concepcion, Eduviges D	Wife	F	Cha	34.0	M		Y	Y	Guam	Guam	Guam	Y	None
	128	132	Concepcion, Delfina D	Daughter	F	Cha	5.0	S				Guam	Guam	Guam		None
	128	132	Concepcion, Prudencio D	Son	M	Cha	1.0	S				Guam	Guam	Guam		None
	128	132	Concepcion, Elizabeth D	Daughter	F	Cha	0.1	S				Guam	Guam	Guam		None
	129	133	Anderson, Juan	Head	M	Cha	30.0	M		Y	Y	Guam	Guam	Guam	Y	Seaman USN
	129	133	Anderson, Concepcion D	Wife	F	Cha	20.0	M		Y	Y	Guam	Guam	Guam	Y	None
	129	133	Anderson, Rosalina C	Daughter	F	Cha	6.0	S				Guam	Guam	Guam		None
	129	133	Anderson, Jose C	Son	M	Cha	4.0	S				Guam	Guam	Guam		None
	130	134	Duenas, Antonio S	Head	M	Cha	52.0	Wd		Y	Y	Guam	Guam	Guam	Y	Farmer
	130	134	Duenas, Soledad C	Daughter	F	Cha	18.0	S	N	Y	Y	Guam	Guam	Guam	Y	None
	130	134	Duenas, Jose C	Son	M	Cha	15.0	S	Y	Y	Y	Guam	Guam	Guam	Y	None
	130	134	Duenas, Carmen C	Daughter	F	Cha	14.0	S	Y			Guam	Guam	Guam	Y	None
	131	135	Ada, Rosa A	Head	F	Cha	42.0	Wd		N	N	Guam	Unknown	Guam	N	Laundress
Togal Street	132	136	Quintanilla, Vicente C	Head	M	Cha	48.0	M		Y	Y	Guam	Guam	Guam	N	Carpenter
	132	136	Quintanilla, Getrudes R	Wife	F	Cha	47.0	M		N	N	Guam	Guam	Guam	N	None
	132	136	Quintanilla, Jose R	Son	M	Cha	26.0	S		Y	Y	Guam	Guam	Guam	Y	Laborer
	132	136	Quintanilla, Ignacio R	Son	M	Cha	20.0	S	N	Y	Y	Guam	Guam	Guam	Y	Laborer
	132	136	Quintanilla, Juan R	Son	M	Cha	16.0	S	N	Y	Y	Guam	Guam	Guam	Y	Farm laborer home farm
	132	136	Quintanilla, Rosalia R	Daughter	F	Cha	15.0	S	N	Y	Y	Guam	Guam	Guam	Y	None
	132	136	Quintanilla, Rita R	Daughter	F	Cha	13.0	S	Y	Y	Y	Guam	Guam	Guam	Y	None
	132	136	Quintanilla, Carmen R	Daughter	F	Cha	10.0	S	Y	Y	Y	Guam	Guam	Guam	N	None
	132	136	Quintanilla, Francisco R	Son	M	Cha	7.0	S	N			Guam	Guam	Guam	N	None
	133	137	Sablan, Pedro D	Head	M	Cha	66.0	D		Y	Y	Guam	Guam	Guam	N	None
	134	138	Santos, Agustin S	Head	M	Cha	40.0	M		Y	Y	Guam	Guam	Guam	Y	Laborer

422

210b

(CHAMORRO ROOTS GENEALOGY PROJECT ™ TRANSCRIPTION)
(COMPILED/TRANSCRIBED BY BERNARD T. PUNZALAN / HTTP://WWW.CHAMORROROOTS.COM)

FOURTEENTH CENSUS OF THE UNITED STATES: 1920-POPULATION
ISLAND OF GUAM

ENUMERATED BY ME ON THE 7th DAY OF April, 1920

Vicente Tydingco ENUMERATOR

DISTRICT 3
NAME OF PLACE Sumay Town

[Proper name and, also, name of class, as city, town, village, barrio, etc]

	PLACE OF ABODE			NAME	RELATION	PERSONAL DESCRIPTION					EDUCATION			NATIVITY				OCCUPATION
Street, avenue, road, etc.	Number of dwelling house is order of visitation	Number of family in order of visitation		of each person whose place of abode on January 1, 1920, was in the family. Enter surname, firs, then given name and middle initial. If any. Include every person living on January 1, 1920. Omit children born since January 1, 1920.	Relationship of this Person to the head of the family.	Sex	Color or race	Age at last birthday	Single, married, widowed or divorced	Attended school any time since sept. 1, 1919	Whether able to read.	Whether able to write.	Place of birth of this person.	Place of birth of father of this person.	Place of birth of mother of this person.	Whether able to speak English.	Trade, profession, or particular kind of work done, as salesman, laborer, clerk, cook, merchant, washerwoman, etc.
1	2	3	4		5	6	7	8	9	10	11	12	13	14	15	16	17
26	134	138	Santos, Teresa M		Wife	F	Cha	35.0	M		Y	Y	Guam	Guam	Guam	N	None
27	134	138	Santos, Maria M		Daughter	F	Cha	14.0	S	N	Y	Y	Guam	Guam	Guam	N	None
28	134	138	Santos, Rosa M		Daughter	F	Cha	10.0	S	N	Y	Y	Guam	Guam	Guam	N	None
29	134	138	Santos, Gil M		Son	M	Cha	3.0	S				Guam	Guam	Guam		None
30	134	138	Santos, Jose M		Brother	M	Cha	20.0	S	N	Y	Y	Guam	Guam	Guam	N	Laborer
31	134	138	Santos, Juana S		Mother	F	Cha	65.0	Wd		N	N	Guam	Guam	Guam	N	None
32	134	138	Mendiola, Ana A		Mother-in-law	F	Cha	70.0	Wd		N	N	Guam	Guam	Guam	N	None
33	135	139	Mendiola, Joaquina C		Head	F	Cha	30.0	Wd		N	N	Guam	Guam	Guam		None
34	135	139	Mendiola, Geronimo C		Son	M	Cha	6.0	S	N			Guam	Guam	Guam		None
35	135	139	Mendiola, Juan C		Son	M	Cha	5.0	S				Guam	Guam	Guam		None
36	135	139	Mendiola, Graviel C		Son	M	Cha	2.0	S				Guam	Guam	Guam		None
37	136	140	Aquiningoc, Juan B		Head	M	Cha	49.0	M		Y	Y	Guam	Guam	Guam	N	None
38	136	140	Aquiningoc, Ana T		Wife	F	Cha	41.0	M		Y	Y	Guam	Guam	Guam	N	None
39	136	140	Aquiningoc, Maria T		Daughter	F	Cha	19.0	S	N	Y	Y	Guam	Guam	Guam	Y	Laundress
40	136	140	Aquiningoc, Joaquin T		Son	M	Cha	16.0	S	N	Y	Y	Guam	Guam	Guam	Y	Servant
41	136	140	Aquiningoc, Antonio T		Son	M	Cha	12.0	S	Y	Y	Y	Guam	Guam	Guam	Y	None
42	137	141	Arceo, Jose M		Head	M	Cha	57.0	M		Y	Y	Guam	Guam	Guam	Y	Farmer
43	137	141	Arceo, Natividad N		Wife	F	Cha	58.0	M		N	N	Guam	Guam	Guam	N	None
44	137	141	Arceo, Guadalupe N		Daughter	F	Cha	18.0	S		Y	Y	Guam	Guam	Guam	Y	None
45	138	142	Perez, Jose C		Head	M	Cha	34.0	M		Y	Y	Guam	Guam	Guam	Y	Seaman USN
46	138	142	Perez, Rafaela C		Wife	F	Cha	36.0	M		Y	Y	Guam	Guam	Guam	Y	None
47	138	142	Perez, Laurion C		Son	M	Cha	14.0	S	Y	Y	Y	Guam	Guam	Guam	Y	None
48	138	142	Perez, Rosario C		Daughter	F	Cha	6.0	S	N			Guam	Guam	Guam		None
49	138	142	Perez, Concepcion C		Daughter	F	Cha	0.1	S				Guam	Guam	Guam		None
50	138	142	Rosa, Carmen Q		Mother-in-law	F	Cha	70.0	Wd		N	N	Guam	Guam	Guam	N	None

Togal Street

423

(CHAMORRO ROOTS GENEALOGY PROJECT™ TRANSCRIPTION)
(COMPILED/TRANSCRIBED BY BERNARD T. PUNZALAN / HTTP://WWW.CHAMORROROOTS.COM)

FOURTEENTH CENSUS OF THE UNITED STATES: 1920-POPULATION
ISLAND OF GUAM

ENUMERATED BY ME ON THE 8th DAY OF April, 1920

Vicente Tydingco ENUMERATOR

DISTRICT 3
NAME OF PLACE **Sumay Town**

[Proper name and, also, name of class, as city, town, village, barrio, etc]

	PLACE OF ABODE			NAME	RELATION	PERSONAL DESCRIPTION					EDUCATION			NATIVITY				OCCUPATION
Street, avenue, road, etc.	Number of dwelling house in order of visitation	Number of family in order of visitation		Name of each person whose place of abode on January 1, 1920, was in the family. Enter surname, first, then given name and middle initial. If any. Include every person living on January 1, 1920. Omit children born since January 1, 1920.	Relationship of this Person to the head of the family.	Sex	Color or race	Age at last birthday	Single, married, widowed or divorced	Attended school any time since Sept. 1, 1919	Whether able to read.	Whether able to write.	Place of birth of this person.	Place of birth of father of this person.	Place of birth of mother of this person.	Whether able to speak English.	Trade, profession, or particular kind of work done, as salesman, laborer, clerk, cook, merchant, washerwoman, etc.
1	2	3	4		5	6	7	8	9	10	11	12	13	14	15	16	17
1	138	142	Reyes, Rosa R		Sister-in-law	F	Cha	47.0	Wd		N	N	Guam	Guam	Guam	N	None
2	138	142	Reyes, Teresa R		Niece	F	Cha	24.0	S		N	N	Guam	Guam	Guam	N	None
3	138	142	Reyes, Ana R		Niece	F	Cha	21.0	S	N	Y	Y	Guam	Guam	Guam	Y	None
4	138	142	Reyes, Laurion R		Nephew	M	Cha	16.0	S	N	Y	Y	Guam	Guam	Guam	Y	Farm laborer home farm
5	138	142	S. Nicolas, Ignacia R		Sister-in-law	F	Cha	30.0	S		N	N	Guam	Guam	Guam	N	Laundress
6	138	142	S. Nicolas, Mariano R		Brother-in-law	M	Cha	29.0	S				Guam	Guam	Guam	Y	Laborer
7	139	143	Concepcion, Maria T		Head	F	Cha	24.0	S		Y	Y	Guam	Guam	Guam	Y	Laundress
8	139	143	Concepcion, Albert		Son	M	Cha	0.5	S				Guam	Unknown	Guam		None
9	139	143	Maekawa, Regina T		Sister	F	Jp	13.0	S	Y	Y	Y	Guam	Japan	Guam	Y	None
10	140	144	Reyes, Luis T		Head	M	Cha	49.0	M		Y	Y	Guam	Guam	Guam	Y	Farmer
11	140	144	Reyes, Dolores P		Wife	F	Cha	44.0	M		Y	Y	Guam	Unknown	Guam	N	None
12	140	144	Reyes, Jose P		Son	M	Cha	26.0	S		Y	Y	Guam	Guam	Guam	Y	Laborer
13	140	144	Reyes, Juan P		Son	M	Cha	21.0	S	N	Y	Y	Guam	Guam	Guam	Y	Farm laborer
14	140	144	Reyes, Joaquin P		Son	M	Cha	19.0	S	N	Y	Y	Guam	Guam	Guam	Y	Servant
15	140	144	Reyes, Maria P		Daughter	F	Cha	17.0	S	N	Y	Y	Guam	Guam	Guam	N	None
16	140	144	Reyes, Ana P		Daughter	F	Cha	15.0	S	N	Y	Y	Guam	Guam	Guam	Y	None
17	140	144	Reyes, Rosa P		Daughter	F	Cha	12.0	S	Y	Y	Y	Guam	Guam	Guam	Y	None
18	140	144	Reyes, Trinidad P		Daughter	F	Cha	7.0	S	Y			Guam	Guam	Guam	N	None
19	140	144	Reyes, Salome P		Daughter	F	Cha	3.0	S				Guam	Guam	Guam	N	None
20	141	145	Sanchez, Teodoro S		Head	M	Cha	28.0	M		Y	Y	Guam	Unknown	Unknown	Y	Farmer
21	141	145	Sanchez, Eliza D		Wife	F	Cha	22.0	M		Y	Y	Guam	Unknown	Unknown	Y	None
22	141	145	Duenas, Maria D		Aunt	F	Cha	53.0	S		N	N	Guam	Unknown	Unknown	N	None
23	142	146	Santos, Emiliana T		Head	F	Cha	34.0	S		N	N	Guam	Guam	Guam	N	None
24	142	146	Santos, Rita T		Sister	F	Cha	32.0	S		Y	Y	Guam	Guam	Guam	N	None
25	142	146	Santos, Luis T		Brother	M	Cha	29.0	S		Y	Y	Guam	Guam	Guam	N	Farmer

Togal Street

(CHAMORRO ROOTS GENEALOGY PROJECT ™ TRANSCRIPTION)
(COMPILED/TRANSCRIBED BY BERNARD T. PUNZALAN / HTTP://WWW.CHAMORROROOTS.COM)

FOURTEENTH CENSUS OF THE UNITED STATES: 1920-POPULATION

ISLAND OF GUAM

211b

SHEET NO. _36B_

ENUMERATED BY ME ON THE 8th DAY OF April, 1920

Vicente Tydingco ENUMERATOR

DISTRICT 3

NAME OF PLACE **Sumay Town**

[Proper name and, also, name of class, as city, town, village, barrio, etc]

	Dwelling #	Family #	NAME	RELATION	Sex	Color/race	Age	Marital	School	Read	Write	Birthplace	Father birthplace	Mother birthplace	English	OCCUPATION
26	142	146	Santos, Luis T jr	Brother	M	Cha	27.0	S		Y	Y	Guam	Guam	Guam	Y	Laborer
27	142	146	Santos, Felix T	Brother	M	Cha	25.0	S		Y	Y	Guam	Guam	Guam	Y	Carpenter
28	142	146	Santos, Dolores T	Sister	F	Cha	21.0	S		Y	Y	Guam	Guam	Guam	Y	Laundress
29	142	146	Santos, Tomas T	Nephew	M	Cha	11.0	S	N	Y	Y	Guam	Unknown	Guam	Y	None
30	143	147	Cruz, Jose C	Head	M	Cha	46.0	M	Y	Y	Y	Guam	Guam	Guam	Y	Farmer
31	143	147	Cruz, Benita C	Wife	F	Cha	44.0	M		N	N	Guam	Guam	Guam	N	None
32	143	147	Cruz, Dolores C	Daughter	F	Cha	14.0	S	N	N	N	Guam	Guam	Guam	N	None
33	143	147	Cruz, Engracia C	Daughter	F	Cha	12.0	S	Y	Y	Y	Guam	Guam	Guam	Y	None
34	144	148	Taitano, Nicolas M	Head	M	Cha	56.0	M		Y	Y	Guam	Guam	Guam	N	Farmer
35	144	148	Taitano, Maria P	Wife	F	Cha	56.0	M		N	N	Guam	Guam	Guam	N	None
36	144	148	Taitano, Rosa P	Daughter	F	Cha	20.0	S	N	Y	Y	Guam	Guam	Guam	Y	None
37	144	148	Taitano, Rosalia P	Daughter	F	Cha	18.0	S	N	Y	Y	Guam	Guam	Guam	Y	Laundress
38	144	148	Taitano, Caridad P	Daughter	F	Cha	15.0	S	N	Y	Y	Guam	Guam	Guam	Y	None
39	144	148	Reyes, Antonio P	Stepson	M	Cha	29.0	S		Y	Y	Guam	Guam	Guam	N	Farm laborer
40	144	148	Lujan, Rosalia L	Boarder	F	Cha	3.0	S				Guam	Unknown	Guam		None
41	145	149	Santos, Antonio M	Head	M	Cha	30.0	M		Y	Y	Guam	Guam	Guam	N	Laborer
42	145	149	Santos, Catalina G	Wife	F	Cha	20.0	M	N	Y	Y	Guam	Luzon	Guam	N	None
43	145	149	Santos, Ignacio T	Son	M	Cha	0.1	S				Luzon	Guam	Guam		None
44	146	150	De Gracia, Ponciano A	Head	M	Fil	59.0	M		N	N	Luzon	Luzon	Luzon	N	Farmer
45	146	150	De Gracia, Rosa A	Wife	F	Cha	32.0	M		N	N	Guam	Unknown	Unknown	N	None
46	146	150	De Gracia, Lorenzo A	Son	M	Fil	8.0	S	Y			Guam	Luzon	Luzon		None
47	146	150	De Gracia, Antonia A	Daughter	F	Fil	6.0	S	N			Guam	Luzon	Luzon		None
48	147	151	Pimley, William	Head	M	W	48.0	M		Y	Y	England	England	England	Y	Superintendent Cable
49	147	152	Paget, Alfred G	Head	M	W	32.0	S		Y	Y	Canada	Canada	Canada	Y	Supervisor
50	148	153	Dias, David	Head	M	W	30.0	M		Y	Y	Honolulu	Portugal	Portugal	Y	Cable operator

Street, avenue, road, etc: Togal Street

(CHAMORRO ROOTS GENEALOGY PROJECT ™ TRANSCRIPTION)
(COMPILED/TRANSCRIBED BY BERNARD T. PUNZALAN / HTTP://WWW.CHAMORROROOTS.COM)

FOURTEENTH CENSUS OF THE UNITED STATES: 1920-POPULATION

ISLAND OF GUAM

212

ENUMERATED BY ME ON THE 8th DAY OF April, 1920

Vicente Tydingco ENUMERATOR

DISTRICT 3

NAME OF PLACE **Sumay Town**

[Proper name and, also, name of class, as city, town, village, barrio, etc]

Street	Dwelling No.	Family No.	NAME	RELATION	Sex	Color or race	Age	Single, married, widowed, divorced	Attended school since Sept. 1, 1919	Able to read	Able to write	Place of birth of this person	Place of birth of father	Place of birth of mother	Able to speak English	OCCUPATION
1	2	3	4	5	6	7	8	9	10	11	12	13	14	15	16	17
	148	153	Dias, Rita	Wife	F	W	23.0	M		Y	Y	Guam	Spain	Guam	Y	None
	148	153	Dias, Walter E	Son	M	W	0.1	S				Guam	Honolulu	Guam		None
	149	154	Oconner, Patrick J	Head	M	W	26.0	S		Y	Y	Ireland	Ireland	Ireland	Y	Cable operator
	149	155	Stroup, Lewis H	Head	M	W	22.0	S		Y	Y	California	California	England	Y	Cable operator
	149	156	Hemeworth, Christopher	Head	M	W	22.0	S		Y	Y	Ireland	Ireland	Ireland	Y	Cable operator
	149	157	Sullivan, Walter T	Head	M	W	22.0	S	N	Y	Y	New York	New York	New York	Y	Cable operator
	149	158	White, Arthur G	Head	M	W	20.0	S	N	Y	Y	British Columbia	England	Nebraska	Y	Cable operator
	149	169	Pitko, Rudolp C	Head	M	W	19.0	S	N	Y	Y	New Jersey	New Jersey	New Jersey	Y	Cable operator
	149	160	Dwyer, Harold B	Head	M	W	19.0	S	N	Y	Y	California	Australlia	California	Y	Cable operator
Cable Station Road	149	161	Keven, Raymund J	Head	M	W	19.0	S	N	Y	Y	Honlulu	Ireland	California	Y	Cable operator
	149	162	Young, Henry	Head	M	W	19.0	S		Y	Y	California	New York	Germany	Y	Cable operator
	149	163	Kemp, Robert	Head	M	W	53.0	M		Y	Y	At sea	Scotland	England	Y	Engineer
	149	164	Carlson, Oscar	Head	M	W	45.0	S		Y	Y	Sweden	Sweden	Sweden	Y	Foreman
	150	165	Winsor, Sheridan P	Head	M	W	26.0	M		Y	Y	California	California	Nevada	Y	Mechanician
	150	165	Winsor, Charlotte Mac	Wife	F	W	25.0	M		Y	Y	California	Canada	Missouri	Y	None
	150	165	Winsor, Keiller M	Son	M	W	1.0	S				California	California	California		None
	150	165	Winsor, Sheridan P jr.	Son	M	W	0.3	S				California	California	California		None
	151	166	Flores, Nieves M	Head	M	Fil	29.0	M		Y	Y	Luzon	Luzon	Luzon	Y	Surveyor of Lands
	151	166	Flores, Guadalupe C	Wife	F	Cha	25.0	M		Y	Y	Guam	Guam	Guam	Y	None
	151	166	Flores, Alejo C	Son	M	Fil	2.0	S				Guam	Luzon	Guam		None
	151	166	Flores, Sabino C	Son	M	Fil	0.1	S				Guam	Luzon	Guam		None
	152	167	Baleto, Sebastian V	Head	M	Cha	55.0	M		N	N	Guam	Guam	Guam	N	Farmer
	152	167	Baleto, Andrea J	Wife	F	Cha	53.0	M		N	N	Guam	Guam	Guam	N	None
	152	167	Baleto, Sixto J	Stepson	M	Cha	28.0	S		Y	Y	Guam	Guam	Guam	N	Laborer
	153	168	Daprosa, Hermoglines	Head	M	Fil	54.0	M		Y	Y	Luzon	Luzon	Luzon	N	Farmer

(CHAMORRO ROOTS GENEALOGY PROJECT ™ TRANSCRIPTION)
(COMPILED/TRANSCRIBED BY BERNARD T. PUNZALAN / HTTP://WWW.CHAMORROROOTS.COM)

FOURTEENTH CENSUS OF THE UNITED STATES: 1920–POPULATION
ISLAND OF GUAM

DISTRICT 3
NAME OF PLACE **Sumay Town**
[Proper name and, also, name of class, as city, town, village, barrio, etc]

ENUMERATED BY ME ON THE 9th DAY OF _April,_ 1920

Vicente Tydingco ENUMERATOR

	Dwelling house no.	Family no.	NAME	RELATION	Sex	Color or race	Age at last birthday	Single, married, widowed or divorced	Attended school since sept. 1, 1919	Able to read	Able to write	Birthplace of person	Birthplace of father	Birthplace of mother	Able to speak English	OCCUPATION
	2	3	4	5	6	7	8	9	10	11	12	13	14	15	16	17
26	153	168	Daprosa, Catalina L	Wife	F	Fil	40.0	M		N	N	Luzon	Luzon	Luzon	N	None
27	154	169	Tolentino, Joaquin T	Head	M	Fil	29.0	M		Y	Y	Guam	Luzon	Guam	N	Laborer
28	154	169	Tolentino, Tomasa DG	Wife	F	Fil	21.0	M	N	Y	Y	Guam	Luzon	Guam	N	None
29	154	169	Tolentino, Rosalia DG	Daughter	F	Cha	2.0	S				Guam	Guam	Guam		None
30	155	170	De Gracia, Manuel B	Head	M	Fil	25.0	M		Y	Y	Guam	Luzon	Guam	Y	Laborer
31	155	170	De Gracia, Dolores T	Wife	F	Fil	26.0	M		Y	Y	Guam	Luzon	Guam	N	None
32	156	171	Gumataotao, Francisco B	Head	M	Cha	35.0	M		Y	Y	Guam	Guam	Guam	Y	Farmer
33	156	171	Gumataotao, Emiliana P	Wife	F	Cha	28.0	M		N	N	Guam	Guam	Guam	N	None
34	156	171	Gumataotao, Mariano P	Son	M	Cha	3.0	S				Guam	Guam	Guam		None
35	157	172	Reyes, Jose G	Head	M	Cha	22.0	S		Y	Y	Guam	Guam	Guam	Y	Cable operator
36	158	173	Salas, Manuel	Head	M	Cha	24.0	S		Y	Y	Guam	Guam	Guam	Y	Cable operator
37	159	174	Charguane, Justo T	Head	M	Cha	20.0	S	N	Y	Y	Guam	Guam	Guam	Y	Servant
38	159	174	Charguane, Guadalupe T	Sister	F	Cha	18.0	S	N	Y	Y	Guam	Guam	Guam	Y	Servant
39	159	174	Charguane, Francisco T	Brother	M	Cha	16.0	S	N	Y	Y	Guam	Guam	Guam	N	Servant
40	159	174	Charguane, Trinidad T	Sister	F	Cha	14.0	S	Y	Y	Y	Guam	Guam	Guam	Y	None
41	160	175	Gogue, Isabel	Head	F	Cha	49.0	S		N	N	Guam	Guam	Guam	N	None
42	160	175	Gogue, Vicente	Son	M	Cha	17.0	S	N	N	Y	Guam	Unknown	Guam	Y	Abstract Clerk
43	160	175	Borja, Juan	Servant	M	Cha	16.0	S	N	N	Y	Guam	Guam	Guam	Y	Servant
44	161	176	Camacho, Juan C	Head	M	Cha	17.0	S	N	Y	Y	Guam	Guam	Guam	Y	Servant
45	162	177	Sablan, Antonio C	Head	M	Cha	19.0	S	N	Y	Y	Guam	Guam	Guam	Y	Servant
46			Here ends the enumeration of Sumay Town													

Street, avenue, road, etc.: Cable Station Road

District 4

(CHAMORRO ROOTS GENEALOGY PROJECT ™ TRANSCRIPTION)
(COMPILED/TRANSCRIBED BY BERNARD T. PUNZALAN / HTTP://WWW.CHAMORROROOTS.COM)

FOURTEENTH CENSUS OF THE UNITED STATES: 1920—POPULATION
ISLAND OF GUAM

DISTRICT 4
NAME OF PLACE **Agat Town**

[Proper name and, also, name of class, as city, town, village, barrio, etc]

ENUMERATED BY ME ON THE 24th DAY OF February, 1920

Albert P. Manley ENUMERATOR

Street, avenue, road, etc.	Dwelling no.	Family no.	NAME	RELATION	Sex	Color or race	Age	Single, married, widowed or divorced	Attended school since Sept. 1, 1919	Read	Write	Birthplace person	Birthplace father	Birthplace mother	English	OCCUPATION
	1	1	Rivera, Antonio D	Head	M	Cha	37.0	M		Y	Y	Guam	Guam	Guam	Y	Shoemaker
	1	1	Rivera, Ana B	Wife	F	Cha	39.0	M		Y	Y	Guam	Guam	Guam	N	None
	1	1	Rivera, Vicente B	Son	M	Cha	11.0	S	Y	Y	Y	Guam	Guam	Guam	Y	None
	1	1	Rivera, Martin B	Son	M	Cha	7.0	S	Y			Guam	Guam	Guam		None
	1	1	Rivera, Filomena B	Daughter	F	Cha	0.9	S				Guam	Guam	Guam		None
	1	1	Pangelinan, Maria B	Servant	F	Cha	53.0	S		Y	Y	Guam	Guam	Guam	N	Servant
	2	2	Charfauros, Mariano T	Head	M	Cha	39.0	M		Y	Y	Guam	Guam	Guam	Y	Farmer
	2	2	Charfauros, Ignacia N	Wife	F	Cha	36.0	M		Y	N	Guam	Guam	Guam	N	None
	2	2	Charfauros, Joaquin N	Son	M	Cha	10.0	S	Y	Y	Y	Guam	Guam	Guam	Y	None
	2	2	Charfauros, Francisco N	Son	M	Cha	9.0	S	Y	Y	Y	Guam	Guam	Guam		None
	2	2	Charfauros, Jose N	Son	M	Cha	2.0	S				Guam	Guam	Guam		None
	2	2	Charfauros, Ignacio N	Son	M	Cha	1.0	S				Guam	Guam	Guam		None
	3	3	Leon Guerrero, Jose D	Head	M	Cha	40.0	M		Y	Y	Guam	Guam	Guam		Farmer
	3	3	Leon Guerrero, Antonia T	Wife	F	Cha	48.0	M		Y	N	Guam	Guam	Guam	N	None
	4	4	Pangelinan, Francisco B	Head	M	Cha	30.0	M		Y	Y	Guam	Guam	Guam	Y	Farmer
	4	4	Pangelinan, Natividad L	Wife	F	Cha	24.0	M		Y	Y	Guam	Guam	Guam	Y	None
	5	5	Charfauros, Felix C	Head	M	Cha	63.0	M		Y	Y	Guam	Guam	Guam	N	Farmer
	5	5	Charfauros, Antonia B	Wife	F	Cha	57.0	M		Y	N	Guam	Guam	Guam	N	None
	5	5	Charfauros, Maria B	Daughter	F	Cha	33.0	S		Y	Y	Guam	Guam	Guam	N	None
	5	5	Charfauros, Jesus B	Son	M	Cha	30.0	S		Y	Y	Guam	Guam	Guam	Y	Farm laborer home farm
Serain Street	5	5	Charfauros, Venancio B	Son	M	Cha	23.0	S	N	Y	Y	Guam	Guam	Guam	Y	Farm laborer home farm
	5	5	Charfauros, Carmen B	Daughter	F	Cha	20.0	S	Y	Y	Y	Guam	Guam	Guam	Y	None
	5	5	Charfauros, Ana B	Daughter	F	Cha	16.0	S	Y	Y	Y	Guam	Unknown	Guam	Y	None
	5	5	Charfauros, Francisca B	Daughter	F	Cha	11.0	S	Y	Y	Y	Guam	Guam	Guam	Y	None
	6	6	Carbullido, Jesus B	Head	M	Cha	49.0	Wd		Y	Y	Guam	Manila, Philippines	Guam	N	Farmer

(CHAMORRO ROOTS GENEALOGY PROJECT ™ TRANSCRIPTION)
(COMPILED/TRANSCRIBED BY BERNARD T. PUNZALAN / HTTP://WWW.CHAMORRROOTS.COM)

FOURTEENTH CENSUS OF THE UNITED STATES: 1920-POPULATION
ISLAND OF GUAM

DISTRICT 4
NAME OF PLACE Agat Town
[Proper name and, also, name of class, as city, town, village, barrio, etc]

ENUMERATED BY ME ON THE 24th DAY OF February, 1920

Albert P. Manley ENUMERATOR

#	Dwelling	Family	NAME	RELATION	Sex	Race	Age	Marital	Attended school since Sept 1, 1919	Read	Write	Birthplace	Father birthplace	Mother birthplace	Speak English	OCCUPATION
26	6	6	Carbullido, Amparo P	Daughter	F	Cha	19.0	S	N	Y	Y	Guam	Guam	Guam	Y	None
27	6	6	Carbullido, Joaquin P	Son	M	Cha	16.0	S	N	Y	Y	Guam	Guam	Guam	Y	Farm laborer home farm
28	6	6	Carbullido, Regina P	Daughter	F	Cha	14.0	S	Y	Y	Y	Guam	Guam	Guam	Y	None
29	7	7	Arceo, Jose B	Head	M	Cha	36.0	M		Y	Y	Guam	Guam	Guam	N	Farmer
30	7	7	Arceo, Ana G	Wife	F	Cha	29.0	M		Y	N	Guam	Guam	Guam	N	None
31	7	7	Arceo, Francisco G	Son	M	Cha	4.0	S				Guam	Guam	Guam		None
32	7	7	Arceo, Vicente G	Son	M	Cha	2.0	S				Guam	Guam	Guam		None
33	7	7	Arceo, Maria G	Daughter	F	Cha	1.0	S				Guam	Guam	Guam		None
34	8	8	Carbullido, Jose B	Head	M	Cha	55.0	M		N	N	Guam	Manila, Philippines	Guam	N	None
35	8	8	Carbullido, Ana M	Wife	F	Cha	49.0	M		Y	Y	Guam	Guam	Guam	N	Washerwoman
36	8	8	Carbullido, Carmen M	Daughter	F	Cha	25.0	S		Y	Y	Guam	Guam	Guam	N	Washerwoman
37	8	8	Carbullido, Ignacio M	Son	M	Cha	11.0	S	Y	Y	Y	Guam	Guam	Guam	Y	None
38	8	8	Carbullido, Rita M	Daughter	F	Cha	6.0	S	N			Guam	Guam	Guam	Y	None
39	9	9	Babauta, Benjamin T	Head	M	Cha	51.0	M		N	N	Guam	Guam	Guam	N	Farmer
40	9	9	Babauta, Dolores T	Wife	F	Cha	50.0	M		Y	N	Guam	Guam	Guam	N	None
41	9	9	Babauta, Consolacion T	Daughter	F	Cha	22.0	S		Y	Y	Guam	Guam	Guam	Y	None
42	9	9	Babauta, Carmen T	Daughter	F	Cha	19.0	S	N	Y	Y	Guam	Guam	Guam	Y	None
43	9	9	Babauta, Rosario T	Daughter	F	Cha	17.0	S		Y	Y	Guam	Guam	Guam	Y	None
44	9	9	Babauta, Vicente T	Son	M	Cha	13.0	S	Y	Y	Y	Guam	Guam	Guam	Y	None
45	9	9	Babauta, Ignacia T	Daughter	F	Cha	5.0	S	Y			Guam	Guam	Guam		None
46	9	9	Babauta, Juana T	Sister	F	Cha	48.0	Wd	N			Guam	Guam	Guam	N	None
47	10	10	Muna, Gregorio D	Head	M	Cha	49.0	M		N	N	Guam	Guam	Guam	N	Farmer
48	10	10	Muna, Josefa S	Wife	F	Cha	47.0	M		Y	Y	Guam	Guam	Guam	N	None
49	10	10	Muna, Pedro S	Son	M	Cha	16.0	S	Y	Y	Y	Guam	Guam	Guam	N	None
50	10	10	Muna, Ana S	Daughter	F	Cha	15.0	S	N	Y	Y	Guam	Guam	Guam	Y	None

Street: Serain Street

(CHAMORRO ROOTS GENEALOGY PROJECT ™ TRANSCRIPTION)

(COMPILED/TRANSCRIBED BY BERNARD T. PUNZALAN / HTTP://WWW.CHAMORROROOTS.COM)

FOURTEENTH CENSUS OF THE UNITED STATES: 1920-POPULATION
ISLAND OF GUAM

ENUMERATED BY ME ON THE 24th DAY OF February, 1920

Albert P. Manley ENUMERATOR

DISTRICT 4
NAME OF PLACE **Agat Town**

[Proper name and, also, name of class, as city, town, village, barrio, etc]

Street, avenue, road, etc.	Number of dwelling house in order of visitation	Number of family in order of visitation	NAME	RELATION	Sex	Color or race	Age at last birthday	Single, married, widowed or divorced	Attended school any time since Sept. 1, 1919	Whether able to read.	Whether able to write.	Place of birth of this person.	Place of birth of father of this person.	Place of birth of mother of this person.	Whether able to speak English.	OCCUPATION
	2	3	4	5	6	7	8	9	10	11	12	13	14	15	16	17
	10	10	Muna, Maria S	Daughter	F	Cha	11.0	S	Y	Y	Y	Guam	Guam	Guam	Y	None
	10	10	Muna, Asemcion S	Daughter	F	Cha	9.0	S	Y			Guam	Guam	Guam		None
	10	10	Muna, Isabel S	Daughter	F	Cha	5.0	S	N			Guam	Guam	Guam		None
	10	10	Muna, Sibera S	Daughter	F	Cha	2.0	S				Guam	Guam	Guam		None
	10	10	Muna, Roque S	Son	M	Cha	0.1	S				Guam	Guam	Guam		None
	11	11	Salas, Ignacia B	Head	F	Cha	33.0	Wd		Y	N	Guam	Guam	Guam	N	Washerwoman
	11	11	Salas, Manuel B	Son	M	Cha	9.0	S	Y	Y		Guam	Guam	Guam		None
	11	11	Salas, Francisco B	Son	M	Cha	6.0	S	N			Guam	Guam	Guam		None
	11	11	Salas, Juan B	Son	M	Cha	1.0	S				Guam	Guam	Guam		None
	12	12	Charfauros, Tomas C	Head	M	Cha	28.0	M		Y	Y	Guam	Guam	Guam	Y	Commissioner
	12	12	Charfauros, Rosa B	Wife	F	Cha	24.0	M		Y	Y	Guam	Guam	Guam	Y	None
	12	12	Charfauros, Antonio B	Son	M	Cha	5.0	S	N			Guam	Guam	Guam		None
	12	12	Charfauros, Jose B	Son	M	Cha	4.0	S				Guam	Guam	Guam		None
	12	12	Charfauros, Tomas B	Son	M	Cha	0.8	S				Guam	Guam	Guam		None
	13	13	Salas, Vicente D	Head	M	Cha	59.0	M		Y	Y	Guam	Guam	Guam	N	Farmer
	13	13	Salas, Maria C	Wife	F	Cha	58.0	M		Y	Y	Guam	Guam	Guam	N	None
	14	14	Taitague, Domingo C	Head	M	Cha	46.0	M		Y	Y	Guam	Guam	Guam	N	Farmer
	14	14	Taitague, Ana Cruz	Wife	F	Cha	56.0	M	N	Y	Y	Guam	Guam	Guam	Y	None
	14	14	Charfauros, Pedro C	Nephew	M	Cha	17.0	S	N	Y	Y	Guam	Guam	Guam	Y	Farm laborer home farm
	14	14	Charfauros, Francisco	Nephew	M	Cha	15.0	S	N	Y	Y	Guam	Manila, Philippines	Guam	N	Farm laborer home farm
	15	15	Carbuillido, Sebastian B	Head	M	Cha	42.0	M	N	Y	Y	Guam	Guam	Guam	N	Farmer
	15	15	Carbuillido, Luisa M	Wife	F	Cha	41.0	M	N	Y	Y	Guam		Guam	N	None
	15	15	Carbuillido, Concepcion M	Daughter	F	Cha	19.0	S	N	Y	Y	Guam	Guam	Guam	N	None
	15	15	Carbuillido, Remedio M	Daughter	F	Cha	16.0	S	N	Y	Y	Guam	Guam	Guam	Y	None
	15	15	Carbuillido, Engracia M	Daughter	F	Cha	15.0	S	N	Y	Y	Guam	Guam	Guam	Y	None

Seraln Street

431

(CHAMORRO ROOTS GENEALOGY PROJECT ™ TRANSCRIPTION)
(COMPILED/TRANSCRIBED BY BERNARD T. PUNZALAN / HTTP://WWW.CHAMORROROOTS.COM)
FOURTEENTH CENSUS OF THE UNITED STATES: 1920-POPULATION
ISLAND OF GUAM

ENUMERATED BY ME ON THE 24th DAY OF February, 1920

Albert P. Manley ENUMERATOR

DISTRICT **4**
NAME OF PLACE **Agat Town**

	Dwelling	Family	NAME	RELATION	Sex	Color or race	Age	Single/married/widowed/divorced	Attended school since Sept. 1, 1919	Able to read	Able to write	Birthplace of person	Birthplace of father	Birthplace of mother	Able to speak English	OCCUPATION
26	15	15	Carbullido, Maria M	Daughter	F	Cha	11.0	S	Y	Y	Y	Guam	Guam	Guam	Y	None
27	15	15	Carbullido, Jose M	Son	M	Cha	8.0	S	Y			Guam	Guam	Guam		None
28	15	15	Carbullido, Francisco M	Son	M	Cha	2.0	S				Guam	Guam	Guam		None
29	16	16	Aguigui, Luis SN	Head	M	Cha	40.0	M		Y	Y	Guam	Guam	Guam	N	Laborer
30	16	16	Aguigui, Trinidad C	Wife	F	Cha	37.0	M		Y	Y	Guam	Guam	Guam	N	None
31	16	16	Aguigui, Concepcion C	Daughter	F	Cha	17.0	S	Y	Y	Y	Guam	Guam	Guam	Y	None
32	16	16	Aguigui, Enrique C	Son	M	Cha	13.0	S	Y	Y	Y	Guam	Guam	Guam	Y	None
33	16	16	Aguigui, Antonia C	Daughter	F	Cha	8.0	S				Guam	Guam	Guam		None
34	16	16	Aguigui, Josefa C	Daughter	F	Cha	6.0	S	N			Guam	Guam	Guam	Y	None
35	17	17	Sablan, Cecilio S	Head	M	Cha	28.0	M		N	N	Guam	Guam	Guam	Y	Farmer
36	17	17	Sablan, Dolores Q	Wife	F	Cha	27.0	M		N	N	Guam	Guam	Guam	N	None
37	17	17	Sablan, Cristobal Q	Son	M	Cha	3.0	S				Guam	Guam	Guam		None
38	17	17	Sablan, Antonia Q	Daughter	F	Cha	2.0	S				Guam	Guam	Guam		None
39	17	17	Sablan, Antonio Q	Son	M	Cha	0.1	S				Guam	Guam	Guam		None
40	17	17	Salas, Jose S	Uncle	M	Cha	35.0	S		N	N	Guam	Guam	Guam	N	Laborer
41	18	18	Nededoc, Vicente S	Head	M	Cha	52.0	M		N	N	Guam	Guam	Guam	N	Farmer
42	18	18	Nededoc, Felicisa C	Wife	F	Cha	56.0	M		Y	Y	Guam	Guam	Guam	N	None
43	18	18	Nededoc, Carmen C	Daughter	F	Cha	23.0	S		Y	Y	Guam	Guam	Guam	Y	None
44	18	18	Nededoc, Jesus C	Son	M	Cha	16.0	S	N	Y	Y	Guam	Guam	Guam	Y	Farm laborer home farm
45	18	18	Nededoc, Jose C	Son	M	Cha	15.0	S	N	Y	Y	Guam	Guam	Guam	Y	Farm laborer home farm
46	18	18	Nededoc, Juan C	Son	M	Cha	12.0	S	Y	Y	Y	Guam	Guam	Guam	Y	None
47	18	18	Nededoc, Joaquin C	Son	M	Cha	9.0	S	N			Guam	Guam	Guam		None
48	19	19	Arceo, Carmen S	Head	F	Cha	48.0	Wd		Y	N	Guam	Guam	Guam	N	Weaver
49	19	19	Arceo, Francisco S	Son	M	Cha	17.0	S	N	Y	Y	Guam	Guam	Guam	Y	Farm laborer home farm
50	19	19	Arceo, Antonia S	Daughter	F	Cha	11.0	S	Y	Y	Y	Guam	Guam	Guam	Y	None

Street (column 1): Serafin Street

(CHAMORRO ROOTS GENEALOGY PROJECT ™ TRANSCRIPTION)
(COMPILED/TRANSCRIBED BY BERNARD T. PUNZALAN / HTTP://WWW.CHAMORROROOTS.COM)

FOURTEENTH CENSUS OF THE UNITED STATES: 1920–POPULATION

ISLAND OF GUAM

SHEET NO. _3A_

DISTRICT **4**
NAME OF PLACE **Agat Town**

[Proper name and, also, name of class, as city, town, village, barrio, etc]

ENUMERATED BY ME ON THE 25th DAY OF February, 1920

Albert P. Manley ENUMERATOR

	PLACE OF ABODE			NAME	RELATION	PERSONAL DESCRIPTION					EDUCATION			NATIVITY				OCCUPATION
Street, avenue, road, etc.	Number of dwelling house is order of visitation	Number of family in order of visitation		Name	Relationship of this Person to the head of the family.	Sex	Color or race	Age at last birthday	Single, married, widowed or divorced	Attended school any time since Sept. 1, 1919	Whether able to read.	Whether able to write.	Place of birth of this person.	Place of birth of father of this person.	Place of birth of mother of this person.	Whether able to speak English.	Trade, profession, or particular kind of work done, as salesman, laborer, clerk, cook, merchant, washerwoman, etc.
1	2	3	4		5	6	7	8	9	10	11	12	13	14	15	16	17
	20	20		Sablan, Juan R	Head	M	Cha	56.0	M		Y	Y	Guam	Guam	Guam	N	Farmer
	20	20		Sablan, Ana P	Wife	F	Cha	54.0	M		Y	Y	Guam	Guam	Guam	N	None
	20	20		Sablan, Rosa P	Daughter	F	Cha	27.0	S		Y	Y	Guam	Guam	Guam	Y	Nurse
	20	20		Sablan, Ignacia P	Daughter	F	Cha	25.0	S		Y	Y	Guam	Guam	Guam	Y	Nurse
	20	20		Sablan, Pedro F P	Son	M	Cha	22.0	S		Y	Y	Guam	Guam	Guam	Y	Farm laborer home farm
	20	20		Sablan, Maria D P	Daughter	F	Cha	21.0	S	N	Y	Y	Guam	Guam	Guam	Y	None
	20	20		Sablan, Juan J P	Son	M	Cha	17.0	S	N	Y	Y	Guam	Guam	Guam	Y	None
	21	21		Reyes, Jose B	Head	M	Cha	30.0	M		Y	Y	Guam	Guam	Guam	Y	Laborer
	21	21		Reyes, Consolacion C	Wife	F	Cha	24.0	M		Y	Y	Guam	Guam	Guam	N	None
	21	21		Reyes, Maria C	Daughter	F	Cha	2.0	S				Guam	Guam	Guam	N	None
	22	22		Sablan, Antonio G	Head	M	Cha	52.0	M		Y	Y	Guam	Guam	Guam	N	Farmer
	22	22		Sablan, Maria G	Wife	F	Cha	36.0	M		N	N	Guam	Guam	Guam	N	None
	22	22		Sablan, Francisco S	Son	M	Cha	25.0	S		Y	Y	Guam	Guam	Guam	Y	Farm laborer home farm
	22	22		Sablan, Diego S	Son	M	Cha	23.0	S		Y	Y	Guam	Guam	Guam	Y	Farm laborer home farm
	22	22		Sablan, Guadalupe B	Daughter	F	Cha	22.0	M		Y	Y	Guam	Guam	Guam	Y	None
	23	23		Palomo, Ignacio D	Head	M	Cha	59.0	M		Y	Y	Guam	Guam	Guam	N	Farmer
	23	23		Palomo, Francisc G	Wife	F	Cha	38.0	M		Y	Y	Guam	Guam	Guam	Y	None
	23	23		Palomo, Carmen G	Daughter	F	Cha	20.0	S	N	Y	Y	Guam	Guam	Guam	Y	None
	23	23		Palomo, Juan G	Son	M	Cha	18.0	S	N	Y	Y	Guam	Guam	Guam	Y	Farm laborer home farm
	23	23		Palomo, Vicente G	Son	M	Cha	15.0	S	Y	Y	Y	Guam	Guam	Guam	Y	None
	23	23		Palomo, Ana A G	Daughter	F	Cha	13.0	S	N	Y	Y	Guam	Guam	Guam	Y	None
	23	23		Palomo, Silvestre G	Son	M	Cha	13.0	S		Y	Y	Guam	Guam	Guam	Y	None
	23	23		Palomo, Jose G	Son	M	Cha	9.0	S	Y	Y		Guam	Guam	Guam	Y	None
	23	23		Palomo, Maria G	Daughter	F	Cha	7.0	S	Y			Guam	Guam	Guam	Y	None
	24	24		Nededoc, Nicolasa N	Head	F	Cha	59.0	S		Y	Y	Guam	Guam	Guam	Y	Weaver

Seraih Street

(CHAMORRO ROOTS GENEALOGY PROJECT ™ TRANSCRIPTION)

(COMPILED/TRANSCRIBED BY BERNARD T. PUNZALAN / HTTP://WWW.CHAMORROROOTS.COM)

215b

FOURTEENTH CENSUS OF THE UNITED STATES: 1920–POPULATION

ISLAND OF GUAM

DISTRICT 4

NAME OF PLACE Agat Town

[Proper name and, also, name of class, as city, town, village, barrio, etc]

ENUMERATED BY ME ON THE 25th DAY OF February, 1920

Albert P. Manley ENUMERATOR

#	Street	No. dwelling	No. family	NAME	RELATION	Sex	Color or race	Age	Single, married, widowed or divorced	Attended school since Sept. 1, 1919	Able to read	Able to write	Place of birth of this person	Place of birth of father	Place of birth of mother	Able to speak English	OCCUPATION
		1	2	3	4	5	6	7	8	9	10	11	12	13	14	15	16	17
26		24	24	Nededoc, Rosa N	Daughter	F	Cha	28.0	S		Y	Y	Guam	Unknown	Guam		Weaver
27		25	25	Terlaje, Baldovino C	Head	M	Cha	46.0	M		Y	Y	Guam	Guam	Guam	N	Farmer
28		25	25	Terlaje, Madalena M	Wife	F	Cha	45.0	M		N	N	Guam	Guam	Guam	N	None
29		25	25	Terlaje, Dolores M	Daughter	F	Cha	17.0	S	N	Y	Y	Guam	Guam	Guam	Y	None
30		25	25	Terlaje, Jose M	Son	M	Cha	15.0	S	Y	Y	Y	Guam	Guam	Guam	Y	Farm laborer home farm
31		25	25	Terlaje, Maria M	Daughter	F	Cha	12.0	S	Y	Y	Y	Guam	Guam	Guam	Y	None
32		26	26	Aguigui, Benedicto SN	Head	M	Cha	42.0	M		Y	Y	Guam	Guam	Guam	N	Farmer
33		26	26	Aguigui, Maria C	Wife	F	Cha	35.0	M			N	Guam	Guam	Guam	N	None
34		26	26	Aguigui, Antonio C	Son	M	Cha	17.0	S	N	Y	Y	Guam	Guam	Guam	Y	Farm laborer home farm
35		26	26	Aguigui, Milagro C	Daughter	F	Cha	15.0	S	Y	Y	Y	Guam	Guam	Guam	Y	None
36		26	26	Aguigui, Ana C	Daughter	F	Cha	13.0	S	Y	Y	Y	Guam	Guam	Guam	Y	None
37		26	26	Aguigui, Juana C	Daughter	F	Cha	11.0	S	Y	Y	Y	Guam	Guam	Guam	Y	None
38		26	26	Aguigui, Luisa C	Daughter	F	Cha	5.0	S	N			Guam	Guam	Guam		None
39		26	26	Aguigui, Donicio C	Son	M	Cha	3.0	S				Guam	Guam	Guam		None
40		27	27	Carbullido, Antonio P	Head	M	Cha	25.0	M		Y	Y	Guam	Guam	Guam	Y	Farmer
41		27	27	Carbullido, Maria T	Wife	F	Cha	26.0	M		Y	Y	Guam	Guam	Guam	N	None
42		27	27	Carbullido, Enriqueta T	Daughter	F	Cha	4.0	S				Guam	Guam	Guam		None
43		27	27	Carbullido, Felix T	Son	M	Cha	3.0	S				Guam	Guam	Guam		None
44		27	27	Carbullido, Alberto E T	Son	M	Cha	1.0	S				Guam	Guam	Guam		None
45	Serain Street	27	27	Meno, Florentino S	Servant	M	Cha	21.0	S	N	Y	Y	Guam	Guam	Guam	Y	Servant
46		27	27	Jesus, Ana S	Servant	F	Cha	13.0	S		Y	Y	Guam	Guam	Guam	Y	Servant
47		28	28	Acfalle, Geronimo SN	Head	M	Cha	44.0	M		N	N	Guam	Guam	Guam	N	Farmer
48		28	28	Acfalle, Maria C	Wife	F	Cha	37.0	M		N	N	Guam	Guam	Guam	N	None
49		28	28	Acfalle, Isabel C	Step-daughter	F	Cha	17.0	S	N	Y	Y	Guam	Guam	Guam	Y	None
50		28	28	Acfalle, Consolacion C	Daughter	F	Cha	7.0	S	Y			Guam	Guam	Guam		None

434

(CHAMORRO ROOTS GENEALOGY PROJECT ™ TRANSCRIPTION)
(COMPILED/TRANSCRIBED BY BERNARD T. PUNZALAN / HTTP://WWW.CHAMORROROOTS.COM)

FOURTEENTH CENSUS OF THE UNITED STATES: 1920-POPULATION

ISLAND OF GUAM

ENUMERATED BY ME ON THE 25th DAY OF February, 1920

Albert P. Manley ENUMERATOR

DISTRICT 4
NAME OF PLACE **Agat Town**

[Proper name and, also, name of class, as city, town, village, barrio, etc]

Street	Dwelling no.	Family no.	NAME	RELATION	Sex	Color or race	Age	Single, married, widowed or divorced	Attended school since Sept. 1, 1919	Able to read	Able to write	Birthplace of person	Birthplace of father	Birthplace of mother	Able to speak English	OCCUPATION
	28	28	Acfalle, Ana C	Daughter	F	Cha	5.0	S	N			Guam	Guam	Guam		None
	28	28	Acfalle, Margarita C	Daughter	F	Cha	2.0	S				Guam	Guam	Guam		None
	29	29	Chaco, Jose Q	Head	M	Cha	49.0	M		Y	Y	Guam	Guam	Guam	N	Farmer
	29	29	Chaco, Joaquina R	Wife	F	Cha	45.0	M		N	N	Guam	Guam	Guam	N	None
	29	29	Chaco, Consolacion R	Daughter	F	Cha	20.0	S	N	Y	Y	Guam	Guam	Guam	Y	None
	29	29	Chaco, Carmen R	Daughter	F	Cha	18.0	S	N	Y	Y	Guam	Guam	Guam	Y	None
	29	29	Chaco, Tomas R	Son	M	Cha	13.0	S	Y	Y	Y	Guam	Guam	Guam	Y	None
	29	29	Chaco, Antonio R	Son	M	Cha	11.0	S	Y	Y	Y	Guam	Guam	Guam	Y	None
	30	30	Chaco, Felipe Q	Head	M	Cha	54.0	M		Y	Y	Guam	Guam	Guam	Y	Farmer
	30	30	Chaco, Trinidad R	Wife	F	Cha	49.0	M		Y	Y	Guam	Guam	Guam	Y	None
	31	31	Okiyama, Francisco K	Head	M	Jp	41.0	M		Y	Y	Japan	Japan	Japan	Y	Retail Merchant dry goods
	31	31	Okiyama, Ana C	Wife	F	Cha	32.0	M		Y	Y	Guam	Guam	Guam	N	None
	31	31	Okiyama, Jesus C	Son	M	Jp	6.0	S	N			Guam	Japan	Guam		None
	32	32	Reyes, Andres B	Head	M	Cha	30.0	M		Y	Y	Guam	Guam	Guam	N	Farmer
	32	32	Reyes, Maria C	Wife	F	Cha	25.0	M		Y	Y	Guam	Guam	Guam	N	None
	32	32	Reyes, Enrique C	Son	M	Cha	6.0	S	N			Guam	Guam	Guam		None
	32	32	Reyes, Felicita C	Daughter	F	Cha	4.0	S				Guam	Guam	Guam		None
	32	32	Reyes, Ignacio C	Son	M	Cha	2.0	S				Guam	Guam	Guam		None
	33	33	Carbullido, Luis B	Head	M	Cha	60.0	Wd		Y	Y	Guam	Manila	Guam	N	Farmer
	33	33	Carbullido, Barbara C	Daughter	F	Cha	28.0	S		Y	Y	Guam	Guam	Guam	N	None
	33	33	Carbullido, Maria C	Daughter	F	Cha	26.0	S		Y	Y	Guam	Guam	Guam	N	None
	33	33	Carbullido, Dolores C	Daughter	F	Cha	23.0	S	N	Y	Y	Guam	Guam	Guam	Y	None
	33	33	Carbullido, Rosa C	Daughter	F	Cha	21.0	S	N	Y	Y	Guam	Guam	Guam	Y	None
	33	33	Carbullido, Josefa C	Daughter	F	Cha	19.0	S	N	Y	Y	Guam	Guam	Guam	Y	None
	33	33	Carbullido, Natividad C	Daughter	F	Cha	17.0	S	N	Y	Y	Guam	Guam	Guam	Y	None

Serain Street

435

(CHAMORRO ROOTS GENEALOGY PROJECT ™ TRANSCRIPTION)
(COMPILED/TRANSCRIBED BY BERNARD T. PUNZALAN / HTTP://WWW.CHAMORROROOTS.COM)
FOURTEENTH CENSUS OF THE UNITED STATES: 1920-POPULATION
ISLAND OF GUAM

DISTRICT 4
NAME OF PLACE **Agat Town**
[Proper name and, also, name of class, as city, town, village, barrio, etc]

ENUMERATED BY ME ON THE 25th DAY OF February, 1920

Albert P. Manley ENUMERATOR

	PLACE OF ABODE		NAME	RELATION	PERSONAL DESCRIPTION				EDUCATION			NATIVITY				OCCUPATION
Street, avenue, road, etc.	Number of dwelling house in order of visitation	Number of family in order of visitation	Name of each person whose place of abode on January 1, 1920, was in the family.	Relationship of this Person to the head of the family.	Sex	Color or race	Age at last birthday	Single, married, widowed or divorced	Attended school any time since Sept. 1, 1919	Whether able to read.	Whether able to write.	Place of birth of this person.	Place of birth of father of this person.	Place of birth of mother of this person.	Whether able to speak English.	Trade, profession, or particular kind of work done, as salesman, laborer, clerk, cook, merchant, washerwoman, etc.
1	2	3	4	5	6	7	8	9	10	11	12	13	14	15	16	17
	33	33	Carbullido, Concepcion C	Daughter	F	Cha	15.0	S	N	Y	Y	Guam	Guam	Guam	Y	None
	33	33	Carbullido, Andres L	Grandfather	M	Cha	86.0	M		N	N	Manila	Manila	Manila	N	None
	33	33	Carbullido, Josefa B	Grandmother	F	Cha	80.0	M		N	N	Guam	Guam	Guam	N	None
	34	34	Terlaje, Filomena B	Head	F	Cha	46.0	Wd		Y	Y	Guam	Guam	Guam	N	Farmer
	34	34	Terlaje, Vicente B	Son	M	Cha	21.0	S	N	Y	Y	Guam	Guam	Guam	N	Laborer
	35	35	Salas, Manuel F	Head	M	Cha	25.0	M		Y	Y	Guam	Guam	Guam	N	Laborer
	35	35	Salas, Caridad B	Wife	F	Cha	26.0	M		Y	Y	Guam	Guam	Guam	N	None
	35	35	Salas, Maria B	Daughter	F	Cha	5.0	S	N			Guam	Guam	Guam		None
	36	36	Quitanoc, Rodevico S	Head	M	Cha	33.0	M		Y	Y	Guam	Guam	Guam	N	Farmer
	36	36	Quitanoc, Rita G	Wife	F	Cha	23.0	M		Y	Y	Guam	Guam	Guam	Y	None
	36	36	Quitanoc, Bartola G	Daughter	F	Cha	3.0	S				Guam	Guam	Guam		None
	36	36	Quitanoc, Vicente G	Son	M	Cha	2.0	S				Guam	Guam	Guam		None
	37	37	Guerrero, Ana R	Head	F	Cha	47.0	Wd		Y	Y	Guam	Guam	Guam	N	Weaver
	37	37	Guerrero, Soledad R	Daughter	F	Cha	16.0	S	N	Y	Y	Guam	Guam	Guam	Y	Weaver
	37	37	Guerrero, Maria R	Daughter	F	Cha	15.0	S	N	Y	Y	Guam	Guam	Guam	Y	Weaver
Serain Street	37	37	Guerrero, Jesus R	Son	M	Cha	13.0	S	Y	Y	Y	Guam	Guam	Guam	Y	Farm laborer home farm
	38	38	Perez, Daniel L	Head	M	Fil	29.0	M		Y	Y	Batangas P.I.	Batangas P.I.	Batangas P.I.	Y	Teacher
	38	38	Perez, Rosa C	Wife	F	Cha	23.0	M		Y	Y	Guam	Guam	Guam	Y	Teacher
	38	38	Perez, Gerardo C	Son	M	Fil	4.0	S				Guam	Guam	Guam		None
	38	38	Perez, Doroteo C	Son	M	Fil	3.0	S				Guam	Guam	Guam		None
	38	38	Perez, Maria C	Daughter	F	Fil	0.3	S				Guam	Guam	Guam		None
	39	39	Babauta, Jose B	Head	M	Cha	37.0	M		Y	Y	Guam	Guam	Guam	N	Farmer
	39	39	Babauta, Juana A	Wife	F	Cha	54.0	M		N	N	Guam	Guam	Guam	N	None
	39	39	Babauta, Antonio A	Son	M	Cha	31.0	S		Y	Y	Guam	Guam	Guam	Y	Farm laborer home farm
	39	39	Babauta, Maria A	Daughter	F	Cha	17.0	S	N	Y	Y	Guam	Guam	Guam	Y	None

(CHAMORRO ROOTS GENEALOGY PROJECT ™ TRANSCRIPTION)
(COMPILED/TRANSCRIBED BY BERNARD T. PUNZALAN / HTTP://WWW.CHAMORROROOTS.COM)

217

FOURTEENTH CENSUS OF THE UNITED STATES: 1920-POPULATION

ISLAND OF GUAM

DISTRICT 4

NAME OF PLACE **Agat** Town

[Proper name and, also, name of class, as city, town, village, barrio, etc]

ENUMERATED BY ME ON THE 26th DAY OF February, 1920

Albert P. Manley ENUMERATOR

	PLACE OF ABODE		NAME	RELATION	PERSONAL DESCRIPTION				EDUCATION			NATIVITY				OCCUPATION
Street, avenue, road, etc.	Number of dwelling house is order of visitation	Number of family in order of visitation	Name of each person	Relationship of this Person to the head of the family	Sex	Color or race	Age at last birthday	Single, married, widowed or divorced	Attended school any time since Sept. 1, 1919	Whether able to read.	Whether able to write.	Place of birth of this person.	Place of birth of father of this person.	Place of birth of mother of this person.	Whether able to speak English.	Trade, profession, or particular kind of work done
1	2	3	4	5	6	7	8	9	10	11	12	13	14	15	16	17
	39	39	Babauta, Jesus A	Son	M	Cha	13.0	S	Y	Y	Y	Guam	Guam	Guam	Y	None
	40	40	Jesus, Magdalena S	Head	F	Cha	49.0	Wd		Y	Y	Guam	Guam	Guam	N	Washerwoman
	40	40	Jesus, Derfina S	Daughter	F	Cha	10.0	S	Y	Y	Y	Guam	Guam	Guam	Y	None
	41	41	Aguigui, Juan A	Head	M	Cha	34.0	M		Y	Y	Guam	Guam	Guam	N	Farmer
	41	41	Aguigui, Josefa R	Wife	F	Cha	38.0	M		N	N	Guam	Guam	Guam	N	None
	41	41	Aguigui, Ignacio R	Son	M	Cha	22.0	S	N	Y	Y	Guam	Guam	Guam	Y	Laborer
	41	41	Aguigui, Geronimo R	Son	M	Cha	16.0	S	N	Y	Y	Guam	Guam	Guam	Y	Farm laborer home farm
	41	41	Aguigui, Amabble R	Daughter	F	Cha	14.0	S	Y	Y	Y	Guam	Guam	Guam	Y	None
Serain Street	41	41	Aguigui, Jose R	Son	M	Cha	6.0	S	N			Guam	Guam	Guam		None
	42	42	Quitanoc, Emelia S	Head	F	Cha	58.0	Wd		Y	Y	Guam	Guam	Guam	N	Weaver
	42	42	Quitanoc, Ramon S	Son	M	Cha	23.0	S		Y	Y	Guam	Guam	Guam	Y	Laborer
	42	42	Quitanoc, Remedio S	Daughter	F	Cha	17.0	S	N	Y	Y	Guam	Guam	Guam	Y	Weaver
	42	42	Cruz, Juana Q	Head	F	Cha	31.0	Wd		Y	Y	Guam	Guam	Guam	N	Weaver
	42	42	Cruz, Jose Q	Son	M	Cha	7.0	S	Y			Guam	Guam	Guam		None
	42	42	Cruz, Maria Q	Daughter	F	Cha	3.0	S				Guam	Guam	Guam		None
	43	43	Babauta, Vicente B	Head	M	Cha	46.0	M		Y		Guam	Guam	Guam	N	Farmer
	43	43	Babauta, Antonia R	Wife	F	Cha	44.0	M		Y	N	Guam	Guam	Guam	N	None
	44	44	Chaco, Manuel Q	Head	M	Cha	50.0	M		N	N	Guam	Guam	Guam	N	Farmer
	44	44	Chaco, Ana C	Wife	F	Cha	51.0	M		N	N	Guam	Guam	Guam	N	None
	44	44	Chaco, Nieves C	Daughter	F	Cha	24.0	S		N	N	Guam	Guam	Guam	N	None
	44	44	Chaco, Juan C	Son	M	Cha	22.0	S		Y	Y	Guam	Guam	Guam	Y	Farm laborer home farm
	44	44	Chaco, Antonio C	Son	M	Cha	20.0	S	N	Y	Y	Guam	Guam	Guam	Y	Farm laborer home farm
	44	44	Chaco, Francisco C	Son	M	Cha	7.0	S	Y			Guam	Guam	Guam		None
	44	44	Chaco, Jesus C	Son	M	Cha	4.0	S				Guam	Guam	Guam		None
	45	45	Babauta, Vicente B	Head	M	Cha	52.0	Wd		N	N	Guam	Guam	Guam	N	Farmer

(CHAMORRO ROOTS GENEALOGY PROJECT ™ TRANSCRIPTION)
(COMPILED/TRANSCRIBED BY BERNARD T. PUNZALAN / HTTP://WWW.CHAMORROROOTS.COM)

FOURTEENTH CENSUS OF THE UNITED STATES: 1920—POPULATION
ISLAND OF GUAM

DISTRICT 4
NAME OF PLACE Agat Town
[Proper name and, also, name of class, as city, town, village, barrio, etc]

ENUMERATED BY ME ON THE 26th DAY OF February, 1920

Albert P. Manley ENUMERATOR

	Dwelling	Family	NAME	RELATION	Sex	Race	Age	Cond.	School	Read	Write	Birth person	Birth father	Birth mother	English	OCCUPATION
	2	3	4	5	6	7	8	9	10	11	12	13	14	15	16	17
26	45	45	Babauta, Francisco R	Son	M	Cha	29.0	Wd		Y	Y	Guam	Guam	Guam	N	Farm laborer home farm
27	45	45	Babauta, Antonia R	Daughter	F	Cha	28.0	S		Y	Y	Guam	Guam	Guam	N	None
28	45	45	Babauta, Jose R	Son	M	Cha	24.0	S		Y	Y	Guam	Guam	Guam	Y	Laborer
29	45	45	Babauta, Antonio R	Son	M	Cha	22.0	Wd		Y	Y	Guam	Guam	Guam	Y	Laborer
30	45	45	Babauta, Catalina R	Daughter	F	Cha	11.0	S	Y	Y	Y	Guam	Guam	Guam	Y	None
31	45	45	Babauta, Josefa R	Daughter	F	Cha	7.0	S	Y			Guam	Guam	Guam	Y	None
32	46	46	Babauta, Rosa B	Head	F	Cha	66.0	Wd		N	N	Guam	Guam	Guam	N	Weaver
33	46	46	Babauta, Rita B	Daughter	F	Cha	54.0	S		N	N	Guam	Guam	Guam	N	Weaver
34	46	46	Babauta, Juan B	Son	M	Cha	20.0	S	N	Y	Y	Guam	Guam	Guam	Y	Farmer
35	46	46	Babauta, Maria R	Niece	F	Cha	14.0	S	Y	Y	Y	Guam	Guam	Guam	Y	None
36	47	47	Chaco, Antonio Q	Head	M	Cha	51.0	M	N	Y	Y	Guam	Guam	Guam	Y	Farmer
37	47	47	Chaco, Milagro R	Wife	F	Cha	36.0	M		Y	Y	Guam	Guam	Guam	N	None
38	47	47	Chaco, Ana R	Daughter	F	Cha	18.0	S	N	Y	Y	Guam	Guam	Guam	Y	Nurse
39	47	47	Chaco, Joaquin R	Son	M	Cha	16.0	S	N	Y	Y	Guam	Guam	Guam	Y	Laborer
40	47	47	Chaco, Juan R	Son	M	Cha	14.0	S	Y	Y	Y	Guam	Guam	Guam	Y	Farm laborer home farm
41	47	47	Chaco, Jose R	Son	M	Cha	12.0	S	Y	Y	Y	Guam	Guam	Guam	Y	None
42	47	47	Chaco, Vicente R	Son	M	Cha	10.0	S	Y	Y	Y	Guam	Guam	Guam	Y	None
43	47	47	Chaco, Regina R	Daughter	F	Cha	8.0	S	Y			Guam	Guam	Guam	Y	None
44	47	47	Chaco, Soledad R	Daughter	F	Cha	6.0	S				Guam	Guam	Guam		None
45	47	47	Chaco, Francisco R	Son	M	Cha	4.0	S				Guam	Guam	Guam		None
46	47	47	Chaco, Jesus R	Son	M	Cha	2.0	S				Guam	Guam	Guam		None
47	47	47	Chaco, Maria R	Daughter	F	Cha	0.3	S				Guam	Guam	Guam		None
48	48	48	Babauta, Jose P	Head	M	Cha	40.0	M		Y	N	Guam	Guam	Guam	N	Farmer
49	48	48	Babauta, Tedora SN	Wife	F	Cha	49.0	M		Y	Y	Guam	Guam	Guam	N	None
50	48	48	Babauta, Juan SN	Son	M	Cha	16.0	S	N	Y	Y	Guam	Guam	Guam	Y	Laborer

Street: Serain Street

(CHAMORRO ROOTS GENEALOGY PROJECT ™ TRANSCRIPTION)
(COMPILED/TRANSCRIBED BY BERNARD T. PUNZALAN / HTTP://WWW.CHAMORROROOTS.COM)

FOURTEENTH CENSUS OF THE UNITED STATES: 1920-POPULATION
ISLAND OF GUAM

ENUMERATED BY ME ON THE 26th DAY OF February, 1920

Albert P. Manley ENUMERATOR

DISTRICT 4
NAME OF PLACE **Agat Town**

[Proper name and, also, name of class, as city, town, village, barrio, etc]

	Number of dwelling house in order of visitation	Number of family in order of visitation	NAME	RELATION	Sex	Color or race	Age at last birthday	Single, married, widowed or divorced	Attended school any time since Sept. 1, 1919	Whether able to read.	Whether able to write.	Place of birth of this person.	Place of birth of father of this person.	Place of birth of mother of this person.	Whether able to speak English.	OCCUPATION
	2	3	4	5	6	7	8	9	10	11	12	13	14	15	16	17
1	48	48	Babauta, Francisco SN	Son	M	Cha	13.0	S	Y	Y	Y	Guam	Guam	Guam	Y	None
2	48	48	Babauta, Felix SN	Son	M	Cha	11.0	S	Y	Y	Y	Guam	Guam	Guam	Y	None
3	48	48	Babauta, Ana SN	Daughter	F	Cha	9.0	S	Y			Guam	Guam	Guam		None
4	48	48	Babauta, Joaquin SN	Son	M	Cha	6.0	S	N			Guam	Guam	Guam		None
5	48	48	Espinosa, Felemona SN	Sister-in-law	F	Cha	43.0	S		Y	N	Guam	Guam	Guam	N	Weaver
6	49	49	Guerrero, Leon C	Head	M	Cha	29.0	M		Y	N	Guam	Guam	Guam	Y	Farmer
7	49	49	Guerrero, Encarnation B	Wife	F	Cha	29.0	M		Y	Y	Guam	Guam	Guam	N	None
8	49	49	Guerrero, Ana B	Daughter	F	Cha	11.0	S		Y	Y	Guam	Guam	Guam	Y	None
9	49	49	Guerrero, Ignacia B	Daughter	F	Cha	9.0	S	Y	Y	Y	Guam	Guam	Guam		None
10	49	49	Guerrero, Baltazar B	Son	M	Cha	4.0	S	Y			Guam	Guam	Guam		None
11	49	49	Guerrero, Felix B	Son	M	Cha	0.2	S				Guam	Guam	Guam		None
12	49	49	Guerrero, Soledad C	Mother-in-law	F	Cha	57.0	Wd		Y	N	Guam	Guam	Guam	N	None
13	49	49	Guerrero, Rosa C	Step-sister	F	Cha	4.0	S				Guam	Guam	Guam		None
14	49	49	Mansapit, Gregorio C	Servant	M	Cha	16.0	S		Y	Y	Guam	Guam	Guam	Y	Servant
15	50	50	Mesa, Juan M	Head	M	Cha	35.0	M		Y	Y	Guam	Guam	Guam	Y	Farmer
16	50	50	Mesa, Tomasa C	Wife	F	Cha	23.0	M		Y	Y	Guam	Guam	Guam	Y	None
17	50	50	Mesa, Rita C	Daughter	F	Cha	3.0	S				Guam	Guam	Guam		None
18	50	50	Mesa, Felix C	Son	M	Cha	2.0	S				Guam	Guam	Guam		None
19	51	51	Mendiola, Graviel S	Head	M	Cha	33.0	M		Y	Y	Guam	Guam	Guam	N	Farmer
20	51	51	Mendiola, Maria G	Wife	F	Cha	34.0	M		Y	Y	Guam	Guam	Guam	N	None
21	51	51	Mendiola, Joaquina G	Daughter	F	Cha	6.0	S	N			Guam	Guam	Guam		None
22	51	51	Mendiola, Maria G	Daughter	F	Cha	5.0	S	N			Guam	Guam	Guam		None
23	51	51	Mendiola, Auria G	Daughter	F	Cha	3.0	S				Guam	Guam	Guam		None
24	51	51	Mendiola, Ignacio G	Son	M	Cha	1.0	S				Guam	Guam	Guam		None
25	51	51	Santos, Polonoria F	Aunt	F	Cha	50.0	S				Guam	Guam	Guam	N	None

Serain Street

(CHAMORRO ROOTS GENEALOGY PROJECT ™ TRANSCRIPTION)
(COMPILED/TRANSCRIBED BY BERNARD T. PUNZALAN / HTTP://WWW.CHAMORROROOTS.COM)

FOURTEENTH CENSUS OF THE UNITED STATES: 1920-POPULATION
ISLAND OF GUAM

218b

DISTRICT 4
NAME OF PLACE **Agat Town**
[Proper name and, also, name of class, as city, town, village, barrio, etc]

ENUMERATED BY ME ON THE 26th DAY OF February, 1920

Albert P. Manley ENUMERATOR

	Number of dwelling house is order of visitation (2)	Number of family in order of visitation (3)	NAME (4)	RELATION: Relationship of this person to the head of the family. (5)	Sex (6)	Color or race (7)	Age at last birthday (8)	Single, married, widowed or divorced (9)	Attended school any time since Sept. 1, 1919 (10)	Whether able to read. (11)	Whether able to write. (12)	Place of birth of this person. (13)	Place of birth of father of this person. (14)	Place of birth of mother of this person. (15)	Whether able to speak English. (16)	OCCUPATION (17)
26	51	51	Pinaula, Juan G	Servant	M	Cha	22.0	S		Y	Y	Guam	Guam	Guam	Y	Servant
27	52	52	Cruz, Maria D	Head	F	Cha	66.0	S		N	N	Guam	Guam	Guam	N	None
28	52	52	Cruz, Antonio D	Son	M	Cha	49.0	Wd		N	N	Guam	Unknown	Guam	N	Farmer
29	52	52	Cruz, Josefina D	Daughter	F	Cha	5.0	S	N			Guam	Unknown	Guam		None
30	52	52	Cruz, Maria D	Sister	F	Cha	64.0	Wd		N	N	Guam	Guam	Guam	N	None
31	52	52	Taitague, Josefa Q	Servant	F	Cha	13.0	S	Y	Y	Y	Guam	Guam	Guam	Y	Servant
32	53	53	Mendiola, Vicente A	Head	M	Cha	33.0	M		Y	Y	Guam	Guam	Guam	Y	Farmer
33	53	53	Mendiola, Barbara S	Wife	F	Cha	28.0	M		Y	Y	Guam	Guam	Guam	Y	None
34	53	53	Mendiola, Regina S	Daughter	F	Cha	6.0	S	N			Guam	Guam	Guam		None
35	53	53	Mendiola, Juan S	Son	M	Cha	5.0	S	N			Guam	Guam	Guam		None
36	53	53	Mendiola, Tomas S	Son	M	Cha	1.0	S				Guam	Guam	Guam		None
37	53	53	Taitano, Maria A	Servant	F	Cha	50.0	Wd		N	N	Guam	Guam	Guam	N	Servant
38	54	54	Onedera, Juan Jito	Head	M	Jp	34.0	M		Y	Y	Japan	Japan	Japan	N	Farm manager
39	54	54	Onedera, Maria S	Wife	F	Cha	25.0	M		Y	Y	Guam	Guam	Guam	Y	None
40	54	54	Onedera, Carmen S	Daughter	F	Jp	6.0	S	N			Guam	Guam	Guam		None
41	54	54	Onedera, Maria S	Daughter	F	Jp	5.0	S	N			Guam	Guam	Guam		None
42	54	54	Onedera, Ana S	Daughter	F	Jp	3.0	S				Guam	Guam	Guam		None
43	54	54	Onedera, Juan S	Son	M	Jp	2.0	S				Guam	Guam	Guam		None
44	55	55	Rivera, Joaquin D	Head	M	Cha	41.0	M		Y	Y	Guam	Guam	Guam	N	Farmer
45	55	55	Rivera, Dolores G	Wife	F	Cha	37.0	M		Y	Y	Guam	Guam	Guam	N	None
46	55	55	Rivera, Antonia G	Daughter	F	Cha	13.0	S	Y	Y	Y	Guam	Guam	Guam	Y	None
47	55	55	Rivera, Jesus G	Son	M	Cha	6.0	S	N			Guam	Guam	Guam		None
48	56	56	Babauta, Antonio C	Head	M	Cha	24.0	M		Y	Y	Guam	Guam	Guam	Y	Farmer
49	56	56	Babauta, Rosa G	Wife	F	Cha	20.0	M		Y	Y	Guam	Guam	Guam	Y	None
50	56	56	Babauta, Jose G	Son	M	Cha	0.8	S				Guam	Guam	Guam		None

Serain Street

440

(CHAMORRO ROOTS GENEALOGY PROJECT ™ TRANSCRIPTION)
(COMPILED/TRANSCRIBED BY BERNARD T. PUNZALAN / HTTP://WWW.CHAMORROROOTS.COM)

FOURTEENTH CENSUS OF THE UNITED STATES: 1920-POPULATION

ISLAND OF GUAM

DISTRICT 4
NAME OF PLACE **Agat Town**

[Proper name and, also, name of class, as city, town, village, barrio, etc]

ENUMERATED BY ME ON THE 27th DAY OF February, 1920

Albert P. Manley ENUMERATOR

	Street, avenue, road, etc.	Number of dwelling house in order of visitation	Number of family in order of visitation	NAME	RELATION	Sex	Color or race	Age at last birthday	Single, married, widowed or divorced	Attended school any time since Sept. 1, 1919	Whether able to read	Whether able to write	Place of birth of this person	Place of birth of father of this person	Place of birth of mother of this person	Whether able to speak English	OCCUPATION
	1	2	3	4	5	6	7	8	9	10	11	12	13	14	15	16	17
1		57	57	San Nicolas, Jose B	Head	M	Cha	41.0	M		Y	Y	Guam	Guam	Guam	Y	Farmer
2		57	57	San Nicolas, Maria S	Wife	F	Cha	32.0	M		Y	Y	Guam	Guam	Guam	Y	None
3		57	57	San Nicolas, Josefa B	Sister	F	Cha	44.0	S		Y	Y	Guam	Guam	Guam	N	Washerwoman
4		57	57	San Nicolas, Vicente B	Brother	M	Cha	26.0	S		Y	Y	Guam	Guam	Guam	Y	Farm laborer home farm
5		58	58	Babauta, Santiago C	Head	M	Cha	29.0	M		Y	Y	Guam	Guam	Guam	N	Farmer
6		58	58	Babauta, Carmen C	Wife	F	Cha	31.0	M		Y	Y	Guam	Guam	Guam	N	None
7		58	58	Babauta, Joaquin C	Son	M	Cha	6.0	S	N			Guam	Guam	Guam		None
8		59	59	Unsiok, Venefacio J	Head	M	Cha	30.0	M		Y	Y	Guam	Guam	Guam	N	Farmer
9		59	59	Unsiok, Maria N	Wife	F	Cha	29.0	M		Y	Y	Guam	Guam	Guam	N	None
10		59	59	Unsiok, Jose N	Son	M	Cha	0.9	S		N	N	Guam	Guam	Guam		None
11		60	60	Charfauros, Francisco A	Head	M	Cha	27.0	M		Y	Y	Guam	Guam	Guam	Y	Farmer
12		60	60	Charfauros, Rosa T	Wife	F	Cha	21.0	M	N	Y	Y	Guam	Guam	Guam	Y	Washerwoman
13		60	60	Charfauros, Rita T	Daughter	F	Cha	0.7	S				Guam	Guam	Guam		None
14		61	61	Taenao, Ignacia M	Head	F	Cha	43.0	Wd		Y	N	Guam	Guam	Guam	Y	Washerwoman
15		61	61	Taenao, Enriquita M	Daughter	F	Cha	15.0	S	N	Y	Y	Guam	Guam	Guam	Y	Washerwoman
16		61	61	Taenao, Maria M	Daughter	F	Cha	11.0	S	Y	Y	Y	Guam	Guam	Guam		None
17	Serafn Street	61	61	Taenao, Carmen M	Daughter	F	Cha	9.0	S	Y	Y	Y	Guam	Guam	Guam		None
18		61	61	Taenao, Conception M	Daughter	F	Cha	6.0	S	N			Guam	Guam	Guam		None
19		62	62	Saluznamnam, Faustina T	Head	F	Cha	49.0	S		N	N	Guam	Guam	Guam	N	Weaver
20		62	62	Gomes, Maria S	Niece	F	Cha	18.0	S	N	Y	Y	Guam	Guam	Guam	Y	Weaver
21		62	62	Saluznamnam, Ignacia T	Niece	F	Cha	14.0	S	Y	Y	Y	Guam	Guam	Guam	Y	None
22		63	63	Charfauros, Consolacion B	Head	F	Cha	50.0	Wd		Y	Y	Guam	Guam	Guam	Y	Washerwoman
23		63	63	Charfauros, Aniceto B	Son	M	Cha	28.0	S		Y	Y	Guam	Guam	Guam	Y	Farm laborer home farm
24		64	64	San Nicolas, Antonio B	Head	M	Cha	30.0	M	N	Y	Y	Guam	Guam	Guam	Y	Farmer
25		64	64	San Nicolas, Maria C	Wife	F	Cha	20.0	M		Y	Y	Guam	Guam	Guam	Y	None

(CHAMORRO ROOTS GENEALOGY PROJECT ™ TRANSCRIPTION)
(COMPILED/TRANSCRIBED BY BERNARD T. PUNZALAN / HTTP://WWW.CHAMORROROOTS.COM)

219b

FOURTEENTH CENSUS OF THE UNITED STATES: 1920-POPULATION

ISLAND OF GUAM

DISTRICT **4**

NAME OF PLACE **Agat Town**

[Proper name and, also, name of class, as city, town, village, barrio, etc]

ENUMERATED BY ME ON THE 27th DAY OF February, 1920

Albert P. Manley ENUMERATOR.

Street	Dwelling No.	Family No.	NAME	RELATION	Sex	Color or race	Age	Single, married, widowed or divorced	Attended school since Sept 1, 1919	Able to read	Able to write	Place of birth of this person	Place of birth of father	Place of birth of mother	Able to speak English	OCCUPATION
	1	2	3	4	5	6	7	8	9	10	11	12	13	14	15	16	17
	64	64	San Nicolas, Vicente C	Son	M	Cha	0.3	S				Guam	Guam	Guam		None
	65	65	Salas, Jose C	Head	M	Cha	33.0	M		Y	Y	Guam	Guam	Guam	N	Farmer
	65	65	Salas, Maria S	Wife	F	Cha	28.0	M		N	N	Guam	Guam	Guam	N	None
	65	65	Salas, Isabel S	Daughter	F	Cha	12.0	S	Y	Y	Y	Guam	Guam	Guam	Y	None
	65	65	Salas, Elestina S	Daughter	F	Cha	0.9	S				Guam	Guam	Guam		None
	66	66	Sablan, Francisco C	Head	M	Cha	24.0	M		Y	Y	Guam	Guam	Guam	Y	Native seaman
	66	66	Sablan, Estfania C	Wife	F	Cha	27.0	M				Guam	Guam	Guam	Y	None
	66	66	Sablan, Alfredo C	Son	M	Cha	1.0	S				Guam	Guam	Guam		None
	67	67	Mansapit, Maria C	Head	F	Cha	35.0	Wd		N	N	Guam	Guam	Guam	N	Washerwoman
	67	67	Mansapit, Dolores C	Daughter	F	Cha	12.0	S	Y	Y	Y	Guam	Guam	Guam	Y	None
	67	67	Mansapit, Juan C	Son	M	Cha	7.0	S	Y	Y	Y	Guam	Guam	Guam	Y	None
Serain Street	67	67	Mansapit, Rosalia C	Daughter	F	Cha	5.0	S	N			Guam	Guam	Guam	Y	None
	68	68	Sablan, Jesus C	Head	M	Cha	22.0	M		Y	Y	Guam	Guam	Guam	Y	Laborer
	68	68	Sablan, Maria B	Wife	F	Cha	16.0	M	N	Y	N	Guam	Guam	Guam	Y	None
	69	69	Reyes, Jose A	Head	M	Cha	59.0	Wd		N	N	Guam	Guam	Guam	N	Farmer
	69	69	Reyes, Maria B	Daughter	F	Cha	29.0	S		Y	Y	Guam	Guam	Guam	Y	None
	69	69	Reyes, Natividad B	Daughter	F	Cha	25.0	S		Y	Y	Guam	Guam	Guam	Y	None
	69	69	Reyes, Cerilo B	Son	M	Cha	20.0	S	N	N	Y	Guam	Guam	Guam	Y	Laborer
	69	69	Babauta, Venancio R	Servant	M	Cha	14.0	S		Y	Y	Guam	Guam	Guam	Y	Servant
	70	70	Borja, Antonio M	Head	M	Cha	42.0	M		Y	Y	Guam	Guam	Guam	Y	Farmer
	70	70	Borja, Maria A	Wife	F	Cha	42.0	M		Y	Y	Guam	Guam	Guam	Y	None
	70	70	Borja, Luis A	Son	M	Cha	20.0	S	N	Y	Y	Guam	Guam	Guam	Y	Farm laborer home farm
	70	70	Borja, Jose A	Son	M	Cha	15.0	S	N	Y	Y	Guam	Guam	Guam	Y	Farm laborer home farm
	70	70	Borja, Rosa A	Daughter	F	Cha	14.0	S	N	Y	Y	Guam	Guam	Guam	Y	None
	70	70	Borja, Martina A	Daughter	F	Cha	11.0	S	Y	Y	Y	Guam	Guam	Guam	Y	None

442

(CHAMORRO ROOTS GENEALOGY PROJECT ™ TRANSCRIPTION)
(COMPILED/TRANSCRIBED BY BERNARD T. PUNZALAN / HTTP://WWW.CHAMORROROOTS.COM)

FOURTEENTH CENSUS OF THE UNITED STATES: 1920-POPULATION

ISLAND OF GUAM

SHEET NO. _8A_

DISTRICT 4
NAME OF PLACE **Agat Town**

[Proper name and, also, name of class, as city, town, village, barrio, etc]

ENUMERATED BY ME ON THE 27th DAY OF February, 1920

Albert P. Manley ENUMERATOR

	PLACE OF ABODE			NAME	RELATION	PERSONAL DESCRIPTION					EDUCATION			NATIVITY				OCCUPATION
Street, avenue, road, etc.	Number of dwelling house is order of visitation	Number of family in order of visitation		of each person whose place of abode on January 1, 1920, was in the family. Enter surname, firs, then given name and middle initial if any. Include every person living on January 1, 1920. Omit children born since January 1, 1920.	Relationship of this Person to the head of the family.	Sex	Color or race	Age at last birthday	Single, married, widowed or divorced	Attended school any time since Sept. 1, 1919	Whether able to read.	Whether able to write.	Place of birth of this person.	Place of birth of father of this person.	Place of birth of mother of this person.	Whether able to speak English.	Trade, profession, or particular kind of work done, as salesman, laborer, clerk, cook, merchant, washerwoman, etc.
1	2	3		4	5	6	7	8	9	10	11	12	13	14	15	16	17
1	70	70		Borja, Asemcion A	Daughter	F	Cha	4.0	S				Guam	Guam	Guam		None
2	70	70		Borja, Antonio A	Son	M	Cha	3.0	S				Guam	Guam	Guam		None
3	71	71		Babauta, Donicio C	Head	M	Cha	24.0	M		Y	Y	Guam	Guam	Guam	Y	Farmer
4	71	71		Babauta, Maria C	Wife	F	Cha	27.0	M		Y	Y	Guam	Guam	Guam	Y	Washerwoman
5	71	71		Babauta, Pedro C	Son	M	Cha	0.3	S				Guam	Guam	Guam		None
6	72	72		Yamashita, Kanzaboro	Head	M	Jp	42.0	M		Y	Y	Japan	Japan	Japan	N	Storekeeper
7	73	73		Rivera, Juan D	Head	M	Cha	32.0	M		Y	Y	Guam	Guam	Guam	N	Farmer
8	73	73		Rivera, Dolores S	Wife	F	Cha	28.0	M		Y	Y	Guam	Guam	Guam	N	None
9	73	73		Rivera, Maria S	Daughter	F	Cha	0.3	S				Guam	Guam	Guam		None
10	73	73		Charfauros, Manuel S	Nephew	M	Cha	9.0	S	Y			Guam	Guam	Guam		None
11	74	74		Terlaje, Joaquin B	Head	M	Cha	25.0	M		Y	Y	Guam	Guam	Guam	N	Farmer
12	74	74		Terlaje, Consolacion B	Wife	F	Cha	18.0	M	N	Y	Y	Guam	Guam	Guam	Y	None
13	74	74		Terlaje, Rosalia B	Daughter	F	Cha	1.0	S				Guam	Guam	Guam		None
14	75	75		Charfauros, Augustin C	Head	M	Cha	37.0	Wd		Y	Y	Guam	Guam	Guam	N	Farmer
15	76	76		Aguigui, Joaquin A	Head	M	Cha	25.0	M		Y	Y	Guam	Guam	Guam	Y	Laborer
16	76	76		Aguigui, Joaquina T	Wife	F	Cha	25.0	M		Y	Y	Guam	Guam	Guam	Y	Nurse
17	77	77	Serain Street	Cruz, Luis D	Head	M	Cha	36.0	M		Y	Y	Guam	Guam	Guam	N	Laborer
18	77	77		Cruz, Simona C	Wife	F	Cha	38.0	M		Y	Y	Guam	Guam	Guam	N	None
19	77	77		Cruz, Ingracia C	Daughter	F	Cha	16.0	S	N	Y	Y	Guam	Guam	Guam	Y	None
20	77	77		Cruz, Ignacia C	Daughter	F	Cha	14.0	S	N	Y	Y	Guam	Guam	Guam	Y	None
21	77	77		Cruz, Jose C	Son	M	Cha	13.0	S	Y	Y	Y	Guam	Guam	Guam	Y	None
22	77	77		Cruz, Carmen C	Daughter	F	Cha	9.0	S	Y			Guam	Guam	Guam		None
23	77	77		Cruz, Josefina C	Daughter	F	Cha	4.0	S				Guam	Guam	Guam		None
24	77	77		Charfauros, Jose S	Nephew	M	Cha	4.0	S				Guam	Guam	Guam		None
25	77	77		Babauta, Vicente C	Nephew	M	Cha	1.0	S				Guam	Guam	Guam		None

443

(CHAMORRO ROOTS GENEALOGY PROJECT ™ TRANSCRIPTION)

(COMPILED/TRANSCRIBED BY BERNARD T. PUNZALAN / HTTP://WWW.CHAMORROROOTS.COM)

FOURTEENTH CENSUS OF THE UNITED STATES: 1920-POPULATION

ISLAND OF GUAM

DISTRICT **4**

NAME OF PLACE **Agat Town**

[Proper name and, also, name of class, as city, town, village, barrio, etc]

ENUMERATED BY ME ON THE 27th DAY OF February, 1920

Albert P. Manley ENUMERATOR

	PLACE OF ABODE			NAME	RELATION	PERSONAL DESCRIPTION				EDUCATION			NATIVITY				OCCUPATION
Street, avenue, road, etc.	Number of dwelling house in order of visitation	Number of family in order of visitation		Name	Relationship of this Person to the head of the family.	Sex	Color or race	Age at last birthday	Single, married, widowed or divorced	Attended school any time since Sept. 1, 1919	Whether able to read.	Whether able to write.	Place of birth of this person.	Place of birth of father of this person.	Place of birth of mother of this person.	Whether able to speak English.	Trade, profession, or particular kind of work done, as salesman, laborer, clerk, cook, merchant, washerwoman, etc.
1	2	3		4	5	6	7	8	9	10	11	12	13	14	15	16	17
			26	Charfauros, Luis A	Head	M	Cha	47.0	M		Y	Y	Guam	Guam	Guam	N	Farmer
	78	78	27	Charfauros, Rosa C	Wife	F	Cha	46.0	M		Y	Y	Guam	Guam	Guam	N	None
	78	78	28	Charfauros, Juan C	Son	M	Cha	22.0	S		Y	Y	Guam	Guam	Guam	Y	Laborer
	78	78	29	Charfauros, Ignacio C	Son	M	Cha	20.0	S	N	Y	Y	Guam	Guam	Guam	Y	Farm laborer home farm
	78	78	30	Charfauros, Consolacion C	Daughter	F	Cha	16.0	S	N	Y	Y	Guam	Guam	Guam	Y	None
	78	78	31	Charfauros, Andres C	Son	M	Cha	13.0	S	N	Y	Y	Guam	Guam	Guam	Y	None
	78	78	32	Charfauros, Dolores C	Niece	F	Cha	14.0	S	N	Y	Y	Guam	Guam	Guam	Y	None
	79	79	33	Santos, Mariano C	Head	M	Cha	28.0	M		Y	Y	Guam	Guam	Guam	N	Farmer
	79	79	34	Santos, Tedora B	Wife	F	Cha	26.0	M		Y	Y	Guam	Guam	Guam	Y	None
	79	79	35	Santos, Josefa B	Daughter	F	Cha	2.0	S				Guam	Guam	Guam		None
	79	79	36	Santos, Juan B	Son	M	Cha	0.2	S				Guam	Guam	Guam		None
Serain Street	80	80	37	San Nicolas, Geronimo S	Head	M	Cha	48.0	M		Y	Y	Guam	Guam	Guam	N	Farmer
	80	80	38	San Nicolas, Josefa A	Wife	F	Cha	46.0	M		Y	Y	Guam	Guam	Guam	N	Weaver
	81	81	39	Nededoc, Andre	Head	M	Cha	60.0	M		Y	Y	Guam	Guam	Guam	N	Farmer
	81	81	40	Nededoc, Nicolasa C	Wife	F	Cha	47.0	M		N	N	Guam	Guam	Guam	N	None
	81	81	41	Nededoc, Candilara C	Daughter	F	Cha	17.0	S	N	Y	Y	Guam	Guam	Guam	Y	None
	81	81	42	Nededoc, Vicente C	Son	M	Cha	15.0	S	N	Y	Y	Guam	Guam	Guam	Y	Farm laborer home farm
	81	81	43	Nededoc, Joaquin C	Son	M	Cha	12.0	S	Y	Y	Y	Guam	Guam	Guam	Y	None
	82	82	44	Jococ, Bartola C	Head	F	Cha	49.0	S		Y	Y	Guam	Manila Philippines	Guam	N	Weaver
	83	83	45	Aguigui, Dolores SN	Head	F	Cha	30.0	S		Y	Y	Guam	Guam	Guam	Y	Weaver
	83	83	46	Aguigui, Juan SN	Son	M	Cha	11.0	S	Y	Y	Y	Guam	Unknown	Guam	Y	None
	83	83	47	Aguigui, Pedro SN	Son	M	Cha	6.0	S	N			Guam	Unknown	Guam	Y	None
	83	83	48	Aguigui, Vicente SN	Son	M	Cha	4.0	S				Guam	Unknown	Guam		None
	83	83	49	Aguigui, Tomasa SN	Daughter	F	Cha	0.3	S				Guam	Guam	Guam		None
	84	84	50	Terlaje, Revostiano B	Head	M	Cha	28.0	M		Y	Y	Guam	Guam	Guam	Y	Farmer

(CHAMORRO ROOTS GENEALOGY PROJECT ™ TRANSCRIPTION)
(COMPILED/TRANSCRIBED BY BERNARD T. PUNZALAN / HTTP://WWW.CHAMORROROOTS.COM)

FOURTEENTH CENSUS OF THE UNITED STATES: 1920-POPULATION

ISLAND OF GUAM

DISTRICT 4
NAME OF PLACE **Agat Town**

[Proper name and, also, name of class, as city, town, village, barrio, etc]

ENUMERATED BY ME ON THE 28th DAY OF February, 1920

Albert P. Manley ENUMERATOR

	PLACE OF ABODE			NAME	RELATION	PERSONAL DESCRIPTION					EDUCATION			NATIVITY				OCCUPATION
	Street, avenue, road, etc.	Number of dwelling house in order of visitation	Number of family in order of visitation	of each person whose place of abode on January 1, 1920, was in the family.	Relationship of this Person to the head of the family.	Sex	Color or race	Age at last birthday	Single, married, widowed or divorced	Attended school any time since Sept. 1, 1919	Whether able to read.	Whether able to write.	Place of birth of this person.	Place of birth of father of this person.	Place of birth of mother of this person.	Whether able to speak English.	Trade, profession, or particular kind of work done, as salesman, laborer, clerk, cook, merchant, washerwoman, etc.
	1	2	3	4	5	6	7	8	9	10	11	12	13	14	15	16	17
1		84	84	Terlaje, Maria C	Wife	F	Cha	27.0	M		Y	Y	Guam	Guam	Guam	Y	None
2		85	85	Cruz, Jose A	Head	M	Cha	21.0	M	N	Y	Y	Guam	Guam	Guam	Y	Farmer
3		85	85	Cruz, Ana B	Wife	F	Cha	30.0	M		Y	N	Guam	Guam	Guam	N	None
4		85	85	Cruz, Felicidad B	Daughter	F	Cha	9.0	S	Y			Guam	Guam	Guam		None
5		85	85	Cruz, Francisca B	Daughter	F	Cha	0.3	S				Guam	Guam	Guam	N	None
6		86	86	Santos, Roque S	Head	M	Cha	37.0	M		Y	Y	Guam	Guam	Guam	Y	Farmer
7		86	86	Santos, Maria C	Wife	F	Cha	33.0	M		Y	Y	Guam	Guam	Guam	Y	None
8		86	86	Santos, Carmen C	Daughter	F	Cha	14.0	S	N	Y	Y	Guam	Guam	Guam	Y	None
9		86	86	Santos, Ascemcion C	Daughter	F	Cha	12.0	S	Y	Y	Y	Guam	Guam	Guam	Y	None
10		86	86	Santos, Juana C	Daughter	F	Cha	11.0	S	Y	Y	Y	Guam	Guam	Guam	Y	None
11		86	86	Santos, Isabel C	Daughter	F	Cha	9.0	S	Y			Guam	Guam	Guam		None
12		86	86	Santos, Maria C	Daughter	F	Cha	7.0	S	Y			Guam	Guam	Guam		None
13		86	86	Santos, Emelia C	Daughter	F	Cha	5.0	S	N			Guam	Guam	Guam		None
14		87	87	Charfauros, Juan L	Head	M	Cha	46.0	M		Y	Y	Guam	Guam	Guam	Y	Farmer
15		87	87	Charfauros, Encarnacion Q	Wife	F	Cha	53.0	M		Y	Y	Guam	Guam	Guam	N	None
16	Pareno Street	87	87	Chargualaf, Ignacio C	Servant	M	Cha	11.0	S	Y	Y	Y	Guam	Guam	Guam	Y	Servant
17		88	88	Reyes, Venancio B	Head	M	Cha	34.0	M		Y	Y	Guam	Guam	Guam	N	Farmer
18		88	88	Reyes, Ignacia C	Wife	F	Cha	22.0	M		Y	Y	Guam	Guam	Guam	Y	None
19		88	88	Reyes, Maria C	Daughter	F	Cha	12.0	S	Y	Y	Y	Guam	Guam	Guam	Y	None
20		88	88	Reyes, Juan C	Son	M	Cha	10.0	S	Y	Y	Y	Guam	Guam	Guam	Y	None
21		88	88	Reyes, Jose C	Son	M	Cha	4.0	S				Guam	Guam	Guam		None
22		89	89	Quintanilla, Betnabe SN	Head	M	Cha	57.0	M		N	N	Guam	Guam	Guam	N	Farmer
23		89	89	Quintanilla, Maria L	Wife	F	Cha	45.0	M		N	N	Guam	Guam	Guam	N	None
24		89	89	Quintanilla, Andres L	Son	M	Cha	12.0	S	Y	Y	Y	Guam	Guam	Guam	Y	None
25		90	90	Mesa, Juan LG	Head	M	Cha	67.0	M		Y	Y	Guam	Guam	Guam	N	Farmer

(CHAMORRO ROOTS GENEALOGY PROJECT ™ TRANSCRIPTION)
(COMPILED/TRANSCRIBED BY BERNARD T. PUNZALAN / HTTP://WWW.CHAMORROROOTS.COM)

FOURTEENTH CENSUS OF THE UNITED STATES: 1920-POPULATION

ISLAND OF GUAM

ENUMERATED BY ME ON THE 28th DAY OF February, 1920

Albert P. Manley ENUMERATOR

DISTRICT 4
NAME OF PLACE Agat Town

	Dwelling	Family	NAME	RELATION	Sex	Color	Age	Cond.	School	Read	Write	Birthplace	Father	Mother	Eng.	OCCUPATION
1	2	3	4	5	6	7	8	9	10	11	12	13	14	15	16	17
	90	90	Mesa, Dolores SN	Wife	F	Cha	47.0	M		Y	Y	Guam	Guam	Guam	N	Weaver
	91	91	Torres, Juan P	Head	M	Cha	43.0	M		Y	Y	Guam	Guam	Guam	Y	Farmer
	91	91	Torres, Ignacia P	Wife	F	Cha	40.0	M		Y	Y	Guam	Guam	Guam	N	None
	91	91	Torres, Jose P	Son	M	Cha	21.0	S	N	Y	Y	Guam	Guam	Guam	Y	Farm laborer home farm
	91	91	Torres, Francisco P	Son	M	Cha	19.0	S	N	Y	Y	Guam	Guam	Guam	Y	Farm laborer home farm
	91	91	Torres, Jesus P	Son	M	Cha	17.0	S	N	Y	Y	Guam	Guam	Guam	Y	Farm laborer home farm
	91	91	Torres, Soledad P	Daughter	F	Cha	13.0	S	Y	Y	Y	Guam	Guam	Guam	Y	None
	91	91	Torres, Maria P	Daughter	F	Cha	5.0	S	N			Guam	Guam	Guam		None
	91	91	Torres, Antonio P	Son	M	Cha	1.0	S				Guam	Guam	Guam		None
	91	91	Chafauros, Juan S	Servant	M	Cha	11.0	S	Y	Y	Y	Guam	Guam	Guam	Y	Servant
	92	92	Ty-dingco, Carlos M	Head	M	Cha	57.0	M		Y	Y	Guam	Guam	Guam	Y	Farmer
	92	92	Ty-dingco, Rosa S	Wife	F	Cha	40.0	M		Y	Y	Guam	Guam	Guam	N	None
	92	92	Ty-dingco, Asemcion S	Daughter	F	Cha	14.0	S	N	Y	Y	Guam	Guam	Guam	Y	None
	92	92	Ty-dingco, Maria S	Daughter	F	Cha	11.0	S	Y	Y	Y	Guam	Guam	Guam	Y	None
	92	92	Ty-dingco, Francisco S	Son	M	Cha	10.0	S	Y	Y	Y	Guam	Guam	Guam	Y	None
	92	92	Ty-dingco, Jose S	Son	M	Cha	9.0	S	Y	Y	Y	Guam	Guam	Guam	Y	None
	92	92	Ty-dingco, Antonio S	Son	M	Cha	8.0	S	Y	Y	Y	Guam	Guam	Guam	Y	None
	92	92	Ty-dingco, Remedio S	Daughter	F	Cha	5.0	S	N			Guam	Guam	Guam		None
	92	92	Ty-dingco, Tomas S	Son	M	Cha	3.0	S				Guam	Guam	Guam		None
	93	93	Herrero, Antonia A	Head	F	Cha	43.0	Wd		Y	Y	Guam	Spain	Guam	Y	Washerwoman
	93	93	Herrero, Jesus S	Nephew	M	Cha	33.0	S		Y	Y	Guam	Guam	Guam	Y	Laborer
	93	93	Herrero, Francisco S	Nephew	M	Cha	17.0	S	N	Y	Y	Guam	Guam	Guam	Y	Farm laborer home farm
	93	93	Herrero, Rita S	Niece	F	Cha	15.0	S	N	Y	Y	Guam	Guam	Guam	Y	Washerwoman
	93	93	Herrero, Manuela S	Niece	F	Cha	5.0	S	Y	N	N	Guam	Guam	Guam	Y	None
	94	94	Aguigui, Ana SN	Head	F	Cha	50.0	S		N	N	Guam	Guam	Guam	N	Weaver

Street: Pareno Street

Line numbers: 26–50

446

(CHAMORRO ROOTS GENEALOGY PROJECT ™ TRANSCRIPTION)
(COMPILED/TRANSCRIBED BY BERNARD T. PUNZALAN / HTTP://WWW.CHAMORROROOTS.COM)

FOURTEENTH CENSUS OF THE UNITED STATES: 1920–POPULATION

ISLAND OF GUAM

222

ENUMERATED BY ME ON THE 1st DAY OF March, 1920

Albert P. Manley ENUMERATOR

DISTRICT 4

NAME OF PLACE Agat Town

[Proper name and, also, name of class, as city, town, village, barrio, etc]

#	Street	Dwelling	Family	NAME	RELATION	Sex	Color or race	Age	Single, married, widowed or divorced	Attended school since Sept 1, 1919	Able to read	Able to write	Birthplace of person	Birthplace of father	Birthplace of mother	Able to speak English	OCCUPATION
1		94	94	Aguigui, Jose SN	Son	M	Cha	23.0	S		Y	Y	Guam	Unknown	Guam	Y	Farm laborer home farm
2		94	94	Aguigui, Carmen SN	Daughter	F	Cha	19.0	S	N	Y	Y	Guam	Unknown	Guam	Y	Teacher
3		94	94	Aguigui, Consolacion SN	Daughter	F	Cha	16.0	S	N	Y	Y	Guam	Unknown	Guam	Y	Weaver
4		94	94	Aguigui, Josefina SN	Daughter	F	Cha	15.0	S	N	Y	Y	Guam	Unknown	Guam	Y	None
5		94	94	Aguigui, Francisco SN	Son	M	Cha	13.0	S	Y	Y	Y	Guam	Unknown	Guam	Y	None
6		94	94	Aguigui, Guadalupe SN	Daughter	F	Cha	11.0	S	Y	Y	Y	Guam	Unknown	Guam	Y	None
7		94	94	Aguigui, Manuel SN	Son	M	Cha	6.0	S	N			Guam	Unknown	Guam	Y	None
8		95	95	San Nicolas, Vicente SN	Head	M	Cha	48.0	M		Y	Y	Guam	Guam	Guam	N	Farmer
9		95	95	San Nicolas, Antonia C	Wife	F	Cha	44.0	M		Y	Y	Guam	Guam	Guam	N	None
10	Pareno Street	95	95	San Nicolas, Joaquin C	Son	M	Cha	19.0	S	N	Y	Y	Guam	Guam	Guam	Y	Farm laborer home farm
11		95	95	San Nicolas, Jose C	Son	M	Cha	13.0	S	Y	Y	Y	Guam	Guam	Guam	Y	Farm laborer home farm
12		95	95	San Nicolas, Felix C	Son	M	Cha	8.0	S	Y			Guam	Guam	Guam	Y	None
13		95	95	San Nicolas, Ana C	Daughter	F	Cha	1.0	S				Guam	Guam	Guam		None
14		96	96	Lizama, Carmelo L	Head	M	Cha	30.0	M		Y	Y	Guam	Guam	Guam	Y	Farmer
15		96	96	Lizama, Isabel C	Wife	F	Cha	29.0	M				Guam	Guam	Guam	N	None
16		97	97	Rivera, Felix T	Head	M	Cha	40.0	M		Y	Y	Guam	Guam	Guam	N	Farmer
17		97	97	Rivera, Soledad S	Wife	F	Cha	39.0	M				Guam	Guam	Guam	N	None
18		97	97	Rivera, Rosa S	Daughter	F	Cha	13.0	S	Y	Y	Y	Guam	Guam	Guam	Y	None
19		97	97	Rivera, Vicente S	Son	M	Cha	10.0	S	Y	Y	Y	Guam	Guam	Guam	Y	None
20		97	97	Rivera, Natividad S	Daughter	F	Cha	8.0	S	Y			Guam	Guam	Guam	Y	None
21		97	97	Rivera, Jose S	Son	M	Cha	6.0	S	N			Guam	Guam	Guam		None
22		97	97	Rivera, Adelia S	Daughter	F	Cha	4.0	S				Guam	Guam	Guam		None
23		97	97	Rivera, Ana S	Daughter	F	Cha	2.0	S				Guam	Guam	Guam		None
24		98	98	Herrero, Manuel A	Head	M	Cha	45.0	Wd		Y	Y	Guam	Spain	Guam	N	Farmer
25		99	99	Nededoc, Juan N	Head	M	Cha	52.0	M		Y	Y	Guam	Guam	Guam	N	Farmer

(CHAMORRO ROOTS GENEALOGY PROJECT ™ TRANSCRIPTION)
(COMPILED/TRANSCRIBED BY BERNARD T. PUNZALAN / HTTP://WWW.CHAMORROROOTS.COM)

FOURTEENTH CENSUS OF THE UNITED STATES: 1920-POPULATION

ISLAND OF GUAM

DISTRICT **4**

NAME OF PLACE **Agat Town**

[Proper name and, also, name of class, as city, town, village, barrio, etc]

ENUMERATED BY ME ON THE 1st DAY OF March, 1920

Albert P. Manley ENUMERATOR

	PLACE OF ABODE		NAME	RELATION	PERSONAL DESCRIPTION				EDUCATION			NATIVITY				OCCUPATION
Street, avenue, road, etc.	Number of dwelling house in order of visitation	Number of family in order of visitation	of each person whose place of abode on January 1, 1920, was in the family. Enter surname, first, then given name and middle initial. If any. Include every person living on January 1, 1920. Omit children born since January 1, 1920.	Relationship of this Person to the head of the family.	Sex	Color or race	Age at last birthday	Single, married, widowed or divorced	Attended school any time since Sept. 1, 1919	Whether able to read.	Whether able to write.	Place of birth of this person.	Place of birth of father of this person.	Place of birth of mother of this person.	Whether able to speak English.	Trade, profession, or particular kind of work done, as salesman, laborer, clerk, cook, merchant, washerwoman, etc.
1	2	3	4	5	6	7	8	9	10	11	12	13	14	15	16	17
	99	99	Nededoc, Antonia P	Wife	F	Cha	52.0	M		Y	N	Guam	Guam	Guam	N	None
	99	99	Nededoc, Jose P	Son	M	Cha	27.0	S		Y	Y	Guam	Guam	Guam	Y	Farm laborer home farm
	99	99	Nededoc, Juan P	Son	M	Cha	25.0	S		Y	Y	Guam	Guam	Guam	Y	Farm laborer home farm
	99	99	Nededoc, Pedro P	Son	M	Cha	21.0	S	N	Y	Y	Guam	Guam	Guam	Y	Laborer
	99	99	Nededoc, Felix P	Son	M	Cha	19.0	S	N	Y	Y	Guam	Guam	Guam	Y	Native seaman
	99	99	Nededoc, Ignacio P	Son	M	Cha	17.0	S	N	Y	Y	Guam	Guam	Guam	Y	Farm laborer home farm
	99	99	Nededoc, Joaquin P	Son	M	Cha	16.0	S	N	Y	Y	Guam	Guam	Guam	Y	Farm laborer home farm
	99	99	Nededoc, Vicente P	Son	M	Cha	14.0	S	Y	Y	Y	Guam	Guam	Guam	Y	Farm laborer home farm
	99	99	Nededoc, Beronica P	Daughter	F	Cha	11.0	S	Y	Y	Y	Guam	Guam	Guam	Y	None
	99	99	Nededoc, Enrique P	Son	M	Cha	10.0	S	Y	Y	Y	Guam	Guam	Guam	Y	None
	99	99	Nededoc, Magdalena P	Daughter	F	Cha	5.0	S	N			Guam	Guam	Guam	Y	None
	100	100	Pineda, Jose A	Head	M	Cha	53.0	M		Y	Y	Guam	Guam	Guam	N	Farmer
	100	100	Pineda, Dolores C	Wife	F	Cha	52.0	M		Y	Y	Guam	Guam	Guam	N	None
Pareno Street	101	101	Pineda, Manuel C	Head	M	Cha	28.0	M		Y	Y	Guam	Guam	Guam	Y	Farmer
	101	101	Pineda, Maxima G	Wife	F	Cha	28.0	M				Guam	Guam	Guam	N	None
	101	101	Pineda, Francisco G	Son	M	Cha	5.0	S	N			Guam	Guam	Guam		None
	101	101	Pineda, Dolores G	Daughter	F	Cha	3.0	S				Guam	Guam	Guam		None
	101	101	Pineda, Victoria G	Daughter	F	Cha	1.0	S				Guam	Guam	Guam		None
	102	102	Charfauros, Mariano A	Head	M	Cha	42.0	M		N	N	Guam	Guam	Guam	N	Farmer
	102	102	Charfauros, Maria SN	Wife	F	Cha	36.0	M		Y	Y	Guam	Guam	Guam	SN	None
	102	102	Charfauros, Francisco SN	Son	M	Cha	6.0	S	N			Guam	Guam	Guam		None
	102	102	Charfauros, Maria SN	Daughter	F	Cha	4.0	S				Guam	Guam	Guam		None
	102	102	Charfauros, Juana SN	Daughter	F	Cha	2.0	S				Guam	Guam	Guam		None
	102	102	Charfauros, Juan SN	Son	M	Cha	0.5	S				Guam	Guam	Guam		None
	102	102	San Nicolas, Francisco A	Servant	M	Cha	18.0	S	N	Y	Y	Guam	Guam	Guam	Y	Servant

(CHAMORRO ROOTS GENEALOGY PROJECT ™ TRANSCRIPTION)
(COMPILED/TRANSCRIBED BY BERNARD T. PUNZALAN / HTTP://WWW.CHAMORROROOTS.COM)

FOURTEENTH CENSUS OF THE UNITED STATES: 1920—POPULATION

ISLAND OF GUAM

DISTRICT 4
NAME OF PLACE **Agat** Town

ENUMERATED BY ME ON THE 2nd DAY OF March, 1920

Albert P. Manley ENUMERATOR

[Proper name and, also, name of class, as city, town, village, barrio, etc]

	PLACE OF ABODE			NAME	RELATION	PERSONAL DESCRIPTION					EDUCATION			NATIVITY				OCCUPATION
Street, avenue, road, etc.	Number of dwelling house is order of visitation	Number of family in order of visitation		Enter surname, first, then given name and middle initial. If any. Include every person living on January 1, 1920. Omit children born since January 1, 1920.	Relationship of this Person to the head of the family.	Sex	Color or race	Age at last birthday	Single, married, widowed or divorced	Attended school any time since Sept. 1, 1919	Whether able to read.	Whether able to write.	Place of birth of this person.	Place of birth of father of this person.	Place of birth of mother of this person.	Whether able to speak English.	Trade, profession, or particular kind of work done, as salesman, laborer, clerk, cook, merchant, washerwoman, etc.
1	2	3		4	5	6	7	8	9	10	11	12	13	14	15	16	17
1	103	103		Babauta, Pedro C	Head	M	Cha	26.0	M		Y	Y	Guam	Guam	Guam	Y	Laborer
2	103	103		Babauta, Dolores S	Wife	F	Cha	25.0	M		Y	Y	Guam	Guam	Guam	Y	None
3	103	103		Babauta, Maria S	Daughter	F	Cha	1.0	S				Guam	Guam	Guam		None
4	103	103		Babauta, Rosalia S	Daughter	F	Cha	0.3	S				Guam	Guam	Guam		None
5	104	104		Muna, Mariano D	Head	M	Cha	54.0	M		Y	Y	Guam	Guam	Guam	N	Farmer
6	104	104		Muna, Carmen P	Wife	F	Cha	51.0	M		N	N	Guam	Guam	Guam	N	None
7	104	104		Muna, Ana P	Daughter	F	Cha	14.0	S	N	Y	Y	Guam	Guam	Guam	Y	None
8	105	105		Babauta, Vicente L	Head	M	Cha	37.0	M		Y	Y	Guam	Guam	Guam	Y	Farmer
9	105	105		Babauta, Remedio A	Wife	F	Cha	29.0	M		N	N	Guam	Guam	Guam	N	None
10	105	105		Babauta, Maria A	Daughter	F	Cha	5.0	S	N			Guam	Guam	Guam		None
11	105	105		Babauta, Jose A	Son	M	Cha	2.0	S				Guam	Guam	Guam		None
12	106	106		Lizama, Francisca A	Head	F	Cha	55.0	Wd		N	N	Guam	Guam	Guam	N	Weaver
13	107	107		Sanchez, Enoveva C	Head	F	Cha	43.0	Wd		N	N	Guam	Guam	Guam	N	Washerwoman
14	106	107		Sanchez, Juan C	Son	M	Cha	16.0	S	N	Y	Y	Guam	Guam	Guam	Y	Farm laborer working out
15	106	107		Sanchez, Maria C	Daughter	F	Cha	7.0	S	Y			Guam	Guam	Guam		None
16	107	108		Charfauros, Carmen A	Head	F	Cha	45.0	Wd		N	N	Guam	Guam	Guam	N	Washerwoman
17	107	108		Charfauros, Jesus A	Son	M	Cha	10.0	S	Y	Y	Y	Guam	Guam	Guam	Y	None
18	107	108		Charfauros, Juan A	Son	M	Cha	2.0	S				Guam	Guam	Guam		None
19	108	109		Rabago, Josefa C	Head	F	Cha	52.0	Wd		N	N	Guam	Guam	Guam	N	Weaver
20	108	109		Rabago, Jose C	Son	M	Cha	24.0	S		Y	Y	Guam	Guam	Guam	Y	Farm laborer home farm
21	108	109		Rabago, Ana C	Daughter	F	Cha	23.0	S		Y	Y	Guam	Guam	Guam	Y	Washerwoman
22	108	109		Rabago, Carmen C	Daughter	F	Cha	21.0	S	N	N	N	Guam	Guam	Guam	N	None
23	108	109		Rabago, Juan C	Son	M	Cha	19.0	S	N	Y	Y	Guam	Guam	Guam	Y	Laborer
24	108	109		Rabago, Vicente C	Son	M	Cha	17.0	S	N	Y	Y	Guam	Guam	Guam	Y	Farm laborer home farm
25	108	109		Rabago, Enrique C	Son	M	Cha	14.0	S	N	Y	Y	Guam	Guam	Guam	Y	Farm laborer home farm

Pareno Street

449

(CHAMORRO ROOTS GENEALOGY PROJECT ™ TRANSCRIPTION)
(COMPILED/TRANSCRIBED BY BERNARD T. PUNZALAN / HTTP://WWW.CHAMORROROOTS.COM)

FOURTEENTH CENSUS OF THE UNITED STATES: 1920-POPULATION
ISLAND OF GUAM

ENUMERATED BY ME ON THE 3rd DAY OF March, 1920

Albert P. Manley ENUMERATOR.

DISTRICT 4
NAME OF PLACE Agat Town
[Proper name and, also, name of class, as city, town, village, barrio, etc]

	Dwelling	Family	NAME	RELATION	Sex	Color or race	Age	Single, married, widowed or divorced	Attended school since Sept. 1, 1919	Able to read	Able to write	Birth of person	Birth of father	Birth of mother	Able to speak English	OCCUPATION
1	2	3	4	5	6	7	8	9	10	11	12	13	14	15	16	17
26	109	110	Taenao, Carmelo M	Head	M	Cha	27.0	M		Y	Y	Guam	Guam	Guam	N	Laborer
27	109	110	Taenao, Joaquina C	Wife	F	Cha	25.0	M		Y	Y	Guam	Guam	Guam	Y	None
28	109	110	Taenao, Jesus C	Son	M	Cha	1.0	S				Guam	Guam	Guam		None
29	109	110	Taenao, Maria C	Daughter	F	Cha	0.5	S				Guam	Guam	Guam		None
30	110	111	Borja, Jose S	Head	M	Cha	34.0	M		Y	Y	Guam	Guam	Guam	Y	Farmer
31	110	111	Borja, Soledad S	Wife	F	Cha	30.0	M		Y	Y	Guam	Guam	Guam	Y	None
32	110	111	Borja, Jose S	Son	M	Cha	6.0	S				Guam	Guam	Guam		None
33	110	111	Borja, Francisco S	Son	M	Cha	4.0	S				Guam	Guam	Guam		None
34	110	111	Borja, Juan V S	Son	M	Cha	2.0	S				Guam	Guam	Guam		None
35	111	112	Cruz, Pedro C	Head	M	Cha	36.0	M		Y	Y	Guam	Guam	Guam	N	Laborer
36	111	112	Cruz, Maria O	Wife	F	Cha	36.0	M		Y	Y	Guam	Guam	Guam	N	None
37	111	112	Cruz, Dolores O	Daughter	F	Cha	12.0	S	Y	Y	Y	Guam	Guam	Guam	Y	None
38	111	112	Cruz, Pedro O	Son	M	Cha	11.0	S	Y	Y	Y	Guam	Guam	Guam	Y	None
39	111	112	Cruz, Raphael O	Son	M	Cha	7.0	S	Y			Guam	Guam	Guam		None
40	111	112	Cruz, Jesus O	Son	M	Cha	5.0	S	N			Guam	Guam	Guam		None
41	111	112	Cruz, Juan O	Son	M	Cha	4.0	S				Guam	Guam	Guam		None
42	111	112	Babauta, Faustino B	Servant	M	Cha	27.0	S		Y	Y	Guam	Guam	Guam	Y	Servant
43	112	113	Sablan, Jose C	Head	M	Cha	28.0	M		Y	Y	Guam	Guam	Guam	Y	Laborer
44	112	113	Sablan, Ana T	Wife	F	Cha	23.0	M		Y	Y	Guam	Guam	Guam	Y	None
45	112	113	Sablan, Maria T	Daughter	F	Cha	5.0	S	N			Guam	Guam	Guam		None
46	112	113	Sablan, Vicente T	Son	M	Cha	3.0	S				Guam	Guam	Guam		None
47	112	113	Sablan, Juan T	Son	M	Cha	1.0	S				Guam	Guam	Guam		None
48	113	114	Cruz, Mariano C	Head	M	Cha	35.0	M		N	N	Guam	Guam	Guam	N	Laborer
49	113	114	Cruz, Maria J	Wife	F	Cha	25.0	M		Y	Y	Guam	Guam	Guam	Y	None
50	113	114	Cruz, Josefa J	Daughter	F	Cha	3.0	S				Guam	Guam	Guam		None

Street: Pareno Street

450

(CHAMORRO ROOTS GENEALOGY PROJECT ™ TRANSCRIPTION)
(COMPILED/TRANSCRIBED BY BERNARD T. PUNZALAN / HTTP://WWW.CHAMORROROOTS.COM)

FOURTEENTH CENSUS OF THE UNITED STATES: 1920—POPULATION

ISLAND OF GUAM

DISTRICT 4

NAME OF PLACE **Agat Town**

[Proper name and, also, name of class, as city, town, village, barrio, etc]

ENUMERATED BY ME ON THE 4th DAY OF March, 1920

Albert P. Manley ENUMERATOR

	PLACE OF ABODE			NAME	RELATION	PERSONAL DESCRIPTION					EDUCATION			NATIVITY				OCCUPATION
Street, avenue, road, etc.	Number of dwelling house in order of visitation	Number of family in order of visitation		Name	Relationship of this Person to the head of the family.	Sex	Color or race	Age at last birthday	Single, married, widowed or divorced	Attended school any time since Sept. 1, 1919	Whether able to read.	Whether able to write.	Place of birth of this person.	Place of birth of father of this person.	Place of birth of mother of this person.	Whether able to speak English.	Trade, profession, or particular kind of work done, as salesman, laborer, clerk, cook, merchant, washerwoman, etc.
1	2	3	4	5	6	7	8	9	10	11	12	13	14	15	16	17
	113	114	Cruz, Miguel J	Son	M	Cha	1.0	S				Guam	Guam	Guam		None
	114	115	Babauta, Jose L	Head	M	Cha	37.0	M		Y	Y	Guam	Guam	Guam	N	Farmer
	114	115	Babauta, Rosa C	Wife	F	Cha	40.0	M		Y	Y	Guam	Guam	Guam	N	None
	114	115	Babauta, Maria C	Daughter	F	Cha	5.0	S	N			Guam	Guam	Guam		None
	114	115	Babauta, Juan C	Son	M	Cha	1.0	S				Guam	Guam	Guam		None
	115	116	Charfauros, Vicente A	Head	M	Cha	44.0	M		Y	Y	Guam	Guam	Guam	N	Farmer
	115	116	Charfauros, Rosa L	Wife	F	Cha	51.0	M		Y	Y	Guam	Guam	Guam	N	None
	115	116	Charfauros, Pedro L	Son	M	Cha	26.0	S		Y	Y	Guam	Guam	Guam	Y	Farm laborer home farm
	115	116	Charfauros, Felix L	Son	M	Cha	21.0	S	N	Y	Y	Guam	Guam	Guam	Y	Laborer
	115	116	Charfauros, Jose L	Son	M	Cha	19.0	S	N	Y	Y	Guam	Guam	Guam	Y	Farm laborer home farm
	115	116	Charfauros, Joaquin L	Son	M	Cha	14.0	S	Y	Y	Y	Guam	Guam	Guam	Y	Farm laborer home farm
	115	116	Charfauros, Juan L	Son	M	Cha	7.0	S	Y			Guam	Guam	Guam	Y	None
	116	117	Babauta, Antonio C	Head	M	Cha	56.0	Wd		Y	Y	Guam	Guam	Guam	N	Farmer
	116	117	Babauta, Jesus L	Son	M	Cha	23.0	S		Y	Y	Guam	Guam	Guam	Y	Farm laborer home farm
	116	117	Babauta, Francisco L	Son	M	Cha	17.0	S	N	Y	Y	Guam	Guam	Guam	Y	Farm laborer home farm
	116	117	Babauta, Roas L	Daughter	F	Cha	14.0	S	N	Y	Y	Guam	Guam	Guam	Y	None
	117	118	Carbullido, Joaquin C	Head	M	Cha	36.0	M		Y	Y	Guam	Guam	Guam	Y	Laborer
	117	118	Carbullido, Trinidad C	Wife	F	Cha	31.0	M		Y	Y	Guam	Guam	Guam	Y	None
	117	118	Carbullido, Maria C	Daughter	F	Cha	11.0	S	Y	Y	Y	Guam	Guam	Guam	Y	None
	117	118	Carbullido, Felicita C	Daughter	F	Cha	3.0	S				Guam	Guam	Guam		None
	117	118	San Nicolas, Jesus SN	Servant	M	Cha	18.0	S	N	Y	Y	Guam	Guam	Guam	Y	Servant
	118	119	Mesa, Jose M	Head	M	Cha	45.0	M		Y	Y	Guam	Guam	Guam	N	Farmer
	118	119	Mesa, Ana P	Wife	F	Cha	32.0	M		Y	Y	Guam	Guam	Guam	N	None
	118	119	Mesa, Enrique P	Son	M	Cha	11.0	S	Y	Y	Y	Guam	Guam	Guam	Y	None
	118	119	Mesa, Francisco P	Son	M	Cha	9.0	S	Y	Y	Y	Guam	Guam	Guam		None

Pareno Street

(CHAMORRO ROOTS GENEALOGY PROJECT ™ TRANSCRIPTION)
(COMPILED/TRANSCRIBED BY BERNARD T. PUNZALAN / HTTP://WWW.CHAMORROROOTS.COM)
FOURTEENTH CENSUS OF THE UNITED STATES: 1920-POPULATION
ISLAND OF GUAM

DISTRICT 4
NAME OF PLACE **Agat Town**
[Proper name and, also, name of class, as city, town, village, barrio, etc]

ENUMERATED BY ME ON THE 5th DAY OF March, 1920

Albert P. Manley ENUMERATOR

	Dwelling	Family	NAME	RELATION	Sex	Color or race	Age	Single/married/widowed/divorced	Attended school since Sept. 1, 1919	Able to read	Able to write	Birthplace of person	Birthplace of father	Birthplace of mother	Able to speak English	OCCUPATION
	2	3	4	5	6	7	8	9	10	11	12	13	14	15	16	17
26	118	119	Mesa, Rosalia P	Daughter	F	Cha	7.0	S	Y			Guam	Guam	Guam		None
27	118	119	Mesa, Maria P	Daughter	F	Cha	5.0	S	N			Guam	Guam	Guam		None
28	118	119	Mesa, Jose P	Son	M	Cha	2.0	S				Guam	Guam	Guam		None
29	119	120	Taienao, Guadalupe M	Head	F	Cha	44.0	Wd		N	N	Guam	Guam	Guam	N	None
30	119	120	Taienao, Vicente M	Son	M	Cha	7.0	S	Y			Guam	Guam	Guam		None
31	119	120	Taienao, Joaquin M	Son	M	Cha	2.0	S				Guam	Guam	Guam		None
32	120	121	Pinaula, Leon B	Head	M	Cha	64.0	M		N	N	Guam	Guam	Guam	N	Farmer
33	120	121	Pinaula, Juliana A	Wife	F	Cha	65.0	M		N	N	Guam	Guam	Guam	Y	None
34	120	121	Pinaula, Soledad G	Daughter	F	Cha	31.0	S		N	N	Guam	Guam	Guam	N	None
35	121	122	San Nicolas, Nieves M	Head	M	Cha	39.0	Wd		Y	Y	Guam	Guam	Guam	N	Washerwoman
36	121	122	San Nicolas, Maria M	Daughter	F	Cha	8.0	S	Y			Guam	Guam	Guam		None
37	121	122	San Nicolas, Amparo M	Daughter	F	Cha	5.0	S	N			Guam	Guam	Guam		None
38	121	122	San Nicolas, Juan M	Son	M	Cha	1.0	S				Guam	Guam	Guam		None
39	121	122	Manebusan, Juan D	Brother	M	Cha	56.0	S		N	N	Guam	Guam	Guam	N	Farm laborer home farm
40	122	123	Cruz, Francisco T	Head	M	Cha	26.0	M		Y	Y	Guam	Guam	Guam	Y	Laborer
41	122	123	Cruz, Carmen SN	Wife	F	Cha	36.0	M		Y	Y	Guam	Guam	Guam	N	None
42	122	123	Cruz, Carmen SN	Daughter	F	Cha	2.0	S				Guam	Guam	Guam		None
43	123	124	Cruz, Vicente G	Head	M	Cha	56.0	M		Y	Y	Guam	Guam	Guam	N	Laborer
44	123	124	Cruz, Loncia T	Wife	F	Cha	56.0	M		N	N	Guam	Guam	Guam	N	None
45	124	125	Salas, Francisco S	Head	M	Cha	25.0	M		Y	Y	Guam	Guam	Guam	Y	Laborer
46	124	125	Salas, Cecelia G	Wife	F	Cha	24.0	M		Y	Y	Guam	Guam	Guam	Y	None
47	124	125	Salas, Trinidad G	Daughter	F	Cha	4.0	S				Guam	Guam	Guam		None
48	124	125	Salas, Joaquin G	Son	M	Cha	1.0	S				Guam	Guam	Guam		None
49	124	125	Salas, Vicente S	Brother	M	Cha	17.0	S	N	Y	Y	Guam	Guam	Guam	Y	Farm laborer home farm
50	124	125	Salas, Vicente C	Nephew	M	Cha	12.0	S	Y	Y	Y	Guam	Guam	Guam	Y	None

Street: Pareno Street

(CHAMORRO ROOTS GENEALOGY PROJECT ™ TRANSCRIPTION)
(COMPILED/TRANSCRIBED BY BERNARD T. PUNZALAN / HTTP://WWW.CHAMORROROOTS.COM)

FOURTEENTH CENSUS OF THE UNITED STATES: 1920-POPULATION
ISLAND OF GUAM

DISTRICT 4
NAME OF PLACE Agat Town

[Proper name and, also, name of class, as city, town, village, barrio, etc]

ENUMERATED BY ME ON THE 6th DAY OF March, 1920

Albert P. Manley ENUMERATOR

	PLACE OF ABODE			NAME	RELATION	PERSONAL DESCRIPTION				EDUCATION			NATIVITY				OCCUPATION
Street, avenue, road, etc.	Number of dwelling house is order of visitation	Number of family in order of visitation		of each person whose place of abode on January 1, 1920, was in the family. Enter surname, first, then given name and middle initial. If any. Include every person living on January 1, 1920. Omit children born since January 1, 1920.	Relationship of this Person to the head of the family.	Sex	Color or race	Age at last birthday	Single, married, widowed or divorced	Attended school any time since Sept. 1, 1919	Whether able to read.	Whether able to write.	Place of birth of this person.	Place of birth of father of this person.	Place of birth of mother of this person.	Whether able to speak English.	Trade, profession, or particular kind of work done, as salesman, laborer, clerk, cook, merchant, washerwoman, etc.
1	2	3	4		5	6	7	8	9	10	11	12	13	14	15	16	17
1	125	126	Taienao, Jose Q		Head	M	Cha	49.0	M		Y	Y	Guam	Guam	Guam	N	Farmer
2	125	126	Taienao, Dolores B		Wife	F	Cha	46.0	M		Y	Y	Guam	Guam	Guam	N	None
3	125	126	Taienao, Maria B		Daughter	F	Cha	20.0	S	N	Y	Y	Guam	Guam	Guam	Y	None
4	125	126	Taienao, Derfina B		Daughter	F	Cha	16.0	S	N	Y	Y	Guam	Guam	Guam	Y	None
5	126	127	Castro, Dolores C		Head	F	Cha	56.0	Wd		N	N	Guam	Guam	Guam	N	None
6	126	127	Castro, Jose C		Son	M	Cha	32.0	S		Y	Y	Guam	Guam	Guam	Y	Farmer
7	126	127	Castro, Manuela C		Daughter	F	Cha	23.0	S		Y	Y	Guam	Guam	Guam	Y	None
8	126	127	Castro, Jesus C		Son	M	Cha	17.0	S	N	Y	Y	Guam	Guam	Guam	Y	Farm laborer home farm
9	126	127	Castro, Ana C		Daughter	F	Cha	17.0	S	N	Y	Y	Guam	Guam	Guam	Y	None
10	126	127	Espinosa, Vicenta E		Grandmother	F	Cha	72.0	Wd		N	N	Guam	Guam	Guam	N	None
11	127	128	Saluznamnam, Juan T		Head	M	Cha	52.0	Wd		Y	Y	Guam	Guam	Guam	N	Farmer
12	127	129	Lizama, Augustin A		Head	M	Cha	27.0	M		Y	Y	Guam	Guam	Guam	Y	Laborer
13	127	129	Lizama, Rosa C		Wife	F	Cha	23.0	M		Y	Y	Guam	Guam	Guam	Y	None
14	127	129	Lizama, Cristina C		Daughter	F	Cha	0.7	S				Guam	Guam	Guam		None
15	128	130	Cruz, Dolores B		Head	F	Cha	53.0	Wd		N	N	Guam	Guam	Guam	N	None
16	128	130	Cruz, Jose C		Son	M	Cha	14.0	S	Y	Y	Y	Guam	Guam	Guam	Y	None
17	129	131	Aquinigoc, Jose B		Head	M	Cha	27.0	M		Y	Y	Guam	Guam	Guam	Y	Farmer
18	129	131	Aquinigoc, Antonia C		Wife	F	Cha	30.0	M		Y	Y	Guam	Guam	Guam	Y	None
19	129	131	Aquinigoc, Carmen C		Daughter	F	Cha	12.0	S	Y	Y	Y	Guam	Guam	Guam	Y	None
20	129	131	Aquinigoc, Juan C		Son	M	Cha	11.0	S	Y	Y	Y	Guam	Guam	Guam	Y	None
21	129	131	Aquinigoc, Enrique C		Son	M	Cha	8.0	S	Y			Guam	Guam	Guam		None
22	129	131	Aquinigoc, Carmelo C		Son	M	Cha	4.0	S				Guam	Guam	Guam		None
23	129	131	Aquinigoc, Felipe C		Son	M	Cha	2.0	S				Guam	Guam	Guam		None
24	129	131	Aquinigoc, Ana B		Mother	F	Cha	40.0	Wd		N	N	Guam	Guam	Guam	N	None
25	130	132	Charfauros, Faustino C		Head	M	Cha	26.0	S		Y	Y	Guam	Unknown	Guam	Y	Laborer

Pareno Street

(CHAMORRO ROOTS GENEALOGY PROJECT ™ TRANSCRIPTION)
(COMPILED/TRANSCRIBED BY BERNARD T. PUNZALAN / HTTP://WWW.CHAMORROROOTS.COM)

225b

FOURTEENTH CENSUS OF THE UNITED STATES: 1920—POPULATION
ISLAND OF GUAM

SHEET NO. _13B_

DISTRICT 4

NAME OF PLACE **Agat Town**

ENUMERATED BY ME ON THE 8th DAY OF March, 1920

Albert P. Manley ENUMERATOR

	PLACE OF ABODE		NAME	RELATION	PERSONAL DESCRIPTION				EDUCATION			NATIVITY				OCCUPATION
Street	Dwelling no.	Family no.	Name	Relation	Sex	Color or race	Age	Single/married	Attended school	Read	Write	Birthplace of person	Birthplace of father	Birthplace of mother	Speak English	Occupation
1	2	3	4	5	6	7	8	9	10	11	12	13	14	15	16	17
	130	132	Charfauros, Dolores L	Mother	F	Cha	49.0	S		N	N	Guam	Unknown	Guam	N	None
	130	132	Charfauros, Maria L	Grandmother	F	Cha	80.0	Wd		N	N	Guam	Guam	Guam	N	None
	131	133	Nededoc, Jose N	Head	M	Cha	33.0	M		Y	Y	Guam	Guam	Guam	Y	Farmer
	131	133	Nededoc, Tedora C	Wife	F	Cha	25.0	M		Y	Y	Guam	Guam	Guam	N	None
	132	134	Babauta, Pedro M	Head	M	Cha	60.0	M		Y	Y	Guam	Guam	Guam	N	Farmer
	132	134	Babauta, Ramona P	Wife	F	Cha	62.0	M		Y	Y	Guam	Guam	Guam	N	None
	133	135	Nededoc, Emelio C	Head	M	Cha	29.0	M		Y	Y	Guam	Guam	Guam	N	Laborer
	133	135	Nededoc, Carmen C	Wife	F	Cha	27.0	M		Y	Y	Guam	Guam	Guam	Y	None
	133	135	Nededoc, Enrique C	Son	M	Cha	5.0	S				Guam	Guam	Guam		None
Parano Street	133	135	Nededoc, Francisco C	Son	M	Cha	2.0	S				Guam	Guam	Guam		None
	133	135	Nededoc, Ana C	Daughter	F	Cha	1.0	S				Guam	Guam	Guam		None
	134	136	Cruz, Manuel C	Head	M	Cha	44.0	Wd		N	N	Guam	Guam	Guam	N	Farmer
	134	136	Cruz, Francisco Q	Son	M	Cha	20.0	S	N	Y	Y	Guam	Guam	Guam	Y	Seaman
	134	136	Cruz, Jose Q	Son	M	Cha	18.0	S	N	Y	Y	Guam	Guam	Guam	Y	Laborer
	134	136	Cruz, Graviel Q	Son	M	Cha	16.0	S	Y	Y	Y	Guam	Guam	Guam	Y	Farm laborer home farm
	134	136	Cruz, Genera Q	Daughter	F	Cha	11.0	S	Y	Y	Y	Guam	Guam	Guam	Y	None
	135	137	Cruz, Ana A	Head	F	Cha	42.0	Wd		Y	Y	Guam	Guam	Guam	N	None
	135	137	Cruz, Jose A	Son	M	Cha	25.0	Wd	N	Y	Y	Guam	Guam	Guam	Y	Farmer
	135	137	Cruz, Mercedes A	Daughter	F	Cha	16.0	S	Y	Y	Y	Guam	Guam	Guam	Y	None
	135	137	Cruz, Enrique A	Son	M	Cha	14.0	S	Y	Y	Y	Guam	Guam	Guam	Y	None
	135	137	Cruz, Magdalena A	Daughter	F	Cha	9.0	S	Y			Guam	Guam	Guam	Y	None
	135	138	Quintanilla, Jesus L	Head	M	Cha	23.0	M		Y	Y	Guam	Guam	Guam	Y	Laborer
	135	138	Quintanilla, Luisa T	Wife	F	Cha	17.0	M	N	Y	Y	Guam	Guam	Guam	N	None
	136	139	Saluznamnam, Vicente T	Head	M	Cha	40.0	M		N	N	Guam	Guam	Guam	N	Laborer
	136	139	Saluznamnam, Maria B	Wife	F	Cha	34.0	M		N	N	Guam	Guam	Guam	N	Weaver

454

(CHAMORRO ROOTS GENEALOGY PROJECT ™ TRANSCRIPTION)
(COMPILED/TRANSCRIBED BY BERNARD T. PUNZALAN / HTTP://WWW.CHAMORROROOTS.COM)

FOURTEENTH CENSUS OF THE UNITED STATES: 1920-POPULATION
ISLAND OF GUAM

SHEET NO. __14A__

DISTRICT 4
NAME OF PLACE **Agat Town**
[Proper name and, also, name of class, as city, town, village, barrio, etc]

ENUMERATED BY ME ON THE 9th DAY OF March, 1920

Albert P. Manley ENUMERATOR

Street, avenue, road, etc.	Number of dwelling house is order of visitation	Number of family in order of visitation	NAME of each person whose place of abode on January 1, 1920, was in the family.	RELATION Relationship of this Person to the head of the family.	Sex	Color or race	Age at last birthday	Single, married, widowed or divorced	Attended school any time since Sept. 1, 1919	Whether able to read.	Whether able to write.	Place of birth of this person.	Place of birth of father of this person.	Place of birth of mother of this person.	Whether able to speak English.	OCCUPATION
1	2	3	4	5	6	7	8	9	10	11	12	13	14	15	16	17
	136	139	Saluznamnam, Ana B	Daughter	F	Cha	11.0	S	Y	Y	Y	Guam	Guam	Guam	Y	None
	136	139	Saluznamnam, Consolacion B	Daughter	F	Cha	8.0	S	Y			Guam	Guam	Guam	Y	None
	137	140	Quintanilla, Juan L	Head	M	Cha	26.0	S		Y	Y	Guam	Guam	Guam	Y	Laborer
	138	141	Jesus, Marcelo B	Head	M	Cha	27.0	M		Y	Y	Guam	Guam	Guam	Y	Laborer
	138	141	Jesus, Francisca B	Wife	F	Cha	24.0	M		Y	Y	Guam	Guam	Guam	Y	None
	138	141	Jesus, Yrestina B	Daughter	F	Cha	1.0	S				Guam	Guam	Guam		None
	139	142	Quituguac, Vicente G	Head	M	Cha	30.0	M		N	N	Guam	Guam	Guam	N	Farmer
	139	142	Quituguac, Maria A	Wife	F	Cha	26.0	M		N	N	Guam	Guam	Guam	N	None
	139	142	Quituguac, Conception A	Daughter	F	Cha	5.0	S				Guam	Guam	Guam	N	None
	139	142	Quituguac, Jose A	Son	M	Cha	1.0	S				Guam	Guam	Guam		None
	140	143	Charfauros, Ramona L	Head	F	Cha	34.0	Wd		N	N	Guam	Guam	Guam	N	Washerwoman
	140	143	Charfauros, Rejina L	Daughter	F	Cha	12.0	S	Y	Y	Y	Guam	Guam	Guam	Y	None
	140	143	Charfauros, Jose L	Son	M	Cha	4.0	S				Guam	Guam	Guam		None
	141	144	Palomo, Pedro G	Head	M	Cha	26.0	M		Y	Y	Guam	Guam	Guam	Y	Laborer
	141	144	Palomo, Patricia C	Wife	F	Cha	29.0	M		Y	Y	Guam	Guam	Guam	N	None
	141	144	Palomo, Maria C	Daughter	F	Cha	1.0	S				Guam	Guam	Guam		None
	142	145	Chaco, Mariano Q	Head	M	Cha	42.0	M		Y	Y	Guam	Guam	Guam	N	Farmer
	142	145	Chaco, Maria L	Wife	F	Cha	46.0	M		Y	Y	Guam	Guam	Guam	N	None
	142	145	Chaco, Ignacio L	Son	M	Cha	17.0	S	N	Y	Y	Guam	Guam	Guam	Y	Farm laborer home farm
	142	145	Chaco, Magdalena L	Daughter	F	Cha	15.0	S	Y	Y	Y	Guam	Guam	Guam	Y	None
	142	145	Chaco, Margarita L	Daughter	F	Cha	12.0	S	Y	Y	Y	Guam	Guam	Guam	Y	None
	143	146	Nededoc, Juan S	Head	M	Cha	45.0	M		Y	Y	Guam	Guam	Guam	N	Farmer
	143	146	Nededoc, Matea R	Wife	F	Cha	52.0	M		N	N	Guam	Guam	Guam	N	None
	143	146	Nededoc, Dolores R	Daughter	F	Cha	15.0	S	N	Y	Y	Guam	Guam	Guam	Y	None
	143	146	Nededoc, Roque R	Son	M	Cha	0.3	S				Guam	Guam	Guam		None

Pareno Street

(CHAMORRO ROOTS GENEALOGY PROJECT ™ TRANSCRIPTION)
(COMPILED/TRANSCRIBED BY BERNARD T. PUNZALAN / HTTP://WWW.CHAMORROROOTS.COM)
FOURTEENTH CENSUS OF THE UNITED STATES: 1920-POPULATION
ISLAND OF GUAM

ENUMERATED BY ME ON THE 10th DAY OF March, 1920

Albert P. Manley ENUMERATOR

DISTRICT 4
NAME OF PLACE Agat Town
[Proper name and, also, name of class, as city, town, village, barrio, etc]

Street, avenue, road, etc.	Number of dwelling house in order of visitation	Number of family in order of visitation	NAME	RELATION	Sex	Color or race	Age at last birthday	Single, married, widowed or divorced	Attended school any time since Sept. 1, 1919	Whether able to read.	Whether able to write.	Place of birth of this person.	Place of birth of father of this person.	Place of birth of mother of this person.	Whether able to speak English.	OCCUPATION
1	2	3	4	5	6	7	8	9	10	11	12	13	14	15	16	17
26	143	146	Perez, Juana R	Mother	F	Cha	80.0	Wd		N	N	Guam	Guam	Guam	N	None
27	144	147	Cruz, Vicente T	Head	M	Cha	29.0	M		Y	Y	Guam	Guam	Guam	N	Farmer
28	144	147	Cruz, Maria S	Wife	F	Cha	32.0	M		N	N	Guam	Guam	Guam	N	None
29	144	147	Cruz, Derfina S	Daughter	F	Cha	9.0	S	Y			Guam	Guam	Guam		None
30	144	147	Cruz, Juan S	Son	M	Cha	7.0	S	N			Guam	Guam	Guam		None
31	144	147	Cruz, Ana S	Daughter	F	Cha	5.0	S				Guam	Guam	Guam		None
32	144	147	Naputi, Eufemira C	Servant	F	Cha	26.0	S		Y	Y	Guam	Guam	Guam	N	Servant
33	144	147	Herrero, Jose S	Servant	M	Cha	13.0	S	Y	Y	Y	Guam	Guam	Guam	Y	Servant
34	145	148	Guerrero, Jose P	Head	M	Cha	27.0	M		Y	Y	Guam	Guam	Guam	Y	Laborer
35	145	148	Guerrero, Ana Q	Wife	F	Cha	19.0	M		Y	Y	Guam	Guam	Guam	Y	None
36	145	148	Guerrero, Antonina Q	Daughter	F	Cha	2.0	S				Guam	Guam	Guam		None
37	146	149	Charfauros, Jose C	Head	M	Cha	26.0	M		Y	Y	Guam	Guam	Guam	Y	Laborer
38	146	149	Charfauros, Maria B	Wife	F	Cha	20.0	M	N	Y	Y	Guam	Guam	Guam	Y	None
39	146	149	Charfauros, Carmela B	Daughter	F	Cha	0.7	S				Guam	Guam	Guam		None
40	147	150	Babauta, Barcelio T	Head	M	Cha	58.0	M		Y	Y	Guam	Guam	Guam	N	Farmer
41	147	150	Babauta, Rita M	Wife	F	Cha	46.0	M		Y	Y	Guam	Guam	Guam	N	None
42	147	150	Babauta, Maria M	Daughter	F	Cha	24.0	S		Y	Y	Guam	Guam	Guam	Y	None
43	147	150	Babauta, Virginia M	Daughter	F	Cha	16.0	S	N	Y	Y	Guam	Guam	Guam	Y	Nurse
44	147	150	Babauta, Francisco M	Son	M	Cha	6.0	S	N			Guam	Guam	Guam		None
45	148	151	Salas, Juan S	Head	M	Cha	46.0	M		N	N	Guam	Guam	Guam	N	Laborer
46	148	151	Salas, Rosalia S	Wife	F	Cha	48.0	M		N	N	Guam	Guam	Guam	N	Washerwoman
47	148	151	Salas, Maria S	Daughter	F	Cha	22.0	S		Y	Y	Guam	Guam	Guam	N	Washerwoman
48	149	152	Mesa, Vicente M	Head	M	Cha	54.0	M		Y	Y	Guam	Guam	Guam	N	Farmer
49	149	152	Mesa, Antonia C	Wife	F	Cha	48.0	M		Y	Y	Guam	Guam	Guam	N	None
50	149	152	Mesa, Juan C	Son	M	Cha	24.0	S		Y	Y	Guam	Guam	Guam	N	Farm laborer home farm

Pareno Street

(CHAMORRO ROOTS GENEALOGY PROJECT ™ TRANSCRIPTION)
(COMPILED/TRANSCRIBED BY BERNARD T. PUNZALAN / HTTP://WWW.CHAMORROROOTS.COM)

FOURTEENTH CENSUS OF THE UNITED STATES: 1920—POPULATION
ISLAND OF GUAM

DISTRICT 4
NAME OF PLACE **Agat Town**
[Proper name and, also, name of class, as city, town, village, barrio, etc]

ENUMERATED BY ME ON THE 11th DAY OF March, 1920

Albert P. Manley ENUMERATOR

	Dwelling No.	Family No.	NAME	RELATION	Sex	Color or race	Age	Marital	Attended school since Sept. 1, 1919	Able to read	Able to write	Birthplace person	Birthplace father	Birthplace mother	Able to speak English	OCCUPATION
1	149	152	Mesa, Carmen C	Daughter	F	Cha	18.0	S	N	Y	Y	Guam	Guam	Guam	N	None
2	149	152	Mesa, Dolores C	Daughter	F	Cha	15.0	S	N	Y	Y	Guam	Guam	Guam	Y	None
3	149	152	Mesa, Mariano C	Son	M	Cha	14.0	S	Y	Y	Y	Guam	Guam	Guam	Y	None
4	149	152	Mesa, Ana C	Daughter	F	Cha	13.0	S	Y	Y	Y	Guam	Guam	Guam	Y	None
5	149	152	Mesa, Rosa C	Daughter	F	Cha	6.0	S	Y			Guam	Guam	Guam		None
6	149	152	Mesa, Ignacio C	Son	M	Cha	5.0	S	N			Guam	Guam	Guam		None
7	150	153	San Nicolas, Vicente F	Head	M	Cha	47.0	M		N	N	Guam	Guam	Guam	N	Farmer
8	150	153	San Nicolas, Conception M	Wife	F	Cha	36.0	M		N	N	Guam	Guam	Guam	N	[illegible]
9	150	153	San Nicolas, Jose M	Son	M	Cha	24.0	S		Y	Y	Guam	Guam	Guam	Y	Washerwoman
10	150	153	Taienao, Carmen M	Niece	F	Cha	23.0	S		Y	Y	Guam	Guam	Guam	Y	Missionary
11	151	154	Larrasoana, Vicente M	Head	M	W	51.0	S		Y	Y	Spain	Spain	Spain	N	Farmer
12	152	155	Bordallo, Baltazar B	Head	M	W	61.0	M		Y	Y	Spain	Spain	Spain	N	None
13	152	155	Bordallo, Rita P	Wife	F	Cha	55.0	M		Y	Y	Guam	Guam	Guam	Y	None
14	152	155	Bordallo, Baltazar P	Son	M	W	19.0	S	Y	Y	Y	Guam	Guam	Guam	Y	None
15	152	155	Bordallo, Delfina P	Daughter	F	W	17.0	S	Y	Y	Y	Guam	Guam	Guam	Y	None
16	152	155	Bordallo, Carlos P	Son	M	W	16.0	S	Y	Y	Y	Guam	Guam	Guam	Y	None
17	152	155	Bordallo, Alfredo P	Son	M	W	14.0	S	Y	Y	Y	Guam	Guam	Guam	Y	Laborer
18	153	156	Salas, Remigio C	Head	M	Cha	31.0	M		Y	Y	Guam	Guam	Guam	N	None
19	153	156	Salas, Locia M	Wife	F	Cha	29.0	M		Y	Y	Guam	Guam	Guam	N	None
20	153	156	Salas, Vicente M	Son	M	Cha	8.0	S	Y			Guam	Guam	Guam		None
21	153	156	Salas, Juan M	Son	M	Cha	7.0	S	Y			Guam	Guam	Guam		None
22	153	156	Salas, Carmen M	Daughter	F	Cha	5.0	S	N			Guam	Guam	Guam		None
23	153	156	Salas, Soledad M	Daughter	F	Cha	1.0	S				Guam	Guam	Guam		None
24	154	157	Taitague, Enocencio C	Head	M	Cha	24.0	M		Y	Y	Guam	Guam	Guam	N	Laborer
25	154	157	Taitague, Candida B	Wife	F	Cha	25.0	M		N	N	Guam	Guam	Guam	N	None

Pareno Street

457

(CHAMORRO ROOTS GENEALOGY PROJECT ™ TRANSCRIPTION)
(COMPILED/TRANSCRIBED BY BERNARD T. PUNZALAN / HTTP://WWW.CHAMORROROOTS.COM)

FOURTEENTH CENSUS OF THE UNITED STATES: 1920-POPULATION

ISLAND OF GUAM

227b

ENUMERATED BY ME ON THE 11th DAY OF March, 1920

Albert P. Manley ENUMERATOR

DISTRICT 4

NAME OF PLACE **Agat Town**

[Proper name and, also, name of class, as city, town, village, barrio, etc]

Street, avenue, road, etc.	Num-ber of dwelling house in order of visi-tation	Num-ber of family in order of visi-tation	NAME	RELATION	Sex	Color or race	Age at last birthday	Single, married, widowed or divorced	Attended school any time since Sept. 1, 1919	Whether able to read.	Whether able to write.	Place of birth of this person.	Place of birth of father of this person.	Place of birth of mother of this person.	Whether able to speak English.	OCCUPATION
1	2	3	4	5	6	7	8	9	10	11	12	13	14	15	16	17
	154	157	Taitague, Ana B	Daughter	F	Cha	5.0	S	N			Guam	Guam	Guam		None
	154	157	Taitague, Tomas B	Son	M	Cha	1.0	S				Guam	Guam	Guam		None
	154	157	Taitague, Antonia C	Mother	F	Cha	69.0	Wd		N	N	Guam	Guam	Guam	N	None
	154	157	Taitague, Felix C	Nephew	M	Cha	8.0	S	Y			Guam	Guam	Guam		None
	155	158	Charfauros, Juan C	Head	M	Cha	23.0	M		Y	Y	Guam	Guam	Guam	Y	Laborer
	155	158	Charfauros, Victoria M	Wife	F	Cha	22.0	M		N	N	Guam	Guam	Guam	N	None
	155	158	Charfauros, Jose M	Son	M	Cha	1.0	S				Guam	Guam	Guam		None
	156	159	Lizama, Joaquin A	Head	M	Cha	32.0	M		Y	Y	Guam	Guam	Guam	Y	Farmer
	156	159	Lizama, Conception S	Wife	F	Cha	34.0	M		N	N	Guam	Guam	Guam	N	None
	156	159	Lizama, Nicolas S	Son	M	Cha	18.0	S	N	Y	Y	Guam	Guam	Guam	Y	Laborer
Pareno Street	156	159	Lizama, Cristina S	Daughter	F	Cha	12.0	S	Y	Y	Y	Guam	Guam	Guam	Y	None
	157	160	Aguigui, Pedro A	Head	M	Cha	56.0	Wd		N	N	Guam	Guam	Guam	N	Farmer
	157	160	Aguigui, Felix A	Son	M	Cha	23.0	S		Y	Y	Guam	Guam	Guam	Y	Farm laborer home farm
	158	161	Carbullido, Vicente C	Head	M	Cha	37.0	M		Y	Y	Guam	Guam	Guam	Y	Laborer
	158	161	Carbullido, Maria A	Wife	F	Cha	26.0	M		N	N	Guam	Guam	Guam	N	None
	158	161	Carbullido, Martina A	Daughter	F	Cha	5.0	S	N			Guam	Guam	Guam		None
	158	161	Carbullido, Francisco A	Son	M	Cha	3.0	S				Guam	Guam	Guam		None
	158	161	Carbullido, Luis A	Son	M	Cha	2.0	S				Guam	Guam	Guam		None
	159	162	Taijito, Antonio T	Head	M	Cha	48.0	M		N	N	Guam	Guam	Guam	N	Farmer
	159	162	Taijito, Maria A	Wife	F	Cha	47.0	M		N	N	Guam	Guam	Guam	N	None
	160	163	Mendiola, Ignacio R	Head	M	Cha	62.0	M		N	N	Guam	Guam	Guam	N	Farmer
	160	163	Mendiola, Carmen S	Daughter	F	Cha	22.0	S	N	Y	Y	Guam	Guam	Guam	Y	None
	160	163	Mendiola, Manuel S	Son	M	Cha	20.0	S	N	Y	Y	Guam	Guam	Guam	Y	Farm laborer home farm
	160	163	Mendiola, Dolores S	Daughter	F	Cha	18.0	S	N	Y	Y	Guam	Guam	Guam	Y	None
	161	164	Hamamoto, Isematsu	Head	M	Jp	41.0	S		Y	Y	Japan	Japan	Japan	N	Farm laborer working out

(CHAMORRO ROOTS GENEALOGY PROJECT ™ TRANSCRIPTION)
(COMPILED/TRANSCRIBED BY BERNARD T. PUNZALAN / HTTP://WWW.CHAMORROROOTS.COM)

FOURTEENTH CENSUS OF THE UNITED STATES: 1920-POPULATION
ISLAND OF GUAM

ENUMERATED BY ME ON THE 12th DAY OF March, 1920

Albert P. Manley ENUMERATOR

DISTRICT 4
NAME OF PLACE **Agat Town**
[Proper name and, also, name of class, as city, town, village, barrio, etc]

	Street, avenue, road, etc.	Number of dwelling house in order of visitation	Number of family in order of visitation	NAME of each person whose place of abode on January 1, 1920, was in the family.	RELATION Relationship of this Person to the head of the family.	Sex	Color or race	Age at last birthday	Single, married, widowed or divorced	Attended school any time since Sept. 1, 1919	Whether able to read.	Whether able to write.	Place of birth of this person.	Place of birth of father of this person.	Place of birth of mother of this person.	Whether able to speak English.	OCCUPATION Trade, profession, or particular kind of work done, as salesman, laborer, clerk, cook, merchant, washerwoman, etc.
	1	2	3	4	5	6	7	8	9	10	11	12	13	14	15	16	17
1	Pateno Street	162	165	Shinazo, Ocha S	Head	M	Jp	26.0	S		Y	Y	Japan	Japan	Japan	N	Storekeeper
2		163	166	Lizama, Jose SN	Head	M	Cha	94.0	Wd		N	N	Guam	Guam	Guam	N	None
3		164	167	English, Maria A	Head	F	Cha	27.0	M		Y	Y	Guam	Guam	Guam	Y	None
4		164	167	English, Carlos A	Son	M	Cha	9.0	S	Y	Y		Guam	Guam	Guam		None
5		164	167	English, Juana A	Daughter	F	Cha	5.0	S	N			Guam	Unknown	Guam		None
6		164	167	English, Maria A	Daughter	F	Cha	3.0	S				Guam	Unknown	Guam		None
7		164	167	English, Conception A	Daughter	F	Cha	1.0	S				Guam	Unknown	Guam		None
8				Here ends the enumeration of Agat Town													
9																	
10																	
11																	
12																	
13																	
14																	
15																	
16																	
17																	
18																	
19																	
20																	
21																	
22																	
23																	
24																	
25																	

(CHAMORRO ROOTS GENEALOGY PROJECT ™ TRANSCRIPTION)
(COMPILED/TRANSCRIBED BY BERNARD T. PUNZALAN / HTTP://WWW.CHAMORROROOTS.COM)

FOURTEENTH CENSUS OF THE UNITED STATES: 1920-POPULATION

ISLAND OF GUAM

ENUMERATED BY ME ON THE 15th DAY OF March, 1920

Albert P. Manley ENUMERATOR.

DISTRICT **4**

NAME OF PLACE **Umatac Barrio**

[Proper name and, also, name of class, as city, town, village, barrio, etc]

Street, avenue, road, etc.	Number of dwelling house in order of visitation	Number of family in order of visitation	NAME	RELATION	Sex	Color or race	Age at last birthday	Single, married, widowed or divorced	Attended school any time since Sept. 1, 1919	Whether able to read	Whether able to write	Place of birth of this person	Place of birth of father of this person	Place of birth of mother of this person	Whether able to speak English	OCCUPATION
	1	1	Aguon, Vicente R	Head	M	Cha	34.0	M		N	N	Guam	Guam	Guam	N	Farmer
	1	1	Aguon, Angela B	Wife	F	Cha	25.0	M		Y	Y	Guam	Guam	Guam	N	None
	1	1	Aguon, Rosa B	Daughter	F	Cha	12.0	S	Y	Y	Y	Guam	Guam	Guam	Y	None
	1	1	Aguon, Manuel B	Son	M	Cha	8.0	S	Y			Guam	Guam	Guam		None
	1	1	Aguon, Maria B	Daughter	F	Cha	4.0	S				Guam	Guam	Guam		None
	1	1	Aguon, Jose B	Son	M	Cha	2.0	S				Guam	Guam	Guam		None
	2	2	Quinata, Antonio I	Head	M	Cha	44.0	M		N	N	Guam	Guam	Guam	N	Farmer
	2	2	Quinata, Vicente M	Wife	F	Cha	43.0	M		N	N	Guam	Guam	Guam	N	None
	2	2	Quinata, Lucio M	Son	M	Cha	23.0	S		Y	Y	Guam	Guam	Guam	Y	Farm laborer home farm
	2	2	Quinata, Jose M	Son	M	Cha	20.0	S	N	N	N	Guam	Guam	Guam	N	Farm laborer home farm
	2	2	Quinata, Baldivino M	Son	M	Cha	18.0	S	N	Y	Y	Guam	Guam	Guam	Y	Farm laborer home farm
	2	2	Quinata, Joaquina M	Daughter	F	Cha	15.0	S	Y	Y	Y	Guam	Guam	Guam	Y	None
	2	2	Tajalle, Enrique R	Servant	M	Cha	30.0	S	N	N	N	Guam	Guam	Guam	N	Servant
	3	3	Sanchez, Antonio S	Head	M	Cha	55.0	M		N	N	Guam	Guam	Guam	N	Farmer
	3	3	Sanchez, Emelia Q	Wife	F	Cha	53.0	M		N	N	Guam	Guam	Guam	N	None
	3	3	Sanchez, Joaquin Q	Son	M	Cha	17.0	S	N	Y	Y	Guam	Guam	Guam	Y	Teacher
	3	3	Sanchez, Ignacio Q	Son	M	Cha	16.0	S	N	Y	Y	Guam	Guam	Guam	Y	Teacher
	3	3	Sanchez, Maria Q	Daughter	F	Cha	10.0	S	Y	Y	Y	Guam	Guam	Guam	Y	None
	4	4	Quinata, Juan Q	Head	M	Cha	30.0	M	N	Y	Y	Guam	Guam	Guam	Y	Farmer
	4	4	Quinata, Tomasa S	Wife	F	Cha	26.0	M		Y	Y	Guam	Guam	Guam	Y	None
	4	4	Quinata, Jesus S	Son	M	Cha	3.0	S				Guam	Guam	Guam		None
	4	4	Quinata, Jose S	Son	M	Cha	0.8	S				Guam	Guam	Guam		None
	5	5	Quinata, Pedro I	Head	M	Cha	47.0	M		N	N	Guam	Guam	Guam	N	Farmer
	5	5	Quinata, Guillerma M	Wife	F	Cha	50.0	M		N	N	Guam	Guam	Guam	N	None
Dionicio Street	5	5	Quinata, Emelia M	Daughter	F	Cha	18.0	S	N	Y	Y	Guam	Guam	Guam	Y	None

(CHAMORRO ROOTS GENEALOGY PROJECT ™ TRANSCRIPTION)
(COMPILED/TRANSCRIBED BY BERNARD T. PUNZALAN / HTTP://WWW.CHAMORROROOTS.COM)

229b

FOURTEENTH CENSUS OF THE UNITED STATES: 1920-POPULATION

ISLAND OF GUAM

DISTRICT 4

NAME OF PLACE Umatac Barrio

[Proper name and, also, name of class, as city, town, village, barrio, etc]

ENUMERATED BY ME ON THE 15th DAY OF March, 1920

Albert P. Manley ENUMERATOR

	PLACE OF ABODE		NAME	RELATION	PERSONAL DESCRIPTION				EDUCATION			NATIVITY				OCCUPATION
	Street, avenue, road, etc.	Number of dwelling house in order of visitation	Number of family in order of visitation	of each person whose place of abode on January 1, 1920, was in the family.	Relationship of this Person to the head of the family.	Sex	Color or race	Age at last birthday	Single, married, widowed or divorced	Attended school any time since Sept. 1, 1919	Whether able to read.	Whether able to write.	Place of birth of this person.	Place of birth of father of this person.	Place of birth of mother of this person.	Whether able to speak English.	Trade, profession, or particular kind of work done
1		2	3	4	5	6	7	8	9	10	11	12	13	14	15	16	17
26		5	6	Babauta, Ignacio G	Head	M	Cha	30.0	M	Y	Y		Guam	Guam	Guam	Y	Farmer
27		5	6	Babauta, Felistina Q	Wife	F	Cha	25.0	M	N	N		Guam	Guam	Guam	N	None
28		6	7	Charfauros, Juan T	Head	M	Cha	37.0	M		Y	Y	Guam	Guam	Guam	Y	Farmer
29		6	7	Charfauros, Calota G	Wife	F	Cha	28.0	M		Y	Y	Guam	Guam	Guam	N	None
30		6	7	Charfauros, Jose G	Son	M	Cha	4.0	S				Guam	Guam	Guam		None
31		6	7	Charfauros, Maria G	Daughter	F	Cha	2.0	S				Guam	Guam	Guam		None
32		6	7	Charfauros, Jesus G	Son	M	Cha	1.0	S				Guam	Guam	Guam		None
33		6	7	Cruz, Dolores G	Grandmother	F	Cha	95.0	Wd		N	N	Guam	Guam	Guam	N	None
34	Dionicio Street	7	8	Aguon, Jesus T	Head	M	Cha	40.0	M		Y	Y	Guam	Guam	Guam	N	Farmer
35		7	8	Aguon, Maria M	Wife	F	Cha	38.0	M		Y	Y	Guam	Guam	Guam	N	None
36		7	8	Aguon, Conception M	Daughter	F	Cha	10.0	S	Y	Y	Y	Guam	Guam	Guam	Y	None
37		7	8	Aguon, Atanacio M	Son	M	Cha	5.0	S	N			Guam	Guam	Guam		None
38		7	8	Aguon, Bernadita M	Daughter	F	Cha	0.8	S				Guam	Guam	Guam		None
39		8	9	Quinata, Faustino M	Head	M	Cha	56.0	M		Y	Y	Guam	Guam	Guam	N	Farmer
40		8	9	Quinata, Maria C	Wife	F	Cha	28.0	M		Y	Y	Guam	Guam	Guam	N	None
41		8	9	Quinata, Jose C	Son	M	Cha	15.0	S	Y	Y	Y	Guam	Guam	Guam	Y	None
42		8	9	Quinata, Ramon C	Son	M	Cha	13.0	S	Y	Y	Y	Guam	Guam	Guam	Y	None
43		8	9	Quinata, Jesus C	Son	M	Cha	11.0	S	Y	Y	Y	Guam	Guam	Guam	Y	None
44		8	9	Quinata, Faustino C	Son	M	Cha	8.0	S	Y	Y	Y	Guam	Guam	Guam	Y	None
45		8	9	Chargulaf, Ana B	Servant	F	Cha	14.0	S	Y	Y	Y	Guam	Guam	Guam	Y	Servant
46		9	10	Aguon, Lucas T	Head	M	Cha	32.0	M		Y	Y	Guam	Guam	Guam	Y	Farmer
47		9	10	Aguon, Joaquina B	Wife	F	Cha	27.0	M		Y	Y	Guam	Guam	Guam	N	None
48		10	10	Babauta, Juan G	Head	M	Cha	31.0	M		Y	Y	Guam	Guam	Guam	Y	Farmer
49		10	10	Babauta, Ana A	Wife	F	Cha	30.0	M		Y	Y	Guam	Guam	Guam	N	None
50		10	10	Babauta, Maria A	Daughter	F	Cha	11.0	S	Y	Y	Y	Guam	Guam	Guam	Y	None

(CHAMORRO ROOTS GENEALOGY PROJECT ™ TRANSCRIPTION)
(COMPILED/TRANSCRIBED BY BERNARD T. PUNZALAN / HTTP://WWW.CHAMORROROOTS.COM)

FOURTEENTH CENSUS OF THE UNITED STATES: 1920–POPULATION
ISLAND OF GUAM

DISTRICT 4
NAME OF PLACE **Umatac Barrio**
[Proper name and, also, name of class, as city, town, village, barrio, etc]

ENUMERATED BY ME ON THE 16th DAY OF March, 1920

Albert P. Manley ENUMERATOR

	Dwelling no. (2)	Family no. (3)	NAME (4)	RELATION (5)	Sex (6)	Color or race (7)	Age (8)	Single, married, widowed or divorced (9)	Attended school since Sept. 1, 1919 (10)	Able to read (11)	Able to write (12)	Birthplace of person (13)	Birthplace of father (14)	Birthplace of mother (15)	Able to speak English (16)	OCCUPATION (17)
1	10	10	Babauta, Florencia A	Daughter	F	Cha	9.0	S	Y			Guam	Guam	Guam		None
2	10	10	Babauta, Jose A	Son	M	Cha	6.0	S	N			Guam	Guam	Guam		None
3	10	10	Babauta, Jesus A	Son	M	Cha	4.0	S				Guam	Guam	Guam		None
4	10	10	Babauta, Manuel M	Father	M	Cha	53.0	Wd		N	N	Guam	Guam	Guam	N	None
5	11	12	Babauta, Robinio G	Head	M	Cha	25.0	M		Y	Y	Guam	Guam	Guam	Y	Farmer
6	11	12	Babauta, Largrimas A	Wife	F	Cha	19.0	M	N	Y	Y	Guam	Guam	Guam	Y	None
7	11	12	Babauta, Joaquina A	Daughter	F	Cha	0.3	S				Guam	Guam	Guam		None
8	12	13	Santiago, Simon Q	Head	M	Cha	32.0	M		Y	Y	Guam	Guam	Guam	N	Farmer
9	12	13	Santiago, Carmen C	Wife	F	Cha	26.0	M		Y	Y	Guam	Guam	Guam	N	None
10	12	13	Santiago, Ana C	Daughter	F	Cha	6.0	S	N	Y	Y	Guam	Guam	Guam		None
11	12	13	Santiago, Dolores C	Daughter	F	Cha	3.0	S				Guam	Guam	Guam		None
12	12	13	Santiago, Jose C	Son	M	Cha	2.0	S				Guam	Guam	Guam		None
13	13	14	Aguon, Felipe L	Head	M	Cha	48.0	M		Y	Y	Guam	Guam	Guam	N	Farmer
14	13	14	Aguon, Maria C	Wife	F	Cha	43.0	M		N	N	Guam	Guam	Guam	N	None
15	13	14	Aguon, Librada C	Daughter	F	Cha	20.0	S	N	Y	Y	Guam	Guam	Guam	Y	None
16	13	14	Aguon, Ana C	Daughter	F	Cha	18.0	S	N	Y	Y	Guam	Guam	Guam	Y	Farm laborer home farm
17	13	14	Aguon, Vicente C	Son	M	Cha	16.0	S	N	Y	Y	Guam	Guam	Guam	Y	None
18	13	14	Aguon, Magdalena C	Daughter	F	Cha	13.0	S	Y	Y	Y	Guam	Guam	Guam	Y	None
19	13	14	Aguon, Trinidad C	Daughter	F	Cha	9.0	S				Guam	Guam	Guam		None
20	13	14	Chigina, Vicente T	Brother-in-law	M	Cha	40.0	S		N	N	Guam	Guam	Guam	N	Weaver
21	14	15	Quinata, Antonio A	Head	M	Cha	33.0	M		Y	Y	Guam	Guam	Guam	N	Farmer
22	14	15	Quinata, Antonia T	Wife	F	Cha	28.0	M		Y	Y	Guam	Guam	Guam	Y	None
23	14	15	Quinata, Sibera T	Daughter	F	Cha	5.0	S	N			Guam	Guam	Guam		None
24	14	15	Quinata, Joaquina T	Daughter	F	Cha	1.0	S				Guam	Guam	Guam		None
25	14	15	Topasna, Rafael E	Servant	M	Cha	49.0	Wd		N	N	Guam	Guam	Guam	N	Servant

Dionlolo Street

(CHAMORRO ROOTS GENEALOGY PROJECT ™ TRANSCRIPTION)
(COMPILED/TRANSCRIBED BY BERNARD T. PUNZALAN / HTTP://WWW.CHAMORROROOTS.COM)

230b

FOURTEENTH CENSUS OF THE UNITED STATES: 1920-POPULATION
ISLAND OF GUAM

ENUMERATED BY ME ON THE 17th DAY OF March, 1920

Albert P. Manley ENUMERATOR

DISTRICT 4
NAME OF PLACE Umatac Barrio

[Proper name and, also, name of class, as city, town, village, barrio, etc]

Street, avenue, road, etc. (1)	No. of dwelling house (2)	No. of family (3)	NAME (4)	RELATION (5)	Sex (6)	Color or race (7)	Age (8)	Single, married, etc (9)	Attended school (10)	Read (11)	Write (12)	Birthplace person (13)	Father (14)	Mother (15)	Speak English (16)	OCCUPATION (17)
	14	15	Topasna, Felix T	Servant	M	Cha	13.0	S	Y	Y	Y	Guam	Guam	Guam	Y	Servant
	15	16	Quinata, Jose G	Head	M	Cha	28.0	M		Y	Y	Guam	Guam	Guam	Y	Farmer
	15	16	Quinata, Francisca C	Wife	F	Cha	21.0	M	N	Y	Y	Guam	Guam	Guam	Y	None
	15	16	Quinata, Gregorio C	Brother	M	Cha	12.0	S	Y	Y	Y	Guam	Guam	Guam	Y	None
	16	17	Sanchez, Enrique Q	Head	M	Cha	38.0	M		Y	Y	Guam	Guam	Guam	N	Farmer
	16	17	Sanchez, Trudes T	Wife	F	Cha	34.0	M		N	N	Guam	Guam	Guam	N	None
	16	17	Sanchez, Felica T	Sister-in-law	F	Cha	43.0	S		N	N	Guam	Guam	Guam	N	None
	16	17	Quinata, Dolores Q	Niece	F	Cha	7.0	S				Guam	Guam	Guam		None
	17	18	Quidachay, Jose T	Head	M	Cha	52.0	M	N	Y	Y	Guam	Guam	Guam	N	Farmer
	17	18	Quidachay, Maria D	Wife	F	Cha	55.0	M		N	N	Guam	Guam	Guam	N	None
Dionicio Street	17	18	Quidachay, Joaquin D	Son	M	Cha	27.0	S		Y	Y	Guam	Guam	Guam	Y	Farm laborer home farm
	17	18	Quidachay, Ramon D	Son	M	Cha	25.0	S		Y	Y	Guam	Guam	Guam	Y	Farm laborer home farm
	17	18	Quidachay, Ana D	Daughter	F	Cha	19.0	S	N	Y	Y	Guam	Guam	Guam	Y	None
	17	18	Quidachay, Elisa D	Daughter	F	Cha	16.0	S	N	Y	Y	Guam	Guam	Guam	Y	None
	17	18	Quinata, Ana Q	Niece	F	Cha	5.0	S	N			Guam	Guam	Guam		None
	18	19	Taitano, Vicente M	Head	M	Cha	53.0	M		Y	Y	Guam	Guam	Guam	Y	Missionary
	18	19	Taitano, Carlina M	Wife	F	Cha	58.0	M		Y	Y	Guam	Guam	Guam	N	None
	18	19	Taitano, Manuel M	Son	M	Cha	17.0	S	N	Y	Y	Guam	Guam	Guam	Y	Farm laborer home farm
	18	20	Quinata, Antonio A	Head	M	Cha	20.0	M	N	Y	Y	Guam	Guam	Guam	Y	Farmer
	18	20	Quinata, Lucia T	Wife	F	Cha	29.0	M		Y	Y	Guam	Guam	Guam	Y	None
	18	20	Salas, Jose T	Nephew	M	Cha	14.0	S	Y	Y	Y	Guam	Guam	Guam	Y	None
	18	20	Salas, Avelina T	Niece	F	Cha	11.0	S	Y	Y	Y	Guam	Guam	Guam	Y	None
	19	21	Taitano, Miguel C	Head	M	Cha	20.0	M	N	N	Y	Guam	Guam	Guam	N	Farmer
	19	21	Taitano, Catalina A	Wife	F	Cha	19.0	M	N	Y	Y	Guam	Guam	Guam	Y	None
	20	22	Sanchez, Manuel S	Head	M	Cha	37.0	M		Y	Y	Guam	Guam	Guam	N	Farmer

463

(CHAMORRO ROOTS GENEALOGY PROJECT ™ TRANSCRIPTION)
(COMPILED/TRANSCRIBED BY BERNARD T. PUNZALAN / HTTP://WWW.CHAMORROROOTS.COM)
FOURTEENTH CENSUS OF THE UNITED STATES: 1920—POPULATION
ISLAND OF GUAM

DISTRICT **4**
NAME OF PLACE **Umatac Barrio**
[Proper name and, also, name of class, as city, town, village, barrio, etc]

ENUMERATED BY ME ON THE 18th DAY OF March, 1920

Albert P. Manley ENUMERATOR

	PLACE OF ABODE		NAME	RELATION	PERSONAL DESCRIPTION				EDUCATION			NATIVITY				OCCUPATION
Street, avenue, road, etc.	Number of dwelling house in order of visitation	Number of family in order of visitation	of each person whose place of abode on January 1, 1920, was in the family.	Relationship of this Person to the head of the family.	Sex	Color or race	Age at last birthday	Single, married, widowed or divorced	Attended school any time since Sept. 1, 1919	Whether able to read.	Whether able to write.	Place of birth of this person.	Place of birth of father of this person.	Place of birth of mother of this person.	Whether able to speak English.	Trade, profession, or particular kind of work done, as salesman, laborer, clerk, cook, merchant, washerwoman, etc.
1	2	3	4	5	6	7	8	9	10	11	12	13	14	15	16	17
	20	22	Sanchez, Teodora Q	Wife	F	Cha	41.0	M		Y	Y	Guam	Guam	Guam	N	None
	20	22	Sanchez, Petronila Q	Daughter	F	Cha	24.0	S		Y	Y	Guam	Guam	Guam	Y	Washerwoman
	20	22	Sanchez, Jose Q	Son	M	Cha	23.0	S		Y	Y	Guam	Guam	Guam	Y	Farm laborer home farm
	20	22	Sanchez, Joaquin Q	Son	M	Cha	17.0	S	N	Y	Y	Guam	Guam	Guam	Y	Farm laborer home farm
	20	22	Sanchez, Joaquina Q	Daughter	F	Cha	13.0	S	N	Y	Y	Guam	Guam	Guam	Y	None
	20	22	Sanchez, Vicente Q	Son	M	Cha	10.0	S	Y	Y	Y	Guam	Guam	Guam	Y	None
	20	22	Sanchez, Elena Q	Daughter	F	Cha	7.0	S	Y	Y	Y	Guam	Guam	Guam	Y	None
	20	22	Sanchez, Ursula Q	Daughter	F	Cha	3.0	S				Guam	Guam	Guam		None
	20	22	Sanchez, Carmela S	Mother	F	Cha	43.0	Wd		N	N	Guam	Guam	Guam	N	None
	20	22	Sanchez, Estaquia S	Sister	F	Cha	25.0	S		Y	Y	Guam	Guam	Guam	Y	None
	20	22	Sanchez, Nicolas S	Brother	M	Cha	20.0	S	N	Y	Y	Guam	Guam	Guam	Y	Farm laborer home farm
Dionicio Street	20	22	Sanchez, Carmen S	Sister	F	Cha	11.0	S	Y	Y	Y	Guam	Guam	Guam	Y	None
	20	22	Sanchez, Caradad S	Sister	F	Cha	9.0	S	Y	Y	Y	Guam	Guam	Guam	Y	None
	20	22	Sanchez, Jose S	Brother	M	Cha	3.0	S				Guam	Guam	Guam		None
	21	23	Quinata, Vicente A	Head	M	Cha	29.0	M		Y	Y	Guam	Guam	Guam	Y	Farmer
	21	23	Quinata, Margarita S	Wife	F	Cha	25.0	M		Y	Y	Guam	Guam	Guam	Y	None
	21	23	Quinata, Antonina S	Daughter	F	Cha	7.0	S	N			Guam	Guam	Guam		None
	21	23	Quinata, Ana S	Daughter	F	Cha	3.0	S				Guam	Guam	Guam		None
	21	23	Quinata, Lidia S	Daughter	F	Cha	0.3	S				Guam	Guam	Guam		None
	22	24	Sanchez, Moises C	Head	M	Cha	25.0	M		Y	Y	Guam	Guam	Guam	Y	Farmer
	22	24	Sanchez, Susana A	Wife	F	Cha	26.0	M		Y	Y	Guam	Guam	Guam	Y	None
	22	24	Sanchez, Maria A	Daughter	F	Cha	4.0	S				Guam	Guam	Guam		None
	22	24	Sanchez, Jesus A	Son	M	Cha	3.0	S				Guam	Guam	Guam		None
	22	24	Sanchez, Estefania Q	Mother	F	Cha	55.0	Wd		N	N	Guam	Guam	Guam	N	None
	22	24	Sanchez, Manuela Q	Sister	F	Cha	30.0	S		Y	Y	Guam	Guam	Guam	Y	None

(CHAMORRO ROOTS GENEALOGY PROJECT ™ TRANSCRIPTION)
(COMPILED/TRANSCRIBED BY BERNARD T. PUNZALAN / HTTP://WWW.CHAMORROROOTS.COM)

FOURTEENTH CENSUS OF THE UNITED STATES: 1920—POPULATION
ISLAND OF GUAM

DISTRICT **4**

NAME OF PLACE **Umatac Barrio**

[Proper name and, also, name of class, as city, town, village, barrio, etc]

ENUMERATED BY ME ON THE 18th DAY OF March, 1920

Albert P. Manley ENUMERATOR

	PLACE OF ABODE			NAME	RELATION	PERSONAL DESCRIPTION				EDUCATION			NATIVITY				OCCUPATION
Street, avenue, road, etc.	Number of dwelling house is order of visitation	Number of family in order of visitation	of each person whose place of abode on January 1, 1920, was in the family. Enter surname, first, then given name and middle initial, if any. Include every person living on January 1, 1920. Omit children born since January 1, 1920.	Relationship of this person to the head of the family.	Sex	Color or race	Age at last birthday	Single, married, widowed or divorced	Attended school any time since Sept. 1, 1919	Whether able to read.	Whether able to write.	Place of birth of this person.	Place of birth of father of this person.	Place of birth of mother of this person.	Whether able to speak English.	Trade, profession, or particular kind of work done, as salesman, laborer, clerk, cook, merchant, washerwoman, etc.
1	2	3	4	5	6	7	8	9	10	11	12	13	14	15	16	17
26	22	24	Sanchez, Francisco Q	Brother	M	Cha	18.0	S	N	Y	Y	Guam	Guam	Guam	Y	Farm laborer home farm
27	22	24	Sanchez, Joaquin Q	Brother	M	Cha	14.0	S	N	Y	Y	Guam	Guam	Guam	Y	None
28	23	25	Quinata, Augustin M	Head	M	Cha	46.0	M		Y	Y	Guam	Guam	Guam	Y	Farmer
29	23	25	Quinata, Dolores A	Wife	F	Cha	42.0	M		Y	Y	Guam	Guam	Guam	N	None
30	23	25	Quinata, Maria A	Daughter	F	Cha	20.0	S	N	Y	Y	Guam	Guam	Guam	N	None
31	23	25	Quinata, Antonio A	Son	M	Cha	18.0	S	N	Y	Y	Guam	Guam	Guam	Y	Farm laborer home farm
32	23	25	Quinata, Joaquin A	Son	M	Cha	16.0	S	N	Y	Y	Guam	Guam	Guam	Y	Farm laborer home farm
33	23	25	Quinata, Felicitas A	Daughter	F	Cha	14.0	S	N	Y	Y	Guam	Guam	Guam	Y	None
34	23	25	Quinata, Rosa A	Daughter	F	Cha	10.0	S	Y	Y	Y	Guam	Guam	Guam	Y	None
35	23	25	Quinata, Isabel A	Daughter	F	Cha	8.0	S	Y	Y	Y	Guam	Guam	Guam	Y	None
36	23	25	Quinata, Mariano A	Son	M	Cha	6.0	S	N			Guam	Guam	Guam		None
37	23	25	Quinata, Vicente A	Son	M	Cha	3.0	S				Guam	Guam	Guam		None
38	24	26	Isezaki, Jose Y	Head	M	Jp	35.0	M		Y	Y	Japan	Japan	Japan	Y	Retail Merchant Dry Goods
39	24	26	Isezaki, Rosa M	Wife	F	Cha	39.0	M		Y	Y	Guam	Guam	Guam	N	None
40	24	26	Isezaki, Rita M	Daughter	F	Jp	3.0	S				Japan	Japan	Guam		None
41	24	26	Isezaki, Francisco M	Son	M	Jp	0.2	S				Guam	Japan	Guam		None
42	24	26	Isezaki, Rosia M	Step-daughter	F	Cha	10.0	S	Y	Y	Y	Guam	Guam	Guam	Y	None
43	24	26	Mariyan, Luisa A	Mother-in-law	F	Cha	70.0	Wd		N	N	Guam	Guam	Guam	N	None
44	25	27	Santiago, Mariano M	Head	M	Cha	57.0	M		Y	Y	Manila Philippines	Manila Philippines	Guam	N	Farmer
45	25	27	Santiago, Marcela Q	Wife	F	Cha	52.0	M		Y	Y	Guam	Guam	Guam	N	None
46	25	27	Santiago, Domingo Q	Son	M	Cha	28.0	S		Y	Y	Guam	Guam	Guam	N	Farm laborer home farm
47	25	27	Santiago, Justo Q	Son	M	Cha	25.0	S		Y	Y	Guam	Guam	Guam	Y	Farm laborer home farm
48	25	27	Santiago, Ana Q	Daughter	F	Cha	20.0	S	N	Y	Y	Guam	Guam	Guam	Y	None
49	25	27	Santiago, Graviela Q	Daughter	F	Cha	15.0	S	N	Y	Y	Guam	Guam	Guam	Y	None
50	25	27	Santiago, Vicente Q	Son	M	Cha	15.0	S	N	Y	Y	Guam	Guam	Guam	Y	Farm laborer home farm

Dionicio Street

465

(CHAMORRO ROOTS GENEALOGY PROJECT ™ TRANSCRIPTION)
(COMPILED/TRANSCRIBED BY BERNARD T. PUNZALAN / HTTP://WWW.CHAMORROROOTS.COM)

FOURTEENTH CENSUS OF THE UNITED STATES: 1920-POPULATION
ISLAND OF GUAM

DISTRICT 4
NAME OF PLACE Umatac Barrio
[Proper name and, also, name of class, as city, town, village, barrio, etc]

ENUMERATED BY ME ON THE 18th DAY OF March, 1920

Albert P. Manley ENUMERATOR

Street	Dwelling No.	Family No.	NAME	RELATION	Sex	Color or race	Age	Condition	Attended school since Sept. 1, 1919	Able to read	Able to write	Birthplace of person	Birthplace of father	Birthplace of mother	Able to speak English	OCCUPATION
	25	27	Santiago, Juan Q	Son	M	Cha	13.0	S	N	Y	Y	Guam	Guam	Guam	Y	Farm laborer home farm
	25	27	Santiago, Teresa Q	Daughter	F	Cha	12.0	S	Y	Y	Y	Guam	Guam	Guam	Y	None
	25	27	Santiago, Jose Q	Son	M	Cha	9.0	S	Y	Y		Guam	Guam	Guam		None
	26	28	Aguon, Ignacio I	Head	M	Cha	53.0	M	Y	Y	Y	Guam	Guam	Guam	N	Farmer
	26	28	Aguon, Milagra Q	Wife	F	Cha	48.0	M		N	N	Guam	Guam	Guam	N	None
	26	28	Aguon, Jose Q	Son	M	Cha	27.0	S	Y	Y	Y	Guam	Guam	Guam	N	Farm laborer home farm
	26	28	Aguon, Jose Q	Son	M	Cha	16.0	S	Y	Y	Y	Guam	Guam	Guam	Y	Farm laborer home farm
	26	28	Aguon, Edevis Q	Daughter	F	Cha	14.0	S	Y	Y	Y	Guam	Guam	Guam	Y	None
	26	28	Aguon, Joaquin Q	Nephew	M	Cha	2.0	S				Guam	Guam	Guam		None
	27	29	Fegurgur, Rosauro C	Head	M	Cha	40.0	M	N	N	N	Guam	Guam	Guam	N	Farmer
	27	29	Fegurgur, Maria S	Wife	F	Cha	50.0	M	N	N	N	Guam	Guam	Guam	N	None
	27	29	Fegurgur, Jesus S	Son	M	Cha	8.0	S	Y			Guam	Guam	Guam		None
	27	29	Fegurgur, Jose S	Son	M	Cha	3.0	S				Guam	Guam	Guam		None
	28	30	Aguon, Juana C	Head	F	Cha	50.0	M	N	N	N	Guam	Guam	Guam	N	None
	28	30	Aguon, Asuncion C	Daughter	F	Cha	23.0	M	Y	Y	Y	Guam	Guam	Guam	Y	None
	28	30	Aguon, Maximo C	Son	M	Cha	21.0	S	N	Y	Y	Guam	Guam	Guam	Y	Farmer
	28	30	Aguon, Milagros C	Daughter	F	Cha	18.0	S	N	Y	Y	Guam	Guam	Guam	Y	None
	28	30	Aguon, Rosalia C	Daughter	F	Cha	6.0	S	N			Guam	Guam	Guam		None
	28	30	Aguon, Cristina C	Daughter	F	Cha	5.0	S				Guam	Guam	Guam		None
	28	30	Aguon, Vicente C	Son	M	Cha	4.0	S				Guam	Guam	Guam		None
	29	31	Quinata, Hermenijildo Q	Head	M	Cha	27.0	S		N	N	Guam	Guam	Guam	N	Farmer
	30	32	Quinata, Josepha T	Head	F	Cha	39.0	S		N	N	Guam	Unknown	Guam	N	None
	30	32	Quinata, Magdalena T	Daughter	F	Cha	4.0	S				Guam	Unknown	Guam		None
	30	32	Quinata, Ana T	Daughter	F	Cha	1.0	S				Guam	Unknown	Guam		None
	30	32	Topasna, Candido T	Servant	M	Cha	10.0	S	Y	Y	Y	Guam	Unknown	Guam	Y	Servant

Street, avenue, road: Dionloto Street

(CHAMORRO ROOTS GENEALOGY PROJECT ™ TRANSCRIPTION)
(COMPILED/TRANSCRIBED BY BERNARD T. PUNZALAN / HTTP://WWW.CHAMORROROOTS.COM)

FOURTEENTH CENSUS OF THE UNITED STATES: 1920-POPULATION

ISLAND OF GUAM

ENUMERATED BY ME ON THE 20th DAY OF March, 1920

Albert P. Manley ENUMERATOR.

DISTRICT 4

NAME OF PLACE Umatac Barrio

[Proper name and, also, name of class, as city, town, village, barrio, etc]

Street, avenue, road, etc.	Number of dwelling house in order of visitation	Number of family in order of visitation	NAME of each person whose place of abode on January 1, 1920, was in the family. Enter surname, firs, then given name and middle initial. If any. Include every person living on January 1, 1920. Omit children born since January 1, 1920.	RELATION Relationship of this Person to the head of the family.	Sex	Color or race	Age at last birthday	Single, married, widowed or divorced	Attended school any time since Sept. 1, 1919	Whether able to read.	Whether able to write.	Place of birth of this person.	Place of birth of father of this person.	Place of birth of mother of this person.	Whether able to speak English.	OCCUPATION Trade, profession, or particular kind of work done, as salesman, laborer, clerk, cook, merchant, washerwoman, etc.
					6	7	8	9	10	11	12	13	14	15	16	17
	31	33	Topasna, Isidoro E	Head	M	Cha	26.0	M		N	N	Guam	Guam	Guam	N	Farmer
	31	33	Topasna, Ascemsion Q	Wife	F	Cha	25.0	M		Y	Y	Guam	Guam	Guam	N	None
	31	33	Topasna, Juan Q	Son	M	Cha	3.0	S				Guam	Guam	Guam	N	None
	31	33	Topasna, Natividad Q	Daughter	F	Cha	1.0	S				Guam	Guam	Guam		None
	32	34	Cheguina, Polocarpio T	Head	M	Cha	29.0	M		N	N	Guam	Guam	Guam	N	Farmer
	32	34	Cheguina, Maxima S	Wife	F	Cha	20.0	M	N	N	N	Guam	Guam	Guam	N	None
	32	34	Cheguina, Calalena S	Daughter	F	Cha	1.0	S				Guam	Guam	Guam		None
	33	35	Sanchez, Polonia A	Head	F	Cha	69.0	Wd		N	N	Guam	Guam	Guam	N	None
	33	35	Sanchez, Regina A	Daughter	F	Cha	48.0	S		N	N	Guam	Guam	Guam	N	None
	33	35	Sanchez, Antonio A	Son	M	Cha	44.0	S		N	N	Guam	Guam	Guam	N	Farmer
	33	35	Sanchez, Lucas A	Son	M	Cha	40.0	S		N	N	Guam	Guam	Guam	N	Farm laborer home farm
	34	36	Cheguina, Antonia S	Head	F	Cha	45.0	Wd		N	N	Guam	Guam	Guam	N	None
	34	36	Cheguina, Jose S	Son	M	Cha	6.0	S	N			Guam	Guam	Guam	N	None
Dionicio Street	34	36	Cheguina, Emiliana S	Niece	F	Cha	20.0	S	N	N	N	Guam	Guam	Guam	N	None
	35	37	Aquiningoc, Manuel A	Head	M	Cha	35.0	M	N	Y	Y	Guam	Guam	Guam	N	Farmer
	35	37	Aquiningoc, Ana Q	Wife	F	Cha	30.0	M		Y	Y	Guam	Guam	Guam	N	None
	35	37	Aquiningoc, Juan Q	Son	M	Cha	10.0	S	Y	Y	Y	Guam	Guam	Guam	Y	None
	35	37	Aquiningoc, Felicidad Q	Daughter	F	Cha	8.0	S	Y			Guam	Guam	Guam		None
	35	37	Aquiningoc, Maria Q	Daughter	F	Cha	7.0	S	Y			Guam	Guam	Guam		None
	35	37	Aquiningoc, Carmen Q	Daughter	F	Cha	5.0	S	N			Guam	Guam	Guam		None
	35	37	Aquiningoc, Jose Q	Son	M	Cha	4.0	S				Guam	Guam	Guam		None
	35	37	Aquiningoc, Dolores Q	Daughter	F	Cha	2.0	S				Guam	Guam	Guam		None
	36	38	Aguon, Sabina R	Head	F	Cha	60.0	Wd		Y	Y	Guam	Guam	Guam	N	None
	36	38	Aguon, Antonio R	Son	M	Cha	19.0	S	N	Y	Y	Guam	Guam	Guam	Y	Farmer
	37	39	Aguon, Filipe R	Head	M	Cha	27.0	M		Y	Y	Guam	Guam	Guam	N	Farmer

(CHAMORRO ROOTS GENEALOGY PROJECT ™ TRANSCRIPTION)
(COMPILED/TRANSCRIBED BY BERNARD T. FUNZALAN / HTTP://WWW.CHAMORROROOTS.COM)

FOURTEENTH CENSUS OF THE UNITED STATES: 1920-POPULATION
ISLAND OF GUAM

ENUMERATED BY ME ON THE 20th DAY OF March, 1920

Albert P. Manley ENUMERATOR

DISTRICT 4
NAME OF PLACE Umatac Barrio
[Proper name and, also, name of class, as city, town, village, barrio, etc]

	PLACE OF ABODE		NAME	RELATION	PERSONAL DESCRIPTION					EDUCATION			NATIVITY				OCCUPATION
Street, avenue, road, etc.	Number of dwelling house is order of visitation	Number of family in order of visitation	of each person whose place of abode on January 1, 1920, was in the family. Enter surname, first, then given name and middle initial. If any. Include every person living on January 1, 1920. Omit children born since January 1, 1920.	Relationship of this Person to the head of the family.	Sex	Color or race	Age at last birthday	Single, married, widowed or divorced	Attended school any time since Sept. 1, 1919	Whether able to read.	Whether able to write.	Place of birth of this person.	Place of birth of father of this person.	Place of birth of mother of this person.	Whether able to speak English.	Trade, profession, or particular kind of work done, as salesman, laborer, clerk, cook, merchant, washerwoman, etc.
1	2	3	4	5	6	7	8	9	10	11	12	13	14	15	16	17
1	37	39	Aguon, Calistra T	Wife	F	Cha	24.0	M		Y	Y	Guam	Guam	Guam	N	None
2	37	39	Aguon, Joaquina T	Daughter	F	Cha	3.0	S				Guam	Guam	Guam		None
3	37	39	Aguon, Jose T	Son	M	Cha	1.0	S				Guam	Guam	Guam		None
4	37	39	Topasna, Ignacio T	Brother-in-law	M	Cha	15.0	S	N	Y	Y	Guam	Guam	Guam	Y	Farm laborer home farm
5	38	40	Quidachay, Juan T	Head	M	Cha	27.0	M		N	N	Guam	Guam	Guam	N	Farmer
6	38	40	Quidachay, Ascemcion T	Wife	F	Cha	26.0	M		Y	Y	Guam	Guam	Guam	N	None
7	38	40	Quidachay, Enriqueta T	Daughter	F	Cha	6.0	S	N			Guam	Guam	Guam		None
8	38	40	Quidachay, Vicente T	Son	M	Cha	5.0	S	N			Guam	Guam	Guam		None
9	38	40	Quidachay, Prodencio T	Son	M	Cha	4.0	S				Guam	Guam	Guam		None
10	38	40	Quidachay, Ana T	Daughter	F	Cha	3.0	S				Guam	Guam	Guam		None
11	38	40	Quidachay, Francisco T	Son	M	Cha	2.0	S				Guam	Guam	Guam		None
12	38	40	Quidachay, Adela T	Daughter	F	Cha	1.0	S				Guam	Guam	Guam		None
13	39	41	Aguon, Petra C	Head	F	Cha	33.0	S		N	N	Guam	Unknown	Guam	N	Washerwoman
14	39	41	Aguon, Juan C	Son	M	Cha	5.0	S	N			Guam	Unknown	Guam		None
15	39	41	Aguon, Isabel C	Daughter	F	Cha	1.0	S				Guam	Guam	Guam		None
16	40	42	Borja, Joaquin T	Head	M	Cha	43.0	M		Y	Y	Guam	Guam	Guam	Y	Farmer
17	40	42	Borja, Dolores A	Wife	F	Cha	35.0	M		Y	Y	Guam	Guam	Guam	N	None
18	40	42	Borja, Julian A	Son	M	Cha	6.0	S	N			Guam	Guam	Guam		None
19	40	42	Borja, Gregorio A	Son	M	Cha	4.0	S				Guam	Guam	Guam		None
20	40	42	Borja, Manuel A	Son	M	Cha	2.0	S				Guam	Guam	Guam		None
21	41	43	Sanchez, Crispin S	Head	M	Cha	50.0	M		N	N	Guam	Guam	Guam	N	Farmer
22	41	43	Sanchez, Maria S	Wife	M	Cha	47.0	M		N	N	Guam	Guam	Guam	N	None
23	41	43	Sanchez, Jose S	Son	M	Cha	20.0	S	N	Y	Y	Guam	Guam	Guam	Y	Farm laborer home farm
24	41	43	Sanchez, Ana S	Daughter	F	Cha	16.0	S	N	Y	Y	Guam	Guam	Guam	Y	None
25	41	43	Sanchez, Manuela S	Daughter	F	Cha	9.0	S	Y			Guam	Guam	Guam		None

Dionicio Street

(CHAMORRO ROOTS GENEALOGY PROJECT ™ TRANSCRIPTION)
(COMPILED/TRANSCRIBED BY BERNARD T. PUNZALAN / HTTP://WWW.CHAMORROROOTS.COM)
FOURTEENTH CENSUS OF THE UNITED STATES: 1920–POPULATION
ISLAND OF GUAM

DISTRICT 4
NAME OF PLACE **Umatac Barrio**
[Proper name and, also, name of class, as city, town, village, barrio, etc]

ENUMERATED BY ME ON THE 22nd DAY OF March, 1920

Albert P. Manley ENUMERATOR

	Number of dwelling house in order of visitation (2)	Number of family in order of visitation (3)	NAME (4)	RELATION (5)	Sex (6)	Color or race (7)	Age at last birthday (8)	Single, married, widowed or divorced (9)	Attended any school since Sept. 1, 1919 (10)	Whether able to read (11)	Whether able to write (12)	Place of birth of this person (13)	Place of birth of father (14)	Place of birth of mother (15)	Whether able to speak English (16)	OCCUPATION (17)
26	41	43	Sanchez, Vicenta T	Head	F	Cha	52.0	S		N	N	Guam	Guam	Guam	N	None
27	41	43	Sanchez, Feliciana T	Daughter	F	Cha	23.0	S		N	N	Guam	Unknown	Guam	N	None
28	41	43	Sanchez, Mariano T	Nephew	M	Cha	2.0	S				Guam	Guam	Guam		None
29	42	45	Quinata, Antonio A	Head	M	Cha	43.0	M		Y	Y	Guam	Guam	Guam	N	Farmer
30	42	45	Quinata, Maria Q	Wife	F	Cha	46.0	M		N	N	Guam	Guam	Guam	N	None
31	42	45	Quinata, Jacinto Q	Son	M	Cha	13.0	S	N	Y	Y	Guam	Guam	Guam	Y	None
32	42	45	Quinata, Vicente Q	Son	M	Cha	9.0	S	Y	Y	Y	Guam	Guam	Guam	Y	None
33	42	45	Quinata, Edwardo Q	Son	M	Cha	6.0	S	N			Guam	Guam	Guam		None
34	42	45	Quinata, Maria Q	Daughter	F	Cha	5.0	S	N			Guam	Guam	Guam		None
35	43	46	Gofigan, Vicenta Q	Head	F	Cha	47.0	Wd		N	N	Guam	Guam	Guam	N	None
36	43	46	Gofigan, Geronimo Q	Son	M	Cha	22.0	S		Y	Y	Guam	Guam	Guam	Y	Farmer
37	43	46	Gofigan, Graviel Q	Son	M	Cha	18.0	S	N	Y	Y	Guam	Guam	Guam	Y	Farm laborer home farm
38	43	46	Gofigan, Vicente Q	Son	M	Cha	16.0	S	N	Y	Y	Guam	Guam	Guam	Y	Farm laborer home farm
39	43	46	Gofigan, Ramon Q	Son	M	Cha	3.0	S				Guam	Guam	Guam		None
40	44	47	Quinata, Anastacio T	Head	M	Cha	24.0	M		N	N	Guam	Guam	Guam	N	Farmer
41	44	47	Quinata, Nieves A	Wife	F	Cha	23.0	M		N	N	Guam	Guam	Guam	N	None
42	44	47	Quinata, Rita A	Daughter	F	Cha	2.0	S				Guam	Guam	Guam		None
43	44	47	Quinata, Vicente A	Son	M	Cha	0.3	S	N			Guam	Guam	Guam		None
44	44	47	Quinata, Vicente T	Brother	M	Cha	19.0	S		Y	Y	Guam	Guam	Guam	Y	Laborer
45	44	47	Quinata, Carlota T	Sister	F	Cha	11.0	S	Y	Y	Y	Guam	Guam	Guam	Y	None
46	45	48	Aguon, Simon C	Head	M	Cha	27.0	M		N	N	Guam	Guam	Guam	N	Farmer
47	45	48	Aguon, Ana A	Wife	F	Cha	26.0	M		N	N	Guam	Guam	Guam	N	None
48	45	48	Aguon, Vicente A	Son	M	Cha	2.0	S				Guam	Guam	Guam		None
49	46	49	Camacho, Manuel C	Head	M	Cha	32.0	M		N	N	Guam	Guam	Guam	N	Farmer
50	46	49	Camacho, Gregoria C	Wife	F	Cha	29.0	M		N	N	Guam	Guam	Guam	N	None

Street, avenue, road, etc. (column 1): Dionicio Street

(CHAMORRO ROOTS GENEALOGY PROJECT ™ TRANSCRIPTION)
(COMPILED/TRANSCRIBED BY BERNARD T. PUNZALAN / HTTP://WWW.CHAMORROROOTS.COM)

234

FOURTEENTH CENSUS OF THE UNITED STATES: 1920—POPULATION

ISLAND OF GUAM

ENUMERATED BY ME ON THE 22nd DAY OF March, 1920

Albert P. Manley ENUMERATOR

DISTRICT 4

NAME OF PLACE Umatac Barrio

[Proper name and, also, name of class, as city, town, village, barrio, etc]

Street, avenue, road, etc.	Number of dwelling house is order of visitation	Number of family in order of visitation	NAME of each person whose place of abode on January 1, 1920, was in this family. Enter surname, first, then given name and middle initial. If any. Include every person living on January 1, 1920. Omit children born since January 1, 1920.	RELATION Relationship of this Person to the head of the family.	Sex	Color or race	Age at last birthday	single, married, widowed or divorced	Attended school any time since Sept. 1, 1919	Whether able to read.	Whether able to write.	Place of birth of this person.	Place of birth of father of this person.	Place of birth of mother of this person.	Whether able to speak English.	OCCUPATION Trade, profession, or particular kind of work done, as salesman, laborer, clerk, cook, merchant, washerwoman, etc.
1	2	3	4	5	6	7	8	9	10	11	12	13	14	15	16	17
	46	49	Camacho, Jesus C	Son	M	Cha	7.0	S	N			Guam	Guam	Guam		None
	46	49	Camacho, Florentina C	Daughter	F	Cha	5.0	S	N			Guam	Guam	Guam		None
	46	49	Camacho, Maria C	Daughter	F	Cha	3.0	S				Guam	Guam	Guam		None
	46	49	Fegurgur, Encarnation T	Servant	F	Cha	40.0	S	N	N	N	Guam	Guam	Guam	N	Servant
	46	49	Fegurgur, Maria T	Servant	F	Cha	18.0	S	Y	Y	Y	Guam	Unknown	Guam	Y	Servant
	46	49	Fegurgur, Ana T	Servant	F	Cha	12.0	S	Y	Y	Y	Guam	Unknown	Guam	N	Servant
	47	50	Topasna, Soledad Q	Head	F	Cha	46.0	Wd	N	Y	N	Guam	Guam	Guam	Y	None
	47	50	Topasna, Eucevio Q	Son	M	Cha	20.0	S	N	Y	Y	Guam	Guam	Guam	Y	Farmer
	47	50	Topasna, Jose Q	Son	M	Cha	18.0	S	N	Y	Y	Guam	Guam	Guam	Y	Farm laborer home farm
	47	50	Topasna, Francisco Q	Son	M	Cha	8.0	S	Y			Guam	Guam	Guam		None
	47	50	Topasna, Juan Q	Son	M	Cha	3.0	S	N			Guam	Guam	Guam		None
	47	50	Topasna, Ana M	Niece	F	Cha	15.0	S	N	Y	Y	Guam	Guam	Guam	Y	None
	48	51	Quinata, Miguel A	Head	M	Cha	25.0	M		Y	Y	Guam	Guam	Guam	Y	Farmer
	48	51	Quinata, Teresa I	Wife	F	Cha	19.0	M	N	Y	Y	Guam	Guam	Guam	N	None
	48	51	Quinata, Antonio I	Son	M	Cha	3.0	S				Guam	Guam	Guam		None
	48	51	Quinata, Francisco I	Son	M	Cha	1.0	S				Guam	Guam	Guam		None
	49	52	Tajalle, Vicenta S	Head	F	Cha	46.0	Wd		Y	Y	Guam	Unknown	Guam	N	Washerwoman
	49	52	Tajalle, Feliciana S	Daughter	F	Cha	29.0	S		N	N	Guam	Unknown	Guam	N	Washerwoman
	49	52	Tajalle, Mariano S	Son	M	Cha	1.0	S				Guam	Unknown	Guam		None
	50	53	Aguon, Maria C	Head	F	Cha	45.0	Wd		Y	Y	Guam	Guam	Guam	N	Washerwoman
	51	54	Aguon, Amparo T	Head	F	Cha	43.0	Wd		N	N	Guam	Guam	Guam	N	Washerwoman
	51	54	Aguon, Amadeo T	Son	M	Cha	23.0	S	N	Y	Y	Guam	Guam	Guam	Y	Farmer
	51	54	Aguon, Maria T	Daughter	F	Cha	20.0	S	N	Y	Y	Guam	Guam	Guam	Y	Washerwoman
	51	54	Aguon, Pedro T	Son	M	Cha	18.0	S	Y	Y	Y	Guam	Guam	Guam	Y	Farm laborer home farm
	51	54	Aguon, Jesus T	Son	M	Cha	13.0	S	Y	Y	Y	Guam	Guam	Guam	Y	None

Dionicio Street

(Numbered rows 1–25 down the left margin)

470

(CHAMORRO ROOTS GENEALOGY PROJECT ™ TRANSCRIPTION)
(COMPILED/TRANSCRIBED BY BERNARD T. PUNZALAN / HTTP://WWW.CHAMORROROOTS.COM)

234b

FOURTEENTH CENSUS OF THE UNITED STATES: 1920-POPULATION

ISLAND OF GUAM

ENUMERATED BY ME ON THE 23rd DAY OF March, 1920

Albert P. Manley ENUMERATOR

DISTRICT **4**

NAME OF PLACE **Umatac Barrio**

[Proper name and, also, name of class, as city, town, village, barrio, etc]

	Street (1)	Dwelling No. (2)	Family No. (3)	NAME (4)	RELATION (5)	Sex (6)	Color or race (7)	Age (8)	Marital (9)	School (10)	Read (11)	Write (12)	Birthplace (13)	Father (14)	Mother (15)	English (16)	OCCUPATION (17)
26		51	54	Aguon, Gregorio T	Son	M	Cha	11.0	S	Y	Y	Y	Guam	Guam	Guam	Y	None
27		51	54	Aguon, Jose T	Son	M	Cha	6.0	S	N			Guam	Guam	Guam		None
28		51	54	Aguon, Felipe T	Son	M	Cha	4.0	S				Guam	Guam	Guam		None
29		51	54	Aguon, Ana T	Daughter	F	Cha	2.0	S				Guam	Guam	Guam		None
30		51	54	Aguon, Vicente T	Son	M	Cha	1.0	S				Guam	Guam	Guam		None
31		52	55	Quinata, Remedio M	Head	F	Cha	29.0	Wd		N	N	Guam	Guam	Guam	N	Washerwoman
32		52	55	Quinata, Trinidad M	Daughter	F	Cha	16.0	S	N	Y	Y	Guam	Guam	Guam	Y	None
33		52	55	Quinata, Engracia M	Daughter	F	Cha	13.0	S	Y	Y	Y	Guam	Guam	Guam	Y	None
34		52	55	Quinata, Joaquin M	Son	M	Cha	11.0	S	Y	Y	Y	Guam	Guam	Guam	Y	None
35	Dioniclo Street	52	55	Quinata, Angelina M	Daughter	F	Cha	9.0	S				Guam	Guam	Guam		None
36		52	55	Quinata, Ana M	Daughter	F	Cha	4.0	S				Guam	Guam	Guam		None
37		52	55	Malijan, Lourdes A	Grand-daughter	F	Cha	2.0	S				Guam	Guam	Guam		None
38		52	55	Malijan, Jose A	Grand-son	M	Cha	1.0	S				Guam	Guam	Guam		None
39		53	56	Aguon, Justo C	Head	M	Cha	30.0	M		Y	Y	Guam	Guam	Guam	N	Farmer
40		53	56	Aguon, Consuelo Q	Wife	F	Cha	26.0	M		Y	Y	Guam	Guam	Guam	N	None
41		53	56	Aguon, Joaquin Q	Son	M	Cha	3.0	S				Guam	Guam	Guam		None
42		53	56	Aguon, Ana Q	Daughter	F	Cha	2.0	S				Guam	Guam	Guam		None
43		53	56	Fegurgur, Rosa A	Servant	F	Cha	50.0	S		N	N	Guam	Guam	Guam	N	Servant
44		54	59	Quinata, Dionisio M	Head	M	Cha	39.0	M		Y	Y	Guam	Guam	Guam	Y	Farmer
45		54	59	Quinata, Ana A	Wife	F	Cha	40.0	M		Y	Y	Guam	Guam	Guam	N	None
46		54	59	Topasna, Juan E	Nephew	M	Cha	18.0	S	N	Y	Y	Guam	Guam	Guam	Y	Farm laborer home farm
47		55	58	Quinata, Jose S	Head	M	Cha	46.0	M		Y	Y	Guam	Guam	Guam	N	Farmer
48		55	58	Quinata, Maria A	Wife	F	Cha	40.0	M		Y	Y	Guam	Guam	Guam	N	None
49		55	58	Quinata, Felisa A	Daughter	F	Cha	23.0	S	N	Y	Y	Guam	Guam	Guam	Y	None
50		55	58	Quinata, Ignacio A	Son	M	Cha	17.0	S	N	Y	Y	Guam	Guam	Guam	Y	Farm laborer home farm

(COMPILED/TRANSCRIBED BY BERNARD T. PUNZALAN / HTTP://WWW.CHAMORROROOTS.COM)

(CHAMORRO ROOTS GENEALOGY PROJECT ™ TRANSCRIPTION)

FOURTEENTH CENSUS OF THE UNITED STATES: 1920-POPULATION
ISLAND OF GUAM

ENUMERATED BY ME ON THE 23rd DAY OF March, 1920

Albert P. Manley ENUMERATOR

DISTRICT 4
NAME OF PLACE Umatac Barrio
[Proper name and, also, name of class, as city, town, village, barrio, etc]

Street, avenue, road, etc.	Number of dwelling house is in order of visitation	Number of family in order of visitation	NAME of each person whose place of abode on January 1, 1920, was in the family.	RELATION Relationship of this Person to the head of the family.	Sex	Color or race	Age at last birthday	Single, married, widowed or divorced	Attended school any time since Sept. 1, 1919	Whether able to read.	Whether able to write.	Place of birth of this person.	Place of birth of father of this person.	Place of birth of mother of this person.	Whether able to speak English.	OCCUPATION Trade, profession, or particular kind of work done, as salesman, laborer, clerk, cook, merchant, washerwoman, etc.
1	2	3	4	5	6	7	8	9	10	11	12	13	14	15	16	17
	55	58	Quinata, Milagro A	Daughter	F	Cha	15.0	S	Y	Y	Y	Guam	Guam	Guam	Y	None
	55	58	Quinata, Josefina A	Daughter	F	Cha	13.0	S	Y	Y	Y	Guam	Guam	Guam	Y	None
	55	58	Quinata, Beatris A	Daughter	F	Cha	11.0	S	Y	Y	Y	Guam	Guam	Guam	Y	None
	55	58	Quinata, Jose A	Son	M	Cha	9.0	S	Y			Guam	Guam	Guam		None
	55	58	Quinata, Vicente A	Son	M	Cha	4.0	S				Guam	Guam	Guam		None
	55	58	Quinata, Juan A	Son	M	Cha	2.0	S				Guam	Guam	Guam		None
	56	59	Quinata, Hilarion A	Head	M	Cha	25.0	M		Y	Y	Guam	Guam	Guam	Y	Farmer
	56	59	Quinata, Josepha A	Wife	F	Cha	27.0	M		Y	Y	Guam	Guam	Guam	N	None
	56	59	Quinata, Jesus S	Son	M	Cha	5.0	S	N			Guam	Guam	Guam		None
	56	59	Quinata, Maria S	Daughter	F	Cha	3.0	S				Guam	Guam	Guam		None
	57	60	Sanchez, Francisco Q	Head	M	Cha	21.0	M	N	Y	Y	Guam	Guam	Guam	Y	Teacher
	57	60	Sanchez, Amparo Q	Wife	F	Cha	23.0	M		Y	Y	Guam	Guam	Guam	Y	None
	57	60	Sanchez, Angelina Q	Daughter	F	Cha	4.0	S				Guam	Guam	Guam		None
	58	61	Quinata, Juan A	Head	M	Cha	35.0	M		Y	Y	Guam	Guam	Guam	Y	Weaving Teacher
	58	61	Quinata, Elogracia D	Wife	F	Cha	30.0	M	N	Y	Y	Guam	Guam	Guam	Y	Weaving Teacher
	58	61	Quinata, Veronica D	Daughter	F	Cha	13.0	S	Y	Y	Y	Guam	Guam	Guam	Y	Weaving Teacher
	58	61	Quinata, Guardalupe D	Daughter	F	Cha	10.0	S	Y	Y	Y	Guam	Guam	Guam	Y	None
	58	61	Quinata, Francisco D	Son	M	Cha	9.0	S	Y			Guam	Guam	Guam		None
	59	62	Babauta, Jose G	Head	M	Cha	31.0	S		N	N	Guam	Guam	Guam	N	Farm laborer working out
	60	63	Aguon, Jose I	Head	M	Cha	37.0	M		N	N	Guam	Guam	Guam	N	Farm laborer working out
	60	63	Aguon, Antonia T	Wife	F	Cha	55.0	M		N	N	Guam	Guam	Guam	N	None
	61	64	Quidachay, Angela T	Head	F	Cha	33.0	Wd	N	N	N	Guam	Guam	Guam		None
	61	64	Quidachay, Maria T	Daughter	F	Cha	6.0	S				Guam	Guam	Guam		None
	61	64	Quidachay, Jose T	Son	M	Cha	2.0	S				Guam	Guam	Guam		None
	62	65	Aguon, Dolores C	Head	F	Cha	20.0	Wd	N	N	N	Guam	Guam	Guam	N	Washerwoman

Dioncio Street

(CHAMORRO ROOTS GENEALOGY PROJECT ™ TRANSCRIPTION)

(COMPILED/TRANSCRIBED BY BERNARD T. PUNZALAN / HTTP://WWW.CHAMORROROOTS.COM)

FOURTEENTH CENSUS OF THE UNITED STATES: 1920—POPULATION

ISLAND OF GUAM

DISTRICT **4**

NAME OF PLACE **Umatac Barrio**

[Proper name and, also, name of class, as city, town, village, barrio, etc]

ENUMERATED BY ME ON THE 23rd DAY OF March, 1920

Albert P. Manley ENUMERATOR

Street, avenue, road, etc.	Number of dwelling house is order of visitation	Number of family in order of visitation	NAME	RELATION	Sex	Color or race	Age at last birthday	Single, married, widowed or divorced	Attended school any time since sept. 1, 1919	Whether able to read.	Whether able to write.	Place of birth of this person.	Place of birth of father of this person.	Place of birth of mother of this person.	Whether able to speak English.	OCCUPATION
1	2	3	4	5	6	7	8	9	10	11	12	13	14	15	16	17
26	62	65	Aguon, Antonio C	Son	M	Cha	0.7	S				Guam	Guam	Guam		None
27	63	66	Barnabas, de Caseda	Head	M	W	27.0	S		Y	Y	Spain	Spain	Spain	N	Missionary
28			Here ends the enumeration of Umatac Barrio													
29																
30																
31																
32																
33																
34																
35																
36																
37																
38																
39																
40																
41																
42																
43																
44																
45																
46																
47																
48																
49																
59																

(CHAMORRO ROOTS GENEALOGY PROJECT ™ TRANSCRIPTION)
(COMPILED/TRANSCRIBED BY BERNARD T. PUNZALAN / HTTP://WWW.CHAMORROROOTS.COM)

FOURTEENTH CENSUS OF THE UNITED STATES: 1920-POPULATION

ISLAND OF GUAM

ENUMERATED BY ME ON THE 24th DAY OF March, 1920

Albert P. Manley ENUMERATOR

DISTRICT 4
NAME OF PLACE Merizo Town

[Proper name and, also, name of class, as city, town, village, barrio, etc]

Street, avenue, road, etc.	Number of dwelling house is order of visitation	Number of family in order of visitation	NAME	RELATION	Sex	Color or race	Age at last birthday	Single, married, widowed or divorced	Attended school any time since Sept. 1, 1919	Whether able to read	Whether able to write	Place of birth of this person	Place of birth of father of this person	Place of birth of mother of this person	Whether able to speak English	OCCUPATION
	1	2	3	4	5	6	7	8	9	10	11	12	13	14	15	16	17
		1	1	Torres, Vicente D	Head	M	Cha	47.0	M		Y	Y	Guam	Guam	Guam	Y	Farmer
	1	1	Torres, Maria F	Wife	F	Cha	43.0	M		Y	Y	Guam	Guam	Guam	N	None
	1	1	Torres, Ascemcion D	Sister	F	Cha	45.0	S		Y	Y	Guam	Guam	Guam	N	None
	1	1	Torres, Jose D	Nephew	M	Cha	16.0	S	Y	Y	Y	Guam	Unknown	Guam	Y	Farm laborer home farm
	1	1	Torres, Gertrudes D	Niece	F	Cha	12.0	S	N	Y	Y	Guam	Unknown	Guam	Y	None
	1	1	Quihene, Juan T	Servant	M	Cha	18.0	S		Y	Y	Guam	Guam	Guam	Y	Servant
	2	2	Tiquengco, Vicente B	Head	M	Cha	54.0	M				Guam	China	Guam	N	Farmer
	2	2	Tiquengco, Nicolasa B	Sister	F	Cha	57.0	Wd				Guam	China	Guam	N	None
	2	3	Manalisay, Jose C	Head	M	Cha	39.0	M		Y	Y	Guam	Unknown	Guam	N	Farmer
	2	3	Manalisay, Soledad C	Wife	F	Cha	35.0	M		Y	Y	Guam	Guam	Guam	N	None
	2	3	Manalisay, Maria C	Daughter	F	Cha	12.0	S	Y	Y	Y	Guam	Guam	Guam	Y	None
	3	4	Cruz, Jose G	Head	M	Cha	33.0	M		Y	Y	Guam	Guam	Guam	N	Farmer
	3	4	Cruz, Rosa C	Wife	F	Cha	29.0	M		Y	Y	Guam	Guam	Guam	N	None
Rosario Street	3	4	Cruz, Vicente C	Son	M	Cha	6.0	S	N			Guam	Guam	Guam		None
	3	4	Cruz, Ramon C	Son	M	Cha	5.0	S	N			Guam	Guam	Guam		None
	3	4	Cruz, Jesus C	Son	M	Cha	3.0	S				Guam	Guam	Guam		None
	3	4	Cruz, Jose C	Son	M	Cha	0.5	S				Guam	Guam	Guam		None
	4	5	Reyes, Lorenzo M	Head	M	Cha	38.0	M		Y	Y	Guam	Guam	Guam	N	Farmer
	4	5	Reyes, Teresa C	Wife	F	Cha	31.0	M		Y	Y	Guam	Guam	Guam	N	None
	4	5	Reyes, Antonio C	Son	M	Cha	8.0	S	Y			Guam	Guam	Guam		None
	4	5	Reyes, Maria C	Daughter	F	Cha	7.0	S				Guam	Guam	Guam		None
	4	5	Reyes, Joaquin C	Son	M	Cha	5.0	S	N			Guam	Guam	Guam		None
	4	5	Reyes, Ignacio C	Son	M	Cha	3.0	S	N			Guam	Guam	Guam		None
	5	6	Cruz, Jose P	Head	M	Cha	27.0	M		Y	Y	Guam	Guam	Guam	Y	Farmer
	5	6	Cruz, Florentina C	Wife	F	Cha	24.0	M		Y	Y	Guam	Guam	Guam	Y	None

(CHAMORRO ROOTS GENEALOGY PROJECT ™ TRANSCRIPTION)
(COMPILED/TRANSCRIBED BY BERNARD T. PUNZALAN / HTTP://WWW.CHAMORROROOTS.COM)

FOURTEENTH CENSUS OF THE UNITED STATES: 1920—POPULATION
ISLAND OF GUAM

DISTRICT 4
NAME OF PLACE **Merizo Town**
[Proper name and, also, name of class, as city, town, village, barrio, etc]

ENUMERATED BY ME ON THE 24th DAY OF March, 1920

Albert P. Manley ENUMERATOR

	Dwelling (2)	Family (3)	NAME (4)	RELATION (5)	Sex (6)	Color or race (7)	Age (8)	Marital (9)	School (10)	Read (11)	Write (12)	Birth person (13)	Birth father (14)	Birth mother (15)	English (16)	OCCUPATION (17)
26	5	6	Cruz, Dolores C	Daughter	F	Cha	4.0	S				Guam	Guam	Guam		None
27	5	6	Cruz, Vicenta C	Daughter	F	Cha	3.0	S				Guam	Guam	Guam		None
28	5	6	Cruz, Josefina C	Daughter	F	Cha	0.2	S				Guam	Guam	Guam		None
29	6	7	Garrido, Nicolas N	Head	M	Cha	30.0	S		Y	Y	Guam	Guam	Guam	Y	Farmer
30	6	7	Garrido, Ana N	Sister	F	Cha	25.0	S		Y	Y	Guam	Guam	Guam	Y	None
31	6	7	Fegurgur, Dolores N	Aunt	F	Cha	37.0	S		Y	Y	Guam	Unknown	Guam	N	None
32	6	7	Garrido, Ramon G	Nephew	M	Cha	7.0	S	N			Guam	Guam	Guam		None
33	7	8	Chargualaf, Juan B	Head	M	Cha	46.0	M		Y	Y	Guam	Guam	Guam	N	Farmer
34	7	8	Chargualaf, Manuela A	Wife	F	Cha	49.0	M		Y	Y	Guam	Guam	Guam	N	None
35	7	8	Meno, Sibera M	Niece	F	Cha	12.0	S	Y	Y	Y	Guam	Unknown	Guam	Y	None
36	8	9	Cruz, Miguel P	Head	M	Cha	30.0	M		Y	Y	Guam	Guam	Guam	N	Farmer
37	8	9	Cruz, Trudes C	Wife	F	Cha	28.0	M		Y	Y	Guam	Guam	Guam	N	None
38	8	9	Cruz, Antonio C	Son	M	Cha	10.0	S	Y	Y	Y	Guam	Guam	Guam	Y	None
39	8	9	Cruz, Jose C	Son	M	Cha	9.0	S	Y	Y	Y	Guam	Guam	Guam	Y	None
40	8	9	Cruz, Jesus C	Son	M	Cha	0.5	S				Guam	Guam	Guam		None
41	8	9	Meno, Maria Q	Servant	F	Cha	16.0	S	N	Y	Y	Guam	Guam	Guam	N	Servant
42	9	10	Quinene, Vicente T	Head	M	Cha	28.0	M		Y	Y	Guam	Guam	Guam	Y	Farmer
43	9	10	Quinene, Librada C	Wife	F	Cha	2.0	M	N	Y	Y	Guam	Guam	Guam	Y	None
44	9	10	Quinene, Ana C	Daughter	F	Cha	1.0	S				Guam	Guam	Guam		None
45	9	10	Cruz, Ramon C	Servant	M	Cha	70.0	Wd		Y	Y	Guam	Unknown	Unknown	N	Servant
46	10	11	Barcinas, Jose S	Head	M	Cha	33.0	M		Y	Y	Guam	Guam	Guam	N	Farmer
47	10	11	Barcinas, Ana C	Wife	F	Cha	35.0	M		Y	Y	Guam	Guam	Guam	N	None
48	10	11	Barcinas, Jesus C	Son	M	Cha	12.0	S	Y	Y	Y	Guam	Guam	Guam	Y	None
49	10	11	Barcinas, Tomas C	Son	M	Cha	11.0	S	Y	Y	Y	Guam	Guam	Guam	Y	None
50	10	11	Barcinas, Martin C	Son	M	Cha	8.0	S	Y	Y	Y	Guam	Guam	Guam	Y	None

Street, avenue, road, etc.: Rosario Street

475

(CHAMORRO ROOTS GENEALOGY PROJECT ™ TRANSCRIPTION)

(COMPILED/TRANSCRIBED BY BERNARD T. PUNZALAN / HTTP://WWW.CHAMORROROOTS.COM)

237

FOURTEENTH CENSUS OF THE UNITED STATES: 1920-POPULATION

ISLAND OF GUAM

ENUMERATED BY ME ON THE 25th DAY OF March, 1920

Albert P. Manley ENUMERATOR

DISTRICT **4**

NAME OF PLACE **Merizo Town**

[Proper name and, also, name of class, as city, town, village, barrio, etc]

Street, avenue, road, etc.	Number of dwelling house in order of visitation	Number of family in order of visitation	NAME	RELATION	Sex	Color or race	Age at last birthday	Single, married, widowed or divorced	Attended school any time since Sept. 1, 1919	Whether able to read	Whether able to write	Place of birth of this person	Place of birth of father of this person	Place of birth of mother of this person	Whether able to speak English	OCCUPATION
1	2	3	4	5	6	7	8	9	10	11	12	13	14	15	16	17
	10	11	Barcinas, Jose C	Son	M	Cha	7.0	S	N			Guam	Guam	Guam		None
	10	11	Barcinas, Grabies C	Son	M	Cha	5.0	S	N			Guam	Guam	Guam		None
	10	11	Barcinas, Ynigo C	Son	M	Cha	3.0	S				Guam	Guam	Guam		None
	10	11	Barcinas, Joaquin C	Son	M	Cha	1.0	S				Guam	Guam	Guam		None
	11	12	Cruz, Pablo C	Head	M	Cha	30.0	M		Y	Y	Guam	Guam	Guam	N	Farmer
	11	12	Cruz, Dolores M	Wife	F	Cha	17.0	M	N	Y	Y	Guam	Guam	Guam	N	None
	11	12	Cruz, Luis M	Son	M	Cha	2.0	S				Guam	Guam	Guam		None
	12	13	Chargulaf, Mariano B	Head	M	Cha	25.0	S		Y	Y	Guam	Guam	Guam	Y	Farmer
	12	13	Chargulaf, Natividad C	Aunt	F	Cha	40.0	S		Y	N	Guam	Unknown	Guam		None
	12	13	Chargulaf, Ynigo C	Cousin	M	Cha	25.0	S		Y	Y	Guam	Unknown	Guam	Y	Farm laborer home farm
	12	13	Chargulaf, Remedio C	Cousin	F	Cha	17.0	S	N	Y	Y	Guam	Unknown	Guam	N	None
	13	14	San Nicolas, Antonio E	Head	M	Cha	37.0	M		Y	Y	Guam	Guam	Guam	N	Farmer
	13	14	San Nicolas, Rosario M	Wife	F	Cha	26.0	M		Y	Y	Guam	Guam	Guam	N	None
	13	14	San Nicolas, Juan M	Son	M	Cha	11.0	S	Y	Y	Y	Guam	Guam	Guam	Y	None
	13	14	San Nicolas, Maria M	Daughter	F	Cha	8.0	S	Y	Y	Y	Guam	Guam	Guam		None
	13	14	San Nicolas, Joaquina M	Daughter	F	Cha	6.0	S	N			Guam	Guam	Guam		None
	13	14	San Nicolas, Jose M	Son	M	Cha	5.0	S	N			Guam	Guam	Guam		None
	13	14	Quinene, Felicita Q	Servant	F	Cha	14.0	S	Y	Y	Y	Guam	Guam	Guam	Y	Servant
	13	14	Quinene, Jose Q	Servant	M	Cha	10.0	S	Y	Y	Y	Guam	Guam	Guam	Y	Servant
	14	15	Babauta, Angel B	Head	M	Cha	55.0	M		Y	Y	Guam	Unknown	Guam	N	Farmer
	14	15	Babauta, Vicenta C	Wife	F	Cha	45.0	M		Y	Y	Guam	Guam	Guam	N	None
	14	15	Nangauta, Emiliana N	Niece	F	Cha	18.0	S	N	Y	Y	Guam	Unknown	Guam	N	None
	14	15	Nangauta, Isabel N	Niece	F	Cha	5.0	S				Guam	Unknown	Guam		None
	15	16	Taeantongo, Geronimo M	Head	M	Cha	44.0	M		Y	Y	Guam	Guam	Guam	N	Farmer
	15	16	Taeantongo, Maria E	Wife	F	Cha	40.0	M		N	N	Guam	Guam	Guam	N	None

Rosatio Street

476

(CHAMORRO ROOTS GENEALOGY PROJECT ™ TRANSCRIPTION)
(COMPILED/TRANSCRIBED BY BERNARD T. PUNZALAN / HTTP://WWW.CHAMORROROOTS.COM)

FOURTEENTH CENSUS OF THE UNITED STATES: 1920-POPULATION
ISLAND OF GUAM

DISTRICT 4
NAME OF PLACE **Merizo Town**

ENUMERATED BY ME ON THE 26th DAY OF March, 1920

Albert P. Manley ENUMERATOR

[Proper name and, also, name of class, as city, town, village, barrio, etc]

1	2	3	4	5	6	7	8	9	10	11	12	13	14	15	16	17
			NAME	RELATION	PERSONAL DESCRIPTION				EDUCATION			NATIVITY				OCCUPATION
Street, avenue, road, etc.	Number of dwelling house in order of visitation	Number of family in order of visitation		Relationship of this Person to the head of the family.	Sex	Color or race	Age at last birthday	Single, married, widowed or divorced	Attended school any time since Sept. 1, 1919	Whether able to read.	Whether able to write.	Place of birth of this person.	Place of birth of father of this person.	Place of birth of mother of this person.	Whether able to speak English.	Trade, profession, or particular kind of work done, as salesman, laborer, clerk, cook, merchant, washerwoman, etc.
	15	16	Taeantongo, Ignacio E	Son	M	Cha	15.0	S	N	Y	Y	Guam	Guam	Guam	Y	Farm laborer home farm
	15	16	Taeantongo, Ana E	Daughter	F	Cha	13.0	S	N	Y	Y	Guam	Guam	Guam	Y	None
	15	16	Taeantongo, Gregorio E	Son	M	Cha	11.0	S	Y	Y	Y	Guam	Guam	Guam	Y	None
	15	16	Taeantongo, Pedro E	Son	M	Cha	9.0	S	Y			Guam	Guam	Guam		None
	15	16	Taeantongo, Catalina E	Daughter	F	Cha	3.0	S				Guam	Guam	Guam		None
	15	16	Taeantongo, Josefa E	Daughter	F	Cha	1.0	S				Guam	Guam	Guam		None
	16	17	Borja, Juan W	Head	M	Cha	44.0	M		Y	Y	Guam	Guam	Guam	Y	Farmer
	16	17	Borja, Dolores B	Wife	F	Cha	33.0	M		Y	Y	Guam	Guam	Guam	N	None
	16	17	Borja, Rita B	Daughter	F	Cha	19.0	S	N	Y	Y	Guam	Guam	Guam	Y	None
	16	17	Champaco, Juan C	Servant	M	Cha	7.0	S	N			Guam	Guam	Guam		None
	17	18	Condaso, Jose F	Head	M	Cha	32.0	M		Y	Y	Guam	Guam	Guam	N	Farmer
	17	18	Condaso, Maria T	Wife	F	Cha	25.0	M		Y	Y	Guam	Guam	Guam	N	None
	17	18	Condaso, Jose T	Son	M	Cha	5.0	S	N			Guam	Guam	Guam		None
	17	18	Condaso, Brijeda T	Daughter	F	Cha	2.0	S				Guam	Guam	Guam		None
	17	18	Condaso, Carmen T	Daughter	F	Cha	1.0	S				Guam	Guam	Guam		None
	18	19	Chagulaf, Geronimo T	Head	M	Cha	25.0	M		Y	Y	Guam	Guam	Guam	N	Farmer
	18	19	Chagulaf, Magdalena T	Wife	F	Cha	21.0	M	N	Y	Y	Guam	Unknown	Guam	Y	None
	19	20	Quinene, Santiago F	Head	M	Cha	24.0	S		Y	Y	Guam	Guam	Guam	Y	Farmer
	19	20	Quinene, Maria F	Sister	F	Cha	30.0	S		Y	Y	Guam	Guam	Guam	N	None
	19	20	Quinene, Ascemcion F	Sister	F	Cha	29.0	S		Y	Y	Guam	Guam	Guam	N	None
	19	20	Quinene, Magdalena F	Niece	F	Cha	11.0	S	Y	Y	Y	Guam	Unknown	Guam	Y	None
	19	20	Quinene, Ana F	Niece	F	Cha	8.0	S	Y			Guam	Unknown	Guam		None
	19	20	Quinene, Jose F	Nephew	M	Cha	5.0	S	N			Guam	Unknown	Guam		None
	20	21	Taijeron, Mariano B	Head	M	Cha	35.0	S		Y	Y	Guam	Guam	Guam	Y	Farmer
	20	21	Taijeron, Maria B	Sister	F	Cha	37.0	S		Y	N	Guam	Guam	Guam	N	None

Rosario Street

477

(CHAMORRO ROOTS GENEALOGY PROJECT ™ TRANSCRIPTION)
(COMPILED/TRANSCRIBED BY BERNARD T. PUNZALAN / HTTP://WWW.CHAMORROROOTS.COM)

238

FOURTEENTH CENSUS OF THE UNITED STATES: 1920—POPULATION
ISLAND OF GUAM

DISTRICT 4
NAME OF PLACE **Merizo Town**
[Proper name and, also, name of class, as city, town, village, barrio, etc]

ENUMERATED BY ME ON THE 26th DAY OF March, 1920
Albert P. Manley ENUMERATOR

Street, avenue, road, etc.	Number of dwelling house in order of visitation	Number of family in order of visitation	NAME	RELATION	Sex	Color or race	Age at last birthday	Single, married, widowed or divorced	Attended school any time since Sept. 1, 1919	Whether able to read	Whether able to write	Place of birth of this person	Place of birth of father of this person	Place of birth of mother of this person	Whether able to speak English	OCCUPATION
1	2	3	4	5	6	7	8	9	10	11	12	13	14	15	16	17
	20	21	Taijeron, Jose B	Nephew	M	Cha	6.0	S	N			Guam	Guam	Guam		None
	21	22	San Nicolas, Frailon S	Head	M	Cha	45.0	M		Y	Y	Guam	Guam	Rota Marianas	N	Farmer
	21	22	San Nicolas, Maria T	Wife	F	Cha	43.0	M		Y	Y	Guam	Unknown	Guam	N	None
	21	22	Naputy, Jesus A	Servant	M	Cha	18.0	S	N	Y	Y	Guam	Guam	Guam	Y	Servant
	21	22	Naputy, Jose A	Servant	M	Cha	15.0	S	N	Y	Y	Guam	Guam	Guam	Y	Servant
	22	23	Quidaguay, Francisco T	Head	M	Cha	44.0	M		Y	Y	Guam	Guam	Guam	N	Weaver
	22	23	Quidaguay, Maria T	Wife	F	Cha	34.0	M		N	N	Guam	Guam	Guam	N	None
	22	23	Quidaguay, Felix T	Son	M	Cha	14.0	S	N	Y	Y	Guam	Guam	Guam	Y	Farm laborer home farm
	22	23	Quidaguay, Dolores T	Daughter	F	Cha	8.0	S	Y	Y	Y	Guam	Guam	Guam	N	None
	22	23	Quidaguay, Pedro T	Son	M	Cha	5.0	S	N			Guam	Guam	Guam	N	None
Rosario Street	22	23	Quidaguay, Jesus T	Son	M	Cha	4.0	S				Guam	Guam	Guam	N	None
	23	24	Champaco, Pedro C	Head	M	Cha	44.0	M		Y	Y	Guam	China	Guam	N	Farmer
	23	24	Champaco, Ana M	Wife	F	Cha	41.0	M		Y	Y	Guam	Guam	Guam	N	None
	23	24	Champaco, Maria M	Daughter	F	Cha	17.0	S	N	Y	Y	Guam	Guam	Guam	N	Farm laborer home farm
	23	24	Champaco, Vicente M	Son	M	Cha	16.0	S	N	Y	Y	Guam	Guam	Guam	Y	None
	23	24	Champaco, Ascemcion M	Daughter	F	Cha	14.0	S	N	Y	Y	Guam	Guam	Guam	Y	None
	23	24	Champaco, Mariano M	Son	M	Cha	12.0	S	Y	Y	Y	Guam	Guam	Guam	Y	None
	23	24	Champaco, Jose M	Son	M	Cha	5.0	S	N			Guam	Guam	Guam	N	None
	24	25	Meno, Rosa C	Head	F	Cha	58.0	Wd		Y	Y	Guam	Guam	Guam	N	None
	24	25	Meno, Dolores C	Daughter	F	Cha	42.0	S		Y	Y	Guam	Guam	Guam	N	Seamstress
	24	25	Meno, Isabel C	Daughter	F	Cha	39.0	S		Y	Y	Guam	Guam	Guam	N	Washerwoman
	24	25	Meno, Candelaria C	Daughter	F	Cha	35.0	S		Y	Y	Guam	Guam	Guam	N	None
	24	25	Meno, Joaquin C	Son	M	Cha	33.0	S		Y	Y	Guam	Guam	Guam	N	Weaver
	24	25	Meno, Jose C	Son	M	Cha	29.0	S		Y	Y	Guam	Guam	Unknown	N	Farm laborer home farm
	24	25	Meno, Vicenta C	Grand-daughter	F	Cha	17.0	S	N	Y	Y	Guam	Unknown	Guam	N	None

(CHAMORRO ROOTS GENEALOGY PROJECT ™ TRANSCRIPTION)
(COMPILED/TRANSCRIBED BY BERNARD T. PUNZALAN / HTTP://WWW.CHAMORROROOTS.COM)

238b

FOURTEENTH CENSUS OF THE UNITED STATES: 1920-POPULATION

ISLAND OF GUAM

ENUMERATED BY ME ON THE 26th DAY OF March, 1920

Albert P. Manley ENUMERATOR

DISTRICT 4

NAME OF PLACE Merizo Town

	Dwelling	Family	NAME	RELATION	Sex	Color	Age	S/M/W/D	School	Read	Write	Birthplace	Father	Mother	English	OCCUPATION
	1	2	3	4	5	6	7	8	9	10	11	12	13	14	15	16	17
26	24	25	Meno, Jose C	Grandson	M	Cha	13.0	S	N	Y	Y	Guam	Unknown	Guam	Y	None
27	24	25	Meno, Maria C	Granddaughter	F	Cha	12.0	S	Y	Y	Y	Guam	Unknown	Guam	Y	None
28	24	25	Meno, Ignacio C	Grandson	M	Cha	11.0	S	Y	Y	Y	Guam	Unknown	Guam	Y	None
29	24	25	Meno, Rosa C	Granddaughter	F	Cha	10.0	S	Y	Y	Y	Guam	Unknown	Guam	Y	None
30	24	25	Meno, Juan C	Grandson	M	Cha	9.0	S	Y	Y		Guam	Unknown	Guam		None
31	24	25	Meno, Vicente C	Grandson	M	Cha	6.0	S	N			Guam	Unknown	Guam		None
32	24	25	Meno, Patricio C	Grandson	M	Cha	6.0	S	N			Guam	Unknown	Guam		None
33	24	25	Meno, Carmen C	Granddaughter	F	Cha	1.0	S				Guam	Unknown	Guam		None
34	25	26	Candaso, Vicente F	Head	M	Cha	31.0	S		Y	Y	Guam	Guam	Guam	Y	Farmer
35	25	26	Candaso, Maria F	Sister	F	Cha	29.0	S		Y	Y	Guam	Guam	Guam	Y	None
36	25	26	Candaso, Jesus F	Brother	M	Cha	27.0	S		Y	Y	Guam	Guam	Guam	Y	Farm laborer home farm
37	25	26	Candaso, Consolacion F	Sister	F	Cha	26.0	S		Y	Y	Guam	Guam	Guam	Y	None
38	25	26	Candaso, Antonio F	Brother	M	Cha	22.0	S		Y	Y	Guam	Guam	Guam	Y	Farm laborer home farm
39	25	26	Candaso, Antonia F	Sister	F	Cha	20.0	S	N	Y	Y	Guam	Guam	Guam	Y	None
40	26	27	Acfalle, Felipe C	Head	M	Cha	30.0	M		Y	Y	Guam	Guam	Guam	N	Farmer
41	26	27	Acfalle, Antonia A	Wife	F	Cha	40.0	M		Y	Y	Guam	Guam	Guam	N	None
42	26	27	Acfalle, Dolores A	Daughter	F	Cha	7.0	S	N			Guam	Guam	Guam		None
43	26	27	Acfalle, Tomasa A	Daughter	F	Cha	5.0	S	N			Guam	Guam	Guam		None
44	27	28	Charfauros, Manuel T	Head	M	Cha	23.0	M	N	Y	Y	Guam	Guam	Guam	Y	Teacher
45	27	28	Charfauros, Joaquina L	Wife	F	Cha	17.0	M	N	Y	Y	Guam	Guam	Guam	N	None
46	27	28	Charfauros, Barbara L	Daughter	F	Cha	1.0	S				Guam	Guam	Guam		None
47	27	28	Babauta, Jesus C	Servant	M	Cha	14.0	S	Y	Y	Y	Guam	Guam	Guam	Y	Servant
48	27	28	Acfalle, Felicidad A	Servant	F	Cha	13.0	S	Y	Y	Y	Guam	Unknown	Guam	Y	Servant
49	28	29	Cruz, Juan G	Head	M	Cha	33.0	M		Y	Y	Guam	Guam	Guam	N	Farmer
50	28	29	Cruz, Maria C	Wife	F	Cha	38.0	M		Y	Y	Guam	Guam	Guam	N	None

Street: Rosario Street

(CHAMORRO ROOTS GENEALOGY PROJECT ™ TRANSCRIPTION)
(COMPILED/TRANSCRIBED BY BERNARD T. PUNZALAN / HTTP://WWW.CHAMORROROOTS.COM)

FOURTEENTH CENSUS OF THE UNITED STATES: 1920-POPULATION

ISLAND OF GUAM

239

SHEET NO. _27A_

ENUMERATED BY ME ON THE 27th DAY OF March, 1920

Albert P. Manley ENUMERATOR

DISTRICT 4
NAME OF PLACE Merizo Town
[Proper name and, also, name of class, as city, town, village, barrio, etc]

Street, avenue, road, etc.	Number of dwelling house is order of visitation	Number of family in order of visitation	NAME of each person whose place of abode on January 1, 1920, was in the family.	RELATION Relationship of this Person to the head of the family.	Sex	Color or race	Age at last birthday	Single, married, widowed or divorced	Attended school any time since Sept. 1, 1919	Whether able to read.	Whether able to write.	Place of birth of this person.	Place of birth of father of this person.	Place of birth of mother of this person.	Whether able to speak English.	OCCUPATION Trade, profession, or particular kind of work done, as salesman, laborer, clerk, cook, merchant, washerwoman, etc.
1	2	3	4	5	6	7	8	9	10	11	12	13	14	15	16	17
	28	29	Cruz, Maria C	Daughter	F	Cha	6.0	S	N			Guam	Guam	Guam		None
	28	29	Cruz, Dolores C	Daughter	F	Cha	4.0	S				Guam	Guam	Guam		None
	28	29	Cruz, Jesus C	Son	M	Cha	3.0	S				Guam	Guam	Guam		None
	28	29	Cruz, Jose C	Son	M	Cha	1.0	S				Guam	Guam	Guam		None
	29	30	Magudoc, Elario N	Head	M	Cha	31.0	M		Y	Y	Guam	Guam	Guam	N	Farmer
	29	30	Magudoc, Victorila N	Wife	F	Cha	32.0	M		Y	Y	Guam	Guam	Guam	N	None
	30	31	Cruz, Ignacio P	Head	M	Cha	51.0	M		Y	Y	Guam	Guam	Guam	N	Farmer
	30	31	Cruz, Maria C	Wife	F	Cha	54.0	M		Y	Y	Guam	Guam	Guam	N	None
	30	31	Cruz, Francisco C	Son	M	Cha	24.0	S		Y	Y	Guam	Guam	Guam	N	Farm laborer home farm
	30	31	Charfauros, Carmen C	Servant	F	Cha	17.0	S	N	Y	Y	Guam	Guam	Guam	N	Servant
	31	32	Taijeron, Jose B	Head	M	Cha	39.0	M		Y	Y	Guam	Guam	Guam	N	Farmer
	31	32	Taijeron, Antonia N	Wife	F	Cha	40.0	M		Y	N	Guam	Guam	Guam	N	None
	32	33	Baza, Venancio T	Head	M	Cha	42.0	M		Y	N	Guam	Guam	Guam	N	Farmer
	32	33	Baza, Maria C	Wife	F	Cha	33.0	M		Y	Y	Guam	Guam	Guam	N	None
	32	33	Baza, Dolores C	Daughter	F	Cha	10.0	S	Y	Y	Y	Guam	Guam	Guam	Y	None
	32	33	Baza, Rosa C	Daughter	F	Cha	4.0	S				Guam	Guam	Guam		None
	32	33	Baza, Josefina C	Daughter	F	Cha	2.0	S				Guam	Guam	Guam		None
	33	34	Cruz, Juan P	Head	M	Cha	35.0	M		Y	Y	Guam	Guam	Guam	Y	Farmer
	33	34	Cruz, Engracio L	Wife	F	Cha	40.0	M		Y	Y	Guam	Guam	Guam	Y	None
	33	34	Cruz, Juan L	Son	M	Cha	14.0	S	Y	Y	Y	Guam	Guam	Guam	Y	None
	33	34	Cruz, Antonio L	Son	M	Cha	11.0	S	Y	Y	Y	Guam	Guam	Guam	Y	None
	33	34	Cruz, Cristobal L	Son	M	Cha	9.0	S	Y	Y		Guam	Guam	Guam		None
	33	34	Cruz, Pedro L	Son	M	Cha	7.0	S	Y			Guam	Guam	Guam		None
	33	34	Cruz, Manuel L	Son	M	Cha	5.0	S	N			Guam	Guam	Guam		None
	33	34	Cruz, Dolores L	Daughter	F	Cha	3.0	S				Guam	Guam	Guam		None

Rosalio Street

(CHAMORRO ROOTS GENEALOGY PROJECT ™ TRANSCRIPTION)
(COMPILED/TRANSCRIBED BY BERNARD T. PUNZALAN / HTTP://WWW.CHAMORROROOTS.COM)

FOURTEENTH CENSUS OF THE UNITED STATES: 1920-POPULATION

ISLAND OF GUAM

DISTRICT 4

NAME OF PLACE Merizo Town

ENUMERATED BY ME ON THE 27th DAY OF March, 1920

Albert P. Manley ENUMERATOR

[Proper name and, also, name of class, as city, town, village, barrio, etc]

	Street	Dwelling house no.	Family no.	NAME	RELATION	Sex	Color or race	Age at last birthday	Single, married, widowed or divorced	Attended school since Sept. 1, 1919	Able to read	Able to write	Place of birth of person	Place of birth of father	Place of birth of mother	Able to speak English	OCCUPATION
		1	2	3	4	5	6	7	8	9	10	11	12	13	14	15	16	17
26		33	34	Cruz, Jose L	Son	M	Cha	0.1	S				Guam	Guam	Guam		None
27		34	35	Tiquengco, Joaquin B	Head	M	Chi n	56.0	Wd		Y	Y	Guam	China	Guam	N	Farmer
28		34	35	Tiquengco, Rosario B	Son	M	Cha	22.0	S		Y	Y	Guam	Guam	Guam	Y	Farm laborer home farm
29		34	35	Tiquengco, Josefina B	Daughter	F	Cha	19.0	S	N	Y	Y	Guam	Guam	Guam	Y	None
30		34	35	Tiquengco, Enrique B	Son	M	Cha	17.0	S	N	Y	Y	Guam	Guam	Guam	Y	Farm laborer home farm
31		34	35	Tiquengco, Francisco B	Son	M	Cha	15.0	S	N	Y	Y	Guam	Guam	Guam	Y	Farm laborer home farm
32		34	35	Tiquengco, Augustina B	Daughter	F	Cha	13.0	S	Y	Y	Y	Guam	Guam	Guam	Y	None
33		35	36	Cruz, Tomas E	Head	M	Cha	35.0	M		Y	Y	Guam	Guam	Guam	N	Farmer
34		35	36	Cruz, Margarita G	Wife	F	Cha	26.0	M		Y	Y	Guam	Guam	Guam	N	None
35		35	36	Cruz, Jose G	Son	M	Cha	8.0	S	Y			Guam	Guam	Guam		None
36	Rosario Street	35	36	Cruz, Jesus G	Son	M	Cha	7.0	S	Y			Guam	Guam	Guam		None
37		35	36	Cruz, Maria G	Daughter	F	Cha	5.0	S	N			Guam	Guam	Guam		None
38		35	36	Cruz, Tomas G	Son	M	Cha	3.0	S				Guam	Guam	Guam		None
39		35	36	Cruz, Ana G	Daughter	F	Cha	1.0	S				Guam	Guam	Guam		None
40		35	36	Champaco, Ana C	Servant	F	Cha	12.0	S	Y	Y	Y	Guam	Guam	Guam	Y	None
41		36	37	Acfalle, Dimas A	Head	M	Cha	49.0	Wd		Y	Y	Guam	Unknown	Guam	N	Farmer
42		36	37	Acfalle, Tedosia B	Daughter	F	Cha	20.0	S	N	Y	Y	Guam	Guam	Guam	Y	Farm laborer home farm
43		36	37	Acfalle, Santiago B	Son	M	Cha	19.0	S	N	Y	Y	Guam	Guam	Guam	Y	Farm laborer home farm
44		36	37	Acfalle, Nicolas B	Son	M	Cha	16.0	S	N	Y	Y	Guam	Guam	Guam	Y	None
45		36	37	Acfalle, Ana B	Daughter	F	Cha	15.0	S	N	Y	Y	Guam	Guam	Guam	Y	None
46		36	37	Acfalle, Ingracia B	Daughter	F	Cha	13.0	S	Y	Y	Y	Guam	Guam	Guam	Y	None
47		36	37	Acfalle, Felicidad A	Niece	F	Cha	14.0	S	N	Y	Y	Guam	Guam	Guam	Y	None
48		37	38	Quinene, Cerilo T	Head	M	Cha	36.0	M		Y	Y	Guam	Guam	Guam	N	Farmer
49		37	38	Quinene, Ana T	Wife	F	Cha	29.0	M		Y	Y	Guam	Guam	Guam	N	None
50		38	39	Hodge, James C	Head	M	B	43.0	M		Y	Y	Massachusetts	Nova Scotia	Vriginia	Y	Farmer

481

(CHAMORRO ROOTS GENEALOGY PROJECT ™ TRANSCRIPTION)
(COMPILED/TRANSCRIBED BY BERNARD T. PUNZALAN / HTTP://WWW.CHAMORROROOTS.COM)

FOURTEENTH CENSUS OF THE UNITED STATES: 1920-POPULATION
ISLAND OF GUAM

ENUMERATED BY ME ON THE 29th DAY OF March, 1920

Albert P. Manley ENUMERATOR

DISTRICT 4
NAME OF PLACE Merizo Town

[Proper name and, also, name of class, as city, town, village, barrio, etc]

Street	Dwelling (2)	Family (3)	NAME (4)	RELATION (5)	Sex (6)	Color or race (7)	Age (8)	Marital (9)	School (10)	Read (11)	Write (12)	Birth person (13)	Birth father (14)	Birth mother (15)	English (16)	OCCUPATION (17)
	38	39	Hodge, Francisca C	Wife	F	Cha	30.0	M		N	N	Guam	Guam	Guam	N	None
	38	39	Taijeron, Carmen C	Mother in law	F	Cha	70.0	Wd		N	N	Guam	Guam	Guam	N	None
	38	39	Taijeron, Ana C	Sister in law	F	Cha	28.0	S		N	N	Guam	Guam	Guam	N	None
	38	39	Taijeron, Margarita C	Sister in law	F	Cha	19.0	S	N	Y	Y	Guam	Guam	Guam	Y	None
	38	39	Taijeron, Joaquina C	Niece in law	F	Cha	3.0	S				Guam	Unknown	Guam		None
	38	39	Taijeron, Francisco C	Nephew in law	M	Cha	2.0	S				Guam	Unknown	Guam		None
	39	40	Delgado, Juan M	Head	M	Cha	35.0	M		Y	Y	Guam	Guam	Guam	N	Farmer
	39	40	Delgado, Ana G	Wife	F	Cha	37.0	M		Y	Y	Guam	Guam	Guam	N	None
	39	40	Delgado, Maria G	Daughter	F	Cha	11.0	S	Y	Y	Y	Guam	Guam	Guam	Y	None
	39	40	Delgado, Concepcion G	Daughter	F	Cha	6.0	S	N	N	N	Guam	Guam	Guam	N	None
Rosario Street	39	40	Delgado, Manuel G	Son	M	Cha	3.0	S				Guam	Guam	Guam		None
	39	40	Delgado, Luis G	Son	M	Cha	2.0	S				Guam	Guam	Guam		None
	39	40	Fuerties, Joaquina T	Mother in law	F	Cha	71.0	Wd		N	N	Guam	Unknown	Guam	N	None
	40	41	Taijeron, Antonio S	Head	M	Cha	43.0	M		Y	Y	Guam	Guam	Guam	N	Farmer
	40	41	Taijeron, Maria D	Wife	F	Cha	42.0	M		Y	Y	Guam	Guam	Guam	N	None
	40	41	Taijeron, Dolores D	Daughter	F	Cha	17.0	S	N	Y	Y	Guam	Guam	Guam	Y	None
	40	41	Taijeron, Jose D	Son	M	Cha	14.0	S	Y	Y	Y	Guam	Guam	Guam	Y	None
	40	41	Taijeron, Jesus D	Son	M	Cha	11.0	S	Y	Y	Y	Guam	Guam	Guam	Y	None
	40	41	Taijeron, Isabel D	Daughter	F	Cha	8.0	S	Y	Y	Y	Guam	Guam	Guam	Y	None
	41	45	Tajalle, Victorina T	Head	F	Cha	42.0	S		N	N	Guam	Unknown	Guam	N	None
	41	45	Tajalle, Jose T	Son	M	Cha	18.0	S	N	Y	Y	Guam	Unknown	Guam	N	Farmer
	41	45	Tajalle, Rosa T	Daughter	F	Cha	15.0	S	N	Y	Y	Guam	Unknown	Guam	Y	None
	41	45	Tajalle, Maria T	Daughter	F	Cha	10.0	S	Y	Y	Y	Guam	Unknown	Guam	Y	None
	41	45	Tajalle, Cerilo T	Son	M	Cha	6.0	S	N			Guam	Unknown	Guam		None
	41	45	Tajalle, Rita T	Daughter	F	Cha	4.0	S				Guam	Unknown	Guam		None

(CHAMORRO ROOTS GENEALOGY PROJECT ™ TRANSCRIPTION)
(COMPILED/TRANSCRIBED BY BERNARD T. PUNZALAN / HTTP://WWW.CHAMORROROOTS.COM)

240b

FOURTEENTH CENSUS OF THE UNITED STATES: 1920—POPULATION

ISLAND OF GUAM

SHEET NO. _28B_

ENUMERATED BY ME ON THE _29th_ DAY OF March, 1920

Albert P. Manley ENUMERATOR

DISTRICT 4

NAME OF PLACE Merizo Town

[Proper name and, also, name of class, as city, town, village, barrio, etc]

Street	Dwelling house no. (2)	Family no. (3)	NAME (4)	RELATION (5)	Sex (6)	Color or race (7)	Age (8)	Single, married, widowed or divorced (9)	Attended school since Sept 1, 1919 (10)	Able to read (11)	Able to write (12)	Birthplace (13)	Father's birthplace (14)	Mother's birthplace (15)	Able to speak English (16)	OCCUPATION (17)
	42	43	Tedpahogo, Aniceto D	Head	M	Cha	25.0	M		Y	Y	Guam	Guam	Guam	Y	Farmer
		43	Tedpahogo, Gabiela M	Wife	F	Cha	26.0	M		Y	Y	Guam	Guam	Guam	N	None
		43	Tedpahogo, Maria M	Daughter	F	Cha	3.0	S				Guam	Guam	Guam		None
		43	Tedpahogo, Manuela T	Mother	F	Cha	45.0	Wd		N	N	Guam	Guam	Guam	N	None
		43	Tedpahogo, Felipe T	Brother	M	Cha	20.0	S	N	Y	Y	Guam	Guam	Guam	Y	Farm laborer home farm
		43	Tedpahogo, Carmen T	Sister	F	Cha	10.0	S	Y	Y	Y	Guam	Guam	Guam	Y	None
		43	Tedpahogo, Angelina T	Sister	F	Cha	4.0	S				Guam	Guam	Guam		None
	43	44	Cruz, Antonio LG	Head	M	Cha	64.0	Wd		Y	Y	Guam	Guam	Guam	N	Farmer
		44	Cruz, Encarnation G	Daughter	F	Cha	34.0	S		Y	Y	Guam	Guam	Guam	N	None
Rosario Street		44	Cruz, Vicente G	Son	M	Cha	30.0	S		Y	Y	Guam	Guam	Guam	Y	Farm laborer home farm
		44	Cruz, Joaquin G	Son	M	Cha	22.0	S		Y	Y	Guam	Guam	Guam	Y	Farm laborer home farm
		44	Cruz, Martina G	Daughter	F	Cha	19.0	S	N	Y	Y	Guam	Guam	Guam	Y	None
	44	45	Tedpahogo, Juana T	Head	F	Cha	60.0	S		N	N	Guam	Unknown	Unknown	N	None
		45	Tedpahogo, Pilar T	Daughter	F	Cha	30.0	S		N	N	Guam	Unknown	Unknown	N	None
		45	Tedpahogo, Ascemcion T	Daughter	F	Cha	25.0	S		N	N	Guam	Unknown	Unknown	N	None
		45	Tedpahogo, Antonia T	Granddaughter	F	Cha	9.0	S	Y			Guam	Unknown	Guam		None
		45	Tedpahogo, Maria T	Granddaughter	F	Cha	2.0	S				Guam	Unknown	Guam		None
	45	46	Chargulaf, Cricencio M	Head	M	Cha	26.0	M		Y	Y	Guam	Guam	Guam	Y	Farmer
		46	Chargulaf, Rosalia T	Wife	F	Cha	25.0	M		Y	Y	Guam	Guam	Guam	Y	None
		46	Chargulaf, Ana T	Daughter	F	Cha	5.0	S				Guam	Guam	Guam		None
		46	Chargulaf, Nicolas T	Son	M	Cha	4.0	S	N			Guam	Guam	Guam		None
	46	47	Quidagua, Ignacio T	Head	M	Cha	39.0	Wd		Y	N	Guam	Guam	Guam	N	Farmer
		47	Quidagua, Antonia T	Sister	F	Cha	41.0	Wd		Y	N	Guam	Guam	Guam	N	None
		47	Quidagua, Maria T	Daughter	F	Cha	14.0	S	Y	Y	Y	Guam	Guam	Guam	Y	None
	47	48	Tajalle, Agapita C	Head	F	Cha	70.0	S		N	N	Guam	Guam	Guam	N	None

(CHAMORRO ROOTS GENEALOGY PROJECT ™ TRANSCRIPTION)
(COMPILED/TRANSCRIBED BY BERNARD T. PUNZALAN / HTTP://WWW.CHAMORROROOTS.COM)

FOURTEENTH CENSUS OF THE UNITED STATES: 1920—POPULATION
ISLAND OF GUAM

DISTRICT 4
NAME OF PLACE Merizo Town
[Proper name and, also, name of class, as city, town, village, barrio, etc]

ENUMERATED BY ME ON THE 30th DAY OF March, 1920

Albert P. Manley ENUMERATOR

Street, avenue, road, etc.	No. of dwelling house	No. of family	NAME	RELATION	Sex	Color or race	Age at last birthday	Single, married, widowed or divorced	Attended school since sept. 1, 1919	Whether able to read	Whether able to write	Place of birth of this person	Place of birth of father	Place of birth of mother	Whether able to speak English	OCCUPATION
1	2	3	4	5	6	7	8	9	10	11	12	13	14	15	16	17
	47	48	Tajalle, Gregorio C	Daughter	F	Cha	30.0	S				Guam	Unknown	Guam	N	None
	47	48	Tajalle, Natividad D	Granddaughter	F	Cha	12.0	S	Y	Y	Y	Guam	Unknown	Guam	Y	None
	47	48	Tajalle, Tomas C	Grandson	M	Cha	9.0	S	Y			Guam	Unknown	Guam		None
	47	48	Tajalle, Dolores C	Granddaughter	F	Cha	2.0	S				Guam	Unknown	Guam		None
	47	48	Tajalle, Gertrudes C	Granddaughter	F	Cha	1.0	S				Guam	Unknown	Guam		None
	48	49	Champaco, Dolores E	Head	F	Cha	38.0	S		N	N	Guam	Guam	Guam	N	None
	48	49	Champaco, Manuela E	Sister	F	Cha	35.0	S		Y	Y	Guam	Guam	Guam	N	None
Rosario Street	48	49	Champaco, Jose E	Nephew	M	Cha	12.0	S	Y	Y	Y	Guam	Unknown	Guam	Y	None
	48	49	Champaco, Ana E	Niece	F	Cha	11.0	S	Y	Y	Y	Guam	Unknown	Guam	Y	None
	48	49	Champaco, Juan E	Nephew	M	Cha	7.0	S	N			Guam	Unknown	Guam		None
	48	49	Champaco, Felicita E	Niece	F	Cha	5.0	S	N			Guam	Unknown	Guam		None
	48	49	Champaco, Joaquina E	Niece	F	Cha	4.0	S				Guam	Unknown	Guam		None
	48	49	Champaco, Rosalia E	Niece	F	Cha	2.0	S				Guam	Unknown	Guam		None
	49	50	Chargulaf, Antonia U	Head	F	Cha	66.0	Wd		Y	Y	Guam	Guam	Guam	N	None
	49	50	Meno, Dolores C	Niece	F	Cha	32.0	S		Y	Y	Guam	Guam	Guam	N	Weaver
	49	50	Meno, Maria C	Niece in law	F	Cha	12.0	S	Y	Y	Y	Guam	Unknown	Guam	N	None
	49	50	Meno, Vicitacion C	Niece in law	F	Cha	10.0	S	Y	Y	Y	Guam	Unknown	Guam	Y	None
	49	50	Meno, Jose C	Nephew in law	M	Cha	7.0	S	N			Guam	Unknown	Guam		None
	49	50	Meno, Joaquina C	Niece in law	F	Cha	5.0	S	N			Guam	Unknown	Guam		None
	49	50	Meno, Filipe C	Nephew in law	M	Cha	3.0	S				Guam	Unknown	Guam		None
	50	51	Meno, Ignacia C	Head	F	Cha	65.0	Wd		N	N	Guam	Guam	Guam	N	None
	50	51	Meno, Maria C	Daughter	F	Cha	40.0	S		N	N	Guam	Guam	Guam	N	None
	50	51	Meno, Carmen C	Daughter	F	Cha	38.0	S		N	N	Guam	Guam	Guam	N	None
	50	51	Meno, Tedora C	Daughter	F	Cha	32.0	S		Y	Y	Guam	Guam	Guam	N	None
	50	51	Meno, Angel C	Son	M	Cha	24.0	S		Y	Y	Guam	Guam	Guam	N	Fisherman

(CHAMORRO ROOTS GENEALOGY PROJECT ™ TRANSCRIPTION)
(COMPILED/TRANSCRIBED BY BERNARD T. PUNZALAN / HTTP://WWW.CHAMORROROOTS.COM)

241b

FOURTEENTH CENSUS OF THE UNITED STATES: 1920-POPULATION

ISLAND OF GUAM

ENUMERATED BY ME ON THE 30th DAY OF March, 1920

Albert P. Manley ENUMERATOR

DISTRICT 4
NAME OF PLACE Merizo Town

[Proper name and, also, name of class, as city, town, village, barrio, etc]

	Street	Dwelling house	Family	NAME	RELATION	Sex	Color or race	Age	S/M/Wd/D	Attended school	Read	Write	Birthplace	Father birthplace	Mother birthplace	Speak English	OCCUPATION
	1	2	3	4	5	6	7	8	9	10	11	12	13	14	15	16	17
26		50	51	Meno, Jose C	Grandson	M	Cha	15.0	S	N	Y	Y	Guam	Unknown	Guam	Y	Farm laborer home farm
27		50	51	Meno, Pedro C	Grandson	M	Cha	12.0	S	Y	Y	Y	Guam	Unknown	Guam	Y	None
28		50	51	Meno, Sabina C	Granddaughter	F	Cha	10.0	S	Y	Y	Y	Guam	Unknown	Guam	Y	None
29		50	51	Meno, Jesus C	Grandson	M	Cha	5.0	S	N			Guam	Unknown	Guam		None
30		50	51	Meno, Antonio C	Grandson	M	Cha	5.0	S	N			Guam	Unknown	Guam		None
31		50	51	Meno, Francisca C	Granddaughter	F	Cha	3.0	S				Guam	Unknown	Guam		None
32		50	51	Meno, Vicente C	Grandson	M	Cha	0.1	S				Guam	Unknown	Guam		None
33		51	52	Chargulaf, Dimas B	Head	M	Cha	54.0	Wd		Y	Y	Guam	Guam	Guam	N	Farmer
34		51	52	Chargulaf, Balentina B	Daughter	F	Cha	23.0	S		Y	Y	Guam	Guam	Guam	Y	None
35		51	52	Chargulaf, Grelerma B	Daughter	F	Cha	20.0	S	N	Y	Y	Guam	Guam	Guam	Y	None
36		51	52	Chargulaf, Carmen B	Daughter	F	Cha	13.0	S	N	Y	Y	Guam	Guam	Guam	Y	None
37		52	53	Borja, Ignacio R	Head	M	Cha	39.0	Wd	N	Y	Y	Guam	Guam	Guam	Y	Farmer
38	Rosarito Street	52	53	Borja, Juan R	Son	M	Cha	17.0	S	N	Y	Y	Guam	Guam	Guam	Y	Cable Operator
39		52	53	Borja, Maraquita R	Daughter	F	Cha	11.0	S	Y	Y	Y	Guam	Guam	Guam	Y	None
40		52	53	Borja, Antonio R	Son	M	Cha	8.0	S	Y			Guam	Guam	Guam	Y	None
41		52	53	Borja, Vicente R	Son	M	Cha	4.0	S				Guam	Guam	Guam		None
42		53	54	Conception, Jose R	Head	M	Cha	20.0	M	N	Y	Y	Guam	Guam	Guam	Y	Farmer
43		53	54	Conception, Carmen C	Wife	F	Cha	24.0	M		Y	Y	Guam	Guam	Guam	Y	None
44		54	55	Quinene, Pedro F	Head	M	Cha	40.0	M		Y	Y	Guam	Guam	Guam	N	Farmer
45		54	55	Quinene, Ana M	Wife	F	Cha	35.0	M		Y	Y	Guam	Guam	Guam	N	None
46		54	55	Quinene, Silvestre M	Daughter	F	Cha	10.0	S	Y	Y	Y	Guam	Guam	Guam	Y	None
47		54	55	Quinene, Mariano M	Son	M	Cha	8.0	S	Y			Guam	Guam	Guam		None
48		54	55	Quinene, Vicente M	Son	M	Cha	4.0	S				Guam	Guam	Guam		None
49		54	55	Quinene, Jesus M	Son	M	Cha	1.0	S				Guam	Guam	Guam		None
50		55	56	Maguadoc, Moises N	Head	M	Cha	38.0	M		Y	Y	Guam	Guam	Guam	N	Farmer

485

(CHAMORRO ROOTS GENEALOGY PROJECT ™ TRANSCRIPTION)
(COMPILED/TRANSCRIBED BY BERNARD T. PUNZALAN / HTTP://WWW.CHAMORROROOTS.COM)

FOURTEENTH CENSUS OF THE UNITED STATES: 1920—POPULATION
ISLAND OF GUAM

DISTRICT **4**
NAME OF PLACE **Merizo Town**
[Proper name and, also, name of class, as city, town, village, barrio, etc]

ENUMERATED BY ME ON THE _31st_ DAY OF March, 1920
Albert P. Manley ENUMERATOR

Street	Dwelling	Family	NAME	RELATION	Sex	Color or race	Age	Marital	Attended school since Sept. 1, 1919	Read	Write	Birthplace of person	Birthplace of father	Birthplace of mother	Speak English	OCCUPATION
	55	56	Maguadoc, Antonia B	Wife	F	Cha	35.0	M		Y	Y	Guam	Guam	Guam	N	None
	56	57	Cruz, Jose P	Head	M	Cha	40.0	M		Y	Y	Guam	Unknown	Guam	N	Farmer
	56	57	Cruz, Maria G	Wife	F	Cha	35.0	M		Y	Y	Guam	Guam	Guam	N	None
	56	57	Cruz, Maria G	Daughter	F	Cha	13.0	S	N	Y	Y	Guam	Guam	Guam	Y	None
	56	57	Cruz, Rosa G	Daughter	F	Cha	9.0	S	N	Y	Y	Guam	Guam	Guam		None
	56	57	Cruz, Isabel G	Daughter	F	Cha	6.0	S	N			Guam	Guam	Guam		None
	56	57	Cruz, Jesus G	Son	M	Cha	4.0	S				Guam	Guam	Guam		None
	56	57	Cruz, Josefa G	Daughter	F	Cha	2.0	S				Guam	Guam	Guam		None
Rosario Street	57	58	Lujan, Dometrio E	Head	M	Cha	30.0	M		Y	Y	Guam	Guam	Guam	Y	Farmer
	57	58	Lujan, Maria R	Wife	F	Cha	24.0	M		Y	Y	Guam	Guam	Guam	Y	None
	57	58	Lujan, Juan R	Son	M	Cha	5.0	S	N			Guam	Guam	Guam		None
	57	58	Lujan, Jose R	Son	M	Cha	4.0	S				Guam	Guam	Guam		None
	57	58	Lujan, Rita R	Daughter	F	Cha	0.6	S				Guam	Guam	Guam		None
	58	59	Leon Guerrero, Pedro R	Head	M	Cha	35.0	M		Y	Y	Guam	Guam	Guam	N	Farmer
	58	59	Leon Guerrero, Estefania R	Wife	F	Cha	30.0	M		Y	Y	Guam	Guam	Guam	N	None
	58	59	Leon Guerrero, Maximimo R	Son	M	Cha	10.0	S	Y	Y	Y	Guam	Guam	Guam	Y	None
	58	59	Leon Guerrero, Jose R	Son	M	Cha	8.0	S	Y	Y	Y	Guam	Guam	Guam		None
	58	59	Leon Guerrero, Carmen R	Daughter	F	Cha	6.0	S	N			Guam	Guam	Guam		None
	58	59	Leon Guerrero, Jesus R	Son	M	Cha	4.0	S				Guam	Guam	Guam		None
	58	59	Leon Guerrero, Vicente R	Son	M	Cha	0.8	S				Guam	Guam	Guam		None
	59	60	Reyes, Ramon A	Head	M	Cha	49.0	Wd		Y	Y	Guam	Guam	Guam	N	Farmer
	59	60	Reyes, Ana A	Sister	F	Cha	46.0	S		Y	Y	Guam	Guam	Guam	N	None
	59	60	Reyes, Jose A	Brother	M	Cha	45.0	S		Y	Y	Guam	Guam	Guam	N	Farm laborer home farm
	59	60	Reyes, Jesus R	Nephew	M	Cha	19.0	S	N	Y	Y	Guam	Guam	Guam	Y	Farm laborer home farm
	59	60	Reyes, Dolores A	Niece	F	Cha	16.0	S	N	Y	Y	Guam	Guam	Guam	Y	None

(CHAMORRO ROOTS GENEALOGY PROJECT ™ TRANSCRIPTION)
(COMPILED/TRANSCRIBED BY BERNARD T. PUNZALAN / HTTP://WWW.CHAMORROROOTS.COM)

FOURTEENTH CENSUS OF THE UNITED STATES: 1920–POPULATION
ISLAND OF GUAM

242b

SHEET NO. _30B_

ENUMERATED BY ME ON THE 31st DAY OF March, 1920

Albert P. Manley ENUMERATOR

DISTRICT 4
NAME OF PLACE Merizo Town

	Dwelling (2)	Family (3)	NAME (4)	RELATION (5)	Sex (6)	Color or race (7)	Age (8)	Single, married, widowed or divorced (9)	Attended school since Sept. 1, 1919 (10)	Able to read (11)	Able to write (12)	Place of birth of this person (13)	Place of birth of father (14)	Place of birth of mother (15)	Speak English (16)	OCCUPATION (17)
26	59	60	Reyes, Francisca A	Niece	F	Cha	14.0	S	N	Y	Y	Guam	Guam	Guam	Y	None
27	59	60	Reyes, Vicente A	Nephew	M	Cha	9.0	S	Y	Y	Y	Guam	Guam	Guam		None
28	59	60	Reyes, Ramon A	Nephew	M	Cha	6.0	S	N			Guam	Guam	Guam		None
29	60	61	Santiago, Filipe M	Head	M	Cha	59.0	M		Y	Y	Guam	Manila Philippines	Guam	N	Farmer
30	60	61	Santiago, Juana S	Wife	F	Cha	61.0	M		Y	Y	Guam	Guam	Guam	N	None
31	60	61	Santiago, Ana S	Daughter	F	Cha	34.0	Wd	N	Y	Y	Guam	Guam	Guam	Y	None
32	60	61	Santiago, Felicidad S	Daughter	F	Cha	20.0	S	N	Y	Y	Guam	Guam	Guam	Y	None
33	60	61	Santiago, Antonia S	Grandaughter	F	Cha	15.0	S	N	Y	Y	Guam	Unknown	Guam	Y	None
34	60	61	Cruz, Juan S	Grandson	M	Cha	11.0	S	Y	Y	Y	Guam	Guam	Guam	Y	None
35	60	61	Cruz, Jose Q	Grandson	M	Cha	9.0	S	Y	Y	Y	Guam	Guam	Guam	Y	None
36	61	62	Cruz, Ramon P	Head	M	Cha	24.0	M		Y	Y	Guam	Guam	Guam	Y	Farmer
37	61	62	Cruz, Justa S	Wife	F	Cha	28.0	M		Y	Y	Guam	Guam	Guam	N	None
38	61	62	Cruz, Jesus S	Son	M	Cha	2.0	S				Guam	Guam	Guam		None
39	61	62	Cruz, Teodoro S	Son	M	Cha	1.0	S				Guam	Guam	Guam		None
40	62	63	Santiago, Rita M	Head	F	Cha	76.0	Wd		Y	Y	Guam	Guam	Guam		None
41	62	63	Manalisay, Carmen C	Daughter	F	Cha	46.0	S		Y	Y	Guam	Unknown	Guam	N	Weaver
42	62	63	Manalisay, Venancio C	Son	M	Cha	42.0	S		Y	Y	Guam	Unknown	Guam	N	Farmer
43	62	63	Manalisay, Nieves C	Daughter	F	Cha	36.0	S		Y	Y	Guam	Unknown	Guam	Y	Nurse
44	62	63	Manalisay, Juan C	Grandson	M	Cha	20.0	S	N	Y	Y	Guam	Unknown	Guam	Y	Farm laborer home farm
45	62	63	Manalisay, Isidro C	Grandson	M	Cha	8.0	S	Y			Guam	Unknown	Guam		None
46	62	63	Manalisay, Beatris C	Cousin	F	Cha	1.0	S				Guam	Guam	Guam		None
47	63	64	Nanguata, Patricio C	Head	M	Cha	31.0	M		Y	Y	Guam	Guam	Guam	N	Farmer
48	63	64	Nanguata, Isabel Q	Wife	F	Cha	36.0	M		Y	Y	Guam	Guam	Guam	N	None
49	63	64	Nanguata, Candalarea C	Sister	F	Cha	35.0	S	N	N	N	Guam	Guam	Guam	N	None
50	63	64	Nanguata, Juan B	Nephew	M	Cha	20.0	S	N	Y	Y	Guam	Guam	Guam	N	Farm laborer home farm

Street: Rosario Street

487

(CHAMORRO ROOTS GENEALOGY PROJECT ™ TRANSCRIPTION)
(COMPILED/TRANSCRIBED BY BERNARD T. PUNZALAN / HTTP://WWW.CHAMORROROOTS.COM)

243

FOURTEENTH CENSUS OF THE UNITED STATES: 1920-POPULATION
ISLAND OF GUAM

ENUMERATED BY ME ON THE 31st DAY OF March, 1920

Albert P. Manley ENUMERATOR

DISTRICT 4
NAME OF PLACE Merizo Town

Street	Dwelling No.	Family No.	NAME	RELATION	Sex	Color or race	Age	S/M/Wd/D	Attended school since Sept. 1, 1919	Able to read	Able to write	Birthplace of person	Birthplace of father	Birthplace of mother	Speak English	OCCUPATION
Rosario Street	63	64	Meno, Dometrio Q	Stepson	M	Cha	10.0	S	N	N	N	Guam	Guam	Guam	N	None
	63	64	Meno, Jose Q	Stepson	M	Cha	5.0	S	N			Guam	Guam	Guam	N	None
	63	64	Nanguata, Soledad C	Niece	F	Cha	10.0	S	Y	Y	Y	Guam	Unknown	Guam	Y	None
	63	64	Nanguata, Vicente C	Nephew	M	Cha	7.0	S	N			Guam	Unknown	Guam	N	None
	63	64	Nanguata, Luis C	Nephew	M	Cha	4.0	S				Guam	Unknown	Guam		None
	63	64	Nanguata, Lucia C	Niece	F	Cha	2.0	S				Guam	Unknown	Guam		None
	64	65	Reyes, Joaquin A	Head	M	Cha	58.0	M		Y	Y	Guam	Guam	Guam	N	Farmer
	64	65	Reyes, Cecilia M	Wife	F	Cha	52.0	M		Y	Y	Guam	Unknown	Guam	N	None
	64	65	Reyes, Jose M	Son	M	Cha	28.0	Wd		Y	Y	Guam	Guam	Guam	Y	Farm laborer home farm
	64	65	Reyes, Juan R	Nephew	M	Cha	14.0	S	Y	Y	Y	Guam	Unknown	Guam	Y	None
Saint Dimas Street	65	66	Reyes, Ignacio A	Head	M	Cha	47.0	M		Y	Y	Guam	Guam	Guam	N	Farmer
	65	66	Reyes, Rosa S	Wife	F	Cha	33.0	M		Y	Y	Guam	Guam	Guam	N	None
	65	66	Reyes, Ana S	Daughter	F	Cha	7.0	S	N			Guam	Guam	Guam	N	None
	65	66	Reyes, Josefina S	Daughter	F	Cha	5.0	S	Y			Guam	Guam	Guam	N	None
	65	66	Reyes, Nicolas S	Son	M	Cha	2.0	S				Guam	Guam	Guam	N	None
	65	66	Taijeron, Maria T	Servant	F	Cha	18.0	S	N	Y	Y	Guam	Unknown	Guam	Y	Servant
	66	67	Nanguata, Antonia C	Head	F	Cha	40.0	M		Y	Y	Guam	Guam	Guam	N	None
	66	67	Nanguata, Maria C	Daughter	F	Cha	13.0	S	Y	Y	Y	Guam	Unknown	Guam	Y	None
	66	67	Nanguata, Mariano C	Son	M	Cha	8.0	S	Y			Guam	Unknown	Guam	N	None
	66	67	Nanguata, Jose C	Son	M	Cha	0.8	S				Guam	Unknown	Guam	N	None
	67	68	Tajamak, Jose	Head	M	Jp	42.0	Wd		Y	Y	Japan	Japan	Japan	N	Storekeeper
	68	69	Quiduagua, Jose B	Head	M	Cha	65.0	M	N	N	N	Guam	Guam	Guam	N	Farmer
	68	69	Quiduagua, Maria T	Wife	F	Cha	65.0	M	N	N	N	Guam	Guam	Guam	N	None
	69	70	Ada, Nicolas B	Head	M	Cha	67.0	M	Y	Y	Y	Guam	Guam	Guam	N	Farmer
	69	70	Ada, Cecilia T	Wife	F	Cha	55.0	M	Y	Y	Y	Guam	Guam	Guam	N	None

(CHAMORRO ROOTS GENEALOGY PROJECT ™ TRANSCRIPTION)
(COMPILED/TRANSCRIBED BY BERNARD T. PUNZALAN / HTTP://WWW.CHAMORROROOTS.COM)

FOURTEENTH CENSUS OF THE UNITED STATES: 1920—POPULATION
ISLAND OF GUAM

ENUMERATED BY ME ON THE 1st DAY OF April, 1920

Albert P. Manley ENUMERATOR

DISTRICT 4
NAME OF PLACE Merizo Town

[Proper name and, also, name of class, as city, town, village, barrio, etc]

	Dwell. no.	Fam. no.	NAME	RELATION	Sex	Color or race	Age	S/M/Wd/D	Attended school since Sept 1, 1919	Able to read	Able to write	Birthplace of person	Birthplace of father	Birthplace of mother	Speak English	OCCUPATION
1	2	3	4	5	6	7	8	9	10	11	12	13	14	15	16	17
26	70	71	Lujan, Manuela E	Head	F	Cha	56.0	Wd		Y	Y	Guam	Unknown	Guam	N	Weaver
27	70	71	Cruz, Francisca E	Daughter	F	Cha	39.0	S		Y	Y	Guam	Guam	Guam	N	Weaver
28	70	71	Lujan, Crecencia E	Daughter	F	Cha	25.0	S		Y	Y	Guam	Guam	Guam	Y	Washerwoman
29	70	71	Lujan, Celidonia E	Daughter	F	Cha	23.0	S		Y	Y	Guam	Guam	Guam	Y	None
30	70	71	Lujan, Juan E	Son	M	Cha	21.0	S	N	Y	Y	Guam	Guam	Guam	Y	Farm laborer home farm
31	70	71	Lujan, Joaquin E	Son	M	Cha	19.0	S	N	Y	Y	Guam	Guam	Guam	Y	Farm laborer home farm
32	70	71	Lujan, Ascemcion E	Daughter	F	Cha	15.0	S	N	Y	Y	Guam	Guam	Guam	Y	None
33	70	71	Babauta, Jose B	Servant	M	Cha	16.0	S	N	Y	Y	Guam	Guam	Guam	Y	Servant
34	71	72	Garrido, Maria R	Head	F	Cha	52.0	Wd		Y	Y	Guam	Guam	Guam	N	None
35	71	72	Garrido, Jose R	Son	M	Cha	23.0	S		Y	Y	Guam	Guam	Guam	Y	Cable operator
36	71	72	Garrido, Juan R	Son	M	Cha	21.0	S	N	Y	Y	Guam	Guam	Guam	Y	Farmer
37	71	72	Garrido, Maria R	Daughter	F	Cha	13.0	S	Y	Y	Y	Guam	Unknown	Guam	Y	None
38	72	73	Reyes, Juan R	Head	M	Cha	40.0	M		N	N	Guam	Unknown	Guam	Y	Farm laborer working out
39	72	73	Reyes, Atilana S	Wife	F	Cha	56.0	M		N	N	Guam	Guam	Guam	N	None
40	72	73	Saluznamnam, Antonia S	Daughter	F	Cha	35.0	S		N	N	Guam	Unknown	Guam	N	None
41	72	73	Saluznamnam, Olimpia S	Daughter	F	Cha	25.0	S		N	N	Guam	Unknown	Guam	N	None
42	72	73	Saluznamnam, Maria S	Daughter	F	Cha	17.0	S	N	N	N	Guam	Unknown	Guam	N	None
43	72	73	Saluznamnam, Maria S	Granddaughter	F	Cha	2.0	S				Guam	Unknown	Guam		None
44	74	74	Diaz, Jose D	Head	M	Cha	48.0	M		Y	Y	Guam	Unknown	Guam	Y	Farm laborer working out
45	74	74	Diaz, Ana C	Wife	F	Cha	45.0	Wd		Y	Y	Guam	Unknown	Guam	N	None
46	74	75	Fegurgur, Alexandra S	Head	F	Cha	42.0	S		N	N	Guam	Guam	Guam	N	None
47	74	75	Fegurgur, Joaquin S	Son	M	Cha	21.0	S	N	Y	Y	Guam	Guam	Guam	Y	Farmer
48	74	75	Fegurgur, Ana S	Daughter	F	Cha	13.0	S	Y	Y	Y	Guam	Guam	Guam	Y	None
49	75	76	Fegurgur, Juan N	Head	M	Cha	58.0	M		Y	N	Guam	Guam	Guam	N	Farmer
50	75	76	Fegurgur, Carmen F	Wife	F	Cha	56.0	M		N	N	Guam	Unknown	Guam	N	None

Street: Saint Dimas Street

(CHAMORRO ROOTS GENEALOGY PROJECT ™ TRANSCRIPTION)
(COMPILED/TRANSCRIBED BY BERNARD T. PUNZALAN / HTTP://WWW.CHAMORROROOTS.COM)

FOURTEENTH CENSUS OF THE UNITED STATES: 1920—POPULATION
ISLAND OF GUAM

DISTRICT 4
NAME OF PLACE **Merizo Town**
[Proper name and, also, name of class, as city, town, village, barrio, etc]

ENUMERATED BY ME ON THE 2nd DAY OF April, 1920

Albert P. Manley ENUMERATOR

	PLACE OF ABODE			NAME	RELATION	PERSONAL DESCRIPTION				EDUCATION			NATIVITY				OCCUPATION
Street, avenue, road, etc.	Number of dwelling house in order of visitation	Number of family in order of visitation	of each person whose place of abode on January 1, 1920, was in the family. Enter surname, first, then given name and middle initial. If any. Include every person living on January 1, 1920. Omit children born since January 1, 1920.	Relationship of this person to the head of the family.	Sex	Color or race	Age at last birthday	single, married, widowed or divorced	Attended school any time since Sept. 1, 1919	Whether able to read.	Whether able to write.	Place of birth of this person.	Place of birth of father of this person.	Place of birth of mother of this person.	Whether able to speak English.	Trade, profession, or particular kind of work done, as salesman, laborer, clerk, cook, merchant, washerwoman, etc.
1	2	3	4	5	6	7	8	9	10	11	12	13	14	15	16	17
	76	77	Aguon, Santiago Q	Head	M	Cha	28.0	M		Y	Y	Guam	Guam	Guam	N	Farmer
	76	77	Aguon, Faustina B	Wife	F	Cha	25.0	M		Y	Y	Guam	Guam	Guam	N	None
	76	77	Aguon, Joaquina B	Daughter	F	Cha	7.0	S	N			Guam	Guam	Guam		None
	76	77	Aguon, Pedro B	Son	M	Cha	3.0	S				Guam	Guam	Guam		None
	76	77	Aguon, Dolores B	Daughter	F	Cha	1.0	S				None	Guam	Guam		None
	76	77	Chargulaf, Jacobo B	Brother in law	M	Cha	23.0	S		Y	Y	Guam	Guam	Guam	Y	Farm laborer home farm
	77	78	Santiago, Gregorio S	Head	M	Cha	32.0	M		Y	Y	Guam	Guam	Guam	N	Farmer
	77	78	Santiago, Consolacion M	Wife	F	Cha	19.0	M		Y	Y	Guam	Guam	Guam	N	None
	77	78	Santiago, Vicente M	Son	M	Cha	0.7	S	N			Guam	Guam	Guam		None
	78	79	Tedpahogo, Vicente B	Head	M	Cha	50.0	M		Y	Y	Guam	Guam	Guam	N	Farmer
	78	79	Tedpahogo, Nicolasa A	Wife	F	Cha	48.0	M		Y	Y	Guam	Guam	Guam	N	None
	78	79	Tedpahogo, Conception A	Daughter	F	Cha	20.0	S	N	Y	Y	Guam	Guam	Guam	Y	None
	78	79	Tedpahogo, Ana A	Daughter	F	Cha	18.0	S	N	Y	Y	Guam	Guam	Guam	Y	None
Saint Dimas Street	78	79	Tedpahogo, Jose A	Son	M	Cha	12.0	S	Y	Y	Y	Guam	Guam	Guam	Y	None
	79	80	Tedpahogo, Eugenio G	Head	M	Cha	22.0	M		Y	Y	Guam	Guam	Guam	Y	Farmer
	79	80	Tedpahogo, Felicita P	Wife	F	Cha	19.0	M	N	Y	Y	Guam	Guam	Guam	N	None
	79	80	Tedpahogo, Jesus G	Brother	M	Cha	25.0	S		Y	Y	Guam	Guam	Guam	N	Farm laborer home farm
	79	80	Tedpahogo, Juan G	Brother	M	Cha	18.0	S	N	Y	Y	Guam	Guam	Guam	Y	Teacher
	80	81	Aguigui, Ignacio B	Head	M	Cha	26.0	M		Y	Y	Guam	Guam	Guam	Y	Farmer
	80	81	Aguigui, Beneda M	Wife	F	Cha	25.0	M		Y	Y	Guam	Guam	Guam	Y	None
	80	81	Aguigui, Rosa M	Daughter	F	Cha	5.0	S				Guam	Guam	Guam		None
	80	81	Aguigui, Margarita M	Daughter	F	Cha	4.0	S				Guam	Guam	Guam		None
	80	81	Aguigui, Carmen M	Daughter	F	Cha	2.0	S				Guam	Guam	Guam		None
	81	82	Barcinas, Benita C	Head	F	Cha	86.0	Wd		Y	Y	Guam	Manila Philippines	Guam	N	None
	81	82	Barcinas, Pedro C	Son	M	Cha	52.0	S		N	N	Guam	Guam	Guam	N	Farmer

244b

(CHAMORRO ROOTS GENEALOGY PROJECT ™ TRANSCRIPTION)
(COMPILED/TRANSCRIBED BY BERNARD T. PUNZALAN / HTTP://WWW.CHAMORROROOTS.COM)

FOURTEENTH CENSUS OF THE UNITED STATES: 1920-POPULATION
ISLAND OF GUAM

ENUMERATED BY ME ON THE 2nd DAY OF April, 1920

Albert P. Manley ENUMERATOR

DISTRICT **4**
NAME OF PLACE **Merizo Town**
[Proper name and, also, name of class, as city, town, village, barrio, etc]

	PLACE OF ABODE			NAME	RELATION	PERSONAL DESCRIPTION				EDUCATION			NATIVITY				OCCUPATION
Street, avenue, road, etc.	Number of dwelling house is order of visitation	Number of family in order of visitation		of each person whose place of abode on January 1, 1920, was in the family. Enter surname, first, then given name and middle initial. If any. Include every person living on January 1, 1920. Omit children born since January 1, 1920.	Relationship of this Person to the head of the family.	Sex	Color or race	Age at last birthday	Single, married, widowed or divorced	Attended school any time since Sept. 1, 1919	Whether able to read.	Whether able to write.	Place of birth of this person.	Place of birth of father of this person.	Place of birth of mother of this person.	Whether able to speak English.	Trade, profession, or particular kind of work done, as salesman, laborer, clerk, cook, merchant, washerwoman, etc.
1	2	3	4		5	6	7	8	9	10	11	12	13	14	15	16	17
	81	82		Barcinas, Ana C	Daughter	F	Cha	46.0	S		Y	Y	Guam	Guam	Guam	N	Weaver
	81	82		Barcinas, Antonia C	Daughter	F	Cha	45.0	S		Y	Y	Guam	Guam	Guam	N	Weaver
	81	82		Barcinas, Tomas LG	Nephew	M	Cha	67.0	Wd		Y	Y	Guam	Guam	Guam	N	Farm laborer home farm
	81	82		Santos, Mariano B	Grandson	M	Cha	15.0	S	N	Y	Y	Guam	Unknown	Guam	Y	Book-keeper
	82	83		Espinosa, Ignacia C	Head	F	Cha	48.0	Wd		Y	Y	Guam	Guam	Guam	N	None
	82	83		Espinosa, Pedro C	Son	M	Cha	22.0	S		Y	Y	Guam	Guam	Guam	Y	Farmer
	82	83		Espinosa, Carmen C	Daughter	F	Cha	19.0	S	N	Y	Y	Guam	Guam	Guam	Y	None
	83	84		Barcinas, Juan S	Head	M	Cha	28.0	M		Y	Y	Guam	Guam	Guam	N	Farmer
	83	84		Barcinas, Tomasa B	Wife	F	Cha	25.0	M		Y	Y	Guam	Guam	Guam	N	None
	83	84		Barcinas, Antonio B	Son	M	Cha	5.0	S	N			Guam	Guam	Guam	N	None
	83	84		Barcinas, Ignacio B	Son	M	Cha	3.0	S				Guam	Guam	Guam	N	None
	83	84		Barcinas, Pedro B	Son	M	Cha	0.8	S				Guam	Guam	Guam	N	None
Saint Dimas Street	84	85		Chargulaf, Fidel N	Head	M	Cha	59.0	M		Y	N	Guam	Guam	Guam	N	Farmer
	84	85		Chargulaf, Barbara N	Wife	F	Cha	66.0	M		N	N	Guam	Guam	Guam	N	None
	85	86		Acfalle, Carmelo C	Head	M	Cha	53.0	M		Y	Y	Guam	Guam	Guam	Y	Farmer
	85	86		Acfalle, Isabel N	Wife	F	Cha	52.0	M		Y	Y	Guam	Guam	Guam	N	None
	85	86		Acfalle, Andrea N	Daughter	F	Cha	25.0	S		Y	Y	Guam	Guam	Guam	N	None
	85	86		Acfalle, Blas N	Son	M	Cha	23.0	S		Y	Y	Guam	Guam	Guam	Y	Farm laborer home farm
	86	87		Tiquengco, Vicente B	Head	M	Cha	27.0	M		Y	Y	Guam	Guam	Guam	Y	Farmer
	86	87		Tiquengco, Petronila P	Wife	F	Cha	29.0	M		Y	Y	Guam	Guam	Guam	Y	None
	86	87		Tiquengco, Rosa P	Daughter	F	Cha	4.0	S				Guam	Guam	Guam	N	None
	87	88		Mansapit, Inez U	Head	F	Cha	90.0	Wd		N	N	Guam	Guam	Guam	N	None
	87	88		Mansapit, Clemente U	Son	M	Cha	52.0	S		N	N	Guam	Guam	Guam	N	None
	87	88		Mansapit, Nicolasa C	Granddaughter	F	Cha	30.0	S		Y	Y	Guam	Guam	Guam	Y	Farmer
	88	89		Manalisay, Felix C	Head	M	Cha	28.0	M		Y	Y	Guam	Guam	Guam	Y	Farmer

(CHAMORRO ROOTS GENEALOGY PROJECT ™ TRANSCRIPTION)
(COMPILED/TRANSCRIBED BY BERNARD T. PUNZALAN / HTTP://WWW.CHAMORROROOTS.COM)

FOURTEENTH CENSUS OF THE UNITED STATES: 1920—POPULATION

ISLAND OF GUAM

ENUMERATED BY ME ON THE 3rd DAY OF April, 1920

Albert P. Manley ENUMERATOR

SHEET NO. _33A_

DISTRICT **4**

NAME OF PLACE **Merizo Town**

[Proper name and, also, name of class, as city, town, village, barrio, etc]

	PLACE OF ABODE			NAME	RELATION	PERSONAL DESCRIPTION					EDUCATION			NATIVITY				OCCUPATION
Street, avenue, road, etc.	Number of dwelling house in order of visitation	Number of family in order of visitation		Name of each person whose place of abode on January 1, 1920, was in the family.	Relationship of this Person to the head of the family.	Sex	Color or race	Age at last birthday	single, married, widowed or divorced	Attended school any time since Sept. 1, 1919	Whether able to read.	Whether able to write.	Place of birth of this person.	Place of birth of father of this person.	Place of birth of mother of this person.	Whether able to speak English.	Trade, profession, or particular kind of work done, as salesman, laborer, clerk, cook, merchant, washerwoman, etc.
1	2	3		4	5	6	7	8	9	10	11	12	13	14	15	16	17
	88	89	1	Manalisay, Alexjandra B	Wife	F	Cha	24.0	M		Y	Y	Guam	Guam	Guam	Y	None
	88	89	2	Manalisay, Gregorio B	Brother	M	Cha	31.0	S		Y	Y	Guam	Guam	Guam	N	Farm laborer home farm
	88	89	3	Babauta, Antonio B	Brother in law	M	Cha	15.0	S	N	Y	Y	Guam	Unknown	Guam	Y	Farm laborer home farm
	88	89	4	Acfalle, Jesus A	Cousin	M	Cha	8.0	S	Y			Guam	Unknown	Guam		None
	89	90	5	Acfalle, Fausto C	Head	M	Cha	27.0	M		Y	Y	Guam	Guam	Guam	Y	Farmer
	89	90	6	Acfalle, Francisca M	Wife	F	Cha	27.0	M		Y	Y	Guam	Guam	Guam	Y	None
	90	91	7	Nangauta, Julian C	Head	M	Cha	46.0	M		Y	Y	Guam	Guam	Guam	N	Farmer
	90	91	8	Nangauta, Gertrudes T	Wife	F	Cha	41.0	M		Y	Y	Guam	Guam	Guam	N	None
	90	91	9	Nangauta, Conception T	Daughter	F	Cha	19.0	S	N	Y	Y	Guam	Guam	Guam	Y	None
	90	91	10	Nangauta, Juan T	Son	M	Cha	17.0	S	N	Y	Y	Guam	Guam	Guam	Y	Farm laborer home farm
	90	91	11	Nangauta, Joaquin T	Son	M	Cha	15.0	S	N	Y	Y	Guam	Guam	Guam	Y	Farm laborer home farm
	90	91	12	Nangauta, Ramon T	Son	M	Cha	10.0	S	Y	Y	Y	Guam	Guam	Guam	Y	None
	90	91	13	Nangauta, Vicente T	Son	M	Cha	7.0	S	N			Guam	Guam	Guam		None
	90	91	14	Nangauta, Josefina T	Daughter	F	Cha	3.0	S				Guam	Guam	Guam		None
	90	91	15	Taijeron, Vicenta A	Sister in law	F	Cha	44.0	S		Y	Y	Guam	Guam	Guam	N	None
	90	91	16	Taijeron, Ana T	Grand daughter	F	Cha	17.0	S	N	Y	Y	Guam	Guam	Guam	Y	None
	91	92	17	Acfalle, Estifania B	Head	F	Cha	43.0	S		Y	Y	Guam	Guam	Guam	Y	None
	91	92	18	Acfalle, Maria B	Sister	F	Cha	41.0	S		Y	Y	Guam	Guam	Guam	Y	None
	91	92	19	Acfalle, Dominga B	Sister	F	Cha	37.0	S		Y	Y	Guam	Guam	Guam	N	None
	91	92	20	Acfalle, Josefa B	Sister	F	Cha	32.0	S		Y	Y	Guam	Guam	Guam	N	None
	91	92	21	Acfalle, Tomasa B	Sister	F	Cha	30.0	S		Y	Y	Guam	Guam	Guam	N	None
	91	92	22	Babauta, Jose B	Nephew	M	Cha	18.0	S	N	Y	Y	Guam	Unknown	Guam	N	Farmer
	91	92	23	Babauta, Vicente B	Nephew	M	Cha	17.0	S	N	Y	Y	Guam	Unknown	Guam	Y	Farm laborer home farm
	91	92	24	Babauta, Joaquina B	Niece	F	Cha	12.0	S	Y	Y	Y	Guam	Unknown	Guam	Y	None
	91	92	25	Babauta, Francisco B	Nephew	M	Cha	11.0	S	Y	Y	Y	Guam	Unknown	Guam	Y	None

Saint Dimas Street

(CHAMORRO ROOTS GENEALOGY PROJECT ™ TRANSCRIPTION)
(COMPILED/TRANSCRIBED BY BERNARD T. PUNZALAN / HTTP://WWW.CHAMORROROOTS.COM)

FOURTEENTH CENSUS OF THE UNITED STATES: 1920—POPULATION

ISLAND OF GUAM

DISTRICT 4
NAME OF PLACE **Merizo Town**
[Proper name and, also, name of class, as city, town, village, barrio, etc]

ENUMERATED BY ME ON THE 3rd DAY OF April, 1920

Albert P. Manley ENUMERATOR

	Street	Dwell. no. (2)	Family no. (3)	NAME (4)	RELATION (5)	Sex (6)	Race (7)	Age (8)	S/M/Wd (9)	School (10)	Read (11)	Write (12)	Birth person (13)	Birth father (14)	Birth mother (15)	Eng. (16)	OCCUPATION (17)
26		91	92	Babauta, Jesus B	Nephew	M	Cha	9.0	S	Y			Guam	Guam	Guam		None
27		92	93	Acfalle, Juan B	Head	M	Cha	31.0	M		Y	Y	Guam	Guam	Guam	N	Farmer
28		92	93	Acfalle, Ana M	Wife	F	Cha	34.0	M		Y	Y	Guam	Guam	Guam	N	None
29		92	93	Acfalle, Rosa M	Daughter	F	Cha	7	S				Guam	Guam	Guam		None
30		92	93	Acfalle, Natividad M	Daughter	F	Cha	6	S	N			Guam	Guam	Guam		None
31		92	93	Acfalle, Miguel M	Son	M	Cha	4	S				Guam	Guam	Guam		None
32		92	93	Acfalle, Trinidad M	Daughter	F	Cha	1	S				Guam	Guam	Guam		None
33		93	94	Acfalle, Conception E	Head	F	Cha	43.0	Wd				Guam	China	Guam	N	Farmer
34		93	94	Acfalle, Vicente E	Son	M	Cha	17.0	S	N	Y	Y	Guam	Guam	Guam	Y	Farm laborer home farm
35		93	94	Acfalle, Jose E	Son	M	Cha	14.0	S	N	Y	Y	Guam	Guam	Guam	Y	Farm laborer home farm
36		93	94	Acfalle, Juan E	Son	M	Cha	11.0	S	Y	Y	Y	Guam	Guam	Guam	Y	None
37		93	94	Acfalle, Ana E	Daughter	F	Cha	10.0	S	Y	Y	Y	Guam	Guam	Guam	Y	None
38		93	94	Acfalle, Felix E	Son	M	Cha	6.0	S	N			Guam	Guam	Guam		None
39		93	94	Acfalle, Mariquita A	Daughter	F	Cha	4.0	S				Guam	Guam	Guam		None
40		94	95	Naputy, Lorenzo E	Head	M	Cha	52.0	M		N	N	Guam	Guam	Guam	N	Farmer
41	Saint Dimas Street	94	95	Naputy, Simona C	Wife	F	Cha	55.0	M		Y	Y	Guam	Guam	Guam	N	None
42		94	95	Naputy, Jose C	Son	M	Cha	28.0	S		Y	Y	Guam	Guam	Guam	N	Farm laborer home farm
43		94	95	Naputy, Antonina C	Daughter	F	Cha	26.0	S		Y	Y	Guam	Guam	Guam	Y	None
44		94	95	Naputy, Narcisa C	Daughter	F	Cha	24.0	S		Y	Y	Guam	Guam	Guam	Y	None
45		94	95	Naputy, Enrique C	Son	M	Cha	20.0	S	N	Y	Y	Guam	Guam	Guam	Y	Farm laborer home farm
46		94	95	Naputy, Juan C	Son	M	Cha	18.0	S	N	Y	Y	Guam	Guam	Guam	Y	Farm laborer home farm
47		94	95	Naputy, Joaquin C	Son	M	Cha	13.0	S	Y	Y	Y	Guam	Guam	Guam	Y	Farm laborer home farm
48		95	96	Tiquengco, Gregorio B	Head	M	Cha	29.0	M		Y	Y	Guam	Guam	Guam	Y	Farmer
49		95	96	Tiquengco, Encarnation C	Wife	F	Cha	28.0	M		Y	Y	Guam	Guam	Guam	N	None
50		95	96	Tiquengco, Maria C	Daughter	F	Cha	2.0	S				Guam	Guam	Guam		None

## 246

SHEET NO. __34A__

(CHAMORRO ROOTS GENEALOGY PROJECT ™ TRANSCRIPTION)
(COMPILED/TRANSCRIBED BY BERNARD T. PUNZALAN / HTTP://WWW.CHAMORROROOTS.COM)

FOURTEENTH CENSUS OF THE UNITED STATES: 1920-POPULATION

ISLAND OF GUAM

ENUMERATED BY ME ON THE 3rd DAY OF April, 1920

Albert P. Manley ENUMERATOR

DISTRICT **4**

NAME OF PLACE **Merizo Town**

[Proper name and, also, name of class, as city, town, village, barrio, etc]

Street, avenue, road, etc.	Number of dwelling house in order of visitation	Number of family in order of visitation	NAME	RELATION	Sex	Color or race	Age at last birthday	Single, married, widowed or divorced	Attended school any time since Sept. 1, 1919	Whether able to read.	Whether able to write.	Place of birth of this person.	Place of birth of father of this person.	Place of birth of mother of this person.	Whether able to speak English.	OCCUPATION
1	2	3	4	5	6	7	8	9	10	11	12	13	14	15	16	17
	95	96	Tiquengco, Jose C	Son	M	Cha	0.8	S				Guam	Guam	Guam		None
	96	97	Eguiguan, Fidel E	Head	M	Cha	50.0	M		N	N	Guam	Unknown	Guam	N	Farmer
	96	97	Eguiguan, Maria B	Wife	F	Cha	45.0	M		N	N	Guam	Guam	Guam	N	None
	96	97	Eguiguan, Ignacio B	Son	M	Cha	18	S	N	Y	Y	Guam	Guam	Guam	Y	Farm laborer home farm
	97	98	Espinosa, Vicente N	Head	M	Cha	43	M		Y	Y	Guam	Guam	Guam	N	Farmer
	97	98	Espinosa, Ignacia F	Wife	F	Cha	44	M		Y	Y	Guam	Guam	Guam	Y	None
	97	98	Espinosa, Joaquina F	Daughter	F	Cha	11	S	Y	Y	Y	Guam	Guam	Guam	Y	None
	97	98	Espinosa, Ysidro F	Son	M	Cha	7.0	S	N			Guam	Guam	Guam		None
	97	98	Espinosa, Francisco F	Son	M	Cha	4.0	S				Guam	Guam	Guam		None
	97	98	Espinosa, Enomisa N	Sister	F	Cha	28.0	S		Y	Y	Guam	Guam	Guam	Y	None
	97	98	Espinosa, Ana N	Niece	F	Cha	6.0	S	N			Guam	Guam	Guam		None
	98	99	Espinosa, Serafin N	Head	M	Cha	45.0	M		N	N	Guam	Unknown	Guam	N	Farmer
	98	99	Espinosa, Dolores B	Wife	F	Cha	43.0	M		N	N	Guam	Guam	Guam	N	None
	98	99	Espinosa, Jacoba B	Daughter	F	Cha	15.0	S	N	Y	Y	Guam	Guam	Guam	Y	None
	98	99	Espinosa, Carmen B	Daughter	F	Cha	14.0	S	N	Y	Y	Guam	Guam	Guam	Y	None
	98	99	Espinosa, Jesus B	Son	M	Cha	7.0	S	N			Guam	Guam	Guam		None
	98	99	Espinosa, Ignacio B	Son	M	Cha	2.0	S				Guam	Guam	Guam		None
	98	99	Espinosa, Vicente b	Son	M	Cha	2.0	S				Guam	Guam	Guam		None
	99	100	Cruz, Venancio T	Head	M	Cha	33.0	M		Y	Y	Guam	Guam	Guam	N	Farmer
	99	100	Cruz, Maria M	Wife	F	Cha	32.0	M		Y	Y	Guam	Guam	Guam	N	None
	99	100	Cruz, Joaquin M	Son	M	Cha	11.0	S	Y	Y	Y	Guam	Guam	Guam	Y	None
	99	100	Cruz, Rosa M	Daughter	F	Cha	10.0	S	Y	Y	Y	Guam	Guam	Guam	Y	None
	99	100	Cruz, Jose M	Son	M	Cha	9.0	S	Y	Y	Y	Guam	Guam	Guam		None
	99	100	Cruz, Josefa M	Daughter	F	Cha	8.0	S	Y			Guam	Guam	Guam		None
	99	100	Cruz, Ana M	Daughter	F	Cha	7.0	S	N			Guam	Guam	Guam		None

Saint Dimas Street

494

(CHAMORRO ROOTS GENEALOGY PROJECT ™ TRANSCRIPTION)
(COMPILED/TRANSCRIBED BY BERNARD T. PUNZALAN / HTTP://WWW.CHAMORROROOTS.COM)

FOURTEENTH CENSUS OF THE UNITED STATES: 1920—POPULATION
ISLAND OF GUAM

ENUMERATED BY ME ON THE 5th DAY OF April, 1920

Albert P. Manley ENUMERATOR

DISTRICT 4
NAME OF PLACE Merizo Town
[Proper name and, also, name of class, as city, town, village, barrio, etc]

Street	Dwelling No.	Family No.	NAME	RELATION	Sex	Color or race	Age	Marital	School since Sept. 1, 1919	Read	Write	Birthplace person	Birthplace father	Birthplace mother	Speak English	OCCUPATION
					6	7	8	9	10	11	12	13	14	15	16	17
26	99	100	Cruz, Manuel M	Son	M	Cha	6.0	S	N			Guam	Guam	Guam		None
27	100	101	Mansapit, Felix C	Head	M	Cha	36.0	M		Y	Y	Guam	Guam	Guam	N	Farmer
28	100	101	Mansapit, Filomena M	Wife	F	Cha	37.0	M		Y	Y	Guam	Guam	Guam	Y	None
29	100	101	Mansapit, Cristobal M	Son	M	Cha	8	S	Y			Guam	Guam	Guam		None
30	100	101	Mansapit, Jose M	Son	M	Cha	6	S	N			Guam	Guam	Guam		None
31	100	101	Mansapit, Jesus M	Son	M	Cha	4	S				Guam	Guam	Guam		None
32	100	101	Mansapit, Joaquin M	Son	M	Cha	2	S				Guam	Guam	Guam		None
33	100	101	Naputy, Carmela	Aunt	F	Cha	40.0	S				Guam	Guam	Guam	N	None
34	101	102	Espinosa, Ignacio N	Head	M	Cha	40.0	M		Y	Y	Guam	Guam	Guam	N	Farmer
35	101	102	Espinosa, Tomasa C	Wife	F	Cha	45.0	M		Y	Y	Guam	Guam	Guam	N	None
36	101	102	Espinosa, Vicente C	Son	M	Cha	17.0	S	N	Y	Y	Guam	Guam	Guam	Y	Farm laborer home farm
37	101	102	Espinosa, Joaquina C	Daughter	F	Cha	15.0	S	Y	Y	Y	Guam	Guam	Guam	Y	None
38	101	102	Espinosa, Jose C	Son	M	Cha	13.0	S	Y	Y	Y	Guam	Guam	Guam	Y	Farm laborer home farm
39	101	102	Espinosa, Estefania C	Daughter	F	Cha	11.0	S	Y	Y	Y	Guam	Guam	Guam	Y	None
40	101	102	Espinosa, Jesus C	Son	M	Cha	9.0	S	Y			Guam	Guam	Guam		None
41	101	102	Espinosa, Jesus C	Daughter	F	Cha	7.0	S	N			Guam	Guam	Guam		None
42	101	102	Espinosa, Ana C	Daughter	F	Cha	2.0	S				Guam	Guam	Guam		None
43	102	103	Baza, Ramon C	Head	M	Cha	66.0	M		Y	Y	Guam	Guam	Guam	N	Farmer
44	102	103	Baza, Faustina T	Wife	F	Cha	40.0	M		Y	Y	Guam	Guam	Guam	N	None
45	102	103	Baza, Pedro T	Son	M	Cha	25.0	S	Y	Y	Y	Guam	Guam	Guam	N	Farm laborer home farm
46	102	103	Baza, Ana T	Daughter	F	Cha	23.0	S		Y	Y	Guam	Guam	Guam	N	None
47	102	103	Baza, Rosa T	Daughter	F	Cha	21.0	S		Y	Y	Guam	Guam	Guam	Y	None
48	103	104	San Nicolas, Vicente E	Head	M	Cha	39.0	M		Y	Y	Guam	Guam	Guam	N	Farmer
49	103	104	San Nicolas, Rita T	Wife	F	Cha	41.0	M		Y	Y	Guam	Guam	Guam	N	None
50	103	104	San Nicolas, Nicolas T	Son	M	Cha	10.0	S	Y	Y	Y	Guam	Guam	Guam	Y	None

Street: Saint Dimas Street

## 247

SHEET NO. _35A_

(CHAMORRO ROOTS GENEALOGY PROJECT ™ TRANSCRIPTION)
(COMPILED/TRANSCRIBED BY BERNARD T. PUNZALAN / HTTP://WWW.CHAMORROROOTS.COM)
FOURTEENTH CENSUS OF THE UNITED STATES: 1920-POPULATION
ISLAND OF GUAM

DISTRICT 4
NAME OF PLACE Merizo Town
[Proper name and, also, name of class, as city, town, village, barrio, etc]

ENUMERATED BY ME ON THE 5th DAY OF April, 1920

Albert P. Manley ENUMERATOR

Street	Dwelling No.	Family No.	Name	Relation	Sex	Color or race	Age	Marital	School	Read	Write	Birthplace of person	Birthplace of father	Birthplace of mother	Speak English	Occupation
	1	2	3	4	5	6	7	8	9	10	11	12	13	14	15	16	17
	103	104	San Nicolas, Juan T	Son	M	Cha	7.0	S	N			Guam	Guam	Guam		None
	103	104	San Nicolas, Maria T	Daughter	F	Cha	4.0	S				Guam	Guam	Guam		None
	103	104	San Nicolas, Rufina T	Daughter	F	Cha	1.0	S				Guam	Guam	Guam		None
	104	105	Mansapit, Filipe B	Head	M	Cha	49	M		Y	Y	Guam	Guam	Guam	N	Farmer
	104	105	Mansapit, Emelia N	Wife	F	Cha	40	M		Y	Y	Guam	Guam	Guam	N	None
	104	105	Mansapit, Cristina N	Daughter	F	Cha	16	S	N	Y	Y	Guam	Guam	Guam	Y	None
	104	105	Mansapit, Santiago N	Son	M	Cha	12	S	Y	Y	Y	Guam	Guam	Guam	Y	None
	104	105	Mansapit, Manuel N	Son	M	Cha	10.0	S	Y	Y	Y	Guam	Guam	Guam	Y	None
	104	105	Mansapit, Venancio N	Son	M	Cha	6.0	S	N			Guam	Guam	Guam		None
	104	105	Mansapit, Pedro N	Son	M	Cha	4.0	S				Guam	Guam	Guam		None
Saint Dimas Street	104	105	Naputy, Pedro N	Father in law	M	Cha	89.0	Wd		Y	Y	Guam	Guam	Guam	N	None
	105	106	Garrido, Vicente C	Head	M	Cha	56.0	M		N	N	Guam	Guam	Guam	N	Farmer
	105	106	Garrido, Ascemcion E	Wife	F	Cha	45.0	M		N	N	Guam	Guam	Guam	N	None
	105	106	Garrido, Antonia E	Daughter	F	Cha	16.0	S	N	Y	Y	Guam	Guam	Guam	Y	None
	105	106	Garrido, Jesus E	Son	M	Cha	13.0	S	N	Y	Y	Guam	Guam	Guam	Y	None
	105	106	Garrido, Rosa E	Daughter	F	Cha	9.0	S	N			Guam	Guam	Guam		None
	105	106	Garrido, Carmen E	Daughter	F	Cha	7.0	S				Guam	Guam	Guam		None
	105	106	Garrido, Vicente E	Son	M	Cha	2.0	S				Guam	Guam	Guam		None
	106	107	Baza, Jose T	Head	M	Cha	36.0	M		Y	Y	Guam	Guam	Guam	N	Farmer
	106	107	Baza, Vicitacion M	Wife	F	Cha	24.0	M		Y	Y	Guam	Guam	Guam	N	None
	106	107	Baza, Dolores M	Daughter	F	Cha	2.0	S				Guam	Guam	Guam		None
	106	107	Baza, Rosa M	Daughter	F	Cha	1.0	S				Guam	Guam	Guam		None
	107	108	Charfauros, Elena L	Head	F	Cha	43.0	Wd		N	N	Guam	Guam	Guam	N	Washerwoman
	107	108	Charfauros, Maria L	Daughter	F	Cha	16.0	S	N	Y	Y	Guam	Guam	Guam	N	Washerwoman
	107	108	Charfauros, Ana L	Daughter	F	Cha	11.0	S	Y	Y	Y	Guam	Guam	Guam	Y	None

(CHAMORRO ROOTS GENEALOGY PROJECT ™ TRANSCRIPTION)
(COMPILED/TRANSCRIBED BY BERNARD T. PUNZALAN / HTTP://WWW.CHAMORROROOTS.COM)

FOURTEENTH CENSUS OF THE UNITED STATES: 1920—POPULATION
ISLAND OF GUAM

DISTRICT 4
NAME OF PLACE **Merizo Town**
[Proper name and, also, name of class, as city, town, village, barrio, etc]

ENUMERATED BY ME ON THE 6th DAY OF April, 1920

Albert P. Manley ENUMERATOR

1 Street	2 Dwelling	3 Family	4 NAME	5 RELATION	6 Sex	7 Color	8 Age	9 Marital	10 School	11 Read	12 Write	13 Birthplace	14 Father	15 Mother	16 English	17 OCCUPATION
	108	109	Manalisay, Julian C	Head	M	Cha	29.0	M		Y	Y	Guam	Guam	Guam	Y	Farmer
	108	109	Manalisay, Dolores N	Wife	F	Cha	20.0	M	N	Y	Y	Guam	Guam	Guam	N	None
	108	109	Manalisay, Francisco T	Son	M	Cha	7.0	S	N			Guam	Guam	Guam	N	None
	109	110	Chargulaf, Ignacio T	Head	M	Cha	52	M		Y	Y	Guam	Guam	Guam	N	Farmer
	109	110	Chargulaf, Juliana T	Wife	F	Cha	46	M		Y	Y	Guam	Guam	Guam	N	None
	109	110	Chargulaf, Jose T	Son	M	Cha	27	S		Y	Y	Guam	Guam	Guam	Y	Farm laborer home farm
	109	110	Chargulaf, Carmen T	Daughter	F	Cha	19	S	N	Y	Y	Guam	Guam	Guam	N	None
Saint Dimas Street	109	110	Chargulaf, Antonio T	Son	M	Cha	17.0	S	N	Y	Y	Guam	Guam	Guam	Y	Farm laborer home farm
	109	110	Chargulaf, Mariano T	Son	M	Cha	8.0	S	Y	Y	Y	Guam	Guam	Guam		None
	109	110	Chargulaf, Dimas T	Son	M	Cha	3.0	S				Guam	Guam	Guam		None
	109	110	Chargulaf, Angelina T	Daughter	F	Cha	2.0	S				Guam	Guam	Guam		None
	110	111	Acfalle, Emelirio C	Head	M	Cha	22.0	S		Y	Y	Guam	Guam	Guam	Y	Farmer
	110	111	Acfalle, Salamon C	Brother	M	Cha	21.0	S	N	Y	Y	Guam	Guam	Guam	Y	Farm laborer home farm
	110	111	Acfalle, Ana C	Sister	F	Cha	15.0	S	N	Y	Y	Guam	Guam	Guam	Y	None
	110	111	Taijeron, Felisa G	Aunt	F	Cha	35.0	S		Y	Y	Guam	Guam	Guam	Y	None
	110	111	Taijeron, Mariano G	Uncle	M	Cha	25.0	S	N	Y	Y	Guam	Guam	Guam	N	Farm laborer home farm
	111	112	Castro, Ramon D	Head	M	Cha	31.0	M		Y	Y	Guam	Guam	Guam	N	Farmer
	111	112	Castro, Ana G	Wife	F	Cha	26.0	M		Y	Y	Guam	Guam	Guam	N	None
	111	112	Castro, Florentina G	Daughter	F	Cha	6.0	S	N			Guam	Guam	Guam		None
	111	112	Castro, Josefa G	Daughter	F	Cha	5.0	S				Guam	Guam	Guam		None
	111	112	Castro, Jose G	Son	M	Cha	0.8	S				Guam	Guam	Guam		None
	111	112	Gusman, Pedro L	Grandfather	M	Cha	92.0	Wd		N	N	Guam	Guam	Guam		None
	112	113	Reyes, Maria L	Head	F	Cha	53.0	Wd		Y	Y	Guam	Guam	Guam	N	Weaver
	112	113	Reyes, Trinidad L	Daughter	F	Cha	23.0	S		Y	Y	Guam	Guam	Guam	Y	None
	112	113	Reyes, Vicente L	Son	M	Cha	12.0	S	Y	Y	Y	Guam	Guam	Guam	Y	None

(CHAMORRO ROOTS GENEALOGY PROJECT ™ TRANSCRIPTION)
(COMPILED/TRANSCRIBED BY BERNARD T. PUNZALAN / HTTP://WWW.CHAMORROROOTS.COM)

FOURTEENTH CENSUS OF THE UNITED STATES: 1920-POPULATION
ISLAND OF GUAM

## 248

SHEET NO. 36A

ENUMERATED BY ME ON THE 6th DAY OF April, 1920

Albert P. Manley ENUMERATOR

DISTRICT 4
NAME OF PLACE Merizo Town

[Proper name and, also, name of class, as city, town, village, barrio, etc]

Street, avenue, road, etc.	Dwelling No.	Family No.	NAME	RELATION	Sex	Color or race	Age at last birthday	Single, married, widowed or divorced	Attended school since Sept. 1, 1919	Able to read	Able to write	Place of birth of this person	Place of birth of father	Place of birth of mother	Able to speak English	OCCUPATION
	1	2	3	4	5	6	7	8	9	10	11	12	13	14	15	16	17
	113	113	Garrido, Joaquin N	Head	M	Cha	27.0	M		Y	Y	Guam	Guam	Guam	Y	Farmer
	113	113	Garrido, Conception S	Wife	F	Cha	27.0	M		Y	Y	Guam	Guam	Guam	Y	None
	114	114	Gogue, Prodencio R	Head	M	Cha	29.0	M		Y	Y	Guam	Guam	Guam	Y	Farmer
	114	114	Gogue, Dolores G	Wife	F	Cha	25	M		Y	Y	Guam	Guam	Guam	Y	Unknown
	114	114	Gogue, Carmen G	Daughter	F	Cha	5	S	N			Guam	Guam	Guam		None
	114	114	Gogue, Joaquina G	Daughter	F	Cha	2	S				Guam	Guam	Guam		None
	114	114	Gogue, Maria R G	Daughter	F	Cha	0.5	S				Guam	Guam	Guam		None
	114	114	Gogue, Isabel R G	Daughter	F	Cha	0.5	S				Guam	Guam	Guam		None
	114	114	Babauta, Ana C	Servant	F	Cha	9.0	S	Y			Guam	Guam	Guam		Servant
Saint Dimas Street	114	114	Espinosa, Joaquina B	Servant	F	Cha	9.0	S	Y			Guam	Guam	Guam		Servant
	115	115	Maguadoc, Maria F	Head	F	Cha	58.0	Wd		Y	Y	Guam	Guam	Guam	N	None
	115	115	Maguadoc, Adela N	Daughter	F	Cha	27.0	S	N	Y	Y	Guam	Guam	Guam	Y	Weaver
	115	115	Maguadoc, Luis N	Son	M	Cha	23.0	S	Y	Y	Y	Guam	Guam	Guam	Y	Farmer
	116	116	Mata, Blas C	Head	M	Cha	43.0	M		Y	Y	Guam	Guam	Guam	N	Farmer
	116	116	Mata, Carmen C	Wife	F	Cha	35.0	M		N	N	Guam	Guam	Guam	N	Farmer
	116	116	Mata, Nieves C	Daughter	F	Cha	13.0	S	N	Y	Y	Guam	Guam	Guam	Y	None
	116	116	Mata, Milagro C	Daughter	F	Cha	12.0	S	Y	Y	Y	Guam	Guam	Guam	Y	None
	116	116	Mata, Maria C	Daughter	F	Cha	11.0	S	Y	Y	Y	Guam	Guam	Guam	Y	None
	116	116	Mata, Jose C	Son	M	Cha	8.0	S	Y	Y	Y	Guam	Guam	Guam	Y	None
	116	116	Mata, Vicente C	Son	M	Cha	6.0	S	N			Guam	Guam	Guam		None
	116	116	Mata, Ignacio C	Son	M	Cha	5.0	S	N			Guam	Guam	Guam		None
	116	116	Mata, Martina C	Daughter	F	Cha	3.0	S				Guam	Guam	Guam		None
	116	116	Mata, Ana C	Daughter	F	Cha	1.0	S				Guam	Guam	Guam		None
	117	117	San Nicolas, Panta L	Head	M	Cha	47.0	M		Y	Y	Guam	Guam	Guam	N	Farmer
	117	117	San Nicolas, Maria C	Wife	F	Cha	44.0	M		Y	Y	Guam	Guam	Guam	N	None

(CHAMORRO ROOTS GENEALOGY PROJECT ™ TRANSCRIPTION)
(COMPILED/TRANSCRIBED BY BERNARD T. PUNZALAN / HTTP://WWW.CHAMORROROOTS.COM)

FOURTEENTH CENSUS OF THE UNITED STATES: 1920-POPULATION
ISLAND OF GUAM

ENUMERATED BY ME ON THE 7th DAY OF April, 1920

Albert P. Manley ENUMERATOR

DISTRICT 4
NAME OF PLACE Merizo Town
[Proper name and, also, name of class, as city, town, village, barrio, etc]

	Number of dwelling house	Number of family	NAME	RELATION	Sex	Color or race	Age at last birthday	Single, married, widowed or divorced	Attended school since Sept. 1, 1919	Whether able to read.	Whether able to write.	Place of birth of this person.	Place of birth of father of this person.	Place of birth of mother of this person.	Whether able to speak English.	OCCUPATION
	2	3	4	5	6	7	8	9	10	11	12	13	14	15	16	17
26	117	118	San Nicolas, Francisco C	Son	M	Cha	17.0	S	N	Y	Y	Guam	Guam	Guam	Y	Farm laborer home farm
27	117	118	San Nicolas, Jose C	Son	M	Cha	13.0	S	Y	Y	Y	Guam	Guam	Guam	Y	Farm laborer home farm
28	117	118	San Nicolas, Maria C	Daughter	F	Cha	8.0	S	Y			Guam	Guam	Guam		None
29	117	118	San Nicolas, Ana C	Daughter	F	Cha	7	S	N			Guam	Guam	Guam		None
30	117	118	San Nicolas, Pedro C	Son	M	Cha	5	S	N			Guam	Guam	Guam		None
31	117	118	San Nicolas, Vicente C	Son	M	Cha	1	S				Guam	Guam	Guam		None
32	118	119	San Nicolas, Felix L	Head	M	Cha	43	M		Y	Y	Guam	Guam	Guam	N	Farmer
33	118	119	San Nicolas, Conception C	Wife	F	Cha	38.0	M		Y	Y	Guam	Guam	Guam	N	None
34	118	119	San Nicolas, Andrea C	Daughter	F	Cha	17.0	S	N	Y	Y	Guam	Guam	Guam	Y	None
35	118	119	San Nicolas, Antonio C	Son	M	Cha	15.0	S	N	Y	Y	Guam	Guam	Guam	Y	None
36	118	119	San Nicolas, Ana C	Daughter	F	Cha	13.0	S	Y	Y	Y	Guam	Guam	Guam	Y	None
37	118	119	San Nicolas, Consuelo C	Daughter	F	Cha	10.0	S	Y	Y	Y	Guam	Guam	Guam	Y	None
38	118	119	San Nicolas, Juan C	Son	M	Cha	8.0	S	Y			Guam	Guam	Guam		None
39	118	119	San Nicolas, Ramona C	Daughter	F	Cha	2.0	S				Guam	Guam	Guam		None
40	119	120	Taeantongo, Ramon M	Head	M	Cha	35.0	S		Y	Y	Guam	Guam	Guam	N	Farmer
41	120	121	Garrido, Jose G	Head	M	Cha	43.0	Wd		Y	Y	Guam	Guam	Guam	N	Farmer
42	120	121	Garrido, Ramona S	Daughter	F	Cha	21.0	S	N	Y	Y	Guam	Guam	Guam	Y	None
43	120	121	Garrido, Antonio S	Son	M	Cha	19.0	S	N	Y	Y	Guam	Guam	Guam	Y	Farm laborer home farm
44	120	121	Garrido, Juan S	Son	M	Cha	17.0	S	Y	Y	Y	Guam	Guam	Guam	Y	Teacher
45	120	121	Garrido, Ana S	Daughter	F	Cha	15.0	S	Y	Y	Y	Guam	Guam	Guam	Y	None
46	120	121	Garrido, Miguel S	Son	M	Cha	13.0	S	Y	Y	Y	Guam	Guam	Guam	Y	None
47	120	121	Garrido, Tomas S	Son	M	Cha	11.0	S	Y	Y	Y	Guam	Guam	Guam	Y	None
48	120	121	Garrido, Augustin S	Son	M	Cha	9.0	S	Y	Y	Y	Guam	Guam	Guam	Y	None
49	121	122	Garrido, Ramon M	Head	M	Cha	67.0	Wd		N	N	Guam	Guam	Guam	N	None
50	121	122	Tiguengco, Nicolasa M	Daughter	F	Cha	48.0	Wd		Y	Y	Guam	Guam	Guam	N	None

Street, avenue, road, etc. — column 1: Saint Dimas Street

(CHAMORRO ROOTS GENEALOGY PROJECT ™ TRANSCRIPTION)
(COMPILED/TRANSCRIBED BY BERNARD T. FUNZALAN / HTTP://WWW.CHAMORROROOTS.COM)

FOURTEENTH CENSUS OF THE UNITED STATES: 1920-POPULATION

ISLAND OF GUAM

ENUMERATED BY ME ON THE 8th DAY OF April, 1920

Albert P. Manley ENUMERATOR

DISTRICT **4**

NAME OF PLACE **Merizo Town**

[Proper name and, also, name of class, as city, town, village, barrio, etc]

	PLACE OF ABODE				NAME	RELATION	PERSONAL DESCRIPTION					EDUCATION			NATIVITY				OCCUPATION	
	Street, avenue, road, etc.	Number of dwelling house in order of visitation	Number of family in order of visitation		Name of each person whose place of abode on January 1, 1920, was in the family. Enter surname, first, then given name and middle initial. If any. Include every person living on January 1, 1920. Omit children born since January 1, 1920.	Relationship of this Person to the head of the family.	Sex	Color or race	Age at last birthday	Single, married, widowed or divorced	Attended school any time since Sept. 1, 1919	Whether able to read.	Whether able to write.	Place of birth of this person.	Place of birth of father of this person.	Place of birth of mother of this person.	Whether able to speak English.	Trade, profession, or particular kind of work done, as salesman, laborer, clerk, cook, merchant, washerwoman, etc.	
	1	2	3		4	5	6	7	8	9	10	11	12	13	14	15	16	17	
1	Saint Dimas Street	121	122		Tiquengco, Maria M	Granddaughter	F	Cha	30.0	S		Y	Y	Guam	Guam	Guam	Y	Weaver	
2		121	122		Tiquengco, Josefina M	Granddaughter	F	Cha	6.0	S	N			Guam	Guam	Guam		None	
3		121	122		Tiquengco, Antonio M	Grandson	M	Cha	4.0	S				Guam	Unknown	Guam		None	
4		122	123		Cristobal, Canali	Head	M	W	52	S		Y	Y	Spain	Spain	Spain	Y	Missionary	
5		122	123		Cruz, Juan P	Servant	M	Cha	20	S	N	Y	Y	Guam	Guam	Guam	Y	Servant	
6					Here ends the enumeration of Merizo Town														
7																			
8																			
9																			
10																			
11																			
12																			
13																			
14																			
15																			
16																			
17																			
18																			
19																			
20																			
21																			
22																			
23																			
24																			
25																			

District 5

(CHAMORRO ROOTS GENEALOGY PROJECT ™ TRANSCRIPTION)
(COMPILED/TRANSCRIBED BY BERNARD T. PUNZALAN / HTTP://WWW.CHAMORROROOTS.COM)
FOURTEENTH CENSUS OF THE UNITED STATES: 1920-POPULATION
ISLAND OF GUAM

DISTRICT **District 5**
NAME OF PLACE **Inarajan Town**
[Proper name and, also, name of class, as city, town, village, barrio, etc]

ENUMERATED BY ME ON THE 24th DAY OF February, 1920

Joaquin Torres ENUMERATOR

			NAME	RELATION	Sex	Color or race	Age at last birthday	Single, married, widowed or divorced	Attended school any time since Sept. 1, 1919	Whether able to read.	Whether able to write.	Place of birth of this person.	Place of birth of father of this person.	Place of birth of mother of this person.	Whether able to speak English.	OCCUPATION
1	2	3	4	5	6	7	8	9	10	11	12	13	14	15	16	17
1	1	1	Zuniga, Alselmo	Head	M	W	26.0	S		Y	Y	Spain	Spain	Spain	Y	Missionary
2	1	1	Paulino, Luis C	Servant	M	Cha	12.0	S	Y	Y	Y	Guam	Guam	Guam	Y	Servant
3	2	2	Combado, Juan P	Head	M	Cha	35.0	M		Y	Y	Guam	Guam	Guam	N	Farmer
4	2	2	Combado, Concepcion SN	Wife	F	Cha	35.0	M		Y	Y	Guam	Guam	Guam	N	None
5	2	2	Combado, Juan SN	Son	M	Cha	10.0	S	Y	Y	Y	Guam	Guam	Guam	Y	None
6	2	2	Combado, Remedios SN	Daughter	F	Cha	5.0	S				Guam	Guam	Guam	Y	None
7	2	2	Combado, Maria SN	Daughter	F	Cha	2.0	S				Guam	Guam	Guam	Y	None
8	2	2	Combado, Guadalupe SN	Daughter	F	Cha	0.6	S				Guam	Guam	Guam		Farmer
9	3	3	Paulino, Jose A	Head	M	Cha	52.0	M		N	N	Guam	Guam	Guam	N	None
10	3	3	Paulino, Pelomena F	Head	M	Cha	52.0	M		Y	Y	Guam	Unknown	Guam	N	Farm Laborer
11	3	3	Paulino, Manuel F	Wife	F	Cha	22.0	S		Y	Y	Guam	Guam	Guam	Y	None
12	3	3	Paulino, Ignacia F	Daughter	F	Cha	18.0	S	N	Y	Y	Guam	Guam	Guam	Y	Farm Laborer
13	3	3	Paulino, Vicente F	Son	M	Cha	15.0	S	N	Y	Y	Guam	Guam	Guam	Y	None
14	3	3	Paulino, Mariano F	Son	M	Cha	12.0	S	Y	Y	Y	Guam	Guam	Guam	Y	None
15	3	3	Paulino, Ramon F	Son	M	Cha	7.0	S	Y			Guam	Guam	Guam		Teacher
16	4	4	Torres, Joaquin	Head	M	Cha	25.0	M		Y	Y	Guam	Guam	Guam	Y	None
17	4	4	Torres, Maria U	Wife	F	Cha	24.0	M				Guam	Guam	Guam		None
18	4	4	Torres, Jose U	Son	M	Cha	3.0	S				Guam	Guam	Guam		None
19	4	4	Torres, Maria O U	Daughter	F	Cha	2.0	S				Guam	Guam	Guam		None
20	4	4	Torres, Joaquin U	Son	M	Cha	1.0	S				Guam	Guam	Guam		None
21	4	4	Torres, Daniel U	Son	M	Cha	0.4	S				Guam	Guam	Guam		Farmer
22	4	4	Un-pingco, Natividad A	Sister-in-law	F	Cha	11.0	S	Y	Y	Y	Guam	Guam	Guam	Y	None
23	5	5	Paulino, Manuel A	Head	M	Cha	63.0	M		Y	Y	Guam	Guam	Guam		None
24	5	5	Paulino, Joaquina T	Wife	F	Cha	38.0	M		N	N	Guam	Guam	Guam	N	
25	5	5	Paulino, Concepcion T	Daughter	F	Cha	6.0	S	N			Guam	Guam	Guam		

(CHAMORRO ROOTS GENEALOGY PROJECT ™ TRANSCRIPTION)
(COMPILED/TRANSCRIBED BY BERNARD T. PUNZALAN / HTTP://WWW.CHAMORROROOTS.COM)

250b

FOURTEENTH CENSUS OF THE UNITED STATES: 1920–POPULATION

ISLAND OF GUAM

ENUMERATED BY ME ON THE 24th DAY OF February, 1920

Joaquin Torres ENUMERATOR

DISTRICT **District 5**
NAME OF PLACE **Inarajan Town**

[Proper name and, also, name of class, as city, town, village, barrio, etc]

Street: Sataljaya Street

#	Dwelling No.	Family No.	NAME	RELATION	Sex	Color or race	Age	Single, married, widowed or divorced	Attended school since Sept. 1, 1919	Able to read	Able to write	Birthplace of person	Birthplace of father	Birthplace of mother	Able to speak English	OCCUPATION
26	5	5	Taimanglo, Mariano C	Step-son	M	Cha	16.0	S	N	Y	Y	Guam	Unknown	Guam	Y	Farm laborer
27	5	5	Taimanglo, Josefa C	Step-daughter	F	Cha	13.0	S	N	Y	Y	Guam	Unknown	Guam	Y	None
28	5	5	Taimanglo, Juan C	Brother-in-law	M	Cha	17.0	S	N	Y	Y	Guam	Guam	Guam	Y	Farm laborer
29	5	6	Taimanglo, Joaquin C	Head	M	Cha	28.0	d		Y	Y	Guam	Guam	Guam	N	Farmer
30	5	6	Taimanglo, Beatris M	Daughter	F	Cha	7.0	S	Y			Guam	Guam	Guam		None
31	6	7	Duenas, Juan T	Head	M	Cha	31.0	M		Y	Y	Guam	Guam	Guam	N	Farmer
32	6	7	Duenas, Ana M	Wife	F	Cha	20.0	M	N	Y	N	Guam	Guam	Guam	N	None
33	6	7	Duenas, Rosalina M	Daughter	F	Cha	1.0	S				Guam	Guam	Guam		None
34	6	7	Duenas, Fredecinda M	Daughter	F	Cha	0.5	S				Guam	Guam	Guam		None
35	7	8	Meno, Felipe N	Head	M	Cha	57.0	M		N	N	Guam	Guam	Guam	N	Farmer
36	7	8	Meno, Soledad P	Wife	F	Cha	55.0	M		Y	N	Guam	Guam	Guam		None
37	7	8	Sugiyama, Manuela M	Daughter	F	Cha	27.0	W d		Y	Y	Guam	Japan	Guam	N	None
38	7	8	Sugiyama, Josefina M	Grand-daughter	F	Jpn	3.0	S				Guam	Japan	Guam		None
39	7	8	Tayama, Gloria M	Grand-daughter	F	Jpn	8.0	S	Y			Guam	Japan	Guam		None
40	7	8	Tayama, Asuncion M	Grand-daughter	F	Jpn	6.0	S	N			Guam	Japan	Guam		None
41	7	8	Tayama, Jose M	Grand-son	M	Jpn	4.0	S				Guam	Japan	Guam		None
42	8	9	Paulino, Cleto C	Head	M	Cha	25.0	M		Y	Y	Guam	Guam	Guam	Y	Carpenter
43	8	9	Paulino, Fabiana C	Mother	F	Cha	52.0	W d		Y	Y	Guam	Guam	Guam	N	None
44	8	9	Paulino, Leocadio C	Brother	M	Cha	22.0	S		Y	Y	Guam	Guam	Guam	Y	Farm laborer
45	8	9	Paulino, Juan C	Brother	M	Cha	18.0	S		Y	Y	Guam	Guam	Guam	Y	Farm laborer
46	8	9	Paulino, Ana C	Sister	F	Cha	15.0	S	N	Y	Y	Guam	Guam	Guam	Y	None
47	8	9	Taitague, Amalia D	Servant	F	Cha	33.0	S		Y	Y	Guam	Guam	Guam	N	Servant
48	8	10	Paulino, Nicolas C	Head	M	Cha	27.0	M		Y	Y	Guam	Guam	Guam	Y	Farmer
49	8	10	Paulino, Carmen D	Wife	F	Cha	18.0	M	N	Y	Y	Guam	Guam	Guam	Y	None
50	8	10	Paulino, Vicenta D	Son	M	Cha	0.5	S				Guam	Guam	Guam		None

(CHAMORRO ROOTS GENEALOGY PROJECT ™ TRANSCRIPTION)
(COMPILED/TRANSCRIBED BY BERNARD T. PUNZALAN / HTTP://WWW.CHAMORROROOTS.COM)

FOURTEENTH CENSUS OF THE UNITED STATES: 1920-POPULATION
ISLAND OF GUAM

DISTRICT District 5
NAME OF PLACE Inarajan Town
[Proper name and, also, name of class, as city, town, village, barrio, etc]

ENUMERATED BY ME ON THE 24th DAY OF February, 1920

Joaquin Torres ENUMERATOR

Street	Dwelling No.	Family No.	NAME	RELATION	Sex	Color or race	Age at last birthday	Single, married, widowed or divorced	Attended school since Sept. 1, 1919	Able to read	Able to write	Place of birth of this person	Place of birth of father	Place of birth of mother	Able to speak English	OCCUPATION
	1	2	3	4	5	6	7	8	9	10	11	12	13	14	15	16	17
	9	11	Duenas, Juan M	Head	M	Cha	57.0	Wd		Y	Y	Guam	Guam	Guam	N	Farmer
	9	11	Duenas, Remedios D	Daughter	F	Cha	17.0	S	N	Y	Y	Guam	Guam	Guam	N	Laundress
	9	11	Duenas, Francisca D	Daughter	F	Cha	16.0	S	N	Y	Y	Guam	Guam	Guam	Y	None
	9	11	Duenas, Josefa D	Daughter	F	Cha	14.0	S	N	Y	Y	Guam	Guam	Guam	Y	None
	9	11	Duenas, Juan D	Son	M	Cha	9.0	S	Y			Guam	Guam	Guam		None
	9	11	Duenas, Vicente D	Son	M	Cha	3.0	S				Guam	Guam	Guam		None
	9	11	Duenas, Maria D	Grand-daughter	F	Cha	9.0	S	Y	Y	Y	Guam	Unknown	Guam		None
	10	12	Duenas, Manuel M	Head	M	Cha	27.0	S		Y	Y	Guam	Unknown	Guam	Y	Farmer
	10	12	Duenas, Maria M	Mother	F	Cha	58.0	S		Y	Y	Guam	Guam	Guam	N	None
Salaljaya Street	10	12	Duenas, Francisco M	Brother	M	Cha	20.0	S	N	N	N	Guam	Unknown	Guam	Y	Farm laborer
	10	12	Chargualaf, Cecilio T	Rancher	M	Cha	42.0	S		Y	N	Guam	Guam	Guam	N	Rancher
	11	13	Quinata, Cayetano A	Head	M	Cha	45.0	M		Y	Y	Guam	Guam	Guam	Y	Teacher
	11	13	Quinata, Ana LG	Wife	F	Cha	44.0	M		Y	Y	Guam	Guam	Guam	Y	None
	12	14	Meno, Jose D	Head	M	Cha	45.0	M		Y	Y	Guam	Unknown	Guam	N	Farmer
	12	14	Meno, Genoveva N	Wife	F	Cha	44.0	M		N	N	Guam	Guam	Guam	N	None
	12	14	Meno, Rosa N	Niece	F	Cha	12.0	S	Y	Y	Y	Guam	Guam	Guam	Y	None
	12	15	Meno, Antonio N	Head	M	Cha	20.0	M	N	N	N	Guam	Guam	Guam	Y	Farmer
	12	15	Meno, Ana C	Wife	F	Cha	19.0	M		Y	Y	Guam	Guam	Guam	Y	None
	13	16	Tedtaotao, Andres M	Head	M	Cha	22.0	S		N	N	Guam	Guam	Guam	N	Farmer
	13	16	Tedtaotao, Consolacion M	Sister	F	Cha	19.0	S		N	N	Guam	Guam	Guam	N	None
	13	16	Meno, Candelaria D	Step-sister	F	Cha	38.0	S		N	N	Guam	Unknown	Guam	N	None
	13	16	Meno, Vicente C	Nephew	M	Cha	8.0	S	Y			Guam	Unknown	Guam	Y	None
	13	16	Meno, Dolores C	Niece	F	Cha	2.0	S				Guam	Unknown	Guam		None
	13	17	Tedtaotao, Pedro M	Head	M	Cha	26.0	M		N	N	Guam	Guam	Guam	N	Farmer
	13	17	Tedtaotao, Angela T	Wife	F	Cha	24.0	M		N	N	Guam	Guam	Guam	N	None

(CHAMORRO ROOTS GENEALOGY PROJECT ™ TRANSCRIPTION)
(COMPILED/TRANSCRIBED BY BERNARD T. PUNZALAN / HTTP://WWW.CHAMORROROOTS.COM)

251b

FOURTEENTH CENSUS OF THE UNITED STATES: 1920-POPULATION
ISLAND OF GUAM

DISTRICT **District 5**

NAME OF PLACE **Inarajan Town**

[Proper name and, also, name of class, as city, town, village, barrio, etc]

ENUMERATED BY ME ON THE 24th DAY OF February, 1920

Joaquin Torres ENUMERATOR

	Dwell	Fam	NAME	RELATION	Sex	Color	Age	S/M/W/D	Sch 1919	Read	Write	Birth person	Birth father	Birth mother	Eng	OCCUPATION
26	13	17	Tedtaotao, Magdalena T	Daughter	F	Cha	4.0	S				Guam	Guam	Guam		None
27	13	17	Tedtaotao, Juan T	Son	M	Cha	1.0	S				Guam	Guam	Guam		None
28	13	18	Tedtaotao, Casiano M	Head	M	Cha	29.0	M		N	N	Guam	Guam	Guam	N	Farmer
29	13	18	Tedtaotao, Leoncia C	Wife	F	Cha	27.0	M		N	N	Guam	Guam	Guam	N	None
30	13	18	Tedtaotao, Jose C	Son	M	Cha	9.0	S	Y			Guam	Guam	Guam		None
31	13	18	Tedtaotao, Dolores C	Daughter	F	Cha	6.0	S	N			Guam	Guam	Guam		None
32	13	18	Tedtaotao, Ana C	Daughter	F	Cha	3.0	S				Guam	Guam	Guam		None
33	13	18	Tedtaotao, Antonia C	Daughter	F	Cha	1.0	S				Guam	Guam	Guam		None
34	14	19	Afaisen, Manuel M	Head	M	Cha	19.0	S	N	Y	Y	Guam	Guam	Guam	Y	Farmer
35	14	19	Afaisen, Pas M	Mother	F	Cha	45.0	W		N	N	Guam	Guam	Guam	N	None
36	14	19	Afaisen, Miguel M	Brother	M	Cha	18.0	S	N	Y	Y	Guam	Guam	Guam	Y	Farm laborer
37	14	19	Afaisen, Maria M	Sister	F	Cha	16.0	S	N	Y	Y	Guam	Guam	Guam	Y	None
38	14	19	Afaisen, Dolores	Sister	F	Cha	11.0	S	Y	Y	Y	Guam	Guam	Guam	Y	None
39	14	20	Chargualaf, Lucas M	Head	M	Cha	25.0	Wd		Y	Y	Guam	Guam	Guam	Y	Farmer
40	14	20	Chargualaf, Josefina C	Daughter	F	Cha	1.0	S				Guam	Guam	Guam		None
41	14	20	Chargualaf, Vicente C	Son	M	Cha	0.2	S				Guam	Guam	Guam		None
42	15	21	Naputi, Vicente T	Head	M	Cha	39.0	M	N	N	N	Guam	Guam	Guam	N	Farmer
43	15	21	Naputi, Nicolasa D	Wife	F	Cha	34.0	M		N	N	Guam	Guam	Guam	N	None
44	15	21	Naputi, Vicente D	Son	M	Cha	14.0	S	Y	Y	Y	Guam	Guam	Guam	Y	None
45	15	21	Naputi, Ana D	Daughter	F	Cha	12.0	S	Y	Y	Y	Guam	Guam	Guam	Y	None
46	15	21	Naputi, Antonia D	Daughter	F	Cha	10.0	S	Y	Y	Y	Guam	Guam	Guam	Y	None
47	15	21	Naputi, Teresa D	Daughter	F	Cha	7.0	S	Y	Y	Y	Guam	Guam	Guam	Y	None
48	15	21	Naputi, Carmen D	Daughter	F	Cha	2.0	S				Guam	Guam	Guam		None
49	16	22	Chargualaf, Froilan M	Head	M	Cha	53.0	M		Y	Y	Guam	Guam	Guam	N	Farmer
50	16	22	Chargualaf, Carmen M	Wife	F	Cha	51.0	M		Y	Y	Guam	Guam	Guam	N	None

Street: Salaijaya Street

(CHAMORRO ROOTS GENEALOGY PROJECT ™ TRANSCRIPTION)
(COMPILED/TRANSCRIBED BY BERNARD T. PUNZALAN / HTTP://WWW.CHAMORROROOTS.COM)

FOURTEENTH CENSUS OF THE UNITED STATES: 1920-POPULATION

ISLAND OF GUAM

ENUMERATED BY ME ON THE 24th DAY OF February, 1920

Joaquin Torres ENUMERATOR

DISTRICT **District 5**

NAME OF PLACE **Inarajan Town**

[Proper name and, also, name of class, as city, town, village, barrio, etc]

	PLACE OF ABODE			NAME	RELATION	PERSONAL DESCRIPTION					EDUCATION			NATIVITY				OCCUPATION
	Street, avenue, road, etc.	Number of dwelling house in order of visitation	Number of family in order of visitation	of each person whose place of abode on January 1, 1920, was in the family.	Relationship of this Person to the head of the family.	Sex	Color or race	Age at last birthday	Single, married, widowed or divorced	Attended school any time since Sept. 1, 1919	Whether able to read.	Whether able to write.	Place of birth of this person.	Place of birth of father of this person.	Place of birth of mother of this person.	Whether able to speak English.	Trade, profession, or particular kind of work done, as salesman, laborer, clerk, cook, merchant, washerwoman, etc.
	1	2	3	4	5	6	7	8	9	10	11	12	13	14	15	16	17
1		16	23	Chargualaf, Jose M	Head	M	Cha	32.0	Wd		Y	Y	Guam	Guam	Guam	N	Farmer
2		16	23	Chargualaf, Juan N	Son	M	Cha	7.0	S	N			Guam	Guam	Guam		None
3		16	23	Chargualaf, Jose N	Son	M	Cha	5.0	S	N			Guam	Guam	Guam		None
4		16	24	Naputi, Enrique P	Head	M	Cha	31.0	M		Y	Y	Guam	Guam	Guam		Carpenter
5		16	24	Naputi, Especiosa C	Wife	F	Cha	25.0	M		Y	Y	Guam	Guam	Guam		None
6		16	24	Naputi, Pio C	Son	M	Cha	8.0	S	Y			Guam	Guam	Guam		None
7		16	24	Naputi, Ana C	Daughter	F	Cha	6.0	S	N			Guam	Guam	Guam		None
8		16	24	Naputi, Jesus C	Son	M	Cha	5.0	S	N			Guam	Guam	Guam		None
9		16	24	Naputi, Maria C	Daughter	F	Cha	1.0	S				Guam	Guam	Guam		None
10		16	24	Meza, Juliana A	Aunt	F	Cha	65.0	Wd		N	N	Guam	Unknown	Guam	N	None
11		17	25	San Nicolas, Francisco C	Head	M	Cha	28.0	M		Y	Y	Guam	Guam	Guam	N	Farmer
12		17	25	San Nicolas, Tomasa M	Wife	F	Cha	29.0	M		N	N	Guam	Guam	Guam	N	None
13		17	25	San Nicolas, Alfonsina M	Daughter	F	Cha	6.0	S	N			Guam	Guam	Guam		None
14		17	25	San Nicolas, Quintin M	Son	M	Cha	2.0	S				Guam	Guam	Guam		None
15		18	26	Castro, Juliana L	Head	F	Cha	26.0	Wd		Y	Y	Guam	Guam	Guam	N	Farmer
16		18	26	Castro, Vicenta L	Son	M	Cha	4.0	S				Guam	Guam	Guam		None
17		18	26	Castro, Maria L	Daughter	F	Cha	2.0	S				Guam	Guam	Guam		None
18		19	27	Lujan, Jose B	Head	M	Cha	58.0	M		Y	Y	Guam	Guam	Guam	N	Farmer
19		19	27	Lujan, Maria C	Wife	F	Cha	69.0	M		N	N	Guam	Guam	Guam	N	None
20		19	28	Lujan, Andres C	Head	M	Cha	25.0	M		Y	Y	Guam	Guam	Guam	Y	Farmer
21		19	28	Lujan, Anunsacion C	Wife	F	Cha	27.0	M		Y	Y	Guam	Guam	Guam	N	None
22		19	28	Lujan, Maria C	Daughter	F	Cha	0.8	S				Guam	Guam	Guam		None
23		19	29	Naputi, Jose T	Head	M	Cha	36.0	M		N	N	Guam	Guam	Guam	N	Farmer
24		19	29	Naputi, Ana L	Wife	F	Cha	27.0	M		N	N	Guam	Guam	Guam	N	None
25		20	30	Lujan, Ignacio C	Head	M	Cha	36.0	M		Y	Y	Guam	Guam	Guam	N	Farmer

Salaljaya Street

(CHAMORRO ROOTS GENEALOGY PROJECT ™ TRANSCRIPTION)

(COMPILED/TRANSCRIBED BY BERNARD T. PUNZALAN / HTTP://WWW.CHAMORROROOTS.COM)

FOURTEENTH CENSUS OF THE UNITED STATES: 1920-POPULATION

ISLAND OF GUAM

DISTRICT **District 5**

NAME OF PLACE **Inarajan Town**　　ENUMERATED BY ME ON THE 24ᵗʰ DAY OF February, 1920

[Proper name and, also, name of class, as city, town, village, barrio, etc]

Joaquin Torres ENUMERATOR

			NAME	RELATION						EDUCATION				NATIVITY				OCCUPATION
26	20	30	Lujan, Dolores F	Wife	F	Cha	30.0	M		Y	Y	Guam	Guam	Guam	N	None	
27	20	30	Lujan, Maria F	Daughter	F	Cha	6.0	S	N			Guam	Guam	Guam		None	
28	20	30	Lujan, Catalina F	Daughter	F	Cha	5.0	S	N			Guam	Guam	Guam		None	
29	21	31	Paulino, Juan N	Head	M	Cha	32.0	M		Y	N	Guam	Guam	Guam	N	Farmer	
30	21	31	Paulino, Ynes L	Wife	F	Cha	37.0	M		N	N	Guam	Guam	Guam	N	None	
31	21	31	Paulino, Angela L	Daughter	F	Cha	22.0	S		Y	Y	Guam	Guam	Guam	Y	None	
32	21	31	Paulino, Margarita L	Daughter	F	Cha	20.0	S	N	Y	Y	Guam	Guam	Guam	Y	None	
33	21	31	Paulino, Concepcion L	Daughter	F	Cha	11.0	S	Y	Y	Y	Guam	Guam	Guam	Y	None	
34	21	31	Paulino, Juan L	Son	M	Cha	9.0	S	Y	Y	Y	Guam	Guam	Guam	N	None	
35	22	32	Meno, Manuel C	Head	M	Cha	46.0	M		Y	Y	Guam	Guam	Guam	N	Farmer	
36	22	32	Meno, Concepcion L	Wife	F	Cha	35.0	M		Y	Y	Guam	Guam	Guam		None	
37	22	32	Meno, Jose L	Son	M	Cha	7.0	S	N			Guam	Guam	Guam		None	
38	22	32	Meno, Jesus L	Son	M	Cha	5.0	S	N			Guam	Guam	Guam		None	
39	22	32	Meno, Maria L	Daughter	F	Cha	3.0	S				Guam	Guam	Guam		None	
40	22	32	Meno, Ana L	Daughter	F	Cha	2.0	S				Guam	Guam	Guam		None	
41	22	32	Meno, Joaquin L	Son	M	Cha	0.5	S				Guam	Guam	Guam		None	
42	22	32	Meno, Alexandra C	Mother	F	Cha	75.0	Wd		N	N	Guam	Guam	Guam	N	None	
43	23	33	Meno, Francisco D	Head	M	Cha	28.0	M		N	N	Guam	Guam	Guam	Y	Farmer	
44	23	33	Meno, Maria P	Wife	F	Cha	29.0	M		Y	Y	Guam	Guam	Guam	N	None	
45	23	33	Meno, Virginia P	Daughter	F	Cha	7.0	S	Y			Guam	Guam	Guam		None	
46	23	33	Meno, Maria P	Daughter	F	Cha	5.0	S				Guam	Guam	Guam		None	
47	24	34	Flores, Manuel D	Head	M	Cha	29.0	M		Y	Y	Guam	Unknown	Guam		Commissioner	
48	24	34	Flores, Joaquina G	Wife	F	Cha	23.0	M		Y	Y	Guam	Unknown	Guam		None	
49	24	34	Quinene, Ignacia F	Boarder	F	Cha	8.0	S	Y	Y	Y	Guam	Guam	Guam	N	None	
50	24	34	Martinez, Jesus R	Farm laborer	M	Cha	21.0	S	N	Y	Y	Guam	Guam	Guam	Y	Farm laborer	

507

(CHAMORRO ROOTS GENEALOGY PROJECT ™ TRANSCRIPTION)
(COMPILED/TRANSCRIBED BY BERNARD T. FUNZALAN / HTTP://WWW.CHAMORROROOTS.COM)

253

FOURTEENTH CENSUS OF THE UNITED STATES: 1920-POPULATION
ISLAND OF GUAM

DISTRICT **District 5**
NAME OF PLACE **Inarajan Town**
[Proper name and, also, name of class, as city, town, village, barrio, etc]

ENUMERATED BY ME ON THE 27th DAY OF February, 1920

Joaquin Torres ENUMERATOR

	PLACE OF ABODE			NAME	RELATION	PERSONAL DESCRIPTION				EDUCATION			NATIVITY				OCCUPATION
Street, avenue, road, etc.	Number of dwelling house in order of visitation	Number of family in order of visitation	Name of each person whose place of abode on January 1, 1920, was in the family.	Relationship of this Person to the head of the family.	Sex	Color or race	Age at last birthday	Single, married, widowed or divorced	Attended school any time since sept. 1, 1919	Whether able to read	Whether able to write	Place of birth of this person.	Place of birth of father of this person.	Place of birth of mother of this person.	Whether able to speak English.	Trade, profession, or particular kind of work done, as salesman, laborer, clerk, cook, merchant, washerwoman, etc.
1	2	3	4	5	6	7	8	9	10	11	12	13	14	15	16	17
	25	35	Naputi, Vicente P	Head	M	Cha	25.0	M		Y	Y	Guam	Guam	Guam	N	Farmer
	25	35	Naputi, Maria F	Wife	F	Cha	28.0	M		Y	Y	Guam	Guam	Guam		None
	25	35	Naputi, Maria N F	Daughter	F	Cha	10.0	S	Y	Y	N	Guam	Guam	Guam		None
	25	35	Naputi, Ramon F	Son	M	Cha	7.0	S	Y			Guam	Guam	Guam		None
	25	35	Naputi, Cristobal F	Son	M	Cha	5.0	S	N			Guam	Guam	Guam		None
	25	35	Naputi, Ana F	Daughter	F	Cha	3.0	S				Guam	Guam	Guam		None
	25	35	Naputi, Juan F	Son	M	Cha	0.9	S				Guam	Guam	Guam		None
	26	36	San Nicolas, Manuel LG	Head	M	Cha	38.0	M		Y	Y	Guam	Guam	Guam	N	Farmer
	26	36	San Nicolas, Andrea C	Wife	F	Cha	42.0	M		Y	Y	Guam	Guam	Guam	N	None
	26	36	San Nicolas, Vicente C	Son	M	Cha	16.0	S	N	Y	Y	Guam	Guam	Guam	Y	None
	26	36	San Nicolas, Ana C	Daughter	F	Cha	13.0	S	N	Y	Y	Guam	Guam	Guam	Y	None
	26	36	San Nicolas, Maria C	Daughter	F	Cha	11.0	S	Y	Y	Y	Guam	Guam	Guam	Y	None
	26	36	San Nicolas, Vicenta C	Daughter	F	Cha	9.0	S	Y	Y	Y	Guam	Guam	Guam		None
	26	36	San Nicolas, Jesus C	Son	M	Cha	6.0	S	N			Guam	Guam	Guam		None
	26	36	San Nicolas, Joaquina C	Daughter	F	Cha	4.0	S				Guam	Guam	Guam		None
	26	36	San Nicolas, Antonio C	Step-son	M	Cha	21.0	S		Y	Y	Guam	Guam	Guam		Farm laborer
Salaljaya Street	27	37	San Nicolas, Ignacio LG	Head	M	Cha	46.0	M		Y	Y	Guam	Guam	Guam	N	Farmer
	27	37	San Nicolas, Trinidad C	Wife	F	Cha	45.0	M		N	N	Guam	Guam	Guam	N	None
	27	37	San Nicolas, Mariano C	Son	M	Cha	21.0	S		Y	Y	Guam	Guam	Guam	Y	Farm laborer
	27	38	Paulino, Juan T	Head	M	Cha	26.0	M		Y	Y	Guam	Guam	Guam	N	Farmer
	27	38	Paulino, Maria SN	Wife	F	Cha	16.0	M	N	Y	Y	Guam	Guam	Guam	Y	None
	27	38	Paulino, Rosalia SN	Daughter	F	Cha	0.9	S				Guam	Guam	Guam		None
	28	39	Concepcion, Jose M	Head	M	Cha	76.0	M		N	N	Guam	Guam	Guam	N	Farmer
	28	39	Concepcion, Dolores C	Wife	F	Cha	74.0	W		N	N	Guam	Guam	Guam	N	None
	29	40	San Nicolas, Antonia LG	Head	F	Cha	71.0	d	Y		N	Guam	Guam	Guam	N	None

(CHAMORRO ROOTS GENEALOGY PROJECT ™ TRANSCRIPTION)

(COMPILED/TRANSCRIBED BY BERNARD T. PUNZALAN / HTTP://WWW.CHAMORROROOTS.COM)

FOURTEENTH CENSUS OF THE UNITED STATES: 1920-POPULATION

ISLAND OF GUAM

DISTRICT **District 5**
NAME OF PLACE **Inarajan Town**

[Proper name and, also, name of class, as city, town, village, barrio, etc]

ENUMERATED BY ME ON THE 27th DAY OF February, 1920

Joaquin Torres ENUMERATOR

	PLACE OF ABODE			NAME	RELATION	PERSONAL DESCRIPTION					EDUCATION			NATIVITY				OCCUPATION
Street, avenue, road, etc.	Number of dwelling house in order of visitation	Number of family in order of visitation	Name of each person whose place of abode on January 1, 1920, was in this family.	Sex	Color or race	Age at last birthday	Single, married, widowed or divorced	Attended school any time since Sept. 1, 1919	Whether able to read.	Whether able to write.	Place of birth of this person.	Place of birth of father of this person.	Place of birth of mother of this person.	Whether able to speak English.	Trade, profession, or particular kind of work done, as salesman, laborer, clerk, cook, merchant, washerwoman, etc.
1	2	3	4	5	6	7	8	9	10	11	12	13	14	15	16	17
26	29	41	Castro, Pedro D	Head	M	Cha	55.0	M		Y	N	Guam	Guam	Guam	N	Farmer
27	29	41	Castro, Joaquina SN	Wife	F	Cha	32.0	M		Y	N	Guam	Guam	Guam	N	None
28	29	41	Castro, Maria SN	Daughter	F	Cha	11.0	S	Y			Guam	Guam	Guam	Y	None
29	29	41	Castro, Antonia SN	Daughter	F	Cha	9.0	S	Y			Guam	Guam	Guam		None
30	29	41	Castro, Jesus SN	Son	M	Cha	6.0	S	N			Guam	Guam	Guam		None
31	29	41	Castro, Rufina SN	Daughter	F	Cha	4.0	S				Guam	Guam	Guam		None
32	29	41	Castro, Ana SN	Daughter	F	Cha	2.0	S				Guam	Guam	Guam		None
33	30	42	Flores, Jesus A	Head	M	Cha	55.0	M		Y	Y	Guam	Guam	Guam	N	Farmer
34	30	42	Flores, Dolores D	Wife	F	Cha	51.0	M		Y	Y	Guam	Guam	Guam	N	None
35	30	42	Flores, Joaquin D	Son	M	Cha	25.0	S		Y	Y	Guam	Guam	Guam	Y	Farm laborer
36	30	42	Flores, Catalina D	Daughter	F	Cha	23.0	S		Y	Y	Guam	Guam	Guam	Y	None
37	30	42	Flores, Juan D	Son	M	Cha	17.0	S	N	Y	Y	Guam	Guam	Guam	Y	Farm laborer
38	30	42	Flores, Vicente D	Son	M	Cha	15.0	S	N	Y	Y	Guam	Guam	Guam	Y	Servant
39	30	42	Flores, Prudencio D	Son	M	Cha	12.0	S	Y	Y	Y	Guam	Guam	Guam	Y	None
40	30	42	Martinez, Maria R	Servant	F	Cha	26.0	S		N	N	Guam	Guam	Guam	N	Servant
41	31	43	Cruz, Jose D	Head	M	Cha	28.0	M		Y	Y	Guam	Guam	Guam	Y	Carpenter
42	31	43	Cruz, Carmen P	Wife	F	Cha	25.0	M		Y	Y	Guam	Guam	Guam	N	None
43	31	43	Cruz, Francisco P	Son	M	Cha	3.0	S				Guam	Guam	Guam		None
44	32	44	Cruz, Leocadio C	Head	M	Cha	53.0	M		Y	Y	Guam	Guam	Guam	N	Farmer
45	32	44	Cruz, Luisa D	Wife	F	Cha	57.0	M		Y	Y	Guam	Guam	Guam	N	None
46	32	44	Cruz, Felix	Son	M	Cha	24.0	S		Y	Y	Guam	Guam	Guam	Y	Farm laborer
47	32	44	Cruz, Maria D	Daughter	F	Cha	16.0	S	N	Y	Y	Guam	Guam	Guam	Y	None
48	33	45	Leon Guerrero, Mariano R	Head	M	Cha	44.0	M		Y	Y	Guam	Guam	Guam	Y	Farmer
49	33	45	Leon Guerrero, Ana D	Wife	F	Cha	37.0	M		Y	Y	Guam	Guam	Guam	N	None
50	33	45	Leon Guerrero, Margarita D	Daughter	F	Cha	20.0	S	N	Y	Y	Guam	Guam	Guam	Y	None

Salaljaya Street

(CHAMORRO ROOTS GENEALOGY PROJECT ™ TRANSCRIPTION)
(COMPILED/TRANSCRIBED BY BERNARD T. PUNZALAN / HTTP://WWW.CHAMORROROOTS.COM)

FOURTEENTH CENSUS OF THE UNITED STATES: 1920-POPULATION

ISLAND OF GUAM

ENUMERATED BY ME ON THE 27th DAY OF February, 1920

Joaquin Torres ENUMERATOR

DISTRICT **District 5**

NAME OF PLACE **Inarajan Town**

[Proper name and, also, name of class, as city, town, village, barrio, etc]

Street, avenue, road, etc.	House No.	Family No.	NAME	RELATION	Sex	Color or race	Age at last birthday	Single, married, widowed or divorced	Attended school since Sept. 1, 1919	able to read	able to write	Place of birth of this person	Place of birth of father	Place of birth of mother	Whether able to speak English	OCCUPATION
	33	45	Leon Guerrero, Maria D	Daughter	F	Cha	16.0	S	N	Y	Y	Guam	Guam	Guam	Y	None
	33	45	Leon Guerrero, Antonia D	Daughter	F	Cha	15.0	S	N	Y	Y	Guam	Guam	Guam	Y	None
	33	45	Leon Guerrero, Teresa D	Daughter	F	Cha	13.0	S	N	Y	Y	Guam	Guam	Guam	Y	None
	33	45	Leon Guerrero, Carmen D	Daughter	F	Cha	12.0	S	N	N	N	Guam	Guam	Guam	N	None
	33	45	Leon Guerrero, Mariano D	Son	M	Cha	11.0	S	Y	Y	Y	Guam	Guam	Guam	Y	None
	33	45	Leon Guerrero, Jose D	Son	M	Cha	8.0	S	Y	Y	Y	Guam	Guam	Guam		None
	33	45	Leon Guerrero, Vicente D	Son	M	Cha	6.0	S	N			Guam	Guam	Guam		None
	33	45	Leon Guerrero, Joaquin D	Son	M	Cha	5.0	S	N			Guam	Guam	Guam		None
	33	45	Leon Guerrero, Jesus D	Son	M	Cha	3.0	S				Guam	Guam	Guam		None
	33	45	Leon Guerrero, Rosa D	Daughter	F	Cha	2.0	S				Guam	Guam	Guam		None
	33	45	Leon Guerrero, Rosario D	Daughter	F	Cha	0.6	S				Guam	Guam	Guam		None
Salaljaya Street	34	46	Cepeda, Vicente C	Head	M	Cha	41.0	M		Y	Y	Guam	Guam	Guam	N	Farmer
	34	46	Cepeda, Antonia C	Wife	F	Cha	36.0	M		N	N	Guam	Guam	Guam	N	None
	34	46	Cepeda, Maria C	Daughter	F	Cha	13.0	S	Y	Y	Y	Guam	Guam	Guam	Y	None
	34	46	Cepeda, Rosa C	Daughter	F	Cha	7.0	S	Y	Y	Y	Guam	Guam	Guam	Y	None
	34	46	Cepeda, Ana C	Daughter	F	Cha	6.0	S	N			Guam	Guam	Guam		None
	34	46	Cepeda, Antonia C	Daughter	F	Cha	1.0	S				Guam	Guam	Guam		None
	35	47	Delgado, Silvano M	Head	M	Cha	38.0	M		Y	Y	Guam	Guam	Guam	N	Farmer
	35	47	Delgado, Maria SN	Wife	F	Cha	35.0	M		N	N	Guam	Guam	Guam	N	None
	35	47	Delgado, Pedro SN	Son	M	Cha	12.0	S	Y	Y	Y	Guam	Guam	Guam	Y	None
	35	47	Delgado, Jose SN	Son	M	Cha	10.0	S	Y	Y	Y	Guam	Guam	Guam	Y	None
	35	47	Delgado, Ana D SN	Daughter	F	Cha	7.0	S	Y			Guam	Guam	Guam		None
	35	47	Delgado, Ana SN	Daughter	F	Cha	2.0	S				Guam	Guam	Guam		None
	35	47	Delgado, Consolacion SN	Daughter	F	Cha	1.0	S				Guam	Guam	Guam		None
	36	48	Naputi, Maria F	Head	F	Cha	31.0	S		N	N	Guam	Guam	Guam	N	Laundress

(CHAMORRO ROOTS GENEALOGY PROJECT ™ TRANSCRIPTION)
(COMPILED/TRANSCRIBED BY BERNARD T. PUNZALAN / HTTP://WWW.CHAMORROROOTS.COM)

254b

FOURTEENTH CENSUS OF THE UNITED STATES: 1920-POPULATION
ISLAND OF GUAM

ENUMERATED BY ME ON THE 28th DAY OF February, 1920

Joaquin Torres ENUMERATOR

DISTRICT **District 5**
NAME OF PLACE **Inarajan Town**

#	Street	Dwell	Fam	NAME	RELATION	Sex	Color	Age	Cond	School	Read	Write	Birthplace	Father	Mother	Eng	OCCUPATION
26		36	48	Naputi, Antonia T	Mother	F	Cha	62.0	Wd		N	N	Guam			N	None
27		37	49	Crisostomo, Vicente C	Head	M	Cha	48.0	M		N	N	Guam	Guam	Guam	N	Farmer
28		37	49	Crisostomo, Rosa M	Wife	F	Cha	42.0	M		N	N	Guam	Guam	Guam	N	None
29		37	49	Crisostomo, Rosario M	Daughter	F	Cha	23.0	S		Y	Y	Guam	Guam	Guam	Y	Midwife
30		37	49	Crisostomo, Maria M	Daughter	F	Cha	17.0	S	N	Y	Y	Guam	Guam	Guam	Y	None
31		37	49	Crisostomo, Antonia M	Daughter	F	Cha	14.0	S	N	Y	Y	Guam	Guam	Guam	Y	None
32		37	49	Crisostomo, Pedro M	Son	M	Cha	13.0	S	Y	Y	Y	Guam	Guam	Guam	Y	None
33		37	49	Crisostomo, Elena M	Daughter	F	Cha	11.0	S	Y	Y	Y	Guam	Guam	Guam	Y	None
34		37	49	Crisostomo, Joaquin M	Son	M	Cha	9.0	S	Y			Guam	Guam	Guam		None
35	Salaljaya Street	37	49	Crisostomo, Jose M	Son	M	Cha	6.0	S	N			Guam	Guam	Guam		None
36		37	49	Crisostomo, Jesus M	Son	M	Cha	5.0	S	N			Guam	Guam	Guam		None
37		37	49	Crisostomo, Manuel M	Son	M	Cha	1.0	S				Guam	Guam	Guam		None
38		37	49	Crisostomo, Ramon M	Step-brother	M	Cha	21.0	S	N	N	Y	Guam	Guam	Guam	N	Farm laborer
39		37	49	Crisostomo, Angel M	Nephew	M	Cha	18.0	S	N	N	N	Guam	Unknown	Guam	N	Farm laborer
40		37	49	Crisostomo, Jose C	Nephew	M	Cha	13.0	S	Y	Y	Y	Guam	Unknown	Guam	N	None
41		38	50	Fejarang, Ramon G	Head	M	Cha	56.0	M		Y	Y	Guam	Guam	Guam	N	Deputy Commissioner
42		38	50	Fejarang, Antonia LG	Wife	F	Cha	55.0	M		Y	Y	Guam	Guam	Guam	N	None
43		38	50	Fejarang, Juan LG	Son	M	Cha	19.0	S	N	Y	Y	Guam	Guam	Guam	Y	Farm laborer
44		38	50	Fejarang, Antonia LG	Daughter	F	Cha	17.0	S	N	Y	Y	Guam	Guam	Guam	Y	None
45		38	50	Fejarang, Rufina LG	Daughter	F	Cha	15.0	S	N	Y	Y	Guam	Guam	Guam	Y	None
46		39	51	Mantanona, Casiano A	Head	M	Cha	45.0	M		N	N	Guam	Guam	Guam	N	Farmer
47		39	51	Mantanona, Rita L	Wife	F	Cha	36.0	M		N	N	Guam	Guam	Guam	N	None
48		39	51	Mantanona, Ignacio L	Son	M	Cha	19.0	S	N	Y	Y	Guam	Guam	Guam	Y	Farm laborer
49		39	51	Mantanona, Dolores L	Daughter	F	Cha	12.0	S	Y	Y	Y	Guam	Guam	Guam	Y	None
50		39	51	Mantanona, Margarita L	Daughter	F	Cha	9.0	S	Y			Guam	Guam	Guam	Y	None

(CHAMORRO ROOTS GENEALOGY PROJECT ™ TRANSCRIPTION)
(COMPILED/TRANSCRIBED BY BERNARD T. FUNZALAN / HTTP://WWW.CHAMORROROOTS.COM)

FOURTEENTH CENSUS OF THE UNITED STATES: 1920-POPULATION
ISLAND OF GUAM

ENUMERATED BY ME ON THE 28th DAY OF February, 1920

Joaquin Torres ENUMERATOR

DISTRICT District 5
NAME OF PLACE Inarajan Town

Street	Dwelling No.	Family No.	NAME	RELATION	Sex	Color or race	Age	Single, married, widowed or divorced	Attended school since Sept. 1, 1919	Able to read	Able to write	Birthplace of person	Birthplace of father	Birthplace of mother	Able to speak English	OCCUPATION
	39	51	Mantanona, Carmen L	Daughter	F	Cha	8.0	S	Y			Guam	Guam	Guam		None
	39	51	Mantanona, Jose L	Son	M	Cha	6.0	S	N			Guam	Guam	Guam		None
	39	51	Mantanona, Manuel L	Son	M	Cha	0.8	S				Guam	Guam	Guam		None
	40	52	San Nicolas, Agustin M	Head	M	Cha	49.0	M		Y	Y	Guam	Guam	Guam	N	Farmer
	40	52	San Nicolas, Martina L	Wife	F	Cha	51.0	M		N	N	Guam	Guam	Guam		None
	40	52	San Nicolas, Carmen L	Daughter	F	Cha	20.0	S	N	Y	Y	Guam	Guam	Guam	Y	None
	40	52	San Nicolas, Maria L	Daughter	F	Cha	17.0	S	N	Y	Y	Guam	Guam	Guam	Y	None
	40	52	San Nicolas, Joaquin L	Son	M	Cha	14.0	S	Y	Y	Y	Guam	Guam	Guam	Y	None
	40	52	San Nicolas, Lucas L	Son	M	Cha	10.0	S	Y	Y	Y	Guam	Guam	Guam	Y	None
	40	52	San Nicolas, Jose L	Son	M	Cha	5.0	S	N			Guam	Guam	Guam	Y	None
	40	53	Flores, Jose D	Head	M	Cha	26.0	M		Y	Y	Guam	Guam	Guam	Y	Farmer
	40	53	Flores, Rafaela SN	Wife	F	Cha	24.0	M		Y	Y	Guam	Guam	Guam	N	None
	40	53	Flores, Alfred SN	Son	M	Cha	3.0	S				Guam	Guam	Guam		None
	40	53	Flores, Alice SN	Daughter	F	Cha	2.0	S				Guam	Guam	Guam		None
	40	53	Flores, Ida SN	Daughter	F	Cha	0.8	S				Guam	Guam	Guam		None
Salaljaya Street	41	54	Taimanglo, Blas T	Head	M	Cha	27.0	M		N	N	Guam	Guam	Guam	N	Farmer
	41	54	Taimanglo, Ana M	Wife	F	Cha	30.0	M		Y	Y	Guam	Guam	Guam	N	None
	41	54	Chargualaf, Maria M	Step-daughter	F	Cha	10.0	S	Y	Y	Y	Guam	Guam	Guam	Y	None
	41	54	Chargualaf, Ramon M	Step-son	M	Cha	5.0	S	N			Guam	Guam	Guam		None
	41	54	Chargualaf, Josefa M	Step-daughter	F	Cha	4.0	S				Guam	Guam	Guam		None
	42	55	Fejarang, Jose LG	Head	M	Cha	28.0	M		Y	Y	Guam	Guam	Guam	Y	Farmer
	42	55	Fejarang, Dolores A	Wife	F	Cha	23.0	M		Y	Y	Guam	Guam	Guam	N	None
	42	55	Fejarang, Antonia A	Daughter	F	Cha	2.0	S				Guam	Guam	Guam		None
	42	55	Fejarang, Tomas A	Son	M	Cha	1.0	S				Guam	Guam	Guam	N	None
	42	55	Cruz, Felix S	Farm laborer	M	Cha	19.0	S	N	Y	Y	Guam	Guam	Guam	Y	Farm laborer

(CHAMORRO ROOTS GENEALOGY PROJECT ™ TRANSCRIPTION)
(COMPILED/TRANSCRIBED BY BERNARD T. PUNZALAN / HTTP://WWW.CHAMORROROOTS.COM)

FOURTEENTH CENSUS OF THE UNITED STATES: 1920-POPULATION

ISLAND OF GUAM

DISTRICT **District 5**
NAME OF PLACE **Inarajan Town**

[Proper name and, also, name of class, as city, town, village, barrio, etc]

ENUMERATED BY ME ON THE 28th DAY OF February, 1920

Joaquin Torres ENUMERATOR

Street, avenue, road, etc.	Num-ber of dwell-ing house is order of visi-tatio n	Num-ber of famil y in order of visi-tatio n	NAME	RELATION	Sex	Color or race	Age at last birthday	Single, married, widowed or divorced	Attended school any time since Sept. 1, 1919	Whether able to read.	Whether able to write.	Place of birth of this person.	Place of birth of father of this person.	Place of birth of mother of this person.	Whether able to speak English.	OCCUPATION
1	2	3	4	5	6	7	8	9	10	11	12	13	14	15	16	17
Salaulago Street	43	56	Mantanona, Luis C	Head	M	Cha	48.0	Wd		N	N	Guam	Guam	Guam	N	Farmer
	43	56	Mantanona, Rita C	Daughter	F	Cha	19.0	S	N	Y	Y	Guam	Guam	Guam	Y	None
	43	56	Mantanona, Jesus C	Son	M	Cha	18.0	S	N	Y	Y	Guam	Guam	Guam	Y	Rancher
	43	56	Mantanona, Cecilio C	Son	M	Cha	14.0	S	Y	Y	Y	Guam	Guam	Guam	Y	None
	43	56	Mantanona, Baldomero C	Son	M	Cha	12.0	S	Y	Y	N	Guam	Guam	Guam	Y	None
	43	56	Chargualaf, Cornelia T	Step-daughter	F	Cha	26.0	S		N	N	Guam	Unknown	Guam	N	None
	44	57	San Nicolas, Dolores N	Head	F	Cha	42.0	S		N	N	Guam	Guam	Guam	N	Farmer
	44	57	San Nicolas, Rosa N	Sister	F	Cha	31.0	S		Y	Y	Guam	Guam	Guam	N	None
	44	57	Quintanilla, Vicente SN	Nephew	M	Cha	16.0	S	Y	Y	Y	Guam	Guam	Guam	N	Farmer
	45	58	Meza, Jose P	Head	M	Cha	37.0	M		N	N	Guam	Guam	Guam	N	None
	45	58	Meza, Caridad M	Wife	F	Cha	41.0	M		Y	Y	Guam	Guam	Guam	N	None
	45	58	Meza, Francisco M	Son	M	Cha	6.0	S	N			Guam	Guam	Guam		None
	45	58	Naputi, Dolores M	Mother-in-law	F	Cha	65.0	Wd		N	N	Guam	Guam	Guam	N	None
	45	58	Crisostomo, Maria M	Niece-in-law	F	Cha	18.0	S	N	N	N	Guam	Guam	Guam	Y	Laundress
	46	59	Diego, Joaquin C	Head	M	Cha	55.0	M		N	N	Guam	Guam	Guam	Y	Farmer
	46	59	Diego, Victorina M	Wife	F	Cha	49.0	M		N	N	Guam	Guam	Guam	N	None
	46	60	Mantanona, Froilan M	Head	M	Cha	41.0	M		N	N	Guam	Guam	Guam	N	Farmer
	46	60	Mantanona, Asuncion M	Wife	F	Cha	52.0	M		N	N	Guam	Guam	Guam	N	None
	46	60	Meno, Vicente C	Step-son	M	Cha	15.0	S	N	Y	Y	Guam	Guam	Guam	Y	Farm laborer
	47	61	Diego, Enemesio SN	Head	M	Cha	21.0	M	N	Y	Y	Guam	Guam	Guam	Y	Farmer
	47	61	Diego, Regina D	Wife	F	Cha	18.0	M	N	Y	Y	Guam	Guam	Guam	Y	None
	47	61	Diego, Florentina D	Daughter	F	Cha	0.9	S				Guam	Guam	Guam		None
	47	61	Chargualaf, Antonio F	Farm laborer	M	Cha	48.0	S		N	N	Guam	Guam	Guam	N	Farm laborer
	48	62	Diego, Romualdo C	Head	M	Cha	46.0	M		Y	Y	Guam	Guam	Guam	Y	Farmer
	48	62	Diego, Dolores SN	Wife	F	Cha	48.0	M		Y	N	Guam	Guam	Guam	N	None

(CHAMORRO ROOTS GENEALOGY PROJECT ™ TRANSCRIPTION)

(COMPILED/TRANSCRIBED BY BERNARD T. PUNZALAN / HTTP://WWW.CHAMORROROOTS.COM)

FOURTEENTH CENSUS OF THE UNITED STATES: 1920-POPULATION

ISLAND OF GUAM

DISTRICT **District 5**

NAME OF PLACE **Inarajan Town**

[Proper name and, also, name of class, as city, town, village, barrio, etc]

ENUMERATED BY ME ON THE 28th DAY OF February, 1920

Joaquin Torres ENUMERATOR

	Street, avenue, road, etc. (1)	Dwelling house No. (2)	Family No. (3)	NAME (4)	RELATION (5)	Sex (6)	Color or race (7)	Age (8)	Single, married, etc. (9)	Attended school since Sept. 1, 1919 (10)	Able to read (11)	Able to write (12)	Place of birth of person (13)	Place of birth of father (14)	Place of birth of mother (15)	Able to speak English (16)	OCCUPATION (17)
1		48	62	Diego, Juan SN	Son	M	Cha	16.0	S	N	Y	Y	Guam	Guam	Guam	Y	Farm laborer home
2		48	62	Diego, Ana SN	Daughter	F	Cha	14.0	S	N	Y	Y	Guam	Guam	Guam	Y	None
3		48	62	Diego, Vicente SN	Son	M	Cha	11.0	S	Y	Y	Y	Guam	Guam	Guam	Y	None
4		48	62	Diego, Jesus SN	Son	M	Cha	10.0	S	Y	Y	Y	Guam	Guam	Guam	Y	None
5		48	62	Diego, Rosa SN	Daughter	F	Cha	8.0	S	Y	Y	Y	Guam	Guam	Guam	Y	None
6		48	62	Diego, Joaquina SN	Daughter	F	Cha	5.0	S	N			Guam	Guam	Guam		None
7		49	63	Kumiyama, Maria M	Head	F	Cha	29.0	Wd		Y	N	Guam	Guam	Guam	N	Farmer
8		49	63	Kumiyama, Rita M	Daughter	F	Jpn	11.0	S	Y	Y	Y	Guam	Japan	Guam	Y	None
9	Salallago Street	49	63	Kumiyama, Juan M	Son	M	Jpn	8.0	S	Y	Y	Y	Guam	Japan	Guam		None
10		49	63	Kumiyama, Margarita M	Daughter	F	Jpn	6.0	S	N			Guam	Japan	Guam		None
11		49	63	Mantanona, Mariano SN	Son	M	Cha	3.0	S				Guam	Unknown	Guam		None
12		50	64	Kamo, Antonio I	Head	M	Jpn	32.0	M		Y	Y	Japan	Japan	Japan	N	Retail merchant
13		50	64	Kamo, Teodora C	Wife	F	Cha	26.0	M		Y	Y	Guam	Guam	Guam	N	None
14		50	64	Kamo, Carmen C	Daughter	F	Jpn	7.0	S	Y			Guam	Japan	Guam		None
15		50	65	Diego, Vicente C	Head	M	Cha	44.0	S	N	Y	Y	Guam	Guam	Guam	N	Farmer
16		51	66	Meno, Juan P	Head	M	Cha	33.0	M		Y	Y	Guam	Unknown	Guam	Y	Farmer
17		51	66	Meno, Patrona C	Wife	F	Cha	23.0	M		Y	N	Guam	Guam	Guam	N	None
18		51	66	Meno, Fraim C	Son	M	Cha	1.0	S				Guam	Guam	Guam		None
19		51	67	Meno, Jose C	Head	M	Cha	45.0	Wd		Y	Y	Guam	Unknown	Guam	N	Farmer
20		51	67	Meno, Antonio M	Son	M	Cha	21.0	S	N	Y	Y	Guam	Guam	Guam	Y	Farm laborer home
21		51	67	Meno, Ramon M	Son	M	Cha	18.0	S	N	Y	Y	Guam	Guam	Guam	Y	Farm laborer home
22		51	67	Meno, Gertrudes M	Daughter	F	Cha	17.0	S	N	Y	Y	Guam	Guam	Guam	Y	None
23		51	67	Meno, Jose T	Son	M	Cha	7.0	S	Y	Y	Y	Guam	Guam	Guam		None
24		51	67	Meno, Engracia T	Daughter	F	Cha	1.0	S				Guam	Guam	Guam		None
25		51	67	Castro, Natividad M	Mother	F	Cha	67.0	M	N	N	N	Guam	Guam	Guam	N	None

(CHAMORRO ROOTS GENEALOGY PROJECT ™ TRANSCRIPTION)

(COMPILED/TRANSCRIBED BY BERNARD T. PUNZALAN / HTTP://WWW.CHAMORROROOTS.COM)

256b

FOURTEENTH CENSUS OF THE UNITED STATES: 1920-POPULATION

ISLAND OF GUAM

ENUMERATED BY ME ON THE 1st DAY OF March, 1920

DISTRICT **District 5**

NAME OF PLACE **Inarajan Town**

Joaquin Torres ENUMERATOR

[Proper name and, also, name of class, as city, town, village, barrio, etc]

	Dwelling no.	Family no.	NAME	RELATION	Sex	Color or race	Age	Single/married	Attended school	Read	Write	Birthplace person	Birthplace father	Birthplace mother	Speak English	OCCUPATION
	2	3	4	5	6	7	8	9	10	11	12	13	14	15	16	17
26	51	68	Naputi, Juan T	Head	M	Cha	41.0	M		N	N	Guam	Guam	Guam	N	Farmer
27	51	68	Naputi, Maria M	Wife	F	Cha	31.0	M		N	N	Guam	Unknown	Guam	N	None
28	51	68	Naputi, Sebastian M	Son	M	Cha	15.0	S	Y	Y	Y	Guam	Guam	Guam	Y	None
29	51	68	Naputi, Remedios M	Daughter	F	Cha	7.0	S	N			Guam	Guam	Guam		None
30	51	68	Naputi, Jose M	Son	M	Cha	5.0	S	N			Guam	Guam	Guam		None
31	51	68	Naputi, Concepcion M	Daughter	F	Cha	1.0	S				Guam	Guam	Guam		None
32	51	68	Naputi, Juan M	Son	M	Cha	0.1	S				Guam	Guam	Guam		None
33	52	69	Chargualaf, Ramon M	Head	M	Cha	53.0	M		Y	Y	Guam	Guam	Guam	N	Farmer
34	52	69	Chargualaf, Estefania SN	Wife	F	Cha	40.0	M	N	Y	Y	Guam	Guam	Guam	N	None
35	52	69	Chargualaf, Margarita SN	Daughter	F	Cha	16.0	S	Y	Y	Y	Guam	Guam	Guam	Y	None
36	52	69	Chargualaf, Jose SN	Son	M	Cha	14.0	S	Y	Y	Y	Guam	Guam	Guam	Y	None
37	52	69	Chargualaf, Vicente SN	Son	M	Cha	10.0	S	Y	Y	Y	Guam	Guam	Guam	Y	None
38	52	69	Chargualaf, Joaquin SN	Son	M	Cha	8.0	S	Y			Guam	Guam	Guam		None
39	52	69	Chargualaf, Pedro SN	Son	M	Cha	5.0	S	Y			Guam	Guam	Guam		None
40	53	70	Taitague, Maria N	Head	F	Cha	35.0	Wd		Y	N	Guam	Guam	Guam		Farmer
41	53	70	Taitague, Jesus N	Son	M	Cha	14.0	S	Y	Y	Y	Guam	Guam	Guam		None
42	53	70	Taitague, Joaquin N	Son	M	Cha	12.0	S	Y	Y	Y	Guam	Guam	Guam		None
43	53	70	Taitague, Josefina N	Daughter	F	Cha	11.0	S	Y	Y	Y	Guam	Guam	Guam		None
44	53	70	Taitague, Daniel N	Son	M	Cha	3.0	S				Guam	Guam	Guam		None
45	53	70	Taitague, Lorenzo N	Son	M	Cha	2.0	S				Guam	Guam	Guam		None
46	53	70	Naputi, Rita D	Mother	F	Cha	69.0	Wd		Y	N	Guam	Guam	Guam		None
47	54	71	San Nicolas, Felipe T	Head	M	Cha	27.0	M		Y	Y	Guam	Guam	Guam	N	Farmer
48	54	71	San Nicolas, Isidora C	Wife	F	Cha	26.0	M		N	N	Guam	Guam	Guam	N	None
49	54	71	San Nicolas, Isabel C	Daugher	F	Cha	0.2	S				Guam	Guam	Guam		None
50	54	71	San Nicolas, Maria T	Sister	F	Cha	17.0	S	N	Y	Y	Guam	Guam	Guam	Y	None

Street: Salailago Street

515

(CHAMORRO ROOTS GENEALOGY PROJECT ™ TRANSCRIPTION)
(COMPILED/TRANSCRIBED BY BERNARD T. PUNZALAN / HTTP://WWW.CHAMORROROOTS.COM)

FOURTEENTH CENSUS OF THE UNITED STATES: 1920-POPULATION

ISLAND OF GUAM

SHEET NO. __8A__

ENUMERATED BY ME ON THE 1st DAY OF March, 1920

Joaquin Torres ENUMERATOR

DISTRICT **District 5**

NAME OF PLACE **Inarájan Town**

[Proper name and, also, name of class, as city, town, village, barrio, etc]

	Num-ber of dwell-ing house is order of visi-tatio n (2)	Num-ber of famil y in order of visi-tatio n (3)	NAME (4)	RELATION (5)	Sex (6)	Color or race (7)	Age at last birthday (8)	Single, married, widowed or divorced (9)	Attended school any time since sept. 1, 1919 (10)	Whether able to read. (11)	Whether able to write. (12)	Place of birth of this person. (13)	Place of birth of father of this person. (14)	Place of birth of mother of this person. (15)	Whether able to speak English. (16)	OCCUPATION (17)
1	55	72	Taitague, Jose D	Head	M	Cha	24.0	S		Y	Y	Guam	Guam	Guam	Y	Farmer
2	55	72	Taitague, Rosario D	Mother	F	Cha	57.0	D		Y	N	Guam	Guam	Guam	N	None
3	55	72	Taitague, Potenciana D	Sister	F	Cha	33.0	S		Y	N	Guam	Guam	Guam	N	None
4	55	72	Borja, Maria T	Sister	F	Cha	31.0	W		Y	N	Guam	Guam	Guam	N	None
5	55	72	Taitague, Jesus D	Nephew	M	Cha	10.0	S	Y	Y	Y	Guam	Unknown	Guam		None
6	55	72	Taitague, Ramon D	Nephew	M	Cha	6.0	S	N			Guam	Unknown	Guam		None
7	55	72	Taitague, Angelina D	Niece	F	Cha	4.0	S				Guam	Unknown	Guam		None
8	55	72	Taitague, Henry D	Nephew	M	Cha	10.0	S	Y	Y	Y	Guam	Unknown	Guam	Y	None
9	55	72	Borja, Juan T	Nephew	M	Cha	1.0	S				Guam	Guam	Guam		None
10	55	73	Taitague, Baldabino B	Head	M	Cha	22.0	M		Y	Y	Guam	Guam	Guam	Y	Farmer
11	55	73	Taitague, Catalina T	Wife	F	Cha	35.0	M		Y	Y	Guam	Guam	Guam	Y	None
12	55	73	Taitague, Gregorio D	Step-son	M	Cha	8.0	S	Y			Guam	Unknown	Guam		None
13	55	73	Chargualaf, Cristina T	Servant	F	Cha	10.0	S	N	N	N	Guam	Guam	Guam	N	Servant
14	55	74	Taitague, Juan D	Head	M	Cha	32.0	M		N	N	Guam	Guam	Guam	N	None
15	55	74	Taitague, Saturnina M	Wife	F	Cha	24.0	M		N	N	Guam	Guam	Guam	N	None
16	55	74	Taitague, Baldabino M	Son	M	Cha	4.0	S				Guam	Guam	Guam		None
17	55	74	Taitague, Gonzalo M	Son	M	Cha	2.0	S				Guam	Guam	Guam		None
18	55	74	Taitague, Aliminda M	Daughter	F	Cha	0.1	S				Guam	Guam	Guam		None
19	56	75	Yamashita, Raymundo H	Head	M	Jpn	39.0	M		Y	Y	Japan	Japan	Japan	Y	Retail merchant
20	56	75	Yamashita, Felicitas C	Wife	F	Cha	23.0	M		Y	Y	Guam	Guam	Guam	Y	None
21	56	75	Yamashita, Luis C	Son	M	Cha	2.0	S				Guam	Japan	Guam		None
22	56	75	Yamashita, Jesus C	Son	M	Jpn	0.5	S				Guam	Japan	Guam		None
23	56	75	Yamashita, Ana O	Niece	F	Jpn	11.0	S	N	N	N	Guam	Japan	Guam	N	None
24	57	76	Naputi, Jesus T	Head	M	Cha	22.0	M		Y	Y	Guam	Guam	Guam	Y	Farmer
25	57	76	Naputi, Dolores M	Wife	F	Cha	25.0	M		Y	N	Guam	Unknown	Guam	N	None

Saitiago Street

(CHAMORRO ROOTS GENEALOGY PROJECT ™ TRANSCRIPTION)
(COMPILED/TRANSCRIBED BY BERNARD T. PUNZALAN / HTTP://WWW.CHAMORROROOTS.COM)

257b

SHEET NO. 8B

FOURTEENTH CENSUS OF THE UNITED STATES: 1920-POPULATION

ISLAND OF GUAM

DISTRICT **District 5**

NAME OF PLACE **Inarajan Town**

[Proper name and, also, name of class, as city, town, village, barrio, etc]

ENUMERATED BY ME ON THE 1st DAY OF March, 1920

Joaquin Torres ENUMERATOR

	1	2	3	4 NAME	5 RELATION	6	7	8	9	10	11	12	13	14	15	16	17 OCCUPATION
26		57	76	Naputi, Albert M	Son	M	Cha	2.0	S				Guam	Guam	Guam		None
27		57	76	Naputi, Maria M	Daughter	F	Cha	1.0	S				Guam	Guam	Guam		None
28		57	76	Naputi, Carmen M	Daughter	F	Cha	0.0	S				Guam	Guam	Guam		None
29		58	77	Taimanglo, Jose C	Head	M	Cha	30.0	M		Y	Y	Guam	Guam	Guam	N	Farmer
30		58	77	Taimanglo, Ana C	Wife	F	Cha	25.0	M		N	N	Guam	Guam	Guam	N	None
31		58	77	Taimanglo, Maria C	Daughter	F	Cha	4.0	S				Guam	Guam	Guam		None
32		58	77	Taimanglo, Jesus C	Son	M	Cha	3.0	S				Guam	Guam	Guam		None
33		58	77	Taimanglo, Silvano C	Brother	M	Cha	21.0	S		Y	Y	Guam	Guam	Guam	Y	Farm laborer home
34	Salatlago Street	58	77	Chiguina, Maria N	Aunt	F	Cha	49.0	S	N	N	N	Guam	Guam	Guam	N	None
35		59	78	Mantanona, Silvestre N	Head	M	Cha	43.0	M		N	N	Guam	Guam	Guam	N	Farmer
36		59	78	Mantanona, Ignacia M	Wife	F	Cha	42.0	M		N	N	Guam	Guam	Guam	N	None
37		59	78	Mantanona, Silvestre M	Son	M	Cha	20.0	S	N	Y	Y	Guam	Guam	Guam	Y	Farm laborer home
38		59	78	Mantanona, Pedro M	Son	M	Cha	6.0	S	Y	Y	Y	Guam	Guam	Guam	Y	None
39		59	78	Mantanona, Dometila M	Daughter	F	Cha	13.0	S	Y	Y	Y	Guam	Guam	Guam	Y	None
40		59	78	Mantanona, Jose M	Son	M	Cha	11.0	S	Y	Y	Y	Guam	Guam	Guam	Y	None
41		59	78	Mantanona, Genoveva M	Daughter	F	Cha	7.0	S	Y			Guam	Guam	Guam		None
42		59	78	Mantanona, Dolores M	Daughter	F	Cha	3.0	S				Guam	Guam	Guam		None
43		59	78	Mantanona, Ana M	Daughter	F	Cha	0.0	S				Guam	Guam	Guam		None
44		60	69	Mantanona, Jose N	Head	M	Cha	28.0	M		N	N	Guam	Guam	Guam	N	Farmer
45		60	69	Mantanona, Josefa M	Wife	F	Cha	41.0	M		N	N	Guam	Guam	Guam	N	None
46		60	69	Mantanona, Ramon M	Son	M	Cha	2.0	S				Guam	Guam	Guam		None
47		60	69	Mantanona, Antonia C	Step-daughter	F	Cha	14.0	S	N	Y	Y	Guam	Unknown	Guam	Y	None
48		60	69	Mantanona, Jose C F	Head	M	Cha	46.0	M		Y	Y	Guam	Guam	Guam	N	Farmer
49		60	69	Mantanona, Felicitas P	Wife	F	Cha	38.0	M		Y	Y	Guam	Guam	Guam	N	None
50		60	69	Mantanona, Manuel P	Son	M	Cha	22.0	S		Y	Y	Guam	Guam	Guam	Y	Farm laborer home

(CHAMORRO ROOTS GENEALOGY PROJECT ™ TRANSCRIPTION)
(COMPILED/TRANSCRIBED BY BERNARD T. PUNZALAN / HTTP://WWW.CHAMORROROOTS.COM)

FOURTEENTH CENSUS OF THE UNITED STATES: 1920-POPULATION
ISLAND OF GUAM

DISTRICT **District 5**
NAME OF PLACE **Inarajan Town**
[Proper name and, also, name of class, as city, town, village, barrio, etc]

ENUMERATED BY ME ON THE 1st DAY OF March, 1920

Joaquin Torres ENUMERATOR

	Street, avenue, road, etc.	Number of dwelling house in order of visitation	Number of family in order of visitation	NAME	RELATION	Sex	Color or race	Age at last birthday	Single, married, widowed or divorced	Attended any school since Sept. 1, 1919	Whether able to read.	Whether able to write.	Place of birth of this person.	Place of birth of father of this person.	Place of birth of mother of this person.	Whether able to speak English.	OCCUPATION
	1	2	3	5	5	6	7	8	9	10	11	12	13	14	15	16	17
1		60	69	Mantanona, Remedios P	Daughter	F	Cha	17.0	S	N	Y	Y	Guam	Guam	Guam	Y	None
2		60	69	Mantanona, Ana P	Daughter	F	Cha	11.0	S	Y	Y	Y	Guam	Guam	Guam	Y	None
3		60	69	Mantanona, Rumio P	Son	M	Cha	7.0	S	Y			Guam	Guam	Guam		None
4		60	69	Mantanona, Angelina P	Daughter	F	Cha	5.0	S	N			Guam	Guam	Guam		None
5		60	69	Mantanona, Silvina P	Daughter	F	Cha	4.0	S				Guam	Guam	Guam		None
6		61	81	Paulino, Santiago N	Head	M	Cha	34.0	W		Y	Y	Guam	Guam	Guam	N	Farmer
7		61	81	Paulino, Jesus D	Son	M	Cha	7.0	S	Y			Guam	Guam	Guam		None
8		61	82	Castro, Jose D	Head	M	Cha	37.0	M		Y	Y	Guam	Guam	Guam	N	Farmer
9		61	82	Castro, Gertrudes LG	Wife	F	Cha	38.0	M		N	N	Guam	Guam	Guam	N	None
10		61	82	Castro, Jose LG	Son	M	Cha	15.0	S	N	Y	Y	Guam	Guam	Guam	Y	Farm labor home
11		61	82	Castro, Jesus LG	Son	M	Cha	13.0	S	Y	Y	Y	Guam	Guam	Guam	Y	None
12		61	82	Castro, Juan LG	Son	M	Cha	9.0	S	Y			Guam	Guam	Guam		None
13		61	82	Castro, Antonia LG	Daughter	F	Cha	7.0	S	Y			Guam	Guam	Guam		None
14		61	82	Castro, Ana LG	Daughter	F	Cha	5.0	S	N			Guam	Guam	Guam		None
15		61	82	Castro, Joaquin LG	Son	M	Cha	3.0	S				Guam	Guam	Guam		None
16		61	82	Castro, Cristobal LG	Son	M	Cha	1.0	S				Guam	Guam	Guam		None
17		61	82	Castro, Margarita LG	Daughter	F	Cha	0.3	S				Guam	Guam	Guam		None
18		62	83	Meno, Felipe Q	Head	M	Cha	22.0	M		Y	Y	Guam	Guam	Guam	Y	Farmer
19		62	83	Meno, Fidela C	Wife	F	Cha	21.0	M	N	Y	Y	Guam	Guam	Guam	Y	None
20		62	83	Meno, Maria C	Daughter	F	Cha	1.0	S				Guam	Guam	Guam		None
21		62	83	Meno, Isabel C	Daughter	F	Cha	0.5	S				Guam	Unknown	Guam		None
22		63	84	Meno, Dolores Q	Head	F	Cha	46.0	W		N	N	Guam	Guam	Guam	N	Farmer
23		63	84	Meno, Josefa Q	Daughter	F	Cha	13.0	d	Y	Y	Y	Guam	Guam	Guam	Y	None
24		63	84	Meno, Jose Q	Son	M	Cha	9.0	S	Y			Guam	Guam	Guam		None
25		63	84	Meno, Maria Q	Grand-daughter	F	Cha	5.0	S	N			Guam	Unknown	Guam		None

Satllago Street

(CHAMORRO ROOTS GENEALOGY PROJECT ™ TRANSCRIPTION)
(COMPILED/TRANSCRIBED BY BERNARD T. PUNZALAN / HTTP://WWW.CHAMORROROOTS.COM)

258b

FOURTEENTH CENSUS OF THE UNITED STATES: 1920-POPULATION

ISLAND OF GUAM

SHEET NO. _9B_

DISTRICT **District 5**

NAME OF PLACE **Inarajan Town**

ENUMERATED BY ME ON THE 2nd DAY OF March, 1920

Joaquin Torres ENUMERATOR

[Proper name and, also, name of class, as city, town, village, barrio, etc]

	Dwelling house number	Family number	NAME	RELATION	Sex	Color or race	Age at last birthday	Single, married, widowed or divorced	Attended school any time since Sept. 1, 1919	Whether able to read	Whether able to write	Place of birth of this person	Place of birth of father of this person	Place of birth of mother of this person	Whether able to speak English	OCCUPATION
	1	2	3	4	5	6	7	8	9	10	11	12	13	14	15	16	17
26	64	85	Diego, Ignacia LG	Head	F	Cha	46.0	Wd		Y	N	Guam	Unknown	Guam	N	Farmer
27	64	85	Diego, Catalina LG	Daughter	F	Cha	18.0	S	N	Y	Y	Guam	Guam	Guam	Y	None
28	64	86	Afaisen, Joaquin SN	Head	M	Cha	26.0	M		Y	Y	Guam	Guam	Guam	Y	Farmer
29	64	86	Afaisen, Maria D	Wife	F	Cha	27.0	M	N	Y	N	Guam	Guam	Guam	N	None
30	64	86	Afaisen, Santiago D	Son	M	Cha	6.0	S				Guam	Guam	Guam		None
31	64	86	Afaisen, Cristina D	Daughter	F	Cha	3.0	S				Guam	Guam	Guam		None
32	64	86	Afaisen, Juan D	Son	M	Cha	1.0	S				Guam	Guam	Guam		None
33	65	87	Quintanilla, Emiterio R	Head	M	Cha	49.0	M		Y	Y	Guam	Unknown	Guam	N	Farmer
34	65	87	Quintanilla, Manuela SN	Wife	F	Cha	44.0	M		Y	N	Guam	Guam	Guam	N	None
35	65	87	Quintanilla, Aniceto SN	Son	M	Cha	21.0	S	N	Y	Y	Guam	Guam	Guam	Y	Farm laborer home
36	65	87	Quintanilla, Jose SN	Son	M	Cha	18.0	S	N	Y	Y	Guam	Guam	Guam	Y	Teacher
37	65	87	Quintanilla, Jesus SN	Son	M	Cha	14.0	S	Y	Y	Y	Guam	Guam	Guam	Y	None
38	65	87	Quintanilla, Maria SN	Daughter	F	Cha	11.0	S	Y	Y	Y	Guam	Guam	Guam	Y	None
39	65	87	Quintanilla, Joaquin SN	Son	M	Cha	8.0	S	Y	Y	Y	Guam	Guam	Guam	N	None
40	66	88	Afaisen, Rita SN	Head	F	Cha	54.0	Wd				Guam	Guam	Guam	N	None
41	66	88	Afaisen, Maria SN	Daughter	F	Cha	14.0	S	N	Y	Y	Guam	Guam	Guam	Y	None
42	66	89	Rivera, Jose LG	Head	M	Cha	29.0	M		Y	Y	Guam	Guam	Guam	Y	Farmer
43	66	89	Rivera, Seledonia A	Wife	F	Cha	25.0	M	N	Y	Y	Guam	Guam	Guam	N	None
44	66	89	Rivera, Maria Raquel A	Daughter	F	Cha	6.0	S				Guam	Guam	Guam		None
45	66	89	Rivera, Pedro A	Son	M	Cha	5.0	S				Guam	Guam	Guam		None
46	66	89	Rivera, Jose A	Son	M	Cha	2.0	S				Guam	Guam	Guam		None
47	66	89	Rivera, Francisco A	Son	M	Cha	0.1	S				Guam	Guam	Guam		None
48	67	90	San Nicolas, Elias N	Head	M	Cha	37.0	M		Y	Y	Guam	Guam	Guam	Y	Farmer
49	67	90	San Nicolas, Maria M	Wife	F	Cha	32.0	M		Y	Y	Guam	Guam	Guam	N	None
50	67	90	San Nicolas, Juan M	Son	M	Cha	11.0	S	Y	Y	Y	Guam	Guam	Guam	Y	None

Street: Sataltago Street

(CHAMORRO ROOTS GENEALOGY PROJECT ™ TRANSCRIPTION)
(COMPILED/TRANSCRIBED BY BERNARD T. PUNZALAN / HTTP://WWW.CHAMORROROOTS.COM)

259

FOURTEENTH CENSUS OF THE UNITED STATES: 1920-POPULATION
ISLAND OF GUAM

ENUMERATED BY ME ON THE 2nd DAY OF March, 1920

Joaquin Torres ENUMERATOR

DISTRICT **District 5**

NAME OF PLACE **Inarajan Town**

Street	Dwelling	Family	Name	Relation	Sex	Color or race	Age	Single, married, widowed or divorced	Attended school since Sept 1, 1919	Able to read	Able to write	Birthplace of person	Birthplace of father	Birthplace of mother	Able to speak English	Occupation
	67	90	San Nicolas, Angelina M	Daughter	F	Cha	8.0	S	Y			Guam	Guam	Guam		None
	67	90	San Nicolas, Soledad A M	Daughter	F	Cha	6.0	S	N			Guam	Guam	Guam		None
	67	90	San Nicolas, Carlos M	Son	M	Cha	4.0	S				Guam	Guam	Guam		None
	67	90	San Nicolas, Aurelia M	Daughter	F	Cha	2.0	S				Guam	Guam	Guam		None
	67	90	San Nicolas, Elizabeth M	Daughter	F	Cha	1.0	S				Guam	Guam	Guam		None
	67	90	Afaisen, Vicenta N	Cousin	F	Cha	38.0	S				Guam	Guam	Guam		Farm laborer
	68	91	Alcantara, Francisco D	Head	M	Cha	20.0	S	N	Y	Y	Guam	Unknown	Guam		Storekeeper
	68	91	Alcantara, Antonia	Mother	F	Cha	63.0	S		N	N	Guam	Guam	Guam		None
Satalago Street	69	92	Meno, Sebastian N	Head	M	Cha	45.0	M		Y	Y	Guam	Unknown	Guam	N	Farmer
	69	92	Meno, Candelaria LG	Wife	F	Cha	43.0	M		Y	Y	Guam	Guam	Guam	N	None
	69	92	Meno, Jesus LG	Son	M	Cha	22.0	S		N	N	Guam	Guam	Guam	N	Farm laborer home
	69	92	Meno, Teresa LG	Daughter	F	Cha	21.0	S		Y	Y	Guam	Guam	Guam	Y	None
	69	92	Meno, Joaquin LG	Son	M	Cha	19.0	S		Y	Y	Guam	Guam	Guam	Y	Farm laborer home
	69	92	Meno, Dolores LG	Daughter	F	Cha	15.0	S		Y	Y	Guam	Guam	Guam	Y	None
	69	92	Meno, Ana LG	Daughter	F	Cha	13.0	S	Y	Y	Y	Guam	Guam	Guam	Y	None
	69	92	Meno, Jose LG	Son	M	Cha	10.0	S	Y	Y	Y	Guam	Guam	Guam	Y	None
	69	92	Meno, Ramon LG	Son	M	Cha	8.0	S	Y			Guam	Guam	Guam	Y	None
	69	92	Meno, Justina LG	Daughter	F	Cha	7.0	S	Y			Guam	Guam	Guam		None
	69	92	Meno, Eduvijes LG	Daughter	F	Cha	5.0	S				Guam	Guam	Guam		None
	69	92	Meno, Juan LG	Son	M	Cha	3.0	S				Guam	Guam	Guam		None
	70	93	Afaisen, Antonio N	Head	M	Cha	45.0	M		N	N	Guam	Guam	Guam	N	Farmer
	70	93	Afaisen, Maria C	Wife	F	Cha	44.0	M		N	N	Guam	Guam	Guam	N	None
	70	93	Chargualaf, Jesus M	Nephew-in-law	M	Cha	12.0	S	Y	Y	Y	Guam	Unknown	Guam	Y	None
	71	94	Meno, Vicente T	Head	M	Cha	30.0	M		Y	Y	Guam	Guam	Guam	N	Farmer
	71	94	Meno, Ana M	Wife	F	Cha	27.0	M		Y	N	Guam	Unknown	Guam	N	None

(CHAMORRO ROOTS GENEALOGY PROJECT ™ TRANSCRIPTION)
(COMPILED/TRANSCRIBED BY BERNARD T. PUNZALAN / HTTP://WWW.CHAMORROROOTS.COM)

FOURTEENTH CENSUS OF THE UNITED STATES: 1920—POPULATION
ISLAND OF GUAM

DISTRICT **District 5**

NAME OF PLACE **Inarajan Town**

[Proper name and, also, name of class, as city, town, village, barrio, etc]

ENUMERATED BY ME ON THE _2nd_ DAY OF MARCH, 1920

Joaquin Torres ENUMERATOR

	Dwelling No. (2)	Family No. (3)	NAME (4)	RELATION (5)	Sex (6)	Color or race (7)	Age (8)	Single/married/widowed/divorced (9)	Attended school (10)	Able to read (11)	Able to write (12)	Place of birth of this person (13)	Place of birth of father (14)	Place of birth of mother (15)	Able to speak English (16)	OCCUPATION (17)
26	71	94	Meno, Jose M	Son	M	Cha	7.0	S				Guam	Guam	Guam		None
27	71	94	Meno, Maria M	Daughter	F	Cha	4.0	M				Guam	Guam	Guam		None
28	71	94	Meno, Dolores M	Daughter	F	Cha	0.3	M				Guam	Guam	Guam		None
29	72	95	Meno, Geronimo SN	Head	M	Cha	51.0	S		Y	Y	Guam	Guam	Guam	N	Farmer
30	72	95	Meno, Ana T	Wife	F	Cha	52.0	S		Y	Y	Guam	Guam	Guam	N	None
31	72	95	Meno, Feliza T	Daughter	F	Cha	29.0	S		Y	Y	Guam	Guam	Guam	N	None
32	72	95	Meno, Petra T	Daughter	F	Cha	26.0	S		Y	Y	Guam	Guam	Guam	N	None
33	72	95	Meno, Maria T	Daughter	F	Cha	19.0	S	N	Y	Y	Guam	Guam	Guam	Y	None
34	72	95	Meno, Juan T	Son	M	Cha	17.0	S	N	Y	Y	Guam	Guam	Guam	Y	Farm laborer home
35	72	95	Meno, Dominga SN	Mother	F	Cha	77.0	Wd				Guam	Unknown	Guam	N	None
36	73	96	Leon Guerrero, Joaquin S	Head	M	Cha	33.0	M		Y	Y	Guam	Unknown	Guam	N	Farmer
37	73	96	Leon Guerrero, Ana A	Wife	F	Cha	34.0	M	N	Y	Y	Guam	Guam	Guam	N	None
38	73	96	Leon Guerrero, Maria A	Daughter	F	Cha	6.0	S		Y		Guam	Guam	Guam		None
39	73	96	Leon Guerrero, Rosario A	Daughter	F	Cha	4.0	S				Guam	Guam	Guam		None
40	73	96	Leon Guerrero, Jesus A	Son	M	Cha	2.0	S	N			Guam	Guam	Guam		None
41	73	96	Leon Guerrero, Luis A	Son	M	Cha	1.0	S				Guam	Guam	Guam		None
42	73	97	Mantanona, Jose C	Head	M	Cha	49.0	M		N	N	Guam	Guam	Guam	N	Farmer
43	73	97	Mantanona, Rosa M	Wife	F	Cha	59.0	M		N	N	Guam	Guam	Guam	N	None
44	73	97	Mantanona, Jose M	Son	M	Cha	21.0	S	N	Y	Y	Guam	Guam	Guam	Y	Farm laborer home
45	73	97	Mantanona, Catlina M	Daughter	F	Cha	17.0	S	N	Y	Y	Guam	Guam	Guam	Y	None
46	73	97	Arriola, Felomena M	Step-daughter	F	Cha	33.0	S		Y	Y	Guam	Guam	Guam	Y	None
47	74	98	Crisostomo, Joaquin M	Head	M	Cha	57.0	M		Y	Y	Guam	Unknown	Guam	N	Farmer
48	74	98	Crisostomo, Maria LG	Wife	F	Cha	47.0	S		Y	N	Guam	Unknown	Guam	N	None
49	74	98	Crisostomo, Ana LG	Daughter	F	Cha	14.0	S	N	Y	Y	Guam	Guam	Guam	Y	None
50	74	98	Crisostomo, Pedro LG	Son	M	Cha	12.0	M	Y	Y	Y	Guam	Guam	Guam	Y	None

Street: Salatlago Street

(CHAMORRO ROOTS GENEALOGY PROJECT ™ TRANSCRIPTION)
(COMPILED/TRANSCRIBED BY BERNARD T. PUNZALAN / HTTP://WWW.CHAMORROROOTS.COM)

FOURTEENTH CENSUS OF THE UNITED STATES: 1920-POPULATION
ISLAND OF GUAM

ENUMERATED BY ME ON THE 2nd DAY OF March, 1920

Joaquin Torres ENUMERATOR

DISTRICT District 5
NAME OF PLACE Inarajan Town

[Proper name and, also, name of class, as city, town, village, barrio, etc]

Street: Satalago Street

#	Dwelling	Family	NAME	RELATION	Sex	Color or race	Age	Marital	Attended school	Read	Write	Birthplace	Father birthplace	Mother birthplace	Speak English	OCCUPATION
1	74	98	Crisostomo, Jose LG	Son	M	Cha	8.0	S	Y	Y	Y	Guam	Guam	Guam	Y	None
2	74	98	Crisostomo, Vicente LG	Son	M	Cha	7.0	S	Y			Guam	Guam	Guam		None
3	74	98	Leon Guerrero, Vicenta S	Mother-in-law	F	Cha	65.0	S		N	N	Guam	Guam	Guam	N	None
4	75	99	Pereda, Nicomedes C	Head	M	Cha	53.0	M		N	N	Guam	Guam	Guam	N	Farmer
5	75	99	Pereda, Ana M	Wife	F	Cha	49.0	M		N	N	Guam	Guam	Guam	N	None
6	75	99	Pereda, Anunsacion M	Daughter	F	Cha	16.0	S	N	Y	Y	Guam	Guam	Guam	N	None
7	76	100	San Nicolas, Vicente C	Head	M	Cha	51.0	M		N	N	Guam	Guam	Guam	N	Farmer
8	76	100	San Nicolas, Nicolasa T	Wife	F	Cha	45.0	M		N	N	Guam	Guam	Guam	N	None
9	76	100	San Nicolas, Agapito T	Son	M	Cha	26.0	S		N	Y	Guam	Guam	Guam	N	None
10	76	100	San Nicolas, Jesus T	Son	M	Cha	19.0	S	N	Y	Y	Guam	Guam	Guam	Y	Farm laborer home
11	76	100	San Nicolas, Jose T	Son	M	Cha	17.0	S	N	Y	Y	Guam	Guam	Guam	Y	Farm laborer home
12	76	100	San Nicolas, Francisco T	Son	M	Cha	13.0	S	Y	Y	Y	Guam	Guam	Guam	Y	None
13	76	100	San Nicolas, Lucia T	Daughter	F	Cha	12.0	S	Y	Y	Y	Guam	Guam	Guam	Y	None
14	76	100	San Nicolas, Maria T	Daughter	F	Cha	9.0	S	Y	Y	Y	Guam	Guam	Guam	Y	None
15	76	100	San Nicolas, Ramon T	Son	M	Cha	4.0	S				Guam	Guam	Guam		None
16	76	100	San Nicolas, Geronimo T	Son	M	Cha	2.0	S				Guam	Guam	Guam		None
17	77	101	Naputi, Juan D	Head	M	Cha	47.0	M		Y	Y	Guam	Guam	Guam	N	Farmer
18	77	101	Naputi, Maria C	Wife	F	Cha	42.0	M		N	N	Guam	Guam	Guam	N	None
19	77	101	Naputi, Soledad C	Daughter	F	Cha	22.0	S		Y	Y	Guam	Guam	Guam	N	None
20	77	101	Naputi, Rosalia C	Daughter	F	Cha	20.0	S	N	Y	Y	Guam	Guam	Guam	N	None
21	77	101	Naputi, Enriqueta C	Daughter	F	Cha	18.0	S	Y	Y	Y	Guam	Guam	Guam	Y	None
22	77	101	Naputi, Elena C	Daughter	F	Cha	17.0	S	Y	Y	Y	Guam	Guam	Guam	N	None
23	77	101	Naputi, Rita C	Daughter	F	Cha	11.0	S	Y	Y	Y	Guam	Guam	Guam	Y	None
24	77	101	Naputi, Antonio C	Son	M	Cha	7.0	S	Y	Y	Y	Guam	Guam	Guam	Y	None
25	77	101	Naputi, Jose C	Son	M	Cha	5.0	S	N			Guam	Guam	Guam		None

(CHAMORRO ROOTS GENEALOGY PROJECT ™ TRANSCRIPTION)
(COMPILED/TRANSCRIBED BY BERNARD T. PUNZALAN / HTTP://WWW.CHAMORROROOTS.COM)

260b

FOURTEENTH CENSUS OF THE UNITED STATES: 1920-POPULATION
ISLAND OF GUAM

ENUMERATED BY ME ON THE 3rd DAY OF March, 1920

Joaquin Torres ENUMERATOR

DISTRICT **District 5**
NAME OF PLACE **Inarajan Town**
[Proper name and, also, name of class, as city, town, village, barrio, etc]

	PLACE OF ABODE		NAME	RELATION	PERSONAL DESCRIPTION					EDUCATION			NATIVITY				OCCUPATION
	Number of dwelling house in order of visitation	Number of family in order of visitation	of each person whose place of abode on January 1, 1920, was in the family.	Relationship of this Person to the head of the family.	Sex	Color or race	Age at last birthday	Single, married, widowed or divorced	Attended school any time since Sept. 1, 1919	Whether able to read.	Whether able to write.	Place of birth of this person.	Place of birth of father of this person.	Place of birth of mother of this person.	Whether able to speak English.	Trade, profession, or particular kind of work done, as salesman, clerk, laborer, cook, merchant, washerwoman, etc.
	2	3	4	5	6	7	8	9	10	11	12	13	14	15	16	17
26	78	102	Naputi, Lucas D	Head	M	Cha	30.0	M		Y	Y	Guam	Guam	Guam	N	Farmer
27	78	102	Naputi, Dolores SN	Wife	F	Cha	31.0	M		Y	Y	Guam	Guam	Guam	N	None
28	78	102	Naputi, Jose SN	Son	M	Cha	3.0	S				Guam	Guam	Guam		None
29	78	102	Naputi, Ana SN	Daughter	F	Cha	2.0	S				Guam	Guam	Guam		None
30	78	102	Naputi, Marcela SN	Daughter	F	Cha	0.1	S				Guam	Guam	Guam		None
31	78	102	San Nicolas, Ana T	Sister-in-law	F	Cha	16.0	S	N	Y	Y	Guam	Guam	Guam	Y	Missionary
32	79	103	Flores, Jose A	Head	M	Cha	60.0	M		Y	Y	Guam	Guam	Guam	Y	Missionary
33	79	103	Flores, Candelaria S	Wife	F	Cha	47.0	M		Y	Y	Guam	Guam	Guam	Y	None
34	79	103	Flores, Jose S	Son	M	Cha	16.0	S	N	Y	Y	Guam	Guam	Guam	Y	Farm laborer home
35	79	103	Atoigue, Jose A	Servant	M	Cha	12.0	S	N	Y	Y	Guam	Unknown	Guam	Y	Servant
36	79	104	Cruz, Jesus D	Head	M	Cha	26.0	M		Y	Y	Guam	Guam	Guam	Y	Farmer
37	79	104	Cruz, Juliana F	Wife	F	Cha	25.0	M		Y	Y	Guam	Guam	Guam	Y	None
38	79	104	Cruz, Robert F	Son	M	Cha	2.0	S				Guam	Guam	Guam		None
39	79	104	Cruz, Albert F	Son	M	Cha	1.0	S				Guam	Guam	Guam		None
40	79	104	Leon Guerrero, Ana N	Servant	F	Cha	12.0	S	Y	Y	Y	Guam	Guam	Guam		Servant
41	80	105	Taimanglo, Jose T	Head	M	Cha	41.0	M		Y	Y	Guam	Guam	Guam	N	Farmer
42	80	105	Taimanglo, Clara M	Wife	F	Cha	34.0	M		N	N	Guam	Guam	Guam	N	None
43	80	105	Taimanglo, Josefa M	Daughter	F	Cha	10.0	S	Y	Y	N	Guam	Guam	Guam	N	None
44	80	105	Taimanglo, Dolores M	Daughter	F	Cha	6.0	S	N			Guam	Guam	Guam		None
45	80	105	Taimanglo, Jesus M	Son	M	Cha	2.0	S				Guam	Guam	Guam		None
46	80	105	Taimanglo, Julia M	Daughter	F	Cha	0.8	S				Guam	Guam	Guam		None
47	80	106	Taimanglo, Victorino T	Head	M	Cha	29.0	S		N	N	Guam	Guam	Guam	N	Farmer
48	81	107	Mantanona, Isaac C	Head	M	Cha	42.0	M		Y	Y	Guam	Guam	Guam	N	Farmer
49	81	107	Mantanona, Manuela M	Wife	F	Cha	38.0	M		Y	N	Guam	Guam	Guam	N	None
50	81	107	Mantanona, Juan M	Son	M	Cha	20.0	S	N	Y	N	Guam	Guam	Guam	Y	Farm laborer home

Salatlago Street

(CHAMORRO ROOTS GENEALOGY PROJECT ™ TRANSCRIPTION)
(COMPILED/TRANSCRIBED BY BERNARD T. PUNZALAN / HTTP://WWW.CHAMORROROOTS.COM)

FOURTEENTH CENSUS OF THE UNITED STATES: 1920-POPULATION

ISLAND OF GUAM

SHEET NO. __12A__

DISTRICT **District 5**

NAME OF PLACE **Inarajan Town**

[Proper name and, also, name of class, as city, town, village, barrio, etc]

ENUMERATED BY ME ON THE 3rd DAY OF March, 1920

Joaquin Torres ENUMERATOR

	Place of Abode (1) Street, avenue, road, etc.	(2) Dwelling house number	(3) Family number	NAME (4)	RELATION (5)	Sex (6)	Color or race (7)	Age (8)	Single, married, widowed or divorced (9)	Attended school since Sept. 1, 1919 (10)	Able to read (11)	Able to write (12)	Place of birth of this person (13)	Place of birth of father (14)	Place of birth of mother (15)	Able to speak English (16)	OCCUPATION (17)
1		81	107	Mantanona, Rosalia M	Daughter	F	Cha	15.0	S	N	Y	Y	Guam	Guam	Guam	Y	None
2		81	107	Mantanona, Jose M	Son	M	Cha	12.0	S	Y	Y	Y	Guam	Guam	Guam	Y	None
3		81	107	Mantanona, Francisco M	Son	M	Cha	9.0	S	Y			Guam	Guam	Guam		None
4		81	107	Mantanona, Martina M	Daughter	F	Cha	7.0	S	Y			Guam	Guam	Guam		None
5		81	107	Mantanona, Petronila M	Daughter	F	Cha	1.0	S				Guam	Guam	Guam		None
6		82	108	Mantanona, Joaquin C	Head	M	Cha	38.0	M		N	N	Guam	Guam	Guam	N	Farmer
7		82	108	Mantanona, Andrea C	Wife	F	Cha	24.0	M		Y	N	Guam	Guam	Guam	N	None
8		82	108	Mantanona, Oliva C	Daughter	F	Cha	4.0	S				Guam	Guam	Guam		None
9		83	109	Chargualaf, Dolores M	Head	F	Cha	39.0	Wd		N	N	Guam	Guam	Guam	N	Farmer
10		83	109	Chargualaf, Lucia M	Daughter	F	Cha	12.0	S	Y	Y	Y	Guam	Guam	Guam	Y	None
11		83	109	Chargualaf, Antonia M	Daughter	F	Cha	10.0	S	Y	Y	N	Guam	Guam	Guam	N	None
12		83	109	Chiguina, Monica C	Aunt	F	Cha	75.0	Wd		N	N	Guam	Guam	Guam	N	None
13		83	109	Chiguina, Magdalena C	Cousin	F	Cha	40.0	S				Guam	Unknown	Guam	N	Farm laborer home
14		84	110	Meno, Regino C	Head	M	Cha	24.0	M		Y	Y	Guam	Guam	Guam	N	Farmer
15		84	110	Meno, Cornelia C	Wife	F	Cha	26.0	M		N	N	Guam	Guam	Guam	Y	None
16	Salallago Street	84	110	Meno, Ana C	Daughter	F	Cha	2.0	S				Guam	Guam	Guam	N	None
17		84	110	Meno, Jesus C	Son	M	Cha	1.0	S				Guam	Guam	Guam		None
18		84	110	Meno, Maria C	Daughter	F	Cha	0.2	S				Guam	Guam	Guam		None
19		85	111	Meno, Vicente C	Head	M	Cha	44.0	M		Y	Y	Guam	Guam	Guam	N	Farmer
20		85	111	Meno, Consolacion N	Wife	F	Cha	49.0	M		Y	Y	Guam	Guam	Guam	N	None
21		85	111	Meno, Jesus N	Son	M	Cha	18.0	S	N	Y	Y	Guam	Guam	Guam	Y	Farm laborer home
22		85	111	Meno, Maria N	Daughter	F	Cha	16.0	S	N	Y	Y	Guam	Guam	Guam	Y	None
23		85	111	Meno, Regina N	Daughter	F	Cha	10.0	S	Y	Y	Y	Guam	Guam	Guam	Y	None
24		85	111	Meno, Jose N	Son	M	Cha	4.0	S				Guam	Guam	Guam		None
25		86	112	Meno, Vicente M	Head	M	Cha	20.0	S	N	Y	Y	Guam	Guam	Guam	Y	Farmer

(CHAMORRO ROOTS GENEALOGY PROJECT ™ TRANSCRIPTION)
(COMPILED/TRANSCRIBED BY BERNARD T. PUNZALAN / HTTP://WWW.CHAMORROROOTS.COM)

FOURTEENTH CENSUS OF THE UNITED STATES: 1920–POPULATION
ISLAND OF GUAM

ENUMERATED BY ME ON THE 3rd DAY OF March, 1920

Joaquin Torres ENUMERATOR

DISTRICT District 5
NAME OF PLACE Inarajan Town

[Proper name and, also, name of class, as city, town, village, barrio, etc]

	Street	Dwelling No.	Family No.	NAME	RELATION	Sex	Color or race	Age	Single/married, widowed/divorced	Attended school since Sept 1, 1919	Able to read	Able to write	Place of birth of person	Place of birth of father	Place of birth of mother	Able to speak English	OCCUPATION
	1	2	3	4	5	6	7	8	9	10	11	12	13	14	15	16	17
26		86	112	Meno, Pedro C	Father	M	Cha	48.0	M		Y	N	Guam	Guam	Guam	N	None
27		86	112	Meno, Encarnacion M	Mother	F	Cha	52.0	M		Y	N	Guam	Unknown	Guam	N	None
28		86	112	Meno, Ramon M	Brother	M	Cha	16.0	S	N	Y	Y	Guam	Guam	Guam	Y	Farm laborer home
29		86	112	Meno, Jose M	Brother	M	Cha	10.0	S	Y	N	N	Guam	Guam	Guam	N	None
30		87	113	Asanoma, Tito R	Head	M	Jpn	46.0	M		Y	Y	Japan	Japan	Japan	N	Farmer
31		87	113	Asanoma, Sabina C	Wife	F	Cha	28.0	M		Y	N	Guam	Guam	Guam	N	None
32		87	113	Asanoma, Francisco C	Son	M	Jpn	6.0	S	N			Guam	Japan	Guam		None
33		87	113	Asanoma, Maria C	Daughter	F	Jpn	3.0	S				Guam	Japan	Guam		None
34		87	113	Asanoma, Jesus C	Son	M	Jpn	2.0	S				Guam	Japan	Guam		None
35		87	113	Asanoma, Jose C	Son	M	Jpn	0.3	S				Guam	Japan	Guam		None
36		87	113	Castro, Francisco N	Father-in-law	M	Cha	59.0	Wd				Guam	Unknown	Guam		None
37		88	114	Taimanglo, Isidoro C	Head	M	Cha	29.0	S		Y	N	Guam	Guam	Guam	N	Farmer
38		88	114	Taimanglo, Guadalupe C	Mother	F	Cha	56.0	Wd		Y	N	Guam	Guam	Guam	N	None
39	Iglesias Street	88	114	Taimanglo, Remedios C	Sister	F	Cha	19.0	S		Y	Y	Guam	Guam	Guam	Y	None
40		88	114	Chargualaf, Francisco M	Cousin	M	Cha	9.0	S	Y			Guam	Unknown	Guam		None
41		88	114	Chargualaf, Lino M	Cousin	M	Cha	7.0	S	Y			Guam	Unknown	Guam		None
42		88	115	Cepeda, Joaquin C	Head	M	Cha	38.0	M		Y	Y	Guam	Guam	Guam	N	Farmer
43		88	115	Cepeda, Dolores T	Wife	F	Cha	25.0	M		Y	Y	Guam	Guam	Guam	N	None
44		88	115	Cepeda, Rosa T	Daughter	F	Cha	2.0	S				Guam	Guam	Guam		None
45		88	115	Cepeda, Fraim T	Son	M	Cha	1.0	S				Guam	Guam	Guam		None
46		89	116	Kamminga, Simeon H	Head	M	Cha	31.0	M		Y	Y	Guam	Holland	Guam	Y	Farmer
47		89	116	Kamminga, Felicidad T	Wife	F	Cha	32.0	M		Y	Y	Guam	Unknown	Guam	N	None
48		89	116	Torres, Jesus T	Step-son	M	Cha	6.0	S	N			Guam	Unknown	Unknown		None
49		90	117	Duenas, Ramon T	Head	M	Cha	32.0	M		Y	Y	Guam	Guam	Guam	N	Farmer
50		90	117	Duenas, Catalina D	Wife	F	Cha	29.0	M		Y	Y	Guam	Guam	Guam	N	None

(CHAMORRO ROOTS GENEALOGY PROJECT ™ TRANSCRIPTION)
(COMPILED/TRANSCRIBED BY BERNARD T. PUNZALAN / HTTP://WWW.CHAMORROROOTS.COM)

FOURTEENTH CENSUS OF THE UNITED STATES: 1920-POPULATION
ISLAND OF GUAM

ENUMERATED BY ME ON THE 3ʳᵈ DAY OF March, 1920

Joaquin Torres ENUMERATOR

DISTRICT **District 5**
NAME OF PLACE **Inarajan Town**
[Proper name and, also, name of class, as city, town, village, barrio, etc]

	Street, avenue, road, etc.	Number of dwelling house in order of visitation	Number of family in order of visitation	NAME	RELATION	Sex	Color or race	Age at last birthday	Single, married, widowed or divorced	Attended school any time since Sept. 1, 1919	Whether able to read	Whether able to write	Place of birth of this person	Place of birth of father of this person	Place of birth of mother of this person	Whether able to speak English	OCCUPATION
	1	2	3	4	5	6	7	8	9	10	11	12	13	14	15	16	17
1		90	117	Duenas, Silvestre D	Son	M	Cha	7.0	S	Y			Guam	Guam	Guam		None
2		90	117	Duenas, Vicente D	Son	M	Cha	5.0	S	N			Guam	Guam	Guam		None
3		90	117	Duenas, Ramon D	Son	M	Cha	4.0	S				Guam	Guam	Guam		None
4		90	117	Duenas, Maria D	Daughter	F	Cha	3.0	S				Guam	Guam	Guam		None
5		90	117	Duenas, Gonzalo D	Son	M	Cha	1.0	S				Guam	Guam	Guam		None
6		91	118	Duenas, Jose M	Head	M	Cha	42.0	M		Y	Y	Guam	Guam	Guam	N	Farmer
7		91	118	Duenas, Teresa T	Wife	F	Cha	55.0	M		Y	Y	Guam	Guam	Guam	N	None
8	Iglesias Street	91	118	Duenas, Jesus T	Son	M	Cha	14.0	S	Y	Y	Y	Guam	Guam	Guam	Y	None
9		91	118	Duenas, Joaquina T	Daughter	F	Cha	34.0	S		N	N	Guam	Guam	Guam	N	None
10		92	119	Santos, Joaquin D	Head	M	Cha	32.0	M		N	N	Guam	Unknown	Guam	N	Farmer
11		92	119	Santos, Felicidad D	Wife	F	Cha	23.0	M		Y	Y	Guam	Guam	Guam	Y	None
12		92	119	Santos, Teresa D	Daughter	F	Cha	1.0	S				Guam	Guam	Guam		None
13				Here ends the enumeration of Inarajan Town.													
14																	
15																	
16																	
17																	
18																	
19																	
20																	
21																	
22																	
23																	
24																	
25																	

(CHAMORRO ROOTS GENEALOGY PROJECT ™ TRANSCRIPTION)
(COMPILED/TRANSCRIBED BY BERNARD T. PUNZALAN / HTTP://WWW.CHAMORROROOTS.COM)

FOURTEENTH CENSUS OF THE UNITED STATES: 1920-POPULATION
ISLAND OF GUAM

ENUMERATED BY ME ON THE 4th DAY OF March, 1920

Joaquin Torres ENUMERATOR

DISTRICT 5
NAME OF PLACE Aga - Inarajan District
[Proper name and, also, name of class, as city, town, village, barrio, etc]

Street: Merizo - Inarajan Road

	Dwelling No.	Family No.	NAME	RELATION	Sex	Color or race	Age	Single/married/widowed/divorced	Attended school since Sept. 1, 1919	Able to read	Able to write	Birthplace of person	Birthplace of father	Birthplace of mother	Able to speak English	OCCUPATION
1	1	1	Paulino, Vicente M	Head	M	Cha	39.0	M		Y	Y	Guam	Guam	Guam	N	Farmer
2	2	2	Naputi, Lucas T	Head	M	Cha	42.0	M		Y	Y	Guam	Guam	Guam	N	None
3	2	2	Naputi, Rosa P	Wife	F	Cha	59.0	M		N	N	Saipan	Guam	Guam	Y	None
4	2	2	Naputi, Ignacia P	Daughter	F	Cha	18.0	S	N	Y	Y	Guam	Guam	Saipan	Y	None
5	2	2	Naputi, Manuel P	Son	M	Cha	16.0	S	Y	Y	Y	Guam	Guam	Saipan	N	None
6	3	3	Chargualaf, Jose T	Head	M	Cha	34.0	M		N	N	Guam	Guam	Guam	N	Farmer
7	3	3	Chargualaf, Dometila M	Wife	F	Cha	30.0	M				Guam	Guam	Guam	N	None
8	3	3	Chargualaf, Damiana M	Daughter	F	Cha	7.0	S	Y			Guam	Guam	Guam		None
9	3	3	Chargualaf, Maria M	Daughter	F	Cha	3.0	S				Guam	Guam	Guam		None
10	3	3	Chargualaf, Dolores M	Daughter	F	Cha	1.0	S				Guam	Guam	Guam		None
11	4	4	Delgado, Jose M	Head	M	Cha	42.0	M		N	N	Guam	Guam	Guam	N	Farmer
12	4	4	Delgado, Josefa C	Wife	F	Cha	48.0	M		N	N	Guam	Guam	Guam	N	None
13	4	4	Delgado, Nicolas M	Nephew	M	Cha	21.0	S		Y	Y	Guam	Unknown	Guam	Y	Farm laborer home
14	4	4	Meno, Soledad D	Niece	F	Cha	20.0	S	N			Guam	Unknown	Guam	Y	None
15	4	4	Meno, Javiel D	Grand-nephew	M	Cha	1.0	S				Guam	Unknown	Guam		None
16	5	5	San Nicolas, Jose C	Head	M	Cha	26.0	M		Y	Y	Guam	Guam	Guam	N	Farmer
17	5	5	San Nicolas, Seferina C	Wife	F	Cha	25.0	M		Y	Y	Guam	Guam	Guam	N	None
18	5	5	San Nicolas, Rosa C	Daughter	F	Cha	3.0	S				Guam	Guam	Guam		None
19	5	5	San Nicolas, Juan C	Son	M	Cha	2.0	S				Guam	Guam	Guam		None
20	5	5	San Nicolas, Maria C	Daughter	F	Cha	0.8	S				Guam	Guam	Guam		None
21	6	6	Meno, Jose C	Head	M	Cha	44.0	M		N	N	Guam	Guam	Guam	N	Farmer
22	6	6	Meno, Francisca N	Wife	F	Cha	40.0	M		N	N	Guam	Unknown	Unknown	N	None
23	6	6	Meno, Joaquina N	Daughter	F	Cha	14.0	S	N	Y	Y	Guam	Guam	Guam	Y	None
24	6	6	Meno, Rosario N	Daughter	F	Cha	12.0	S	Y	Y	Y	Guam	Guam	Guam	Y	None
25	6	6	Meno, Ursula N	Daughter	F	Cha	6.0	S	N			Guam	Guam	Guam		None

(CHAMORRO ROOTS GENEALOGY PROJECT ™ TRANSCRIPTION)

(COMPILED/TRANSCRIBED BY BERNARD T. PUNZALAN / HTTP://WWW.CHAMORROROOTS.COM)

263b

FOURTEENTH CENSUS OF THE UNITED STATES: 1920-POPULATION

ISLAND OF GUAM

ENUMERATED BY ME ON THE 4th DAY OF March, 1920

Joaquin Torres ENUMERATOR

DISTRICT **5**

NAME OF PLACE **Aga - Inarajan District**

[Proper name and, also, name of class, as city, town, village, barrio, etc]

	PLACE OF ABODE		NAME	RELATION	PERSONAL DESCRIPTION					EDUCATION			NATIVITY				OCCUPATION
Street, avenue, road, etc.	Number of dwelling house in order of visitation	Number of family in order of visitation	of each person whose place of abode on January 1, 1920, was in the family. Enter surname, first, then given name and middle initial. If any. Include every person living on January 1, 1920. Omit children born since January 1, 1920.	Relationship of this Person to the head of the family.	Sex	Color or race	Age at last birthday	Single, married, widowed or divorced	Attended school any time since Sept. 1, 1919	Whether able to read.	Whether able to write.	Place of birth of this person.	Place of birth of father of this person.	Place of birth of mother of this person.	Whether able to speak English.	Trade, profession, or particular kind of work done, as salesman, laborer, clerk, cook, merchant, washerwoman, etc.
1	2	3	4	5	6	7	8	9	10	11	12	13	14	15	16	17
26	6	6	Meno, Luis N	Son	M	Cha	1.0	S				Guam	Guam	Guam		None
27	7	7	Camacho, Vicente C	Head	M	Cha	69.0	D		N	N	Guam	Guam	Guam	N	Farmer
28			Here ends the enumeration of Aga - Inarajan District													
29																
30																
31																
32																
33																
34																
35																
36																
37																
38																
39																
40																
41																
42																
43																
44																
45																
46																
47																
48																
49																
50																

(CHAMORRO ROOTS GENEALOGY PROJECT ™ TRANSCRIPTION)
(COMPILED/TRANSCRIBED BY BERNARD T. PUNZALAN / HTTP://WWW.CHAMORROROOTS.COM)

FOURTEENTH CENSUS OF THE UNITED STATES: 1920-POPULATION

ISLAND OF GUAM

DISTRICT 5

NAME OF PLACE Malolos - Inarajan District

[Proper name and, also, name of class, as city, town, village, barrio, etc]

ENUMERATED BY ME ON THE 4th DAY OF March, 1920

Joaquin Torres ENUMERATOR

Street, avenue, road, etc.	Dwelling house number	Family visitation number	NAME	RELATION	Sex	Color or race	Age at last birthday	Single, married, widowed or divorced	Attended school any time since Sept. 1, 1919	Whether able to read	Whether able to write	Place of birth of this person	Place of birth of father of this person	Place of birth of mother of this person	Whether able to speak English	OCCUPATION
	1	1	Afaisen, Manuel T	Head	M	Cha	42.0	M		Y	Y	Guam	Guam	Guam	N	Farmer
	1	1	Afaisen, Ana SN	Wife	F	Cha	42.0	M		Y	N	Guam	Guam	Guam	N	None
	1	1	Afaisen, Natividad SN	Daughter	F	Cha	14.0	S	N	Y	Y	Guam	Guam	Guam	Y	None
	1	1	Afaisen, Elisa SN	Daughter	F	Cha	13.0	S	N	Y	Y	Guam	Guam	Guam	Y	None
	2	2	Paulino, Carmen N	Head	F	Cha	60.0	Wd				Guam	Guam	Guam	N	Farmer
	2	2	Paulino, Ana N	Daughter	F	Cha	31.0	S		Y	Y	Guam	Guam	Guam	N	Farm laborer home
	2	2	Mantanona, Juan P	Grand-son	M	Cha	14.0	S	Y	Y	Y	Guam	Guam	Guam	Y	None
	3	3	Martinez, Clemente R	Head	M	Cha	48.0	M		N	N	Guam	Guam	Guam	N	Farmer
	3	3	Martinez, Josefa R	Wife	F	Cha	49.0	M		N	N	Guam	Unknown	Guam	N	None
	3	3	Martinez, Jose R	Son	M	Cha	23.0	S		N	N	Guam	Guam	Guam	N	Farm laborer home
	3	3	Martinez, Joaquin R	Son	M	Cha	17.0	S	N	N	N	Guam	Guam	Guam	Y	Farm laborer home
	3	3	Martinez, Concepcion R	Daughter	F	Cha	13.0	S	N	N	N	Guam	Guam	Guam	N	None
	3	3	Martinez, Carmen R	Daughter	F	Cha	9.0	S				Guam	Guam	Guam	N	None
	3	3	Martinez, Caridad R	Grand-step-daughter	F	Cha	3.0	S				Guam	Unknown	Guam		None
	4	4	Meno, Joaquin C	Head	M	Cha	39.0	M		Y	Y	Guam	Guam	Guam	N	Farmer
	4	4	Meno, Rosa T	Wife	F	Cha	21.0	M	N	N	N	Guam	Guam	Guam	N	None
	4	4	Meno, Ramon T	Son	M	Cha	2.0	S				Guam	Guam	Guam		None
	4	4	Meno, Margarita T	Daughter	F	Cha	0.1	S				Guam	Guam	Guam		None
	5	5	Chargualaf, Justo T	Head	M	Cha	38.0	S		N	N	Guam	Guam	Guam	N	Farmer
	5	5	Paulino, Maria Q	Cook	F	Cha	38.0	M		N	N	Guam	Guam	Guam	N	Cook
	5	5	Quidachay, Amanda T	Boarder	F	Cha	2.0	S				Guam	Unknown	Unknown	N	None
	6	6	Taimanglo, Joaquin T	Head	M	Cha	39.0	M		Y	Y	Guam	Guam	Guam	N	Farmer
	6	6	Taimanglo, Dolores T	Wife	F	Cha	38.0	S	N	N	N	Guam	Unknown	Guam	N	None
	6	6	Taimanglo, Jose T	Son	M	Cha	9.0	S				Guam	Guam	Guam		None
	7	7	Mangliona, Paulino S	Head	M	Cha	37.0	M		Y	Y	Guam	Guam	Guam	Y	Farmer

Inarajan - Talofofo Road

(CHAMORRO ROOTS GENEALOGY PROJECT ™ TRANSCRIPTION)
(COMPILED/TRANSCRIBED BY BERNARD T. PUNZALAN / HTTP://WWW.CHAMORROROOTS.COM)

264b

FOURTEENTH CENSUS OF THE UNITED STATES: 1920-POPULATION

ISLAND OF GUAM

ENUMERATED BY ME ON THE 4th DAY OF March, 1920

Joaquin Torres ENUMERATOR

DISTRICT 5

NAME OF PLACE Malolos - Inarajan District

Street: Inarajan - Talofofo Road

Line	Dwell. (2)	Fam. (3)	NAME (4)	RELATION (5)	Sex (6)	Race (7)	Age (8)	Marital (9)	School (10)	Read (11)	Write (12)	Birth (13)	Father (14)	Mother (15)	Eng. (16)	OCCUPATION (17)
26	7	7	Manglona, Leoncia C	Wife	F	Cha	27.0	M		Y	Y	Guam	Guam	Guam	N	None
27	7	7	Manglona, Jesus C	Son	M	Cha	0.4	S				Guam	Guam	Guam		None
28	8	8	Aguon, Rosa T	Head	F	Cha	54.0	W d		Y	Y	Guam	Guam	Guam	N	Farmer
29	8	8	Pinaula, Vicente A	Grand-son	M	Cha	15.0	S	N	Y	Y	Guam	Unknown	Guam	Y	Farm laborer home
30	8	8	Martinez, Enrique	Farm laborer	M	Cha	13.0	S	N	N	N	Guam	Guam	Guam	N	Farm laborer
31	8	9	Cruz, Francisco D	Head	M	Cha	22.0	M		Y	Y	Guam	Unknown	Guam	Y	Farmer
32	8	9	Cruz, Maria T	Wife	F	Cha	18.0	M	N	N	N	Guam	Guam	Guam	Y	None
33	8	9	Cruz, Edward T	Son	M	Cha	0.0	S				Guam	Guam	Guam		None
34	9	10	Aguon, Juan T	Head	M	Cha	33.0	M		Y	Y	Guam	Guam	Guam	N	Farmer
35	9	10	Aguon, Dolores F	Wife	F	Cha	23.0	M		Y	Y	Guam	Guam	Guam	N	None
36	9	10	Aguon, Vicente F	Son	M	Cha	3.0	S				Guam	Guam	Guam		None
37	9	10	Aguon, Concepcion F	Daughter	F	Cha	2.0	S					Guam	Guam		None
38	9	10	Aguon, Rosa F	Daughter	F	Cha	0.3	S					Guam	Guam		None
39	10	11	Martinez, Manuel R	Head	M	Cha	25.0	W d		Y	Y	Guam	Unknown	Guam	Y	Farmer

Here ends the enumeration of Malolos - Inarajan District.

(CHAMORRO ROOTS GENEALOGY PROJECT ™ TRANSCRIPTION)
(COMPILED/TRANSCRIBED BY BERNARD T. PUNZALAN / HTTP://WWW.CHAMORROROOTS.COM)

FOURTEENTH CENSUS OF THE UNITED STATES: 1920-POPULATION

ISLAND OF GUAM

SHEET NO. __16A__

DISTRICT **5**

NAME OF PLACE **Bubulao - Inarajan District**

[Proper name and, also, name of class, as city, town, village, barrio, etc]

ENUMERATED BY ME ON THE 5th DAY OF March, 1920

Joaquin Torres ENUMERATOR

	Dwelling No. (2)	Family No. (3)	NAME (4)	RELATION (5)	Sex (6)	Color or race (7)	Age (8)	Marital (9)	School (10)	Read (11)	Write (12)	Birthplace (13)	Father birthplace (14)	Mother birthplace (15)	Speak English (16)	OCCUPATION (17)
1	1	1	Chiguina, Jesus D	Head	M	Cha	37.0	M		Y	Y	Guam	Unknown	Guam	N	Farmer
2	1	1	Chiguina, Soledad M	Wife	F	Cha	37.0	M		N	N	Guam	Guam	Guam	N	None
3	1	1	Chiguina, Juan M	Son	M	Cha	13.0	S	N	Y	Y	Guam	Guam	Guam	Y	None
4	1	1	Chiguina, Antonia M	Daughter	F	Cha	11.0	S	Y	Y	Y	Guam	Guam	Guam	Y	None
5	2	2	Leon Guerrero, Inocencio	Head	M	Cha	25.0	S		Y	Y	Guam	Unknown	Guam	N	Farmer
6	3	3	Leon Guerrero, Vicente S	Head	M	Cha	34.0	M		Y	Y	Guam	Unknown	Guam	N	Farmer
7	3	3	Leon Guerrero, Carlotta T	Wife	F	Cha	26.0	M		Y	Y	Guam	Guam	Guam	N	None
8	3	3	Leon Guerrero, Lagrimas N	Daughter	F	Cha	15.0	S	N	Y	Y	Guam	Guam	Guam	N	None
9	3	3	Leon Guerrero, Joaquina N	Daughter	F	Cha	4.0	S				Guam	Guam	Guam		None
10	3	3	Leon Guerrero, Vicenta N	Daughter	F	Cha	2.0	S				Guam	Guam	Guam	N	None
11	4	4	Chargualaf, Sebastian S	Head	M	Cha	48.0	M		N	N	Guam	Guam	Guam	N	Farmer
12	4	4	Chargualaf, Isabel D	Wife	F	Cha	38.0	M		Y	Y	Guam	Guam	Guam	N	None
13	4	4	Chargualaf, Jose T	Son	M	Cha	12.0	S	N	N	Y	Guam	Guam	Guam	Y	F.I. working
14	4	4	Chargualaf, Rita T	Daughter	F	Cha	7.0	S	Y	Y	Y	Guam	Guam	Guam	N	None
15	4	4	Chargualaf, Consolacion T	Daughter	F	Cha	5.0	S	N	N	N	Guam	Guam	Guam	N	None
16	4	4	Delgado, Tomasa M	Step-daughter	F	Cha	11.0	S	Y	Y	Y	Guam	Unknown	Guam	Y	None
17	4	4	Delgado, Jose M	Step-son	M	Cha	3.0	S				Guam	Unknown	Guam		None
18	5	5	Rosario, Domingo Q	Head	M	Cha	58.0	M		N	N	Guam	Guam	Guam	N	Farmer
19	5	5	Rosario, Dolores T	Wife	F	Cha	40.0	M		N	N	Guam	Guam	Guam	N	None
20	5	5	Rosario, Francisco T	Son	M	Cha	17.0	S		N	N	Guam	Guam	Guam	N	Rancher
21	5	5	Rosario, Trinidad T	Daughter	F	Cha	16.0	S		N	N	Guam	Guam	Guam	N	None
22	5	5	Rosario, Antonio T	Son	M	Cha	12.0	S		N	N	Guam	Guam	Guam	N	Farm laborer home
23	5	5	Rosario, Jose T	Son	M	Cha	2.0	S				Guam	Guam	Guam		None
24	5	5	Rosario, Catalina T	Daughter	F	Cha	1.0	S				Guam	Guam	Guam		None
25	5	5	Rosario, Juan T	Son	M	Cha	0.5	S				Guam	Guam	Guam		None

Bubulao- Inarajan District

(CHAMORRO ROOTS GENEALOGY PROJECT ™ TRANSCRIPTION)
(COMPILED/TRANSCRIBED BY BERNARD T. PUNZALAN / HTTP://WWW.CHAMORROROOTS.COM)

265b

FOURTEENTH CENSUS OF THE UNITED STATES: 1920—POPULATION

ISLAND OF GUAM

DISTRICT **5**

NAME OF PLACE **Bubulao - Inarajan District**

[Proper name and, also, name of class, as city, town, village, barrio, etc]

ENUMERATED BY ME ON THE 5th DAY OF March, 1920

Joaquin Torres ENUMERATOR

	Number of dwelling house in order of visitation (2)	Number of family in order of visitation (3)	NAME (4)	RELATION (5)	Sex (6)	Color or race (7)	Age at last birthday (8)	Single, married, widowed or divorced (9)	Attended school any time since Sept. 1, 1919 (10)	Whether able to read. (11)	Whether able to write. (12)	Place of birth of this person. (13)	Place of birth of father of this person. (14)	Place of birth of mother of this person. (15)	Whether able to speak English. (16)	OCCUPATION (17)
26	6	6	Barcinas, Isaac LG	Head	M	Cha	50.0	M		Y	Y	Guam	Guam	Guam	N	Farmer
27	6	6	Barcinas, Magdalena D	Wife	F	Cha	47.0	M		Y	Y	Guam	Guam	Guam	N	None
28	6	6	Barcinas, Mercedes D	Daughter	F	Cha	22.0	S		Y	Y	Guam	Guam	Guam	Y	None
29	6	6	Barcinas, Jose D	Son	M	Cha	17.0	S	N	Y	Y	Guam	Guam	Guam	Y	Rancher
30	6	6	Barcinas, Josefa D	Daughter	F	Cha	10.0	S	N	N	N	Guam	Guam	Guam	N	None
31	7	7	Barcinas, Juan D	Head	M	Cha	26.0	M		Y	Y	Guam	Guam	Guam	Y	Farmer
32	7	7	Barcinas, Rita A	Wife	F	Cha	25.0	M		Y	Y	Guam	Guam	Guam	Y	None
33	7	7	Barcinas, Jose A	Son	M	Cha	1.0	S				Guam	Guam	Guam		None
34	7	7	Barcinas, Maria A	Daughter	F	Cha	0.2	S				Guam	Guam	Guam		None
35	8	8	Quidachay, Jose D	Head	M	Cha	23.0	S		Y	Y	Guam	Guam	Guam	Y	Rancher
36	9	9	Quidachay, Antonio Q	Head	M	Cha	78.0	M		N	N	Guam	Guam	Guam	N	Farmer
37	9	9	Quidachay, Maria G	Wife	F	Cha	30.0	M		N	N	Guam	Unknown	Guam	N	None
38	9	9	Quidachay, Mariano G	Son	M	Cha	17.0	S	N	Y	Y	Guam	Guam	Guam	Y	Farm laborer home
39	9	9	Quidachay, Jesus G	Son	M	Cha	12.0	S	N	N	N	Guam	Guam	Guam	N	Farm laborer home
40	9	9	Quidachay, Francisco Q	Nephew	M	Cha	20.0	S	N	Y	Y	Guam	Unknown	Guam	Y	Farm laborer home
41	10	10	Quidachay, Jose T	Head	M	Cha	28.0	M		Y	Y	Guam	Guam	Guam	N	Farmer
42	10	10	Quidachay, Teresa B	Wife	F	Cha	35.0	M		N	N	Guam	Guam	Guam	N	None
43	10	10	Quidachay, Juan B	Son	M	Cha	10.0	S	Y	Y	Y	Guam	Guam	Guam	Y	None
44	10	10	Quidachay, Caridad B	Daughter	F	Cha	8.0	S	N			Guam	Guam	Guam		None
45	10	10	Quidachay, Maria B	Daughter	F	Cha	4.0	S				Guam	Guam	Guam		None
46	10	10	Quidachay, Ana B	Daughter	F	Cha	0.6	S				Guam	Guam	Guam		None
47	10	11	Babauta, Ignacio G	Head	M	Cha	32.0	M		Y	N	Guam	Guam	Guam	N	Farmer
48	11	11	Babauta, Rosa Q	Wife	F	Cha	26.0	M		Y	N	Guam	Guam	Guam	N	None
49	11	11	Babauta, Engracia Q	Daughter	F	Cha	10.0	S	N	N	N	Guam	Guam	Guam	N	None
50	11	11	Babauta, Rita Q	Daughter	F	Cha	4.0	S				Guam	Guam	Guam		None

Street, avenue, road, etc. (1): Bubulao Inarajan District

(CHAMORRO ROOTS GENEALOGY PROJECT ™ TRANSCRIPTION)
(COMPILED/TRANSCRIBED BY BERNARD T. PUNZALAN / HTTP://WWW.CHAMORROROOTS.COM)

FOURTEENTH CENSUS OF THE UNITED STATES: 1920-POPULATION

ISLAND OF GUAM

ENUMERATED BY ME ON THE 5th DAY OF March, 1920

Joaquin Torres ENUMERATOR

DISTRICT **5**

NAME OF PLACE **Bubulao - Inarajan District**

[Proper name and, also, name of class, as city, town, village, barrio, etc]

Street, avenue, road, etc.	Number of dwelling house in order of visitation	Number of family in order of visitation	NAME of each person whose place of abode on January 1, 1920, was in the family.	RELATION Relationship of this Person to the head of the family.	Sex	Color or race	Age at last birthday	Single, married, widowed or divorced	Attended school any time since Sept. 1, 1919	Whether able to read.	Whether able to write.	Place of birth of this person.	Place of birth of father of this person.	Place of birth of mother of this person.	Whether able to speak English.	OCCUPATION Trade, profession, or particular kind of work done, as salesman, laborer, clerk, cook, merchant, washerwoman, etc.
1	2	3	4	5	6	7	8	9	10	11	12	13	14	15	16	17
Bubulao Inarajan District	10	11	Babauta, Dolores Q	Daughter	F	Cha	2.0	S				Guam	Guam	Guam		None
	10	11	Babauta, Vicente Q	Son	M	Cha	0.3	S				Guam	Guam	Guam		None
	11	12	Taitague, Jose C	Head	M	Cha	34.0	M		Y	Y	Guam	Guam	Guam	N	Laborer
	11	12	Taitague, Catalina C	Wife	F	Cha	26.0	M		Y	Y	Guam	Unknown	Guam	Y	None
	11	12	Taitague, Agueda C	Daughter	F	Cha	0.3	S				Guam	Guam	Guam		None
	12	13	Chargualaf, Agustin T	Head	M	Cha	49.0	M		Y	Y	Guam	Guam	Guam	N	Farmer
	12	13	Chargualaf, Ana A	Wife	F	Cha	41.0	M		N	N	Guam	Guam	Guam	N	None
	12	13	Chargualaf, Joaquina A	Daughter	F	Cha	19.0	S	N	Y	Y	Guam	Guam	Guam	Y	Farm laborer home
	12	13	Chargualaf, Jose A	Son	M	Cha	9.0	S	Y			Guam	Guam	Guam		None
	13	14	Cruz, Pedro G	Head	M	Cha	45.0	S		N	N	Guam	Guam	Guam	N	Farmer

Here ends the enumeration of Bubulao - Inarajan District.

(CHAMORRO ROOTS GENEALOGY PROJECT ™ TRANSCRIPTION)

(COMPILED/TRANSCRIBED BY BERNARD T. PUNZALAN / HTTP://WWW.CHAMORROROOTS.COM)

FOURTEENTH CENSUS OF THE UNITED STATES: 1920—POPULATION

ISLAND OF GUAM

ENUMERATED BY ME ON THE 8th DAY OF March, 1920

Joaquin Torres ENUMERATOR

DISTRICT 5

NAME OF PLACE Talofofo Barrio

[Proper name and, also, name of class, as city, town, village, barrio, etc]

Street, avenue, road, etc.	Number of dwelling house is order of visitation	Number of family in order of visitation	NAME	RELATION	Sex	Color or race	Age at last birthday	Single, married, widowed or divorced	Attended school any time since Sept. 1, 1919	Whether able to read	Whether able to write	Place of birth of this person	Place of birth of father of this person	Place of birth of mother of this person	Whether able to speak English	OCCUPATION
1	2	3	4	5	6	7	8	9	10	11	12	13	14	15	16	17
	1	1	Garrido, Vicente L	Head	M	Cha	48.0	Wd		Y	Y	Guam	Guam	Guam	N	Farmer
	1	1	Garrido, Felis S	Son	M	Cha	21.0	S	N	Y	Y	Guam	Guam	Guam	Y	Farm laborer home
	1	1	Garrido, Antonia S	Daughter	F	Cha	19.0	S	N	Y	Y	Guam	Guam	Guam	N	None
	1	1	Garrido, Jose S	Son	M	Cha	17.0	S	N	Y	Y	Guam	Guam	Guam	Y	Farm laborer home
	1	1	Garrido, Ignacio S	Son	M	Cha	15.0	S	Y	Y	Y	Guam	Guam	Guam	Y	None
	1	1	Garrido, Maria S	Daughter	F	Cha	13.0	S	Y	Y	Y	Guam	Guam	Guam	N	None
	1	1	Garrido, Enrique S	Son	M	Cha	11.0	S	Y	Y	Y	Guam	Guam	Guam	N	None
	1	1	Garrido, Rosalia S	Daughter	F	Cha	9.0	S	N			Guam	Guam	Guam		None
	1	1	Garrido, Concepcion S	Daughter	F	Cha	2.0	S				Guam	Guam	Guam		None
	2	2	Pablo, Trinidad A	Head	F	Cha	36.0	Wd		N	N	Guam	Guam	Guam	N	Farmer
	2	2	Pablo, Maria A	Daughter	F	Cha	14.0	S	N	N	N	Guam	Guam	Guam	N	None
	2	2	Pablo, Rosa A	Daughter	F	Cha	11.0	S	N	N	N	Guam	Guam	Guam	N	None
	2	2	Pablo, Elena A	Daughter	F	Cha	8.0	S	N			Guam	Guam	Guam		None
	2	2	Pablo, Serafin A	Son	M	Cha	6.0	S				Guam	Guam	Guam		None
	2	2	Pablo, Benjamin A	Son	M	Cha	4.0	S				Guam	Guam	Guam		None
	2	2	Pablo, Ramon A	Son	M	Cha	2.0	S				Guam	Guam	Guam		None
	3	3	Yamanaka, Diego	Head	M	Jp	32.0	M		Y	Y	Japan	Japan	Japan	N	Farmer
	3	3	Yamanaka, Catalina M	Wife	F	Cha	31.0	M		Y	N	Guam	Guam	Guam	N	None
	3	3	Yamanaka, Josefina M	Daughter	F	Jp	4.0	S				Guam	Japan	Guam		None
	3	3	Yamanaka, Juan M	Son	M	Jp	2.0	S				Guam	Japan	Guam		None
	3	3	Yamanaka, Maria M	Daughter	F	Jp	0.8	S				Guam	Japan	Guam		None
	4	4	Diego, Jose SN	Head	M	Cha	19.0	S	N	Y	Y	Guam	Guam	Guam	Y	Teacher
	5	5	Santos, Manuel U	Head	M	Cha	47.0	M		Y	Y	Guam	Guam	Guam	N	Farmer
	5	5	Santos, Ramona M	Wife	F	Cha	43.0	M		N	N	Guam	Guam	Guam	N	None
	5	5	Santos, Rosa M	Daughter	F	Cha	21.0	S	N	Y	Y	Guam	Guam	Guam	Y	None

Talofofo Barrio

534

(CHAMORRO ROOTS GENEALOGY PROJECT ™ TRANSCRIPTION)
(COMPILED/TRANSCRIBED BY BERNARD T. PUNZALAN / HTTP://WWW.CHAMORROROOTS.COM)

FOURTEENTH CENSUS OF THE UNITED STATES: 1920-POPULATION

ISLAND OF GUAM

ENUMERATED BY ME ON THE 8th DAY OF March, 1920

Joaquin Torres ENUMERATOR

DISTRICT 5

NAME OF PLACE Talofofo Barrio

[Proper name and, also, name of class, as city, town, village, barrio, etc]

	Dwell	Fam	NAME	RELATION	Sex	Color	Age	Cond.	School	Read	Write	Birthplace	Father	Mother	Eng.	OCCUPATION
26	5	5	Santos, Juan M	Son	M	Cha	12.0	S	Y	Y	Y	Guam	Guam	Guam	N	None
27	5	5	Santos, Jose M	Son	M	Cha	10.0	S	Y	Y	N	Guam	Guam	Guam	N	None
28	5	5	Santos, Juana M	Daughter	F	Cha	8.0	S	N			Guam	Guam	Guam		None
29	5	5	Santos, Jesus M	Son	M	Cha	6.0	S	N			Guam	Guam	Guam		None
30	5	5	Santos, Adela M	Daughter	F	Cha	2.0	S					Guam	Guam		None
31	6	6	Santos, Vicente U	Head	M	Cha	31.0	S		Y	Y	Guam	Guam	Guam	N	Farmer
32	7	7	San Nicolas, Antonio SN	Head	M	Cha	40.0	M		Y	Y	Guam	Guam	Guam	N	Farmer
33	7	7	San Nicolas, Trinidad S	Wife	F	Cha	39.0	M		Y	Y	Guam	Guam	Guam	N	None
34	7	7	San Nicolas, Enrique S	Son	M	Cha	15.0	S	Y	Y	Y	Guam	Guam	Guam	Y	None
35	7	7	San Nicolas, Venancio S	Son	M	Cha	13.0	S	Y	Y	Y	Guam	Guam	Guam	Y	None
36	7	7	San Nicolas, Maria S	Daughter	F	Cha	12.0	S	Y	Y	Y	Guam	Guam	Guam	Y	None
37	7	7	San Nicolas, Carmen S	Daughter	F	Cha	10.0	S	Y	Y	Y	Guam	Guam	Guam	N	None
38	7	7	San Nicolas, Concepcion S	Daughter	F	Cha	8.0	S	N	N	N	Guam	Guam	Guam		None
39	7	7	San Nicolas, Tomasa S	Daughter	F	Cha	6.0	S	N			Guam	Guam	Guam		None
40	7	7	San Nicolas, Francisca S	Daughter	F	Cha	4.0	S				Guam	Guam	Guam		None
41	7	7	San Nicolas, Ana S	Daughter	F	Cha	1.0	S				Guam	Guam	Guam		None
42	8	8	Santos, Antonio U	Head	M	Cha	35.0	M		Y	Y	Guam	Guam	Guam	N	Farmer
43	8	8	Santos, Soledad I	Wife	F	Cha	26.0	M		Y	Y	Guam	Guam	Guam	N	None
44	8	8	Santos, Antonia I	Daughter	F	Cha	8.0	S	N			Guam	Guam	Guam		None
45	8	8	Santos, Maria I	Daughter	F	Cha	0.0	S				Guam	Guam	Guam		None
46	9	9	Sahagon, Manuel C	Head	M	Cha	44.0	Wd		Y	Y	Guam	Philippine Islands	Guam	N	Farmer
47	9	9	Sahagon, Ignacio R	Son	M	Cha	23.0	S		Y	Y	Guam	Guam	Guam	Y	Laborer
48	9	9	Sahagon, Jose R	Son	M	Cha	19.0	S	N	Y	Y	Guam	Guam	Guam	Y	Farm laborer home
49	9	9	Sahagon, Felicitas R	Daughter	F	Cha	16.0	S	N	Y	Y	Guam	Guam	Guam	Y	None
50	9	9	Sahagon, Vicenta R	Daughter	F	Cha	14.0	S	N	N	N	Guam	Guam	Guam	N	Farm laborer home

Talofofo Barrio

(CHAMORRO ROOTS GENEALOGY PROJECT ™ TRANSCRIPTION)

(COMPILED/TRANSCRIBED BY BERNARD T. PUNZALAN / HTTP://WWW.CHAMORROROOTS.COM)

FOURTEENTH CENSUS OF THE UNITED STATES: 1920–POPULATION

ISLAND OF GUAM

DISTRICT 5

NAME OF PLACE Talofofo Barrio

[Proper name and, also, name of class, as city, town, village, barrio, etc]

ENUMERATED BY ME ON THE 8th DAY OF March, 1920

Joaquin Torres ENUMERATOR

	PLACE OF ABODE			NAME	RELATION	PERSONAL DESCRIPTION					EDUCATION			NATIVITY				OCCUPATION
	Street, avenue, road, etc.	Number of dwelling house in order of visitation	Number of family in order of visitation	Name of each person whose place of abode on January 1, 1920, was in the family. Enter surname, first, then given name and middle initial. If any. Include every person living on January 1, 1920. Omit children born since January 1, 1920.	Relationship of this Person to the head of the family.	Sex	Color or race	Age at last birthday	Single, married, widowed or divorced	Attended school any time since Sept. 1, 1919	Whether able to read.	Whether able to write.	Place of birth of this person.	Place of birth of father of this person.	Place of birth of mother of this person.	Whether able to speak English.	Trade, profession, or particular kind of work done, as salesman, laborer, clerk, cook, merchant, washerwoman, etc.
	1	2	3	4	5	6	7	8	9	10	11	12	13	14	15	16	17
1		9	9	Sahagon, Joaquina R	Daughter	F	Cha	9.0	S	N			Guam	Guam	Guam		None
2		9	9	Sahagon, Ana R	Daughter	F	Cha	4.0	S				Guam	Guam	Guam		None
3		10	10	Reyes, Jose R	Head	M	Cha	22.0	M		Y	Y	Guam	Unknown	Guam	N	Farmer
4		10	10	Reyes, Maria P	Wife	F	Cha	21.0	M	N	Y	Y	Guam	Guam	Guam	N	None
5		10	10	Reyes, Lourdes P	Daughter	F	Cha	1.0	S				Guam	Guam	Guam		None
6		10	10	Reyes, Jose P	Son	M	Cha	0.0	S				Guam	Guam	Guam		None
7		10	10	Pablo, Bernadita A.	Sister-in-law	F	Cha	10.0	S	N			Guam	Guam	Guam	N	None
8		11	11	Pablo, Juan SN	Head	M	Cha	45.0	M		N	N	Guam	Guam	Guam	N	Farmer
9		11	11	Pablo, Maria D	Wife	F	Cha	35.0	M		N	N	Guam	Guam	Guam	N	None
10	Talofofo Barrio	11	11	Pablo, Antonia D	Daughter	F	Cha	16.0	S	N	N	N	Guam	Guam	Guam	N	None
11		11	11	Pablo, Joaquina D	Daughter	F	Cha	13.0	S	N	N	N	Guam	Guam	Guam	N	None
12		11	11	Pablo, Jose D	Son	M	Cha	9.0	S	N			Guam	Guam	Guam		None
13		11	11	Pablo, Jesus D	Son	M	Cha	7.0	S				Guam	Guam	Guam		None
14		11	11	Pablo, Antonio D	Son	M	Cha	5.0	S				Guam	Guam	Guam		None
15		11	11	Pablo, Engracia D	Daughter	F	Cha	2.0	S				Guam	Guam	Guam		None
16		12	12	Ogo, Jose O	Head	M	Cha	29.0	M		N	N	Guam	Unknown	Guam	N	Farmer
17		12	12	Ogo, Andrea D	Wife	F	Cha	25.0	M		N	N	Guam	Guam	Guam	N	None
18		12	12	Ogo, Ana D	Daughter	F	Cha	3.0	S				Guam	Guam	Guam		None
19		12	12	Ogo, Antonia D	Daughter	F	Cha	2.0	S				Guam	Guam	Guam		None
20		12	12	Ogo, Jose D	Son	M	Cha	0.3	S				Guam	Guam	Guam		None
21		13	13	Sakuras, Luis C	Head	M	Jp	38.0	S		Y	Y	Japan	Japan	Japan	N	Farm laborer
22		14	14	Duenas, Manuel D	Head	M	Cha	43.0	M		N	N	Guam	Guam	Guam	N	Farmer
23		14	14	Duenas, Magdalena S	Wife	F	Chn	42.0	M		N	N	Guam	China	Guam	N	None
24		15	15	Duenas, Juan T	Head	M	Cha	38.0	W		N	N	Guam	Guam	Guam	N	Farmer
25		15	15	Duenas, Jose M	Son	M	Cha	11.0	S		N	N	Guam	Guam	Guam	N	None

536

(CHAMORRO ROOTS GENEALOGY PROJECT ™ TRANSCRIPTION)
(COMPILED/TRANSCRIBED BY BERNARD T. PUNZALAN / HTTP://WWW.CHAMORROROOTS.COM)

FOURTEENTH CENSUS OF THE UNITED STATES: 1920-POPULATION

ISLAND OF GUAM

DISTRICT 5
NAME OF PLACE Talofofo Barrio
[Proper name and, also, name of class, as city, town, village, barrio, etc]

ENUMERATED BY ME ON THE 9th DAY OF March, 1920

Joaquin Torres ENUMERATOR

	Dwelling	Family	NAME	RELATION	Sex	Color or race	Age	Single, married, widowed or divorced	Attended school since Sept. 1, 1919	Able to read	Able to write	Birthplace of person	Birthplace of father	Birthplace of mother	Able to speak English	OCCUPATION
	2	3	4	5	6	7	8	9	10	11	12	13	14	15	16	17
26	15	15	Duenas, Isabel M	Daughter	F	Cha	9.0	S	N			Guam	Guam	Guam		None
27	15	15	Duenas, Pedro M	Son	M	Cha	6.0	S	N			Guam	Guam	Guam		None
28	16	16	Duenas, Antonia T	Head	F	Cha	58.0	Wd		N	N	Guam	Unknown	Guam	N	Farmer
29	16	16	Duenas, Tomasa T	Daughter	F	Cha	27.0	S		N	N	Guam	Guam	Guam	N	Farm laborer home
30	16	16	Duenas, Rita T	Daughter	F	Cha	25.0	S		Y	Y	Guam	Guam	Guam	N	Farm laborer home
31	16	16	Duenas, Benita T	Daughter	F	Cha	23.0	S		N	N	Guam	Guam	Guam	N	Farm laborer home
32	16	16	Duenas, Vicente T	Grand-son	M	Cha	3.0	S				Guam	Unknown	Guam		None
33	17	17	Duenas, Felix D	Head	M	Cha	29.0	M		N	N	Guam	Unknown	Guam	N	Farmer
34	17	17	Lizama, Paula D	Mother	F	Cha	60.0	M		N	N	Guam	Unknown	Guam	N	None
35	17	17	Lizama, Benito S	Step-father	M	Cha	79.0	M		N	N	Guam	Guam	Guam	N	None
36	18	18	Toves, Jose A	Head	M	Cha	38.0	S		N	N	Guam	Guam	Guam	N	Rancher
37	19	19	Toves, Ramon A	Head	M	Cha	45.0	M		N	N	Guam	Guam	Guam	N	Rancher
38	19	19	Toves, Ana M	Wife	F	Cha	53.0	M		N	Y	Guam	Guam	Guam	N	None
39	19	19	Toves, Catlina M	Daughter	F	Cha	17.0	S	N	Y	Y	Guam	Guam	Guam	N	None
40	19	19	Toves, Ana M	Daughter	F	Cha	15.0	S	N	Y	N	Guam	Guam	Guam	N	None
41	19	19	Toves, Ramon T	Grand-son	M	Cha	0.4	S				Guam	Unknown	Guam		None
42	20	20	Cabrera, Joaquin V	Head	M	Cha	49.0	M		Y	Y	Guam	Guam	Guam	N	Farmer
43	20	20	Cabrera, Ana D	Wife	F	Cha	45.0	M		N	N	Guam	Guam	Guam	N	None
44	20	20	Cabrera, Consolacion D	Daughter	F	Cha	22.0	S	N	Y	Y	Guam	Guam	Guam	Y	None
45	20	20	Cabrera, Jose D	Son	M	Cha	19.0	S	N	Y	Y	Guam	Guam	Guam	Y	Servant
46	20	20	Cabrera, Pedro D	Son	M	Cha	18.0	S	N	Y	Y	Guam	Guam	Guam	Y	Farm laborer home
47	20	20	Cabrera, Juan D	Son	M	Cha	17.0	S	N	Y	Y	Guam	Guam	Guam	Y	Farm laborer home
48	20	20	Cabrera, Maria D	Daughter	F	Cha	15.0	S	N			Guam	Guam	Guam	N	None
49	20	20	Cabrera, Ana D	Daughter	F	Cha	13.0	S	N			Guam	Guam	Guam	N	None
50	20	20	Cabrera, Soledad D	Daughter	F	Cha	8.0	S	N			Guam	Guam	Guam		None

Street, avenue, road, etc.: Talofofo Barrio

(CHAMORRO ROOTS GENEALOGY PROJECT ™ TRANSCRIPTION)
(COMPILED/TRANSCRIBED BY BERNARD T. PUNZALAN / HTTP://WWW.CHAMORROROOTS.COM)
FOURTEENTH CENSUS OF THE UNITED STATES: 1920-POPULATION
ISLAND OF GUAM

DISTRICT 5
NAME OF PLACE Talofofo Barrio
[Proper name and, also, name of class, as city, town, village, barrio, etc]

ENUMERATED BY ME ON THE 9th _ DAY OF March, 1920

Joaquin Torres ENUMERATOR

	Place of Abode			NAME	RELATION	Personal Description				Education			Nativity				Occupation
Street, avenue, road, etc.	Number of dwelling house is order of visitatio n	Number of famil y in order of visitatio n	of each person whose place of abode on January 1, 1920, was in the family.	Relationship of this Person to the head of the family.	Sex	Color or race	Age at last birthday	Single, married, widowed or divorced	Attended school any time since Sept. 1, 1919	Whether able to read.	Whether able to write.	Place of birth of this person.	Place of birth of father of this person.	Place of birth of mother of this person.	Whether able to speak English.	Trade, profession, or particular kind of work done, as salesman, laborer, clerk, cook, merchant, washerwoman, etc.
1	2	3	4	5	6	7	8	9	10	11	12	13	14	15	16	17
	20	20	Cabrera, Benita D	Daughter	F	Cha	6.0	S	N			Guam	Guam	Guam		None
	20	20	Cabrera, Isabel D	Daughter	F	Cha	4.0	S				Guam	Guam	Guam		None
	21	21	Materne, Ynes S	Head	F	Cha	35.0	M		Y	N	Guam	Guam	Guam	N	Laundress
	21	21	Materne, Jose S	Son	M	Cha	14.0	S	Y	Y	Y	Guam	Guam	Guam	Y	None
	21	21	Santos, Jose C	Father	M	Cha	64.0	d		N	N	Guam	Guam	Guam	N	None
	22	22	Aguero, Vicente SN	Head	M	Cha	29.0	M		Y	Y	Guam	Guam	Guam	N	Farmer
	22	22	Aguero, Maria SN	Daughter	F	Cha	6.0	S	N			Guam	Guam	Guam		None
	22	22	Aguero, Juana SN	Daughter	F	Cha	5.0	S				Guam	Guam	Guam		None
	23	23	Pablo, Mariano A	Head	M	Cha	49.0	M		N	N	Guam	Guam	Guam	N	Farmer
	23	23	Pablo, Dolores B	Wife	F	Cha	46.0	M		N	N	Guam	Guam	Guam	N	None
	23	23	Pablo, Ana B	Daughter	F	Cha	16.0	S	Y	Y	Y	Guam	Guam	Guam	Y	None
	23	23	Pablo, Joaquin B	Son	M	Cha	14.0	S	Y	Y	Y	Guam	Guam	Guam	Y	None
	23	23	Pablo, Vicente B	Son	M	Cha	9.0	S	N			Guam	Guam	Guam		None
	23	23	Pablo, Tomas B	Son	M	Cha	4.0	S				Guam	Guam	Guam		None
	23	23	Pablo, Gregorio B	Son	M	Cha	1.0	S				Guam	Guam	Guam		None
	23	23	Pablo, Amable B	Niece	F	Cha	17.0	S				Guam	Guam	Guam		None
	24	24	Tenorio, Leonardo C	Head	M	Cha	20.0	M		N	N	Guam	Guam	Guam	Y	Farmer
	24	24	Tenorio, Lucia C	Wife	F	Cha	16.0	M		Y	Y	Guam	Guam	Guam	N	None
	25	25	Ulloa, Vicente LG	Head	M	Cha	49.0	M		Y	Y	Guam	Unknown	Unknown	Y	Farmer
	25	25	Ulloa, Maria R	Wife	F	Cha	36.0	M		Y	N	Guam	Guam	Guam	N	None
	25	25	Ulloa, Preciosa R	Daughter	F	Cha	9.0	S	N			Guam	Guam	Guam		None
	25	25	Ulloa, Teresa R	Daughter	F	Cha	7.0	S				Guam	Guam	Guam		None
	25	25	Ulloa, Rosa R	Daughter	F	Cha	5.0	S				Guam	Guam	Guam		None
	25	25	Ulloa, Soledad R	Daughter	F	Cha	2.0	S				Guam	Guam	Guam		None
	25	25	Castro, Juana R	Mother-in-law	F	Cha	70.0	d		N	N	Guam	Guam	Guam	N	None

Talofofo Barrio

(CHAMORRO ROOTS GENEALOGY PROJECT ™ TRANSCRIPTION)
(COMPILED/TRANSCRIBED BY BERNARD T. PUNZALAN / HTTP://WWW.CHAMORROROOTS.COM)

269b

FOURTEENTH CENSUS OF THE UNITED STATES: 1920—POPULATION
ISLAND OF GUAM

ENUMERATED BY ME ON THE 9th DAY OF March, 1920

Joaquin Torres ENUMERATOR

DISTRICT **5**
NAME OF PLACE **Talofofo Barrio**
[Proper name and, also, name of class, as city, town, village, barrio, etc]

Line	Street	Dwelling No. (2)	Family No. (3)	NAME (4)	RELATION (5)	Sex (6)	Color or race (7)	Age (8)	Marital (9)	School (10)	Read (11)	Write (12)	Birthplace person (13)	Birthplace father (14)	Birthplace mother (15)	Speak English (16)	OCCUPATION (17)
26		26	26	Cepeda, Vicente A	Head	M	Cha	58.0	M		Y	Y	Guam	Guam	Guam	Y	Farmer
27		26	26	Cepeda, Concepcion A	Wife	F	Cha	54.0	M		Y	Y	Guam	Guam	Guam	N	None
28		27	27	Aguon, Joaquin C	Head	M	Cha	33.0	M		Y	Y	Guam	Guam	Guam	N	Farmer
29		27	27	Aguon, Joaquina C	Wife	F	Cha	28.0	M		Y	Y	Guam	Guam	Guam	N	None
30		27	27	Aguon, Jose C	Son	M	Cha	8.0	S	N			Guam	Guam	Guam		None
31		27	27	Aguon, Teresa C	Daughter	F	Cha	5.0	S	N			Guam	Guam	Guam		None
32		27	27	Aguon, Concepcion C	Daughter	F	Cha	3.0	S				Guam	Guam	Guam		None
33		27	27	Aguon, Joaquin C	Son	M	Cha	1.0	S				Guam	Unknown	Guam		None
34		28	28	Quidachay, Vicente Q	Head	M	Cha	52.0	M		Y	Y	Guam	Guam	Guam	N	Farmer
35		28	28	Quidachay, Andrea R	Wife	F	Cha	49.0	M		Y	Y	Guam	Guam	Guam	N	None
36		28	28	Quidachay, Francisco R	Son	M	Cha	23.0	S		Y	Y	Guam	Guam	Guam	N	Farm laborer home
37		28	28	Quidachay, Candelaria R	Daughter	F	Cha	15.0	S	N	Y	Y	Guam	Guam	Guam	N	None
38	Talofofo Barrio	28	28	Quidachay, Ana R	Daughter	F	Cha	9.0	S	N			Guam	Guam	Guam		None
39		28	28	Quidachay, Juan R	Son	M	Cha	5.0	S	N			Guam	Guam	Guam		None
40		29	29	Mantanona, Antonia P	Head	F	Cha	40.0	Wd		N	N	Guam	Guam	Guam	N	None
41		29	29	Mantanona, Teresa P	Daughter	F	Cha	14.0	S	N	Y	Y	Guam	Guam	Guam	Y	None
42		29	29	Mantanona, Manuel P	Son	M	Cha	12.0	S	N	Y	Y	Guam	Guam	Guam	N	None
43		29	29	Mantanona, Juan P	Son	M	Cha	8.0	S	N			Guam	Guam	Guam		None
44		29	29	Mantanona, Milagros P	Daughter	F	Cha	5.0	S				Guam	Guam	Guam		None
45		29	29	Mantanona, Carmen P	Daughter	F	Cha	2.0	S				Guam	Unknown	Guam		None
46		30	30	Babauta, Jose D	Head	M	Cha	48.0	M		N	N	Guam	Guam	Guam	N	Farmer
47		30	30	Babauta, Dolores Q	Wife	F	Cha	38.0	M		N	N	Guam	Guam	Guam	N	None
48		30	30	Babauta, Joaquin Q	Son	M	Cha	17.0	S	N	Y	Y	Guam	Guam	Guam	Y	Laborer
49		30	30	Babauta, Maria Q	Daughter	F	Cha	13.0	S	N	N	N	Guam	Guam	Guam	N	None
50		30	30	Babauta, Concepcion Q	Daughter	F	Cha	10.0	S	N	N	N	Guam	Guam	Guam	N	None

(CHAMORRO ROOTS GENEALOGY PROJECT ™ TRANSCRIPTION)

(COMPILED/TRANSCRIBED BY BERNARD T. FUNZALAN / HTTP://WWW.CHAMORROROOTS.COM)

FOURTEENTH CENSUS OF THE UNITED STATES: 1920—POPULATION

ISLAND OF GUAM

270

DISTRICT **5**

NAME OF PLACE **Talofofo Barrio**

[Proper name and, also, name of class, as city, town, village, barrio, etc]

ENUMERATED BY ME ON THE 9th DAY OF March, 1920

Joaquin Torres ENUMERATOR

			NAME	RELATION	Sex	Color or race	Age at last birthday	Single, married, widowed or divorced	Attended school any time since Sept. 1, 1919	Whether able to read.	Whether able to write.	Place of birth of this person.	Place of birth of father of this person.	Place of birth of mother of this person.	Whether able to speak English.	OCCUPATION
1	2	3	4	5	6	7	8	9	10	11	12	13	14	15	16	17
1	30	30	Babauta, Rosalia Q	Daughter	F	Cha	8.0	S	N				Guam	Guam	Guam		None
2	30	30	Babauta, Jose Q	Son	M	Cha	5.0	S	N				Guam	Guam	Guam		None
3	30	30	Babauta, Francisco Q	Son	M	Cha	3.0	S					Guam	Guam	Guam		None
4	31	31	Tenorio, Pedro C	Head	M	Cha	26.0	M		Y	Y	Guam	Guam	Guam	N	Farmer
5	31	31	Tenorio, Ana M	Wife	F	Cha	19.0	M	N	Y	N	Guam	Guam	Guam	N	None
6	31	31	Tenorio, Maria M	Daughter	F	Cha	1.0	S					Guam	Guam	Guam		None
7	31	31	Tenorio, Maria C	Mother	F	Cha	65.0	W		Y	N	Guam	Guam	Guam	N	None
8	31	31	Pablo, Esperanza A	Niece	F	Cha	15.0	S	N	N	N	Guam	Guam	Guam	N	None
9	32	32	Tenorio, Manuel C	Head	M	Cha	22.0	M		Y	Y	Guam	Guam	Guam	N	Farmer
10	32	32	Tenorio, Maria Q	Wife	F	Cha	17.0	M	N	Y	Y	Guam	Guam	Guam	N	None
11	33	33	Castro, Ignacio P	Head	M	Cha	29.0	M		Y	Y	Guam	Guam	Guam	Y	Farmer
12	33	33	Castro, Rita C	Wife	F	Cha	21.0	M	N	Y	Y	Guam	Guam	Guam	N	None
13	33	33	Castro, Consolacion C	Daughter	F	Cha	4.0	S					Guam	Guam	Guam		None
14	33	33	Castro, Jose C	Son	M	Cha	2.0	S					Guam	Guam	Guam		None
15	33	33	Castro, Joaquin C	Son	M	Cha	1.0	S					Guam	Guam	Guam		None
16	34	34	Castro, Jose L	Head	M	Cha	55.0	M		Y	N	Guam	Guam	Guam	N	Farmer
17	34	34	Castro, Maria P	Wife	F	Cha	50.0	M		N	N	Guam	Unknown	Guam	N	None
18	34	34	Castro, Amparo P	Daughter	F	Cha	20.0	S	N	Y	Y	Guam	Guam	Guam	Y	None
19	34	34	Castro, Maria P	Daughter	F	Cha	18.0	S	N	Y	Y	Guam	Guam	Guam	Y	None
20	34	34	Castro, Enrique P	Son	M	Cha	15.0	S	N	Y	Y	Guam	Guam	Guam	Y	F.I.—Working out
21	34	34	Castro, Jesus P	Son	M	Cha	13.0	S	Y	Y	Y	Guam	Guam	Guam	N	None
22	34	34	Castro, Jose P	Son	M	Cha	10.0	S	N	Y	N	Guam	Guam	Guam	N	No
23	35	35	Castro, Antanasio P	Head	M	Cha	23.0	M		Y	Y	Guam	Guam	Guam	Y	Farmer
24	35	35	Castro, Librada P	Wife	F	Cha	18.0	M	N	N	N	Guam	Guam	Guam	N	None
25	36	36	Castro, Vicente P	Head	M	Cha	28.0	M		Y	Y	Guam	Guam	Guam	Y	Farmer

Talofofo Barrio

(CHAMORRO ROOTS GENEALOGY PROJECT ™ TRANSCRIPTION)
(COMPILED/TRANSCRIBED BY BERNARD T. PUNZALAN / HTTP://WWW.CHAMORROROOTS.COM)

FOURTEENTH CENSUS OF THE UNITED STATES: 1920-POPULATION

ISLAND OF GUAM

270b

DISTRICT 5
NAME OF PLACE Talofofo Barrio
[Proper name and, also, name of class, as city, town, village, barrio, etc]

ENUMERATED BY ME ON THE 10th DAY OF March, 1920

Joaquin Torres ENUMERATOR

	2	3	NAME (4)	RELATION (5)	Sex (6)	Color or race (7)	Age (8)	Single, married, widowed or divorced (9)	Attended school since Sept. 1, 1919 (10)	read (11)	write (12)	Birthplace of person (13)	Birthplace of father (14)	Birthplace of mother (15)	Speak English (16)	OCCUPATION (17)
26	36	36	Castro, Elena G	Wife	F	Cha	23.0	M		Y	Y	Guam	Guam	Guam	Y	None
27	36	36	Castro, Concepcion G	Daughter	F	Cha	1.0	S				Guam	Guam	Guam		None
28	37	37	Arse, Ki	Head	M	Jp	29.0	S		Y	Y	Japan	Japan	Japan	N	Farm laboror
29	38	38	Pablo, Felix A	Head	M	Cha	38.0	M		N	N	Guam	Unknown	Guam	N	Farmer
30	38	38	Pablo, Dolores A	Wife	F	Cha	38.0	M		Y	N	Guam	Guam	Guam	N	None
31	38	38	Pablo, Felicidad A	Daughter	F	Cha	13.0	S	N	N	N	Guam	Guam	Guam	N	None
32	38	38	Pablo, Antonio A	Son	M	Cha	12.0	S	N	N	N	Guam	Guam	Guam	N	None
33	38	38	Pablo, Dolores A	Daughter	F	Cha	3.0	S				Guam	Guam	Guam		None
34	38	38	Pablo, Regina A	Step-daughter	F	Cha	16.0	S	N	N	N	Guam	Guam	Guam	N	None
35	38	38	Pablo, Joaquin A	Step-son	M	Cha	8.0	S	N	N	N	Guam	Guam	Guam	N	None
36	39	39	Kiga, Y	Head	M	Jp	42.0	M		Y	Y	Japan	Japan	Japan	N	Farm laboror
37	39	39	Kiga, Yioshi	Wife	F	Jp	32.0	M		Y	Y	Japan	Japan	Japan	N	None
38	39	39	Kiga, Jesus	Son	M	Jp	0.0	S				Guam	Japan	Japan		None
39	40	40	Taitague, Victoriano L	Head	M	Cha	50.0	M		Y	Y	Guam	Guam	Guam	N	Farmer
40	40	40	Taitague, Magdalena B	Wife	F	Cha	42.0	M		N	N	Guam	Guam	Guam	N	None
41	40	40	Taitague, Felix B	Son	M	Cha	20.0	S	N	Y	Y	Guam	Guam	Guam	Y	Farm laboror
42	40	40	Taitague, Josefina B	Daughter	F	Cha	18.0	S	N	Y	Y	Guam	Guam	Guam	N	None
43	40	40	Taitague, Felipe B	Son	M	Cha	13.0	S	Y	Y	Y	Guam	Guam	Guam	Y	None
44	40	40	Taitague, Genoveva B	Daughter	F	Cha	10.0	S	N	N	N	Guam	Guam	Guam	N	None
45	40	40	Taitague, Maria B	Daughter	F	Cha	9.0	S	N			Guam	Guam	Guam		None
46	41	41	Duenas, Ignacio T	Head	M	Cha	26.0	M		N	N	Guam	Guam	Guam	N	Farmer
47	41	41	Duenas, Anunsacion T	Wife	F	Cha	30.0	M		Y	N	Guam	Guam	Guam	N	None
48	41	41	Duenas, Pedro T	Son	M	Cha	2.0	S				Guam	Guam	Guam		None
49	41	41	Duenas, Vicente T	Son	M	Cha	1.0	S				Guam	Guam	Guam		None
50	41	41	Duenas, Fernando T	Son	M	Cha	0.0	S				Guam	Guam	Guam		None

Street, avenue, road, etc. (1): Talofofo Barrio

(CHAMORRO ROOTS GENEALOGY PROJECT ™ TRANSCRIPTION)
(COMPILED/TRANSCRIBED BY BERNARD T. PUNZALAN / HTTP://WWW.CHAMORROROOTS.COM)

FOURTEENTH CENSUS OF THE UNITED STATES: 1920—POPULATION
ISLAND OF GUAM

SHEET NO. 22A

ENUMERATED BY ME ON THE 10th DAY OF March, 1920

Joaquin Torres ENUMERATOR

DISTRICT 5
NAME OF PLACE Talofofo Barrio
[Proper name and, also, name of class, as city, town, village, barrio, etc]

Street, avenue, road, etc.	Number of dwelling house in order of visitation	Number of family in order of visitation	NAME	RELATION	Sex	Color or race	Age at last birthday	Single, married, widowed or divorced	Attended school any time since Sept. 1, 1919	Whether able to read.	Whether able to write.	Place of birth of this person.	Place of birth of father of this person.	Place of birth of mother of this person.	Whether able to speak English.	OCCUPATION
	1	2	3	4	5	6	7	8	9	10	11	12	13	14	15	16	17
1	41	41	Taitague, Francisco D	Step-son	M	Cha	9.0	S		Y			Guam	Unknown	Guam		None
2		42	Taijeron, Pedro T	Head	M	Cha	30.0	M		N	N	Guam	Unknown	Guam	N	Farmer
3		42	Taijeron, Remedios T	Wife	F	Cha	24.0	M		N	N	Guam	Guam	Guam	N	None
4		42	Taijeron, Vicente T	Son	M	Cha	4.0	S				Guam	Guam	Guam		None
5		42	Taijeron, Jose T	Son	M	Cha	0.3	S				Guam	Guam	Guam		None
6		43	Castro, Vicente C	Head	M	Cha	26.0	M		Y	Y	Guam	Guam	Guam	Y	Deputy Commissioner
7		43	Castro, Concepcion C	Wife	F	Cha	25.0	M		Y	Y	Guam	Guam	Guam	N	None
8		43	Castro, Delfina C	Daughter	F	Cha	4.0	S				Guam	Guam	Guam		None
9		43	Castro, Ester C	Daughter	F	Cha	2.0	S				Guam	Guam	Guam		None
10		43	Castro, Concepcion C	Daughter	F	Cha	0.1	S				Guam	Guam	Guam		None
11		43	Castro, Dolores C	Mother	F	Cha	50.0	Wd	N	N	Y	Guam	Guam	Guam	N	None
12		43	Castro, Jose C	Brother	M	Cha	10.0	S	N	N	N	Guam	Guam	Guam	N	None
13	44	44	Babauta, Domingo D	Head	M	Cha	35.0	S		N	N	Guam	Guam	Guam	N	Farm laborer
14	45	45	Materne, Juan D	Head	M	Cha	34.0	S		Y	Y	Guam	Guam	Guam	N	Laborer
15	45	45	Materne, Andres D	Brother	M	Cha	30.0	S		Y	Y	Guam	Guam	Guam	N	Laborer
16			Here ends the enumeration of Talofofo Barrio														
17																
18																
19																
20																
21																
22																
23																
24																
25																

Talofofo Barrio

(CHAMORRO ROOTS GENEALOGY PROJECT ™ TRANSCRIPTION)
(COMPILED/TRANSCRIBED BY BERNARD T. PUNZALAN / HTTP://WWW.CHAMORROROOTS.COM)

FOURTEENTH CENSUS OF THE UNITED STATES: 1920-POPULATION
ISLAND OF GUAM

DISTRICT 5
NAME OF PLACE Yona Municipality
[Proper name and, also, name of class, as city, town, village, barrio, etc]

ENUMERATED BY ME ON THE 11th DAY OF March, 1920

Joaquin Torres ENUMERATOR

	PLACE OF ABODE			NAME	RELATION	PERSONAL DESCRIPTION					EDUCATION			NATIVITY				OCCUPATION
Street, avenue, road, etc.	Number of dwelling house in order of visitation	Number of family in order of visitation		Name of each person whose place of abode on January 1, 1920, was in the family.	Relationship of this Person to the head of the family.	Sex	Color or race	Age at last birthday	Single, married, widowed or divorced	Attended school any time since Sept. 1, 1919	Whether able to read	Whether able to write	Place of birth of this person.	Place of birth of father of this person.	Place of birth of mother of this person.	Whether able to speak English.	Trade, profession, or particular kind of work done, as salesman, laborer, clerk, cook, merchant, washerwoman, etc.
1	2	3	4		5	6	7	8	9	10	11	12	13	14	15	16	17
	1	1	Lujan, Manuel O		Head	M	Cha	32.0	M		Y	Y	Guam	Unknown	Guam	Y	Commissioner
	1	1	Lujan, Carmen U		Wife	F	Cha	43.0	M		Y	Y	Guam	Unknown	Guam	Y	None
	1	1	Lujan, William U		Son	M	Cha	9.0	S	Y			Guam	Guam	Guam		None
	1	1	Lujan, Manuel U		Son	M	Cha	7.0	S	Y			Guam	Guam	Guam		None
	1	1	Lujan, Francisco U		Son	M	Cha	5.0	S	N			Guam	Guam	Guam		None
	1	1	Lujan, Antonio U		Son	M	Cha	3.0	S				Guam	Guam	Guam		None
	1	1	Lujan, Henry U		Son	M	Cha	0.8	S				Guam	Guam	Guam		
	1	1	Aguon, Felix P		Farmer laborer	M	Cha	24.0	S		Y	N	Guam	Guam	Guam	Y	Farm laborer
	1	1	Aguon, Vicente P		Farmer laborer	M	Cha	19.0	S	N	N	N	Guam	Guam	Guam	N	Farm laborer
	2	2	Benavente, Jesus R		Head	M	Cha	46.0	M		Y	Y	Guam	Unknown	Guam	N	Deputy Commissioner
	2	2	Benavente, Nicolasa Q		Wife	F	Cha	47.0	M		N	N	Guam	Guam	Guam	N	None
	2	2	Benavente, Ramon Q		Son	M	Cha	15.0	S	N	Y	Y	Guam	Guam	Guam	Y	Farm laborer home
	2	2	Benavente, Dolores Q		Daughter	F	Cha	13.0	S	N	Y	Y	Guam	Guam	Guam	Y	None
	2	2	Duenas, Joaquin D		Farmer laborer	M	Cha	23.0	S		Y	Y	Guam	Guam	Guam	Y	Farm laborer
	2	2	Quichocho, Jose Q		Boarder	M	Cha	3.0	S				Guam	Unknown	Guam		None
	3	3	Cruz, Vicente B		Head	M	Fil	52.0	M		Y	Y	Guam	Philippine Islands	Guam	N	Farmer
	3	3	Cruz, Baltasara M		Wife	F	Cha	29.0	M		Y	Y	Guam	Guam	Guam	N	None
	3	3	Cruz, Magdalena M		Daughter	F	Fil	12.0	S	Y	Y	Y	Guam	Guam	Guam	Y	None
	3	3	Cruz, Jose M		Son	M	Fil	9.0	S	Y			Guam	Guam	Guam		None
	3	3	Cruz, Maria M		Daughter	F	Fil	6.0	S	N			Guam	Guam	Guam		None
	3	3	Cruz, George M		Son	M	Fil	4.0	S				Guam	Guam	Guam		None
	3	3	Cruz, Engracia M		Daughter	F	Fil	2.0	S				Guam	Guam	Guam		None
	4	4	Quitaro, Agustin P		Head	M	Cha	29.0	M		N	N	Guam	Unknown	Guam	N	Farmer
	4	4	Quitaro, Soledad B		Wife	F	Cha	33.0	M		N	N	Guam	Guam	Guam		None
	4	4	Quitaro, Jesus B		Son	M	Cha	7.0	S	Y			Guam	Guam	Guam		None

Yona Municipality

(CHAMORRO ROOTS GENEALOGY PROJECT ™ TRANSCRIPTION)
(COMPILED/TRANSCRIBED BY BERNARD T. PUNZALAN / HTTP://WWW.CHAMORROROOTS.COM)

FOURTEENTH CENSUS OF THE UNITED STATES: 1920-POPULATION

ISLAND OF GUAM

272b

DISTRICT **5**

NAME OF PLACE **Yona Municipality**

ENUMERATED BY ME ON THE __11th__ DAY OF March, 1920

Joaquin Torres ENUMERATOR

[Proper name and, also, name of class, as city, town, village, barrio, etc]

	PLACE OF ABODE		NAME	RELATION	PERSONAL DESCRIPTION				EDUCATION			NATIVITY				OCCUPATION
Line	Number of dwelling house in order of visitation	Number of family in order of visitation	of each person whose place of abode on January 1, 1920, was in the family. Enter surname, first, then given name and middle initial. If any.	Relationship of this Person to the head of the family.	Sex	Color or race	Age at last birthday	Single, married, widowed or divorced	Attended any school since Sept. 1, 1919	Whether able to read.	Whether able to write.	Place of birth of this person.	Place of birth of father of this person.	Place of birth of mother of this person.	Whether able to speak English.	Trade, profession, or particular kind of work done
1	2	3	4	5	6	7	8	9	10	11	12	13	14	15	16	17
26	4	4	Quitaro, Jose B	Son	M	Cha	6.0	S	N			Guam	Guam	Guam		None
27	4	4	Quitaro, Juan B	Son	M	Cha	0.2	S				Guam	Guam	Guam		None
28	5	5	Mafnas, Serafin B	Head	M	Cha	30.0	M		Y	Y	Guam	Unknown	Guam	N	Farmer
29	5	5	Mafnas, Maria C	Wife	F	Cha	26.0	M		Y	Y	Guam	Guam	Guam	N	None
30	5	5	Mafnas, Maria C	Daughter	F	Cha	7.0	S	N			Guam	Guam	Guam		None
31	5	5	Mafnas, Juan C	Son	M	Cha	0.2	S				Guam	Guam	Guam		None
32	5	5	Mafnas, Vicenta B	Mother	F	Cha	65.0	S		N	N	Guam	Guam	Guam	N	None
33	6	6	Taitingfong, Daniel C	Head	M	Cha	21.0	S		N	N	Saipan	Unknown	Saipan	Y	Farmer
34	6	6	Taitingfong, Rosa C	Mother	F	Cha	53.0	S	N	Y	Y	Guam	Guam	Guam	N	None
35	6	6	Taitingfong, Juan C	Brother	M	Cha	18.0	S		N	N	Guam	Unknown	Saipan	N	Farm laborer home
36	6	6	Taitingfong, Remedios C	Sister	F	Cha	16.0	S		N	N	Guam	Unknown	Saipan	N	None
37	6	6	Taitingfong, Felipa C	Sister	F	Cha	12.0	S	Y	Y	Y	Guam	Unknown	Saipan	Y	None
38	7	7	Quidachay, Juan Q	Head	M	Cha	68.0	Wd		N	N	Guam	Unknown	Guam	N	Farmer
39	7	7	Quidachay, Vicente B	Son	M	Cha	21.0	S		N	N	Guam	Guam	Guam	N	Farm laborer home
40	7	7	Quidachay, Jesus B	Son	M	Cha	16.0	S		Y	Y	Guam	Guam	Guam	Y	Farm laborer home
41	7	7	Quidachay, Concepcion B	Daughter	F	Cha	14.0	S		N	N	Guam	Guam	Guam	N	None
42	7	7	Quidachay, Remedios B	Daughter	F	Cha	11.0	S		N	N	Guam	Guam	Guam	N	None
43	7	7	Quidachay, Antonio B	Daughter	F	Cha	7.0	S	Y			Guam	Guam	Guam		None
44	8	8	Aqualo, Juana Q	Head	F	Cha	67.0	Wd		N	N	Guam	Guam	Guam	N	None
45	9	9	Quifunas, Jose C	Head	M	Cha	26.0	M		N	N	Guam	Guam	Guam	N	Farmer
46	9	9	Quifunas, Felicitas F	Wife	F	Cha	23.0	M		N	N	Guam	Guam	Guam	N	None
47	9	9	Quifunas, Maria F	Daughter	F	Cha	4.0	S				Guam	Guam	Guam		None
48	9	9	Quifunas, Jose F	Son	M	Cha	1.0	S				Guam	Guam	Guam		None
49	9	9	Quifunas, Manuel A	Father	M	Cha	57.0	M		N	N	Guam	Guam	Guam	N	None
50	10	10	Aguon, Jose T	Head	M	Cha	70.0	M		N	N	Guam	Guam	Guam	N	Farmer

Yona Municipality

544

(CHAMORRO ROOTS GENEALOGY PROJECT ™ TRANSCRIPTION)

(COMPILED/TRANSCRIBED BY BERNARD T. PUNZALAN / HTTP://WWW.CHAMORROROOTS.COM)

FOURTEENTH CENSUS OF THE UNITED STATES: 1920-POPULATION
ISLAND OF GUAM

DISTRICT **5**

NAME OF PLACE **Yona Municipality**

[Proper name and, also, name of class, as city, town, village, barrio, etc]

ENUMERATED BY ME ON THE 12th DAY OF March, 1920

Joaquin Torres ENUMERATOR

	Street, avenue, road, etc.	Number of dwelling house is order of visitation	Number of family in order of visitation	NAME	RELATION	Sex	Color or race	Age at last birthday	Single, married, widowed or divorced	Attended school any time since Sept. 1, 1919	Whether able to read	Whether able to write	Place of birth of this person	Place of birth of father of this person	Place of birth of mother of this person	Whether able to speak English	OCCUPATION
	1	2	3	4	5	6	7	8	9	10	11	12	13	14	15	16	17
1		10	10	Aguon, Maria P	Wife	F	Cha	60.0	M		N	N	Guam	Guam	Guam	N	None
2		10	10	Aguon, Ramon P	Son	M	Cha	18.0	S	N	N	N	Guam	Guam	Guam	N	Farm laborer home
3		10	10	Aguon, Jesus P	Son	M	Cha	16.0	S	N	Y	N	Guam	Guam	Guam	Y	Servant
4		10	10	Aguon, Milagros P	Daughter	F	Cha	12.0	S	Y	Y	Y	Guam	Guam	Guam	Y	None
5		10	10	Aguon, Jose P	Son	M	Cha	10.0	S	Y	N	Y	Guam	Guam	Guam	N	None
6		11	11	Peredo, Camilo J	Head	M	Cha	44.0	M		Y	Y	Guam	Unknown	Guam	N	Farmer
7		11	11	Peredo, Ana B	Wife	F	Cha	43.0	M		N	N	Guam	Unknown	Guam	N	None
8		11	11	Peredo, Jose B	Son	M	Cha	18.0	S	N	Y	Y	Guam	Guam	Guam	Y	Laborer
9		11	11	Peredo, Juan B	Son	M	Cha	16.0	S	N	Y	Y	Guam	Guam	Guam	Y	Laborer
10		11	11	Peredo, Maria B	Daughter	F	Cha	14.0	S	N	Y	Y	Guam	Guam	Guam	Y	None
11		11	11	Peredo, Francisco B	Son	M	Cha	12.0	S	Y	Y	Y	Guam	Guam	Guam	Y	None
12		11	11	Peredo, Joaquin B	Son	M	Cha	10.0	S	Y	Y	Y	Guam	Guam	Guam	Y	None
13		11	11	Peredo, Ignacio B	Son	M	Cha	8.0	S	Y			Guam	Guam	Guam		None
14		11	11	Peredo, Pedro B	Son	M	Cha	1.0	S				Guam	Guam	Guam		None
15		12	12	Sayama, Jesus S	Head	M	Jp	27.0	M		Y	Y	Japan	Japan	Japan	N	Farm laborer
16		12	12	Sayama, Joaquina B	Wife	F	Cha	26.0	M		Y	Y	Guam	Guam	Guam	N	None
17		12	12	Sayama, Jose B	Son	M	Cha	0.7	S				Guam	Japan	Guam		None
18		13	13	Balajadia, Jose J	Head	M	Cha	35.0	M		Y	Y	Guam	Unknown	Guam	N	Farmer
19		13	13	Balajadia, Cornelia I	Wife	F	Cha	31.0	M		Y	Y	Guam	Guam	Guam	N	None
20		13	13	Balajadia, Pedro I	Son	M	Cha	12.0	S	Y	Y	Y	Guam	Guam	Guam	Y	None
21		13	13	Balajadia, Juan I	Son	M	Cha	10.0	S	Y	Y	Y	Guam	Guam	Guam	Y	None
22		13	13	Balajadia, Francisca I	Daughter	F	Cha	8.0	S	Y			Guam	Guam	Guam		None
23		13	13	Balajadia, Manuel I	Son	M	Cha	6.0	S	N			Guam	Guam	Guam		None
24		13	13	Balajadia, Catalina I	Daughter	F	Cha	2.0	S				Guam	Guam	Guam		None
25		13	13	Balajadia, Jose I	Son	M	Cha	1.0	S				Guam	Guam	Guam		None

Yona Municipality

(CHAMORRO ROOTS GENEALOGY PROJECT ™ TRANSCRIPTION)
(COMPILED/TRANSCRIBED BY BERNARD T. PUNZALAN / HTTP://WWW.CHAMORROROOTS.COM)

FOURTEENTH CENSUS OF THE UNITED STATES: 1920-POPULATION
ISLAND OF GUAM

273b

SHEET NO. 24B

ENUMERATED BY ME ON THE 12th DAY OF March, 1920

Joaquin Torres ENUMERATOR

DISTRICT 5
NAME OF PLACE Yona Municipality
[Proper name and, also, name of class, as city, town, village, barrio, etc]

	1	2	3	4	5	6	7	8	9	10	11	12	13	14	15	16	17
	Street, avenue, road, etc.	Number of dwelling house	Number of family	Name	Relation	Sex	Color or race	Age at last birthday	Single, married, or divorced	Attended school since Sept. 1, 1919	read	write	Place of birth of this person.	Place of birth of father	Place of birth of mother	speak English	Occupation
26		13	13	Balajadia, Antonio I	Son	M	Cha	0.1	S				Guam	Guam	Guam		None
27		14	14	San Nicolas, Juan A	Head	M	Cha	26.0	M		Y	Y	Guam	Guam	Guam	N	Farmer
28		14	14	San Nicolas, Soledad M	Wife	F	Cha	26.0	M		N	N	Guam	Guam	Guam	N	None
29		15	15	Pangelinan, Maria Q	Head	F	Cha	44.0	Wd		N	N	Guam	Guam	Guam	N	Farmer
30		15	15	Pangelinan, Carmen Q	Daughter	F	Cha	18.0	S	N	Y	Y	Guam	Guam	Guam	N	Cook
31		15	15	Pangelinan, Jose Q	Son	M	Cha	15.0	S	N			Guam	Guam	Guam	Y	Farm laborer home
32		15	15	Pangelinan, Antonia Q	Daughter	F	Cha	11.0	S	Y	Y	Y	Guam	Guam	Guam	Y	None
33		15	15	Pangelinan, Emiliana Q	Daughter	F	Cha	9.0	S	Y			Guam	Guam	Guam		None
34		15	15	Pangelinan, Ramon Q	Son	M	Cha	6.0	S	N			Guam	Guam	Guam		None
35		15	15	Pangelinan, Maria Q	Daughter	F	Cha	4.0	S				Guam	Guam	Guam		None
36		15	15	Pangelinan, Jesus Q	Son	M	Cha	2.0	S				Guam	Guam	Guam		None
37		16	16	Benavente, Vicente R	Head	M	Cha	46.0	M		N	N	Guam	Unknown	Guam	N	Farmer
38		16	16	Benavente, Dolores P	Wife	F	Cha	59.0	M		N	N	Guam	Unknown	Guam	N	None
39		17	17	Quidachay, Juan M	Head	M	Cha	25.0	M		N	N	Guam	Unknown	Guam	N	Farmer
40		17	17	Quidachay, Ana T	Wife	F	Cha	14.0	S	N	N	N	Guam	Guam	Guam	N	None
41		18	18	Quidachay, Mariano P	Head	M	Cha	23.0	M		N	N	Guam	Unknown	Guam	N	Farmer
42		18	18	Quidachay, Rita S	Wife	F	Cha	28.0	M		N	N	Guam	Unknown	Guam	N	None
43		18	18	Quidachay, Delgadina S	Daughter	F	Cha	1.0	S				Guam	Guam	Guam		None
44		19	19	Pangelinan, Jose C	Head	M	Cha	53.0	Wd		Y	Y	Guam	Unknown	Guam	N	Farmer
45		19	19	Pangelinan, Jesus R	Son	M	Cha	29.0	S		Y	Y	Guam	Guam	Guam	Y	Farm laborer home
46		20	20	Taitingfong, Manuel C	Head	M	Cha	24.0	M		N	N	Guam	Unknown	Saipan	N	Farmer
47		20	20	Taitingfong, Carmen A	Wife	F	Cha	23.0	M		N	N	Guam	Guam	Guam	N	None
48		21	21	Quichocho, Josefa P	Head	F	Cha	28.0	Wd		N	N	Guam	Philippine Islands	Guam	N	Farmer
49		21	21	Quichocho, Maria P	Daughter	F	Cha	10.0	S	Y	Y	Y	Guam	Guam	Guam	N	None
50		21	21	Quichocho, Jose P	Son	M	Cha	7.0	S	Y			Guam	Guam	Guam	N	None

Yona Municipality

546

(CHAMORRO ROOTS GENEALOGY PROJECT ™ TRANSCRIPTION)
(COMPILED/TRANSCRIBED BY BERNARD T. PUNZALAN / HTTP://WWW.CHAMORROROOTS.COM)

FOURTEENTH CENSUS OF THE UNITED STATES: 1920-POPULATION
ISLAND OF GUAM

ENUMERATED BY ME ON THE 13th DAY OF March, 1920

Joaquin Torres ENUMERATOR

DISTRICT 5
NAME OF PLACE Yona Municipality
[Proper name and, also, name of class, as city, town, village, barrio, etc]

	PLACE OF ABODE			NAME	RELATION	PERSONAL DESCRIPTION					EDUCATION			NATIVITY				OCCUPATION
Street, avenue, road, etc.	Number of dwelling house in order of visitation	Number of family in order of visitation		of each person whose place of abode on January 1, 1920, was in the family. Enter surname, firs, then given name and middle initial. If any. Include every person living on January 1, 1920. Omit children born since January 1, 1920.	Relationship of this Person to the head of the family.	Sex	Color or race	Age at last birthday	Single, married, widowed or divorced	Attended school any time since Sept. 1, 1919	Whether able to read.	Whether able to write.	Place of birth of this person.	Place of birth of father of this person.	Place of birth of mother of this person.	Whether able to speak English.	Trade, profession, or particular kind of work done, as salesman, laborer, clerk, cook, merchant, washerwoman, etc.
1	2	3	4		5	6	7	8	9	10	11	12	13	14	15	16	17
1	21	21	Quichocho, Soledad P		Daughter	F	Cha	5.0	S	N			Guam	Guam	Guam		None
2	21	21	Quichocho, Rosario P		Daughter	F	Cha	3.0	S				Guam	Guam	Guam		None
3	21	21	Quichocho, Ana P		Daughter	F	Cha	2.0	S				Guam	Guam	Guam		None
4	22	22	Fernandez, Antonio Q		Head	M	Cha	18.0	S	N	Y	Y	Guam	Guam	Guam	Y	Farmer
5	22	22	Fernandez, Gabriela Q		Mother	F	Cha	44.0	Wd		N	N	Guam	Guam	Guam	N	None
6	22	22	Fernandez, Potenciana Q		Sister	F	Cha	17.0	S	N	Y	Y	Guam	Guam	Guam	Y	None
7	22	22	Fernandez, Cristina Q		Sister	F	Cha	14.0	S	N	Y	Y	Guam	Guam	Guam	Y	None
8	22	22	Fernandez, Roque Q		Brother	M	Cha	12.0	S	Y	Y	Y	Guam	Guam	Guam	Y	None
9	22	22	Fernandez, Carmen Q		Sister	F	Cha	10.0	S	Y	Y	Y	Guam	Guam	Guam	Y	None
10	22	22	Fernandez, Ana Q		Sister	F	Cha	8.0	S	Y			Guam	Guam	Guam	N	None
11	22	22	Fernandez, Maria Q		Sister	F	Cha	6.0	S				Guam	Guam	Guam		None
12	22	22	Fernandez, Jesus Q		Brother	M	Cha	3.0	S				Guam	Guam	Guam		None
13	22	22	Fernandez, Jose Q		Brother	M	Cha	2.0	S				Guam	Guam	Guam		None
14	22	22	Fernandez, Joaquin Q		Brother	M	Cha	0.8	S				Guam	Guam	Guam		None
15	23	23	Baza, Ramon S		Head	M	Cha	28.0	S		Y	Y	Guam	Guam	Guam	Y	Farmer
16	23	23	Baza, Ana S		Sister	F	Cha	36.0	S		Y	N	Guam	Unknown	Guam	N	None
17	24	24	Balajadia, Joaquin J		Head	M	Cha	28.0	M		N	N	Guam	Guam	Guam	N	Farmer
18	24	24	Balajadia, Susana P		Wife	F	Cha	26.0	M		N	N	Guam	Guam	Guam	N	None
19	24	24	Balajadia, Vicente P		Son	M	Cha	8.0	S				Guam	Guam	Guam		None
20	24	24	Balajadia, Remedios P		Daughter	F	Cha	3.0	S				Guam	Guam	Guam		None
21	24	24	Balajadia, Jose P		Son	M	Cha	0.8	S				Guam	Guam	Guam		None
22	25	25	Camacho, Vicente S		Head	M	Cha	37.0	Wd		N	N	Guam	Guam	Guam	N	Farmer
23	25	25	Camacho, Maria B		Daughter	F	Cha	9.0	S	Y			Guam	Guam	Guam		None
24	25	25	Camacho, Rosario B		Daughter	F	Cha	8.0	S	Y			Guam	Guam	Guam		None
25	25	25	Camacho, Ana B		Daughter	F	Cha	6.0	S	N			Guam	Guam	Guam		None

Yona Municipality

(CHAMORRO ROOTS GENEALOGY PROJECT ™ TRANSCRIPTION)
(COMPILED/TRANSCRIBED BY BERNARD T. PUNZALAN / HTTP://WWW.CHAMORROROOTS.COM)
FOURTEENTH CENSUS OF THE UNITED STATES: 1920-POPULATION
ISLAND OF GUAM

ENUMERATED BY ME ON THE 15th DAY OF March, 1920

Joaquin Torres ENUMERATOR

DISTRICT 5
NAME OF PLACE Yona Municipality

[Proper name and, also, name of class, as city, town, village, barrio, etc]

	Dwelling No. (2)	Family No. (3)	NAME (4)	RELATION (5)	Sex (6)	Color or race (7)	Age (8)	Single, married, widowed or divorced (9)	Attended school since Sept. 1, 1919 (10)	Read (11)	Write (12)	Birthplace person (13)	Birthplace father (14)	Birthplace mother (15)	English (16)	OCCUPATION (17)
26	25	25	Camacho, Roque B	Son	M	Cha	5.0	S	N			Guam	Guam	Guam		None
27	25	25	Balajadia, Rosa I	Mother-in-law	F	Cha	60.0	S		N	N	Guam	Unknown	Guam	N	None
28	25	25	Balajadia, Joaquina B	GrandMother-in-law	F	Cha	80.0	S		N	N	Guam	Unknown	Guam	N	None
29	26	26	Aguero, Jose SN	Head	M	Cha	21.0	S	N	Y	Y	Guam	Guam	Guam	Y	Farmer
30	26	26	Aguero, Maria SN	Mother	F	Cha	56.0	Wd		N	N	Guam	Guam	Guam	N	None
31	26	26	Aguero, Juan SN	Brother	M	Cha	20.0	S	N	Y	Y	Guam	Guam	Guam	Y	Farmer laborer ome
32	26	26	Aguero, Maria SN	Sister	F	Cha	17.0	S	N	Y	Y	Guam	Guam	Guam	Y	None
33	26	26	Aguero, Jesus SN	Brother	M	Cha	14.0	S	Y	Y	Y	Guam	Guam	Guam	Y	Servant
34	27	27	Baza, Jose C	Head	M	Cha	29.0	M		Y	Y	Guam	Guam	Guam	Y	Farmer
35	27	27	Baza, Manuela C	Wife	F	Cha	24.0	M	Y			Guam	Guam	Guam	Y	None
36	27	27	Baza, Maria C	Daughter	F	Cha	7.0	S				Guam	Guam	Guam		None
37	27	27	Baza, Vicente C	Son	M	Cha	4.0	S				Guam	Guam	Guam		None
38	27	27	Baza, Adela C	Daughter	F	Cha	1.0	S				Guam	Guam	Guam		None
39	28	28	Pocahigui, Pedro	Head	M	Fil	75.0	M		N	N	Philippine Islands	Philippine Islands	Philippine Islands	N	Farmer
40	28	28	Pocahigui, Maria P	Wife	F	Cha	60.0	M		N	N	Guam	Guam	Guam	N	None
41	28	28	Pocahigui, Francisco P	Son	M	Fil	17.0	S	N	Y	Y	Guam	Philippine Islands	Guam	Y	Laborer
42	28	28	Pocahigui, Isabel P	Daughter	F	Fil	15.0	S	N	Y	Y	Guam	Philippine Islands	Guam	Y	None
43	29	29	Quidachay, Vicente P	Head	M	Cha	32.0	M		Y	Y	Guam	Guam	Guam	N	Farmer
44	29	29	Quidachay, Ana P	Wife	F	Cha	24.0	M		Y	Y	Guam	Guam	Guam	N	None
45	29	29	Quidachay, Joaquin P	Son	M	Cha	6.0	S	N			Guam	Guam	Guam	N	None
46	29	29	Quidachay, Jose P	Son	M	Cha	5.0	S	N			Guam	Guam	Guam		None
47	29	29	Quidachay, Cornelio P	Son	M	Cha	2.0	S				Guam	Guam	Guam		None
48	30	30	Balajadia, Vicente M	Head	M	Cha	36.0	M		N	N	Guam	Unknown	Guam	N	Farmer
49	30	30	Balajadia, Ana S	Wife	F	Cha	36.0	M		N	N	Guam	Unknown	Guam	N	None
50	30	30	Balajadia, Felix S	Son	M	Cha	6.0	S				Guam	Guam	Guam		None

Yona Municipality

(CHAMORRO ROOTS GENEALOGY PROJECT ™ TRANSCRIPTION)
(COMPILED/TRANSCRIBED BY BERNARD T. PUNZALAN / HTTP://WWW.CHAMORROROOTS.COM)

FOURTEENTH CENSUS OF THE UNITED STATES: 1920-POPULATION
ISLAND OF GUAM

DISTRICT 5
NAME OF PLACE Yona Municipality
[Proper name and, also, name of class, as city, town, village, barrio, etc]

ENUMERATED BY ME ON THE 16th DAY OF March, 1920

Joaquin Torres ENUMERATOR

	2	3	4 NAME	5 RELATION	6 Sex	7 Race	8 Age	9	10	11	12	13	14	15	16	17 OCCUPATION
1	30	30	Balajadia, Joaquina S	Daughter	F	Cha	4.0	S				Guam	Guam	Guam		None
2	30	30	Balajadia, Enrique S	Son	M	Cha	2.0	S				Guam	Guam	Guam		None
3	30	30	Balajadia, Jesus S	Son	M	Cha	0.2	S				Guam	Guam	Guam		None
4	30	30	Balajadia, Vicenta R	Mother	F	Cha	63.0	S		N	N	Guam	Unknown	Guam	N	None
5	31	31	Taimanglo, Mariano F	Head	M	Cha	42.0	M		N	N	Guam	Guam	Guam	N	Farmer
6	31	31	Taimanglo, Soledad SN	Wife	F	Cha	41.0	M		N	N	Guam	Guam	Guam	N	None
7	31	31	Taimanglo, Isabel SN	Daughter	F	Cha	18.0	S	N	Y	Y	Guam	Guam	Guam	Y	None
8	31	31	Taimanglo, Ana SN	Daughter	F	Cha	15.0	S	N	N	N	Guam	Guam	Guam	N	None
9	31	31	Castro, Ignacio J	Farm laborer	M	Cha	30.0	Wd		N	N	Guam	Unknown	Guam	N	Farm laborer
10	32	32	Chargiliya, Rita B	Head	F	Cha	57.0	Wd		N	N	Guam	Unknown	Guam	N	Farmer
11	32	32	Chargiliya, Rosa B	Boarder	F	Cha	15.0	S	N	Y	Y	Guam	Unknown	Guam	Y	None
12	32	32	Meno, Nieves M	Cook	F	Cha	42.0	Wd		N	N	Guam	Unknown	Guam	N	Cook
13	32	32	Cepeda, Concepcion M	Servant	F	Cha	13.0	S		N	N	Guam	Guam	Guam	N	Servant
14	33	33	Baza, Telesforo Q	Head	M	Cha	55.0	M		Y	Y	Guam	Guam	Guam	N	Farmer
15	33	33	Baza, Margarita C	Wife	F	Cha	53.0	M		N	N	Guam	Guam	Guam	N	None
16	33	33	Baza, Vicente C	Son	M	Cha	18.0	S	N	Y	Y	Guam	Guam	Guam	Y	Farm laborer home
17	34	34	Agualo, Ramon T	Head	M	Cha	60.0	Wd		N	N	Guam	Guam	Guam	N	Farmer
18	34	34	Taitingfong, Ana T	Niece	F	Cha	36.0	S		Y	Y	Guam	Unknown	Guam	N	None
19	35	35	Cruz, Santiago LG	Head	M	Cha	52.0	M		Y	Y	Guam	Guam	Guam	N	Farmer
20	35	35	Cruz, Josefa B	Wife	F	Cha	45.0	M		Y	N	Guam	Guam	Guam	N	None
21	35	35	Cruz, Rosa B	Daughter	F	Cha	2.0	S				Guam	Guam	Guam	Y	None
22	35	35	Cruz, Jesus B	Son	M	Cha	22.0	S		Y	Y	Guam	Guam	Guam	Y	Farm laborer home
23	35	35	Cruz, Juan B	Son	M	Cha	19.0	S	N	Y	Y	Guam	Guam	Guam	Y	Farm laborer home
24	35	35	Cruz, Ana B	Daughter	F	Cha	15.0	S		Y	Y	Guam	Guam	Guam	Y	None
25	35	35	Cruz, Maria B	Daughter	F	Cha	13.0	S	Y	Y	Y	Guam	Guam	Guam	Y	None

(CHAMORRO ROOTS GENEALOGY PROJECT ™ TRANSCRIPTION)
(COMPILED/TRANSCRIBED BY BERNARD T. PUNZALAN / HTTP://WWW.CHAMORROROOTS.COM)

FOURTEENTH CENSUS OF THE UNITED STATES: 1920—POPULATION
ISLAND OF GUAM

275b

ENUMERATED BY ME ON THE 16th DAY OF March, 1920

Joaquin Torres ENUMERATOR

DISTRICT 5
NAME OF PLACE Yona Municipality

[Proper name and, also, name of class, as city, town, village, barrio, etc]

	Dwelling (2)	Family (3)	NAME (4)	RELATION (5)	Sex (6)	Color or race (7)	Age (8)	Condition (9)	Attended school (10)	Read (11)	Write (12)	Birthplace (13)	Father birthplace (14)	Mother birthplace (15)	Speak English (16)	OCCUPATION (17)
26	35	35	Cruz, Isabel B	Daughter	F	Cha	9.0	S	Y			Guam	Guam	Guam		None
27	35	35	Cruz, Luisa B	Daughter	F	Cha	7.0	S	Y			Guam	Guam	Guam		None
28	35	35	Cruz, Loria B	Daughter	F	Cha	5.0	S	N			Guam	Guam	Guam		None
29	36	36	Cruz, Manuel B	Head	M	Cha	24.0	M		Y	Y	Guam	Guam	Guam	Y	Farmer
30	36	36	Cruz, Dometila F	Wife	F	Cha	20.0	M	N	Y	Y	Guam	Unknown	Guam	Y	None
31	37	37	Dimapan, Vicente I	Head	M	Cha	51.0	M		Y	Y	Guam	Guam	Guam	N	Farmer
32	37	37	Dimapan, Antonia A	Wife	F	Cha	45.0	M		Y	Y	Guam	Guam	Guam	N	None
33	37	37	Tenorio, Magdalena D	Boarder	F	Cha	1.0	S				Guam	Unknown	Guam		None
34	37	37	Tenorio, Maria I	Cook	F	Cha	22.0	S		N	N	Guam	Unknown	Guam	N	Cook
35	38	38	Cruz, Juan IG	Head	M	Cha	42.0	S		Y	Y	Guam	Guam	Guam	N	Farmer
36	39	39	Baza, Vicente S	Head	M	Cha	33.0	M		N	N	Guam	Guam	Guam	N	Farmer
37	39	39	Baza, Teresa C	Wife	F	Cha	32.0	M		Y	Y	Guam	Guam	Guam	Y	None
38	39	39	Baza, Rosa C	Daughter	F	Cha	10.0	S	Y	Y	Y	Guam	Guam	Guam	N	None
39	39	39	Baza, Biatris C	Daughter	F	Cha	8.0	S	Y	Y	Y	Guam	Guam	Guam		None
40	39	39	Baza, Tito C	Son	M	Cha	5.0	S	Y			Guam	Guam	Guam		None
41	39	39	Baza, Pilar C	Daughter	F	Cha	2.0	S				Guam	Guam	Guam		None
42	39	39	Baza, Maria C	Daughter	F	Cha	1.0	S				Guam	Guam	Guam		None
43	40	40	Meno, Jose J	Head	M	Cha	43.0	M		Y	Y	Guam	Unknown	Guam	N	Farmer
44	40	40	Meno, Rita C	Wife	F	Cha	48.0	M		N	N	Guam	Guam	Guam	N	None
45	40	40	Meno, Vicente C	Son	M	Cha	17.0	S	N	Y	Y	Guam	Guam	Guam	Y	Farmer laborer home
46	40	40	Meno, Isabel C	Daughter	F	Cha	13.0	S	N	Y	Y	Guam	Guam	Guam	Y	None
47	41	41	Duenas, Vicente M	Head	M	Cha	27.0	M		N	N	Guam	Unknown	Guam	N	Farmer
48	41	41	Duenas, Dolores S	Wife	F	Cha	26.0	M		Y	Y	Guam	Guam	Guam	N	None
49	41	41	Duenas, Maria S	Daughter	F	Cha	8.0	S	Y	Y	Y	Guam	Guam	Guam	N	None
50	42	42	Pangelinan, Manuel C	Head	M	Cha	48.0	M		Y	Y	Guam	Guam	Guam	N	Farmer

Yona Municipality

(CHAMORRO ROOTS GENEALOGY PROJECT ™ TRANSCRIPTION)
(COMPILED/TRANSCRIBED BY BERNARD T. PUNZALAN / HTTP://WWW.CHAMORROROOTS.COM)

FOURTEENTH CENSUS OF THE UNITED STATES: 1920–POPULATION

ISLAND OF GUAM

ENUMERATED BY ME ON THE 18th DAY OF March, 1920

Joaquin Torres ENUMERATOR

DISTRICT **5**

NAME OF PLACE **Yona Municipality**

[Proper name and, also, name of class, as city, town, village, barrio, etc]

	PLACE OF ABODE			NAME	RELATION	PERSONAL DESCRIPTION					EDUCATION			NATIVITY				OCCUPATION
Street, avenue, road, etc.	Number of dwelling house is order of visitation	Number of family in order of visitation		of each person whose place of abode on January 1, 1920, was in the family. Enter surname, firs, then given name and middle initial. If any. Include every person living on January 1, 1920. Omit children born since January 1, 1920.	Relationship of this Person to the head of the family.	Sex	Color or race	Age at last birthday	Single, married, widowed or divorced	Attended school any time since sept. 1, 1919	Whether able to read.	Whether able to write.	Place of birth of this person.	Place of birth of father of this person.	Place of birth of mother of this person.	Whether able to speak English.	Trade, profession, or particular kind of work done, as salesman, laborer, clerk, cook, merchant, washerwoman, etc.
1	2	3	4		5	6	7	8	9	10	11	12	13	14	15	16	17
1	42	42	Pangelinan, Herminichilda M		Wife	F	Cha	4.0	M		Y	N	Guam	Guam	Guam	N	None
2	42	42	Pangelinan, Rosa M		Daughter	F	Cha	7.0	S	Y			Guam	Guam	Guam		None
3	42	42	Pangelinan, Jesus M		Son	M	Cha	6.0	S	N			Guam	Guam	Guam		None
4	42	42	Pangelinan, Jose M		Son	M	Cha	4.0	S				Guam	Guam	Guam		None
5	42	42	Pangelinan, Maria M		Niece	F	Cha	12.0	S				Guam	Unknown	Guam	Y	None
6	43	43	Pangelinan, Jose C		Head	M	Cha	29.0	M		N	N	Guam	Guam	Guam	N	Farmer
7	43	43	Pangelinan, Magdalena F		Wife	F	Cha	20.0	M	N	N	N	Guam	Guam	Guam	N	None
8	43	43	Pangelinan, Francisco F		Son	M	Cha	4.0	S				Guam	Guam	Guam		None
9	43	43	Pangelinan, Ana F		Daughter	F	Cha	0.7	S				Guam	Guam	Guam		None
10	43	43	Quichocho, Ana D		Mother-in-law	F	Cha	48.0	Wd				Guam	Guam	Guam		None
11	44	44	Pocahigui, Domingo P		Head	M	Fil	36.0	M		N	N	Guam	Philippine Islands	Guam	N	Farmer
12	44	44	Pocahigui, Dolores O		Wife	F	Cha	31.0	M		N	N	Guam	Guam	Guam	N	None
13	44	44	Pocahigui, Jose O		Son	M	Fil	9.0	S				Guam	Guam	Guam		None
14	44	44	Pocahigui, Felix O		Son	M	Fil	8.0	S				Guam	Guam	Guam		None
15	44	44	Pocahigui, Rafael O		Son	M	Fil	5.0	S				Guam	Guam	Guam		None
16	44	44	Pocahigui, Maria O		Daughter	F	Cha	4.0	S				Guam	Guam	Guam		None
17	44	44	Pocahigui, Jesus O		Son	M	Fil	1.0	S				Guam	Guam	Guam		None
18	45	45	Cruz, Joaquin C		Head	M	Cha	32.0	M		Y	Y	Guam	Guam	Guam	N	Farmer
19	45	45	Cruz, Concepcion R		Boarder	F	Cha	9.0	S	Y			Guam	Unknown	Unknown		None
20	45	45	Cruz, Rosalia R		Boarder	F	Cha	7.0	S	Y			Guam	Unknown	Unknown		None
21	45	45	Cruz, Pedro R		Boarder	M	Cha	3.0	S				Guam	Unknown	Unknown		None
22	46	46	Cruz, Raymundo C		Head	M	Cha	30.0	M		N	N	Guam	Guam	Guam	N	Farmer
23	46	46	Cruz, Ana T		Wife	F	Cha	31.0	M		N	N	Guam	Guam	Guam	N	None
24	46	46	Cruz, Maria T		Daughter	F	Cha	6.0	S	N			Guam	Guam	Guam		None
25	46	46	Cruz, Vicente T		Son	M	Cha	3.0	S				Guam	Guam	Guam		None

Yona Municipality

(CHAMORRO ROOTS GENEALOGY PROJECT ™ TRANSCRIPTION)
(COMPILED/TRANSCRIBED BY BERNARD T. PUNZALAN / HTTP://WWW.CHAMORROROOTS.COM)
FOURTEENTH CENSUS OF THE UNITED STATES: 1920-POPULATION
ISLAND OF GUAM

ENUMERATED BY ME ON THE 18th DAY OF March, 1920

Joaquin Torres ENUMERATOR

DISTRICT 5
NAME OF PLACE Yona Municipality

[Proper name and, also, name of class, as city, town, village, barrio, etc]

	Dwelling No. (2)	Family No. (3)	NAME (4)	RELATION (5)	Sex (6)	Color or race (7)	Age (8)	Single, married, etc (9)	Attended school (10)	Able to read (11)	Able to write (12)	Birthplace of person (13)	Birthplace of father (14)	Birthplace of mother (15)	Able to speak English (16)	OCCUPATION (17)
26	46	46	Taisague, Feliza C	Sister-in-law	F	Cha	48.0	S		N	N	Guam	Guam	Guam	N	None
27	46	46	Taisague, Rosalia C	Niece-in-law	F	Cha	3.0	S				Guam	Unknown	Guam	N	None
28	47	47	Concepcion, Ignacio C	Head	M	Cha	41.0	M		N	N	Guam	Guam	Guam	N	Farmer
29	47	47	Concepcion, Enriqueta C	Wife	F	Cha	39.0	M		Y	N	Guam	Guam	Guam	N	None
30	47	47	Concepcion, Francisco C	Son	M	Cha	20.0	S	N	Y	Y	Guam	Guam	Guam	Y	Laborer
31	47	47	Cruz, Francisco C	Step-son	M	Cha	12.0	S	Y	Y	Y	Guam	Unknown	Guam	Y	None
32	48	48	Quichocho, Joaquin D	Head	M	Cha	36.0	M		N	N	Guam	Guam	Guam	N	Farmer
33	48	48	Quichocho, Josefa C	Wife	F	Cha	43.0	M		N	N	Guam	Guam	Guam	N	None
34	48	48	Quichocho, Jose C	Son	M	Cha	19.0	S	N	Y	Y	Guam	Guam	Guam	Y	Famer laborer home
35	48	48	Quichocho, Mercedes C	Daughter	F	Cha	9.0	S	Y	Y	Y	Guam	Guam	Guam		None
36	48	48	Quichocho, Jesus C	Son	M	Cha	7.0	S	Y			Guam	Guam	Guam		None
37	48	48	Quichocho, Ignacio C	Son	M	Cha	2.0	S				Guam	Guam	Guam		None
38	49	49	Atoigue, Vicente T	Head	M	Cha	34.0	M		N	N	Guam	Guam	Guam	N	Farmer
39	49	49	Atoigue, Rosa M	Wife	F	Cha	34.0	M		N	N	Guam	Guam	Guam	N	None
40	49	49	Atoigue, Francisco M	Son	M	Cha	10.0	S	N	N	N	Guam	Guam	Guam	N	None
41	49	49	Atoigue, Tomas M	Son	M	Cha	8.0	S	N			Guam	Guam	Guam		None
42	49	49	Atoigue, Joaquin M	Son	M	Cha	6.0	S	N			Guam	Guam	Guam		None
43	49	49	Atoigue, Juan M	Son	M	Cha	1.0	S				Guam	Guam	Guam		None
44	49	49	Atoigue, Manuel T	Brother	M	Cha	36.0	S		N	N	Guam	Guam	Guam	N	Famer laborer home
45	50	50	Tenorio, Francisco I	Head	M	Cha	38.0	M		N	N	Guam	Guam	Guam	N	Farmer
46	50	50	Tenorio, Emiliana A	Wife	F	Cha	48.0	M		N	N	Guam	Guam	Guam	N	None
47	50	50	Atoigue, Antonio A	Nephew-in-law	M	Cha	7.0	S	N	N	N	Guam	Unknown	Guam	N	None
48	51	51	Salas, Juan J	Head	M	Cha	27.0	M		N	N	Guam	Unknown	Guam	N	Farmer
49	51	51	Salas, Selestina T	Wife	F	Cha	30.0	M		N	N	Guam	Unknown	Guam	N	None
50	51	51	Salas, Jose T	Son	M	Cha	1.0	S				Guam	Guam	Guam	N	None

Yona Municipality

(CHAMORRO ROOTS GENEALOGY PROJECT ™ TRANSCRIPTION)
(COMPILED/TRANSCRIBED BY BERNARD T. PUNZALAN / HTTP://WWW.CHAMORROROOTS.COM)

SHEET NO. _28A_

FOURTEENTH CENSUS OF THE UNITED STATES: 1920—POPULATION

ISLAND OF GUAM

DISTRICT 5
NAME OF PLACE **Yona Municipality**
[Proper name and, also, name of class, as city, town, village, barrio, etc]

ENUMERATED BY ME ON THE 19th DAY OF March, 1920

Joaquin Torres ENUMERATOR

Street, avenue, road, etc.	Number of dwelling house in order of visitation	Number of family in order of visitation	NAME	RELATION	Sex	Color or race	Age at last birthday	Single, married, widowed or divorced	Attended school any time since Sept. 1, 1919	Whether able to read	Whether able to write	Place of birth of this person	Place of birth of father of this person	Place of birth of mother of this person	Whether able to speak English	OCCUPATION
	1	2	3	4	5	6	7	8	9	10	11	12	13	14	15	16	17
	52	52	Reyes, Vicente G	Head	M	Cha	53.0	M		N	N	Guam	Guam	Guam	N	Farmer
	52	52	Reyes, Joaquina G	Wife	F	Cha	24.0	M		Y	N	Guam	Guam	Guam	N	None
	53	53	Ogo, Francisco M	Head	M	Cha	37.0	M		Y	Y	Guam	Unknown	Guam	N	Farmer
	53	53	Ogo, Magdalena O	Wife	F	Cha	37.0	M		N	N	Guam	Guam	Guam	N	None
	53	53	Ogo, Maria O	Daughter	F	Cha	15.0	S	N	Y	Y	Guam	Guam	Guam	Y	None
	53	53	Ogo, Ramon O	Son	M	Cha	7.0	S	Y	Y	Y	Guam	Guam	Guam		None
	53	53	Ogo, Jesus O	Son	M	Cha	5.0	S	N			Guam	Guam	Guam		None
	53	53	Ogo, Dolores S	Mother-in-law	F	Cha	80.0	Wd		N	N	Guam	Guam	Guam	N	None
	54	54	Hara, Jose H	Head	M	Jp	41.0	M		Y	Y	Japan	Japan	Japan	N	Retail merchant
	54	54	Hara, Romana C	Wife	F	Cha	33.0	M		Y	Y	Guam	Japan	Guam	N	None
	54	54	Hara, Manuel C	Son	M	Jp	12.0	S	Y	Y	Y	Guam	Japan	Guam	Y	None
	54	54	Hara, Francisca C	Daughter	F	Jp	10.0	S	Y	Y	Y	Guam	Japan	Guam	Y	None
	54	54	Hara, Jose C	Son	M	Jp	8.0	S	Y			Guam	Japan	Guam		None
	54	54	Hara, Maria C	Daughter	F	Jp	3.0	S				Guam	Japan	Guam		None
	55	55	Campos, Jose SN	Head	M	Cha	40.0	M		Y	Y	Guam	Unknown	Guam	N	Farmer
	55	55	Campos, Dominga G	Wife	F	Cha	44.0	M		Y	Y	Guam	Unknown	Guam	N	None
	55	55	Campos, Maria G	Daughter	F	Cha	16.0	S	N	Y	Y	Guam	Guam	Guam	Y	None
	56	56	Lizama, Ignacio C	Head	M	Cha	26.0	M		Y	Y	Guam	Guam	Guam	Y	Farmer
	56	56	Lizama, Regina F	Wife	F	Cha	18.0	M	N	Y	Y	Guam	Guam	Guam	Y	None
	56	56	Lizama, Pedro F	Son	M	Cha	1.0	S				Guam	Guam	Guam		None
	56	56	Lizama, Vicenta F	Daughter	F	Cha	0.1	S				Guam	Guam	Guam		None
	56	56	Lizama, Raymundo L	Father	M	Cha	62.0	Wd				Guam	Unknown	Guam	N	None
	56	56	Ogo, Manuel L	Nephew	M	Cha	6.0	S				Guam	Guam	Guam		None
	57	57	Toves, Juan G	Head	M	Cha	20.0	M		Y	Y	Guam	Guam	Guam	Y	Farmer
	57	57	Toves, Ana M	Wife	F	Cha	15.0	M	N	N	N	Guam	Guam	Guam	N	None

Yona Municipality

(CHAMORRO ROOTS GENEALOGY PROJECT ™ TRANSCRIPTION)
(COMPILED/TRANSCRIBED BY BERNARD T. PUNZALAN / HTTP://WWW.CHAMORROROOTS.COM)

FOURTEENTH CENSUS OF THE UNITED STATES: 1920—POPULATION
ISLAND OF GUAM

DISTRICT 5
NAME OF PLACE **Yona Municipality**
[Proper name and, also, name of class, as city, town, village, barrio, etc]

SHEET NO. __28B__

ENUMERATED BY ME ON THE __20th__ DAY OF March, 1920

Joaquin Torres ENUMERATOR

	PLACE OF ABODE		NAME	RELATION	PERSONAL DESCRIPTION					EDUCATION			NATIVITY				OCCUPATION
Street, avenue, road, etc.	Number of dwelling house in order of visitation	Number of family in order of visitation	of each person whose place of abode on January 1, 1920, was in the family. Enter surname, firs, then given name and middle initial. If any. Include every person living on January 1, 1920. Omit children born since January 1, 1920.	Relationship of this Person to the head of the family.	Sex	Color or race	Age at last birthday	Single, married, widowed or divorced	Attended any school any time since Sept. 1, 1919	Whether able to read.	Whether able to write.	Place of birth of this person.	Place of birth of father of this person.	Place of birth of mother of this person.	Whether able to speak English.	Trade, profession, or particular kind of work done, as salesman, laborer, clerk, cook, merchant, washerwoman, etc.
1	2	3	4	5	6	7	8	9	10	11	12	13	14	15	16	17
	57	57	Toves, Jesus M	Son	M	Cha	0.9	S				Guam	Guam	Guam		None
	58	58	Mantanona, Benito M	Head	M	Cha	26.0	Wd		Y	N	Guam	Unknown	Guam	N	Farm laborer
	59	59	Cruz, Juan M	Head	M	Cha	24.0	M		Y	Y	Guam	Guam	Guam		Farmer
	59	59	Cruz, Maria C	Wife	F	Cha	22.0	M		Y	Y	Guam	Guam	Guam		Farmer
	59	59	Cruz, Margarita C	Daughter	F	Cha	0.8	S				Guam	Guam	Guam		None
	60	60	Camacho, Francisco B	Head	M	Cha	36.0	M		N	N	Guam	Guam	Guam	N	Farmer
	60	60	Camacho, Maria O	Wife	F	Cha	48.0	M		N	N	Guam	Guam	Guam	N	None
	60	60	Camacho, Jose O	Son	M	Cha	20.0	S	N	Y	Y	Guam	Guam	Guam	Y	None
Yona Municipality	60	60	Camacho, Josefa O	Daughter	F	Cha	16.0	S	N	Y	Y	Guam	Guam	Guam	Y	None
	60	60	Camacho, Vicente O	Son	M	Cha	14.0	S	N	Y	Y	Guam	Guam	Guam	Y	None
	60	60	Camacho, Rosa O	Daughter	F	Cha	13.0	S	Y	Y	Y	Guam	Guam	Guam	Y	None
	60	60	Camacho, Pedro O	Son	M	Cha	9.0	S	Y			Guam	Guam	Guam		None
	60	60	Camacho, Ramon O	Son	M	Cha	6.0	S	N			Guam	Guam	Guam		None
	60	60	Camacho, Josefina O	Daughter	F	Cha	3.0	S				Guam	Guam	Guam		None
	61	61	Aguon, Jose T	Head	M	Cha	56.0	Wd		Y	Y	Guam	Guam	Guam	N	Farmer
	62	62	Toves, Pedro S	Head	M	Cha	47.0	M		N	N	Guam	Guam	Guam	N	Farmer
	62	62	Toves, Vicenta G	Wife	F	Cha	48.0	M		N	N	Guam	Guam	Guam	N	None
	62	62	Toves, Joaquin G	Son	M	Cha	17.0	S	N	Y	Y	Guam	Guam	Guam	N	Farm laborer home
	63	63	Mantanona, Atanasio I	Head	M	Cha	24.0	M		Y	Y	Guam	Unknown	Guam	N	Farmer
	63	63	Mantanona, Natividad T	Wife	F	Cha	24.0	M		Y	Y	Guam	Guam	Guam	N	None
	63	63	Mantanona, Maria T	Daughter	F	Cha	0.3	S				Guam	Guam	Guam		None
	63	63	Mantanona, Joaquina M	Sister	F	Cha	15.0	S	N	N	N	Guam	Unknown	Guam	N	None
	64	64	Pangelinan, Juan B	Head	M	Cha	26.0	M		Y	Y	Guam	Guam	Guam	N	Farmer
	64	64	Pangelinan, Maria B	Wife	F	Cha	26.0	M		Y	Y	Guam	Guam	Guam	N	None
	65	65	Rodriges, Maria R	Head	F	Cha	45.0	S		N	N	Guam	Unknown	Guam	N	Farm laborer

(CHAMORRO ROOTS GENEALOGY PROJECT ™ TRANSCRIPTION)
(COMPILED/TRANSCRIBED BY BERNARD T. PUNZALAN / HTTP://WWW.CHAMORROROOTS.COM)
FOURTEENTH CENSUS OF THE UNITED STATES: 1920-POPULATION
ISLAND OF GUAM

SHEET NO. _29A_

ENUMERATED BY ME ON THE _22nd_ DAY OF March, 1920

Joaquin Torres ENUMERATOR

DISTRICT 5
NAME OF PLACE Yona Municipality

[Proper name and, also, name of class, as city, town, village, barrio, etc]

Street, avenue, road, etc.	Number of dwelling house in order of visitation	Number of family in order of visitation	NAME	RELATION	Sex	Color or race	Age at last birthday	Single, married, widowed or divorced	Attended school any time since Sept. 1, 1919	Whether able to read	Whether able to write	Place of birth of this person	Place of birth of father of this person	Place of birth of mother of this person	Whether able to speak English	OCCUPATION
1	2	3	4	5	6	7	8	9	10	11	12	13	14	15	16	17
	65	65	Rodriges, Vicente M	Son	M	Cha	13.0	S	N	N	N	Guam	Unknown	Guam	N	Servant
	65	65	Rodriges, Carmen D	Daughter	F	Cha	8.0	S	Y			Guam	Unknown	Guam		None
	66	66	Toves, Ramon S	Head	M	Cha	23.0	M		Y	Y	Guam	Guam	Guam	N	Laborer
	66	66	Toves, Isabel G	Wife	F	Cha	22.0	M		Y	Y	Guam	Guam	Guam	N	None
	66	66	Toves, Vicente G	Son	M	Cha	0.2	S				Guam	Guam	Guam		None
	66	66	Toves, Maria S	Mother	F	Cha	68.0	Wd				Guam	Guam	Guam	N	None
	66	66	Cruz, Jose T	Nephew	M	Cha	12.0	S		Y	Y	Guam	Unknown	Guam		Rancher
	67	67	Ogo, Jose C	Head	M	Cha	23.0	M		Y	N	Guam	Guam	Guam	N	Rancher
	67	67	Ogo, Ana M	Wife	F	Cha	24.0	M		Y	Y	Guam	Unknown	Guam	N	None
	67	67	Ogo, Isabel M	Daughter	F	Cha	0.8	S				Guam	Guam	Guam		None
	68	68	Cepeda, Juan C	Head	M	Cha	48.0	M		N	N	Guam	Guam	Guam	N	Farmer
	68	68	Cepeda, Josefa B	Wife	F	Cha	49.0	M		N	N	Guam	Guam	Guam	N	None
	68	68	Cepeda, Jose B	Son	M	Cha	23.0	S		Y	Y	Guam	Guam	Guam	Y	Enlisted man USN
	68	68	Cepeda, Dolores B	Daughter	F	Cha	18.0	S	N	Y	Y	Guam	Guam	Guam	Y	None
	68	68	Cepeda, Rosa B	Daughter	F	Cha	16.0	S	N	Y	Y	Guam	Guam	Guam	Y	None
	68	68	Cepeda, Ana B	Daughter	F	Cha	12.0	S	Y	Y	Y	Guam	Guam	Guam	Y	None
	68	68	Cepeda, Manuel B	Son	M	Cha	10.0	S	Y	Y	Y	Guam	Guam	Guam	Y	None
	69	69	Cepeda, Jose C	Head	M	Cha	46.0	M		Y	N	Guam	Guam	Guam	N	Farmer
	69	69	Cepeda, Maria R	Wife	F	Cha	43.0	M		Y	N	Guam	Unknown	Guam	N	None
	69	69	Cepeda, Jesus R	Son	M	Cha	16.0	S	Y	Y	Y	Guam	Guam	Guam	Y	None
	69	69	Cepeda, Vicente R	Son	M	Cha	7.0	S	Y			Guam	Guam	Guam		None
	69	69	Cepeda, Paz R	Daughter	F	Cha	3.0	S				Guam	Guam	Guam		None
	70	70	Quichocho, Joaquina Q	Head	F	Cha	45.0	M		N	N	Guam	Unknown	Guam	N	Salt maker
	70	70	Quichocho, Teresa Q	Daughter	F	Cha	20.0	S	N	Y	Y	Guam	Guam	Guam	Y	Salt maker
	70	70	Quichocho, Tomasa Q	Daughter	F	Cha	17.0	S	N	N	N	Guam	Guam	Guam	N	Servant

Yona Municipality

(CHAMORRO ROOTS GENEALOGY PROJECT ™ TRANSCRIPTION)
(COMPILED/TRANSCRIBED BY BERNARD T. PUNZALAN / HTTP://WWW.CHAMORROROOTS.COM)

FOURTEENTH CENSUS OF THE UNITED STATES: 1920—POPULATION
ISLAND OF GUAM

ENUMERATED BY ME ON THE 23rd DAY OF March, 1920

Joaquin Torres ENUMERATOR

DISTRICT **5**
NAME OF PLACE **Yona Municipality**
[Proper name and, also, name of class, as city, town, village, barrio, etc]

Street, avenue, road, etc.	Number of dwelling house in order of visitation	Number of family in order of visitation	NAME	RELATION	Sex	Color or race	Age at last birthday	Single, married, widowed or divorced	Attended school any time since Sept. 1, 1919	Whether able to read	Whether able to write	Place of birth of this person	Place of birth of father of this person	Place of birth of mother of this person	Whether able to speak English	OCCUPATION
1	2	3	4	5	6	7	8	9	10	11	12	13	14	15	16	17
	70	70	Quichocho, Francisca Q	Daughter	F	Cha	12.0	S	N	N	N	Guam	Guam	Guam	N	None
	70	70	Quichocho, Biatris Q	Daughter	F	Cha	11.0	S	Y	N	N	Guam	Guam	Guam	N	None
	70	70	Quichocho, Francisco Q	Son	M	Cha	9.0	S	N	N	N	Guam	Guam	Guam	N	None
	71	71	Aguon, Venancio T	Head	M	Cha	40.0	M		N	N	Guam	Guam	Guam	N	Farmer
	71	71	Aguon, Tomasa O	Wife	F	Cha	36.0	M		N	N	Guam	Guam	Guam	N	None
	71	71	Aguon, Ignacio O	Son	M	Cha	13.0	S	Y	Y	Y	Guam	Guam	Guam	Y	None
	71	71	Aguon, Jose O	Son	M	Cha	6.0	S	N	N	N	Guam	Guam	Guam		None
	71	71	Aguon, Maria O	Daughter	F	Cha	3.0	S				Guam	Guam	Guam		None
	71	71	Aguon, Ana O	Daughter	F	Cha	1.0	S				Guam	Guam	Guam		None
	72	72	Toves, Maria T	Head	F	Cha	30.0	M	N	N	N	Guam	Unknown	Guam	N	Rancher
	72	72	Toves, Luis S	Husband	M	Cha	45.0	M		N	N	Guam	Guam	Guam	N	None
	72	72	Toves, Rosario T	Daughter	F	Cha	15.0	S	N	Y	Y	Guam	Guam	Guam		None
	72	72	Toves, Soledad T	Daughter	F	Cha	8.0	S	N	N	N	Guam	Guam	Guam		None
	72	72	Toves, Vicente T	Son	M	Cha	6.0	S	N	N	N	Guam	Guam	Guam		None
	72	72	Toves, Pedro T	Step-son	M	Cha	18.0	S	N	Y	Y	Guam	Guam	Guam	Y	Servant
	73	73	Quichocho, Juan P	Head	M	Cha	41.0	M	N	N	N	Guam	Unknown	Guam	N	Farmer
	73	73	Quichocho, Maria I	Wife	F	Cha	38.0	M	N	Y	Y	Guam	Unknown	Guam	N	None
	73	73	Quichocho, Maria N	Daughter	F	Cha	21.0	S	N	N	N	Guam	Guam	Guam	N	None
	73	73	Quichocho, Rosa N	Daughter	F	Cha	17.0	S	N	N	N	Guam	Guam	Guam	N	None
	73	73	Quichocho, Trinidad I	Daughter	F	Cha	13.0	S	N	Y	Y	Guam	Guam	Guam	N	None
	73	73	Quichocho, Manuel I	Son	M	Cha	10.0	S	Y	Y	Y	Guam	Guam	Guam	Y	None
	73	73	Quichocho, Dolores I	Daughter	F	Cha	8.0	S	Y			Guam	Guam	Guam		None
	74	74	San Nicolas, Ignacio A	Head	M	Cha	25.0	M		Y	Y	Guam	Guam	Guam	Y	Farmer
	74	74	San Nicolas, Dolores N	Wife	F	Fil	25.0	M		Y	Y	Guam	Philippine Islads	Guam	N	None
	74	74	San Nicolas, Jose N	Son	M	Cha	2.0	S				Guam	Guam	Guam		None

Yona Municipality

(CHAMORRO ROOTS GENEALOGY PROJECT ™ TRANSCRIPTION)

(COMPILED/TRANSCRIBED BY BERNARD T. PUNZALAN / HTTP://WWW.CHAMORROROOTS.COM)

FOURTEENTH CENSUS OF THE UNITED STATES: 1920—POPULATION

ISLAND OF GUAM

ENUMERATED BY ME ON THE 24th DAY OF March, 1920

Joaquin Torres ENUMERATOR

DISTRICT 5

NAME OF PLACE Yona Municipality

[Proper name and, also, name of class, as city, town, village, barrio, etc]

	Dwell. No.	Family No.	NAME	RELATION	Sex	Color/race	Age	Condition	School	Read	Write	Birthplace	Father	Mother	English	OCCUPATION
1	74	74	San Nicolas, Vicente N	Son	M	Cha	0.5	S				Guam	Guam	Guam		None
2	75	75	San Nicolas, Jesus A	Head	M	Cha	22.0	S		Y	Y	Guam	Guam	Guam	Y	Farmer
3	75	75	San Nicolas, Maria A	Mother	F	Cha	49.0	Wd		N	N	Guam	Guam	Guam	N	None
4	75	75	San Nicolas, Ana A	Sister	F	Cha	15.0	S	N	Y	Y	Guam	Guam	Guam	N	None
5	76	76	Rodriges, Lucas S	Head	M	Cha	28.0	M		Y	Y	Guam	Guam	Guam	Y	Farmer
6	76	76	Rodriges, Dolores B	Wife	F	Cha	24.0	M		Y	Y	Guam	Guam	Guam	N	None
7	76	76	Rodriges, Jesus B	Son	M	Cha	5.0	S	N			Guam	Guam	Guam		None
8	76	76	Rodriges, Maria B	Daughter	F	Cha	4.0	S				Guam	Guam	Guam		None
9	76	76	Rodriges, Jose B	Son	M	Cha	2.0	S				Guam	Guam	Guam		None
10	76	76	Rodriges, Antonia B	Cousin	F	Cha	10.0	S	Y	N	N	Guam	Unknown	Guam		None
11	76	76	Baza, Pedro T	Father-in-law	M	Cha	52.0	M		Y	Y	Guam	Guam	Guam		None
12	76	76	Baza, Ana P	Mother-in-law	F	Cha	53.0	M		N	N	Guam	Guam	Guam	N	None
13	76	76	Baza, Rosa T	Aunt-in-law	F	Cha	55.0	S		N	N	Guam	Guam	Guam	N	None
14	77	77	Rosario, Lorenzo C	Head	M	Cha	19.0	S	N	Y	Y	Guam	Guam	Guam	Y	Teacher
15	78	78	Rodriges, Mariano L	Head	M	Cha	63.0	M		N	N	Guam	Guam	Guam	N	Farmer
16	78	78	Rodriges, Fermina S	Wife	F	Cha	44.0	M		N	N	Guam	Guam	Guam	N	None
17	78	78	Rodriges, Jose S	Son	M	Cha	17.0	S	N	Y	Y	Guam	Guam	Guam	Y	Farmer laborer home
18	78	78	Rodriges, Ana R	Grand-niece	F	Cha	13.0	S	N	Y	Y	Guam	Unknown	Guam	N	None
19	79	79	Taisipig, Gregorio M	Head	M	Cha	31.0	M		Y	Y	Guam	Guam	Guam	N	Farmer
20	79	79	Taisipig, Ana T	Wife	F	Cha	30.0	M		N	N	Guam	Unknown	Guam	N	None
21	79	79	Taisipig, Jesus T	Son	M	Cha	8.0	S	Y			Guam	Guam	Guam		None
22	79	79	Taisipig, Hermina T	Daughter	F	Cha	6.0	S	N			Guam	Guam	Guam		None
23	79	79	Taisipig, Antonia T	Daughter	F	Cha	5.0	S	N			Guam	Guam	Guam		None
24	79	79	Taisipig, Dolores T	Daughter	F	Cha	3.0	S				Guam	Guam	Guam		None
25	79	79	Taisipig, Rosa T	Daughter	F	Cha	1.0	S				Guam	Guam	Guam		None

Yona Municipality

(CHAMORRO ROOTS GENEALOGY PROJECT ™ TRANSCRIPTION)
(COMPILED/TRANSCRIBED BY BERNARD T. PUNZALAN / HTTP://WWW.CHAMORROROOTS.COM)

279b

FOURTEENTH CENSUS OF THE UNITED STATES: 1920-POPULATION

ISLAND OF GUAM

SHEET NO. _30B_

ENUMERATED BY ME ON THE _25th_ DAY OF _March_, 1920

Joaquin Torres ENUMERATOR

DISTRICT **5**

NAME OF PLACE **Yona Municipality**

[Proper name and, also, name of class, as city, town, village, barrio, etc]

	PLACE OF ABODE			NAME	RELATION	PERSONAL DESCRIPTION					EDUCATION			NATIVITY				OCCUPATION
	Street, avenue, road, etc.	Number of dwelling house in order of visitation	Number of family in order of visitation	of each person whose place of abode on January 1, 1920, was in the family. Enter surname, first, then given name and middle initial. If any. Include every person living on January 1, 1920. Omit children born since January 1, 1920.	Relationship of this Person to the head of the family.	Sex	Color or race	Age at last birthday	Single, married, widowed or divorced	Attended school any time since Sept. 1, 1919	Whether able to read.	Whether able to write.	Place of birth of this person.	Place of birth of father of this person.	Place of birth of mother of this person.	Whether able to speak English.	Trade, profession, or particular kind of work done, as salesman, laborer, clerk, cook, merchant, washerwoman, etc.
	1	2	3	4	5	6	7	8	9	10	11	12	13	14	15	16	17
26		79	79	Taisipiq, Carmen M	Mother	F	Cha	58.0	Wd				Guam	Guam	Guam		None
27		80	80	Quichocho, Ana Q	Head	F	Cha	30.0	S		N	N	Guam	Unknown	Unknown	N	Laundress
28		80	80	Quichocho, Maria Q	Daughter	F	Cha	15.0	S	N	Y	Y	Guam	Unknown	Unknown	N	None
29		80	80	Quichocho, Rita Q	Daughter	F	Cha	12.0	S	Y	Y	Y	Guam	Unknown	Unknown	Y	None
30		80	80	Quichocho, Juan Q	Son	M	Cha	0.8	S				Guam	Unknown	Unknown	Y	None
31		81	81	Taitingfong, Manuel T	Head	M	Cha	36.0	M		Y	Y	Guam	Unknown	Guam	N	Farm laborer
32		81	81	Taitingfong, Francisca T	Mother	F	Cha	60.0	S		N	N	Guam	Unknown	Guam	N	None
33		82	82	Taitingfong, Maria C	Head	F	Cha	57.0	Wd		Y	Y	Guam	Guam	Guam	Y	Farmer
34		82	82	Baza, Ramon C	Son	M	Cha	18.0	S	N	Y	Y	Guam	Guam	Guam	Y	Farmer
35		82	82	Baza, Jose C	Son	M	Cha	16.0	S	N	N	N	Guam	Guam	Guam	Y	Farm laborer home
36		82	82	Baza, Francisca C	Daughter	F	Cha	14.0	S	Y	Y	Y	Guam	Guam	Guam	Y	None
37		82	82	Taitingfong, Juan C	Son	M	Cha	9.0	S	Y	Y	N	Guam	Guam	Guam	N	None
38		82	82	Taitingfong, Vicente S	Step-son	M	Cha	24.0	S				Guam	Guam	Guam	N	Farm laborer home
39		82	82	Atoigue, Ana C	Niece	F	Cha	23.0	S				Guam	Guam	Guam	Y	None
40		82	82	Atoigue, Leonardo C	Nephew	M	Cha	3.0	S				Guam	Unknown	Guam	N	None
41		83	83	Ogo, Vicente J	Head	M	Cha	28.0	M		Y	Y	Guam	Unknown	Guam	N	Laborer
42		83	83	Ogo, Ana C	Wife	F	Cha	25.0	M		N	N	Guam	Guam	Guam	N	None
43		83	83	Ogo, Joaquina O	Daughter	F	Cha	3.0	S				Guam	Guam	Guam		None
44		83	83	Ogo, Antonia O	Daughter	F	Cha	1.0	S				Guam	Guam	Guam		None
45		84	84	Pangelinan, Pedro R	Head	M	Cha	59.0	M		N	N	Guam	Guam	Guam	N	Farmer
46		84	84	Pangelinan, Nives C	Wife	F	Cha	44.0	M		N	N	Guam	Guam	Guam	N	None
47		85	85	Aguon, Ignacio T	Head	M	Cha	18.0	S		Y	Y	Guam	Guam	Guam	N	None
48		86	86	Usodo, Gregorio	Head	M	Jp	38.0	M		Y	Y	Japan	Japan	Japan	Y	Farmer
49		86	86	Usodo, Ana B	Wife	F	Cha	23.0	M		Y	Y	Guam	Guam	Guam	Y	None
50		86	86	Usodo, Jose B	Son	M	Jp	3.0	S				Guam	Japan	Guam	N	None

Yona Municipality

558

(CHAMORRO ROOTS GENEALOGY PROJECT ™ TRANSCRIPTION)
(COMPILED/TRANSCRIBED BY BERNARD T. PUNZALAN / HTTP://WWW.CHAMORROROOTS.COM)

FOURTEENTH CENSUS OF THE UNITED STATES: 1920–POPULATION
ISLAND OF GUAM

DISTRICT **5**
NAME OF PLACE **Yona Municipality**

ENUMERATED BY ME ON THE 25th DAY OF March, 1920

Joaquin Torres ENUMERATOR

[Proper name and, also, name of class, as city, town, village, barrio, etc]

1	2	3	4	5	6	7	8	9	10	11	12	13	14	15	16	17
PLACE OF ABODE			NAME	RELATION	PERSONAL DESCRIPTION				EDUCATION			NATIVITY				OCCUPATION
Street, avenue, road, etc.	Number of dwelling house is order of visitation	Number of family in order of visitation	of each person whose place of abode on January 1, 1920, was in the family. Enter surname, firs, then given name and middle initial. If any. Include every person living on January 1, 1920. Omit children born since January 1, 1920.	Relationship of this Person to the head of the family.	Sex	Color or race	Age at last birthday	Single, married, widowed or divorced	Attended school any time since Sept. 1, 1919	Whether able to read.	Whether able to write.	Place of birth of this person.	Place of birth of father of this person.	Place of birth of mother of this person.	Whether able to speak English.	Trade, profession, or particular kind of work done, as salesman, laborer, clerk, cook, merchant, washerwoman, etc.
1	86	86	Usodo, Dolores B	Daughter	F	Cha	1.0	S				Guam	Japan	Guam		None
2	86	86	Usodo, Maria B	Daughter	F	Cha	0.0	S				Guam	Japan	Guam		None
3	87	87	Aguon, Pedro T	Head	M	Cha	46.0	M		Y	Y	Guam	Guam	Guam	N	Farmer
4	87	87	Aguon, Maria L	Wife	F	Cha	47.0	M		N	N	Guam	Unknown	Guam	N	None
5	87	87	Aguon, Luis L	Son	M	Cha	22.0	S		Y	Y	Guam	Guam	Guam	Y	Farm laborer home
6	87	87	Aguon, Juan L	Son	M	Cha	18.0	S	N	Y	Y	Guam	Guam	Guam	Y	Laborer
7	87	87	Aguon, Jesus L	Son	M	Cha	14.0	S	N	Y	Y	Guam	Guam	Guam	Y	Servant
8	87	87	Aguon, Joaquin L	Son	M	Cha	13.0	S	Y	Y	Y	Guam	Guam	Guam	Y	None
9	87	87	Aguon, Trinidad L	Daughter	F	Cha	11.0	S	Y	Y	Y	Guam	Guam	Guam	Y	None
10	87	87	Aguon, Jose L	Son	M	Cha	9.0	S	Y			Guam	Guam	Guam		None
11	87	87	Aguon, Vicente L	Son	M	Cha	7.0	S	Y			Guam	Guam	Guam		None
12	87	87	Aguon, Manuel L	Son	M	Cha	5.0	S	N			Guam	Guam	Guam		None
13	87	87	Aguon, Francisco L	Son	M	Cha	3.0	S				Guam	Guam	Guam		None
14	88	88	Baza, Jesus C	Head	M	Cha	24.0	M		Y	Y	Guam	Guam	Guam	Y	Laborer
15	88	88	Baza, Maria LG	Wife	F	Cha	25.0	M				Guam	Guam	Guam	N	None
16	88	88	Baza, Concepcion LG	Daughter	F	Cha	1.0	S				Guam	Guam	Guam		None
17	89	89	Hataguchi, Okidia	Head	M	Jp	41.0	S		Y	Y	Japan	Japan	Japan	N	Farm laborer
18	90	90	Cruz, Joaquin R	Head	M	Cha	40.0	M		Y	Y	Guam	Unknown	Guam	N	Farmer
19	90	90	Cruz, Rosa T	Wife	F	Cha	32.0	M		N	N	Guam	Guam	Guam	N	None
20	90	90	Cruz, Isabel T	Daughter	F	Cha	9.0	S	N			Guam	Guam	Guam		None
21	90	90	Cruz, Maria T	Daughter	F	Cha	7.0	S	N			Guam	Guam	Guam		None
22	90	90	Cruz, Jesus T	Son	M	Cha	5.0	S	N			Guam	Guam	Guam		None
23	90	90	Cruz, Catalina T	Daughter	F	Cha	3.0	S				Guam	Guam	Guam		None
24	90	90	Cruz, Tomasa T	Son	M	Cha	1.0	S				Guam	Guam	Guam		None
25																

Yona Municipality

Here ends the enumeration of Yona Municipality.

References

Bureau of the Census. (1975, September). *Historical Statistics of the United States: Colonial Times to 1970 Part I*. Retrieved on March 21, 2011 from:
http://www2.census.gov/prod2/statcomp/documents/CT1970p1-01.pdf

National Archives and Records Administration (NARA). (n.d.). *1920 Federal Population Censuses*. Retrieved March 21, 2011 from:
http://www.archives.gov/research/census/publications-microfilm-catalogs-census/1920/part-01.html

Rodgers, R. (1995). *Destiny's Landfall: a history of Guam*. University of Hawai'i Press: Honolulu, HI.

US Census Bureau. (1920). *Instructions to Enumerators*. Retrieved on March 21, 2011 from:
http://www2.census.gov/prod2/decennial/documents/1920Instructions toEnumerators.pdf

US Census Bureau. (n.d.). *History: 1920 Overview*. Retrieved on March 21, 2011 from:
http://www.census.gov/history/www/through_the_decades/overview/19 20.html

www.ingramcontent.com/pod-product-compliance
Lightning Source LLC
Chambersburg PA
CBHW052129020426

42334CB00023B/2655